THE VISIONS OF Anne Catherine Emmerich

BOOK I

THE VISIONS OF Anne Catherine Emmerich

BOOK I

Dramatis Personae • Creation • Antiquity
Old Testament Times • Youth of Mary • Birth and
Early Years of Jesus • First Journeys of Jesus
With a Day-by-Day Chronicle
April AD 29 to August AD 30

From the Notes of
CLEMENS BRENTANO

Revised and Supplemented
by James Richard Wetmore
General Editor

*Introductory Material, Chronology,
& Daily Summaries*
by Robert Powell, Ph.D.

First published in the USA
by Angelico Press 2015
Revised Text, New Text, Supplements,
Translations, and Layout
© James Richard Wetmore, 2015
Introductory Material, Chronology,
and Daily Summaries
© Robert Powell, 2015

All rights reserved

No part of this book may be reproduced
or transmitted, in any form or by
any means, without permission

For information, address:
Angelico Press
169 Monitor St.
Brooklyn, NY 11222
www.angelicopress.com

Book I: ISBN 978-1-59731-146-5 (pbk)
Book I: ISBN 978-1-59731-467-1 (hbk)
Book II: ISBN 978-1-59731-147-2 (pbk)
Book II: ISBN 978-1-59731-468-8 (hbk)
Book III: ISBN 978-1-59731-148-9 (pbk)
Book III: ISBN 978-1-59731-469-5 (hbk)

Cover Images:
J. James Tissot (French, 1836–1902)
Front: *The Magnificat* (detail)
Back: *The Annunciation* (detail)
Brooklyn Museum, purchased by
public subscription: 00.159.19, 00.159.16
Reproduced by permission
of the Brooklyn Museum
Cover Design: Michael Schrauzer

Acknowledgments

As general editor of this series, I owe a debt of gratitude to many people, past and present, whose devotion to Anne Catherine Emmerich, and to her visions, has made this new edition possible. Of course, it is to Anne Catherine herself—and to the spiritual gifts with which she was graced—that we owe everything. And without the total dedication of Clemens Brentano, who sat by her side year after year, we would have no written record at all. Over the past two centuries many others have labored selflessly at arranging and translating the visions. Two German authors, the Very Reverend Carl E. Schmöger and Fr. Helmut Fahsel, provided ground-breaking studies on Anne Catherine's life and visions. Fr. Fahsel in particular provided a temporal and geographical framework that proved indispensable for this edition. And then, in 2009, at a time when the project had been in full swing for many years, the dedicated labors of the Belgian Jozef De Raedemaeker came to full fruition with his publication in full of the 38 notebooks Brentano filled during his time with Anne Catherine. These notebooks hold untold treasures, and a fourth volume of this series, drawn largely from them, is nearing completion. But it was left to the extraordinary research of Dr. Robert Powell to pull together the temporal indications, using the best of the modern science of chronology, to establish the reliable day-by-day itinerary of the life of Jesus according to which this edition is organized. Much of the introductory material is also based upon his work. The appendices are his work also, as are the daily summaries (in italics) placed at the outset of most daily entries, as well as much of the gazetteer. His generous enthusiasm, dedication, and commitment to this project pervade every aspect of the final result. To be acknowledged also are J. James Tissot, whose providential paintings—clearly inspired by his reading of Anne Catherine's visions—bring the text to life in a way no other illustrations could, and the Brooklyn Museum, curator of many of Tissot's paintings, who provided the necessary permissions.

I gratefully acknowledge for their contributions to the project also the following individuals, without whose help and support many more years may have elapsed before this priceless text could be brought before the world in so complete a form: Robert Ledwidge, Jackie Sohn, Mado Spiegler, Edita Zacharr, Richard Bloedon, Lynne Klugman, Eileen Sullivan, Philip Mees, Lacquanna Paul, John Clarke, and John Riess. I offer special thanks to Marcia Burchard, whose understanding, encouragement, patience, and deep appreciation of the full significance of Anne Catherine and her visions helped sustain me over the past decade.

Lastly, I dedicate this work to the memory of my parents, Thomas T. Wetmore, III and Joan Marie Hancock, whose loving, selfless, virtuous, and spiritually informed lives touched me and many others in ways that offered guidance and touchstones that only grow more clear to the heart and mind with the passage of years.

Ex Deo Nascimur, In Christo Morimur, Per Spiritum Sanctum Reviviscimus

This Edition Offered in Special Veneration of:
St. Michael, the Archangel

Mary, Our Lady of the Sign
Sophia, The Holy Wisdom

Christ of the Apocalypse

Michaël-Sophia, in Nomine Christi

CONTENTS

Introductory

Endorsements i
General Introduction 1 — Biographical Glimpses 5

Dramatis Personae

Introduction 29 — The Holy Men [John the Baptist, Apostles, Lazarus & Friends, Other Male Figures] 31— Temporal Sequence of Contacts Between Jesus and His Apostles and Disciples 62 — The Disciples Chosen by Jesus in the Course of His Ministry Organized by Geographic or Family Association 64 — The Holy Women at Christ's Death and Resurrection 66 — Other Holy Women and Those Previously Described Considered Again, Organized by Geographic or Family Association 90 — Table of Genealogy and Close Relations of Jesus 94 — Enemies and Adversaries of Jesus 97

Beginnings

THE CREATION: Fall of the Angels 113 — Creation of the Earth 113 — Adam and Eve 114 — The Tree of Life and the Tree of Knowledge 115

ANTIQUITY AND OLD TESTAMENT TIMES: The Fall 116 — The Promise of the Redeemer 119 — Adam and Eve Driven from Paradise 120 — The Family of Adam 121 Cain • The Children of God • The Giants 122 — Noah and His Posterity • Hom and Djemschid, Leaders of the People 123 — The Tower of Babel 128 —Derketo 130 — Semiramis 132 — Melchizedek 134 — Job 136 — Abraham 138 — Melchizedek's Sacrifice of Bread and Wine 140 — Abraham Receives the Sacrament of the Old Covenant 141 — Jacob 142 — Joseph and Asenath 145 — The Ark of the Covenant 149

The Messiah Comes

MARY AND HER ANTECEDENTS: Genealogy, Birth, and Marriage of Anne 153 — The Immaculate Conception of Mary 157 —Symbols of the Mystery of the Immaculate Conception 162 —Symbolical Vision 164 — Eve of Mary's Birth 164 — Birth of Mary 165 —The Child Receives the Name of Mary 167 — Preparations for Mary's Presentation 168 —The Journey to the Temple 170 — The Entrance into Jerusalem 172 — Mary's Entrance into the Temple and Her Offering 174 — A Glance at the Obduracy of the Pharisees 177 — John Promised to Zechariah 177

BIRTH, CHILDHOOD, AND YOUTH OF JESUS: Mary Espoused to Joseph 178 — The Holy House of Nazareth 182 — Mary's Annunciation 182 — Mary's Visitation 183 —

Feast Pictures 187 — The Blessed Virgin's Preparations for the Birth of Christ • Journey to Bethlehem 188 — The Arrival in Bethlehem 192 — Birth of the Child Jesus 195 — Adoration of the Shepherds • Devout Visits to the Crib 198 — The Circumcision 200 — Journey of the Three Kings to Bethlehem 202 — Genealogy of the Kings 205 — The Kings before Herod 206 — The Kings Arrive at Bethlehem 208 — The Second Day of the Kings at the Crib • Their Departure 211 — The Return of Anne 213 — Mary's Purification 215 — Feast Picture 217 — Death of Holy Simeon 218 — Return of the Holy Family to Nazareth 218 — The Flight into Egypt 219 — The Holy Family among Robbers 222 — The Balsam Garden 224 — The Holy Family Reaches Heliopolis 224 — The Murder of the Innocent Children 225 — The Holy Family Goes to Matarea 226 — The Return of the Holy Family from Egypt 229 — John as a Child Growing Up in the Desert 230 — Feast Picture of John the Baptist 231 — The Holy Family at Nazareth • Jesus at the Age of Twelve in the Temple of Jerusalem 232 — Death of Joseph • Jesus and Mary in Capernaum 235

Day-by-Day Chronicle of the Life, Travels, and Teaching of Jesus During His Public Ministry

Year 1: AD 29

April 16–September 22, AD 29: *Jesus Begins His Public Teaching • From Capernaum to the Baptism*

Jesus on His Way to Hebron 292 — The Family of Lazarus 294 — Jesus in Hebron, Dothaim, and Nazareth 296 — Jesus Journeys over Lebanon to Sidon and Sarepta 300 — Jesus in Bethsaida and Capernaum 303 — Jesus in Sepphoris, Bethulia, Kishion, and Jezreel 305 — Jesus among the Publicans 310 — Jesus in Chisloth-Tabor 310 — Jesus in the Shepherd Village of Kimki 311 — Jesus in a Shepherd Village near Nazareth 312 — Jesus with Eliud, the Essene 313 — Jesus Discourses with Eliud the Essene upon the Mysteries of the Old Testament and the Incarnation 314 — Jesus and Eliud Walking and Conversing Together 316 — Jesus in Nazareth 318 — Jesus Rejects Three Rich Youths • He Confounds Many Learned Men in the Synagogue of Nazareth 319 — Jesus with Eliud in the Leper Settlement 321 — Jesus Transfigured before Eliud 321 — A Glance at the Disciples Going to the Baptism 322 — Jesus in Gophna 323 — Jesus Condemns Herod's Adultery • The Journey of the Holy Women 325 — Jesus in Bethany 326 — Jesus's Interview with Silent Mary • His Conversation with His Mother 329 — Jesus Journeys with Lazarus to the Place of Baptism 331

September 23–October 21, AD 29: *John Preaching Penance & Baptizing • Baptism in the Jordan • Retracing Journeys of Mary and Joseph • Beginning of 40 Days' Fast*

John Leaves the Desert 332 — Herod's Soldiers • Deputies from the Sanhedrin • Crowds of Neophytes Come to John 336 — John Receives an Admonition to Go to Jericho 337 — Herod's Interview with John • The Celebration of a Festival at the Place of Baptism 339 — The Island upon which Jesus Received Baptism Rises out of the Jordan 340 — New Embassy from Jerusalem • Herod again Seeks an Interview with John 341 — Jesus Baptized by John 342 — Jesus Travels over Luz and Ensemes to Visit the Two Inns at which the Holy Family Rested on Their

Journey to Bethlehem and Flight into Egypt 345 — Jesus in the Valley of Shepherds near Bethlehem 349 — The Crib Cave, a Place of Devotion among the Shepherds 352 — Jesus Visits Certain Inns, the Halting Places of the Holy Family on Their Flight into Egypt 353 — Jesus Goes toward Mizpah to Visit a Relative of Joseph 354 — Jesus Visits an Inn at which Mary Stopped on Her Journey to Bethlehem 356 — "Behold the Lamb of God" 356 — Jesus in Gilgal, Dibon, Succoth, Aruma, and Bethany 357

Years 1–2: AD 29–30

October 22, AD 29–May 2, AD 30: *Jesus in the Desert • Marriage Feast of Cana • Jesus Celebrates Passover in Jerusalem for the First Time*

The Forty Days' Fast of Jesus 364 [*Jesus Tempted in Many Ways by Satan 367 — Satan Tempts Jesus by Magical Arts 369 — Satan Tempts Jesus to Turn Stones into Bread 369 — Satan Carries Jesus to the Pinnacle of the Temple, and then to Mount Quarantania • Angels Minister unto Jesus 369*] — Jesus Goes to the Jordan, and Orders Baptism to be Administered 371 — Jesus in Shiloh, Kibzaim, and Thebez 376 — First Formal Call of Peter, Philip, and Nathaniel 379 — The Wedding at Cana 384 [*The Nuptial Ceremony • The Women's Game • The Men's Lottery 386*] —Jesus in Capernaum and at the Sea of Galilee 390 — Jesus Permits Baptism to be Given at the Jordan 394 — Jesus in Adummin and Nebo 398 — Jesus Cures in Phasael the Daughter of Jairus the Essene • Magdalene's First Call to Conversion 401 — Jesus in Capernaum, Gennabris, and Chisloth-Tabor 402 — Jesus in Shunem, Ulama, and Capernaum 407 — Jesus in Dothaim and Sepphoris • From a Distance, He Helps the Shipwrecked 411 — Jesus in Nazareth • The Three Youths • The Feast of Purim 412 — Jesus at Lazarus's Estate near Thirza and at His Home in Bethany 414 — Jesus's First Passover Celebration in Jerusalem 416 — Jesus Turns the Vendors out of the Courts of the Temple • The Paschal Supper • Death of Mary the Silent 421

May 3–August 2, AD 30: *From the Close of the First Passover to the Conversion of the Samaritan Woman at Jacob's Well and Travels in North Galilee*

The Letter of King Abgar 458 — Jesus on the Confines of Sidon and Tyre 459 — Jesus in Amichores-Libnath 462 — Jesus in Adama • Miraculous Conversion of an Obstinate Jew 465 — The Parable of the Unjust Steward 469 — Jesus and the Disciples Invited to Teach and Baptize in Seleucia 470 — Jesus Preaching on the Mountain near Berotha 473 — Jesus Passes through Gath-Hepher to Capernaum 477 — John the Baptist Arrested by Herod and Imprisoned at Machaerus 478 — Jesus in Bethany • Inns Established for the Accommodation of Jesus and the Disciples on their Journeys • The Pearl Lost and Found 480 — Jesus in Beth-Horon • Hardships and Privations of the Disciples 484 — Jesus at Jacob's Well near Sichar • Dinah the Samaritan Woman 486 — Jesus in Ginea and Ataroth • He Confounds the Wickedness of the Pharisees 492 — Jesus in Engannim and Nain 496

Supplements

Mysticism, Miracles, and Wonders 499 — Gazetteer 517

ILLUSTRATIONS

INTRODUCTORY
Portrait & Signature of Anne Catherine ····· Pt div.
Painting of Anne Catherine, M. Max, 1885 ·· Pt div.

General Introduction

Anne Catherine in her room (Brentano) ········ 1
Anne Catherine in her bed (Brentano) ········ 1
Distant View of House of Mary (Brentano) ····· 2
Distant View from House of Mary ············· 3
Floor Plan of House of Mary ················· 3
House of Mary before Restoration ············ 3
The House of Mary at Ephesus ················ 3

Biographical Glimpses

Birthplace of Anne Catherine ················ 5
The Cow Barn ································ 6
Flecks on Anne Catherine's Headcloth ········ 7
Augustinian Convent in Dülmen ··············· 7
Impression of Double Cross ·················· 8
Dr. Franz Wilhelm Wesener ··················· 9
Sketch of Clemens Brentano ················· 10
Sketch of Christian Brentano ··············· 10
Anne Catherine's Sleeping & Sewing Rooms ···· 11
Anne Catherine's Living Room ··············· 11
Cl. A. von Droste-Vischering ··············· 12
Bernard Overberg ··························· 12
Luise Hensel ······························· 13
Drawing of Anne Catherine by L. Hensel ····· 13
Passage from Brentano's Notebook ··········· 14
Letter in Anne Catherine's Hand ············ 15

DRAMATIS PERSONAE
Baptism in the Jordan (by Brentano) ······ Pt div.
9 Drawings from Brentano's Notes ········· Pt div.

Holy Men

The Exhortation to the Apostles ············ 31
Discourse with the Disciples ··············· 32
Childhood of John the Baptist ·············· 33
The Voice of One Crying in the Wilderness ·· 33
John the Baptist Teaching the Pharisees ···· 34
Herod Antipas ······························ 34
John the Baptist Sees Jesus from Afar ······ 35
The Baptism of Jesus ······················· 35
Herodians at the Castle of Machaerus ······· 35
More Herodians ····························· 36
Salome Dancing before Herod Antipas ········ 36
The Head of John the Baptist on a Platter ·· 36

Disciples at John's Second Place of Baptism ····· 37
Simon Peter ································ 38
Simon Peter with Jesus Teaching ············· 38
With Jesus Teaching in the Portico of Solomon ··· 39
With Jesus Healing in the Streets of Jerusalem ·· 39
The Primacy of Peter ······················· 40
Second Miraculous Draught of Fishes ········ 40
"Feed my Lambs" ··························· 40
Andrew ··································· 41
The Calling of Peter and Andrew ············ 41
John of Zebedee ··························· 42
Prophecy of Destruction of the Temple ······ 42
At the Last Supper ························· 43
James the Greater ························· 43
John and James Espy the Risen One ·········· 44
Listening to Jesus When Tempted ············ 44
James the Less ···························· 45
Water Bearer at Washing of Feet ············ 46
Bartholomew ······························· 46
Thomas ··································· 47
The Disbelief of Thomas ···················· 48
Judas Iscariot ···························· 49
Mary Magdalene Anoints Jesus ··············· 50
Judas Meets with the Pharisees ············· 50
Judas Betrays Jesus with a Kiss ············ 51
Judas Scatters the 60 Pieces of Silver ····· 52
Judas Hangs Himself ························ 52
Philip ··································· 53
Address to Philip ·························· 53
Matthew ·································· 54
The Calling of Matthew ····················· 54
Simon ···································· 55
Judas Thaddeus ···························· 56
Lazarus ·································· 58
Ordaining of the Twelve Apostles ··········· 61

Holy Women

The Holy Women ····························· 66
Holy Women Watch Crucifixion from afar ····· 67
Washing the Body of Jesus ·················· 67
Following the Body to the Anointing Stone ·· 68
Preparing the Body ························· 68
Following the Body to the Sepulcher ········ 68
Magdalene and Mary, Mother of Joses ········ 69
Magdalene and Two Holy Women at Sepulcher ·· 70
Risen One Appears to Three Holy Women ······ 71
"Touch Me Not" ···························· 72

Mary Receives the Magnificat · · · · · · · · · · 73	
Elizabeth and Mary at Visitation · · · · · · · · · · · 74	
Mary Looks up from Foot of Cross · · · · · · · · · 75	
Mary Kisses Jesus before Enshrouding · · · · · · · · · 75	
Mary Looks up at Ascension Angels · · · · · · · · 76	
Mary's Final Visit to Jerusalem & Golgotha · · · · · 76	
Mary Heli · 77	
Mary Cleophas · 78	
Mary Salome Holding Virgin Mary at Cross · · · · · 78	
Mary Salome and John at Nailing · · · · · · · · · · 79	
Martha · 79	
Martha Cooking · 79	
Magdalene Repentant · · · · · · · · · · · · · · · · · · · 80	
Magdalene Anoints Jesus's Head · · · · · · · · · · · 81	
Magdalene Listens to Jesus Teach · · · · · · · · · · · 82	
Magdalene Listens to Jesus in Bethany · · · · · · · · 82	
Maroni at Raising of the Youth of Nain · · · · · · · 83	
Veronica Holds Out Her Scarf to Jesus · · · · · · · · · 84	
The Holy Face of the Scarf of Veronica · · · · · · · · 84	
Susanna of Jerusalem · · · · · · · · · · · · · · · · · · · 85	
Salome of Jerusalem · 85	
Mary Mark · 86	
Johanna Chusa · 87	
Dinah the Samaritan Woman · · · · · · · · · · · · · 87	
Dinah Drawing Water at Jacob's Well · · · · · · · · · 88	
Mara the Suphanite · 89	
Anna Cleophas · 89	
Mother and Child Carrying Water · · · · · · · · · · · 96	

Enemies and Adversaries of Jesus

Murder of the Innocents · · · · · · · · · · · · · · · · · · 97
Twelve-Year-Old Jesus Teaching in the Temple · · · 97
Some Pharisees Ridicule Jesus · · · · · · · · · · · · · · 98
Pharisees ask 'By what right do you these things?' · 98
Uproar with Pharisees in the Temple · · · · · · · · · 99
Pharisees Gather in Council · · · · · · · · · · · · · · · 100
Pharisees Spy on Jesus and the Disciples · · · · · · · 100
Pharisees Interrupt Jesus at Synagogue · · · · · · · · 101
Pharisees Tempt Jesus at Banquet · · · · · · · · · · · 101
Pharisees' Hirelings Hurl Stones at Jesus · · · · · · · 102
Sanhedrin Priests in Assembly · · · · · · · · · · · · · · 102
The Pharisees Do Not Lay Hands on Him · · · · · · 103
Healed Blind Man Tells His Story · · · · · · · · · · · 104
They Sought to Cast Him from the Mountain · · · 104
Jesus Chases Out the Money-Changers · · · · · · · · 105
Sadducees of Ataroth with Jesus · · · · · · · · · · · · 105
Jesus Teaches Some Priests · · · · · · · · · · · · · · · · 106
A Scribe Speaks with Jesus · · · · · · · · · · · · · · · · 106
An Herodian · 107
Pharisees and Herodians Conspire · · · · · · · · · · · 107
Disciples of John the Baptist · · · · · · · · · · · · · · · 108
They Watch the Disciples of Jesus Baptize · · · · · · 108
Herod Antipas · 109
Pontius Pilate and His Wife Claudia · · · · · · · · · · 110
Fall of the Tower of Siloam · · · · · · · · · · · · · · · 110
Annas and Caiphas · 111

BEGINNINGS
Creation, Antiquity, and Old Testament Times

Adam & Eve Driven from Paradise · · · · · · · · · Pt div.
The Ark Passes over the Jordan · · · · · · · · · · · Pt div.
Building the Ark · Pt div.
Abraham's Oak, Hebron · · · · · · · · · · · · · · · · · 139

THE MESSIAH COMES

4 Drawings from Brentano's Notes · · · · · · · · Pt div.
Cave of the Nativity (by Brentano) · · · · · · · · Pt div.

Mary and Her Antecedents

Jerusalem from the Mount of Olives · · · · · · · · · 154
Mount Hermon · 159
Approaching Jerusalem from the South · · · · · · · 171
Jerusalem from Scopus · · · · · · · · · · · · · · · · · · · 173

Birth, Childhood, and Youth of Jesus

View over Nazareth · 180
Hilltop near Nazareth · · · · · · · · · · · · · · · · · · · 185
Galilean Hamlet near Nazareth · · · · · · · · · · · · · 186
The High Road to Bethlehem · · · · · · · · · · · · · 189
Farmhouse Inn on the Way to Bethlehem · · · · · · 191
Cave of the Nativity · 195
Birth Grotto among Caves Outside Bethlehem · · 196
Hebron at Sunrise · 213
Kidron from Jehosaphat · · · · · · · · · · · · · · · · · 216
Temple Scrolls · 219
A Spring by the Way · 224
Well of the Virgin · 228
Jerusalem in Distance from the Olives · · · · · · · · · 233

TISSOT SECTION A—*The Virgin Mary and the Childhood of Jesus*: 28 Paintings · · · · · · · · 237–292

CHRONICLE
OF THE LIFE, TRAVELS, & TEACHING OF JESUS

Jesus Begins His Public Teaching

Village of Siloam · Pt div.
Bethany in the Distance · · · · · · · · · · · · · · · · · 295
View toward Sidon · 301

Temple Garden, Ancient Jezreel · · · · · · · · · · · · · 308
River Kishon · 321
Fields and Vineyards on the Road to Bethany · · · 327
Plain of Jericho, Aqueducts in the Distance · · · · 331

John Teaching Penance & Baptizing
River Jordan at Dan · 335
Stream in Jezreel Valley · · · · · · · · · · · · · · · · · · 337
Threshing Grain · 348

Jesus in the Desert • Marriage Feast of Cana • Jesus Celebrates Passover in Jerusalem for First Time
Under the Arches · 377
Fishing in the Sea of Galilee near Bethanat · · · · · 392
Synagogue Lamp · 407

TISSOT SECTION B—*The Public Teaching of Jesus*:
16 Paintings · 425–457

First Passover to Conversation with Samaritan Woman at Jacob's Well • Travels in North Galilee
Lake Merom in the Distance · · · · · · · · · · · · · · · 466
Parable of the Pharisee and the Publican · · · · · · · 474
The Sower · 476
Shechem at the Foot of Mount Garizim · · · · · · · 486
Hill of Samaria · 489
Women Carrying Water · · · · · · · · · · · · · · · · Pt div.
Olive Trees in Hinnom Valley · · · · · · · · · · · · Pt div.
North Walls of Jerusalem · · · · · · · · · · · · · · · Pt div.

SUPPLEMENTS
Mysticism, Miracles, & Wonders
The Baptism in the Jordan · · · · · · · · · · · · · · · · · 499
Theophany in Temple: Voice from on High · · · · 499
Jesus Transfigured · 500
John, Peter, and James at Transfiguration · · · · · · 501
With Arms Extended · 502
Luminous Figure of Jesus Walking on Sea · · · · · · 502
Stilling a Storm · 503
Walking on the Sea, Peter Sinks · · · · · · · · · · · · · 503
Multiplying of Food · 504
Abundant Catch of Fish · · · · · · · · · · · · · · · · · · 505
Healing the Sick along the Road · · · · · · · · · · · · 505
Healing the Sick before a City Gate · · · · · · · · · · 506
Healing Lepers in the Open Air · · · · · · · · · · · · · 507
Healing the Man with a Withered Hand · · · · · · · 508
Healing Two Blind Men in Capernaum · · · · · · · · 508
Enue Touches the Seam of Jesus's Cloak · · · · · · · 509
Curing a Raging Possessed · · · · · · · · · · · · · · · · 510
"Satan, depart!" · 511
Raising of the Daughter of Jairus · · · · · · · · · · · · 512
Raising of Lazarus · 513
Blessing Mother and Child · · · · · · · · · · · · · · · · 514
Blessing a Young Boy · 514
The Disciples Baptize · 515
Jesus Sends the Disciples Out in Pairs · · · · · · · · · 516

MAPS

The Journey of the Three Kings · · · · · · · · · · · · · 203
Flight of the Holy Family in Egypt · · · · · · · · · · · 221
Area around Capernaum during Time of Christ · · 236

MAP 1: *Journey to the Place Where John the Baptist Grew Up* (May 29–June 20, AD 29) · · · 293
MAP 2: *Journey to Sidon, Mount Carmel, and Jacob's Well* (June 30–July 31, AD 29) · · · · · · · 299
MAP 3: *Travels in Southern Galilee* (August 4–26, AD 29) · · · · · · · · · · · · · · · · · · · 304
MAP 4: *Travels with Eliud in Lower Galilee* (August 27–September 17, AD 29) · · · · · · · · · · 309
MAP 5: *Journey to the Baptism in the Jordan* (September 18–28, AD 29) · · · · · · · · · · · · · · · 324
MAP 6: *Visit to the Valley of the Shepherd's near Bethlehem* (September 28–Oct. 10, AD 29) · · · 350
MAP 7: *The Forty Days in the Wilderness* (October 11–November 30, AD 29) · · · · · · · · 361
MAP 8: *At the Second Place of Baptism* (December 1–19, AD 29) · · · · · · · · · · · · · · · · 372

MAP 9: *The Wedding at Cana* (December 19–January 2, AD 30) · · · · · · · · · 381
MAP 10: *The First Sermon on the Mount* (January 3–11, AD 30) · · · · · · · · · · · · · · · · · · 391
MAP 11: *At the Place of Baptism* (January 11–26, AD 30) · · · · · · · · · · · · · · · · · 395
MAP 12: *A Raising from the Dead* (January 27–February 9, AD 30) · · · · · · · · · · · 400
MAP 13: *First Journey with the Future Apostles* (February 10–23, AD 30) · · · · · · · · · · · · · · · · 404
MAP 14: *Travels in Galilee* (February 24–March 15, AD 30) · · · · · · · · · · · 410
MAP 15: *The First Passover* (March 16–May 26, AD 30) · · · · · · · · · · · · · · · 417
MAP 16: *Travels in Northern Galilee* (End of May–July 19, AD 30) · · · · · · · · · · · · · 461
MAP 17: *The Conversation at Jacob's Well* (July 20–29, AD 30) · 481
MAP 18: *The Healing of the Nobleman's Son* (July 29–August 7, AD 30) · · · · · · · · · · · · · · · 495

ABBREVIATIONS
Books frequently referred to in the text

BL: *Das bittere Leiden unseres Herrn Jesu Christi nach den Betrachtungen der gottseligen Anna Katharina Emmerich, Clemens Brentano* [Complete Works, vol. 26], (Stuttgart: Kohlhammer, 1980)

HDK: *Die heiligen Drei Könige, Helmut Fahsel* (Basel: Ilionverlag, 1941)

LBVM: *The Life of the Blessed Virgin Mary from the Visions of Anne Catherine Emmerich*, transl. Sir Michael Palairet (Rockford, Illinois: Tan Books, 1970)

LHHJC: *Das Leben unseres Herrn and Heilandes Jesu Christi nach den Geschichten der gottseligen Anna Katarina Emmerich* aufgeschrieben von Clemens Brentano, 3 volumes (Regensburg, 1858–1860)

LIFE: *The Life of Anne Catherine Emmerich,* by the Very Reverend Carl E. Schmöger, C.SS.R., 2 volumes (Rockford, Illinois: Tan Books, 1976)

LJ i: *Lehrjahre Jesu. Teil I: Mai 1821 bis Juli 1822*, Clemens Brentano [Complete Works vol. 24.1], (Stuttgart: Kohlhammer, 1983)

LJ ii: *Lehrjahre Jesu. Teil II: August bis Dezember 1822*, Clemens Brentano [Complete Works vol. 24.2], (Stuttgart: Kohlhammer, 1985)

LJC: *The Life of Jesus Christ, and Biblical Revelations, From the Visions of the Venerable Anne Catherine Emmerich*, 4 volumes (Rockford, Illinois: Tan Books, 1979)

MKF: *Offnet Eure Herzen MARIA, der Königen des Friedens*, Slavko Barbaric and Tomislav Vlasic (Jestetten, Germany: Rosenkranz Aktion, 1987)

TC: *The Time of Christ*, Ormond Edwards (Edinburgh: Floris Books, 1986)

WJW: *Der Wandel Jesu in der Welt*, Helmut Fahsel (Basel: Ilionverlag, 1942)

ENDORSEMENTS
By Notable Authors

THE VISIONS of Anne Catherine have merited the recommendations of numerous learned prelates and theologians like Father Poulain, Dom Guéranger, and Cardinals Gibbons and Ehrle, and they have been a source of profound spiritual benefit to many persons, including such distinguished writers as J.K. Huysmans, Father Gerard Manley Hopkins, S.J., Léon Bloy, Jacques and Raïssa Maritain, and Paul Claudel, as the following quotations will demonstrate:

J.J. Goerres: "I know of no revelations richer, more profound, more wonderful, or more thrilling in their nature than those of Sister Emmerich."

Dom Prosper Guéranger, O.S.B.: "In the publication of this work (*The Life of Jesus Christ*) we must recognize a disposition of Divine Providence, who has deigned to console Catholic Germany in the midst of the most dreadful blasphemies that have been and still are uttered against the holy Gospels, by thus placing before our eyes the facts of the Gospel narratives. Indeed Catherine Emmerich has her mission! God does not lavish the extraordinary gifts which have been revealed in her. Not in vain has He placed her in the heart of Germany just before the outbreak of the most frightful infidelity.... I shall allow no favorable opportunity to pass without paying Anne Catherine Emmerich the tribute she deserves. Her revelations have found no reader who has perused them with greater diligence and appreciation than I, and I have ever been most eager to communicate my impressions concerning them to all my acquaintances.

Father Gerard Manley Hopkins, S.J.: "One day in the Long Retreat (which ended on Christmas Day) they were reading in the refectory Sister Emmerich's account of the Agony in the Garden and I suddenly began to cry and sob and could not stop. I put it down for this reason, that if I had been asked a minute beforehand I should have said that nothing of the sort was going to happen and even when it did I stood in a manner wondering at myself."

Léon Bloy and the *Maritains*: "At the very beginning [of the latter's conversion], Léon Bloy made us read Schmöger's three thick volumes on the life and visions of Anne Catherine Emmerich . . . one of the greatest mystics of the nineteenth century . . . the religious beauty of the visions and spiritual illuminations . . . is so great that there must have been at least one mystic involved—either Catherine or Brentano. No mere poet could have given a picture of such depth, coherence and theological value, of the inner life of a co-sufferer in Christ's Passion.... The *Revelations* of Anne Catherine Emmerich gave us a picture of Catholicism that was crowded and vivid, moving and yet familiar. They taught us countless things—we, who knew nothing of Catholic history, dogmas, theology, liturgy, mysticism. At that time a sober catechism would probably have done nothing to make us understand. In our ignorance we had the greatest need for the help of images, for that sort of portrait of the Church, drawn in the four dimensions of height and length, of width and depth. And at the same time we were shown heroic Catholicism—sanctity in its terrible trials, in its humility and divine charity, in its asceticism, in the beatitude wherein it reaches it fulfillment, in its pure harmony, in its power, in its beauty."

Paul Claudel: "The books which proved very helpful during that period [of his conversion] were ... Pascal ... Bossuet ... Dante ... not to forget the marvelous private revelations of Catherine Emmerich.

J.K. Huysmans: "[T]he tonic, the stimulant in weakness, the strychnine for failure of faith, the goad which drives you in tears to the feet of Christ, the *Dolorous Passion* of Sister Emmerich."

Émile Baumann: "We find that Catherine Emmerich's originality is most valuable in her visions, thanks to the ability which she had of revealing their essential elements. Theologically hers are inferior to those of St. Teresa and of many others.... The three books of her revelations nevertheless constitute ... one of the most beautiful supernatural poems that can be described as inspired."

Georges Goyau: "Henceforth, too, the veneration of the humanity of Christ was to play an increasingly important role in religious fervour. The visions of Catherine Emmerich deserve to be taken as a landmark in the development of this worship.

"All the detail which they add to the dramatic story of Christ is an enrichment, not indeed of the deposit of faith itself ... but of Christian piety. They do not impose themselves on belief, still less on erudition; but the light they cast, the emotions they arouse, bear up the wings of meditation.

"Clement Brentano, by making himself, at the bedside of the stigmatized woman, the assiduous chronicler of all that Catherine saw and said, thereby brought a fresh source of sustenance to the devout curiosity of believing souls. Before the eyes of that Germany in which certain schools were beginning to regard the story of Christ as a kind of myth, he developed scenes of pathos, scenes picturesque in their tragedy, in which the face of Christ became animated by a new life, more troubled, more poignant, one might almost say more in the raw, than the one which the sobriety of the Gospel narrative shows us.

"And thanks to Brentano, she who, through her stigmata, let herself become 'in conformity with Christ,' was to lead coming Christian generations, if not to know Christ better, at least to feel for Him better, in a compassion in which faith and love mingle and kneel together."

Father Poulain: "It may also be that the revelation can be regarded as Divine in its broad outlines, but doubtful in minor details. Concerning the revelations of Mary of Agreda and Anna Catherine Emmerich, for example, contradictory opinions have been expressed: some believe unhesitatingly everything they contain, and are annoyed when anyone does not share their confidence; others give the revelations no credence whatsoever (generally on *a priori* grounds); finally there are many who are sympathetic, but do not know what to reply when asked what degree of credibility is to be attributed to the writings of these two ecstatics. The truth seems to be between the two extreme opinions.... In particular instances these visionaries have been mistaken.... If there be question of the general statement of facts given in these works, we can admit with probability that many of them are true. For these two visionaries led lives that were regarded as very holy. Competent authorities have judged their ecstasies divine. It is therefore prudent to admit that they received a special assistance from God, preserving them not absolutely, but in the main, from error.

INTRODUCTORY

⊕

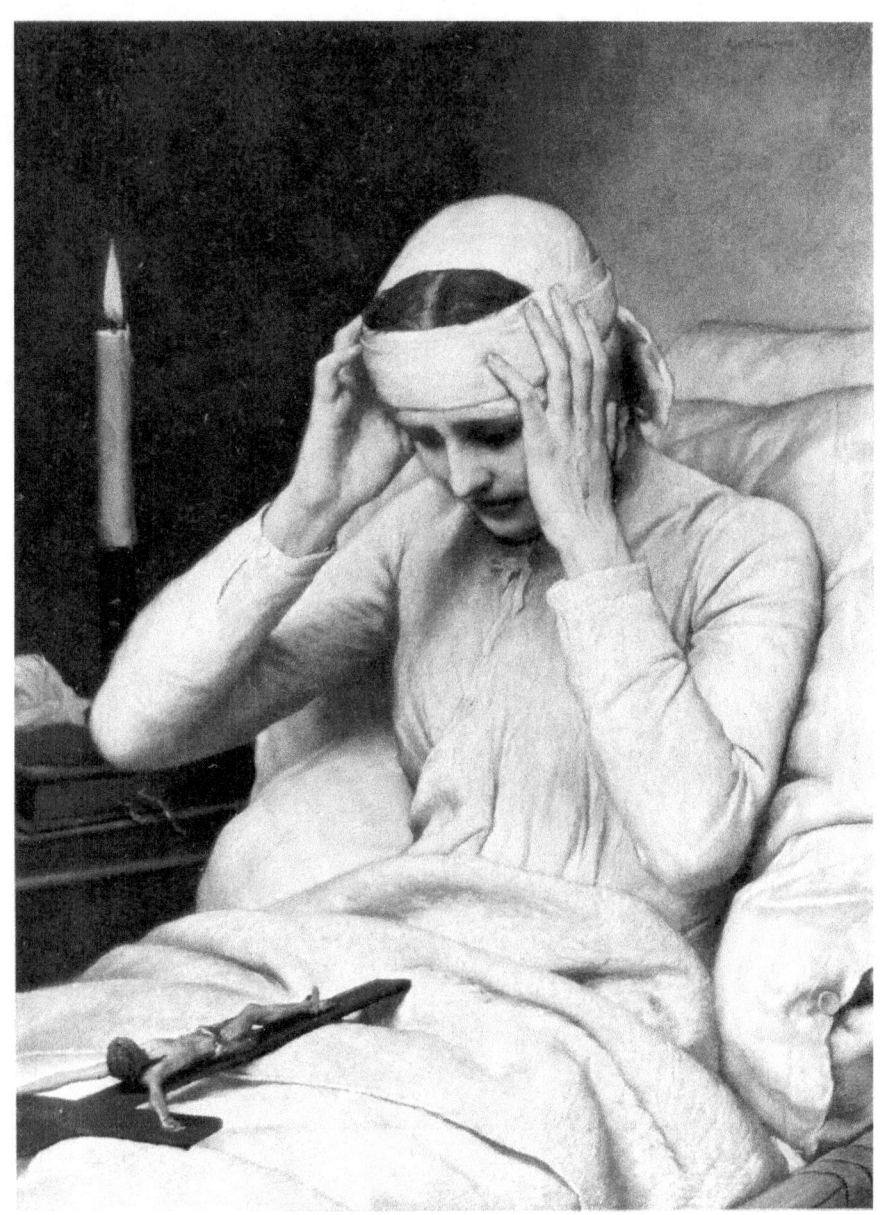

Anne Catherine Emmerich
Gabriel von Max (1840–1915), 1885

GENERAL INTRODUCTION

ANNE CATHERINE EMMERICH was born on September 8, 1774, at Flamske, near Coesfeld, Germany. From early childhood she was blessed with the gift of spiritual sight and lived almost constantly in inner vision of scenes of the Old and New Testaments. As a child, her visions were mostly of pre-Christian events, but these grew less frequent with the passing years, and, by the time she had become, at twenty-nine, an Augustinian nun at the Order's convent in Dülmen, Germany, her visions had become concerned primarily with the life of Christ. Because of difficult political circumstances, her convent was disbanded on December 3, 1811, and one by one the nuns in residence were obliged to leave. Anne Catherine—already very ill—withdrew to a small room in a house in Dülmen.

Anne Catherine in her room, by Cl. Brentano

By November, 1812, her illness had grown so severe that she was permanently confined to bed. Shortly thereafter, on December 29, 1812, she received the stigmata, a manifesting of the wounds suffered by Christ on the Cross, and the highest outward sign of inner union with Christ. Unable to assimilate any form of nourishment, for the rest of her life she was sustained almost exclusively by water and the Eucharist.

As news spread that she bore the stigmata (which bled on Fridays), more and more people came to see her. For us, the most significant of these was the poet Clemens Brentano, who first visited her on the morning of Thursday September 24, 1818. He was so impressed by the radiance of her being that he decided to move nearby in order to record her visions. Anne Catherine had already had a presentiment that someone—whom she called "the pilgrim"—would one day come to preserve her revelations. The moment Clemens Brentano entered her room, she recognized him as this "pilgrim."

Brentano, a novelist and romantic poet then living in Berlin, was associated with leading members of the Romantic Movement in Germany. Earlier (1806–1808), his association with Achim von Arnim had resulted in their famous compilation of folk literature, *Des Knaben Wunderhorn* (*The Boy's Magic Horn*). He settled his affairs and moved from Berlin to Dülmen early in 1819. Thereafter, he visited Anne Catherine every morning, noting down briefly all that she related to him; then, after writing out a full report at home, he returned later the same day to read it back to her. She would then often expand upon certain points, or, if necessary, correct details.

On July 29, 1820, Anne Catherine began to communicate visions concerning the day-to-day life of Christ Jesus that she had witnessed each preceding day. These visions encompassed the better part of Christ's ministry, and she was able to describe in extraordinary detail the places Christ visited, his miracles and healings, his teaching activity in the synagogues and elsewhere, and the people around him. She not only named and described many of these people with astonishing concreteness, but spoke also of their families, their occupations, and other intimate, biographical details.†

Anne Catherine in her bed, by Cl. Brentano

Anne Catherine was called to relate the day-by-day details of the life and ministry of Christ Jesus, and Brentano was called to record all that she communicated of her visions. They worked together daily until her death on February 9, 1824, except for one period of six months, during which Brentano was away, and several shorter periods when, mainly due to illness, it was impossible for Anne Catherine to communicate her visions. Although

---

† As mentioned in *Dramatis Personae*, in 2009 Jozef De Raedemaeker of Belgium completed and published in 38 volumes his monumental edition of Brentano's complete notes of the visions of Anne Catherine at which he was present. The third volume of the current work will include extensive material, especially on the holy men and women mentioned therein, drawn from this invaluable resource.

she had already recounted various details—the life of the Virgin Mary and the visit of the three kings, among other things, during 1819 and the early part of 1820—the real start of the revelation bestowed on Anne Catherine was July 29, 1820, when she began describing the ministry of Christ Jesus *day by day*. This revelation continued until her death some three and one-half years later—although only three years were actually recorded because of Clemens Brentano's six month absence from Dülmen in 1823.

Brentano (and others) believed that the three years of Christ's ministry had been revealed almost in their entirety in the daily chronicle, extending from four months before the Baptism to the Ascension. As we shall see, however, the revelation was not complete.†

This introduction would not be complete without mentioning the contribution made to this edition by the French painter J. James Tissot, who was born in 1836 in the town of Nantes. Tissot was influenced by the styles of painting then in vogue and formed friendships especially with the Impressionists Edgar Degas and Edouard Manet. An early preoccupation with medieval themes gave way during the 1860s to a penchant for depictions of modern life. Political events in France then led Tissot to England, where he arrived nearly penniless in 1871, but soon rose to considerable fame. In 1876 he returned to France, where in 1885, as the result of a vision he claimed to have had, Tissot returned to the Catholic faith. He then formed the intention in 1886 of illustrating the bible, to some extent under the influence of his reading of the visions of Anne Catherine, which had by then been translated into French and were quite popular. To this end, Tissot made three trips to Palestine to gather material, and by 1894 was mounting exhibitions. He himself collected his New Testament paintings into a three-volume work, including gospel extracts along with his own commentaries. In 1898 these paintings were acquired by the Brooklyn Museum of Art. As the current edition of the visions of Anne Catherine was nearing completion, Tissot's paintings came to the attention of the editor, who soon realized that many of them were inspired by Anne Catherine's descriptions, sometimes down to the least detail,‡ and so arrangements were made to include them, more than 350 in all, in this edition. These paintings are organized in inserts and cross-referenced with the texts to which they refer. Numerous of Tissot's sketches made in Palestine are included also.

ENCOUNTERING the visions of Anne Catherine Emmerich's work can raise the question: How is it possible that this woman, who never left the German region in which she was born, could describe in such detail the geography and topography of Palestine, and the customs and habits of people living there? To answer this, the researcher upon whose work the chronological aspects of this new edition is largely based—Dr. Robert Powell—undertook an exhaustive analysis of her work, gradually penetrating the historical reality underlying Christ's life. But his work was not done in isolation, for others had earlier laid some of the groundwork in various ways.

For example, the French priest, Abbé Julien Gouyet of Paris, after reading an account of Anne Catherine's visions concerning the death of the Virgin Mary near

Distant View of the House of Mary, by Cl. Brentano

Ephesus traveled there and searched the whole area. On October 18, 1881, guided by various particulars in her account, he discovered the ruins of a small stone building on a mountain (Bulbul Dag, "Mount Nightingale") overlooking the Aegean Sea, with a view across to the remains of the ancient city of Ephesus. Abbé Gouyet was convinced that this was the house described in Anne Catherine's visions as the dwelling place of the Virgin Mary during the last years of her life. He was at first ridiculed, but several years later the ruins were independently discovered again by two Lazarist missionaries who had undertaken a similar search on the basis of Anne Catherine's visions.†† They ascertained that the building had been a place of pilgrimage in earlier times for Christians descended from the church of Ephesus, the community referred to by St. John (Rev. 2:1–7). The building had been known in those days as *Panaya Kapulu*, the House of the Blessed Virgin, and

---

† As long as the belief persisted—as it has until now—that the account as recorded was more or less complete, it was not possible to establish a full chronology of Jesus Christ's life. Only now, with the discovery of a gap in the visionary account, are we in a position to establish the actual chronology of Christ's ministry, insofar as we can take Anne Catherine's indications to be accurate as to place and time (see Appendix I: *Chronology of the Life of Jesus Christ*).

‡ During the course of integrating Tissot's paintings into the text, the editor learned of an M.A. thesis taking as its subject precisely the connection between Tissot's paintings and the descriptions of Anne Catherine. This thesis, by Lori Stewart, is entitled *The Holy Alliance: The Visions of Anne Katherine Emmerich and the Art of J. James Tissot*.

†† This story is told in *Our Lady of Ephesus*, by Fr. Bernard F. Deutsch (Milwaukee: Bruce Publishing Co., 1965).

General Introduction

Distant View from House of Mary

was revered as the place where she had died. Traditionally, the date of her death, August 15, was the very day of the annual pilgrimage to Panaya Kapulu.

Following this discovery, a commission from the nearby

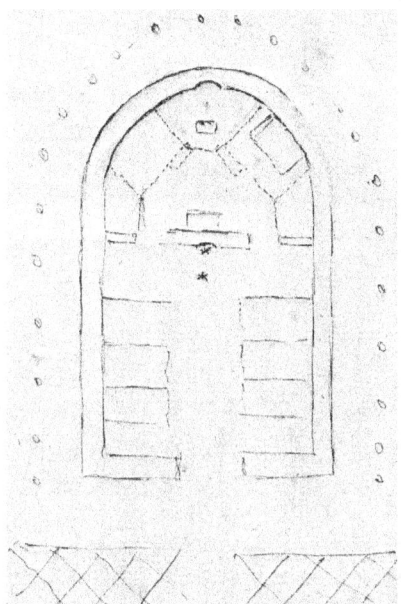
Floor Plan of House of Mary, by Cl. Brentano

Turkish city of Izmir determined that the foundation of the original house dated back to the first century AD. It noted that the structure of the house conformed exactly to Anne Catherine's detailed description. The house has since been restored and is now a place of pilgrimage. At a ceremony to commemorate the hundredth anniversary of its restoration, Archbishop Bernardini made this statement: "Dear brothers and sisters, all our bishops agree that the Virgin Mary died here. September 28 and May 12 are very significant holy days for us, for on September 28, 1890, it was confirmed that the Blessed Virgin lived and died here, and on May 12, 1891, the first religious ceremony was held here in her honor. This house is the only known surviving building in which the Blessed Virgin lived."

This remarkable example demonstrates the authenticity of Anne Catherine's visions. That her visions provide spiritual nourishment had long been the experience of many spiritual seekers, but the discovery of Panaya Kapulu con-

House of Mary before Restoration

firmed that her visions were objectively authentic and accessible (at least in part) to corroboration along conventional lines of research.†

The House of Mary at Ephesus

THE LIFE of Jesus Christ has been the subject of untold thousands of books, each with its own perspective and intent; but most of these have ignored the conditions that actual knowledge of the spiritual reality of Christ's life inevitably imposes upon a sincere researcher in this field. As is clear from the foregoing, one of those who has made

---

† This latter point will be more fully demonstrated in Appendix I, which with the help of Anne Catherine's account proposes to establish an accurate historical dating of the life of Christ.

real and significant contributions to our understanding of the spiritual conditions surrounding this historical reality is she whose visions you now hold in your hand—Anne Catherine Emmerich—to whom it was given to be so attuned to the life of Christ as a mystical reality that her comprehensive visions encompassed even minute details of time and place—testable "coordinates," in fact. This edition of the visions of Anne Catherine incorporates in many places a day-by-day chronology, and, during the days of the Passion, a nearly hour-by-hour itinerary. It also contains 40 detailed maps depicting Jesus Christ's journeys and local movements.† This degree of precision was made possible by the many temporal details, as well as the many geographical descriptions and references, contained in the visions—such as those already mentioned in connection with the discovery of the House of the Blessed Virgin. Many chronologies of the life of Jesus Christ have been put forward, but the dates given in the current work differ from all previous efforts in that they derive from the application of modern chronological and astro-chronological science to the whole of Anne Catherine's visions—which constitute a vast body of data that is internally consistent as to time and place to an extraordinary degree. Granted, the accuracy of this dating hinges upon the accuracy of Anne Catherine's visions, but close study proves these visions to be so reliable and so specific that, taking the generally agreed upon time period of Jesus's life, results of an extraordinary degree of reliability can be determined.

Naturally, the overriding value of the visions lies in the additional insight they offer into the life of Jesus Christ, so that for some the day-by day breakdown and the maps may function as no more than a convenient framework for study and meditation. Those primarily concerned with the visions as inspirational reading need not trouble themselves about the specific dates, although they may, as just mentioned, nevertheless find that the day-by-day chronology is a useful way to maintain their orientation as they make their way gradually through this lengthy work. But some will wish to assess for themselves the method by which specific dates and geographical movements have been thought reliable enough to include here. Such readers will find told in the following *Chronology* the dramatic story (though necessarily abbreviated) of what we believe to be the determination—at least within the world of Anne Catherine's visions—of a precise chronology of the life of Christ. This subject would of course require a separate work to expound at full length.

IN VIEW of the vast compass of Anne Catherine's visions, the present text is organized in such a manner that the reader can move through it in several ways. The primary one, of course, is to read through the text in its entirety. Since the story during the years of the ministry—from the baptism in the Jordan up to the events of the Passion—is divided in most cases into a day-by-day itinerary, the breaks in the text between consecutive days provide useful points to leave off, or recommence, reading. In addition, since the length of the account for any given day can vary considerably (and in some cases extend for many pages), in most cases an italicized summary of the day's events is provided at the outset. These summaries often include additional material, including gospel references. One could, then, read from summary to summary as the days unfold as a means to gain an overview, or as a way to return to refresh one's memory of the story after a full reading. Finally, opposite the paintings by Tissot, which are organized chronologically in extended sets, will be found passages from the visions relevant to the painting in question, along with gospel references, and in most instances also descriptive material Tissot himself provided, illuminating various aspects of his depictions. The shortest route through the visions, then, would be a sequential viewing of the paintings, along with a reading of the texts associated with them. Even though there are over 350 such paintings, it of course remains true that many scenes in the visions are not illustrated, especially those scenes (and there are many) where there is no gospel parallel, so that this pathway through the visions, while offering a visual complement to many of the essential and best-known events, will be the least complete. Nonetheless, it has its fascination. In the end, it is the editor's hope that readers will enjoy and benefit from all these ways to deepen into the text, and thereby into the spiritual content conveyed.

---

† Due recognition must be given here to Fr. Helmut Fahsel for his monumental work *Der Wandel Jesu in der Welt* (Basel: Ilionverlag, 1942), in which he made a first attempt at a day-by-day account of Christ's ministry (as revealed by Anne Catherine) back in time to the years AD 31–34. Despite a fallacy in Fahsel's transposition of dates, we take this opportunity to express grateful acknowledgment and deep indebtedness to him for arranging Anne Catherine's visions of the ministry according to weekdays and calendar dates. In his work, Fahsel also reckoned the duration of Jesus's travels from town to town. His chronicle proved an indispensable resource for the chronological research into Christ's ministry presented in this edition of the visions. Fahsel also gathered together all Anne Catherine's geographical and topological descriptions, and found that they were mutually consistent and agreed precisely with the actual topography of Palestine. On the basis of these descriptions, Fahsel was then able to construct the detailed maps of Palestine at the time of Christ—including minute details of Jesus's journeys during his ministry—that have been adapted for the current work.

BIOGRAPHICAL GLIMPSES

by Helmut Fahsel
(Revised and Supplemented)

Looking into the Past

THE SUN'S light travels just over eight minutes before it reaches our eyes. The light we receive today from the Pleiades left that constellation over three hundred years ago. And if we turn our gaze to the great Andromeda galaxy, what we actually see is how it looked millions of years ago. We may thus look directly into the past, but unfortunately our eyes are too weak, and even our telescopes too limited, to gather sufficient beams of light to reveal fully all that has transpired over the centuries among the stars. Nonetheless, on the basis of what was just described, we may envision at least the possibility of attaining a direct view of the time when Jesus walked the Earth, if only we possessed an instrument that might gather together the scattered light, whether outward or inward, that went out from that time and place and bring it back to our vision.

That the All-Knowing and All-Powerful Creator has it in His Power to grant just such a capacity to a living human being would be difficult to deny. Indeed, He has made manifest this gift even now among our contemporaries,[†] though not to the degree and extent of a simple farmer's daughter from Dülmen in Westphalia who lived at the time of Napoleon Bonaparte.

The Child Visionary

The favorite recreation of this child's father, Bernhard Emmerich, as he sat by the fire after his day's toil, was to take his little daughter on his knee and listen to the marvelous things she would relate at his bidding.

"Anna Kathrinchen," he would say, "now here we are! tell me something!" Then she would describe to him the pictures shown her from the Old Testament, until the good man would exclaim, with tears in his eyes: "But, child, where did you get all that?" And the little one would answer earnestly: "Father, it is all true! That is the way I saw it!" Whereupon the astonished father would grow silent and forbear to question further.

Later on Anne Catherine would say: "When I was a little girl, I was continually absorbed in God. I performed all my duties without interfering with this absorption. I was always in contemplation. Working with my parents in the fields, or engaged in any other labor, I was as it were lifted above the Earth. Exterior things were like a confused and painful dream, but within all was heavenly light and truth.

"I thought everybody saw such inner things just as we see other things around us. I spoke of them freely to my parents, my brothers and sisters, and to my playmates, until I found that they laughed at me, asking if I had a book in which all these things were written. Then I began to be more reserved on such subjects, thinking I ought not to mention them, though why I could not tell.

*Birthplace of Anne Catherine, with
Stall, Barn, and her Small Sewing Room*

"I had these visions by day and by night, in the fields, and going about my different occupations. One day at school I spoke with childish simplicity of the Resurrection, using other terms than those taught us. I thought every one knew the same, never suspecting that I was saying anything strange. But the children wondered and told the master, who gravely warned me not to indulge such imaginations. I still had visions, but I kept silence concerning them.

"I never studied anything from the Gospels, or the Old Testament, for I have myself seen all in the course of my life. I see them every year; sometimes they are alike, or again they are attended by new scenes. I have often been present with the spectators, assisting as a contemporary, even taking part in the scene, though I did not always remain in the same place. I was often borne up into the air and beheld the scene from on high. Other things, mysteries especially, I saw interiorly. I had an inward consciousness of them, pictures apart from the outward scene. In all

---

† The reference is to Theresa Neumann (April 8, 1898–September 18, 1962), from Konnersreuth in Bavaria, Germany.

cases I saw through and through, one body never hid another, and yet there was no confusion.

"While a child, before I entered the convent, I had many visions principally from the Old Testament, but afterward they became rare and the life of our Lord took their place."

A Journey with my Angel

"The angel calls me and I follow him to various places; I often journey with him. He takes me among persons whom I know either well or slightly, and again among others who are entire strangers to me. We cross the sea as quickly as thought travels. I can see far, far away!

"It was he who took me to the Queen of France (*Marie Antoinette*) in her prison. When he comes to take me on a journey I generally see first a glimmering of light, then his luminous form appears suddenly before me like a flash from a lantern opened in the dark.

"As we journey along in the darkness, a faint light floats over our path. We pass over countries familiar to me to far distant regions. Sometimes our way lies over roads; sometimes across deserts, mountains, rivers, and seas. I travel always on foot, and I often have to climb rugged mountains. My knees ache from fatigue, and my bare feet burn.

"My guide is sometimes ahead of me, sometimes at my side. I never see his feet move. He is silent, he makes few motions, but sometimes he accompanies his short replies by a gesture of the hand or an inclination of the head.

"O how bright and transparent he is! He is grave but very kind. His hair is smooth, flowing, and shining. His head is uncovered, and his robe long and dazzlingly white like that of a priest. I address him freely, but I can never look him full in the face. I incline before him. He gives me all kinds of signs. I never ask him many questions; the satisfaction I take in being near him prevents me. He is always very brief in his words. I see him also in the moment of my waking."

Once Anne Catherine said: "When in contemplation, or in the discharge of some spiritual labor, I am often suddenly recalled into our present world of darkness by a sacred and irresistible power. I hear the word 'obedience,' as if uttered from afar. It is a sad sound to me at such moments, but obedience is the living root of the tree of contemplation."

St. Jane of Valois

"I was only a tiny child, and I used to mind the cows, a most troublesome and quite fatiguing duty. One day the thought occurred to me, as indeed it had often done before, to quit my home and the cows, and go serve God in some solitary place where no one would know me. I had a vision in which I went to Jerusalem, where I met a religious in whom I afterward recognized St. Jane of Valois.† She looked very grave. At her side was a lovely little boy about my own size. St. Jane did not hold him by the hand, and I knew from that that he was not her child. She asked me what was the matter with me, and when I told her, she comforted me, saying: 'Never mind! Look at this little boy! Would you like him for your companion?' I said: 'Yes!' Then she told me not to be discouraged, but to wait until the little boy would come for me, assuring me that I would be a religious, although it seemed quite unlikely then. She told me that I should certainly enter the cloister, for nothing is impossible to my affianced.

The Cow Barn

Then I returned to myself and drove the cows home. From that time I looked forward to the fulfilment of her promise. I had this vision at noon. Such things never disturbed me. I thought every one had them. I never knew any difference between them and real intercourse with creatures."

The Crown of Thorns is Received

"One day about noon, during the last year of my residence with the Soentgen family, about four years before I joined the convent, I was kneeling near the organ in the Jesuits' church at Coesfeld. Immersed in contemplation, I beheld the tabernacle door open and Jesus issue from it under the form of a radiant youth. In his left hand he held a garland, in his right a crown of thorns, which he graciously presented to my choice. I chose the crown of thorns. Then Jesus laid it lightly on my brow; and, putting up both hands, I pressed it firmly down. From that instant, I experienced inexpressible pains in my head. The

---

† Jane of Valois (1464–1505), daughter to Louis XI, king of France, and founder of the Sisters of the Annunciation.

apparition vanished, and I awoke from my rapture to hear the clicking of the sacristan's keys as he closed the church.... Next day my forehead and temples were very much inflamed, and I suffered fearful pain."†

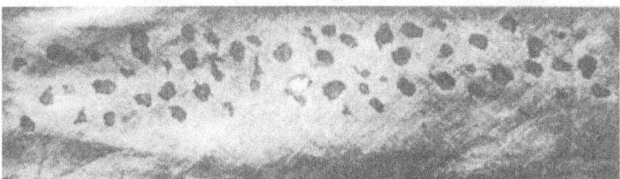
Flecks of Blood from the Wound of the Crown of Thorns on Anne Catherine's Headcloth

Ecstatic Raptures

Anne Catherine often had ecstasies in the convent, especially during the last four years of its existence. She said: "In my duties as sacristan I was often lifted up suddenly, and I stood on the highest points of the church, on the windows, the carving, and the cornices, cleaning and dusting where humanly speaking no one could go. I was not frightened when I felt myself thus raised and held up in the air, for I had always been accustomed to my angel's assistance. Sometimes when I awoke, I found myself sitting in a large closet in which were kept things belonging to the sacristy; sometimes I was in a corner near the altar where not a soul could see me, and I cannot understand how I squeezed into it without tearing my habit. But sometimes, on awaking, I found myself seated on the highest rafter of the roof. This generally happened when I had hidden myself to weep.

"When I lived in the convent, my hands were always hurting. When I held them in front of the sun, they were so thin that the rays of the sun went through them like arrows.

"I often found myself seized by a vision while working or when sick in bed, yet all the while still among the other nuns, hearing and seeing everything they said or did; or I was in church before the holy sacrament, even though I had not left my cell. How this could have happened, I cannot tell. The first time I became aware of such a thing, I thought it was a dream; I was about fifteen then. Later on, similar things would occur quite often. It also happened that one of the other nuns might see me in the kitchen or in the garden, but immediately afterward find me lying in my cell, deathly ill. These things made my presence quite strange to the other nuns, and they didn't know what to make of me.

"Very often when taking communion I see my Lord approach, and when I swallow the host he disappears and I feel his ineffably sweet presence. When he enters the person who receives communion, he rises up all through the soul, as when sugar dissolves. The more intense the desire, the more fully inward is he present."

Augustinian Convent in Dülmen

The Stigmatization

No precise knowledge would have been had on Anne Catherine's reception of the wounds if it were not for the visions relative to it which she had at various times during the last years of her life. On Oct. 4, 1820, the Feast of St. Francis of Assisi, she had the following vision:

"I saw the saint among some bushes on a wild mountain in which were scattered grottoes like little cells. Francis had opened the Gospel several times. Each time it chanced to be at the history of the Passion, and so he begged to feel his Lord's sufferings. He used to fast on this mountain, eating only a little bread and roots. He knelt, his bare knees on two sharp stones, and supported two others on his shoulders.

"It was after midnight and he was praying with arms extended, half kneeling, half sitting, his back resting against the side of the mountain. I saw his angel near him holding his hands, his countenance all on fire with love.

---

† A fuller account of this episode will be found further on in the *Autobiographical Vision*, with which this section concludes.

He was a slight man. He wore a brown mantle, open in front with a hood like those worn at the time by shepherds. A cord bound his waist.

"At the moment in which I saw him he was as if paralyzed. A bright light shot from heaven and descended upon him. In it was an angel with six wings, two above his head, two over his feet, and two with which he seemed to fly. In his right hand he held a cross, about half the usual size, on which was a living body glowing with light, the feet crossed, the five wounds resplendent as so many suns.

"From each wound proceeded three rays of rosy light converging to a point. They shot first from the hands toward the palms of the saint's hands; then from the wound in the right side toward the saint's right side (these rays were larger than the others); and lastly, from the feet toward the soles of the saint's feet. In his left hand the angel held a blood-red tulip in whose center was a golden heart, which I think he gave to the saint.

"When Francis returned from ecstasy, he could only with difficulty stand, and I saw him going back to his monastery suffering cruelly and supported by his angel-guardian. He hid his wounds as well as he could. There were large crusts of brownish blood on the back of his hands, for they did not bleed regularly every Friday; but his side often bled so profusely that the blood flowed down on the ground. I saw him praying, the blood streaming down his arms.

"I saw many other incidents of his life. Once, even before he knew him, the pope beheld Francis in vision supporting the Lateran on his shoulders when it was ready to fall.

"Then I had a vision of myself receiving the wounds. I never knew before how it was. Three days before the new year, and about three o'clock in the afternoon, I was lying alone in the little room I used to have at the widow Roters',† my arms extended. I was contemplating the Passion of Jesus Christ and asking to be allowed to feel his pains.

"I said five Our Fathers in honor of the five wounds. I experienced great sweetness, with an intense desire that my prayer might be granted, when suddenly I beheld descending obliquely upon me a great light. It was a crucified body, living and transparent, with extended arms but no cross. The wounds more resplendent than the body, like five circles of brilliant light. I was rapt out of myself, and I yearned with mingled pain and sweetness to share my savior's sufferings.

"As my desire grew still more vehement at the sight of his wounds, it shot, so to speak, from my breast, hands,

† On the Münster Road in Dülmen, where she had lived since the closure of the convent.

feet, and side toward them. At the same moment, triple rays of red light, converging to a point, darted first from the hands, then from the side and feet of the image upon my hands, side, and feet. I lay for a time unconscious, until Mrs. Roters' little girl lowered my hands. She told the family that I had cut them and that they were bleeding, but I implored them to say nothing about it.

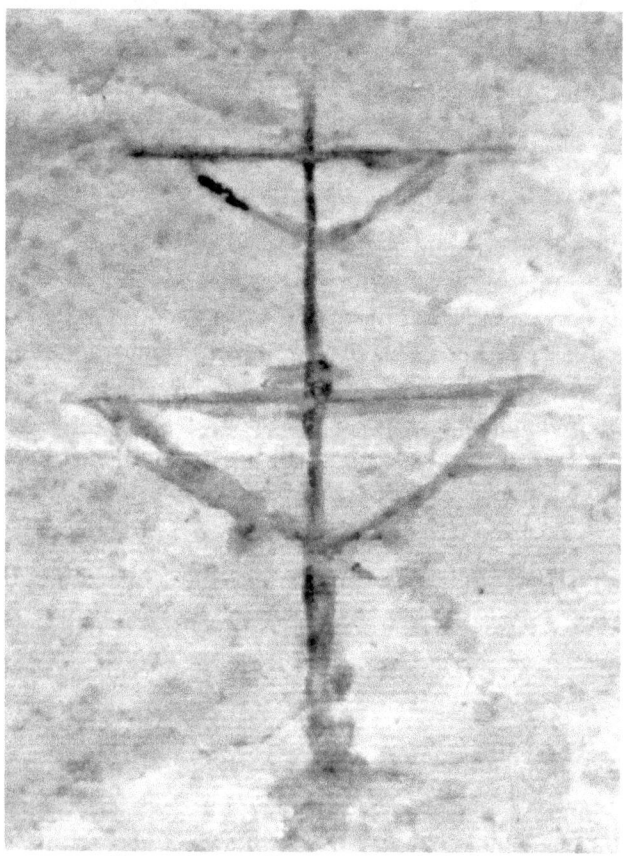

Impression on Blotting Paper of Bleeding Double Cross on Anne Catherine's Breast

"I had had the double cross [*Gabelkreuz*] on my breast for some time, since the Feast of St. Augustine when, as I was praying on my knees, my arms extended, my Lord signed me with it. After I received these wounds, I felt a great change in my whole person; my blood circulated toward these points with a painful twitching sensation. St. Francis appeared to me that night, consoled me, and spoke of the violence of interior pains."

Official Investigation

Three months later the stigmatist Anne Catherine, now thirty-eight years of age, was subjected by religious authorities to an investigation of her condition. After a full three months' of careful scrutiny, the three participating physicians declared that they could ascertain no natural cause for the wounds, nor for the fact that they appeared only at specific times.

When six years later Anne Catherine was transferred to a new residence, there followed a further detailed study, this time conducted by lay authorities over a period of twenty-two days. The results so plainly excluded the possibility that the wounds could be explained either by natural causes or by fraud, that even the most dubious and provoked among those present could offer no plausible rebuttal.

The Phenomenon of Requiring No Food

At the time the stigmata appeared, Anne Catherine underwent a further change whereby she no longer had need of any nourishment—a condition that lasted for the remaining eleven years of her life. Throughout these eleven years she was under the close personal care of Dr. Franz Wilhelm Wesener, who recorded his observations in considerable detail in a medical journal throughout the period

Dr. Franz Wilhelm Wesener (1782–1832)

extending from March 23, 1813 to November 3, 1819. He also provided a full report of the official investigation of Anne Catherine's wounds, as well as a "necessarily brief account of the life of the stigmatic Augustinian nun." All three of these texts were published in 1925 by the St. Rita Verlag, located in Würzburg. It is in the medical journal that Dr. Wesener attests to the fact that Anne Catherine took no nourishment, as well as to the authenticity of her visionary gift, and to the many visits paid her daily, or sometimes weekly, by various people.

Other Freely Granted Graces

Among the other gifts Anne Catherine received, as witnessed by frequent visitors, let us mention the gift of seeing into the hearts and minds of strangers (without any possibility of natural communication) and the gift of distinguishing consecrated persons from unconsecrated ones. Furthermore, she started to develop and retained the gift of so-called mystical translocation to a very exceptional degree. She was often moved by an inner impulse to offer her sufferings for sick people or for people living in sin. And her prayers were heard. She manifested transient illnesses, similar to and connected in remarkable ways to the condition of particular persons, who then experienced either a sudden improvement or a sudden conversion. This gift had already manifested itself when she was young, and it could be applied not only to living persons but also to the dead, to whom she was able to transmit relief in the afterlife.

The Purpose of the Visions

There was probably no one who, having become personally acquainted with Anne Catherine, was not astounded, deeply touched, and convinced by her saintly change of life. Quite apart from her love of God, expressed in words as well as in deeply infused contemplation and ecstasy, her love for others grew in proportion to the persecutions and calumnies of some enemies of the supernatural; so also did her humility grow in proportion to the wide notoriety occasioned by her stigmatization. No surprise, then, that she often prayed God that her special visionary gift might be taken from her.

"Yesterday [December 31, 1821] I begged almighty God to withdraw my visions, that I may not be forced to communicate them, but I was not heard. As usual, I was told to relate all that I could recall, even if I should be laughed at, or even if I do not see any use in it. I was again told that no one has ever seen all that I have seen or in the same way, but that this is not my affair, it is the Church's. So much being allowed to go to waste will entail great accountability and do much harm. They who deprive me of leisure, and the clergy who have no faith and who find no one to take down my visions, will have to render a severe account of their negligence. I saw, too, how the demon raises obstacles."

One day Anne Catherine, overwhelmed by suffering, entreated our Lord to withdraw those visions in which she beheld so much that was incomprehensible to her. But she received the following reply: "I give you visions not for yourself, but that you may collect and communicate them. The present is not the time for outward miracles; therefore, I give you visions. I have done the same at all times to show that I am with my Church to the consummation of ages. But visions alone secure not any one's salvation. You must practice charity, patience, and the other virtues."

Sketch of Clemens Brentano Around Age 40

"Long ago I was ordered to tell all, even if I should be looked upon as a fool. But no one wanted to listen to me, and the holiest things that I had seen and heard were so misunderstood and derided that through timidity I shut all up in my own heart, though not without pain. Then I used to see in the distance the figure of a stranger who was to come to write by me. I have found him, I recognize him in the Pilgrim.

"The many wonderful communications from the Old and the New Testament and the innumerable pictures from the lives of the saints have been given me, through God's mercy, not for my instruction alone—for there is much that I cannot understand—but that I may communicate them, that they may revive what is now forgotten. This duty has again been continually imposed upon me. I have explained this fact as well as I could, but no one will take the trouble even to listen to me, and so I must keep it to myself and forget much of it. I hope God will send me what is necessary."

The Arrival of Clemens Brentano

Anne Catherine's hope was to be fulfilled in her twenty-fourth year, when the forty-year-old Clemens Brentano, already a famous writer, came for the first time to see her in Dülmen. Brentano had become aware of Anne Catherine already five years previously through his friend the young Count Stolberg, and then also by his own brother Christian Brentano, who had himself already traveled to Dülmen.

Brentano records in his journal for Thursday, Sept. 24, 1818, "I arrived in Dülmen about ten o'clock in the morning, and Dr. Wesener announced my approaching visit to Anne Catherine, which she warmly approved. We had to pass through a barn and some old store-rooms before reaching the stone steps leading to her room. Her sister answered our knock at the door, and we entered the little kitchen back of which is her small apartment. She saluted me graciously, remarking that she would recognize me from my resemblance to my brother.

Sketch of Christian Brentano Around Age 34

"Her countenance wears the imprint of purity and innocence. It charmed me, as did also the vivacity of her manner, in which I could detect no trace of effort or excitement. She does not sermonize, there is none of that mawkish sweetness about her that can be so disgusting. She speaks simply and to the point, but her words are full of depth, charity, and life. She put me at my ease at once. I understood everything, I felt everything.

View into Anne Catherine's Sleeping and Sewing Rooms

"After the passage of only a few weeks, Anne Catherine said: 'I am amazed at myself, speaking to you with so much confidence, communicating so much that I cannot disclose to others. From the first glance, you were no stranger to me; indeed, I knew you before seeing you. In visions of my future, I often saw a man of very dark complexion sitting by me writing, and when you first entered the room I said to myself, Ah! there he is!'"

At that time Clemens Brentano wrote in his journal, "I shall try to note down what I learn from the invalid. I hope to become her biographer."

Brentano's Conversion

But notwithstanding all his observations, conversations, experiences, and notes, it was not to be that Brentano would undertake such a biographical task as he envisioned until—through the effect of all he came to see and undergo through Anne Catherine's gifts of grace, and also through her discussions on religion—he had first passed through his own personal conversion.

"The marvels that surround me, the childlike innocence, the peace, patience, and wonderful intuition of spiritual things I behold in this poor, illiterate peasant-girl, by whom a new world has been opened up to me, make me feel keenly the misery of my own life of sin and trouble, as well as the folly of the generality of mankind. I see in another light the value of perishable goods, and I shed tears of bitter repentance over my soul's lost beauty and innocence!

"I feel again that the Church is for her something that I, in my blindness, cannot yet comprehend; and I ponder over all that I have here received, upon all that I have learned for the first time. I compare with it my past disorderly life, and a new longing for conversion is aroused in my soul.

"The kindness and confidence shown me by this privileged creature encourage me, do me the greatest good, for she is so truly, so sincerely Christian. None ever knew as she the misery of my soul, the enormity of my sins. I myself know them not as they really are, but she knows them, she weighs and measures with a clear-sightedness unknown to me. She consoles and helps me.

"Now I understand the Church. I see that she is infinitely more than an assemblage of individuals animated by the same sentiments. Yes, she is the body of Jesus Christ who, as her head, is essentially united to her, and who maintains with her intimate and constant relations. And now, too, do I see what an immense treasure of gifts and graces the Church has received from God who communicates Himself to men only in and by her."

Toward the end of this same year, Dr. Wesener wrote in his medical journal: "Mr. Clemens Brentano has embarked on a study of the inner life of the invalid. The results of his work flow most readily from his pen, and he will communicate the essentials of his findings to me."

Anne Catherine's Living Room, Where She Died

Brentano's Extended Residence in Dülmen

In January of the following year (1819) Brentano traveled back to Berlin to set his affairs in order, with the intention of returning almost immediately to Dülmen, to set up a residence there. In the meanwhile, however, some of those closest to Anne Catherine had conceived no little opposition to Brentano's continuing presence, no doubt owing to the sort of jealousy and love of power that so often affects those who form a circle around a mystic.

Cl. A. von Droste-Vischering (1773–1845)

However, when in the new year Vicar-General Clemens August von Droste-Vischering returned to Dülmen, Anne Catherine revealed to him the instruction she had so often received from God to communicate her visions to Brentano, together with the request that the Vicar-General, as her religious superior, should render this decision. To this request the good man responded "Brentano must not be kept from her."

Shortly after Brentano's return, Anne Catherine sent her father confessor Limberg (who until now had been both indifferent to her visions and opposed to Brentano's continued presence) to Münster to her spiritual director, the famous pedagogue and now seminary dean Bernhard Overberg, to whom she had for years entrusted deep insight into her mystical visions. Anne Catherine had charged Limberg to set both his and her conscience clearly at rest by asking Dean Overberg for his opinion regarding Brentano and his wish to record her visions. The Dean stated that in his view it was according to God's desire that Brentano remain by Anne Catherine and record her visions. And upon his return to Dülmen in June of that year, Dean Overberg reaffirmed his position on the matter.

The Vision of the Garden

Anne Catherine related a vision in which, under the appearance of a garden, she had seen many things of Brentano's past life, his present work, and its fulfillment after her own death.

"I saw," she said, "the Pilgrim far away, sad and lonely in his room. He could interest himself in nothing, all was distasteful to him. I wanted to fly to him, to help him, but I could not. Then I saw a garden, a large garden divided into two parts by a hedge over which some people were looking, but who were unable to cross it. My guide took me where the vegetation was rich, beautiful, luxuriant, but all overrun with weeds. I saw beans and peas, and there were blossoms and flowers in abundance, but no fruit. Many people were walking about apparently well pleased with themselves.

"My guide said to me as we walked around: 'See, what it means: beautiful flowers of rhetoric, brilliant but sterile; abundant, but producing no harvest; plentiful, but yielding nothing!' 'Ah!' I exclaimed, 'must all the labor be lost?' 'No,' was the answer, 'nothing will be lost! It will all be turned under to make manure,' at which I felt glad and yet sorry too.

"When I came again, the garden was all ploughed up and the Pilgrim was setting out plants in beds. It was a pleasing sight. At last he left the garden, and some people entered whom I knew only by sight, I knew not their names. They fell upon me in a rage and abused me terribly, inveighing against my communications to the Pilgrim, complaining that a new sect would arise from it, and

Bernhard Overberg (1754–1826)

asking what they were to think of me! I took it all in silence. Then they broke out against the Pilgrim who, I thought, was within hearing. Then I went and sat down on a stone in a neighboring grove.

"And now a priest came along, an active, energetic man. He expressed surprise at my not defending myself; but after a little reflection, he said: 'This person endures bad treatment very coolly, and yet he is both intelligent and sensitive! The Pilgrim's conduct is probably very different from what we imagine; the confessor, too, is a good man who would not permit anything wrong.' As the unknown ecclesiastic continued thus speaking in favor of the Pilgrim, the brawlers began to slink away and I noticed how diligently the Pilgrim had worked and how much the plants had grown and flourished.

"My guide said: 'Make good use of this heavenly instruction. You shall in truth endure these injuries and outrages. Be prepared! For awhile you shall live at peace with the Pilgrim; but lose not time, squander not the graces given you, for your end will soon come. What the Pilgrim gathers he will bear far away, for here there is no desire to have it. But it will produce fruit where he goes, and that same fruit will one day return and make itself felt even here.'"

The Providential Nature of the Writings

"Clemens Brentano made it his habit," so wrote the well-known author Luise Hensel† in her recollections of Anne Catherine Emmerich, "to come to her side each morning between the hours of nine and ten o'clock and note down what she would relate to him. I was often present with them, engaged in sewing. Upon arriving home, Brentano would during the course of the day expand on his notes of what Anne Catherine had said, returning in evening to read out to her all he had written, so that she could correct or amend his words as she felt necessary.

Drawing of Anne Catherine Made Under Direction of Luise Hensel

"I would like to take this opportunity also to testify that this holy woman Anne Catherine once said to me that she had received from God the command to convey her visions to Clemens Brentano and that he record them in writing."

Luise Hensel (1798–1876)

† Luise Hensel, the sister of Wilhelm Hensel and the sister-in-law of the composer Fanny Mendelssohn was born on March 30, 1798 in Prussia. After the death of her father in 1809, she moved to Berlin with her mother. Around this time, Clemens Brentano and the composer Ludwig Berger shared an unrequited love for Luise. However, she still influenced the romantic style of Brentano quite significantly; Brentano wrote the following to his brother in 1817: "These songs (referring to 20 songs sent him by Hensel) at first broke my heart, causing me to burst into tears, their truth and simplicity striking me as the holiest that man could produce." Another author, Wilhelm Müller, was also unlucky in love with Hensel. The story of this unfulfilled love is recorded in two works composed by Franz Schubert, the song cycle *Die schöne Müllerin* ("The pretty mill-girl") and *Winterreise* ("Winter Journey"). The love of another man, casual friend Ludwig von Gerlach, who would later become a teacher of Otto von Bismarck, led to Luise enjoying a high political position, but this conflicted with her religious feelings, and in an emotional crisis, she joined the Catholic Church. These circumstances weighed heavily on her, and in 1819 she left Berlin for Münster, where, under the influence of the religious teacher Bernhard Overberg, her convictions deepened. In 1821, she took a job as a teacher for the widow of the poet Count Friedrich Leopold zu Stolberg in the town of Sondermühlen, where she stayed until 1823. During these years she was a regular visitor at the bedside of Anne Catherine, often in the company of Brentano. Luise lived a quiet life until the year 1827. From then on, she led a life of pilgrimage, a life of self-imposed poverty and privation. This began with her teaching at a church in Aachen, where she taught for six years, teaching, among others, the eventual founder of the "Sisters of the Poor Children of Jesus," Clara Fey. Her religious convictions were once again tested by love, this time in the form of a marriage proposal from a doctor, Clemens August Alertz, who would later become the personal physician to Pope Pius IX. She spent the rest of her life conducting religious teachings, and writing religious works, moving several times. She died in Paderborn on December 18, 1876, at the age of 78.

Biographical Glimpses

On December 30, 1819, while in a visionary state, Anne Catherine said something quite remarkable. Lying in ecstasy, quite still and stiff in her dark room, Brentano held before her a page from his notes, whereupon she suddenly pronounced "these pages are written in a shining script; they were written by the man whom I saw sitting at his writing yesterday night. This man writes not of himself only, but with grace from God. No other man than he could do this; it is as though he saw all himself."

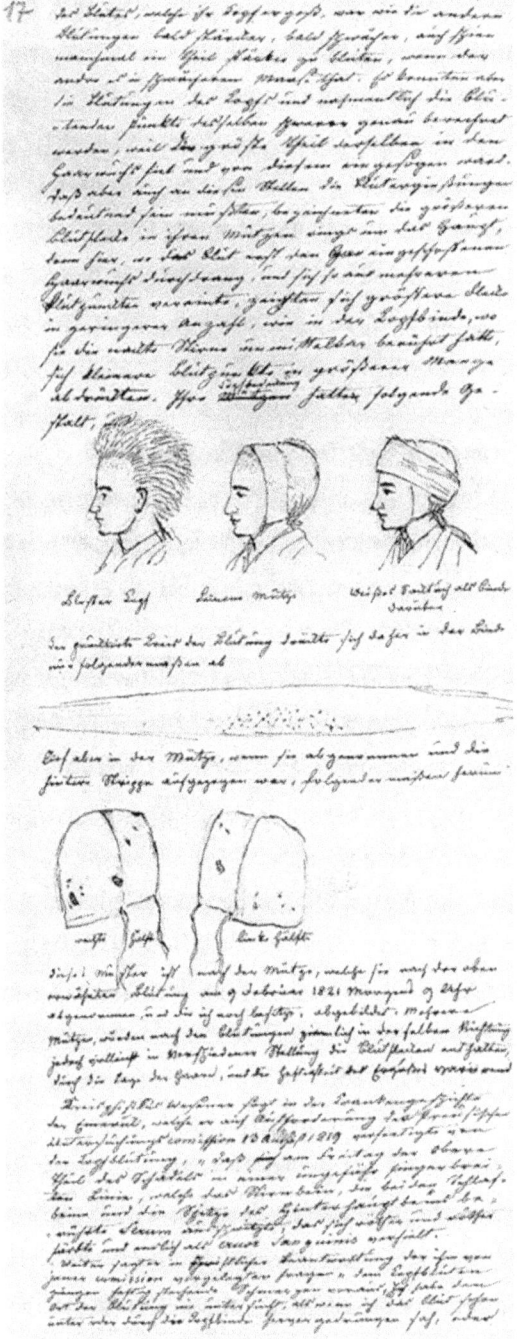

Page from Brentano's Notebooks Showing Anne Catherine's Head and Headbands

The Travels of Jesus

On March 11, 1820 Anne Catherine said, "My time is at an end; I live now only because there is something I must yet do, and the time to accomplish this has been granted me. And on July 29 of that same year she began to relate to Brentano—sometimes right in the moment, and sometimes recalling visions received only hours previously—events from the travels of Jesus in the world.

Regarding these visions, Brentano wrote, "Day by day she beheld and reported the events of the years of Jesus's ministry right up to his Ascension. She described all in great detail, often giving exact names for places, people, festivals, specific customs of the time, teachings, and miracles in a manner exceeding all expectation.

"Now, Anne Catherine had read neither the Old Testament nor the New, and so on occasions when she was exhausted and would have preferred to be spared the need to keep speaking—and she would say to me 'Just read about it in the bible'—she was astonished that something she had been relating was not to be found in the bible, and would add 'but one hears it said over and over again that one need read only the bible, for all is to be found therein.'"

Autobiographical Vision

On the evening of December 15, as Anne Catherine lay in ecstasy, the Pilgrim placed on her breast a little parcel, containing a relic, previously designated by her as belonging to St. Ludgarde. She was instantly aware of his action and, without awaking from ecstasy, she exclaimed; "Ah! what a good shepherd! He has come over the broad waters! His body lies in the old church in my country.... But there is another person! I have not seen her for a long time. Strange! There is something in it I cannot understand! She has the stigmata, she is an Augustinian! She is clothed as I used to be and as I still am, partly as a little nun. It is singular! She must be still alive, she is hidden in some corner. I cannot understand it! How much she has suffered! I can take her for a model, for all my sufferings are nothing to hers! And, strange to say, she is outwardly joyous! No one knows what she endures. It would seem almost as if she knew it not herself!

"I see by her so many poor people and children. I think I know them. Someone must have hidden this person from me. My friends and acquaintances must know her. Ah! how her heart is wounded! It is encircled by a crown of thorns full of sharp points. She has very curious surroundings, and how many people are secretly spying and calumniating her! How bright and joyous she is under it! She bounds along like a deer! She is truly an example for me. Now I see clearly how miserable I am!"

After these words, the Pilgrim retired, leaving the relic in the parcel! Next morning, she related the following: "I had last night a most wonderful vision which I cannot understand. There must be a person hidden here who is frequently placed in circumstances similar to mine. She had the stigmata too, but she has now lost them. I watched her all night in her pains. She must have lived in our convent, for I saw around her all the nuns excepting myself. No one ever guessed the terrible secret suffering that oppressed her, as she was always so cheerful. I cannot imagine what it all means. I have never had such graces or such sufferings, and I could not help feeling very much ashamed at my own cowardice. Perhaps, before my time, such a person lived in our convent; but the circumstances are so like unto my own that it puzzles me. I cannot understand it, it is all very strange!"

The Pilgrim here remarked; "Perhaps, it was a picture of yourself, of how you would have supported your sufferings, were you perfect; and you may also have seen graces received of which you may have been unconscious or forgetful."

She thought that this might possibly be the case and, at the Pilgrim's request, she continued the recital of this vision of herself:

"I saw a religious, who had been very ill even before her entrance, forced to leave her convent. From the very beginning of her novitiate, she was a prey to indescribable secret sufferings. Once I saw her heart surrounded by roses that changed suddenly to thorns and tore it cruelly, while sharp points and darts entered her breast.

"People far and near suspected her, calumniated her in the most odious manner. All their thoughts against her, though not passing into deeds, flew toward her like steel-pointed arrows and wounded her on all sides. Plots hatched afar entered her flesh like sharp darts, and once I saw her heart literally cut to pieces. Still was she cheerful, kind toward all, as if unconscious of her wrongs.

"My compassion for her was so great that I felt her pains in my own breast. Her soul was perfectly transparent, and when fresh sufferings assailed her, I saw in her fiery red rays and wounds, especially in her breast and heart. Around her head was a crown of thorns of three different kinds of branches; one of small white flowers with yellow stamens; the second with flowers like the first, but longer leaves; the third of roses and buds. She often pressed it down on her head, and then the thorns penetrated more deeply.

"I saw her at work in the convent, going here and there, the birds alighting familiarly upon her shoulders. Sometimes she stood perfectly rigid or lay prostrate on the ground, when a man often came and bore her to her cell. I could never see into her cell; he seemed to put her in through the wall. A protecting spirit was ever by her, while the devil constantly prowled around, stirred up minds against her, raised loud noises in her room, and even assaulted her person; but she seemed to be always abstracted, her mind elsewhere.

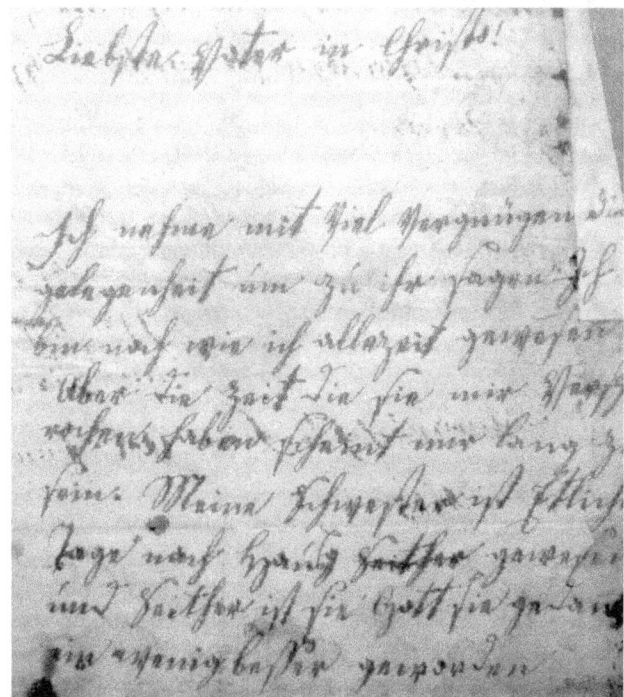

Page from Letter in Anne Catherine's Hand

"I saw her sometimes in the church, mounting in the most extraordinary manner upon the altar, clambering up the walls and windows where she had any cleaning to do. She was raised and upheld by spirits in places where another could not possibly stand. On several occasions I saw her in two places at once: in the church before the blessed sacrament, and at the same time either upstairs in her cell, in the kitchen, or elsewhere—and once I saw evil spirits maltreating her most cruelly.

"She used to be surrounded by the saints, and sometimes she held the infant Jesus in her arms for hours together. When with her sister-religious, he was always at her side. Once I saw her at table, and weapons of all kinds being hurled at her; but she was shielded by the blessed, who crowded around her. I saw her at another time making hosts, although quite ill, and a blessed spirit aiding her. Once, when she lay sick and neglected, I saw two of the deceased religious making up her bed and carrying her here and there. They lifted her from her bed and placed her in the middle of the room, where she lay on her back without support in the air. When someone entered the room unexpectedly she fell heavily to the floor.

"I saw her very often reduced to extremity by the use of certain remedies, and then I saw the apparitions with which she was favored: a beautiful woman all resplendent with light, or a youth like my celestial Lord, who brought her remedies in little phials, or herbs, or morsels of something which they put on a little shelf at the head of her bed.

"Once, as she knelt by her table in ecstasy, she received from an apparition a little statue of Mary; and at another time, her heavenly Lord placed on her finger a ring containing a precious stone on which was carved a figure of his blessed Mother. After some time he returned and took it away from her.

"I often saw blessed spirits laying pictures and all sorts of things on her breast when she was ill, and taking them away when she got better; and I often beheld her miraculously protected from imminent and serious danger. One day she stood by the trap-door of the drying-loft, helping to raise a basket of wet linen, while another sister worked the rope below. When the basket had almost reached the top, she made an effort to draw it toward her with one hand, the other grasping the rope. Just then the devil raised a frightful din in the courtyard. The sister below turned her head and slackened her hold on the rope, to the imminent peril of the one above, who was nearly precipitated, basket and all, upon her companion. Had not God protected her and allowed someone to seize the rope, she would certainly have been killed; as it was, she dislocated her hip, from which accident she afterward endured terrible tortures.

"I saw her wonderfully protected by her angel on many other occasions and under circumstances perilous to both soul and body, and I beheld her driven almost to despair by her persecutors. Once, when sick unto death, she was borne away from her convent by two persons who would never have succeeded in preserving her life during the short journey, had not some more powerful beings come to their aid.

"I saw her, when out of her convent, dressed as I was at that time, a prey to secret sufferings, but favored by the same graces as before. She was often without assistance and sick unto death.

"Again, I saw her at the hermitage, where she fainted. She was brought home to her lodgings by a friend who discovered the cross on her breast. And again, I saw her in two places at one and the same time, lying in bed and walking around her room, several persons keeping watch at the door. I saw her very ill in bed, her whole person rigid, her arms extended, her color brilliant as a rose. A resplendent cross descended from on high toward the right of the bed. On it was the Savior, from whose wounds shot luminous red rays piercing her hands, feet, and side.

"From each wound darted three rays fine as the finest thread, which united in a point as they entered her body. The three from the wound of the side were larger and further apart than the others and terminated in a point like a lance. At the instant of contact, I saw drops of blood spurting from her hands, feet, and right side. When the circumstance became known, the whole town was in excitement, but soon the affair was hushed up and kept secret.

"I saw her confessor ever true to her, but timid, scrupulous, and suspicious, submitting her to endless trials. An Ecclesiastical Commission was deputed to examine into her case. It was conducted most rigorously, and I rejoiced to see the members soon convinced of her truth. I saw her afterward undergoing the surveillance of some citizens, during which she was, as usual, supported by supernatural beings, her angel ever by her side. Later, I saw near her a man writing in secret; but he was not an ecclesiastic.

"I saw her subjected to another investigation, which began with every appearance of good faith and kindness, but the devil was at the bottom of it. She was often in danger of death during it, but she was supported and strengthened by heavenly apparitions. Her persecutors did not want to allow her to return to her friends, and there were others expecting her, desiring to have her in other places. She was betrayed and ill-treated. Her heart was torn by men's malice, but she was throughout the whole affair cheerful, even gay, so much so that even the nurse guessed nothing of what she endured interiorly.

"I saw her, thanks to supernatural intervention, restored to her own home. I saw her afterward in still greater danger, her enemies assembled for the purpose of carrying her off by force; but they disputed among themselves and gave up their design. I saw her chief persecutor entering her presence in a rage, as if about to attack her, when suddenly, by some interior movement, he became calm and withdrew. Meanwhile her sister, whose hidden malice and perversity were quite incomprehensible, caused her great anxiety. I saw her spiritual relations with certain ecclesiastics. She excited my pity. I felt her sufferings in my own breast, and I wanted to ask her how she could bear so many afflictions. I inquired of my guide if I might question her, if I might speak familiarly with her, and he said I might. Then I asked how she could support her secret sufferings so uncomplainingly, to which she answered in these few words: 'As you do!'—which greatly astonished me. I saw once that the Mother of God also endured incomprehensible sufferings in secret.

"Then I saw that this person once lived with a seamstress, a good though strict woman. I saw her once take off a garment in the street and bestow it upon a poor beggar.

"The devil laid snares for her; he did not approach her

himself, but he sent wicked men, among them a married man; but she understood not the drift of their intentions.

"Three different times I saw the evil one attempting her life. Twice he tried to hurl her down the ladder that led to the garret in which she slept. She used to rise by night to pray, and twice I beheld a horrible black figure push her to the edge of the landing; but her angel interposed and saved her.

"On another occasion, as she was making the Way of the Cross in a lonely place near the river, I saw the enemy trying to cast her into a deep pit near the citadel; but again her angel rescued her.

"I saw her conversing frequently and lovingly with her dear celestial Lord, to whom one day she pledged her troth, though I cannot say whether there was an exchange of rings or not. Their interviews were full of childlike simplicity.

"Once, when I saw her at midday absorbed in prayer, languishing with divine love, in the Jesuits' church, Clara Soentgen by her side, a resplendent youth, her Affianced, issued from the blessed sacrament in the tabernacle and presented her two crowns, one of roses, the other of thorns. She chose the latter. He placed it on her head and she pressed it down to her own great pain. She was so absorbed as not to perceive that the sacristan was rattling his keys to attract her attention. Clara Soentgen may have seen something strange in her exterior, but the interior signification was unknown to her. She herself was unconscious of her blood having flowed until one of her companions remarked to her that her binder† was stained. She hid these effusions of blood until after she entered the convent, when they became known to one of the sisters. I saw her at Clara Soentgen's, where she gladly gave all that she earned to maintain the household in peace.

"Again, I beheld her working in the fields. So great was her desire to enter a convent that she fell sick. She firmly resolved to go. She had constant vomitings and went about so sad that her mother anxiously questioned her as to the cause; on learning it she expressed disapprobation, saying that such a project was not feasible on account of her daughter's poverty and delicate health. When she informed her father of it, he also disapproved and reprimanded her severely. But she told her parents that God was rich, He would help her.

"She fell ill, and I saw her confined to her bed. About noon, one day, when no one was home but her mother, I saw her lying—as I thought, asleep—the sun shining through her little window. A man and two female religious radiant with light entered her room. They approached her bed bearing a large book written upon parchment in letters of red and gold, and bound in yellow with clasps. The frontispiece was a picture of a man, and there were several other pictures in it. They presented it to her, saying, if she would study it, she would learn all that a religious ought to know. She replied that she would be only too glad to do so, and she took it on her knees. It was in Latin, but she understood it all and read it eagerly.

"She took this same book with her to the convent and often studied it earnestly; whenever she had perused a certain portion of it, it was withdrawn from her. Once I saw it lying on her table, whence some of the religious tried to steal it away, but they could not remove it.

"I saw her in another part of the convent when the priest found her in prayer perfectly unconscious of all around, as if paralyzed. I saw the Lord appear to her on the Feast of St. Augustine, make the sign of the cross on her breast, and then give her a cross, which she pressed to her heart before returning it to him. It was white and soft like wax. After this she was sick unto death till Christmas, and she received all the sacraments.

"She dreamed that she saw Mary sitting under a tree at Bethlehem; she conversed with her and ardently longed to die and remain with our Lady. Mary told her that she too had longed to die with her divine Son, but that she had to live and suffer many years after his death. Then she awoke.

"I saw the luminous cross descending toward her and her reception of the stigmata. I saw her during the investigation, and I understood that she was far advanced in the reading of her book. I saw her afterward in the house in which I now am, and in Mersmann's house where, too, she had the book.

"She was often in danger of death, from which however she was always supernaturally saved. Lastly, I saw her future. There was an ecclesiastical inquiry, and they seemed to be drawing up papers concerning her."‡

On June 15, 1821, Anne Catherine had a vision of St. Ludgarde, in connection with which she saw another series of pictures drawn from her own life:

"I had also visions of the life of a person who, as I afterward discovered, was none other than myself. Sometimes they were presented in union with those of St. Ludgarde's

---

† "Binder," a pointed covering for the forehead worn by peasants.

‡ Brentano was so astonished at her words that he wrote in his journal; "Ah! If we had not these hateful interruptions! If we could only get her whole history from her own lips, what a treasure should we possess! What a faithful portrait of this admirable soul!"

life, that I might note the points of resemblance in God's gifts to each, and the manner of their bestowal.

"From her infancy this person was persecuted by the evil one. She used to pray in the fields in places in which she instinctively felt the influence of a malediction, the presence of the powers of darkness. The devil at such times raged around the child, struck her, and hurled her to the ground; at first she ran away in terror but soon returned, animating her courage by faith and confidence in God. 'How can you chase me away, miserable wretch! There is nothing in common between us. You have never had any power over me, neither shall you have it in this place!'—and kneeling down again in the same spot, she would continue her prayer until Satan withdrew.

"Unable to make her relax her fervor, the devil urged her to weaken and destroy her health by excessive austerities, but the child defied him and redoubled her mortifications. One day, her mother left her alone, charging her to mind the house, and the demon sent an old woman from the neighborhood to tempt her. Having some bad object in view, the old woman said to the child: 'Go get some ripe pears from my garden! Be quick before your mother comes back!'—and off she ran in all haste. A plough half-hidden under the straw lay in her path. She stumbled and struck her breast so violently against it that she fell senseless to the ground. Her mother, returning home, found the child in this condition and brought her to her senses by a sound correction. But the child long felt the effects of the accident.

"I saw how satan misled the mother. For a long time she had erroneous ideas of her child, and often punished her undeservedly; but the little girl bore all patiently, offered it to God, and so overcame the enemy.

"I saw her praying at night and the devil inciting a boy to distract her in an unseemly manner; but she drove him off and continued her prayer.

"I saw the devil cast the child down from a high ladder, but her angel protected her; and once, as she crept along the narrow edge of a deep ditch to avoid treading on the wheat, he tried to push her in, but again she escaped the danger. Once, satan threw her into a pond about twelve feet deep and thrust her to the bottom three times, but her angel brought her each time to the surface.

"I saw the child on another occasion about to step into her little bed, her heart raised to God in prayer, when the evil one from under the bed seized her by the ankles with icy-cold hands and tumbled her over on the floor. I remember very well that she was neither terrified nor did she cry aloud; she remained quite still and, though no one had ever taught her to do so, she redoubled her prayers and conquered her enemy.

"She was always surrounded by suffering souls, who were visible to her; she prayed for them earnestly, notwithstanding the devil's attacks. Last night, during this vision, the soul of a peasant woman came to me and thanked for her deliverance.

"I saw the child, now arrived at girlhood, attacked by a young man instigated thereto by the devil; but she was protected by the ministry of two angels. I saw her praying in the cemetery of Coesfeld. The devil dashed her from side to side and, as she returned home, he cast her into a tan-pit. I beheld all the attacks, all the persecutions leveled against her in the convent. I saw satan cast her down the trap-door where she remained hanging by both hands in a most wonderful manner. I never saw him rouse in her the least temptation contrary to purity, indeed he never even attempted to do so. I saw the investigation to which she was subjected and satan taking an active part in the whole affair. I should not have comprehended how she could have endured so much, had I not seen angels and saints constantly by her. I saw, too, the interior dispositions of all the assistants, their continual touching of her wounds, and I heard their discourse. They gave her repose neither by day nor by night, for they were continually approaching her with a light. I saw their rage when they could discover nothing. I saw the Pilgrim's book, from which many things were taken for publication."

The Nature of Her Visions

Anne Catherine tried several times to give the Pilgrim some idea of her contemplation, but in vain; she could never satisfactorily explain the spiritual activity of her visions. We quote what the Pilgrim was able to write on different occasions:

"I see many things that I cannot possibly express. Who can say with the tongue what he sees not with the bodily eyes?"

"I see it not with the eyes. It seems as if I saw it with my heart in the midst of my breast. It makes the perspiration start! At the same time I see with my eyes the objects and persons around me; but they concern me not, I know not who or what they are. I am in contemplation even now while I am speaking"

"For several days I have been constantly between the state of vision and the natural waking state. I have to do violence to myself. In the middle of a conversation I suddenly see before me other things and pictures and I hear my own words as if proceeding from another, as if coming out of an empty cask. I feel as if I were intoxicated and reeling. My conversation goes on coolly and often more animatedly than usual, but when it is over I know not what I have said, though I have been speaking connectedly. It costs me an effort to maintain this double state. I see passing objects dimly and confusedly like a sleeper awaking out of a dream. The second sight attracts me more powerfully, it is clearer than the natural, but it is not through the eyes."

After relating a vision one day, she laid aside her work, saying: "All this day I have been flying and seeing; sometimes I see the Pilgrim, sometimes not. Does he not hear the singing? It seems to me that I am in a beautiful meadow, the trees forming arches over me. I hear wondrously sweet singing like the clear voices of children. All around me here below is like a troubled dream, dim and confused, through which I gaze upon a luminous world perfectly distinct in all its parts, intelligible even in its origin and connected in all its wonders. In it the good and holy delight more powerfully, since one sees his way from God to God; and what is bad and unholy troubles more deeply, as the way leads from the demon to the demon in opposition to God and the creature. This life in which nothing hinders me, neither time nor space, neither the body nor mystery, in which all speaks, all enlightens, is so perfect, so free, that the blind, lame, stammering reality appears but an empty dream. In this state I always see the relics by me shining, and sometimes I see little troops of figures floating over them in a distant cloud. When I return to myself, the boxes and caskets in which the shining relics lie reappear."

Once the Pilgrim gave her a little parcel into which without her knowledge he had slipped a relic. She took it with a significant smile, as if to say she could not be so deceived, and laying it on her heart, she said: "I knew directly what you were giving me. I cannot describe the impression it produces. I not only see, I feel a light like the will-o'-the-wisp, sometimes bright, sometimes dull, blowing toward me as if directed by a current of wind. I feel, too, a certain connecting link between the light and the shining body, and between the latter and a luminous world, itself born of light. Who can express it?—The light seizes me, I can not prevent it from entering my heart; and, when I plunge in deeper, it seems as if I passed through it into the body from which it emanates, into the scenes of its life, its struggles, its sufferings, its triumphs! Then I am directed in vision as is pleasing to God. There is a wonderful, a mysterious, relation between our body and soul. The soul sanctifies or profanes the body; otherwise there could be no expiation, no penance by means of the body. As the saints while alive worked in the body, so even when separated from it they continue to act by it upon the faithful. But faith is essential to the reception of holy influences.

"Often while speaking with others on quite different subjects I see far in the distance the soul of a deceased person coming toward me and I am forced to attend to it at once. I become silent and thoughtful. I have apparitions also of the saints in the same way. I once had a beautiful revelation on this point, in which I learned that seeing with the eyes is no sight, that there is another, an interior sight, that is clear and penetrating. But when deprived of daily Communion a cloud obscures my clear inward sight, I pray less fervently, with less devotion, I forget important things, signs, and warnings, and I see the destructive influence of exterior things that are essentially false. I feel a devouring hunger for the Blessed Sacrament and, when I look toward the church, feel as if my heart were about to escape from my breast and fly to my Redeemer…"

"When I was in trouble, because in obedience to my guide's orders I refused to be removed to another abode, I cried to God to direct me. I was overwhelmed with trials, and yet I saw so many holy visions that I knew not what to do. In my prayer I was calm. I saw a face, a countenance approach me and melt, as it were, into my breast as if uniting with my being. It seemed as if my soul becoming one with it returned into itself and grew smaller and smaller, while my body appeared to become a great massive substance large as a house. The countenance, the apparition in me, appeared to be triple, infinitely rich and varied, but at the same time always one. It penetrated (that is, its beams, its regards) into all the choirs of angels and saints. I experienced joy and consolation from it, and I thought: Could all this come from the evil spirit? And while I was thus thinking, all the pictures, clear and distinct like a series of bright clouds, passed again before my soul, and I felt that they were now out of me, at my side in a luminous sphere. I felt also that although I was larger, yet I was not so massive as before. There was now, as it were, a world outside of me into which I could peer through a luminous opening. A maiden approached who explained this world of light to me, directed my attention here and there, and pointed out to me the vineyard of the holy bishop in which I now had to labor.

"But I saw too on my left a second world full of deformed figures, symbols of perversity, calumny, raillery, and injury. They came like a swarm, the point directed toward me. Of all that came to me from this sphere I could accept nothing, for the just, the good were in the pure, luminous sphere on my right. Between these two spheres I hung by one arm poor and abandoned, floating, so to say, between heaven and earth. This state lasted long and caused me great pain; still I was not impatient.

"The way in which a communication from the blessed is received, is hard to explain. What is said is incredibly brief; by one word from them I understand more than by thirty from others. I see the speaker's thought, but not with the eyes; all is clearer, more distinct than in the present state. One receives it with as much pleasure as he hails a breeze in summer. Words cannot well express it."

"All that the poor soul said to me was, as usual, brief. To understand the language of the souls in purgatory is difficult. Their voice is smothered, as if coming through something that dulls the sound; it is like one speaking from a pit or a cask. The meaning, also, is more difficult to grasp. Closer attention is required than when our Lord, or my guide, or a saint speaks to me, for their words penetrate like a clear current of air; one sees and knows all they say.

The Value of Prayer

The following vision on the value of prayer was vouchsafed to Anne Catherine:

"I was in a great, bright place that extended on every side as far as the eye could reach, and there it was shown me how it is with men's prayers before God. They seemed to be inscribed on large white tablets that were divided into four classes: some were written in magnificent golden letters; others in shining silver; some in darker characters; and others again in black, streaked lines. I gazed with delight, but as I thought myself unworthy of such a favor, I hardly dared ask my guide what it all meant. He told me: 'What is written in gold is the prayer of those who have united their good works to the merits of Jesus Christ and who often renew this union; they aim at observing his precepts and imitating his example.'

"'What is written in silver is the prayer of those who think not of union with the merits of Jesus Christ; but who are, notwithstanding, pious and who pray in the simplicity of their hearts.

"'What is written in darker colors is the prayer of those who have no peace unless they frequently confess and communicate and daily say certain prayers; but who are, however, tepid and perform their good works through habit.

"'Lastly, what is written in black, streaked characters is the prayer of such as place all their confidence in vocal prayers and pretended good works, but who do not keep God's commandments nor curb their evil desires. Such prayer has no merit before God, therefore is it streaked. So also would the good works of a man be streaked who indeed gives himself much trouble to help on some charity, but with a view to the honor or temporal advantage attached to it.'"

She relates another symbolical vision on prayer: "I was kneeling in my accustomed place in church, and I saw by the brilliant light that shone around two beautifully dressed ladies in prayer at the foot of the High Altar. With heartfelt emotion I watched them praying so devoutly, when two dazzling crowns of gold were let down as if by a cord over their heads. I drew near and saw that one crown rested on the head of one of the ladies, while the other remained suspended in the air a little above the head of the second. At last they both arose and I remarked to them that they had been praying earnestly. 'Yes,' replied the second, 'it is a long time since I prayed as devoutly and with as much consolation as I have done today.' But the first, on whose head the crown had rested, complained that although she had wanted to pray fervently, yet all kinds of thoughts and distractions had assailed her, against which she had to fight the whole time. Now I saw clearly by this that the dear God looks only at the heart in time of prayer."

This vision had been vouchsafed Anne Catherine to teach her that her own prayer, so often disturbed and interrupted by the presence of visitors and other annoyances, was now no less agreeable to God than the tranquil devotion formerly hers in the cloister. We may recognize a similar intention in a later vision, simple apparently and of no great significance, but which is a striking proof of God's constant care over His chosen one:

"I had to cross a narrow bridge. In terror I gazed on the deep waters flowing below, but my angel led me over in safety. On the bank was a mouse-trap around which a little mouse kept running and running, and at last it slipped in to get the bait. 'Foolish little animal!' I cried, 'you are sacrificing your liberty, your life for a mouthful!' 'Are men more reasonable?' asked my angel, 'when for a momentary gratification they endanger their soul's salvation?'"

Her compassion for the poor little mouse was turned by her angel to men blindly rushing to their own destruction, that she might help them from afar by her prayers and supplications. The vision appeared to imply what seemed to her impossible, that the hidden, peaceful life of former years was never to return, and so God willed. That happiness so longed-for was never again to be hers. The time had arrived for the last and most painful part of her mission. As the Church was bereft of her asylums of peace, in which piety could be practiced unmolested and contemplation sheltered from the vulgar gaze, so was Anne Catherine torn from that sacred abode in which she had hoped to end her days, a trial which she shared with Holy Church up to the last instant of her life.

How Jesus Healed

On one occasion, when asked how Jesus healed, Anne Catherine said:

"Jesus healed in various ways, each one having its own signification. I cannot now, however, repeat them as I saw them. Each had reference to the meaning and the secret cause of the malady, also to the spiritual needs of the invalid. In the anointing with oil, for instance, there was a certain spiritual strength and energy denoted by the signification of the oil itself. No one of these actions was without its own peculiar meaning. With these forms, Jesus instituted all those ceremonies that the saints and priests who exercised their healing power would afterward make use of in his name. They either received them from tradition, or were used in the name of Jesus through an inspiration of the Holy Spirit. As the Son of God, in order to become man, chose the body of a most pure creature—thus to correspond to the requirements of man's nature—so did he frequently use in effecting his cures pure and simple created substances that had been blessed by his Spirit, as, for instance, oil. He afterward gave to the cured bread to eat with some juice of the grape. At other times he healed by a mere command uttered at a distance, for he had come upon Earth to cure the most varied ills and that in the most varied ways. He had come to satisfy, for all that believed in him, by his own great sacrifice upon the cross, in which sacrifice were contained all pains and sorrows, all penances and satisfactions. With the various keys of his charity he first opened the fetters and bonds of temporal misery and chastisement, instructed the ignorant in all things necessary for them to know, healed all kinds of maladies, and aided the needy in every way; then with that chief key of his love, the key of the cross, he opened heaven's expiatory door as well as the door of Limbo.

Spiritual Attacks

Once, having found Anne Catherine enduring a martyrdom, Brentano wrote:

"It would be vain to attempt a description of her sufferings. To understand it even slightly, one would have to watch the various phases of her inexplicable state." The cause of her pains none could divine. Her life glided by in this daily struggle without sympathy or support. She never appeared to lose the remembrance of her thorny crown; even when the rest of her person became rigid, she retained command over her head, supporting it in such a way that the thorns might not penetrate too deeply. Sometimes her whole body was slashed and torn with whips, her hands were tied, she was bound with cords; the torture she endured forced the cold sweat from every pore, and yet she related all without a sign of impatience. Suddenly she extended her arms in the form of a cross with an effort so violent that one would have thought the distended nerves were about to snap. She lowered them again, her head gradually sank upon her breast as if she were dead, her limbs were motionless, she lay like a corpse. 'I am with the poor souls,' she murmured, and on returning to consciousness, she related the following, though with an effort":

"I have had three violent attacks, and I have suffered everything just as my Lord did in his Passion. When I was about to yield, when I groaned in agony, I beheld the same suffering undergone by him. Thus I went through the whole Passion as I see it on Good Friday. I was scourged, crowned with thorns, dragged with ropes, I fell, I was nailed to the cross, I saw the Lord descend into hell, and I, too, went to purgatory. I saw many detained therein; some I knew, others I knew not. I saw souls saved who had been buried in darkness and forgetfulness, and this afforded me consolation.

"The second attack I endured for all that were not in a state to bear patiently what falls to their lot, and for the dying who were unable to receive the Blessed Sacrament. I saw many whom I helped.

"The third attack was for the Church. I had a vision of a church with a high, elaborate tower, in a great city on a mighty river. The patron of the church is Stephen, by whom I saw another saint who was martyred after him. Around the church I saw many very distinguished people, among them some strangers with aprons and trowels who appeared about to pull down the church with the beautiful tower and slate roof. People from all parts were gathered there, among them priests and even religious, and I was so distressed that I called to my Lord for assistance. Xavier with the cross in his hand had once been all powerful, the enemy ought not to be allowed to triumph now! Then I saw five men going into the church, three in heavy antique vestments like priests, and two very young ecclesiastics who seemed to be in Holy Orders. I thought these two received Holy Communion, and that they were destined to infuse new life into the Church.

"Suddenly a flame burst from the tower, spread over the roof, and threatened to consume the whole church. I thought of the great river flowing by the city—could they not extinguish the flames with its waters? The fire injured many who aided in the destruction of the church and drove them away, but the edifice itself remained standing, by which I understood that the Church would be saved only after a great storm. The fire, so frightful to behold, indicated in the first place a great danger; in the second, renewed splendor after the tempest. The Church's destruction is already begun by means of infidel schools.

"I saw a great storm rising in the north and sweeping in a half-circle to the city with the high tower, and then off to the west. I saw combats and streaks of blood far and wide in the heavens over many places, and endless woes and misery threatening the Church, with everywhere snares being laid to entrap her. The servants of the Church are so slothful. They use not the power they possess in the priesthood! I shed bitter tears at the sight."—She wept while recounting this vision, imploring Almighty God to deliver her from such spectacles. She mourned also over the flocks without shepherds, and counseled prayer, penance, and humility to avert a portion of the impending danger.

On another occasion, during the first week of Advent, Anne Catherine spoke further, after a vision, of attacks and persecution:

"I had to struggle all night; I am worn out with the sad pictures I saw. My guide took me all around the earth through immense black caverns built by the powers of darkness, and filled with people wandering about in sin. It was as if I went over all the habitable points of the globe and saw nothing but sin. I often saw new troops of men falling from on high into the blindness of vice. I saw nothing good. I saw in general more men than women, the children were few. Often when I was overcome by the sight, my guide brought me for a little while out into the light, into a meadow or beautiful region where the sun shone, but where there were no people; afterward I had to return into the darkness and see again the malice, blindness, pride, deceit, envy, avarice, discord, murders, luxury, snares, passions, the horrible wickedness of men—all plunging them into greater misery, deeper darkness. I was under the impression that whole cities were built upon a thin crust that would soon cave in and precipitate them into the abyss. I saw people digging ditches for one another's destruction; but there were no good people here, none falling into the ditches. All these wicked people were in a great dark place, running about at random as in a great fair, grouping together, and enticing one another to sin. Sometimes the darkness grew deeper, and the road led down a steep crag, frightful to behold, extending around the whole earth.

"I saw people of all nationalities, all costumes, and all sunk in crime. At times I awoke in terror, and saw the moon shining brightly in at my window. I groaned in anguish, and begged God to send me no more such frightful pictures; but I had soon again to descend into those terrible regions of darkness and behold their abomination. Once I found myself in a sphere so horrible that I thought myself in hell, and I began to weep aloud. My guide said: 'I am by thee, hell cannot be where I am.'

"Then, turning longingly to the poor souls in purgatory, I was transported into the midst of them. It seemed like a place near the earth, and there too I saw inexpressible torments; but they were God-fearing souls who sinned not, who perpetually sighed, hungered, thirsted for deliverance. They could all see what they longed for and for which they had to wait in patience. Their suffering was full of resignation; their acknowledgment of their faults and their utter inability to help themselves peculiarly touching. I saw all their sins. They were in different depths, different degrees of abandonment; some up to the neck, some to the breast, etc., and they implored aid. After I had prayed for them, I awoke and again begged God to deliver me from these visions.

"But scarcely had I fallen asleep than I was led once more into the dark regions. Satan threatened me and placed horrible pictures before me. Once I met an insolent devil who said something like the following: 'There was no necessity for your coming down here and seeing everything—now you'll go up above, boast of your trip, and write something about it!' I told him to cease his stupid talk.

"Once I thought I saw a great, wicked city being undermined by devils who were already far advanced with the work. I thought as it had so many heavy buildings, it must now soon fall in. I had often felt that Paris would sink in, for I see so many caves under it, but not cut out purposely like those in Rome.

"At last, I reached a large place like one of our own cities. In it was a little more light, and there I was shown a horrible sight, our Lord Jesus Christ crucified! My whole soul shuddered, for the executioners were men of our own time, and our Lord was suffering much more cruelly from them than he did from the Jews. Thank God, it was only a picture! 'So would they,' said my guide, 'now treat the Lord, could he still suffer.' I saw with horror among his tormentors men whom I knew, even priests. This place was connected with the dark regions by many veins and ramifications. I saw, too, my own persecutors and how they would treat me, if I fell into their hands; they would by torture try to make me confirm their false statements."

The remembrance of this horrible vision made Anne Catherine's heart beat with fright. Nothing could induce her to give it entire; she concluded with these words:

"My guide said to me, 'Now you have seen the horrible blindness and darkness of men. Murmur no more at your own lot, but pray! Your lot is very sweet.' This vision was followed by that inquietude I so often feel, that of being accountable for something, since so many sins are committed on my account. The dread of disobedience haunts me. My guide said, 'It is pride that makes you think that only good should happen through you! And if you are not obedient, it is my fault and not yours!'"

The Gray Robe

On Christmas Eve, 1819, Anne Catherine was shown in a vision new sufferings in store for her. The following is her account of it:

"There came three holy nuns, among them Frances of Rome, who brought me a clean white robe with a scalloped border; on the left side was a red heart surrounded by roses. I touched them and the thorns pricked me to blood. The nuns threw the robe around me quickly, saying that I must wear it until the New Year, when it would be exchanged for a gray one with a heavy iron cross. If at the New Year I returned the present one spotless, the cross on the second one would, perhaps, be much lightened.

"I thought this referred to my death, and I said, 'Is it true that I am going to die?'—But they answered, 'No, thou hast still much to suffer,' and then they disappeared. My guide announced those bitter sufferings in severe words that cut into my soul like swords. He told me that I should not succumb, that I drew them on myself by undertaking so much for others, that I should be more moderate, not so eager to do so much good, that Jesus alone can do such things. Then sharp pains racked me until two hours past midnight. I lay upon a harrow covered with thorns that penetrated into my very bones."

She had at short intervals three attacks of these same sufferings. On Dec. 29th, the Pilgrim found her quite changed in appearance by physical and mental pain, her features drawn, her forehead knit, her whole frame twitching convulsively. "I have not slept all night," she said, "I am almost dead; still I had exterior consolation. The sweetness of suffering spread itself through my inmost soul, it came from God. The blessed Virgin also consoled me. I saw her inexpressible sufferings on the night the Lord was seized, and particularly that caused her by Peter's denial. I saw how she lamented it to John; it was only to him that she told her grief.

"I asked her why my sister's state gave me so much pain, wounded me so deeply, yes, almost distracted me, while I supported courageously far worse than it. I was told: 'As you perceive light from the relics of the saints by your intuition of the union existing among Christ's members, so do you perceive more clearly the blindness, the anger, the disunion of your sister's state, because it comes from the root of your sinful flesh in fallen Adam, in a direct line through your ancestors. You feel their sins in your flesh through your parents and earliest ancestors. It is sin proceeding from the share you have in the fall.'

"I suffered, I watched, I fainted away, I regained consciousness, I counted the hours, and when morning dawned I cried out to my Lord not to abandon me. I saw him taking leave of his mother. I saw Mary's grief. I saw him upon the Mount of Olives, and he said to me: 'Do you wish to be treated better than Mary, the most pure, the most beloved of all creatures? What are your sufferings compared with hers?'—Then he showed me endless miseries, the dying unprepared, etc., and my guide said to me: 'If you would help them, suffer for them, else how can justice be satisfied?'—He showed me future sorrows, and told me that few pray and suffer to avert evils. I became thankful and courageous, I suffered joyously for I had seen him! He again said, 'See, how many dying souls! In what a state!'—and showed me a dying priest of my own country, one who had fallen so low that he could not receive Holy Communion with faith and purity of heart. I did not know him. My guide said, 'Suffer for all these until midday'—Then I suffered joyously. I still suffer, but I shall soon be relieved."

Toward noon her countenance changed, the heart-rending expression faded, her pains seemed to leave her gradually like water evaporating under the sun's rays. Her drawn features relaxed, and precisely at noon became sweet and peaceful as those of a sleeping child—the paroxysm had passed. Her members became torpid, and she fell into a state of insensibility exempt from suffering.

The last evening of the year she was completely absorbed by her journey to the Heavenly Jerusalem, and she occasionally repeated some verses from the breviary referring to the City of God. Once she said: "I must be trodden under foot, my garden is too flourishing, it will produce nothing but flowers." She beheld herself in all possible situations, her heart cruelly lacerated. She exclaimed: "O how much that person afflicts me! I can hardly endure the sight of her sufferings! I beg God to hide them from me!"

On a later night in January the three little nuns came again and took off her white robe, which was still spotless. They put on her the promised gray one with the heavy black cross which she was to wash white with her tears. A number of poor souls came to thank her for their deliverance, among them an old woman of her own hamlet for whom she had prayed much. She felt that she had delivered them through the spotlessness of her white robe, and that affected her deeply.

"When I received the gray robe," she said, "I saw again all the torments in reserve for me. I had, besides, an apparition of St. Teresa, who consoled me greatly by speaking of her own sufferings. She also reassured me on the score of my visions, telling me not to be troubled but to disclose all; that with her it so happened that the more open she was in this respect the clearer did her visions become.

"My Lord also spoke lovingly with me and explained the gray robe. 'It is of silk,' he said, 'because I am wounded in my whole person, and you are not to tear it by impatience. It is gray, because it is a robe of penance and humiliation.' He told me, too, that when I was sick, he was satisfied with me; but that when I was well, I was too condescending. He said, moreover, that I should tell all that was shown me even though I might be ridiculed for it, for such was his will. Everything is of use. Then I felt as if I were borne from one bed of thorns to be laid on another, but I offered all for the poor souls."

Anne Catherine's Care for Brentano's Soul

Brentano committed to paper many words regarding Anne Catherine's solicitude for his soul, and concern for his conversion. One occasion of special significance in this regard was a conversation during the course of which Anne Catherine had unquestionably established the purity and truth of the Catholic faith. Having succumbed to a false mysticism, which made him look upon the Church "as a community of the children of God without distinction of outward profession," Brentano had one day, shortly after his arrival, expressed himself in glowing terms "of brethren separated in body but united in soul, since all belong to the universal Church."

He was not a little surprised, then, to receive the following grave and conclusive reply: "The Church is only one, the Catholic! And if there were left upon earth but one Catholic, he would be the one, universal Church, the Catholic Church, the Church of Jesus Christ against which the gates of hell shall never prevail."

When Brentano objected that all that believe in Jesus Christ are sons of God, she replied, "If Jesus Christ declares that the children of God should love and honor Him as their Father, they should also call the dear Mother of God their mother and love her as their mother. The Our Father is—for him who does not understand this, who does not do it—simply a vain formula; he is far from being a child of God."

Then, returning to the subject of the Church, she continued: "The knowledge of the greatness and magnificence of this Church—in which the sacraments are preserved in all their virtue and inviolable sanctity—is, unhappily, rare in these our days, even among the clergy. It is because so many priests are ignorant of their own dignity that so many of the faithful forget theirs and comprehend not the expression to belong to the Church! That no human power may ever destroy it, Almighty God has attached an indelible character to Holy Orders. Were there but a single priest on earth rightly ordained, Jesus Christ would live in his Church as God and Man in the Most Holy Sacrament of the altar; and whoever would receive this sacrament, after being absolved by the priest, would alone be truly united to God.

"It is something grand, but at the same time something impossible without true interior light—without purity and simplicity of heart—to live in accordance with the faith of this Holy Church; to celebrate with her the divine worship and thereby participate in the infinite treasure of grace and satisfaction she possesses in the merits of her divine head; and, through his merits, to share in the blood of her innumerable martyrs, in the penance and sufferings of her saints, in the prayers and good works of the devout faithful. This treasure she communicates without diminishing to all in union with her, to all her true children. It is from it that she draws wherewith to satisfy the justice of God, to liquidate for the living as well as for the souls in purgatory the debts that they themselves could never cancel.

"Every hour has its own particular grace; he who rejects it languishes and perishes. As there is an earthly year with its seasons, an earthly nature with its creatures, its fruits, and its peculiar properties, so also does there exist an economy of a higher order for the restoration of our fallen race. It has innumerable graces and means of salvation all linked together in the course of the spiritual year which, too, has its different seasons. Each year, each day, each hour, ripens these fruits for our eternal salvation. The children of the Catholic Church that piously celebrate the spiritual year with its feasts and ceremonies, that regulate their life according to its prescriptions, that recite the holy canonical hours, alone are faithful laborers in the vineyard, they alone will reap abundant benedictions.

"It is sad to behold in our times so few that understand this economy of divine grace and conform their life thereto. But a day will come on which, conscience-stricken, they will at last comprehend what the ecclesiastical year is, with its feasts and seasons and days consecrated to God, its public and private devotions, its canonical hours, its breviary recited by priests and religious. It is the divine Savior himself who abides with us in this order of things, who gives himself to us at all times as food and victim, that we may become one with him.

"How strikingly do not his untiring mercy and solicitude for us shine forth in the thousands of masses in which the propitiatory sacrifice, his bloody death upon the cross, is daily renewed in an unbloody manner and offered for us to the heavenly Father! This sacrifice of the cross is an eternal sacrifice, a sacrifice of infinite efficacy, unalterable and ever new. But men must profit by it in time, which is finite, and during which all things are taken into account. In accordance with the precept of the Son of God made man, this thrice holy Sacrifice shall be daily renewed until the account is filled up and the temporal existence of the world shall reach its term, for it is Jesus Christ himself who, by the hands of lawfully ordained priests (even were they otherwise unworthy) offers himself to his heavenly Father under the species of bread and wine for our reconciliation."

When Anne Catherine held such conversations with the Pilgrim, she profited by the opportunity to exhort him to prayer, to the practice of penance, to Christian charity, to self-victory and renunciation, and all in so simple and natural a manner that her remarks penetrated his soul less as words of exhortation than of consolation, or as the necessary consequence of what she had previously said and which he had recognized to be true.

When unable to hold long conversations, she begged his prayers as a spiritual alms for herself or some intention recommended to her, or prescribed to him certain pious exercises, certain prayers, encouraging him to hope in God and thus unite himself more closely with the Church.

She would use arguments like the following: "We enjoy the goods left us by our parents and ancestors, but we forget what we owe them in return. How they sigh for our gratitude! How much they need our help! They cry: 'Suffer, pray, give alms for us! Offer the Holy Mass for us!'"

When he asked what he could do for his deceased parents, she advised him, besides prayers and alms-giving, to impose upon himself for a certain time determinate practices of self-renunciation, patience, sweetness, and interior mortification.

The Pilgrim could not, indeed, resist the force of Anne Catherine's words. But there was one opinion dear to his heart and of which he scarcely wished to be disabused: that is, the possibility of practicing piety, of being very agreeable to Almighty God, even without actual and exterior union with the Church. He alleged as a proof of this that numbers of non-Catholics are better than some Catholics living in communion with the Church, whose sad state in many countries he painted so eloquently that Anne Catherine dared not reply. She saw plainly that her arguments would have no effect upon him at the time. One day she herself turned the conversation on this point:

"My spiritual guide has reproached me severely for having listened with too much complaisance to your eulogy of pious heretics. He asked whether I had forgotten who I am and to whom I belong. He says that I am a virgin of the Catholic Church, consecrated to God and bound by holy vows; I ought to praise God in the Church and pray with sincere pity for heretics. I know better than others what the Church really is, and I ought on that account to praise the members of Jesus Christ in the Church, his Body.

"As to those who are separated from this Body and who inflict cruel wounds upon it, I ought to commiserate them and pray for their conversion. In praising the disobedient, one participates in their faults. Such praises are not charitable, since true zeal for the salvation of souls is cooled by them. It is well for me that I have been reproved on this head, for we must not be too indulgent when there is question of things so holy.

"I indeed behold many good people among heretics who inspire me with great compassion, but I see also that they are children whose origin dates back no further than their own times. They are drifting about without helm or pilot, and they are incessantly splitting up into parties one against the other. A movement toward piety that at times affects them emanates from the Catholic stock to which they formerly belonged; but it is soon counteracted by another in an opposite direction, a spirit of ignorance and indocility that urges them to rise in rebellion against their common Mother. They are eager to practice piety, but not Catholicity. Although they pretend that ceremonies and lifeless forms are of no importance, and that Almighty God must be served in spirit and in truth, yet do they obstinately hold to their own forms that are in reality dead, to forms of their own invention, which are in consequence ever changing.

"These forms are not the result of internal development, a body animated by a soul; they are mere skeletons. It is for this reason that they who practice them are infected with pride and cannot bend their necks to the yoke. How, in truth, could they possess humility of heart —they who are not taught from their infancy to humble themselves, who confess not their sins and their miseries, who are not accustomed, like the children of the Church, to accuse themselves in the sacrament of penance before the representative of God?

"Behold, then, why I see even in the best among such people only defects, presumption, obstinacy, and pride. The only heretics that are not in a positively dangerous position, are they who, wholly ignorant of the Church out of which there is no salvation, practice piety as far as they know how; but as soon as God gives them the least doubt, they should regard it as a call from heaven and seek to know the truth. Heretics become members of the Church by holy baptism, if validly administered. They live only by the Church and have, in point of spiritual nourishment, only what falls to them from the Church; but they do not sit at table with the children of the house, they are outside insulting and boasting, or dying of starvation. When in vision I behold baptized heretics returning to the Church, they appear to come in through the walls before the altar and the most blessed sacrament; while the non-baptized, Jews, Turks, and pagans, are shown to me as entering by the door."

One day she expressed her thoughts by means of the following symbolical picture.

"I beheld two cities, the one on the right, the other on the left. A beautiful avenue of flowering trees led to the city on the left, but the flowers fell to the ground one after another; no fruit was to be seen. My guide said to me: 'Notice how much poorer this new city is than the old one on the right.' The city itself was full of windings and streets, but all within was dead. Then my guide drew my attention to the old city on the right. In many parts it presented a more irregular and dilapidated appearance than the other, but all around arose magnificent trees covered with fruit. In it there were no poor, save those who neglected to gather the fruit or take care of the trees, which were of great age and rose majestically to heaven. The trees on the left appeared neglected, their branches broken, and the fruit fallen; but on the right, they were healthy, vigorous, and laden with fruit."

The Pilgrim was still more disconcerted when he saw how uncompromisingly Anne Catherine condemned the false mysticism of Boos and Gossner,† their secret practices, and their adherents. As she herself had once been looked upon as a clairvoyant by the supporters of mesmerism, so now in the early stage of his acquaintance with her, the Pilgrim was tempted to see in her an illustration of his pet mysticism. But a closer study of her demeanor, her purity of faith, her respect for ecclesiastical authority, soon led to a more just appreciation.

One day he spoke warmly in praise of the sect. She replied: "Yes, I know Gossner. He is abominable to me! He is a dangerous man! The hard, obstinate Boos, too, is abhorrent to me! It would take a great deal to save him."

The Pilgrim then spoke of Marie Oberdorfer, one of the foremost in the circle of false mystics, as of a woman highly favored by heaven, and he supported his opinion upon that of an ecclesiastic whom he greatly esteemed. Anne Catherine suddenly exclaimed: "Enlightened! What is that?" And upon his explaining that it meant light for the understanding of the Holy Scriptures, she replied: "Such light as you speak of is of no account, but great is the grace of the true children of the Church! They alone, by their sincere and obedient confession of the only true Catholic faith, by their living communion with the visible Church, are on the right road to the Heavenly Jerusalem. As to those who presume to revolt against the Church and her spiritual authority, who pretend that they alone possess understanding, who call themselves 'the communion of saints,' they have no real light, for they are not of the faithful; they wander, separated from God and His Church.

"I behold even among the best of them neither humility, simplicity, nor obedience, but only pride, frightful pride. They are terribly vain of the separation in which they live. They speak of faith, of light, of living Christianity, but they disdain and outrage the Holy Church in which alone light and life should be sought. They exalt themselves above the ecclesiastical power and hierarchy, paying neither submission nor respect to spiritual authority; they presumptuously pretend that they comprehend everything better than the heads of the Church, better than her holy Doctors; they reject good works, but at the same time are eager to possess perfection, they who, with all their so-called light, deem neither obedience, nor mortification, nor penance, nor disciplinary rules necessary. I see them straying ever further and further from the Church, and I see of how much evil they are productive."

As the Pilgrim was shocked by her severe condemnation, which grated harshly upon his own opinions, she returned, again and again, to the same subject:

"I always see these 'illuminati' in a certain connection with the coming of Antichrist; for by their secrets, by their injustice, they forward the accomplishment of that mystery of iniquity."

Brentano dared not contradict her words, but it was long before he fully understood that they attacked false mysticism in its very essence. No errors entail consequences so disastrous as that pride of intellect which impels men to aim at union with the divinity apart from the painful road of penance, without the practice of Christian virtue, and with no other guide than that interior sentiment which they regard as an infallible sign of Christ's workings in the soul. "Christ for us! Christ in us!" such is the watchword of these sectaries. They reject the decisions of the Church, they shake off the yoke of faith and the commandments, and they level every barrier between them and the baneful influence of their theories.

Brentano had not, indeed, fully accepted these teachings, but he had looked upon them favorably, and their pet expressions, "Spirit, Love, Light, Way to God, Dwelling in God, Operations of God, the Word of God in us, etc.," held out to him the possibility of attaining their end in the sweetest and easiest way. But in the vicinity of this true servant of God his delusions vanished. With all the energy of his soul he now began to cultivate that pure, strong faith which he saw to be the fundamental principle, the essential element, whence she herself drew the strength to accomplish the work assigned her.

---

† Martin Boos (1762–1825) was a German Roman Catholic theologian. He was born at Huttenried in Bavaria. He followed the extreme practises of asceticism as a penance for sin, all to no avail, as he believed, and then developed a doctrine of salvation by faith which came very near to pure Lutheranism, which he preached with great effect. After serving as priest in several Bavarian towns, he was driven from Bavaria by the opposition of the ecclesiastical authorities and other priests. However, his pietistic movement won considerable way among the Catholic laity, and even attracted some fifty or sixty priests. Johannes Evangelista Gossner (1773–1858), was German divine and philanthropist, born at Hausen near Augsburg. He, like Martin Boos and others, came under the spell of the Evangelical movement. Some time after taking priests' orders, Gossner's evangelical tendencies brought about his dismissal, and in 1826 he formally left the Roman Catholic for the Protestant communion.

DRAMATIS PERSONAE

⊕

Baptism in the Jordan
(l-r: John the Baptist, Jesus, Andrew, Saturnin)
Drawn by Cl. Brentano after Anne Catherine's description

Drawings from Brentano's Notes (clockwise from bottom):
Folk of the Land of the Three Kings • Daniel • Mary Dressed for the Way of Sorrows
Peter • Mark • Datula (see Book IV) • Mary Radiating • Elijah • (Center) Raising of Lazarus

DRAMATIS PERSONAE

The HOLY MEN (John the Baptist, Apostles, and Lazarus & Friends)
and the HOLY WOMEN (Before and at Christ's Death and Resurrection)

Introduction

ANNE CATHERINE EMMERICH's visionary descriptions of the life of Christ and of the apostles, disciples, and holy women—the most accurate and far-reaching we have—offer a profound comprehension not only of the life of Jesus, but also of those closest to him. Nearly two centuries of research (both biblical and archeological) have established that the historical accuracy of these visions is remarkable. The following summaries, based upon these visions, offer much for further contemplation. We first consider the apostles and disciples, and then the holy women. These summaries are by no means exhaustive: a complete description of the apostles, disciples, holy women, and many other secondary figures who come to life as presented in Anne Catherine's visions would require a full-length book.† Most of this material, translated from the original German, is published here in English for the first time.

Only since the year 2009 have the complete works of Anne Catherine (that is, her visions as transcribed by Clemens Brentano) been available, for it was in this year that Jozef De Raedemaeker completed the monumental task of transcribing all of Brentano's original diaries of these visions (extending month-by-month from 1818 until Anne Catherine's death in 1824) and publishing them in 38 volumes. This was a private initiative, not the project of a publishing house.

As an example of the treasures scattered throughout these 38 volumes, let us consider the following excerpt taken from the volume for the month of July 1820, being Brentano's transcription made on Saturday, July 15 of that year. Italicized comments were made by Clemens Brentano and comments in parentheses are by the editor:

> Yesterday I saw Jesus telling the apostles how they should go out into the whole world. Today I saw this taking place. This was long after his death, because Paul was there with them. I saw them gathered in the same house where they were when Peter was freed from prison and came to them. They often gathered there. This was not the house where the Last Supper took place and where the Holy Spirit descended upon them. (*It belonged to the mother of John Mark.*) I saw that night all twelve gathered, with many of their disciples. They were all prepared for travel. They stood beneath the lamp, Peter at the head of the circle. Each of the twelve apostles was carrying a curved shepherd's staff. When they prayed, the staff rested in the crook of their arm. The many disciples standing behind them had shorter staffs.... Peter spoke, and I believe that I recall Peter and John—and, if I am not mistaken, James the Less—indicating the regions to which they should go.
>
> Each had one or two disciples with him. Perhaps some of them had three. Prior to departing they embraced one another, and each blessed the other with a laying-on of hands. The one being blessed did not kneel. Thereupon they parted company, and the vision came to an end.... It was daybreak when they separated, and I now received images of the various regions of the world to which they traveled. Some I saw going overseas. I saw Andrew and Judas Thaddeus ... especially clearly. They were gathered, ready to set off....
>
> I did not see them take the holy sacrament.... Not all twelve apostles were present. I saw about nine of them.... Among the disciples present were many who went only part of the way.... I definitely remember that Peter and John were present, and a small dark-haired (apostle) who was related to Jesus and did not leave (Jerusalem)—I believe this was James (*James the Less was bishop of Jerusalem*)—as well as Paul, Andrew, Judas Thaddeus, Bartholomew, who was tall, and Barnabas, who was very handsome, slim, and nimble.... I do not recall that Matthew the publican, who was the smallest of them all, was there. The one who was martyred together with Judas Thaddeus, Simon, was there. They had not all been in Jerusalem. They came together there. I saw that they journeyed from far and wide to meet together.
>
> I saw that it was mainly Peter who spoke. John and James the Less were his helpers, as it were. He turned to the one or the other (apostle) and seemed to say something to them that was known to him from the Lord. The apostles each chose some of the disciples standing behind them, whom they loved or trusted. It seemed that they had chosen them already in advance, because they were all ready to travel. There was a laying-on of hands by Peter and others for the departing apostles. I recall only the apostles (in relation to the laying-on of hands). At dawn they took leave of one another, and I had visions of how they went here and there in pairs or threesomes and how some individuals went on ahead and others lagged behind. It seemed to me that from time to time some returned. At this gathering, so it seemed to me, they spread

---

† Such a book is in preparation, and will constitute an extensive fourth volume in addition to the three volumes of visions already published. It will contain further background information from traditional apostolic histories, a wide selection of Anne Catherine's visions on other subjects of the greatest possible interest, more on her life, and other supplemental material.

out more and more, going to various distant lands. This had to be quite a time after the freeing of Peter from prison by the angel, because much had changed in the city and in the house where they gathered. Also, Mary was no longer in Jerusalem. And I did not see any of the women whom I would normally have seen at this "taking leave." Much had changed, also, in the house of the Last Supper.

Apart from the information given in the Acts of the Apostles, next to nothing is known from the Bible about the lives of the apostles after the event of Pentecost, the descent of the Holy Spirit, in the year AD 33. However, there are ancient traditions about their travels and deeds, constituting a voluminous literature. In the above vision Anne Catherine offers a glimpse into the reality of the words of Christ, "Lo, I am with you always, even unto the end of time." For Jesus was present—not physically of course, but in his resurrection body—at the gathering of the apostles in Jerusalem that she describes. As she states, not all twelve were there. She explicitly mentions the presence of seven apostles (reporting also that Paul and Barnabas were there), saying that "about nine" were together. Traditionally, this gathering of the apostles in Jerusalem, with Paul present also, is thought to have taken place around AD 50—that is, after the death of the apostle James the Greater in the year AD 44.

For our present purpose, regarding male figures, we have limited ourselves (apart from some brief references at the end) to short descriptions of John the Baptist and the twelve apostles, as well as Matthias, who replaced Judas Iscariot outwardly, and Lazarus (with a quick glance at his friends Nicodemus and Joseph of Arimathea), who might in a sense be said to have replaced him inwardly. As regards the female figures, their selection will be explained in the introduction to the section where they are described. In the fourth volume of the present work, as noted before, extensive material will be provided, translated from Brentano's notes, on those individuals presented here (but at far greater length), and many others besides—in fact, virtually all those Anne Catherine mentions by name, both men and women.

Regarding the following descriptions based on Anne Catherine's visions as recorded by Clemens Brentano, three possibilities are to be distinguished: (*a*) sometimes the descriptions exactly reproduce Anne Catherine's words as given in their published form by Clemens Brentano and translated into English by the anonymous nun whose (further revised) version is also used in this book, in which case it is a matter of Brentano's *edited version* of Anne Catherine's words; (*b*) sometimes the descriptions are taken directly from Brentano's diaries as translated into English by the editors from the above-mentioned 2009 edition, which means these are the words spoken by Anne Catherine as recorded by Clemens Brentano *prior to being edited* (the above passage about the gathering of the apostles in Jerusalem providing an example of this); and (*c*) sometimes they are a paraphrase of (*a*) or of (*b*), or of a mixture of both.

In the case of several of the disciples and holy women whose life sketches follow, Anne Catherine did not describe the circumstances relating to their death. Thus, in the following account we have in some instances drawn upon tradition. In such cases we always preface with relevant section with the words such as "According to tradition…"

Anne Catherine often reported words Jesus spoke, words that can also be found in the gospels in more or less the same form, and in such instances the corresponding biblical reference is indicated in parentheses. Comments in parentheses are by the editors, and all the specific dates given are based on the chronological research presented in Appendices I–V.

James Tissot painted full figure portraits of most of the apostles, and depicted them also in many other scenes, dressed always in the same way, so that they can be readily recognized as one becomes more familiar with his paintings. The same applies to the holy women. Where such portraits exist, they have been placed at the head of the appropriate section, and in some cases details of larger paintings that include the individual concerned—who can be easily identified therein by his or her attire—have also been included.

THE HOLY MEN

John the Baptist, Apostles, Lazarus (& Friends), Other Male Figures

⊕

John the Baptist · 33	Judas Iscariot · 48
Simon, *called* Peter · 38	Philip · 52
Andrew · 41	Matthew · 53
John · 42	Simon · 55
James the Greater · 43	Judas Thaddeus · 56
James the Less · 45	Matthias · 57
Bartholomew · 46	Lazarus (*and* Friends) · · · · · · · · · · · · · · · · · 58
Thomas · 47	Other Male Figures · · · · · · · · · · · · · · · · · · · 60

The Exhortation to the Apostles (Luke 9:1–5)

Discourse with the Disciples

JOHN THE BAPTIST

The Prophetic Character

ALREADY in the womb John, a relative of Jesus,† was moved by the eternal, and brought by the Holy Spirit into extra-temporal communication with his Lord. As a little boy he was withdrawn from the world and his education left to the higher influences of a Nature permeated by God. Withdrawn thus from his time and contemporaries, he lived until the age of thirty deep in the remote wilderness of Judah, which he then left, impelled by God.

Childhood of John the Baptist

As if reborn, he then went forth and took up his mission, seriously, forcefully, and without worldly cares. All of Palestine became now his desert, and just as previously he had kept company with springs, rocks, trees, and animals—living with and speaking to them—so now did he keep company with good men and sinners, never thinking of himself.

Outer Appearance

When from his last wandering place above the source of the Jordan he appeared from out of the desert, John made

The Voice of One Crying in the Wilderness

a most wonderful impression. He was tall, and lean as a result of much fasting and mortification of the flesh, but strong and muscular. He was uncommonly noble, pure and simple, upright and commanding. His skin was dark, his face gaunt, stern, and strong. His hair was reddish brown and curly; he had a short beard. Around the middle of his body was wrapped a loin-cloth, which hung to his knees. He wore a coarse brown coat of three parts. It was of one piece in the back and tied at the waist with a strap. His arms and chest were uncovered. He carried a tall staff, shaped at the top like a shepherd's crook.

---

† The relationship of Mary of Nazareth to John's mother Elizabeth was that of a first cousin once removed. Thus, the relationship of John to Jesus was that of a second cousin once removed

The Establishment of the Three Baptismal Sites

Twice in the year AD 29, during the three months prior to the baptism of Jesus, John traveled for three months the length and breadth of Palestine. His gait was uncommonly powerful, and his pace vigorous but unrushed. His was not the serene walking of Jesus. If he had no business in a place he simply wandered on from field to field. He entered houses and schools to teach, and on public squares and streets people would cluster around him. Now and then priests and authorities confronted him, but then—full of astonishment and pondering—let him pass on.

John the Baptist Teaching the Pharisees

His saying that he was to "prepare the way for the Lord" was no mere figure of speech, for in truth he did visit beforehand the places and tread the paths that Jesus and his disciples would later travel. He cleared the roads of stones and weeds and opened new pathways. He laid planks across brooks and dug out small reservoirs and springs. He built benches and resting places, and awnings for shade. He aroused astonishment when he entered houses to borrow tools for his work, or to recruit volunteers to help him in his labors. Wherever he went, crowds formed around him, and he proceeded straightway to call for repentance, announcing the coming Messiah and himself as his forerunner.

In May or June, AD 31, he established his first baptismal pool on the east bank of the Jordan at a bend in river near Ainon (a short distance north of the present ferry of Ed-Damije). A few weeks later (June 21–23), Herod Antipas visited him and offered to build him a house, which offer he rejected. Immediately after he began his baptizing activity, more and more people went to receive his

Herod Antipas

baptism—among them many of those who later became apostles and discip;les of Jesus. Because John the Baptist was attracting so many people, on July 26, AD 29, the first envoys of the Sanhedrim appeared and confronted him, asking why he did not first present himself to the Temple, and questioning his poor clothing and crude appearance. Many Jews took him to be Elijah, returned from heaven.

The Holy Men

John the Baptist Sees Jesus from Afar

Around July 19, John and his disciples struck their tents at the Ainon baptismal site and proceeded southward along the Jordan's east bank, drawing up in due course diagonally across the river from Jericho, where they founded a new baptismal site (between what is now Wadi Nimrin and Wadi el-Kafren). At this his second baptismal site, John spent only a few weeks. When Jesus returned from his forty-day fast early in December AD 29, he had his disciples rebuild this site, and it was there that he for the first time allowed the disciples to baptize.

By mid-August, John was already teaching and baptizing at his third baptismal site, on the west bank of the Jordan between Ono and Bethagla (a short distance south of the second site). It was on September 23, AD 29 that Jesus came to the River Jordan at this third site to be baptized by John. The baptism of Jesus by John at 10 AM that morning was the fulfillment of John's life mission. After December, when Jesus started having his own disciples baptize, the stream of people coming to John diminished, which filled John's disciples with resentment, all the more so when some of John's disciples joined with those of Jesus. Yet all the while John bore witness to Jesus and announced unceasingly that soon he would step back.

The Imprisonment and Death of the Baptist

After Passover, AD 30, John was again at his first site near Ainon, teaching and baptizing. Late in May, some soldiers

The Baptism of Jesus

Herodians at the Castle in Machaerus

More Herodians

of Herod from Succoth came to fetch him under the pretext of a pressing invitation to Kallirrhoe (on the east bank of the Dead Sea). There he was imprisoned for six weeks in the castle vaults and then released. Herod had great respect for John and asked only that he not preach in public against his adulterous marriage.

On the night of July 17–18, AD 30, John was again incarcerated by Herod's soldiers, first in the jail of Hesebon (35 km east of Jericho) and then, two days later, in the fortress of Machaerus (35 km to the southwest). There he was interrogated several times during the month of August by Herod, who was worried on account of the upheavals caused by the newly-baptized, and also by the news he heard from his followers, the Herodians, about miracles wrought by Jesus.

Here, at this castle, John met his death (by beheading) on the evening of Antipas's birthday celebration (January 3–4, AD 31). That evening Herod Antipas, spell-bound by the dancing of his step-daughter Salome in celebration of his birthday, declared that he would offer her anything she requested of him, even up to half his kingdom. Instigated by her mother, however, Salome requested the head of John the Baptist on a plate. Although he fulfilled this request, it was devastating for Antipas, who had hoped to release John from captivity. On January 18, John's friends

Salome Dancing Before Herod Antipas

transported his body to Jutta, followed by his head several weeks later.

The Head of the Baptist on a Platter

Jesus and the Baptist

It is striking that during their years of wandering neither Jesus nor John cultivated personal contact with each other. In fact they spoke only once, and very briefly. When Jesus (September 4–5, and then late September/early October, AD 30) taught for several days in Ainon, and even traveled with John's disciples, he never once visited John.

Immediately after the Baptist's death, Jesus provided the reason for this unusual friendship devoid of any personal contact. Talking to friends in Jutta on January 9, AD 31, he said that although John had longed to see him, he had constrained himself not to do so, demanding of himself nothing more than to accomplish his own mission—which was to be a precursor and maker of the way, not a fellow traveler or collaborator. Even at the time of the Baptism on September 23, AD 29, John remained within the bounds of acting as ceremonial witness, even though his heart was almost bursting with yearning and love; and later he slipped humbly away rather than yield to his desire to approach Jesus.

As the greatest witness to the Messianic nature of Jesus, John's testimony would hold more weight for his contemporaries in that from birth to death he had *not* been in personal contact with Jesus: for this would make it all the more difficult to claim that his witness had been in any way influenced by him on whose behalf he stood testimony.

It is striking also that John did not call for the help of the all-powerful Messiah during his imprisonment, and that the all-loving Master did not liberate his greatest herald from jail, and thus prevent his murder. Indeed, some of John's followers considered it reprehensible that Jesus withheld his help, and told him so. Jesus answered that he knew well that John longed to be freed from his dungeon, and confirmed that in the end he would be truly freed. But John did not believe that Jesus would himself come to Machaerus to liberate the one who had prepared the way for him.

Another time, Jesus announced quite clearly that John would have to diminish, in order that he (Jesus) might bring his mission to fulfillment. This reminds us of the passage (John 16:7) in which Jesus announces that he must disappear from the world in order that the Consoler (the Holy Spirit) might come.

That is, just as his human presence would have been an obstacle to the disciples receiving the Holy Spirit (cf. Thomas Aquinas, *Theol. III*, q.57, a.1, and q.75, a.1), so for contemporaries of Jesus, the Baptist's physical presence would have constituted an interior obstacle to the full reception of the Messiah, and his teaching and work.

Obviously John knew this also, for as Jesus entered upon his public teaching and baptizing, John lessened his own activity proportionately, speaking increasingly of his own imminent and complete withdrawal. John went on bearing witness to Jesus; and when it was no longer possible for him to do so from his jail, he sent repeated messages to Jesus, imploring him to go to Jerusalem and announce himself before all the world.

For his part, Jesus repeatedly and effusively praised John, especially on November 15, AD 30 at the tax collectors' suburb of Megiddo (Matt. 11:7–15), where he declared that John the Baptist, though lesser in God's eyes than the least spirit in heaven, was yet the greatest of all who have walked the earth. (Thomas Aquinas, *Lectur. Super Matth.*, ibid.)

Disciples at John's Second Place of Baptism

SIMON, *called* PETER

AFTER the death of his wife, Jonah, the owner of a fishery near Capernaum at the northwest end of the Sea of Galilee, handed it over to his younger son, Simon, and moved together with his older son Andrew further south on the

Simon Peter

Sea of Galilee. Simon, referred to as Simon Bar-Jonas (*bar* signifying "son"), was later named Peter by Jesus. Simon had a housekeeper, his older sister, who was very industrious, but rather sickly. After three years, Simon-Peter married a widow whose husband had been a fisherman from Bethsaida, near Capernaum, on the Sea of Galilee. The widow was older than Simon-Peter, and from her previous marriage had two sons and a daughter. The daughter was later martyred, and, as the step-daughter of Peter, is known to us as Petronella. The widow's mother also moved into the home of the newly-wedded couple. Shortly after the wedding, Jonah, together with Andrew and a niece moved into the house vacated by the widow who was now Jonas's daughter-in-law. This house was located at Bethsaida next to a little stream.

Through this marriage Simon-Peter was now distantly related to Jesus of Nazareth through Maroni, the wealthy widow of Nain, whose son Martialis Jesus raised from the dead on November 13, AD 30. As described in the section on the holy women, Maroni was a cousin of Peter's wife and also the sister of the wife of the later apostle James the Greater, who was a second cousin of Jesus. James and his brother John, the two sons of Mary Salome (a cousin of Mary of Nazareth), both worked at Simon-Peter's fishery, as did Andrew also.

Simon-Peter first heard about Jesus from James and John. Shortly after this, Peter's wife, accompanied by Peter's sister, met the Virgin Mary at a gathering of the women in Nazareth. On December 19, AD 29, just prior to the wedding at Cana (on December 28), John and Andrew introduced Peter to Jesus, who spoke the words: "Thou art Simon, the son of Jonah. Thou shalt be called Cephas" (John 1:42). (Cephas = Peter = "the rock".)

Simon Peter with Jesus Teaching

Unlike his brother Andrew, who had a fiery nature, Peter was shy and sensitive, also modest and humble. Whereas Andrew was the first chosen of those who later became the twelve apostles, it was a great step for Simon-Peter to abandon his fishery and his family life in order to become a

With Jesus Teaching in the Portico of Solomon

disciple of Jesus. During a conversation with Jesus on the day (August 19, AD 30) he healed Peter's mother-in-law, Peter was still anxious and concerned about leaving the fishery to follow him. However, this conversation and the healing of his mother-in-law marked a turning point, as thereafter Peter started adjusting to taking the momentous step of joining the company of Jesus, which became explicit on November 21, AD 30, when Jesus called from the shore of the Sea of Galilee, as Peter and Andrew were casting their net from Peter's boat into the water, "Come and follow me; I will make you fishers of men" (Matt. 4:19).

Peter's leading role among the twelve disciples who later became the twelve apostles was highlighted on March 19, AD 31, when on a hill outside the town of Sogane, just before sunrise, Jesus addressed the disciples with the question, "Who do people say that I am?" followed by the further question, "Who do you say that I am?" To which, just as the sun was rising, Peter responded, "Thou art Christ, the Son of the living God!" Jesus then spoke the words, "Blessed are you, Simon Bar-Jonas! For flesh and blood has not revealed this to you, but my Father who is in heaven. And I tell you, you are Peter, and on this rock I will build my church, and the powers of death shall not prevail against it. I will give you the keys of the kingdom of heaven, and whatever you bind on earth shall be bound in heaven, and whatever you loose on earth shall be loosed in heaven" (Matt. 16:13–20).

This pronouncement by Jesus gains in significance in light of the event of Peter's empowerment through the Risen Christ that took place shortly after Easter Sunday (April 5, AD 33), on which day Christ Jesus rose from the dead. It was on the evening of Saturday, April 11, AD 33, as the disciples together with the Virgin Mary and Mary Magdalene were gathered in the Cenacle, or Hall of the Last Supper, that the Risen One appeared to the twelve and placed Thomas's forefinger and middle finger in the wound on his right side. After this, the Risen One related how he had said to Peter that he should strengthen his brothers and why he had said this to him. He said why he wanted to give Peter to them as their leader, even though Peter had denied him—that there had to be a shepherd for the flock—and he spoke about Peter's zeal.

Thereupon John went into the sanctuary of the Cenacle and returned with a colored, embroidered mantle over his arm and a staff in his hand. The staff was bent at the top, like a shepherd's crook. Peter knelt before the Risen One, who gave him something small and round to eat—something radiant with light. Thereby Peter received a special power. Jesus also breathed upon Peter a power, which poured into him. It was not so much a breath as a force, an essence, that Peter received—and he received also words of essence, not merely spoken words. Drawing close first to Peter's mouth and then to each ear in turn, the Risen One poured this force into each of these three orifices. This was not the Holy Spirit as such, but something that the Holy Spirit at Pentecost would then wholly enliven within Peter.

With Jesus Healing in the Streets of Jerusalem

The Primacy of Peter

The Risen One then placed his hands upon Peter and bestowed upon him power and might over the others, draping the mantle around him and placing the staff in his hand. Jesus said to him also that the mantle should hold together in him all the power and might he had given him, indicating when this mantle was to be used, namely, whenever he wished to make use of his power.

Peter then addressed them all in the capacity of the dignity of his new status. He had become a different man, one full of power. The others listened to him and were moved to tears at his speech. He consoled them and spoke of much that Jesus had prophesied and of how it had now been fulfilled. During Peter's speech, the Risen One vanished from the Cenacle.

In deep winter eleven years later (January 18, AD 44), Peter arrived in Rome together with two disciples: Apollinaris and Martialis, the son of Maroni, the widow of Nain.

Second Miraculous Draught of Fishes

Martialis had been raised from the dead by Christ (November 13, AD 30). The three were also accompanied by a servant, whose name was Marcion.

Peter had set off from Antioch, traveling first to Jerusalem, where Christians were being persecuted, journeying then to Naples, and from there to Rome. He had been in Antioch for seven years. Prior to that he had been in Palestine—in Jerusalem, Sarona, and Joppe. Before he went to Joppe he had been in Samaria with the apostle Simon. Altogether he was in Joppe three times.

From Rome he traveled to Ephesus that summer to be present at the death and assumption of the Virgin Mary (August 15, AD 44). After his stay in Ephesus, he returned to Jerusalem, where he was imprisoned, but then miraculously released by an angel (as described in the section on Mary Mark). He then returned to Rome, where he was

"Feed My Lambs"

bishop of the fledgling community of Christians there for twenty-five years, until he was crucified in AD 69 at the age of 99.†

---

† This age indication by Anne Catherine, given that she stated also that he was "five years older than Jesus" (a statement that appears to be accurate, when considered in light of other statements she made concerning the ages of the apostles relative to Jesus's age) should be modified to read "he was crucified in AD 69 at approximately 75 years of age. It was evening and already dark when Peter died on the cross. When friends took his body down from the cross, it radiated with light."

ANDREW

ANDREW, born about 10 BC, was three years older than his brother Peter. He was smaller than Peter in stature and his appearance was one of honesty, openness, and simplicity. He had a bald pate, with snow-white, curly hair hanging

Andrew

down on both sides of his head. He was very industrious, trustworthy, faithful, and generous. He was married, with two sons and two daughters. Already in June AD 29, some three months prior to meeting Jesus, Andrew had been baptized by John the Baptist. He belonged to the small group of about twenty who were the first disciples of John. On September 23, AD 29 Andrew was present at the baptism of Jesus, assisting John the Baptist. After the baptism, John told Andrew to announce the baptism of the Messiah throughout Galilee. That same day Andrew accompanied Jesus to Bethel, and, following Jesus's instructions, began to baptize people there—a baptism differing in several respects from that of John.

Andrew, who was the eldest of the twelve later apostles, was the first to give up everything and follow Jesus. Whereas the other disciples who came from time to time to be with Jesus generally returned then to their homes and occupations, Andrew traveled tirelessly and was continuously involved with teaching and baptizing. He especially enjoyed teaching the children while Jesus was teaching in the synagogue.

Andrew was extremely zealous in spreading the word. He was the first to relate, and with great enthusiasm, to the others who worked at the fishery—Peter, James, John, James the Less, and Judas Thaddeus—the news about Jesus. And he would undertake long journeys to spread the good news to others.

Andrew's wife was very industrious also. She did not get around much. She had a small business at their home, making fishing nets. Several poor girls were employed by her to help with this work. She gave moral instruction to these girls and taught them how to pray. After Christ's ascension, when Andrew went on his apostolic journeys, she continued to live for a time in their house in Bethsaida. Then, however, she moved to Ephesus, to the region where the Virgin Mary lived.

After Christ's ascension, Andrew moved constantly from place to place on his travels through Greece and Asia, performing many miracles in the name of Christ. In Nicomedia, for example, he raised a boy from the dead, and in Hellespont he calmed a storm.

Prior to his death Andrew traveled through Arabia to Egypt. He donated everything he possessed to the fledgling community of Christians. He was sentenced to death by a judge, Aegeas, and was crucified upside down. To the central staff of the cross upon which he was crucified was affixed an X-cross (now called the "St. Andrew's cross").

The Calling of Peter and Andrew

For two days and nights he hung upside down from the cross, all the while preaching the word of God. A number of people, who loved him dearly, sought to free him. But Andrew prayed to die, and they were unable to release him from the cross. Thus did his life end, in his ninety-third year. (If this age indication given by Anne Catherine is accurate, Andrew died around AD 84.)

JOHN

JOHN and his older brother James, the sons of Zebedee and Mary Salome, a cousin of Mary of Nazareth, were second cousins to Jesus. Often the two brothers are referred to as

John of Zebedee

the "sons of Zebedee." They were born in the little town of Japha, about one hour south of Nazareth. Being related to Jesus, and because the family at that time lived not so far from Nazareth, Jesus, James, and John were known to one another already as children. As a young man, John, together with his brother James, joined Peter's fishery, working together with Peter and his brother Andrew as fishermen. On December 19, AD 29, Andrew introduced Peter and John to Jesus, who said to Peter (as we have mentioned): "Thou art Simon, the son of Jonah. Thou shalt be called Cephas" (John 1:42). To John, whom he had known since childhood, he spoke about seeing him again. By September, AD 30, John was—like Andrew—traveling in the company of Jesus as one of his disciples.

The experiences the disciples underwent were often difficult. They were fatigued from the long journeys undertaken by Christ and inwardly exhausted by the masses of people wanting to see Jesus, as well as feeling irked and downcast by the attacks of his enemies, the scribes and the Pharisees. John, however, took everything in his stride. He was open and intrinsically obedient by nature, and inwardly immersed in loving admiration of the Master. In fact, John was more childlike and naturally trusting of Jesus than the others. He was ever kind and loving, and completely accepting, without care or worry. Nevertheless, he was very sensitive.

When on the evening January 9, AD 31 (addressing them in the room of the house in Jutta where John the Baptist had been born), Jesus, in the company of the Virgin Mary, Peter, Judas Thaddeus, Simon, and James the Less, told them that Herod Antipas had killed John the Baptist, John cast himself down to the ground, weeping bitterly.

At the time of his last great teaching in the temple (March 31, AD 33), Jesus instructed John and his brother James to write down anything of his teaching that they had not understood. However, neither of them wrote for very long. So enchanted were they by Jesus's teaching, so immersed in what he was saying, so focused in their attention, that they forgot to write.

Prophecy of the Destruction of the Temple (James, Peter, John)

At the Last Supper, Christ sat between Peter and John: Peter to his left, and John to his right. Into the sacred chalice the Lord received water and wine, the water poured by

At the Last Supper (John, Jesus, Peter)

John and the wine by Peter. After the communion, Christ anointed Peter and John, laying his hands on their heads. Then he gave them detailed instructions relating to the holy sacrament. Later that evening, it was Peter, James, and John who accompanied Jesus to the Garden of Gethsemane, just as they had accompanied him also to the summit of Mt. Tabor on the night of the transfiguration (April 3/4, AD 31), and just as they were present at the raising of the daughter of Jairus from the dead (December 1, AD 30).

John was the only male disciple present at Christ's crucifixion. Jesus spoke to him from the cross, saying, "Behold thy mother" (John 19:27), referring to the Virgin Mary, whom John later accompanied to Ephesus, where he built for her a house.

At the resurrection, on the morning of April 5, AD 33, it was Peter and John who ran to Christ's tomb to find it empty. And it was Peter, James, and John who—together with Thomas, Nathaniel of Cana, John Mark, and Silas—were present at the northeast end of the Sea of Galilee on the morning of April 15, AD 33, when from the shore the Risen One appeared to this group of seven, who were in a boat, having fished unsuccessfully throughout the night.

Later, in Ephesus, John remained with the Virgin Mary for the rest of her life, never leaving her. He gave her the holy sacrament, prayed with her the Way of the Cross, blessed her, and received blessing in turn from her. John was like a son to her, closer to her than anyone else. After the Blessed Virgin's death and assumption, John stayed on in Ephesus for a time after the other apostles left, first together and then each going his separate way. Eventually, John also returned to Jerusalem and was present at the gathering of the apostles referred to in the Acts of the Apostles (Acts 15:6), thought to have taken place around the year AD 50. According to tradition, John died a martyr's death, like his brother James the Greater.

JAMES THE GREATER

JAMES was the elder of the two "sons of Zebedee." Whereas John was thin and delicately constituted, James was tall and broad-shouldered. He had dark hair and a brownish beard, but his face was pale. His mood generally was serious, yet he could also be very light-hearted and joyous. He was married and, until his final call to become a disciple (November 21, AD 30), he and his wife lived in a house not

James the Greater

far from Capernaum. They had no children. His wife was a sister of the widow of Nain (Maroni), the mother of the youth Martialis, raised from the dead by Jesus on November 13, AD 30.

Together with John, James worked as a fisherman at Peter's fishery. When Jesus taught in the more intimate circle of the disciples, James often put questions to him, and the Lord enjoyed answering his questions. Because Peter, James, and John were allowed by Jesus to be present at significant miraculous events, such as the transfiguration and other events listed under *John of Zebedee* above, these three apostles came to represent *faith* (Peter), *hope* (James), and *love* (John), the three cardinal virtues.

Some time after Christ's ascension, when the persecutions of the Christians began, James the Greater went to live in the cave of the nativity in Bethlehem. Then he went to Ephesus, where he visited the Virgin Mary, and then to Spain, where he remained only for about one-quarter of a year, having to flee for his life. He returned to Palestine, traveling via Marseille and Rome, having been absent altogether for about one year. He went to Joppe in Samaria, where he had a confrontation with Hermogenes, who was practicing magic there. Through miracles, he converted Hermogenes, and then, before leaving Palestine again spent some time in Joppe, where he met up with Peter, performing some miracles together with him there.

From Joppa, James traveled by boat back to Spain, where he spent about three years. During this time he faced great difficulties. After many disputes, he was put in

Listening to Jesus When Tempted by Pharisees & Sadducees (James the Greater, James the Less, John, Peter)

prison, but an angel freed him. When he was in Saragossa, he again faced persecution. Not knowing what to do, he lay on his back with his arms spread out in the form of a cross and prayed to Mary. There took place then the first appearance of the Virgin Mary—and *prior* to her assumption. In his vision, James saw a radiance streaming upon the water (of the River Ebro) and above the city. From this light a great pillar formed. James beheld the Virgin Mary—indescribably beautiful—standing upon the pillar, streaming out rays of light in all directions. The largest and brightest ray, however, streamed between the north and the west to the region where James was later buried. At this location in Saragossa, where he had the vision, he set up a stone to commemorate the apparition. Later a church was built at this site, and again there was a miracle confirming that this had indeed been the place of the apparition.

John and James the Greater Espy the Risen One on the Shore

From Saragossa, guided by Mary, James traveled to Braga and then to Compostela, where his remains were later buried. Then he received an interior summons to visit the Virgin Mary in Ephesus. She said to him there that he would soon die in Jerusalem, and she strengthened and comforted him.

When James took leave of Mary and his brother John in Ephesus, he went to Jerusalem, where he was indeed martyred. On this account he was not present in Ephesus at the death and assumption of the Virgin Mary (August 15, AD 44). He was represented in Ephesus by Joseph Barsabbas, the son of Mary Cleophas and Sabbas, who was the second husband of Mary Cleophas.

The death of James in Jerusalem took place shortly after the new moon. When he was captured and bound, he said "You can bind my hands, but not the blessing and not my tongue." At his execution a great tumult arose and many were converted. James the Less wanted to receive his corpse, but the Jews instructed soldiers to take it away. His body was initially buried in the vicinity of Jerusalem. But it was later found and exhumed by some of the disciples, and transported back to Spain by the disciples Saturnin, Ctesiphon, and Joseph of Arimathea. According to tradition, the relics of James the Greater were later found at Santiago de Compostela, which became one of the greatest pilgrimage sites in Christendom.

According to Acts 12:1–2, James the Greater, not long after he returned from Spain to Jerusalem, was killed "with the sword" by King Herod Agrippa I (just before Easter AD 44). Thus captured by the king and beheaded, he became the first apostle to be martyred, and on account of his martyrdom came to represent the suffering Church. He is also looked upon as a great upholder of the true faith against those who deny the faith.

JAMES THE LESS

JAMES THE LESS, brother of Judas Thaddeus and Simon, was the youngest of the three sons of Alpheus and Mary Cleophas. He was an Essene. His mother, even though she was a niece of Mary of Nazareth, was about four years older than her (see the section on the holy women). In turn, James the Less was about eight years younger than Jesus. On account of his great similarity in appearance to Jesus, he was often called "the brother of the Lord." However, his actual relationship to Jesus of Nazareth was not that of brother but that of first cousin once removed.

Like Jesus, James the Less was extraordinarily handsome. He also worked at Peter's fishery as a fisherman, and received the baptism of John the Baptist not long after

James the Less

John started baptizing (in the year AD 29). On account of their family relationship, Jesus and James the Less knew each other during childhood, but did not see each other thereafter for many years until they met again on May 29, AD 29, when Jesus, on his first journey to Hebron, visited together with the Virgin Mary the home of Mary Cleophas in Nazareth. Some months later (August 12, AD 29) James the Less for the first time heard Jesus preach. This was at a small place in the Zebulon valley between Nazareth and Sepphoris. The holy women of Nazareth were present there also, as well as the future apostles Peter, Andrew, and Philip, all of whom, like James the Less, were already disciples of John the Baptist. James was also present four-and-a-half months later at the wedding at Cana and experienced there the miracle of the changing of water into wine (December 28, AD 29). He then accompanied Jesus on his journey from Judea to Galilee, taking part for the first time in a longer journey in the company of the Master.

After Christ's ascension, James the Less played a leading role in the community of Christians in Jerusalem. After Peter left Jerusalem, James the Less became head of the community there, the first bishop of Jerusalem. He died a martyr's death in Jerusalem some years after the martyrdom of the apostle James the Greater (AD 44). In the seven days leading up to his death he was tried and every day beaten for an hour or so. In the end James the Less was pushed from the temple, stoned, and beaten to death.

James the Less, Water Bearer at the Washing of the Feet

BARTHOLOMEW

Known also as NAPHTALI, BARTHOLOMEW was an Essene also. Good-looking and intelligent, he had a high forehead and a pale face set with large dark eyes. His hair was dark, and he wore a modest beard split down the middle. He was well-built and of all the apostles the most refined in terms of appearance. There was a nobility and delicacy in his manner. He moved quickly, and his upright bearing gave the impression of a well-educated nobleman.

On May 29, AD 29, on his way from Capernaum to Nazareth, Jesus passed through Bethulia. As he did so, he glanced at Bartholomew, who received a stream of grace through Jesus's gaze. This gaze, which touched him deeply, Bartholomew never forgot. From that moment he felt inwardly drawn to Jesus. He worked in the town of Debbaseth, west of Nazareth, as a clerk with an official position. Through this employment he had become friends with the future apostles Thomas and Simon, and also with Nathaniel Chased (John 1:45–51), who worked as a clerk in Gennabris, near the southern end of the Sea of Galilee.

Bartholomew went to hear Jesus teach, and also witnessed miraculous healings, but at this point he did not yet speak with Jesus. In late May AD 30, as Jesus was in West Galilee on his way back from the place of baptism (Ono, near the mouth of the River Jordan), he was introduced to Bartholomew by Andrew. At this encounter Jesus said to Andrew concerning Bartholomew, "I know him; he will follow me. I see good in him, and in due course of time I shall call him."

Bartholomew

Not long after this, when Jesus was again in the area of Debbaseth, he visited Bartholomew and received him as one of the twelve chosen disciples, the later apostles. He blessed Bartholomew, laying his hand upon him. Bartholomew immediately gave up his position and followed Jesus. He was the ninth disciple of the twelve—the summons of Matthew, Thomas, and Judas taking place later that year. Although his given name was Naphtali, he received the name Bartholomew, because Jesus referred to him always as the son (*bar*) of Thomai (the name of his father).

Following Christ's ascension, Bartholomew traveled and preached in Asia as far away as Armenia and India. He then journeyed through Arabia and crossed the Red Sea on his way to Abyssinia, where he converted the king, whose name was Polymius. In Abyssinia Bartholomew raised someone from the dead and also cast out demons from many people. Polymius and his family, and many others, were baptized by Bartholomew, who also consecrated the temple there as a church. He healed many and was much loved by the people of Abyssinia.

Then, in the year AD 44, Bartholomew received an interior call to go to Ephesus to the Virgin Mary. He arrived there in time to be present at her death and assumption together with the other apostles (excepting Thomas, who arrived one day late). Upon his return to Abyssinia, Bartholomew was betrayed by the heathen priests of the temple, who denounced him to Polymius' brother Afthages as a magician. Afthages accused Bartholomew, saying: "You led my brother astray to pray to your God. I will teach you to worship mine." Bartholomew replied: "The God who gave me the power to show satan (in the temple prior to its consecration as a church) to your brother and to cast him (satan) into hell, gives me the power also to destroy your idols and to convert you to the faith." Following immediately upon these words, a messenger brought Afthages the news that his idol had plunged to the ground and shattered. Afthages angrily commanded that Bartholomew be scourged. He was bound to a tree and flayed. The whole time he taught in a loud voice, until they plunged a sword through his throat. They flayed him from the feet up and placed his own skin in his hand. After his death, they cast his body to the animals. However, at night some who were newly converted to the faith removed the body. King Polymius, accompanied by many people, fetched the body and buried it. Later they built a chapel above the grave. Thirteen days later, Afthages and the pagan priests who had betrayed Bartholomew went mad and rushed to the grave, crying aloud for help. Thereupon, Afthages experienced an act of grace and converted to Christianity. The pagan priests, however, died a hideous death.

Bartholomew can be of special help to those in despair and those suffering from lameness or paralysis.

THOMAS

The parents of THOMAS lived in Apheke, south of Nazareth. Thomas was born with a twin brother (the name Thomas means "a twin") and their mother died in childbirth. His father, who was a tradesman, married again, and Thomas's stepmother gave birth to a daughter and two sons. After the death of the father, the stepmother married again, so that Thomas now had a stepfather as well as a stepmother. He was given then into the care of his

Thomas

uncle, who belonged to a sect, and Thomas received a severe upbringing.

On account of his father's activity as a tradesman, Thomas had come at an early age into contact with foreigners. In this way he had learned to speak foreign languages and become acquainted with the customs of other peoples outside Palestine. Through his education he had grown quite obstinate, wanting always to have things proved to him. He tried various occupations: sailor, tradesman, and fisherman on the Sea of Galilee. It was through the latter that he first came into contact with the first disciples, the subsequent apostles.

Later, Thomas went to Saphet, where he studied Jewish tradition, attending a school of the Pharisees, although without becoming one. He got to know Nathaniel Chased and Bartholomew, from whom he learned the trade of being a clerk. Thomas (born about 5 BC) was some three years older than Jesus of Nazareth. During his twenties he came to know James the Less, who was an Essene and very pious, and who spoke to Thomas about Jesus. Through this, Thomas was changed inwardly, becoming more pious and also more serious.

The Disbelief of Thomas

In his thirtieth year, Thomas was living at Arimathea as a clerk. From there he went to the town of Dothan, to the home of Issachar, who had recently married his brother's widow. It was there that he met Jesus and some of the disciples. Thus did Thomas ask Jesus if he could become a disciple: "I want to follow you and to do whatever you ask of me. Through your teaching and through your miracles, which I have seen, I am convinced that John and all your disciples known to me have spoken the truth about you. Please allow me to enter your kingdom."

As a disciple, Thomas enjoyed entering into discussion with the Pharisees and disputing with them concerning Jesus's teaching.

Three years after Christ's ascension, accompanied by the apostle Judas Thaddeus and some other disciples, Thomas traveled to the land of the three kings, of whom only two were still living, and whom during the final year of his ministry Jesus had also visited. Thomas baptized the two kings and all their entourage. Thomas then journeyed further east, whereas Judas Thaddeus moved on to Edessa, where he healed King Abgar.

Thomas was accompanied by an old servant from the East. Everywhere Thomas went, he performed miracles. He, like the other apostles, died a martyr's death, Anne Catherine giving his age as 93. According to tradition, it was in the city of Madras (present-day Chennai), India, that he died. As he knelt in prayer upon a stone, a pagan priest plunged a spear into him from behind. At the time of his death his coloring was brown; he was thin and haggard, and he had reddish hair. At his death the Lord appeared to him. His relics were later sent to Edessa.

Thomas had a half-sister named Lysia. His older twin-brother (Thomas was the younger twin) came into the community of Christians through Peter. This was after Christ's ascension. Peter related to him that Thomas, on account of his disbelief at the appearance of the Risen One, had been allowed to place his fingers in the wounds. This took place six days after the resurrection (April 11, AD 33). It was on this Saturday evening, as the disciples together with the Virgin Mary and Mary Magdalene were gathered in the Hall of the Last Supper, that the Risen One appeared to the twelve and, taking first Thomas's right hand in his right hand, placed the tip of his forefinger into the wound on his left hand, then took Thomas's left hand in his left hand, placed the tip of his forefinger into the wound on his right hand, and then with his right hand guided Thomas's right hand, placing his forefinger and middle finger in the wound on his right side. Thomas's brother, who was tall, accompanied the apostle Peter to Damascus. Lysia converted to the faith around the time of the stoning to death of Stephen. She was a rich widow and donated all she possessed to the community of holy women in Jerusalem. Her two sons later became disciples.

JUDAS ISCARIOT

The parents of JUDAS had lived for a time in the little town of Iscariot, twelve miles west of the Jordan and ten miles northeast of Sychar, and this is how Judas came to be called Judas Iscariot. His mother was a dancer and a singer, also a poet. She wrote songs and verses and sang them, accompanying on the harp. She taught dance to young women. Her husband, a Jew, did not live together with her. Judas was an illegitimate child born to his mother from a relationship she had with Judas's natural father, who was a military commander from Damascus.

The Holy Men

Judas Iscariot

He did not continue the relationship with Judas's mother much longer, and soon distanced himself from her altogether.

After his birth, the mother of Judas set him out in a basket upon the water, similar to what took place with Moses after his birth. A well-to-do woman, who wanted a child, received him. She and her husband were a wealthy, childless couple. Through them, Judas received an excellent upbringing. Later, on account of his misbehavior after an act of deception, he landed back in the care of his natural mother. Her husband, upon learning about Judas's background, cursed him.

After the death of his mother and stepfather, Judas lived primarily in Iscariot at the home of his uncle Simon, toward whom he was very considerate and well-behaved, and whom he helped a great deal. When Judas met Jesus, (October 24, AD 30), he may have been twenty-five years old, about six years younger than Jesus. He was of middle height and rather handsome. His hair was deep black and his beard somewhat reddish. In his attire he was perfectly neat and more elegant than the majority of Jews.

Judas was affable, obliging, and fond of making himself important. He talked with an air of confidence of the great, or of persons renowned for holiness, affecting familiarity with such persons when he found himself among those that did not know him. But if anyone who knew better convicted him of untruth, he retired confused. He was avaricious of honors, distinctions, and money. He was ever in pursuit of good luck, longing always for fame, rank, high position, and wealth, though not seeing clearly how all this was to be achieved. The appearance of Jesus in public, however, greatly encouraged him to hope for the realization of his dreams. After all, the disciples were provided for; the wealthy Lazarus took part with Jesus, of whom everyone thought he was about to establish a kingdom; and he was spoken of on all sides as a king, as the Messiah, as the prophet of Nazareth. His miracles and wisdom were on every tongue.

Judas consequently conceived a great desire to be numbered among the disciples of Jesus and to share in his greatness, which, he thought, was to be of this world. For a long time previously he had picked up, wherever he could, information concerning Jesus and had in turn carried around tidings of him. He had sought out acquaintance with several of the disciples, and was now nearing the object of his desires. A chief motive influencing him to follow Jesus was that he (Judas) had no settled occupation and but half an education. He had embarked on trade and commerce, but without success, and had squandered the fortune left him by his natural father. Lately he had been executing all kinds of commissions, carrying on all sorts of business and brokerage for others. In the discharge of such affairs he proved himself both zealous and intelligent.

Judas had made the acquaintance of Bartholomew and Simon already prior to October 23, AD 30, on which date, in the evening, Bartholomew and Simon undertook to speak to Jesus about Judas, recommending that he be accepted as a disciple. Prior to this, Judas had begged them to present him to Jesus as one desirous of discipleship. They were well pleased to do so, for they took delight in his cleverness, his readiness to render service, and his courteous manner.

When Bartholomew and Simon spoke of Judas with Jesus, they said they knew him to be an active, well-informed man, very willing to be of service, and very desirous of a place among the disciples. Jesus sighed as they spoke and appeared troubled. When they asked him the cause of his sadness, he answered: "It is not yet time to speak, but only to think of it."

Already on the afternoon of the next day, Simon and Bartholomew introduced Judas to Jesus. Bartholomew and Simon presented him with the words: "Master, here is Judas, of whom we have spoken to thee." Jesus looked at him graciously but with indescribable sorrow. Judas, bowing, said: "Master, I pray thee allow me to share thy instructions." Jesus replied sweetly and in words full of prophetic meaning: "You may have a place among my disciples, unless you prefer to leave it to another."

Because he was so obliging, the disciples initially appreciated Judas. He even cleaned their shoes. He was able to run great distances on errands for the community of the disciples. He was adept at business dealings and paid close attention to the monetary exchanges made by the disciples.

It was in the town of Meroz that Judas became a disciple. Immediately afterward, as he was teaching on the mount of Meroz, Jesus instructed that the money which some of the disciples had brought with them from Capernaum should be distributed among the poor—to which Judas paid special attention.† Soon after, some of the disciples began to dislike Judas. Thomas spoke out to the Lord that Judas did not particularly please him, because Judas was so opportunistic, and he asked Jesus why he had taken him into the circle of disciples. For, he added, in comparison with others, Judas was a difficult person. Jesus did not give Thomas a direct answer, but said that everyone was included in the eternal providence of God.

The Blessed Virgin often warned Judas, who, however, was always vacillating. Although he did display repentance for his errors, he seemed to be incapable of lasting remorse. He was thinking always of money and worldly things. Whereas the other disciples (the later apostles) performed miracles, Judas never did. He was full of jealousy and envy. Toward the end of Jesus's ministry, he grew weary of the continual travels. Much that Jesus taught remained a mystery to him, and he no longer felt that he needed to be obedient to the Lord.

The culmination of Judas's discontent came to expression on the evening prior to the Last Supper. On that Wednesday evening (April 1, AD 33), at the festive gathering at the house of Simon the Pharisee in Bethany, Mary Magdalene anointed Jesus. As Magdalene was leaving the room, and just passing before him, Judas stretched forth his hand to stay her as he indignantly addressed to her some words on her extravagance, saying that the purchase money might better have been given to the poor. Magdalene made no reply. She was weeping bitterly. Then Jesus spoke, bidding Judas and some others let her pass, and saying that she had anointed him for his death, for later

† Judas took a close interest in the financial dealings of the community of Christians and, in fact, later became minder of the pursestrings of the community.

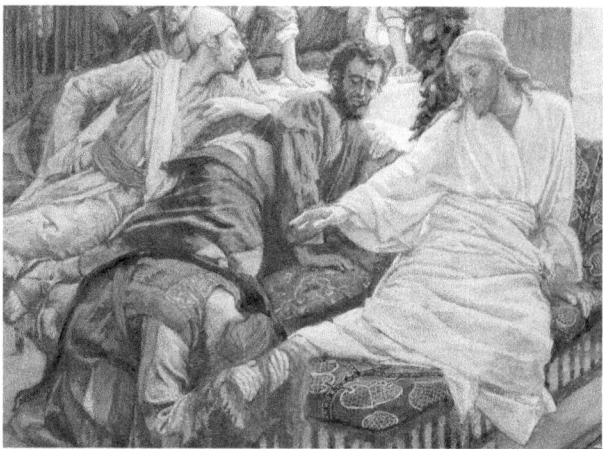

Mary Magdalene Anoints Jesus

she would not be able to do it, and that wherever this gospel would be preached, her action and their murmuring would be recounted also.

Magdalene retired then, her heart full of sorrow. The rest of the meal was disturbed by the displeasure of the apostles and the reproaches of Jesus. When it was over, all returned to Lazarus's home. Judas, full of wrath and avarice, thought within himself that he could no longer put up with such things. But, concealing his feelings, he laid aside his festal garment and pretended he had to go back to the public house to see that what remained of the meal was distributed to the poor. Instead of this, however, he ran full speed to Jerusalem, the devil with him all the while, red, thin-bodied, and angular—before him and

Judas Meets in Jerusalem with the Pharisees

behind him, as if lighting the way. Judas saw through the darkness. He stumbled not, but ran along in perfect safety.

When he arrived in Jerusalem he ran into the house of Caiaphas in which, later on, Jesus was exposed to scorn and derision. The Pharisees and high priests were still together, but Judas did not enter their assembly. Two of their number came out and spoke with him in the courtyard below. When Judas told them he was ready to deliver Jesus and asked what they would give for him, they showed great joy and returned to announce the news to the rest of the council. After a while, one came out again and made an offer of thirty pieces of silver. Judas wanted to receive them at once, but they would not yet give them to him.

After receiving the holy sacrament at the Last Supper, Judas did not return to his place, but immediately left the Cenacle. The others thought Jesus had given him some commission to execute. He left without prayer or thanksgiving. When outside the door, three devils pressed around him. One entered into his mouth, one urged him on, and the third ran in front of him. It was night. They seemed to be lighting his way as he hurried on like a madman to complete his betrayal.

Around midnight Judas arrived at the Garden of Gethsemane, accompanied by twenty soldiers and six officials. Judas went up to Jesus and kissed him, saying: "Hail, Master!" Jesus replied: "Judas, would you betray the Son of

Judas Betrays Jesus with a Kiss

Man with a kiss?" (Luke 22:47–48). Now, at the beginning of his act of treason Judas had really never considered what its result would be. He wanted to obtain the traitor's reward and please the Pharisees by pretending to deliver Jesus into their hands, but he had never counted on things going so far, he never dreamed of Jesus being brought to judgment and crucified. He was thinking only of the money, and had for a long time been in communication with some sneaking, spying Pharisees and Sadducees who by flattery had incited him to treason.

Judas had grown tired of the fatiguing, wandering, persecuted life led by the apostles. Several months past he had begun his downward course by stealing from the alms committed to his care; and his avarice, excited by Magdalene's lavish anointing of Jesus, urged him on to extremes. He had always counted upon Jesus establishing a temporal kingdom, in which he hoped for some brilliant and lucrative post. But as this was not forthcoming, he turned his thoughts to amassing a fortune. He saw that hardships and persecution were on the increase; and so, he reasoned, before things came to the worst, he would ingratiate himself with some of the powerful and distinguished among Jesus's enemies. He saw that Jesus would not become a king, whereas the high priests and prominent men of the temple were people very attractive in his eyes. And so he allowed himself to be drawn into closer communication with their agents, who flattered him in every way and told him in the greatest confidence that under any circumstances an end would soon be put to Jesus's career. During the last few days they followed him to Bethany, and thus did he sink deeper and deeper into depravity.

Judas almost ran his legs off trying to induce the high priests to come to some conclusion. But they would not come to terms and treated him with great contempt. They told him that the time now intervening before the feast was too short. If any action were taken now, it would create trouble and disturbance during the feast. The Sanhedrin alone paid some degree of attention to his proposals.

After Judas's sacrilegious reception of the sacrament, satan had taken complete possession of him, and he went off at once to complete his horrible crime. But after hearing that Jesus had been sentenced to death, anguish, despair, and remorse began to struggle in the soul of Judas—though all too late. Satan instigated him to flee. The bag of silver pieces hanging from the girdle under his mantle was for him like a hellish spur. He grasped it tightly in his hand to prevent its rattling and striking against him at every step. On he ran at full speed, not after the procession, not to cast himself in Jesus's path to implore mercy and forgiveness, not to die with Jesus. No, not to confess with contrition before God his awful crime, but to unburden himself of his guilt and of the price of his treachery before men.

Like one bereft of his senses, Judas rushed into the temple, whither several of the council, as superintendents of the priests whose duty it was to serve, and also some of the elders, had gone directly after the condemnation of Jesus. They glanced wonderingly at one another, and then fixed their gaze with proud and scornful smiles upon Judas, who stood before them, his countenance distorted by despairing grief. He ripped the bag of silver pieces from his girdle and held it toward them with his right hand, while in a voice of agony he cried: "Take back your money! By it you have led me to betray the just one. Take back your money! Release Jesus! I recall my contract. I have sinned grievously by betraying innocent blood!"

The priests poured out upon him the full measure of their contempt. Raising their hands, they stepped back before the proffered silver, as if to preserve themselves from pollution, and said: "What is it to us that you have sinned? Think you to have sold innocent blood? Look you to it! It is your own affair! We know what we have bought from you, and we find him deserving of death. You have your money. We want none of it!" With these and similar words spoken quickly and in the manner of men that have business on hand and that wish to get away from an importunate visitor, they turned from Judas.

Their treatment inspired Judas with such rage and despair that he became like one insane. His hair stood on end, with both hands he rent asunder the chain that held the silver pieces together, scattered them in the temple, and fled from the city. He ran like a maniac to the Valley of Himmon, with Satan under a horrible form at his side. The evil one, to drive him to despair, was whispering into his ear all the curses the prophets had ever invoked upon this valley, wherein the Jews had once sacrificed their own children to idols. From the city came repeated sounds of noisy tumult, and Satan whispered again: "Now he is being led to death! Thou hast sold him! Knowest thou not how the law runs: he who sells a soul among his brethren, and receives the price thereof, let him die! Put an end to thyself, thou wretched one! Put an end to thyself!"

Judas Scatters the Silver Pieces in the Temple

Overcome by despair, Judas took his girdle and hung himself on a tree. The tree was one that consisted of several trunks, and rose out of a hollow in the ground. As he hung, his body burst asunder, and his bowels poured out upon the earth. (It was around sunrise on Good Friday, April 3, AD 33, that Judas put an end to his life.)

Judas Hangs Himself

PHILIP

PHILIP worked as a clerk in the fishing village of Bethsaida. His manner was polite and refined. Andrew also lived in Bethsaida and was acquainted with Philip. Already in June AD 29 the two of them went to John the Baptist and were baptized. Several weeks later, on August 5, in Bethsaida's synagogue, Philip heard Jesus preaching for the first time. One week later, in a school in the Zebulon Valley, he heard him preach a second time. Andrew, after becoming a disciple, came to Philip several times to relate to him his experiences of the Lord. He also invited

The Holy Men

Philip

Philip to the wedding at Cana (which took place on December 28, AD 29). On December 24, two days prior to the start of the three-day wedding celebration, Andrew took Philip to go on a walk with Jesus, who had just arrived in Capernaum and, after teaching at the synagogue, was walking with a group of about eleven people in a valley near the synagogue. Shy and hesitant, Philip hung back, not pressing forward to be at Jesus's side. The Lord turned to him and said, "Follow me!" (John 1:43). Joyfully Philip joined the company of Jesus. The Master had called him, and Philip experienced inwardly the spiritual reality of this call. The next day Philip visited his friend the clerk Nathaniel Chased in Gennabris and described his experience. Nathaniel then went with Philip to find the Lord, who was now on his way to Cana for the wedding. The subsequent exchange that took place between Jesus and Nathaniel is described in John 1:45–51. Some time after Christ's ascension, Philip went to Egypt. It was from there that he traveled to Ephesus for the death and assumption of the Blessed Virgin Mary (which took place August 15, AD 44). Prior to her death, Philip received the Virgin Mary's blessing, he weeping bitterly. On that occasion he received the holy sacrament from Peter after the other apostles. Later, Philip was in the city of Hieropolis in Phrygia. Bartholomew was there with him. (At Hieropolis a Martyrium named after the apostle Philip stands on top of the hill outside the northeastern section of the city walls. It dates from the fifth century AD. It is said that Philip is buried in the center of the building, but his grave has not been discovered. The Martyrium burned down at the end of the fifth or early sixth century AD, as attested by fire marks on the columns. Philip is said to have been martyred in Hieropolis by being crucified upside-down, or by being hung upside down by his ankles from a tree.)

Address to Philip (John 14:5–20)

MATTHEW

Originally called LEVI, Jesus named him MATTHEW. He was the stepson of Mary Cleophas who, in turn, was the niece of Mary of Nazareth. Levi was the son of Alpheus, Mary Cleophas's first husband, who brought his son Levi with him into the marriage. When Levi chose to become a publican, this was a matter of great concern for Mary

Cleophas and the rest of her family, as this profession was very much looked down upon.

Matthew

Through his stepmother, Levi was a second cousin (by marriage rather than blood) of Jesus. Mary Cleophas's other sons were second cousins of Jesus by way of their blood relationship with him. On September 6, AD 29, Mary Cleophas spoke with Jesus about her sons. One was a clerk, or a kind of magistrate, named Simon; two were fishermen—James the Less and Judas Thaddeus. These three were the sons of her first marriage. As stated above, Alpheus, her first husband, was a widower with one son when she married him, and this was Levi (later Matthew). Mary Cleophas wept bitterly when she spoke of Matthew, for he was a publican. Joseph Barsabbas, who—like James the Less and Judas Thaddeus—was employed at Peter's fishery, was her son by her second husband Sabbas. Furthermore, by her third marriage with the fisherman Jonah, she had another son, the young Simeon, still a boy.

During this conversation Jesus consoled Mary Cleophas, promising that all her sons would one day follow him. Of Matthew, whom he had already seen when on his way to Sidon, he spoke words of comfort, foretelling that he would one day be one of his best disciples.

Matthew was aware of the notoriety of his profession as a publican. At the northeastern shore of the Sea of Galilee (on November 19, AD 30), when from the top of a little eminence Matthew beheld Jesus and the disciples coming toward him, he became confused and withdrew into his private office. But Jesus continued to approach, and from the opposite side of the road called out to him. Then Matthew came hurrying out, prostrated himself face to the ground before Jesus, and protested that he did not esteem himself worthy that Jesus should speak to him. But Jesus said: "Matthew, arise, and follow me!" Matthew arose, saying he would instantly and joyfully abandon all things and follow him, and accompanied Jesus back to where stood the disciples, who greeted him and extended their hands in welcome. Thaddeus, Simon, and James the Less particularly rejoiced at his coming, as they and Matthew were half-brothers.

The Calling of Matthew

Matthew at once procured a substitute in his business, an excellent man who was to discharge his duties until further arrangements could be made.

Matthew was a married man, with four children. He joyfully imparted to his wife the good fortune that had befallen him, as well as his intention to abandon all and follow Jesus, and she received his announcement with corresponding joy. Then he directed her to see to the preparing of a reception for Jesus for the next morning, he himself taking charge of the invitations and other arrangements.

In stature Matthew was the smallest of the twelve who were later the twelve apostles; and he was one of the eldest. He was older than Jesus, but not quite as old as Peter who, in turn, was younger than Andrew. (Andrew was three years older than Peter.) One might easily have taken Matthew for the father of his young half-brother Joseph Barsabbas. Matthew was a man of heavy, bony frame with black hair and beard. Since his acquaintance with Jesus on the way to Sidon, he had received John's baptism and regulated his whole life most conscientiously.

Toward noon the next day Jesus returned with the disciples to Matthew's, where many publicans who had been invited were already assembled. Some Pharisees and some of John's disciples had joined Jesus on the way, but they did not enter Matthew's. They stayed outdoors, sauntering around the garden with the disciples, to whom they put the question: "How can you tolerate your Master's making himself so familiar with sinners and publicans?" They received for answer: "Ask himself why he does so!" But the Pharisees responded: "One cannot speak with a man who always maintains that he is right."

Matthew received Jesus and his followers most lovingly and humbly, and washed their feet. His half-brothers warmly embraced him, and then he presented his wife and children to Jesus. Jesus spoke to the mother and blessed the children, who then retired. When Jesus was seated, Matthew went down on his knees before him. Jesus laid his hand upon him, blessed him, and addressed to him some words of instruction. It was then that Matthew, formerly called Levi, received the name Matthew.

(According to tradition, after Christ's ascension Matthew stayed for a time in Judea, where he wrote his gospel in the Hebrew language, primarily for the sake of the community of Christians in Jerusalem.) He later traveled with Peter to Antioch to spread the good news there. Subsequently, in the city of Mirmide (in Macedonia?), Matthew was taken captive, blinded, and thrown into prison, where he awaited death. But then Andrew, summoned by an angel, came from the region of Achaia in the Peloponnese (Greece) to Matthew, healed him of blindness, and released him from his prison chains. Then, preaching the gospel, the city was converted to Christianity. (According to tradition, Matthew was put to death at Naddabar, a city in Asia (or in Ethiopia?), with a halberd (a pike fitted with an axe head.)

SIMON

SIMON was younger than Jesus. In stature he was thin, and he looked similar to John, the son of Zebedee. Simon was the second of the three sons of Alpheus and Mary Cleophas. Judas Thaddeus was his elder brother, and James the Less his younger. Matthew, who was also older than him, was his half-brother—the son of Alpheus from a previous marriage, before he married Mary Cleophas. The brothers were not among Jesus's playmates as children, for they lived in another place. However, they knew him and saw him when their parents visited with one another.

Simon

As a young man, Simon worked in the court at Tiberias as an arbiter and clerk. Because of his passionate engagement for upholding justice, he was called "zealous" (Simon the Zealot).

On December 20, AD 29, when Jesus was teaching in the vicinity of Tarichea at the southern end of the Sea of Galilee, Simon was at work in the courthouse of Tiberias. His brother James the Less went there to seek him out and encourage him to come see and hear the Master. Simon was so deeply struck by his encounter with the Lord that he did not return to the courthouse but instead set about putting his affairs in order, including handing over his official position at the courthouse to an acquaintance. He immediately followed Jesus, who accepted him as a disciple. A few days later there took place the wedding at Cana, at which Simon was also present.

The fact of Simon's being taken on as a disciple, and the almost simultaneous summoning by Jesus of the two clerks Philip (on December 24, AD 29) and Nathaniel Chased (on the following day) to follow him, made a deep impression on Thomas and Bartholomew, who were longtime friends with Simon, Philip, and Nathaniel Chased.

It was Simon who, together with Bartholomew, had suggested (on October 23, AD 30) to Jesus that Judas Iscariot be accepted as a disciple.

Simon, together with his elder brother Judas Thaddeus, died a martyr's death. They died in Persia. Prior to this, Simon had been together with Peter in Samaria. Simon had also been in Egypt. He performed miracles there, and converted many people in places where the holy family had sojourned during their flight to Egypt. In Memphis an idol of Isis fell at his command. This figure of Isis had seven breasts and was veiled. She wore a tiara on her head and held a sheath of wheat in one hand and an upside-down vessel in the other. Simon was also in the Egyptian town of Matarea, where the holy family—and earlier Abraham, and earlier still Job—had lived. He built a chapel in the home of the holy family, with an altar, and opened a well that had been covered.

After the gathering of the apostles in Jerusalem referred to in the Introduction, Simon and Judas Thaddeus initially went together to the place (Beth-Horon, approximately ten miles northwest of Jerusalem) where on his last journey Jesus had cursed the fig tree. Traveling further with their disciples, the brothers first went together, and then separated. One of the places they went to together was Babylon. (This visit to Babylon is described in the section on Judas Thaddeus.) Before they left Babylon, they instituted a disciple named Abdias† as bishop there. Simon journeyed thence to the Black Sea and then on to Scythia.

Later, through God's guidance, the two brothers found their way together again in a far-distant, war-torn city in Persia. There they cast out many demons. There were many pagan priests in this city, and the brothers caused golden and silver idols of the sun and the moon to fall down from their pedestals.

Simon was killed in a terrible tumult in front of the temple, murdered with a kind of ploughshare of the sort the people there used (a plough without wheels). The man in whose house Simon and Judas Thaddeus lived was also murdered, as was Thaddeus (see following description).

JUDAS THADDEUS

JUDAS THADDEUS was the eldest son of Mary Cleophas, and, like Peter, was five years older than Jesus (and thus born about 7 BC). Like his younger brother James the Less, Judas Thaddeus worked at Peter's fishery. However Thaddeus was more a merchant than a fisherman. He traveled around trading with fishing nets, sail cloth, and tackling. He joined the disciples for the first time on July 24, AD 30.

Judas Thaddeus

His half-brother Matthew did not become a disciple until November 19 of that year. However, his younger brothers Simon and James the Less had become disciples already in AD 29, having both been present at the wedding at Cana in December of that year. All the brothers were second cousins of Jesus. Because they were accustomed to traveling and had also a facility in communicating with foreigners, when Jesus returned from his journey to Cyprus he sent

---

† More will be said about this important figure in Volume IV.

Judas Thaddeus together with his brother James the Less to Gessur to meet seven pagan philosophers from Cyprus who were to arrive there. These seven pagan philosophers had been converted by Jesus in Salamis in the course of his journey to Cyprus. Jesus had advised them to come and settle in Palestine.

As described in the section on the apostle Thomas, three years after Christ's ascension Thomas and Thaddeus went to the land of the three kings to baptize the two kings then still living. Thaddeus had with him the veil of Veronica, upon which the miraculous image of the face of Christ was imprinted. This veil was later brought to Rome. Thomas had a vision of Jesus in which he dictated a letter addressed to King Abgar of Edessa, which Thaddeus was to bring to the king. And so Thaddeus traveled to Edessa and went to see the king with the letter in hand. As he entered the king's chamber, the radiant figure of Jesus was alongside him. The king looked neither at the apostle nor at the letter, but bowed down in face of the radiant figure of Jesus.

King Abgar was a man of integrity, who was very ill with leprosy. After Abgar spoke with Thaddeus, the apostle laid his hands upon the king and healed him. Later the king taught and healed many, who all became Christians.

On his further journey Judas Thaddeus was accompanied by Silas, one of the three youths who had traveled with Jesus on his long journey outside Israel, traversing the route to Ur and then to Heliopolis. Thaddeus taught and baptized as he went. In the mountainous region around Kedar, he baptized all the people, and they formed a Christian shepherd people living in tents, most of whom later suffered martyrdom through raiding pagan peoples.

Judas Thaddeus retraced the entire journey that Jesus had made from Kedar to the land of the three kings, and from there to Ur and then across the Arabian desert to Heliopolis in Egypt. In one city where Thaddeus was put in prison by its rulers, the people were so fond of him that they stormed the prison and released him from captivity. However, one disciple—not Silas—died in this prison.

After the meeting of the apostles in Jerusalem referred to in the Introduction, the brothers Simon and Judas Thaddeus traveled together (as described in the section on Simon). Judas Thaddeus had his priestly staff with him, like all the apostles. In one region Thaddeus had a shocking encounter. He and Simon, accompanied by many others, arrived at a kind of "tent city." Upon their arrival, many rough looking naked rogues ran out, one of them charging in a rage at Thaddeus with his snout-like nose sticking up and sneering. Then he ran off. After this hostile reception from the people, Simon and Thaddeus were taken and presented to their leader. The leader, however, treated them in a friendlier manner. They were moved to a place that was more securely built than a tent. There were more people there. Some, who were not soldiers, started to incite the crowd against Simon and Thaddeus, and a tumult broke out. And so they left, still accompanied by many people.

In due course they arrived at a great city on a river (Babylon). Many canals cut across the land and in the city were many huge, heavy buildings. Things went well for them there until, in an assembly of the people in the presence of the king, pagan priests stepped forward in opposition to the apostles. In both of their hands they held snakes, many that were as long as an arm. These snakes were poisonous, and in some mysterious way the priests had power over them. When the snakes were released against the two brother apostles, the priests lost their power over the snakes, which then turned against them, coiling around and biting them, so that they cried out until the apostles commanded the snakes to stop.

Many in the city became Christians, including the king. A disciple named Abdias remained behind as bishop of the community of Christians when Simon and Thaddeus left.

They traveled then to Persia, to another great city, where they were guests of a man who converted to Christianity. Accompanied by this man, they went to the temple, where golden and silver idols of the sun and moon were set on a throne upon wheels at the temple center. A huge crowd was gathered in the temple and also outside. Through the apostles presence the idols fell down and shattered, and a great tumult broke out. The two brothers, without defending themselves, were attacked and seized. In the midst of a great crowd of priests and others wielding all manner of weapons, they were roughly used and finally killed. Simon's death has already been described in his section. Thaddeus also died a martyr's death at the same time, his head split open by an axe during the uproar in front of the temple. The man accompanying them, in whose house they were guests, was murdered also.

MATTHIAS

Mary Heli, as described in the section on the holy women, was the older sister of Mary of Nazareth. She was about twenty years older. Her husband Cleophas, a nephew of Joseph, brought a son from a previous marriage with him into the marriage with Mary Heli. This son, who came originally from Bethlehem, was MATTHIAS, who was later elected by the apostles to take the place of Judas Iscariot in the circle of twelve, as described below.

After Christ's ascension there was a gathering of the

disciples in the Cenacle, and "Peter stood up among the brethren—the company of persons was in all about a hundred and twenty." (Acts 1:15) There were many there who would have liked to take the place of Judas. Of the many disciples present, two had no such ambition or intention, and they were suggested by Peter as candidates to replace Judas in the circle of the apostles. These two were Joseph Barsabbas[†] and Matthias. For this reason—that they had no ambition to take the place of Judas—they were the two who came into consideration to take Judas's place.[‡]

Matthias and Jesus were first cousins—not by blood, but by virtue of the marriage of Matthias's father to Mary Heli. At the time of the choice of a replacement for Judas, Joseph Barsabbas was young, thirteen years younger than Jesus. (Anne Catherine states that at this time Matthias was also young, but this seems unlikely, given that he was the older half-brother of Mary Cleophas, the mother of Judas Thaddeus, Simon, and James the Less.)

Matthias was of slender build, with sandy hair. After Christ's ascension he went with Thomas to the two remaining kings (of the three kings). Some time after the death of James the Less, while in Armenia, Matthias died a martyr's death by being hit over the head with an iron bar.

LAZARUS (*and* FRIENDS)

LAZARUS looked older than Jesus. At the time of the Lord's baptism, Lazarus had extensive possessions, landed property, gardens, and many servants. His sister Martha had her own house, and another sister named Mary, who lived entirely alone, had also her separate dwelling. His sister Mary Magdalene, the youngest of the three sisters, lived in her castle at Magdala.

Lazarus was already long acquainted with the holy family. His aunt Naomi, his mother's sister, had been the teacher of the Virgin Mary in the temple. He had from early on aided Joseph and Mary with copious alms and, from first to last, did much for the community. The purse of Jesus's disciples and all their expenses he supplied out of his own wealth.

The father of Lazarus, of very noble Egyptian descent, was named Zarah, or Zerah. He had dwelt in Syria, on the confines of Arabia, where he held a position under the Syrian king; but for services rendered in war he had received from the Emperor Augustus property near Jerusalem and in Galilee. He was like a prince, and was very rich. He then acquired still greater wealth through his wife Jezebel, a Jewess of the sect of the Pharisees. He became a Jew, and was pious and strict according to the Pharisaical laws. He owned part of the city on Mount Zion, on the side upon which the brook near the temple heights flows through the ravine. But the greater part of this property he had bequeathed to the temple, retaining, however, in his family, some ancient privilege on its account. This property was on the road by which the apostles went up to the Cenacle, but the latter itself formed no longer a part of it.

Lazarus

Zarah's castle in Bethany was very large. It featured numerous gardens, terraces, and fountains, and was surrounded by double ditches.

The prophecies of Anna and Simeon were known to the family of Zarah, who were waiting for the Messiah. And even in Jesus's youth they were acquainted with the holy

---

[†] Joseph Barsabbas was the son of Mary Cleophas and her second husband, Sabbas, and thus half-brother to the apostles Judas Thaddeus, Simon, and James the Less, and—like them—first cousin once removed to Jesus. Like his half-brothers, the three apostles, Joseph Barsabbas worked also at Peter's fishery.

[‡] "Therefore it is necessary to choose one of the men who have been with us the whole time the Lord Jesus went in and out among us, beginning from John's baptism to the time when Jesus was taken up from us. For one of these must become a witness with us of his resurrection." So they proposed two men: Joseph called Barsabbas (also known as Justus) and Matthias. Then they prayed, "Lord, you know everyone's heart. Show us which of these two you have chosen to take over this apostolic ministry, which Judas left to go where he belongs." Then they cast lots, and the lot fell to Matthias; so he was added to the eleven apostles. (Acts 1:21–26)

family, just as pious, noble people are wont to be with their humble, devout neighbors.

The parents of Lazarus had in all fifteen children, of whom six died young. Of the nine that survived, only four were living at the time of Christ's teaching. These four were: Lazarus; Martha, about two years younger; Mary, looked upon as simple-minded (whom we shall call Silent Mary), two years younger than Martha; and Mary Magdalene, five years younger than Silent Mary. The latter is not named in scripture, nor reckoned among the Lazarus family; but she is known to God. She was always put aside in her family, and lived altogether unknown. Magdalene, the youngest child, was very beautiful and, even in her early years, tall and well-developed like a girl of more advanced age.

After the death of their father, lots were cast as to how the inheritance should be apportioned. The castle at Magdala and other properties in that area of the Sea of Galilee fell to Magdalene; the castle at Bethany to Martha and Silent Mary; and the property on Mt. Zion as well as a large number of properties in Southern Galilee and the castle near Herodium fell to Lazarus. However, Martha made the main part of the castle at Bethany available to her brother, who preferred to stay there. Here in Bethany, and also in Lazarus's house on Mt. Zion, Jesus was frequently a guest, and often met with Lazarus's close friends.

Among those belonging to this circle of friends were the quarry owner and stone-cutter Joseph of Arimathea and the sculptor Nicodemus. There was also Obed, who was occupied at the temple (and who was a son of the old priest Simeon), as well as the Pharisee Simon of Bethany, who owned a hotel with a festival hall in Bethany, and, lastly, John Mark, the son of Mary Mark (not to be confused with Mark who wrote the Gospel of St Mark).

Lazarus was everywhere greatly honored and admired as a very wealthy yet pious—even enlightened—man. His demeanor was quite different from that of everyone else. He was very serious and moderate in all things; he spoke little, but when he did speak it was with a gentleness that nonetheless carried weight. His manner with friends bore the stamp of familiarity and yet at the same time he was always refined and distinguished in his bearing and in conversation. He was tall and fair-haired, bearing a resemblance to St Joseph, except that his features were more stern and striking. Like Nicodemus and many other friends, he believed at first that Jesus's mission was—together with his disciples—to seize Jerusalem, to free the country from the yoke of Roman rule, and to restore the kingdom of the Jews—although this belief was never spoken out. Gradually, however, he realized from the Lord's sermons that Jesus's kingdom was not of this world.

During the night of September 22/23, AD 29, Lazarus accompanied Jesus to his baptism in the River Jordan. After Jesus was baptized by John the Baptist, Lazarus and his friends received John's baptism also. Lazarus was present at the wedding at Cana in late December AD 29, and provided for the second course of the wedding feast, which the Master had taken on. Indeed, the expenses incurred by Jesus and the disciples on their travels, and also the alms they handed out to the poor, were taken care of by Lazarus, who entrusted Simeon's son Obed with such payments on behalf of the community.

After the second and final conversion of his sister Mary Magdalene, who then joined the circle of holy women around the Virgin Mary, Lazarus saw to Magdalene's request that her castle at Magdala and her properties in that region be sold, and that the money thus raised be put at the disposal of the Lord for the payment of alms.

In July, AD 32 Lazarus fell ill and he died on either the 14th or 15th day of that month. One week later he was entombed in Bethany. On the morning of the sabbath (July 26) Jesus raised Lazarus from the dead. Then, as Lazarus knelt before him in the hall of the castle, Jesus placed his right hand on his head and breathed on him seven times, imbuing him with the seven gifts of the Holy Spirit. Herewith he initiated Lazarus, purifying him of all earthly connections and sins, strengthening him through the gifts of the Holy Spirit already ten months before the apostles were similarly blessed at Pentecost (May 24, AD 33). (Through his death Lazarus had beheld the spiritual world, and through his raising he became the first Christian initiate.)

After having been raised from the dead, Lazarus was under threat of death from the enraged Pharisees, "For the chief priests planned to put also Lazarus to death" (John 12:10). Therefore he was obliged to keep a low profile, remaining for the most part hidden at his home in Bethany. Indeed, he concealed himself in subterranean apartments there throughout the persecution that arose against him.

About three years after Pentecost, persecution of Christians by the Jews intensified, and while Mary Magdalene was visiting her brother and sister in Bethany, the three were arrested. On this occasion Lazarus, Martha, and Mary Magdalene were taken into custody, as well as the sisters' maidservants Marcella and Sarah and two other people who were visiting Lazarus at the time: one of the seventy-two disciples, named Maximin, and the man born blind who was healed by Jesus, Celidonius, sometimes known as Sidonius. These seven were arrested and taken to the Mediterranean coast (somewhere close to present-day Tel-Aviv), where they were put into a little boat, towed far out to the sea, and cut loose. The intention was that they should perish, but this did not happen. Through divine providence the little boat made it across the Mediterranean, the family, servants, and companions coming ashore at a place in the south of France now called St. Maries-de-la-Mer.

Having been raised from the dead, Lazarus possessed an extraordinary power, as did Mary Magdalene, and Martha too, after having spent so much time in the presence of Jesus. When Lazarus spoke, it was a powerful experience for all who heard.

While Sarah stayed behind in St. Maries-de-la-Mer, the rest of the group went to the town of Massilia (present-day Marseille), further eastward along the coast. There they lived, and because of Lazarus's presence and the power of his speech, a whole community was soon converted to the new religion of Jesus Christ, the Messiah, who had died and risen from the dead. Lazarus baptized them and became the bishop of this first community of Christians in Europe.

Lazarus remained as bishop of Marseille, Magdalene retired to lead the life of a hermit in a cave at Saint-Baume, east of Marseille, and Martha traveled with her maidservant Marcella north of Marseille and founded a community there.

OTHER MALE FIGURES

Eliud the Essene

JESUS visited a venerable old man named *Eliud* on Tuesday, September 6, AD 29, just outside of Nazareth. He was a widower, the son of a brother of Zechariah, and looked after by his daughter and a nephew of Zechariah. Jesus is with him for twelve days, conversing in his home and undertaking together a private journey through Southern Galilee, during which they visit a leper settlement, a healing pool, and several towns. They never leave each other's side, and on the last night, in the field of Jezreel, Jesus appears to Eliud in transfigured form. Why this singular distinction and preference for one person? Anne Catherine received an answer to this question which can shed its clarifying light also upon all other such private conversations that Jesus held: all the private individuals whom the evangelists mention by name, and with whom the Master spent extended periods of time, are "types" of humanity, representing very specific groups in human history, as also certain states that recur ever and again in human souls as well as specific gifts and vocations (even misdirected ones, as in the case of Judas Iscariot). Eliud is the type of a mystic living in a state of mature private illumination, as a result of which he is granted a particularly intimate contact with Jesus. Accordingly, Jesus's conversations with Eliud deal with things he did not share with the public at large, or even in a small circle. When they part company, Jesus gives Eliud a special blessing and accepts him into the community of his new kingdom. And shortly before his death, the weakened Eliud receives the divine consolation of speaking one last time with Jesus, who passes an entire night in his Capernaum lodging.

Respected Civic Leaders

Jesus is much gratified when men who are respected in their town and region prove free of envy and any desire for power, and in their quest for holiness remain unafraid of other men and their devious talk. To this sort of men belong *Jairus of Phasael, Dinotus, Jairus of Capernaum, Simeon the Samaritan, Obed*, and *Simeon of Gath-Hepher*, whose stories are briefly told below.

First there is the married Essene and headman Jairus of Phasael, with whom Jesus visits the sick of the town in October, AD 29, and whose sixteen-year-old daughter he brings back from the dead on Tuesday, February 7, AD 30 (this being the first occasion on which he calls the dead back to life).

Then there is the thirty-year-old widower and Pharisee Dinotus (or Dinocus) in Gennabris, a friend of Andrew, who gives lodging to Jesus for several days at the end of August, AD 30.

Another is the leader of the synagogue at Capernaum—named Jairus also—whose daughter Salome is raised from the dead twice and who courageously sides with Jesus even though he must resign his position in consequence.

There is then the independently wealthy Samaritan Simeon, who has settled with his family near Amichores-Libnath ("city of waters") and who offers Jesus the use of his gardens to teach and baptize in July, AD 30.

Again, we have the patriarchal Obed, a great landowner near Michmethath who at the end of October, AD 30, shows his properties to Jesus and, in the circle of his family and laborers, listens carefully to his teachings.

And finally, there is the married Essene and Pharisee's son Simeon of Gath-Hepher, who in late December, AD 30, donates his land and possessions to Jesus's community.

Pagan Officials

Jesus honors also those holders of public office who, though pagan, often show greater faith than the Jews, for instance: the Roman centurions *Cornelius* and *Zorobabel*, whom we know through the gospels; also the Roman garrison-commander *Achias* (father of Jephthah, whom Jesus healed) from the military town of Gischala, where he resides in the home where Paul was born; and the chief magistrate *Ozias* in Antipatris, whose paralyzed daughter Michol he heals. Then again there are the centurions *Cassius* (later called Longinus, after the lance with which he pierced the side of Jesus upon the cross), and *Abenadar*, who shortly before the piercing gave over command of the garrison to Cassius, in order to go join the disciples, and who after the Passion assists John, Nicodemus, and Joseph of Arimathea in taking the body of Jesus down from the cross and bearing it with them to the holy women to be washed and prepared for burial—and then, together with the same three, carries the body on a litter to the holy sepulcher.

Merchants

Furthermore, there are among the merchants men who can legitimately call themselves friends of Jesus, for despite their wealth and worldly success they have found the priceless pearl of supernatural salvation—men like the wood-merchant *Issachar* in Dothan and the shipper *Israel* in Cana (father of the bride of Cana, and a descendent of Ruth of Bethlehem), who knows the holy family from long ago; also the cloth manufacturer *Jesse* in Dabrath and his trading partner, the merchant *Cyrinus* from Salamis in Cyprus.

Shepherds and Customs Officials

Finally, Jesus feels at home as among friends when he is in the company of certain shepherds, whose childlike and open-hearted dispositions give him great joy, and also among certain customs officials, such as *Zacchaeus* in Jericho, and those in the commercial districts of Dibon, Jezreel, Gilead, and Gessur, who become committed converts and renounce any dishonest gain.

Ordaining of the Twelve Apostles

TEMPORAL SEQUENCE

Of Contacts Between Jesus and His Apostles and Disciples

AD 29

May 29: As Jesus passes through Bethulia he casts a grace-filled glance at Nathaniel Chased and Bartholomew.

May 30: Parmenas and Jonadab accompany Jesus from Nazareth to Hebron, but at this early stage do not remain faithful to him.

July 2 or *July 3*: While journeying together, the tax collector *Levi* (the later apostle Matthew), and the son Kolaya of Lea the widow, and the Essene Eustachius [son of Seba of Nazareth?] speak with Jesus about John the Baptist.

July 6: Peter and Andrew speak briefly with Jesus about the Baptist.

August 4: Jesus receives Amandor, Eustachius, and Kolaya as his first disciples.

August 8: Peter and Andrew hear Jesus in the synagogue at Nazareth.

August 12: Peter, Andrew, James the Less, and Philip hear Jesus on the sabbath at a village in the Zebulon valley.

August 14: Jesus receives the two sons Arastaria and Cocharia of his great-aunt Maraha as disciples.

September 13: In addition to his five disciples, in Nazareth Jesus receives as disciples four friends and relatives of the holy family.

September 23: On this day of the baptism in the River Jordan, which took place at about 10 AM that morning, Andrew and Saturnin, as disciples of John the Baptist, and also *Lazarus,* follow Jesus and his nine disciples to Bethel, and baptize there in a hospital. After the close of the sabbath around sunset the next day, Andrew, the first of the future twelve apostles, leaves for Capernaum to proclaim the baptism of the Messiah in Galilee.

October 5: The two brothers Aminadab and Manasseh, relatives of Joseph, become disciples of Jesus in secret.

October 7: Two disciples of John, the brothers Aram and Themeni, nephews of Joseph of Arimathea, become disciples of Jesus not far from Ono, the place of his baptism. Later this day, when Jesus and his disciples reach a holy site not far from Gilgal, Saturnin and two other disciples baptize at this historically sacred place.

December 1: After the forty days in the wilderness, Jesus was again near Ono, the place of his baptism. Andrew and Saturnin and a few other disciples of John left the place where John was baptizing and teaching and caught up with Jesus. When Jesus declared his intention to gather more disciples, Andrew mentioned his brother Peter and also Philip and Nathaniel Chased.

December 4: Andrew and Saturnin baptize people north of Bethabara, at the second place where John had baptized before going to Ono.

December 19: Andrew presents Peter and John to Jesus, who says to Peter "You are Simon, son of Jonah, and in future shall be called Cephus." (John 1:41) Peter and John are the second and third disciples of the future twelve.

December 20: Lazarus, Saturnin, the son of Simeon, and the bridegroom Nathaniel come to see Jesus.

December 22: Jesus stayed at Capernaum in the house of Nathaniel the bridegroom. Here he meets with Sadoch, James, and Heliachim, the three sons of Cleophas and Mary Heli, the elder sister of Mary of Nazareth. The three are cousins of Jesus. As was customary at the time, they were referred to as "brothers of the Lord."

December 24: Jesus calls Philip in the valley of Capernaum. (John 1:43).

December 25: Jesus calls Nathaniel Chased on the way to Cana, near Gennabris. (John 1:45)

December 26–29: At the four-day celebration of the wedding in Cana, as was Jesus's intention, all the future apostles—with the exception of Bartholomew, Thomas, and Judas—as well as a large number of the disciples, including Nathaniel Chased, Obed, and Jonathan, become better acquainted.

AD 30

February 6: In Ono, east of Jericho, Jesus calls twenty new disciples. Ono is the small town close to the place of baptism of Jesus in the River Jordan.

April 5: With about thirty disciples Jesus celebrates Passover at Lazarus's house in Jerusalem. Among the thirty are all the future apostles—excepting Bartholomew, Thomas, Judas Iscariot, and Matthew. He teaches them how to bless the baptismal water and permits them already now and then to teach and heal, although for want of sufficient faith their healings are not always successful.

April 8–9: The "night conversation" between Jesus and Nicodemus took place. (John 3:1–21).

May 4–18: At the second place of baptism—of the three places where John the Baptist baptized—Jesus permits Andrew, Saturnin, Peter, and James the Greater to baptize. A great many people are baptized in the course of these two weeks. (John 3:22)

Second Half of May: In the second half of May many disciples are arrested and interrogated. Also John the Baptist is arrested by Herod and put in prison toward the end of May. Around this time, in Gennabris, Peter, Andrew, and John break their shackles and in the wake of this miracle they and all the other disciples taken into custody in Gennabris by the Pharisees are allowed to go free to return to the area of Bethsaida and Capernaum, the region of Peter's fishery.

June 21: Approximately twenty Galilean disciples, among them six of the future apostles—Peter, Andrew, James the Greater, John, James the Less, and Thaddeus—meet with Jesus in secret on the outskirts of Tyre, in various outlying inns. Nathaniel Chased, Nathaniel the bridegroom, and others who had been at the wedding at Cana were also present. That evening they all met together at an inn close by the city that was on an island accessible by way of a breakwater. Jesus lovingly greeted each disciple, extending to each one, in turn, his hand. They were filled with an indescribable joy.

July 24: Nearly all the disciples thus far called, along with seven of the future apostles—Peter, Andrew, James, John, James the Lesser, Judas Thaddeus, and Philip—meet with Jesus in the valley of upper Beth-Horon and then embark upon a strenuous journey with him. Jesus teaches along the way.

July 26: Jesus went with Andrew, James, and Saturnin to Jacob's well near Sychar. He sent the three disciples into the town to buy provisions. Then the Samaritan woman, Dinah, came for water. (John 4:9–26).

October 23: While in Meroz, Bartholomew, Simon the Zealot, Judas Thaddeus, and Philip come to visit Jesus. Bartholomew and Simon the Zealot are taken into the circle of disciples, and also recommended to Jesus as a possible disciple Judas Iscariot, who was staying nearby.

October 24: Judas Iscariot is received as a disciple.

October 29: Thomas is received as a disciple.

November 2: In Dabrath, Caleb and Aaron, the sons of Jesse (a nephew of Joseph), are received as disciples.

November 8: With the exception of Matthew, all the future apostles and many other disciples, about sixty in all, are present near Gabara at the Sermon on the Mount.

November 18: Andrew and Saturnin baptize some fifty people in Capernaum, after which Thomas, Bartholomew, and John lay hands upon the newly-baptized.

November 19: Jesus calls Matthew from his toll station. (Matthew 9:9)

November 21: Jesus's final calling† of Peter, Andrew, James the Greater, and John by the seashore near Matthew's toll station. (Matthew 4:18) Later that day, near Bethsaida-Julias, Peter, Andrew, and Saturnin baptize.

November 26: Peter's miraculous catch of fish. (Luke 5:4)

December 4: Jesus brings the apostles together and bestows upon them the power to heal and to cast out demons. (Matthew 10:1)

December 7: Jesus and Peter walk for the first time upon the sea. (Matthew 14:2)

December 10: The first formal sending out of the twelve apostles and the disciples, from the teaching Mount by Hanathon. (Matthew 10:5) Six apostles and eighteen disciples were sent.

December 21: The returning apostles and disciples relate their experiences, and some twenty or thirty Jews, who they brought with them, are baptized.

December 28: The apostles on the way with Jesus to Chisloth-Tabor are strengthened in their gifts of grace. Jesus takes three Egyptian disciples.

December 31: The second sending out of the apostles and disciples (excepting Peter, John, and several disciples), this time from the teaching Mount by Tabor.

AD 31

January 27: The returning apostles and disciples describe to Jesus their apostolic journeys. (Mark 6:30)

January 28: Jesus sets the twelve apostles over the seventy-two disciples.

January 29: For the second time Jesus and Peter walk upon the sea. (Matt. 14:24–33)

February 5: Jesus arranges the apostles in three rows,

---

† At the first calling, these four became disciples of Christ, but continued to work at Peter's fishery. With this second call, they stopped working at the fishery and became full-time disciples.

according to their inner disposition and temperament: Peter, Andrew, John, James the Greater, Matthew
Thaddeus, Bartholomew, James the Less
Thomas, Simon the Zealot, Philip, Judas Iscariot

February 7: Jesus bestows upon the apostles in greater measure the power to work healing miracles. All weep, and Jesus also is very moved.

March 7: Jesus sends forth the apostles a third time, on this occasion to distant places both east and west, even to Damascus and Arabia. Already within the week they begin to return to Jesus.

March 19: In Gaulanitis, south of Sogane, Peter receives from Jesus the keys to the heavenly kingdom. (Matt. 16:13–20)

March 28: During the second Passover festival in Jerusalem, the theological student Stephen (the later deacon and martyr) becomes personally acquainted with John.

April 3–4: Jesus is transfigured on Mount Tabor in the presence of Peter, James the Greater, and John. (Matt. 17:1)

April 23: In the lonely mountain regions northwest of Garisima there took place the fourth sending out of the apostles and disciples, after Jesus laid his hands upon them to fill them with new strength. This time five apostles and some fifty disciples stayed with him and accompanied him on the journey to Ornithopolis.

THE DISCIPLES CHOSEN BY JESUS IN THE COURSE OF HIS MINISTRY

Organized by Geographic or Family Association

[1–4] *The Four Male Cousins of Jesus*
The so-called "brothers of the Lord," the sons of Cleophas and Mary Heli, the eldest sister of the blessed Virgin: Sadoch, James, Heliachim, and Matthias (who was later chosen to replace Judas Iscariot in the circle of the apostles).

[5–8] *Four Close Relatives of Jesus*
Arastaria and Cocharia, the two sons of Maraha of Sepphoris, Mary's aunt, were among the first disciples of Jesus. Joseph Barsabbas, the son of Sabbas and Mary Cleophas, and Nathaniel (called the lesser Cleophas), the son of Anna Cleophas, the daughter of Cleophas from an earlier marriage, were employed at the fishery of Zebedee.

[9–10] *The Two Sons of Widows distantly related to Jesus*
Kolaya, son of the widow Lea, and Eustachius, son of one of the three Essene widows related to Jesus, who lived on Mount Carmel.

[11–14] *The Four Nephews of Cleophas*
The four sons of Sebadja of Nazareth: Cleophas (the disciple from Emmaus), Jacob, Judas, and Japhet, childhood playmates of Jesus, and later disciples of John the Baptist, who came to follow Jesus only after John's death.

[15–18] *The Four related to Jesus through Sobe*
Nathaniel of Capernaum, who knew Jesus in his youth (and was the bridegroom at the wedding of Cana), and the three sons of the aunt of this Nathaniel. Sobe was the sister of Anne, and so an aunt of the blessed Mary.

[19–22] *The Four Related to Jesus through John the Baptist*
Veronica's son Amandor, one of the first disciples, as well as another relative of Veronica in Jerusalem, who remained a secret disciple, and the half-Greek Parmenas, son of Jonah, the Greek third husband of Mary Cleophas born to the sister of her second husband, Sabbas. And finally, Joseph (or Joses) Barsabbas, a relation of Zechariah of Hebron.

[23–26] *The Four Related to Jesus through Joseph*
The two sons of a relative of Joseph: Manasseh and Aminadab, initially secret disciples who later stepped forward as public disciples. Two of the six children (three boys and three girls) of Jesse, a son of Joseph's brother Elijah: Caleb and Aaron, from Dabrath in Southern Galilee.

[27–28] *The Two Childhood Playmates of Jesus*
Jonadab and Silvanus, both from Nazareth.

[29–31] *The Three Galilean Disciples*
Nathaniel Chased, the clerk from Gennabris; Jonathan, the half-brother of Peter; and the evangelist Mark, who was temporarily a leaseholder of a fishery near Bethsaida, but was frequently away on journeys to other lands, and who only remained close to Jesus during the year AD 33, in the last few months of his ministry.

32–39] *The Eight Jerusalem Disciples*
John Mark, the son of Mary Mark; a son of Johanna Chusa and also another of her relatives; then the two nephews of Joseph of Arimathea: Aram and Themeni; and finally, the three sons of Obed (the son of the aged priest Simeon) who served in the Temple.

[40–64] *The Twenty-Five Disciples from Judea*
Annadias, son of the chief tax collector Zacchaeus of Jericho, four disciples from Beersheba, whom Jesus received on January 8, AD 33, and twenty disciples from Ono, south of Jericho.

[65–66] *The Two Disciples from Samaria*
The blind-born but prophetically-gifted Essene Manahem of Coreae, whom Jesus healed, and a certain Azor, who accompanied Jesus on his journey to Cyprus.

[67–69] *The Three Greek Disciples*
Saturnin of Patras, of royal lineage, one of the first disciples both of John the Baptist and of Jesus, and a prolific baptizer of new disciples; and the brothers Tharzissus and Aristobolus, whom Lazarus brought to Jesus.

[70–81] *The Twelve Disciples from Cyprus*
Barnabas of Kythria, son of a landowner and timber merchant, who had studied in Jerusalem; Jonas of Salamis on Cyprus, son of an Essene; Mnason, son of a strictly orthodox Jew; the two sons of the wholesale merchant Cyrinus of Salamis: Aristarchus and Trophimus; and seven pagan philosophers whom Jesus converted while on Cyprus.

[82–84] *The Three Unreported Disciples*
The three sons of the Mesopotamians from the entourage of the three kings who remained behind with the shepherds of Bethlehem—each marrying one of their daughters—and then settled in Samaria. It was these three young men whom Jesus took with him on his journey to Mesopotamia. From eldest to youngest: Eliud, Silas, and Eremenzear. The latter came from the city of Atom, on the Euphrates.

[85–89] *The Five Other Disciples from the East*
Selam (or Sela) of Kedar, from the region of Hauran; the temple server Caisar of Atom, in Mesopotamia; and three Chaldeans from Sikdor, all of whom joined the other disciples only in the year AD 33, during the last few months of his ministry.

[90–100] *The Eleven Egyptian Disciples*
Three friends of Jesus's youth from Egypt; also Deodatus, whose mother was the wealthy Mira of Heliopolis; and seven other disciples, whom Jesus brought back from Heliopolis and Matarea on his last Egyptian journey.

Herewith, however, the tally of the disciples of Jesus is by no means complete.

THE HOLY WOMEN

At Christ's Death and Resurrection

(Then Considered Again, along with Other Holy Women,
Organized by Geographic or Family Association)

⊕

Holy Women at Christ's Death & Resurrection · · 67	Susanna of Jerusalem · · · · · · · · · · · · · · · · · · 85
The Virgin Mary · 73	Salome of Jerusalem · · · · · · · · · · · · · · · · · · · 85
Mary Heli · 77	Mary Mark · 86
Mary Cleophas · 78	Johanna Chusa · 86
Mary Salome · 78	Dinah the Samaritan · · · · · · · · · · · · · · · · · · · 87
Martha · 79	Mara the Suphanite · 88
Mary Magdalene · 80	Anna Cleophas · 89
Maroni · 83	Other Holy Women · 90
Veronica · 83	

The Holy Women

THE HOLY WOMEN AT CHRIST'S DEATH & RESURRECTION

AT THE CONCLUSION of this article concerning the holy women present at Christ's death and resurrection, short descriptions are given for the fifteen women named. Clarifications, where needed, are given in brackets. The reason

Holy Women Watch Crucifixion from Afar, with John

for focusing upon the holy women present at the Mystery of Golgotha is that these women—along with the only male apostle present, John of Zebedee—bore witness to the great sacrifice of the Son of God, Christ.

According to Anne Catherine, during the night Thursday/Friday of Christ's Passion, the blessed Virgin Mary, who was the center of the circle of holy women, was accompanied by the following nine women: Martha, Mary Magdalene, Mary Cleophas, Mary Salome, Mary Mark, Susanna (of Jerusalem), Johanna Chusa, Veronica (Seraphia), and Salome (of Jerusalem).

All of these holy women—and several more—were present at the crucifixion. Altogether, according to Anne Catherine, there were seventeen women present at the scene of the crucifixion—arranged in three groups: *four* who were directly beneath the cross; *six* who were a relatively short distance from the cross; and *seven* somewhat further away.

That there were *four* directly beneath the cross is confirmed by comparing the accounts of the four gospels:

Anne Catherine: Virgin Mary, Mary Magdalene, Mary Cleophas, and Salome (Mary Salome)

Matthew: Mary Magdalene, Mary the mother of James and Joses (Mary Cleophas), the mother of the sons of Zebedee (Mary Salome)

Mark: Mary Magdalene, Mary the mother of James the Less and Joses (Mary Cleophas), Salome (Mary Salome)

Luke: His mother the Virgin Mary, Mary Magdalene, Mary the wife of Cleophas [Mary Cleophas]

John: No information given

The *six* holy women who according to Anne Catherine were a relatively short distance from the cross were:

Martha, Mary Heli, Veronica (Seraphia), Johanna Chusa, Susanna (of Jerusalem), and Mary Mark.

Finally, Anne Catherine says that there were *seven* holy women present at the crucifixion who were somewhat further from the cross. Although she does not name these holy women, from her subsequent descriptions, it can be deduced that five of this group were:

Salome (of Jerusalem), Anna Cleophas (daughter of a brother of Joseph), Maroni (the mother of the youth of Nain [Luke 7:11–17]), Dinah (the Samaritan woman with whom Jesus conversed at Jacob's well [John 4:4–42]), and Mara (the Suphanite, who had been possessed and had been healed by Jesus, who then spoke of the parable of the lost sheep in reference to herself. [Matt. 18:10–14])

Taking these three groups together, it can be said that there were *fifteen* holy women present at the crucifixion (perhaps there were two more, still to be identified).

Magdalene, John, and the Virgin Mary with Body of Jesus

Christ's body was taken down from the cross by Joseph of Arimathea, Nicodemus, and Abenadar (the Roman centurion of Arab descent who dipped a sponge in vinegar and raised it on the end of his lance to the mouth of Jesus on the cross [John 19:28–30]).

After the body was taken down, it was prepared for burial. Anne Catherine describes how the Virgin Mary attended especially to the head and chest region and Mary

Magdalene to the feet of Jesus.[K21] All the remaining holy women who were still present helped or watched the preparation of the body for burial. Especially helpful were Mary Cleophas, Salome (probably Mary Salome, rather than Salome of Jerusalem), and Veronica (Seraphia).

Holy Women Follow the Body to the Anointing Stone

Anne Catherine explicitly mentions that Mary Heli, who was already old, watched this activity on the part of the holy women in preparing the body for burial. She also mentions that a small group of holy women had left the hill of Golgotha after the crucifixion and gone to the home of Lazarus in Bethany to relate to him all that had happened. These holy women were Martha (Lazarus's sister), Maroni, Dinah, and Mara.

Mary and the Holy Women Prepare the Body

After the body had been prepared, it was carried to the tomb, about a seven-minute walk east of Golgotha. The body of Jesus was borne on a makeshift stretcher by four men: Nicodemus and Joseph of Arimathea at the front, and John and Abenadar at the rear. The tomb (*holy sepulcher*) was situated in a cave in the rocks of a beautiful garden, and the garden and tomb both belonged to Joseph of Arimathea. The garden with the holy sepulcher was located outside the city wall, close to the Bethlehem gate in the city wall, and also close to the little gate of Nicodemus. According to Anne Catherine, when on Easter Sunday morning Mary Magdalene discovered that the holy sepulcher was empty, "She hurriedly rushed through the little gate of Nicodemus into the city," to find the disciples and to tell them that, "They have taken the Lord from the tomb."

Holy Women Follow the Body to the Sepulcher

There was a procession of eleven or twelve holy women following the four men bearing the body.[K24] Anne Catherine names twelve women. However, two of the names appear to refer to the same woman, namely Mary Salome, who was married to Zebedee. When the "wife of Zebedee" and "Mary Salome" are both named (and they are named consecutively in the list), it would appear that Anne Catherine referred to this woman in two different ways, in which case there would have been eleven holy women in the procession.

Anne Catherine quite exactly describes the procession of the holy women following the four men. Although she does not say so explicitly, the impression she gives is that the women are arranged in pairs, headed by the Virgin Mary and Mary Heli, followed by Mary Magdalene and Mary Cleophas, and so on. Since Mary Salome is the same as Salome (the wife of Zebedee)—as the name is here given by Anne Catherine—the order of the procession was:

Virgin Mary, Mary Heli, Mary Magdalene, Mary Cleophas, Veronica (Seraphia), Johanna Chusa, Mary Mark, Mary

Salome, Salome of Jerusalem, Susanna (of Jerusalem), and Anna—a niece of Joseph (the husband of Mary).

Anne Catherine describes that a group of five women went into the city on Holy Saturday to purchase all kinds of herbs, little flasks of ointment, and nard water. They wanted to go early next morning to the holy sepulcher to scatter the herbs over the body of Jesus in its winding sheet and pour upon it the perfumed water.

These five women were Mary Magdalene, Mary Cleophas, Salome (of Jerusalem), Johanna Chusa, and Mary Salome. This is the order in which they are mentioned in the original German text of the visions of Anne Catherine written down by Clemens Brentano. In the English translation, the name Salome (of Jerusalem) is erroneously omitted from this list, indicating only Mary Magdalene, Mary Cleophas, Johanna Chusa, and Mary Salome.

Anne Catherine's description of Easter Sunday morning initially describes only four of this group of five holy women going to the garden of the holy sepulcher. As can be seen from the accounts in the four gospels (see summary below), four women are also named as having gone on Easter Sunday morning to the garden of the holy sepulcher. These four women named in the gospels are Mary Magdalene, Salome, Johanna (Chusa), and Mary the mother of James. Anne Catherine's account helps to clarify that the Salome named here is indeed Salome of Jerusalem (rather than Mary Salome). However, there is some ambiguity in the gospel designation "Mary the mother of James," since on the one hand *Mary Cleophas* was the mother of the disciples *James* the Less, Judas Thaddeus, and Simon, while on the other *Mary Salome* was the mother of the disciples *James* the Greater and John.

As we shall see in the following, the most probable solution to this ambiguity is that with "Mary the mother of James"—the designation occurring in both Mark and Luke—is meant Mary Cleophas, noting also that in the section above summarizing the gospel accounts of the women under the cross, Mary Cleophas is referred to as "Mary the mother of James and Joses." On account of this ambiguity, however, there remains the slight possibility that the fifth woman mentioned in Anne Catherine's account, Mary Salome, is the "Mary mother of James" mentioned in one of the gospel accounts—either in Mark or Luke—in which case the other gospel reference using this designation would be referring to Mary Cleophas who, according to Anne Catherine, was definitely one of the four women. However, it seems most unlikely that "Mary the mother of James" in one gospel would refer to Mary Salome, but in another gospel to Mary Cleophas.

For our considerations, it is the case that Mary Salome *is* mentioned later in Anne Catherine's account in the original German version. Given that Mary Salome was part of this group that went to buy the herbs, ointment, and perfumed water on Holy Saturday, and that the five women did this with the intention of going together to the holy sepulcher early the next morning, it seems a reasonable supposition that Mary Salome was indeed there, but that perhaps she followed the other four later and so was not initially mentioned in the description by Anne Catherine (although, as stated already, she *is* mentioned *later* in the original German edition).

Whereas Mary Salome's name is clearly stated later on in the description in the original German edition, only the simpler name "Salome" is indicated in the English edition. Anne Catherine described that this Salome was *not* the mother of John and his brother James. In other words, this Salome was *not* Mary Salome. This Salome (Salome of Jerusalem) is thus clearly distinguished from Mary Salome, who *was* the mother of James and John. "She was not the mother of John, but another Salome, a rich lady of Jerusalem, a relative of Joseph," who was wealthy enough to cover the major part of the cost of purchasing the herbs, ointments, and perfumed water. Anne Catherine added that it was Mary Magdalene and Salome who had shared in defraying most of the cost of the purchase.

Now let us consider more closely what is confusing in the original German text. First we read:

Mary Magdalene and Mary "the Mother of Joses"
Watch Over the Sepulcher (Mark 15:47)

Magdalene forgot all danger and hurried into the garden, and Salome followed her at some distance. It was primarily these two who had purchased the ointments. The other two women were more afraid and hung back at the entrance to the garden.

Here the first two women are clearly identified as Magdalene and Salome (of Jerusalem), who went on ahead of the other two women (Mary Cleophas and Johanna Chusa in Anne Catherine's account). After describing that Magdalene and Salome went together to the holy sepulcher and that Magdalene then—after seeing that the body of Jesus was not there—ran back to the Cenacle to tell the disciples, Anne Catherine says:

Concerning Mary Salome, who did not go further than the entrance to the sepulcher, I do not know whether she heard anything spoken by the angel (in the sepulcher). I saw her, right after Magdalene, flee in fright from the sepulcher and the garden and seek out the other women who had remained behind outside the garden, in order to let them know what had taken place.

Mary Magdalene and Two Holy Women at the Sepulcher

The translator of this text into English clearly thought that Anne Catherine had made a mistake in saying "Mary Salome" instead of "Salome," and therefore concluded that "Mary Salome" should be corrected to "Salome." Moreover, later in the German text it is stated:

The other women, when told by Mary Salome, were shocked and joyful at the same time, and hesitated a while before going into the garden.

Thus, in the original German text of Anne Catherine's description there are *two* references to Mary Salome in the garden of the holy sepulcher that morning. The following is a comparison with the gospel accounts of the holy women present in the garden of the holy sepulcher on Easter Sunday morning:

Emmerich: Magdalene, Mary Cleophas, Johanna Chusa, Salome (of Jerusalem), (later she refers to) Mary Salome
Matthew: Magdalene, the other Mary*
Mark: Magdalene, Salome (of Jerusalem) Mary the Mother of James*
Luke: Magdalene, Johanna (Chusa), Mary the mother of James*
John: Magdalene
(* *most likely* Mary Cleophas)

The naming of Mary Salome (twice) in the original German text of Anne Catherine's description of the holy women in the garden of the holy sepulcher on Easter Sunday morning appears, then, to be a mistake—a mistake that was corrected in the English translation, where in the two places in the German text that the name Mary Salome appears, the name is given instead simply as Salome. Thus, from the English translation it appears that there were four (not five) holy women who bore witness to the resurrection early that Sunday morning, whereas from Anne Catherine's description it is evident that originally five holy women had planned to go to the garden of the holy sepulcher on Easter Sunday morning, but that only four of this group of holy women set off together (Mary Magdalene, Mary Cleophas, Johanna Chusa, and Salome of Jerusalem).

Of course, there is the possibility already referred to, that the fifth woman belonging to the original group, Mary Salome, followed later and joined the other four in the garden of the holy sepulcher, by which time Mary Magdalene had already left and run back to the Cenacle to find the disciples in order to tell them about the empty tomb. However, since (as indicated in the following) the holy women had been afraid to go out while it was still dark—fearing that the enemies of Jesus might waylay them—it seems unlikely that Mary Salome would have dared proceed alone to the garden. In this case, the corrective given in the English translation (twice changing the name "Mary Salome" to "Salome") is appropriate.

Given the significance of the holy women bearing witness to the resurrection, which is the most significant event of the life of the Earth, it is worthwhile to consider this in detail. The details presented in the following are based on the original German edition.

Anne Catherine describes that in the night preceding the resurrection,

My gaze turned again to the holy women [who] wanted to go to Jesus's tomb before daybreak. Several times they had given voice to their concern about this undertaking, for they were very afraid that the enemies of Jesus might waylay them when they went out. However, the blessed Virgin ... consoled them, that after some rest they should take courage and go to the tomb, and no harm would befall them.

Here the Virgin Mary, at the center of the entire group of holy women, counseled the five to proceed with their plan to go to the holy sepulcher before daybreak. The Virgin Mary knew of the significance of bearing witness to this great event that was about to take place—the event that would signify the crowning of creation through the birth of the "first born of the dead" as the archetype for all humanity.

> As the morning sky lightened with a white streak of light, I saw Magdalene, Mary Cleophas, Johanna Chusa, and Salome ... leave their dwelling place near the Cenacle.

Although not described in the four gospels, the Virgin Mary herself—according to Anne Catherine—was the first to bear witness to the risen Lord:

> It was about eleven o'clock at night when the blessed Virgin, moved by love and ardent desire, could no longer remain in the house.... She traversed alone the whole way passed over by Jesus bearing the cross.... She went through the deserted streets and paused at every spot upon which some special suffering or outrage had befallen the Lord.... She was in an elevated state of love ... entirely immersed in love and contemplation.... She completed her way to the top of Mt. Golgotha.... I saw in vision the soul of Jesus in dazzling splendor between two warrior angels.... Now I saw the Lord arise in glory through the rock. There was an earthquake, and a warrior angel descended like lightning from heaven down to the tomb, rolled the stone to the right side and sat upon it....

The Risen One Appears to Three Holy Women in the Garden of the Sepulcher

> In the very moment when the angel descended to the tomb and there was an earthquake, I saw the risen Lord appear to his mother on Golgotha. He was extraordinarily beautiful and glorious, his manner serious.... His wounds were large and radiant.... He showed her his wounds, and as she sank to the ground to kiss his feet, he took her by the hand, raised her up, and disappeared.... Looking east, I saw on the horizon above Jerusalem a white streak of light.... The holy women were near to the little gate of Nicodemus when the Lord rose from the dead.... Magdalene forgot all danger and hurried into the garden, and Salome followed her at some distance.... The other two women were more anxious and remained behind at the entrance to the garden. As she approached the guards, I saw Magdalene in a state of shock hurry back some distance toward Salome. Then, however, both went together ... into the sepulcher.... The whole place was resplendent with light, and an angel sat to the right of the tomb. Magdalene was deeply troubled, and I do not know if she

heard any of the angel's words. I saw her immediately rush out hurriedly from the garden through the little gate of Nicodemus into the city.... Concerning Mary Salome, who did not go further than the entrance to the sepulcher, I do not know whether she heard anything spoken by the angel. I saw her, right after Magdalene, flee in fright from the sepulcher and the garden and seek out the other women who had remained behind outside the garden, in order to let them know what had taken place.... The other women, when told by Mary Salome, were shocked and joyful at the same time, and hesitated a while before going into the garden.

Careful consideration of these words seem to indicate that Anne Catherine did indeed twice refer to Salome of Jerusalem as "Mary Salome," so that it would appear, here again, that the corrective made in the English translation is appropriate. Since in the subsequent description by Anne Catherine there is no further mention of the names of the holy women present in the garden of the holy sepulcher, nor of their number, it is not possible to draw a definite conclusion regarding this. However, without further evidence to the contrary, it would seem that there were actually four holy women (Mary Magdalene, Mary Cleophas, Johanna Chusa, and Salome of Jerusalem) in the garden of the holy sepulcher on Easter Sunday morning. Continuing with Anne Catherine's description:

> I saw Magdalene arrive at the Cenacle.... Peter and John opened the door. Magdalene merely uttered the words, "They have taken the Lord from the tomb! We do not know where"—and ran back with great haste to the garden of the holy sepulcher.... Magdalene hurried...to the tomb.... She saw two angels in white priestly robes sitting at the head and the foot of the tomb.... She looked around and saw in the east about ten steps from the sepulcher...a long white-clad figure in the dawn twilight.... Jesus said to her "Mary!" Recognizing the voice and forgetting the crucifixion, death, and burial, as if he were still living, she turned quickly... and exclaimed, "Rabuni! (Master!)" She fell upon her knees in front of him and stretched out her arms toward his feet. Jesus, however, raised his hand in a defensive gesture toward her and said, "Do not touch me! For I have not yet ascended to my Father. Go to my brothers and say to them: I shall ascend to my Father and your Father, to my God and your God." Thereupon the Lord disappeared.... Magdalene found the holy women and related to them that she had spoken with Peter and had seen the angels and now the Lord in the garden, and the women replied that they had also seen the angels. Magdalene now hurried off to the city...and the women went again toward the garden.... Close by the garden of the holy sepulcher Jesus appeared to the holy women in a flowing white robe...and said, "Hail to you!" Trembling they fell at his feet....The Lord, addressing some words to them, gestured in a certain direction, and then vanished, whereupon the holy women hurried through the Bethlehem gate to Mt. Zion, to tell the disciples in the Cenacle that they had seen the Lord....

"Touch Me Not"

In addition to Mary Magdalene, the holy women Mary Cleophas, Johanna Chusa, and Salome of Jerusalem also bore witness to the miracle of the resurrection on Easter Sunday morning (and perhaps also Mary Salome).†

What does Anne Catherine say about these women, and the other holy women, who are otherwise simply names from the bible to us?

---

† In vision on Easter night, Saturday/Sunday, March 29/30, 1823, Anne Catherine referred to *five* holy women present at the Resurrection (including Mary Salome), rather than the *four* usually mentioned as having been there.

THE VIRGIN MARY

Mary's Nature and Appearance

The VIRGIN MARY was the second daughter of Anne and Joachim. She was always composed, serious, and deeply inward. She was attuned to everything connected with Jesus and the community of disciples, and also the community of holy women. She carried the whole in her heart. Her love was boundless and her wisdom unfathomable.

Mary Magdalene was taller and more beautiful than the other holy women, including even the beautiful Dinah the Samaritan, but the Virgin Mary was the most beautiful of all. Although the beauty of her form was not unmatched by others, and in some respects Magdalene's beauty was even more striking, Mary stands out among them all, more especially through an indescribable silent blessing that emanated from her, and through her simplicity, meekness, youthfulness, earnestness, and purity.

Mary was always composed, serious, and deeply inward. She was purity itself, so lacking in any extraneous qualities that she seems no more nor less than the reflection of God in a human being. No other is like her in this respect, except for her son. She, like her son, was in the image and likeness of God—the one expressing the feminine side of God, and the other the masculine side. Exalted beyond all others, she was at the same time the most humble of human beings, completely guileless, like an innocent child.

In terms of physical appearance, Mary was slender, tall, and ever youthful. She had a high forehead, a long well-proportioned nose, large eyes (usually cast down), a beautiful red mouth, and a pleasantly tanned skin with shimmering rosy cheeks. She was serious, quiet, and often sad (but never over-distraught). When she wept, her tears ran gently across her exquisitely peaceful face.

Everyone who beheld her saw that she was beyond all other women in her unspeakable purity, innocence, and wisdom. Peaceful serenity and loving-kindness emanated from her gaze as a blessing toward all human beings with whom she came into connection.

Mary's Permanent Residence

During the 3½ years of Jesus's ministry, Mary resided with her maid in the house she had moved to after Joseph's death, located between Capernaum and Bethsaida, at the north end of the Sea of Galilee. It belonged to the wealthy Levi, who lived in a large house nearby. Peter's family had leased it from Levi and put it at the disposal of Jesus and Mary. The house was roomy and included several outbuildings where occasional visitors would stay, including Mary's relatives and friends—most of whom came from Nazareth, Sepphoris, and Jerusalem—and later the disciples of Jesus. The house was ideally suited for this purpose.

It was to this house that Jesus returned again and again from his teaching and healing journeys throughout Palestine. Mary also often traveled on these journeys, in the company of some of the holy women, in order to be present at the teachings of her son.

Mary at the Time She Received the Magnificat

Mary did not maintain her own household, and possessed neither fields nor cattle of her own. She lived as a widow from the gifts of friends and relatives (especially those from Sepphoris). Levi's servant stopped by regularly, bringing food from Capernaum, looking after the house and garden, and house-sitting when Mary was away.

Mary occupied herself with sewing, spinning, and crocheting. She prayed much, and converted and taught other women. There were almost always guests in the house, so much so that often she had no room even for additional visitors who had traveled the long distance there from Nazareth or Jerusalem.

Jesus's Comportment with his Mother

Even at home Mary was not spared many a stress and strain. It started with all manner of gossip from neighbors whereby, under the guise of consoling her, they accused Jesus of living the life of a vagrant, telling her that he was neglecting her and that it should be his first concern to learn a trade in order to support her, now that Joseph was dead. Whether for or against him, people throughout the land were constantly talking about Jesus.

Mary was very poised and inwardly restrained, but even so, not free of some inner agitation, premonitions, and anxiety whenever her son was away. Every vile rumor his enemies let loose was reported to her, just as all the fears and worries of his well-meaning acquaintances came also to her ear. As a result, she often waited with fearful longing for his return.

Elizabeth and Mary at the Time of the Visitation

Jesus's behavior toward Mary was ever loving and respectful. Whenever they met, he extended to her both his hands; and if she knelt before him to kiss them, he kissed hers in return when she arose. When they were alone, he often embraced her consolingly. When he was teaching, she treated him as a saint and prophet. She never embraced him, but extended her hand when he offered his.

Jesus put recent converts under Mary's wing, for instance Dinah the Samaritan woman, Mara the Suphanite, and Mary Magdalene. He introduced all the apostles and disciples to her personally, and whenever he returned to Capernaum, hers was always the first house he visited.

There was an unspoken covenant between the two that Mary take the disciples into her heart, her prayers, and her blessing—to some extent even into her very self—as her children and as siblings to Jesus. She was their spiritual mother, even as she was the actual mother of Jesus in the flesh. She fulfilled this agreement always to her utmost and in the most intimate fashion; and Jesus also accorded this covenant great solemnity. There was in its fulfillment something inexpressibly holy, a deep interiority—for Mary was as the rootstock and fruiting vine of the flesh and blood of Jesus.

Mary's Wisdom

At the high point of Jesus's teaching activity—at the time of the great crowds that came to hear him speak at Capernaum in early AD 30, when the great Mountain Sermons began—Mary attended all his sermons, for although she had prior awareness of the mysteries he revealed, as yet she had not fully understood them: for instance, how the Second Person of the Divinity was received by her body and there became flesh, both as her child and as Divine Humanity. All these deep knowings were embraced within her humble and respectful motherly love for Jesus.

But when—much to the fury of the deluded—Jesus taught more openly the secrets of his origin, his earthly mission, and his approaching return to the Father, Mary's attention was recalled to these mysteries.

After one such teaching, while at prayer in her lodgings later that evening, Mary had an intellectual vision of the angel's salutation, the birth and childhood of Jesus, the reality of her motherhood and of his truly being a child—and she consciously assimilated the fact that she bore and raised as her own child he who is the son of God.

She was so overcome with awe that she dissolved into tears. And yet these revelations were cloaked still in her feeling of motherly love for her Divine Son, just as in the sacrament the form of the bread cloaks the living God.

Some Aspects of Mary's Behavior

Altogether, Mary was indescribably simple in nature. Jesus never let on before others that she was an especially worthy person. She herself never involved herself with any but the sick and unlearned. She appeared always earnest and unutterably modest.

All respected her, even her son's enemies, although she sought no one out and always maintained her reserve. The only time she stepped forward was at the head of the procession when Jesus made his triumphant entry into Jerusalem.

At the gathering in Jutta immediately after the Baptist's beheading, as those present visited his birth room, Mary showed them a large blanket covered with embroidered sayings of the Prophets, and recounted the circumstances of her making the blanket with Elizabeth. She told of having prophesied to Elizabeth that John would see Jesus only three times, and noted that this indeed proved true.

Mary Looking up from the Foot of the Cross

At this point Jesus spoke up, and after carefully introducing the subject, told the story of the decapitation—and in consequence the blanket was drenched in the mourners' tears.

At the great Mountain Sermons of October, AD 30, Mary took charge of the care of the sick among the women and children, as well as the distribution of charitable gifts to the poor. With her friends and the disciples she oversaw the practical accomplishment of all these things.

Afterward, she and her friends continued their work, making blankets, clothing, sandals, and belts; preparing food stocks, baking bread—all for the poor—and visiting the sick. Throughout all this activity she remained uncommonly silent, simpler and more serious than the others.

She also visited Judas Iscariot to caution him, for he had shown himself to be envious and avaricious. On one occasion she wept over him. He was moved and repeatedly tried to change his ways, but always fell back.

While Jesus taught at the last community meal before the Passion, Mary wept at the women's table as she carved the lamb.

Mary's Death and Assumption

About one year after the crucifixion, Stephen was stoned and the rising settlement of new converts around Jerusalem was dissolved, the Christians dispersed, and some murdered. A few years later, a new storm arose against them. Then it was that Mary, who until that time had dwelt in the small house near the Cenacle and in Bethany, allowed herself to be conducted by John to the region of Ephesus, where the Christians had already made settlements. This happened a short time after the imprisonment of Lazarus and his sisters by the Jews, and their setting out over the sea.

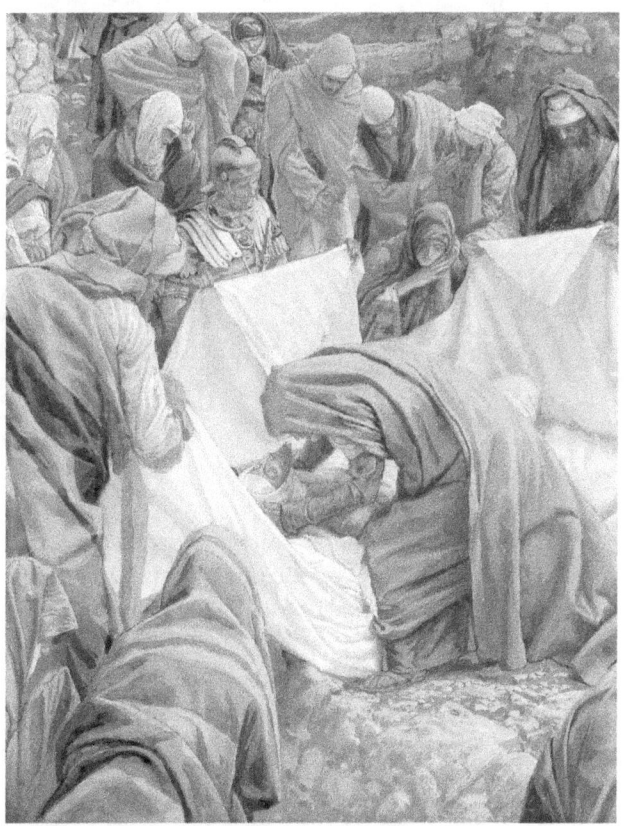

Mary Kisses Jesus Before the Enshrouding

Mary's dwelling was not in Ephesus itself, but from three to four hours distant. It stood on a height upon which several Christians from Judea, among them some of the holy women related to her, had taken up their abode. In the neighborhood of her dwelling, the blessed Virgin had herself erected the stations of the Holy Way of the Cross. Though by now very advanced in years, Mary had in her appearance no other mark of age than that of a great longing, which at length effectuated her glorification. She was inexpressibly grave. The older she grew, the whiter and more transparent became her face. She was thin, but with no wrinkle, no sign of decay in her. She was like a spirit.

Mary Looks Up at Ascension Angels

After Mary had lived three years in the settlement near Ephesus, she conceived a great desire to visit Jerusalem, so John and Peter escorted her thither. Several apostles were there assembled, and Mary assisted them with her advice.

On her arrival, before she entered the city, she visited the Mount of Olives, Mount Golgotha, the Holy Sepulcher, and all the holy places around Jerusalem. Mary was so sad, so moved by compassion, that she could scarcely walk. Peter and John supported her under the arms.

A year and a half before her death, she made one more journey from Ephesus to Jerusalem, where she again visited the holy places. When she came to the back gate of that palace where she had first seen Jesus passing with the cross and where he fell, she was so agitated by the painful remembrance that she too sank to the ground. Her companions thought she was dying.

As Mary felt her end approaching, in accordance with the directions of her divine son, she called the apostles to her by prayer. She was now in her sixty-fourth year.

When the apostles went all together into Mary's little sleeping chamber in order to take leave of her, the disciples and holy women remained standing in the front apartment. Mary sat upright, and as the apostles knelt in turn at the side of her couch, she prayed over each and blessed him with her hands laid upon him crosswise. She did the same to the disciples and to the women. Mary then addressed them in a body, and did all that Jesus had in Bethany directed her to do.

Mary's Final Visit to Jerusalem and Golgotha

Peter then celebrated the Holy Mass in the Virgin's own oratory. Mary was in a sitting posture on her couch during the whole celebration. Peter first gave the blessed Virgin the last anointing, just as that sacrament is administered at the present day. Next he administered holy communion, which she received sitting up without support. Then she sank back again on her pillow, and after the apostles had offered a short prayer, she received the chalice from John, but not now in so upright a posture.

After communion, Mary spoke no more. Her countenance, blooming and smiling as in youth, was raised above. The roof of her chamber was no longer visible, and the lamp appeared to be suspended in the open air.

A pathway of light arose from Mary up to the heavenly Jerusalem, up to the throne of the most holy Trinity. On either side of this pathway were clouds of light out of which gazed angelic faces.

Mary raised her arms to the Heavenly Jerusalem. Her body with all its wrappings was floating high above the couch. A figure of light, also with upraised arms, appeared to issue from Mary. The two choirs of angels united under this figure and soared up with it, as if separating it from the body, which now sank back upon the couch, the hands crossed upon the breast.

Many holy souls, among them Joseph, Anne, Joachim, John the Baptist, Zechariah, and Elizabeth, came to meet her. But up she soared, followed by them, to her son, whose wounds were flashing light far more brilliant than that which surrounded him. He received her and placed in her hand a scepter, pointing at the same time over the whole circumference of the earth. At last a multitude of souls was released from Purgatory and soared up to heaven.

On the night following the burial there took place the bodily assumption of the blessed Virgin into heaven, which Anne Catherine describes thus:

"I saw on this night several of the apostles and holy women in the little garden, praying and singing psalms before the grotto. I saw a broad pathway of light descend from heaven and rest upon the tomb. In it were circles of glory full of angels, in the midst of whom the resplendent soul of the blessed Virgin came floating down. Before her went her divine son, the marks of his wounds flashing with light.

In the innermost circle, that which surrounded the holy soul of Mary, the angels appeared like the faces of very young children; in the second circle, they were like those of children from six to eight years old; and in the outermost, like the faces of youths, I could clearly distinguish only the face, the rest of the figure consisting of perfectly transparent light. Encircling the head of the blessed Virgin like a crown was a choir of blessed spirits.

I know not what those present saw of all this. But I saw that some gazed up in amazement and adoration, while others cast themselves prostrate in fright upon the earth.

These apparitions, becoming more and more distinct as they approached nearer, floated over the grotto, and another pathway of light issued from it and arose to the heavenly Jerusalem.

The blessed soul of Mary, floating before Jesus, penetrated through the rock and into the tomb, out of which she again arose radiant with light in her glorified body and, escorted by the entire multitude of celestial spirits, returned in triumph to the heavenly Jerusalem."

The assumption of the blessed Virgin Mary took place on August 15, AD 44.†

MARY HELI

MARY HELI‡ was the first daughter of Anne and Joachim, the parents, later, of Mary of Nazareth, the Virgin Mary. Mary Heli was not the child of promise. She was born too early, and for this reason led a somewhat reserved life. She lived mostly with her grandparents in the town of Sepphoris, when Anne and Joachim began a new life in Nazareth.

Mary Heli was about twenty years older than her sister Mary of Nazareth.†† Her husband, Cleophas, was a nephew of Joseph, who brought a son from a previous marriage with him into the marriage with Mary Heli.‡‡ This son was Matthias, who later was elected by the disciples to take the place of Ju-das Iscariot in the circle of twelve. From her union with Cleophas, Mary Heli bore three sons —Sadoch, James, and Heliachim (Joachim)—

Mary Heli

and one daughter, Mary Cleophas, who was therefore a niece of Mary of Nazareth. Sadoch, James, Heliachim, and Matthias were known as the "brothers of the Lord," although in fact they were cousins of Jesus. All four were among the earliest disciples of John the Baptist, and after the death of John they became disciples of Jesus.

---

† An account of Mary's lineage, birth, and childhood, and a more complete description of her life after the Passion, including her residence in Ephesus and Assumption, will be found in Volume III.

‡ She is called Mary (of) Heli, to distinguish her from her younger sister (Mary of Nazareth) of the same name, because she was the daughter of Joachim, or Heliachim.

†† Nineteen years and five months later, at the age of approximately 43, Anne conceived her long-awaited second child, Mary (of Nazareth).

‡‡ Anne Catherine states also that Joachim brought to this marriage a daughter, Anna Cleophas, who had been born out of wedlock.

Later, after the death of Cleophas, Mary Heli married a priest named Obed, to whom she bore a son, Jairus.† She lived at Japha, a small place about one hour south of Nazareth, where Zebedee had lived earlier, and his sons James and John were born.

MARY CLEOPHAS

MARY CLEOPHAS was the daughter of Mary Heli. Because of the age difference between Mary Heli and her younger sister Mary of Nazareth, Mary Cleophas—although a niece of Mary of Nazareth—was about four years older than her, and a frequent playmate of their youth.

In the course of her life, Mary Cleophas had three husbands. The first was called Alpheus, who had been married before and already had a son, who thus became the stepson of Mary Cleophas, and who grew up in their home. This son was Matthew, who later became one of the twelve disciples. To Alpheus, Mary Cleophas bore one daughter, Susanna Alpheus, and three sons: Judas Thaddeus, Simon, and James the Less, all three of whom went on to become part of the circle of the twelve disciples of Jesus.

Mary Cleophas

Her second marriage was to Sabbas, to whom she bore another son, Joseph Barsabbas, who also later became a disciple—however, unlike his four brothers, not one of the twelve apostles.

Her third husband was a Greek, Jonah, who brought with him a son, Parmenas, from an earlier marriage. Parmenas also became a disciple of Jesus. To Jonah, Mary Cleophas bore a son, Simeon Justus, who was about ten years old at the time of Christ's Resurrection. Simeon Justus, after the death of James the Lesser, became the second bishop of Jerusalem.

At the start of Jesus's ministry, Mary Cleophas settled in the neighborhood of Capernaum close to the house of the blessed Virgin. Later she lived in Cana. On November 25, AD 30, Mary Cleophas, who lay desperately ill with fever at the home of Peter in Bethsaida, was healed by Christ Jesus. She died five years after Christ's ascension.

MARY SALOME

MARY SALOME was a cousin of Mary of Nazareth and the wife of the fisherman Zebedee: Mary of Nazareth was the daughter of Anne and Joachim, and Mary Salome was the daughter of Sobe and Solomon‡—and Anne and Sobe were sisters, daughters of the Essenes Ismeria and Eliud. (There was a third daughter, Maraha, who was younger than Sobe and older than Anne). Mary Salome, Anne's niece, was about the same age as Anne's eldest daughter, Mary Heli. She was, then, the daughter of the aunt of the mother of God.

Zebedee and Mary Salome had two sons, James and John, sometimes referred to as the "sons of Zebedee." In their early years, James and John did not know Jesus personally, but they later became disciples of Jesus—John being the only one of the twelve who was present at the death and burial of Christ and who, together with Peter,

Mary Salome Holding the Virgin Mary at the Cross

---

† Anne Catherine states that Obed had sons from an earlier marriage, who were also disciples of John the Baptist.

‡ Mary Salome took her name from her father Solomon (Salome), just as Mary Cleophas took hers from her father Cleophas.

was in the garden of the Holy Sepulcher on Easter Sunday morning. Peter, James, and John were the three disciples who witnessed the Transfiguration of Jesus on Mt. Tabor in the night April 3/4 of the year AD 31. They were also present with Jesus in the garden of Gethsemane in the night April 2/3 of the year AD 33 after the Last Supper. These three—

Mary Salome & John at Nailing

Peter, James, and John—represent faith, hope, and love.

Near the beginning of Jesus's ministry, Mary Salome lived in the house which previously had been the home of the holy family in Nazareth. Later she lived near Capernaum. As referred to above, Mary Salome is named in the Gospel of Matthew as one of the holy women at the foot of the cross. She was one of the four Marys directly beneath the cross, the others being the Virgin Mary, Mary Magdalene, and Mary Cleophas. She is also referred to in the Gospel of Matthew for requesting of Jesus, "Command that these two sons of mine [James and John] may sit, one at your right hand and one at your left, in your kingdom." (Matt. 20:20–28)

MARTHA

Martha

MARTHA, who was about two years younger than her brother Lazarus,† was the eldest of his three sisters. Not only did she come from a wealthy family but also she was gifted with a talent for organization. She applied this gift with apostolic fervor as a true servant of the community of disciples and the community of holy women. She lived simply and sought always to do good works. Initially together with her brother, and then increasingly with the help of some of the holy women, she was constantly occupied with caring for the needs of Jesus and the community of the disciples and holy women. About three years after

Martha Cooking

Christ's Resurrection, Martha and her brother Lazarus and her sister Magdalene were captured by the Jews and set adrift on the Mediterranean Sea together with four others in a small boat. Through providence they landed in the south of France, where she began missionary activity. Whereas Lazarus remained as bishop of Marseille, and her sister Mary Magdalene retired to lead the life of a hermit in a cave at Saint-Baume, east of Marseille, Martha went with her maidservant Marcella north of Marseille and founded a community there.

After witnessing Martha raise someone who had died of drowning, many people converted to Christianity. So close was her bond with her younger sister, Mary Magdalene,

† More on Martha will be found under *Lazarus*, in the section on the Holy Men.

that Martha, although in a different region of the south of France, died about one week after her death. According to tradition, it was at the town of Tarascon, Provence, that she passed away.

MARY MAGDALENE

MARY MAGDALENE, the youngest sister of Lazarus, belonged to the intimate circle of Jesus and his mother, and heads the list of converted sinners as the "type" of all saintly sinners. She grew up at the family castle in Bethany, just northeast of Jerusalem. This is also where Lazarus was later raised from the dead by Jesus.

Magdalene was the youngest of four children and was very beautiful. She was about nine years younger than Lazarus and approximately seven years younger than Martha. The third sister was referred to as Silent Mary who, in modern terminology, would be called handicapped or impaired. She did not speak, but had profound inner visions. She was about five years older than Magdalene. However, she died at a relatively early age on April 8, AD 30, about six months after the ministry of Jesus began on September 23, AD 29, the day of the baptism in the Jordan. As described in the section on Lazarus, the family was quite wealthy. Lazarus had inherited from his father and shared his wealth with his three sisters.

At the age of seven Magdalene lost her parents,† who had spoilt their youngest and extremely beautiful and precocious daughter. By the age of nine she already had admirers. As her talents and qualities blossomed, so did the rumors and astonishment surrounding her. She had a very active social life, was well-educated, and wrote aphorisms about love on little parchment rolls, which she exchanged with her suitors. When she was eleven, she moved with a large retinue of maids and servants to her own castle (which had fallen to her by lot at her parents' death) on the southwest shore of the Sea of Galilee in the town of Magdala, located a few miles north of Tiberias. In her new lodgings she was soon entertaining officers from the garrisons of Magdala and surroundings. Initially she associated with witty men, but gradually the character of her intimate male and female friends sank lower.

Magdalene was taller than all the other women, robust, but yet graceful. She had very beautiful, tapering fingers, a small, delicate foot, a wealth of beautiful long hair, and there was something imposing in all her movements. Being wealthy and beautiful, she enjoyed life and, corre-

Mary Magdalene Repentant

spondingly, lived sumptuously. This was a source of great concern for her brother Lazarus and sister Martha, both of whom had in the meantime become disciples of Jesus of Nazareth. Lazarus and Martha were praying for guidance as to how to go about introducing their sister to Jesus.‡

---

† For a full account of Magdalene's parents, see the article on her brother Lazarus in *The Apostles and Disciples*.

‡ James the Greater also took an early and special interest in bringing Magdalene to listen to Jesus.

Magdalene received the first ray of grace on the final day of Jesus's forty-day fast, as he was being ministered to by the angels. She was wonderfully agitated. At the time she was busied with finery for some amusement. Suddenly anxiety about her life seized upon her, and a longing rose in her soul to be freed from the chains that bound her. She cast the finery from her hands, but was laughed at by those around her.† However this inner motivation did not last long.

In January, AD 30, Martha convinced Magdalene to join her on a trip to Jezreel to see the new prophet from Nazareth. Although Jesus had already left by the time they arrived on the tenth day of the month, Magdalene heard from eyewitnesses about the miracles he had just performed. One month later, on February 9, Magdalene was again in Jezreel at the instigation of her brother Lazarus and her sister Martha, as well as of Veronica and Johanna Chusa, who had been visiting with her. From the window of the inn where she was staying she caught a glimpse of Jesus entering the town with his disciples, and he blessed her with a glance.

Shaken and overcome, she rushed into a leper-hostel and then returned to Magdala with her siblings. But she soon reverted to her old ways. On July 19, AD 30, in the circle of his followers, Jesus told them to pray for Magdalene, saying she would soon come and become an example for others.

Then one day Martha received guidance to go to Magdalene because she knew that Jesus was going to be teaching in the area of Magdala, in a place called Gabara—northwest of Tiberias—not far from the Sea of Galilee. Martha managed to persuade her sister to come and hear Jesus preach on a hill near Gabara on November 8, AD 30.‡

Magdalene arrived dressed in her finest clothes with an attitude of curiosity to see the new prophet, but not with any sense of belief. She brought some friends who enjoyed living the high life with her. Around ten o'clock Jesus arrived at the mountain, where there was a teacher's chair. He delivered a powerful discourse, culminating with the words: "Come! Come to me, all who are weary and laden with guilt! Do penance, believe, and share the kingdom with me!" At these words, Mary Magdalene was deeply moved inwardly, and Jesus, perceiving her agitation, addressed his hearers with some words of consolation—words actually meant for Mary Magdalene—and she was converted. That evening, a Pharisee named Simon Zabulon invited Jesus to a banquet. During the meal, Magdalene entered the room carrying a flask of ointment, with which she anointed Jesus's head. (This scene and the ensuing dispute with Simon Zabulon is described in Luke 7:36–50.)

Mary Magdalene Anoints Jesus's Head

However, while Jesus was speaking, Magdalene had an extraordinary experience. She became riveted by everything Jesus said, to the point that—and this is an event that is difficult for us to understand—Jesus cast a demon out from Mary Magdalene. In modern parlance we might call it some kind of obsession, but in those days it was said that the person was possessed by a demon. The following words spoken by Christ apply to her:

> When the unclean spirit has gone out of a man, he passes through waterless places seeking rest; and finding none, he says: "I will return to my house from which I came." And when he comes he finds it swept and put in order. Then he goes and brings seven other spirits more evil than himself, and they enter and dwell there; and the last state becomes worse than the first. (Luke 11:24)

In fact, this is exactly what happened. Magdalene did have a relapse; for she returned to her former lifestyle and became possessed again, this time by seven demons. Martha and Lazarus, who witnessed this, were of course now deeply concerned and kept praying for guidance as to what to do. This new condition lasted for almost exactly seven weeks. (Again and again we find this period of seven weeks in the life of Christ. For instance, Pentecost came seven weeks after the Resurrection.)

Magdalene was soon again in her old track, receiving the visits of men who spoke in the usual disparaging way

---

† Regarding this event, Jesus later consoled Lazarus on the subject of Magdalene, of whom he said that already there had fallen upon her soul a spark of salvation, which would entirely consume her.

‡ To further encourage Magdalene to hear Jesus preach at the mountain, Martha told her that Dinah the Samaritan Woman and Mara the Suphanite invited her there also.

of Jesus, his journeys, his doctrine, and of all who followed him. They ridiculed what they heard of Magdalene's visit to Gabara, and looked upon it as a very unlikely story. As for the rest, they declared that they found Magdalene more beautiful and charming than ever.

It was by such speeches that Magdalene allowed herself to be infatuated and her good impressions dissipated. She soon sank deeper than before, and her relapse into sin gave the devil greater power over her. He attacked her more vigorously when he saw that he might possibly lose her. She became possessed, and often fell into cramps and convulsions.

Mary Magdalene Listens to Jesus Teach

And so, seven weeks after the encounter with Jesus at Gabara, on December 26, AD 30, Martha again managed to persuade Magdalene to come and hear Jesus speak, this time in a place called Azanoth, a few miles northwest of Gabara. On this occasion Jesus cast out all seven demons, as described in great detail by Anne Catherine, and as is referred to briefly also in the Gospel: "Mary, called Magdalene, from whom seven demons had gone out" (Luke 8:2).

Mary Magdalene Listens to Jesus in Bethany, While Martha Prepares a Meal

This was, of course, an event of great importance in the life of Mary Magdalene. Something truly extraordinary had taken place through which she was able more and more to find her true calling.

After he had cast out the demons, Jesus advised Magdalene to abide in the company of the Virgin Mary. Just as Jesus himself had a circle of disciples, who were all men—remembering that it was a patriarchal culture—so the Virgin Mary had a circle of women around her which Anne Catherine refers to as the holy women. Magdalene joined this circle of holy women and played an important role therein.

This was all preparation for the great event, later, when she was the one who, on the morning of the resurrection, came to the empty tomb. There, in the garden of the Holy Sepulcher, she turned around and saw someone whom she thought to be the gardener—until she heard him speak. Then she knew: this is the Risen One; he has risen from the dead.

Christ then spoke with her and said that she should go to the disciples and tell them that he would be ascending to the Father. He gave her the task of being a messenger.

One of the Greek words for messenger is "apostle." Because it was Mary Magdalene who brought the news of the resurrection to the apostles, particularly to Peter and John, she is called the "apostle to the apostles."

MARONI

MARONI was a wealthy widow from the town of Nain. She was the sister of the wife of the apostle James the Greater and the mother of the youth of Nain,† who at the age of twelve Jesus raised from the dead at the entrance to the city of Nain around 9 AM on Monday, November 13, AD 30 (as described in Luke 7:11–17), and who, after this miracle had taken place, not only lodged Jesus and the disciples both at her summer estate and her great house in Nain, but also generously placed a portion of her wealth at the disposal of the community—in which she became then one of the most active women. At her request and with the help of his own mother, Jesus then healed from a distance Maroni's friend, the widow Mary of Nain, from possession, after which she also entered the circle of holy women.

Maroni at the Raising of the Youth of Nain

Maroni was the daughter of an uncle, on the father's side, of Peter, and so was a cousin of Peter's wife. Her first husband was the son of a sister of Elizabeth, who herself was the daughter of a sister of the mother of Anne. Maroni's first husband having died without children, she had married Eliud,‡ a relation of Anne, and had left Chisloth, near Tabor, to take up her abode at Nain, which was not far off, and where she soon lost her second husband.

---

† According to Anne Catherine, the youth's name was Martialis. He later became a disciple and was one of the group of disciples who accompanied the apostle Peter to Rome.

VERONICA

VERONICA, earlier called SERAPHIA, was from Jerusalem, the daughter of a brother of Zechariah of Hebron (the father of John the Baptist), into whose ancestral house near the Jerusalem fish market Joachim and Anne had moved when they brought their little daughter Mary to the Temple. Thus, Veronica was a cousin of John the Baptist. She was related also to the old priest Simeon, and a friend of his sons, who had acquired from their father an inclination, or secret love, for the Messiah.

Veronica was a tall, beautiful, and courageous woman, with a great love for Jesus. She was already an adult, though not yet married, when the twelve-year-old Jesus was teaching in the temple. At that time Jesus's parents had searched for him everywhere among his relatives, but he had remained behind with four older boys. During those days, when not at the temple, Jesus had stayed in the same house by the Jerusalem gate where Mary had stayed the day before her purification, and again for two nights with some elderly people when Jesus was a small child. While the twelve-year-old Jesus was staying there, it was Veronica who sent him meals. This small house or inn of elderly people was a kind of establishment. It was situated east of the Mount of Olives, and often used later as a refuge by Jesus and the disciples. Later, in fact the very last time Jesus was to teach in the temple, Veronica secretly brought him food there.

Later, Veronica married Sirach, a member of the Sanhedrin who was descended from the chaste Susanna, whose story is told in Chapter 13 of the Book of Daniel. To begin with, he was hostile toward Jesus and his followers, and would keep Veronica locked up at home whenever he noticed she was helping Jesus and the disciples. But then

---

‡ Regarding this connection, Anne Catherine provides the following background: "To the north of Mount Tabor was situated the city of Tabor, whence the mountain derived its name, and about an hour westward in the direction of Sepphoris was another fortified place, Casaloth [Chisloth], which was in the valley on the south side of the mountain, northward from Nain, and in the direction of Apheke. I have heard a more modern name given to this place, and I saw that relatives of Jesus once dwelt there, namely, a sister of Elizabeth, who, like the maidservant of Mary Mark, bore the name of Rhoda. She had three daughters (Sobe, Anne, and Maraha) and two sons. Maraha was one of the three widows, friends of Mary, and her two sons—Arastaria and Cocharia—were later among the disciples. One of Rhoda's sons married Maroni, and died without issue. His widow, in obedience to the law, entered into a second marriage with one of her first husband's family named Eliud, a young nephew of Anne. Thereafter she lived at Nain, and by her second husband had one son, who was called Martialis. She was now a widow for the second time, the so-called widow of Nain whose son Martialis was raised from the dead by Jesus.

Sirach received instruction from Joseph of Arimathea and Nicodemus—members of the Sanhedrin also—and on this account his attitude toward Jesus changed. He then allowed Veronica to follow Jesus and serve the community of the disciples. They had three children, two of whom later became disciples, while the third fell away. Her son Amandor was one of the first disciples of Jesus.†

It was Veronica who purchased the holy vessel from the Temple and gave it to be used at the Last Supper. Thus did this vessel (later called the Grail cup), which had been given originally by Melchizedek to Abraham and was then handed down through the ages as a most holy and sacred artifact, eventually come into the hands of Jesus for the institution of the Eucharist at the Last Supper.

Veronica Holds Out Her Scarf to Jesus

Seraphia, after her death, received the Latin name Veronica, that is, *vera icon*, meaning "true icon," because of her veil, which on Good Friday received an imprint of the face of Jesus. It was not so much a veil as a linen neck scarf,‡ which she had hanging around her shoulders at the time when Jesus on that Friday was carrying the

The Holy Face on the Scarf of Veronica

cross through the streets of Jerusalem. When she beheld his battered and bloody face, she offered her veil, reaching out with it toward Jesus's face, as a sign of her empathy for his suffering. He pressed it to his face and the veil miraculously received an imprint thereof.

Veronica's scarf remained at first with the holy women, but when Magdalene, Martha, Lazarus, and some others were exiled (arriving ultimately at Marseilles), it was passed on to Mary, and later brought to Rome by some apostles. There is another account that the scarf remained with the holy women, that the apostle Thaddeus took it with him to King Abgar, and that it came later to Constantinople, and is now in Turin, where the burial sheet of Christ is also.††

---

† Amandor was received as a disciple by Jesus in Bethsaida on Thursday, August 4, AD 29, along with the Essene youth Eustachius, and the son of the widow Lea, Kolaya. Amandor, Eustachius, and Kolaya were the first three disciples of Jesus.

‡ Such scarfs were traditionally worn at the time as a sign of sympathy with another's sorrow.

†† Anne Catherine beheld yet another episode in the history of this scarf, in which Veronica takes it to Rome, along with Nicodemus and Epaphras.

The Holy Women at Christ's Death and Resurrection

During the persecution of the Christians in Jerusalem, toward the end of the third year after their return—when Lazarus and his sisters were driven into exile—I saw Veronica flee with some other women. But she was overtaken and cast into prison, where she was tortured as a martyr for the truth, for Jesus. Veronica, who had so often fed Jesus (in both the early and the final years of his life) with earthly bread—even as with his own flesh and blood he had nourished her to eternal life—died of starvation.

SUSANNA OF JERUSALEM

SUSANNA OF JERUSALEM was a daughter of Cleophas, born to him out of wedlock. Cleophas was an older brother of Joseph. Born in Gophna, she lived in the Temple as a little girl, like the Virgin Mary. From her grandfather, a Persian nobleman, she acquired wealth and later married a government official named Matthias, a relative of the later apostle Matthias who took the place of Judas Iscariot in the circle of twelve at Pentecost. Right at the start of Christ's ministry, Susanna of Jerusalem belonged to the circle of friends around Lazarus and Martha in Bethany, often accompanying Martha on her travels to help the disciples. Susanna also supported the community with generous donations.

When Dinah the Samaritan woman first converted, on on July 26, AD 30, she repaired to an inn lying between Jerusalem and Jericho where many other holy women resided at that time, among them Susanna. Dinah sought Susanna out to help her remain upright in her faith and teach her, for she was still struggling mightily against fleshly desires. She remained with Susanna for a considerable time, and in the end achieved a full conversion.

The Virgin Mary placed much trust in certain women, such as Susanna and Johanna Chusa, to the extent that she entrusted them with certain personal details about Jesus and herself.

Susanna was present at the foot of the cross and at the entombment.

SALOME OF JERUSALEM

SALOME OF JERUSALEM was a widow at the time of the crucifixion on Golgotha. Like Susanna of Jerusalem, Salome was related to the holy family through a brother of Joseph.

Salome of Jerusalem

Salome lived at the home of Martha in Bethany. In the company of Mary Magdalene, Mary Cleophas, and Johanna Chusa. She was in the garden of the holy sepulcher on Easter Sunday morning and experienced the Risen Christ there.

Susanna of Jerusalem

MARY MARK

MARY MARK was a relative of the old priest Simeon, who blessed the baby Jesus in the temple (Luke 2:22–35). She lived with her son John Mark† northeast of Jerusalem.

Mary Mark

Their house lay beyond the city, about a quarter of an hour from the Temple, on the eastern side and opposite the Mount of Olives.‡ It was not far from the home of Joseph of Arimathea, and near a stone-cutter's yard, in a retired quarter of the city little frequented by Pharisees. Jesus was often a guest at Mary Mark's home, often with several disciples. It was not necessary to enter the city in order to reach it, and was the site of many gatherings of the holy women during the years of the ministry. The virgin Mary stayed there frequently, and also directly prior to the Passion.

Mary Mark was very active among the holy woman, seeing after the needs of Jesus and the disciples through the ministry, and was present at Golgotha, helped with the preparation of Jesus's body for burial, and at the entombment stood facing the Virgin.

JOHANNA CHUSA

JOHANNA CHUSA was a tall and pale woman, very serious in her manner. She was a niece of the prophetess Anna, who was in the temple when Simeon blessed the child Jesus (Luke 2:36–38). Johanna Chusa's son had already made the acquaintance of the twelve-year-old Jesus when he (Jesus) remained behind in the temple and later was one of Jesus's secret disciples in Jerusalem.

Johanna Chusa was frequently at the home of Lazarus and Martha in Bethany and was one of Martha's most industrious helpers. Jesus often dined at the home of Johanna Chusa with his disciples. It was Johanna Chusa who, together with Veronica and Mary of Hebron, a niece of Elizabeth, went to Herod's castle at Machaerus to retrieve the head of Elizabeth's son, John the Baptist.

Johanna was also one of the four holy women to bear witness to the Risen Christ in the garden of the holy sepulcher on Easter Sunday morning, which Anne Catherine describes thus:

> When the morning sky began to clear with a streak of white light, I saw Magdalene, Mary Cleophas, Johanna Chusa, and Salome, enveloped in mantles, leaving their abode near the Cenacle. They carried spices packed in linen cloths, and one

---

† John Mark was a close friend of Lazarus, Nicodemus, Simeon's son, and Obed.

‡ Elsewhere, Anne Catherine says of the house of Mary Mark and her son John Mark that their house stood a quarter of an hour outside the gate through which the cattle were led to the cattle market on the north side of the temple. It was built upon a high hill which, at a later period, was covered with houses. It was from here to Gethsemane one-half hour; and from Gethsemane across the Mount of Olives to Bethany, something less than an hour. The last-named place lay almost in a straight line east of the temple and, by the direct route, it may have been only one hour from Jerusalem. From certain points of the temple and from the castles in the rear, one could descry Bethany. Bethphage, however, was not in sight, as it lay low; and the view was, besides, up to the point at which the temple could be seen through a defile of the mountain road, obstructed by the Mount of Olives.

Johanna Chusa

of them had a lighted lantern.... The holy women walked anxiously to the little gate belonging to Nicodemus.... During the dispersion of the disciples and the Passion of the Lord, Martha had a heavy duty to fulfill and she still discharged it. Though torn with grief, she had to see to everything, to lend a helping hand everywhere. She had to feed the dispersed and wandering, attend to their wants, provide nourishment for all. Her assistant in all this, as well as in the cooking, was Johanna Chusa, a widow whose husband had been a servant of Herod.

Johanna did not live long after the Passion, for some Jews out of malice began immediately to pursue and secretly put away the early Christians. Johanna was imprisoned on one occasion, but then released. She was killed sometime later as the result of such persecution.

DINAH THE SAMARITAN

The first of the holy women to have been converted by Jesus was DINAH the Samaritan woman, who is known to us through her lengthy conversation with Jesus and subsequent conversion at Jacob's well in Sichar† on Wednesday, July 26, AD 30. (John 4:4–42) Dinah was an uncommonly gifted, open-hearted, easily influenced, pleasing woman of great vivacity and impetuosity, but she was always disturbed in conscience. She was living now more respectably, that is with this her reputed husband, in a house that stood alone and surrounded by a moat, near the gate leading from Shechem to the spring house. Though not held in contempt by the inhabitants, still they did not have much communication with her. Her manners were different from theirs, her costume elaborate and studied, all which, however, they pardoned in her as she was a stranger.

Dinah was an intelligent woman of some standing in the world, the offspring of a mixed marriage—a Jewish mother and a pagan father—born at a country seat near Damascus. She lost her parents at an early age, and was cared for by a dissolute nurse by whom her wayward passions had been fostered.

Dinah the Samaritan Woman

Later Dinah had five husbands, one after the other. Some died of grief, others were put out of the way by her new lovers. The last of these, a rich merchant who was a relative of one of her former husbands, lived in Shechem, whither she followed him and superintended his household, for purposes of convenience calling herself Salome. They were not espoused, but the fact that they were not

---

† There remains some uncertainty regarding the name of the town nearest to Jacob's well. Most commentators have supposed that Shechem, now called Nablus, was the town here called Sichar. But Shechem lies a mile and a half west of Jacob's well, whereas Sichar, now called Askar, lies scarcely half a mile north of the well. It was a small town, loosely called a city, and adjoined the land that Jacob gave to Joseph, Joseph's tomb being about one hundred yards east of it. It may be presumed for the purpose of nomenclature in these visions that Sichar was nearest the actual well, whereas the larger town of Shechem was the scene of most of the other events Anne Catherine relates regarding Dinah and other Samaritans.

married was not known to the people of Shechem, who on account of her intelligence, beauty, and good nature held Dinah in high esteem. The husband was a vigorous man of about thirty-six years with a ruddy face and a reddish beard. Dinah was living with this man at the time of her conversion at Jacob's well.†

Dinah Drawing Water at Jacob's Well

From her marriages Dinah had three daughters and two half-grown sons, all of whom had remained with the relatives of their respective fathers when their mother was obliged to leave Damascus. Dinah's sons at a later period joined the seventy-two disciples.

Following her conversion, Jesus introduced Dinah to the Virgin Mary and she joined the circle of holy women, becoming one of the most industrious helpers in the community. Along with Magdalene, Mary Cleophas, Seraphia (Veronica), and Mara the Suphanite, she was among the most beautiful women of the community, although the Virgin Mary outshone them all.

After the crucifixion, when the body of Jesus was taken down from the cross and prepared for burial and the body carried by litter to the sepulcher, with many of the other holy women in train behind, Dinah the Samaritan, Maroni of Nain, and Mara the Suphanite were with Martha and Lazarus in Bethany. Later Anne Catherine saw the blessed Virgin and her companions knocking at the Cenacle and being admitted. The holy women retired to the apartments occupied by the blessed Virgin. The holy women also prayed with Mary under a lamp. Later, when it had grown quite dark, Lazarus, Martha, the widow Maroni of Nain, Dinah the Samaritan, and Mara the Suphanite were admitted. They had come from Bethany to keep the sabbath.

Anne Catherine had much to say about Dinah at the time of her conversion, and in her later role as one of the holy women. She also expanded at some length on how the life of Dinah was prophetic—that Jesus had spoken to the entire sect of Samaritans in her person, that they were attached to their errors by as many ties as she had committed adulteries.

Anne Catherine had also a special love for Dinah, who it seems must have reciprocated, for on three occasions—even while busied with visions of the daily life of Jesus—she reports that Dinah visited her. She appeared as a bride dressed in white, with a crown upon her head, bowing in deep humility before Jesus. On one occasion Anne Catherine suddenly perceived Dinah in this form as though looking in at her through the window as she lay upon her sickbed. And on another, while distracted by some domestic disturbance, Anne Catherine looked up suddenly through her tears and said:

> See! There stands the Samaritan woman. And Jesus also! She bows ever before him on his way, and with such humility. She is so different now, white as snow and nobly dressed. This is not yet, however, but still to come.

MARA THE SUPHANITE

About a month after Dinah's conversion there came to the city of Ainon a woman named MARA the Suphanite. She was a Jewess and rich, but an adulteress, and came from the region of Supha in the land of the Moabites (who were descendants of Lot). It was because she was from the region of Supha that she was called the Suphanite. She was a descendant of Orpah, the widow of Chilion (the son of

---

† There were many things in Dinah's life similar to those of Magdalene's, but she had fallen more deeply than the latter. Still, I once saw that in the beginning of Magdalene's dissolute career at Magdala, one of her lovers lost his life at the hand of a rival.

Naomi and Elimelech of Bethlehem, so that Orpah was the daughter-in-law of Naomi).†

Mara the Suphanite

Mara's Jewish husband, who lived in Damascus, had rejected her because she had had four lovers, one after the other. Through these liaisons she had given birth to three illegitimate children—a son and two daughters—whom she had with her in Ainon at the time of her conversion. Her legitimate children had been retained by their father when he repudiated his unfaithful wife, their mother.

Mara was living at this time in a house of her own at Ainon. For a long time she had conceived sentiments of sorrow for her disorders and had done penance—her conduct being so reserved and proper that she had won the esteem of even the most respectable women of Ainon.

Hearing the preaching of John the Baptist against adultery had intensified Mara's sense of wanting to do penance. She was often possessed by five devils. They had again seized upon her when, as a last resource, she had gone to the court where Jesus was curing the sick. The Pharisees rebuffed her and their words—which in her deep dejection she had taken as true—had driven her to the brink of despair.

Mara was converted in Ainon on Monday, September 4, AD 30, through her encounter with Jesus. On that day Jesus delivered Mara from the demonic influence and granted her forgiveness, blessing also her three illegitimate children, whose hands he placed in those of their healed and fully converted mother. Mara then bestowed upon Jesus many gifts at a banquet held in his honor in her festive house.

Upon his later return to Ainon, Jesus helped Mara reconcile with her husband. Following her conversion, Dinah and Veronica welcomed Mara warmly into the circle of holy women.

As was described at the close of the article on Dinah the Samaritan, at the time when the body of Jesus was taken down from the cross, washed and prepared, and carried on a litter to the sepulcher, Mara—along with Dinah and Maroni of Nain—were with Martha and Lazarus in Bethany. Similarly, when it had grown quite dark, she and these same others, having traveled from Bethany together, were admitted into the Cenacle that same night.

ANNA CLEOPHAS

ANNA was a niece of St Joseph, being the eldest daughter of his brother Cleophas (by his first marriage), and so referred to by Anne Catherine as Anna Cleophas. By late AD 30, Anna was living with Martha. She was the mother of Nathaniel. Nathaniel was the youngest of Anna's sons engaged at Zebedee's fishery. He was about twenty years old at this time, gentle and amiable, with something of the appearance of John. He had been reared in the house of his grandfather, and was nicknamed "Little Cleophas," in order to distinguish him from the other Nathaniels.‡ I learned that on this sabbath when I heard Jesus say: "Call little Cleophas to me!" Jesus was very fond of him.

Anna Cleophas

---

† Upon Naomi's advice, Orpah did not accompany her to Bethlehem. Instead, Ruth—the widow of Orpah's other son Mahlon—accompanied Naomi thither. Orpah married again in Moab, and from that union sprang the family of Mara the Suphanite, which was thereby connected with the House of David, the ancestral line of Jesus. "I saw," said Anne Catherine elsewhere, "how a stray branch of the stock of David was purified within Mara by the grace of Jesus, and admitted into the bosom of the church. I cannot express how many of these roots and offshoots I see become intertwined with each other, lost to view, and then once more brought to light."

‡ The disciple Nathaniel Chased (whom Jesus saw beneath the fig tree), and Nathaniel the Bridegroom of Cana.

OTHER HOLY WOMEN

And Those Previously Described Considered Again, Organized by Geographic or Family Association

Jesus's Conversations with Silent Mary

LIKE the aged Essene Eliud of Nazareth—the type of the mystic living in contemplative solitude—we find among the holy women Lazarus's middle sister, *Silent Mary*. She has her own quarters with an enclosed garden on the grounds of the Bethany estate of Martha. Her family considers her mentally handicapped, but Jesus judges differently, telling Eliud "She is not for this world, therefore is she now altogether secluded from it. But she has never committed a sin. If I should speak to her, she would perfectly comprehend the greatest mysteries."

Jesus has with her two long private and very profound conversations, in which she speaks ecstatically of the mysteries of the Trinity and of the Incarnation. Jesus interrupts her now and then with a prayer of gratitude to the heavenly Father, then blesses her and predicts her impending liberation from earthly life; this occurs in April, AD 30, in the presence of the blessed Virgin and the other holy women.

The Three Closely-Related Marys

Among the holy women in Galilee we find first and foremost *three Marys*, all close relatives of Jesus:

The first, *Mary Heli*, is the daughter of Joachim and Anne, born nearly twenty years before Mary of Nazareth. She is not the child of promise, and is called Mary of Heli—by which she is distinguished from the other of the same name—because she is the daughter of Joachim (or Heliachim). Her husband, Cleophas, is a nephew of Joseph, who brought a son from a previous marriage with him into the marriage with Mary Heli. This son is Matthias, who is later elected by the disciples to take the place of Judas Iscariot in the circle of twelve. To her husband Cleophas, Mary Heli bears three sons—Sadoch (Zadok), James, and Heliachim (Joachim)—and one daughter, Mary Cleophas, who is therefore a niece of Mary of Nazareth (although older than her aunt). Sadoch, James, Heliachim, and Matthias are known as the "brothers of the Lord," although in fact they are cousins to Jesus. All four become disciples of John the Baptist, and after the death of John become disciples of Jesus. Later, after the death of Cleophas, Mary Heli marries a priest named Obed, to whom she bears a son, Jairus. She lives at Japha, a small place about one hour south of Nazareth. Mary Heli is the firstborn child of her parents, Anne and Joachim. Anne is about twenty-four years old when she gives birth to Mary Heli. Nineteen years and five months later, at the age of approximately forty-three, she conceives her long-awaited second child, Mary. She is present at the burial of Christ Jesus.

The second, *Mary Salome*, is a cousin of Mary of Nazareth and the wife of the fisherman Zebedee. Mary of Nazareth is the daughter of Anne and Joachim, and Mary Salome is the daughter of Sobe and Solomon—and Anne and Sobe are sisters, daughters of the Essenes Ismeria and Eliud.† Zebedee and Mary Salome have two sons, James and John, sometimes referred to as the sons of Zebedee. They became disciples of Jesus—John being the only one of the twelve present at the death and burial of Christ and who, together with Peter, is in the garden of the holy sepulcher on Easter Sunday morning.

Near the beginning of Jesus's ministry, Mary Salome lives in the house which previously had been home to the holy family in Nazareth. Later she lives near Capernaum. Mary Salome is named in the gospel as one of the four Marys directly beneath the cross, the others being the Virgin Mary, Mary Magdalene, and Mary Cleophas.

The third, *Mary Cleophas*, niece and childhood playmate of the Virgin, is the daughter of Mary Heli. Because of the age difference between Mary Heli and Mary of Nazareth—the second daughter, or child of promise—Mary Cleophas, although a niece of Mary, is about four years older than her. Mary Cleophas is wife, first, of Alpheus, whose children she bears: Judas Thaddeus (or just Thaddeus), Simon the Zealot, James the Less, and Susanna (or Susanna Alpheus). From his first marriage, Alpheus had brought his son Levi (latter called Matthew). Thaddeus, Simon, James the Less, and Matthew all later become one of the twelve apostles of Jesus. Later still, Mary Cleophas will marry Sabba, by whom she has a son, the disciple Joseph Barsabbas (or Joses Barsabbas). Mary Cleophas's third and final marriage is to the Greek Jonah, who comes

---

† There is a third daughter, Maraha, who is younger than Sobe and older than Anne.

with a son by a first marriage, the disciple Parmenas. With Jonah she bears one more son, Simon the Just.[†]

At the start of Jesus's teaching travels, Mary Cleophas settles in the neighborhood of Capernaum, close by the house of the blessed Virgin. She recommends her sons to Jesus as disciples, and later she lives in Cana. On November 25, AD 30, Mary Cleophas, who is lying desperately ill with fever at the home of Peter in Bethsaida, is healed by Jesus. She is very active in the care of the sick and the poor at the time of the mountain sermons. Mary Cleophas stands also at the cross, and dies five years after the Ascension.

Three Other Women Relatives of Jesus

The second group of three Galilean women who are close relatives of Jesus include *Mahara*, youngest sister of Anne (that is, an aunt of the Virgin), living in Sepphoris in the former home of Anne's parents, where she often lodges Jesus and his mother. Her two sons, Arastaria and Cocharia, are among the very first disciples of Jesus, being received on August 14, AD 29. Then there is *Susanna*, wife of Alpheus of Nazareth, daughter of Alpheus and Mary Cleophas, and thus sister of the apostles Thaddeus, Simon the Zealot, and James the Less (and step-sister of Matthew, Parmenas, and Simon the Just). And finally, *Anna Cleophas*, Cleophas's daughter by his first marriage. She is the mother of Nathaniel. To differentiate him from the other two Nathaniels,[‡] he is sometimes called the Little Cleophas, and Jesus is very fond of him.

The Five Holy Widows

To the so-called five holy widows belong first and foremost the three mothers of the earliest disciples of Jesus: *Lea* and *Seba* of Nazareth, whose sons Kolaya and Eustachius, respectively, are received by Jesus on August 4, AD 29; and *Sobe*, daughter of the elder Sobe and cousin to the blessed Virgin, who on many occasions lodged Jesus and his mother in Cana, and whose nephew is Nathaniel, the bridegroom at the wedding of Cana, who lives in Capernaum and, at about the same time as the other two, becomes a disciple of Jesus. Then there is the wealthy widow *Maroni* of Nain, sister of James the Greater's wife and mother of Martialis—the youth of Nain whom Jesus raises from the dead—and who, after this miracle has taken place, lodges Jesus and the disciples both at her summer estate and her great house in Nain, and places a portion of her wealth at the disposal of the community, in which she then becomes one of the most active women. At her request and with the help of his own mother, Jesus then heals from a distance Maroni's friend the widow *Mary of Nain* from possession, after which she also enters the circle of the holy women.

The Jerusalem Women

Due to her organizing talents and apostolic zeal, Lazarus's oldest sister *Martha* stands at the head of the Jerusalem women. At first, she is ever underway with her brother and the women assistants, establishing new hostels, supervising the established ones, and ensuring that all of them are regularly provided with household implements, fresh food, and blankets for the disciples and apostles.

Then we have *Seraphia* from Jerusalem, daughter of a brother of John the Baptist's father Zechariah (and thus a cousin to John the Baptist), in whose ancestral house near the Jerusalem fishmarket Joachim and Anne had moved when they brought their little daughter to the Temple. Seraphia is related also to the old priest Simeon, and a friend of his sons. At the time of Jesus's teaching travels, she is married to Sirach, a member of the Temple Council, and suffers much from his initial hostility toward Jesus. Following his conversion by Joseph of Arimathea and Nicodemus, Sirach becomes better disposed and allows his wife to follow Jesus and serve him and the disciples. She is a tall, beautiful, and courageous woman, and is the one who with a cloth wipes the brow of Jesus on his way to the cross. The cloth acquires thereby an image of the face of Jesus, and for this reason she is given the name *Veronica* (from *vera icon,* or 'true image'). Her son Amandor is one of Jesus's earliest followers.

Third, there is *Susanna of Jerusalem*, the illegitimate daughter of Joseph's brother Cleophas. From her grandfather, a Persian nobleman, she has acquired wealth and has married the government official Matthias, relative of the later apostle Matthias. Born in Gophna, she lives in the temple as a little girl, like the Virgin Mary. From the beginning she is part of Lazarus's circle in Bethany and accompanies Martha on her rounds, supporting her with generous offerings. Later, she is present at the burial of Jesus.

Fourth, the widow *Salome* (like Susanna, related to the holy family on Joseph's side) has lived for a long time with Martha in Bethany, is present at the burial of Jesus, and accompanies Magdalene, Mary Cleophas, and Johanna

---

[†] Mary Cleophas is distantly related to Peter through her third husband.

[‡] The early disciple Nathaniel Chased, and Nathaniel, the bridegroom of Cana (sometimes called by his baptismal name Amandor—derived from the word "Amen"—but not to be confused with Amandor, the son of Seraphia).

Chusa when they go to the sepulcher on the morning of the Resurrection.

Fifth, *Mary Mark*, a relative of the old priest Simeon, lives with her son John Mark northeast of Jerusalem and often has Jesus stay at her house. The virgin Mary stays with her before the Crucifixion, and she stands facing the Virgin at the burial.

Sixth, *Johanna Chusa*, is a tall, pale, stern woman, but strong and energetic. She is a niece of the prophetess Anna of the Temple, and her son is acquainted with the twelve-year-old Jesus when the latter remains behind in Jerusalem. Later he is one of the secret disciples in Jerusalem. Johanna is often at the Bethany estate and collaborates with Martha on maintaining the hostels. Jesus often dines at her house with his disciples; and she is the one who, with Veronica and *Mary of Hebron* (Elizabeth's niece), travels to Machaerus with a few servants from Jutta to find and retrieve the Baptist's head. She is also one of the four holy women who bear witness to the Risen Christ in the garden of the holy sepulcher on Easter Sunday morning.

The Converted Sinners

Mary Magdalene, youngest sister of Lazarus, belongs to the intimate circle of Jesus and his mother, and heads the list of converted sinners as the "type" of all saintly sinners. At the age of seven she loses her parents, who have spoiled their youngest and extremely beautiful and precocious daughter. By the age of nine she already has admirers. As her talents and qualities grow and blossom, the rumors and astonishment surrounding her grow in equal measure. She has a very active social life, is well educated, and writes aphorisms about love on little parchment rolls, which she exchanges with her suitors. When she is eleven, she moves with her large retinue of maids and servants to the castle of Magdalum, which falls to her by lot at her parents' death. In her new lodgings she is soon entertaining officers from the garrisons of Magdalum and surroundings. Initially she associates with witty men, but over time the level of her intimate male and female friends sinks ever lower.

Magdalene receives the first ray of grace on the final day of Jesus's forty-day fast. She is moved and overcome by a sudden foreboding about her life and a longing for salvation. However the inner motivation does not last long. In January, AD 30, Martha convinces Magdalene to join her on a trip to Jezreel to see the new prophet from Nazareth. When they arrive, Jesus has already left, but Magdalene hears from eyewitnesses about the miracles he has just performed. One month later Magdalene is again in Jezreel at the instigation of her brother and her sister Martha, as well as of Veronica and Johanna Chusa, who had visited her.

From the window of the inn she catches a glimpse of Jesus entering the town with his disciples and he blesses her with a glance. Shaken and overcome, she rushes into a leper-hostel and then returns to Magdalum with her siblings. But she soon reverts to her old ways. On July 19, AD 30, in the circle of his followers, Jesus tells them to pray for Magdalene, saying she will soon come and become an example for others. On November 8th, at the mountain sermon near Gabara, she experiences a second conversion, and on December 26th, her final conversion.

From then on she lives in the residence of her deceased sister Silent Mary in Bethany, repeatedly asks Jesus to help their dying brother Lazarus, anoints him several times at table (the last time being at the Last Supper), stands under the cross, accompanies the body to the burial, and is the first to experience the resurrected Christ at the sepulcher.

The *first* to have been converted by Jesus is *Dinah the Samaritan woman*, who is known to us through her lengthy conversation with Jesus at Jacob's well. The daughter of a mixed marriage (her mother Jewish and her father pagan), she was born on an estate not far from Damascus. Orphaned at an early, she has five husbands in a row, from whom she separates, partly out of grief, partly because she has found new lovers. From these marriages, she has three daughters and two sons, who all reside with their fathers when she must leave Damascus. At the time of the meeting at Jacob's well she is living out of wedlock with a relative of one of her husbands, a rich Sichem merchant. The people of Sichem know nothing about the illegitimacy of this union and appreciate Dinah for her charming and witty ways. Following her conversion, Jesus introduces Dinah to his mother, and she becomes one of the most active helpers in the Christian community. Along with Magdalene, Mary Cleophas, Veronica, and Mara, she is among the most beautiful women of the community, although the Virgin outshines them all.

About a month after Dinah's conversion, there comes to Ainon a wealthy woman from Suphan in the land of the Moabites, *Mara the Suphanite*. Her Jewish husband lives in Damascus and has thrown her out after she has had four consecutive lovers, from whom she bears three children. She has lived in Ainon for a good while, full of contrition. She behaves well and listens to the Baptist's preaching against adultery, which leaves her shaken. However she is often possessed by a demon, and this happens again upon the arrival into town of Jesus, in whom she has placed her last hope. Jesus frees her from the demonic influence, blesses her illegitimate children, places the children's hands in that of their healed and fully-converted mother, and is rewarded with many gifts at a banquet in his honor in the festive house. Upon his return to Ainon, Jesus helps

Mara reconcile with her husband. Dina and Veronica accept her kindly into the circle of the helping women.

On October 25, AD 30, the rich pagan widow *Lais* from Nain comes to hear Jesus teach on the preaching mountain in Meroz, where she asks for his help with her two daughters, Athalia and Sabia—both conceived out of wedlock—who are at her home, possessed by a demon. Jesus hears her tearful prayer and immediately heals her daughters from a distance. All three women join the circle of the helping women and accompany the mother of Jesus when she goes and teaches among the pagan caravans, mid-November of the same year.

Other Women Converts

That same month, October AD 30, while making her rounds visiting the sick, the blessed Virgin makes the acquaintance of *Enue*, the pagan widow of a Caesarea Philippi Jew, and does much to strengthen her faith. Enue suffers from an issue of blood. On December 1, AD 30, while in a crowd, she touches the hem of Jesus's tunic and is immediately healed (Matt. 9:20). Two days later, Enue's sister-in-law *Lea*, the wife of a Pharisee (Paneas) very hostile to Jesus,[†] sings the Lord's praises to Mary during a sermon (Luke 11:27), and on March 6, AD 31, Jesus is a guest in the house of Enue's pagan uncle in Caesarea-Philippi; at table, Enue's grateful daughter anoints Jesus in the presence of her well-pleased mother.

Similarly to Lais of Nain, there appears in mid-February, AD 31, the widowed pagan owner of a factory in Ornithopolis, who in the gospel (Matt. 15:22 and Mark 7:26) is designated as the woman from Canaan and Syrophoenicia—or *the Syrophoenician woman*. She encounters Jesus in the city of Dan and, in tears, resolutely asks for the healing of her possessed daughter. The Lord is touched by her faith, and not only heals the daughter at a distance but also heals the mother of a spinal deformation; and on the following day he heals her deaf-mute relative. The grateful and generous Syrophoenician woman now puts herself at the service of Jesus's interests among the Diaspora Jews in Syrophoenicia. Each time he visits Ornithopolis (twice a year) she organizes a banquet in his honor. During one such banquet, her daughter donates to Jesus all her jewels and artworks, which precious objects Jesus immediately redeems for the benefit of the poor in the Diaspora communities.

By the end of the second year of Jesus's teaching, the holy women assisting the community number approximately thirty-seven. By the end of his wanderings, counting all the maids and caretakers in the hostels, the number has mounted to seventy.

[†] This Lea is to be distinguished from the holy woman of the same name mentioned above in the section "The Five Holy Widows."

Table of Genealogy and

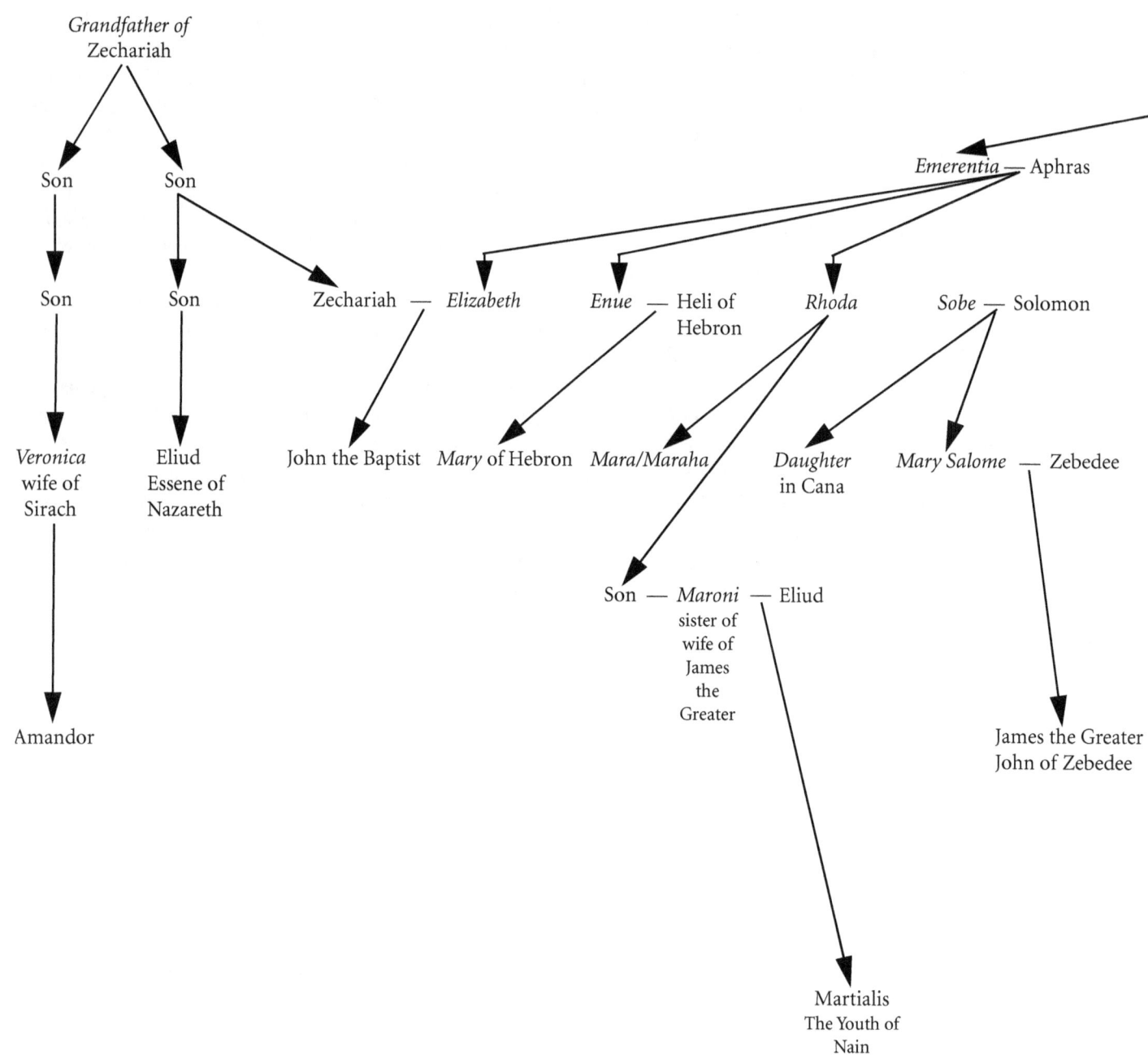

Close Relations of Jesus

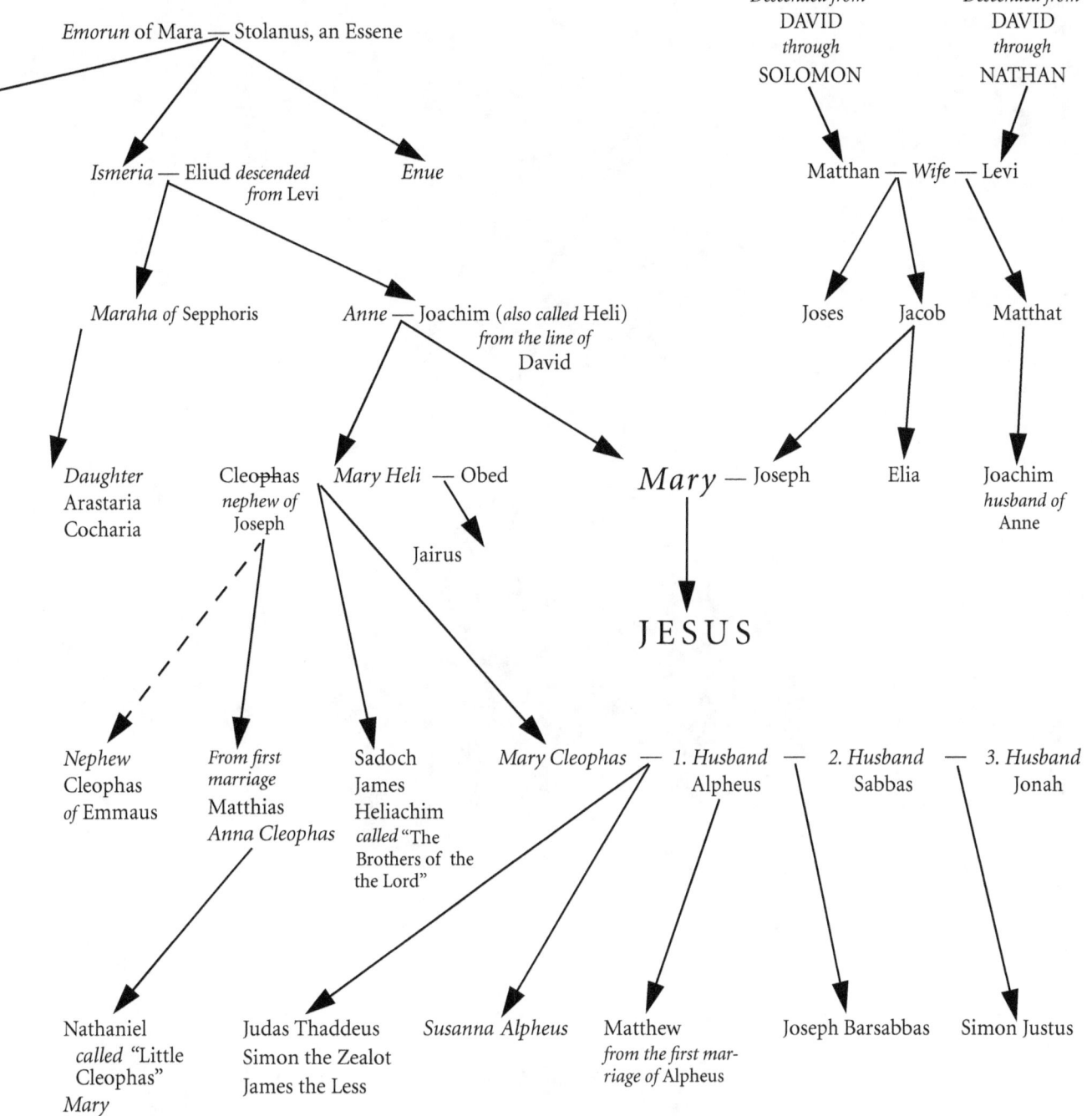

Mother and Child Carrying Water

ENEMIES AND ADVERSARIES OF JESUS

The Earliest Adversaries of Jesus

Adversaries as a Child

Foes of Jesus stepped forward right from the beginning. Such was: the opposition of Herod and his minions, set in motion by the appearance of the three kings—which led to Herod's attempt to apprehend them; the interrogation of Joseph in Bethlehem; the attempt to shut off access to the crib cave; and finally, the preparations for, and accomplishment of, the murder of the innocents.

Murder of the Innocents

Adversaries as a Youth

Opposition to Jesus during the years of his youth set in especially when, as a twelve-year-old, he taught in the Temple, exploding the pride and vanity of the older scribes and Pharisees who gathered around him. They regarded Jesus at that time as a gifted boy whose pert and saucy attitude needed amending. Some would later accuse Jesus of hypocrisy for the way he disputed with and undermined the scholars present, addressing them as though he sought their instruction—saying such things as "What do you mean by that?" or "Do tell us, if you will, when the Messiah will come"—but in truth mocking for the benefit of others by demonstrating for all to see that he knew better.

Twelve-Year-Old Jesus Teaching in the Temple

Adversaries as a Young Man

In Nazareth, Mary and Joseph suffered much from the shenanigans of many mean-spirited Jews who were envious of this wise son of a carpenter who seemed to know far more than they fancied they themselves did, and whose holy manner of life put them to shame. In order that he might be better protected from such persecution after his father Joseph had died, Levi—a close friend of considerable means from Capernaum—offered Jesus and Mary a house, to which they then removed. But even here miscreants soon began to provoke him as he set out on short journeys with friends.

Primary Adversary as an Adult—The Pharisees

Accusations of Disrespect

The first teaching journeys of Jesus's ministry had scarcely begun when groups of his primary adversary, the Pharisees, began to appear. At first their opposition took the form of accusations of such offenses as that he and his companions whispered among themselves and spread seeds of discontent. At his first public sermon in Nazareth, on July 31, AD 29, they mocked the poverty of his parents, saying "Little butter and honey have we seen you eat with your father, the poor carpenter." (see Isa. 7:15) And when in his sermons Jesus spoke of his Father—Who had sent him and Whose will he was to fulfill—the Pharisees, not understanding that he spoke of God, would ridicule him, saying among themselves (but loudly enough for all to hear), "He speaks always of his father, but is he not from Nazareth and the son of a poor carpenter?" In the same way they ridiculed his parable of the owner of the vineyard who sent his son among the vine-dressers, saying of him, "Did his father, the poor carpenter from Nazareth, own a vineyard?"

Some Pharisees Ridicule Jesus

They would scornfully point out his lack of education, saying, "Just three months ago his father the carpenter was still living, and they were working together; yet now, after a few brief travels abroad, he returns and straightaway imparts his wisdom." Their insinuations grew all the more severe as—hard as they may knock their heads together—they could not ascertain from what source of instruction Jesus could have obtained his knowledge, saying "Whence has he such expositions of Holy Writ? Was not his time in the elementary school at Nazareth but short? How came he by such understanding of art and science? What is to be done with him?"

Accusations of Social Impropriety

To disdain for Jesus's modest origins and limited education were soon added criticisms regarding his personal and civic responsibilities. He was accused of neglecting his filial duties: "If he were even marginally righteous, he would stay at home and look after his mother. After his father the poor carpenter Joseph died, he should have assured his mother's livelihood by taking up a trade—and yet, with his father now gone, the son lets his father's carpentry business go."

Pharisees Ask "By What Right Do You These Things?"

In a similar vein they reviled him on account of his itinerancy: "He is ever underway, one knows not whither nor whence. But be assured that when he does appear—whether in town or countryside—commotion is sure to follow. Why does he not stay by his mother's side?" At the same time they reprove him for his manner on those occasions when he does appear: "How comes it that he speaks with such bold certainty? By what right does he make his demands and call others to repentance?"

More hostile still were the accusations the Pharisees leveled against his religious conduct: "He profanes the sabbath by causing disturbances, inciting crowds, and healing the sick. He forgives sins! But whence has he the authority to do such a thing? He does not keep the fast and grants his disciples also far too much latitude in this regard, thereby showing disrespect for the Law. He shows himself willing to take gold from those enamored of him and then distributes the monies received to the poor upon his own discretion—thereby depriving the synagogue of rightful alms. He attracts wealthy widows in order to gain their inheritance. Indeed, he says plainly that he is the Son of God, the Messiah, thereby blaspheming God Himself."

Finally, the Pharisees complain of his civic and social behavior in associating with tax collectors, Samaritans, and especially Sichemites—not to mention his doings in their own communities with pagans, and also among Diaspora Jews.

Not only this, but he is accused of going about in the countryside with women of ill repute, for it is common knowledge that some among those whom he has converted were formerly profligate sinners.

Above all they decry how the people are agitated whenever and wherever Jesus appears: how at his mountain sermons he propagandizes; how he blesses children, visits people in their homes, addresses women so directly; how he chooses without proper sanction which cities and towns he will visit, and when he joins gatherings in the places he visits, avoids those considered the leading figures and dignitaries of the place; and how, despite the fact that he lacks any authorization from the Temple—as well as any diploma or scholarly training of any sort—he nonetheless teaches publicly.

Allegations of Disruptive Actions

When Jesus left Capernaum after his first major period of teaching, the town elders and Pharisees came together, saying "Such uproar and unrest this man leaves in his wake! Normal routine is disturbed and people abandon their tasks to gather around him. He casts insults and reprimands upon all and sundry with the severest of words. He seeks out simple folk as against the lettered, and admits even pagans to the kingdom he never ceases to announce.

"Never does he consult with men of learning, nor speak with town officials to make arrangements before he heals the sick. In whatever city or town he may be, he acts as though its synagogue belongs to him, teaching now by the sea, now among fishermen, now in the mountains—however might suit him best, coming and going with no notice, as though there were no civic order to be maintained."

The Pharisees were sorely tried when, in the city of Dothan, Jesus gave his sanction and blessing to the marriage of the elderly merchant Issachar to the young Salome, a union that could not be blessed with children and so was contrary to the Law. But Jesus made plain their true, malevolent motive: they had hoped Issachar's ancestral estate would fall to them upon his death, but now there would be other heirs on the newly-wedded wife's side. And so they caused a rumor to be spread abroad that Jesus had benefitted much from Issachar's largesse and that his disciples were spent and lazy men whom Jesus let feed and revel at other men's tables. All this, and the uproar that followed him wherever he went, were—according to the Pharisees—to be seen as the pernicious effects of his teaching, for which the teacher himself should be held accountable.

Suspicions of the Pharisees

In addition to accusations fabricated from events such as those just mentioned, the Pharisees also carefully promulgated suppositions and suspicions of all sorts. "He must have entered into some sort of liaison with foreigners, for he is always talking about the coming of a new kingdom, the nearness of the Messiah, and the destruction of Jerusalem. Yes, his father Joseph was of noble lineage, but see how low the family has fallen. Perhaps Jesus is secretly the son of another and very powerful father who is seeking to clandestinely mobilize a cohort of followers with whom to seize control of Judea when a suitable opportunity presents itself. However that may be, we may be sure an impressive apparatus and source of support must stand behind him, for how otherwise could he so boldly step forward as though within his rights to controvert all custom and overturn all legal authority? Not only this, but recall how often he is absent. What might this not augur as to some sinister alliance?"

The Pharisees in Capernaum, furious when, on November 17, AD 30, Jesus not only healed two scribes suffering

Uproar With Pharisees in the Temple

from leprosy but then forgave them their sins, screamed "He heals on the sabbath? And how is it that he forgives sins? It must be that the devil helps him. Clearly he is a madman, for see how he runs around hither and yon—scarcely has he finished creating a spectacle here before he appears of a sudden in Nain, awakening the dead; and then he is in Megiddo, only to reappear here shortly thereafter. This is not the way of a man in his right mind. Some great and evil spirit animates him—some devil who evokes in him the highest devil of all. Why does he spend his nights alone and in the open upon the mountains? He must be cavorting with Beelzebub himself, and from thence drawing his knowledge and power."

The Fears of the Pharisees

Notwithstanding all their blustering reproaches, in truth many of Jesus's adversaries among the Pharisees harbored a real fear of the future. "What if this carpenter's son really

Pharisees Gather in Council

is the Messiah, and not only no Pharisee, but in fact our enemy? What would become of us? What part would we have in his kingdom? What if one of these days he proclaims himself king and has on his side not only the people but the Romans as well? He says Caesar is owed his taxes, and Pontius Pilate lets him be. Is he perhaps using Jesus as a foil against his greatest opponent, Herod Antipas? Yet Herod is himself so superstitious that he regards Jesus as perhaps the risen Baptist, whom in his heart he always honored and feared!"

One night, after Jesus had finished teaching, the Pharisees gathered together to study ancient writings concerning the Messiah. They openly confessed their misgivings, for in truth many associations could be drawn between the wisdom sayings regarding the Messiah and Jesus. The following day Jesus set their anxiety at rest, reminding them of God's benevolent Providence and that anyone of good will who put their trust in God had nothing to fear.

Surveillance

Gradually the Pharisees moved beyond accusation, suspicion, and fear, and found ways to restrict the movements of Jesus—even impede his activity altogether. On one occasion the major centers of learning in Judea and Jerusalem

Pharisees Spy on Jesus and the Disciples

sent a commission of fifteen Pharisees to Capernaum to listen in on his teachings and document his actions. Another time fifty Pharisees were dispatched, on the pretext of visiting the synagogue. Once arrived, they broke into smaller groups and followed Jesus wherever he went in order to report back their findings to Capernaum and Jerusalem.

Disputation and Interrogation

It was customary that those present in the synagogue while a sermon was being held might interrupt the speaker to

Pharisees Interrupt Jesus at Synagogue

put questions and start a discussion—a practice that, through collusion, was put to good and frequent use by the Pharisees. For the most part their efforts were aimed at enticing the despised teacher Jesus onto thin ice in hopes of catching him in some contradiction with the Law. Then, after the sermon, they would surround Jesus and one would step forward to speak, the others then following suit—as had been previously arranged—in order to provoke an indignant outcry and thereby intimidate the common people standing by.

Pharisees Tempt Jesus at Banquet

Even banquets came to be used as opportunities to tempt Jesus into taking a false step. Now and then a high-ranking Pharisee would invite Jesus to dine at his house, where beforehand plans had been laid as to what questions would be asked and what objections raised, all with a view to glean from what Jesus said some incriminating words to send on to the Sanhedrin in Jerusalem. Likewise, as Jesus was preaching in synagogues, certain Pharisees would upon an agreed-upon signal mutter and generally set off a disturbance, sometimes suddenly and with great ostentation quitting the room as well.

Conspicuous Impediments

One of the most obvious obstacles put in the way of Jesus and his teaching was the outright closure of the synagogue where he was to teach, and the withholding of the keys. Under such circumstances Jesus would then teach either in the nearby marketplace or on the town's teaching hill. Or again, it might happen that merely by laying his hands on the synagogue door, it would swing instantly open in response to his spiritual power. Something similar occurred on March 1, AD 33, in the Temple in the case of a locked grating surrounding the teaching seat. Years earlier, on September 4, AD 29, in Kimki, as furious Pharisees went so far as to extinguish the temple lamps while Jesus was speaking, the Master slipped away unnoticed during the ensuing commotion.

Another method the Pharisees employed was to send letters to the chiefs of all the synagogues, forbidding them to permit Jesus to preach on their premises. However this ploy rarely worked, for fear of the people's reaction. To counter this latter, messages would be distributed among the people admonishing them, for the sake of public order and safety, not to congregate in crowds, not to bring forward the sick, not to rejoice should they encounter the Prophet, not to leave their regular employments, not to accept invitations by the disciples of Jesus to participate in the sermons on the mount—and to always keep women and children at home. Already at the time of the first Passover (April 6, AD 30) during the ministry of Jesus, the Pharisees—slinking about among the people—had let it be known that during the festival no one was to associate with Jesus, follow after him, or chatter and gossip about him.

Worse still were the disturbances set in motion, after Jesus had spoken, by individuals hired for the purpose and who would afterward lie in wait for Jesus and his disciples, hurling stones at them as they passed by. We know also (Luke 4:29) that a plan was set in motion when Jesus was in Nazareth on August 12, AD 30, to cast him down from a nearby mountain.

On the occasion of their festival journey (January 25,

AD 31), sixty-four Pharisees from all the regions around Capernaum met together to set up a commission to closely interrogate those who had been healed by Jesus. They investigated the best known healings, and also intentionally caught off-guard some of the recently-healed, whom they sequestered and quizzed about their alleged former ailments, harshly disputing the reality of their supposed healings and raising a hue and cry about things for which they had in public but recently shown tolerance.

Pharisees' Hirelings Hurl Stones at Jesus

Appeal to the Sanhedrin

The Pharisees' final and greatest hope in their campaign against Jesus lay in the High Court—or Sanhedrin—in Jerusalem. Already on July 27, AD 29, the Sanhedrin had sent letters to all major municipal centers of Palestine (those with schools of law and leading politicians) enjoining them to pay special heed to one whom the Baptist had pronounced to be he whose coming had long been looked for, and who would soon seek his baptism. They were to keep a keen lookout, for—so they said—if this man truly were the Messiah, he should have no need of John's baptism. They were especially vexed, moreover, because it was said the one of whom the Baptist spoke was the same who as a mere twelve-year-old lad had taught in the Temple.

In October AD 29, the Sanhedrin for the first time promulgated a high decree regarding the troublesome new prophet out of Nazareth. Prior to this, reports from bribed informants planted throughout the region had been gathered together.

Now the Sanhedrin, consisting of seventy-one priests and scribes, was called to assembly. Twenty of these were selected to form a commission, and then five of these chosen to meet as representatives in council. They consulted the family registers and could not dispute the fact that both Joseph and Mary were in the line of David, and Mary's mother Anne in that of Aaron.

But the families had fallen into some obscurity—and Jesus was known to associate with servants, common laborers, and other such rabble. He defiled himself mixing with tax collectors and pagans, and even associated with slaves. It was reported that only recently Jesus had been in the vicinity of Bethlehem among some Sichemites who had left their day-labors and come to a house where Jesus discoursed with them (September 28, AD 29, in Beth-Arabah) in so intimate and familiar a manner that it was put forward that with such a following he might well foment an uprising.

Sanhedrin Priests in Assembly

Some held the view that he was quite likely a changeling who at the right moment would proclaim himself the son of a king. In addition, it seemed Jesus must have received secret instruction—no doubt from the devil—for it was reported that he would often leave the company of others and wander alone into the desert or, as has already been said, among the high hills and mountains.

It was such deliberations as these that led to the high decree, broadcast far and wide, that Jesus was clearly a student of the devil. Yes, his healings could not be denied, nor his teaching repudiated—but questions remained as to how all this was possible.

During the period May 4–18, AD 30, the throngs seeking baptism at Ono—now that Jesus had bestowed this capacity also on Andrew, Saturnin, Peter, and James the

Greater—stirred up yet more of a sensation among the Pharisees. They caused letters to be sent to the heads of synagogues throughout the land, instructing them to seize Jesus wherever he might appear and to arrest and interrogate his disciples regarding his teachings—and where they erred, to set them right.

It was at this time, the beginning of June, AD 30, that with scarcely any effort Peter, Andrew, and John—who had been apprehended and hand-cuffed in Gennabris—broke their chains and, to their astonishment, escaped. At this juncture Jesus withdrew for about two months from his public teaching.

On June 5, AD 32, the Pharisees in Jericho sent messengers to the Sanhedrin in Jerusalem in order to obtain full legal authority to arrest Jesus, as well as guidance on how best to accomplish this. The disciples were concerned for Jesus, and begged him to retreat, but he continued peacefully on his way.

A month later, on July 26, AD 32, the raising of Lazarus from death brought on a great commotion in the vicinity of the castle in Bethany. A multitude came to the place from Jerusalem, among them many guards. In Jerusalem, the Sanhedrin conferred through the night on the matter. It was feared that Jesus might awaken many more from the dead, which would cause chaos regarding questions of inheritance. And around noon that same day a tumult broke out in Bethany itself. Lazarus was obliged to conceal himself in a cellar beneath the castle.

Jesus, meanwhile, had during the night reached Perea on the far side of the Jordan, and shortly thereafter left Capernaum on a three-month journey to Mesopotamia, Chaldea, and Egypt.

Upon his return, the Sanhedrin was quickly notified that the Nazarene was again active in full view. The Pharisees in Sichem threatened him with arrest or extradition, but Jesus told them there was no need, as he was just then leaving for Jerusalem anyway.

That Jesus at this time, as well on other occasions, escaped arrest, and that—with a few minor exceptions—was able to teach unhindered through February and March, AD 33, can only be explained by the same powerful will that already long before—and also right up to his final arrest in the Garden of Gethsemane—led all things to pass in union with the will of the heavenly Father.

The Decision to Put Jesus to Death

The Pharisees' initial decision to kill Jesus was taken after he healed the man with the withered hand in Capernaum on December 2, AD 30. At that time the Pharisees met with the Herodians and planned how best to waylay Jesus at the coming Passover. (Mark 3:6) For its part, the Sanhedrin had decided already by dawn of July 27, AD 32—the day after the raising of Lazarus—that Jesus must die. (John 11:47–53)

After Jesus delivered a sermon in the Temple, on March 7, AD 33, those gathered at the time in the house of the high priest Caiaphas let it be known that none were hereafter to take Jesus or his disciples into house or inn. And it was when they learned—notwithstanding this decree—that Jesus was lodged with Lazarus in Bethany, that they took the decision to kill Lazarus also. (John 12: 9–11)

The Pharisees Do Not Lay Hands on Him

After Jesus cleansed the Temple for the second time (March 13, AD 33), the priests and scribes considered with great care how they might put an end to him. And yet they feared Jesus also, for his teachings had made a great impression on the people. (Mark 11:18) The following day they tried to lay hold of him, but in the end their fear of the people got the upper hand and they abandoned their plan to arrest him. (Luke 20:19)

Then on March 26 they gathered together again in the palace of Caiaphas to work out some stratagem whereby they might apprehend and kill Jesus—but, as they said, "not during the feast, lest a tumult arise among the people." (Matt. 26:3–5) Here it was that Judas came to their aid. (Matt. 26:14)

Unexpected Incidents

Among the stumbling-blocks Jesus in his wisdom and power set in the way of the measures taken by the Pharisees—and that so angered them—belong first and foremost the many occasions when unanticipated incidents would abruptly undo the plans and expectations of these malefactors.

In Chisloth-Tabor, for example, on September 1, AD 29, Jesus foiled their scheme to engage him in debate by suddenly causing the poor of the city to be invited to the banquet, while at the same time reminding the quarrelsome priests and scribes of the rights of the poor—which both disconcerted and disarmed them.

Healed Blind Man Tells His Story to the Pharisees

On another occasion, when the Pharisees were spying on him in hopes of finding cause to rightly accuse him of violating the sabbath, Jesus performed no healings. Then again, during a discussion on questions of divorce, Jesus exposed their unlawful interpolations into marital law, even offering concrete evidence of what lay behind their machinations.

Scheduled inquiries Jesus sometimes circumvented by not appearing at meals to which he had been invited for that purpose, but instead healing the sick in front of the house in which the dinner was to be held—so that the Pharisees where thereby made to bear unwilling witness to the jubilations of the healed. Even more—and against all law and custom—women and children would appear also, expressing their joy even more loudly than the rest.

Those who had been healed would go to the Temple or a nearby synagogue and proclaim their testimony before the Pharisees—who would forthwith contest their healing and accuse them of disturbing the peace. Here and there one possessed would appear without warning in the midst of a discussion and be healed by Jesus. In short, matters often took a very different turn than the antagonists had intended.

Failed Threats and Apprehendings

In many cases the failure of assailants and attempted arrests can be attributed to perfectly straightforward causes. For example, Jesus might prove he was in the right by appeal to the custom of the land or to Mosaic Law, so that fear of breaking those laws on the part of the Pharisees or other adversaries would prevent his capture—an equally effective deterrent being that the multitude was often on the side of Jesus, as for example on such joyful occasions as the cleansing of the Temple and the major sermons or healings. At such times even his adversaries could not but be in awe of Jesus. Or again, he might disarm them with answers that left them speechless, or with parables that revealed the true character of an auditor, whereby others among them would take malicious pleasure at the unmasking of their companion. Yet before long they would fall back, full of annoyance, into their former wrath.

They Sought to Cast Him Down from the Mountain

However, most such cases of fending off threats and provocation can only be explained by the supernatural power of the God-Man. Already through nightly prayers to his heavenly Father, Jesus was in truth directing the events of the coming days, intercepting the schemes of his adversaries, and as often as not leaving them totally perplexed.

Jesus Chases Out the Money-Changers

Then again, his appearance was often enough to disarm his opponents, for he could at will stand before them on one occasion as the purest, most humble and peaceful of men, and on another evoke awe in all present—in some, even an enigmatic respect. At such times Jesus might pass unmolested among his adversaries despite the fact that he was ready to hand, and they could so easily have apprehended him. Or else he might disappear entirely from their sight, as he had done in Nazareth on August 12, AD 30, when they sought to cast him down from the mountain.

These supernatural gifts were apparent at the cleansings of the Temple also, when the money-changers shrank back from Jesus—and not only on account of the strap he wielded—as the priests hurrying to the scene shortly thereafter did not interfere either, out of shame for the disarray they had let take hold.

The two remarkable theophanies that gave witness to Jesus in the Temple through a darkening of the sky, or eclipse, and an enigmatic voice from on high (which in both cases again silenced his adversaries) are among the public miracles considered elsewhere.†

Other Adversaries

Hostile Sadducees

On account of their Epicurean worldview, the Sadducees were naturally antagonistic to Jesus. In conformity with the tenets of Epicureanism, however, they tended to avoid most public duties, functions, and events. For them the miracles of Jesus were to be explained on the basis of natural causes, with the proviso that all such natural causes were not yet fully understood. Only in those few cities with sufficient Sadducees to support a synagogue of their own did they occasionally come into conflict with Jesus. But here again, they were no friends of violence, so that when a tumult erupted in Sepphoris on August 18, AD 29, after the healing of a possessed man, and Jesus with his disciples had to flee, the fault was not due to any instigation on the part of the Sadducees—even though the shocking healing that had taken place in their synagogue was to them a shameful insult.

Sadducees of Ataroth with Jesus

When the Sadducees of Ataroth invited the new prophet Jesus of Nazareth—whose wonders were on everyone's lips—to their synagogue on July 30, AD 30, it was more for the sake of amusement than anything else: they hoped to lure him into a trap, and, should he fall for it, have a good

† See *Miracles and Wonders* in *Supplements*.

laugh at his expense. To this end they brought Jesus to a dead man whose chest they had in secret cut open and filled with balsam—but who they said publicly was a living madman—and invited Jesus to raise him from the dead. Their strategy was that if Jesus did indeed raise him, they could claim that the man had not actually been dead.

Jesus directed that the chest of the man lying there all stiff and still be opened, revealing by the worms of decay therein that he was indeed dead. He then told those present that he would not raise this man, as he had not believed in the resurrection.

Priests and Scribes

As with the Sadducees, so also those priests antagonistic to Jesus did not confront him in nearly so rude and violent a manner as did the Pharisees. Many laid aside their envy and truly were in awe of the new prophet—although they were still hard-pressed to believe the Messiah would come forward in such a manner. They gladly attended his teachings and sermons in order to learn from him. When alone with Jesus, their questions were courteous, and they said little in response; they did not enter into debates with him, but wondered at his command of the Scriptures.

Jesus Teaches Some Priests

They sought to profit from his insights and put them to good use in their own sermons. But in public they dared not take his part or be counted among his disciples, for they feared the authorities and were loath to put their official positions in jeopardy.

For their part, the scribes enjoyed discussing with Jesus the topic of marriage, as they were themselves not entirely clear on the latest innovations in this domain. They were pleased when Jesus came to visit them among their own peers in teaching centers in some of the principal cities. They were curious both of what, and how, he taught, but reluctant to enter into conversation on matters of theology for fear of displaying ignorance before their fellow-scribes. They would listen quietly and later discuss what they had heard privately among themselves.

A Scribe Speaks with Jesus

They were offended however when Jesus permitted their discussions to be interrupted abruptly by common people or the sick, taking this as a sign of disrespect and a breach of decorum. If on occasion they questioned whether they had erred in inviting the unrefined disciples to their sessions also, Jesus stood firm that they remain by him.

The most antagonistic among the scribes would say among themselves: truly, Jesus is a most gifted and wondrous man, but is he not arrogant for a carpenter's son? His wisdom dazzles but is not well-grounded, for he has not our training—and who can say how he may have acquired other, more advanced, schooling? Not only that, but what need is there for his innovations? We have the Promise and the Law, and these suffice.

Finally, they regarded his manner of itinerant teaching and sermonizing on mountain-tops unworthy of the modesty proper to a true savant, and as serving to unnecessarily raise up opponents.

The Sect of the Herodians

The Herodians were not an avowed religious party in Palestine, but a secular, politically-motivated group based upon mutual interest. They took their name from Herod the Great and acted as partisans on his behalf—for which reason they enjoyed his support.

Many Herodians were architects, or engaged in related occupations, and so owed their livelihoods to Herod's passion for building. It is not entirely clear whether during

Enemies and Adversaries of Jesus

the time of Jesus's itinerant teaching the Herodians were working toward Roman rule, or on behalf of an independent, secular kingdom under the rule of Herod Antipas. In either case, Jesus had nothing good to say about them, censured them for their secrecy and hypocrisy, and made them blanch when, in the company of others, he exposed their clandestine intrigues and shadowy codes of conduct, and condemned their shameful deeds.

The Herodians' headquarters were located in Jotopata, on the west side of the Sea of Galilee, and it was here—when he was teaching in the nearby spa town of Bethulia on August 22, AD 30—that they invited Jesus.

When he arrived at the synagogue in Jotopata, Jesus sharply criticized Herod and spoke openly to all assembled there of the Herodians' intrigues. He spoke against them again two days later, on August 24, AD 30, in the vicinity of Dothaim, revealing even by what signs Herodians might be identified—for many in this region had long complained of their pervasive espionage.

Pharisees and Herodians Conspire

An Herodian

The following day, in Gennabris, together with some Pharisees and Sadducees with whom they had formed an alliance, the Herodians put to Jesus the most cunning of questions regarding the approach of the new kingdom of which he was always speaking, in order to throw suspicion on him in the eyes of the Romans, of Herod, and of the Sanhedrin—for the candor and supernatural conviction Jesus displayed was for them all a thorn in their sides, and they would gladly have been rid of him. But in his answers Jesus gave the lie all the more powerfully to their stratagems.

Then he spoke of the call of pagans also to the work of salvation, likening the present teachers among the Jews to mute dogs, who are not vigilant but instead fatten themselves on food and drink while misleading to this same end also the Herodians and Sadducees. He said they stalk about but let out no bark when the people—even their true shepherds—are set upon.

Later, the Herodians asked Jesus—as usual in their deceptively polite and deferential way—how great a number would be admitted into his kingdom. Jesus called their attention to the as yet incomplete conquest of the land of Canaan, which they had still to share with so many pagans, finally explaining that none would come into his kingdom without first walking the strait path and entering in through the bridal door—which he then clearly distinguished from the wrongly hung side-door of secondary worldly aims.

On this occasion, as on so many others, it was astonishing how, when such adversaries were among themselves, they would bluster about capturing Jesus as he taught, but, when Jesus was actually among them, how they could in fact do nothing, but were rather quite astonished—even in some measure convinced—by what Jesus said, although their anger remained unabated nonetheless.

Disaffected Disciples of John the Baptist

When Jesus returned from his forty-day fast and invested some of his disciples with the power to baptize, many streamed to the place of baptism on the Jordan, including also many of the Baptist's former disciples. It is quite understandable then that those who elected to remain with John complained bitterly of what they saw as the success of Jesus and his disciples at their expense. Nonetheless, the Baptist himself never tired of making clear to them his relationship with the coming Messiah, and regularly sent groups of his own disciples wherever Jesus was then teaching and healing in order that they might satisfy themselves as to who was the greater.

Disciples of John the Baptist

But there were some among John's disciples who would not concede that their own master could be the lesser of the two; and after John's death some of these deteriorated to the point of succumbing to the Herodians' view of Jesus. Filled with jealousy of his deeds and also those of his disciples, the disgruntled disciples accused Jesus of not coming to the Baptist's aid in order that his own reputation might thereby be magnified. They also reproved the disciples of Jesus for the liberties they took. And finally, they claimed that John's testimony regarding Jesus was nothing more than a case of exaggerated humility on his part.

For all these reasons Jesus warned his disciples about the disaffected disciples of the Baptist and—alluding to their habit of wearing wool strips around their necks and waists—said "Beware of false prophets, who come to you in sheep's clothing, but inwardly are ravenous wolves." (Matt. 7:15) It seems the sheepskin worn by the Baptist had for these disciples become a sort of ritual woolen stole, facsimiles of which they also wore in emulation of him—indicating thereby how to them his teaching had become the basis of a sect.

Apart from the thoroughly disaffected disciples of the Baptist, there were others less prejudiced who in the third year of Jesus's ministry had taken his part as disciples, but who on February 1, AD 31, along with many other recent disciples, began to murmur and waver as Jesus spoke of the eucharistic bread of life. (John 6:48–71) And when for several days (January 31–February 3, AD 31) he preached about eating his flesh and drinking his blood, about thirty of the newer disciples and other hangers-on—especially the least secure converts among the former disciples of the Baptist—took a step toward the Pharisees.

Disciples of John the Baptist (top)
Watch Disciples of Jesus as they Baptize

Regarding this, Jesus proclaimed it well that they had revealed of whom they regarded themselves spiritual children before they might cause even more mischief. It was on this occasion—indeed that same night—while speaking about this trouble with his twelve apostles that Jesus asked whether they also would leave him, to which Peter replied "Lord, to whom shall we go? You have the words of eternal life." Jesus responded, "Did I not choose you, the twelve, and one of you is a devil?" (John 6:67–71) By this he meant of course Judas Iscariot, the greatest adversary of all.†

---

† The story of Judas Iscariot, as revealed in Anne Catherine's visions, is told in considerable detail in his entry in *The Holy Men*.

Herod Antipas and Pontius Pilate

King Herod Antipas

On August 24, AD 30, during the second year of Jesus's ministry, Herod asked the imprisoned Baptist during an inquisition at his fortress in Machaerus to tell him plainly

Herod Antipas

what he thought of the man Jesus who was causing such an uproar in Galilee: who he was, and whether he was not taking John's own rightful place. Herod said he knew John had proclaimed Jesus earlier, but that he had not taken particular notice at the time—and so would like now to fully and truly know his mind on the subject, for it had been reported to him that Jesus delivered awe-inspiring sermons, spoke of a kingdom, referred to himself in parables as a king's son, and other such things, whereas in fact he was but the son of a carpenter. How could this be reconciled?

John then addressed those present so openly and with such enthusiasm about Jesus that Herod became greatly alarmed and covered his ears. In consequence, he several days later called together some Pharisees and Herodians to advise him how best to restrain Jesus. The upshot of this meeting was that eight were chosen to go to Jesus and, as diplomatically as possible, give him to understand that he must cease his wonder-working and teaching in Upper Galilee and the further side of the Sea of Galilee. Neither should he undertake the same in the region of Galilee over which Herod ruled, or in his lands further south along the Jordan. They further warned Jesus, by the example of John, that Herod could be easily convinced of the need to arrest him and imprison him alongside the Baptist.

Already on August 26, AD 30, that is, before the delegation mentioned had yet met with him—Herod's envoys having only just departed Machaerus—Jesus spoke publicly at the synagogue in Gennabris of their spying and slinking about, saying "When they come, let the fox kits tell that fox (Herod) he need not worry himself on my account. Neither shall I worry over him, but will teach whithersoever I am sent. For see, I will keep on driving out demons and healing today and tomorrow—and on the third day I will reach my goal (cp. Hosea 6:2). I must press on today and tomorrow and the next day,† for surely no prophet can die outside Jerusalem. Jerusalem, Jerusalem! you who kill the prophets and stone those sent to you!" (Luke 13:32–34)

When on January 23, AD 31, Jesus freed those imprisoned at Thirza, news of their release reached the ears of Herod, directing his attention again even more acutely to Jesus, especially as he had been much troubled and full of doubts and uneasiness since the Baptist's death.

He took counsel with the Herodians and summoned some Sadducees from Jerusalem to question them regarding the raising of the dead. Regarding Jesus, Herod said "John the Baptist has been raised from the dead; that is how these powers have come to work in him." Some were of the view that Jesus was Elijah come again, while others regarded him as just one prophet among many. But Herod held fast to his conviction, saying "John, whom I beheaded, has been raised." (Mark 6:14–16)

---

† Fr. Fahsel here suggests that by this reference to three days Jesus is alluding also to the three years of his ministry.

Accordingly, over the next few months Herod despatched from Hesebon to Capernaum several officers who upon their arrival asked (first the headman Zorobabel, and then the Pharisees) who Jesus was and what he taught, demanding also that they arrange to have him brought to Herod, who wished to see him.

Zorobabel of course spoke only good of Jesus, describing as well as he could the miraculous healing of his son on August 3, AD 30 (John 4:50–53) and many other great miracles that had taken place throughout Galilee. The Pharisees however told a very different tale, adding that they had no power over Jesus, who was a vagrant of humble descent roving about the countryside in the company of a rag-tag band, preaching unheard-of doctrines, and no doubt working his miracles with the help of the devil. In any event, they said, there was no cause to fear him, for his following was made up of the poor, mostly ignorant men and infatuated women sinners.

With this report in hand the officers returned to Herod. These soldiers constituted a new militia personally loyal to Herod, who had acquired them through the uncle of his unfaithful wife Herodias. This was deemed necessary, as the soldiers who had served in Machaerus when John the Baptist was imprisoned there had distanced themselves from Herod.

The Roman Governor Pontius Pilate

During the second year of the ministry of Jesus, Herod offered Pilate for his building project on the Temple Mount some high-quality stone and mortar as well as a number of master masons from his region—an offer Pilate was pleased to accept.

This was however a ruse on Herod's part to incite the population against Pilate. All eighteen of the architects Herod assigned to the task were in fact Herodians. They intentionally misbuilt the walls to cave in upon each other at a time when they might crush as many as three hundred laborers, for most of whom—being disciples of the Baptist—Herod harbored great hatred. The calamity, which in the event claimed approximately one hundred lives, took place on January 1, AD 31. (Luke 13:4)

Fall of the Tower of Siloam (Luke 13:1–5)

Pilate was beside himself, and a great enmity arose between the two leaders that came to an end only at the time of the Passion. For now, however, Pilate sent messengers to Machaerus to formally protest Herod's actions. But after the beheading of John, Herod had left Machaerus and removed to Hesbon. For his part, Pilate traveled by way of Bethzur and Antipatris on his way to Appolonia to take ship for Rome with the object of personally lodging a complaint there against Herod.

Pontius Pilate and His Wife Claudia

Shortly before he set off for Rome, Pilate called a meeting with his government officials. They spoke of the Galilean Jesus and the great miracles he worked. It was reported that he was now active in the neighborhood of Jerusalem. Pilate asked, "Do many march with him? Are they armed?" and was told "No, those who accompany him are peaceful disciples and people of no official standing, or of low station—and often he travels alone. He teaches in the heights and in synagogues, heals the sick, and gives alms. When he teaches, many gather to hear him, sometimes in the thousands."

Pilate asked, "Does he speak against Caesar?" and was answered, "No, he advocates improved morals and compassion. He says Caesar should be given his due, and likewise God. But it is said that he speaks often of his kingdom and its near approach."

At the conclusion of this discussion Pilate said, "So long as he does not tramp around with a militia, or others bearing arms, and only works miracles, there is nothing to fear from him. If he works a miracle in one place and then leaves for another, he will soon be forgotten or abandoned—and in any case, I hear the Jewish priests are always scolding him. He poses no threat. But should he ever consort with a crowd bearing arms, he must be stopped in his tracks."

Annas and Caiaphas

As for the actions of Herod and Pilate, as well as of the high priest Caiaphas and his father-in-law Annas, at the time of the Passion—this is described in detail by the evangelists, and the more so in Anne Catherine's visions.

Adam and Eve Driven from Paradise (Gen. 3:24)

BEGINNINGS

⊕

The Ark Passes over the Jordan (Jos. 3:17)

Building the Ark (Gen. 6:14)

THE CREATION

Fall of the Angels

I SAW spreading out before me a boundless, resplendent space, above which floated a globe of light shining like a sun. I felt that it was the Unity of the Trinity. In my own mind, I named it the ONE VOICE, and I watched it producing its effects. Below the globe of light arose concentric circles of radiant choirs of spirits, wondrously bright and strong and beautiful. This second world of light floated like a sun under that higher Sun.

These choirs came forth from the higher Sun, as if born of love. Suddenly I saw some of them pause, rapt in the contemplation of their own beauty. They took complacency in self, they sought the highest beauty in self, they thought but of self, they existed but in self.

At first all were lost in contemplation out of self, but soon some of them rested in self. At that instant, I saw this part of the glittering choirs hurled down, their beauty sunk in darkness, while the others, thronging quickly together, filled up their vacant places. And now the good angels occupied a smaller space. I did not see them leaving their places to pursue and combat the fallen choirs. The bad angels rested in self and fell away, while those that did not follow their example thronged into their vacant places. All this was instantaneous.

Then rising from below, I saw a dark disc, the future abode of the fallen spirits. I saw that they took possession of it against their will. It was much smaller than the sphere from which they had fallen, and they appeared to me to be closely crowded together.

I saw the Fall of the angels in my childhood and ever after, day and night, I dreaded their influence. I thought they must do great harm to the earth, for they are always around it. It is well they have no bodies, else they would obscure the light of the sun. We should see them floating around us like shadows.

Immediately after the Fall, I saw the spirits in the shining circles humbling themselves before God. They did homage to him and implored pardon for the fallen angels.

At that moment I saw a movement in the luminous sphere in which God dwelt. Until then it had been motionless and, as I felt, awaiting that prayer.

After that action on the part of the angelic choirs, I felt assured that they would remain steadfast, that they would never fall away. It was made known to me that God in his judgment, in his eternal sentence against the rebel angels, decreed the reign of strife until their vacant thrones are filled. But to fill those thrones seemed to me almost impossible, for it would take so long. The strife will, however, be upon the earth. There will be no strife above, for God has so ordained.

After I had received this assurance, I could no longer sympathize with Lucifer, for I saw that he had cast himself down by his own free, wicked will. Neither could I feel such anger against Adam. On the contrary, I felt great sympathy for him because I thought: It has been thus ordained.

Creation of the Earth

IMMEDIATELY after the prayer of the faithful choirs and that movement in the Godhead, I saw below me, not far from and to the right of the world of shadows, another dark globe arise.

I fixed my eyes steadily upon it. I beheld it as if in movement, growing larger and larger, as it were, bright spots breaking out upon it and encircling it like luminous bands. Here and there, they stretched out into brighter, broader plains, and at that moment I saw the form of the land setting boundaries to the water. In the bright places I saw a movement as of life, and on the land I beheld vegetation springing forth and myriads of living things arising. Child that I was, I fancied the plants were moving about.

Up to this moment, there was only a gray light like the sunrise, like early morning breaking over the earth, like nature awakening from sleep.

And now all other parts of the picture faded. The sky became blue, the sun burst forth, but I saw only one part of the earth lighted up and shining. That spot was charming, glorious, and I thought: There is Paradise!

While these changes were going on upon the dark globe, I saw, as it were, a streaming forth of light out of that highest of all the spheres, the God-sphere, that sphere in which God dwelt.

It was as if the sun rose higher in the heavens, as if bright morning were awakening. It was the first morning. No created being had any knowledge of it, and it seemed as if all those created things had been there forever in their unsullied innocence. As the sun rose higher, I saw the plants and trees growing larger and larger. The waters became clearer and holier, colors grew purer and brighter—all was unspeakably charming. Creation was not then as it is now. Plants and flowers and trees had other forms. They are wild and misshapen now compared with what they were, for all things are now thoroughly degenerate.

When looking at the plants and fruits of our gardens, apricots, for instance, which in southern climes are, as I have seen, so different from ours, so large, magnificent, and delicious, I often think: As miserable as are our fruits compared with those of the South, are the latter when compared with the fruits of Paradise. I saw there roses, white and red, and I thought them symbols of Christ's Passion and our Redemption. I saw also palm trees and others, high and spreading, which cast their branches afar, as if forming roofs.

Before the sun appeared, earthly things were puny; but in his beams they gradually increased in size, until they attained full growth.

The trees did not stand close together. Of all plants, at least of the largest, I saw only one of each kind, and they stood apart like seedlings set out in a garden bed. Vegetation was luxuriant, perfectly green, of a species pure, sound, and exempt from decay. Nothing appeared to receive or to need the attention of an earthly gardener. I thought: How is it that all is so beautiful, since as yet there are no human beings! Ah! Sin has not yet entered. There has been no destruction, no rending asunder. All is sound, all is holy. As yet there has been no healing, no repairing. All is pure, nothing has needed purification.

The plain that I beheld was gently undulating and covered with vegetation. In its center rose a fountain, from all sides of which flowed streams, crossing one another and mingling their waters. I saw in them first a slight movement as of life, and then I saw living things. After that I saw, here and there among the shrubs and bushes, animals peeping forth, as if just roused from sleep. They were very different from those of a later day, not at all timorous. Compared with those of our own time, they were almost as far their superior as men are superior to beasts. They were pure and noble, nimble, and joyous. Words cannot describe them. I was not familiar with many of them, for I saw very few like those we have now. I saw the elephant, the stag, the camel, and even the unicorn. This last I saw also in the ark. It is remarkably gentle and affectionate, not so tall as a horse, its head more rounded in shape. I saw no asses, no insects, no wretched, loathsome creatures. These last I have always looked upon as a punishment of sin. But I saw myriads of birds and heard the sweetest notes as in the early morning. There were no birds of prey that I could see, nor did I hear any animals bellowing.

Paradise is still in existence, but it is utterly impossible for humankind to reach it. I have seen that it still exists in all its splendor. It is high above the earth and in an oblique direction from it, like the dark globe of the angels fallen from heaven.

Adam and Eve

I saw Adam created, not in Paradise, but in the region in which Jerusalem was subsequently situated. I saw him come forth glittering and white from a mound of yellow earth, as if out of a mold. The sun was shining and I thought (I was only a child when I saw it) that the sunbeams drew Adam out of the hillock. He was, as it were, born of the virgin earth. God blessed the earth, and it became his mother. He did not instantly step forth from the earth. Some time elapsed before his appearance. He lay in the hillock on his left side, his arm thrown over his head, a light vapor covering him as with a veil. I saw a figure in his right side, and I became conscious that it was Eve, and that she would be drawn from him in Paradise by God. God called him. The hillock opened, and Adam stepped gently forth. There were no trees around, only little flowers. I had seen the animals also, coming forth from the earth in pure singleness, the females separate from the males.

And now I saw Adam borne up on high to a garden, to Paradise. God led all the animals before him in Paradise, and he named them. They followed him and gamboled around him, for all things served him before he sinned. All that he named, afterward followed him to earth. Eve had not yet been formed from him.

I saw Adam in Paradise among the plants and flowers, and not far from the fountain that played in its center. He was awaking, as if from sleep. Although his person was more like to flesh than to spirit, yet he was dazzlingly white. He wondered at nothing, nor was he astonished at his own existence. He went around among the trees and the animals, as if he were used to them all, like a man inspecting his fields.

Near the tree by the water arose a hill. On it I saw Adam reclining on his left side, his left hand under his cheek. God sent a deep sleep on him and he was rapt in vision. Then from his right side, from the same place in which the side of Jesus was opened by the lance, God drew Eve. I saw her small and delicate. But she quickly increased in size until full-grown. She was exquisitely beautiful. Were it not for the Fall, all would be born in the same way, in tranquil slumber.

The hill opened, and at Adam's side arose a crystalline rock, formed apparently of precious stones; at Eve's, lay a white valley covered with something like fine white pollen.

When Eve had been formed, I saw that God gave something, or allowed something to flow upon Adam. It was as if there streamed from the Godhead, apparently in human form, currents of light from forehead, mouth, breast, and hands. They united into a globe of light, which entered Adam's right side whence Eve had been taken. Adam alone received it. It was the germ of God's Blessing, which was threefold. The Blessing that Abraham received from the angel was one. It was of similar form, but not so luminous. Eve arose before Adam, and he gave her his hand. They were like two unspeakably noble and beautiful children, perfectly luminous, and clothed with beams of light as with a veil. From Adam's mouth I saw issuing a broad stream of glittering light, and upon his forehead was an expression of great majesty. Around his mouth played a sunbeam, but there was none around Eve's. I saw Adam's heart very much the same as in men of the present day, but his breast was surrounded by rays of light. In the middle of his heart I saw a sparkling halo of glory. In it was a tiny figure as if holding something in its hand. I think it symbolized the Third Person of the Godhead. From the hands and feet of Adam and Eve shot rays of light. Their hair fell in five glittering tresses, two from the temples, two behind the ears, and one from the back of the head.

I have always thought that by the wounds of Jesus there were opened anew in the human body portals closed by Adam's sin. I have been given to understand that Longinus opened in Jesus's side the gate of regeneration to eternal life; therefore no one entered heaven while that gate was closed.

The glittering beams on Adam's head denoted his abundant fruitfulness, his glory, his connection with other radiations. And all this shining beauty is restored to glorified souls and bodies. Our hair is the ruined, the extinct glory; and as is this hair of ours to rays of light, so is our present flesh to that of Adam before the Fall. The sunbeams around Adam's mouth bore reference to a holy posterity from God, which, had it not been for the Fall, would have been effectuated by the spoken word.

Adam stretched forth his hand to Eve. They left the charming spot of Eve's creation and went through Paradise, looking at everything, rejoicing in everything. That place was the highest in Paradise. All was more radiant, more resplendent there than elsewhere.

The Tree of Life and the Tree of Knowledge

IN THE CENTER of the glittering garden, I saw a sheet of water in which lay an island connected with the opposite land by a pier. Both island and pier were covered with beautiful trees, but in the middle of the former stood one more magnificent than the others. It towered high over them as if guarding them. Its roots extended over the whole island as did also its branches, which were broad below and tapering to a point above. Its boughs were horizontal, and from them arose others like little trees. The leaves were fine, the fruit yellow and sessile in a leafy calyx like a budding rose. It was something like a cedar. I do not remember ever having seen Adam, Eve, or any animal near that tree on the island. But I saw beautiful noble-looking white birds and heard them singing in its branches. That tree was the Tree of Life.

Just before the pier that led to the island, stood the Tree of Knowledge. The trunk was scaly like that of the palm. The leaves, which spread out directly from the stem, were very large and broad, in shape like the sole of a shoe. Hidden in the forepart of the leaves, hung the fruit clustering in fives, one in front, and four around the stem. The yellow fruit had something of the shape of an apple, though more of the nature of a pear or fig. It had five ribs uniting in a little cavity. It was pulpy like a fig inside, of the color of brown sugar, and streaked with blood-red veins. The tree was broader above than below, and its branches struck deep roots into the ground. I see a species of this tree still in warm countries. Its branches throw down shoots to the earth where they root and rise as new trunks. These in turn send forth branches, and so one such tree often covers a large tract of country. Whole families dwell under the dense foliage.

At some distance to the right of the Tree of Knowledge I saw a small, oval, gently sloping hill of glittering red grains and all kinds of precious stones. It was terraced with crystals. Around it were slender trees just high enough to intercept the view. Plants and herbs grew around it, and they, like the trees, bore colored blossoms and nutritious fruits.

At some distance to the left of the Tree of Knowledge I saw a slope, a little dale. It looked like soft clay, or like mist, and it was covered with tiny white flowers and pollen. Here too were various kinds of vegetation, but all colorless, more like pollen than fruit.

It seemed as if these two, the hill and the dale, bore some reference to each other, as if the hill had been taken out of the dale, or as if something from the former was to be transplanted into the latter. They were to each other what the seed is to the field. Both seemed to me holy, and I saw that both—but especially the hill—shone with light. Between them and the Tree of Knowledge arose different kinds of trees and bushes. They were all, like everything else in nature, transparent as if formed of light.

These two places were the abodes of our first parents. The Tree of Knowledge separated them. I think that God, after the creation of Eve, pointed out those places to them.

I saw that Adam and Eve were little together at first. I saw them perfectly free from passion, each in a separate abode. The animals were indescribably noble-looking and resplendent, and they served Adam and Eve. All had, according to their kind, certain retreats, abodes, and walks apart. The different spheres contained in themselves some great mystery of the divine Law, and all were connected with one another.

ANTIQUITY AND OLD TESTAMENT TIMES

The Fall

I SAW Adam and Eve walking through Paradise for the first time. The animals ran to meet and follow them, but they appeared to be more familiar with Eve than with Adam. Eve was in fact more taken up with the earth and created things. She glanced below and around more frequently than Adam. She appeared the more inquisitive of the two. Adam was more silent, more absorbed in God. Among the animals was one that followed Eve more closely than the others. It was a singularly gentle and winning, though artful creature. I know of none other to which I might compare it. It was slender and glossy, and it looked as if it had no bones. It walked upright on its short hind feet, its pointed tail trailing on the ground. Near the head, which was round with a face exceedingly shrewd, it had little short paws, and its wily tongue was ever in motion. The color of the neck, breast, and underpart of the body was pale yellow, and down the back it was a mottled brown very much the same as an eel. It was about as tall as a child of ten years. It was constantly around Eve, and so coaxing and intelligent, so nimble and supple that she took great delight in it. But to me there was something horrible about it. I can see it distinctly even now. I never saw it touch either Adam or Eve. Before the Fall, the distance between man and the lower animals was great, and I never saw the first human beings touch any of them. They had, it is true, more confidence in man, but they kept at a certain distance from him.

When Adam and Eve returned to the region of shining light, a radiant figure like a majestic man with glittering white hair stood before them. He pointed around, and in few words appeared to be giving all things over to them and to be commanding them something. They did not look intimidated, but listened to him naturally. When he vanished, they appeared more satisfied, more happy. They appeared to understand things better, to find more order in things, for now they felt gratitude, but Adam more than Eve. She thought more of their actual bliss and of the things around them than of giving thanks for them. She did not rest in God so perfectly as did Adam; her soul was more taken up with created things. I think Adam and Eve went around Paradise three times.

Again I saw Adam on the shining hill upon which God had formed the woman from a rib of his side as he lay buried in sleep. He stood alone under the trees lost in gratitude and wonder. I saw Eve near the Tree of Knowledge, as if about to pass it, and with her that same animal more wily and sportive than ever. Eve was charmed with the serpent; she took great delight in it. It ran up the Tree of Knowledge until its head was on a line with hers. Then clinging to the trunk with its hind feet, it moved its head toward hers and told her that, if she would eat of the fruit of that tree, she would no longer be in servitude, she would become free, and understand how the multiplication of the human race was to be effected. Adam and Eve had already received the command to increase and multiply, but I understood that they did not know as yet how God willed it to be brought about. I saw, too, that had they known it and yet sinned after that knowledge, Redemption would not have been possible. Eve now became more thoughtful. She appeared to be moved by desire for what the serpent had promised. Something degrading took possession of her. It made me feel anxious. She glanced toward Adam, who was still quietly standing under the trees. She called him, and he came.

Eve started to meet him, but turned back. There was a restlessness, a hesitancy about her movements. Again she started, as if intending to pass the tree, but once more hesitated, approached it from the left, and stood behind it, screened by its long, hanging leaves. The tree was broader above than below, and its wide, leafy branches drooped to the ground. Just within Eve's reach hung a remarkably fine bunch of fruit.

And now Adam approached. Eve caught him by the arm and pointed to the talking animal, and he listened to its words. When Eve laid her hand on Adam's arm, she touched him for the first time. He did not touch her, but the splendor around them grew dim.

I saw the animal pointing to the fruit, but he did not venture to snap it off for Eve. But when the longing for it arose in her heart, he broke off and handed her the central and most beautiful piece of the clustering five.

And now I saw Eve draw near to Adam, and offer him the fruit. Had he refused it, sin would not have been committed. I saw the fruit break, as it were, in Adam's hand. He saw pictures in it, and it was as if he and Eve were instructed upon what they should not have known. The interior of the fruit was blood-red and full of veins. I saw Adam and Eve losing their brilliancy and diminishing in stature. It was as if the sun went down. The animal glided down the tree, and I saw it running off on all fours. I did not see the fruit taken into the mouth as we now take food in eating, but it disappeared between Adam and Eve.

I saw that while the serpent was still in the tree, Eve sinned, for her consent was with the temptation. I learned also at that moment what I cannot clearly repeat; namely, that the serpent was, as it were, the embodiment of Adam

The Fall

and Eve's will, a being by which they could do all things, could attain all things. Here it was that Satan entered.

Sin was not completed by eating the forbidden fruit. But that fruit from the tree which, rooting its branches in the earth thus sent out new shoots, and which continued to do the same after the Fall, conveyed the idea of a more absolute propagation, a sensual implanting in self at the cost of separation from God. So, along with disobedience, there sprang from their indulgence that severing of the creature from God, that planting in self and through self, and those selfish passions in human nature. One that uses the fruit solely for the enjoyment it affords, must accept as the consequence of the act the subversion, the debasement of nature as well as sin and death.

The blessing of a pure and holy multiplying out of God and by God, which Adam had received after the creation of Eve was, in consequence of that indulgence, withdrawn from him; for I saw that the instant Adam left his hill to go to Eve, the Lord grasped him in the back and took something from him. From that something, I felt that the world's salvation would come.

Once on the Feast of the Holy and Immaculate Conception, God gave me a vision of that mystery. I saw enclosed in Adam and Eve the corporal and spiritual life of all humankind. I saw that by the Fall it became corrupted, mixed up with evil, and that the bad angels had acquired power over it. I saw the Second Person of the Godhead come down and, with something like a crooked blade, take the Blessing from Adam before he had sinned. At the same instant, I saw the Virgin issuing from Adam's side like a little luminous cloud, and soaring all resplendent up to God.

By the reception of the fruit, Adam and Eve became, as it were, intoxicated, and their consent to sin wrought in them a great change. It was the serpent in them. Its nature pervaded theirs, and then came the tares among the wheat.

As punishment and reparation, circumcision was instituted. As the vine is pruned that it may not run wild, may not become sour and unfruitful, so must it be done to man that he may regain his lost perfection. Once when the reparation of the Fall was shown me in symbolical pictures, I saw Eve in the act of issuing from Adam's side, and even then stretching out her neck after the forbidden fruit. She ran quickly to the tree and clasped it in her arms. In an opposite picture, I saw Jesus born of the Immaculate Virgin. He ran straight to the cross and embraced it. I saw posterity obscured and ruined by Eve, but again purified by the Passion of Jesus. By the pains of penance must the evil love of self be rooted out of the flesh. The word of the Epistle that the son of the handmaid shall not be joint heir, I always understood to mean the flesh and slavish subjection thereto, typified under the figure of the handmaid.

Marriage is a state of penance. It calls for prayer, fasting, alms-deeds, renunciation, and the intention to increase the kingdom of God.

Adam and Eve before sin were very differently constituted from what we, poor, miserable creatures now are. With the reception of the forbidden fruit, they imbibed a material existence. Spirit became matter; flesh, an instrument, a vessel. At first they were one in God, they sought self in God; but afterward they stood apart from God in their own will. And this self-will is self-seeking, a lusting after sin and impurity. By eating the forbidden fruit, man turned away from his Creator. It was as if he drew creation into himself. All creative power, operations, and attributes, their commingling with one another and with all nature, became in man material things of different forms and functions.

Once man was endowed with the kingship of nature, but now all in him has become nature. He is now one of its slaves, a master conquered and fettered. He must now struggle and fight with nature—but I cannot clearly express it. It was as if man once possessed all things in God, their Creator and their Center; but now he made himself their center, and they became his master.

I saw the interior, the organs of man as if in the flesh, in corporeal, corruptible images of creatures, as well as their relations with one another, from the stars down to the tiniest living thing. All exert an influence on man. He is connected with all of them; he must act and struggle against them, and from them suffer. But I cannot express it clearly since I, too, am a member of the fallen race.

Man was created to fill the choirs of the fallen angels. Were it not for the Fall of Adam, the human race would have increased only till the number of the fallen angels was reached, and then the world would have come to an end. Had Adam and Eve lived to see even one sinless generation, they would not have fallen. I am certain that the world will last until the number of the fallen angels has been filled, until the wheat shall have been reaped from the chaff.

Once I had a great and connected vision of sin and the whole plan of Redemption. I saw all mysteries clearly and distinctly, but it is impossible for me to put all into words. I saw sin in its innumerable ramifications from the Fall of the angels and from Adam's Fall down to the present day, and I saw all the preparations for the repairing and redeeming down to the coming and death of Jesus. Jesus showed me the extraordinary blending, the intrinsic uncleanness of all creatures, as well as all that he had done from the very beginning for their purification and restoration.

At the Fall of the angels, myriads of bad spirits descended to earth and into the air. I saw many creatures under the influence of their wrath, possessed by them in many ways.

The first man was an image of God, he was like heaven; all was one in him, all was one with him. His form was a reproduction of the divine Prototype. He was destined to possess and to enjoy earth and all created things, but holding them from God and giving thanks for them. Man was, however, free; therefore was he subjected to trial, therefore was he forbidden to eat of the Tree of Knowledge. In the beginning, all was smooth and level. When the little mound, the shining hill upon which Adam stood arose, when the white, blooming valley by which I saw Eve standing was hollowed out, the corruptor was already near.

After the Fall, all was changed. All forms of creation were produced in self, dissipated in self. What had been one became many, creatures no longer looked to God alone, each was concentrated in self.

Humankind at first numbered two, then three, and at last they became innumerable. They had been images of God; but after the Fall they became images of self, which images originated in sin. Sin placed them in communication with the fallen angels. They sought all their good in self and the creatures around them with all of whom the fallen angels had connection; and from that interminable blending, that sinking of their noble faculties in self and in fallen nature, sprang manifold wickedness and misery.

My Lord showed me this clearly, distinctly, intelligibly, more clearly than one beholds the things of daily life. At the time, I thought that a child might comprehend it, but now I cannot repeat it. He showed me the whole plan of Redemption with the way in which it was to be effected, as also all that he himself had done. I saw that it is not right to say that God need not have become man, need not have died for us upon the cross; that he could, by virtue of his omnipotence, have redeemed us otherwise. I saw that he did what he did in conformity with his own infinite perfection, his mercy, and his justice; that there is indeed no necessity in God, he does what he does, he is what he is!

I saw Melchizedek as an angel and a type of Jesus, as a priest upon the earth; inasmuch as the priesthood is in God, he was an angel priest of the eternal hierarchy. I saw him preparing, founding, building up, and separating the human family, and acting toward them as a guide. I saw too, Enoch and Noah, what they represented, what they effected; on the other side, I saw the ever-active empire of hell and the infinitely varied manifestations and effects of an earthly, carnal, diabolical idolatry. And I saw in all these manifestations similar pestilential forms and figures leading, so to say, by a secret, inborn necessity and an uninterrupted process of dissolution to sin and corruption. In this manner I saw sin and the prophetic, foreshadowing figures of Redemption which, in their way, were images of divine power as man himself in the image of God. All were shown me from Abraham to Moses, from Moses to the prophets, also the way in which they were connected and their reference to similar types in our own day.

Thus, for instance, with these visions of the Old Testament was connected the instruction I received upon the reason priests no longer relieve or cure, why it is either not in their power, or why it is now effected so differently from what it used to be. I saw this gift of the priesthood possessed by the prophets, and the signification of the form under which it was exercised was shown me. I saw, for example, the history of Elisha giving his staff to Gehazi to lay upon the dead child of the Sunamitess. In this staff lay spiritually Elisha's mission and power. It was, as it were, his arm, the prolongation of his arm. And here I saw the interior signification and power of a bishop's crozier and a monarch's scepter. If used with faith, they unite both bishop and monarch in a certain way with him from whom they hold their dignity, with God, marking them out at the same time as distinct from all others. But Gehazi's faith was not firm, and the mother thought that only through Elisha himself could help be obtained; and so between Elisha's power from God and his staff, the questionings of human presumption intervened, and the staff cured not. Then I saw Elisha praying and stretching himself, hand to hand, mouth to mouth, breast to breast, upon the boy, and the soul of the boy returned to his body. It was explained to me that this manner of healing referred to and prefigured the death of Jesus. In Elisha, by faith and the power conferred by God, were opened again in man all the avenues of grace and expiation that had been closed after the Fall; that is, the head, the breast, the hands, and the feet. Elisha stretched himself as a living, symbolical cross upon the dead, closed cross of the boy's form, and through his prayer of faith life was restored. He expiated, he atoned for the sins the parents had committed by their head, heart, hands, and feet—sins that had brought death to their boy.

Side by side with the above I saw pictures of the wounds of Jesus and of his death upon the cross, by which I traced the harmony between Jesus and his prophet. Since the crucifixion of Jesus, the gift of healing and repairing has existed in full measure among the priests of his church and in general among faithful Christians; for in the same proportion as we live in him and are crucified with him, are those avenues of grace, his sacred wounds, opened to us. I learned many things of the imposition of hands, the efficacy of a benediction, and the influence exerted by the hand, even at a distance—all was explained by the staff of Elisha, which symbolized the hand. That priests of the present day so seldom cure and bless, was shown me in an example significant to that conformity to Jesus upon which depend all such effects. I saw three artists making figures of wax. The first used beautiful white wax, and he was both skillful and intelligent. But he was self-conceited, the image of Christ was not in him, and his work was of no value. The second used wax not so white as that of the first, and his indolence and self-will spoiled all. He did nothing at all. The third was awkward and unskillful; but he worked away in his simplicity and with great diligence on common yellow wax. His work was excellent, a speaking likeness, although the features were coarse. I saw renowned preachers vaunting their worldly wisdom, but effecting nothing; while many a poor, unlettered man exercises by the priestly power alone the gift of healing and blessing.

It seemed to me, while all this was shown me, that I was in school. My Lord made me see how he had suffered from his conception to his death, always expiating, always satisfying for sin. I saw this in distinct visions of his life. I saw too that, by prayer and the offering of sufferings for others, many souls that have done no good upon earth may be converted and saved at the hour of death.

I saw also that the apostles were sent over the greater part of the earth to crush the power of Satan and to scatter benedictions. It was just those regions into which they went that had been most thoroughly infected by the evil one. Jesus, by his perfect atonement, acquired that power against Satan for such as had received or such as would receive his Holy Spirit, and he secured it to them forever. I was given to understand that the power to withdraw various regions of the earth from Satan's dominion by means of a blessing is signified by the words: "Ye are the salt of the earth." For the same reason is salt one of the ingredients of holy water.

I saw, too, in this vision that the meticulous details of sensual, worldly life are most scrupulously observed. I saw the malediction following the reversed blessing. I saw the pretended miracles in the kingdom of Satan. I saw that the worship of nature, superstition, magic, mesmerism, worldly arts and science, and all the means employed to smooth death over, to make sin attractive, to lull the conscience, are practiced with rigorous exactitude, even with fanaticism by the very men who regard the ceremonies of the Holy Church as superstitious forms, for which any other may be indifferently substituted. And yet these men subject their whole life and all their actions to certain ceremonious observances. It is only of the kingdom of the God-Man that they make no account. The world is served with perfection, but the service of God is shamefully neglected!

The Promise of the Redeemer

AFTER the fall of Man, God made known to the angels his plan for the restoration of the human race.

I saw the throne of God. I saw the most holy Trinity and a movement in the divine Persons. I saw the nine choirs of angels and God announcing to them the way by which he would restore the fallen race. I saw the inexpressible joy and jubilation of the angels at the announcement.

I saw Adam's glittering rock of precious stones arise before the throne of God, as if borne up by angels. It had steps cut in it, it increased in size, it became a throne, a tower, and it extended on all sides until it embraced all things. I saw the nine choirs of angels around it, and above the angels in heaven I saw the image of the Virgin. It was not Mary in time; it was Mary in eternity, Mary in God. The Virgin entered the tower, which opened to receive her, and she appeared to become one with it. Then I saw issuing from the most holy Trinity an apparition which, likewise, went into the tower.

Among the angels, I noticed a kind of monstrance at which all were working. It was in shape like a tower, and on it were all kinds of mysterious carving. Near it on either side stood two figures, their joined hands embracing it. At every instant it became larger and more magnificent. I saw something from God passing through the angelic choirs and going into the monstrance. It was a shining holy thing, and it became more clearly defined the nearer it drew to the monstrance. It appeared to me to be the germ of the divine Blessing for a pure offspring which had been given to Adam, but withdrawn when he was on the point of hearkening to Eve and consenting to eat the forbidden fruit. It was the Blessing that was again bestowed upon Abraham, withdrawn from Jacob, by Moses deposited in the Ark of the Covenant, and lastly received by Joachim, the father of Mary, in order that Mary might be as pure and stainless in her conception as was Eve upon coming forth from the side of the sleeping Adam. The monstrance, likewise, went into the tower.

I saw, too, a chalice prepared by the angels. It was of the same shape as that used at the Last Supper, and it also went into the tower. To the right of the tower I saw, as if on the edge of a golden cloud, grapevines and wheat intertwining like the fingers of clasped hands. From them sprang a branch, a whole genealogical tree upon whose boughs were little figures of males and females reaching hands to one another. Its highest blossom was the crib with the child.

Then I saw in pictures the mystery of Redemption from the Promise down to the fullness of time, and in side pictures I saw counteracting influences at work. At last, over the shining rock, I saw a large and magnificent church. It was the one, holy, catholic church, which bears living in itself the salvation of the whole world. The connection of these pictures one with another and their transition from one to another was wonderful. Even what was evil and opposed to the end in view, even what was rejected by the angels as unfit, was made subservient to the development of Redemption. And so I saw the ancient temple rising from below; it was very large and like a church, but it had no tower. It was pushed to one side by the angels, and there it stood slanting. I saw a great mussel shell make its appearance and try to force its way into the old temple; but it, too, was hurried aside.

I saw appear a broad, lopped-off tower through whose numerous gateways figures like Abraham and the children of Israel entered. It was significant of their bondage in Egypt. It was shoved aside, as well as another Egyptian tower in staircase form. The latter was symbolical of astrology and soothsaying. Then appeared an Egyptian temple. It was pushed aside like the others, and remained standing crooked.

At last, I saw a vision on earth such as God had shown to Adam; that is, that a Virgin would arise and restore to him the salvation he had forfeited. Adam knew not when it would take place, and I saw his deep sadness because Eve bore him only sons. But at last she had a daughter.

I saw Noah and his sacrifice at the time in which he received from God the Blessing. Then I had visions of Abraham, of his Blessing, and of the promise of a son Isaac. I saw the Blessing descending from firstborn to firstborn, and always transmitted with a sacramental action. I saw Moses on the night of Israel's departure from Egypt, getting possession of the mystery, the holy thing, of which none other knew save Aaron. I saw it afterward in the Ark of the Covenant. Only the high priests and certain saints, by a revelation from God, had any knowledge of it. I saw the transmitting of this mystery through the ancestry of Jesus Christ down to Joachim and Anne, the purest and holiest couple that ever existed, and from whom was born Mary, the spotless Virgin. And then I saw Mary becoming the living Ark of God's Covenant.

Adam and Eve Driven from Paradise

AFTER some time I saw Adam and Eve wandering about in great distress. They were no longer beaming with light, and they went about, one here, the other there, as if seeking something they had lost. They were ashamed of each other. Every step they took led them downward, as if the ground gave way beneath their feet. They carried gloom wherever they went; the plants lost their bright colors and turned gray, and the animals fled before them. They sought large leaves and wove them into a cincture for their loins. They always wandered about separate.

After they had thus fled for a considerable time, the region of refulgent light whence they had come began to look like the summit of a distant mountain. Among the bushes of a gloomy-looking plain they hid themselves, but apart. Then a voice from above called them, but they would not obey the call. They were frightened, they fled still further, and hid still deeper among the bushes. It made me sad to see that. But the voice became more imperative, and, in spite of their desire to flee and hide, they were compelled to come forth.

The majestic figure shining with light again appeared. Adam and Eve with bowed head stepped from their hiding places, but they dared not look upon their Lord. They glanced at each other, and both acknowledged their guilt. And now God pointed out to them a plain still lower than the one on which they stood. On it were bushes and trees. On reaching it, they became humble, and for the first time, rightly understood their miserable condition. I saw them praying when left there alone. They separated, fell on their knees, and raised up their hands with tears and cries. I thought as I gazed upon them how good it is to be alone in prayer.

Adam and Eve were at this time clothed in a garment that reached from the shoulders to the knee, and which was girded at the waist by a strip of the inner bark of a tree.

While our first parents were descending lower and lower from the place of their creation, Paradise itself appeared, like a cloud, to be mounting higher and higher above them. Then a fiery ring, like the circle sometimes seen around the sun and moon, came down from heaven and settled around the height upon which was Paradise.

Adam and Eve had been only one day in Paradise. I now see Paradise far, far off like a strip of land directly under the point of sunrise. When the sun rises, it mounts up from the right of that strip of land which lies east of the Prophet Mountain† and just where the sun rises. It looks to me like an egg hanging over indescribably clear water which separates it from the earth. The Prophet Mountain is, as it were, a promontory rising up through that water. On that mountain one sees extraordinarily verdant regions broken here and there by deep abysses and ravines full of water. I have, indeed, seen people climbing up the Prophet Mountain, but they did not go far.

I saw Adam and Eve reach the earth, their place of

---

† Anne Catherine's detailed visions of the "Prophet Mountain," or "Mountain of the Prophets," and certain of its mysteries, will be found in Book IV.

penance. Oh, what a touching sight—those two creatures expiating their fault upon the naked earth! Adam had been allowed to bring an olive branch with him from Paradise, and now he planted it. Later on, the cross was made from its wood. Adam and Eve were unspeakably sad. Where I saw them, they could scarcely get a glimpse of Paradise, and they were constantly descending lower and lower. It seemed as if something revolved and they came at last, through night and darkness, to the wretched, miserable place upon which they had to do penance.

The Family of Adam

IT WAS to the region of the Mount of Olives that I saw Adam and Eve come. The country was very different from what it is at present, but I was assured that it was the same. I saw Adam and Eve living and doing penance on that part of the Mount of Olives upon which Jesus sweat blood. They cultivated the soil. I saw them surrounded by sons. They were in great distress, and they implored God to bestow upon them a daughter, for they had received the Promise that the woman's seed should crush the serpent's head.

Eve bore children at stated intervals. After each birth a number of years was always devoted to penance. It was after seven years of penance that Seth, the child of promise, was born of Eve in the grotto of the crib, where, also, an angel announced to Eve that Seth was the seed given her by God in the place of Abel. For a long time, Seth was concealed in that grotto, likewise in the cave in which Abraham was afterward suckled, for his brothers like those of Joseph sought his life.

Once I saw about twelve people: Adam, Eve, Cain, Abel, two sisters, and some young children. All were clothed in skins thrown over their shoulders like a scapular and girded at the waist. The female dress was large and full around the breast where it served as a pocket. It fell down around the limbs, and was fastened at the sides and once under the arm. The men wore shorter dresses, which had a pocket fastened to them. The skins from which their dresses were made were, from the neck to the elbow, exceedingly fine and white. They all looked very noble and beautiful in their clothing. They had huts in those days, partly sunk in the earth and covered with plants. Their household was quite well-arranged. I saw orchards of low, but tolerably vigorous fruit trees. There was grain also, such as wheat, which God had given to Adam for seed.

I do not remember having seen either grapevines or wheat in Paradise. None of the productions of Paradise had to be prepared for eating. Such preparation is a consequence of sin and, therefore, a symbol of labor and suffering. God gave to Adam whatever it was necessary for him to sow. I remember having seen men who looked like angels taking something to Noah when he went into the ark. It appeared to me to be a vine branch stuck in an apple.

A certain kind of grain grew wild at that time, and among it Adam had to sow the good wheat. That improved it for awhile, but it again degenerated and became worse and worse. The wild grain was excellent in those early times. It was most luxuriant further to the east, in India or China, where as yet there were but few inhabitants. It does not thrive where wine is largely made and fish abound.

The milk of animals was drunk in those days, and they likewise ate cheese dried in the sun. Among the animals, I noticed sheep in particular. All that Adam had named followed him from Paradise, but afterward they fled from him. He had to entice them back with food, that is the domestic animals, and familiarize them to himself. I saw birds hopping about, little animals running around, and all sorts of bounding creatures, such as antelopes and deer.

The household order was quite patriarchal. I saw Adam's children in their separate huts, reclining around a stone at meals. I saw them also praying and giving thanks.

God had taught Adam to offer sacrifice; he was the priest in his family. Cain and Abel also were priests. I saw that even the preparations for their sacrifice took place in a separate hut.

On the head they wore caps made of leaves and their stalks woven together. They were shaped like a ship and had a rim in front by which they could be raised from the head. Those first human beings had beautiful skin of a yellowish tinge, which shone like silk, and their hair was reddish-yellow like gold. Adam wore his hair long. His beard was short at first, but later he let it grow. Eve at first wore her long hair hanging around her; but later on she wound it around her head in a coil like a cap.

Fire I always saw like a hidden flame, and it appeared to be in the earth. It was given to man from heaven, and God himself taught him the use of it. They burned for fuel a yellow substance that looked like earth. I saw no cooking going on. In the beginning the food was merely dried in the sun; and the wheat, after being crushed, was exposed under twisted covers to the heat of the sun to dry. God gave them wheat, barley, and rye, and taught them how to cultivate them. He guided man in all things.

I saw no large rivers in the beginning as, for instance, the Jordan; but fountains sprang forth whose waters were conducted into reservoirs.

Flesh meat was not eaten before Abel's death.

I once had a vision of Mount Calvary. I saw on it a prophet, the companion of Elijah. The mount was at that time full of caves and sepulchers. The prophet entered one of the caves and from a stone coffin filled with bones he took up the skull of Adam. Instantly an angel appeared before him, saying: "That is Adam's skull," and he forbade its removal. Scattered over the skull was some thin yellow hair. From the prophet's account of what had occurred, the spot was named "The Place of Skulls" (Golgotha). Christ's cross stood in a straight line above that skull at the time of his crucifixion. I was interiorly instructed that the spot upon which the skull rests is the middle point of the earth. I was told the distance east, south, and west in numbers, but I have forgotten them.

Cain • The Children of God • The Giants

I SAW that Cain conceived on the Mount of Olives the design to murder Abel. After the deed, he wandered about the same spot frightened and distracted, planting trees and tearing them up again. Then I saw a majestic figure in the form of a man refulgent with light appear to him. "Cain," he said, "where is thy brother Abel?" Cain did not at first see the figure; but when he did, he turned and answered: "I know not. He has not been given in charge to me." But when God replied that Abel's blood cried to him from the earth, Cain grew more troubled, and I saw that he disputed long with God. God told him that he should be cursed upon the earth, that it should bring forth no fruit for him, and that he should forthwith flee from the land in which he then dwelt. Cain responded that everywhere his fellow men would seek to kill him. There were already many people upon the earth. Cain was very old and had children. Abel also left children, and there were other brothers and sisters, the children of Adam. But God replied that it would not be so; that whoever should kill Cain should himself be punished sevenfold, and he placed a sign upon him that no one should slay him. Cain's posterity gradually became colored. Ham's children also were browner than those of Shem. They who were distinguished by a particular mark engendered children of the same stamp; and as corruption increased, the mark also increased until at last it covered the whole body, and people became darker and darker. But yet in the beginning there were no people perfectly black; they became so only by degrees.

God pointed out to Cain a region to which he should flee. And because Cain said: "Then, wilt thou let me starve?"—(the earth was for him accursed)—God answered no, that he should eat the flesh of animals. He told him likewise that a nation would arise from him, and that good also would come from him. Before this men ate no flesh.

Cain went forth and built a city, which he named after his son Enoch.

Abel was slain in the valley of Jehosaphat opposite Mount Calvary. Many murders and evil deeds took place there at a subsequent period. Cain slew Abel with a kind of club that he used to break soft stones and earth when planting in the fields. The club must have been of hard stone, for it was shaped like a pickaxe, the handle of wood.

We must not picture to ourselves the earth before the Deluge as it is now. Palestine was by no means so broken up by valleys and ravines. Plains were far more extensive, and single mountains less lofty. the Mount of Olives was at that time only a gentle rising. The crib cave of Bethlehem was as later a wild cavern, but the surroundings were different.

The people of those early times were larger, though not out of proportion. We would regard them with astonishment, but not with fright, for they were far more beautiful in form than people of a later period. Among the old marble statues that I see in many places lying in subterranean caves, may be found similar figures.

Cain led his children and grandchildren to the region pointed out to him, and there they separated. Of Cain himself, I have never seen anything more that was sinful. His punishment appeared to consist in hard, but fruitless labor. Nothing in which he was personally engaged succeeded. I saw that he was mocked and reviled by his children and grandchildren, treated badly in every way. And yet they followed him as their leader, though as one accursed. I saw that Cain was severely punished, but not damned.

One of Cain's descendants was Tubalcain, the originator of numerous arts, and the father of the giants. I have frequently seen that, when the angels fell, a certain number had a moment of repentance and did not in consequence fall as low as the others. Later on, these fallen spirits took up their abode on a high, desolate, and wholly inaccessible mountain whose site at the time of the Deluge became a sea, the Black Sea, I think. They were permitted to exercise their evil influence upon men in proportion as the latter strayed further from God. After the Deluge they disappeared from that region, and were confined to the air. They will not be cast into hell before the last day.

I saw Cain's descendants becoming more and more godless and sensual. They settled further and further up that mountain ridge where were the fallen spirits. Those spirits took possession of many of the women, ruled them completely, and taught them all sorts of seductive arts. Their children were very large. They possessed a quickness, an aptitude for everything, and they gave themselves up entirely to the wicked spirits as their instruments. And so arose on this mountain and spread far around, a wicked race which by violence and seduction sought to entangle

Seth's posterity likewise in their own corrupt ways. Then God declared to Noah his intention to send the Deluge. During the building of the ark, Noah had to suffer terribly from those people.

I have seen many things connected with the race of giants. They could with ease carry enormous stones high up the mountain, they could accomplish the most stupendous feats. They could walk straight up trees and walls just as I have seen others possessed by the devil doing. They could effect the most wonderful things, they could do whatever they wished; but all was pure jugglery and delusion due to the agency of the demon. It is for that reason that I have such horror of every species of jugglery and fortune-telling. These people could form all kinds of images out of stone and metal; but of the knowledge of God they had no longer a trace. They sought their gods in the creatures around them. I have seen them scratch up a stone, form it into an extravagant image, and then adore it. They worshipped also a frightful animal and all kinds of ignoble things. They knew all things, they could see all things, they were skilled in the preparing of poisons, they practiced sorcery and every species of wickedness. The women invented music. I saw them going around among the better tribes trying to seduce them to their own abominations. They had no dwelling houses, no cities, but they raised massive round towers of shining stone. Under those towers were little structures leading into great caverns wherein they carried on their horrible wickedness. From the roofs of these structures, the surrounding country could be seen, and by mounting up into the towers and looking through tubes, one could see far into the distance. But it was not like looking through tubes made to bring distant objects into view. The power of the tubes to which I here allude was effected by satanic agency. They that looked through them could see where the other tribes were settled. Then they marched against them, overcame them, and lawlessly carried all before them. That same spirit of lawlessness they exercised everywhere. I saw them sacrificing children by burying them alive in the earth. God overthrew that mountain at the time of the Deluge.

Enoch, Noah's ancestor, opposed that wicked race by his teachings. He wrote much. Enoch was a very good man and one very grateful to God. In many parts of the open fields he raised altars of stone and there the fruits of the earth flourished. He gave thanks to God and offered sacrifice to him. Chiefly in his family was religion preserved and handed down to Noah. Enoch was taken up to Paradise. There he waits at the entrance gate, whence with another (Elijah) he will come again before the last day.

Ham's descendants likewise had similar relations with the evil spirits after the Deluge, and from such connection sprang so many demoniacs and necromancers, so many mighty ones of the world, so many great, wild, daring men.

Semiramis herself was the offspring of demoniacs, consequently she was apt at everything save the working out of her salvation.

Later on, there arose another people esteemed as gods by the pagans. The women that first allowed themselves to be ruled by evil spirits were fully conscious of the fact, though others were ignorant of it. These women had it (the principle of possession) in them like flesh and blood, like original sin.

Noah and His Posterity • Hom and Djemschid, Leaders of the People

I SAW Noah, a simple-hearted old man, clothed in a long white garment. He was walking about in an orchard and pruning the trees with a crooked bone knife. A cloud hovered over him and in it was a human figure. Noah fell on his knees. I saw that he was, then and there, interiorly instructed upon God's design to destroy humankind, and he was commanded to build an ark. I saw that Noah grew sad at the announcement, and that he prayed for the punishment to be averted. He did not begin the work at once. Again the Lord appeared to him, twice in succession, commanding him to begin the building, otherwise he should perish with the rest of humankind. At last, I saw Noah removing with all his family to the country in which Zoroaster, the Shining Star, subsequently dwelt. Noah settled in a high, woody, solitary region where he and his numerous followers lived under tents. Here he raised an altar and offered sacrifice to the Lord. Neither Noah nor any of his family built permanent houses, because they put faith in the prophecy of the Deluge. But the godless nations around laid massive foundations, marked off courts, and erected all kinds of buildings designed to resist the inroads of time and the attacks of an enemy.

There were frightful deeds upon the earth in those days. Men delivered themselves up to all kinds of wickedness, even the most unnatural. They plundered one another and carried off whatever suited them best, they laid waste homes and fields, they kidnapped women and maidens. In proportion to their increase in numbers, was the wickedness of Noah's posterity. They even robbed and insulted Noah himself. They had not fallen into this state of base degradation from want of civilization. They were not wild and barbarous; rather, they lived commodiously and had well-ordered households—but they were deeply imbued with wickedness. They practiced the most shameful idolatry, everyone making his own god of whatever pleased him best. By diabolical arts, they sought to seduce Noah's immediate family. Mosoch, the son of Japhet and grandson of Noah, was thus corrupted after he had, while working in the field, taken from them a poisonous beverage which intoxicated him. It was not wine, but the juice of a plant which they were accustomed to drink in small quantities during their work, and whose leaves and fruit they chewed. Mosoch became the father of a son, who was named Hom.

When the child was born, Mosoch begged his brother Tubal to take it, and thus hide his guilt. Tubal did so out of fraternal affection. The child, with the stalks and sprouts of a certain viscous root, was laid by his mother before Tubal's tent. She hoped thereby to acquire a right over his inheritance; but the Deluge was already at hand, and so her plans were fruitless. Tubal took the boy and had him reared in his family without betraying his origin. And so it happened in this way that the child was taken into the ark. Tubal called the boy Hom, the name of the root whose sprouts lay near him as the only sign. The child was not nourished with milk, but with the same root. If that plant is allowed to grow up straight, it will reach the height of a man; but when it creeps along the ground, it sends up shoots like the asparagus, hard with tender tops. It is used as food and as a substitute for milk. The root is bulbous, and from it rises a crown of a few brown leaves. Its stem is tolerably thick and the pith is used as meal, cooked like pap or spread in thin layers and baked. Wherever it thrives, it grows luxuriantly and covers leagues of ground. I saw it in the ark.

It was long before the ark was completed, for Noah often discontinued it for years at a time. Three times did God warn him to proceed with it. Each time Noah would engage workmen, recommence and again discontinue in the hope that God would relent. But at last the work was finished.

I saw that in the ark, as in the cross, there were four kinds of wood: palm, olive, cedar, and cypress. I saw the wood felled and hewed upon the spot, and Noah bearing it himself upon his shoulders to the place of building, just as Jesus afterward carried the wood of his cross. The spot chosen for the construction of the ark was a hill surrounded by a valley. First the bottom was put in.

The ark was rounded in the back and the keel, shaped like a trough, was smeared with pitch. It had two stories supported on hollow posts, which stood one above another. These posts were not round trunks of trees; they were in oval sections filled with a white pith which became fibrous toward the center. The trunk was knotty, or furrowed, and the great leaves grew around it without branches. (Probably a species of palm.) I saw the workmen punching the pith out with a tool. All other trees were cut into thin planks. When Noah had carried all the materials to the appointed spot and arranged them in order, the building was begun. The bottom was put in and pitched, the first row of posts raised, and the holes in which they stood filled up with pitch. Then came the second floor with another row of posts for the third floor, and then the roof. The spaces between the posts were filled in with brown and yellow laths placed crosswise, the holes and chinks being stuffed with a kind of wool found on certain trees and plants, and a white moss that grows very abundantly around some trees. Then all was pitched inside and outside. The roof was rounded. The entrance between the two windows was in the center of one side, a little more than halfway up. In the middle of the roof likewise was a square opening. When the ark had been entirely covered with pitch, it shone like a mirror in the sun. Noah went on working alone and for a long time at the different compartments for the animals, as all were to be separate. Two passages extended through the middle of the ark, and back in the oval part, concealed by hangings, stood a wooden altar, the table of which was semicircular. A little in the front of the altar was a pan of coals. This was their fire. Right and left were spaces partitioned off for sleeping apartments. All kinds of chests and utensils were carried into the ark, and numerous seeds, plants, and shrubs were put into earth around the walls, which were soon covered with verdure. I saw something like vines carried in, and on them large yellow grapes, the bunches as long as one's arm.

No words can express what Noah endured from the malice and ill will of the workmen during the whole time that the ark was building. They mocked him, they insulted him in every way, they called him a fool. He paid them well in cattle, but that did not prevent their reviling him. No one knew why he was building the ark, therefore did they ridicule him. When all was finished, I saw Noah giving thanks to God, who then appeared to him. He told him to take a reed pipe and call all the animals from the four corners of the globe. The nearer the day of chastisement approached, the darker grew the heavens. Frightful anxiety took possession of the whole earth; the sun no longer showed his face, and the roar of the thunder was unceasingly heard. I saw Noah going a short distance north, south, east, and west, and blowing upon his reed pipe. The animals came flocking at the sound and entered the ark in order, two by two, male and female. They went in by a plank laid from the entrance to the ground. When all were safe inside, the plank also was hoisted in. The largest animals, white elephants and camels, went in first. They were restless as at the approach of a storm, and it took several days for them all to enter. The birds flew in through the skylight and perched under the roof on poles and in cages, while the waterfowl went into the bottom of the vessel. The land animals were in the middle story. Of such as are slaughtered, there were seven couples.

The ark, lying there by itself on the top of the hill, shone with a bluish light. At a distance, it looked as if it were descending from the clouds. And now the time for the Deluge drew nigh. Noah had already announced it to his family. He took with him into the ark Shem, Ham, and Japhet with their wives and their children. There were in the ark grandsons from fifty to eighty years old with their children small and large. All that had labored at its construction and who were good and free from idolatry entered with Noah. There were over one hundred people in the ark, and they were necessary to give daily food to the animals and to clean after them. I must say, for I always see it so, that Shem's, Ham's and Japhet's children all went into the ark. There were many little boys and girls in it, in fact all of Noah's family that were good. Holy scripture mentions only three of Adam's children, Cain, Abel, and Seth; and yet I see many others among them, and I always see them in pairs, boys and girls. And so too, in 1 Peter 3:20, only eight souls are mentioned as saved in the ark; that is, the four ancestral couples by whom, after the Deluge, the earth was to be peopled. I also saw Hom in the ark. The child was fastened by a skin into a bark cradle formed like a trough. I saw many infants cradled in a similar way, floating on the waters of the Deluge.

When the ark rose on the waters, when crowds of people upon the surrounding mountains and in the high trees were weeping and lamenting, when the waters were covered with the floating bodies of the drowned and with uprooted trees, Noah and his family were already safe inside. Before he and his wife, his three sons and their wives entered the ark, he once more implored God's mercy. When all had entered, Noah drew in the plank and made fast the door. He left outside near relatives and their families who, during the building of the ark, had separated from him. Then burst forth a fearful tempest. The lightnings played in fiery columns, the rains fell in torrents, and the hill upon which the ark stood soon became an island. The misery was great, so great that I trust it was the means of many a soul's salvation. I saw a devil, black and hideous, with pointed jaws and a long tail, going to and fro through the tempest and tempting men to despair. Toads and serpents sought a hiding place in the crevices of the ark. Flies and vermin I saw not. They came into existence later to torment men.

I saw Noah offering sacrifice in the ark upon an altar covered with red over which was a white cloth. In an arched chest were preserved the bones of Adam. During prayer and sacrifice, Noah laid them on the altar. I saw on the altar, likewise, the chalice of the Last Supper which, during the building of the ark, had been brought to Noah by three figures in long white garments. They looked like the three men that announced to Abraham the birth of a son. They came from a city that was destroyed at the time of the Deluge. They addressed Noah as one whose fame had reached them, and told him that he should take with him into the ark a mysterious something that they gave him, in order that it might escape the waters of the Deluge. The mysterious thing was that chalice. In it lay a grain of wheat, large as a sunflower seed, and a vine branch. Noah stuck both into a yellow apple and put it into the chalice. The chalice had no cover, for the branch was to grow out of it. After the dispersion of men at the building of the Tower of Babel, I saw that chalice in the possession of one of Shem's descendants in the country of Semiramis. He was the ancestor of the Samanenses, who were established at Canaan by Melchizedek. Hither they took the chalice.

I saw the ark driving over the waters, and dead bodies floating around. It rested upon a high rocky peak of a mountain chain far to the east of Syria, and there it remained for a long time. I saw that land was already appearing. It looked like mud covered with a greenish mold.

Immediately after the Deluge, fish and shellfish began to be eaten. Afterward, as people multiplied, they ate bread and birds. They planted gardens, and the soil was so fruitful that the wheat which they sowed produced ears as large as those of maize. The root from which Hom received his name was also planted. Noah's tent stood on the spot where, at a later period, was that of Abraham. In the plain and in the surrounding country, Noah's sons had their tents.

I saw the cursing of Ham. But Shem and Japhet received from Noah on their knees the Blessing. It was delivered to them with ceremonies similar to those used by Abraham when giving over the same Blessing to Isaac. I saw the curse pronounced by Noah upon Ham moving toward the latter like a black cloud and obscuring him. His skin lost its whiteness, he grew darker. His sin was the sin of sacrilege, the sin of one who would forcibly enter the Ark of the Covenant. I saw a most corrupt race descend from Ham and sink deeper and deeper in darkness. I see that the dark, idolatrous nations are the descendants of Ham.

It would be impossible for me to say how I beheld the nations increasing and extending and, in many different ways, falling into darkness and corruption. But with all that, many luminous rays streamed forth from them and sought the light.

When Tubal, the son of Japhet, with his own children and those of his brother Mosoch, sought counsel of Noah as to the country to which they should migrate, they were fifteen families in number, Noah's children already extended far around, and the families of Tubal and Mosoch also dwelt at some distance from Noah. But when Noah's children began to quarrel and oppress one another, Tubal desired to remove still farther off. He wanted to have nothing to do with Ham's descendants, who were already thinking of building the Tower. He and his family heeded not the invitation received later to engage in that undertaking, and it was declined also by the children of Shem.

Tubal with his troop of followers appeared before Noah's tent, asking for directions as to whither he should go. Noah dwelt upon a mountain range between Libanus and Caucasus. He wept when he saw Tubal and his followers, for he loved that race, because it was better, more God-fearing than others. He pointed out a region toward the northeast, charged them to be faithful to the commands of God and to the offering of sacrifice, and made them promise to guard the purity of their descent, and not to intermingle with the descendants of Ham. He gave them girdles and breastpieces that he had had in the ark. The heads of the families were to wear them when engaged in divine service and performing marriage ceremonies, in order to guard against malediction and a depraved posterity. The ceremonies used by Noah when offering sacrifice reminded me of the Holy Sacrifice of the Mass. There were alternate prayers and responses, and Noah moved from place to place at the altar and bowed reverently. He gave them likewise a leathern bag containing a vessel made of bark, in which was an oval golden box enclosing three other smaller vessels. They also received from him the roots or bulbs of that Hom plant, rolls of bark or skins upon which were written characters, and round wooden blocks upon which signs were engraved.

These people were of a bright, reddish-yellow complexion, and very beautiful. They were clothed in skins and woolen garments girdled at the waist, the arms alone bare. The skins they wore were scarcely drawn from the animal when they were clapped, still bloody, on the limbs. They fitted so tightly that my first thought was: Those people are hairy. Not so, however, for their own skin was smooth as satin. With the exception of various kinds of seed, they did not take much baggage with them, since they were departing for a high region toward the northeast. I saw no camels, but they had horses, asses, and animals with spreading horns like stags. I saw them, Tubal's followers, on a high mountain where they dwelt one above another in long, low huts like arbors. I saw them digging the ground, planting, and setting out trees in rows. The opposite side of the mountain was cold. Later on the whole region became much colder. In consequence of this change in the climate, one of the grandsons of Tubal, the ancestor Djemschid, led them further toward the southwest. With a few exceptions, all who had seen Noah and had taken leave of him died in this place, that is, on the mountain to which Tubal had led them. They who followed Djemschid were all born on the same mountain. They took with them the few surviving old men who had known Noah, carrying them very carefully in litters.

When Tubal with his family separated from Noah, I saw among them that child of Mosoch, Hom, who had gone with Tubal into the ark. Hom was already grown, and later on I saw him very different from those around him. He was of large stature like a giant, and of a very serious, peculiar turn of mind. He wore a long robe, he was like a priest. He used to go alone to the summit of the mountain and there spend night after night. He observed the stars and practiced magic. He was taught by the devil to arrange what he saw in vision into a science, a religion, and thereby he vitiated and counteracted the teaching of Enoch. The evil inclinations inherited from his mother mingled in him with the pure hereditary teachings of Enoch and Noah, to which the children of Tubal clung. Hom, by his false visions and revelations, misinterpreted and changed the ancient truth. He studied and pondered, watched the stars and had visions which, by Satan's agency, showed him deformed images of truth. Through their resemblance to truth, his doctrine and idolatry became the mothers of heresy. Tubal was a good man. Hom's manner of acting and his teaching were very displeasing to Tubal, who was greatly grieved to see one of his sons, the father of Djemschid, attach himself to Hom. I heard Tubal complaining: "My children are not united. Would that I had not separated from Noah!"

Hom conducted the waters of two springs from the higher part of the mountain down to the dwellings. They soon united into one stream which, after a short course, swelled into a broad torrent. I saw Djemschid and his followers crossing it at their departure. Hom received almost divine homage from his followers. He taught them that God exists in fire. He had also much to do with water, and with that viscous root from which he derived his name. He planted it and solemnly distributed it as a sacred medicine and nourishment. This distribution at last became a ceremony of religion. He carried its juice or pap around with him in a brown vessel like a mortar. The axes were of the same material. They got them from people of another tribe that lived far away in a mountainous country and forged such implements by means of fire. I saw them on a mountain from which fire burst forth, sometimes in one place, sometimes in another. I think the vessel which Hom carried around with him was made out of the melted metal or rock that flowed from the mountain, and which was caught in a mold. Hom never married nor did he live to be very old. He published many of his visions referring to his own death. He himself put faith in them as did also Derketo and his other followers at a later period. But I saw him dying a frightful death, and the evil one carried him off body and soul; nothing remained of him. For that reason his followers thought, that, like Enoch, he had been taken up to a holy dwelling place. The father of Djemschid had been a pupil of Hom, and Hom left him his spirit in order that he might then be the one who would succeed him.

On account of his knowledge, Djemschid became the leader of his people. They soon became a nation, and were led by Djemschid still further south. Dsemchid was very distinguished; he was well-educated, and had embraced Hom's teachings. He was unspeakably lively and vigorous, much more active and better also than Hom, who was of a dark, rigid disposition. He practiced the religion formulated by Hom, added many things of his own thereto, and gave much attention to the stars. His followers regarded fire as sacred. They were all distinguished by a certain sign which denoted their race. People at that time kept together in tribes; they did not intermingle then as now. Djemschid's special aim was to improve the races and maintain them in their original purity; he separated and transplanted them as seemed best to him. He left them perfectly free, and yet they were very submissive to him. The descendants of those races, whom I now see wild and barbarous in distant lands and islands, are not to be compared with their progenitors in point of personal beauty or manly character; for those early nations were noble and simple, yet withal most valiant. The races of the present day are also far less skillful and clever, and possess less bodily strength.

On his marches, Djemschid laid the foundations of tent cities, marked off fields, made long roads of stone, and formed settlements here and there of certain numbers of men and women, to whom he gave animals, trees, and plants. He rode around large tracks of land, striking into the earth with an instrument which he always carried in his hand, and his people then set to work in those places, grubbing and hacking, making hedges and digging ditches. Djemschid was remarkably strict and just. I saw him as a tall old man, very thin and of a yellowish-red complexion. He rode a surprisingly nimble little animal with slender legs and black and yellow stripes, very much like an ass.

Djemschid rode around a tract of land just as our poor people go around a field on the heath by night, and thus appropriated it for cultivation. He paused here and there, plunged his grubbing axe into the ground or drove in a stake to mark the sites of future settlements. The instrument, which was afterward called Djemschid's golden plowshare, was in form like a Latin cross. It was about the length of one's arm and, when drawn out, formed with the shaft a right angle. With this instrument, Djemschid made fissures in the earth. A representation of the same appeared on the side of his robe where pockets generally are. It reminded me of the symbol of office that Joseph and Asenath always carried in Egypt, and with which they also surveyed the land, though that of Djemschid was more like a cross. On the upper part was a ring into which it could be run.

Djemschid wore a mantle that fell backward from the front. From his girdle to the knee hung four leathern flaps, two behind and two before, strapped at the side and fastened under the knee. His feet were bound with leather and straps. He wore a golden shield on his breast. He had several similar breastplates to suit various solemnities. His crown was a pointed circlet of gold. The point in front was higher and bent like a little horn, and on the end of it waved something like a little flag.

Djemschid constantly spoke of Enoch. He knew that he had been taken away from the earth without undergoing death. He taught that Enoch had delivered over to Noah all goodness and all truth, had appointed him the father and guardian of all blessings, and that from Noah all these blessings had passed over to himself. He wore about him a golden egg-shaped vessel in which, as he said, was contained something precious that had been preserved by Noah in the ark, and which had been handed down to himself. Wherever he pitched his tent, there the golden vessel was placed on a column, and over it, on elegant posts carved with all kinds of figures, a covering was stretched. It looked like a little temple. The cover of the vessel was a crown of filigree work. When Djemschid lighted fire, he threw into it something that he took out of the vessel. The vessel had indeed been used in the ark, for Noah had preserved the fire in it; but it was now the treasured idol of Djemschid and his people. When it was set up, fire burned before it to which prayers were offered and animals sacrificed, for Djemschid taught that the great God dwells in light and fire, and that he has many inferior gods and spirits serving him.

All submitted to Djemschid. He established colonies of men and women here and there, gave them herds and permitted them to plant and build. They were now allowed to follow their own pleasure in the matter of marriage, for Djemschid treated them like cattle, assigning wives to his followers in accordance with his own views. He himself had several. One was very beautiful and of a better family than the others. Djemschid destined his son by her to be his successor. By his orders, great round towers were built, which were ascended by steps for the purpose of observing the stars. The women lived apart and in subjection. They wore short garments, the bodice and breast of material like leather, and some kind of stuff hung behind. Around the neck and over the shoulders they wore a full, circular cloak, which fell below the knee. On the shoulders and breast, it was ornamented with signs or letters. From every country that he settled, Djemschid caused straight roads to be made in the direction of Babel.

Djemschid always led his people to uninhabited regions, where there were no nations to expel. He marched everywhere with perfect freedom, for he was only a founder, a settler. His race was of a bright reddish-yellow complexion like ochre, very handsome people. All were marked in order to distinguish the pure from those of mixed descent. Djemschid marched over a high mountain covered with ice. I do not remember how he succeeded in crossing, but many of his followers perished. They had horses or asses; Djemschid rode on a little striped animal. A change of climate had driven them from their country. It became too cold for them, but it is warmer there now. Occasionally he met on his march a helpless tribe either escaping from the tyranny of their chief, or awaiting in distress the advent of some leader. They willingly submitted to Djemschid, for he was gentle, and he brought them grain and blessings. They were destitute exiles who, like Job, had been plundered and banished. I saw some poor people who had no fire and who were obliged to bake their bread on hot stones in the sun. When Djemschid gave them fire, they looked upon him as a god. He fell in with another tribe that sacrificed children who were deformed or who did not reach their standard of beauty. The little ones were buried up to the waist, and a fire kindled around them. Djemschid abolished this custom. He delivered many poor children, whom he placed in a tent and confided to the care of some women. He afterward made use of them, here and there, as servants. He was very careful to keep the genealogical line pure.

Djemschid first marched in a southwesterly direction, keeping the Prophet Mountain to the south on his left; then he turned to the south, the mountain still on his left, but to the east. I think he afterward crossed the Caucasus. At that period, when those regions were swarming with human beings, when all was life and activity, our countries were but forests, wildernesses, and marshes; only off toward the east might be met a small, wandering tribe.

The Shining Star (Zoroaster), who lived long after, was descended from Djemschid's son, whose teachings he revived. Djemschid wrote all kinds of laws on bark and tables of stone. One long letter often stood for a whole sentence. Their language was as yet the primitive one, to which ours still bears some resemblance. Djemschid lived just prior to Derketo and her daughter, the mother of Semiramis. He did not go to Babel himself, though his career ran in that direction.

I saw the history of Hom and Djemschid as Jesus spoke of it before the pagan philosophers, at Lanifa in the isle of Cyprus. These philosophers had in Jesus's presence spoken of Djemschid as the most ancient of the wise kings who had come from far beyond India. With a golden dagger received from God, he had divided off and peopled many lands, and had scattered blessings everywhere. They questioned Jesus about him and the various wonders related to him. Jesus responded to their questions by saying that Djemschid was by nature a prudent man, a man wise according to flesh and blood; that he had been a leader of the nations; that upon the dispersion of men at the building of the Tower of Babel, he had led one race and settled countries according to a certain order; that there had been other leaders of that kind who had, indeed, led a worse life than he, because his race had not fallen into so great ignorance as many others. But Jesus showed them also what fables had been written about him and that he was a false side picture, a counterfeit type of the priest and king Melchizedek. He told them to notice the difference between Djemschid's race and that of Abraham. As the stream of nations moved along, God had sent Melchizedek to the best families, to lead and unite them, to prepare for them lands and abiding places, in order that they might preserve themselves unsullied and, in proportion to their degree of worthiness, be found more or less fit to receive the grace of the Promise. Who Melchizedek was, Jesus left to themselves to determine; but of one thing they might be certain, he was an ancient type of the future, but then fast approaching, fulfillment of the Promise. The sacrifice of bread and wine which he had offered would be fulfilled and perfected, and would continue till the end of time.

The Tower of Babel

THE BUILDING of the Tower of Babel was the work of pride. The builders aimed at constructing something according to their own ideas, and thus resist the guidance of God. When the children of Noah had become very numerous, the proudest and most experienced among them met to resolve upon the execution of some work so great and so strong as to be the wonder of all ages to come and cause the builders to be spoken of as the most skillful, the most powerful of men. They thought not of God, they sought only their own glory. Had it been otherwise, as I was distinctly told, God would have allowed their undertaking to succeed. The children of Shem took no active part in the work. They dwelt in a level country where palm trees and similar choice fruit grow. They were, however, obliged to contribute something toward the building, for they did not dwell so far distant at that period as they did later. The descendants of Ham and Japhet alone were engaged in the work; and because the Semites refused to join them, they called them a stupid race. The Semites were less numerous than the children of Ham and Japhet, and among them the family of Heber and the ancestors of Abraham studiously refrained from encouraging the enterprise. Upon Heber who, as we have said, took no part in the work, God cast his eyes; and amid the general disorder and corruption, he set him and his posterity apart as a holy nation. God gave him also a new and holy language possessed by no other nation, that thereby his race should be cut off from communication with all others. This language was the pure Hebrew, or Chaldaic. The first tongue, the mother tongue, spoken by Adam, Shem, and Noah, was different, and it is now extant only in isolated dialects. Its first pure offshoots are the Zend, the sacred tongue of India, and the language of the Bactrians. In those languages, words may be found exactly similar to the Low German of my native place. The book that I see in modern Ctesiphon, on the Tigris, is written in that language. Heber was still living at the time of Semiramis. His grandfather Arphaxad was the favorite son of Shem. He was a man of great judgment and full of profound wisdom. But a good deal of idolatrous worship and sorcery may have been handed down by him. The Magi derive their origin from him.

The Tower of Babel was built upon rising ground, about two leagues in circumference, around which lay an extensive plain covered with fields, gardens, and trees. To the foundations of the Tower, that is up to its first story, twenty-five very broad stone walks led from all sides of the plain. Twenty-five tribes were engaged in the building, and each tribe had its own road to the Tower. Off in the distance, where these roads began, each tribe had its own particular city that, in time of danger or attack, they might flee to the Tower for shelter. The Tower was intended likewise to serve as a temple for their idolatrous worship. The stone roads were, where they took their rise in the plain, tolerably far apart; but around the Tower, they lay so close that the intervening spaces were not greater than the breadth of a wide street. Before reaching the Tower, they were connected by cross arches, and between every two there opened a gateway about ten feet wide into its base.

When these gently inclined roads had reached a certain height, they were pierced by single arcades. Near the Tower the arcades were double, one above the other, so that through them one could make the circuit of the building, even around the lowest part, under all the roads. Above the arches that connected the inclined roads were walks, or streets, running horizontally around the Tower.

Those gently rising roads extended like the roots of a tree. They were designed in part as supporting counter-pillars to strengthen the foundation of the immense building, and partly as roads for the conveyance from all points of building materials and other loads to the first story of the Tower.

Between these extended bases were encampments upon substructures of stone. In many places the tops of the tents rose above the roads that ran through them. From every encampment, steps cut in the walls led up to the walks. One could go all around the Tower through the encampments and arches and under the stone roads.

Besides the occupants of the encampments, there were others who lived in the vaults and spaces on either side of the stone roads. In and around the whole building swarmed innumerable living beings. It was like a huge anthill. Countless elephants, asses, and camels toiled up and down the roads with their heavy burdens. Although these burdens were far broader than the animals themselves, yet several could with ease pass one another on the roads. On them were halting places for feeding and unloading the animals, also tents on the level spaces and even factories. I saw animals without a guide bearing their burdens up and down. The gateways in the basement of the Tower led into a labyrinth of halls, passages, and chambers. From this lower part of the Tower, one could mount by steps cut out on all sides. A spiral walk wound from the first story around the exterior of the polygonal building. The interior at this point consisted of cellars, immense and secure, covered chambers and passages.

The building was begun on all sides at once. All tended to one central point where at first stood a large encampment. They used tiles, also immense hewed stones, which they hauled to the site. The surface of the walks was quite white, and it glistened in the sun. At a distance, the sight it presented was wonderful. The Tower was planned most skillfully. I was told that it would have been finished and would now be standing as a magnificent monument of human skill, had it been erected to the honor of God. But the builders thought not of God. Their work was the offspring of presumption. The names of those that had contributed to the grandeur and magnificence of the building were inscribed with words of praise in the vaults and on the pillars; in the former by means of different colored stones, and on the latter in large characters. There were no kings, but only the heads of the different families, and they ruled according to common counsel. The stones employed in the building were skillfully wrought. They fitted into one another, held one another together. There were no raised figures on the building, but many parts of it were inlaid with colored stones, and here and there were figures hewn in niches. Canals and cisterns were constructed for water supplies. All lent a helping hand, even the women trod the clay with their feet. The men worked with breast and arms bare, the most distinguished wearing a little cap with a button. Even in very early times, women kept the head covered.

The building so increased in bulk and height that, on account of the shade it cast, it was quite cold on one side, while on the other the reflection of the sun's rays made it very hot. For thirty years, the work went on. They were at the second story. They had already encircled and walled in the interior with towerlike columns, had already recorded their names and races thereon in colored stones when the confusion broke forth. I saw one sent by God, Melchizedek, going around among the leaders and the masters of the building. He called upon them to account for their conduct, and he announced to them the chastisement of God. And now began the confusion. Many who had up to this time worked on peaceably, now boasted of their skill and the great services they had rendered in the undertaking. They formed parties, they laid claim to certain privileges. This occasioned contradictions, animosities, and rebellion. There were at first only two tribes among the disaffected and these, it was resolved, should be put down; but soon it was discovered that disunion existed among all. They struggled among themselves, they slew one another, they could no longer make themselves understood by one another, and so at last they separated and scattered over the whole earth. I saw Shem's race going farther southward where later on was Abraham's home. I saw one of Shem's race. He was a good man, but he did not follow his leader. On account of his wife, he preferred staying among the wicked ones of Babel he became the leader of the Samanenses, a race that always held themselves aloof from others. Under the cruel Semiramis, Melchizedek transplanted them to Palestine.

When in my childhood I had the vision of the building of the Tower, I used to reject it because I could not understand it. I had, of course, seen nothing like it, no buildings but our farmhouses whence the cows go out by the fireplace, and the city of Coesfeld. More than once I thought it must be heaven. But I had the vision again and again, and always in the same way I see it still, and I have also seen how it looked in Job's time.

One of the chief leaders in the Tower building was Nimrod. He was afterward honored as a deity under the name of Belus. He was the founder of the race that honored Derketo and Semiramis as goddesses. He built Babylon out of the stones of the Tower, and Semiramis greatly embellished it. He also laid the foundation of Nineveh, and built substructures of stones for tent dwellings. He was a great hunter and tyrant. At that period savage animals were very numerous, and they committed fearful ravages. The hunting expeditions fitted out against them were as grand as military expeditions. They who slew these wild animals, were honored as gods. Nimrod also drove men together and subdued them. He practiced idolatry, he was full of cruelty and witchcraft, and he had many descendants. He lived to be about two hundred and seventy years old. He was of sallow complexion, and from early youth he had led a wild life. He was an instrument of Satan and very much given to star worship. Of the numerous figures and pictures that he traced in the planets and constellations, and according to which he prophesied concerning the different nations and countries, he sought to reproduce representations, which he set up as gods. The Egyptians owe their Sphinx to him, as also their many-armed and many-headed idols. For seventy years, Nimrod busied himself with the histories of these idols, with ceremonial details relative to their worship and the sacrifices to be offered them, also with the forming of the pagan priesthood. By his diabolical wisdom and power, he had subjected the races that he led to the building of the Tower. When the confusion of tongues arose, many of those tribes broke away from him, and the wildest of them followed Mizraim into Egypt. Nimrod built Babylon, subjected the country around, and laid the foundation of the Babylonian Empire. Among his numerous children were Ninus and Derketo. The last-mentioned was honored as a goddess.

Derketo

FROM Derketo to Semiramis, I saw three generations of daughters. Derketo was a tall, powerful woman. I saw her clothed in skins with numerous straps and animals' tails hanging about her. Her head was covered by a cap made of the feathers of birds. I saw her with a great train of followers, male and female, sallying forth from the neighborhood of Babylon. She was constantly in vision, or engaged in prophesying, offering sacrifice, founding cities, or roving about. She and her followers drove before them scattered tribes with their herds, prophesied on the subject of good dwelling places, piled up stones some of which were immense, offered sacrifice, and practiced all kinds of wickedness. She drew all to herself. She was sometimes here, sometimes there. She was everywhere honored. She had in her old age a daughter, who played a part similar to her own. I saw this vision in a plain, by which was signified the origin of the abomination. Lastly, I saw Derketo as a frightful old woman in a city by the sea. She was again carrying on her sorcery by the seashore. She was in a state of diabolical ecstasy, and she was proclaiming to her people that she must die for them, give her life for them. She told them that she could remain with them no longer, but that she would be transformed into a fish and as such be always near them. She gave directions for the worship to be paid her and, in presence of the assembled multitude, plunged into the sea. Soon after a fish arose above the waves, and the people saluted it with sacrifices and abominations of all kinds. Their divinations were full of mysteries, signs, etc., connected with water. Through Derketo's instrumentality, an entire system of idolatry arose.

After Derketo, I saw another woman, the daughter of Derketo. She appeared to me on a low mountain, which signified that her position was more powerful than that of her mother. This was still in Nimrod's time, for they belonged to the same age. I saw this daughter leading a life even wilder and more violent than her mother's had been. She was engaged most of her time in hunting, attended by crowds of followers. She often went to a distance of three hundred miles, pursued wild animals, offered sacrifice, practiced witchcraft, and prophesied. In this way numerous places were founded and idolatrous worship established. I saw this woman fall into the sea while struggling with a hippopotamus.

Her daughter Semiramis I saw upon a lofty mountain surrounded by all the kingdoms and treasures of the world, as if Satan were showing them to her, giving them to her. I saw that Semiramis put the finishing touch to every abomination of the Babylonian race.

In the earliest times power over others was held more peaceably and was vested in many; later on unlimited jurisdiction was possessed by single individuals. These latter then became the leaders, the gods of their followers, and they formulated various systems of idolatrous worship, each according to his own ideas. They could also perform wonders of skill, valor, and invention, for they were full of the spirit of darkness. Thence arose whole tribes, first rulers and priests combined, later of priests alone. I have seen that, in those days, women of this stamp were more numerous than men. They were all in interior communication, connected with one another by feelings, thoughts, and influence. Many things narrated of them are imperfect recitals of their ecstatic, or mesmeric expressions relative to themselves, their origin, their doings uttered sometimes by themselves, at others by their devilish clairvoyants. The Jews also had many secret arts in Egypt. But Moses, the seer of God, rooted them out. Among the rabbis, however, many such things existed as points of learning. Later on these secret arts became low, vulgar practices among wandering tribes, and they still exist in witchcraft and superstition. But they have all sprung from the same tree of corruption, from the same low kingdom of darkness. I see the visions of all that engage in such practices either just above or entirely under the earth. There is an element of the same in magnetism.

Water was held specially sacred by those early idolaters. It entered into all their service. Whether divinations or ecstasies, they always began by gazing into water. They had ponds consecrated to that purpose. After some time, their ecstatic state became habitual, and even without the aid of water they had their evil visions. I have seen the way in which they had those visions and it was indeed singular. The whole earth with all that it contains seemed to be once more under water, but veiled as in a dark sphere. Tree stood under tree, mountain under mountain, water under water. I saw that those enchantresses beheld all that was going on: wars, nations, perils, etc., just as is done at the present day, only with this difference that the former put what they saw into effect, made good what they saw. Here was a nation to be subdued, here one to be taken by surprise, there a city to be built. Here were famous men and women, and there was the plan by which they might be outwitted; in fine, every item of their diabolical worship was seen before reduced to practice by those females. Derketo saw in vision that she should cast herself into the sea and be transformed into a fish, and what she saw, she hesitated not to carry into effect. Even the abominations practiced in their worship were all mirrored in the water before they put them into execution.

In the age in which Derketo's daughter lived, dykes and roads began to be constructed. She raided down into Egypt itself. Her whole life was one series of movings and hunting expeditions. Her adherents belonged to the tribe that had plundered Job in Arabia. The diabolical worship of Derketo's people became systematized first in Egypt. Here it took such hold that, while the witches sat in the temples and in chambers on strange-looking seats before various kinds of mirrors, their visions, communicated while actually seen, were reported by the priests to hundreds of men who engraved them upon the stone walls of caverns.

Strange that I should see all those abominable chief instruments of darkness always in unconscious communion with one another! I saw similar actions and things going on in different places among similar instruments of the evil one. The only difference among them was that which arose from the diversity of manners and customs among the several nations and the different degrees of depravity into which they had fallen. Some had not as yet sunk so deep in these abominations, and were not so far removed from the truth; those, for instance, from whom the family of Abraham and the races of Job and the three kings sprang, as also the star worshippers of Chaldea, and they that had the Shining Star (Zoroaster).

When Jesus Christ came upon earth, when the earth was soaked with his blood, the fierce influence of such practices was considerably diminished, and witchcraft lost much of its power. Moses was a seer from his cradle, but he was according to God and he always practiced what he saw.

Derketo, her daughter, and her granddaughter Semiramis lived to be very old, according to the general age of that time. They were tall, powerful, mighty, such as would almost frighten us in our day. They were inconceivably bold, fierce, shameless, and they carried out with astonishing assurance whatever the evil one had shown them in vision. They felt their own power, they thought themselves divinities; they were facsimiles of those furious sorcerers on the high mountain that perished in the Deluge.

It is touching to see how the holy patriarchs, although they had frequent revelations from God, had nevertheless to suffer and to struggle unremittingly in order to keep clear of the abominations that surrounded them. And again, it is affecting to remember in what secret, what painful ways salvation at last came upon earth, while all went well with demonolatry, while all things were made to subserve its interests.

When I saw all this, the immense influence exercised by those goddesses and the high worship they received over all the earth; and, on the other side, when I contemplated Mary's little band with whose symbolical picture in the cloud of Elijah the philosophers of Cyprus sought to couple their lying abominations; when I saw Jesus, the fulfillment of all promises, poor and patient, standing before them teaching and afterward going to meet his cross—ah, that made me inexpressibly sad! But after all, this is the history of the truth and the light ever shining in the darkness, and the darkness not comprehending it. And so it has been and so it is still, the same old story even down to our own day.

But the mercy of God is infinite. I have seen that at the time of the Deluge, many, very many were saved from eternal punishment. Fright and anguish converted them to God. They went to purgatory, and Jesus freed them on his descent into hell.

Numbers of trees escaped being uprooted by the waters of the Deluge. I saw them thriving again, but most of them were covered, choked up by mud.

Semiramis

THE MOTHER of Semiramis was born in the region of Nineveh. Outwardly demure, in secret she was cruel and dissolute. The father of Semiramis was a native of Syria and, like her mother, sunk in the most detestable idolatry. He was put to death after the child's birth, his murder being in some way connected with, or in consequence of, their divinations. Semiramis was born far away at Ascalon, in Palestine, and then taken by pagan priests to some shepherds in a wilderness. She spent much of her time during her childhood alone on a mountain. I saw her mother and the pagan priests turning aside, when on their hunting expeditions, to visit her. I saw too the devil under various forms playing with her, like John in the desert going around with angels. I saw near her birds of brilliant plumage. They brought her all kinds of curious toys. I do not remember all that went on connected with her, but it was the most horrible idolatry. She was beautiful, full of intelligence and seductive arts, and everything succeeded with her. In obedience to certain divinations, she became the wife of one of the chief shepherds of the king of Babylon, and later on she married the king himself. This king had conquered a nation far to the north, and had dragged a part of them to his own country as slaves. Some time after when Semiramis reigned alone, many of them were oppressed by her and forced to labor at her extravagant buildings. Semiramis was looked upon as a goddess by her nation.

The hunting expeditions carried on by Semiramis's mother were wilder than those which she herself conducted. She, the mother, went about with a little army mounted on camels, striped asses, and horses. Once I saw them in Arabia toward the Red Sea, on a great hunt, at the time when Job dwelt in his city there. The huntresses were very dexterous, and they sat on horseback like men. They were fully clothed to the knee, below which the limbs were laced with straps. On the feet they wore soles with two high heels upon which were colored figures. They wore short, closely fitting jackets made of fine feathers of the most diverse hues and patterns. Crossed over the arms and breast were straps trimmed with feathers. The shoulders were covered with a cape, likewise of feathers, and set with glittering stones and pearls. On the head, they wore a kind of hat of red silk or wool. Over the face fell a veil in two halves, either of which could be used as a protection from wind and dust. A short mantle completed their costume. Their hunting weapons consisted of spears, bows, and arrows; at their side hung a shield. The savage animals had multiplied astonishingly. The hunters drove them together from all parts of immense districts and slew them. They also dug pits and covered them as snares. When the beasts fell into them, they were soon dispatched with hatchets and clubs. I saw the mother of Semiramis hunting the animal described by Job under the name of behemoth, also tigers, lions, etc. I saw no monkeys in those early times. I saw similar hunts upon the water, upon which idolatry and numerous abominations were generally practiced. The mother was outwardly not so dissolute as Semiramis, but she possessed a diabolical nature with amazing strength and temerity. What a frightful thing, to plunge into the sea in her struggle with that mighty monster! Mounted on a dromedary, she pursued the animal, until dromedary and rider plunged into the waves. She was honored as the goddess of the chase and a benefactress to humankind.

Semiramis returning home from Africa after one of her hunting or military expeditions, went to Egypt. This kingdom had been founded by Mizraim, the grandson of Ham, who at his coming had found there already several scattered tribes of degenerate neighboring races. Egypt was peopled by several races, and ruled sometimes by one, sometimes by another. When Semiramis went to Egypt four cities were in existence. The oldest was Thebes, where a lighter, a more slender, and agile race lived than in the city of Memphis, whose inhabitants were short and thickset. It lay upon the left bank of the Nile, over which was a long bridge. On the right bank was the place where in Moses's time Pharaoh's daughter lived. The darker inhabitants with woolly hair were even in those first ages slaves, and they had never ruled in Egypt. They that first went thither and built Thebes came, I think, from Africa; the others from over the Red Sea and from where the Israelites entered. A third city was called Chume, later Heliopolis. It lies toward the north below Thebes.

When Mary and Joseph fled to Egypt with Jesus, I saw extraordinarily large buildings still around this city. Lower down than Memphis, not very far from the sea, lay the city of Saïs. I think it is still older than Memphis. Each of these four cities had its own king.

Semiramis was very highly honored in Egypt where, by her intrigues and diabolical arts, she greatly contributed to the spread of idolatry. I saw her in Memphis, where human sacrifices were common, plotting and practicing magic and astrology. I did not at this period see the bull Apis, but I saw idols with tails and a head like the sun. It was Semiramis who here planned the first pyramid; it was built on the eastern bank of the Nile, not far from Memphis. The whole nation had to assist at its construction. When it was completed, I saw Semiramis again journeying thither with about two hundred followers. It was for the consecration of the building. Semiramis was honored almost as a divinity.

The pyramid happened to be constructed on marshy ground; consequently a foundation of stupendous pillars was built for it. It was like an immense broad bridge. The pyramid was raised upon it. One could go around under it, as if into an immense temple formed of columns. It was divided off into innumerable rooms, dungeons, and spacious halls. The pyramid itself up to the very summit also contained numerous apartments, large and small, with openings like windows from which I saw flags of cloth hanging and waving. All around the pyramid were baths and gardens. This building was the real center of Egyptian idolatry, astrology, witchcraft, and abominable impurity. Here children and the aged were offered in sacrifice. Astrologers and necromancers dwelt in the pyramid and there had their diabolical visions. Near the baths was immense machinery for purifying the muddy waters of the Nile. The baths witnessed the most infamous horrors of idol worship. I saw later on Egyptian women practicing the greatest abominations in them. This pyramid did not long exist; it was destroyed.

The nation was frightfully superstitious. The pagan priests were in darkness so great and so given to divination that in Heliopolis even the dreams of the people were collected, recorded, and referred to the stars. Numerous mesmerists arose who, in their diabolical visions, confounded truth with falsehood. According to their visions, idolatry was formulated, and even the cycles of time computed. I saw that the idols Isis and Osiris were no other than Joseph and Asenath whose coming into Egypt the astrologers foresaw in their demoniacal visions. They consequently incorporated them into their religion. When they did come, they were honored as divinities. I saw that Asenath wept over such impiety, and wrote against it.

The scholars of the present day who write about Egypt are in gross error. They accept so many things concerning the Egyptians as history, science, and learning, which nevertheless have no other foundation than astrology and false visions. That any nation could remain as stupid and beastly as the Egyptians is a proof of it. But these savants reject such demoniacal inspirations and practices as impossible. They esteem the Egyptians more ancient than they really are, because in those early times they appear to have possessed such knowledge of abstruse and hidden things.

But I saw that, even at the coming of Semiramis to Memphis, these people in their pride had designedly confused their calendar. Their ambition was to take precedence of all other nations in point of time. With this end in view they drew up a number of complicated calendars and royal genealogical tables. By this and frequent changes in their computations, order and true chronology were lost. That this confusion might be firmly established, they perpetuated every error by inscriptions and the erection of great buildings. For a long time they reckoned the ages of father and son, as if the date of the former's demise were that of the latter's birth. The kings, who waged constant war with the priests on the subject of chronology, inserted among their forefathers the names of persons that never existed. Thus the four kings of the same name who reigned simultaneously in Thebes, Heliopolis, Memphis, and Saïs, were in accordance with this design, reckoned one after the other. I saw too that once they reckoned nine hundred and seventy days to a year, and again, years were computed as months. I saw a pagan priest drawing up a chronological table in which for every five hundred years, eleven hundred were set down.

I saw these false computations of the pagan priests at the same time that I beheld Jesus teaching on the sabbath at Aruma. Jesus, speaking before the Pharisees of the Call of Abraham and his sojourn in Egypt, exposed the errors of the Egyptian calendar. He told them that the world had now existed 4028 years. When I heard Jesus say this, he was himself thirty-one years old.

I saw in those times, also, a people who honored Seth as a god. They made distant and perilous journeys into Arabia where they supposed his grave to be. It seems to me that the descendants of this people are still in existence, and that the Turks suffer them to pass freely through their territory on their pilgrimages to that grave.

Melchizedek

I HAVE often seen Melchizedek, but never as a human being. I have always seen him as a being of another nature, as an angel, as one sent by God. I have never at any time seen any determinate dwelling place, any home, any family, any associates connected with him. I never saw him eating, drinking, or sleeping, and never did the thought occur to me that he was a mortal. He was clothed as no priest at the time on the earth, but like the angels in the Heavenly Jerusalem. His robes were such as Moses, upon the command of God, afterward ordained the priestly vestments should be. I have seen Melchizedek appearing here and there, interposing and legislating the affairs of nations; as, for instance, at the celebration of victories after war, at that time waged with such cruelty.

Wherever he appeared, wherever he was, he exercised an irresistible influence by his mere presence. No one opposed him, and yet he never resorted to harsh measures; even the idolaters cheerfully accepted his decisions and acted upon his advice. He had no companion of his own nature; he was entirely alone. Sometimes he had two hired couriers. They were clothed in short white garments, and they ran on before him to announce his coming. He dismissed them when their mission was over. All that he needed, he had without trouble of acquiring. They from whom he received anything could always spare what they gave. They bestowed it upon him with joy. They regarded him with reverential fear, but esteemed themselves happy to be in his company. Although the wicked found fault with him, yet they humbled themselves in his presence. Melchizedek, that being of a higher order, was regarded by the great ones of the pagan world, those sensuous, godless men, in much the same light that an extraordinarily holy man would be looked upon at the present day, if he suddenly appeared amongst us as a stranger doing good to all around.

Thus I saw Melchizedek at the court of Semiramis in Babylon, where she reigned with indescribable grandeur and magnificence. She caused immense buildings to be erected by her slaves, whom she oppressed far more severely than did Pharaoh the children of Jacob in Egypt. The most horrible idolatry was practiced among the Babylonians. Human victims were buried up to the neck in the earth, and thus offered in sacrifice. It is hardly credible to what a degree all kinds of luxury, magnificence, opulence, and the arts were carried. Semiramis also waged great wars; her armies were composed of countless warriors. But these wars were almost always against nations off toward the east. She went not much westward. The nations toward the north were dark and sinister-looking people.

As time went on, there arose in the kingdom of Semiramis a numerous people of the Semitic race. After the building of the Tower, their ancestors had remained in Babylon. They lived as a little pastoral tribe under tents, raised cattle, and celebrated their religious ceremonies by night, either in an open tent or under the starry sky. Many blessings attended them, they were prosperous in all things, and their cattle were always remarkably fine. Semiramis, the diabolical woman, resolved to exterminate this tribe and she had already destroyed a great many belonging to it. She knew from the blessing attending them that God had merciful designs over them; therefore would she, as an instrument of the devil, oppress them. When the distress of these people was at its height, Melchizedek appeared. He went to Semiramis, demanded permission for them to depart, and rebuked her for her cruelty. Semiramis yielded to his desires, and he led them in different bands toward Palestine. Melchizedek dwelt in a tent near Babylon, and here he broke that bread to the good people from which they received strength to depart. He pointed out to them, here and there in Canaan, places suitable for settlements, and they received from him lands of various quality. He divided them off according to their purity in order that they should not mix with others. Their name sounded like Samanen, or Semanen. Melchizedek pointed out to some of them as suitable for a settlement the region which was afterward the site of the Dead Sea, but their city was destroyed with Sodom and Gomorrha.

Semiramis received Melchizedek with great reverence. She secretly dreaded him on account of his wisdom. He appeared before her as the king of the Morning Star, that is of the most distant eastern land. She fancied that he might perhaps woo her for his bride. But he spoke to her sternly, reproached her with her cruelty, and foretold to her the destruction of her pyramid at Memphis. Semiramis grew speechless from terror, and I saw the punishment that fell upon her. She became like a beast. She was for a long time penned up, and they cast to her in derision grass and straw in a manger; only one servant was faithful to her and furnished her with food. She was freed from the chastisement, but she carried on her disorders anew. She came at last to a frightful end, her intestines being torn from her body. She was aged one hundred and seventeen years.

Melchizedek came to be regarded as a prophet, as a teacher, as a being from a higher sphere, with whom all things succeeded. There were at that time, as also later, many such apparitions of beings of a higher order. They were to the people of that age as familiar as were the angels in Abraham's time. But diabolical apparitions also were frequent, in the same way as false prophets rose up by the side of the true. The departure of the Semitic race from Babylon bears some analogy to that of the Israelites from Egypt, although the former were by no means so numerous as the latter.

Of the Samanenses whom Melchizedek settled in Palestine, I saw long before the coming of Abraham three men on the so-called Bread Mountain, in the neighborhood of Tabor. They lived in caves. They were of a browner complexion than Abraham, and were clothed in skins. They bound a great leaf on their head to protect them from the sun. Their life, modeled on that of Enoch, was a holy one. Their religion was simple, though full of mysterious signification, and they had visions and revelations which they easily interpreted. Their religion taught that God would unite himself with man and for that union they must prepare in every possible way. They also offered sacrifice. A third part of their daily allowance they exposed to the sun, either to be consumed by it or, perhaps, for the benefit of other needy creatures. That the latter was the case, I also saw. These people lived quite solitary, apart from the rest of the inhabitants of the country. The latter were not yet numerous and lived scattered, here and there, in abodes built in the style of fortified tent cities. I saw those three men going through the country digging wells, cutting down forests, and laying the foundations of subsequent cities. I saw them driving the evil spirits from the air around whole regions and banishing them to other places, to poor, swampy, foggy districts. I saw again that the wicked spirits prefer such wretched abodes. I often saw these men wrestling with them. At first, I wondered how cities could arise where they laid stones, which so soon became overgrown, and then I had another vision in which I was shown a number of places built on these sites; for instance, Saphat, Bethsaida, Nazareth (where those three men worked on the spot upon which afterward stood the house in which the angel delivered the message to Mary); Gath-Hepher, Sepphoris (in the region near Nazareth, where Anne's house afterward stood); Megiddo, Nain, Ainon, the caves of Bethlehem and Hebron. I also saw them founding Michmethath and many other places that I have now forgotten.

I saw them every month assembling on this mountain where Melchizedek broke a large four-cornered loaf (three feet square, perhaps, and tolerably thick) into numerous little pieces which he divided among them. The loaf was of a brownish color and had been baked in the ashes. I saw that Melchizedek always went to them without a companion. Sometimes he bore the loaf quite lightly, as if it merely floated above his hand; and again when he drew near to the mountain, I saw it as a weight upon his shoulders. I think he took this precaution on approaching them that they might look upon him as merely a man. Still they met him with great reverence, prostrating before him. He taught them how to plant vines on Tabor. He also gave them all kinds of seeds, which they scattered in many parts of the country and which now grow wild there. I saw these people every day cutting a piece off the loaf with the brown spades they used at work. They also ate birds, which flew toward them in great numbers. They had festival days, and they were familiar with the stars. They celebrated the eighth day with prayer and sacrifice, also some days in the course of the year. I saw them also making numerous roads through the still wild country to the places where they had laid foundations, dug wells, and sowed seed. This they did that the people coming after them might, by following these roads, make settlements near the wells and fertile places prepared for them. I saw these three men often surrounded while at work by crowds of evil spirits, whom they could see. I saw these spirits, by prayer and the word of command, banished to swampy wastes. They departed instantly, and the men went quietly on with their work, clearing and purifying.

They made roads to Cana, Megiddo, and Nain, and in this way they prepared the birthplace of most of the prophets. They laid the foundations of Abel-Mehola and Dothan, and dug out the beautiful baths at Bethulia. Melchizedek still scoured the country alone and as a stranger; no one knew where he lived.

The three Samanenses were old, but still very active. On the site of the Dead Sea and in Judea, cities already existed. There were some also further north but none as yet in the central regions.

The Samanenses dug their own graves and sometimes stretched themselves in them; one made his near Hebron, another on Tabor, and the third in the caves not far from Saphet. They were, in a certain sense, for Abraham what John was for Jesus. They purified the country, they prepared the land and the ways, they sowed good fruit, and they brought water for the leader of God's people. But John prepared the heart for penance and for a second birth in Jesus Christ. The Samanenses did for Israel what John did for the church. I have seen such men in other places also, where they had been introduced by Melchizedek.

I often saw Melchizedek as he appeared in Palestine long before the time of Semiramis and Abraham, when the country was still a wilderness. He seemed to be laying it out, marking off and preparing certain districts. I saw him entirely alone, and I thought: What is this man doing here so early? There is not a human being in this place! I saw him near a mountain, boring a well. It was the source of the Jordan. He had a long fine instrument which, like a ray of light, pierced the mountainside. I saw him in the same way opening fountains in different parts of the earth. In those early times, that is, before the Deluge, I never saw the rivers gushing forth and flowing as they do now, but I saw volumes of water pouring down from a high mountain in the east.

Melchizedek took possession of many parts of Palestine by marking them off. He measured off the site for the pool of Bethesda, and long before Jerusalem existed he laid a stone where the temple was to stand. I saw him planting in the bed of the Jordan the twelve precious stones upon which the priests stood with the Ark of the Covenant at the departure of the children of Israel. He planted them like seeds, and they increased in size.

I always saw Melchizedek alone, save when he had to busy himself with the uniting, the separating, or the guiding of nations and families.

I saw that Melchizedek built a castle at Salem. But it was rather a tent with galleries and steps around it, like the castle of Mensor, in Arabia. The foundation alone was solid, for it was of stone. I think the four corners where the principal posts stood were still to be seen even in John's time. It had only a very strong foundation of stone, which looked like a fortification overrun with verdure. John had there his little hut of rushes.

That tent castle was a resort for strangers and travelers, a kind of safe and convenient inn near the pleasant waters. Perhaps Melchizedek, whom I have always seen as the guide and counselor of the still unsettled races and nations, kept this castle as a place in which to harbor and instruct them. But even at that time, it bore some reference to baptism.

This was Melchizedek's central point. From it he started on his journeys to lay out Jerusalem, to visit Abraham, and to go elsewhere. Here also he gathered together and distributed families and peoples, who settled in various places. All this took place previously to the offering of bread and wine which, I think, was made in a valley south of Jerusalem. Melchizedek built Salem before he built Jerusalem. Wherever he labored and constructed, he seemed to be laying the foundation of a future grace, to be drawing attention to that particular place, to be beginning something that would be perfected in the future.

Melchizedek belongs to the choir of angels that are set over countries and nations, that brought messages to Abraham and the other patriarchs. They stand opposite the archangels Michael, Gabriel, and Raphael.

Job

THE FATHER of Job, a great leader of the nations, was brother to Peleg, the son of Heber. Shortly before his time occurred the dispersion of men at the building of the Babylonian Tower. Job was the youngest of thirteen sons. They dwelt north of the Black Sea near a mountain chain which was warm on one side, and on the other cold and covered with ice. Job was forefather of Abraham. Abraham's mother was a great granddaughter of Job, who had married into the family of Heber. Job may have still been alive at the time of Abraham's birth. He dwelt in different places, and his afflictions came upon him in three different abodes. Between the first and the second, there intervened a period of nine years' prosperity; between the second and the third, seven years; and after the third, twelve years. His sufferings always befell him in a different dwelling place. But he never was so absolutely ruined as to have nothing left; he merely became quite poor when compared with his former circumstances. He always had enough left to pay all his debts.

Job could not remain in his parents' house. His ideas and inclinations did not accord with theirs. Job adored in nature the one only God, especially in the stars and in the change from day to night. He spoke frequently of God's wonderful works, and offered to him a worship purer than that of those around him. He moved with his followers northward from the Caucasus to a very miserable swampy region. I think it is now inhabited by a nation distinguished by their flat noses, high cheekbones, and small eyes. Here Job first settled, and things went well with him. He gathered around him all kinds of poor, abandoned creatures who dwelt in caves and bushes, and who lived exclusively upon the raw flesh of birds and animals taken in hunting. Job was the first who taught them how to cook their food. With their help he dug up and cultivated the land. He and his people wore at that time but little clothing and they dwelt in tents. Job soon found himself the owner of immense herds in this place, among them numerous striped asses and spotted animals. Once three sons were born to him at one birth, and three daughters at another. He had as yet no city here, but went around among his fields which extended to a distance of seven leagues. No grain was cultivated in those marshy districts; but they raised a large sedge, which grows also in water, and whose pith was eaten either boiled or roasted. They dried their meat in holes dug in the earth, and exposed to the sun, until Job taught them how to cook it. They planted many species of gourds for food.

Job was unspeakably gentle, affable, just, and benevolent. He assisted all in need. He was, too, exceedingly pure and very familiar with God, who communicated with him through an angel, or "a white man," as the people of that period expressed it. These angelic apparitions were like radiant, but beardless, youths in long white garments that fell in heavy folds or strips around them, I could not distinguish which. They were girded, and they took food and drink. God consoled Job during his sufferings by means of these apparitions, and they passed sentence on his friends, his nephews, and his other relatives. He did not, like the nations around him, worship idols. They made for themselves images of all kinds of animals and adored them. But Job fabricated for himself a representation of the Almighty God, the figure of a child crowned with rays. The hands were held one above the other, and in one was a globe upon which was depicted a little vessel riding on the waves. I think it was to represent the Deluge of which, as well as of the wisdom and mercy of God, Job often spoke to his two confidential servants. The figure was portable and shone like metal. Job prayed before it, and burned grain before it as a sacrifice. The smoke arose from the top of it as through a funnel.

It was in this place that Job's first affliction befell him. The time that intervened between the different misfortunes recorded of him, was not for him a time of peace. He always had to combat and struggle against the wicked races by whom he was surrounded. After his first affliction, he removed further up the mountain range, the Caucasus, where he again began anew and where prosperity again followed him. He and his followers now began to clothe themselves less scantily, and their mode of life exhibited more refinement.

From this, his second dwelling place, Job went, accompanied by a numerous train of followers, to Egypt where at that time strangers called shepherd kings, and who were from his own native land, governed a part of the country. These shepherd kings were afterward expelled by an Egyptian monarch. Job's mission to Egypt was to conduct thither one of his own relatives, who was to be the bride of one of the shepherd kings. He took with him rich presents, about thirty camels, and many servants. When I saw him in Egypt, Job was a large, powerful man of agreeable appearance; he had a yellowish-brown complexion and reddish hair. Abraham was fairer. The Egyptians were of an earthy brown. Job was not contented in Egypt. I used to see him looking back longingly toward the east, toward his fatherland which lay more to the south than the most distant country of the three kings. I heard him complaining bitterly to his servants, telling them that he would rather live with wild beasts than with the people of Egypt. The horrible idolatry that everywhere prevailed in that country afflicted him. The Egyptians worshipped a frightful idol with an upraised head, like that of an ox, and broad open jaws. They heated it intensely, and laid living children as offerings on its glowing arms.

The shepherd king, for whose son Job conducted the bride into Egypt, would fain have kept him there, and he assigned to him Matarea as a dwelling place. The region was at that time very different from what it was at a later period when the holy family sojourned there. Still I saw that Job dwelt on the spot afterward occupied by them, and that the Fountain of Mary was already shown him by God. When Mary discovered this well, it was already lined with stone, though still covered over. Job used the stone by the well for religious worship. By prayer he freed the country around his dwelling place from wild and venomous animals. Visions referring to man's salvation were vouchsafed him here, and he saw, too, the trials in store for him. With burning zeal he exclaimed against the infamous practices of the Egyptians and their human sacrifices. I think these latter were in consequence abolished.

When Job had returned to his native country, his second misfortune overtook him; and when, after twelve years of peace, the third came upon him, he was living more toward the south and directly eastward from Jericho. I think this country had been given to him after his second calamity, because he was everywhere greatly revered and loved for his admirable justice, his knowledge, and his fear of God. This country was a level plain, and here Job began anew. On a height, which was very fertile, noble animals of various kinds were running around, also wild camels. They caught them in the same way as we do the wild horses on the heath.

Job settled on this height. Here he prospered, became very rich, and built a city. The foundations were of stone; the dwellings were tents. It was during this period of great prosperity that his third calamity, his grievous distemper, overtook him. After enduring this affliction with great wisdom and patience, he entirely recovered, and again became the father of many sons and daughters. I think Job did not die till long after, when another nation intruded itself into the country.

Although in the Book of Job this narrative is given very differently, yet many of Job's own words are therein recorded. I think I could distinguish them all. Where the story says that the servants came quickly one after another to Job with news of his losses, it must be remarked that the words: "And as he still spoke of it," signify, "And while the last calamity was not yet effaced from the mind of men," etc.

That Satan appeared before God with the sons of God and brought an action against Job, is told in this way only for the sake of brevity. There was at that time much communication between the evil spirits and idolaters to whom they appeared in angelic form. In this way, Satan incited his wicked neighbors against Job, and they calumniated him. They said that he did not serve God properly, that he had a superfluity of possessions, and that it was very easy for him to be good. Then God resolved to show that afflictions are often only trials, etc.

The friends who spoke around Job symbolized the reflections of his kinsmen upon his fate. But Job longingly awaited the Savior, and he was one of the ancestors of the race of David. He was to Abraham, through the mother of the latter (who was one of his descendants), what the ancestors of Anne were to Mary.

The history of Job, together with his dialogues with God, was circumstantially written down by two of his most trusty servants who seemed to be his stewards. They wrote upon bark, and from Job's own dictation. These two servants were named respectively Hay and Uis, or Ois. These narratives were held very sacred by Job's descendants. They passed from generation to generation down to Abraham. In the school of Rebecca, the Canaanites were instructed in them on account of the lessons of submission under trials from God that they inculcated.

Through Jacob and Joseph, they descended to the children of Israel in Egypt. Moses collected and arranged them differently for the use of the Israelites during their servitude in Egypt and their painful wanderings in the wilderness; for they contained many details that might not have been understood, and which would have been of no service in his time. But Solomon again entirely remodelled them, omitting many things and inserting many others of his own. And so, this once authentic history became a sacred book made up of the wisdom of Job, Moses, and Solomon. One can now only with difficulty trace the particular history of Job, for the names of cities and nations were assimilated to those of the land of Canaan, on which account Job came to be regarded as an Edomite.

Abraham

ABRAHAM and his forefathers belonged to a very peculiar type of a mighty race. They led a pastoral life. They were not really natives of Ur, in Chaldea, but they had removed there. They exercised special authority and jurisdiction. Here and there, they took possession of certain regions where good pasturage was found. They marked off the boundaries, erected an altar of stones, and the land thus enclosed became their property. Something happened to Abraham in his early childhood similar to that which occurred to the child Moses by which his nurse saved his life. It had been prophesied to the ruler of the country that a wonderful child would be born whose birth would be very fatal to his interests. The ruler took measures accordingly, on which account Abraham's mother concealed herself before his birth in the same cave in which Seth had been hidden by Eve. There Abraham was born, and there secretly reared by his nurse, Maraha. She passed for a poor slave who worked in the wilderness. Her hut was near this cave, which was named after her the Milk Cave. She was, after her death and in accordance with her own request, buried there by Abraham.

Abraham was a remarkably large child. When, on account of his unusual size, he was of an age to pass for a child born before the prophecy alluded to, his parents took him home. But his precocious wisdom exposed him to danger, so the nurse fled with him, and again concealed him a long time in the same cave. Many children of his age were massacred at that time. Abraham tenderly loved Maraha, his nurse. In after years, in all his wanderings he took her with him on a camel. She also dwelt with him at Succoth. She died at the age of one hundred years. Abraham hewed out a tomb for her in the white stone which, like a hill, enclosed the cave in which he was born. The cave became a place of devotion, especially for mothers. Throughout the whole of this history, we discover a mysterious prefiguring of the early persecutions which Mary with the child Jesus had to endure. It was, too, in this same cave that they hid from Herod's soldiers when they sought the child.

The father of Abraham received great graces from heaven, and understood many mysteries. His race possessed the gift of discovering gold in the earth, and he fab-ricated out of it little idols similar to those that Rachel purloined from Laban. Ur is a place in the north of Chaldea. I perceived in many parts of this region, on mountains and plains, white flames arising, as if the ground were on fire. I know not whether this fire was spontaneous or kindled by man.

Abraham was a great astronomer. He understood the properties of things, and the influence of the stars upon birth. He saw all kinds of things in the stars, but he turned all to God. He followed God in all things and served him alone. He imparted his knowledge to others in Chaldea, but he traced all back to God.

I saw that in a vision he received from God the order to depart from his own country. God showed him another land, and Abraham next morning, without asking any questions, led forth all his people and departed. I afterward saw him pitching his tent in a region of Palestine which seemed to me to lie around the place where Nazareth subsequently stood. Abraham himself erected here an oblong altar of stone with a tent over it. Once when kneeling before the altar, a light descended from heaven upon him. An angel, a messenger from God, appeared, said something to him, and presented to him a shining, transparent gift. The angel spoke with Abraham, and the latter received the mysterious Blessing, the holy thing from heaven; he opened his garment and laid it upon his breast. I was told that this was the sacrament of the Old Testament. Abraham, as yet, knew not what it contained. It was hidden from him, as from us is concealed the substance of the most holy Sacrament. But it was given to him as a sacred thing, as a pledge of the promised posterity. The angel was exactly of the same kind as the one that announced to the blessed Virgin the conception of the Messiah. He was also as gentle and tranquil as Gabriel in the execution of his commission, not so hasty and rapid as I see other angels under similar circumstances. I think Abraham always carried the mysterious gift about with him. The angel spoke to him of Melchizedek who was to celebrate before him the sacrifice which, after the coming of the Messiah, would be accomplished, and which should be continued forever.

Abraham then took from a casket five large bones which he laid upon the altar in the form of a cross. A light burned before it, and he offered sacrifice. The fire burned like a star, the center white and the rays red.

I also saw Abraham with Sarah in Egypt. He went thither in obedience to a command from God; first, on account of the famine; and, secondly, to take possession of a treasure which had been carried there by one of Sarah's relatives. The treasure consisted of triangular pieces of gold strung together to form a genealogical table of the children of Noah, and especially of Shem down to Abraham's own time. It had been taken into Egypt by a daughter of Sarah's maternal aunt, who had gone thither with a pastoral tribe, some of Job's lateral descendants, who afterward degenerated into a wild state. She had there hired herself as a servant. She had stolen that treasure as later on

Abraham's Oak, Hebron

Rachel did the gods of Laban. The genealogical table was made like the scales of a balance hanging on cords. The latter consisted of small triangular pieces strung together, and from them depended single collateral strings. On the gold pieces were figures and letters denoting Noah's, and especially Shem's, descendants. When the cords were let down, the various pieces all lay together in the dish. I heard, but I have forgotten, the number of shekels (so the sum is called) to which the whole amounted. This family register had fallen into the hands of Pharaoh and the priests. They made on it various reckonings connected with their own unending chronological calculations, but they never rightly understood it.

When Pharaoh was visited by heavy afflictions he consulted with his idolatrous priests, and granted to Abraham all he demanded.

Upon Abraham's return to Palestine, I saw Lot by him in a tent. Abraham was pointing all around with his hand. In his bearing there was something of the deportment of the three kings. He wore a long white, woolen garment with sleeves; a plaited white girdle with tassels; and a sort of cowl hanging down the back. On his head was a small cap, and upon his breast a shield in the shape of a heart made of metal or precious stones. His beard was long. I have no words to say how kind and generous Abraham was. If he had anything that pleased another, especially if it were cattle, he offered it to him at once, for he was a declared enemy to envy and covetousness. Lot's clothing was almost like that of Abraham, but he was not so tall, nor so noble-looking. He was indeed good, but at the same time a little covetous. I often saw the servants of the two disputing, and I saw Lot separating from Abraham. But as he went, I saw him enveloped in fog. Over Abraham, I saw light. I saw him take down his tents and wander about. He built an altar of field stones, and raised a tent over it. The people of that time were skillful in building out of rough stones, and the master with the servant put his hand to the work. The altar just mentioned was in the region of Hebron, the subsequent dwelling place of Zechariah, the father of the Baptist. The region to which Lot removed was very good, as was all this part of the country toward the Jordan. I saw the cities around Lot's dwelling place plundered, and Lot himself with all his goods and chattels carried off. I saw a fugitive bear the news to Abraham, who immediately invoked the aid of heaven. Then gathering his servants together, he surprised the enemy and freed his brother. The latter thanked him gratefully, and was full of regret for having separated from him. The enemy and the warriors in general, especially the giants, were not clothed like Abraham's followers. Their garments were narrower and shorter; their dress was in many pieces, covered with buttons, stars, and other ornaments. The giants were extraordinarily large people. They brutally and insolently carried off all they could lay their hands upon, but they were often obliged to yield their booty to others who plundered them in turn.

Melchizedek's Sacrifice of Bread and Wine

I OFTEN saw Melchizedek with Abraham. He appeared to him in the same way as did the angels at different times. Once he commanded him a triple sacrifice of doves and other birds, and he prophesied concerning Sodom and Lot. He told him that he would come to him again to sacrifice bread and wine, and he indicated to him, also, for what he should pray to God. Abraham was full of reverence before Melchizedek, and he eagerly awaited the promised sacrifice. As a preparation for it, he built a very beautiful altar and surrounded it with an arbor. When about to come for the sacrifice of bread and wine, Melchizedek sent messengers to command Abraham to make his coming known and to announce him as the king of Salem. Abraham went out to meet him. He knelt before him and received his blessing. This took place in a valley southward from the fertile valley that lies toward Gaza.

Melchizedek came from the region where Jerusalem afterward stood. He had with him a very nimble animal of a gray color. It had a short, broad neck, and it was laden on both sides. On one was a vessel of wine, flat on the side that lay against the beast; on the other, was a box containing rows of flat, oval loaves, likewise the chalice that I afterward saw used at the Last Supper for the institution of the blessed sacrament. It had cups in the shape of little barrels. These vessels were neither of gold, nor silver, but transparent as of brownish precious stones. They did not appear to me to have been fabricated by man, they looked as if they had grown. The impression made by Melchizedek was similar to that produced by the Lord during his teaching life. He was very tall and slight, remarkably mild and earnest. He wore a long garment so white and shining that it reminded me of the white raiment that surrounded the Lord at his Transfiguration. Abraham's white garment was quite dingy compared with it. He wore also a girdle with letters similar to that worn later by the Jewish priests, and like them his head was covered with a small gothic miter during the sacrifice. His hair was shining yellow like long glittering strands of silk, and his countenance was luminous.

Upon Melchizedek's arrival, he found the king of Sodom already with Abraham in his tent, and around were numbers of people with animals, sacks, and chests. All were very grave and solemn, full of reverence for Melchizedek whose presence inspired awe. He stepped to the altar, which was a kind of tabernacle, wherein he placed the chalice. There was also a recess in it, I think for the sacrifice. Abraham had laid upon the altar the bones of Adam which Noah had had in the ark. They now prayed before them that God would fulfill the Promise made to Adam of a future Messiah. Melchizedek spread upon the altar first a red cover, which he had brought with him, and over that a white transparent one. The ceremony reminded me of the Holy Mass. I saw him elevate the bread and wine, offer, bless, and break. He reached to Abraham the chalice used afterward at the Last Supper in order that he might drink. All the rest of those present drank from the little vessels which were handed around by Abraham and the most distinguished personages. The bread, too, was passed around in morsels larger than those given at Holy Communion in the early times. I saw these morsels shining. They had only been blessed, not consecrated. The angels cannot consecrate. All that partook of the food were filled with new life and drawn nearer to God.

Melchizedek gave bread and wine to Abraham, the former more luminous than that received by the others.

Abraham derived from it great strength and such energy of faith that later on at the command of God, he did not hesitate to sacrifice his child of promise. He prophesied in these words: "This is not what Moses upon Sinai gives the Levites." I know not whether Abraham also offered the sacrifice of bread and wine, but I do know that the chalice from which he drank was the same used by Jesus at the institution of the most holy Sacrament.

When Melchizedek at the sacrifice of bread and wine blessed Abraham, he at the same time ordained him a priest. He spoke over him the words: "The Lord said to my Lord, sit thou at my right hand. Thou art a priest forever according to the order of Melchizedek. The Lord hath sworn, and he will not repent."

He laid his hands upon Abraham, and Abraham gave him tithes. I understood the deep signification of Abraham's giving tithes after his ordination. But the reason of its importance, I no longer recollect.

I saw also that David, when composing this Psalm, had a vision of Abraham's ordination by Melchizedek, and that he repeated the last words prophetically. The words, "Sit thou at my right hand," have a peculiar signification. When the eternal generation of the Son from the Father was shown me in vision, I saw the Son issuing from the right side of the Father as a luminous form surrounded by a triangle, as the Eye of God is depicted, and in the upper corner I saw the Holy Spirit. But it is inexpressible!

I saw that Eve came from the right side of Adam, that the patriarchs carried the Blessing in their right side, and that they placed the children to whom they delivered it upon their right. Jesus received the stroke of the lance in his right side, and the church came forth from the same right side. When we enter the church, we go into the right side of Jesus, and we are in him united to his heavenly Father.

I think that Melchizedek's mission upon earth was ended with this sacrifice and the ordination of Abraham, for after that I saw him no more. The chalice with the six cups he delivered to Abraham.

Abraham Receives the Sacrament of the Old Covenant

ABRAHAM sat in front of his tent under a large tree by the roadside. He was in prayer. He often sat thus waiting to show hospitality to travelers. As he prayed, he raised his eyes to heaven and saw, as in a sunbeam, an apparition from God that announced to him the coming of the three white men. He arose and sacrificed a lamb on the altar, before which I saw him kneeling in ecstasy begging for the Redemption of humankind. The altar stood to the right of the large tree in a tent open at top. Further on was a second tent in which the vessels and other utensils for sacrifice were kept. It was to this last that Abraham generally retired when superintending the shepherds who dwelt around here. Still further on, and on the opposite side of the road, was the tent of Sarah and her household. The females always lived apart.

Abraham's sacrifice was almost accomplished when he beheld the three angels appear on the highroad. On they came in their girded garments, one after another, an even distance between them. Abraham hurried out to meet them. Bowing low before God, he saluted them, and led them to the tent of the altar. Here they let down their garments and commanded Abraham to kneel. I saw the wonderful things that now happened to Abraham through the ministry of the angels. He was in ecstasy, and all the actions were rapid, as is usual in such states. He heard the first angel announce to Abraham as he knelt that God would bring forth from his posterity a sinless, an immaculate maiden who, while remaining an inviolate virgin, should be the mother of the Redeemer, and that he was now to receive what Adam had lost through sin. Then the angel offered him a shining morsel and made him drink a luminous fluid out of a little cup. After that he blessed him, drawing his right hand in a straight line down from Abraham's forehead, then from the right and the left shoulder respectively down under the breast, where the three lines of the blessing united. Then with both hands the angel held something like a little luminous cloud toward Abraham's breast. I saw it entering into him, and I felt as if he were receiving the blessed sacrament.

The second angel told Abraham that he should before his death impart the mystery of this Blessing to Sarah's firstborn, in the same way that he had himself received it. He informed him also that his future grandson, Jacob, would be the father of twelve sons from whom twelve tribes should spring. The angel told him also that this Blessing would be withdrawn from Jacob; but that after Jacob had become a nation, it should be again restored and placed in the Ark of the Covenant as a holy thing belonging to the whole nation. It should be theirs as long as they gave themselves to prayer. The angel explained to Abraham that, on account of the wickedness of men, the mystery would be removed from the Ark and confided to the patriarchs and that at last it would be given over to a man who would be the father of the promised Virgin. I heard also in this promise that by six prophetesses and through star pictures it had been made known to the pagans that the Redemption of the world should be accomplished through a virgin.

All this was made known to Abraham in vision, and he

saw the Virgin appear in the heavens, an angel hovering at her right and touching her lips with a branch. From the mantle of the Virgin issued the Church.

The third angel foretold to Abraham the birth of Isaac. I saw Abraham so full of joy over the promised holy Virgin and the vision he had had of her that he gave no thought to Isaac, and I think that this same promise made the command he subsequently received to sacrifice Isaac easy to him. After these holy communications, I saw first the entertainment of the angels and then the laughing of Sarah. I saw Abraham escorting the angels at their departure, and I heard him supplicating for Sodom.

When Abraham awoke from ecstasy, he led the angels under the tree and placed stools around it. The angels sat down, and he washed their feet. Then Abraham hurried to Sarah's tent to tell her to prepare a meal for his guests. This she did and, veiling herself, she carried it halfway to them. The meal over, Abraham accompanied the angels a short distance on their journey. It was then that Sarah heard them speak to him of the birth of a son. She had approached them behind the enclosure of the tent. She laughed. I saw numbers of doves tame as hens before the tents. The meal consisted of the same kind of birds, round loaves, and honey.

Abraham at his departure from Chaldea had already received the mystery of the Blessing from an angel, but it was given to him in a veiled manner, and was more like a pledge of fulfillment of the promise that he should be the father of an innumerable people. Now, however, the mystery was resuscitated in him by the angels, and he was enlightened upon it.

Jacob

REBECCA knew that Esau had no share in the divine mystery. Esau was dull, rough, and slothful; Jacob was very active and shrewd, more like his mother. Isaac, however, was more partial to Esau as his firstborn. Esau was often away from home hunting. Rebecca often pondered how she could procure the birthright, the Blessing, for Jacob, and she taught him how to go about buying it. The mess of pottage for which Esau sold it was composed of vegetables, meat, and green leaves like lettuce. Esau came home tired from the chase. Jacob coaxed him, and received the surrender of the birthright.

Isaac was at this time very old and blind. He feared he would soon die, and consequently he was anxious to give his Blessing over to Esau. Rebecca, who knew that Jacob should and must have it, could not persuade Isaac to give it to him. She was on that account very much afflicted, and went around quite anxious. When she found that Isaac would no longer be withheld from imparting the Blessing, and that he called to him Esau who was in the neighborhood, she laid her plans. She told Jacob to hide when his brother came in that he might not be seen. Isaac ordered Esau to go bring him something of his hunting. Then Rebecca sent Jacob to get a kid from the flock, and hardly was Esau gone when the dish for Isaac was prepared.

Esau's best clothes, which Rebecca now put upon Jacob, consisted of a jacket very like Jacob's own, only stiffer and embroidered on the breast in colors. Esau's arms and breast were covered with thick, black hair like wool, his skin being like the skin of an animal; therefore Rebecca wrapped a part of the kid's skin around Jacob's arms and put a piece upon his breast where the jacket lay open. This jacket differed from the one usually worn only by the amount of work upon it. It was slit at the sides, and passed over the head by a hole which was bound with soft, brownish leather. The side slits were fastened together with leather strings, and when a girdle was worn over it, the fullness around the breast served as a pocket. No garment was worn under this jacket, which was sleeveless and left the breast bare. The headgear and apron worn with the jacket were brownish, or gray.

I saw Isaac feeling Jacob's breast and hands where Esau was full of hair. I saw that he wavered a little, he was troubled and doubting. But then came the thought that, notwithstanding his doubts, it was certainly Esau and that God willed him to have the Blessing. And so he made over to Jacob that Blessing which he had received from Abraham, and Abraham from the angel. He had, with Rebecca's assistance, previously prepared something mystical which was connected with it; that is, a drink in a cup.

The other children of the patriarchs knew not of it. Only the one that received the Blessing knew of the mystery which, however, still remained to him, as to us the blessed sacrament, a mystery. The cup was rather flat on one side. It was transparent and shone like mother-of-pearl. It was filled with something red, something like blood, and I felt that it was Isaac's blood. Rebecca had helped to prepare it.

When Isaac blessed Jacob, they were alone. Jacob bared his breast and stood before his father. Isaac drew the hand with which he gave the Blessing from Jacob's forehead straight down to the abdomen, from the right shoulder to the same point, and the same from the left shoulder. Then he laid his right hand on Jacob's head and his left upon the pit of his stomach, and Jacob drank the contents of the little cup. And now it seemed as if Isaac delivered to him all things, all power, all strength, while with both hands he took, as it were, something out of his own person and placed it in that of Jacob. I felt that this something was his own strength, that it was the Blessing. All this time, Isaac was praying aloud. While giving over the Blessing, Isaac sat erect on his couch; he became animated, and rays of light streamed from him. When Isaac drew his hand down in giving the Blessing, Jacob held both of his open and half-raised, as the priest does at the Dominus vobiscum; but when the father merely prayed, Jacob kept them crossed on his breast. When Isaac delivered the Blessing to Jacob, the latter received it and crossed his hands under his breast like one who is holding something. At the close of the ceremony, Isaac laid his hands upon Jacob's head and upon the region of the stomach, and then Jacob received the cup out of which he had drunk.

When the imparting of the Blessing had been accomplished, I saw Isaac swooning, either from exertion or from having actually given over and parted with his strength. But Jacob was radiant, quickened, full of life and strength. And now came Esau from the hunt.

When Isaac discovered that the Blessing had been transferred to the wrong one, he had no regret, he recognized it to be God's will. But Esau was mad with rage, he tore his hair. Still, in his fury there seemed to be more envy of Jacob than grief for the lost Blessing.

Both Esau and Jacob were full-grown men, over forty years old at the time of the transfer of the Blessing. Esau already had two wives who were not much liked by his parents. When Rebecca saw Esau's rage, she sent Jacob away secretly to her brother Laban. I saw his departure. He wore a jacket that reached to the waist, an apron as far as the knees, sandals on his feet, and a band wrapped round his head. In his hand was a shepherd's staff, a small sack containing bread hung from his shoulder, and under his arm was a flask. This was all he took with him. I saw him hurrying off, followed by the tears of his mother. Isaac had blessed him a second time, and commanded him to go to Laban, and to take a wife in his new home. Isaac and Rebecca had much to endure from Esau. Rebecca especially had much sorrow.

I saw Jacob, on his journey to Mesopotamia, lying asleep on the spot where Bethel afterward stood. The sun had set. Jacob lay stretched on his back, a stone under his head, his staff resting on his arm. Then I saw the ladder that Jacob beheld in his dream, and which in the Bible is described as "standing upon the earth, and the top thereof touching heaven." I saw this ladder rising up to heaven from Jacob where he lay upon the earth. It was like a living genealogical tree of his posterity. I saw below on the earth, just as those genealogical trees are represented, a green trunk as if growing out of the sleeping Jacob. It divided into three branches which arose in the form of a triangular pyramid whose apex reached the heavens. The three branches were connected by other smaller ones that formed a three-sided pyramidal ladder. I saw this ladder surrounded by numerous apparitions. I saw on it Jacob's descendants, one above another; they formed the ancestry of Jesus according to the flesh. They often crossed over from side to side, stepping past and even before one another. Some stood back and others from the opposite side stepped before them, according as the germ of the sacred humanity was clouded by sin and then again purified by continence until at last the pure flower, the holy Virgin in whom God willed to become Man appeared on the highest point of the ladder touching the heavens. I saw heaven open above her and disclose the splendor of God. God spoke thence to Jacob.

I saw Jacob awake the next morning. First, he built a round foundation of stone on which he laid a flat stone, then he raised upon this the stone which he had placed under his head the preceding night. Lastly he made a fire and offered something in sacrifice; he also poured something into the fire on the stone. He knelt while praying, and I think he kindled the fire as the three kings did, that is, by friction.

I saw Jacob in many other places also, at Bethel for instance, as he journeyed to Laban, staff in hand. I saw him at Ainon, where he had been before and where he repaired a cistern that later on became John's fountain of baptism. I saw him even at that early period praying at the spot Mahanaim. He begged almighty God to protect him and also to keep his clothes from becoming shabby lest, on his arrival in Mesopotamia, his uncle Laban on account of his miserable appearance might not acknowledge him. Then he beheld two troops of angels hovering on either side of him like two armies. This was shown him as a sign of God's protection over him, and of the power which should be given unto him. The fulfillment of this vision he saw on his return journey.

Then I saw him going further eastward, along the south side of the river Jabbok, and passing a night on the spot where he afterward wrestled with the angel. Here too he had a vision.

On Jacob's return from Mesopotamia, his encampment lay east of the encampment of the subsequent Jabesh-Gilead. I saw Laban, his father-in-law, following him in pursuit of his lost idols. He overtook him, and words ran high between them on the score of the idols, for Jacob did not know that Rachel had secretly brought them with her. When Rachel saw that her father, who had been searching the whole encampment for his lost treasures, would soon reach her tent, she took the stolen idols and hid them under a heap of fodder not far from her own tent. The idols were metal dolls, about two and a half arms long in swaddling clothes. The heaps of fodder were on a slope of the valley south of the Jabbok, and were for the use of the camels. Rachel muffled herself up and sat down on one of them, as if she were sick and had retired for awhile. Many other women sat like her on the other heaps. On a similar, though somewhat larger straw heap, I have seen the leprous Job sitting. That on which Rachel sat was of the size of a full harvest wagon. They brought quantities of fodder with them on the camels, and on the way often laid in fresh supplies of it. These idols had long been a subject of scandal to Rachel, and she carried them off merely to disengage her father from them.

Jacob had sent messengers to Esau, of whom he was in dread. They returned with the news that Esau was at hand with four hundred men. Then Jacob divided his whole train into two bands. His best flocks he divided into several and sent them on to Esau. He led his followers to Mahanaim where he had for the second time the vision which he had seen on his setting out; that is, the vision of the angelic armies. He said: "With my staff did I set out, but I am now richer by two armies." He now understood the signification of that first vision.

When his whole train had crossed the Jabbok, Jacob sent his wives and children over by night, and remained alone. Then he ordered his tent to be erected on the spot where, on his journey from Palestine, he had seen the face of God. He wanted to pray there by night. He ordered his tent to be closed on all sides, and bade his servants retire to some distance. Then I saw him crying with his whole heart to God. He laid all things before him, especially his great anxiety with regard to Esau. The tent was open above, that he might better send forth his sighs to heaven.

Then I saw him wrestling with the angel. It took place in a vision. Jacob arose and prayed. Then there descended from above a light in which was a great luminous figure, which began to wrestle with Jacob, as if wanting to push him out of the tent. They wrestled here and there, up and down, in all directions through the tent. The apparition acted as if wanting to draw Jacob toward all the cardinal points, but Jacob always faced about to the center of the tent. This struggle prefigured the fact that Israel, though pressed on all sides, should not be forced from Palestine.

But when Jacob once again faced to the middle of the tent, the angel grasped him by the hip. I saw this take place when Jacob, who was wrestling in vision, wanted to cast himself upon his couch, or sink back upon it. When the angel touched Jacob's hip and at the same time did what he wanted to do, he said to the latter who was holding him fast: "Let me go, for the dawn is breaking!" Then Jacob ceased struggling and awoke from his vision. Seeing the angel of God still standing before him, he cried: "No, I will not let thee go until thou bless me!" He felt the need of God's blessing, for he knew that strength had departed from him and that Esau was at hand. Then spoke the angel: "How art thou called?" (This belonged to the Blessing. Abram also at his Blessing was named Abraham). He answered: "Jacob." Then said the angel: "Thou shalt be called Israel, for thou hast wrestled with God and men and hast not been vanquished." Then Jacob said: "How art thou called?" And the angel answered: "Why dost thou ask me how I am called?"—which words signified: "Dost thou not know me? Hast thou not already learned who I am?" And Jacob knelt before him, and received the blessing. The angel blessed him as Abraham had been blessed by God, as Abraham had imparted the blessing to Isaac, and Isaac to Jacob; that is, in three lines.

This blessing was especially to ensure patience and perseverance. And now the angel vanished. Jacob saw that the dawn was breaking, and he named the place Phanuel. He ordered his tent to be taken down, and he crossed the Jabbok to his family. And now the sun arose upon him. He limped on the right side, for he had there been deprived of strength.

When Esau turned off, Jacob went with all his family, his servants, and his herds, to Mahanaim and took possession of the country from Succoth to the hill Ainon. He dwelt ten years at Ainon. He afterward extended his settlement westward from Ainon and over the Jordan to Salem. His tents reached to where Shechem dwelt, for there he bought a field.

I saw Dinah walking around there with her maids, and conversing out of curiosity with the Shechemites. I saw Shechem caressing her, for which reason her maids went away, and he took her with him into the city. This was the cause of great sorrow to Dinah, while bloodshed and slaughter accrued from it to the Shechemites. Shechem at that time was not yet a great city. It was built of large, square stones and had only one gate.

The patriarchs, Abraham, Isaac, and Jacob, had more strength in their right side than in their left; it was not, however, noticeable, for their garments were wide and full. There was in their right side a certain fullness like a swelling. It was the holy thing, the Blessing, the mystery. It was luminous, in shape like a bean, and it contained a germ. The firstborn received it from the father, hence the prerogatives of primogeniture. Jacob received it instead of Esau, because Rebecca knew that he was the one destined for it. In his struggle with the angel, it had been taken away from Jacob, though without producing a wound. It was like a drying up of the swelling. But after the removal of the Blessing, Jacob no longer lived so securely, so immediately under God's protection. While he possessed the Blessing, he was like one strengthened by a sacrament; afterward, however, he felt himself humiliated, he was careworn and he experienced great troubles. He was conscious of the Blessing's having been withdrawn from him, therefore he would not let the angel go until, by a benediction, he had strengthened him. Joseph later on, when in the prison of Pharaoh, in Egypt, received that same Blessing from an angel.

Joseph and Asenath

JOSEPH was sixteen years old when he was sold into Egypt. He was of middle height, very slender and agile, active both in body and mind. He was indeed very different from his brothers, and all felt drawn to love him. Were it not for the marked preference shown him by his father, his brothers also would have loved him. Reuben was of a more lively disposition than the others. Benjamin was a large, ungainly man, but very good-natured, easily led. Joseph wore his hair divided into three, one part on either side of his head, the third falling down behind in long curls. When ruler over Egypt, he wore it short, but afterward allowed it again to grow.

When Jacob bestowed the many-colored coat upon Joseph, he gave over to him also some of the bones of Adam, without telling him, however, what they were. Jacob gave them to Joseph as a precious talisman, for he knew well that his brothers did not love him. Joseph carried the bones on his breast in a little leathern bag rounded on top. When his brothers sold him, they took from him only the colored coat and his customary outer garment, but left the band and a sort of scapular on his breast beneath which he had hung the little bag.

The colored coat was white with broad red stripes. It had on the breast three rows of black cord crossing one another, in the center of which were yellow ornaments. It was full around the breast. When bound at the waist, the fullness served as a pocket. It was narrower toward the lower part of the skirt and had slits at the side, to render motion easier. It fell below the knee, was somewhat longer in the back and open in front. Joseph's ordinary dress did not reach to the knees.

Joseph was known to Pharaoh and his wife before his imprisonment. Potiphar's affairs were so flourishing under Joseph's management, Potiphar himself was so blessed during Joseph's stay under his roof, since he conducted all things so well for Pharaoh, that the latter was eager to see the faithful servant. Pharaoh's wife, who was religiously inclined and very desirous of salvation and who had, at the same time, like all the Egyptians, a great hankering after new gods, was so astounded at the wise, intelligent, extraordinary young stranger, that she honored him interiorly as a divinity. She said repeatedly to Pharaoh: "This man has been sent by our gods. He is not a human being like ourselves." Hence it came to pass that he was thrown, not into the common dungeon, but into the prison reserved for the nobility, and there he was made the overseer. Pharaoh's wife sincerely deplored his conviction as a malefactor, and thought that she had been mistaken in him. But when he was liberated and again appeared at court, she treated him with great distinction. The cup that Joseph ordered to be placed in Benjamin's sack was the first present the queen had made to him. I know it well; it had two handles, but no foot. It seemed to have been cut out of one precious stone or one solid transparent mass, I know not which, and was in shape exactly like the upper part of the chalice used at the Last Supper. It was also among the vessels that the children of Israel took away with them from Egypt, and it was afterward preserved in the Ark of the Covenant.

Joseph was seven years in prison. During his greatest affliction, he received the mysterious Blessing of Jacob in the same manner as the patriarchs had done. He had a vision also of a numerous posterity.

I know all about Potiphar's wife. I saw how desirous she was to pervert Joseph, but after his elevation, she did penance and became chaste and devout. She was a tall, powerful woman, her skin of a yellowish-brown and shining like silk. She wore a colored robe over which was one of figured gauze. The lower one shone through it as if through lace. Joseph had frequent contact with her, since his master's affairs were all entrusted to him. But when he became aware of the fact that she had grown more familiar in her manner toward him, he no longer remained in the house overnight during his master's absence. She often intruded herself upon him when he was busy at his writing. Once I saw her enter his presence in immodest attire. He was standing writing in one corner of a hall. (In those days they used to write upon rolls of parchment that hung on the wall. The writer either sat or stood before them.) She addressed him and he replied. Then she grew bolder, seeing which he turned hurriedly away. She grasped his mantle, but he fled leaving it in her hand.

I saw Joseph with Potiphar's pagan priests at Heliopolis. Asenath, the daughter of Dinah and the Shechemite, lived with them as a prophetess and a decorator of the idols. Seven other maidens were her companions. Potiphar had bought her from her nurse in her fifth year. This nurse had fled with her to the Red Sea by order of Jacob, that the child might not be murdered by his sons. Asenath possessed the spirit of prophecy, and was esteemed by Potiphar as a prophetess. Joseph knew her, but he knew not that she was his niece. She was of a very earnest character, she sought seclusion, and in spite of her great beauty, she abhorred the society of men. She was favored with significant visions, was familiar with the Egyptian star worship, and had a secret presentiment of the religion of the patriarchs. I saw no witchcraft connected with her. She saw in vision the whole mystery of life, the transplanting, the coming to, and the departure of Israel from Egypt, even the long journey through the wilderness. She wrote many rolls on the leaves of a water-plant or on skin. The letters were strange-looking, they were like the heads of birds and animals. These writings were, even during her lifetime, misunderstood by the Egyptians and misconstrued into a sanction for their wicked abominations. Asenath grieved deeply over this misconception brought about by the evil one, and she shed many tears. She had more numerous visions than any other of her time, and she was filled with wondrous wisdom. She conducted herself gravely, and refused advice to none. She could weave also and embroider. Her enlightened spirit detected man's corruption of truth, therefore was she grave, reserved, retiring, and silent.

I saw that the misconception of Asenath's visions and writings led to her being worshipped under the name of Isis, and Joseph under that of Osiris. This perhaps was the cause of her abundant tears. She also wrote against their erroneous conception of her visions, which had led to their proclaiming her the mother of all the gods.

When Potiphar offered sacrifice, Asenath ascended a tower upon which she seemed to be, as it were, in a little garden. Here she gazed upon the stars by moonlight. She fell into ecstasy, and read all things clearly in the stars. The truth was shown her in pictures, because she was chosen of God. I have seen the pagan priests introduced into strange, diabolical worlds where they beheld the most abominable things. By such diabolical visions were the secret communications of Asenath disfigured and made to contribute to the abominations of idolatry.

Asenath introduced many useful arts and domestic animals into Egypt, among the latter, for instance, the cow. She taught the art of making cheese, that of weaving, and many others hitherto unknown to the inhabitants. She also healed many diseases. The plow was introduced by Joseph, who was himself skilled in its use. There was one thing that seemed truly wonderful to me. Asenath ordered the flesh of the numerous animals slaughtered for sacrifice to be boiled down until it became a gelatinous mass, which served for food on campaigns and in times of scarcity. The operation was carried on in the open air and in caldrons in the earth. The Egyptians were rejoiced and amazed at this new mode of procuring food.

When Joseph met Asenath at the pagan priest's dwelling, she approached to embrace him. This she did not through boldness, but impelled by the Spirit. It was in her a kind of prophetic action, and took place in presence of the pagan priest. Asenath was looked upon as holy. But I saw Joseph keep her off with outstretched hand and address earnest words to her. Then Asenath, deeply agitated, retired to her own room where she remained in tears and penance.

I saw her in her chamber. She stood concealed by a curtain, her wealth of long and beautiful hair falling around her and curling at the ends. There was impressed on the skin of the pit of her stomach a wonderful sign. In a figure like a heart-shaped shell stood a child with outstretched arms, holding in one hand a small dish, in the other a cup, or chalice. In the dish, were three young ears of corn that appeared to be just breaking out of the husk, and the figure of a dove which seemed to peck after the grapes in the cup held by the child. Jacob knew of this sign; but notwithstanding, he had to send the child away in order to shield her from the rage of his sons. But when he came down into Egypt, and Joseph told him all things, he recognized his granddaughter by this mark. Joseph, too, had a mark of the same kind upon his breast, a very full bunch of grapes.

Now I saw an angel appear in resplendent raiment, holding a lotus in his hand. He saluted Asenath. She glanced at him and drew her veil around her. He commanded her to dry her tears, to adorn herself in festal robes, and he also requested her to bring him food. She left the room and returned adorned as directed, bringing with her a low table, small and light, upon which were wine and little flat loaves that had been baked in ashes. Asenath evinced no fear. She was not shy, but simple and humble, just like Abraham and the other patriarchs when treating with apparitions. When the angel now spoke to her, she unveiled. He asked her for some honey, but she replied that, unlike other maidens who are fond of it, she had none. Thereupon the angel told her that she would find some among the idols that stood in the chamber. These idols were of various forms; they had heads of animals and for bodies serpents coiled downward.

Asenath looked, and found a beautiful, coarse-celled honeycomb, white as the Host of our altars. She set it before the angel, who bade her eat of it. He blessed it, and I saw it shining and flashing between them. I cannot now express the signification of this heavenly honey; for when one sees such things, it is just as they actually are, one knows all. But now, when I try to recall it, the honey appears to be what is called honey, yet I know not what the flowers, the bees, and the honey properly signified. I can only say this much: Asenath really possessed in herself only bread and wine (or that which is typified by bread and wine), but she had no honey. By the reception of this honey, she issued from idolatry into the light of Israel, into salvation through the Old Law. It signified also that she should aid many souls, that many like bees should build around her. I heard her say that she would drink no more wine, for that now she was more in need of honey. I saw numbers of bees and vast stores of honey in Midian near Jethro.

In blessing the honeycomb, the angel directed his finger toward all regions of the world, which signified that, by her presence, her types, and the mystery of its own, the honey's signification, Asenath should be a mother and a leader. When later on she was honored as a divinity and represented with numerous breasts, it was in consequence of the misconception of her vision that she should nourish many.

The angel told her that she was destined to be united with Joseph, that she should be his bride, and he blessed her as Isaac had blessed Jacob and as the angel had blessed Abraham. The three lines that constituted the formula of the blessing, were drawn upon her twice, once to the pit of the stomach and once to the abdomen.

After this, I saw in vision Joseph going to Potiphar to demand Asenath for his wife; but I can only remember that, like the angel, he carried a lotus in his hand. Joseph knew of Asenath's wonderful wisdom, but their mutual relationship was hidden from both.

I saw that Pharaoh's son likewise was in love with Asenath, on which account she had to remain secluded. He had persuaded Dan and Gad to espouse his cause, and all three lay in ambush to slay Joseph. But Judah (obeying a divine inspiration, I think) warned Joseph to take another route. Benjamin also conducted himself nobly in this affair, and defended Asenath. Dan and Gad were punished by the death of their children; for even before it was known to anyone, they had been warned not to enlist in the murderous design.

When Joseph and Asenath appeared in public, like the pagan priests of Potiphar, they bore in their hand a sign regarded as sacred and emblematic of the highest authority. The upper part was a ring; the lower, a Latin cross, a T. It served as a seal, and when grain was measured and divided the heaps were marked with it. It was used in the same way for the building of granaries and canals, also for the rising and falling of the Nile. Writings were sealed with it after they had first been marked with a red vegetable juice. When Joseph discharged any official duty, this symbol of authority, the cross being clasped in the ring, lay on a cushion at his side. It seemed to me also like a distinctive sign of the mystery of the Ark of the Covenant still enclosed in Joseph.

Asenath also had an instrument like a wand. When in vision, she followed wherever it led. Where it quivered she struck the earth, and so discovered springs and water. It was made under the influence of the stars.

In the processions of high festivals, Joseph and Asenath rode upon a glittering chariot. Asenath wore an ancient shield which enclosed the whole person from below the arms. On it were numerous signs and figures. Her dress reached to her knees, below which the limbs were tightly laced. A wide mantle fell over the back, the sides of which were clasped together over the knees. The toes of her shoes were turned up like skates, and her headdress of colored feathers and pearls was shaped like a helmet.

Joseph wore a tight-fitting coat with sleeves, and over it a golden breastplate covered with figures. Straps with golden knots were crossed around the hips, and from his shoulders fell a mantle. His head ornament was of feathers and precious stones.

When Joseph went to Egypt, New Memphis was being built about seven leagues north of Old Memphis. Between the two cities, built on a dyke, was a highway with walks. Scattered among the trees were idols with grave, sad female faces and bodies of dogs. They sat upon stone slabs. There were as yet no beautiful buildings, only great, long ramparts and artificial stone mountains (pyramids) full of vaults and chambers. The dwellings were slight with a superstructure of wood. There were still great forests and marshes all around. At the flight of Mary into Egypt, the Nile had already changed its course.

The Egyptians worshipped all kinds of animals, toads, serpents, crocodiles. They looked on quite coolly while a person was being devoured by a crocodile. At Joseph's coming, the worship of the bull had not yet come into practice. It was introduced in consequence of Pharaoh's dream of the seven fat and the seven lean cows. They had numerous kinds of idols; some like swaddled children, others like coiled serpents, some of which could be made longer or shorter at pleasure. A great many of the idols were adorned with breastplates on which the plans of cities and the course of the Nile were curiously inscribed. These shields were made in accordance with the pictures which the pagan priests traced in the stars, and after whose plan they built cities and canals. New Memphis was founded in this way.

The evil spirits at that time must have possessed a different, a more material power, for I saw that Egyptian sorcery came out of the earth, out of the abyss. When a pagan priest began his enchantments, I saw figures of all kinds of ugly animals arise out of the ground around the sorcerer and enter his mouth in a current of black vapor. He became thereby entranced and clear-sighted. It was as if, at the entrance of each spirit, a world hitherto closed was opened up to him and he saw things far and near, the abysses of the earth, countries, human beings, in fine, all things over which each particular spirit exerted an influence. Modern witchcraft always appears to me to be more under the influence of the spirits of the air. What the wizard saw by the aid of these spirits appeared like a delusion, a mirage, which they conjured up before him. I could see far beyond these pictures, for they were like shadows. It was as if one looked behind a curtain.

When the Egyptian pagan priests intended to read the stars, they fasted as a preparation, performed certain purifications, clothed themselves in sackcloth, and sprinkled themselves with ashes. While they gazed upon the stars from their tower, sacrifices were offered. The pagans of those times had a confused knowledge of the religious mysteries of the true God which had been handed down from Seth, Enoch, Noah, and the patriarchs to the chosen people, therefore were there so many abominations in their idolatry. The devil made use of them, as later on of heresy, to weave the pure, unclouded, authentic revelations of God into a snare for man's destruction. Therefore God enveloped the mystery of the Ark of the Covenant in fire in order to preserve it. The women of Egypt in Joseph's time were still clothed like Semiramis.

When Jacob went into Egypt to Joseph, he pursued the same route through the wilderness by which later on Moses journeyed to the Promised Land. Jacob knew that he would see Joseph again; he always had a presentiment of this in his heart. He had even on this journey to Mesopotamia at the place upon which he erected the altar (not where he saw the ladder) a vision of his future sons. One he saw, in the region where Joseph was sold, sink from sight and like a star rise again in the south. He exclaimed therefore when they brought him the blood-stained coat, the foregoing circumstance almost forgotten recurring to him: "I shall weep for Joseph until I find him again."

Jacob had, through Reuben, made many inquiries as to whom Joseph had married, but had not yet been entirely enlightened on the point that Joseph's wife was his own niece. Rueben and Potiphar were old acquaintances. Owing to the influence of the former, the latter received circumcision and served the God of Jacob.

Jacob dwelt about a day's journey distant from Joseph. When he fell sick, Joseph drove in a chariot to see him. Jacob questioned him closely about Asenath and, when he heard of the sign on her person, he exclaimed: "She is flesh of thy flesh. She is bone of thy bone!" and he revealed to Joseph who she was. Joseph was so deeply affected that he almost lost consciousness. On his return home, he told his wife, and both shed tears to their heart's content over the news.

Some time after, Jacob grew worse, and Joseph was again by his side. Jacob put his feet from the couch to the floor, and Joseph had to lay his hand under his father's hip, and swear to bury him in Canaan. While Joseph swore, Jacob adored the Blessing hidden in him, for he knew that Joseph had received from an angel the Blessing that had been withdrawn from himself. Joseph bore this Blessing in his right side until death. Even after death, it lay enclosed in his body until the night before the departure of the Israelites, when Moses took possession of it and placed it in the Ark of the Covenant, together with the remains of Joseph, as the Sacred Thing of the chosen people.

Three months after his visit, Jacob died. Both Jews and Egyptians celebrated his obsequies and sounded his praises, for he was greatly loved.

Asenath bore to Joseph first Manasseh and Ephraim, then other children, in all eighteen, among them several twins. She died three years before Joseph, and was embalmed by Jewish women. As long as Joseph lived, her body stood in his own monument. But the ancients of the people had taken some part of her intestines which they preserved in a little golden figure; and as the Egyptians also aspired to its possession, it was entrusted to the Jewish midwives. One of these women placed it in a reed box smeared with pitch and concealed it in the bulrushes near the canal. On the night of the departure, a nurse of the tribe of Asher brought this secret thing to Moses. The woman's name was Sarah.

Joseph, at his death, was embalmed by the Jews in presence of the Egyptians. Then were placed together the remains of Joseph and Asenath in compliance with the notes that the latter had made from her visions and had left to the Jews. The Egyptian priests and astrologers had placed Joseph and Asenath among their own divinities. They had some inkling of the notes left by Asenath and a presentiment of the high influence, the blessing that she and Joseph would be for Israel. But that blessing they coveted for themselves, and therefore they sought to oppress Israel. It was on this account that the Israelites, who multiplied astonishingly after Joseph's death, were so harassed by Pharaoh. The Egyptians knew well that the Israelites would not leave the country without the bones of Joseph; consequently at several different times they stole some of the remains of Joseph and at last got entire possession of them. The Jewish people at large knew only of Joseph's corpse, but not of the mystery that it contained. That was known to only a few. But the entire nation grieved deeply when the ancients found out and made known to them that the holy thing upon which the Promise rested had been stolen. Moses, who had been reared at Pharaoh's court in all the Egyptian wisdom, visited his people and learned the cause of their grief. When he murdered the Egyptian, God ordained that as a fugitive he should go to Jethro, since the latter by his connection with the priestess Segola would be able to help him to discover the purloined mystery. Moses had, also, at the command of God, married Sephora in order to incorporate that family into the house of Israel.

Segola was the natural daughter of Pharaoh by a Jewish mother. Although reared in the Egyptian star worship, she was very fond of the Jews. It was she that had divulged to Moses while still at court that he was not a son of Pharaoh.

Aaron, after the death of his first wife, had to marry a daughter of this Segola, in order that the mother's influence with the Israelites might be increased. The children of this marriage went with the Israelites at their departure from Egypt. But Aaron was obliged to separate from his wife, that the Aaronic priesthood might spring from a purely Jewish stock. Segola's daughter, after her separation from Aaron, married again. Her descendants, at the time of the Savior, dwelt at Abila whither her mummy had been brought by them.

Segola was very enlightened and possessed great influence over Pharaoh. She had on her forehead a bump such as many of the prophets had in olden times. She was led by the Spirit to procure numerous favors and gifts for the Israelites.

On the night upon which the angel of the Lord struck the firstborn of the Egyptians, Segola, wrapped in her veil, accompanied Moses, Aaron, and three other Israelites to two sepulchral mounds that were separated by a canal over which lay a bridge. The canal flowed between Memphis and Goshen into the Nile. The entrance into the mounds was under the bridge and below the surface of the water. Steps led from the bridge down to it. Segola descended alone with Moses. She cast into the water a scrap of paper upon which was inscribed the name of God. The water retreated and left the entrance to the monument free. They struck on the stone door and it opened inward. Then they called to the others to come down. When they did so, Moses bound their hands together with his stole and made them swear to protect the mystery. After the oath, he loosed their hands, and all entered the vault where they struck a light, which showed all kinds of passages with images of the dead standing therein.

Joseph's body, with the remains of Asenath, lay in an Egyptian tauriform, metal coffin, which shone like polished gold. The back formed a cover. This they lifted off, and Moses took the mystery out of the hollow body of Joseph, wrapped it in cloths, and handed it to Segola, who carried it in her arms concealed under her garments. The remaining bones were placed together upon a stone, wrapped in cloths, and carried away by the men. Now that they had gained possession of the Sacred Thing, Israel could depart from the country. Segola wept, but Israel was full of joy.

Moses concealed a relic of Joseph's body in the top of his staff. This top was in form like a medlar, or persimmon; it was yellowish and surrounded by leaves. It was different from the shepherd's staff that Moses was commanded to cast on the ground before God and which was there changed to a serpent. It was a reed: the upper and the lower end could be pushed in and drawn out. With the lower point, which appeared to me to be of metal and which was in form like a sharp pencil, Moses touched the rock as if tracing words upon it. The rock opened under the point, and water gushed forth. Water flowed also from the sand wherever Moses made signs upon it with this staff. The upper part of the reed staff, in shape like a medlar, could be pushed in and drawn out; before it the Red Sea divided.

From Joseph's death to the departure of Israel from Egypt, there were about one hundred and seventy years according to our manner of reckoning. But they had at that time another way of reckoning, other weeks and years. This was often explained to me, but I cannot now recall it.

While the Israelites lived in Egypt, they had no temple, but only tents. They piled up stones, poured oil over them, sacrificed grain and lambs, sang, and prayed.

The Ark of the Covenant

ON the same night that Moses took possession of the holy thing, a golden casket shaped like a coffin was prepared, in which at their departure the Israelites took it with them. It must have been large enough for a man to rest in it, for it was to become a church, a body. This was the night upon which the doorposts were signed with blood. As I witnessed the rapid working at the chest, I thought of the holy cross which, too, was hurriedly put together on the night before the death of Jesus. The chest was of gold plate and shaped like an Egyptian mummiform coffin, broad above and narrow below. On the upper part was a picture of a face surrounded by beams. On the sides were marked the length of the arms and the position of the ribs.

In the center of this coffin-like chest, was placed a little golden casket wherein was contained the holy thing which Segola had taken out of the sepulchral vault. In the lower part of the chest were sacred vessels, among them the chalice and cups of the patriarchs which Abraham had received from Melchizedek and which with the Blessing had been entailed upon the firstborn. This was the first form of the Ark of the Covenant, and these were its first contents. It had two covers, the lower one red, the upper one white.

Only afterward, on Mount Sinai, was made the chest inlaid with gold inside and outside, and in it the golden mummiform coffin with the holy thing was placed. The coffin did not fill the chest. It reached only about halfway up the chest and it was not so long; for at the head and foot there was still room for two small compartments in which were placed relics of Jacob's and Joseph's family and later on the rod of Aaron. When the Ark of the Covenant was placed in the temple upon Zion, its interior had undergone a change. The golden mummiform coffin had been removed, and in its place was a little mass of whitish substance shaped like the coffin.

Even when a child, I often saw the Ark of the Covenant. I saw it inside and outside, and I knew of all that was put into it from time to time. All the precious holy things that the Israelites preserved were kept in it, but it could not have been heavy, since it was easily carried.

The chest was longer than broad, its height being equal to its width. It had below a projecting ledge. The top was wrought skillfully in gold for about two feet in breadth: flowers, scrolls, faces, suns, and stars, all in different colors. All was magnificent, although the ornamentation was not very much raised. The apex and leaves arose only a little above the top of the chest. At the corners below this border, at either end, were the two rings through which ran the bars for carrying it. The whole chest was of setim wood [acacia] covered with gold and beautifully inlaid with figures of different colors.

In the middle of the Ark was a small but unnoticeable door, by which the high priest, when alone in the Most Holy, could take out the holy thing for blessing or for prophesying. It opened in two parts toward the interior right and left, and was large enough to admit of the high priest's reaching in easily. Where the bars for carrying it extended over these doors, they were slightly curved. When the doors were opened, the golden casket, in which was preserved the holy thing in its precious coverings, also opened like a book.

Above the top of the Ark arose the Throne of Grace. It consisted of a hollow table covered with gold-plate, and in it lay holy bones. It was as large as the roof of the Ark, but only deep enough to rise a little above it. It was fastened to the Ark by eight setim wood screws, four at either end. It did not rest exactly on the Ark; there was space enough between them to afford a sight from side to side. The heads of the screws were of gold and shaped like fruit. The four outer ones fastened the table to the four corners of the Ark, the four inner ones ran into the interior. Each end of the Throne of Grace was concave, and in each cavity was securely fastened a golden cherub about the size of a boy. In the center of the Throne was a round opening by which a tube ran through the roof of the Ark. One could see it in the space between the roof and the hollow table. This basket-shaped opening was surrounded by a golden crown. Four transverse pieces fastened the crown to the rod, which from the holy thing in the Ark arose through the tube and the crown and, like the petals of a flower, spread out into seven points. The right hand of one of the cherubs and the left of the other clasped the rod, while their outspread wings, the right of the one and the left of the other, met behind it. The two other wings, only slightly expanded, did not meet, but left the sight of the crown from the front of the Ark free.

Under these wings, the cherubs extended their arms with warning hands. One knee only of each cherub touched the Ark; the other limb was in a hovering attitude. The cherubs turned their faces a little to one side with a slightly agitated expression, as if they felt a holy awe before the radiant crown. They were clothed around the middle portions of the body only. On long journeys, they were removed and carried separately.

I saw on the petal-like points of the rod flames burning, which had been enkindled by the priests. The substance used for these lights was brown. I think it was a sacred resin. They kept it in boxes. But I have often seen great streams of light shooting up out of the crown, and similar streams descending from heaven into it, also oblique currents breaking out of it in fine rays. These last signified the route by which the people should journey.

On the lower end of the rod inside the Ark were hooks from which hung the two Tables of the Law, and below them the holy thing. Below the latter, though not resting on the floor of the Ark, was a ribbed vessel of gold containing manna. When I looked sidewise into the Ark, I could not see the altar, nor the holy thing. I always regarded the Ark of the Covenant as a church, the holy thing as the altar with the most blessed sacrament, and the vessel of manna as the lamp before the altar. When I entered a church in my childhood, I used to associate its different parts with the corresponding parts of the Ark of the Covenant. The mystery, the holy thing of the Ark, was to me what the blessed sacrament is to us, only not so full of grace, although it was something full of strength and reality. It made upon me a more obscure, a more awe-inspiring impression, but still one very sacred and full of mystery. It always seemed to me that all in the Ark of the Covenant was holy, that all our salvation was in it, as if rolled up in a ball, as if in a germ.

The holy thing of the Ark was more mysterious than the most blessed sacrament. The former seemed to be the germ of the latter; the latter, the fulfillment of the former. I cannot express it. The holy thing of the Ark was a mystery as hidden as is Jesus in the most holy Sacrament to us. I felt that only a few of the high priests knew what it was, that only the pious among them knew it by divine enlightenment and made use of it. To many it was unknown and they profited not by it, just as with us so many graces and wonders of the church pass unheeded. They are lost as all salvation would be, were it founded on human will and intellect, instead of upon a rock.

I could weep over the sad state, the blindness of the Jews. They once possessed all in the germ; but the fruit, they would not recognize. First, they had the mystery, the holy thing; it was the Pledge, the Promise. Then came the Law and afterward the Grace. When I saw the Lord teaching in Sichar, the people questioned him as to what had become of the holy thing of the Ark of the Covenant. He answered them that humankind had already received a great deal of it, that it was even then among them. The fact of their no longer possessing it as they once did, was a proof that the Messiah was born.

I saw the mystery, the holy thing, in a form, in a kind of veil, as a substance, as an essence, as strength. It was bread and wine, flesh and blood; it was the germ of the Blessing before the Fall. It was the sacramental presence of that holy propagation of man before he fell. It was preserved to man by religion. It was possible for it to be ever more and more realized in subsequent generations by a continuous purification through piety, which purification was perfected in Mary, thus rendering her fit to receive through the Holy Spirit the long-awaited Messiah. Noah, in planting the vineyard, had made the preparation; but here in the holy thing were contained already the reconciliation and protection. Abraham had received it in that blessing which I saw bestowed upon him as something tangible, as a substance. It was a mystery entrusted to one family, therefore the great prerogative of the firstborn.

Before the departure from Egypt, Moses took possession of the holy thing. As before this it had been the religious mystery of one family, so now it became the mystery of the whole nation. It was placed in the Ark of the Covenant as the most holy Sacrament in the tabernacle and in the monstrance.

When the children of Israel worshiped the golden calf and fell into gross errors, Moses doubted the power of the holy thing. For this he was punished by not being allowed to enter into the Promised Land. When the Ark fell into the hands of the enemy, the holy thing, the bond of union among the Israelites, was removed by the high priest, as was always done when danger threatened. And yet was the Ark still so sacred that the enemy under the pressure of God's chastising anger were forced to restore it. Few comprehended the holy thing or the influence it exerted. It often happened that one man by his sins could interrupt the stream of grace, could break the direct genealogical line that was to end in the Savior, or rather in that pure vessel that was to receive him from God. In this way, the Redemption of the human race was long delayed. But penance could again restore continuity to that line. I do not know for certain whether this sacrament were in itself divine, whether it came forth simply and purely what it was, directly from God, or whether it owed its sacred character to a kind of priestly, supernatural consecration. I think, however, that the first proposition is the true one, for I know for certain that priests often opposed its action and thus retarded Redemption. But they were heavily punished for it, yes, oftentimes even with death itself. When the holy thing operated, when prayer was heard, it became bright and increased in size, shining through the cover with a reddish glow. The blessing proceeding from it increased and diminished at different times according to the purity and piety of humankind. By prayer, sacrifice, and penance, it appeared to grow larger.

I saw Moses expose it before the people only twice: at the passage through the Red Sea and at the worshipping of the golden calf; but even then it was covered. It was removed from the golden casket and veiled as the blessed sacrament is on Good Friday. Like it, it was carried before the breast, or raised up for a blessing or a malediction, as if exerting its influence even at a distance. By it, Moses restrained many of the Israelites from idolatry and saved them from death.

I often saw the high priest making use of it when he was alone in the Holy of Holies. He turned it in a certain direction, as if to strengthen, to protect, to shield, sometimes to shower a blessing, to grant a petition, sometimes even to punish. He never touched it with uncovered hands.

The holy thing was also plunged by him into water. This he did with a religious intention, and the water was given as a sacred draught. Deborah, the prophetess, Anna the mother of Samuel in Shiloh, and Emerentia, the mother of St. Anne, drank of this water. By this holy drink, Emerentia was prepared for the conception of St. Anne. St. Anne drank not of this water, since the Blessing was in her.

Joachim, through an angel, received the holy thing out of the Ark of the Covenant, and Mary was conceived under the Golden Gate of the temple. At her birth, she herself became the Ark of the holy thing which then reached its destination, and the wooden Ark in the temple was deprived of its presence.

When Joachim and Anne met under the Golden Gate, they were surrounded by dazzling light, and the blessed

The Ark of the Covenant

Virgin was conceived without original sin. A wonderful sound was heard; it was like a voice from God.

Men cannot comprehend this mystery of Mary's sinless conception in Anne, therefore is it hidden from them.

The ancestors of Jesus received the germ of the Blessing for the Incarnation of God; but Jesus Christ himself is the sacrament of the New Covenant, the Fruit, the Fulfillment of that Blessing, to unite men again to God.

When Jeremiah at the time of the Babylonian Captivity hid the Ark of the Covenant and other precious objects on Mount Sinai, the mystery, the holy thing, was no longer in it; only its coverings were buried by him with the Ark. He knew, however, what it had contained and how holy it was. He wanted, therefore, to speak of it publicly and of the abomination of treating it irreverently. But Malachi restrained him, and took charge of the holy thing himself. Through him it fell into the hands of the Essenes, and afterward was placed by a priest in the second Ark of the Covenant. Malachi was, like Melchizedek, an angel, one sent by God. I saw him not as an ordinary man. Like Melchizedek, he had the appearance of a man, differing from him only inasmuch as was suited to his time.

Shortly after Daniel's being led to Babylon, I saw Malachi as a boy of seven years, wearing a reddish garment, and wandering around with a staff in his hand. He seemed to have lost his way, and he took shelter with a pious couple at Sapha of the tribe of Zebulon. They thought him a lost child of one of the captive Israelites, and they kept him with them. He was very amiable, and so extraordinarily patient and meek that everyone loved him; he could therefore teach and do what he pleased without molestation. He had much contact with Jeremiah, whom he assisted with advice when in the greatest perils. It was through him also that Jeremiah was freed from prison in Jerusalem.

The ancient Ark of the Covenant, hidden by Jeremiah on Mount Sinai, was never again discovered. The second one was not so beautiful as the first, and it did not contain so many precious things. Aaron's rod was in possession of the Essenes on Horeb, where also a part of the holy thing was preserved. The family that Moses appointed as the immediate protectors of the Ark of the Covenant, existed till the time of Herod.

All will come to light on the last day. Then will the mystery become clear, to the terror of all that have made a bad use of it.

THE MESSIAH COMES

Drawings from Brentano's Notes (clockwise from bottom):
Mary Crowned by the Father, Offering Palm with her Crucified Son • Young Mary Veiled
for the Temple • Mary as Virgo, the Moon Beneath her Feet • Mary's Gesture, as the Betrothed

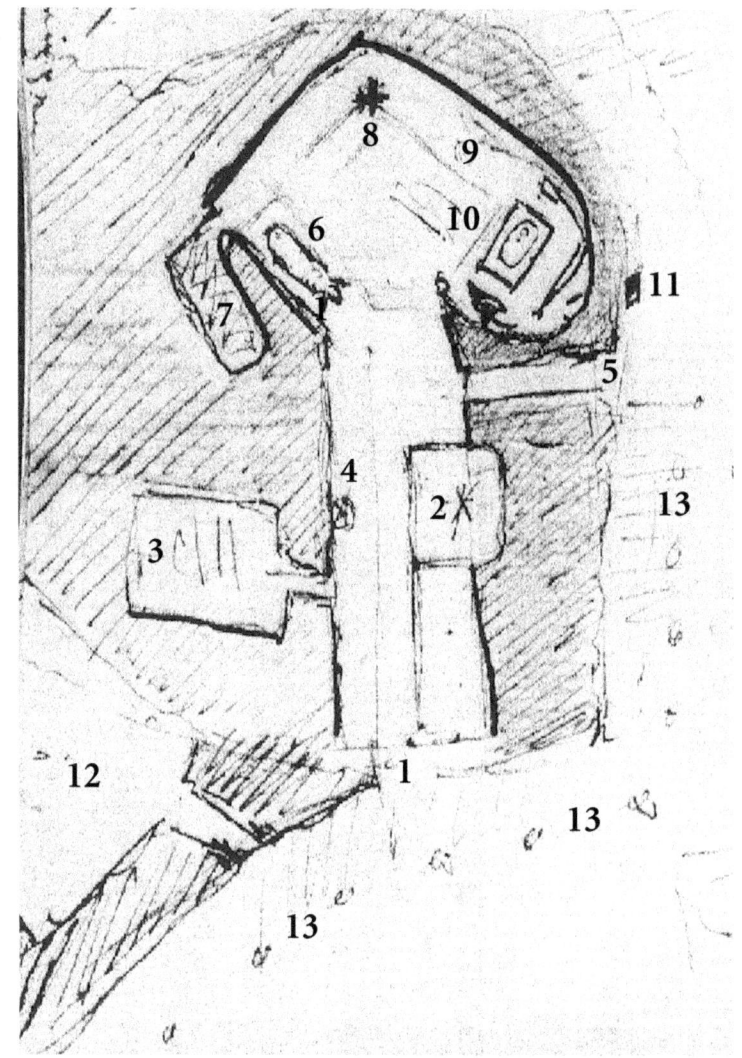

Cave of the Nativity
(drawing by Cl. Brentano, after Anne Catherine)

1. Cave Entrance 2. Sectioned-Off Bedroom of Joseph 3. A Side Cave 4. Fireplace 5. Southern Side-Entrance 6. Location of the Donkey 7. Fodder Storage 8. Birthplace of Jesus 9. Where the Three Kings Worshipped Jesus 10. Location of the Crib 11. Entrance to an Adjacent Cave 12. Another Cave 13. Reed Roof on Posts

MARY AND HER ANTECEDENTS

Genealogy, Birth, and Marriage of Anne

THE ANCESTORS of St. Anne were Essenes. These extraordinarily pious people were descended from those priests who, in the time of Moses and Aaron, carried the Ark, and who received precise rules in the days of Isaiah and Jeremiah. They were not numerous in the beginning. Later on in Palestine they lived in communities occupying a tract about forty-eight miles long and thirty-six wide. Some time after, they migrated to the region of the Jordan where they dwelt chiefly on Mount Horeb and on Mount Carmel.

In early times, before Isaiah gathered them together, the Essenes lived scattered as pious, ascetic Jews. They neither changed nor repaired their garments until they actually fell to pieces. They married, but observed great continence in the married state. With mutual consent, husband and wife frequently lived apart in distant huts. They also ate apart, first the husband and on his departure the wife. Even in those early times some of the forefathers of Anne and of other members of the holy family were found among them. From them sprang those that are called the children of the prophets. They dwelt in the desert and around Mount Horeb. There were many of them likewise in Egypt. For a long time war drove them from Mount Horeb, but they were gathered together again by their superiors. The Maccabees belonged to this sect. They greatly revered Moses. They had a piece of his garment. He had given it to Aaron, through whom it came into the Essenes' possession. They preserved it as a sacred thing, and I had a vision in which I saw that fifteen of the Essenes had perished in its defense. Their superiors knew of the mystery, the holy thing, in the Ark of the Covenant. The unmarried among the Essenes formed a special congregation like a religious order. They had to undergo a probation of long years before being admitted to it, and then they were received for a longer or a shorter time as the prophetical inspiration of superiors might dictate. The married Essenes, who exercised strict vigilance over their children and household, bore to the real Essene community the same spiritual relationship that the Franciscan Tertiaries do to the Franciscan Order. In all affairs they were guided by the counsel of their spiritual superior on Horeb.

The unmarried Essenes were unspeakably chaste and devout. They wore long white garments, which they kept scrupulously clean. They received children to educate. The aspirant to their rigid life had to be fourteen years old. Postulants of advanced piety were kept only one year on probation; others, two years. They lived in perfect chastity and carried on no kind of business; they exchanged their agricultural products for the various necessaries of life. If anyone of their number were so unfortunate as to sin grievously, he was excommunicated, which excommunication was followed by consequences such as attended St. Peter's malediction against Ananias—he died. The superior of the Essenes knew by divine inspiration whenever anyone had fallen into sin. I saw also some who lived only to do penance; one, for instance, stood in a sort of stiff coat, with outstretched, inflexible sleeves, lined with prickles.

They had caves on Mount Horeb which served as cells. Attached to them by wicker-work was a large cave for general assembly. At the eleventh hour all met here for a meal. Each had before him a small loaf and cup. The superior went around and blessed the loaf of each. The meal over, all returned to their own cells. In the large hall was an altar upon which lay blessed loaves. They were covered and intended for distribution to the poor. There were numbers of tame pigeons around which fed out of the hand. The Essenes used these doves for food, also for religious ceremonies. They uttered some words over them, and they let them fly away. I saw them also performing the same ceremony over lambs; they spoke some words over them and then let them run into the wilderness.

I saw that they went three times every year to the temple of Jerusalem. They had among them priests, whose special care was the preservation of the sacred vestments; they cleaned them and prepared new ones, to the purchase of which they had contributed. I saw these people engaged in agriculture, in cattle raising, and especially in gardening. That part of Mount Horeb which lay around their cells was covered with gardens and fruit trees. I saw many of them engaged likewise in weaving and platting, and in embroidering the sacerdotal garments. I saw that they did not manufacture the silk themselves. It came in bundles for sale, and they exchanged their products for it.

In Jerusalem, they had a special dwelling place, also a particular part of the temple assigned to them. They were objects of dislike to the other Jews. I saw them sending offerings to the temple for sacrifice, huge bunches of grapes that two men carried between them on a pole, and lambs. But these lambs were not slaughtered; they were allowed to run. I never saw them bringing offerings for slaughter. Before going up to the temple, they prepared themselves by prayer, rigid fasting, disciplines, and other penitential exercises. He who with unatoned sins ventured to the temple might fear a sudden death; and indeed, this happened to some. If on their way to the temple they met a person sick or helpless, they paused and went no further until they had in some manner assisted him. I saw them gathering herbs and preparing teas. They healed the sick by the imposition of hands, or by stretching themselves upon them with extended arms. I saw them also exerting their healing power at a distance. If a sick person could not

Moruni, or Emorun, that is, noble mother. She married Stolanus upon the advice of Archos, the prophet, who was the superior of the Essenes for about ninety years. He was a very holy man with whom counsel was always taken by those intending to enter upon the married state, that they might make a good choice. It seemed to me strange that this divinely enlightened superior always prophesied

Jerusalem from the Mount of Olives

go himself to the Essenes, he sent to them another as his representative. All that would have been done for the sick person himself, had he really been present, was done for his representative, and the sick man was cured at the same hour.

The superior at the time of Anne's grandparents was a prophet named Archos. He had visions in the cave of Elijah on Horeb, which visions referred to the coming of the Messiah. Archos knew from what family the Messiah would come and, when he prophesied to Anne's grandparents concerning their posterity, he saw that the time was drawing near. He knew not exactly how far off it was nor how it might still be retarded by sin; but he exhorted them to penance and sacrifice.

Anne's grandfather, an Essene, was before his marriage called Stolanus; but by his wife and in consideration of her dowry, he received the name Garescha, or Sarziri. Anne's grandmother was of Mara in the desert. Her name was

respecting the female descendants, and that the ancestors of Anne, as well as Anne herself, always had daughters. It was as if the religious education of the pure vessels that were to conceive the holy children destined to be the precursors of the disciples, of the apostles, and of the Lord himself, devolved upon them.

I saw Emorun going to Archos before her marriage. She entered the hall on Horeb, passed thence into a side apartment, and conferred with the superior through a grating like that of a confessional. Then Archos went up a long flight of steps to the summit of the mountain where was found the cave of the prophet Elijah. The entrance was narrow, and a few steps led down into the cave, which was neatly hollowed out. The light fell through an opening in the vaulted roof. I saw by the wall a small stone altar, upon which was the rod of Aaron and a shining chalice as of one precious stone. In this chalice lay a portion of the Ark of the Covenant. The Essenes had come into possession of it at a time when the Ark had fallen into the hands of the enemy. The rod of Aaron stood in a little tree as in a box. The tree had yellowish leaves wreathed in spirals. I cannot say whether this little tree was really growing or whether it was artificial. It was, for instance, something like a root of Jesse. If the superior prayed concerning a marriage, he took the rod of Aaron into his hand. If the union in question would contribute to Mary's lineage, the rod put forth a bud from which sprang one or more blossoms bearing the sign of the choice. The forefathers of Anne were legitimate descendants of this lineage, and their chosen daughters had been by such signs designated. New blossoms burst forth whenever a chosen daughter was to enter the married state. The little tree with its spiral leaves was like a genealogical table, like the root of Jesse, and by it could be seen how far the advent of Mary was distant. There were on the altar, also, some small bunches of herbs in pots. Their flourishing or withering denoted something. I saw all around on the walls grated compartments wherein were preserved ancient holy bones very beautifully encased in silk and wool. They were the bones of prophets and holy Israelites who had lived upon the mountain and in its vicinity. I saw such bones in the cells or caves of the Essenes. They used to place lighted lamps and flowers before them, and there offer prayers.

When Archos prayed in this cave, he was vested precisely like the high priest in the temple. His clothing consisted of about eight pieces. First, he placed upon his breast a kind of broad scapular such as Moses used to wear next to his person. It had an opening in the middle for the neck and fell in equal length before and behind. Over this, he wore a white alb of twisted silk bound by a cincture that fastened also the wide stole which, crossing on the breast, reached down to the knee. Over the alb was a kind of chasuble of white silk. It reached to the ground behind, and had two little bells at the lower edge. Around the neck was a standing collar buttoned in front. The beard was parted over this collar. Last of all came a small, shining mantle of white untwisted silk. It was fastened in front by three stone clasps upon which something was engraved. From either shoulder toward the breast ran a row of six precious stones, upon which also signs were engraved. On the back of it and in the center, was a shield upon which were inscribed some letters. This mantle was also adorned with fringes, tassels, and artificial fruit. On one arm he wore a short maniple. The headdress was of white silk rolled in puffs one above another and ending in a silken tuft. Over the forehead was a plate of gold set with precious stones.

Archos prayed prostrate on the earth before the altar. I saw that he had a vision of a rose tree with three branches springing from Emorun. On each branch was a rose, and that of the second was marked with a letter. He saw also an angel writing letters on the wall. In consequence of this vision, Archos told Emorun that she should marry her sixth suitor, that she should bring forth a chosen child who would bear a sign and who would be a vessel of the approaching Promise. The sixth suitor was Stolanus. The married pair did not dwell long in Mara; they removed to Ephron. Again I saw their daughters, Emerentia and Ismeria, consulting with Archos. He commanded them to embrace the married state, for they also were cooperating vessels of the Promise. The elder one, Emerentia, married a Levite named Aphras, and became the mother of Elizabeth, who gave birth to John the Baptist. A third daughter was named Enue. Ismeria was the second daughter of Stolanus and Emorun. She had at her birth the mark that Archos, in his vision of Emorun, had seen on the rose of the second branch. Ismeria married Eliud, of the tribe of Levi. They were wealthy, as I judged from their great household. They owned many herds, but they kept nothing for themselves, they gave all to the poor. They dwelt in Sepphoris, four leagues from Nazareth, where they possessed property. They had property also in the valley of Zebulon whither they used to remove in the warm season. After Ismeria's death, Eliud took up his abode there permanently. Joachim's father with his family had likewise settled in the same valley.

The eminent chastity and mortification of Stolanus and Emorun had descended to Ismeria and Eliud. Ismeria's first daughter was called Sobe. She married Solomon, and became the mother of Mary Salome who married Zebedee and gave birth to the future apostles, James the Greater and John. When at Sobe's birth the sign of the Promise was not found on her, her parents were greatly troubled. They journeyed to the prophet on Horeb. He exhorted them to prayer and sacrifice, and promised them consolation. For about eighteen years they were without children, and then Anne was born. Both father and mother had the same vision one night upon their couch. Ismeria saw an angel near her writing on the wall. On awakening she told her husband, who also had had the same vision, and both still saw the written character on the wall. It was the letter M. At her birth Anne brought with her into the world the same sign upon the region of the stomach.

Anne was especially dear to her parents. I saw her as a child. She was not strikingly beautiful, though prettier than some others. Her beauty was not to be compared with Mary's, but she was extraordinarily pious, childlike, and innocent. She was the same at every age, as I have seen, as a maiden, as a mother, and as a little old grandmother. Whenever I happened to see a very childlike old peasant woman, I always thought: "She is like Anne."

When in her fifth year, Anne was taken to the temple, as Mary was later. There she remained twelve years, returning home in her seventeenth year. Meantime, her mother had had a third daughter, whom she named Maraha, and Anne found also in the paternal house a little son of her eldest sister Sobe, who was called Eliud. Maraha afterward inherited the paternal property of Sepphoris and became the mother of the subsequent disciples, Arastaria and Cocharia. The young Eliud was afterward the second husband of Maroni of Nain.

One year later, Ismeria fell sick and died. She called her household around her deathbed, gave them her parting advice, and appointed Anne as their future mistress. Then she spoke alone with Anne, saying that she must marry, for that she was a vessel of the Promise. About eighteen months after, Anne, then in her nineteenth year, married Heli, or Joachim. This she did in obedience to the spiritual direction of the prophet. On account of the approach of the Savior's advent, she married Joachim of the House of David, for Mary was to belong to the House of David; otherwise she would have had to choose her spouse from among the Levites of the tribe of Aaron, as all of her race had done. She had had many suitors and, at the time of the prophet's decision, she was not yet acquainted with Joachim. She chose him only upon supernatural direction.

Joachim was poor and a relative of Joseph. Joseph's grandfather Matthan had descended from David through Solomon. He had two sons, Joses and Jacob. The latter was Joseph's father. When Matthan died, his widow married a second husband named Levi, descendant of David through Nathan. The fruit of this marriage was Matthat, the father of Heli, or Joachim. Joachim was a short, broad, spare man. Joseph, even in his old age, was very handsome compared with him. However, in disposition and morals, Joachim was a superior man. Like Anne, he had something very distinguished about him. Both were true Israelites; but there was something in them that they themselves knew not, a yearning, a wonderful earnestness. I have rarely seen either of them laugh, although in the early part of their married life they were not particularly grave. Both possessed a calm, uniform disposition; even in early youth, they were something like sedate old people.

They were married in a small town that possessed only one obscure school, and only one priest presided at the ceremony. Courtship in those days was carried on very simply. The lovers were very reserved. They consulted each other on the subject and regarded their marriage merely as something inevitable. If the young girl said yes, her parents were satisfied; if no, and if she could give good reasons for her refusal, they looked upon the affair as ended. First the matter was settled before the parents, and then the promises were made before the priest in the synagogue. The priest prayed in the sanctuary before the rolls of the Law, the parents in their accustomed place, while the young couple in an adjoining apartment deliberated in private over their intention and contract. When they had taken their determination, they declared it to their parents. The latter again conferred with the priest, who now went to meet the couple outside the sanctuary. The nuptial ceremony was celebrated the next day.

Joachim and Anne lived with Eliud, Anne's father. There reigned throughout his household the severe usages and discipline of the Essenes. The house lay in the environs of Sepphoris. It formed one of a group of houses of which it was the largest. Here Joachim and Anne dwelt seven years.

Anne's parents were in good circumstances. They had numerous herds and a house handsomely furnished with beautiful carpets, table furniture, etc. The servants, men and women, were many. I never saw them engaged in agriculture, but herding cattle on the pasture grounds. Ismeria and Eliud were pious, devout, charitable, and just. They frequently divided their herds and other possessions into three parts: one part for the temple, whither they drove it themselves and where it was received by the servants of the temple; a second part they gave to the poor or to their needy relatives, some of whom were generally present to receive it; and the third part they reserved for their own use. They lived very frugally and gave to all that asked help. When I saw all this, even in childhood, I thought: Giving lasts long. He who gives gets back double, for I perceived that the third part again rapidly increased. It was soon so large that it could be again divided into three parts as before. They had many relatives who upon all solemn occasions assembled at their house. But I never even on those occasions saw much feasting. Food was indeed distributed among the poor, but grand entertainments I never saw. At these assemblies the guests generally reclined in circles on the ground, and conversed of God with earnest expectancy. It frequently happened that some of these relatives were bad people. They looked angry and displeased when Eliud and Ismeria, full of heavenly longing, glanced upward as they spoke of God. But to these evil-minded people the holy couple were ever kind; they never omitted to invite them to their reunions, and they gave twice as much to them as to others. I used to see that they, with bitter feelings, impatiently coveted what Eliud and Ismeria gave them with so much good will. It was no uncommon thing for the holy couple to give sheep, sometimes one, sometimes more, to the poor belonging to them.

Here in her father's house, Anne gave birth to her first

daughter, who was called Mary. I saw her full of joy over her newborn babe. It was a lovely child. I saw it growing stout and strong. It was gentle and pious, and the parents loved it. But yet, there was something about the child that I could not understand, something that indicated that it was not the one looked forward to by the parents as the fruit of their union. There was always a shade of trouble and anxiety about them, as if they had offended God, therefore they did penance, lived in continence, and multiplied their good works. I often saw them going apart to pray.

They had lived in this way with their father, Eliud, seven years (which I could guess by the age of their first child), when they resolved to withdraw from the paternal house. Their design was to live in privacy, to begin their married life anew and, by performing actions pleasing to God, to draw down his benediction upon their union. I saw them take this resolution in the paternal home and I also saw Eliud setting aside a portion of his riches for them. The herds were divided, oxen, asses, and sheep set apart for the new household. The animals named were much larger than those of our country. On the asses and oxen were packed all kinds of movables, furniture and clothing. The good people were as skillful in packing as were the animals ready to receive and carry away their loads.

We do not pack our goods so skillfully on our wagons as these people could upon their beasts. They had beautiful vessels, all more highly ornamented than those of the present day. Beautiful, fragile, curiously-shaped pitchers, upon which were all kinds of ornamentation like carving, were stuffed with moss, enveloped in wrappings, fastened to the ends of a strap, and hung over the back of the animals upon which were laid bundles of colored covers and garments. Some of the covers were embroidered in gold and were very costly. Father Eliud gave the departing couple a small but heavy lump of something in a bag; it was like a lump of gold, of precious metal. When all was ready, the servant men and maids formed in procession and drove the herds and beasts of burden before them toward the new dwelling, about five or six leagues distant.

The house stood upon a hill between the valley of Nazareth and the valley of Zebulon. A terebinthine walk led to it. In front of it, on a bare, stony foundation, was a courtyard surrounded by a low stone wall, upon or behind which grew a hedge. On one side of this courtyard were sheds for the cattle. The door of the house, which was tolerably large, was in the center of the building and hung upon hinges. Through it one entered a kind of anteroom, which extended the whole breadth of the house. Right and left of the hall were small apartments cut off by lightly woven partitions, or screens, that could be removed at pleasure. It was in this hall that the principal meals were laid on feasts as, for instance, when Mary was taken to the temple. Opposite the entrance, a light wicker door led from the hall into a passage upon either side of which were four apartments lying right and left. They were separated by movable wicker partitions, the upper part ending in gratings. These partitions were so placed as to form a rounded, or rather a kind of triangular space, in the middle of whose central side, just opposite the door, was the fireplace. Behind the two oblique sides, right and left, were other chambers. In the center of this kitchen there hung from the ceiling a many-branched lamp. Around the house were fields and orchards.

When Joachim and Anne entered their new abode, they found everything in order, owing to the diligence of the domestics who had preceded them. They had unpacked all things as nicely and carefully as they had packed them, and everything was in its place. Anne's servants were so handy, they did everything quietly and intelligently. They were not like the servants of our day, who have to be told every single thing.

And now the holy couple began here a new married life. They made a sacrifice to God of all the preceding years, and began again as if they had only just now been united. Their only aim was, by a life pleasing to God, to attract upon themselves that blessing for which alone they sighed. I saw them both going to and fro among their herds. They divided them into three parts, and drove the best to the temple. The poor received the second part, and the worst was retained for themselves. They acted in the same manner with all that belonged to them.

The Immaculate Conception of Mary

ANNE had the assurance, the firm belief that the coming of the Messiah was very near, and that she herself would be of the number of his relatives according to the flesh. Her prayer was continuous and she constantly aimed at greater purity. It had been revealed to her that she was to bring forth a child of benediction. Her firstborn daughter, who had remained with her grandfather Eliud, Anne recognized and loved as her own and Joachim's child; but she felt certain that she was not the child whom, by interior enlightenment, she knew that she was to bear. For nineteen years and five months after the birth of this first child, Joachim and Anne were childless. They lived in continued prayer and sacrifice, in mortification and continency. I frequently saw them dividing their herds, which rapidly multiplied again. Joachim often remained far away with his flocks in humble supplication to God.

The anxiety of both and their longing after the promised blessing had reached their height. Many of their acquaintances upbraided them because of their sterility, which they attributed to some wickedness. They said that the child living with Eliud was not really Anne's daughter, otherwise she would have it with her. When Joachim, absent with the herds, went again to the temple to offer sacrifice, Anne used to send servants out to the fields to him with various things, doves, and other birds in baskets and cages. Joachim loaded two asses from the meadow with them, also with three little long-necked animals, white and nimble, and lambs and kids in wicker baskets. He carried a lantern at the end of a stick; it looked like a light in a scooped-out gourd. I saw him with his offerings journeying over a beautiful green field between Bethany and Jerusalem. I often saw Jesus in the same spot. Toward evening, Joachim reached the temple. The asses were stabled in the same place as subsequently at Mary's presentation, and the offerings were carried up the steps of the mount that led to the temple. When they had been received by the attendants, Joachim's servants returned while he himself went on into the hall in which were the water basins for the cleansing of the gifts. Thence he passed through a long corridor to a hall upon the left of the sanctuary where were the altar of incense, the table of showbread, and the seven-branched candlestick. The hall was filled with those that had brought offerings. Joachim was received in a very contemptuous manner by a priest named Reuben, who would scarcely admit him. He was shoved into a corner behind a grating, and his offerings were not, like those of others, conspicuously placed behind the gratings to the right of the courtyard, but indifferently set on one side. The priests were around the altar of incense, upon which an offering was being made. Lamps were burning, and lights were lit on the seven branched candlestick, but not all seven at once. I have often noticed that different arms of the candlestick were lighted on different occasions.

I saw Joachim leaving the temple in great trouble. He went from Jerusalem through Bethany, and into the country of Machaerus, where he sought consolation in the house of an Essene. The prophet Manahem had once dwelt here, and also in the family of an Essene at Bethany. This prophet had foretold to Herod while still a child his future kingdom and wickedness. From this place, Joachim went to his most distant herds on Mount Hermon. The way led through the wilderness of Gaddi and over the Jordan. Hermon is a long, narrow, unbroken mountain whose sunny side is green and blooming when the other is still covered with snow. Joachim was so dejected, so mortified that he would not allow his people to inform Anne where he was staying, while the trouble of the latter when she heard how things had gone at the temple and saw that Joachim did not return home, was indescribable. For five months Joachim thus remained in concealment on Hermon. I saw him praying and weeping. When he went to look after his flocks and his lambs, he was often so overcome by sadness that he cast himself with covered face prostrate on the ground. His servants questioned him upon the cause of his grief. But he did not tell them that it was because he was childless. Again he divided his magnificent herds into three parts. The best he sent to the temple, the second to the Essenes, and the least he kept for himself.

Anne, in the midst of her anxiety, had much to endure also from an insolent maidservant who bitterly taunted her with her sterility. She bore with her a long time, but at last she sent her from the house. The maid had requested permission to go to a feast. This was not in accordance with the strict discipline of the Essenes. Anne refused the permission, and then the maid reproached her, telling her that she deserved to be sterile and abandoned by her husband on account of her harsh and unreasonable temper. Then Anne sent her, with gifts and accompanied by two servants, back to her parents, that they might receive her safe and sound as she had come to her. She sent them also the message that she could no longer take charge of their daughter. After the girl's departure, Anne went in sadness to her chamber and prayed. When evening closed, she threw a long scarf over her head and enveloped herself entirely in it, took a covered light beneath her mantle, went out under a spreading tree that stood in the courtyard, lit the lamp, and prayed. This tree was one of those whose branches strike root again and again, and thus form a whole tract of covered walk under their foliage. Its leaves are very large. I think it was with such that Adam and Eve clothed themselves in Paradise. The whole tree had the characteristics of that of the forbidden fruit. The pear-shaped fruit hung usually in fives at the end of the branches. It was fleshy inside with blood-colored veins; in its center was a hollow space in which reposed the kernel. The Jews made use of the large leaves chiefly at the Feast of Tabernacles. They adorned the walls with them, laying them like the scales of a fish, so that their edges closely fitted together. The tree was surrounded by groves and seats.

When Anne had long besought God not to separate her from Joachim, her pious husband, although he had been pleased to deprive her of children, an angel appeared to her. He hovered above her in the air. He told her to set her heart at rest, for the Lord had heard her prayer; that she should on the following morning go with two of her maidservants to the temple of Jerusalem; that there under the Golden Gate, entering by the side of the valley of Jehosaphat, she should meet Joachim, who was even now on his way thither, that Joachim's offering would be accepted, that his prayer would be heard, that he (the angel) had

Mount Hermon

appeared also to him. The angel likewise directed Anne to take some doves with her as an offering, and promised that the name of the child she was soon to conceive should be made known to her.

Anne thanked the Lord and returned to the house. When, after her lengthy prayer, she lay on her couch asleep I saw light descending upon her. It surrounded her, yes, even penetrated her. I saw her, upon an interior perception, tremblingly awake and sit upright. Near her, to the right, she saw a luminous figure writing on the wall in large, shining Hebrew characters. I read and understood the writing word for word. It was to this effect: that she should conceive, that the fruit of her womb should be altogether special, and that the Blessing received by Abraham was to be the source of this conception. I saw Anne's anxiety as to how she should communicate all that to Joachim; but the angel reassured her by telling her of Joachim's vision. I received then a clear explanation of Mary's Immaculate Conception. I saw that, in the Ark of the Covenant, a sacrament of the Incarnation, of the Immaculate Conception, a mystery for the restoration of fallen humanity, was contained. I saw Anne, with surprise and joy, reading the red and golden letters of this luminous writing. Her gladness increased to such a degree that, when she arose to set out for Jerusalem, she looked far younger than before. I saw on Anne's person at the instant the angel appeared to her a beam of light and in her a shining vessel. I cannot better describe it than by saying that it was like a cradle, or a tabernacle which had been closed but was now opened, and made ready to receive a holy thing. How wonderfully I saw this is not to be expressed; for I saw it as if it were the cradle of salvation for the whole human race, and also as a kind of sacred vessel now opened, and the veil withdrawn. I saw it quite naturally as if one and the same holy thing.

I saw, too, the apparition of the angel to Joachim. The angel commanded him to take his offering up to the temple, promised that his prayer should be heard, and told him that he should pass under the Golden Gate. At this announcement, Joachim was troubled. He felt very timid about going again to the temple. But the angel assured him that the priests had already been enlightened with regard to him. It was the time of the Feast of Tabernacles. Joachim and his shepherds had already erected their tabernacles. With a large herd of cattle as an offering, Joachim reached Jerusalem on the fourth day of the festival, and put up near the temple. Anne arrived in Jerusalem also on the fourth day of the festival. She stopped with the family of Zechariah near the fish market, and met Joachim for the first time only at the end of the festival.

When Joachim approached the temple, two of the priests came out to meet him. They did this acting upon a divine inspiration. Joachim had brought with him two lambs and three kids. His offering was accepted, slaughtered, and burned at the customary place in the temple. But a part of it was taken and burned at another place to the right of the entrance porch, in the center of which stood the large teacher's desk.

When the smoke arose, I saw a beam of light descend upon Joachim and the officiating priest. There was a pause, the beholders looked on in amazement, and I saw two priests go out to Joachim and lead him through the side apartments into the sanctuary before the altar of incense. Then the priests laid incense upon the altar, not in grains but in the lump; it kindled of itself. The priests immediately retired to a distance and left Joachim alone before the altar. I saw him on his knees, his arms extended, while the incense offering slowly consumed itself. He remained shut up in the temple all night, praying with great and ardent desires. I saw that he was in ecstasy. A luminous figure appeared to him in the same manner as to Zechariah, and gave him a roll written in shining letters. On it were the three names: Helia, Hanna, Mirjam, and near the last one the picture of a little Ark of the Covenant, or a tabernacle. Joachim laid the roll on his breast under his garment. The angel spoke: "Anne will conceive an immaculate child from whom the Redeemer of the world will be born." The angel told him moreover not to grieve over his sterility which was not a disgrace to him, but a glory, for that what his spouse would conceive should not be from him but through him, a fruit from God, the culminating point of the Blessing given to Abraham. I saw that Joachim could not comprehend these words. Then the angel led him behind the curtain that concealed the grating before the Holy of Holies. The space between the curtain and the grating afforded standing room. Then the angel held up before Joachim's face a shining ball that reflected like a mirror. Joachim breathed upon it and gazed into it. When I saw the angel holding the ball so close to Joachim's face, I thought of a custom in use at our country weddings, where one kisses a painted head and gives fourteen pennies to the sexton. And now, as if called up by the breath of Joachim, appeared all kinds of pictures in the globe. He saw them clearly, for his breath did not dim them. It seemed to me that the angel then said to him that Anne should conceive although remaining just as unsullied by him as this ball. The angel then took it from Joachim and raised it on high. I saw it hovering in the air and, as if through an opening, innumerable and wonderful pictures went into it. They were like a whole world, one picture growing out of another. Up in the highest point appeared the most holy Trinity, and below, to one side, were Paradise, Adam and Eve, the Fall, the Promise of a Redeemer, Noah, the Ark, scenes connected with Abraham and Moses, the Ark of the Covenant, and numerous symbols of Mary. I saw cities, towers, gateways, flowers, all wonderfully connected together by beams of light like bridges. They were all assaulted and combated by beasts and spirits, which, however, were everywhere beaten back by the streams of light that burst upon them.

I saw also a garden enclosed by a dense thornhedge. All kinds of horrible animals were trying to enter, but could not. I saw a tower stormed by numerous warriors who were, however, always repulsed.

And in this way I saw innumerable pictures all bearing some reference to Mary. They were bound together by passages or bridges. In them I saw obstacles, hindrances, struggles, all of which were overcome, and the pictures disappeared successively on the opposite side of the globe, as if they had entered into the Heavenly Jerusalem. But as I gazed at them dissolving in the interior of the globe, the globe itself mounted on high and I saw it no more.

The angel now removed something from the Ark of the Covenant, though without opening the door. It was the mystery of the Ark, the sacrament of the Incarnation, the Immaculate Conception, the Consummation of the Blessing of Abraham. I beheld it under the appearance of a luminous body. The angel blessed or anointed Joachim's forehead with the tip of his thumb and forefinger; then he slipped the shining body under Joachim's garment and it entered into him, how I cannot say. He also gave him something to drink out of a glittering chalice which he held supported by two fingers. The chalice was of the same shape as that used at the Last Supper, but without a foot. Joachim was directed to take it with him and keep it at his home.

I understood that the angel forbade Joachim to reveal anything about this holy mystery; and then, too, I understood why Zechariah, the father of the Baptist, was struck mute after receiving the blessing and the promise of Elizabeth's fruitfulness through the mystery of the Ark of the Covenant. Not till later was this mystery missed from the Ark by the priests. Then were they at first confounded; afterward they became altogether pharisaical. The angel now led Joachim out of the Holy of Holies and vanished. Joachim lay on the ground like one stupefied.

I saw the priests enter the sanctuary, lead Joachim out reverently, and place him upon a seat that stood on a raised platform where usually only priests sat. The seat was almost like that used by Magdalene in her grandeur. They bathed his face, held something to his nose, and gave him to drink; in short, they treated him as one in a swoon. Joachim was, by virtue of what he had received from the angel, quite radiant. He looked as if he had returned to the bloom of youth.

Joachim was afterward conducted by the priests to the entrance of the subterranean passage that ran under the temple and under the Golden Gate. This was a passage set aside for special purposes. Under certain circumstances, penitents were conducted by it for purification, reconciliation, and absolution. The priests parted from Joachim at the entrance, and he went alone into the narrow, gradually widening, and almost imperceptibly descending passage. In it stood pillars twined with foliage. They looked like trees and vines, and the green and gold decorations of the walls sparkled in the rosy light that fell from above. Joachim had accomplished a third part of the way when Anne met him in the center of the passage directly under the Golden Gate, where stood a pillar like a palm tree with hanging leaves and fruit. Anne had been conducted into the subterranean passage through an entrance at the opposite end by the priest to whom she and her maid had brought the offering of doves in baskets, and to whom also she had told what the angel had revealed to her. She was also accompanied by some women, among them the prophetess Anna.

I saw Joachim and Anne embrace each other in ecstasy. They were surrounded by hosts of angels, some floating over them carrying a luminous tower like that which we see in the pictures of the Litany of Loretto. The tower vanished between Joachim and Anne, both of whom were encompassed by brilliant light and glory. At the same moment the heavens above them opened, and I saw the joy of the most holy Trinity and of the angels over the Conception of Mary. Both Joachim and Anne were in a supernatural state. I learned that, at the moment in which they embraced and the light shone around them, the Immaculate Conception of Mary was accomplished. I was also told that Mary was conceived just as conception would have been effected, were it not for the fall of man.

After this, Joachim and Anne, praising God, turned toward the outer gate of the passage. They went under an arch into a space like a chapel where numerous lights were burning. Thence they passed to the gate where they were received by the priests who accompanied them back. The temple was all thrown open and decorated with garlands of leaves and fruit. Divine service was performed under the open sky. In one place stood eight pillars at some distance from one another, and over them were twined garlands of green.

Joachim and Anne went for awhile to one of the priests' houses in Jerusalem, and then immediately journeyed homeward. I saw them in Nazareth holding an entertainment at which many of the poor were fed and presented with alms. Joachim received numerous congratulations upon the acceptance of his offering.

Upon their arrival home, the holy couple made known the mercy of God with feeling, joy, and devotion. From that time they lived in perfect continence and in great fear of God. I received at this time an instruction upon the great influence exerted upon children by the purity, the continence, and the mortification of parents.

Four and one-half months less three days after St. Anne had conceived under the Golden Gate, I saw the soul of Mary, formed by the most holy Trinity, in movement. I saw the divine Persons interpenetrating one another. It became a great shining mountain, and still like the figure of a man. I saw something from the midst of the three divine Persons rising toward the mouth and issuing from it like a beam of light. This beam hovered before the face of God and assumed a human shape, or rather it was formed to such. As it took the human form, I saw it, as if by the command of God, most beautifully fashioned. I saw God showing the beauty of this soul to the angels, and from it they experienced unspeakable joy.

I saw that soul united to the living body of Mary in Anne's womb. Anne lay asleep upon her couch. I saw a light hovering over her and from it a beam descending toward the middle of her side. I saw that beam enter into her in the form of a small, luminous, human figure. At the same instant Anne sat up. She was entirely surrounded by light, and she had a vision. She saw her own person open, as it were, and in it, as if in a tabernacle, a holy, luminous virgin from whom proceeded all salvation. I saw, too, that this was the instant that Mary first moved in her mother's womb.

Anne arose and announced to Joachim what had taken place. Then she went out to pray under the tree beneath which a child had been promised to her. I learned that Mary's soul animated her body five days earlier than is customary with ordinary children, and that she was born twelve days sooner.

Symbols of the Mystery of the Immaculate Conception

I SAW the whole earth parched and dried up. I saw Elijah with two servants climbing up Mount Carmel. They first crossed a high ridge, then went up steps cut in the rock to a terrace; from this terrace they ascended by similar steps to a level place from which arose a hill. The hill contained a cave, and up to this Elijah mounted alone. He left his servants on the borders of the level place, that they might look down upon the Sea of Galilee. Its waters were dried up, and its bed lay full of holes, mud, and putrefied carcasses. Elijah sat down, his head resting upon his knees, covered himself with his mantle and prayed earnestly to God. Seven times did he call to his servants as to whether no cloud out of the sea had yet arisen. At last I saw in the middle of the sea a white vapor out of which came a little black cloud. In the latter was a small, shining figure which, rising on high, gradually increased in size. As the cloud rose, Elijah perceived in it the figure of a radiant virgin. Her head was surrounded by rays, her arms were outstretched in the form of a cross, one hand grasping a victor's wreath, and her long garments fell as if bound below her feet. She appeared to be hovering over Palestine. In this vision, Elijah learned four mysteries relative to the blessed Virgin. One was that she would come in the seventh age, and another was the family to which she should belong. He also saw on one shore of the sea a low, spreading tree, and on the other a very lofty one whose summit drooped over upon the lower one.

I saw the cloud break up and fall in fleecy vapors upon certain holy places and upon the abodes of certain pious people who were in prayer. These vapors were bordered by rainbow edges, and in them was the blessing like a pearl in its shell. I was told that this, though typical, was a true representation of how the preparation for the coming of the blessed Virgin would develop from those various blessed points.

Soon after this vision, Elijah enlarged the cave in which he was accustomed to pray. He made new regulations for the prophet children, of whom from that time some in that cave constantly supplicated for the coming of Mary and honored her advent.

Elijah had by his prayer called up the clouds, and he directed them according to interior enlightenment; otherwise a sudden and destructive rain gust might have resulted from them. At first I saw these clouds dropping down dew, settling in white plains, forming eddies with rainbow-colored edges, and finally dissolving in drops. I recognized some connection between them and the manna in the desert which in the morning lay brittle and thick like a skin upon the ground. It could be gathered in rolls. I saw the vapors floating along the Jordan. They did not fall in all places indiscriminately, but only here and there, at Salem, for instance, where John baptized at a later period, and at the spot where subsequently his pool of baptism stood. I asked for the signification of the colored edges, and it was explained to me by a certain shell of the sea which, too, has shining colored margins. The shell under the sun's rays absorbs the light, reflects its colors at the edges, thus purifying the ray as it were, until in its own center the pure, white pearl is formed. I cannot express it, but I understood that that dew and the rain following it did more than what is commonly signified by a refreshing, a watering of the earth. I received the clear assurance that, without this dew, Mary's advent would have been delayed one hundred years longer; while through that watering and blessing of the earth, the different families living on its produce were quickened and enlivened. Thus their flesh received a new blessing by which it became more purified and ennobled by propagation. The vision of the pearl in its shell bore reference to Jesus and Mary.

The drought that I saw was not confined to the earth alone; there was also a great drought, great sterility among men. But the spray of the fructifying dew descended from generation to generation down to the flesh of Mary. I cannot express it. At times, there appeared upon the colored edges of the cloud one or several pearls, and upon these a human figure, breathing forth something spirit-like which again seemed to amalgamate in the others.

I saw also that, by the great mercy of God, the pious pagans of that age knew that the Messiah would be born of a virgin of Judea. This knowledge was imparted to the star worshippers of Chaldea by the appearance of a vision either in a star or in the heavens. They prophesied concerning it. I saw the same tidings of salvation proclaimed in Egypt.

Elijah was commanded by God to bring together into Judea several pious families scattered to the north, east, and south. He sought for three prophet scholars suited to the mission, and he implored a sign from God by which he might recognize them, for it was a distant and very hazardous undertaking.

One went north; the second, east; and the third, south. This last route led to Egypt where Israelites could not enter without risk. I saw the third messenger journeying along the road subsequently traversed by the holy family, and also at Heliopolis. He came, at last, to a great pagan temple surrounded by numerous buildings and situated in a wide plain. A live bull was worshipped in this temple, and in it were also the image of a bull and other idols. Deformed children were sacrificed to the animal. As the prophet was passing the temple, he was seized and led before the priests. Fortunately for him, they were exceedingly inquisitive, else perhaps they would have murdered him at once. They questioned him as to whence he came. He answered fearlessly, telling them that a virgin would be born from whom should proceed the salvation of the world, then would all their idols be shattered. They were amazed and impressed by what they heard, and allowed him to go on his way. But they afterward took counsel together and resolved to make the image of a virgin. When it was finished, they placed it high in the center of the temple roof, and in a position as if in the act of floating down.

The virgin's headdress was like that of so many of the other idols, half-woman, half-lion, that were in the temple. The upper part of the arms was close to the body, the forearms extended as if warding off something. Feathers radiated from both upper and lower arms, two clasping together like crests, or combs; similar feathers ran down the sides and the middle of the body to the tiny feet.

The Egyptians honored this image and offered sacrifice to it, that thereby the virgin might not destroy their god Apis and their other idols. But they still continued in their usual abominations. The only change the prophet's communication wrought was that they thenceforth invoked the image of the virgin and honored it according to the various interpretations they put upon his words.

I saw much of the history of Tobias and the marriage brought about by the angel, between young Tobias with Sarah. The latter was a type of St. Anne. The old Tobias represented the race of pious Jews that yearned after the Messiah. His blindness signified that he was to be the father of no more children, and that he should devote himself entirely to meditation and prayer. His quarrelsome wife was an image of the vain and troublesome ceremonies of the pharisaical doctors of the Law. The swallow, a messenger of spring, heralded the coming salvation. Tobias's blindness chiefly betokened the faithful, though obscure, waiting and longing for salvation and the ignorance of whence it should come.

The angel had indeed spoken truly when he said that he was Azarias, the son of Ananias, for this word signifies the help of the Lord out of the cloud of the Lord. This angel was the guide of the races, the protector and administrator of the Blessing even unto the Conception of the blessed Virgin. In the prayer offered together by young Tobias and Sarah, and which I saw carried by angels to the throne of God where it was favorably received, I recognized the supplications of the pious Israelites and the daughters of Zion for the coming of the Savior, also the simultaneous prayers of Joachim and Anne for the child promised to them. The blindness of Tobias and the reproaches of his wife signified also the contempt shown to Joachim and the slighting of his offerings. The seven murdered husbands of Sarah represented those among the ancestors of Mary who had placed obstacles to her coming and, consequently, to the salvation of man. They likewise denoted the suitors dismissed by Anne before her marriage with Joachim. The reproaches of Sarah's maid signified the derision of pagans, of unbelievers, and of godless Jews upon the delay in the coming of the long-looked-for Messiah. Such impious taunts drove the pious to still more earnest prayer. It was also and very particularly a symbol of the scorn that Anne endured from her maid, at which being confused, she had recourse to prayer with so great earnestness that she was heard. The fish about to devour the young Tobias typified the prolonged sterility of Anne; but the removal of its heart, liver, and gall denoted good works and mortification. The little kid brought home by Tobias's wife as the wages of her work, was really a stolen one that the people had given to her cheap. Tobias knew the people as well as the whole transaction, and that was the reason that they despised him. It bore also some signification to the relations that existed between the pious Jews and the Essenes on the one hand, and the Pharisees and merely ceremonious Jews on the other, also the scorn felt by the latter for the former; but what that signification was, I cannot now recall. The gall, by which the blind Tobias was restored to sight, symbolized the suffering and bitterness by which the elect among the Jews arrived at the knowledge of salvation and attained to a participation in the same. It signified the entrance of light into darkness, Jesus entering upon his bitter Passion from his very birth.

Symbolical Vision

I SAW a slender pillar arise out of the earth. It was like the stalk of a flower, and like the calyx, or the capsule, of the poppy, I saw the octagonal church upon the top of this pillar. The pillar arose through the center of the church and there, like a tree, divided into several branches. Upon these branches stood the members of the holy family and their relatives. They were indeed the central objects of veneration in this vision. They stood as if on the stamens of flowers. Anne stood above between two holy men, Joachim and her father, or some other member of her family. Below St. Anne's breast I saw a brilliant space almost in the shape of a heart. In this light, I saw the figure of a shining child unfolding as it were, becoming larger. Its hands were clasped upon its breast, its head inclined, and it constantly shed toward one quarter of the globe numerous rays of light. I noticed with surprise that the rays did not stream in all directions. On the surrounding branches and inclining toward this middle one, were adorers, and all around in the church, in groups and choirs innumerable, were saints inclining in prayer toward the holy central point. The sweetness, fervor, and simplicity of this sacred service can be compared to nothing but a flowery field swayed toward the sun by a gentle breeze, and sending its perfumes and colors to those beams to which all flowers owe their gifts, yes, their existence itself. Above this picture of the Immaculate Conception arose the stem of grace. It extended above Anne, and upon this stem, crown-like, sat Mary and Joseph. Below them in adoration sat Anne. But above them all, on the very summit of the tree, sat the child Jesus in unfading splendor, the imperial globe in his hand. In adoration around these groups, were first the choirs of the apostles and disciples and, in more distant circles, those of the other saints. High above all, I saw in the brightest light, figures and powers of indeterminate form, and over them something like a half-sun rayed out its beams. This second picture seemed to signify the Advent. First I saw the region below and around the pillar, then I saw the church and its adorers, and lastly the child developing in the shining heart. I received at the same time an unspeakable assurance of the sinless Conception. I read it plainly as if in a book, and I comprehended it. I was also informed that a church had once stood on this spot, but on account of its being the scene of many scandalous disputes on the subject of the Immaculate Conception, it had been given over to destruction. The Church Triumphant, however, still celebrates the festival on its site. I heard also the words: "Every vision contains some mystery until its fulfillment."

Eve of Mary's Birth

WHAT gladness throughout all nature! Birds are singing, lambs and kids are gamboling, and swarms of doves are fluttering with joy around the spot upon which once stood Anne's abode. I see only a wilderness there at the present day… But I had a vision of pilgrims in the far-off times who, girded and with long staves in their hands, wended their way through the country to Mount Carmel. On their head they wore a covering wound around like a turban. They, too, participated in the joy of nature. And when in their astonishment they asked the hermits that dwelt in the neighborhood the cause of this remarkable exultation, they received for answer that such manifestations of gladness were customary. They were always observed upon the eve of the anniversary of Mary's birth around that spot where once stood Anne's house. The hermits told them of a holy man of the early times who had been the first to notice these wonders in nature. His account gave rise to the celebration of the Feast of Mary's Nativity which soon became general throughout the church: And now I, too, beheld how this came to pass.

I saw a pious pilgrim, two hundred and fifty years after Mary's death, traversing the Holy Land, visiting and venerating all places connected with the actions of Jesus while on earth. He was supernaturally guided. Sometimes he tarried several days together in certain places in which he tasted extraordinary consolation. There he prayed and meditated, and there also he received revelations from on high. For several years he had, from the seventh to the eighth of September, noticed a great jubilation in nature and heard angelic voices singing in the air. He prayed earnestly to know the meaning of all this, and it was made known to him in a vision that that was the birth night of the blessed Virgin Mary. He was on his way to Mount Sinai when he had this vision. In it he was informed also of the existence of a chapel built in Mary's honor in a cave of the prophet Elijah. He was told to reveal this, as well as the circumstance of Mary's birth night, to the hermits on Mount Sinai.

I saw him again when he arrived at the mount. Where the convent now stands there dwelt, even at that early period, hermits scattered here and there. It was then as inaccessible from the valley as it is now. To reach the top of the mountain from that side, hoisting machines were used. I saw that in consequence of the pilgrim's communication, the eighth of September was here first celebrated in the year 250, and that later it was introduced into other parts of the church.

I saw hermits accompanying the pilgrim to the cave of Elijah to visit the chapel that had been built therein to Mary's honor. But it was not easy to find, for the mountain was covered with gardens that still produced magnificent fruits, though long allowed to run wild, and there were numerous caves of hermits and Essenes. The pilgrim who had had the vision told them to send a Jew into the different caves, and that the one out of which he should be thrust would be the cave of Elijah. He had been thus instructed in vision. I then saw them sending an old Jew into the caves; but, as often as he tried to enter a certain one that had a narrow entrance built up before it, he was repulsed. By this miracle the cave of Elijah was recognized. On entering it they found another cave, the entrance to which had been closed by masonry; this was the chapel in which the prophet Elijah had in prayer honored the future mother of the Savior. Many holy relics were still preserved in it, bones of the prophets and patriarchs, screens and vessels that had once been used in ceremonies of the Old Law. These latter were appropriated to the use of the church.

The spot upon which the thorn bush had stood was called in the language of that country: The Shadow of God. It was entered only barefoot. The Elijah chapel was walled up with beautiful large stones through which ran flower-like veinings. They were afterward employed for the erection of the church. In the vicinity is a mountain entirely of red sand on which, nevertheless, there is very beautiful fruit.

I learned from St. Bridget that if pregnant women fast on the eve of Mary's birth and say fervently nine Hail Marys to honor the nine months she passed in Anne's womb; if they frequently repeat these prayers during their pregnancy, and especially on the eve of their delivery, receiving then the holy sacraments devoutly, she will offer their prayer to God herself and bring them through even very critical circumstances to a happy delivery.

I saw the blessed Virgin on the eve of her nativity. She said to me: "Whoever says this evening," (Sept. 7th) "nine times the Hail Mary lovingly and devoutly to honor the nine months spent in my mother's womb as also my birth, and continues the same devotion for nine consecutive days, daily gives to the angels nine flowers for a bouquet. This bouquet they bear to heaven and offer to the most holy Trinity to obtain some favor for the one that prays."

I was transported to a high place between heaven and earth. I saw the earth below me gray and somber, and above me heaven where, among the choirs of angels and the orders of the blessed, was the blessed Virgin before the throne of God. I saw prepared for her two thrones of honor, two buildings of honor, which finally became churches, yes, whole cities, and they were formed out of the prayers of earth. They were built entirely of flowers, leaves, garlands, the various species typical of the different value and characteristics of the prayers of individuals and of whole congregations. Angels and saints took them from the hands of those that offered them and bore them up to heaven.

Birth of Mary

SEVERAL days previously, Anne informed Joachim that the time of her delivery was at hand. She sent messengers to her sister Maraha, at Sepphoris, also to the widow Enue, Elizabeth's sister, in the valley of Zebulon, and to her sister Sobe's daughter Salome, the wife of Zebedee, of Bethsaida. The sons of Sobe and Zebedee, James the Greater and John, were not yet born. Anne sent for these three women to come to her. I saw them on their journey. Two of them were accompanied by their husbands, who returned, however, when they had reached the neighborhood of Nazareth. Joachim had sent the menservants off to the herds, and had otherwise disposed of the domestics not absolutely needed in the house. Mary Heli, Anne's eldest daughter, now the wife of Cleophas, took charge of the household affairs.

On the evening before the birth of the child, Joachim himself went to his herds in the field nearest his home. I saw him with some of his servants who were related to him. He called them brothers, but they were only his brother's children. The pasture grounds were beautifully divided off and hedged in. In the corners were huts wherein the servants were provided with food supplied from Anne's house. There was also a stone altar before which they prayed. Steps led down to it, and the space around it

Birth of Mary

was neatly paved with triangular stones. Behind the altar was a wall with steps at the sides. The whole place was surrounded by trees.

Joachim, after praying here awhile, selected the finest lambs, kids, and bullocks from his herds, and sent them by his servants to the temple as offerings. He did not return to his home before night.

I saw the three women approaching Anne's abode toward evening. When they arrived, they went straight to her apartment back of the fireplace. Anne embraced them, told them that her time drew near, and standing intoned with them a Psalm. "Praise God, the Lord. He has had pity on his people and has freed Israel. Truly, he has fulfilled the Promise that he made to Adam in Paradise: 'The seed of the woman shall crush the serpent's head.'" I do not remember all, verse for verse, but Anne rehearsed the different types of Mary, and said: "The germ that God gave to Abraham has ripened in me. The promise made to Sarah and the blossom of Aaron's rod are fulfilled in me." During all this time, Anne was shining with light. The room was full of glory, and over Anne hovered Jacob's ladder. The women around her were amazed, entranced. I think they too saw the ladder.

And now a slight refreshment was placed before the visitors. They ate and drank standing and toward midnight lay down to rest. But Anne remained up in prayer. After awhile she went and roused the women. She felt that her time was near, and she desired them to pray with her. They all withdrew behind a curtain that concealed an oratory. Anne opened the doors of a little closet built in the wall. In it was a box containing sacred treasures, and on either side lights so contrived that they could be raised in their sockets at pleasure, and rested on upright supports. These lamps were now lighted. At the foot of the little altar was a cushioned stool. The box contained some of Sarah's hair, which Anne held in great reverence; some of the bones of Joseph, which Moses had brought with him out of Egypt; something belonging to Tobias, relics of clothing, I think; and the little, white, shining, pear-shaped cup from which Abraham drank when he received the Blessing from the angel, and which was later on taken from the Ark of the Covenant and given to Joachim along with the Blessing. This Blessing was like wine and bread, like a sacrament, like a supernatural, invigorating food. Anne knelt before the shrine, one of the women on either side, and the third behind her. Again I heard them reciting a Psalm. I think that the burning bush on Horeb was mentioned in it. And now a supernatural light began to fill the chamber and to hover around Anne. The three women fell prostrate as if stunned. Around Anne the light took the exact form of the thornbush on Horeb, so that I could no longer see her.

The flame streamed inward, and all at once I saw Anne receiving into her arms the shining child Mary. She wrapped it in her mantle, pressed it to her heart, laid it on the stool before the relics, and went on with her prayer.

Then I heard the child crying, and I saw Anne drawing forth some linen from under the large veil that enveloped her. She swathed the child first in gray and then in red, leaving the breast, arms, and head bare, and then the luminous thornbush vanished. The holy women arose and in glad surprise received the newborn child into their arms. They wept for joy. All intoned a hymn of praise while Anne held the child on high. I saw the chamber again filled with light and myriads of angels. They announced the child's name, singing: "On the twentieth day, this child shall be called Mary." Then they sang Gloria and Alleluia. I heard all these words.

Anne went to her chamber, and lay down upon her couch. The women bathed and swathed the child, and laid it by the mother. Next to the bed was a little portable basket-crib furnished with wooden pegs, by means of which it could be stuck into holes on the right or left, or at the foot of the bed as might be desired. One of the women went and called Joachim. He entered, knelt by Anne's couch, and his tears fell in torrents over the child. Then he took it up, held it aloft, and intoned a canticle of praise like unto that of Zechariah. He spoke words expressive of his longing now to die, and he alluded to the germ given by God to Abraham and perfected in himself, also to the root of Jesse. I noticed, though not till afterward, that Mary Heli was not among the first to see the child. She must at this time have been for some years the mother of Mary Cleophas. Still she was not present at Mary's birth, because the Jewish custom does not permit the daughter to be with the mother at such a time.

When Mary was born, I saw her at one and the same time before the most holy Trinity in heaven and on earth in Anne's arms. I saw the joy of the whole heavenly court. I saw all her gifts and graces in a supernatural way revealed to her. I often have such visions, but they are for me inexpressible, for others unintelligible, therefore am I silent with regard to them. Mary was also instructed in innumerable mysteries. As this vision ended, the child cried upon earth.

I saw the news of Mary's birth announced also in Limbo, and I beheld the transports of joy with which it was received by the patriarchs, especially by Adam and Eve, who rejoiced that the Promise made them in Paradise was now fulfilled. I saw also that the patriarchs increased in grace, their abode became lighter and less constrained, and that they began to exercise a greater influence on earth. It was as if all their good works, all their penance, all the efforts of their life, all their desires and aspirations had at last brought forth fruit.

All nature, animate and inanimate, men and beasts, were stirred to joy, and I heard sweet singing. But sinners were filled with anguish and remorse. I saw, especially around Nazareth and in other parts of Palestine, many possessed souls who at the hour of Mary's birth became perfectly furious. They uttered horrible cries, and they were tossed and dashed about. The devils cried out of them: "We must withdraw! We must go out!"

My greatest delight was to see the old priest Simeon in the temple on this night of Mary's birth. He was aroused by the fearful cries of the possessed confined in one of the streets on the temple mountain. Simeon with others had charge of them. He went that night to the house in which they were, and asked the cause of those shrieks that roused everyone from sleep. The possessed man nearest to the entrance cried out fiercely that he must get out. Simeon released him, and then the devil cried out: "I must go forth! We must go forth! A virgin is born, and there are upon earth so many angels who torment us. We must go forth, and never again shall we dare possess a human being!" Then I saw the poor creature horribly tossed to and fro by the devil, who at last went out of him. Simeon was in prayer. I rejoiced greatly at seeing old Simeon then.

I saw, too, Anna, the prophetess, and another one of Mary's future teachers in the temple aroused and instructed in vision upon the birth of the child. They told each other what had happened. I think they knew of Anne.

In the country of the three holy kings, certain prophetesses had visions of the birth of the blessed Virgin. They told their priests that a virgin was born, to welcome whom many spirits had come down upon earth, but that other spirits were troubled. The star-gazing kings also saw pictures of it in their stars.

In Egypt, on the night of the birth, an idol was hurled from its temple into the sea, and another fell from its place and was dashed to pieces.

Next morning I saw a great crowd from the neighborhood around the house along with Anne's servants, male and female. The women in charge showed the child to them. Many of them were very much affected, and many wicked hearts were changed. They had gathered around the house because they had seen a light over it during the night and also because the birth of Anne's child was looked upon as a great blessing.

Later on other relatives of Joachim from the valley of Zebulon arrived, also the servants from a distance. The child was shown to all, and a repast was prepared in the house.

On the following days people flocked in numbers to see the child Mary. Her little cradle, which was in the form of a boat, was placed upon a raised pedestal, something like a sawing jack, in the front apartment. The lower coverlet was red, the upper one white, and on them lay the child swathed up to the armpits in red and transparent white. She had tiny, golden curls.

I saw also Mary Cleophas, the child of Mary Heli and Cleophas, the grandchild of Anne. She was then a little girl of only a few years. She was playing with the infant Mary and caressing her. She was a stout, healthy child. She wore a little white, sleeveless dress bordered with red from which hung tiny red balls, like apples. Around her little bare arms were twined rows of white stuff, maybe feathers or silk or wool. The child Mary had also a little transparent scarf around her neck.

The Child Receives the Name of Mary

I SAW a great feast in Anne's house; all was gladness. The wicker partitions in the front of the house had been taken away, and a large room was thusly made ready. All around it ran a low table upon which stood plates, glasses, etc., but as yet no food. In the middle of the room was an altar covered with red and white, and a stand upon which scrolls were laid. A small basket-cradle stood on the altar. It was shaped like a shell and woven in white and red; the coverlet was sky-blue. Priests from Nazareth were present in their sacred vestments; among them was one robed more magnificently than the rest. Many of the female guests, relatives of Anne, were also in their holiday garments. Among them were Anne's eldest daughter Mary Heli, espoused to Cleophas, Anne's sister from Sepphoris, and others. Several of Joachim's relatives also were present. Anne was up, but she did not appear. She remained in her chamber behind the fireplace. Enue, Elizabeth's sister, brought the infant Mary, swathed as described in red and transparent white, and gave her to Joachim. The priests approached the altar, the attendants bearing the chief priest's train, and prayed from the scrolls. Joachim placed the child on the arms of the chief priest, who held her aloft, prayed for awhile, and then laid her in the little cradle on the altar. Then he took a pair of scissors, furnished with a little box at the end for catching the clippings, (something like a pair of snuffers), and cut a little hair from both sides and from the middle of the child's head. The hair thus removed, he burned it upon a pan of coals. Then he took a box of oil and anointed the five senses of the child. With his thumb, he pressed the ointment upon the ears, the eyes, the nose, the mouth, and the heart of the child. He wrote the name Mary on a scrap of parchment, and laid it on the child's breast. Then the little Mary was, by Joachim, given back to Enue, who took her to Anne. The women stood back during the ceremony, at the end of which other psalms were sung. I saw then all kinds of table furniture, dishes, etc., that I had not before noticed. There were vessels on the table that were quite light, their covers pierced with holes. I think they were baskets into which flowers were put. On a side table I saw numbers of little white rods, as if of bone, also spoons. There were also bent tubes lying on it, but I know not for what use. I saw no more of the meal itself.

Preparations for Mary's Presentation

MARY was three years and three months old when she made the vow to join the virgins in the temple. She was very delicately built and had golden hair inclined to curl at the ends. She was already as tall as a child of five or six here in our country. Mary Heli's daughter was a few years older than Mary, and much stronger and stouter. I saw in Anne's house the preparations for Mary's admittance into the temple. It was made the occasion of a great festival. Five priests had assembled from Nazareth, Sepphoris, and other places, among them Zechariah and a son of the brother of Anne's father. They were about to perform a sacred ceremony over the child Mary, a kind of examination as to whether she was sufficiently mature in mind to be admitted to the temple. Besides the priests, there were present Anne's sister from Sepphoris with her daughter Mary Heli and her child, and several other little girls and relatives.

The robes worn by the child at this feast were cut out by the priests themselves and the different parts quickly sewed together by the women present. The child was clothed in them at certain periods when subjected to a series of interrogatories. The ceremony was in itself very grave and solemn, although the faces of the aged priests were at times lit up by smiles of admiration at the expressions and answers of the little Mary, and it was frequently interrupted by the tears of Joachim and Anne. Three entire suits were prepared for Mary and put on her at different times during the ceremony, the questioning and answering going on in the meantime. All this took place in a large room next to the dining hall. Light entered through a square opening in the center of the roof, which opening was often covered by a net. The floor was covered with a red carpet. In the middle of the room stood a table, intended for an altar, with a red cover, and over that a white transparent one. Upon it lay a case with rolls of writings and a curtain upon which the picture of Moses was either embroidered or laid on and sewed down. He was represented in the large mantle in which he used to pray, the tables of the Law hanging on his arm. I have always seen Moses represented as a tall, broad-shouldered man. He had a high, somewhat pyramidal head, a large hooked nose, and upon his broad, high forehead, were two bumps inclining toward each other and giving him a very remarkable appearance. In his childhood, they were like little warts. His complexion was brown, bright and ruddy, his hair inclined to red. I saw many such protuberances as those possessed by Moses on the foreheads of the ancient prophets and hermits; sometimes only one such excrescence appeared upon the middle of the forehead.

On the altar lay the three outfits for the child Mary along with various materials, etc., presented by the relatives for her dowry. A kind of throne stood upon steps before the altar. The priests entered the hall with naked feet. Three of them only proceeded to the examination and blessed the child, who was as yet in her usual clothing. Joachim and Anne were present with their relatives; the women stood back, the little girls at Mary's side. One of the priests took the garments from the altar, explained their signification, and handed them to Anne's sister, from Sepphoris, who put them on the child.

First came a little, yellow, knitted robe, and then a colored, laced bodice, which was put on over the head and fastened around the body. It had on the breast something like cords. Over that came a brownish mantle with armholes, from the upper part of which hung lappets. It was cut out around the neck, and closed under the breast.

On her feet were brown sandals with thick, green soles. Her reddish-yellow curls were arranged, and a silken crown with feathers in it placed upon them. The feathers were a finger in length, and they bent over toward the inside of the crown. I know to what bird in that country they belonged. A large square, ash-colored kerchief was thrown over her head like a large veil. It could be drawn together under the arms in such a way that they might rest in it as in slings. It appeared to be a mantle used in time of prayer and penance, also in traveling.

The priests now put to the child all sorts of questions relative to the discipline enforced in the temple. Among other things, they said to her: "Thy parents, having promised thee to the temple, have made a vow that thou shouldst drink no wine nor vinegar, shouldst eat no grapes nor figs. Now what wilt thou add to this vow? Think upon this during thy meal." The Jewish people, and especially the young maidens were accustomed to drink vinegar. Mary, too, was fond of it. On these and similar things, was she interrogated.

And now the second suit was put upon the child. It consisted of a sky-blue body, a mantle of the same color, but of a lighter shade, a richer bodice, and a white veil, glossy like silk, which fell behind in folds something like the consecrated veil of a nun. Over this was a fine, closely-fitting wreath of colored flowerbuds made of silk and intermixed with small green leaves. Then the priests threw over her face a white veil gathered on top like a cap. It was caught by three clasps, one below the other, by means of which the veil could be raised upon the head, either one third, or one half, or even the whole.

The child was instructed upon the use of this veil, when to be raised or lowered in eating or answering questions. In this array, Mary went to table where she sat between two of the priests, the third opposite to her. The women and children sat at one end of the table apart from the men. During the meal, the priests practiced the child in many points upon the use of the veil, asking questions and receiving her answers, and also in many other of the customary ceremonies. They reminded her that she still could partake of everything, and they offered her different dishes, tempting her in order to see how far her abstinence would go. But Mary excited their admiration by all that she did and said. She tasted sparingly of only a few dishes, and answered all their questions with simplicity and wisdom. During the meal and the whole of the examination, I saw angels hovering around her, directing and assisting her in all things.

After the repast, she was clothed anew before the altar in the next room. Anne's sister from Sepphoris assisted the priest in the ceremony, during which the latter explained the signification of the garments and spoke of spiritual things. The robes now put on the child were the most beautiful of all. A violet-blue bodice, and over it a breastpiece embroidered in colors. The latter was now fastened to the piece that covered the back, caught to the plaited skirt, and fell below in a point. Over this fell a violet-blue mantle, full and magnificent, rounded in the back very much like a chasuble. When it was closed on the breast, it formed puffs on the arms, like arches, wherein they could rest, and yet be exposed to view. It had five rows of gold embroidery down the front, the middle one furnished with the buttons or hooks that fastened the mantle. It was also embroidered around the edge. A large changeable-colored veil was then put on, which glanced from white to violet-blue. Upon this veil rested a crown, closed on top by five clasps. It was a thin, broad circlet lined with gold, the upper edge spreading into points tipped with little balls. A network of silk covered the outside, which was ornamented with small roses of the same material in whose center were fastened five pearls. The five points also were of silk and surmounted by a ball. The breastpiece was fastened behind, yet had cords also in front as if for lacing. Her mantle was caught first over the breast by a crossband, which was prevented from pressing upon the breast ornament by a button with a long shank; it closed again under the bodice and fell behind the arms in folds.

In this festive attire, Mary was placed upon the steps before the altar, the little girls at her side. She now repeated her resolve to abstain from flesh, fish, and milk, to make use of only a certain drink prepared from the pith of a reed soaked in water. This was much used by the poor of Palestine, just as here in our own country rice or barley water is drunk by them. To this beverage, Mary proposed to add occasionally some terebinthine juice. This juice is like a white, viscid oil and is very refreshing, though not in the same degree as balsam. Mary expressed her resolution to refrain also from spices and fruits, with the exception of a kind of yellow berry that grows in bunches. I know them well. Children and poor people eat them in that country. She said also that she would lie on the bare ground and nightly rise three times to pray. The other maidens rose but once.

Upon hearing this, Anne and Joachim shed tears, and the aged Joachim pressed his child in his arms, saying: "Ah, my child, that is too hard! If thou livest so mortified a life, I, thy poor old father, shall never see thee again." This scene was very affecting.

But the priests replied to the child that she should, like the others, rise once only during the night, and they laid down other and milder conditions for her. Finally, they said, "Many of the other virgins enter the temple without a dowry or even wherewith to pay their board. On this account and with their parents' consent, they engage to wash the blood-besprinkled garments of the priests and the rough woolen cloths. This is a very heavy work, and not accomplished without bleeding hands. But thou wilt never be called upon for such services, since thy parents are able to maintain thee at the temple."

But Mary quickly replied that she was ready even for this work, were she esteemed worthy to perform it. At this speech, Joachim again betrayed his emotion.

During these holy ceremonies, I beheld Mary becoming at times so tall that she even rose above the heads of the priests. This was for me a sign of her wisdom and grace. The priests were filled with amazement, at once solemn and joyful.

At last, Mary was blessed by the priests. I saw her radiant with light as she stood on the little altar throne, two priests on either side of her and one opposite. They held rolls of writing, and prayed over the child, their hands outstretched above her. At that moment, I saw a wonderful vision in the child Mary. She seemed, by virtue of the blessing, to become transparent. In her was a glory, a halo of unspeakable splendor, and in that halo appeared the mystery of the Ark of the Covenant, as if in a glittering crystal vessel. I saw Mary's heart open like the doors of a temple, and the holy thing of the Ark of the Covenant, around which a tabernacle of precious stones of multiplied signification had been formed like a heavenly throne, going into her heart through that opening, like the Ark of the Covenant into the Holy of Holies, like the monstrance into the tabernacle. I saw that by this the child Mary was glorified; she hovered above the earth. With the entrance of this sacrament into Mary's heart, which immediately closed over it, the vision faded, and I saw the child all penetrated by glowing fervor. During this wonderful vision I saw that Zechariah received an interior assurance, a heavenly intimation that Mary was the chosen vessel of the mystery. From it he had received a ray that had appeared figuratively in Mary.

And now the priests led the child to her parents. Anne caught her child to her breast and kissed her, but Joachim —deeply affected—reverenced Mary and only took her hand. The elder sister Mary Heli embraced the favored child with much more gaiety than did Anne, who was a very serious, practical, moderate, and self-possessed woman. The little niece, Mary Cleophas, acted as any child would, and fondly embraced the little Mary.

Then the priests took the child again, disrobed her, and led her forth in her customary dress. I saw them standing drinking out of a cup, and then departing.

The Journey to the Temple

I SAW Joachim, Anne, and their elder daughter busied during the night packing and preparing for a journey. A lamp with several wicks was burning, and I saw Mary Heli busily going about with a light. Some days before, Joachim had sent his servants up to the temple with offerings of cattle, five of the finest of every kind. They made a nice herd. Now he saddled two of the beasts of burden, and loaded them with all kinds of baggage: clothes for the child and presents for the temple. A broad package was laid on the back of each beast, and formed a comfortable seat. The baggage was all in bundles. On both sides of one of the beasts platter-shaped baskets with arched covers were fastened. In them were birds as large as partridges. There were also oval baskets containing fruit. A cover with heavy tassels was thrown over the whole load.

Two of the priests were still present. One was very old. He wore a cap pointed on the forehead and with lappets over the ears. His upper garment was shorter than the under one, and over it was a kind of stole. He had much to do with the child. The other priest was younger.

I saw also two boys present. They were not human. They appeared there supernaturally and with a spiritual signification. They carried long standards rolled upon staffs furnished with knobs at both ends. The larger of the two boys came to me with his standard unfurled, read, and explained it to me. The writing appeared entirely strange to me, the single, golden letters all inverted. One letter represented a whole word. The language sounded unfamiliar, but I understood it all the same. He showed me in his roll the passage referring to the burning thornbush of Moses. He explained to me how the thornbush burned, and yet was not consumed; so now was the child Mary inflamed with the fire of the Holy Spirit, but in her humility she knew nothing of it. It signifies also the divinity and humanity in Jesus, and how God's fire united with the child Mary. The putting-off of the shoes, he explained thus: "The Law will now be fulfilled. The veil is withdrawn and the essence appears." By the little standard on his staff was signified, as he told me, that Mary now began her course, her career, to become the mother of the Redeemer. The other boy seemed to be playing with his standard. He jumped about and ran around with it. By this was signified Mary's innocence. The great Promise is to be fulfilled in her, rests upon her, and yet she plays like a child in this holy destiny. I cannot express the loveliness of those boys. They were different from all others present, and these latter did not appear to see them.

There were besides Anne about six female relatives with their children and some men who accompanied them. Joachim guided the beast, upon which the child Mary sometimes rode. He carried a light, for it was still dark when they set out. A servant led the other. The little procession was also accompanied by the other apparitions of the prophets. As Mary hastened from the house, they pointed out to me a place in their rolls, wherein it was declared that, although the temple was indeed magnificent, yet Mary contained in herself still greater magnificence. Mary wore the little yellowish gown and the large veil so fastened around her that her arms could rest in it.

When she rode, the prophet boys followed behind her; but when she walked, they were at her side, singing the Psalms 44 and 49. I knew that the same would be sung at her reception in the temple. The child Mary saw those boys, but she said nothing about it. She was perfectly silent, wholly recollected in self.

The journey was difficult, over mountain and valley. In the latter lay chilling mists and dew. Once I saw the travelers resting at a fountain under some balsam trees, and again stopping overnight at an inn at the foot of a mountain.

Twelve leagues from Jerusalem, they came up at an inn

with the herd that had been sent on in advance as an offering, and which was just about starting anew. Joachim was well known here, and was quite at home. When taking his offerings up to Jerusalem, he had always stopped at this inn; and when, from his penitential stay among the shepherds he returned to Nazareth, he had also put up here.

I again saw the holy travelers in the city Beth-Horon, six leagues from Jerusalem. They had crossed a rivulet, had passed Gophna and Ozensara, and were still distant about two leagues from a road whence Jerusalem could be descried. At Beth-Horon they put up at a Levitical school. Relatives of Joachim and Anne from Nazareth, Sepphoris, Zebulon, and the country around, had come hither with their daughters, and there was quite a little festival in Mary's there. Several times she reclined by Anne's side at table, or stood behind her with her arm around her neck.

On the following day, accompanied by the teacher of the Levitical school and his family, they started very early for Jerusalem. The young girls carried beautiful fruits and garments as presents for the child. It looked to me as if there was going to be a real festival in Jerusalem. The nearer they approached the Holy City, the more eager and desirous became Mary. She generally ran on before her parents.

I saw the arrival of the procession in Jerusalem, and also beheld the roads and paths and buildings more distinctly than I had done for a long time. Jerusalem was a very singular-looking city. We must not represent it to ourselves

Approaching Jerusalem from the South

honor. She was conducted with many other children to a hall in which a special place had been prepared for her on an elevated seat like a throne. She was then crowned. The teachers questioned her, and were struck with all her answers. Mention was made of the wisdom of another maiden who not long since had returned from the temple to her home at Gophna. She was called Susanna, and I think that it was her place Mary was going to take in the temple. Susanna was then fifteen; later, she joined the holy women that followed Jesus.

Mary rejoiced at being now so near to the temple. Joachim embraced her, weeping and saying, "I shall never see thee again!" During the repast, Mary went here and with its streets thronged as the great cities of the present day. Many steep and hilly streets ran around behind the city walls, from which no gates led. The houses lying high behind those walls faced the opposite side, for many parts of the city were built at subsequent periods, new ridges of hills being taken in accordingly. The old city walls, however, were always allowed to remain standing. Many of the deep valleys were spanned by massive stone arches. The courtyards and rooms of the houses all opened toward the back of the building, the entrance only being on the street. The walls were surmounted by terraces or balconies. The houses were kept closed the greater part of the time. When the inhabitants had no affairs to call them to the public places of the city or to the temple, they remained for the most part in their own houses and courts. It was tolerably quiet on the streets, excepting in the neighborhood of the markets and palaces, where there was much going to and fro of soldiers and travelers. On certain days, at the time when all were gathered in the temple for worship, the city in many localities was entirely deserted. On this account and the seclusion of the people in their houses, Jesus and his disciples were enabled to go undisturbed through the solitary streets and deep valleys. Water was not plentiful in the city; one often sees high buildings to and from which it was conveyed, also towers in which it was pumped. They were very careful of water at the temple where such quantities were needed for washing and purifying the various vessels, etc. They had great engines for pumping it up. There were numbers of shopkeepers and merchants in the city; they had their booths all together in the markets and open squares. So stood, for instance, not far from the sheepgate, many dealers in all kinds of gold trinkets and shining stones. Their booths were round and light, and quite brown as if streaked with something, pitch or resin, probably. Though light, they were very strong. There they carried on their business and, under tents stretched from one to another, they exposed their different wares. There were also certain localities, near the palaces for instance, where there was more life in the streets, where it was more brisk. Old Rome was indeed more pleasantly situated. It was not so steep, and its streets were more lively. On one side of the mountain upon which the temple was situated, the declivity was more gentle. Here there were several streets upon terraces and on top of the thick walls, where some of the priests and servants of the temple dwelt, as did some laboring people who performed the lowest services, such as purifying the ditches wherein was thrown the offal of the cattle slaughtered for the temple. On the other side, the mountain was very steep, and the ditch quite black. Around the summit of the mountain was a green ledge whereon the priests had all kinds of little gardens. Even in Christ's time there was upon certain parts of the temple work constantly going on.

There were quantities of ore in the mountain upon which stood the temple, and much was dug out and used in the building. Inside the meadow were numbers of smelting vaults and furnaces. I never felt at home in the temple, for I never could find in it a place well-suited for prayer. It was all so immensely solid, so massive, so high, the numerous courts were so narrow, dark, and obstructed by so many elevated platforms and seats, that, when the people were in it, it presented a somewhat frightful spectacle, and even looked confined with its high, massive walls and lofty pillars. The constant slaughtering going on and the quantities of blood flowing in consequence, I found most repulsive, though words cannot express the wonderful order and cleanliness that reigned in everything connected with it.

The Entrance into Jerusalem

I SAW the caravan that conducted Mary approaching Jerusalem from the north, and winding toward the east around the outlying gardens and palaces of the city. They crossed the valley of Jehosaphat and, leaving the road to Bethany on the left, entered the city by the sheepgate leading to the cattle market. There was a pool here in which the sheep were washed. Thence their way turned to the right and ran between walls to another section of the city. Then they followed a long road through a valley, and at last reached the neighborhood of the fish market at the west side of the city. Here stood the house at which Zechariah, when engaged in the service of the temple, always put up. Out of this inn came men, women, and children with garlands to meet the caravan and to conduct them in ceremony to the house, about a quarter of an hour's distance, at which they were to stop. Zechariah was not present, but I saw a very old man there, his father's brother I think; and among those that came out to welcome Mary were relatives with their children from the country around Hebron and Bethlehem. There was a fine feast prepared for them in the house at which they stopped. The child Mary wore the second festival suit with the little blue mantle.

Zechariah called here for them, in order to take them to the feast inn that he had hired for them. This was an inn which could be hired on festival occasions like the present. There were four such inns on the northeast side of the mountain on which stood the temple. That hired by Zechariah was very large. Four halls surrounded a large court, along whose walls were sleeping places and long, low tables. A spacious saloon and a kitchen were also prepared for the guests. On two sides of this feast inn dwelt some of the servants of the temple, whose duty it was to see to the animals intended for sacrifice. The court wherein was placed the herd that Joachim had brought as an offering lay hard by.

A procession was formed when Zechariah was about to lead the travelers into the inn hired for the feast. He himself walked first with Joachim and Anne; then came Mary surrounded by four little girls in white, followed by the other children and relatives. Their way led to Herod's palace and passed that of the Roman governor, leaving the citadel of Antonia behind; at last they reached a high wall, up which there was a flight of more than fifteen steps. Mary, to the astonishment of all, mounted them without

Jerusalem from Scopus

assistance. Her friends wanted to help her, but she refused. Upon their entrance into the inn, their feet were washed. Then they were shown into a large hall in the center of which a lamp was suspended from the ceiling over a large, metal basin of water. Here they washed their face and hands.

Joachim and Anne then went up with Mary to the dwelling of some of the priests. Here, likewise urged by an interior spirit, the child hurried to mount the steps. The two priests cordially received them into the house. Both had been present at Mary's examination in Nazareth. They called one of the women belonging to the temple, where she executed all kinds of works common to females, and educated little girls. Her abode was at some distance from the temple, among the added rooms forming the sleeping apartments of the temple virgins. Out of these rooms, one could—unseen—look down into the sanctuary. The widow was so enveloped in her mantle that one could see only a little of her face. The priests and the parents delivered the child Mary over to her as her future pupil. She received her gravely, but cordially, while the child was all submission and reverence. She (the widow) accompanied the party to the feast inn, and received a package as the child's dowry.

The following day was taken up with preparations for Joachim's sacrifice and for Mary's entrance into the temple.

Joachim went early with his offering of cattle to the temple, in front of which the animals for the sacrifice were selected. Those not chosen were at once led back to the cattle market. Joachim had to lay his hand upon the head of each animal before it was slaughtered and he afterward received some of the flesh and blood of each. There were in this place many pillars, tables, and vessels, where the sacrifices were cut up, divided, and arranged. The scum of the blood was put aside, the fat, the spleen, and the liver separated, and all parts were salted. The entrails of the lambs were cleaned, filled with something, and again restored to the animal so that it looked like a whole lamb. The feet were bound crosswise. A great portion of the meat was taken to a court in which were some of the temple virgins. They seemed to have something to do connected with it; perhaps they had to prepare it either for themselves or for the priests. All was carried on with indescribable order. The priests and Levites came and went, two and two; and during the difficult and multifarious work, all progressed as if by line and level. The pieces prepared for sacrifice lay over till the next day.

In the inn was held a feast, and there was also a repast, at which about one hundred people assisted along with the children, among them twenty-four girls of different ages. Among others, I saw Seraphia, who was called Veronica after the death of Jesus. She was already well-grown, probably from ten to twelve years old. They prepared garlands and wreaths for Mary and her companions, and ornamented for them seven scepter-shaped lamps on whose summit burned a flame. During the feast many priests and Levites went in and out of the inn, taking part also in the repast. When they expressed surprise at the greatness of Joachim's offering, he bade them recall the ignominy he had endured at the temple when his former offerings were rejected, and the great mercy of God who had heard his supplications, and he asked them whether he should not now express his gratitude according to the extent of his power. I saw the child Mary and the other girls taking a walk in the neighborhood of the house.

Mary's Entrance into the Temple and her Offering

ZECHARIAH and the other men had already gone to the temple, and now Mary was led thither by the women and the virgins. Anne and her elder daughter Mary Heli, with the little daughter of the latter, Mary Cleophas, walked first; then came Mary in her second suit, the sky-blue dress and mantle, her neck and arms adorned with garlands, and the flower-wreathed candlestick in her hand. On either side walked three little maidens with similarly trimmed candlesticks. They were dressed in white embroidered with gold, and wore bluish mantles. They were quite covered with garlands, even their arms were twined with flowers. Then followed the other virgins and little girls, about twenty in number, all dressed beautifully, but somewhat differently, though all wore mantles. Then came the elderly females. They could not proceed straight to the temple from this point; they had to take a circuitous route of nearly half an hour. They passed through some streets and before Veronica's house. From many of the dwellings the procession was saluted, the spectators gazing in wonder at the child and her beautiful train of attendants. There was something very extraordinary in Mary's appearance. At the temple, men were busy opening a large and wonderfully beautiful gate upon which were carved grapevines, ears of wheat, and heads of various kinds. It was the Golden Gate. The priests led the holy Virgin up numerous steps to this gate. Joachim and Zechariah met them at the gate, which opened into a long archway, and led them through several passages into a hall. Here Mary was again questioned by the priests, after which she was clothed in the third holiday suit, the violet-blue, embroidered one.

And now Joachim went with the priests to offer sacrifice. He took fire from a certain place and stood between two priests at the altar. The approach to the altar from three sides was free, but not so on the fourth. At the four corners of the altar stood small copper pillars and a pipe of the same metal, shaped like a large inverted funnel, which ended in a spiral tube. By this arrangement the smoke from the burning sacrifice rose and escaped over the head of the priest. On three sides of the altar a shelf could be drawn out to receive what was to be laid on the middle of it, since to reach that far would be impossible.

When the sacrifice was kindled, Mary went with the women and children to her place of prayer in the women's porch, where she and her young companions stood in the front row. The porch was separated from the court of the altar of burnt offerings by a wall, in which was a gate with a grating above. Through this gate Joachim entered the subterranean passage when, upon the day of Mary's Immaculate Conception, he met Anne under the Golden Gate. The women back in the court could see the altar better when mounted on steps raised in tiers. In another court was standing a crowd of white-robed boys belonging to the temple, playing upon flutes and harps.

After the sacrifice, a portable altar was set up under the arched gateway, and before it were placed a couple of steps. Zechariah and Joachim, with some priests and two Levites, entered from the court of the altar of burnt offerings, carrying rolls and writing materials, while Anne led Mary to the steps before the altar. Mary knelt upon the steps, while Joachim and Anne, laying their hands on her head, uttered some words bearing reference to the offering of their child, which words were written down by the two Levites. Then one of the priests cut a lock of hair from the child's head, and cast it upon a pan of live coals, after which he threw around her a brown veil. During this ceremony, the girls sang Psalm 44, *Eructavit cor meum*; the priests, Psalm 49, *Deus deorum Dominus*; and the boys played on their musical instruments.

And now the priests led the holy Virgin up a long flight of steps in the wall that separated the sanctuary from the rest of the temple. They stood her in something like a niche, from which she could see into the temple where were ranged numbers of men who seemed to be consecrated to its service. Two priests stood at Mary's side, and several others on the steps praying and reading aloud from rolls. Behind Mary and on the other side of the wall, a priest was standing at the altar of incense, only half of his person visible from the point at which Mary and her attendants were placed. Through an opening contrived for the purpose, one could cast incense upon the altar without entering the court. The priest now at the incense altar was a holy old man. While he offered sacrifice and the cloud of incense arose around Mary, I saw a vision, which grew in magnitude until at last it filled the whole temple and obscured it.

I saw above the heart of Mary the glory and the mystery of the Ark of the Covenant. At first it looked exactly like the Ark of the Covenant; and lastly like the temple itself. Out of the mystery, and before Mary's breast, arose a chalice similar to that of the Last Supper; above it and just in front of her mouth appeared bread marked with a cross. Beams of light radiated around her, and in them shone her various types and symbols. The mysterious pictures of the Litany of Loretto and the other names and titles of Mary, I saw ranged up the whole flight of steps and around her.

From her shoulders, right and left, stretched an olive and a cedar branch crosswise above an elegant palm tree with a small tuft of leaves that stood directly behind her. In the intervening spaces of this verdant cross, appeared all the instruments of Christ's Passion. Over the vision hovered the Holy Spirit, a figure winged with glory, in appearance more human than dovelike. The heavens opened above Mary and the central point of the Heavenly Jerusalem, the City of God, floated over her with all the gardens, the palaces, and the dwellings of the future saints. Angels in myriads hovered around, and the glory that encircled her was full of angelic faces.

Ah, who can express it! Infinite variety, unceasing change, all these pictures following quickly upon and, as it were, growing out of one another. Innumerable points of this vision, I have forgotten. All the splendor and magnificence of the temple, the richly ornamented wall before which Mary was standing—all grew dark and somber. The whole temple disappeared, for Mary and her glory alone was visible.

In this vision, symbolic of Mary's spiritual signification, I saw her not as a child, but full-grown. She hovered in the air. And through and through the vision I still saw the priests, the incense offering, and everything else. Then the priest at the altar appeared to prophesy, and to call upon the people to thank God and to pray, for that great things were to come upon the child. The crowd in the temple, greatly awed—although they had not seen the vision that I saw—maintained a solemn stillness. The vision faded away just as gradually as it had unfolded. At last, the mystery of the Ark of the Covenant shone again in its glory over her heart, and the child once more stood there alone in her rich attire.

Then the priests, among whom Zechariah was one of those standing on the lower steps, led Mary down by the hand. One of them took the light from her and the little garlands off her arms, and handed them to the other girls. Mary was then led through a door into another hall where six other temple virgins, their mistress Naomi (who was

Mary's Entrance into the Temple and her Offering

the sister of Lazarus's mother), Anna, and another female met them and scattered flowers before her. To them the priest delivered the child.

When the singing was ended, Mary took leave of her parents. Joachim was especially affected. He took the little child up in his arms, pressed her to his heart, and said weeping: "Remember my soul before God."

Mary now accompanied the women and children belonging to the temple to their dwelling on the north side, from which passages and winding stairs led up to little chambers adjoining the sanctuary and the Holy of Holies, where they went to pray. The others (that is, Mary's relatives and friends) returned to the apartments near the entrance and took a repast with the priests, the women apart. There were still in the temple some devout adorers. Many had followed the procession to the entrance. There were numbers among those present who knew that Mary was a child of promise in her family. I remember, though not distinctly, that Anne had dropped some such expressions to her friends as: "Now does the vessel of the Promise enter the temple. Now is the Ark of the Covenant in the temple." It was by a special manifestation of the divine Will that this feast was so solemnly and magnificently celebrated.

Joachim and Anne were indeed wealthy, but they lived very frugally. They gave all to the temple and to the poor. I do not now remember how long it was that Anne took for herself nothing but cold victuals, but she treated her domestics generously and provided them with dowries. I think she and Joachim returned that same day with their whole company to Beth-Horon.

I saw also a feast among the temple children. They had a meal at which Mary had to question first the mistresses and then the maidens separately as to whether they were willing to have her among them. This was the custom. Then the girls had a dance among themselves. They stood two and two opposite one another and danced, changed places across, and formed figures in and out. There was no leaping, but certain swaying movements of the whole person, which seemed somewhat expressive of the Jewish character. Some of the girls accompanied the dance with the music of flutes, triangles, chimes, and an instrument that gave forth sounds at once strange and agreeable. It consisted of a little box with oblique sides, over which were stretched strings which the players touched with their fingers. The center of the box contained bellows out of which projected several pipes, some crooked, others straight. The performer pressed sometimes here, sometimes there on the center of the bellows, which mingled its sounds with those of the strings. The instrument was rested either upon the knee of the performer or upon a stool under which the knee was placed. In the evening, Naomi took Mary to her cell, from which she could see down into the temple. Here Mary mentioned to Naomi her desire to get up more frequently in the night to pray, but Naomi refused her request for the present. The women belonging to the temple wore white robes, long and wide, girdled at the waist. Their flowing sleeves were turned up when at work.

Far back in the temple were numerous chambers built in the wall and connected with the dwellings of the women. Mary's cell was one of the most distant, one nearest the Holy of Holies. From the passage that led to it, one raised a curtain and stepped into an apartment, a sort of antechamber separated from the cell by a light, semicircular, movable screen. Here in the corners, right and left, were shelves for clothing and other things. Opposite the door in the screen that led into the cell was an opening hung with gauze and tapestry, and looking down into the temple. It was rather high in the wall; one had to mount upon steps to reach it. On the left of the cell lay a cover rolled into a bundle, which Mary unrolled at night for a couch. A branched lamp stood in a niche of the wall. I saw the holy child standing on a stool near it and praying out of a roll with red knobs on the rod. It was indeed a touching sight. The child wore a little coarsely woven, striped dress, blue and white, with yellow flowers. A small round table like a stool stood in the room, and on it I saw Anna setting a dish of fruit the size of beans, and a little jug. The child was skillful far beyond her years. She could already work on little white cloths for the service of the temple. The wall of her cell was inlaid with colored, triangular stones.

I often saw the child Mary seized with holy longing for the Messiah and saying to Anna: "Oh, will the promised child be born soon? Oh, if I could only see that child! Oh, if only I am living when he is born!" Then Anna would give this reply: "Think how old I am and how long I have waited for that child! And you, you are still so young!" And Mary would shed tears of longing for the promised Savior.

The maidens reared in the temple under the care of the matrons occupied themselves with embroidery, with all kinds of ornamental work, and with cleansing the priestly garments and the vessels belonging to the temple. From their cells, they could see into the temple, pray, and meditate. They were, by the fact of their parents' having placed them there, entirely dedicated to the Lord. Upon reaching a certain age, they were given in marriage, for there was among the more enlightened Israelites the pious, though secret hope that from such a virgin dedicated to God the Messiah would be born.

I never saw that Herod built the temple anew. Under him there were indeed many changes made in it; but at the time of Mary's entrance, eleven years before the birth of Christ, the temple itself had not been touched. The additions and changes had been made as heretofore on the outbuildings alone.

A Glance at the Obduracy of the Pharisees

HOW obdurate and obstinate the priests and the Pharisees of the temple were may be discovered from the small esteem in which they held the distinctions bestowed upon the holy family.

First Joachim's offering was rejected; but after some months both his own and his wife's were, by God's command, received. Joachim was admitted even into the presence of the Holy of Holies and he, as well as Anne, was—though unknown to each other—led into the passage under the temple. There they met, Mary was conceived, and priests awaited them at the entrance of this cave under the temple—all that took place by God's command. I have seen that sometimes, though not often, the sterile were commanded to be led in there.

Mary entered the temple in her fourth year, and in all things was she distinguished and remarkable. The sister of Lazarus's mother was her teacher and nurse. Her whole manner of acting was so remarkable, so marvelous, that I have seen great rolls written by aged priests about her. I think they still lie hidden with other writings.

Then came the wonderful manifestations at Joseph's espousals and the blossoming of his rod, the accounts of the three kings and of the shepherds, the presentation of Jesus, Anna's and Simeon's testimony, and the teaching of Jesus at the age of twelve in the temple.

But all this the priests and Pharisees noticed not. Their mind was preoccupied by business and court affairs. Because the holy family lived in voluntary retirement and poverty, they were forgotten in the crowd. The more enlightened, however, such as Simeon, Anna, and others, knew of them.

But when Jesus appeared and John bore witness to him, the teaching of the Pharisees was so directly contradictory that, even if the signs of his coming had not been forgotten by them, they would certainly not have made them known. Herod's reign and the Roman yoke had so involved them in quarrels and intrigues that their taste for spiritual things was weakened. They did not esteem John's testimony, and they soon forgot him after he was beheaded. They cared little for the teaching and miracles of Jesus, and their ideas of the prophets and the Messiah were altogether erroneous. It is not surprising, therefore, that they so shamefully treated Jesus, and put him to death, that they disavowed his resurrection, the wonderful signs that followed it, and even the fulfillment of his prophecy respecting the destruction of Jerusalem. Nor is it to be wondered at that they neglected the signs that heralded his advent, since he had not at that time either taught or wrought miracles. Were the blindness, the obduracy of these men not so incomprehensibly great, could it have lasted even to this day?

When I go over the Way of the Cross in Jerusalem of the present day, I frequently see under a certain ruined building a large vault, or many adjoining vaults, which are partly fallen in and filled with water. Standing in the midst of the water, which rises almost to a level with it, is a table. From the center of the table to the roof of the vault, rises a pillar around which are hung little coffers filled with rolls of writings. Under the table also I saw rolls lying in the water. Perhaps these vaults were once burial places. They lie under Mount Calvary. I think the ruined building is the house wherein Pilate once dwelt, and the treasure will after some time be discovered.

John Promised to Zechariah

I SAW Zechariah conversing with Elizabeth.[A1] He was telling her how sad he was because his turn to offer sacrifice in the temple was drawing near, and how he dreaded the contempt that would there await him on account of his being childless. Zechariah went twice a year to the temple. He did not live at Hebron itself, but at a place called Jutta about fifteen minutes' walk from Hebron. The ruins of former buildings still lay between the two places, leading one to fancy that they had once been connected. Many such ruins were to be found on the other side of Hebron, for the place was once as large as Jerusalem. At Hebron dwelt priests of a lower degree; in Jutta, those of a higher rank. Zechariah seemed to be the superior of them all. He and Elizabeth were regarded with extraordinary veneration from the fact of both having descended in a direct line from the race of Aaron.

I saw Zechariah with many people of this locality, going to a little property that he owned in the neighborhood of Jutta. It consisted of a house, an orchard, and a spring. I saw him there also with the holy family at the time of Mary's Visitation. At the period of which I am speaking, Zechariah was teaching the people and praying with them. It seemed to be a preparation for a feast. He told them of his great dejection, and of his presentiment that something remarkable was going to happen to him.

Again I saw Zechariah with the same people going to Jerusalem, where he had to wait four days before his turn to sacrifice came round. Until that time, he prayed in the forepart of the temple. At last when his turn came, he went into the sanctuary outside the entrance to the Holy of Holies. The roof over the altar of incense was opened so that the sky could be seen. The priest offering sacrifice was not visible to those outside. A partition concealed him, but the smoke of the incense could be seen rising. I think Zechariah told the other priests that he must be left alone, for I saw them leaving the sanctuary. Zechariah went into the Holy of Holies, where it was dark. It appeared to me that he took the Tables of the Law out of the Ark of the Covenant, and laid them upon the golden altar of incense. When he kindled the incense, I saw to the right of the altar a light coming down on him and in it a luminous figure. Zechariah, frightened, stepped back and sank, as if in ecstasy, at the right side of the altar. The angel raised him up and spoke some words to him.[A2] Zechariah replied.

Then I saw something like a ladder let down from heaven, and two angels ascending and descending to him. One took something from him; but the other—after Zechariah had opened his garment—inserted a shining little body in his side. Zechariah had become mute. I saw him before leaving the Holy of Holies, writing on a little tablet that lay there. This tablet he sent at once to Elizabeth, who likewise had had a vision at that same hour.

I saw that the people outside were troubled and anxious on account of Zechariah's remaining so long in the sanctuary. They were even moving toward the door to open it, when Zechariah replaced the Tables in the Ark and came forth. The crowd questioned him about his long stay in the sanctuary. He tried to answer, but could not. He signified to them by signs that he had become mute, and went away. Zechariah was a tall and exceedingly majestic old man.

BIRTH, CHILDHOOD, AND YOUTH OF JESUS

Mary Espoused to Joseph

JOSEPH was the third of six brothers. His parents dwelt in a large mansion outside of Bethlehem. It was the ancient birthplace of David, but in Joseph's time only the principal walls were in existence. His father's name was Jacob. In front of the house was a large courtyard, or garden. In it was a stone spring house built over a spring whose waters gushed forth out of faucets, each of which represented some animal's head. The garden was enclosed by walls and surrounded by covered walks of trees and shrubbery.

The lower story of the dwelling had a door, but no windows. In the upper story there were circular openings, over which ran around the whole top of the house a broad gallery with four little pavilions capped by cupolas. From these cupolas, a view far into the surrounding country was afforded. David's palace in Jerusalem was provided with similar towers and cupolas. It was out of one of them that he saw Bathsheba. Above the center of the flat roof arose another smaller story, likewise crowned by a tower and cupola.

Joseph and his brothers occupied that last story with an aged Jew, their preceptor. The latter occupied the highest room in the story, while the brothers slept in one chamber, their sleeping places separated from one another by mats, which in the daytime were rolled up against the walls. I have seen them playing up there, each in his own separate space. They had toys shaped like animals, like little pugs. Their preceptor gave them all sorts of strange instructions that I could not understand. He laid sticks on the ground in various figures and stood the boys in them. The latter stepped into other figures which they had formed by rearranging the sticks. They laid sticks also in various positions, as if for measurement. I saw too the father and mother of the boys. They did not appear to trouble themselves much about their children, for they paid very little attention to them. They, the parents, appeared to me to be neither good nor bad.

Joseph was perhaps eight years old. He was very different from his brothers, very talented, and he learned quickly; but he was simple in his tastes, gentle, pious, and unambitious. The other boys used to play him all kinds of tricks and knock him around at will. They had little enclosed gardens, at whose entrance there stood on pillars covered images like swaddled infants. I often saw similar figures on the curtains of oratories, those of Anne and the blessed Virgin, for instance. The only difference was that Mary's picture held in its arms a chalice above which something arose. In Joseph's parental home these images were like swathed infants with round faces environed by rays of light. There were many such pictures in Jerusalem, especially in the olden times, and also among the decorations of the temple. I have seen them in Egypt also; and among the idols that Rachel purloined from her father were similar figures though smaller. Many of the Jews had swathed puppets like them lying in little chests and baskets. They were intended to represent the child Moses in his little basket, and the swathing signified the binding power of the Law. When gazing at these figures, I used to think: The Jews honored the little image of the child Moses, but we have the images of the child Jesus.

In the boys' little gardens grew bushes, small trees, and plants. I saw that his brothers often slyly trod down and tore up the plants in Joseph's little garden. They always treated him roughly, but he bore all patiently. Sometimes, when kneeling in prayer in the colonnade that ran around the courtyard, his face turned to the wall, his brothers would push him over. Once I saw one of them, when Joseph was thus praying, kick him in the back; but Joseph appeared not to notice it. The other repeated his blows, until at last Joseph fell to the ground. Then I saw that he had been absorbed in God. But he did not revenge himself; he merely turned away quietly and sought another secluded spot.

Outside and adjoining the garden wall were some small, low dwellings. In them dwelt two elderly, veiled females, as is often the case near the schools. They were servants. I saw them carrying water into the house. The domestic arrangements were similar to those of Joachim and Anne's house, the beds rolled up and wicker partitions before them. I often saw Joseph's brothers talking with the servant maids and helping them in their work; but Joseph never interchanged words with them; he was always very reserved. I think there were also some daughters in the family.

Joseph's parents were not well-satisfied with him. They would have wished him, on account of his talents, to fit himself for a position in the world. But he was too unworldly for such aims, he had no desire whatever to shine. He may have been about twelve years old when I often saw him beyond Bethlehem opposite the crib cave, praying with some very pious, old, Jewish women. They had an oratory hidden in a vault. I do not know whether these women were relatives of Joseph or not; I think that they were connected with Anne. Joseph often went to them in his troubles and shared their devotions. Sometimes he dwelt in their neighborhood with a master carpenter, to whom he lent a helping hand. The carpenter taught him his trade, and Joseph found his geometry of use. The hostility of his brothers at last went so far that, when eighteen, Joseph fled from his father's house by night. A friend, who lived outside of Bethlehem, had brought him clothes in which to make his escape. I saw him in Lebona carrying on carpentry. He worked for his living in a very poor family. The man supported himself by making such rough wicker partitions as those Joseph knew how to put together. The latter humbly assisted the family as far as he could. I saw him gathering wood and carrying it to the house. His parents, in the meantime, believed that he had been kidnapped; but his brothers discovered him, and then he was again persecuted. Joseph, however, would not leave the poor people nor desist from the humble occupation of which his family was ashamed. I saw him afterward in another place (Thaanach). There he did better work for a well-to-do family. Though a small place, it had a synagogue. Joseph lived very piously and humbly, loved and esteemed by all. At last he worked for a man in Tiberias, at which place he lived alone near the water.

Joseph's parents were long since dead, and his brothers scattered; only two of them still dwelt in Bethlehem. The paternal mansion had passed into other hands, and the whole family had rapidly declined. Joseph was deeply pious; he prayed much for the coming of the Messiah. I noticed, too, his great reserve in the presence of females. Shortly before his call to Jerusalem for his espousals with Mary, he entertained the idea of fitting up a more secluded oratory in his dwelling. But an angel appeared to him in prayer and told him not to do it; that, as in ancient times, the patriarch Joseph became by God's appointment the administrator of the Egyptian granaries, so now to him was the granary of Redemption to be wedded. In his humility Joseph could not comprehend the meaning of this and so he betook himself to prayer. At last he was summoned to Jerusalem to be espoused to the blessed Virgin.

There were seven other virgins who were with Mary to be dismissed from the temple and given in marriage. On this account St. Anne went to Jerusalem to be with Mary, who grieved at the thought of leaving the temple. But she was told that she must be married. I saw one of the distinguished old priests, who was no longer able to walk, borne into the Holy of Holies. An incense offering was enkindled. The priest prayed sitting before a roll of writings, and in vision his hand was placed upon that verse in the prophet Isaiah (Is. 11:1.) in which it is written that there shall come forth a rod out of the root of Jesse and a flower shall rise up out of his root. Thereupon I saw that all the unmarried men in the country of the House of David were summoned to the temple. Many of them made their appearance in holiday attire, and Mary was conducted to their presence. I saw one among them, a very pious youth from the region of Bethlehem, who had always ardently prayed to be allowed to minister to the advent of the Messiah. Great was his desire to wed Mary. But Mary wept; she wished not to take a husband. Then the high priest gave to each of the suitors a branch which was to be held in the hand during the offering of prayer and sacrifice.[A3] After that, all the branches were laid in the Holy of Holies with the understanding that he whose branch should blossom was to be Mary's husband. Now when that youth who so ardently desired to wed Mary found that this branch, along with all the others, had failed to blossom, he retired to a hall outside the temple and, with arms raised to God, wept bitterly. The other suitors left the temple, and that youth hurried to Mount Carmel where, since the days of Elijah, hermits had dwelt. He took up his abode on the mount, and there spent his days in prayer for the coming of the Messiah.

I saw the priests, after this, hunting through different rolls of writing in their search for another descendant of the House of David, one that had not presented himself among the suitors for Mary's hand. And there they found that, among the six brothers of Bethlehem, one was unknown and ignored. They sought him out and so discovered Joseph's retreat, six miles from Jerusalem, near Samaria. It was a small place on a little river. There Joseph dwelt alone in a humble house near the water, and carried on the trade of a carpenter under another master. He was told to go up to the temple. He went, accordingly, arrayed in his best. A branch was given him. As he was about to lay it upon the altar, it blossomed on top into a white flower like a lily. At the same time I saw a light like the Holy Spirit hovering over him. He was then led to Mary, who was in her chamber, and she accepted him as her spouse. [A4]

The espousals took place, I think, upon our 23rd of January. They were celebrated in Jerusalem, on Mount Zion in a house often used for such feasts. The seven virgins that were to leave the temple with Mary had already departed. They were recalled to accompany Mary on her festal journey to Nazareth, where Anne had already prepared her little home. The marriage feast lasted seven or eight days. The women and the virgins, companions of Mary in the temple, were present, also many relatives of Joachim and Anne, and two daughters from Gophna. Many lambs were slaughtered and offered in sacrifice.

I have had a clear vision of Mary in her bridal dress. She wore a colored, woolen underdress without sleeves, her arms encircled by white, woolen fillets. On the breast and as high as the neck, lay a white collar ornamented with jewels, pearls, etc. Then came a kind of gown open in front, wide like a mantle from top to bottom, and with flowing sleeves. This gown was blue, embroidered with large red, white, and yellow roses and green leaves, something like the ancient vestments worn at Mass. It fastened around the neck on the white collar, and the lower border was edged with fringes and tassels. Over this was a kind of scapular of white-and-gold-flowered silk, set over the breast with pearls and shining stones. It lay upon the front opening of the dress, and reached to the edge of the same; it was about two feet wide and was fringed with tassels and balls. A corresponding strip hung down the back,

View over Nazareth

while shorter and narrower ones fell over the shoulders and arms. These lappets were caught under the arms from front to back with the gold cords, or delicate chains, with which the broad upper piece of the bodice was fastened, as also the breastpiece that was placed over the upper body. By this arrangement, the flowered stuff of the dress was puffed out between the cords. The wide sleeves were tightly fastened in the middle of the upper and the lower arm by buckles, puffing out around the shoulders, the elbows, and the wrists.

Over this costume fell a long sky-blue mantle. It was fastened at the neck by an ornament, and over it was a white ruffle seemingly of feathers or silk dots. The mantle fell back from the shoulders, forming a large fold on the sides, and hung behind in a pointed train. It was embroidered around the edge in flowers of gold.

Mary's hair was arranged with such skill as is difficult to describe. It was parted on top of the head and divided into numerous fine strands, which were caught together with pearls and white silk. It formed a large net that fell over the shoulders and down the back to the middle of the mantle. It looked like a web. The ends of the hair were rolled in, and the whole net edged with fringe and pearls.

On her head was placed, first a wreath of white raw silk or wool, closing on top with three bands of the same meeting in a tuft. On this rested a crown about the breadth of one's hand, set with many colored jewels. Three pieces arose from the circlet and met together in the center, where they were surmounted by a ball.

In her left hand Mary carried a little garland of red and white roses made of silk, and in the right a beautiful candlestick covered with gold. It had no foot, but was furnished like a scepter with knobs above and below the point at which it was to be grasped by the hand. The stem began to swell out in the middle and ended in a little dish upon which burned a white flame.

On her feet she wore heavy sandals about two fingers in thickness under which, before and behind, was a support like a heel. They were green, and gave the foot the appearance of standing upon sods. Two straps, white and gold, went over the foot and held them in their place.

The virgins at the temple arranged Mary's skillfully woven hairnet. I saw them thus engaged. There were many busied with it, and the work went more swiftly than one could imagine. Anne brought all the beautiful clothes, but Mary was so modest that it was only with reluctance that she allowed herself to be arrayed in them.

After the nuptial ceremony, her braided hair was wound around her head, a milk-white veil reaching up to the elbows thrown over her, and the crown placed upon it.

The blessed Virgin had auburn hair, dark eyebrows, fine and arched, a very high forehead, large downcast eyes with long, dark lashes, a straight nose, delicate and rather long, a lovely mouth around which played a most noble expression, and a pointed chin. She was of medium height, and she moved very gently and gravely, looking very bashful in her rich attire. After the marriage feast, she wore another dress. It was striped and less magnificent than the one described. I have a scrap of it among my relics. This striped dress she wore at Cana and on other holy occasions. She wore her wedding suit once again in the temple.

The very wealthy among the Jews changed their dress three or four times during a marriage feast. Mary in her magnificent apparel presented an appearance somewhat similar to the richly adorned women of a much later period, the Empress Helena, for instance, and even Cunegundes herself. The usual clothing of the Jewish women enveloped them closely, giving them an appearance of being wrapped up; but Mary's wedding dress was very different; it was something on the Roman style.

Joseph wore a long, wide, blue coat fastened from the breast down with loops and buttons. The wide sleeves were laced at the sides, a broad cuff turned up at the wrist, the inside provided, as it were, with pockets. Around the neck was something like a brown collar, over which lay a kind of stole, and upon the breast hung two white bands.

After the marriage, Joseph went to Bethlehem on some business, and Mary with twelve or fifteen women and maidens went on foot to Anne's house near Nazareth. When Joseph returned, I saw at Anne's house a feast at which, besides the usual household, there were about six guests and several children present. Cups were on the table. The blessed Virgin wore a mantle embroidered with red, white, and blue flowers. Her face was covered with a transparent veil over which was a black one.

I afterward saw Joseph and Mary in the house of Nazareth. Joseph had a separate apartment in the front of the house, a three-cornered chamber this side of the kitchen. Both Mary and Joseph were timid and reserved in each other's presence. They were very quiet and prayerful.

Once I saw Anne making preparations to go to Nazareth. Under her arm she carried a bundle that contained some things for Mary. To reach Nazareth, which lay in front of a hill, she had to go over a plain and through a grove. Mary wept very much when Anne was leaving and accompanied her a part of the way. Joseph was alone in his apartment in the front of the house.

Mary and Joseph had, properly speaking, no regular housekeeping affairs; they received from Anne all that they needed. I saw Mary spinning and sewing too, but yet with wide stitches. The clothes then worn had not many seams and were entirely in strips. I saw her embroidering also, and with little white sticks knitting or working. The cooking she did was very simple and, while it was going on, the bread was baking in the ashes. They used sheep's milk, and of meat generally pigeons only.

The Holy House of Nazareth

THE LITTLE house at Nazareth which Anne fitted up for Mary and Joseph, belonged to Anne. From her own dwelling, she could, unnoticed, reach it in about half an hour by a crosspath. It lay not far from the gate. It had a small courtyard in front and nearby was a well, a couple of steps leading down to it. It was near a hill, but not built on it. A narrow path dug out of the hill separated it from the back of the house, in which there was one little window. It was darker on this side of the house than on the other. The back part was triangular and built on higher ground than the front. The foundations were cut in the rock; the upper part was a light masonry. Mary's sleeping compartment was in the back, and there it was that the angelic Annunciation took place. This chamber had a semicircular form, on account of the movable partitions placed around the walls and which were of coarser wickerwork than that ordinarily used for the light screens. The patterns in which these screens were woven were similar to wafers, and the colors used were designed to bring the figures out. Mary's sleeping place was on the side just behind a wicker screen. On the left was a little closet with a small table and stool. This was the blessed Virgin's oratory.

This back room was separated from the rest of the house by a fireplace, which consisted of a graded wall from whose center over the slightly raised hearth a chimney rose up to the roof and ended in a tube above it. Over the opening through which the tube projected was built a little roof. On top of the chimney, I saw in after years two little bells hanging. To the right and left of the chimney and opening into Mary's rooms were doors up to which three steps led. In the chimney wall were all kinds of nooks in which stood the little vessels that I still see at Loretto. Behind was a rafter of cedarwood, upon which the wall of the chimney rested. From this upright rafter ran a crossbeam to the center of the back wall, and into this there were others dovetailed from the two side walls. These beams were of a bluish cast with yellow ornaments. Between them one could see up through the roof, which was hung with large leaves and matting, and in three places, namely in the three corners, adorned with stars. The star in the middle corner was large like the morning star. Later on the ceiling was adorned with numerous stars. Over the horizontal rafter, which extended from the chimney to the back of the wall, was an opening in the center for the window, and under this was hung a lamp. There was a rafter under the chimney also. The roof was not high and pointed, but so level that one might walk around the edge. It was flat on top, and there rose the chimney with its tubes, protected by the little roof.

When after Joseph's death the blessed Virgin removed to the neighborhood of Capernaum, the Holy House was left beautifully adorned like a sacred shrine. Mary often went from Capernaum to visit the scene of the Incarnation and to pray there. Peter and John, whenever they went to Palestine, visited the House of Nazareth and celebrated Mass in it. An altar was erected where the fireplace used to be. The little cupboard once used by Mary was placed as a tabernacle upon the altar.

I have often in vision witnessed the transporting of the Holy House to Loretto. For a long time, I could not believe it, and yet I continued to see it. I saw the Holy House borne over the sea by seven angels. It had no foundation, but there was under it a shining surface of light. On either side was something like a handle. Three angels carried it on one side and three on the other; the seventh hovered in front of it, a long train of light after him.

I remember that it was the back of the house, the part that contained the fireplace, the altar of the apostles, and the little window, that was transported to Europe. It seems to me when I recall it that the rest of the building was in some danger of falling. I see in Loretto the crucifix also that the blessed Virgin had when in Ephesus. It was formed of different kinds of wood. Later on, it came into the possession of the apostles. Many miracles take place before that crucifix.

The wall of the Holy House of Loretto is entirely the original one. Even the rafter under the chimney is still in its place. The miraculous picture of the Mother of God stands on the altar of the apostles.

Mary's Annunciation

ON THE day upon which the church celebrates the feast, I had a vision of Mary's Annunciation.

I saw the blessed Virgin a short time after her marriage in the house of Nazareth. Joseph was not there. He was at that moment journeying with two beasts of burden on the road to Tiberias, whither he was going to get his tools. But Anne was in the house with her maid and two of the virgins who had been with Mary in the temple. Everything in the house had been newly arranged by Anne. Toward evening, they all prayed standing around a circular stool from which they afterward ate vegetables that had been served. Anne seemed to be very busy about the household affairs, and for a time she moved around here and there, while the blessed Virgin ascended the steps to her room. There she put on a long, white, woolen garment, such as it was customary to wear during prayer, a girdle around her waist, and a yellowish-white veil over her head. The maid entered, lighted the branched lamp, and retired. Mary drew out a little, low table, which stood folded by the wall, and placed it in the center of the room. It had a semicircular leaf, which could be raised on a movable support so that when ready for use the little table stood on three legs. Mary spread upon it a red and then a white, transparent cover, which hung down on the side opposite the leaf. It was fringed at the end and embroidered in the center. A white cover was spread on the rounded edge. When the little table was prepared, Mary laid a small, round cushion before it and, resting both hands on the leaf, she gently sank on her knees, her back turned to her couch, the door of the chamber to her right. The floor was carpeted. Mary lowered her veil over her face, and folded her hands, but not the fingers, upon her breast. I saw her praying for a long time with intense fervor. She prayed for redemption, for the promised king, and that her own supplications might have some influence upon his coming. She knelt long, as if in ecstasy, her face raised to heaven; then she drooped her head upon her breast and thus continued her prayer. And now she glanced to the right and beheld a radiant youth with flowing, yellow hair. It was the archangel Gabriel. His feet did not touch the ground. In an oblique line and surrounded by an effulgence of light and glory, he came floating down to Mary. The lamp grew dim, for the whole room was lighted up by the glory.

The angel, with hands gently raised before his breast, spoke to Mary. I saw the words like letters of glittering light issuing from his lips. Mary replied, but without looking up. Then the angel again spoke and Mary, as if in obedience to his command, raised her veil a little, glanced at him, and said, "Behold the handmaid of the Lord. May it be done unto me according to thy word!"[A5] I saw her now in deeper ecstasy. The ceiling of the room vanished, and over the house appeared a luminous cloud with a pathway of light leading up from it to the opened heavens. Far up in the source of this light I beheld a vision of the most holy Trinity. It was like a triangle of glory, and I thought that I saw therein the Father, the Son, and the Holy Spirit.

As Mary uttered the words: "May it be done unto me according to thy word!" I saw an apparition of the Holy Spirit. The countenance was human and the whole apparition environed by dazzling splendor, as if surrounded by wings. From the breast and hands, I saw issuing three streams of light. They penetrated the right side of the blessed Virgin and united into one under her heart. At that instant Mary became perfectly transparent and luminous. It was as if opacity disappeared like darkness before that flood of light.

While the angel and with him the streams of glory vanished, I saw down the path of light that led up to heaven, showers of half-blown roses and tiny green leaves falling upon Mary. She, entirely absorbed in self, saw in herself the Incarnate Son of God, a tiny, human form of light with all the members, even to the little fingers, perfect. It was about midnight that I saw this mystery.

Some time elapsed, and then Anne and the other women entered Mary's room, but when they beheld her in ecstasy they immediately withdrew. The blessed Virgin then arose, stepped to the little altar on the wall, let down the picture of a swathed child that was rolled above it, and prayed standing under the lamp before it. Only toward morning did she lie down. Mary was at this time a little over fourteen years old.

An intuitive knowledge of what had taken place was conferred upon Anne. Mary knew that she had conceived the Redeemer, yes, her interior lay open before her, and so she already understood that her Son's kingdom should be a supernatural one, and that the House of Jacob, the church, would be the reunion of regenerate humankind. She knew that the Redeemer would be the king of his people, that he would purify them and render them victorious; but that in order to redeem them he must suffer and die.

It was explained to me likewise why the Redeemer remained nine months in his mother's womb, why he was born a little child and not a perfect man like Adam, and why also he did not take the beauty of Adam in Paradise. The Incarnate Son of God willed to be conceived and born that conception and birth, rendered so very unholy by the Fall, might again become holy. Mary was his mother, and he did not come sooner because Mary was the first and the only woman conceived without sin. Jesus when put to death was thirty-three years, four months, and two weeks old.

I thought all the while: Here in Nazareth, things are different from what they are in Jerusalem. There the women dare not set foot in the temple, but here in this church at Nazareth, a virgin is herself the temple and the Most Holy rests in her.

Mary's Visitation

MARY's annunciation took place before Joseph's return. He had not yet settled at Nazareth when, with Mary, he started on the journey to Hebron. After the Conception of Jesus, the blessed Virgin experienced a great desire to visit her cousin Elizabeth. I saw her traveling with Joseph toward the south. Once I saw her passing the night in a hut made of wickerwork and which was all overrun with vines and beautiful white blossoms. From that point to Zechariah's house it was a journey of about twelve hours. Near Jerusalem they turned off to the north in order to take a more solitary route. They made the circuit of a little city two leagues from Emmaus, and took a road traversed by Jesus in after years. Although it was a long journey, they made it very quickly. They now had to cross two hills. I saw them resting between them, eating some bread and refreshing themselves with some balsam drops which they had collected on the way, and which they mingled with their drinking water. The hill was formed of overhanging rocks and caves. The valleys were very fertile. I remarked on the road one particular flower. It had fine green leaves and a cluster of nine tiny bell-shaped blossoms, white, lightly flushed with red.

Mary wore a brown, woolen underdress over which was a gray one with a girdle, and a yellowish covering on her head. Joseph carried in a bundle a long brownish garment with a cowl, and bands in front. It was one that Mary was accustomed to wear whenever she went either to the temple or the synagogue.

Zechariah's house stood upon a solitary hill, and other dwellings were scattered around. Not far from it, a tolerably large brook flowed down from the mountain.

Elizabeth had learned in vision that one of her race was to give birth to the Messiah; she had dwelt in thought upon Mary, had very greatly desired to see her, [A6] and had indeed beheld her journeying to Hebron. In a little room to the right of the entrance to the house she placed seats, and here she tarried, often looking long and anxiously down the road in the hope of catching the first glimpse of Mary. When Zechariah was returning from the Passover, I saw Elizabeth, urged by an impetuous desire, hurrying from the house and going a considerable distance on the road to Jerusalem. When Zechariah met her, he was alarmed to find her so far from home and that, too, in her present condition. But she told him of her anxiety and that she could not help thinking that her cousin Mary was coming from Nazareth to see her. Zechariah, however, thought it improbable that the newly-married couple would at that time undertake so great a journey. On the following day I saw Elizabeth taking the road again under the influence of the same impression, and now I saw the holy family coming to meet her.

Elizabeth was advanced in years. She was tall, her face small and delicate, and she wore something wrapped around her head. She was acquainted with Mary only by hearsay. As soon as the blessed Virgin saw Elizabeth, she knew her and hurried on to meet her, while Joseph purposely held back. Mary had already reached the houses in the neighborhood of Zechariah's home. Their occupants were enraptured at her beauty, and filled with such reverence by her demeanor that they stood back modestly. When the cousins met, they saluted each other joyfully with outstretched hands. I saw a light in Mary and issuing from her a ray which entered into Elizabeth, who thereby became wonderfully agitated. They did not pause long in sight of the beholders, but arm in arm passed up the courtyard to the door of the house, where Elizabeth once more bade Mary welcome. Joseph went around to the side of the house and into an open hall where sat Zechariah. He respectfully saluted the aged priest, who responded in writing on his tablet.

Mary and Elizabeth entered the room in which was the fireplace. Here they embraced, clasping each other in their arms and pressing cheek to cheek. I saw light streaming down between them. Then it was that Elizabeth, becoming interiorly inflamed, stepped back with uplifted hands, and exclaimed, "Blessed art thou among women, and blessed is the fruit of thy womb.

"And whence is this to me, that the mother of my Lord should come to me?

"For behold, as soon as the voice of thy salutation sounded in my ears, the infant in my womb leaped for joy.

"And blessed art thou that hast believed, because those things shall be accomplished that were spoken to thee by the Lord."

At these last words, Elizabeth took Mary into the little room prepared for her that she might sit down and rest. It was only a few steps from where they then were. Mary released her hold upon Elizabeth's arm, crossed her hands on her breast, and divinely inspired, uttered her canticle of thanksgiving: "My soul doth magnify the Lord, and my spirit hath rejoiced in God, my Savior.

"Because he hath regarded the humility of his handmaid; for behold from henceforth all generations shall call me blessed.

"Because he that is mighty hath done great things to me: and holy is his name.

"And his mercy is from generation unto generations, to them that fear him.

"He hath showed might in his arm: he hath scattered the proud in the conceit of their heart.

"He hath put down the mighty from their seat, and hath exalted the humble.

"He hath filled the hungry with good things: and the rich he hath sent empty away.

"He hath received Israel his servant, being mindful of his mercy.

"As he spoke to our fathers, to Abraham, and to his seed forever."

I saw Elizabeth, moved by similar emotion, reciting the whole canticle with Mary. Then they seated themselves on low seats. A small goblet was on the little table. And, oh, I was so happy! I sat nearby and prayed with them the whole time.

I saw Joseph and Zechariah still together. They were conversing by means of the tablet, and always about the coming of the Messiah. Zechariah was a tall, handsome

Hilltop near Nazareth

old man clothed like a priest. He and Joseph sat together at the side of the house that opened on the garden, in which Mary and Elizabeth were now sitting on a rug under a high, spreading tree. [A7] Behind the tree was a fountain from which gushed water when a spigot was pressed. I saw grass and flowers around, and trees bearing little, yellow plums. Mary and Elizabeth were eating rolls and small fruits out of Joseph's traveling pouch. What touching simplicity and moderation! Two maids and two men servants were in the house. They prepared a table under the tree. Joseph and Zechariah came out and ate something. Joseph wanted to return home at once, but they persuaded him to stay eight days. He knew not of Mary's conception. The women were silent on that subject. They had a secret understanding together about their interior sentiments.

When all, Mary and Elizabeth, Joseph and Zechariah, were together, they prayed making use of a kind of litany. I saw a cross appear in their midst, and still there was no cross at that time. Yes, it was as if two crosses visited each other.

In the evening they all sat together again in the garden near a lamp under the tree. A cover like a tent was stretched under the tree, and low stools with backs stood around. After that I saw Joseph and Zechariah going to an oratory, while Mary and Elizabeth retired to their little chamber. They were inflamed with divine ardor, and together they recited the Magnificat. The blessed Virgin wore a transparent white veil which she lowered when speaking to men.

Zechariah took Joseph on the following day to another garden at some distance from the house. He was in all things most exact and methodical. This second garden was set out with beautiful bushes and trees full of fruit. In the center was an avenue of trees, and at the end of it a small house whose entrance was on the side. Above were openings with slides like windows. A woven couch filled with moss or some other fine plant stood in one room in which there were also two white figures as large as children. I have no clear knowledge of how they came there nor what they signified, but they appeared to me to be very like Zechariah and Elizabeth, only much younger.

I saw Mary and Elizabeth much together. Mary helped with everything around the house and prepared all kinds of necessaries for the child. Both she and Elizabeth knit on a large coverlet for the latter, and they worked also for the poor.

During Mary's absence, Anne frequently sent her maid to see after Mary's house at Nazareth, and once I saw her there herself.

I saw Zechariah and Joseph spending the night of the next day in the garden at some distance from the house. They slept part of the time in the little summer house, and prayed during the other part in the open air. They returned quite early in the morning to the house where Mary and Elizabeth had passed the night. Mary and Elizabeth recited together morning and evening the hymn of thanksgiving, the Magnificat, which Mary had received from the Holy Spirit at the salutation of Elizabeth. During its recital they stood opposite each other against the wall, as if in choir, their hands crossed upon their breast, the black veil of each covering her face. At the second part, which refers to God's promise, I saw the previous history of the most holy Incarnation and the mystery of the most holy sacrament of the Altar, from Abraham down to Mary. I saw Abraham sacrificing Isaac, also the mystery of the Ark of the Covenant, which Moses received on the night before the departure from Egypt, and by which he was enabled to escape and conquer. I recognized its connection with the holy Incarnation, and it seemed to me as if this mystery were now fulfilled or living in Mary. I saw also the prophet Isaiah and his prophecy of the Virgin, and from him to Mary visions of the approach of the most blessed sacrament. I still remember that I heard the words: "From father to father down to Mary, there are more than fourteen generations." I saw also Mary's blood taking its rise in her ancestors and flowing nearer and nearer to the

Incarnation. I have no words to describe this clearly. I can say only that I saw, sometimes here, sometimes there, the people of different races. There seemed to issue from them a beam of light which always terminated in Mary as she appeared at that moment with Elizabeth. I saw this beam issuing first from the mystery of the Ark of the Covenant and ending in Mary. Then I saw Abraham and from him a ray, which again ended in Mary, etc. Abraham must have dwelt quite near to Mary's abode at that time; for during the Magnificat I saw that the beam which proceeded from

Galilean Hamlet near Nazareth

him came from no great distance, while those from persons nearer to the Mother of God in point of time seemed to come from afar. Their rays were as fine, as clear as those of the sun when they shine through a narrow opening. In such a beam I beheld Mary's blood glancing red and bright, and it was said to me: "Behold, as pure as this red light must the blood of that Virgin be from whom the Son of God will become incarnate."

Once I saw Mary and Elizabeth going in the evening to Zechariah's country place. They took with them rolls and fruit in little baskets, for they intended to stay overnight. Joseph and Zechariah followed them later. I saw Mary going to meet them as they entered. Zechariah had brought his little tablet, but it was too dark for writing. I saw Mary speaking to him. She was telling him that he should speak on that night. He laid aside his tablet and conversed orally with Joseph. I saw all this to my own great astonishment. Then my guide said to me: "Why, what is that?" and he showed me a vision of St. Goar, who hung his mantle on the sunbeams as on a hook. I received then the instruction that lively, childlike confidence makes all things real and substantial. These two expressions gave me great interior light upon all kinds of miracles, but I cannot explain it.

They, Mary, Elizabeth, Joseph, and Zechariah, all spent the night in the garden. They sat or walked two by two, prayed now and then, or retired into the little summer house to rest. I heard them say that Joseph would return home on the evening of the sabbath, and that Zechariah would go with him as far as Jerusalem. The moon shone bright in a starry sky. It was indescribably calm and lovely near those holy souls.

Once also I had a peep into Mary's little chamber. It was night, and she was at rest. She was lying on her side with one hand under her head. Over her brown underdress she wound from head to foot a strip of white, woolen stuff about four feet in width. When preparing for rest, she took one end of this strip under her arm and wound it tightly around her head and the upper part of her person, then down to the feet and up again; so that she was entirely enveloped, and could not take a long step. She did this near the couch, at the head of which was a little roll of something for a pillow. The arms from the elbow down were left free, and the veiling of the head opened on the breast.

I often saw under Mary's heart a glory in whose center burned an indescribably clear little flame, and over Elizabeth's womb a similar glory, but the light in it was not so clear.

When the sabbath began, I saw in Zechariah's house, in a room that I had not before seen, lamps lighted and the sabbath celebrated. Zechariah, Joseph, and about six other men from the neighborhood were standing and praying under a lamp and around a little chest upon which lay rolls of writing. They had on their heads something like a small veil. They did not make so many distorted movements of the body as do the latter-day Jews, although like them they frequently bowed the head and raised the arms.

Mary, Elizabeth, and two other women stood apart in a grated partition from which they could see into the oratory. They were entirely enveloped, their prayer mantles over their heads.

Zechariah wore his festive robes the whole of the sabbath. They consisted of a long, white garment with rather narrow sleeves. He was girdled with a broad cincture, wound many times around him. On it were letters, and from it hung straps. This garment was provided with a cowl, which hung in plaits from the head down the back like a folded veil. When he moved or performed any action, he threw this garment rolled together with the ends of the girdle up over one shoulder, and stuck it into the girdle under his arm. His lower limbs were loosely bound, and the strip enveloping them fastened by the straps that kept the soles in place upon his naked feet. He showed his priestly mantle to Joseph. It was sleeveless, wide and heavy and very beautiful, flashing with white and purple intermixed. It was closed on the breast with three jeweled clasps.

When the sabbath was over, I saw them eating again for the first time. They took their repast together under the trees in the garden near the house. They ate green leaves previously dipped into something, and sucked little bunches of herbs which too had been soaked. There were little bowls of small fruits on the table and other dishes, from which they partook of something with brown, transparent spatulas. It may have been honey that they were eating with horn spatulas. There were also little rolls, and I saw them eating them.

After the meal, Joseph accompanied by Zechariah started on his journey home. The night was calm, the moon shining, and the sky studded with stars. Before parting, all prayed separately. Joseph took with him his little bundle in which were a few rolls and a small jug of something. Both the travelers had staves; but Joseph's was hooked on top, while Zechariah's was long and ended in a knob. Both had traveling mantles which they wore over their head. Before starting, they embraced Mary and Elizabeth, alternately pressing them to their heart. But I saw no kissing at that time. The parting was calm and cheerful. The two women accompanied them a short distance, and then the travelers proceeded alone. The night was unspeakably lovely.

Mary and Elizabeth now returned to the house and went into Mary's chamber. A lamp was burning upon a bracket on the wall, as was usual while Mary slept or prayed. The two women stood facing each other, and recited the Magnificat. They spent the whole night in prayer, for what reason I cannot now say. Through the day I saw Mary busy with all kinds of work, weaving covers, for instance.

I saw Joseph and Zechariah still on the road. They spent the night under a shed. They took very circuitous roads and, I think, visited many people, for they were three days on their journey.

Again I saw Joseph at Nazareth. Anne's maid took charge of the house for him, going to and fro between the two houses. With this exception, Joseph was entirely alone.

I also saw Zechariah returning home, and I saw Mary and Elizabeth reciting as usual the Magnificat, and doing all kinds of work. Toward evening they used to walk in the garden. There was a well in it, a rare occurrence in this part of the country; therefore travelers always took with them in a little jug some kind of juice to drink. Sometimes also, and generally toward evening when it grew cool, Mary and Elizabeth walked some distance from the house, for it stood alone in the midst of fields. They usually retired about nine o'clock, and always rose again before the sun.

The blessed Virgin remained with Elizabeth three months, until after the birth of John, but she returned to Nazareth before his circumcision. Joseph went to meet her halfway on the journey, and for the first time noticed that she was pregnant. But he gave no sign of his knowledge, and struggled with his doubts. [A8] Mary, who had feared this, was silent and preoccupied, thus increasing his uneasiness. When arrived in Nazareth, Mary went to the parents of the deacon Parmenas and remained some days with them. Joseph's anxiety had meanwhile increased to such a degree that, when Mary returned home, he determined to flee from the house. Then the angel appeared to him and consoled him.

Feast Pictures

I SAW a wonderful and almost indescribable vision of a feast. I saw a church that looked like a slender, delicate, octangular fruit, the roots of whose stem touched the earth over a bubbling fountain. The stem was not high, one could just see between the church and the earth. The entrance was over the spring which bubbled and bubbled, casting out something white like earth or sand, and rendering all around green and fruitful. There were no roots over the spring in front of the church. The center of the interior was like the capsule in an apple, the cells formed of many delicate white threads. In these cells were little organs like the kernels of an apple. Through an opening in the floor, one could look straight down into the bubbling spring. I saw some kernels that looked withered and decayed, falling into it. But while I gazed, the fruit seemed to be developing more and more into a church; and the capsule at last appeared something like a piece of machinery, like a loose artificial nosegay in the center of it. And now I saw the blessed Virgin and Elizabeth standing on that nosegay and looking again like two tabernacles, the one the tabernacle of a saint, the other that of the Most Holy. The two blessed women turned toward each other and offered mutual felicitations. Then there issued from them two figures, Jesus and John. John, the larger of the two, lay coiled on the earth, his head in his lap; but Jesus was like a tiny child formed of light, just as I so often see him in the blessed sacrament. Upright and hovering, he moved toward John and passed over him like a white vapor as he lay there with his face upon the earth. The reflection from the snowy vapor glanced through the opening in the floor down into the spring, and by it was swallowed up. Then Jesus raised the little John and embraced him, after which each returned to the womb of his mother, who meantime had been singing the Magnificat.

I saw also during that singing Joseph and Zechariah issuing from the walls on opposite sides of the church and followed by an ever-increasing flow of people, while the whole building continued unfolding, as it were, taking more and more the appearance of a church and the occasion that of a sacred festival. Vines with luxuriant foliage were growing around the church, and they became so dense that they had to be trimmed.

The church now rested on the earth. In it was an altar, and through an opening over the bubbling spring arose a baptismal font. Many people entered by the door, and there was at last a grand and perfect festival. All that took place therein, both in form and in action, was a silent growth. I cannot relate all; words fail me.

On John's feast, I had another vision of a festival. The octangular church was transparent, as if formed of crystal or jets of water. In the center was a well spring above which arose a little tower. I saw John standing by it and baptizing. The vision changed. Out of the spring grew a flower stalk, around which arose eight pillars supporting a pyramidal crown. Upon the crown stood the grandparents of Anne, Elizabeth, and Joseph; a little distant from the main stem were Mary and Joseph with the parents of the latter and those of Zechariah. Up on the central stem stood John. A voice seemed to proceed from him, and I saw nations and kings entering the church and receiving the blessed Eucharist from the hands of a bishop. I heard John saying that their happiness was greater than his.

The Blessed Virgin's Preparations for the Birth of Jesus • Journey to Bethlehem

I SAW the blessed Virgin for many days with Anne, while Joseph remained alone in Nazareth, one of Anne's maids taking charge of the house for him. They, Mary and Joseph, received their principal support from Anne's house as long as she lived. I saw the blessed Virgin near Anne sewing and embroidering bands and tapestry. They seemed to be very busy in the house. Joachim must long since have been dead, for I saw Anne's second husband there and a little girl of from six to seven years old. She was helping Mary and being taught by her. If not a daughter of Anne, it must have been one of Mary Cleophas's children also called Mary.

I saw Mary sitting in a room with other women and preparing covers large and small. Some were embroidered with gold and silver. There was one large coverlet in a box in the midst of the women, at which all were working, knitting with two little wooden needles and balls of colored wool. Anne was very busy. She went around from one to another, receiving and giving wool. All expected Mary to be delivered in Anne's house, and these covers and other things were being prepared partly for the birth of the child and partly as gifts for the poor. Everything was of the best, and all abundantly, and richly provided. They knew not that Mary would, of necessity, have to journey to Bethlehem.

Joseph was at that moment on his way to Jerusalem with cattle for sacrifice.

I saw Joseph returned from Jerusalem. He had taken thither cattle for sacrifice, and had put up at the house before the Bethlehem gate. It was at this same inn that he and Mary stopped later on, before Mary's Purification. The keeper of the inn was an Essene. Joseph went from there to Bethlehem, but did not visit his relatives. He was looking around after a place to build, also for some means of procuring lumber and tools, for in the spring after Mary's delivery, which he thought would take place in Nazareth, he intended to remove with her to Bethlehem, as he did not care for Nazareth. He wanted to get a place near the inn of the Essene. From Bethlehem he went again to Jerusalem, to offer sacrifice. When he was returning from this journey to Jerusalem, and about midnight was crossing the field of Kimki, six hours from Nazareth, an angel appeared to him and said that he should set out at once with Mary for Bethlehem, as it was there that her child was to be born.[A9] The angel told him, moreover, that he should provide himself with a few necessaries, but no laces nor embroidered covers, and he mentioned all the other things he was to take. Joseph was very much surprised. He was told also that, besides the ass upon which Mary was to ride, he was to take with him a little she-ass of one year which had not yet foaled. This little animal they were to let run at large, and then follow the road it would take.

I saw Joseph and Mary in their house at Nazareth; Anne too was present. Joseph informed them of the commands he had received, and they began to prepare for the journey. Anne was very much troubled about it. The blessed Virgin had had all along an interior admonition that she should bring forth her child in Bethlehem; but in her humility she had kept silence. She knew it, also, from the prophecies. She had all the prophecies referring to the birth of the Messiah in her little closet at Nazareth; she read them very often and prayed for their fulfillment. She had received them from her teachers at the temple, and by the same holy women had been instructed upon them. Her prayer was always for the coming of the Messiah. She esteemed her happy of whom the child should be born, and she desired to serve her as her lowest handmaid. In her humility, she had never conceived the thought that she herself was to be the one. From those prophecies she knew that the Savior would be born in Bethlehem, therefore she lovingly submitted to the divine Will and began her journey. It was a very painful one for her, since at that season it was cold among the mountains. Mary had an inexpressible

The High Road to Bethlehem

feeling that henceforth she must and could be only poor. She could possess no exterior goods, for she had all in herself. She knew that she was to be the mother of the Son of God. She knew and she felt that, as by a woman sin had entered into the world, so now by a woman the Expiation was to be born. It was under the influence of this feeling that she had exclaimed: "Behold the handmaid of the Lord!" I understood, likewise, that Jesus was conceived of the Holy Spirit about the hour of midnight, and about midnight should be born.

I saw Joseph and Mary with Anne, Mary Cleophas, and some servants silently setting out upon their journey. They started from Anne's. An ass bore a comfortable cross-seat for Mary and her baggage. On the field of Kimki, where the angel had appeared to Joseph, Anne had a pasture ground; and here the servants went to get the little she-ass of one year which Joseph had to take with him. She ran after the holy family. Anne, Mary Cleophas, and the servants now parted from Joseph and Mary after a touching leave-taking. I saw the two travelers going some distance further and putting up at a house that lay on very high ground. They were well received. I think the proprietor was the lease holder of a farm called the House of Kimki and to which the field belonged. From it one could see far into the distance, yes, even to the mountains near Jerusalem.

I again saw the holy family in a very cold valley, through which they were making their way toward a mountain. The ground was covered with frost and snow.

It was about four hours from the house of Kimki. Mary was suffering exceedingly from the cold. She halted near a pine tree, and exclaimed: "We must rest. I can go no farther." Joseph arranged a seat for her under the tree, in which he placed a light. I often saw that done at night by travelers in those parts. The blessed Virgin prayed fervently, imploring God not to allow them to freeze; and at once so great a warmth passed into her that she stretched out her hands to Joseph that he might warm himself by them. She took some food to renew her strength. The little ass, their guide, came up with them here and stood still. The actions of the little animal were truly astonishing. On straight roads, between mountains, for instance, where they could not go astray, she was sometimes behind, sometimes far ahead of them; but where the road branched, she was sure to make her appearance and run on the right way. Whenever they reached a spot at which they should halt, the little creature stood still. Joseph here spoke to Mary of the good lodgings that he expected to find in Bethlehem. He told her that he knew the good people of an inn at which, for a moderate sum, they could get a comfortable room. It was better, he said, to pay a little than to depend upon free quarters. He praised Bethlehem in order to console and encourage her.

After that, I saw the holy family arrive at a large farmhouse, about two hours' distance from the pine tree. The woman was not at home, and the man refused Joseph admittance, telling him that he might go on further. On they went until they came to a shepherd's shed where they found the little ass, and where they too halted.

There were some shepherds in it; but they soon vacated after showing themselves most friendly and supplying straw and faggots, or bundles of reeds, for a fire. The shepherds then went to the house from which Mary and Joseph had been sent away. They mentioned having met them, and said: "What a beautiful, what an extraordinary woman! What an amiable, pious, benevolent man! What wonderful people those travelers are!" The man's wife had now returned home, and she scolded at their having been sent away. I saw her going to the shepherd's hut at which they had put up, but she was timid and dared not enter. This hut was on the north side of that mountain on whose southern declivity lay Samaria and Thebez. Toward the east of this region and on this side of the Jordan, Salem and Ainon are situated, and on the opposite side, Succoth. It was about twelve hours from Nazareth. The woman came again with her two children. She was quite friendly, and seemed to be very much touched by what she saw. The husband also came and begged pardon. After Mary and Joseph had refreshed themselves a little, he showed them to an inn about an hour further up the mountain.

The host, however, excused himself to Joseph, pleading the numbers already there. But when the blessed Virgin entered and begged for shelter, the wife of the innkeeper, as also the innkeeper himself, changed their bearing toward them. The man at once arranged a shelter for them under a neighboring shed, and took charge of the ass. The little she-ass was not with them. She was running around the fields; for when not needed, she did not make her appearance. This inn was a tolerably fine one, and consisted of several houses. Although situated on the north side of the mountain, it was surrounded by orchards, pleasure gardens, and balsam trees. Mary and Joseph remained overnight and the whole of the next day, for it was the sabbath.

On the sabbath the hostess with her three children visited Mary, also the woman of that other house with her two children. Mary talked to the little ones and instructed them. They had little rolls of parchment from which they read. I, too, made bold to speak confidently to Mary. She told me how extremely well it was with her in her present condition. She felt no weight. But sometimes she experienced a sensation of being so immensely large internally and as if she were hovering in her own person. She felt that she encompassed God and man, and that he whom she encompassed carried her.

Joseph went out with the host to his fields. Both host and hostess had conceived great love for Mary; they sympathized with her condition. They pressed her to remain, and showed her a room which they would give her. But very early the next morning she started with Joseph on their journey. They went forward, a little more to the east, along the mountain and into a valley, increasing the distance between them and Samaria to which they seemed at first to be going. The temple upon Gerizim was in sight. On the roof were numerous figures like lions or other animals, which shone with a white light in the sun.

The road led down into a plain, or the field of Shechem. After a journey of about six leagues, they came to a solitary farmhouse where they were made welcome. The man was an overseer of fields and orchards belonging to a neighboring city. It was warmer here and vegetation more luxuriant than at any place they had been, for it was the sunny side of the mountain, and that makes a great difference in Palestine at this season. The house was not exactly in the valley, but on the southern declivity of the mountain which stretches from Samaria to the east. The occupants belonged to those shepherds with whose daughters later on the servants remaining behind from the caravan of the three kings had married. In after years also Jesus often tarried here and taught. Before departing, Joseph blessed the children of the family.

I saw him and Mary journeying over the plain beyond Shechem. The blessed Virgin sometimes went on foot. They rested occasionally and refreshed themselves. They had with them little rolls and a cool, strengthening drink in nice little jugs, brown and shining like metal. The seat that Mary used on the ass was furnished with a pad on either side as a support for the limbs, which were thereby brought more into a sitting posture. The support was over the neck of the ass, and Mary sat sometimes to the right, sometimes to the left. Berries and other fruits were still hanging on the bushes and trees that were exposed to the sun, and these they gathered on the way. The first thing that Joseph always did on arriving at an inn was to prepare a comfortable seat or couch for Mary; then he washed his feet, as did Mary also. Their ablutions were frequent.

It was quite dark one evening when they reached a lonely inn. Joseph knocked and begged for shelter, but the owner would not open the door. Joseph explained to him his position, telling him that his wife could go no farther. But the man was inflexible; he would not interrupt his own rest. And when Joseph told him that he would pay him, he received for answer: "This is not an inn, I will not have that knocking." The door remained closed. Mary and Joseph went on for a short distance and found a shed. He struck a light, and prepared a couch for Mary, she herself assisting him. He brought the ass in, and found some straw and fodder for it. Here they rested a few hours. I saw them departing early the next morning while it was still dark. They may now have been distant from their last halting place about six hours, about six and twenty from Nazareth, and ten from Jerusalem. The last house stood on level ground, but the road from Gabatha to Jerusalem began again to grow steep. Up to this time Mary and Joseph traveled no great highroads, though they crossed several commercial routes which ran from the Jordan to Samaria and to the roads that lead from Syria down into Egypt. So far, the roads by which they came, with the exception of that single broad one, were very narrow and ran over the mountains. One had to be very cautious in walking, but the ass could tread its way securely.

Now I saw the travelers arrive at a house whose owner was at first uncivil to Joseph. He threw the light on Mary's face, and twitted Joseph on having so young a wife. But the man's wife took them in, gave them shelter in an outhouse, and offered them some little rolls.

When they left this place, they next sought lodging in a large farmhouse where also they were not received in a manner especially cordial. The innkeepers were young, and paid little heed to Mary and Joseph. They were not simple shepherds, but rich farmers, such as we have here, mixed up with the world, with trade, etc. I saw one old man going about the house with a walking stick. From here they had still seven hours' journey to Bethlehem, but they did not take the direct route thither, because it was mountainous and at this season too difficult. They followed the little she-ass across the country between Jerusalem and the Jordan. I saw them arrive about noon at a large shepherd's house, about two hours from John's place of baptism on the Jordan. Jesus once passed a night there after his baptism. Near the house was another for the farm and sheep utensils, and in the yard was a spring from which the water was conducted through pipes to the bathtubs. There was a large public house here; and numbers of servants who took their meals at it were going and coming. The host received the travelers very kindly and he was very obliging. He insisted upon one of the servant's washing Joseph's feet at the spring. He also supplied him with fresh garments while he aired and brushed those he took off. A maid-servant rendered the same services to Mary, for the mistress of the house was backward in making her appearance; she lived retired. She is the same that Jesus afterward healed of a thirty years' sickness. He told her that her malady had come upon her as a punishment for her want of hospitality toward his relatives. But I know the reason of her nonappearance to Mary and Joseph. She was young and rather frivolous. She had caught a glance of the blessed Virgin, had spoken a word to her, perhaps (I do not now recall all the circumstances), and had conceived a feeling of jealousy on account of her beauty. It was for that reason that she kept herself secluded on this occasion. There were some children in the house.

Farmhouse Inn on the Way to Bethlehem

At their departure about noon, Mary and Joseph were accompanied part of the way by some of the people belonging to the inn. They proceeded westward toward Bethlehem, and arrived after a journey of about two hours at a little village consisting of a long row of houses with gardens and courts lying on both sides of a broad highroad. Joseph had connections here such as spring from the second marriage of a stepfather or stepmother. Their house was finely situated and very handsome. But Mary and Joseph did not enter. They passed through the place and went straight on toward Jerusalem for half an hour, when they came to a public house in which a crowd was gathered for a funeral. The frame partitions in the house had been removed from before the chimney and hearth. The fireplace was draped with black, and before it rested a coffin enveloped in the same somber hue. The male mourners wore long black robes with short, white ones over them and some had rough, black maniples on their arms. All were praying. In another apartment sat the women, entirely enveloped in their large veils. There was in the yard a large fountain with several faucets. The proprietors of the house, who were taken up with the charge of the obsequies, left to the servants the duty of receiving Mary and Joseph. This was done, accordingly, and the customary services rendered the holy travelers.

Tapestry, or mats, were let down from their rollers near the ceiling, and a curtained space arranged for them. After some time I saw the people of the house in conversation with them. The white garments had been laid aside. I saw a great many beds rolled up against the walls. They could be entirely separated from one another by means of the mats let down from the ceilings. Early the following morning Mary and Joseph again started off. The good wife of the house told them they might stay, because Mary appeared in hourly expectation of her delivery. But Mary said with lowered veil that she had yet six or eight and thirty hours. The woman was anxious to keep them, though not in her own house. I saw the husband, as Joseph and Mary were departing, talking to the former about his beasts. Joseph praised the ass very much, and told him that he had brought the other with him in case of necessity. When the people spoke of the difficulty of getting lodgings in Bethlehem, Joseph replied that he had friends there and that Mary and he would certainly be well received. This made me feel so sorry. Joseph always spoke of this with so much confidence. I heard him again making the same remark to Mary on their way.

It so happened on the last days of the journey, when they were nearing Bethlehem, that Mary sighed longingly for rest and refreshment. Joseph turned aside from the road for half an hour to a place where, upon a former occasion, he had discovered a beautiful fig tree laden with fruit. It had seats around it for weary wayfarers to rest upon. But when they reached it they found, to their great disappointment, that it was at that time quite destitute of fruit. In after years something connected with Jesus happened near that tree. It nevermore had fruit, though it continued green. Jesus cursed it, and it withered.

The Arrival in Bethlehem

THE DISTANCE from the last public house to Bethlehem may have been three hours. Mary and Joseph went around by the north and approached the city on the west. A short distance outside the city, about a quarter of an hour's walk brought them to a large building surrounded by courtyards and smaller houses. There were trees in front of it, and all sorts of people encamped in tents around it. This house was once the paternal home of Joseph, and ages before it had been the family mansion of David. It was at this period used as the custom house of the Roman taxes.

Joseph still had in the city a brother, who was an innkeeper. He was not his own brother, but a stepbrother. Joseph did not go near him. Joseph had had five brothers, three own-brothers and two stepbrothers. Joseph was five and forty years old. He was thirty years and, I think, three months older than Mary. He was thin, had a fair complexion, prominent cheekbones tinged with red, a high, open forehead, and a brownish beard.

The little she-ass was not with them here. She had run away around the south side of the city, where it was somewhat level, a kind of valley.

Joseph went straight into the custom house, for all newcomers had to present themselves there and obtain a ticket for entrance at the city gate. The city had properly no gate, but the entrance lay between two ruined walls that looked like the remains of a gate. Although Joseph was somewhat late in presenting himself for assessment, he was well received.

Mary remained in a small house in the courtyard among the women, who were very attentive to her, and offered her something to eat. These women cooked for the soldiers. The latter were Romans, as I could tell by the straps hanging around their hips. The weather was lovely, not at all cold, the sun lighting up the mountain between Jerusalem and Bethany. One can see it very well from here. Joseph went up to a large room in an upper story, where he was interrogated, who he was, etc., and his questioners examined long rolls of writing, numbers of which were hanging on the walls. They unrolled them and read to him his ancestry, also that of Mary. Joseph knew not before that through Joachim, Mary had descended in a straight line from David. The official asked him, "Where is thy wife?"

For seven years the inhabitants of this part of the country were not regularly assessed, owing to various political troubles. I saw the numbers V and II, and that certainly makes seven. The tax collecting had already been going on for many months, but two payments were still to be made. The people had to remain almost three months. They had indeed paid something here and there during those seven years, but there had been no regular collection of taxes. Joseph did not pay anything on that first day, but his circumstances were inquired into. He told the official that he possessed no real estate, that he lived by his trade and the assistance of his wife's parents. Mary also was summoned to appear before the clerk, but not upstairs. She was interrogated in a passage on the first floor, and nothing was read to her.

There were numbers of clerks and functionaries in the house, scattered throughout the different rooms, and a great many Romans and soldiers were to be met in the upper stories. There were also Pharisees and Sadducees, priests and elders, and all sorts of clerks and officials of both Jewish and Roman extraction. There was no such payment of taxes going on in Jerusalem. But in many other places, in Magdala on the Sea of Galilee, for instance, taxes were being received. The Galileans had to pay there, and the people from Sidon, too, partly on account of their commercial connections, I think. Only those that had no establishments, that possessed no estates, had to report at their birthplace.

The receipts for the next three months were to be divided into three parts. The Emperor Augustus, Herod, and another king who dwelt in the neighborhood of Egypt, had a share in them. The king near Egypt, having gained some advantage in war, had a claim upon a certain district far up the country; consequently, they had to give him something. The second payment had some reference to the building of the temple; it was something like a payment on money advanced. The third was for the poor and for widows, who had received nothing for a long time. But it all went as such things do in our own day—a little to the right man. Good reasons were easily found for its remaining in the hands of the great. Incessant writing and moving to and fro were kept up.

Joseph then went with Mary straight to Bethlehem on whose outskirts the houses stood scattered, and into the heart of the city. At the different streets they met, he left Mary and the ass standing while he went up and down in search of an inn.[A10] Mary often had to wait long before Joseph, anxious and troubled, returned. Nowhere did he find room; everywhere was he sent away. And now it began to grow dark. Joseph at last proposed going to the other side of the city, where they would surely find lodgings. They proceeded down a street, which was more of a country road than a regular street, for the houses stood scattered along the hills, and at the end of it reached a low, level space, or field. Here stood a very beautiful tree with a smooth trunk, its branches spreading out like a roof. Joseph led Mary and the beast under it, and there left them to go again in quest of an inn. He went from house to house, his friends, of whom he had spoken to Mary, unwilling to recognize him. Once during his quest, he returned to Mary, who was waiting under the tree. He wept, and she consoled him. He started afresh on his search. But whenever he brought forward the approaching delivery of his wife as a pressing reason for receiving hospitality, he was dismissed still more quickly.

Meantime it had grown dark. Mary was standing under the tree, her ungirdled robe falling around her in full folds, her head covered with a white veil. The ass was nearby, its head turned toward the tree, at the foot of which Joseph had made a seat for Mary with the baggage. Crowds were hurrying to and fro in Bethlehem, and many of the passersby gazed curiously at Mary, as one naturally does on seeing a person standing a long time in the dark. I think also that some of them addressed her, and asked her who she was. Ah, they little dreamed that the Savior was so near! Mary was so patient, so tranquil, so full of hope. Ah, she had indeed long to wait! At last she sat down, her hands crossed on her breast, her head lowered. After a long time, Joseph returned in great dejection. I saw that he was shedding tears and, because he had failed again to find an inn, he hesitated to approach. But suddenly he bethought him of a cave outside Bethlehem used as a storing place by the shepherds when they brought their cattle to the city. Joseph had often withdrawn thither to conceal himself from his brothers and to pray. It was very likely to be deserted at that season or, if any shepherds did come, it would be easy to make friends with them. He and Mary might there find shelter for awhile, and after a little rest he would go out again on his search.

And now they went around to the left, as if through the ruined walls, tombs, and ramparts of a country town. They mounted a rampart or hill, and then the road began again to descend. At last, they reached a hill before which stood trees, firs, pines, or cedars, and trees with small leaves like the box tree. In this hill was the cave or vault spoken of by Joseph. There were no houses around. One side of the cave was built up with rough masonry through which the open entrance of the shepherds led down into the valley. Joseph opened the light wicker door and, as they entered, the she-ass ran to meet them. She had left them near Joseph's paternal house, and had run around the city to this cave. She frolicked around and leaped gaily about them, so that Mary said: "Behold! It is surely God's will that we should be here." But Joseph was worried and, in secret, a little ashamed, because he had so often alluded to the good reception they would meet in Bethlehem. There was a projection above the door under which he stood the ass and then proceeded to arrange a seat for Mary. It was quite dark, about eight o'clock, when they reached this place. Joseph struck a light and went into the cave. The entrance was very narrow. The walls were stuffed with all kinds of coarse straw, like rushes, over which hung brown mats. Back in the vaulted part were some airholes in the roof, but here also everything was in disorder. Joseph cleared it out and prepared as much space in the back part as would afford room for a couch and seat for Mary, who had seated herself on a rug with her bundle for a support. The ass was then brought in, and Joseph fastened a lamp on the wall. While Mary was eating, he went out to the field in the direction of the Milk Cave, and laid a leathern bottle in the rivulet that it might fill. He went also to the city where he procured some little dishes, a bundle of other things, and I think, some fruit. It was indeed the sabbath, but on account of the numerous strangers in the city and their need of various necessaries, provisions and utensils were exposed for sale on tables placed at the street corners. The price was paid down on the spot. I think servants or pagan slaves guarded the tables, but I cannot remember for certain.

When Joseph returned, he brought with him a small bundle of slender sticks beautifully bound up with reeds, and a box with a handle in which were glowing coals. These he poured out at the entrance of the cave to make a fire. He next brought the water bottle, which he had filled at the rivulet, and prepared some food. It consisted of a stew, made of yellow corn, some kind of large plant that contained a great many seeds, and a little bread. After they had eaten and Mary had lain down to rest upon her rush couch over which was spread a cover, Joseph began to prepare his own resting place at the entrance of the cave. When this was done, he went again into the city. Previously to setting out, he had stopped up all the openings of the cave, in order to keep out the air. Then for the first time, I saw the blessed Virgin on her knees in prayer, after which she lay down upon the carpet on her side, her head resting on her arm, her bundle serving for a pillow.

This cave lay at the extremity of the mountain ridge of Bethlehem. A clump of beautiful trees stood in front of the entrance, and thence could be descried some of the towers and roofs of the city. Over the entrance, which was closed by a door made of wickerwork, was a shed. From the door, a moderately wide passage led into the cave, an irregularly formed vault, half-round, half-triangular. On one side of the passage was a recess rather lower than the general surface, and this Joseph had enclosed by curtains for his own sleeping place. The rest of the passage, from the recess to the entrance, he cut off by hangings, and there had a kind of storeroom.

The passage was not so lofty as the cave itself, which was vaulted by nature. The inner walls of the cave, where they were formed entirely by nature, though not perfectly even, yet were pleasing and clean; indeed to my eye, there was something about them quite charming. They pleased me more than did those parts upon which some attempts had been made at masonry, for these latter were coarse and rough. The foundation of the right side of the entrance appeared for some distance to have been hewn out of the rock; only the upper part seemed to have been made by the hand of man. There were also some holes in this passage. In the middle of the vaulted roof was an opening and, I think, three others cut obliquely halfway up the same. These oblique openings presented a smoother appearance than the topmost one; they looked like the handiwork of man. The floor of the cave was deeper than that of the entrance, and was on three sides surrounded by a stone seat somewhat raised, broad in some places, in others narrow. At one of the broad parts, the ass took its stand. It had no trough, but a large leathern bag was placed before it or hung in the corner. Behind was a small side cave just large enough to allow the animal to stand upright. There the fodder was stored. A gutter ran along by this corner, and I saw Joseph cleaning the cave out every day.

Where Mary reposed before the birth of the child and where I beheld her elevated above the ground at the moment of her delivery, there was a similar seat of stone. The spot in which the crib stood was a deep recess, or side vault. Near it was a second entrance into the cave, which was in the ridge of a hill that ran toward the city. In the rear, the hill sank into a very charming valley planted with rows of trees. This valley led to the Suckling Cave of Abraham, situated in a projection of the opposite hill. The valley may have been one-eighth of an hour in width, and through it flowed that little rivulet from which Joseph had procured the water.

Besides the real crib cave, there were in the same hill, but lying somewhat deeper, two other caves, in one of which the blessed Virgin often remained hidden.

When in after years St. Paula laid the first foundation of her convent at Bethlehem, I saw a small, lightly-built chapel erected in the valley and on the east side of the cave. It was so constructed as to be contiguous to the rear of the crib cave and directly back of the spot upon which Jesus was born. This little chapel of wood and wicker walls was hung inside with tapestry. Four rows of cells opened into it, which were built as lightly as the shepherds' cots generally are in Palestine. In every row were separate cells, each surrounded by its own little garden, and all connected by covered passages leading to the chapel. Here Paula and her daughter gathered around them their first companions. In the chapel and free from the wall, stood an altar with its little tabernacle. Behind it hung a red and white silk curtain, which concealed the facsimile of the crib cave that St. Paula had caused to be made. It was separated from the real cave, from the exact spot upon which Jesus was born, only by the rocky wall. This crib was made of white stone, and was a faithful imitation of that of Jesus. The manger also was represented, and even the hay hanging through its sides. The infant in it was likewise of white stone, and closely swathed in a blue veil. The figure was hollow and not very heavy. I saw St. Paula often taking it up into her arms while she prayed. Upon the wall over this crib hung a banner upon which was represented the ass with its head turned toward the crib. It was embroidered in colors, and the hair made of thread, so natural that it looked like real hair. Above the crib was a hole in which a star was fastened. I saw that the child Jesus often appeared here to St. Paula and her daughter. In front of the curtain and right and left of the altar were hanging lamps.

Birth of the Child Jesus

I SAW Joseph on the following day arranging a seat and couch for Mary in the so-called Suckling Cave of Abraham, which was also the sepulcher of Maraha, his nurse. It was more spacious than the cave of the crib. Mary remained there some hours, while Joseph was making the latter more habitable. He brought also from the city many different little vessels and some dried fruits.

Mary told him that the birth hour of the child would arrive on the coming night. It was then nine months since her conception by the Holy Spirit. She begged him to do all in his power that they might receive as honorably as possible this child promised by God, this child supernatu-

Cave of the Nativity

rally conceived; and she invited him to unite with her in prayer for those hard-hearted people who would afford him no place of shelter. Joseph proposed to bring some pious women whom he knew in Bethlehem to her assistance; but Mary would not allow it, she declared that she had no need of anyone. It was five o'clock in the evening when Joseph brought Mary back again to the crib cave. He hung up several more lamps, and made a place under the shed before the door for the little she-ass, which came joyfully hurrying from the fields to meet them.

When Mary told Joseph that her time was drawing near and that he should now betake himself to prayer, he left her and turned toward his sleeping place to do her bidding. Before entering his little recess, he looked back once toward that part of the cave where Mary knelt upon her couch in prayer, her back to him, her face toward the east. He saw the cave filled with the light that streamed from Mary, for she was entirely enveloped as if by flames. It was as if he were, like Moses, looking into the burning bush. He sank prostrate to the ground in prayer, and looked not back again. The glory around Mary became brighter and brighter, the lamps that Joseph had lit were no longer to be seen. Mary knelt, her flowing white robe spread out before her. At the twelfth hour, her prayer became ecstatic, and I saw her raised so far above the ground that one could see it beneath her. Her hands were crossed upon her breast, and the light around her grew even more resplendent. I no longer saw the roof of the cave. Above Mary stretched a pathway of light up to heaven, in which pathway it seemed as if one light came forth from another, as if one figure dissolved into another, and from these different spheres of light other heavenly figures issued. Mary continued in prayer, her eyes bent low upon the ground. At that moment she gave birth to the infant Jesus. I saw him like a tiny, shining child, lying on the rug at her knees, and brighter far than all the other brilliancy.[A11] He seemed to grow before my eyes. But dazzled by the glittering and flashing of light, I know not whether I really saw that, or how I saw it. Even inanimate nature seemed stirred. The stones of the rocky floor and the walls of the cave were glimmering and sparkling, as if instinct with life.

Mary's ecstasy lasted some moments longer. Then I saw her spread a cover over the child, but she did not yet take it up, nor even touch it. After a long time, I saw the child stirring and heard it crying, and then only did Mary seem to recover full consciousness. She lifted the child, along with the cover that she had thrown over it, to her breast and sat veiled, herself and child quite enveloped. I think she was suckling it. I saw angels around her in human form prostrate on their faces. It may, perhaps, have been an hour after the birth when Mary called Joseph, who still lay prostrate in prayer. When he approached, he fell on his knees, his face to the ground, in a transport of joy, devotion, and humility. Mary again urged him to look upon the Sacred Gift from heaven, and then did Joseph take the child into his arms. And now the blessed Virgin swathed the child in red and over that in a white veil up as far as under the little arms, and the upper part of the body from the armpits to the head she wrapped up in another piece of linen. She had only four swaddling cloths with her. She laid the child in the crib, which had been filled with rushes and fine moss over which was spread a cover that hung down at the sides. The crib stood over the stone trough, and at this spot the ground stretched straight and level as far as the passage, where it made a broader flexure toward the south. The floor of this part of the cave lay somewhat deeper than where the child was born, and down to it steps had been formed in the earth. When Mary laid the child in the crib, both she and Joseph stood by it in tears, singing the praises of God.

The seat and the couch of the blessed Virgin were near the crib. I saw her on the first day sitting upright and also resting on her side, though I noticed in her no special signs of weakness or sickness. Both before and after the birth, she was robed in white. When visitors came, she generally sat near the crib more closely veiled.

On the night of the birth there gushed forth a beautiful spring in the other cave that lay to the right. The water ran forth their fragrance. In Bethlehem it was misty, and the sky above shone with a murky, reddish glare. But over the valley of the shepherds, around the crib, and in the valley of the Suckling Cave floated bright clouds of refreshing dew.

I saw the herds of the three oldest shepherds near the hill under sheds; but those further on near the shepherds' tower were partly in the open air. The three eldest shepherds, roused by the wonders of the night, I saw standing together before their huts, gazing around and pointing out the magnificent light that shone over the crib. The shep-

Birth Grotto among Caves along Ridge outside Bethlehem

out, and the next day Joseph dug a course for it and formed a spring.

In those visions to which the event itself, and not the feast of the church, gave rise, I saw, indeed, no such sparkling joy in nature as I sometimes see at holy Christmastide. Then the joy has an interior signification. But yet, I saw extraordinary gladness, and in many places, even in the most distant regions of the world, something marvelous on that midnight. By it the good were filled with joyful longings, and the bad with dread. I saw also many of the lower animals joyfully agitated. I saw fountains gushing forth and swelling, flowers springing up in many places, trees and plants budding with new life, and all sending

herds at the distant tower were also in full movement. They had climbed up the tower and were looking toward the crib over which they, too, saw the light. I saw something like a cloud of glory descend upon the three shepherds. I saw in it figures moving to and fro, and heard the approach of sweet, clear voices singing softly. At first, the shepherds were frightened. Soon there stood before them five or seven lovely, radiant figures holding in their hands a long strip like a scroll upon which were written words in letters a hand in length. The angels were singing the Gloria. [A12]

The angels appeared also to the shepherds on the tower and where else, I do not now recall. I did not see them hurrying off at once to the cave. The first three were indeed an hour and a half distant from it, and those on the tower as far again. But I saw that they began at once to reflect upon what gifts they should take to the newborn Savior, and to get them together as quickly as possible. The three shepherds went to the crib early next morning.

I saw that Anne at Nazareth, Elizabeth in Jutta, Naomi, Anna, and Simeon in the temple—all had on this night visions from which they learned the birth of the Savior. The child John was unspeakably joyous. But only Anne knew where the newborn child was; the others, and even Elizabeth, knew indeed of Mary and saw her in vision, but they knew nothing of Bethlehem.

I saw something very wonderful taking place in the temple. The writings of the Sadducees were more than once hurled by an invisible force from the places in which they were kept, which circumstance gave rise to unaccountable dread. The fact was ascribed to sorcery, and large sums of money were paid to hush the matter up.

I saw that in Rome, across the river where numbers of Jews dwelt, a well of oil gushed forth spontaneously, to the wonder of all the witnesses. And when Jesus was born, a magnificent statue of the god Jupiter fell with violence from its place. All were struck with fear. Sacrifices were offered and another idol, I think Venus, was interrogated as to the cause. The devil was forced to speak by its mouth, and he proclaimed that it had happened because a virgin unmarried had conceived and brought forth a son. He told them also of the miracle of the oil well. Where this took place now stands a church in honor of the Mother of God. I saw that the pagan priests were deeply perplexed at the whole affair. They searched their writings, and discovered the following history. About seventy years previously, this idol (Jupiter) had been greatly venerated. It was magnificently ornamented with gold and precious stones, grand ceremonies were held in its honor, and numerous sacrifices offered to it. But there was in Rome at that time an extraordinarily pious woman who lived on her own means. I know not for certain whether she was a Jewess or not; but she had visions, uttered prophecies, and informed many persons as to the cause of their sterility. This woman had thrown out words to this effect that they should not honor the idol at so great a cost, for that they would one day behold it burst asunder in their midst. This speech proved so offensive that she was imprisoned and tormented until by her prayers she obtained from God the information as to when that misfortune would happen. The pagan priests demanded what had been revealed to her, and when at last she replied: "The idol will be shattered when an immaculate virgin shall bring forth a son," they hooted at her, and released her as a fool. And now the people recalled the fact and declared that the woman had spoken truly. I saw also that the Roman consuls, of whom one was named Lentulus and who was a friend of St. Peter and an ancestor of the martyr-priest Moses, made notes of this occurrence, as well as that of the bursting forth of the oil well.

On this night, I saw the Emperor Augustus at the Capitol where he had an apparition of a rainbow upon which sat the virgin and child. From the oracle that he caused to be interrogated upon what he had seen, he received the answer: "A child is born, and before him we must all flee!" The emperor at once erected an altar and offered sacrifice to the Son of the Virgin, as to the "First-born of God."

I had also a vision of Egypt far beyond Matarea, Heliopolis, and Memphis. There was in that region a large idol that used to give answers to all kinds of questions. Suddenly it became mute. The king ordered immense sacrifices to be offered throughout his whole dominions. Then was the devil, upon the command of God, forced to say: "I have become silent, I must give place to another. The Son of the Virgin is born, and a temple will be here erected to his honor." Upon hearing this, the king wanted to raise a temple to the newborn child next to that of the god, but I do not clearly recall the story. I know, however, that the idol was put aside and that a temple was erected to the virgin and child whom it had proclaimed, and who were afterward honored with pagan rites.

I beheld a great wonder in the country of the three kings. There was a tower on a mountain to which the kings retired in turn with a retinue of priests, in order to observe the stars. What they saw they committed to writing and communicated to one another. On this night there were two of them there, Mensor and Sair. The third, who dwelt toward the east side of the Caspian Sea, was called Theokeno. He was not present. There was a certain constellation at which they always gazed, and whose variations they noted. In it they saw visions and pictures. Upon this night also they had several visions of various kinds. It was not in one star alone that they saw those visions, but in several that formed a figure, and there seemed to be a movement in them. They saw the vision of the moon over which arose a beautiful rainbow-colored arch on which was seated a virgin. The left limb was drawn up in a sitting posture, the right hung a little lower and rested on the moon. To the left of the virgin and rising above the arch, was a grapevine, and on her right a sheaf of wheat. In front of the virgin was a chalice like that used at the Last Supper. It appeared to issue, but with greater clearness and brightness, from the brilliancy that emanated from her. Out of the chalice arose a child, and over the child shone a bright disk like an empty monstrance. It was surrounded by radiating beams.

It reminded me of the blessed sacrament. On the virgin's right was an octangular church with a golden door and two small side-doors. With the right hand, the virgin put the child and the host into the church which, meanwhile, grew larger and larger, and in which I saw the most holy Trinity. Above the church arose a tower. Theokeno, the third king, had similar visions in his own home.

Over the head of the virgin sitting on the arch shone a star, which suddenly shot from its place and skimmed along the heavens before the kings. It was for them a voice announcing as never before that the child, so long awaited by them and by their ancestors, was at last born in Judea, and that they were to follow that star. For some nights immediately preceding that blessed one, they had from their tower seen all kinds of visions in the heavens, kings journeying to the child and offering their homage to it. So now they hurriedly gathered together their treasures and with gifts and presents began the journey, for they did not want to be the last. I saw all three after a few days meeting on the way.

Adoration of the Shepherds • Devout Visits to the Crib

IN THE early dawn after the birth of Jesus, the three oldest of the shepherds came to the crib cave with the gifts they had gathered together. These consisted of little animals bearing some resemblance to deer. They were very lightly built and nimble, had long necks and clear, beautiful eyes. They followed or ran along beside the shepherds who led them with fine, guiding cords. The shepherds carried also large, live birds under their arms, and dead ones slung over their shoulders.

They told Joseph at the entrance of the cave what the angel had announced to them, and that they had come to do homage to the Child of Promise and to offer him gifts. Joseph accepted their presents and allowed them to lead the animals into the space that formed a kind of cellar near the side entrance of the cave. Then he conducted them to the blessed Virgin, who was sitting on the ground near the crib, a rug under her, the infant Jesus on her lap. [A13] The shepherds, their staves resting on their arms, fell on their knees and wept with joy. They knelt long, tasting great interior sweetness, and then intoned the angelic canticle of praise, and a psalm that I have forgotten. When they were about to take leave, Mary placed the child in their arms.

Some of the other shepherds came in the evening, accompanied by women and children, and bringing gifts. They sang most sweetly before the crib the Gloria, some psalms, and short refrains of which I remember the words: "O Child, blooming as a rose art thou! As a herald thou comest forth!" They brought gifts of birds, eggs, honey, woven stuffs of various colors, bundles of raw silk, and ears of corn, also several bundles of a corn with heavy grains growing on a stalk with large leaves like those of rushes.

The three oldest shepherds came back in turn and helped Joseph to make the crib cave and its surroundings more comfortable. I saw also several pious women with the blessed Virgin, performing some services for her. They were Essenes, and lived in the valley, not far from the crib cave, in little rocky cells adjoining one another. They owned little gardens near their cells, and they taught the children of their community. Joseph had invited them to come, for he was acquainted with them even in early youth. When he was hiding in the crib cave, from his brethren, he visited these pious women who dwelt in the side of the rock. They now came in turn to the blessed Virgin, bringing little necessaries and bundles of wood. They cooked and washed for the holy family.

Some days after the birth of Jesus, I saw a touching scene in the crib cave. Joseph and Mary were standing by the crib and gazing with emotion upon the infant Jesus, when suddenly the ass fell upon its knees and lowered its head to the ground. Mary and Joseph shed tears. I saw Mary at another time standing by the crib. As she gazed upon the child, the deep conviction stole upon her that it had come upon earth to suffer. That reminded me of a vision I had had at an earlier period in which I had been shown how Jesus, while still in his mother's womb and from the movement of his birth, had suffered. I saw under the heart of Mary a glory and in it a bright shining child. As I gazed upon it, it seemed as if Mary were hovering over it and surrounding it. I beheld the child growing and all the torments of the crucifixion inflicted upon it. It was a sad, a fearful sight! I wept and sobbed aloud. I saw other forms around it beating and pushing, scourging and crowning it. Then they laid the cross upon it, next nailed it to the same, and pierced it in the side. I saw the whole Passion of Christ in the child. It was a frightful sight! As the child hung on the cross, It said to me: "All this did I suffer from my conception until my thirty-fourth year, when my Passion was outwardly consummated." (The Lord died when he was thirty-three years and three months old.) "Go and announce it to men!" But how can I announce it to men?

I saw Jesus also as the newborn child, and I saw how many of the children that went to the crib ill-treated the infant Jesus. The Mother of God was not there to protect the child, and the children went with all kinds of switches and rods, and struck it in the face until the blood flowed. The child meekly extended its little hands before its face, in order to ward off the blows. The smallest children were they that struck the most maliciously. The parents of some even twisted and wrapped the rods for them. They brought thorns, nettles, whips, little rods of all kinds, each having its own signification. One came with a very slender rod, like a reed. But when it was about to strike the child, the rod snapped, and fell back upon itself. I knew several of the children. Some went about boasting in their fine clothes, but I stripped them, and whipped some of them well.

While Mary was still standing by the crib in deep meditation, some shepherds drew near with their wives, in all about five persons. To give them room to approach the crib, the blessed Virgin withdrew a little to the spot upon which she had given birth to the child. The people did not actually adore, but they gazed down upon the child deeply moved, and before leaving they bowed low over it as if kissing it.

It was day. Mary sat in her usual place with the infant Jesus on her lap. He was swathed, the hands and face alone free. Mary had something like a piece of linen in her hands with which she was busied. Joseph was at the fireplace near the entrance of the cave, and appeared to be making a shelf to hold some vessels. I was standing next to the ass. And now came in three aged female Essenes, who were cordially welcomed, though Mary did not rise. They brought quite a number of presents: small fruits, birds with red, awl-shaped beaks as large as ducks, which they carried by the wings, oval rolls about an inch in thickness, some linen, and other stuff. All were received with rare humility and gratitude. The women were very silent and recollected. Deeply moved, they gazed down upon the child, but they did not touch it. When they withdrew, it was without farewells or ceremony. Meanwhile, I was taking a good look at the ass. It had a very broad back, and I thought to myself: "You good beast! You have carried a great burden!" and I wanted to feel it, to see if it were real. I ran my hand over its hair, and it felt as smooth as silk.

Now came two married women with three little girls about eight years old. They appeared to be strangers and people of distinction, who had come in obedience to a call more miraculous than that received by any previous visitor. Joseph welcomed them very humbly. They brought presents less in size than the others, but of greater value: grain in a bowl, small fruits, and a cluster of thick, triangular, gold leaves on which was a stamp like a seal. I thought: "Strange! That looks like the representation of the eye of God! But no! How can I compare the eye of God with red earth!" Mary arose and placed the child in the ladies' arms. Both held him a little while, praying silently with uplifted heart, and then kissed him. The three little girls were silent and deeply impressed. Joseph and Mary conversed with their visitors and when they left, Joseph accompanied them part of the way. Ah! Could we, like these women, behold the beauty, the purity, the innocent wisdom of Mary! She knew all things! But in her humility, she appears unconscious of her gifts. Like a child, she casts down her eyes; and when she raises them, her glance, like a flash of lightning, like the truth, like a ray of unsullied light, pierces one through and through. That is because she is perfectly pure, perfectly innocent, full of the Holy Spirit, and without any reflection on self. No one can resist her glance.

These people appeared to have come at least some miles and that secretly, for they avoided being seen in the city. Joseph behaved with great humility during such visits, retiring and looking on from some distant corner.

I saw also Anne's maid and an old manservant coming from Nazareth to the crib. The maid was a widow and related to the holy family. She brought all sorts of necessaries from Anne to Mary, with whom she took up her abode. The old man shed tears of joy, and returned with news to Anne.

The day after, I saw the blessed Virgin and the infant Jesus leave the crib cave with the maid for some hours. Stepping from the door of the cave, Mary turned toward the shed on the right, went some steps forward, and concealed herself in that side cave in which, at the birth of Jesus, a spring had welled up. She remained there four hours, because some men, spies of Herod, had come from Bethlehem, in consequence of the rumor set afloat by the words of the shepherds, that a miracle had there taken place in connection with a child. These men met Joseph in front of the crib cave. After exchanging a few words with him, they left him with a contemptuous smile at his humility and simplicity.

The crib cave was retired, and very pleasantly situated. No one from Bethlehem went there, only the shepherds whose duties called them thither. No one in Bethlehem took any interest in what was going on outside for, in consequence of the influx of strangers, the city was all alive, and much buying and selling going on. Cattle were being bought and slaughtered, for many people paid their taxes in cattle. There were numbers of pagans in the city in the capacity of servants.

The wonderful apparition of the angels was soon noised among the dwellers of the mountain valleys far and near, and with it the birth of the child in the cave. The innkeepers from whom the holy family on their journey had received hospitality now came, one after another, to do homage to him whom unknown they had entertained. I saw that hospitable keeper of the last inn, first sending presents by a servant, and then coming himself to honor the child. I saw also the good wife of that man who had been so cross to Joseph, and other shepherds and good people coming to the crib. They were very much affected by what they saw. All were in holiday attire, and were going up to Bethlehem for the sabbath. The good wife might have gone to Jerusalem which was nearer, but she preferred coming here to Bethlehem.

A relative of Joseph, and father of that Jonadab who, at the crucifixion of Jesus, presented a strip of linen to him, had also come to the crib cave on his way to Bethlehem for the sabbath. Joseph was very kind to him. This relative had heard from people of his place of Joseph's wonderful situation; he came therefore to bring him gifts and to visit the infant Jesus and Mary. But Joseph would not accept anything, although he pawned the little she-ass to this relative with the understanding that she might be redeemed for the same amount of money received. After that, Mary, Joseph, the maid, and two of the shepherds who were standing in front of the entrance celebrated the sabbath in the crib cave. A lamp with seven wicks was lighted, and upon a small table covered with white and red, lay the prayer rolls.

The numerous eatables presented by the shepherds were either given to the poor or handed around for the entertainment of others. The birds were hung on a spit before the fire, turned from time to time, and sprinkled with the flour of a reed-like plant which was very plentiful around the area of Bethlehem and Hebron. From its grain a shining, white jelly was prepared and cakes baked. I saw under the fireplace very hot and clean holes in which birds could be roasted.

After the sabbath, the Essene women got a meal ready under the arbors which Joseph, with the help of the shepherds, had put up at the entrance of the cave. Joseph went into the city to engage priests for the circumcision of the child. The cave was cleared and put in order. The partition that Joseph had put up in the passage was removed, and the ground spread with carpets, for in this passage near the crib cave, the place for the ceremony was prepared.

The Circumcision

JOSEPH returned from Bethlehem with five priests and a woman whose services were necessary on such occasions. They brought with them the circumcision stool and an octangular slab with all that was needed for the ceremony. All this was placed in order in the passage. The stool was hollow and formed a chest, which could be taken apart, thus affording a kind of low seat with a support on the side. It was covered with red. The circumcision stone was, perhaps, over two feet in diameter. In the center was a metal plate under which, in a hollow of the stone, were all kinds of little boxes containing fluids. These boxes were in separate compartments, and at one side lay the circumcision knife. The stone was laid upon the little stool which, covered with a cloth, always stood on the spot upon which Jesus was born, and the circumcision stool was placed next to it.

That evening a repast was spread under the arbor at the entrance to the cave. A crowd of poor people had followed the priests, as is usual on such occasions, and during the meal they were continually receiving something both from the priests and from Joseph. The priests went to Mary and the child, spoke with the mother, and took the child in their arms. They also spoke to Joseph about the name the child was to receive. They prayed and sang the greater part of the night, and circumcised the child at daybreak. Mary was very much troubled, very anxious about it. After the ceremony, the infant Jesus was swathed in red and white as far as under the little arms, which also were bound and the head wrapped in a cloth. The child was again laid on the octangular stone, and prayers recited over it. If I remember rightly, the angel had already told Joseph that the child should be called Jesus, and I have a faint recollection that one of the priests did not at first approve the name, consequently, they still continued in prayer.

Then I saw a radiant angel standing in front of the priest and holding before him a tablet like that above the cross, upon which was inscribed the name of Jesus. I saw the priest writing the name upon a scrap of parchment. I know not whether he or any of the others saw the angel, but deeply moved, he wrote the name under divine inspiration. After that, Joseph received the child back and handed it to the blessed Virgin who, with two other women, was standing back in the crib cave. Mary took the weeping child into her arms and quieted it. Some shepherds were standing at the entrance of the cave. Lamps were burning, and the dawn was breaking. There was some more praying and singing and, before the priests departed, they took a little breakfast. I saw that all present at the circumcision were good people. The priests were enlightened and later attained salvation. Alms were distributed the whole morning to many poor people who presented themselves. Afterward followed a crowd of beggars, filthy, black creatures, very repulsive to me. They carried bundles and, coming up from the valley of the shepherds, passed the crib as if going to Jerusalem for the celebration of a feast. They were very boisterous, cursing and scolding horribly, because they did not receive by way of alms as much as they wanted. I do not know exactly what was the matter with them. During the ceremony of circumcision, the ass was tied further back than usual; at other times, it stood in the crib cave.

The Circumcision

During the day, I saw the nurse again with Mary attending to the child. That night, the child was very restless from pain. It cried, and Mary and Joseph tried to soothe it by carrying it up and down the cave.

While reflecting upon the mystery of the circumcision, I had a vision. I saw two angels with little tablets in their hands, standing under a palm tree. Upon one tablet were pictured various instruments of martyrdom, of which I remember one, a pillar which stood in the middle. On it was a mortar, which had two rings. On the other tablet were letters denoting the seasons and years of the church. On the palm tree and as if growing out of it, was kneeling a virgin, her flowing mantle, or veil, for it was fastened over her head, floating around her. In her hands was a heart upon which I saw a tiny, shining child. I saw an apparition of God the Father draw near to the palm tree, break off a heavy branch that formed a cross, and lay it on the child. Then I saw the child raised, as it were, on the cross, and the virgin reaching the palm branch with the crucified child on it to God the Father, the heart alone remaining in her hand.

On the evening of the following day I saw Elizabeth on an ass and accompanied by an old servant, coming from Jutta to the cave. Joseph received her most cordially. The joy of Mary and Elizabeth was extremely great as they embraced each other. Elizabeth pressed the child to her heart. She slept in Mary's cave next to the place in which Jesus was born. Before the sacred spot stood a stool upon which they often laid the child.

Mary told Elizabeth all that had happened to her, and when Elizabeth heard of their difficulty in getting a lodging on their arrival in Bethlehem, she wept heartily. Mary gave her all the details of the infant Jesus's birth. I remember hearing her say that she had been in ecstasy ten minutes at the time of the Annunciation, that it appeared to her as if her heart had grown double its size and that she was filled with unspeakable happiness. But at the child's birth she had experienced an intense longing. She felt while kneeling that she was upheld by angels, and as if her heart was broken asunder and one-half taken from her. She had also been ten minutes in ecstasy at the time of the birth. She had been conscious of an emptiness within her, a longing after something outside of herself. Suddenly a light shone before her, and the figure of the child seemed to grow before her eyes. Then she saw it moving and heard it crying and, coming to herself, she raised it from the rug to her breast, for at first seeing it environed with glory, she had hesitated to take it up.

Elizabeth said: "Thou hast not given birth in the same way as other mothers. The birth of John was sweet also, but it was not like that of thy child."

Once I saw Elizabeth with Mary and the child concealing themselves toward evening in the side cave. They remained there the whole night, for visitors from Bethlehem were approaching by whom they did not want to be seen.

The Jewish women do not leave their children long without other nourishment than the breast; and so the infant Jesus was fed in those first days on pap made of the sweet, light, nutritious pith of a certain rush-like plant.

As in the temple at Jerusalem, the holy Feast of the Maccabees began at this time; it was also celebrated by Joseph in the crib cave. He fastened three lamps with seven little lights on the walls of the cave and, during a whole week, lighted them morning and evening. Once I saw in the cave one of the priests who had been present at the child's circumcision. He had a roll of writings from which he prayed with Joseph. It seemed to me that he wanted to find out whether Joseph kept that feast or not. I think, too, that he announced to him another, for a fast-day was near at hand. I saw the preparations for it in Jerusalem. Food was prepared the day before the feast, the fire was covered, servile work was put aside, the doors and windows were hung with tapestry.

Anne often sent servants with gifts of provisions and utensils, all of which Mary soon distributed to the poor. Once Anne sent a beautiful little basket of fruit with large, newly-blown roses stuck in among it. The pink roses were paler than ours, almost flesh-colored, and there were some yellow, and some white. Mary was very much pleased, and placed it beside her.

And now came Anne herself, accompanied by her second husband and a servant. The infant Jesus stretched out his little arms to her, and great was her joyful emotion. Mary gave her a full account of all as she had done to Elizabeth. They mingled their tears together, pausing at times to fondle the infant Jesus.

Anne had brought with her many things for Mary and the child, coverlets, swathing-bands, etc. Although Mary had already received so many things from her, yet the crib cave was still quite poor in appearance, since whatever was at all unnecessary was given away at once. Mary told Anne that the kings from the East were approaching with rich gifts, and that their coming would attract much attention. Anne, therefore, resolved to go and stay with her sister, who dwelt at some hours' distance, and to return after the departure of the royal visitors. Then I saw Joseph set to work to clear out the crib cave as well as those in its vicinity, in order to prepare for the arrival of the kings whom Mary in spirit had seen coming. He went also to Bethlehem to make the second payment of taxes and to look around for a dwelling, for he intended to settle in Bethlehem after Mary's Purification.

Journey of the Three Kings to Bethlehem

SOME days after their departure from home, I saw the caravan of Theokeno come up with those of Mensor and Sair at a ruined city. Rows of tall pillars were still standing here and in many places large beautiful statues. A band of wild robbers had taken up their quarters among the ruins. They were clothed in the skins of beasts and armed with spears; they were of a brownish color, short and stout, but very agile. The three caravans left this city together at daybreak and, after journeying half a day, rested in a very fertile district where there was a spring around which were many roomy sheds. This was an ordinary halting place for caravans. Each of the kings had in his train, as companions, four nobles of his own race; but he himself was like a patriarch over all. He took care of all, commanded all, dispensed to all. [A14] In each caravan were to be found people of different color. Mensor's race was of a pleasing brownish color; Sair's was brown; and Theokeno's of a bright yellow. I saw no shining black, saving the slaves, of whom each king possessed some.

The nobles, holding staves in their hands, sat upon their dromedaries high among the piled-up packages, which were covered with hangings. These were followed by other animals almost as large as horses, on which servants and slaves rode among the baggage. On their arrival, they unloaded the animals and watered them at the spring. This spring was surrounded by a little mound upon which was a wall with three open entrances. In this enclosed space was a cistern, somewhat lower than the surrounding surface. It had a pump with three pipes furnished with faucets. Over the cistern was a cover usually kept locked. But a man from the ruined city had accompanied the travelers, and he, on payment of a tax, unlocked the reservoir. The travelers had leathern vessels, which could be folded perfectly flat. They were divided into four compartments, which when filled afforded drink to four of the camels at once. These people were extremely careful of the water; not a drop was suffered to go to waste. Then the beasts were put up in an enclosed, but uncovered space close to the spring, the stall of each animal being separated from its neighbor's by a partition. There were some troughs before them, into which was poured the feed which had been brought with them. It consisted of corn, the grains of which were as large as acorns. Among the baggage were bird baskets, high and narrow, which hung on the sides of the animals among the broad packages. In the separate compartments of these baskets, either singly or in pairs, according to their different sizes, were birds like doves or hens. They served for food on the way. In leathern chests they had loaves, all of the same size, like single plates, closely packed together. Only as many as were needed were taken out at once. They had with them very costly vessels of yellow metal set with precious stones. They were almost exactly of the shape of our sacred vessels, some like chalices, some like little boats and dishes, out of which they drank and upon which they handed around the food. The rims of most of these vessels were set with precious stones.

The three races were somewhat different in costume. Theokeno and his followers, as well as Mensor, wore high caps embroidered in colors, and white bands wound thickly around their heads. Their short coats reached to the calf of the leg, and were very simple with only a few buttons and ornaments on the breast. They were enveloped in light, wide, and very long mantles which trailed behind. Sair and his followers wore caps with little white pads and round cowls embroidered in colors. They had shorter mantles, which were, however, longer behind than in front. Under their mantles were short tunics buttoning down to the knee and ornamented on the breast with laces, spangles, and innumerable glittering buttons, button on button. On one side of the breast was a little sparkling shield like a star. All had bare feet bound with laces to which soles were fastened. The nobles wore short swords or large knives in their girdles, and they had many bags and boxes hanging about them. Among the kings and their relatives were men about fifty, forty, thirty, and twenty years old. Some wore their beard long, others short. The servants and camel drivers were much more simply clothed; indeed, some had only a strip of stuff or an old garment around them.

When the beasts had been fed, watered, and stalled, and the attendants themselves had drunk, a fire was made in the middle of the enclosure in which they had encamped. The wood used for that purpose consisted of sticks about two and a half feet long which the poor people of the surrounding country had brought hither in well-arranged bundles, as if prepared expressly for travelers. The kings constructed a three-cornered log pile and laid the sticks around the top, leaving an opening on one side to admit air. The pile was very skillfully put together. But I cannot say for certain how they lit the fire. I saw one of them put one piece of wood into another, as if into a box, swing it round and round a little while, and then draw it forth burning. And so they kindled a fire, and then I saw them killing some birds and roasting them.

The three kings and the ancients acted, each one in his own family, like the father of the house, cutting up the food and helping it around. The carved birds and little loaves were laid on small dishes, or plates, which stood upon little feet, and passed around; and in the same way,

The Journey of the Three Kings

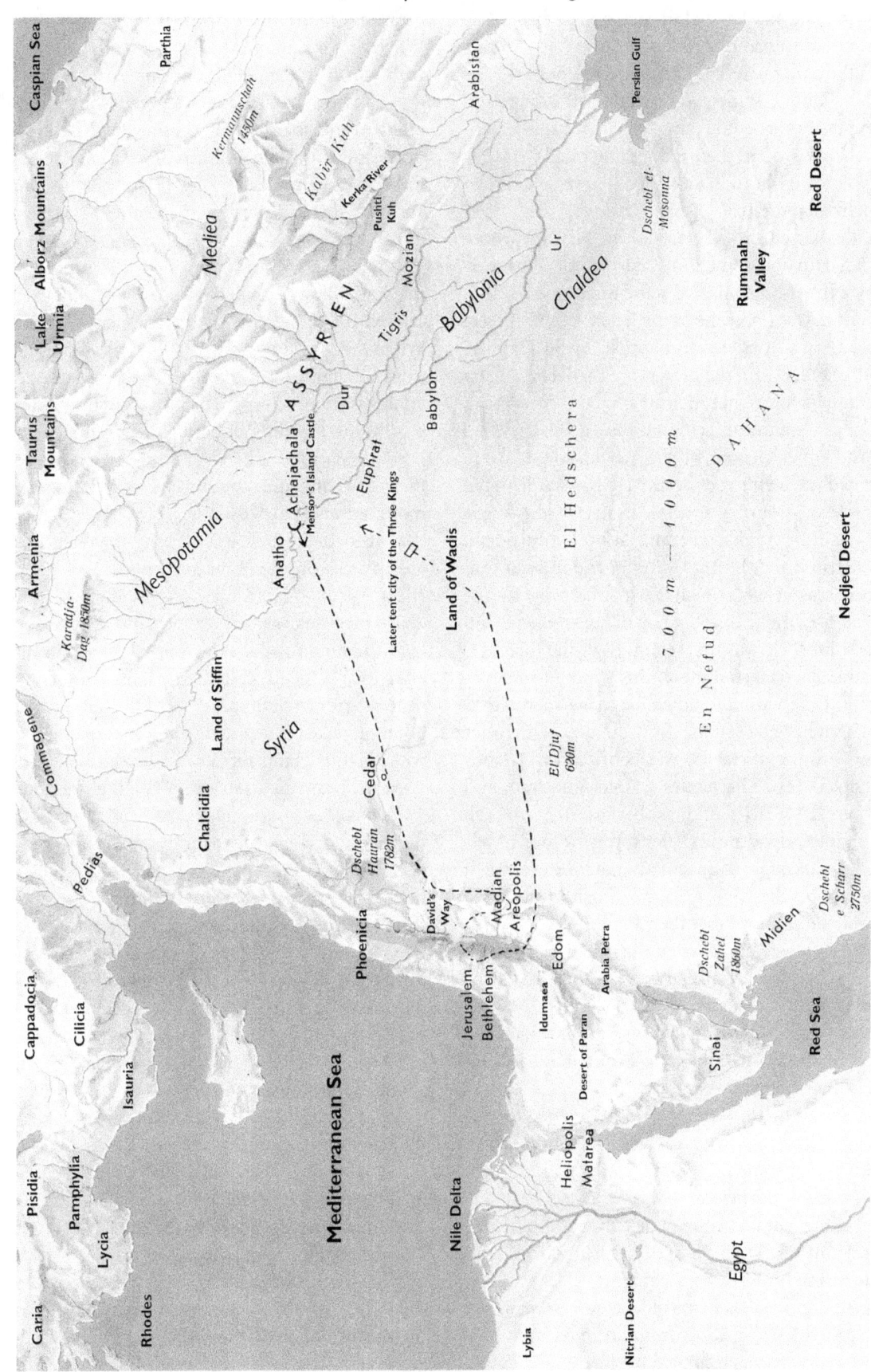

Achajachala (Acajaja)—Kedar—David's Way—Madian—Jerusalem
Bethlehem—Future Site of the Kings' Tent City

the cups were filled and handed to each one to drink. The lowest among the servants, of whom some were Moors, reclined on the bare earth. They appeared to be slaves. The simplicity, the kindness, the good nature of the kings and nobles, were unspeakably touching. They gave to the people who gathered around them something of all that they had; they even held out to them the golden vessels and let them drink like children.

Mensor, the brownish, was a Chaldean. His city, whose name sounded to me something like Acajaja, was surrounded by a river, and appeared to be built on an island. Mensor spent most of his time in the fields with his herds. After the death of Christ, he was baptized by St. Thomas, and named Leander. Sair, the brown, on that very Christmas night stood prepared at Mensor's for the expedition. He and his race were the only ones so brown, but they had red lips. The other people in the neighborhood were white. Sair had the baptism of desire. He was not living at the time of Jesus's journey to the country of the kings. Theokeno was from Media, a country more to the north. It lay like a strip of land further toward the interior and between two seas. Theokeno dwelt in his own city; its name I have forgotten. It consisted of tents erected on stone foundations. He was the wealthiest of the three. He might, I think, have taken a more direct route to Bethlehem, but in order to join the others he made a circuitous one. I think that he had even to pass near Babylon in order to come up with them. He also was baptized by St. Thomas and named Leo. The names Caspar, Melchior, and Balthasar were given to the kings, because they so well suited them, for Caspar means "He is won by love"; Melchior, "He is so coaxing, so insinuating, he uses so much address, he approaches one so gently"; Balthasar, "With his whole will, he accomplishes the will of God."

From Mensor's city, Sair dwelt at the distance of a three days' journey, each day counting twelve hours; and Theokeno further on, at a distance of five such days. Mensor and Sair were together when they saw in the stars the vision of the birth of Jesus, and both set out on the following day with their respective caravans. Theokeno, also, had the same vision in his own home, and he hurried to join the other two. Their journey to Bethlehem was about seven hundred and some odd hours. In the odd number, six occurs. It was a journey of about sixty days, each day twelve hours long; but they accomplished it in thirty-three days, on account of the great speed of their camels, and because they often traveled day and night.

The star that guided them was like a ball from whose lower surface light streamed as from an open mouth. It always appeared to me as if guided by an apparition that held it by a thread of light. By day I saw walking before the caravan a figure more brilliant than the light of the sun. When I reflect upon the length of the journey, the rapidity with which they made it appears to me astonishing. But those beasts have so light and even a step that their march looks to me as orderly and as swift, their movements as uniform, as the flight of birds of passage. The homes of the three kings formed a triangle with one another. Mensor and Sair dwelt nearest to each other; Theokeno was the most distant.

When the caravan had rested till evening, the people that had followed helped to load the beasts again, and then carried off home all that the travelers left behind them. When the caravan set out, the star was visible, shining with a reddish light, like the moon in windy weather. Its train of light was pale and long. The kings and their followers went part of the way on foot beside their animals, praying with heads uncovered. The road here was such as to prevent their traveling quickly; but when it became level, they mounted and pushed on at a swift rate. Sometimes they slackened their pace and all sang together, the sound of their voices on the night air producing a most touching effect. When I gazed upon them riding forward in such order, their hearts filled with joy and devotion, I could not help thinking: "Ah, if our processions could only pattern after this!" Once I saw them passing the night in a field near a spring. A man from one of the huts in the neighborhood unlocked it for them. They watered their beasts and, without unpacking, refreshed themselves by a short rest.

Again I saw the caravan upon a high plateau. On their right extended a mountain chain, and it seemed to me that they were drawing near to a point in the road where it again made a descent to a thickly settled district whose houses lay among trees and fountains. The inhabitants of this place wove covers out of threads stretched from tree to tree, and adored images of oxen. They bountifully supplied food to the crowd that followed the caravan, but the dishes out of which they ate were used no more. I was surprised at that.

The next day I saw the kings near a city whose name sounded like Causur, and which was built of tents on stone foundations. They stopped to rest with the king to whom the city belonged, and whose tent palace lay at a little distance. The three kings had since their meeting traveled fifty-three or sixty-three hours. They told the king of Causur all that they had seen in the stars. He was very greatly astonished. He looked through a tube at the star that was guiding them, and in it he saw a little child with a cross.

He begged them, in consequence, to inform him on their return of all that they discovered, that he might erect altars and offer sacrifice to the child. On the kings' departure from Causur, they were joined by a considerable train of nobles, who were going to travel the same way. Later they rested at a spring and made a fire, but they did not unload their camels. When again on their way, I heard them softly and sweetly singing together short verses, such as: "Over the mountains we shall go. And before the new king kneel!"

One of them began and the others took up and sang with him the verses, which they in turn composed and intoned. In the center of the star was plainly visible a little child with a cross.

Mary had a vision of the kings' approach when they were resting a day in Causur, and she told it to Joseph and Elizabeth.

At last I saw the kings arrive at the first Jewish city, a small, straggling place where many of the houses were surrounded by high hedges. They were here in a straight line from Bethlehem, notwithstanding which they proceeded along toward the right as the streets ran in that direction. As they entered this place, they sang more sweetly than ever and were full of joy, for the star was here shining upon them with unusual brilliancy, although the moonlight was so bright that one could see shadows distinctly. The inhabitants of the city, however, either did not see the star, or they took no special notice of it. They were exceedingly obliging. When some of the cavalcade dismounted, they assisted them greatly in watering their camels. It reminded me of Abraham's time, for then people were all so good and ready to assist one another. Many of them, bearing branches in their hands, led the caravan through the city and even went a part of the way with them. The star was not constantly shining before them; sometimes it was quite dull. It appeared to shine out more clearly wherever good people lived; and when the travelers beheld it more brilliant than usual, their hearts were filled with emotion thinking that there, perhaps, they would find the Messiah. The kings were not without apprehension lest their large caravan would create notice and comment.

The next day they went without halting around a dark, foggy city and, at a short distance from it, crossed a river which empties into the Dead Sea. That evening, I saw them enter a city whose name sounded like Manathea, or Madian. Their caravan was now perhaps two hundred strong, so great was the crowd their generosity drew after them. A street ran through this last place, the inhabitants of which consisted partly of Jews, partly of pagans. The caravan was led into the space between the city and its surrounding wall, and there the kings pitched their tents. I saw here, as in the former city, how anxious they became when they discovered that no one knew anything of the newborn king, and I heard them telling how long the star had been looked for among them.

Genealogy of the Kings

I HEARD that the three kings traced their genealogy back to Job, who had dwelt on the Caucasus and had jurisdiction over other districts far and wide. Long before Balaam, and before Abraham's sojourn in Egypt, they had the prophecy of the star and the hope of its fulfillment. The leaders of a race from the land of Job had upon an expedition to Egypt, in the region of Heliopolis, received from an angel the revelation that from a virgin the Savior would be born whom their descendants would honor. They were also instructed to go no farther, but to return to their homes and watch the stars. They celebrated festivals in memory of the event, erected altars and triumphal arches which they adorned with flowers, and then turned back home. There may, perhaps, have been three thousand of these people collected together at this time. They were dwellers in Media and star worshippers, of a beautiful, yellowish-brown color and of tall and noble stature. They roamed from place to place with their herds, ruling wherever they pleased by their irresistible power. They had, as the kings now related, been the first to announce the prophecy to their people, and the first to introduce among them the observation of the stars. When both the prophecy and the study had fallen into general oblivion, they were received first by one of Balaam's scholars, and long after him by three prophetesses, the daughters of the three kings' forefathers. And now at last, five hundred years since the time of those prophetesses, the star had appeared which they were to follow.

Those three prophetesses were contemporary. They were deeply versed in the stars; they had visions and the spirit of prophecy. They foresaw that a star would arise out of Jacob and that an inviolate virgin would bring forth the Savior. Clothed in long garments, they went about the country announcing this prophecy, exhorting to good, foretelling the future down to the most remote ages, and promising that messengers from the Savior would come to their people and lead them to the worship of the true God. The fathers of these virgins built a temple to the promised Mother of God on the spot where their lands joined, and in its vicinity a tower from which to observe the constellations and their various changes. From these three princes, about five hundred years after and through a lineal descent of fifteen generations, sprang the holy kings. It was by their intermingling with other races that they became so different in color. For a length of time, some of their ancestors were constantly on the tower observing the stars. What they saw was noted down and taught orally; and, in consequence of these observations, many changes gradually crept into their temple and worship.

All periods remarkable on account of their reference to the coming of the Messiah were pointed out to them by visions in the stars. During the last year since Mary's Conception, these visions were more and more significant, and the coming of salvation more explicitly shown. At the time of the blessed Virgin's Conception, they saw the virgin with the scepter and the scales in whose evenly balanced plates lay wheat and grapes. They saw, too, a prefiguration of the bitter Passion itself, for they beheld the newborn king involved in a war from which he came out victorious over all his enemies.

This observing of the stars was accompanied by religious ceremonies, fasting, prayer, purification, and self-denial. They watched not one star alone, but a whole constellation; by certain coincidences among the different stars as they gazed, were formed the visions and pictures that they saw. The wicked, engaging in this star worship, were affected by evil influences and thrown into convulsions by their demoniacal visions. It was by the agency of such people that the practice arose of sacrificing the aged and little children. But such cruelties gradually fell into disuse. The kings saw the visions clearly and from them tasted sweet, interior consolation, without feeling the effects of any malign influence. They became, on the contrary, better and more pious. With great simplicity and candor, they described what they saw to their inquisitive auditors; but when they perceived that what their forefathers had so patiently awaited for two thousand years was not received with implicit belief, they became sad. The star was hidden by a cloud; but when it again appeared, looking so large among the drifting clouds and so near to the earth, the kings arose from their couches, called the people of the city together, and pointed it out to them. The people gazed awestruck; some were deeply impressed, others were vexed at the kings for disturbing their rest, while the majority sought but to profit by the princely bounty.

I heard the royal travelers saying how far they had journeyed up to this time. They reckoned the day's journey on foot as one of twelve hours. Before reaching their place of meeting, one had made a journey of three such days, the other five of twelve hours. But on their beasts, which were dromedaries, subtracting the night and the hours of rest, they could treble that distance; therefore the three days' journey on foot up to the place of meeting were equivalent to only one, and the five days counted but for two. From that place to where they were at present they had made a fifty-six days' journey of twelve hours, or six hundred and seventy-two hours. They had, therefore, from Christ's birth up to the present, counting the days that passed until they met and those devoted to resting, consumed about twenty-five days. At this place also, they took a day to rest.

The people here were singularly importunate and shameless; they pressed around the kings like swarms of wasps. The royal travelers dealt out to them freely small triangular yellow pieces like tin and also darker grains. They must have possessed unnumbered treasures. When the caravan was departing, it wound around the city, in which I saw idols standing in the temple. On the opposite side they crossed a bridge and went through a little Jewish place that contained a synagogue. And now they were on a good road, hastening toward the Jordan. About one hundred persons had joined their caravan. They had still a journey of about twenty-four hours to Jerusalem. But I saw them passing through no more cities, and they were met but by few people, as it was the sabbath. The nearer they drew to Jerusalem, the more disheartened they became; for the star no longer shone with its usual brightness and, since their entrance into Judea, they saw it but seldom. They had hoped also to find the people on their route exulting with joy and celebrating with magnificence the birth of the newborn Savior, to honor whom they themselves had come so far. But beholding no sign of excitement, they grew anxious and perplexed, thinking that, perhaps, after all they had made a mistake.

It may have been midday when they crossed the Jordan. They paid the ferrymen, though only two of them lent a helping hand. They held back and let them attend to their transportation themselves. The Jordan was not broad at that time and it was full of sandbanks. Boards were laid over crossbeams, and the dromedaries stood upon them. The passage across the river was made expeditiously. The kings first appeared to be going toward Bethlehem, but soon they turned and went on to Jerusalem. I saw the city towering up high against the sky. The sabbath was over before the caravan arrived outside the city.

The Kings before Herod

THE CARAVAN OF the kings took about a quarter of an hour to pass any given point. When it halted before Jerusalem, the star had become invisible; consequently, the travelers were very much troubled. The kings rode upon dromedaries, and three other dromedaries were laden with the baggage. The rest of the cavalcade were mounted upon nimble animals of a yellowish color with small heads, I know not whether they were horses or asses, but they were very different in appearance from our horses. The animals upon which the nobles rode were very handsomely caparisoned and hung with golden stars and little chains. Some of the followers went to the gate of the city, and returned with officers and soldiers.

The arrival of the kings at that time when no feast was

being celebrated, when no special commercial interest seemed to bring them, and also by that particular road, was something remarkable. They explained to the officials why they had come, and spoke of the star and the child. But their hearers were ignorant on the subject, and so the kings began again to think that they had surely erred, since they could not find one person who looked as if he knew anything connected with the Redemption of the world. The people gazed at them in wonder, unable to conceive what they wanted. The kings explained that they were ready to pay for whatever they got from them, and that they wished to confer with their king.

And now arose great hurrying to and fro, the travelers meantime interchanging questions and answers with the crowd gathered around them. Some had indeed heard of a child that was to be born at Bethlehem; but they were poor, ignorant people, and their words had no weight. Others laughed derisively and the kings grew troubled and disheartened; and then they perceived by the expressions of the people that Herod knew nothing of what they sought and that he was by no means beloved by his subjects. They became anxious as to how they should address him. They had recourse to prayer, their courage revived, and they said to one another: "He who has brought us so quickly here by means of the star will also lead us home in safety."

They now led the caravan around the city and brought it in at the side nearer Mount Calvary. Not far from the fish market, they and their animals were conducted into a circular court, which was surrounded by halls and dwellings, and before whose gates guards were standing. In the middle of the court was a well, at which they watered the beasts, and all found quarters in the stalls and places under the arches. On one side of the court arose the mountain on which it lay; on the other, it was free and shaded by trees. I saw people coming with torches and examining the baggage.

Herod's palace stood higher up the mountain not far from this court. I saw the road leading to it lighted up by torches and lanterns hung on poles. I saw officials going down from the palace and conducting thither Theokeno, the eldest of the kings. He was received under an archway and ushered into a hall. There he made known his errand to a courtier, who reported it to Herod. Herod became almost insane at the news, and gave orders for the kings to present themselves before him on the following morning. He also sent word to them to rest while he made inquiries, and he would inform them of the result.

When Theokeno returned, he and his two royal companions became still more uneasy, and ordered the baggage that had been unpacked to be packed again. They slept none that night. I saw some of them going around the city with guides. It seemed to me that they suspected Herod of knowing all, but of being unwilling to disclose the truth to them. They still sought the star. In Jerusalem itself all was quiet, but there was much running to and fro and questioning among the sentinels at the court.

It may have been about eleven o'clock at night when Theokeno was sent for by Herod. There appeared to be some kind of festivity going on, for the palace was ablaze with lights, and I saw females in it. The news brought by Theokeno threw Herod into the greatest terror. He dispatched servants to the temple and also into the city, and I saw priests and scribes and aged Jews going to him with rolls of writings under their arms. They wore their priestly garments, also their breastplates, and their girdles on which letters were inscribed. There were about twenty around him, expounding the writings. I saw them also mounting with him to the roof of the palace and gazing at the stars. Herod was very uneasy and perplexed. But the scribes tried to divert him, by endeavoring to prove that there was nothing in the talk of the kings; that those Eastern people were always superstitiously raving about the stars; and that, if there was any truth in what they said, surely the priests of the temple and the dwellers in the Holy City would have known it long ago.

Next morning at daybreak, I saw one of the courtiers going down to the caravan and bringing up all three of the kings to Herod's palace. They were ushered into an apartment around which were pots of foliage and bushes. Refreshments were spread at the entrance. But the kings declined the proffered food, and remained standing until Herod entered. They approached him with an obeisance, and without preamble put to him the question as to where they should find the newborn king of the Jews, for they had seen his star and they were come to do him homage. Herod was very much troubled, but he concealed his fears.[A15] Some of the scribes were still with him. He questioned the kings closely concerning the star, and told them that of Bethlehem Ephrata ran the Promise. But Mensor related to him the last vision they had seen in the star, whereupon Herod's anxiety became almost too great for concealment. Mensor said that they had seen a virgin with a child lying before her. From the right side of the child issued a branch formed of light, upon which stood a tower with many gates, which tower increased in size until it became a city. The child appeared standing above it with sword and scepter; and they had seen not only themselves, but all the kings of the earth, coming to bow down before and adore that child, for its kingdom was to vanquish all other kingdoms. Herod advised them to go quietly and without delay to Bethlehem, and when they had found the child to return and inform him that he too might go and adore him. I saw the kings going down from the palace, and leaving Jerusalem at once. The day was dawning, and the lights on the way leading up to the palace were still burning. The crowd that had followed the royal caravan had passed the night in the city.

Herod who, about the time of Christ's birth, had gone to his palace at Jericho, had been even before the coming of the kings very restless and uneasy. Two of his illegitimate sons had been raised by him to high positions in the temple. They were Sadducees, and by them he was kept informed of all that transpired, as well as of all who were opposed to his designs. Among these he was told of one, a man good and upright, a distinguished functionary of the temple. Herod sent him a courteous and friendly invitation to come to him in Jericho. When the good man was on his way to comply with the invitation, Herod's creatures fell upon him and murdered him in the desert, making it appear as if robbers had perpetrated the awful deed. Some days later, Herod returned to Jerusalem, in order to take part in the Feast of the Consecration of the temple. Then he thought he would, in his own way, give pleasure to the Jews and show them honor. He caused to be made a golden figure something like a lamb, though still more like a goat, for it had horns. This figure was to be erected above the gate leading from the outer court of the women into the court of sacrifice. Herod insisted upon this and, moreover, expected to be thanked for what he had done. But the priests resisted. Herod threatened them with a fine. They replied that the fine indeed they would pay; but that the figure, according to their Law, they could never accept. Herod fell into a rage, and ordered it to be set up secretly. Thereupon, one of the officers of the temple, fired with zeal, seized it as it was being brought in, cleft it in twain, and hurled it to the ground. This gave rise to a tumult, and Herod ordered the offender to be imprisoned. Herod was, on account of this affair, extremely displeased, and regretted having come to the feast; but his courtiers sought by all kinds of diversions to remove the impression from his mind.

There was among some pious people in Judea the expectation of the near advent of the Messiah, and the circumstances attendant on the birth of Jesus had been noised abroad by the shepherds. Herod had heard all and had at Bethlehem made secret inquiries into it. His spies, however, having found only poor Joseph, and having besides orders not to attract attention, reported that it was nothing, that they had found only a poor family buried in a cave, and the whole affair not worth talking about. But now, all of a sudden, appeared the great caravan of the kings. Their questioning after the king of Judah was marked by such confidence and precision, they spoke with such certainty of the star, that Herod could scarcely hide his anxious perplexity. He hoped to learn the particulars of the affair from the kings themselves, and then take measures accordingly. But when the kings, warned by God, did not return, he explained their flight as a consequence of their falsehood and disappointment; they were, he thought, ashamed to come back and be looked upon as fools. He therefore caused to be proclaimed in Bethlehem and in a general way, that the people should have nothing to do with the strangers. When he thought to make away with Jesus, he found that he was no longer in Nazareth. He caused search to be made after him for a long time. When he had to give up all hope of finding him and his anxiety was, in consequence, so much the more increased, he took the desperate resolution to murder all the children. He was so cautious in executing his measures that he transported his troops beforehand, in order to avoid any insurrection.

The Kings Arrive at Bethlehem

I SAW the kings leaving Jerusalem in the same order in which they had come. They left by a gate to the south: first, Mensor, the youngest; then Sair, and lastly, Theokeno. They were followed by a crowd as far as a brook outside the city, and here the rabble left them and turned back home. On the opposite side of the brook, the kings halted and looked for their star. To their great joy, they saw it, and on again they went, singing sweetly. But what I wondered at was, that the star did not guide them by a direct route from Jerusalem to Bethlehem; they went more to the west and passed a little city that is well known to me. Beyond the same, I saw them halting at a beautiful place to pray. A well sprang up before them; they dismounted and dug a basin for the water, surrounding it with sand and sods. They remained here several hours and watered their beasts; for in Jerusalem, on account of their anxiety and trouble, they had had no rest.

The star, which by night looked like a globe of light, now had the appearance of the moon when seen by day; but still it did not appear exactly round, but somewhat pointed. I saw that it was often hidden behind the clouds.

The highroad that lay between Bethlehem and Jerusalem swarmed with people, travelers with their baggage on asses. They were, perhaps, on account of the census, returning from Bethlehem to distant homes, or going up to Jerusalem to the temple or the markets. But on the route taken by the kings, it was very quiet. Perhaps the star guided them that way, that they might escape notice, and arrive in Bethlehem in the evening.

It was twilight when the caravan drew up before Bethle-

The Kings Arrive at Bethlehem

hem at the same gate at which Mary and Joseph had stopped. When the star had disappeared, the kings went to the house, the former abode of Joseph's parents, and in which Joseph and Mary had recently been inscribed. Here they thought they were to find the newborn king. It was a spacious mansion with numerous small buildings around it, an enclosed courtyard in front, and stretching beyond that a lawn with trees and a fountain. I saw on the lawn Roman soldiers, because of the tax offices in the house. Crowds of people thronged around the newcomers whose beasts were being watered under the trees near the fountain. The kings and their followers dismounted. The people showed them every mark of respect; they were not rude to them as they had been to Joseph. They presented green branches, and supplied them with food and drink; but I could see that that was principally in consideration of the gold pieces which the kings were freely disbursing.

I saw the travelers tarrying long in doubt and anxiety. At last, I saw a light rising in the heavens on the opposite side of Bethlehem over the region of the crib. The light was like that of the rising moon. I saw the caravan again set out and wind around the south side of Bethlehem toward the east, thus bringing on one hand the field in which Christ's birth had been announced to the shepherds. They had to go around a ditch and some ruined walls. They had made choice of this route, because they had while in Bethlehem been directed to the valley of the shepherds as a good place for encamping. Some of the Bethlehemites followed the cavalcade, but the kings said nothing to them of the object of their search.

Joseph appeared to know of their arrival. Whether he had learned it through someone from Jerusalem, or in vision, I know not; but I saw him during the day bringing all kinds of things from Bethlehem, fruit, honey, and vegetables. I saw him also clearing out the cave, making more room, taking away the partitions that cut off his own little sleeping place from the passage, and stowing away the wood and the cooking utensils under the shed before the door.

When the caravan had filed down into the valley of the crib cave, all dismounted and began to set up their tents while the people that had crowded after them from Bethlehem returned to the city. The encampment was partly pitched when over the cave shone out the star and in it a child plainly visible. It stood directly above the crib, its stream of light falling straight down upon it. The kings and their followers uncovered their heads and watched it sinking lower and lower, increasing in size as it approached the earth. It looked to me as large as a sheet, I think. All were at first amazed. It was already dark; no dwelling was to be seen around, only the hill of the crib cave, looking like a rampart on the plain. But soon their amazement turned to joy, and they sought the entrance of the cave. Mensor pushed back the door and there, in the upper end of the cave, which was resplendent with light, he beheld Mary sitting with the child, and looking just like the virgin they had so often seen in the star pictures. Mensor stepped back and told his companions what he had seen, then all three entered the passage. I saw Joseph coming out to them with an old shepherd, and speaking to them in quite a friendly way. The kings told him in a few words that they had come to adore the newborn king of the Jews whose star they had seen, and bring him gifts. Joseph humbly bade them welcome, and they went back to their tents, in order to prepare themselves for the ceremony of their presentation. The old shepherd accompanied the kings' servants to the little valley behind the hill, where there were sheds and shepherd stalls, in order to care for the beasts. The caravan filled the whole of the little valley.

And now I saw the kings taking down from the camels and putting on their wide, flowing mantles of yellow silk. They fastened around their girdles with little chains, bags, and golden boxes with knobs, that looked to me like sugar bowls. They, along with the flowing mantles, made them look quite broad. They took also a little table with low feet that could be opened and folded at pleasure. It served as a salver. A cloth with tasselled fringe was thrown over it, and on it placed the boxes and dishes containing the gifts.

Each king was accompanied by his four relatives. All followed Joseph with some of their servants to the shed before the entrance to the cave. Here they spread the cloth over the table and stood on it several of the boxes they had hanging at their girdles, to be presented as their gifts in common. Then two youths of Mensor's train went in at the door, laid down strips of carpet all the way up to the crib, and withdrew to a distance. And now Mensor and his four companions entered, having previously laid aside their sandals. Two servants bore the table with the gifts through the passage up to the crib cave; but at the entrance, Mensor took it from them, carried it in himself, and on bended knee placed it at Mary's feet. The other kings and their companions remained standing at the entrance.

I saw the cave filled with supernatural light. Opposite the entrance and on the spot where Jesus was born, was Mary leaning on one arm in a posture more reclining than sitting; by her side was Joseph, and on her right, in a raised trough with a cover thrown over it, lay the infant Jesus. At Mensor's entrance, Mary rose to a sitting posture, drew her veil around her, and took the child, which she enveloped in its folds, upon her lap. But she drew the veil aside sufficiently to allow the child to be seen as far as below the little arms. She held it upright leaning against her breast, its little head supported by her hand. The infant folded its little hands upon its breast as if in prayer. It was shining with light, was very gracious, and at times extended its little hands, as if grasping something. Mensor fell on his knees before Mary, bowed his head, crossed his hands on his breast, and offered the gifts with some reverent words. [A16] Then he took from the bag at his girdle a handful of little metal bars, about a finger in length, thick and heavy. They were pointed at the upper end, granular in the middle, and shone like gold. He laid them humbly on Mary's lap by the child, as his gift to her. Mary accepted them graciously and humbly, and covered them with the end of her mantle. Mensor's companions stood behind him with heads lowly bowed. Mensor gave gold, because he was full of love and confidence, and had always with unshaken devotion and untiring efforts, sought after salvation.

When Mensor and his companions withdrew, Sair with his four relatives entered and knelt. He carried in his hand a golden censer, in shape like a boat, filled with small, greenish grains like resin. He gave incense, for he was the one that clung to God, voluntarily, reverently, and lovingly following his will. He placed his gift upon the little table, and knelt long in adoration.

After Sair came Theokeno, the eldest of the kings. He could not kneel, because he was too old and stout. He stood bowing low, and laid upon the table a little golden ship in which was a fine, green herb. It was fresh and living, stood erect like a delicate green bush, and had small white flowers. Theokeno offered myrrh, for myrrh is typical of mortification and vanquished passions. This good man had had to struggle against severe temptations to idolatry and polygamy. He remained very long before the infant Jesus, so long that I felt anxious for the good people, the kings' followers, who at the entrance were so patiently awaiting their turn to see the child.

The words of the kings and their followers were extraordinarily simple and childlike; they were as if inebriated with love. They always began: "We have seen his star and that he is king over all kings. We have come to adore him and to bring him gifts." With the tenderest tears and most fervent prayers, they commended to the child Jesus themselves, their goods, and property, all that they valued on earth. They begged him to take their hearts, their souls, their actions, their thoughts; they entreated him to enlighten them, to bestow upon them all the virtues, and to the whole earth to grant peace, happiness, and love. They were glowing with love. No words could depict their ardor and humility, nor the tears of joy that bathed their cheeks and flowed down the beard of the eldest. They were perfectly happy; they believed that, at last, they had entered into the star after which their forefathers had so long legitimately sighed, and at which they themselves had so longingly gazed. All the joy of the promise of many hundreds of years now fulfilled, welled up in their hearts.

Joseph and Mary also wept. I never before had seen them so full of joy. The honor paid their child and Savior and the recognition of him by the kings, of that child for whom their poverty could afford so poor a couch, of that child the knowledge of whose high dignity lay hidden in the silent humility of their own hearts—all that comforted them immeasurably. They saw brought to him from so great a distance by God's almighty power, and in spite of the machinations of man, what they themselves could not procure for him, viz., the adoration of the great, and magnificent gifts offered with holy profusion. Ah! They adored with those great ones, and the honor their child received inundated their heart with exceedingly great joy.

The Mother of God accepted everything most humbly and thankfully. She spoke not, but the movement of her veiled head told all. The infant Jesus lay on her mantle and covered by her veil, through which his little form shone brightly. It was only at the close of their visit that the blessed Virgin addressed some kind words to each, throwing her veil back a little as she spoke.

The kings now returned to their tents, which were lighted up and looked very beautiful.

At last, the good servants arrived at the crib. During the adoration of the kings, they had with Joseph's help erected a white tent on the hill toward the shepherd field to the left of the crib cave. They had brought with them on their beasts of burden the tent with all its covers and poles, the latter of which fitted into one another. At first I thought that Joseph had put it up, and I began to wonder where he had got it so quickly and opportunely; but when the caravan was about to leave, I saw that tent taken down and packed up with the rest. There was a kind of shed of straw matting put up in it, under which the chests were placed. After the servants had pitched the tent and arranged all things in it, they took their stand at the door of the crib cave, humbly awaiting admittance.

And now they began to enter, five at a time, accompanied by one of the nobles to whom they belonged. They knelt before Mary, and silently adored the child. Lastly, came the boys in their little mantles, and then there may have been in all about thirty persons present.

When all had withdrawn, the kings again came in together. They had changed their mantles for others of raw silk, white and flowing, and they carried censers and incense. Two servants had previously laid down over the floor of the cave a carpet of a deep red color, on which Mary sat with the child while the kings offered incense.

This carpet Mary kept ever afterward. She walked on it, and took it with her on the ass to Jerusalem when she went there for her Purification. The kings incensed the child, Mary, Joseph, and the whole cave. This was with them a ceremony expressive of veneration.

I saw the kings afterward in the tent reclining on a carpet around a little low table. Joseph brought in little plates of fruit, rolls, honeycomb, and small dishes of vegetables. Then he sat down and ate with them. He was so delighted, and not at all shamefaced; he wept for joy almost the whole time. When I saw that, I thought of my own father, and how, at my profession in the convent, he had to sit among so many fine people. In his humility and simplicity, he had indeed felt intimidated, but it did not prevent his giving vent to his feelings in tears of joy.

When Joseph returned to the crib cave, he removed all the rich gifts to a recess at the right of the crib, where he had screened a little corner from sight. Anne's maid, who had remained to wait upon Mary, retired to the little cellar-like cave on the left of the crib cave, and did not come forth until all the visitors had departed. She was a quiet, modest person. I saw neither Mary nor Joseph nor the maid examining the gifts or showing any worldly pleasure on their account. They were accepted with thanks, and with liberality were again distributed to the needy. That maid was a relative of Anne, and a robust and very serious person.

On this evening and during the night, I saw in Bethlehem only at Joseph's paternal house a noisy bustling to and fro and, when the kings entered the city, there was some little excitement; around the crib cave all was, at first, very quiet. After awhile, I saw here and there in the distance Jews lurking and whispering together, and giving notice in the city of what they saw. I saw also in Jerusalem on this day many old Jews and priests hurrying to and fro with writings to Herod, and then all became quiet as if they wished the subject dropped.

At last, the kings with their people held, under the cedar over the Suckling Cave, a religious service. The singing was most touching, the boys' sweet voices mingling with those of the elders. After the service, the kings went with a part of their followers to a large inn at Bethlehem. The others slept in the tents between the crib and the Suckling Cave, which latter they had also taken possession of for the storing of part of their treasures. The white tent before the crib was occupied by some of the most distinguished of the nobles.

The Second Day of the Kings at the Crib • Their Departure

ON the next day, the kings again visited the crib cave separately. During the whole day, I saw much given away by them, especially to the shepherds out in the field where the beasts had been sheltered. I saw poor old women bent with age going around with mantles over their shoulders given them by the kings' generosity. I saw crowds of Jews from Bethlehem thronging around the good people, trying by every means in their power to extort presents from them, and looking through all that they had with a design to cheat. I saw the kings freeing several of their people who wanted to remain among the shepherds. They gave them some of the beasts of burden with all kinds of covers and vessels packed on them, also golden grains, or gold dust, and they parted from them most cordially. I know not why their number was so diminished; perhaps many went away, or were sent home the preceding night.

There was also a quantity of bread given away. I do not know where they got so much, but true it is that they had it. They were accustomed to bake wherever they encamped. I think they must already have received a warning to diminish their luggage as much as possible on their return journey.

That evening I saw the kings in the crib cave, taking leave. Mensor entered first alone, and the blessed Virgin gave him the child in his arms. He shed abundant tears, and his face was beaming with joy. Then followed the others and took leave with many tears. They again offered numerous gifts: a great roll of precious stuff; pieces of silk, some whitish, others red; also flowered stuffs, and many very fine covers. They left their large mantles also with the holy family. They were fine wool of a pale delicate color, and so light that they floated on the breeze. They brought also numerous dishes piled one above the other, boxes of grain, and a basket full of pots containing delicate green plants bearing tiny leaves and white blossoms. About three of these small pots stood in the middle of a larger one; still another could have found room between them and the rim of the large pot. They were arranged in the basket, one above the other. There were also long, narrow baskets containing birds, such as I had seen hanging on the dromedaries, and which they used for food. They all wept much when parting from the child and Mary. I saw the blessed Virgin standing by them when they took their leave. The kings' gifts were received by Mary and Joseph with touching humility and sincere thanks to the donors, but without any manifestations of pleasure. During the whole of this wonderful visit, I never saw in Mary the least shadow of self-interest. In her love for the child Jesus and compassion for Joseph, she thought that the possession of these treasures would, perhaps, prevent their being treated in Bethlehem with such contempt as had been shown them upon their arrival, for Joseph's trouble and mortification on that account had been to her a source of suffering.

The Second Day of the Kings at the Crib • Their Departure

Lamps were already lighted in the crib cave when the kings took leave. They went out behind the hill toward the east, to the field in which were their people and beasts. In it stood a high tree whose spreading boughs shaded a wide circumference. The tree was very old and had a legend of its own, for Abraham and Melchizedek had met under its branches. The shepherds and the people around regarded it as sacred. A spring gushed up before it, the waters of which the shepherds used at certain seasons on account of their healing qualities. There was near the tree a furnace which could be covered, and at both sides huts affording shelter at night. A hedge surrounded the whole tract. Thither went the kings, and found all the followers still remaining to them gathered together. A light was suspended from the tree, and under it they prayed, and sang with indescribable sweetness.

Joseph entertained the kings again in the tent by the crib, and then they and their nobles returned to their inn at Bethlehem. Meanwhile, the governor of the city (acting on a secret order from Herod or moved by a spirit of officiousness, I know not), had resolved to arrest the kings then in Bethlehem, and accuse them to Herod as disturbers of the peace. I know not when he was going to execute his resolve, but to the kings that night in Bethlehem and to their followers in their tents near the crib, an angel appeared in sleep, warning them to depart forthwith and to hasten home by another way. Those in the tents immediately awakened Joseph, and told him the order just received. While they proceeded to arouse the whole encampment and order the tents to be taken down, which was done with incredible speed, Joseph hurried off to Bethlehem to announce it to the kings. But they, leaving most of their baggage behind them, had already started from the city. Joseph met them on the way and told them his errand. They informed him that they, too, had received similar instructions from an angel. Their hurried departure was unnoticed in Bethlehem. Issuing forth quietly and without their baggage, an observer might have concluded that they were going to their people, perhaps for prayer. While they were still in the cave, weeping and taking leave, their followers were already starting in separate bands in order to be able to travel more quickly, and were hurrying to the south, by a route different from that by which they had come, through the desert of Engaddi along the Dead Sea.

The kings implored the holy family to flee with them. On their refusal, they begged Mary at least to conceal herself with Jesus in the Suckling Cave, that she might not on their account be molested.

They left many things to Joseph to give away. The blessed Virgin, taking the veil from her head, bestowed it upon them. She had been accustomed to envelope the infant Jesus in its folds when holding him in her arms. The kings still held the child in their arms. They were shedding tears and uttering most touching words. At last they gave their light silk mantles to Mary, mounted their dromedaries, and hurried away. I saw the angel by them in the field, pointing out the way they should take. The caravan was now much smaller, and the beasts but lightly burdened. Each king rode at about a quarter of an hour's distance from the others. They seemed to have vanished all of a sudden. They met again in a little city, and then rode forward less rapidly than they had done on leaving Bethlehem. I always saw the angel going on before them, and sometimes speaking with them.

Mary, wrapping the child Jesus in her mantle, at once withdrew to the Suckling Cave. The gifts of the kings and all that they had left were also taken thither by the shepherds who had tarried around the encampment in the valley. The kings' people who had preferred to remain behind their masters lent a helping hand.

The three oldest of the shepherds, who had been the first to do homage to Jesus, received very rich presents from the kings. When it was discovered in Bethlehem that the caravan had departed, the travelers were already near Engaddi, and the valley in which they had encamped was, with the exception of some tentpoles left standing and the footprints in the grass, lonely and still as before.

The appearance of the royal caravan had caused great excitement in Bethlehem. Many now regretted that they had refused lodgings to Joseph; some spoke of the kings and their followers as of a swarm of adventurers, while others connected their advent with the accounts they had heard of the wonderful apparitions to the shepherds. I saw from the city hall a proclamation made to the assembled citizens; viz., that they should beware of all preposterous opinions and superstitious reports, and go no more to the abode of those people outside the city.

When the crowd had dispersed, I saw Joseph at two different times conducted to the city hall. The second time, he took with him some of the gifts of the kings, which he presented to the old Jews who had taken him to task, and he was set at liberty. There was another way leading from the city to the neighborhood of the crib cave, not by the city gate, but from that place where Mary, on the evening of her arrival with Joseph in Bethlehem, had rested under the tree while waiting for Joseph to find a lodging. This point of egress I saw the Jews blocking up with a fallen tree. They also erected a watchhouse with a bell from which was a rope stretched across the road. Thus anyone trying to go that way would soon be discovered.

I saw also about sixteen soldiers with Joseph at the crib

cave. But when they found besides himself only Mary and the child, they returned to the city to report.

Joseph had carefully concealed the royal gifts. There were other caves in the hill under that of the crib. No one knew of them but Joseph, who had discovered them long

Fodder was scattered under the trees, and from their branches hung little boxes. Out of these boxes the weavers took chrysalides, about a finger in length, from which they wound off a web like that of a spider. They fastened a number of these chrysalides before the breast, and spun

Hebron at Sunrise

ago in his boyhood. They had existed from the time of Jacob who, when Bethlehem counted only a couple of huts, had there a tent with his followers.

The gifts of the kings, the woven stuffs, the mantles, the golden vessels—all after the resurrection were consecrated to religious uses. Each king had three light mantles and one, thick and heavy, for bad weather. The thin ones were of very fine wool, yellow and red mixed, and so light that they floated on the breeze as the wearers moved along. On festive occasions, they were exchanged for mantles of silk; they were not dyed, but of the original, lustrous shade. The train was embroidered around the edge with gold, and it was so long that it had to be carried. I had also a vision of the raising of silkworms. In a region between the country of Sair and Theokeno I saw trees full of silkworms. Every tree was surrounded by a little ditch of water, in order to prevent the worms from crawling away.

from them a fine thread which they rolled on a piece of wood provided with a hook. I saw the silk weavers among the trees at their looms, which were very simple. The strips of stuff woven were as wide, perhaps, as my bed.

The Return of Anne

AFTER the departure of the kings, the holy family went over into the other cave, and I saw the crib cave quite empty, the ass alone still standing there. Everything, even the hearth, had been cleared away. I saw Mary peaceful and happy in her new abode, which had been arranged somewhat comfortably. Her couch was near the wall and by her rested the child Jesus in an oval basket made of broad strips of bark. The upper end of the basket, where the head of the infant Jesus lay, was arched over with a cover. The basket itself stood on a woven partition, before which Mary sometimes sat with the child beside her. Joseph had a separate space at a little distance. Above the movable partition there projected from the wall a pole to which a lamp was suspended. I saw Joseph bringing in a pitcher of water and something in a dish. But he did not go any more to Bethlehem for necessaries; the shepherds brought him all that he needed.

And now I saw Zechariah coming for the first time from Hebron to visit the holy family. He wept for joy as he held the child in his arms, and recited, with some little changes, the canticle of thanksgiving that he had uttered at John's circumcision. He spent the following day with Joseph, and then took his departure.

Many persons going up to Bethlehem for the sabbath called also at the crib cave; but when they no longer found Mary there, they went on to the city.

Anne now came back to the Mother of God. She had been eight days with her youngest sister, who had married into the tribe of Benjamin. She lived about three hour's distance from Bethlehem, and had several sons who later became disciples of Jesus; among them was the bridegroom of Cana. Anne's eldest daughter was with her. She was taller than Anne and looked almost as old. Anne's second husband also was with her. He was older and taller than Joachim, was named Eliud, and was engaged at the temple, where he had something to do with the cattle intended for sacrifice. Anne had a daughter by this marriage, and she, too, was called Mary. At the time of Christ's birth, the child may have been from six to eight years old. By her third husband, Anne had a son, who was known as the brother of Christ. There is a mystery connected with Anne's repeated marriages. She entered into them in obedience to the divine command. The grace by which she had become fruitful with Mary had not yet been exhausted. It was as if a blessing had to be consumed.

Mary told Anne all about the kings, and she was very much touched at God's bringing those men so far to adore the child. She was filled with emotion on seeing their gifts, upon which she looked as expressions of their adoration. She helped to arrange and pack them, and she also gave many of them away. Anne's maid was still with Mary. When in the crib cave, she stayed in the little cellar-like cave to the left, and now she slept under a shed that Joseph had put up for her just in front of their present abode. Anne and her daughters slept in the crib cave. I saw that Mary let Anne take care of the child Jesus, a favor she had not granted to anyone else. I saw something that very much affected me. The hair of the infant Jesus, which was yellow and crisp, ended in very fine rays of light which glistened and sparkled through one another. I think they curled the child's hair, for they twisted it over the little head when they washed it. Then they put a little cloak around him. I always saw Mary, Joseph, and Anne full of devout emotion for the child Jesus; but their expression of it was quite unaffected and simple, as is always the case among holy, chosen souls. The child displayed a love in turning toward its mother such as is by no means usual in young children. Anne was so happy when she was nursing the child. Mary always laid it in her arms.

The kings' gifts were now hidden in the cave in which Mary had taken up her abode. They were in a wicker chest placed in a recess of the wall and perfectly concealed from sight.

Anne's husband with her daughters and maid soon returned home, taking with them many of the royal gifts. Anne was now all alone with Mary and Joseph, and she remained until Eliud and the maid came back. I saw her and Mary weaving or embroidering covers. She slept in the cave with Mary, but separate.

There were again in Bethlehem soldiers seeking in many houses after the king's son newly-born. They especially importuned with their questions a noble Jewish lady who was in childbed, but they went no more to the crib cave. It was now reported that only a poor, Jewish family had been there, but of them nothing more could be learned. Two of the old shepherds went to Joseph (two of those that had first gone to the crib) and warned him of what was going on in Bethlehem. Then I saw Joseph, Mary, and Anne with the child Jesus making their way from the cave to the tomb under that large cedar tree beneath which I had heard the kings singing one evening. It was distant from the cave about seven and a half minutes. The tree stood upon a hill at the foot of which was an obliquely lying door opening into a passage that led to a perpendicular door which closed the entrance to the tomb. The shepherds often stayed in the forepart of it. In front of the tomb was a spring. The tomb cave itself was not square, but rather rounded in form. At the upper end, which was somewhat broader, something like a scalloped stone coffin stood on heavy supports upon a foundation of stone; one could see between it and the coffin. The interior of the cave was of soft, white stone. I saw the holy family entering it by night with a covered light. In the cave that they had vacated nothing now was to be seen which could attract notice. The beds had been rolled up and taken away, as well as all their household effects. It looked like an abandoned dwelling place. Anne carried the child in her arms, Joseph and Mary at her side, while the shepherds led the way as guides. And now I had a vision, but I do not know whether it was seen by the holy family or not. I saw around the child Jesus in the arms of Anne a glory made up of seven angelic figures entwined together and leaning one upon the other. There were, besides, many other figures in this aureola, and on either side of Anne, of Joseph, and of Mary, I saw figures of light supported by them, held up, as it were, under the arms. Passing through the first entrance, they shut it and went on into the interior of the tomb cave.

A couple of days before Anne's return home, I saw some shepherds entering the tomb cave and speaking to Mary; they told her that government officials were coming to seek her child. Joseph hurried off with the child Jesus wrapped in his mantle, and I saw Mary, for half a day perhaps, sitting in the cave very anxious and without the child.

When Eliud with Anne's maid came again from Nazareth to take Anne home, I saw a very beautiful ceremony celebrated in the crib cave. Joseph had taken advantage of Mary's withdrawal to the tomb cave, and with the help of the shepherds had adorned the whole interior of the crib cave. It was festooned with flower garlands, both walls and roof, and in the center stood a table. All the beautiful carpets and stuffs of the kings that had not yet been removed, were spread over the floor and hung in festoons from the walls. A cover was spread on the table, and on it was placed a pyramid of flowers and foliage that reached to the opening in the roof. On top of the pyramid hovered a dove. The whole cave was full of light and splendor. The child Jesus in his little basket cradle was placed upon a stool on the table. He sat upright as he had done on the lap of his mother at the adoration of the kings. Joseph and Mary were standing on either side of him. They were adorned with wreaths, and they drank something out of a glass. I saw choirs of angels in the cave. All were very happy and full of emotion. It was the anniversary of Joseph and Mary's espousals.

When the celebration was over, I saw Anne and Eliud going away and taking with them on two asses what still remained of the kings' gifts.

The holy family immediately set about preparing for their own departure. Their household effects had steadily diminished. The portable partitions and other pieces of furniture made by Joseph were now bestowed upon the shepherds, who removed them at once.

I saw the blessed Virgin going twice by night to the crib cave with the child Jesus, and laying it on a carpet on the spot upon which it was born. Then she knelt down at its side and prayed. I saw the whole cave filled with light as at the moment of the birth. It was now entirely cleared out, for Anne on reaching home had dispatched two of her servants to get whatever the holy family would not need on their journey. I saw them returning with the two asses on which they rode laden with goods. The cave to which the holy family had removed, as well as the crib cave, were now quite empty; they had also been swept out, for Joseph wanted to leave everything perfectly clean.

On the night preceding their departure for the temple, I saw Mary and Joseph taking formal leave of the crib cave. They spread the deep red cover of the kings first over that spot upon which the child Jesus was born, laid the child on it, and kneeling beside it, prayed. Then they laid the child in the crib and again prayed beside it; and, lastly, on the place where it had been circumcised where, too, they knelt in prayer. Joseph had caused the young she-ass to be pawned among his relatives, for he was still resolved to return to Bethlehem and build himself a house in the valley of the shepherds. He had mentioned his intention to the shepherds, saying that he would take Mary for awhile to her mother, that she might recover from the hardships undergone in her late abode. He left all kinds of things with them.

Mary's Purification

BEFORE the break of day, Mary seated herself on the ass, the child Jesus on her lap. She had only a couple of covers and one bundle. She sat upon a side seat that had a little footboard. They started to the left around the crib hill and off by the east side of Bethlehem unperceived by anyone.

I saw them at midday resting at a spring that was roofed in and surrounded by seats. A couple of women came out here to Mary, bringing to her little mugs and rolls.

The offering that the holy family had with them was hanging in a basket on the ass. The basket had three compartments; two contained fruit, and in the third, which was of open wickerwork, were doves. Toward evening, when about a quarter of an hour's distance from Jerusalem, they turned and entered a small house that lay next to a large inn. The owners were a married couple without children, and by them the holy travelers were welcomed with extraordinary joy. The house lay between the brook Kidron and the city. I saw Anne's manservant and the maid stopping with these people on their journey home, at which time also they engaged quarters for the holy family. The husband was a gardener; he clipped the hedges and kept the road in order. The wife was a relative of Johanna Chusa. They appeared to me to be Essenes.

The whole of the next day I still saw the holy family with the old people outside Jerusalem. The blessed Virgin was almost all the time alone in her room with the child, which lay upon a low, covered projection of the wall. She was always in prayer, and appeared to be preparing herself for the sacrifice. I received at that moment an interior instruction as to how we should prepare for the Holy Sacrifice. I saw in her room myriads of angels adoring the child Jesus. Mary was wholly absorbed in her own interior. The old people did out of pure love all they could for the Mother of God. They must have had some presentiment of the child's holiness.

I had a vision also of the priest Simeon. He was a very aged, emaciated man with a short beard. He had a wife and three grown sons, the youngest of whom was already to his prayer. I have seen that the pious priests and Israelites of those times did not sway to and fro so much when at prayer as the Jews of our days; but I saw them scourging themselves. Anna in her temple cell was also rapt in prayer; and she, too, had a vision.

Early in the morning while it was still quite dark, I saw the holy family accompanied by the two old people going into the city and to the temple. The ass was laden as if for a journey, and they had with them the basket of offerings.

Kidron from Jehosaphat

twenty years old. Simeon dwelt at the temple. I saw him going through a narrow, dark passage in the wall of the temple to a little cell which was built in the thick walls. It had only one opening, from which he could look down into the temple. Here I saw the old man kneeling and praying in ecstasy.[A17] The apparition of an angel appeared before him, telling him to notice particularly the first child that would, early the next morning, be brought for presentation, for that it was the Messiah whom he had now awaited so long. The angel added that, after seeing the child, he would die. Oh, what a beautiful sight that was to me! The little cell was so bright, and the old man radiant with joy! He went home full of gladness, announced to his wife the good tidings of the angel, and then returned

They first entered a court that was surrounded by a wall, and there the ass was tied under a shed. The blessed Virgin and child were received by an old woman and conducted along a covered walk up to the temple. The old woman carried a light, for it was still dark. Here in this passage came Simeon full of expectation to meet Mary. He spoke a few joyous words with her, took the child Jesus, pressed him to his heart, and then hurried to another side of the temple. Since the preceding evening, when he had received the announcement of the angel, he had been consumed by desire. He had taken his stand in the women's passage to the temple, hardly able to await the coming of Mary and her child.

Mary was now led by the woman to a porch in that part

of the temple in which the ceremony of presentation was to take place. Anna and another woman (Naomi, Mary's former directress) received her. Simeon came out to the porch and conducted Mary with the child in her arms into the hall to the right of the women's porch. It was in this porch that the treasure box stood by which Jesus was sitting when the widow cast in her mite. Old Anna, to whom Joseph had handed over the basket of fruit and doves, followed with Naomi, and Joseph retired to the standing place of the men.

It was understood at the temple that several women were coming today to offer sacrifice, and preparations had been made accordingly. Numerous pyramidal lamps were burning round the walls, the little flames rising out of a disk supported upon an arm in the form of an arch, which shone almost as brightly as the light itself. On the disk hung extinguishers which, when struck together above the flame, put it out. Before the altar, from whose corners projected horns, was placed a chest, the doors of which opened outward and afforded supports for a tolerably large slab, the whole forming a table. This surface was covered first with a red cloth and over that a white transparent one, both of which fell to the floor. On the four corners burned lamps with several branches; in the center of the table was a cradle-shaped basket, and near it two oval dishes and two small baskets. All these objects, as also the priests' vestments, which were lying on the horned altar, were kept in the chest whose open doors formed the table. A railing enclosed the whole. On both sides of this hall were rows of seats in tiers where priests were sitting in prayer.

Simeon conducted Mary through the altar rail and up to the table of sacrifice. The infant Jesus, wrapped in his sky-blue dress, was laid in the basket cradle. Mary wore a sky-blue dress, a white veil, and a long, yellowish mantle. When the child had been placed in the cradle, Simeon led Mary out again to the standing place of the women. He then proceeded to the altar proper, whereon lay the priestly vestments and at which, besides himself, three other priests were vesting. And now one of them went behind, one before, and two on either side of the table, and prayed over the child, while Anna approached Mary, gave her the doves and fruit in two little baskets, one on top of the other, and went with her to the altar rail. Anna remained there while Mary, led again by Simeon, passed on through the railing and up to the altar. There upon one of the dishes she deposited the fruit, and into the other laid some coins; the doves she placed upon the table in the basket. Simeon stood before the table near Mary while the priest behind it took the child from the cradle, raised it on high and toward the different parts of the temple, praying all the while. [A18] Simeon next received the child from him, laid it in Mary's arms, and, from a roll of parchment that lay near him on a desk, prayed over her and the child.

After that Simeon again led Mary to the railing, whence Anna accompanied her to the place set apart for the women. In the meantime, about twenty mothers with their firstborn had arrived. Joseph and several others were standing back in the place assigned to the men.

Then two priests at the altar proper began a religious service accompanied by incense and prayers, while those in the rows of seats swayed to and fro a little, but not like the Jews of the present day.

When these ceremonies were ended, Simeon went to where Mary was standing, took the child into his arms and, entranced with joy, spoke long and loud. When he ceased, Anna also filled with the Spirit, spoke a long time. I saw that the people around heard them indeed, but it caused no interruption to the other ceremonies. Such praying aloud appeared not to be unusual. But all were deeply impressed, and regarded Mary and the child with great reverence. Mary shone like a rose. Her public offerings were indeed the poorest; but Joseph in private gave to Simeon and to Anna many little, yellow, triangular pieces to be employed for the use of the temple, and chiefly for the maidens belonging to it who were too poor to meet their own expenses. It was not everyone that could have his children reared in the temple. Once I saw a boy in Anna's care. I think he was the son of a prince, or king, but I have forgotten his name.

I did not witness the purification ceremonies of the other mothers; but I had an interior conviction that all the children offered on that day would receive special grace, and that some of the martyred innocents were among them. When the most holy child Jesus was laid upon the altar in the basket cradle, an indescribable light filled the temple. I saw that God was in that light, and I saw the heavens open up as far as the most holy Trinity.

Mary was now led back into the court by Anna and Naomi. Here she took leave of them, and was joined by Joseph and the old people with whom she and Joseph had lodged. They went with the ass straight out of Jerusalem, and the good, old people accompanied them a part of the way. They reached Beth-Horon the same day, and stayed overnight in the house which had been Mary's last stopping place on her journey to the temple thirteen years before. Here some of Anne's people were waiting to conduct them home.

Feast Picture

I SAW the festival of the Purification celebrated also in the spiritual church. It was filled with angelic choirs and in the center above them I saw the most holy Trinity and in it something like a void. In the middle of the church stood an altar and on it a tree with broad, pendent leaves, similar to the tree in Paradise by which Adam fell.

I saw the blessed Virgin with the child Jesus in her arms floating up from the earth to the altar, while the tree on the same inclined low before her and began to wither. A magnificent angel in priestly garments, a halo round his head, approached Mary. She gave him the child, and he laid it upon the altar. At that instant I saw the most holy Trinity as ever before in its fullness. I saw the angel give to Mary a little shining ball whereon was the figure of a swathed child, and I saw her with this gift hovering over the altar. From all sides, I saw crowds of poor people approaching Mary with lights. She reached those lights to the child on the ball into which they seemed to pass, and then to reappear. I saw that all these lights united into one, which spread over Mary and the child, and illumined all things. Mary had extended her wide mantle over the whole earth. And now there was a festival.

I think that the withering of the Tree of Knowledge at Mary's appearance and the offering of the child to the most holy Trinity signified the reuniting of the human race with God, and through Mary those scattered lights became one light in the light of Jesus, and illumined all things.

Death of Holy Simeon

I SAW that Simeon, after prophesying in the temple, returned home and fell sick. I saw him on his couch giving his last advice to his wife and sons, and imparting to them his joy. Then I saw him die. There were several old Jews and priests praying around him.

When he had breathed his last, they carried the body into another room where, without stripping it, it was washed. The body was laid on a board pierced with holes, under which was a copper basin to receive the water as it fell. A large sheet was thrown over the corpse, and under that the washing was performed. Green leaves and herbs were then strewn plentifully over it and a wide cloth bound firmly around it, as is done in the swathing of a child. The corpse was so stiff and straight that I was tempted to think it was bound to a board. The burial took place in the evening. Six men with lights carried the corpse on a board with low, curved sides to the sepulcher hewn in a hill not far from the temple. It was entered through an oblique door; the interior walls were ornamented with stars and various figures like the blessed Virgin's cell at the temple. I noticed the same kind of ornamentation in St. Benedict's first cloister. The corpse was deposited in the center of the little cave, the passage around it being left free; then some religious rites were solemnized. They laid all kinds of things around the corpse: coins and little stones and leaves, I think. I do not now remember all distinctly. Simeon was related to Veronica and, through his father, with Zechariah also. His sons served in the temple, and were always, though in secret, on terms of friendship with Jesus and his relatives. Some of them before and some after the Ascension of our Lord, joined the disciples. At the time of the first persecution they did much for the community.

Return of the Holy Family to Nazareth

I SAW the holy family returning to Nazareth by a much more direct route than that by which they had gone to Bethlehem. On their first journey they had shunned the inhabited districts and seldom put up at an inn; but now they took the straight route, which was much shorter.

Joseph had in his cloak pocket some little rolls of thin, yellow, shining leaves on which were letters. He had received them from the holy kings. The shekels of Judas were thicker, and in the form of a tongue.

I saw the holy family arrive at Anne's, in Nazareth. The eldest sister of Mary, Mary Heli, with her daughter Mary Cleophas, a woman from Elizabeth's place, and that one of Anne's maids who had been with Mary in Bethlehem were there. A feast was held such as had been celebrated at the departure of the child Mary for the temple. Lamps burned above the table, and there were some old priests present. Things went on quietly. Though there was great joy over the child Jesus, yet it was a calm, inward joy. I have never seen much excitement among those holy souls. They partook of a slight repast, the women as usual eating apart from the men. I can remember no more of this vision, although I must have been present in a very real way, for I had to accomplish in it a work of prayer. In Anne's garden, notwithstanding the season, I saw numbers of pears, plums, and other fruits still on the trees, although the leaves had already fallen.

I have always forgotten to say a word about the weather in Palestine during the winter season, because being so accustomed to it myself, I think that everyone else knows it too. I often see rain and fog, and sometimes snow, but it soon melts away, and I see many trees upon which fruit is still hanging. There are in the year several harvests, the first in what corresponds to our spring. In the present season, winter, I see the people on the roads wrapped up in mantles which are thrown over the head also. On the sacred night of Christmas I always see everything green, blossoming, and full of flowers, the animals frolicsome, the vineyards laden with luscious grapes, and I hear the sweet caroling of birds; but immediately after, it is again quiet and just as it usually is there at this season. The tree outside of Bethlehem and under which Mary stood while Joseph was seeking an inn was, as long as she remained under it, quite green. It afforded ample shelter. But when she left it, it resumed its wintry nakedness. This was perhaps only a mark of reverence; but the blessed Virgin was fully conscious of it. The shepherd field was, however, already green at this season, for they watered it.

The road from Anne's house to Joseph's in Nazareth was about one half-hour's distance, and ran between gardens and hills. I saw Joseph at Anne's loading two asses with many different things, and going on before with Anne's maid to Nazareth. Mary followed with Anne, who carried the child Jesus.

Mary and Joseph had no care of the housekeeping. They were provided with all things by Anne, who often went to see them. I saw her maid carrying provisions to them in two baskets, one on her head, the other in her hand.

I saw the blessed Virgin knitting, or crocheting little robes. To her right side was fastened a ball of wool and she had in her hands two short needles of bone, I think, with little hooks at the end; one was about a foot long, the other shorter. The stitches were arranged on the needles above the hooks, over which in doing the work the thread was thrown, and the stitch thus formed. The finished web hung between the two needles. I saw Mary thus working, either standing or sitting by the child Jesus, who lay in his little basket cradle.

I saw Joseph, out of long strips of bark—yellow, brown, and green—plaiting screens, large surfaces, and covers for ceilings. He had a stock of this woven board-like work piled under a shed near the house. He wove into them all kinds of patterns, stars, hearts, etc. I thought as I looked at them that he had no idea how soon he would have to leave all.

I saw the holy family while at Nazareth visited also by Mary Heli. She came with St. Anne, bringing with her her grandson, a boy of about four years, the child of her daughter Mary Cleophas. I saw the holy women sitting together, caressing the child Jesus, and laying it in the little boy's arms; they acted just as people do nowadays. Mary Heli lived in a little town about three hours east of Nazareth. She had a house almost as large as her mother's. It had a courtyard surrounded by a wall, and in it a well with a pump. On pressing with the foot at the base of the pump, the water flowed out into a stone basin before it. Mary Heli's husband was named Cleophas. Their daughter Mary Cleophas, who had married Alpheus, lived at the other end of the town.

That evening I saw the holy women praying together. They were standing in front of a little table, which was fastened to the wall and covered with red and white. On it lay a roll which Mary unfolded and hung upon the wall. A figure was embroidered on it in pale colors; it was like a corpse entirely enveloped in a long, white mantle. It had something in its arms. I saw a picture like it at Anne's during the festival before Mary's departure for her presentation in the temple. A lamp was burning during their prayer. Mary stood a little in front of the table with Anne and Mary Heli on either side. At certain times they crossed their hands upon their breast, folded them together, or stretched them forth. Mary read out of a roll that lay before her. They prayed in measured and steady tones; it reminded me of choir chanting.

The Flight into Egypt

WHEN Herod saw that the kings did not return, he thought they had failed to find Jesus, and the whole affair seemed to be dying out. But after Mary's return to Nazareth, Herod heard of Simeon's and Anna's prophecies at the presentation of the child in the temple, and his fears were reawakened. I saw him in as great disquietude as at the time of the kings' stay in Jerusalem. He was conferring with some aged Jews who read to him from long rolls of

Temple Scrolls

writings mounted on rods. He had given orders for a number of men to be gathered together in a large court, and there provided with weapons and uniforms. Things went on as they do with us when soldiers are recruited. I

The Flight into Egypt

saw that he sent these troops to various places around Jerusalem, from which the mothers were to be summoned to the Holy City. He caused their numbers to be everywhere ascertained. He took these precautions in order to prevent the tumult that would necessarily follow if the news of the projected slaughter of the children was spread. I saw those soldiers in three different places, in Bethlehem, in Gilgal, and in Hebron. The inhabitants were in great consternation, because not able to divine why a garrison was placed in their towns. The soldiers remained about nine months in those places, and the murder of the little ones began when John was about two years old.

Anne and Mary Heli were still at the home of the holy family in Nazareth. Mary, with her child, slept in the apartment to the right behind the fireplace; Anne, to the left; and between hers and that of Joseph, Mary Heli. These rooms were not so high as the house itself, and were cut off from one another only by wicker partitions. The ceiling also was of wickerwork. Mary's couch was surrounded by a curtain, or screen. At her feet, in his own little bed, lay the infant Jesus within Mary's reach when she sat upright. I saw a radiant youth standing at the side of Joseph's couch and speaking to him. Joseph sat up, but overcome by sleep, again lay down. Then the youth caught him by the hand and raised him up. Joseph, now thoroughly aroused, stood up and the youth vanished. Then I saw Joseph going to the lamp that burned in the center of the house, and getting a light. He proceeded to Mary's chamber, knocked, and asked permission to enter. I saw him going in and speaking to Mary who, however, did not open her screen. After this he went out to the stable for the ass, and returning, went into a room wherein were stored all kinds of household goods. He was getting things ready for a journey. Mary arose, quickly clothed herself for traveling, and went to arouse Anne, who got up at once along with Mary Heli and the little boy. I cannot express how touching was the trouble of Anne and the sister. Anne embraced Mary over and over again with many tears, clasping her to her heart as if she were never again to see her. The sister threw herself flat on the floor, and wept. Only just before setting out, did they take the infant Jesus from his little bed. They all pressed the child to their heart, and it was given to the little boy to embrace. Mary then took the child upon her breast, resting it in a strip of stuff that fastened over her shoulders. A long mantle enveloped both mother and child, and Mary wore over her head a large veil, which hung down on both sides of her face. She made but few preparations for the journey, and all she did was done quietly and quickly. I did not see her even swathing the child afresh. The holy travelers took only a few things with them, far fewer than they had brought from Bethlehem, only a little bundle and some coverings. Joseph had a leathern bottle filled with water and a basket with compartments in it, in which were loaves, little jugs, and live birds. There was a cross seat for Mary and the child on the ass, also a little footboard. They went forward a short distance with Anne, for they took the road in the direction to her house, only somewhat more to the left. When Joseph approached with the ass, Anne again embraced and blessed Mary, who then mounted and rode off. It was not yet midnight when they left the house. The child Jesus was twelve weeks old. I had seen three times four weeks.

I saw Mary Heli going to her mother's house in order to send Eliud with a servant to Nazareth, after which she returned with the boy to her own home. I next saw Anne in Joseph's house packing everything up for Eliud and the servant to remove to her own house.

The holy family passed by many places that night, and not till morning did I see them resting under a shed and taking a little refreshment.

I saw them taking their first night's lodgings in the little village of Nazara, between Legio and Massaloth. The poor, oppressed people of this place who lodged the holy family were not, properly speaking, Jews. They had to go far over a mountainous road to Samaria to worship, for their temple was on Mount Garizim, and they always had to work like slaves on the temple of Jerusalem and other public buildings. The holy family could go no further. They were well received by these outcasts with whom they remained the whole of the following day. On their return from Egypt, they again visited those poor people. They did the same both going and returning from the temple the first time that the child Jesus made the journey to it. The whole family at a later period was baptized by John, and they afterward joined the disciples of Jesus.

The holy family on their flight met only three inns at which to spend the night: here, at Nazara; again at Anim, or Engannim, among the camel dealers; and lastly, among the robbers. At other times, they rested during their tiresome wanderings in valleys and caves and the most out-of-the-way places. Further on from Nazara, I saw them hidden under the great pine tree near which Mary, on her journey to Bethlehem, had been so cold. The persecution of Herod was known in these parts and it was, consequently, unsafe for them. The Ark of the Covenant had once rested under this tree, when Joshua assembled the people and made them renounce their idols.

Later, I saw the holy family by a well and balsam bush resting and refreshing themselves. The branches of the bush were notched, and out of them oozed the balsam in drops. The child Jesus lay on Mary's lap, his little feet bare. To the left behind them, lay Jerusalem far up above the level of the country in which they then were.

Flight of the Holy Family to Egypt

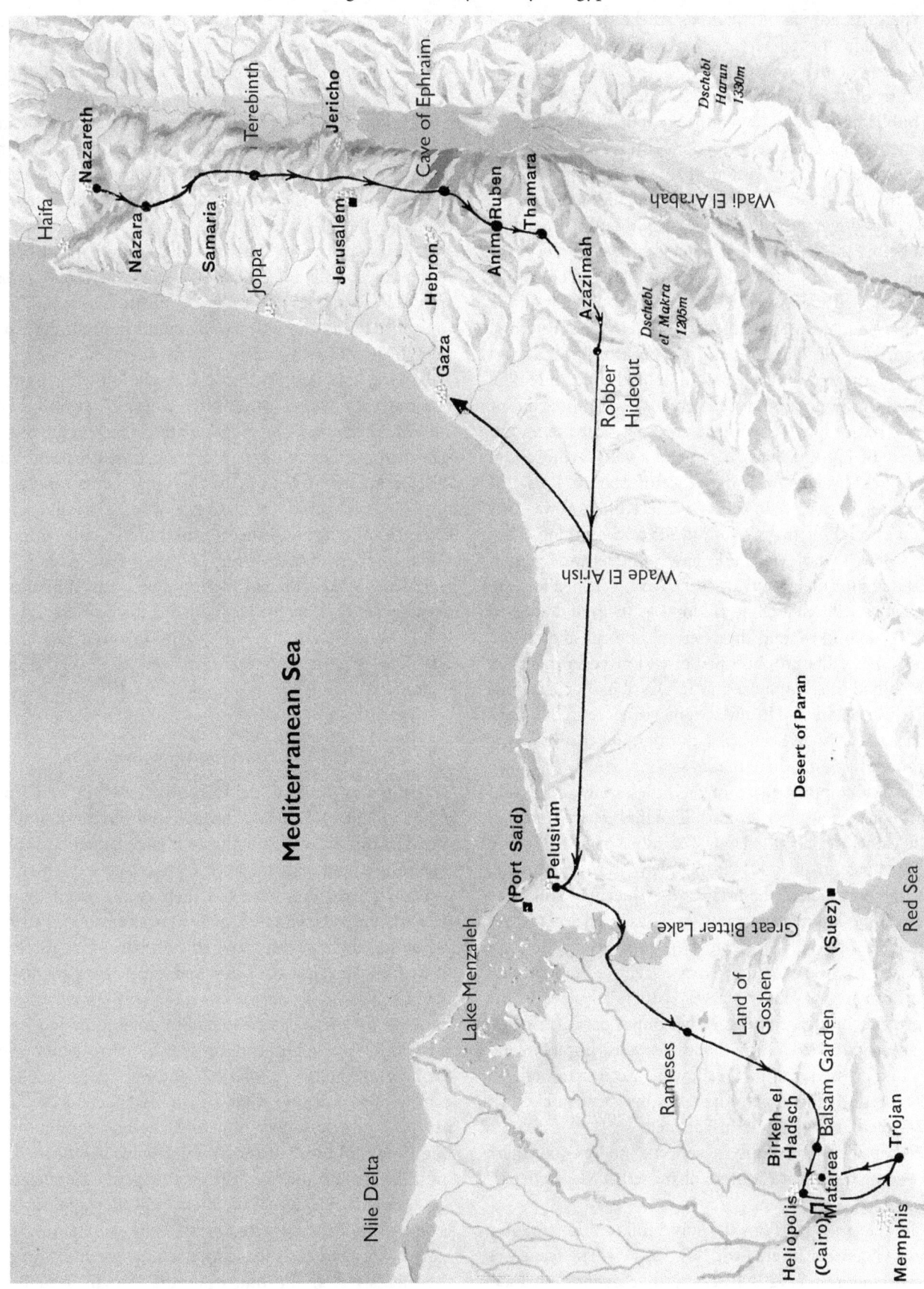

Nazareth—Nazara—Terebinthe Moreh—Caves of Ephraim—Pelusium
Heliopolis—Trojan—Matarea—Pelusium—Gaza—Nazareth

When the holy family had passed the walls of Gaza, I saw them in the wilderness. No words can depict the difficulties of this journey. They always traveled a mile eastward of the ordinary highway and, as they shunned the public inns, they suffered the want of all necessaries. I saw them quite exhausted with not a drop of water (the little jug was empty) drawing near to a low bush some distance from the road. The blessed Virgin alighted from the ass and sat down upon the dry grass. Suddenly there jetted high before them a spring of water, which spread over the plain. I witnessed their joy. Joseph dug a hole at a little distance, and led the ass to it. The poor beast gladly drank from it as it filled. Mary bathed the child in the spring, and refreshed herself. The sun shone out beautifully for a short time, and the weary travelers were strengthened and full of grateful emotion. They tarried here for two or three hours. On the sixth night, I saw them in a cave near the mount and city of Ephron. The cave was in a wild ravine, about one hour's distance from the grove of Mamre. I saw the holy family arrive, worn-out and dejected. Mary was very sad; she wept, for they were in want of everything. They rested here a whole day and many wonders were vouchsafed them for their refreshment. A spring gushed forth in the cave, a wild goat came running to them and allowed itself to be milked, and they were visibly consoled by an angel. One of the prophets had often prayed in this cave. Samuel had once sojourned in it, David had guarded his father's sheep around it, and to it had often retired to pray. He had, in this cave, received through angels the divine commands, among them that to slay Goliath.

The last stopping place of the holy family in Herod's dominion was near its confines. The innkeepers appeared to be camel dealers, for I saw a number of camels in an enclosed pasture ground. The people were rude and wild, and they enriched themselves by thieving; still they received the holy family most graciously. This place was distant a couple of hours from the Dead Sea.

Once I saw Mary sending a messenger to Elizabeth, who then brought her child to a very concealed place in the desert. Zechariah accompanied her only a part of the way. When they reached a certain body of water, Elizabeth and the child crossed over on a raft, while Zechariah went on to Nazareth by the same route taken by Mary on her visit to Elizabeth. I saw him on his journey.

Perhaps he was going to make some inquiries, for there were some friends at Nazareth distressed at Mary's departure.

On a starry night, I saw the holy family going through a sandy wilderness covered with low thickets. The scene was as vivid before me, as if I were really crossing the desert with them. Here and there under the copsewood, venomous snakes lay coiled. With loud hissing, they approached the path and darted their heads angrily toward the holy family. But they, shielded by the light that environed them, stepped securely along. I saw other animals with immense fins like wings on their blackish body, with short feet, and a head like that of a fish. They darted along, flying over the ground. At last, the holy family came behind the bushes to a deep fissure in the ground, like the walls of a narrow defile, and here they rested.

The last place in Judea by which they passed, had a name that sounded like Mara. I thought of Anne's ancestral place, but it was not it. The people were very rude and uncivilized, and the holy family could get nothing from them by way of refreshment.

Leaving this last place and scarcely knowing how to proceed, they pressed on through a desolate region. They could find no road, and a dark, pathless mountain-height stretched out before them. Mary was exhausted and very sad. She knelt with Joseph, the child in her arms, and cried to God. And behold! Several large, wild beasts, like lions, came running around them, exhibiting friendly dispositions. I understood that they had been sent to show the way. They looked toward the mountain, ran thither and then turned back again, just like a dog that wants someone to follow it. At last the holy family followed them and, after crossing the mountain, arrived at a very dismal region.

The Holy Family among Robbers

AT some distance from the road by which they were traveling, a light glimmered through the darkness. It proceeded from a hut belonging to a gang of robbers, who had hung a light on a neighboring tree, thus to allure travelers. The road too, here and there, was broken by pits over which cords with little bells were stretched. The ringing of these bells gave notice to the robbers of the presence of luckless wayfarers. All of a sudden, I saw a man with about five comrades surrounding the holy family. All were actuated by wicked intentions. But when they looked at the child, I saw a glittering ray like an arrow penetrating the heart of the leader, who straightaway commanded his comrades to offer no injury to the strangers. Mary also saw the ray. The robber now took the holy family to his home, and told his wife how strangely his heart had been moved. The people were at first shy and shamefaced, something very unusual for them; still they approached, little by little, and gathered around the holy family, who had seated themselves in a corner on the ground. Some of the men went in and out, while the woman brought to Mary little rolls, fruits, honeycomb, and cups containing something to drink. The ass also was placed under shelter. The woman cleared out a small room for Mary and brought her a little tub of water in which to bathe the child. She also dried the swathing bands for her at the fire. The husband was deeply impressed by the demeanor of the holy family, and especially the appearance of the child. He said to his wife, "This Hebrew child is no ordinary child. Beg the lady to allow us to wash our leprous child in his bathing water. It may, perhaps, do it some good." The wife went to request the favor of the blessed Virgin; but before she had time to speak, Mary bade her take the water she had used for Jesus's bath, wash the sick child in it, and it would become cleaner than it was before attacked by the disease. The boy was about three years old and stiff from leprosy. His mother carried him in and put him into the bath. Wherever the water touched him, the leprosy fell like scales to the bottom of the tub; the boy became clean and well. The mother was out of herself with joy; she wanted to embrace Mary and the child Jesus. But Mary, stretching out her hand, warded her off; she would allow neither the child nor herself to be touched by her. She told her to dig a hole deep down to a rock, and pour the water just used into it, that she might always have it for similar purposes. Mary spoke with her long, and exacted from her a promise to embrace the first opportunity of escape from her present abode. The people were all delighted; they stood around the holy family gazing at them in wonder. During the night, other members of their band came to the hut, and to them the boy's cure was related. The robbers' reverential bearing toward the holy family was so much the more remarkable, since I saw that night many travelers, attracted to their hut by the light immediately taken prisoner and carried deep into the forest to an immense cave that served for their special storehouse. It lay under a thicket, the entrance closely concealed. In it were clothes, carpets, meat, goats, sheep, and innumerable other stolen things, all in profusion. I saw also boys about seven or eight years old whom the robbers had kidnapped. They were cared for by an old woman who lived in the cave.

Mary slept none that night; she sat upon her couch on the floor perfectly still. At early dawn the holy family started again on their journey in spite of the robber and his wife, who wanted them to stay longer. They took with them a supply of provisions put up by their grateful host and hostess who also accompanied them a part of the way, that they might escape the snares.

The robber and his wife took leave of the holy family with expressions of deep feeling, uttering these remarkable words: "Remember us wherever you go!" Upon hearing them, I had a vision in which I saw that the cured boy afterward turned out to be the good thief who on the cross said to Jesus: "Remember me when thou comest into thy kingdom." The robber's wife, after some time, joined those that dwelt around the balsam garden.

The holy family went from here further on into the desert. When they had again lost all trace of anything like a path, they were a second time surrounded by all kinds of animals, among them huge winged lizards and even serpents, which pointed out the way to them. [A19]

At a later period, when unable to advance through the sandy plain in which they were, I saw a very lovely miracle. On either side of the road sprouted up the plant Rose of Jericho, with its crisped branches, its tiny flowers in the center, and its straight root. On they went now right joyously, watching as far as the eye could see these plants springing up, and so across the whole plain. I saw that it was revealed to the blessed Virgin that, at some future day the people of the country would gather these roses and sell them to travelers in exchange for bread. The name of this region sounded like Gaza, or Goze.

I saw the holy family arrive at a town and district called Lepe or Lape, in which were numerous canals and ditches with high dams. I saw them crossing the water on a raft. Mary sat on a log, and the ass was standing in something like a trough, or tub. Two brown-complexioned, half-naked men with flat noses and protruding lips, ferried them over. Our holy travelers came now to the house on the outskirts of the town; but the occupants were so rough and pitiless that, without saying a word, Mary and Joseph moved further on. I think this was the first pagan Egyptian city they had yet reached. They had made, up to this time, ten days' journey in the Jewish country and then in the wilderness.

I next saw the holy family on Egyptian territory, in a level, green country full of pasture grounds. In the trees were stationed idols like swathed dolls, or like fishes wrapped in broad bands upon which were figures or letters. Occasionally, I saw people fat, but short in stature, approaching these idols and venerating them. The holy family sought a little rest under the cattle shed, the cattle going out of their own accord to make room for them. They were in want of food, having neither bread nor water. Mary no longer had nourishment for her child, and no one gave them anything. Every kind of human misery was experienced by them during this flight.

At last, some shepherds drew near to water their cattle. They, too, would have gone away without giving them anything, had not Joseph's entreaties moved them to unlock the well and allow them to have a little water.

Again, I saw the holy family weary and exhausted in a forest, at whose egress stood a slender date tree, the fruit all clustered on top. Mary approached the tree, the child Jesus on her arm, prayed and raised the child up to it. Instantly the tree bowed down its top as if kneeling, so that Mary could gather all its fruit. It afterward remained in that position. I saw Mary dividing a quantity of the fruit among the naked children who had run after them from the last village.

At a quarter of an hour's distance from this tree stood another unusually large one of the same kind, very high, and hollow like an old oak. In it the holy family lay concealed from the people that followed them. That evening I saw them taking shelter within the walls of a ruined place, where they stayed overnight.

The Balsam Garden

ON the next day, the holy family continued their journey through a sandy, desolate wilderness. Famishing for water and exhausted by weariness, they sat down on one of the sandhills, and the blessed Virgin sent up a cry to God.

A Spring by the Way

Suddenly, a stream of pure water gushed forth at her side. Joseph removed the sandhill that was over it, and a clear, beautiful, little fountain jetted up. He made a channel for it, and it flowed over quite a large space, disappearing again near its source. Here they refreshed themselves, and Mary bathed the child Jesus, while Joseph gave drink to the ass and filled the water bottles. I saw all kinds of animals like turtles drinking at the gushing waters. They did not appear at all afraid of the holy family.

The soil over which the water had flowed soon began to clothe itself with verdure, and numbers of balsam trees afterward grew there. When the holy family returned from Egypt, those trees were large enough to furnish balsam for their refreshment. The place soon grew into a little settlement. Wherever the pagans planted these trees they withered. They thrived only when the Jews whom the holy family had known in this country went to live there. I think the wife of that robber whose boy had been cured of leprosy by the bath of the child Jesus went there, too, for she soon escaped from the robbers. Her boy, however, remained with them some time longer.

A balsam hedge surrounded the garden, and in its center were several large fruit trees. At a subsequent period, another large well was dug, out of which quantities of water were raised by means of a wheel turned by oxen. This water mingled with that of Mary's spring and watered the whole garden; unmixed, it would have proved injurious. I have seen that the oxen employed in turning the wheel could not by any means be forced to work from Saturday noon till early on Monday morning.

The Holy Family Reaches Heliopolis

I SAW the holy family on their way to Heliopolis. From their last night lodgings they were accompanied thither by a good man who, I think, was one of the workmen on that canal over which they had been ferried. They now crossed a long and very high bridge over a wide river (the Nile), which appeared to have several branches, and came to a place before the city gate which was surrounded by a kind of promenade. Here, on a tapering pedestal, stood a great idol with the head of an ox, and in its arms something like the figure of a swathed child. The idol was encompassed by a circle of benches, or tables of stone upon which the worshippers laid their sacrifices. Not far off was a very large tree, under which the holy family sat down to rest.

They had scarcely seated themselves when the earth began to quake, the idol tottered, and tilted over. A hue and cry instantly arose from the people, and many of the workmen on the canal in the neighborhood came rushing up. But the good man who had accompanied the holy family started with them for the city. They were already at the opposite side of the idol place when the terrified crowd, with menacing and abusive words, angrily surrounded them. Suddenly the earth heaved, the huge tree fell, its roots breaking up out of the ground, and there arose a lake of muddy water into which the idol splashed. It sank so deep that one could scarcely see its horns, and some of the most wicked of the bystanders sank with it. The holy family now entered the city unmolested, and put up near an idolatrous temple, a large stone building containing many rooms. Some of the idols in the temples of the city were likewise overturned.

Heliopolis is also called On. Asenath, wife of the Egyptian Joseph, resided here with the pagan priest Potiphar, and here also Dionysius the Areopagite studied. The city extends to a great distance around the many-branched river. One sees it from afar lying high above the general level. The river flows through it under the arches that support some of the buildings. Great logs lie in some parts of the river branches, placed there to enable the inhabitants to cross. I saw the ruins of enormous buildings, huge masses of heavy masonry, towers half standing, and even temples almost entire. I saw, too, pillars like towers, around the outside of which one could mount to the top. [A20]

The holy family dwelt under a low colonnade, in which there were other dwellings besides their own. The supporting pillars were rather low, some round, some square, and above ran a highway for the accommodation of vehicles and pedestrians. Opposite this colonnade was a pagan temple with two courts. Joseph put up before their little abode a screen of light woodwork. There was room for the ass, also. The screen, or light wall that Joseph put up, was of the same kind as he was accustomed to make. I remarked behind a similar screen and set up against the wall an altar consisting of a small table covered with red and over that a white, transparent cloth; on it stood a lamp.

I saw Joseph working at home, and often also abroad. He made long rods with round knobs at the ends, little three-legged stools with a handle by which to grasp them, and a certain kind of basket. He made, also, a great many light, wicker partitions, and little, light towers, some hexagonal, others octagonal. They were formed of long, thin boards, tapering toward the top and ending in a knob. They had an entrance, and were large enough to allow a man to sit inside as in a sentry box; they had steps outside, up which one could mount. I saw little towers like these standing here and there before the pagan temples, also on the flat roofs of the houses. People used to sit in them; perhaps they were watch houses, or maybe they were intended as screens from the sun.

I saw the blessed Virgin weaving tapestry and doing another kind of work. For the latter she used a staff on the top of which a knot was fastened. I cannot say whether she was spinning or not. I often saw people visiting her and the little infant Jesus. The child lay on the ground by Mary's side, in a kind of cradle like a little boat. Sometimes I saw it raised on a frame like a sawing jack. There were not many Jews in Heliopolis, and I saw them going about with a downcast look as if they had no right to live there.

North of Heliopolis, between it and the Nile, which there divides into several branches, lay the little territory of Goshen, and in it a little place cut up by canals, among which dwelt numbers of Jews whose religious ideas were very much confused. Several of them became acquainted with the holy family, and Mary did all kinds of feminine work for them, receiving as payment bread and other provisions. The Jews in the land of Goshen had a temple, which they compared with the temple of Solomon; but it was very different.

Not far from his dwelling, Joseph built an oratory where the resident Jews, who possessed no such place of their own, used to assemble with the holy family for prayer. It was surmounted by a light cupola which could be thrown open, thus enabling the worshippers to stand under the open sky. In the center of the hall stood an altar, or table of sacrifice, covered, as usual, with red and white; on it lay rolls of parchment. The priest, or teacher, was a very old man. The men and women were not so separated from one another at prayer as in Palestine; the men stood on one side, the women on the other.

The holy family dwelt a little more than a year at Heliopolis. They had much to suffer from the Egyptians who hated and persecuted them, on account of their overturned idols; and as the houses were all solidly built, Joseph could not find work at his trade. They left Heliopolis, therefore, but not before they had learned from an angel of the slaughter of the Bethlehemite babes. Both Mary and Joseph were deeply grieved, and the child Jesus, who was now able to walk, being a year and a half old, shed tears the whole day.

The Murder of the Innocent Children

I SAW the mothers with their boys, from infants in the arms up to the age of two years, going to Jerusalem. They were from those different places around the Holy City, in which Herod had placed garrisons and in which, by means of officials, he had issued a proclamation to that effect; viz. from Bethlehem, Gilgal, and Hebron. I saw many women even from the Arabian frontiers taking their children to Jerusalem, and these had more than a day's journey to make. The mothers went in bands, some with two children and riding on asses. On their arrival in the city, they were all conducted to a large building, and the husbands who accompanied some of them dismissed. The mandate was joyously obeyed, for the poor people imagined they were going to receive a reward.

The building into which the mothers and their children were ushered was not far from the house occupied by Pilate at a later period. It stood alone, and so encompassed by walls that no one outside could hear anything going on within. A gateway through double walls led into a large court enclosed on all sides by buildings. Those to the right and left were of one story; that in the middle, which looked like an old, deserted synagogue, was two stories in height. From all three, doors opened into the court. The middle building was a hall of justice, for I saw in the court before it a stone block, pillars with chains, and such trees as could be bound together by their branches and then suddenly snapped asunder, in order to tear people to pieces.

The mothers were led through the court and into the two side buildings, where they were shut up. It looked to me at first as if they were in a sort of hospital, or lazar-house. When they saw themselves thus unexpectedly deprived of liberty, they began to fear, to cry, and to lament.

The lower story of the court of justice was a great hall like a prison, or guardroom; the upper one was also a large hall from which windows opened upon the court. The officers of justice were assembled in the latter, rolls of writing lying before them on tables. Herod himself was there. He wore his crown and a purple mantle bordered with black and lined with white fur. He stood at the windows with many others, looking down upon the slaughter of the Innocents.

The mothers, one by one, with their boys, were summoned from the side buildings into the great hall under the judgment hall. On their entrance, the children were taken from them by the soldiers and carried out into the court where about twenty others were actively at work with swords and lances, piercing the little creatures through throat and heart. Some of the children were still in swaddling clothes, infants in the mothers' arms; while others, able to run around, wore little woven dresses. The soldiers did not remove the children's clothing but, having pierced them through the heart and throat, they grasped them by one arm or leg and slung them together in a heap. It was a terrible sight![A21]

The mothers were, one after another, pushed back into the large hall by the soldiers. When the fate of their little ones dawned upon them, they raised a frightful cry, tore their hair, and clung to one another. There were so many of them and, toward the last, they were so crowded together that they could scarcely stir. I think the slaughter lasted till near evening. The bodies of the murdered children were buried together in a great pit in the court. I saw the mothers that night fettered, and taken back to their homes by the soldiers. Similar scenes were enacted in other places, for the massacre was carried on during several days.

The number of the Holy Innocents was indicated to me by another number which sounded like ducen, and which I had to repeat until, I think, the whole amounted to seven hundred and seven, or seven hundred and seventeen.

The place of the children's massacre in Jerusalem was the subsequent hall of justice, and not far from that of Pilate; but it was at his time very greatly changed. At Christ's death, I saw the pit in which the murdered children were buried fall in. Their souls appeared and left the place.

Elizabeth had fled with John into the desert. After a long search, she found a cave, and there she remained with him for forty days. After that, I saw that an Essene belonging to the community on Mount Horeb and a relative of Anna the prophetess, brought food to John, at first every eight, afterward every fourteen days, and otherwise provided for him. Before Herod's persecution, John could have been hidden in the neighborhood of his parents' house; but he had made his escape into the desert impelled by divine inspiration. He was destined to grow up in solitude, apart from contact with his fellow beings, and destitute of the customary nourishment of man. I saw that that wilderness produced certain fruits, berries, and herbs.

The Holy Family Goes to Matarea

THE holy family left Heliopolis on account of the persecution they there endured and because Joseph could not obtain work. They took byroads and went still further into the country, journeying southward toward Memphis. Passing through a little town not far from Heliopolis, they halted in the forecourt of an open, pagan temple, and sat down to rest; when, all of a sudden, down tumbled the idol and fell to pieces. It had the head of an ox with triple horns, and several cavities in the body to receive the sacrifices that were to be consumed. At once arose a tumult among the pagan priests; they seized the holy family and threatened them with punishment. But one of them represented to his companions, as they were consulting what measures to take, that the best thing for them to do would be to commend themselves to the God of these strangers; for he remembered, he said, what plagues had come upon their forefathers when they had persecuted those people, and that upon the night of their departure from Egypt the firstborn in every house had died. These words were effectual, and the holy family was left in peace. The pagan priest who had spoken them went soon after to Matarea with several of his people, and there joined the holy family and the Jewish community.

Mary and Joseph next went to Troja, a place on the eastern side of the Nile, opposite Memphis. It was large and very dirty. They had some idea of remaining there, but they were not well received; indeed, they could get not even a drink of water, much less a few dates for which they begged. Memphis lay west of the Nile, which was at that point very broad and contained some islands.

A part of the city lay also on this side of the river and, in Pharaoh's time, a large palace with gardens and high towers, from which Pharaoh's daughter often looked out on the country around. I saw the spot upon which, among the tall bulrushes, the child Moses was found. Memphis was like three cities in one, for it was built on both sides of the Nile, and appeared also to be connected with Babylon, a city lying eastward of the river and nearer to its mouth. In Pharaoh's time, the country in general around the Nile between Heliopolis, Babylon, and Memphis, was so covered with high stone dams and buildings, and so linked together by canals, that those three cities presented the appearance of one large city. But at the time of the holy family, all were separate, immense wastes intervening between them.

The holy travelers proceeded northward from Troja along the river toward Babylon, a dirty, low-lying city. Between the Nile and Babylon, they took the route by which they had come and returned a distance of about two hours. Buildings in ruins were scattered here and there along the whole road. After crossing a small branch of the river, or a canal, they reached Matarea, which was built upon a tongue of land jutting out into the Nile. The river bathed the city on two sides. It was, in general, a wretched enough place, built only of date-wood and solid mud covered with rushes. Joseph found plenty of work here. He built more substantial houses of wickerwork with galleries around them, to which the occupants could go for air and recreation.

Here the holy family dwelt in a dark, vaulted cave that lay in a retired spot on the land side, not far from the gate by which they had entered. Joseph, as at Heliopolis, built a light screen before it. One of the idols in a little temple fell at their arrival and later all the others did the same. The people were in consternation, but one of the priests quieted them by recalling to their remembrance the plagues of Egypt. After some time, as a little community of Jews and converted pagans gathered around the holy family, the priests gave over to them the little temple whose idol had fallen at their coming, and Joseph turned it into a synagogue. Joseph was like the patriarch of the community. He taught them how to sing the psalms correctly, for Judaism in those parts had greatly deteriorated.

Only the poorest Jews dwelt here in Babylon, and that in the most wretched dens and caves. But in the Jewish settlement between On and the Nile they were numerous and better off. They had a regular temple, for they had lapsed into frightful idolatry. They had a golden calf, a figure with an ox's head, around which were ranged other representations of animals like polecats, or ferrets. These last mentioned animals defend people against the crocodile. They had, too, an imitation of the Ark of the Covenant and horrible things in it. The idolatry they practiced was of the most shameful kind and, in a subterranean hall, they carried on the most infamous wickedness, deluded by the hope that from it their Messiah should come forth. They were exceedingly stiff-necked, and would not be converted. Later on, however, many of them left that settlement and went to Babylon, about two hours distant. In doing so, they could not, on account of the numerous dykes and canals, travel by a straight road; they had to make a detour around On.

These Jews of the land of Goshen had already made the acquaintance of the holy family, while the latter abode in On. Mary while there had done various kinds of work for them, such as knitting and embroidering covers and bands. She would never undertake works for vanity or extravagance, but only useful things and religious vestments. I saw women bringing work to her, which they wanted done in accordance with the requirements of vanity and fashion, and Mary returning it although so much in need of the pay she would have received for it. The women mocked and scornfully derided her.

The holy family at first suffered greatly from want. Good water could not be had and wood failed; the inhabitants used only dried grass and reeds for their cooking. The holy family generally ate cold food. Joseph had plenty to do. He improved the poor huts for the people; but they treated him almost like a slave, giving him for his labor only what they themselves thought proper. Sometimes he brought home something as a remuneration for his work, and sometimes he brought nothing. The people were very unskillful in building their huts. They had no wood, excepting here and there a log or two; and even if they had had wood, they had no tools to shape it, for they had only knives of bone or stone. Joseph had brought the most necessary tools with him.

The holy family was soon settled somewhat comfortably. They had little stools and tables, wicker screens, and a well-ordered fireplace also. The Egyptians ate sitting flat on the ground. In the wall of Mary's sleeping place I saw a recess that Joseph had hollowed out, and in it was Jesus's little bed. Mary's couch was beside it, and I have often seen her by night kneeling in prayer to God before that little bed. Joseph slept in another enclosed corner.

The oratory of the holy family was in a passage outside. Joseph and the blessed Virgin had separate places in it and Jesus, too, had his little corner, where he prayed sitting, standing, or kneeling. There was a kind of little altar before the blessed Virgin's place, a small table covered with red and white. This table was like a leaf on hinges that could be let down from or put up against the wall. When let down, it disclosed a shelf in the wall itself and on the shelf were various objects, among them something that was held as sacred. I saw little bushes in pots formed like chalices; a withered, though still whole branch, on top of which was the lily that had blossomed in Joseph's hand when he had been chosen by lot in the temple for Mary's spouse; and something like fine, thin, white sticks that were placed crosswise in the rounded part of the recess. The blossoming lily branch was the top of Joseph's staff; it was stuck in a box about one and a half inches in diameter. The little sticks that were arranged crosswise were also in a box, a transparent one. There were about five of those little white sticks of the thickness of a coarse straw. They were crossed and bound in the middle to a kind of little sheaf. But one pays very little attention to such things when in vision; one's thoughts are chiefly intent upon the holy personages there presented.

I saw that the holy family had to subsist on fruits and bad water. They had been so long without good water that Joseph resolved to saddle the ass, take his leathern bottle, and start for the balsam spring in the desert in order to get some. But the blessed Virgin was told in prayer by an angelic apparition that she should seek and find a spring at the back of their present abode. I saw her going over the hill in which they dwelt to a deep vacant lot that lay at some distance between ruined walls. A large, old tree stood on that ground. Mary had in her hand a rod provided with a little scoop, such as the people of that country commonly carry on journeys. She stuck it into the ground near the tree, and a beautiful, clear stream of water instantly gushed forth. She hurried back joyfully to call Joseph, who soon removed the upper crust of earth and disclosed a well which had long ago been dug out and lined with masonry, but which for some time had been choked up and dry. He soon restored it and paved it around very beautifully with stones.[A22] At the side of the well toward which Mary had approached lay a great stone almost like an altar. I think it was used for that purpose in former times.

The blessed Virgin after that often washed Jesus's clothes and bands here, and dried them in the sun. The well remained unknown and was used only by the holy family until Jesus had grown large enough to go on little errands and even to bring water for his mother. Once I saw him taking other children to the well and giving them a drink of the water, which he scooped up in a hollow, crooked leaf. The little ones told this to their parents, and so the well became known. Others now began to go to it, though it remained principally in the use of the Jews. Even in the time of the holy family it possessed healing properties for the leprous. Later, when a little chapel had been built over the dwelling of the holy family, there was near the high altar a flight of steps leading down to their first abode. There I saw the spring. It was surrounded by dwellings, and its waters used for the cure of leprosy and similar diseases. Even the Turks kept a light burning in the little chapel, and dreaded being overtaken by some misfortune if they neglected it. But the last I saw of the spring, it was lying solitary, surrounded only by trees.

I saw the boy Jesus bringing water from the well for his mother for the first time. Mary was in prayer when the boy slipped to the well with a bottle and brought it back full of water. Mary was unspeakably affected when she saw him coming back with the water. She knelt down and implored him never to do that again, for he might fall into the well. But Jesus replied that he would take care, and that he wanted to render her that service whenever she needed it.

Well of the Virgin

If Joseph happened to be working at a little distance from home, and left a tool lying behind him, I used to see the boy Jesus running after it and bringing it to him. The boy noticed everything. I think the joy that Mary and Joseph experienced on his account must have outweighed all their sufferings. Though perfectly childlike, he was very wise, skilled in everything; he knew and understood everything. I often saw Mary and Joseph filled with unspeakable admiration.

When the boy Jesus took to their owners the covers embroidered or woven by his mother, who hoped to receive bread in return for her work, I often saw him teased at first, and consequently sad. But after awhile the holy family was very much loved by the people. I saw other children giving Jesus figs and dates, while many of their elders sought the holy family for help and consolation. All in trouble said, "Let us go to the Jewish child." I saw the boy going on all kinds of errands, even to a Jewish town a mile distant, to get bread in exchange for his mother's work. The wild animals, numerous on his route, did him no harm; on the contrary, they and even the serpents showed him affection. Once I saw him going with other children to the Jewish town; he was weeping bitterly over the degradation of the Jews.

When he went for the first time alone to that Jewish town, he wore, also for the first time, the brown robe woven by Mary. It was trimmed around the border with yellowish flowers. I saw him kneeling and praying on the way. Two angels appeared to him and spoke of Herod's death, but he said nothing of it to his parents.

The Return of the Holy Family from Egypt

I SAW the holy family's departure from Egypt. Herod was long since dead, but danger still threatened and they could not return. I saw Joseph, who was always busy at his trade, very much troubled one evening. The people for whom he had been working had given him nothing; consequently, he had nothing to take home where there was so much need. He knelt down in the open air and prayed. He was greatly afflicted; his sojourn among these people was becoming intolerable. They practiced infamous idolatry, even sacrificing deformed children. The parent that sacrificed a healthy, well-formed child, was thought to be very pious. They had, besides, still more shameful rites that they carried on in secret. Even the Jews in the Jewish towns were to Joseph objects of horror.

While in his trouble he prayed to God for help, I saw an angel appear to him. He bade him arise, and on the following morning depart from Egypt by the public highroad. He told him also not to fear, for he would accompany him. I saw Joseph hastening with the news to the blessed Virgin and Jesus, and all setting to work to get their few movables packed together on the ass.

Next morning, their intention to depart having become known, crowds of sorrowing neighbors came to them, bringing with them all kinds of gifts in little vessels of bark. Several mothers brought their children. There was among them a noble lady with a little boy of several years. She called him Mary's son, because having long abandoned the hope of having a boy, this child had been vouchsafed to her at Mary's prayer. She gave to the boy Jesus triangular coins, yellow, white, and brown. Jesus first looked at them and then at his mother. This lady's little son was later on admitted by Jesus into the number of his disciples, and was named Deodatus. The mother's name was Mira.

The people of the place, of whom there were more pagans than Jews, were sincerely grieved at the holy family's departure, though a few were glad. These last looked upon them as sorcerers who obtained all they desired through the help of Lucifer, the prince of devils. The Jews could no longer be recognized as Jews, so deeply were they sunk in idolatry.

The holy family started, accompanied by all their friends. They took the direction between On and the Jewish town, turning away from On a little to the south, in order to reach the balsam garden. They wanted to rest there awhile and replenish their water supply. The garden was already flourishing. The balsam trees were as tall as moderately large grapevines and in four rows surrounded the garden, which had an entrance. There were sycamores and all kinds of fruit trees, some like dates. The spring sent a stream around the whole garden. The friends that had accompanied them here took leave, but the holy family remained for some hours. Joseph had made some little vessels out of bark; they were covered with pitch, very smooth and nice. He snapped from the reddish balsam twigs the clover-like leaves, and hung the flasks underneath, in order to gather the balsam drops for the journey. When they stopped to rest, he often made, for their ordinary use, vessels and flasks of that kind out of bark. The blessed Virgin washed and dried some things here. After having rested and refreshed themselves, they proceeded on their way by the common highroad.

I had many visions of their journey, which was made without any special danger to them. Mary was often very much distressed, because walking through the hot sand was so painful for the boy Jesus. Joseph had made for him, out of bark, shoes that reached above the ankle where they were firmly fastened; still I saw the holy travelers frequently pausing while Mary shook the sand out of the child's shoes. She herself wore only sandals. Jesus was dressed in his little brown robe, and they often had to seat him on the ass. [A23] For protection against the scorching rays of the sun, all three wore very broad hats made of bark and fastened under the chin with a string.

I saw them passing by many cities, but I now recall only the name Rameses. At last, I saw them in Gaza, where they stopped for three months. There were many pagans in that city. Joseph did not want to return to Nazareth, but to go to Bethlehem; still he was undecided, because he heard that Archelaus was now reigning over Judea, and he, too, was very cruel. But an angel appeared and put an end to his doubts by telling him that he should return to Nazareth. Anne was still living. She and some of her relatives were the only ones that knew where the holy family was during all those years.

I had a glimpse of the boy Jesus, now seven years old, as he walked between Mary and Joseph on their journey back to Judea from Egypt. I did not see the ass with them then, and they were carrying their bundles themselves. Joseph was about thirty years older than Mary. I saw them on a road in the desert, about two hours' distant from John's cave. The boy Jesus, as he walked, gazed in that direction, and I saw that his soul was turning to John. At the same time, I saw John at prayer in his cave. An angel in the form of a boy appeared to him, telling him that the Savior was passing by. John ran out of the cave and, with outstretched arms, flew toward the point that his Savior was passing. He hopped about and danced with joy. This vision was most touching. John's cave lay deeply buried in a hill. It was not much wider than his own little bed, though it extended some distance in length. The entrance was only a little opening, through which he used to swing himself out. In the top was an oblique aperture that admitted light. I saw in it a reed stand, upon which lay some honeycomb and dried locusts. The latter were yellow and speckled, as large, perhaps, as crabs. The desert in which Jesus fasted is four hours' distance from here. John was clothed in his camel's skin. The angel that appeared to him was like a boy of his own age. I saw him at different periods, small at first and then larger, just as if he were growing up with John. He was not always with him; he used to appear and disappear.

John as a Child Growing Up in the Desert

JOHN had already been long in the desert before the holy family's return from Egypt. That he had retired there at so young an age was due principally to divine inspiration and partly to his own inclinations, for he was of a meditative nature and loved solitude. He was never in a school; the Holy Spirit himself taught him in the desert. He was much talked of even from his childhood, for the wonders attendant on his birth were known and a light was often seen around the child. Herod soon laid snares for him, and even before the children's massacre, Elizabeth was obliged to flee with him into the desert. He could walk and help himself at the time. He took refuge not far from the first cave of Magdalene, and Elizabeth visited him sometimes.

When in his sixth or seventh year, I saw him again led into the desert by his mother. When Elizabeth left the house with the boy, Zechariah was not home. He loved John so much and his grief at losing him was so great that he was obliged to absent himself in order not to witness his departure. He had, however, given him his blessing; for he was in the habit of blessing both mother and child whenever he left home. John wore a garment of skin. It passed from left to right over the shoulder and breast, was fastened under the right arm, and hung down behind. This was his only garment. His hair was brownish and darker than that of Jesus. He bore in his hand a white staff which he had brought with him from home, and which he always kept in the desert.

I saw him as just described hastening across the country by the hand of his mother. Elizabeth was a tall, active, old woman with a small, delicate face, and she was completely enveloped in a large mantle. John often ran on before her, hopping and jumping, perfectly unrestrained and childlike in action, though not distracted in soul. I saw them crossing a river. There was no bridge at that point, and so they crossed on a raft that was floating on the water. Elizabeth was a very resolute person, no difficulty daunted her; she herself rowed the raft across, using for that purpose the branch of a tree. They now turned eastward and entered a ravine, rocky and desolate above, but lower down covered with bushes and overgrown with strawberries. John now and then ate one. After going some distance into the ravine, Elizabeth took leave of John. She blessed him, pressed him to her heart, kissed him on the cheeks and forehead, and turned away, looking back at him as she retraced her steps, weeping. But the boy appeared wholly unconcerned, and quietly walked on deeper into the ravine. I followed the child with a feeling of uneasiness at his going so far from his mother, and fearing that he would not be able to find his way home again. But just then, a voice said to me, "Be not uneasy. The child knows well what he is about." I went with him and, in several visions, saw his whole after life in the desert. He often told me himself how he denied himself in every way and mortified his senses, his understanding becoming clearer and clearer, learning in an unexplainable way something from everything around him. I saw him when a child playing with flowers and animals. The birds were particularly familiar with him. They lighted upon his head when he was walking or praying, and perched upon his staff when he laid it across the branches. There they sat in numbers, while he watched them and played with them. I saw him also going after other animals, following them into their dens, feeding them, playing with them, or earnestly watching them.

At the opposite extremity of this rocky ravine, the country was somewhat more open, and John pressed on until he reached a little lake with a low shore covered with white sand. I saw him there wading far out into the water. The fish swam up and gathered around him; he seemed quite at home with them. He lived in this region a long time, and I saw that he wove for himself out of branches a sleeping hut among the bushes. It was very low and only large enough to allow him to lie in it.

Both here and afterward in other places I often saw by him radiant figures, angels, with whom he treated fearlessly and confidently, though most reverently. They appeared to be teaching him, directing his attention to different things. He had fastened a piece of wood to his staff, thus giving it the form of a cross, also a strip of broad grass, or bark, or leaves like a little flag. He often played with it, waving it here and there. [A24] While he lived in this part of the desert, I saw his mother visiting him twice, but they did not meet at this spot. He must have known when she was coming, for he always went some distance to meet her. Elizabeth brought him a tablet with a slender reed for writing.

After his father's death, John went secretly to Jutta, to console Elizabeth. He remained concealed with her for some time. She told him many things of Jesus and the holy family, some of which he noted down with strokes on his tablet. Elizabeth wanted him to go with her to Nazareth, but he would not. He returned again to the desert.

Once when Zechariah had gone with a herd to the temple, he was set upon by Herod's soldiers and rudely maltreated in a narrow pass on the side of Jerusalem nearest to Bethlehem, at a spot whence the city could not be seen. The soldiers dragged him into a prison on that side of Mount Zion by which, at a later period, the disciples used to ascend. Zechariah was frightfully maltreated, tortured, and at last pierced with a sword, because he would not disclose John's retreat. Elizabeth was at the time in the desert with John. When she returned to Jutta, he accompanied her part of the way, and then went back to the desert. On reaching Jutta, Elizabeth learned of the murder of her husband and great were her lamentations.

Zechariah was buried by his friends in the vicinity of the temple. He is not that Zechariah who was slain between the altar and the temple and whom I saw at the time of the crucifixion with the other risen dead. He issued from that part of the wall in which the aged Simeon once had his cell for prayer, and walked about the temple. The last Zechariah was murdered in a struggle that had taken place among many at the temple, concerning the genealogy of the Messiah and certain privileges and places of individual families.

Elizabeth's sorrow was so great that she could no longer bear to remain in Jutta, without John; consequently, she returned to him in the desert. She soon after died there and was buried by an Essene, a relative of Anna the prophetess. The house in Jutta, a very handsomely ordered one, was occupied by her sister's daughter. John secretly returned to it once after his mother's death, after which he buried himself still deeper in the desert and thenceforth was altogether alone. I saw him journeying to the south around the Dead Sea, then up the eastern side of the Jordan, from wilderness to wilderness toward Kedar and even toward Gessur. When he passed from one wilderness to another, I saw him running through broad fields by night. He went to that region where long after I saw John the Evangelist sitting and writing under the high trees. Under those trees grew bushes with berries, of which he sometimes ate. I saw him also eating a certain herb that bears a white flower and has five round leaves like clover. We have at home herbs like them, only smaller. They grow under the hedges, and the leaves have a sourish taste. When I was a child I used to love to chew them while minding the cattle off in the solitary fields, because I had seen John eating them. I also saw him drawing forth from holes in the trees and picking out of moss on the ground lumps of some brownish-looking stuff, which he ate. I think it was wild honey, for it was very plentiful there. The skin that he had brought with him from home, he now wore around his loins, and over his shoulders hung a brown, shaggy cover which he had woven himself. There were in the desert wool-bearing animals which ran tamely around John, and camels with long hair on their neck. They stood most patiently and allowed him to pull it out. I saw him twisting the hair into cords and weaving from them that covering which he wore hanging around him when he appeared among men and baptized.

I saw him in continual and familiar communication with angels, by whom he was instructed. He slept upon the hard rock and under the open sky, ran over rough stones through thorns and briers, disciplined himself with thistles, wore himself out working on trees and stones, and lay prostrate in prayer and contemplation. He levelled roads, made little bridges, and changed the course of well springs. I often saw him writing in the sand with a reed, kneeling and standing motionless in ecstasy, or praying with outstretched arms. His penance and mortification became more and more severe, his prayer longer and more fervent. He saw the Savior only three times face to face with his bodily eyes. But Jesus was with him in spirit; and John, who was constantly in the prophetic state, saw in spirit the actions of Jesus.

I saw John when full grown. He was a powerful, earnest man. He was standing by a dry well in the desert, and appeared to be in prayer. A light hovered over him like a cloud, and it seemed to me as if it came from on high, from the water above the earth. Then a light, shining stream fell over him into the basin below. While gazing on this torrent, I saw John no longer at the edge of the basin; he was in it, the shining water flowing over him, and the basin filled by the sparkling stream. Then again, I saw him, as at first, standing on the basin's edge; but I did not see him out of it, nor coming out. I think that the whole was perhaps a vision which John himself had had, and by which he was instructed to begin to baptize; or it may have been a spiritual baptism bestowed upon him in vision.

Feast Picture of John the Baptist

I SAW in the desert in which John dwelt a spiritual church rising up out of the waters that flowed in streams from on high, from Paradise, that floated in clouds, and welled up in fountains. The church was immeasurably vast; it seemed to be symbolical of baptism, and it grew with the baptized. It was perfectly transparent like crystal. An octagonal tower arose from the interior and reached up far out of sight. Under it was a great fountain like the baptism fountain of John which he had formed in the desert after a model shown him in vision. In the tower grew a genealogical tree upon which appeared John and his ancestors. There was also an altar, and a wonderful representation of John's conception, birth, circumcision, and life in the desert, of the baptism of Jesus and John's beheading. Far up in the tower, as if on a ladder reaching to heaven, were seen in admirable order the whole host of saints, the entire history of the Promise and the Redemption, and the abodes of the blessed, endless in number. High above all the rest hovered the blessed Virgin in a mantle so wide as to cover all. All these representations were white and transparent. And now came immense crowds from all sides, kings and peoples in all kinds of costumes; they looked like nations that were migrating. Many passed by the baptism church and went into the desert, where there is no water of life. Many others entered the church and knelt down by the baptism fountain, by the side of which stood John under the appearance that he presented as a child in the desert. He struck the water with his little staff and sprinkled it over them. And, no matter how tall they were on entering the church, all that were thus sprinkled became small. But many only passed in and out of the church. They who had become little ones, like unto those that enter the heavenly kingdom, ascended the high, wonderful tower on the ladder that reached to heaven. There were at the baptism holy godparents. The whole church, which appeared to be a building and still was formed of water, floated on high as if supported by a cord let down from heaven.

The Holy Family at Nazareth • Jesus at the Age of Twelve in the Temple of Jerusalem

THERE were three separate rooms in the house at Nazareth, that of the Mother of God being the largest and, most pleasant; in it Jesus, Mary, and Joseph met to pray. I very seldom saw them together at other times. They stood at prayer, their hands crossed upon their breast, and they appeared to speak aloud. I often saw them praying by a light. They stood under a lamp that had several wicks, or near a kind of branched candlestick fastened to the wall, and upon which the flame burned. They were most of the time alone in their respective rooms, Joseph working in his. I saw him cutting sticks and laths, planing wood, and carrying up a beam, Jesus helping him. [A25] Mary was generally engaged sewing or knitting with little needles, at which she sat on the ground, her feet crossed under her, and a little basket at her side. They slept alone, each in a separate room. The bed consisted of a cover which in the morning was rolled up.

I saw Jesus assisting his parents in every possible way, and also on the street and wherever opportunity offered, cheerfully, eagerly, and obligingly helping everyone. He assisted his foster-father in his trade, or devoted himself to prayer and contemplation. He was a model for all the children of Nazareth; they loved him and feared to displease him. When they were naughty and committed faults, their parents used to say to them: "What will Joseph's son say when I tell him this? How sorry he will be!" Sometimes they gently complained to him before the little ones, saying, "Tell them not to do such or such a thing anymore." And Jesus took it playfully and like a little child. He would beg the children affectionately to do so and so, would pray with them to his heavenly Father for strength to become better, and would persuade them to acknowledge their faults and ask pardon on the spot.

About an hour's journey from Nazareth toward Sepphoris, is a little place called Ophna. There, during the boyhood of Jesus, dwelt the parents of James the Greater and of John. In those early years, they associated with Jesus, until their parents removed to Bethsaida and they themselves went to the fishery.

There lived in Nazareth an Essene family related to Joachim. They had four sons, a few years older or younger than Jesus, named respectively, Cleophas, James, Judas, and Japhet. They, too, were playmates of Jesus, and with their parents were in the habit of making the journey to the temple along with the holy family. These four brothers became, at the time of Jesus's baptism, disciples of John, and after his murder, disciples of Jesus. When Andrew and Saturnin crossed the Jordan to Jesus, they followed them and spent the whole day with him. They were among those disciples of John whom Jesus took with him to the marriage feast at Cana. Cleophas is the same to whom, in company with Luke, Jesus appeared at Emmaus. He was married and dwelt at Emmaus. His wife afterward joined the women of the community.

Jesus was tall and slender with a delicate face and a beaming countenance and though pale, he was healthy-looking. His perfectly straight, golden hair was parted over his high, open forehead and fell upon his shoulders. He wore a long, light-brownish gray tunic, which reached to his feet, the sleeves rather wide around the hand.

At the age of eight years, Jesus went for the first time with his parents to Jerusalem for Passover, and every succeeding year he did the same.

In those first visits, Jesus had already excited attention in Jerusalem among the friends with whom he and his parents stayed, also among the priests and doctors. They spoke, of the pious, intelligent child, of Joseph's extraordinary son, just as amongst us one might, at the annual pilgrimages, notice in particular this or that modest, holy-looking person, this or that clever peasant child, and recognize him again the next year. So Jesus had already some acquaintances in the city when, in his twelfth year, with their friends and their sons, he accompanied his parents to Jerusalem. His parents were accustomed to walk with the people from their own part of the country, and they knew that Jesus, who now made the journey for the fifth time, always went with the other youths from Nazareth.

But this time Jesus had, on the return journey not far from the Mount of Olives, separated from his companions, who all thought that he had joined his parents who were following. Jesus had, however, gone to that side of Jerusalem nearest to Bethlehem, to the inn at which the holy family before Mary's Purification had put up. Mary and Joseph thought him on ahead with the other Nazarenes, while these latter thought that he was following with his parents. When at last they all met at Gophna, the anxiety of Mary and Joseph at his absence was very great.[A26] They returned at once to Jerusalem, making inquiries after him on the way and everywhere in the city itself. But they could not find him, since he had not been where they usually stayed. Jesus had slept at the inn before the Bethlehem gate, where the people knew him and his parents. [A26]

There he had joined several youths and gone with them to two schools of the city, the first day to one, the second

Jerusalem in the Distance from Among the Olives

to another. On the morning of the third day, he had gone to a third school at the temple, and in the afternoon into the temple itself where his parents found him. These schools were all different, and not all exactly schools of the Law. Other branches were taught in them. The last mentioned was in the neighborhood of the temple and from it the Levites and priests were chosen.

Jesus by his questions and answers so astonished and embarrassed the doctors and rabbis of all these schools that they resolved, on the afternoon of the third day, in the public lecture hall of the temple and in presence of the rabbis most deeply versed in the various sciences "to humble the boy Jesus." The scribes and doctors had concerted the plan together; for, although pleased at first, they had in the end become vexed at him. They met in the public lecture hall in the middle of the temple porch in front of the sanctuary, in the round place where later Jesus also taught. There I saw Jesus sitting in a large chair which he did not, by a great deal, fill. Around him was a crowd of aged Jews in priestly robes. They were listening attentively and appeared to be perfectly furious. [A27] I feared they would lay hands upon him. On the top of the chair in which Jesus was sitting were brown heads like those of dogs. They were greenish brown, the upper parts glistening and sparkling with a yellow light. There were similar heads and figures upon several long tables, or benches, that stood in the temple sideways from this place, covered with offerings. The place was very large and so crowded that one could scarcely imagine himself in a church.

As Jesus had in the schools illustrated his answers and explanations by all kinds of examples from nature, art, and science, the scribes and doctors had diligently gathered together masters in all these branches. They now began, one by one, to dispute with him. He remarked that although, properly speaking, such subjects did not appear appropriate to the temple, yet he would discuss them since such was his Father's will. But they understood not that he referred to his heavenly Father; they imagined that Joseph had commanded him to show off his learning.

Jesus now answered and taught upon medicine. He described the whole human body in a way far beyond the reach of even the most learned. He discoursed with the same facility upon astronomy, architecture, agriculture, geometry, arithmetic, jurisprudence and, in fine, upon every subject proposed to him. He applied all so skillfully to the Law and the Promise, to the prophecies, to the temple, to the mysteries of worship and sacrifice that his hearers, surprised and confounded, passed successively from astonishment and admiration to fury and shame. They were enraged at hearing some things that they never before knew, and at hearing others that they had never before understood.

Jesus had been teaching two hours, when Joseph and Mary entered the temple. They inquired after their child of the Levites whom they knew, and received for answer that he was with the doctors in the lecture hall. But as they were not at liberty to enter that hall, they sent one of the Levites in to call Jesus. Jesus sent them word that he must first finish what he was then about. Mary was very much troubled at his not obeying at once, for this was the first time he had given his parents to understand that he had other commands than theirs to fulfill. He continued to teach for another hour, and then he left the hall and joined his parents in the porch of Israel, the women's porch, leaving his hearers confounded, confused, and enraged. Joseph was quite awed and astonished, but he kept a humble silence. [A28] Mary, however, drawing near to Jesus, said, "Child, why hast thou done this to us? Behold, thy father and I have sought thee sorrowing!" But Jesus answered gravely, "Why have you sought me? Do you not know that I must be about my Father's business?" But they did not understand. They at once began with him their journey home. The bystanders gazed at them in astonishment, and I was in dread lest they should lay hands upon the boy, for I saw that some of them were full of rage. I wondered at their allowing the holy family to depart so peaceably. Although the crowd was dense, yet a wide path was made to permit the holy family to pass. I saw all the details and heard almost the whole of Jesus's teaching, but I cannot remember all. It made a great impression upon the scribes. Some recorded the affair as a notable event, while here and there it was whispered around, giving rise to all kinds of remarks and false reports. But the true statement, the scribes kept to themselves. They spoke of Jesus as of a very forward boy, possessed indeed of fine talents, but said those talents required to be cultivated.

I saw the holy family again leaving the city, outside of which they joined a party of about three men, two women, and some children. I did not know them, but they appeared to be from Nazareth. They went together to different places around Jerusalem, also to the Mount of Olives. They wandered around the beautiful pleasure grounds there found, occasionally standing to pray, their hands crossed on their breast. I saw them also going over a bridge that spanned a brook. This walking around and praying of the little party reminded me forcibly of a pilgrimage.

When Jesus had returned to Nazareth, I saw a feast in Anne's house, at which were gathered all the youths and maidens among their friends and relatives. I know not whether it was a feast of rejoicing at Jesus's having been found, a feast solemnized upon the return from the Passover journey, or a feast customary upon the completion of a son's twelfth year. Whatever it may have been, Jesus appeared to be the object of it.

Beautiful bowers were erected over the table, from which hung garlands of vine leaves and ears of corn. The children were served with grapes and little rolls. There were present at this feast thirty-three boys, all future disciples of Jesus, and I received an instruction upon the years of Jesus's life. During the whole feast, Jesus instructed the other boys, and explained to them a very wonderful parable which, however, was only imperfectly understood. It was of a marriage feast at which water could be turned into wine and the lukewarm guests into zealous friends; and again, of a marriage feast where the wine could be changed into blood and the bread into flesh, which blood and flesh would abide with the guests until the end of the world as strength and consolation, as a living bond of union. He said also to one of the youths, a relative of his own named Nathaniel: "I shall be present at thy marriage."

From his twelfth year, Jesus was always like a teacher among his companions. He often sat among them instructing them or walked about the country with them.

Death of Joseph • *Jesus and Mary in Capernaum*

AS the time drew near for Jesus to begin his mission of teaching, I saw him ever more solitary and meditative; and toward the same time, the thirtieth year of Jesus, Joseph began to decline. I saw Jesus and Mary often with him. Mary sometimes sat on the ground by his couch, or upon a low, round three-legged stool, which served also for a table. I seldom saw them eating; but when they did, or brought some refreshment to Joseph's bedside, it consisted of three, white, rather long, four-cornered pieces, about two fingers in breadth, that lay side by side on a little plate, and I saw also some little fruits in a dish. They gave him something to drink out of a mug.

When Joseph was dying, Mary sat at the head of his bed, holding him in her arms. Jesus stood just below her near Joseph's breast. The whole room was brilliant with light and full of angels. After his death, his hands were crossed on his breast, he was wrapped from head to foot in a white winding sheet, laid in a narrow casket, and placed in a very beautiful tomb, the gift of a good man. Only a few men followed the coffin with Jesus and Mary; but I saw it accompanied by angels and environed with light. Joseph's remains were afterward removed by the Christians to Bethlehem, and interred. I think I can still see him lying there incorrupt.

Joseph had of necessity to die before the Lord, for he could not have endured his crucifixion; he was too gentle, too loving. He had already suffered much from the persecution Jesus had had to support from the malice of the Jews from his twentieth to his thirtieth year; for they could not bear the sight of him. Their jealousy often made them exclaim that the carpenter's son thought he knew everything better than others, that he was frequently at variance with the teachings of the Pharisees, and that he always had around him a crowd of young followers.

Mary never ceased to suffer from these persecutions. Such pains always seem to me sharper than those of martyrdom. Unspeakable was the love with which Jesus in his youth bore the jealous persecution of the Jews.

After Joseph's death, Jesus and Mary removed to a little village of only a few houses between Capernaum and Bethsaida. A man named Levi, who was very much attached to the holy family, had given Jesus a house there in which to dwell. It stood alone surrounded by a ditch of standing water. A couple of Levi's people also were in the house in the capacity of servants, and Levi himself supplied all necessaries from Capernaum. It was to this little place that Peter's father retired when he gave over to him the fishery at Bethsaida.

Jesus had already many followers among the young people of Nazareth, but they were not faithful to him. He walked with them in the country around the lake and went up to Jerusalem with them for the feasts. The Lazarus family in Bethany were already acquainted with the holy family. The Pharisees of Nazareth were against Jesus; they called him a vagrant. Levi gave him that house that he might, without fear of disturbance, live in it and gather his followers around him.

There was on the lake around Capernaum a region of extraordinarily fertile and charming valleys. There were several harvests during the year, and uncommonly beautiful leaves, blossoms, and fruits—all at the same time. Many distinguished Jews had gardens and castles there, Herod among their number. The Jews of Jesus's time were no longer like their fathers; through commerce and their contact with pagans, they had become very corrupt. One never saw the women in public nor at work in the fields, excepting the very poorest gleaning some ears of corn. They were to be seen only on pilgrimages to Jerusalem and other holy places. Husbandry and all kinds of traffic were carried on mostly through slaves. I have seen all the cities of Galilee. Where now scarcely three villages are in existence, there were then almost a hundred and an innumerable crowd of people.

Mary Cleophas, who with her third husband, the father of Simeon of Jerusalem, dwelt in Anne's house near Nazareth, afterward removed with her boy Simeon to Mary's in Nazareth. The rest of her family and her servants remained at Anne's.

When Jesus, a short time after, went from Capernaum by way of Nazareth to the region of Hebron, he was accompanied by Mary as far as Nazareth, where she awaited his return. She was always so solicitous about him. There came also to comfort the holy family on the death of Joseph and to see Jesus again, Joseph Barsabbas, the son of Mary Cleophas by her second marriage with Sabbas, and the three sons of her first marriage with Alpheus: Simon, James the Less, and Thaddeus, all three of whom already carried on business away from home. They had had no close communication with Jesus since his childhood. They knew in general of Simeon's and Anna's prophecies on the occasion of his presentation in the temple, but they attached no importance to them. They preferred to follow John the Baptist, who soon after passed through these parts.

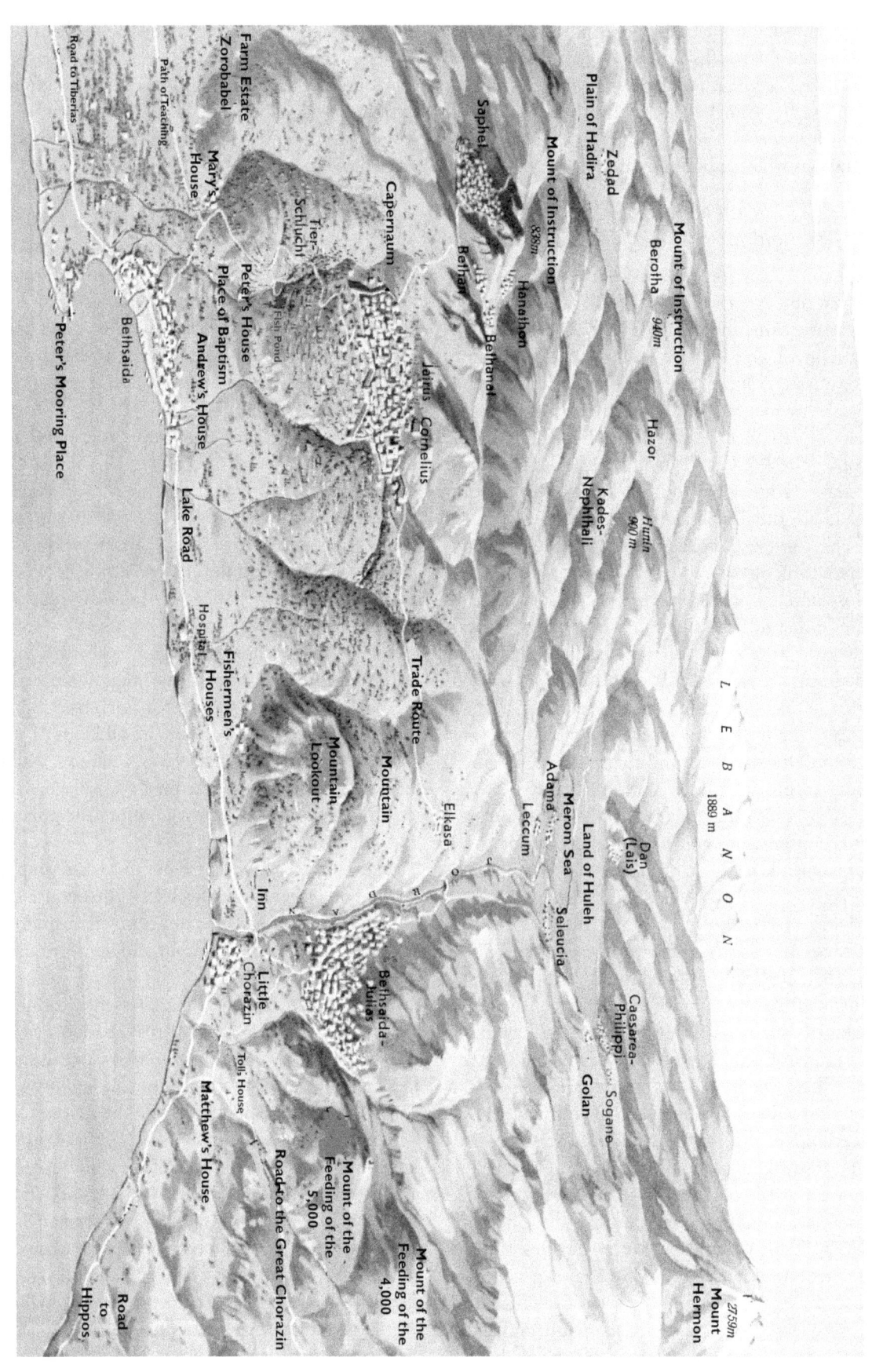

Area around Capernaum during Time of Christ

TISSOT ILLUSTRATIONS
[Section A]

The Virgin Mary & The Childhood of Jesus

⊕

Zechariah and Elizabeth · · · · · · · · · · · · · · · · · 238	The Magi in the House of Herod · · · · · · · · · · · · 266
The Vision of Zechariah · · · · · · · · · · · · · · · · · · 240	The Adoration of the Magi · · · · · · · · · · · · · · · · 268
The Testing of the Suitors of the Holy Virgin · · · 242	The Aged Simeon · 269
Betrothal of the Holy Virgin and Joseph · · · · · · · 244	The Presentation of Jesus in the Temple · · · · · · · 270
The Annunciation · 246	The Flight into Egypt · 272
The Visitation · 248	The Sojourn in Egypt · 274
The Magnificat · 250	The Massacre of the Innocents · · · · · · · · · · · · · · 276
The Anxiety of Joseph · 252	Jesus and his Mother at the Spring · · · · · · · · · · · 278
The Vision of Joseph · 254	The Return from Egypt · · · · · · · · · · · · · · · · · · · 280
Joseph Seeks a Lodging in Bethlehem · · · · · · · · 256	The Childhood of John the Baptist · · · · · · · · · · · 282
The Birth of Jesus · 258	The Youth of Jesus · 284
The Angel and the Shepherds · · · · · · · · · · · · · · 260	It is Noticed that Jesus is Lost · · · · · · · · · · · · · · · 286
The Adoration of the Shepherds · · · · · · · · · · · · 262	Jesus Among the Doctors · · · · · · · · · · · · · · · · · · 288
The Magi Journeying · 264	Jesus Found in the Temple · · · · · · · · · · · · · · · · · 290

Zechariah and Elizabeth [A1]

⊕

I SAW Zechariah conversing with Elizabeth. He was telling her how sad he was because his turn to offer sacrifice in the temple was drawing near, and how he dreaded the contempt that would there await him on account of his being childless. He owned a little property in the neighborhood of Jutta. It consisted of a house, an orchard, and a spring. I saw him there also with the holy family at the time of Mary's Visitation. [177]

The Vision of Zechariah [A2]

⊕

ZECHARIAH went into the Holy of Holies, where it was dark. It appeared to me that he took the Tables of the Law out of the Ark of the Covenant, and laid them upon the golden altar of incense. When he kindled the incense, I saw to the right of the altar a light coming down on him and in it a luminous figure. Zechariah, frightened, stepped back and sank, as if in ecstasy, at the right side of the altar. The angel raised him up and spoke some words to him. Zechariah wore his festive robes the whole of the sabbath. They consisted of a long, white garment with rather narrow sleeves. He was girdled with a broad cincture, wound many times around him. On it were letters, and from it hung straps. This garment was provided with a cowl, which hung in plaits from the head down the back like a folded veil. When he moved or performed any action, he threw this garment rolled together with the ends of the girdle up over one shoulder, and stuck it into the girdle under his arm. His lower limbs were loosely bound, and the strip enveloping them fastened by the straps that kept the soles in place upon his naked feet. [178]

[LUKE 1:8–22] 8 Now while he was serving as priest before God when his division was on duty, 9 according to the custom of the priesthood, it fell to him by lot to enter the temple of the Lord and burn incense. 10 And the whole multitude of the people were praying outside at the hour of incense. 11 And there appeared to him an angel of the Lord standing on the right side of the altar of incense. 12 And Zechariah was troubled when he saw him, and fear fell upon him. 13 But the angel said to him, "Do not be afraid, Zechariah, for your prayer is heard, and your wife Elizabeth will bear you a son, and you shall call his name John. 14 And you will have joy and gladness, and many will rejoice at his birth; 15 for he will be great before the Lord, and he shall drink no wine nor strong drink, and he will be filled with the Holy Spirit, even from his mother's womb. 16 And he will turn many of the sons of Israel to the Lord their God, 17 and he will go before him in the spirit and power of Elijah, to turn the hearts of the fathers to the children, and the disobedient to the wisdom of the just, to make ready for the Lord a people prepared." 18 And Zechariah said to the angel, "How shall I know this? For I am an old man, and my wife is advanced in years." 19 And the angel answered him, "I am Gabriel, who stand in the presence of God; and I was sent to speak to you, and to bring you this good news. 20 And behold, you will be silent and unable to speak until the day that these things come to pass, because you did not believe my words, which will be fulfilled in their time." 21 And the people were waiting for Zechariah, and they wondered at his delay in the temple. 22 And when he came out, he could not speak to them, and they perceived that he had seen a vision in the temple; and he made signs to them and remained dumb.

The Testing of the Suitors of the Holy Virgin [A3]

⊕

THEREUPON I saw that all the unmarried men in the country of the House of David were summoned to the temple. Many of them made their appearance in holiday attire. Then the high priest gave to each of the suitors a branch which was to be held in the hand during the offering of prayer and sacrifice. After that, all the branches were laid in the Holy of Holies with the understanding that he whose branch should blossom was to be Mary's husband. But all the branches failed to blossom. I saw the priests, after this, hunting through different rolls of writing in their search for another descendant of the House of David, one that had not presented himself among the suitors for Mary's hand. And there they found that, among the six brothers of Bethlehem, one was unknown and ignored. They sought him out and so discovered Joseph's retreat, six miles from Jerusalem, near Samaria. He was told to go up to the temple. He went, accordingly, arrayed in his best. A branch was given him. As he was about to lay it upon the altar, it blossomed on top into a white flower like a lily. At the same time I saw a light like the Holy Spirit hovering over him. He was then led to Mary, who was in her chamber, and she accepted him as her spouse. [179]

ACCORDING to the Apocryphal Gospels, the claims of the various suitors of the holy Virgin were tested in the following manner. The suitors, who had all to be of the race of David, and must none of them have contracted any other alliance, each brought with him a rod. All these rods were placed in the Holy of Holies, and the owner of the rod which should flower would be the one chosen to be the husband of Mary. The legend tells us that there were three thousand suitors, but that Joseph, dreading the test, held himself aloof on the appointed day; however, the high priest, Abiathar, wearing the sacerdotal robes with the twelve bells, came forth from the Holy of Holies, bearing in his hand the rod of Joseph, which had been pointed out to him by an angel. When it was given to Joseph, a white dove issued from it, and soaring up to heaven, disappeared.

Betrothal of the Holy Virgin and Joseph [A4]

⊕

THE espousals were celebrated in Jerusalem, on Mount Zion in a house often used for such feasts. The marriage feast lasted seven or eight days. The women and the virgins, companions of Mary in the temple, were present, also many relatives of Joachim and Anne, and two daughters from Gophna. I have had a clear vision of Mary in her bridal dress. She wore a colored, woolen underdress without sleeves, her arms encircled by white, woolen fillets. On the breast and as high as the neck, lay a white collar ornamented with jewels, pearls, etc. Then came a kind of gown open in front, wide like a mantle from top to bottom, and with flowing sleeves. This gown was blue, embroidered with large red, white, and yellow roses and green leaves, something like the ancient vestments worn at Mass. It fastened around the neck on the white collar, and the lower border was edged with fringes and tassels. Over this was a kind of scapular of white- and gold-flowered silk, set over the breast with pearls and shining stones. It lay upon the front opening of the dress, and reached to the edge of the same; it was about two feet wide and was fringed with tassels and balls. A corresponding strip hung down the back, while shorter and narrower ones fell over the shoulders and arms. The wide sleeves were tightly fastened in the middle of the upper and the lower arm by buckles, puffing out around the shoulders, the elbows, and the wrists.... The blessed Virgin had auburn hair, dark eyebrows, fine and arched, a very high forehead, large downcast eyes with long, dark lashes, a straight nose, delicate and rather long, a lovely mouth around which played a most noble expression, and a pointed chin. She was of medium height, and she moved very gently and gravely, looking very bashful in her rich attire. After the marriage feast, she wore another dress. It was striped and less magnificent than the one described. I have a scrap of it among my relics. This striped dress she wore at Cana and on other holy occasions. She wore her wedding suit once again in the temple. [180]

[LUKE 1:26–27] 26 In the sixth month the angel Gabriel was sent from God to a city of Galilee named Nazareth, 27 to a virgin betrothed to a man whose name was Joseph, of the house of David; and the virgin's name was Mary.

JEWISH *weddings were celebrated on the fourth day of the week, or the fifth if the bride were a widow. It must, therefore, have been on a Wednesday or a Thursday that the marriage of Joseph and Mary took place. The bride always entered her new home at sunset. This part of the ceremony was looked upon as most important; and the marriage itself was also sometimes spoken of as the Reception or Introduction of the wife. The bride and bridegroom often each wore a crown. They advanced to the sound of a drum and other instruments of music, beneath a canopy of painted material, from which, in the case of wealthy families, ornaments of gold were suspended.*

The Annunciation [A5]

⊕

I SAW the blessed Virgin a short time after her marriage in the house of Nazareth. Joseph was not there. He was at that moment journeying with two beasts of burden on the road to Tiberias, whither he was going to get his tools. But Anne was in the house with her maid and two of the virgins who had been with Mary in the temple. Everything in the house had been newly arranged by Anne. Toward evening, they all prayed standing around a circular stool from which they afterward ate vegetables that had been served. Anne seemed to be very busy about the household affairs, and for a time she moved around here and there, while the blessed Virgin ascended the steps to her room. There she put on a long, white, woolen garment, such as it was customary to wear during prayer, a girdle around her waist, and a yellowish-white veil over her head. She gently sank on her knees, her back turned to her couch, the door of the chamber to her right. The floor was carpeted. Mary lowered her veil over her face and folded her hands, but not the fingers, upon her breast. I saw her praying for a long time with intense fervor. She knelt long, as if in ecstasy, her face raised to heaven; then she drooped her head upon her breast and thus continued her prayer. And now she glanced to the right and beheld a radiant youth with flowing, yellow hair. It was the archangel Gabriel. His feet did not touch the ground. In an oblique line and surrounded by an effulgence of light and glory, he came floating down to Mary. The lamp grew dim, for the whole room was lighted up by the glory. The angel, with hands gently raised before his breast, spoke to Mary. I saw the words like letters of glittering light issuing from his lips. Mary replied, but without looking up. Then the angel again spoke and Mary, as if in obedience to his command, raised her veil a little, glanced at him, and said, "Behold the handmaid of the Lord. May it be done unto me according to thy word!" [183]

[LUKE 1:28–38] 28 And he came to her and said, "Hail, O favored one, the Lord is with you!" 29 But she was greatly troubled at the saying, and considered in her mind what sort of greeting this might be. 30 And the angel said to her, "Do not be afraid, Mary, for you have found favor with God. 31 And behold, you will conceive in your womb and bear a son, and you shall call his name Jesus. 32 He will be great, and will be called the Son of the Most High; and the Lord God will give to him the throne of his father David, 33 and he will reign over the house of Jacob for ever; and of his kingdom there will be no end." 34 And Mary said to the angel, "How shall this be, since I have no husband?" 35 And the angel said to her, "The Holy Spirit will come upon you, and the power of the Most High will overshadow you; therefore the child to be born will be called holy, the Son of God. 36 And behold, your kinswoman Elizabeth in her old age has also conceived a son; and this is the sixth month with her who was called barren. 37 For with God nothing will be impossible." 38 And Mary said, "Behold, I am the handmaid of the Lord; let it be to me according to your word." And the angel departed from her.

The Visitation [A6]

⊕

ZECHARIAH'S house stood upon a solitary hill, and other dwellings were scattered around. Not far from it, a tolerably large brook flowed down from the mountain. Elizabeth had learned in vision that one of her race was to give birth to the Messiah; she had dwelt in thought upon Mary, had very greatly desired to see her. Elizabeth was advanced in years. She was tall, her face small and delicate, and she wore something wrapped around her head. She was acquainted with Mary only by hearsay. [184]

[LUKE 1:39–45, 56–64] 39 In those days Mary arose and went with haste into the hill country, to a city of Judah, 40 and she entered the house of Zechariah and greeted Elizabeth. 41 And when Elizabeth heard the greeting of Mary, the babe leaped in her womb; and Elizabeth was filled with the Holy Spirit 42 and she exclaimed with a loud cry, "Blessed are you among women, and blessed is the fruit of your womb! 43 And why is this granted me, that the mother of my Lord should come to me? 44 For behold, when the voice of your greeting came to my ears, the babe in my womb leaped for joy. 45 And blessed is she who believed that there would be a fulfilment of what was spoken to her from the Lord." . . . 56 And Mary remained with her about three months, and returned to her home. 57 Now the time came for Elizabeth to be delivered, and she gave birth to a son. 58 And her neighbors and kinsfolk heard that the Lord had shown great mercy to her, and they rejoiced with her. 59 And on the eighth day they came to circumcise the child; and they would have named him Zechariah after his father, 60 but his mother said, "Not so; he shall be called John." 61 And they said to her, "None of your kindred is called by this name." 62 And they made signs to his father, inquiring what he would have him called. 63 And he asked for a writing tablet, and wrote, "His name is John." And they all marvelled. 64 And immediately his mouth was opened and his tongue loosed, and he spoke, blessing God.

The Magnificat [A7]

⊕

ZECHARIAH was a tall, handsome old man clothed like a priest. He and Joseph sat together at the side of the house that opened on the garden, in which Mary and Elizabeth were now sitting on a rug under a high, spreading tree. Behind the tree was a fountain from which gushed water when a spigot was pressed. I saw grass and flowers around, and trees bearing little, yellow plums. In the evening they all sat together again in the garden near a lamp under the tree. [185]

[LUKE 1:46–56] 46 And Mary said, "My soul magnifies the Lord, 47 and my spirit rejoices in God my Savior, 48 for he has regarded the low estate of his handmaiden. For behold, henceforth all generations will call me blessed; 49 for he who is mighty has done great things for me, and holy is his name. 50 And his mercy is on those who fear him from generation to generation. 51 He has shown strength with his arm, he has scattered the proud in the imagination of their hearts, 52 he has put down the mighty from their thrones, and exalted those of low degree; 53 he has filled the hungry with good things, and the rich he has sent empty away. 54 He has helped his servant Israel, in remembrance of his mercy, 55 as he spoke to our fathers, to Abraham and to his posterity for ever." 56 And Mary remained with her about three months, and returned to her home.

THE journey from Nazareth to Aïn-Karim, where Elizabeth dwelt, must have taken about four days, the way having been both steep and rough. The hills of Samaria and Judea, cutting right across the road thither, and the wild valley, known as the Wady-el-Arimaïeh, or that of Robbers, which had to be traversed in going from Samaria to Jerusalem, must have made the journey extremely arduous, especially for the holy Virgin, in the state she was then in. It is natural to suppose that they passed the last night at Jerusalem, and that they arrived at Aïn-Karim, three hours' journey beyond that town, early on the next day.—Was it at the first interview with Elizabeth that the Virgin uttered the hymn of the Magnificat? Was it not more likely at the time of the private out-pouring of confidences between the two, which must have taken place later on? It seems to us much more natural that it should have been then, and we have therefore chosen, as the setting of the scene fraught with such sacred mystery, the secluded garden of Elizabeth. In the midst of an exchange of their strange and wonderful experiences, Mary was suddenly possessed by the Spirit of God, and, in a kind of prophetic ecstasy, she poured forth her joy at her coming maternity, her humble acceptance of the will of the Almighty, her inspired insight into the grandeur of the Divine plan.

The Anxiety of Joseph [A8]

⊕

THE blessed Virgin remained with Elizabeth three months, until after the birth of John, but she returned to Nazareth before his circumcision. Joseph went to meet her halfway on the journey, and for the first time noticed that she was pregnant. But he gave no sign of his knowledge, and struggled with his doubts. Mary, who had feared this, was silent and preoccupied, thus increasing his uneasiness. When arrived in Nazareth, Mary went to the parents of the deacon Parmenas and remained some days with them. Joseph's anxiety had meanwhile increased to such a degree that, when Mary returned home, he determined to flee from the house. Then the angel appeared to him and consoled him. [187]

[MATTHEW 1:18–19] 18 Now the birth of Jesus Christ took place in this way. When his mother Mary had been betrothed to Joseph, before they came together she was found to be with child of the Holy Spirit; 19 and her husband Joseph, being a just man and unwilling to put her to shame, resolved to divorce her quietly.

IN chapter sixteen of the so-called Protevangelium of St. James the Less, in the collection of the Apocryphal Gospels, we are told that Joseph was struck with stupor, and thought to himself: "What shall I do with her? And he said: If I hide her sin, I shall be guilty according to the Law of God; and if I accuse her and betray her to the Sons of Israel, I fear that I shall be unjust and deliver the blood of the innocent to the condemnation of death. What shall I do with her? I will leave her secretly." Such were the thoughts which haunted the mind of Joseph and hindered him in his work.—To explain the point of view of my picture, I must add that I have imagined the following scene. Joseph is in his workshop, which is on the way leading to the well. It is early morning, when the women go to fetch the water needed for the day, and Joseph's tender affection for her to whom he has recently become betrothed leads him to watch for the moment when she will pass. Certain alarming signs about his young bride, though he had been vaguely conscious of them, had not as yet shaken his confidence in her. But now, as he watches her pass his workshop day by day, these signs of something unusual recur to his memory, his anxiety is aroused and at last the truth is forced on his mind beyond a doubt. He can no longer hope that he has been mistaken, he understands it all now; he can work no more; he abandons the task he had begun, and gives himself up to his painful forebodings. I have accepted the tradition that Saint Joseph practiced the trade of a carpenter or something similar to it. According to some traditions he made the yokes of ploughs and the wood-work of implements of husbandry. Others, founded probably on his sojourn in Egypt, say that he made the trellis-work used, especially in that country, to make partitions between the rooms of houses, to take the place of windows and to ornament balconies. However this may be, there is no doubt that Joseph occupied a very humble position. Though he was of royal lineage, his family had retained none of its ancient splendor, and he himself lived in a quiet secluded way, congenial, doubtless, to the humility and modesty of his character.

The Vision of Joseph [A9]

⊕

I SAW Joseph returned from Jerusalem. He had taken thither cattle for sacrifice, and had put up at the house before the Bethlehem gate. It was at this same inn that he and Mary stopped later on, before Mary's Purification. The keeper of the inn was an Essene. Joseph went from there to Bethlehem, but did not visit his relatives. He was looking around after a place to build, also for some means of procuring lumber and tools, for in the spring after Mary's delivery, which he thought would take place in Nazareth, he intended to remove with her to Bethlehem, as he did not care for Nazareth. He wanted to get a place near the inn of the Essene. From Bethlehem he went again to Jerusalem, to offer sacrifice. When he was returning from this journey to Jerusalem, and about midnight was crossing the field of Kimki, six hours from Nazareth, an angel appeared to him and said that he should set out at once with Mary for Bethlehem, as it was there that her child was to be born. The angel told him, moreover, that he should provide himself with a few necessaries, but no laces nor embroidered covers, and he mentioned all the other things he was to take. Joseph was very much surprised. [188]

[MATTHEW 1:20–25] 20 But as he considered this, behold, an angel of the Lord appeared to him in a dream, saying, "Joseph, son of David, do not fear to take Mary your wife, for that which is conceived in her is of the Holy Spirit; 21 she will bear a son, and you shall call his name Jesus, for he will save his people from their sins." 22 All this took place to fulfill what the Lord had spoken by the prophet: 23 "Behold, a virgin shall conceive and bear a son, and his name shall be called Emmanuel" (which means, God with us). 24 When Joseph woke from sleep, he did as the angel of the Lord commanded him; he took his wife, 25 but knew her not until she had borne a son; and he called his name Jesus.

Joseph Seeks a Lodging in Bethlehem [A10]

⊕

JOSEPH then went with Mary straight to Bethlehem, on whose outskirts the houses stood scattered, and into the heart of the city. At the different streets they met, he left Mary and the ass standing while he went up and down in search of an inn. Mary often had to wait long before Joseph, anxious and troubled, returned. [193]

[LUKE 2:3–5] 3 And all went to be enrolled, each to his own city. 4 And Joseph also went up from Galilee, from the city of Nazareth, to Judea, to the city of David, which is called Bethlehem, because he was of the house and lineage of David, 5 to be enrolled with Mary, his betrothed, who was with child.

IT is three days' walk, by the direct road from Nazareth to Bethlehem; and if you go by way of Jerusalem, four days are required. The travelers summoned to be taxed by the decree of Caesar Augustus, when Cyrenius was Governor of Syria, must have been very numerous, and the one caravansary the town could boast must have been quite insufficient to accommodate them all. As a matter of fact we must understand by the "diversorium" used in the Vulgate a simple caravansary and not a regular hostelry properly so called, such as is implied in most translations of the Gospels. The sort of establishment to which we apply the term of hostelry, or inn, would have been altogether foreign to the Oriental usages of the time

The Birth of Jesus [A11]

⊕

WHEN Mary told Joseph that her time was drawing near and that he should now betake himself to prayer, he left her and turned toward his sleeping place to do her bidding. Before entering his little recess, he looked back once toward that part of the cave where Mary knelt upon her couch in prayer, her back to him, her face toward the east. He saw the cave filled with the light that streamed from Mary, for she was entirely enveloped as if by flames. It was as if he were, like Moses, looking into the burning bush. He sank prostrate to the ground in prayer, and looked not back again. The glory around Mary became brighter and brighter, the lamps that Joseph had lit were no longer to be seen. Mary's flowing white robe spread out before her.

At the twelfth hour, her prayer became ecstatic, and I saw her raised so far above the ground that one could see it beneath her. Her hands were crossed upon her breast, and the light around her grew even more resplendent. I no longer saw the roof of the cave. Above Mary stretched a pathway of light up to heaven, in which pathway it seemed as if one light came forth from another, as if one figure dissolved into another, and from these different spheres of light other heavenly figures issued. Mary continued in prayer, her eyes bent low upon the ground.

At that moment she gave birth to the infant Jesus. I saw him like a tiny, shining child, lying on the rug at her knees, and brighter far than all the other brilliancy. He seemed to grow before my eyes. But dazzled by the glittering and flashing of light, I know not whether I really saw that, or how I saw it. Even inanimate nature seemed stirred. The stones of the rocky floor and the walls of the cave were glimmering and sparkling, as if instinct with life. Mary's ecstasy lasted some moments longer. Then I saw her spread a cover over the child, but she did not yet take it up, nor even touch it. [195]

[LUKE 2:6–7] 6 And while they were there, the time came for her to be delivered. 7 And she gave birth to her first-born son and wrapped him in swaddling cloths, and laid him in a manger, because there was no place for them in the inn.

IT will be well to say a few words about this town of Bethlehem where the first years of Jesus's childhood were passed. Beth-leem or Bethlehem is also known by the Hebrew name of Ephrata. These words mean the "House of Bread" and "the land or country." The origin of this town dates from the most remote antiquity. Moses speaks of it in the 35th chapter of Genesis in connection with the birth of Benjamin, which took place, he tells us, when his parents had but a little way to come to Ephrath (which is the same as Bethlehem), Rachel dying immediately afterward. At the time of the conquest of Palestine by Joshua, Bethlehem was, like Jerusalem, inhabited by the Canaanites, and in the division of the conquered districts, it fell to the lot of the tribe of Judah.

The situation of Bethlehem, moreover, is most beautiful. Built on the crest of the mountains of Judea, about two leagues to the south of Jerusalem, its form is that of a crescent, one end of which is marked by the Wells of David, the other by the Grottoes of the Nativity. Between the two horns of the crescent stretches a fertile valley, the Wady-el-Karoubeh. The descent of this valley is very steep, and resembles a circus, with low, parallel walls, which keep the earth from sliding down, representing the tiers of seats. This valley presents a most charming appearance, clothed, as it is, with an abundant vegetation, in which vines, fig, olive, and almond trees abound. The view from the top of the plateau is bounded on the north by the Hill of Mar-Elias, and on the west by the Mountains of the Desert where St. John dwelt. On the east, Beit-Saour rises from the little hill where Ruth gleaned the ears of corn in the field of Boaz, while beyond can be seen the sterile stony hills, called the Wilderness. Yet further to the east the rocks of Mount Moab stretch along like a wall, the base of which is bathed by the waters of the Dead Sea. On the south, Mount Herodion forms a regular cone, on the summit of which a few ruins indicate the site of the castle of Herod.

The Grottoes of the Nativity are a series of natural caves, extending for a considerable distance in the mountains, forming chambers connected with each other. As a matter of fact, shepherds, watching their flocks on the hills, availed themselves of these shelters in cold or bad weather, and it was in them that Mary and Joseph, finding no place in the caravansary, decided to take refuge.

The Angel and the Shepherds [A12]

⊕

I SAW the herds of the three oldest shepherds near the hill under sheds; but those further on near the shepherds' tower were partly in the open air. I saw something like a cloud of glory descend upon the three shepherds. I saw in it figures moving to and fro, and heard the approach of sweet, clear voices singing softly. At first, the shepherds were frightened. Soon there stood before them five or seven lovely, radiant figures holding in their hands a long strip like a scroll upon which were written words in letters a hand in length. The angels were singing the *Gloria*. [196]

[LUKE 2:8–14] 8 And in that region there were shepherds out in the field, keeping watch over their flock by night. 9 And an angel of the Lord appeared to them, and the glory of the Lord shone around them, and they were filled with fear. 10 And the angel said to them, "Be not afraid; for behold, I bring you good news of a great joy which will come to all the people; 11 for to you is born this day in the city of David a Savior, who is Christ the Lord. 12 And this will be a sign for you: you will find a babe wrapped in swaddling cloths and lying in a manger." 13 And suddenly there was with the angel a multitude of the heavenly host praising God and saying, 14 "Glory to God in the highest, and on earth peace among men with whom he is pleased!"

THE place where the shepherds were when the angels appeared to them is supposed to have been what is now called Beit-Saour, a word signifying "the house of the Shepherds." The Old Testament (Micah 4:8) refers to a "Tower of the flock, the stronghold of the daughter of Sion," which served as a refuge to the shepherds and their charges, in cases of nocturnal surprise. Similar towers were to be seen in more than one place on hills in country districts. Even at the present day, the Arabs have recourse to such towers to protect them from the attacks of the Bedouins, but there was one special peculiarity of the shelters between Bethlehem and the Holy City, and that was, the rearing in them of the ewes, rams, and young bulls, destined for the daily sacrifices of the Temple.

    The Gospels tell us that when the shepherds were surprised by the angels, they were "abiding in the field, keeping watch over their flock by night." The shepherds on guard gathered round a camp fire, while waiting their turn to rest, and it must have been to those thus waiting that the angels appeared.

The Adoration of the Shepherds [A13]

⊕

THEY told Joseph at the entrance of the cave what the angel had announced to them, and that they had come to do homage to the Child of Promise and to offer him gifts. Joseph accepted their presents and allowed them to lead the animals into the space that formed a kind of cellar near the side entrance of the cave. Then he conducted them to the blessed Virgin, who was sitting on the ground near the crib, a rug under her, the infant Jesus on her lap. The shepherds, their staves resting on their arms, fell on their knees and wept with joy. They knelt long, tasting great interior sweetness, and then intoned the angelic canticle of praise, and a psalm that I have forgotten. When they were about to take leave, Mary placed the child in their arms.

Some of the other shepherds came in the evening, accompanied by women and children, and bringing gifts. They sang most sweetly before the crib the *Gloria*, some psalms, and short refrains of which I remember the words: "O Child, blooming as a rose art thou! As a herald thou comest forth!" They brought gifts of birds, eggs, honey, woven stuffs of various colors, bundles of raw silk, and ears of corn, also several bundles of a corn with heavy grains growing on a stalk with large leaves like those of rushes. [198]

[LUKE 2:15–19] 15 When the angels went away from them into heaven, the shepherds said to one another, "Let us go over to Bethlehem and see this thing that has happened, which the Lord has made known to us." 16 And they went with haste, and found Mary and Joseph, and the babe lying in a manger. 17 And when they saw it they made known the saying which had been told them concerning this child; 18 and all who heard it wondered at what the shepherds told them. 19 But Mary kept all these things, pondering them in her heart.

The Magi Journeying [A14]

⊕

EACH of the kings had in his train, as companions, four nobles of his own race; but he himself was like a patriarch over all. He took care of all, commanded all, dispensed to all. In each caravan were to be found people of different color. Mensor's race was of a pleasing brownish color; Sair's was brown; and Theokeno's of a bright yellow. I saw no shining black, saving the slaves, of whom each king possessed some.

The nobles, holding staves in their hands, sat upon their dromedaries high among the piled-up packages, which were covered with hangings. These were followed by other animals almost as large as horses, on which servants and slaves rode among the baggage. [202]

[MATTHEW 2:1–2] 1 Now when Jesus was born in Bethlehem of Judea in the days of Herod the king, behold, wise men from the East came to Jerusalem, saying, 2 "Where is he who has been born king of the Jews? For we have seen his star in the East, and have come to worship him."

THE Book of Daniel speaks of Magi or soothsayers who were in the service of King Nebuchadnezzar, who studied astronomy and interpreted dreams. Those referred to in the Gospels seem to have been not only wise men, but Kings or Sheiks of Chaldea and its neighborhood.

Had the travelers exchanged ideas previous to their arrival? It is very probable that they had. No doubt their caravans, though they started from different points, met beyond the Jordan, on the side of the Mountains of Moab, whence they entered the Promised Land, still preceded by the star. This is the moment represented in my picture. The district they are crossing is near the Holy City; it shows the volcanic hills on the shores of the Dead Sea, between Jericho, the Kidron valley, and Jerusalem.

The Magi in the House of Herod [A15]

⊕

NEXT morning at daybreak I saw one of the courtiers going down to the caravan and bringing up all three of the kings to Herod's palace. They were ushered into an apartment around which were pots of foliage and bushes. Refreshments were spread at the entrance. But the kings declined the proffered food, and remained standing until Herod entered. They approached him with an obeisance, and without preamble put to him the question as to where they should find the newborn king of the Jews, for they had seen his star and they were come to do him homage. Herod was very much troubled, but he concealed his fears. Some of the scribes were still with him. He questioned the kings closely concerning the star, and told them that of Bethlehem Ephrata ran the Promise. But Mensor related to him the last vision they had seen in the star, whereupon Herod's anxiety became almost too great for concealment. Herod advised them to go quietly and without delay to Bethlehem, and when they had found the child to return and inform him that he too might go and adore him. [207]

[MATTHEW 2:3–9] 3 When Herod the king heard this, he was troubled, and all Jerusalem with him; 4 and assembling all the chief priests and scribes of the people, he inquired of them where the Christ was to be born. 5 They told him, "In Bethlehem of Judea; for so it is written by the prophet: 6 'And you, O Bethlehem, in the land of Judah, are by no means least among the rulers of Judah; for from you shall come a ruler who will govern my people Israel.'" 7 Then Herod summoned the wise men secretly and ascertained from them what time the star appeared; 8 and he sent them to Bethlehem, saying, "Go and search diligently for the child, and when you have found him bring me word, that I too may come and worship him." 9 When they had heard the king they went their way; and lo, the star which they had seen in the East went before them, till it came to rest over the place where the child was.

THE advisers consulted by Herod belonged to the Sanhedrin, the supreme national tribunal of the Jewish people. This Sanhedrin consisted of seventy-one members divided into three classes, or, as we should say now, chambers. The first chamber consisted of the Chief-Priests, also called Princes, who either were or had been in office, and the heads of the twenty-four sacerdotal families; the second included the scribes and doctors of the law; and the third the elders or notable men of the Jewish nation.

The Adoration of the Magi [A16]

⊕

I SAW the cave filled with supernatural light. Opposite the entrance and on the spot where Jesus was born, was Mary leaning on one arm in a posture more reclining than sitting; by her side was Joseph, and on her right, in a raised trough with a cover thrown over it, lay the infant Jesus. The infant folded its little hands upon its breast as if in prayer. It was shining with light, was very gracious, and at times extended its little hands, as if grasping something. Mensor fell on his knees before Mary, bowed his head, crossed his hands on his breast, and offered the gifts with some reverent words. [210]

[MATTHEW 2:9–11] 9 When they had heard the king they went their way; and lo, the star which they had seen in the East went before them, till it came to rest over the place where the child was. 10 When they saw the star, they rejoiced exceedingly with great joy; 11 and going into the house they saw the child with Mary his mother, and they fell down and worshiped him. Then, opening their treasures, they offered him gifts, gold and frankincense and myrrh.

The Aged Simeon [A17]

⊕

I HAD a vision also of the priest Simeon. He was a very aged, emaciated man with a short beard. He had a wife and three grown sons, the youngest of whom was already twenty years old. Simeon dwelt at the temple. I saw him going through a narrow, dark passage in the wall of the temple to a little cell which was built in the thick walls. It had only one opening, from which he could look down into the temple. Here I saw the old man kneeling and praying in ecstasy. [216]

The Presentation of Jesus in the Temple [A18]

MARY was now led by the woman to a porch in that part of the temple in which the ceremony of presentation was to take place. Anna and another woman (Naomi, Mary's former directress) received her. Simeon came out to the porch and conducted Mary with the child in her arms into the hall to the right of the women's porch. It was in this porch that the treasure box stood by which Jesus was sitting when the widow cast in her mite. Old Anna, to whom Joseph had handed over the basket of fruit and doves, followed with Naomi, and Joseph retired to the standing place of the men. Simeon stood before the table near Mary while the priest behind it took the child from the cradle, raised it on high and toward the different parts of the temple, praying all the while. [217]

[LUKE 2:22–38] 22 And when the time came for their purification according to the law of Moses, they brought him up to Jerusalem to present him to the Lord 23 (as it is written in the law of the Lord, "Every male that opens the womb shall be called holy to the Lord") 24 and to offer a sacrifice according to what is said in the law of the Lord, "a pair of turtledoves, or two young pigeons." 25 Now there was a man in Jerusalem, whose name was Simeon, and this man was righteous and devout, looking for the consolation of Israel, and the Holy Spirit was upon him. 26 And it had been revealed to him by the Holy Spirit that he should not see death before he had seen the Lord's Christ. 27 And inspired by the Spirit he came into the temple; and when the parents brought in the child Jesus, to do for him according to the custom of the law, 28 he took him up in his arms and blessed God and said, 29 "Lord, now lettest thou thy servant depart in peace, according to thy word; 30 for mine eyes have seen thy salvation 31 which thou hast prepared in the presence of all peoples, 32 a light for revelation to the Gentiles, and for glory to thy people Israel." 33 And his father and his mother marveled at what was said about him; 34 and Simeon blessed them and said to Mary his mother, "Behold, this child is set for the fall and rising of many in Israel, and for a sign that is spoken against 35 (and a sword will pierce through your own soul also), that thoughts out of many hearts may be revealed." 36 And there was a prophetess, Anna, the daughter of Phanuel, of the tribe of Asher; she was of a great age, having lived with her husband seven years from her virginity, 37 and as a widow till she was eighty-four. She did not depart from the temple, worshiping with fasting and prayer night and day. 38 And coming up at that very hour she gave thanks to God, and spoke of him to all who were looking for the redemption of Jerusalem.

THE *Presentation of Jesus in the Temple must have taken place at the top of the steps which led up from the Court of the Women (Azarath naschim) to the Court of the Men and to that of the Priests, where was the Altar of Burnt Sacrifice. In the background can be seen a terrace overlooking the court above the three entrance gateways, from which the women looked on at important ceremonies. On these occasions this terrace was supplemented by a kind of trellis-work balcony, which to some extent concealed from those outside what was going on.*

The Court of the Women was entered on the east of the Temple by the Beautiful or Corinthian Gate; crossing this Court, which was about sixty-five and a half yards long, the worshipper found himself opposite the doorway, where the presentations took place. It was reached by a semicircular staircase of fifteen steps, corresponding with the fifteen Psalms called the "Degrees" chanted one on each step during the libations.

The greater number of those who have endeavored to restore the plan of the Temple of Herod place the Nicanor Gate between the Court of the Women and that of the Men, at the head of the semicircular staircase of the fifteen steps or of the Psalms, of which we have just spoken. They indicate on the east, as the Entrance to the Court of the Women, the Beautiful or Corinthian Gate, spoken of in the Acts of the Apostles in the account of the healing of the lame man by Saint Peter and Saint John. . . . On this last point they are right; but they ignore what is nevertheless certain, that the three names: Beautiful, Corinthian, and Nicanor all denote one and the same entrance. . . . The actual gates of the Gateway in question were of Corinthian brass, hence the name of Corinthian Gate. They were brought from Alexandria by a certain Nicanor and it is said miraculously saved from shipwreck. This was the only Gateway not overlaid with plaques of gold, because, as the Talmud tells us, the brass of which it was made itself gleamed as brightly as gold; hence the name of Beautiful.

The Flight into Egypt [A19]

⊕

THE holy family went from here further on into the desert. When they had again lost all trace of anything like a path, they were a second time surrounded by all kinds of animals, among them huge winged lizards and even serpents, which pointed out the way to them. [223]

[MATTHEW 2:13–14] 13 Now when they had departed, behold, an angel of the Lord appeared to Joseph in a dream and said, "Rise, take the child and his mother, and flee to Egypt, and remain there till I tell you; for Herod is about to search for the child, to destroy him." 14 And he rose and took the child and his mother by night, and departed to Egypt.

TO get to Egypt the holy family, after leaving Bethlehem, must have gone by way of Hebron or Bersabea where there remains to this day a little mosque dedicated by the Muslims to "Saint Joseph the carpenter" in memory of the passage of the holy family. From it a distant view can be obtained of the mountain slopes, and of the Mediterranean Sea near Gaza. It was in this direction that the fugitives bent their steps. They must have entered Egypt by way of Pelusium and have reached Heliopolis and then the Egyptian Babylon, where old Cairo now stands. We will indicate further on the route taken by the holy family on their way back from Egypt.

The Sojourn in Egypt [A20]

⊕

I SAW the holy family on their way to Heliopolis. From their last night lodgings they were accompanied thither by a good man who, I think, was one of the workmen on that canal over which they had been ferried. They now crossed a long and very high bridge over a wide river (the Nile), which appeared to have several branches, and came to a place before the city gate which was surrounded by a kind of promenade.

Heliopolis is also called On. Asenath, wife of the Egyptian Joseph, resided here with the pagan priest Potiphar, and here also Dionysius the Areopagite studied. The city extends to a great distance around the many-branched river. One sees it from afar lying high above the general level. The river flows through it under the arches that support some of the buildings. I saw the ruins of enormous buildings, huge masses of heavy masonry, towers half standing, and even temples almost entire. I saw, too, pillars like towers, around the outside of which one could mount to the top. [225–226]

[MATTHEW 2:15] 15 and remained there until the death of Herod. This was to fulfil what the Lord had spoken by the prophet, "Out of Egypt have I called my son."

THE *Church of the Copts in Old Cairo (the ancient Egyptian Babylon) is one of the very oldest Christian churches of Egypt. It dates from the sixth century, and was built above a cave or kind of natural crypt, which is reached at the present day by a few steps, and in which, according to tradition, the holy family took shelter during their exile. The little Babylonian colony was a very busy one at the time of which we are writing, and there must have been many dahabeahs laden with corn and other produce on the banks of the Nile, with crowds of fellahs occupied about them.*

The water of the Nile, though rather muddy, was good, and was used for drinking and other domestic purposes by the inhabitants. At certain hours of the day the women went in long files to draw water at a very convenient part of the port, and the very spot is still shown where the Virgin often came, carrying the infant Jesus in her arms. Indeed, it seems likely that Mary would be very unwilling, especially in a foreign land, to leave her divine son alone; moreover Joseph, occupied as he was with his trade of a carpenter, would probably be frequently absent. It will be remembered that he was employed, at least so tradition says, in making the woodwork used in Egyptian houses, especially the wainscotting so much in vogue in Egypt.

Beyond the spot just mentioned, and in the background of my picture, can be seen the island of Rhodes, sacred to the memory of Moses, for it is said that it was on it that he was found amongst the flags by the daughter of Pharaoh.

Another goal of pilgrimage, and one of the most venerated of all the spots connected with the sojourn in Egypt, is near the town of Heliopolis. This is the so-called sanctuary of Matarea, where, according to tradition, the Virgin, weary with her long journey, rested beneath the shade of a sycamore tree. The tree itself is no longer there, but a shoot from it, dating from about the fifteenth century, still marks the spot. Here, says the legend, the heat being great, the Virgin was thirsty, and a spring gushed forth for her refreshment; hence the name of Matarea, which signifies clear water, given to the venerated site. At Heliopolis, if yet another tradition is to be believed, the idols in a temple suddenly fell down when the holy family passed.

The Massacre of the Innocents [A21]

⊕

I SAW the mothers with their boys, from infants in the arms up to the age of two years, going to Jerusalem. I saw many women even from the Arabian frontiers taking their children to Jerusalem, and these had more than a day's journey to make. The mothers went in bands, some with two children and riding on asses. On their arrival in the city, they were all conducted to a large building, and the husbands who accompanied some of them dismissed. The mandate was joyously obeyed, for the poor people imagined they were going to receive a reward.

The building into which the mothers and their children were ushered was not far from the house occupied by Pilate at a later period. It stood alone, and so encompassed by walls that no one outside could hear anything going on within. A gateway through double walls led into a large court enclosed on all sides by buildings. Those to the right and left were of one story; that in the middle, which looked like an old, deserted synagogue, was two stories in height. From all three, doors opened into the court. The middle building was a hall of justice, for I saw in the court before it a stone block, pillars with chains, and such trees as could be bound together by their branches and then suddenly snapped asunder, in order to tear people to pieces.

The mothers were led through the court and into the two side buildings, where they were shut up. It looked to me at first as if they were in a sort of hospital, or lazar-house. When they saw themselves thus unexpectedly deprived of liberty, they began to fear, to cry, and to lament.

The lower story of the court of justice was a great hall like a prison, or guardroom; the upper one was also a large hall from which windows opened upon the court. The officers of justice were assembled in the latter, rolls of writing lying before them on tables. Herod himself was there. He wore his crown and a purple mantle bordered with black and lined with white fur. He stood at the windows with many others, looking down upon the slaughter of the Innocents.

The mothers, one by one, with their boys, were summoned from the side buildings into the great hall under the judgment hall. On their entrance, the children were taken from them by the soldiers and carried out into the court where about twenty others were actively at work with swords and lances, piercing the little creatures through throat and heart. Some of the children were still in swaddling clothes, infants in the mothers' arms; while others, able to run around, wore little woven dresses. The soldiers did not remove the children's clothing but, having pierced them through the heart and throat, they grasped them by one arm or leg and slung them together in a heap. It was a terrible sight!

The place of the children's massacre in Jerusalem was the subsequent hall of justice, and not far from that of Pilate; but it was at his time very greatly changed. At Christ's death, I saw the pit in which the murdered children were buried, fall in. Their souls appeared and left the place. [226]

[MATTHEW 2:16–18] 16 Then Herod, when he saw that he had been tricked by the wise men, was in a furious rage, and he sent and killed all the male children in Bethlehem and in all that region who were two years old or under, according to the time which he had ascertained from the wise men. 17 Then was fulfilled what was spoken by the prophet Jeremiah: 18 "A voice was heard in Ramah, wailing and loud lamentation, Rachel weeping for her children; she refused to be consoled, because they were no more."

ACCORDING to tradition, the Massacre of the Innocents took place in the following manner: all the mothers who had children under two years of age were gathered together, under the pretext of a fête to be held in honor of the birth of one of Herod's own sons. Not a mother would have liked to miss it, and all the poor women came, bringing their little ones decked out in their best. To avoid a tumult when the broken-hearted mothers gave vent to their shrieks of despair on discovering the cruel deception, the women were made to enter one by one a porch opening into a court. There the child was torn from the mother's arms and flung into the gloomy court, while she was driven out at the other end of the porch or gallery, so that the group of waiting mothers, still in happy ignorance and eager for their own turn to come, had no suspicion of what awaited them.

Jesus and His Mother at the Spring [A22]

⊕

I SAW that the holy family had to subsist on fruits and bad water. They had been so long without good water that Joseph resolved to saddle the ass, take his leathern bottle, and start for the balsam spring in the desert in order to get some. But the blessed Virgin was told in prayer by an angelic apparition that she should seek and find a spring at the back of their present abode. I saw her going over the hill in which they dwelt to a deep vacant lot that lay at some distance between ruined walls. A large, old tree stood on that ground. Mary had in her hand a rod provided with a little scoop, such as the people of that country commonly carry on journeys. She stuck it into the ground near the tree, and a beautiful, clear stream of water instantly gushed forth. She hurried back joyfully to call Joseph, who soon removed the upper crust of earth and disclosed a well which had long ago been dug out and lined with masonry, but which for some time had been choked up and dry. He soon restored it and paved it around very beautifully with stones. At the side of the well toward which Mary had approached lay a great stone almost like an altar. I think it was used for that purpose in former times. [228]

[LUKE 2:39–40] 39 And when they had performed everything according to the law of the Lord, they returned into Galilee, to their own city, Nazareth. 40 And the child grew and became strong, filled with wisdom; and the favor of God was upon him.

IN the Holy Land there are a certain number of wells, called Wells of the Virgin Mary (Aïn-sitti Mariam). The most celebrated is that of Siloam, situated on the south-east of the Temple, in the Valley of Jehosaphat. This was the well which partly supplied with water the Pool of Siloam, to which Jesus Christ sent the man who had been born blind to purify himself after he had given him sight by anointing his eyes with clay made by mixing earth with his own spittle.

Another of these wells is that of Aïn-Karim. It is situated near what is known as the Desert of John the Baptist. According to tradition, the Virgin Mary went to this well during her visit to Elizabeth whose house was near it. Yet another is shown at Nazareth, which is evidently the one to which the Holy Virgin went most frequently, and according to a Greek legend, it was there that the Angel Gabriel first appeared to her who was to be the mother of the Redeemer, to prepare her to receive him on his later mission, when he was to give her his more definite and, so to speak, official message.

In our picture, the holy Child wears the garment without seam, made of a kind of woven linen of a purplish brown color. The legend about this garment is well known. It tells how Mary wove it herself for her son, and that it grew with his growth, so that it lasted him until the time of his passion and death. Over the seamless garment Jesus wears what was called a "gibbeh," a loose robe open at the neck, kept in place by a sash which he wore as a Jew of pure descent, for it was part of the Rabbinical law that the upper or nobler part of the human body should be thus separated from the lower.

The Return from Egypt [A23]

⊕

I HAD many visions of their journey, which was made without any special danger to them. Mary was often very much distressed, because walking through the hot sand was so painful for the boy Jesus. Joseph had made for him, out of bark, shoes that reached above the ankle where they were firmly fastened; still I saw the holy travelers frequently pausing while Mary shook the sand out of the child's shoes. She herself wore only sandals. Jesus was dressed in his little brown robe, and they often had to seat him on the ass. For protection against the scorching rays of the sun, all three wore very broad hats made of bark and fastened under the chin with a string. [229]

[MATTHEW 2:19–21] 19 But when Herod died, behold, an angel of the Lord appeared in a dream to Joseph in Egypt, saying, 20 "Rise, take the child and his mother, and go to the land of Israel, for those who sought the child's life are dead." 21 And he rose and took the child and his mother, and went to the land of Israel.

THE return of the holy family was doubtless far less fatiguing than the journey to Egypt. In the first place Jesus was older and the road was now a little better. On leaving Old Cairo to go toward Pelusium, the travelers first traversed sandy districts, passing salt marshes, and then followed the coast by way of Gaza and Jaffa, till they entered Samaria. There they left the open country, and made their way through the numerous valleys beyond it.

The Childhood of John the Baptist [A24]

⊕

JOHN had already been long in the desert before the holy family's return from Egypt. That he had retired there at so young an age was due principally to divine inspiration and partly to his own inclinations, for he was of a meditative nature and loved solitude.

He had fastened a piece of wood to his staff, thus giving it the form of a cross, also a strip of broad grass, or bark, or leaves like a little flag. He often played with it, waving it here and there. [230]

[LUKE 1:80] 80 And the child grew and became strong in spirit, and he was in the wilderness till the day of his manifestation to Israel.

TRADITION indicates as the desert in which the child who was to be called the "Prophet of the Highest" spent his early years, that on the west of Aïn-Karim, among the rugged rocks skirting the Terebinth valley. It was from the bed of the torrent which flows through this valley that David took the stones for the sling with which he went forth to meet and slay Goliath. There grew the so-called locust-tree or Saint John's bread-tree with various shrubs and roots, and there, too, were plenty of the locusts and wild honey which we are told formed the food of the prophet.

The Youth of Jesus [A25]

⊕

THERE were three separate rooms in the house at Nazareth, that of the Mother of God being the largest and most pleasant; in it Jesus, Mary, and Joseph met to pray. I very seldom saw them together at other times. They stood at prayer, their hands crossed upon their breast, and they appeared to speak aloud. I often saw them praying by a light. They stood under a lamp that had several wicks, or near a kind of branched candlestick fastened to the wall, and upon which the flame burned. They were most of the time alone in their respective rooms, Joseph working in his. I saw him cutting sticks and laths, planing wood, and carrying up a beam, Jesus helping him. Mary was generally engaged sewing or knitting with little needles, at which she sat on the ground, her feet crossed under her, and a little basket at her side. They slept alone, each in a separate room. The bed consisted of a cover which in the morning was rolled up.

I saw Jesus assisting his parents in every possible way, and also on the street and wherever opportunity offered, cheerfully, eagerly, and obligingly helping everyone. He assisted his foster-father in his trade. [232]

[LUKE 2:51–52] 51 And he went down with them and came to Nazareth, and was obedient to them; and his mother kept all these things in her heart. 52 And Jesus increased in wisdom and in stature, and in favor with God and man.

THE special idea of the picture called "The Youth of Jesus" is the following: As already stated, Jesus practiced the trade of a carpenter, or some other similar to it, and in the course of his daily work he must sometimes have performed actions foreshadowing certain details of the tragic and bloody drama which was to terminate his earthly career. It is improbable, especially after the prophecy of the aged Simeon, that Joseph and Mary had no inkling of what the future of their child was to be. With some such inkling in their minds the smallest detail, a mere nothing, would be enough to arouse their anxiety and sadden them. We have imagined some such incident: Jesus is carrying a piece of wood on his shoulder; while Mary and Joseph watch him thoughtfully with some vague presentiment of the future cross.

On Return from Jerusalem, It is Noticed that Jesus is Lost [A26]

⊕

BUT this time Jesus had, on the return journey not far from the Mount of Olives, separated from his companions, who all thought that he had joined his parents who were following. Jesus had, however, gone to that side of Jerusalem nearest to Bethlehem, to the inn at which the holy family before Mary's Purification had put up. Mary and Joseph thought him on ahead with the other Nazarenes, while these latter thought that he was following with his parents. When at last they all met at Gophna, the anxiety of Mary and Joseph at his absence was very great. They returned at once to Jerusalem, making inquiries after him on the way and everywhere in the city itself. But they could not find him, since he had not been where they usually stayed.

Jesus had slept at the inn before the Bethlehem gate, where the people knew him and his parents. There he had joined several youths and gone with them to two schools of the city, the first day to one, the second to another. On the morning of the third day, he had gone to a third school at the temple, and in the afternoon into the temple itself where his parents found him. These schools were all different, and not all exactly schools of the Law. Other branches were taught in them. The last mentioned was in the neighborhood of the temple and from it the Levites and priests were chosen. [233]

[LUKE 2:41–45] 41 Now his parents went to Jerusalem every year at the feast of the Passover. 42 And when he was twelve years old, they went up according to custom; 43 and when the feast was ended, as they were returning, the boy Jesus stayed behind in Jerusalem. His parents did not know it, 44 but supposing him to be in the company they went a day's journey, and they sought him among their kinsfolk and acquaintances; 45 and when they did not find him, they returned to Jerusalem, seeking after him.

ACCORDING to one tradition, it was at Beeroth, the modern El Bireh, an hour and a half's march from Jerusalem, that Mary and Joseph noticed that Jesus was no longer with them. Great crowds of Galileans must have been returning from Jerusalem, one huge caravan succeeding another, each made up of natives from one part of the country. At the first issue from the Holy City, the various parties would, of course, get mixed together, but they divided into groups, growing ever smaller and smaller as the people branched off at the various cross roads. No doubt Joseph and Mary thought Jesus had stayed behind with friends in the rear of their own caravan. Full of anxiety Mary and Joseph went a little further, probably to Jifnah, the first halting-place, and there waited, but the child did not appear. Then they turned back to Jerusalem seeking him.

Jesus Among the Doctors [A27]

⊕

JESUS by his questions and answers so astonished and embarrassed the doctors and rabbis of all these schools that they resolved, on the afternoon of the third day, in the public lecture hall of the temple and in presence of the rabbis most deeply versed in the various sciences, "to humble the boy Jesus." The scribes and doctors had concerted the plan together; for, although pleased at first, they had in the end become vexed at him.

They met in the public lecture hall in the middle of the temple porch in front of the sanctuary, in the round place where later Jesus also taught. There I saw Jesus sitting in a large chair which he did not, by a great deal, fill. Around him was a crowd of aged Jews in priestly robes. They were listening attentively and appeared to be perfectly furious.

As Jesus had in the schools illustrated his answers and explanations by all kinds of examples from nature, art, and science, the scribes and doctors had diligently gathered together masters in all these branches. They now began, one by one, to dispute with him. He remarked that although, properly speaking, such subjects did not appear appropriate to the temple, yet he would discuss them since such was his Father's will. But they understood not that he referred to his heavenly Father; they imagined that Joseph had commanded him to show off his learning.

Jesus now answered and taught upon medicine. He described the whole human body in a way far beyond the reach of even the most learned. He discoursed with the same facility upon astronomy, architecture, agriculture, geometry, arithmetic, jurisprudence and, in fine, upon every subject proposed to him. He applied all so skillfully to the Law and the Promise, to the prophecies, to the temple, to the mysteries of worship and sacrifice that his hearers, surprised and confounded, passed successively from astonishment and admiration to fury and shame. They were enraged at hearing some things that they never before knew, and at hearing others that they had never before understood.

Jesus had been teaching two hours, when Joseph and Mary entered the temple. [234]

[LUKE 2:46–47] 46 After three days they found him in the Temple, sitting among the teachers, listening to them and asking them questions; 47 and all who heard him were amazed at his understanding and his answers.

Jesus Found in the Temple [A28]

⊕

JESUS had been teaching two hours, when Joseph and Mary entered the temple. They inquired after their child of the Levites whom they knew, and received for answer that he was with the doctors in the lecture hall. But as they were not at liberty to enter that hall, they sent one of the Levites in to call Jesus. Jesus sent them word that he must first finish what he was then about. Mary was very much troubled at his not obeying at once, for this was the first time he had given his parents to understand that he had other commands than theirs to fulfill. He continued to teach for another hour, and then he left the hall and joined his parents in the porch of Israel, the Women's Court, leaving his hearers confounded, confused, and enraged. Joseph was quite awed and astonished, but he kept a humble silence. [234]

[LUKE 2:48–50] 48 And when they saw him they were astonished; and his mother said to him, "Son, why have you treated us so? Behold, your father and I have been looking for you anxiously." 49 And he said to them, "How is it that you sought me? Did you not know that I must be in my Father's house?" 50 And they did not understand the saying which he spoke to them.

THE Women's Court, where, as already stated, the meeting between Jesus and his parents probably took place, was of considerable size and adjoined that of the men. It was reached, as we said above, by a semicircular staircase on which the Levites, bearing harps, dulcimers, cymbals, and other instruments of music, chanted the fifteen Psalms called the Songs of the Degrees. During the offering of sacrifices they chanted near the Altar. . . . In the background of the picture through the door can be seen the altar of burnt offerings; a red band was painted all round it to indicate where the sprinklings with blood were to cease.

Village of Siloam

YEAR 1

Day-by-Day
CHRONICLE

OF THE LIFE, TRAVELS, & TEACHING OF JESUS

Jesus Begins His Public Teaching
From Capernaum to the Baptism
April 16–September 22, AD 29

John Preaching Penance and Baptizing
Baptism in the Jordan—Jesus Retraces Journeys
of Mary and Joseph—Beginning of Forty Days' Fast
September 23–October 21, AD 29

Jesus in the Desert—Marriage Feast of Cana
Jesus Celebrates Passover in Jerusalem for the First Time
October 22, AD 29–May 2, AD 30

From the Close of the First Passover
to the Conversion of the Samaritan Woman
at Jacob's Well—Travels in North Galilee
May 3–August 2, AD 30

JESUS BEGINS HIS PUBLIC TEACHING: FROM CAPERNAUM TO THE BAPTISM

YEAR 1

Nisan 15, AD 29, to Nisan 14, AD 30
April 16/17, AD 29, to April 4/5, AD 30

NISSAN (*30 days*): *April 2/3 to May 1/2 AD 29*
Nisan New Moon: April 2 at 10:30 PM Jerusalem time

Around the start of the month of Nisan, Joseph died, signifying Jesus's spiritual coming of age. Since the age of eight, Jesus had attended the Passover festival in Jerusalem every year with Joseph and Mary. Now, twenty-one years later, in AD 29 (aged 29), he went to Jerusalem accompanied only by Mary. We can imagine what a solemn event this visit to the temple must have been and how, from this time on, the heavenly Father filled his attention, his earthly father having passed away.

The Passover festival lasted a week, from Nisan 15 to Nisan 21. On the day corresponding historically to the last day of the Passover festival (April 24, AD 29), Anne Catherine had a vision of John the Baptist in the wilderness, not far from Mount Lebanon. The "word of God" came to John. It was the fifteenth year of the reign of Tiberius. John left the wilderness and "he went into all the region about the Jordan, preaching a baptism of repentance for the forgiveness of sins" (Luke 3:3).

In a subsequent vision, relating to June, AD 29, which was about the time John attained the age of 30, Anne Catherine saw him travel through Galilee and Samaria, visiting Bethsaida, Capernaum, Tiberias, Nazareth, Jericho, and his birthplace Jutta, near Hebron. Everywhere he introduced himself as Zechariah's son, and spoke of himself as a forerunner of Jesus. He traveled back up the east side of the River Jordan to the Sea of Galilee. Crossing the Jordan, he visited Bethsaida, Capernaum, and Nazareth again. Then he returned through Samaria to a place on the banks of the Jordan near where the River Zarqa flows into the Jordan, between Ainon and Salem. Here he remained, teaching and baptizing.

Thus, about three months before the baptism, John traveled twice through Palestine, proclaiming the one who was to come, whose way he prepared.

IYYAR (*29 days*): *May 2/3 to May 30/31, AD 29*
Iyyar New Moon: May 2 at 1:20 PM Jerusalem time

After returning from the Passover, around the start of the month of Iyyar, Jesus and Mary moved from Nazareth to a house near the town of Capernaum. The house was made available to them by a wealthy friend, a man called Levi, who lived in Capernaum. Levi saw that Jesus had difficulties in Nazareth because he was frequently at variance with the teachings of the Pharisees there. Levi provided Jesus with a house so that he could have a place to go where, without fear of disturbance, he could gather his followers around him. The house was situated outside the town, between Capernaum and Bethsaida, not far from the Sea of Galilee. The house was large enough to accommodate not only Jesus and Mary but also guests. It was even possible to hold small gatherings there. Levi also saw to it that his servants regularly brought provisions for Jesus and Mary from Capernaum and that the house was properly cared for, and that it was protected when both Jesus and Mary went away.

Toward the end of the month of Iyyar, Jesus began his travels, which, from this time on and for almost four years, were to take him through the length and breadth of Palestine and beyond. On the first journey, which signified the start of his public teaching, he went by way of Nazareth to the region of Hebron in the south, where John the Baptist had grown up. It was with this journey that Anne Catherine's day-by-day communications concerning the ministry of Jesus Christ began. Although, strictly speaking, the ministry began some four months later, with the baptism in the Jordan, the daily chronicle of Jesus' public teaching starts here.

(Follow Map 1)

Jesus on His Way to Hebron

Sunday, May 29, AD 29 (Iyyar 27)

This morning Jesus set off from Capernaum on his journey to the region of Hebron in Judea. For the first part of the journey, as far as Nazareth, he was accompanied by Mary. Between Capernaum and Nazareth, they passed through Bethulia. There Nathaniel Chased was deeply moved by the gaze that Jesus cast in his direction. Mary then remained in Nazareth with her niece, Mary Cleophas. She would await Jesus's return there. Jesus continued on his way that same evening,

Map 1: Journey to the Place Where John the Baptist Grew Up
May 29–June 20, AD 29

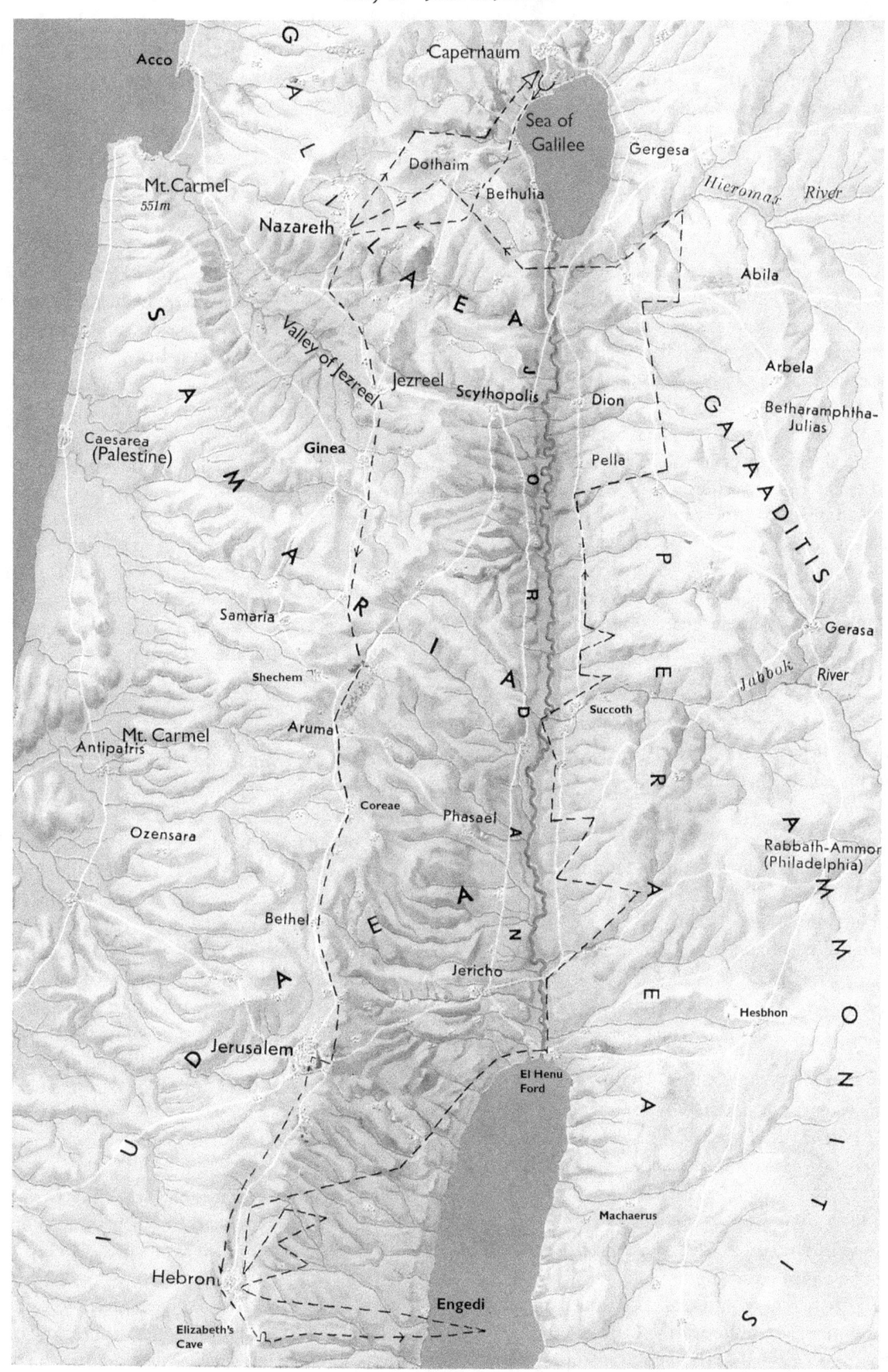

Capernaum—Bethulia—Nazareth—Bethany—Jerusalem—Hebron—Elizabeth's Cave
Dead Sea—Hebron—Perea—Hieromax—Dothaim—Nazareth—Capernaum

accompanied by two young friends from Nazareth, Parmenas and Jonadab.

JESUS went through Nazareth in going from Capernaum to Hebron, passing through the indescribably beautiful country of Galilee and by the hot baths of Emmaus. These baths were on the declivity of a mountain, about an hour further on from Magdala in the direction of Tiberias.

The meadows were covered with very high, thick grass, and on the declivity stood the houses and tents between rows of fig trees, date palms, and orange trees. The road was crowded, for a kind of national feast was going on. Men and women in separate groups were playing for wagers, the prize consisting of fruit. There Jesus saw Nathaniel, called also Chased, standing among the men under a fig tree. Just at the moment when Nathaniel was struggling against a sensual temptation that had seized him and was glancing over at the women's game, Jesus passed and cast upon him a warning look. Without knowing Jesus, Nathaniel was deeply moved by his glance, and thought: "That man has a sharp eye." He felt that Jesus was more than an ordinary man. He became conscious of his guilt, entered into himself, overcame the temptation, and from that time kept a stricter guard over his senses.[B1] I think I saw there, also, Naphtali, known as Bartholomew, and that a glance from Jesus touched him also.

Monday, May 30, AD 29 (Iyyar 28)
Jesus and his two friends traveled the whole day, without stopping, through Samaria, directing their steps toward Jerusalem.

Jesus journeyed with two of his young friends to Hebron in Judea. They did not remain faithful to him. They separated from him, but after his resurrection, converted by his apparition on Mount Thebez in Galilee, they once again joined his followers.

SIVAN (30 days): May 31/June 1 to June 29/30, AD 29
Sivan New Moon: June 1 at 2:15 AM Jerusalem time

Tuesday, May 31, AD 29 (Iyyar 29)
Today, they arrived at Lazarus's castle in Bethany. After talking with Lazarus, Jesus and his two friends visited the temple in Jerusalem. That evening (the start of the first day of Sivan) they traveled further, journeying through the night to Hebron.

In Bethany Jesus visited Lazarus, who looked much older than Jesus; he appeared to me to be fully eight years his senior. Lazarus had large possessions, landed property, gardens, and many servants. Martha had her own house, and another sister named Mary, who lived entirely alone, had also her separate dwelling. Magdalene lived in her castle at Magdala. Lazarus was already long acquainted with the holy family. He had at an early period aided Joseph and Mary with large alms and, from first to last, did much for the community. The purse that Judas carried and all the early expenses, he supplied out of his own wealth.

From Bethany Jesus went to the temple in Jerusalem.

The Family of Lazarus

THE FATHER of Lazarus was named Zarah, or Zerah, and was of very noble Egyptian descent. He had dwelt in Syria, on the confines of Arabia, where he held a position under the Syrian king; but for services rendered in war, he received from the Roman emperor property near Jerusalem and in Galilee. He was like a prince, and was very rich. He had acquired still greater wealth by his wife Jezebel, a Jewess of the sect of the Pharisees. He became a Jew, and was pious and strict according to the Pharisaical laws. He owned part of the city on Mount Zion, on the side upon which the brook near the height on which the temple stands flows through the ravine. But the greater part of this property he had bequeathed to the temple, retaining, however, in his family some ancient privilege on its account. This property was on the road by which the apostles went up to the Cenacle, but the Cenacle itself formed no longer a part of it. Zarah's castle in Bethany was very large. It had numerous gardens, terraces, and fountains, and was surrounded by double ditches. The prophecies of Anna and Simeon were known to the family of Zarah, who were waiting for the Messiah. Even in Jesus's youth they were acquainted with the holy family, just as pious, noble people are wont to be with their humble, devout neighbors.

The parents of Lazarus had in all fifteen children, of whom six died young. Of the nine that survived, only four were living at the time of Christ's teaching. These four were: Lazarus; Martha, about two years younger; Mary, looked upon as a simpleton, two years younger than Martha; and Mary Magdalene, five years younger than the simpleton. The simpleton is not named in scripture, not reckoned among the Lazarus family; but she is known to God. She was always put aside in her family, and lived altogether unknown.

Magdalene, the youngest child, was very beautiful and, even in her early years, tall and well-developed like a girl of more advanced age. She was full of frivolity and seductive art. Her parents died when she was only seven years old. She had no great love for them even from her earliest age, on account of their severe fasts. Even as a child she was vain beyond expression, given to petty thefts, proud, self-willed, and a lover of pleasure. She was never faithful, but clung to whatever flattered her most. She was, therefore, extravagant in her pity when her sensitive compassion was aroused, and kind and condescending to all that appealed to her senses by some external show. Her mother had had some share in Magdalene's faulty education, and that sympathetic softness the child had inherited from her.

Magdalene was spoiled by her mother and her nurse. They showed her off everywhere, caused her cleverness and pretty little ways to be admired, and sat much with her dressed up at the window. That window-sitting was the chief cause of her ruin. I saw her at the window and on the terraces of the house upon a magnificent seat of carpets and cushions, where she could be seen in all her splendor from the street. She used to steal sweetmeats and take them

Bethany in the Distance

to other children in the garden of the castle. Even in her ninth year she was engaged in love affairs.

With her developing talents and beauty increased also the talk and admiration they excited. She had crowds of companions. She was taught, and she wrote love verses on little rolls of parchment. I saw her while so engaged counting on her fingers. She sent these verses around, and exchanged them with her lovers. Her fame spread on all sides, and she was exceedingly admired.

But I never saw that she either really loved or was loved. It was all, on her part at least, vanity, frivolity, self-adoration, and confidence in her own beauty. I saw her a scandal to her brother and sisters whom she despised and of whom she was ashamed on account of their simple life.

When the patrimony was divided, the castle of Magdala fell by lot to Magdalene. It was a very beautiful building. Magdalene had often gone there with her family when she was a very young child, and she had always entertained a special preference for it. She was only about eleven years old when, with a large household of servants, men and maids, she retired thither and set up a splendid establishment for herself.

Magdala was a fortified place, consisting of several castles, public buildings, and large squares of groves and gardens. It was eight hours east of Nazareth, about three from Capernaum, one and a half from Bethsaida toward the south, and about a mile from the Sea of Galilee. It was built on a slope of the mountain and extended down into the valley which stretches off toward the lake and around its shores. One of those castles belonged to Herod. He possessed a still larger one in the fertile region of Galilee. Some of his soldiers were stationed in Magdala, and they contributed their share to the general demoralization. The officers were on intimate terms with Magdalene. There were, besides the troops, about two hundred people in Magdala, chiefly officials, master builders, and servants. There was no synagogue in the place; the people went to the one at Bethsaida.

The castle of Magdala was the highest and most magnificent of all; from its roof one could see across the Sea of Galilee to the opposite shore. Five roads led to Magdala, and on every one at one half-hour's distance from the well-fortified place stood a tower built over an arch. It was like a watchtower whence could be seen far into the distance. These towers had no connection with one another; they rose out of a country covered with gardens, fields, and meadows. Magdalene had menservants and maids, fields and herds, but a very disorderly household; all went to rack and ruin.

Through the wild ravine at the head of which Magdala lay far up on the height, flowed a little stream to the lake. Around its banks was a quantity of game, for from the three deserts contiguous to the valley the wild beasts came down to drink. Herod used to hunt here. He had also near his castle in the country of Galilee a park filled with game.

The country of Galilee began between Tiberias and Tarichea, about four hours' distance from Capernaum; it extended from the sea three hours inland and to the south around Tarichea to the mouth of the Jordan. The rising valley with the baths near Bethulia, artificially formed from a brook nearby, lay contiguous to this region, and was watered by streams flowing to the sea. This brook formed in its course several artificial lakes and waterfalls in different parts of the beautiful district which consisted entirely of gardens, villas, castles, parks, walks, orchards, and vineyards. The whole year round found it teeming with blossoms and fruits. The rich ones of the land, and especially of Jerusalem, had here their villas and gardens.

Every portion was under cultivation, or laid off in pleasure grounds, groves, and verdant labyrinths, and adorned with walks winding around pyramidal hillocks. There were no large villages in this part of the country. The permanent residents were mostly gardeners and custodians of the property, also shepherds whose herds consisted of fine sheep and goats. There were besides all kinds of rare animals and birds under their care. No street ran through Magdala, but two roads from the sea and from the Jordan met here.

Jesus in Hebron, Dothaim, and Nazareth

Wednesday, June 1, AD 29 (Sivan 1)

In Hebron, Jesus, saying he wanted to visit a friend, parted company with Parmenas and Jonadab. They did not become Jesus's disciples until much later. Jesus then went into the desert region south of Hebron and found his way to the cave ("Elizabeth's cave") where the young John the Baptist had stayed, having been brought thither by his mother Elizabeth.

WHEN Jesus arrived at Hebron, he left there his companions, saying that he was desirous of visiting a friend. Zechariah and Elizabeth were no more. Jesus then went to the wilderness which lay to the south of Hebron, between it and the Dead Sea, whither Elizabeth had taken the boy John. To reach it, one had to climb a mountain covered with white pebbles, and then cross a lovely valley of palm trees.

Thursday, June 2, AD 29 (Sivan 2)

In the wilderness south of Hebron, Jesus remained alone in prayer, preparing for his mission.

I saw Jesus entering the wilderness, and going into the cave to which John was first taken by Elizabeth. Then he crossed a little brook over which John also had passed. I saw him alone and in prayer, as if preparing for his teaching mission.

Friday, June 3, AD 29 (Sivan 3)

Traveling eastward, Jesus came to the shores of the Dead Sea. There was a storm, and some people were in difficulty on their raft. Jesus helped them to land. He then made his way to Hebron for the sabbath. That evening, he visited the synagogue for the evening sabbath celebration.

When he left the desert, he went again to Hebron. I saw him as he journeyed lending a helping hand everywhere along the road. At the Dead Sea he helped some people who were on a kind of raft formed of beams and covered by an awning. On it were men, cattle, and merchandise. Jesus called to them and shoved a plank out to them from the shore. He helped them to land and stood by while they repaired their raft. They were at a loss as to who he was; for though there was nothing remarkable in his dress, yet his charming graciousness and dignity of bearing greatly impressed them. At first they thought it must be John the Baptist, who had already made his appearance at the Jordan; but they soon discovered their mistake, for John's complexion was brown, much darker than that of Jesus, and his whole appearance rough.

Saturday, June 4, AD 29 (Sivan 4)

After the morning service at the synagogue, Jesus visited the sick to console and help them, but he did not heal anyone. Wherever he went, he evoked wonder and amazement, for he appeared to all as a wonderful and benevolent person. Even those possessed grew quiet in his presence. Some people thought at first that he was John the Baptist, but then they realized that he was another prophet, as yet unknown. That evening, Jesus left Hebron and traveled by night to the Jordan.

Jesus celebrated the sabbath in Hebron, and there dismissed his traveling companions. He visited the sick in their homes, consoling and assisting them in every way. He raised them in his arms, carried them, and made their beds; but I did not see him curing anyone. To all he appeared to be a benevolent, a wonderful person. He visited the possessed and they grew calm in his presence, though as yet he drove no devil out. Wherever he went, he rendered aid when aid was needed. He raised the fallen, he refreshed the thirsty, he guided the traveler, over bridge and brook—and all looked in astonishment upon the kind-hearted wayfarer.

Sunday, June 5, AD 29 (Sivan 5)

From Hebron he went to the spot where the Jordan flows into the Dead Sea. Here he crossed the river in a boat, and journeyed along its eastern bank to Galilee.

Monday, June, 6 AD 29 (Sivan 6)

In the region north of Pella, on the east side of the Jordan, Jesus visited many sick people, consoling them, and exhorting them to prayer. In response to a question, he taught concerning the nearness of the Messiah and gave indications as to how one would be able to recognize him.

I saw him traveling on between Pella and the country of Gergesa, making short journeys and helping all in need.

He went to all the sick, even to the lepers, consoling them, raising them in his arms, making their beds, exhorting them to prayer, and pointing out, to the admiration of all, what treatment was necessary, what remedies to use in the different cases. At one place, some people knew of the prophecies of Simeon and Anna and they questioned him as to whether he was the one to whom they referred. It was a common thing for people to follow him from one place to another out of the love he inspired. The possessed were calm when near him.

Tuesday, June 7, AD 29 (Sivan 7)

Today, he reached a place south of Gergesa, east of the Sea of Galilee, through which the Hieromax flows. There, he helped some men who were at work repairing their boats.

He went also to the rapid little stream that flows into the Jordan below the Sea of Galilee (the Hieromax), not far from that steep mountain from which he subsequently cast the swine into the sea. Near the river stood a row of little mud huts like shepherds' huts, which were occupied by the men who were at that moment on the shore laboring at their barks. They could not succeed in their work. I saw Jesus go up to them, make some suggestions in a friendly way, drag a beam to the spot, and put his hand to the work. He pointed out various expedients and, as he worked, exhorted them to patience and charity.

Wednesday, June 8, to Tuesday, June 14, AD 29 (Sivan 8–14)

For several days, Jesus remained on the east side of the Jordan. Everywhere he went, he helped others. Then he crossed the Jordan and went to the little town of Dothaim, west of the Sea of Galilee.

Wednesday, June 15, AD 29 (Sivan 15)

Jesus visited the madhouse in Dothaim. There a number of people were raging uncontrollably. As Jesus began to speak to them, they became quiet. When they were thus calmed, Jesus sent them back to their homes. The people of Dothaim were astonished and invited him to attend a wedding on the following day.

After that I saw Jesus in Dothaim, a scattered little place northeast of Sepphoris, and in which there was a synagogue. The inhabitants were not bad, though very much neglected. Abraham had once owned fields there for his cattle intended for offerings. Joseph and his brethren used to guard their flocks in this same region, and it was here that the former was sold. Dothaim, at the time of our Lord, was but a sparsely settled place, but its soil was good and its meadows extended down to the Sea of Galilee. It contained a large building like a madhouse, in which many possessed lived. On Jesus's arrival, they became perfectly furious and dashed themselves almost to death. The keepers could not bind them. Jesus entered and spoke to them, and they became quite calm. He addressed to them a few more words, after which they quietly left the house and repaired to their several homes. The people were amazed at what they saw. They were unwilling for Jesus to depart, and one of them invited him to a marriage feast.

Thursday, June 16, AD 29 (Sivan 16)

Jesus attended the wedding in Dothaim, speaking at the celebration in a friendly manner. Afterward, he addressed some words of wisdom to the bride and groom, who later, after the resurrection, joined the community of Christians.

I saw all the wedding ceremonies as at Cana. Jesus was like an honored stranger at the feast. He spoke wisely and graciously, giving the bride and groom good advice. They afterward joined the disciples when Jesus appeared upon Thebez.

Friday, June 17, AD 29 (Sivan 17)

When Jesus returned to Nazareth, he went around among his parents' acquaintances, but he was everywhere coldly received. When he sought to enter the synagogue in order to teach, they turned him away. Then he repaired to the public marketplace and spoke of the Messiah to the crowd, of whom some were Sadducees, others Pharisees. He told them that the Messiah would be different from what each one's ideas pictured. John the Baptist, he called "The voice in the wilderness."[B2] Two youths, clothed in long garments and wearing girdles like priests, had followed Jesus from the country of Hebron; but they went not always with him.

Saturday, June 18, and Sunday, June 19, AD 29 (Sivan 18–19)

Jesus kept the sabbath in Nazareth.

Monday, June 20, or Tuesday, June 21, AD 29 (Sivan 20–21)

After that I saw Jesus and Mary, Mary Cleophas, the parents of Parmenas, in all about twenty persons, leave Nazareth and go to Capernaum. They had with them asses laden with baggage.

Wednesday, June 22, AD 29 (Sivan 22)

Jesus and Mary were at their house between Capernaum and Bethsaida. Mary Cleophas stayed at a house nearby, and Parmenas's parents also stayed in the neighborhood. At this time, John the Baptist was becoming renowned throughout the land, owing to his activity of teaching and baptizing on the east bank of the Jordan between Ainon and Salem. He had already been baptizing for several weeks, and his fame had spread to Herod Antipas, who sent messengers to him from his castle at Kallirhoe, east of the Dead Sea, where he was staying. Herod invited John to visit him, but John turned the invitation down. About this time Herod traveled in his coach, together with some of his soldiers, to a place about five hours south of Ainon, and invited John to visit him there. John came to a hut nearby, and Herod went alone to talk to him. Herod asked John why he chose to live in a miserable hut (near Ainon), saying that he would have a large house built for him. John replied that he did not need a house; he had all that he needed, and his sole will was to serve God. He spoke solemnly and decisively, standing at some distance from Herod, and then left to return to the place of baptism.

The house in Nazareth had been cleaned and adorned. It was so well arranged that, with its rich hangings, it reminded me of a church. It was left unoccupied. The third husband of Mary Cleophas and some of her sons still carried on business in Anne's abode, and they took care of that house of the holy family. Mary Cleophas with her youngest sons, Joseph Barsabbas and Simeon, dwelt at this time quite near to the small house not far from Capernaum which Levi had fitted up for the Lord, and the parents of Parmenas lived at no great distance.

Thursday, June 23, to Wednesday, June 28, AD 29 (Sivan 23–29)

Jesus went from place to place, especially visiting those places through which John the Baptist had passed several weeks earlier on his journey through Palestine. Everywhere he went, Jesus taught in the synagogues and consoled the sick but did not perform any healing miracles. During the first part of this one-week period, Anne Catherine saw Jesus teaching at the synagogue of a small place concerning the nearness of the Messiah, the baptism of John, and the need for repentance. The people started to voice their disapproval. They whispered, mockingly, "Three months ago his father, the carpenter, was still alive. He worked with him. Now he has traveled about and returned to impart his wisdom."

Jesus journeyed again from place to place, and appeared chiefly where John had been when he left the desert. He entered the synagogue and instructed, he consoled and relieved the sick. When he taught in the synagogue of a certain little town and spoke of John's baptism, of the coming of the Messiah, and of penance, the people murmured. They mocked him, and I heard some of them say:

"Three months ago, his father, the carpenter, was still alive. Then he worked with him. Now he has traveled a little and back he comes to impart to us his wisdom."

On Saturday, June 25, AD 29, Anne Catherine saw John baptizing the three sons of Mary Cleophas—the future apostles Simon, James the Less, and Judas Thaddeus—at Ainon. These three were the sons of Mary Cleophas by her first marriage to Alpheus, who had died. Their half-brother Joseph Barsabbas—the son of Mary Cleophas and her second husband, Sabbas was also baptized then. Two other future apostles, Andrew and Philip, had already become followers of John the Baptist, and Andrew (and probably Philip) had also been baptized. Andrew and Philip had since returned to their place of work at Bethsaida. By now, John had about twenty disciples.

Wednesday, June 29, AD 29 (Sivan 29)

Today, Jesus was in Cana, where he visited his widowed cousin Mary, the daughter of Sobe and the sister of Mary Salome. (Mary Salome was married to Zebedee—their children, James and John, afterward became apostles—whereas Mary of Cana was also the aunt of the bridegroom Nathaniel who, six months hence, married the daughter of the wealthy Israel of Cana. See Wednesday, December 28, AD 29 for the wedding at Cana, which Jesus attended.) Here, in Cana, Jesus was not accompanied by any of those who were to become disciples.

Jesus went also to Cana and taught. He had relatives there whom he visited. At this time he was not yet accompanied by any of his future disciples. It looked as if he were studying men, and building upon the foundation that John had laid. Sometimes a good man accompanied him from place to place.

TAMMUZ (29 days): June 30/July 1 to July 28/29, AD 29
Tammuz New Moon: June 30 at 1:30 PM Jerusalem time

(Follow Map 2)

Friday, July 1, AD 29 (Tammuz 1)

Once I saw four men, among them some of his future disciples, on the highroad between Samaria and Nazareth. They were in a shady place waiting for Jesus who, with one companion, was coming that way. When he arrived in sight, they set forward to meet him. They told him that they had been baptized by John, and that he had spoken of the near coming of the Messiah. They told him also of John's severe language toward the soldiers, only a few of whom he had baptized. Among other things, he had said

Map 2: Journey to Sidon, Mount Carmel, and Jacob's Well
June 30–July 31, AD 29

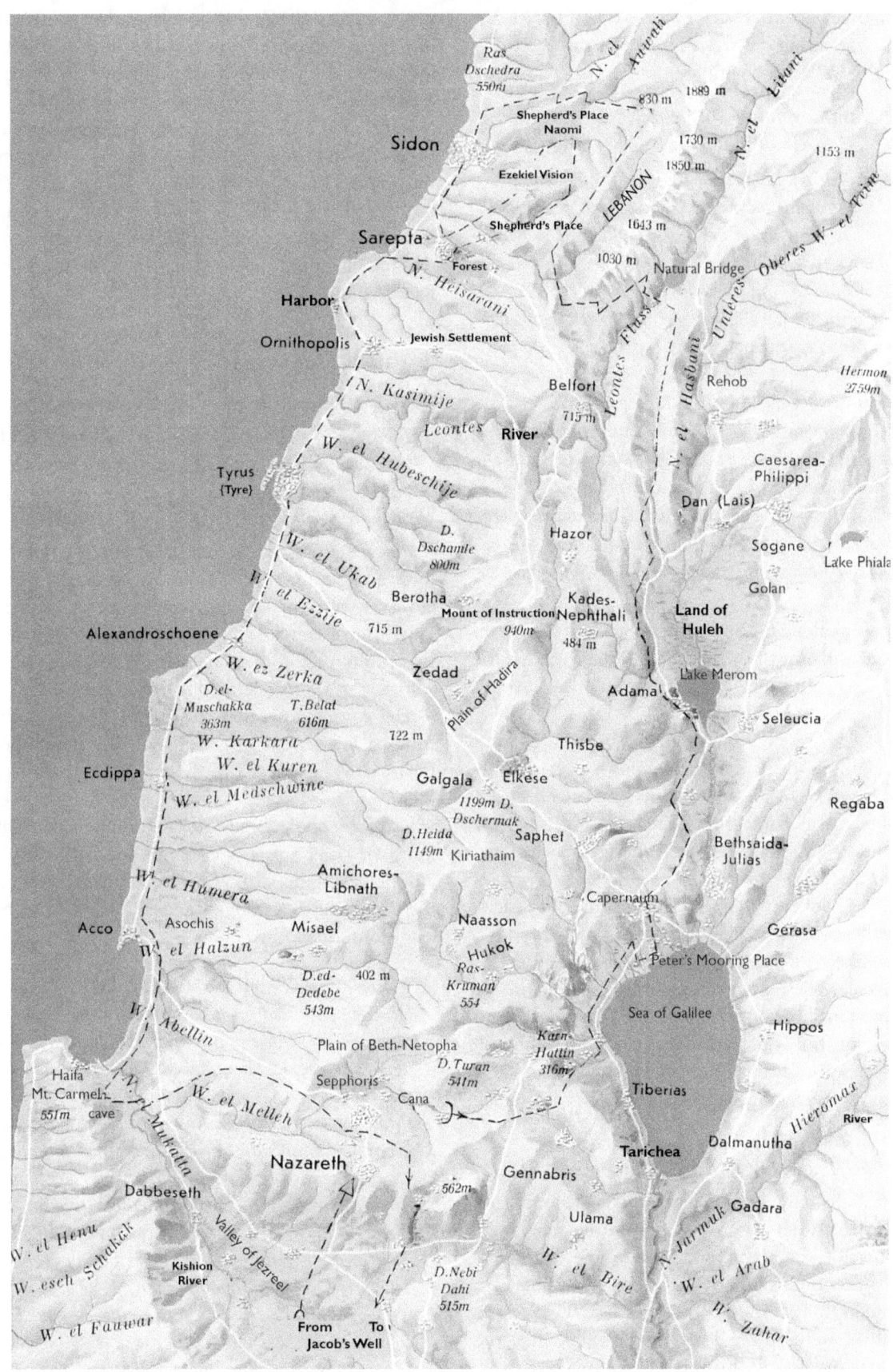

Cana—Peter's Fishery—Nazareth—South End of Lebanon—Jerusalem—Sidon—Sarepta—Battlefield of Ezekiel's Vision—Naomi's Shepherd's Place—Sarepta—Carmel—Chisloth-Tabor—Jacob's Well—Nazareth

that it would be better to take the stones out of the Jordan and baptize them rather than such as they. I saw these disciples of John walking on with Jesus.

Saturday, July 2, to Tuesday, July 5, AD 29 (Tammuz 2–5)

During this period, Jesus made his way through Galilee in the direction of Capernaum. Here and there, in the region on the west side of the Sea of Galilee, he taught about the Messiah. From time to time, too, one of the possessed would call out after him. He cast out a demon from one of them. On the way, he met six more of the Baptist's disciples, among whom was Levi, who later became an apostle and was named Matthew. Kolaya and Eustachius, who were distantly related to Jesus, were also among these six. They had heard of Jesus, and suspected that he might be the one of whom the Baptist prophesied. Kolaya and Eustachius accompanied Jesus along the way, speaking to him of John, and of Lazarus and his sisters. They marveled at Jesus and were filled with wonder both at his manner of speaking and at what he said.

Jesus then went along the Sea of Galilee toward the north. He spoke very plainly of the Messiah. In many places, the possessed cried after him. Out of one man he drove a devil, and he taught in the schools.

Six men who were coming from the baptism of John met Jesus. Among them were Levi, known later as Matthew, and two sons of the widowed relatives of Elizabeth. They all knew Jesus, some through relationship, others by hearsay; and they strongly suspected, though they had had no assurance of it, that he was the one of whom John had spoken. They spoke of John, of Lazarus and his sisters, especially of Magdalene. They supposed she had a devil, for she was already living apart from her family in the castle of Magdala. These men accompanied Jesus, and were filled with astonishment at his discourse. The aspirants to baptism going from Galilee to John used to tell him all that they knew and heard of Jesus, while they that came from Ainon, where John baptized, used to tell Jesus all they knew of John.

Wednesday, July 6, AD 29 (Tammuz 6)

Jesus went alone to the sea, passing through a fence into an enclosed fishery where lay five ships. On the shore were several huts for the accommodation of the fishermen. Peter, the owner of this fishery, was in one of the huts with Andrew; John and James, with their father Zebedee and several others, were on the boats. In the middle one was Peter's father-in-law with his three sons. I once knew all their names, but now I have forgotten them. The father was surnamed the Zealot, because he had gained his point in a dispute with the Romans concerning the right of navigation on the lake. There were about thirty men on the boats.

Jesus went along the shore by the fenced-off way between the huts and the boats, speaking with Andrew and the others. I know not whether he spoke to Peter. They did not know him as yet. He spoke of John and of the near coming of the Messiah. Andrew was already a baptized disciple of John. Jesus told them that he would come to them again.

Jesus Journeys over Lebanon to Sidon and Sarepta

Thursday, July 7, AD 29 (Tammuz 7)

Today, Jesus was on his way northward through Galilee, accompanied by about half-a-dozen people. People were impressed by his teaching on the way. Some felt he might be the one spoken of by John the Baptist.

JESUS turned off from the lake, and went further on toward Lebanon. This he was led to do chiefly by the numerous reports current throughout the country and the great excitement to which they gave rise. Many looked upon John as the Messiah, but others spoke of another whom John's words seemed to designate.

The companions of Jesus on this journey numbered from six to twelve. Some turned off at different points on the road, while others joined him. His instructions pleased them, and they began to think that he must be the one of whom John spoke. Jesus attached himself particularly to none. He was properly speaking alone, but he was sowing and preparing. In all that he did I saw many relations to the actions of the prophets and to their fulfillment, especially to those of Elijah.

Friday, July 8, AD 29 (Tammuz 8)

Having continued on his way northward through the night, Jesus went on this morning, accompanied by about ten people. He taught as he went, stopping now and then to address people in various places they passed through. Later in the day, they crossed a spur of the Lebanon foothills and beheld the city of Sidon on the coast of the Mediterranean. The city was large and bustling with life; there were innumerable ships on the sea. Jesus and his group made their way toward the city. Not only pagans—gentiles—lived there, but also some Jews. That evening the sabbath began. Jesus taught in the synagogue of the Jewish community. He spoke of the coming of the Messiah and of the downfall of idolatry. Leaving his companions behind, Jesus left the city, proceeding southward to the town of Sarepta, where he stayed overnight in a dwelling built into the city walls. An elderly man lived there. This was the same dwelling where the widow had lived who had once given food to Elijah (1 Kings 17:9).

Jesus went with his companions over a spur of the Lebanon mountains toward the great city Sidon lying along the sea. From the mountain height, the view was indescribably beautiful. The city was apparently quite close to the sea; but viewed from its own plane, one could see that it

Messiah and of the downfall of idolatry. Queen Jezebel who so persecuted Elijah was from this city.

Jesus left his companions in Sidon, and went to a little place more to the south and away from the sea. He wanted to be alone to pray. On one side it was entirely flanked by a wood. It had thick walls, and was surrounded by vineyards. It was Sarepta, the place in which Elijah was fed by the widow. The Jews, as also the pagans, had a superstition connected with that fact. They always allowed pious

View toward Sidon

was fully forty-five minutes distant from the shore. It was a large, busy place. Gazing down upon it from on high, one might fancy that he was looking upon an innumerable fleet of ships; for from the numerous flat roofs arose a forest of high poles and flagstaffs, with long streamers of red and other colors, while white canvas was stretched from pole to pole, or floated in the breeze. These booths were swarming with people at their different avocations. Between the houses, I saw all kinds of shining vessels being prepared. The country around was dotted with exceedingly fertile spots, all teeming with fruit. In and around these gardens were numbers of immense trees, some surrounded by seats. Steps led up into others, so that quite a company could sit in their branches as in a summer house. The plain in which the city lay between the mountain and the sea was not very broad.

There were both Jews and pagans in the city. They carried on business with one another, and idolatry was general. The Lord on his way taught and preached in the shady places under the great trees, speaking of John, of his baptism, and of penance.

Jesus was well received in the city. He had been there once before. In the school he taught of the coming of the

widows to live in the city walls. They thought by so doing they secured themselves from every danger, and could practice every sort of vice in the city. Old men dwelt in the walls at the time of which I am now speaking.

Saturday, July 9, AD 29, to Tuesday, July 19, AD 29 (Tammuz 9–19)

Jesus decided to remain in Sarepta for several days. He stayed with the pious old Jews living in the city walls who revered Elijah and were occupied with interpreting the prophecies concerning the coming of the Messiah. Jesus also visited the synagogue and taught the children. He spent much time, too, alone in prayer in the forest around the town. Sometimes he remained there all night. He also visited some of the surrounding pagan places and admonished the Jews not to mix with the pagans. Toward the end of this period, John the Baptist and his followers left the place of baptism near Ainon and went south to a new place, near Gilgal. After baptizing there only for a short time, John then continued on to a third place of baptism on the west side of the Jordan, near a village called Ono. It was here that Jesus himself was later baptized.

Jesus lodged with an old man in the city wall, in the house once occupied by that widow who fed Elijah. The old men who then dwelt in the walls were something like hermits. They lived there in accordance with an ancient custom honoring Elijah, meditating and explaining the prophecies, and chiefly engaged in prayer for the coming of the Messiah. Jesus taught them concerning the Messiah and the baptism of John. They were pious, but entertained many erroneous ideas, of which one was that the Messiah was to come in worldly splendor. Jesus often retired to the wood near Sarepta and there prayed alone. He taught in the synagogue, and occupied himself also in instructing the children. In the villages around, in which there were numbers of pagans, he exhorted the people not to mix with them. There were some good people here, and some very bad ones. Jesus had no companions, excepting occasionally some resident of the place. I saw him teaching men and women in the open air, often on hillocks and under trees.

The climate here is such that it always seems to me we are in May, because in Palestine the grain for the second harvest is as far advanced as it is with us in that month. They do not cut the grain so close to the ground as we do. They grasp the stalk below the ear, and cut it off a little under four feet long. They do not thrash it. They stand the little sheaves upright and pass over them a roller fastened between two oxen. The grain is much drier than ours, and falls out readily. They separate it in the open air, or in a kind of circular barn with a thatched roof, but open on all sides.

Wednesday, July 20, AD 29 (Tammuz 20)

Around this time, Jesus left Sarepta and went north to a place not far from a battlefield where in a vision Ezekiel had beheld the bones of the dead that were gathered together and restored to life (Ezekiel 37). Jesus taught and consoled the people living there, teaching them that Ezekiel's vision was about to be fulfilled (meaning that the breathing of new life into the dead was a vision referring to the sending of the Holy Spirit).

From Sarepta Jesus went to a place lying to the northeast, not far from the plain upon which Ezekiel, caught up in spirit, had the vision of the dry bones coming together. Sinews and flesh took possession of them, the winds passed over them, spirit and life entered into them. I was told that the coming together of the bones and their clothing with flesh were fulfilled by the teaching and baptism of John. But the spirit and life breathed into them was accomplished by Jesus through Redemption and by the descent of the Holy Spirit. Jesus consoled the people, who were very poor and oppressed, and explained to them the vision of Ezekiel.

Thursday, July 21, AD 29 (Tammuz 21)

Jesus traveled further north to a little shepherd community situated close to a small stream. Naomi and her daughter Ruth had stayed here for a length of time (Ruth 1:19). Jesus taught the shepherds, and then set off back toward Sarepta again, passing by Sidon on the way.

When he left this place, he went northward to the country which John had first visited on leaving the desert. It was a little sheep-rearing place. Naomi and her daughter Ruth dwelt there a long time. Naomi had so good a name among the people that she is still spoken of in those parts. Later she removed to Bethlehem. The Lord taught very zealously here. The time approached for him to retrace his steps southward and thence to Samaria for his baptism. Jacob also owned fields up here. Through this place ran a little river, back of which far up in the desert lay John's spring. From this spring the road became very steep, reminding me of that which Adam and Eve took when driven from Paradise. It led down to the battlefield of Ezekiel. On Adam and Eve's route, the trees became smaller and smaller and quite misshapen until at last they reached a desolate region where grew some miserable bushes. Paradise was as high above the earth as is the sun. After the Fall it disappeared behind a mountain which seemed to rise before it.

The Savior, on his return from the shepherds' country to Sarepta, followed the route trodden by the prophet Elijah when going from the brook Kerith to Sarepta. Jesus taught here and there as he journeyed on, passing by Sidon.

Friday, July 22, and Saturday, July 23, AD 29 (Tammuz 22–23)

Jesus taught and celebrated the sabbath in Sarepta. Then he departed and walked through the night, traveling southward toward Mount Carmel, where the prophet Elijah had once been.

From Sarepta he was soon to go southward for his baptism. He kept the sabbath in Sarepta. After the sabbath Jesus started for Nazareth, teaching at various points on the road. He was sometimes attended by companions, and sometimes alone. He went barefoot, putting his sandals on only when about to enter any town or village.

Sunday, July 24, and Monday, July 25, AD 29 (Tammuz 24–25)

Jesus continued on his way. After visiting Mount Carmel, he traveled eastward toward Mount Tabor. At the foot of the west side of Mount Tabor was the little town Chisloth-Tabor. Here Jesus taught in the synagogue concerning the baptism of John. Five people accompanied

Jesus here, among them some future disciples. One of the holy women, Veronica, together with her son Amandor and her friend Johanna Chusa, left Jerusalem at this time to travel to Capernaum. From there they were to go with Mary to Nazareth, where they expected Jesus to arrive when he returned from his journey to Lebanon.

He passed through the valleys toward Mount Carmel, and once he was near the road leading down into Egypt, but he turned off to the east.

The Mother of God, Mary Cleophas, the mother of Parmenas, and two other women, I saw going to Nazareth, while Seraphia (afterward Veronica), Johanna Chusa, and the son of Veronica, who later on joined the disciples, were on their way to the same place from Jerusalem. They were going to visit Mary, with whom they had become acquainted on their yearly journeys to the Holy City.

Mary and Joseph, as also other pious families, were in the habit of visiting through devotion three places during the year; viz., the temple of Jerusalem, the pine tree near Bethlehem, and Mount Carmel. Anne's family and other pious people usually went to the last named place in May when returning from Jerusalem. There were on the mountain a well and a cave of Elijah, the latter like a chapel. Devout Jews were constantly visiting these hallowed places. They came, not at fixed times, but whenever it best suited them, and prayed for the coming of the Messiah. Jewish hermits dwelt on the mountain, and later on Christian cenobites had there their cells.

In a little town on the west side of Mount Tabor, Jesus taught in the school, and spoke of John's baptism. There were five followers around him, among them some future disciples.

Wednesday, July 27, AD 29 (Tammuz 27)

The Sanhedrin of Jerusalem dispatched couriers with letters to all the principal places of Palestine in which were Jewish schools and rabbis, telling them to be on their guard against a certain man, of whom the Baptist said that he was the one that was to come and that he would soon present himself for baptism. They should have an eye upon the man and give information of his actions; for if he were indeed the Messiah, he needed not the baptism of John. The members of the Sanhedrin also were very much annoyed when they learned that Jesus was he who as a boy had taught in the temple. The couriers went likewise to a city on the road near Hebron, four hours from the sea, in that country wherein the spies of Aaron and Moses found the huge bunches of grapes. The city is called Gaza. There was a very long row of tents reaching from the city to the sea, and under them different kinds of woolen and silk stuffs exposed for sale.

AB (30 Days): July 29/30 to August 27/28, AD 29 Ab
New Moon: July 29 at 11:10 PM Jerusalem time

Friday, July 29, and Saturday, July 30, AD 29 (Tammuz 29—Ab 1)

Before returning to Nazareth, Jesus, with his five traveling companions, visited Jacob's well near Sychar in Samaria. He taught here and there as he went, celebrating the sabbath in the neighborhood.

Jesus with five followers taught, here and there, down to the country around Jacob's well, where he celebrated the sabbath.

Sunday, July 31, and Monday, August 1, AD 29 (Ab 2–3)

When he and his companions were returning to Nazareth, the blessed Virgin went out to meet her son. But when she saw that he was not alone, she paused at a distance and went back without saluting him. I wondered at her self-denial. Jesus taught in the school at Nazareth, the holy women being present.

Tuesday, August 2, AD 29 (Ab 4)

The next day, when Jesus taught in the synagogue before a large audience, the holy women were not present. He was attended by five disciples and about twenty of the young Nazarenes, companions of his boyhood. His hearers murmured at his teaching. They whispered among themselves that he would now, perhaps, take possession of the place of baptism that John had abandoned and there baptizing give himself out for one like unto John. But, they continued, he was very different from John. John had dwelt in the desert preparing for his mission, but this Jesus they knew well, and they declared that they would not allow him to deceive them.

Wednesday, August 3, AD 29 (Ab 5)

Today, Anne Catherine saw a group of about twenty arrive at John's place of baptism near Ono. They had been sent from Jerusalem by the Sanhedrin. They told John that he should present himself in Jerusalem. But John replied that soon the one he proclaimed would come to him. He described the one-to-come quite clearly, saying that he had been born in Bethlehem and raised in Nazareth but that he had never seen him.

(Follow Map 3)

Jesus in Bethsaida and Capernaum

Thursday, August 4, AD 29 (Ab 6)

Jesus spoke with his mother at the house where she was staying and where the other holy women and friends

Map 3: Travels in Southern Galilee
August 4–26, AD 29

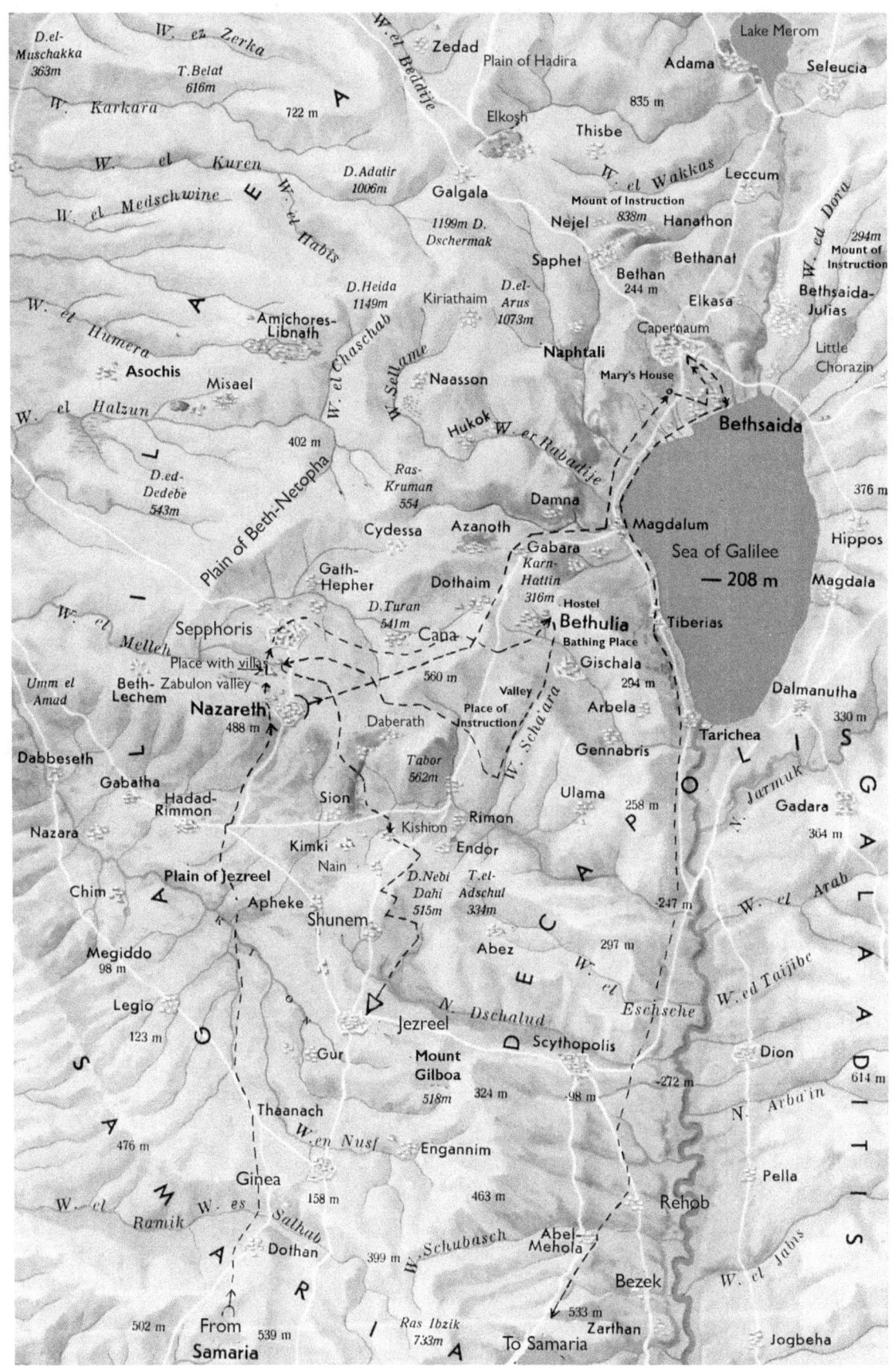

Nazareth—Capernaum—Bethsaida—Land of Samaria—Zebulon Valley—Sepphoris—Bethulia
Wadi Scha'ara—Zebulon Valley—Kision—Jezreel

were also gathered. Jesus explained that, because of the hostility and rejection he had encountered in Nazareth, he would return to Capernaum and Bethsaida to teach. He left the house with Veronica's son Amandor, the Essene youth Eustachius, and the son of the widow Lea, Kolaya. Amandor, Eustachius, and Kolaya were his first three disciples.*

JESUS left Nazareth to go to Bethsaida where he aimed at rousing some of the people by his teaching. The blessed Virgin and his followers remained behind. During his stay in Nazareth, Jesus had stopped with his friends in his mother's house. But so much discontent and murmuring arose in the little town on his account that he resolved to go to Bethsaida for awhile, and return to Nazareth at some future time. He was accompanied by Amandor, the son of Veronica; a son of one of the three widowed relatives of Jesus, whose name sounds like Sirach; and one of Peter's relatives known later as one of the disciples.

Friday, August 5, AD 29 (Ab 7)

As the sabbath began this evening, Jesus went to the synagogue in Bethsaida. He spoke very powerfully, advocating repentance and the baptism by John. Many people were present, including the future apostle Philip.

At Bethsaida, Jesus taught very forcibly in the synagogue on the sabbath. He told his hearers that they should now enter into themselves, repair to the baptism of John, and purify themselves by penance; otherwise a time would come when they would cry woe! woe! There were many people in the synagogue, but none of the future apostles, excepting, I think, Philip. The others, belonging to Bethsaida and the country around, were celebrating the sabbath elsewhere. They were in a house near the fishery in the neighborhood of Capernaum. During this preaching of Jesus, I prayed that the people would go to the baptism of John and be truly converted. Thereupon I had a vision in which I saw that John was the preparer, who washed from the people their rawness, their coarseness. I saw him working so actively, so vigorously, preaching so vehemently that his camel skin slipped from shoulder to shoulder. This, I think, was merely symbolical, for at the same time I saw something like scales falling from some of the newly baptized, black vapors issuing from others, and light, shining clouds descending upon others.

Sunday, August 7, AD 29 (Ab 9)

Jesus made his way from Bethsaida to Capernaum, teaching on the way. He was accompanied by Amandor, Eustachius, and Kolaya.

Monday, August 8, AD 29 (Ab 10)

In Capernaum also Jesus taught in the school. Crowds came from all sides to hear him, among them Peter, Andrew, and many others who had already been baptized by John.

Tuesday, August 9, AD 29 (Ab 11)

Jesus stayed in Capernaum.

Wednesday, August 10, AD 29 (Ab 12)

Today, Jesus taught at a place on the west shore of the Sea of Galilee, two hours south of Capernaum. The three disciples who had accompanied him to Bethsaida and Capernaum were still with him.

When Jesus left Capernaum, I saw him teaching two hours distant from the city toward the south. His hearers were numerous. He had with him only the three disciples, for the future apostles who had heard him in Capernaum had, without exchanging words with him, gone again to the sea. Jesus spoke here also of John's baptism and the fulfilled Promise.

Thursday, August 11, AD 29 (Ab 13)

Jesus traveled southward through Lower Galilee toward Samaria. Then he turned toward the north again.

Friday, August 12, and Saturday, August 13, AD 29 (Ab 14–15)

Jesus kept the sabbath in a school between Nazareth and Sepphoris. The holy women from Nazareth were present, also Peter's wife and the wives of some others of the future apostles.

The place consisted of only a few houses and a school. It was separated from Anne's former residence by a field. Of the future apostles, Peter, Andrew, James the Less, and Philip, all disciples of John, came to hear Jesus. Philip belonged to Bethsaida; he was tolerably well educated, and was much engaged in writing. Jesus did not tarry long here. He took no meal, but only taught. The apostles had, probably, celebrated the sabbath in the neighborhood, for the Jews often visited other places on the sabbath. Being informed of Jesus's presence, they had come to hear him. He had not yet spoken to any of them in particular.

Jesus in Sepphoris, Bethulia, Kishion, and Jezreel

Sunday, August 14, AD 29 (Ab 16)

FROM the last place, Jesus crossed a mountain with the three disciples and went to Sepphoris, four hours' distance from Nazareth. He stopped at his great-aunt's. She was Anne's youngest sister Maraha, and the mother of a daughter and two sons. These sons were clothed in long, white garments. They were named respectively Arastaria and Cocharia, and later on they joined the disciples.

The blessed Virgin, Mary Cleophas, and other women

had also come hither. The feet of Jesus were washed, and a repast prepared in his honor. He passed the night in Maraha's house, which had been the home of Anne's parents. Sepphoris was a large city, and in it were three different sects: the Pharisees, the Sadducees, and the Essenes, each with its own school. This city often suffered severely from war. At the present day, it is scarcely in existence.

Monday, August 15, to Wednesday, August 17, AD 29 (Ab 17–19)

Jesus stayed some days here, preaching and exhorting his hearers to go to the baptism of John. He taught in two synagogues on the same day, in a large, high one, and in a small one. The large one belonged to the Pharisees. They listened indignantly to his words, and murmured against him. The women were present at this instruction; but in the other synagogue, the small one that belonged to the Essenes, there was no place for women. Jesus was kindly received by the Essenes.

Thursday, August 18, AD 29 (Ab 20)

Today, Jesus taught at the synagogue of the Sadducees in Sepphoris. Next to the synagogue was a madhouse, and inmates were obliged to attend the synagogue, accompanied by custodians. As Jesus taught, one or the other of the inmates began to speak out loud: "This is Jesus of Nazareth, born in Bethlehem, visited by wise men from the east." "His mother is with Maraha." "He is bringing a new teaching," and so on. Jesus spoke the words: "The spirit that speaks this is from below and should return there." At this, all the inmates became quiet and were healed. Afterward a great uproar broke out in Sepphoris, forcing Jesus to hide in a house. That night, he left the town, as did his three disciples and the two sons of Maraha (Arastaria and Cocharia). Later, the five met up with Jesus by some trees outside the town, on the way from Sepphoris to Bethulia. They then proceeded together to Bethulia.

As Jesus was teaching in the school of the Sadducees, something very wonderful took place. There were in Sepphoris numbers of demoniacs, simpletons, lunatics and possessed. They were instructed in a school near the synagogue, which latter place they were obliged to attend when prayer and teaching were going on. They had a hall in the rear reserved for themselves, and they were made to listen attentively. Custodians armed with whips stood among them, each with few or more under his charge, according as they were more or less troublesome. Before Jesus entered, I saw these poor creatures during the teaching of the Sadducees distorting their countenance and falling into convulsions. Their keepers had to bring them to order with the lash. When Jesus made his appearance, they were at first quite still; but after a little while one began and then another to cry out: "That is Jesus of Nazareth, born in Bethlehem and visited by wise men from the east. His mother is now with Maraha. He is preaching new doctrine, which we must not tolerate." And so they went on recounting aloud the whole life of Jesus and all that had happened to him up to the present time. Now this one began, then that one took it up. The lashes of the custodians availed naught, for soon all began to cry out together and the confusion became general. Then Jesus commanded them to be brought to him outside the synagogue, and he sent two disciples to collect all the other insane from the different quarters of the city and bring them also. Soon there was a crowd, fully fifty such unfortunates around him, and multitudes of others, all eager to see what would happen. The insane kept up their cries. Then Jesus spoke, saying: "The spirit that speaks through these, is from below. Let it again go below!" And at the same instant, all became quiet. They were cured, and I saw several fall to the ground.

And now a great tumult, excited by the cure, broke out in the city, and Jesus and his followers were in great danger. The excitement became so great that Jesus escaped into a house and left the city that night. The blessed Virgin, the three disciples, with Cocharia and Arastaria, the sons of Anne's sister, left the city also. The mother of Jesus was in great trouble and anxiety, for this was the first time she had seen her son so violently persecuted. Jesus had appointed some trees outside the city as a meeting place, and from there all went on together to Bethulia.

The majority of those cured by Jesus in Sepphoris, went to John's baptism. Later on they were the principal ones of the city who followed Jesus.

Bethulia is that city at whose siege Judith slew Holofernes. It was built on a mountain southeast of Sepphoris. The view from it extended far around into the distance. Magdalene's castle in Magdala was not far off, and Magdalene herself was at this time at the height of her glory. Bethulia, too, possessed a castle and the place was rich in springs.

Friday, August 19, AD 29 (Ab 21)

Mary and the holy women also made their way to Bethulia. The town was much visited on account of its springs; it was a kind of bathing resort. Jesus and his five companions went to an inn on the outskirts of town. Mary went to see him there. That evening, as the sabbath began, Jesus taught in Bethulia.

Jesus and his disciples entered an inn outside Bethulia, and thither came Mary and the holy women again to meet him. I heard Mary talking to him, begging him not to teach here again, for she was afraid there might be another insurrection. But Jesus replied that he knew what he had to accomplish. Mary asked: "Shall we not now go to John's baptism?" To which Jesus answered gravely: "Why shall we now go to John's baptism? Have we need of it? I shall journey and reap still a while longer, and I shall say when it is time to go to the baptism." As afterward at Cana, Mary kept silence. I have seen that the holy women received baptism not till after Pentecost, and then in the pool of Bethesda. The holy women went on into the city.

Saturday, August 20, AD 29 (Ab 22)

Jesus taught on the sabbath in the synagogue, and many from the country around came to hear him. Here in Bethulia, also, I saw numbers of insane and possessed on the highroad outside the city and, here and there, on the streets through which Jesus passed. They were quieted and freed from their paroxysms. The people said among themselves: "This man must possess a power like unto that of the ancient prophets, since those unfortunates grow calm on his appearance." They felt benefitted by his presence, even though apparently he did nothing special for them; and so they sought him in the inn to thank him. He taught and exhorted to John's baptism, and spoke with as much vehemence as did John himself.

Sunday, August 21, AD 29 (Ab 23)

The people of Bethulia gave to Jesus and his followers a most honorable reception. They would not allow him to put up at the inn outside the city, but strove among themselves as to who should have the honor of entertaining him in their houses. They that had not Jesus, at least wanted one of the five disciples who were with him. But they, the disciples, would not leave their Master. At last, Jesus promised to make the inn and the houses of the good people his headquarters alternately. Their great enthusiasm and love for him were not altogether disinterested, and Jesus charged them with it during his instruction in the synagogue. They had a secondary design.

They wanted, by entertaining the new prophet, to attract to their city that esteem which they had lost by their trade and other dealings with pagans. They were also destitute of a pure love of truth.

Monday, August 22, AD 29 (Ab 24)

When Jesus left Bethulia, I saw him in a valley teaching under the trees. Besides the five disciples, there were now about twenty others following him. The holy women had already returned to Nazareth. Jesus had left Bethulia because he was so much besieged by the people. Numbers of sick and possessed from the country around had gathered in the city, hoping to be cured; but Jesus did not as yet wish to heal so openly.

Tuesday, August 23, and Wednesday, August 24, AD 29 (Ab 25–26)

During the day, Jesus taught in the same valley south of Bethulia to a group of about thirty people. Here there was a place for teaching, used by the Essenes, that went back to the days of the prophets. Toward sunset, Jesus went to a small place in the valley of Zebulon consisting of a number of villas. It was about an hour north of Nazareth. There, Jesus taught that evening in the synagogue, where he received a friendly welcome.

As he journeyed away from Bethulia, he left the Sea of Galilee behind. The place in which he next taught was an old place of instruction formerly used by the Essenes, or prophets. It consisted of an elevated, grassy mound, surrounded by little parapets against which the audience could rest comfortably. There were about thirty people around Jesus in this place.

That evening I saw him with his followers arrive at the little village with its synagogue, a small place in the valley of Zebulon consisting of a number of villas, about one hour's distance from Nazareth, whence not long before he had set out to go to Sepphoris. The inhabitants received him with every mark of kindness. They conducted him to a large house in front of which was a courtyard, washed his feet, as also those of the disciples, cleaned and brushed his traveling garments, and prepared for him and his followers a repast. Jesus taught here in the synagogue. The holy women were in Nazareth.

Thursday, August 25, AD 29 (Ab 27)

Today, Jesus was in the neighborhood of Kishion. He preached on a hill and spoke of his coming baptism.

Next day he went about two miles further on toward the Levitical city, Kishion, a small place southeast of Nazareth, near Mount Tabor. He was followed by about seven possessed, who still more plainly than those of Sepphoris proclaimed his mission and history. Aged priests and youths in long, white garments came forth from the city to meet him, for some of his followers had already gone before him into the city.

Jesus did not free the possessed here. They were confined in a house by the priests, that they might not create disorder. But he freed them later after his baptism. He was quite well received and entertained in this place, but when he proposed to teach, they questioned him: What call had he? What mission? Was he merely Joseph and Mary's son? Jesus answered evasively that he who had sent him and to whom he belonged would make all that known at his baptism. He taught many other things on this point and also of the baptism of John. His instructions were given on a hill in the center of the place where, as at Thebez, a stand had been prepared for the purpose, not exactly in the open air, but under a rush-covered tent or shed.

Friday, August 26, AD 29 (Ab 28)
Speaking here and there, Jesus wandered through an area where there were many shepherds. As the sabbath began, he arrived in the town Jezreel, south of Mount Tabor.

Jesus went from here through the pastoral region where later, after the second Passover, he healed a leper. He taught in the different little villages around. But for the sabbath he went with his companions to Jezreel, a scattered place, the houses, which were built in groups, being

Temple Garden, Ancient Jezreel

separated from one another by ruins, towers, and gardens. A highroad ran through the city, called King's street. Jesus had with him only three of his companions, several having gone on before.

Jezreel was the home of strict observers of the Jewish Law. They were not Essenes, however, but Nazarites. They made vows for a time, longer or shorter, and practiced various kinds of mortification. They had a large institution, comprising different sections. The unmarried men occupied one part exclusively, the unmarried women another. The married also made vows of continency for a certain period, during which the husbands lived in a house next to that of the unmarried men, while the wives retired to that of the single women. They were all clothed in gray and white. Their superior wore a long, gray garment edged with fringe and little white ornaments like fruit, and bound by a gray girdle on which were inscribed white letters. Around one arm was a band of coarse, gray and white woven fabric as thick as a twisted napkin, one end of which—ornamented with tufted fringe—hung down a little. He wore a collar, or little mantle, almost like that of Archos, the Essene, excepting that it was gray and open behind instead of in front. A blank shield was fastened on it in front, while behind it was tied or laced. On the shoulders hung slit lappets. All wore black, shining, puffed caps, with some words stamped on the front; three bands met on top forming a ball, which, like the rim, was white and gray. The Nazarites had long, thick curly hair and beards. I tried to think which of the apostles looked like them and, at last, I remembered that it was Paul. His hair and garments, when he persecuted the Christians, were in the style of the Nazarites. I saw him afterward, also, with the Nazarites, for he was one of them. They used to let their hair grow until their vow was accomplished, when they cut it off and burned it in sacrifice. They sacrificed pigeons, also. One could assume and fulfill the unfulfilled vows of another. Jesus celebrated the sabbath with them. Jezreel is separated from Nazareth by a mountain range. Not far from it is a well near which Saul once encamped with his army.

(Follow Map 4)

Saturday, August 27, AD 29 (Ab 29)
In his sabbath teaching, Jesus warned against setting oneself apart from others through pride. His attention was directed especially to those of the Nazarite sect, many of whom were living in Jezreel, who had set themselves apart from others living in the town who had married pagans.

Jesus taught on the sabbath of the baptism of John. He said that, although their piety was praiseworthy, yet excess was dangerous; that there are different ways to salvation; that splits in the community would easily give rise to sects; that, in their pride, they looked down upon their weaker brethren who could not do so much as they themselves, but who should be succored by the stronger. Such teaching as his was very necessary here, for in the outskirts there were people who had mixed with the pagans, and who were destitute of rule or direction, because the Nazarites had separated from them. Jesus visited these people in their homes, and invited them to his instruction on baptism.

Sunday, August 28, AD 29 (Ab 30)
The Nazarites invited Jesus to eat with them. During the course of the meal, some Nazarites spoke about circumcision. Jesus declared that circumcision would soon be replaced by baptism (through the Holy Spirit) as the sign of the new covenant.

Map 4: Travels with Eliud in Lower Galilee
August 27–September 17, AD 29

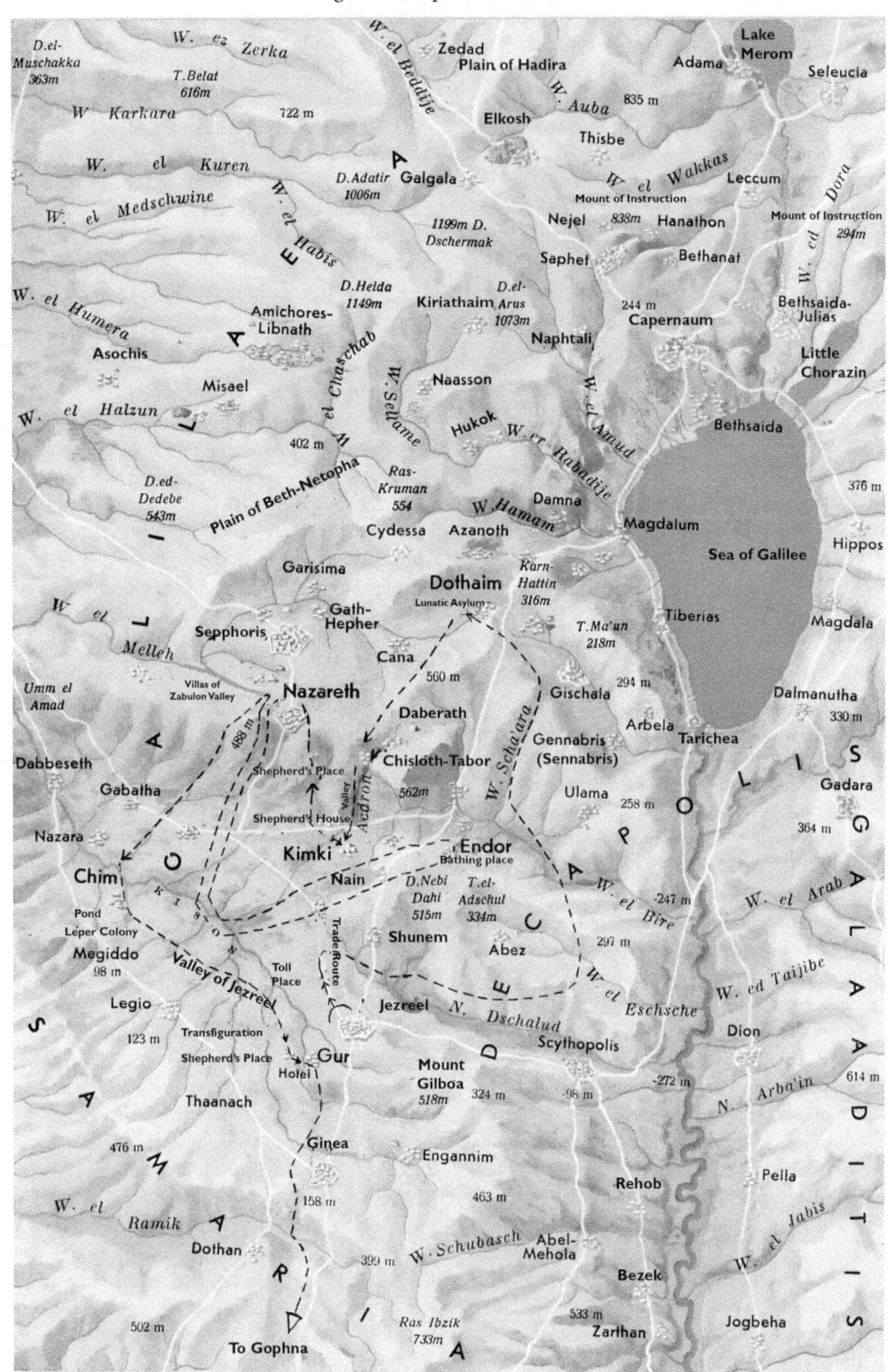

Jezreel—Publicans' Place—Dothaim—Chisloth-Tabor—Edron Valley—Kimki—Nazareth
Endor—Nazareth—Chim—Plain of Jezreel—Gur

Next day Jesus was present at a repast given him by the Nazarites, at which circumcision was spoken of in connection with baptism. For the first time I heard Jesus speaking of circumcision, but I cannot exactly recall his words.

He said something to this effect, that the law of circumcision had a reason for its existence which would soon be taken away, when the people of God would come forth no longer according to the flesh from the family of Abraham, but spiritually from the baptism of the Holy Spirit.

Great numbers of the Nazarites became Christians; but they clung so tenaciously to Judaism that many of them, seeking to combine Christianity with it, fell into heresy.

ELUL (29 Days): August 28/29 to September 25/26, AD 29 Elul New Moon: August 28 at 8:00 AM Jerusalem time

Jesus Among the Publicans

Monday, August 29, AD 29 (Elul 1)
Today, Jesus visited a group of rich tax collectors living between Jezreel and Apheke. They had their own synagogue, where Jesus taught.

WHEN Jesus left Jezreel, he journeyed awhile toward the east, then went around the mountain which lay between Jezreel and Nazareth and, about two hours from the former place, reached a number of houses standing in rows on either side of the highroad. They were occupied by publicans. Some poor Jews dwelt under tents at a little distance from the road. That road, along which the dwellings of the publicans stood, was fenced in by wickerwork, the entrance at either end being closed. Rich publicans lived here who rented many tolls in the country and again leased the same to under-collectors. Matthew was one of these latter tax gatherers, but belonging to another place. Mary, the niece of Elizabeth, once dwelt here, I think. Having become a widow, she went to Nazareth and afterward to Capernaum. She was the same that was present at the blessed Virgin's death. The commercial highroad to Egypt from Syria, Arabia, and Sidon passed through this place. Great bales of white silk in bundles like flax were brought this way on camels and asses; also fine woolen stuffs both white and colored; great, heavy, woven strips of carpet; and lastly spices. When the camels arrived in this district, the gates were closed and the merchants had to unpack their goods, which were carefully examined. They had to pay a tax, partly in merchandise and partly in money. The latter was mostly three- or four-cornered yellow, white, or reddish pieces, on which was stamped a figure, raised on one side and hollow on the other. They gave also coins different from these. I saw on those coins little towers, a virgin, also an infant in a little ship. Little bars of gold, such as were offered by the kings at the crib, I never saw again excepting with some strangers who came to John the Baptist.

The publicans were all leagued together. When one received more than his fellows, he divided with the rest. They were wealthy and lived well. Their homes were surrounded by courtyards, gardens, and walls, reminding me of those of our well-to-do peasants. They lived entirely among themselves, for others would not associate with them. They had a school of their own and a teacher.

Tuesday, August 30, AD 29 (Elul 2)
Jesus continued to teach the tax collectors, exhorting them to receive the baptism of John.

Jesus was well received by them, his followers also. I saw several women arrive here; I think Peter's wife was among them. One of them spoke with Jesus, and they soon went away. Perhaps they were either coming from or going to Nazareth, and were executing some commission for the Mother of God. Jesus stayed first with one, then with another of the publicans, and taught in their school. He especially pointed out to them the fact that they often extorted from travelers more toll than was just. They became very much confused, and could not divine how he knew that. They were more humble than the other Jews, and took his words better. Jesus urged them to receive baptism.

Jesus in Chisloth-Tabor

Wednesday, August 31, AD 29 (Elul 3)
JESUS left the publicans after having taught among them the whole night. Many of them desired to make him presents, but he would accept nothing. Several followed him, for they wanted to go with him to baptism. On this day he journeyed through the country by Dothaim and passed the madhouse where, on his first journey from Nazareth, he had calmed the raving and the possessed. As he was passing it, they called him by name and clamored violently to be released. Jesus commanded their custodians to free them, promising that he would answer for the consequences. They were all set at liberty. Jesus cured them all, and they followed him. Toward evening, he arrived at Chisloth, a city on Mount Tabor, inhabited mainly by Pharisees. They had heard of Jesus; but they were displeased at seeing him followed by publicans (whom they looked upon as malefactors), possessed known to be such, and a motley crowd of others. He entered their school and taught of the baptism of John; then, addressing his followers, he exhorted them before attaching themselves to him to think seriously whether they would be able to persevere

or not, for they must not think his path an easy one. He expounded to them also several parables on building. If a man desired to build himself a house, he should consider first whether the owner of the ground would allow him to use it for that purpose; in like manner, they that would follow him should first expiate their offences and do penance. Again, if a man would erect a tower, he must first estimate the cost. And many other things Jesus taught that were not well received by the Pharisees. They listened only to catch him in his words. I saw them concerting together to give him an entertainment at which they hoped to ensnare him in his speech.

Thursday, September 1, AD 29 (Elul 4)

The Pharisees invited Jesus to a meal, so that they could ensnare him with his own words. On arriving, the first thing that Jesus did was to ask where the poor were. To the displeasure of the Pharisees, Jesus then sent out his disciples to round up the poor of the town and bring them to the meal. The same night, he left Chisloth.

They prepared a great feast in a public hall, down which stood three tables, side by side, and right and left burned lamps. Over the middle table, at which Jesus, some of the disciples, and the Pharisees sat, the aperture, customary in the roofs of that country, stood open. The followers of Jesus were seated at the side tables. In this city there must have been an ancient custom commanding the poor, of whom there were numbers dwelling in the greatest abandonment, to be invited; for as soon as Jesus sat down at table, he turned to the Pharisees asking where were the poor, and whether it was not their right to take part in the feast. The Pharisees were embarrassed, and they answered that the custom had long fallen into disuse. Then Jesus commanded his disciples Arastaria and Cocharia, the sons of Maraha, and Kolaya, the son of the widow Lea, to go gather together the poor of the city and bring them to the feast. The Pharisees were highly displeased at the command, for it gave rise to much comment throughout the city. Many of the poor were already in bed and asleep. I saw the disciples rousing them. Numerous and varied were the joyous scenes I then witnessed in the huts and haunts of the poor. At last they arrived and were received and welcomed by Jesus and his disciples. The latter served them while Jesus addressed to them a very beautiful instruction. The Pharisees, though greatly irritated, had not a word to say, for Jesus was in the right, and at this the people rejoiced. Great excitement prevailed in the city. After partaking plentifully of the various good things, the poor people departed, taking with them a supply for their friends at home. Jesus had blessed the food for them, prayed with them, and exhorted them to go to John's baptism. He would not tarry longer in the city, and left that night with his followers. Many of the latter, however, discouraged partly by his exhortations, left him for their homes while others went to prepare for John's baptism.

Jesus in the Shepherd Village of Kimki

Friday, September 2, AD 29 (Elul 5)

After leaving Chisloth, Jesus passed through the Edron valley, accompanied by some followers. He came to the shepherd village of Kimki. That evening, he celebrated the sabbath and taught in the synagogue there.

JESUS journeyed during the night between two valleys. I saw him sometimes conversing with his followers, then again falling behind and praying on his knees to his Father, after which he again rejoined them. On the following afternoon I saw him arrive at a shepherd village whose houses lay scattered here and there. It possessed a school, but no resident priest; the people were attended by one from a distance. When Jesus arrived, the school was closed. He assembled the shepherds in an apartment of the inn and there instructed them. As the sabbath was approaching, there came that evening several priests of the sect of the Pharisees, some of them from Nazareth. Jesus spoke of baptism and the near advent of the Messiah. The Pharisees were very hostile toward him; they spoke of his humble origin, and tried to make little of him. Jesus slept here that night.

Saturday, September 3, AD 29 (Elul 6)

Jesus again taught in the synagogue, expounding several parables, which the Pharisees mocked as childish. That night, Jesus stayed with a poor family and healed the mistress of the house who was suffering from edema.

Jesus, in his instructions on the sabbath, expounded many parables. He called for a grain of mustard seed and, when they brought it to him, he spoke for some time of it, saying that if they had faith equal only to a grain of that seed, they would be able to transport the pear tree before them into the sea. A large pear tree laden with fruit stood nearby. The Pharisees mocked at his teaching, which they considered childish. Jesus explained at length, but I have forgotten. He also recounted the parable of the unjust steward.

The people of this place and of the whole country around were in admiration of Jesus. They related what they had heard from their fathers of the teaching and works of the last prophets, and they compared this new teacher to them with this exception, however, that he was much milder. The shepherd settlement was named Kimki.

The hills of Nazareth could be discerned in the distance, for they were only about two hours off. It was a scattered little place, a few houses only around the synagogue. Jesus took up his abode in a poor family, the mistress of which lay sick of the edema. He had compassion upon her and cured her, laying his hand upon her head and stomach. She was perfectly restored, and served her guest at table. Jesus forbade her to speak of what had happened until he should have returned from the baptism. Whereupon she asked why she might not tell it everywhere. Jesus answered: "If thou wilt publish it everywhere, thou shalt become mute," and she did become mute, and remained so until his return from baptism. At this time it may have been about fourteen days until then, for at Bethulia or Jezreel he had spoken of three weeks.

Sunday, September 4, AD 29 (Elul 7)

This evening, in the synagogue, the Pharisees were greatly angered at Jesus' teaching, which warned against taking life too lightly as had been done at the time of Noah or Lot. The Pharisees accused Jesus of speaking as if he were the Messiah himself, and—amid uproar—they put out the lights. That night, Jesus and his disciples left Kimki and went northward.

Jesus taught three days in the synagogue of this place. The Pharisees were greatly incensed against him. He spoke of the coming of the Messiah, saying, "Ye are expecting him to appear surrounded by worldly glory. But he is already come, and he will make his appearance as a poor man. He will teach truth. He will get more blame than praise, for he wills justice. But separate not from him, that ye may not be lost. Be ye not like those children of Noah who mocked him when he so laboriously built the ark that was to save them from the flood. All they that derided not went into the ark and were saved." Then turning to his disciples, he addressed them, saying, "Separate not from me like Lot from Abraham when, seeking more fertile regions, he went to Sodom and Gomorrha. And look not around after the glory of the world which fire from heaven shall destroy, that ye may not be turned into pillars of salt! Remain with me under every trial. I will always help you," etc. The Pharisees, still more irritated, exclaimed: "What is this that he promises them, seeing that he has nothing himself?" Then turning to him, they asked: "Art thou not from Nazareth? The son of Joseph and Mary?" But Jesus answered evasively that he whose son he was, would manifest it. Then they continued: "Why dost thou speak here as elsewhere of the Messiah? We have heard of thy teaching. Thinkest thou indeed that we shall imagine that thou meanest Thyself?" Jesus answered: "Upon that question I have nothing to say, excepting these words, yes, ye do think it." The excitement in the synagogue became great, the Pharisees extinguished the lights, while Jesus and the disciples, although it was night, left the place and journeyed some distance along the highroad. I saw them sleeping under a tree.

Jesus in a Shepherd Village near Nazareth

Monday, September 5, AD 29 (Elul 8)

Jesus and his traveling companions went to a shepherd village between the Edron valley and Nazareth. There they ate with some shepherds. Jesus healed two people who had been smitten with leprosy. He and his five disciples then went on to Nazareth and put up in a community of Essenes on the outskirts of the town. Jesus stayed with the venerable Eliud, an elderly Essene widower, who was cared for by his daughter.

ON the following morning I saw crowds of people on the road waiting for Jesus. They had not been with him in that last place, but had gone on ahead of him. I saw him turning aside from the road with them and, about three o'clock in the afternoon, coming up to another shepherd field. In it were only some light huts occupied by the shepherds in grazing time. There were no women here. The shepherds went forward to meet Jesus; they must have been informed of his coming by those that had gone on before. While some of their number went to meet him, the others busied themselves killing birds and lighting a fire in order to prepare a meal. This took place in an open hall, something like an inn, the fireplace being separated from the guest room by a wall. All around the hall ran a mossy bank with a platted support for the back overgrown by green foliage. The hosts led the Lord and his followers in, about twenty in number, equal to that of the shepherds themselves. All washed their feet, a separate basin being assigned to Jesus. He asked for more water and, after using it, commanded it not to be thrown out. When all were ready for table, Jesus questioned the shepherds, who appeared anxious about something, as to the cause of their trouble, and asked if there were not some of their number absent. In answer to his questions, they acknowledged that they were sad on account of two of their companions who were lying sick of leprosy. Fearing that it might be the unclean leprosy, and dreading lest Jesus might not come to them on that account, they had taken care to conceal them. Then Jesus ordered them to be brought before him, and he sent some of his disciples after them. At last, they appeared, so closely enveloped from head to foot in sheets that it was with great difficulty they could walk, though each was supported on either side. Jesus addressed them, telling them that their leprosy had come not from within, but from an outward infection. While he spoke, I was spiritually enlightened that, not through malice, but through temptation they had sinned. Jesus commanded them to wash in the water which he had used for his feet. They obeyed, and I saw the crusts falling from them leaving the scars behind. The water was then poured into a hole in the ground and covered with earth. Jesus strictly commanded the good people to say not a word of their cure until he should have returned from the baptism.

He afterward gave an instruction upon John, the baptism, and the coming of the Messiah. His hearers questioned him very simply as to which they should follow, himself or John, and they desired to know which was the greater. Jesus answered: "The greatest is he who serves as the least and last of all. He who for the love of God humbles himself as the least—he is the greatest." He exhorted them also to go to the baptism, spoke of the difficulties to be encountered in following him, and sent away all that had done so excepting the five disciples. He appointed a meeting place in the desert, not far from Jericho, I think in the region of Ophra. Joachim had owned a pasture ground in those parts. Some of Jesus's hearers left him entirely, some went straight to John, while others returned home to prepare for their journey to the baptism.

Jesus and the five disciples afterward went on to Nazareth, which at most was only about a short hour's distance. They approached by the side whose gate opens to the east on the road leading to the Sea of Galilee, but they went not into the city.

Nazareth had five gates. A little less than a quarter of an hour's distance from the city rose the mountain from whose steep summit they often hurled people, and whence, at a later period, they wanted to cast Jesus. At the foot of this mountain lay some huts. Jesus directed the five disciples to seek lodgings in them, as he did himself. They were supplied with water to wash their feet, a piece of bread, and a place in which to sleep. Anne's property lay to the east of Nazareth. The shepherds had bread baked in the ashes, also a well dug in the earth, but without masonry.

Jesus with Eliud, the Essene

THE VALLEY through which Jesus went by night from Chisloth-Tabor is called Edron, and the shepherd village in whose synagogue the Pharisees of Nazareth had so derided him was named Kimki. The people with whom Jesus and the five disciples put up outside of Nazareth were Essenes and friends of the holy family. The Essenes, both men and women, dwelt around here in the ruins of old stone vaults, solitary and unmarried. The former wore long white garments, the latter mantles, and both cultivated little gardens. They had once dwelt near Herod's castle in the valley of Zebulon but out of friendship for the holy family had come hither.

He with whom Jesus stayed was named Eliud. He was a very venerable, gray-haired old man with a long beard. He was a widower, and his daughter took care of him. He was the son of a brother of Zechariah. The Essenes lived very retired around here, attended the synagogue at Nazareth, and were very devoted to the holy family. The care of Mary's house during her absence had been entrusted to them.

Tuesday, September 6, AD 29 (Elul 9)

While the five disciples visited friends and relatives in Nazareth, Jesus talked with the aged Eliud, who had had many deep mystical experiences. The holy Virgin and Mary Cleophas visited Jesus. In the course of conversation with his mother, Jesus told her that he would go to Jerusalem four times for the Passover festival, but that the last time would be one of great affliction for her.

Next morning the five disciples of Jesus went into Nazareth to visit their relatives and acquaintances, also the school. Jesus, however, stayed with Eliud, with whom he prayed and very confidentially conversed, for to that simple-hearted, pious man many mysteries had been revealed.

There were four women in Mary's house besides herself: her niece, Mary Cleophas; Johanna Chusa, a cousin of Anna the prophetess; the relative of Simeon, Mary, mother of John Mark; and the widow Lea. Veronica was no longer there, nor was Peter's wife, whom I had lately seen at the place where the publicans lived.

The blessed Virgin and Mary Cleophas came to Jesus in the morning. Jesus stretched out his hand to his mother, his manner to her being affectionate, though very earnest and grave. Mary was anxious about him. She begged him not to go to Nazareth, for the feeling against him there was very bitter. The Pharisees belonging to Nazareth, who had heard him in the synagogue of Kimki, had again roused indignation against him. Jesus replied to his mother's entreaties that he would await where he was the multitude that were to go with him to the baptism of John, and then pass through Nazareth. Jesus conversed much with his mother on this day, for she came to him two or three times. He told her that he would go up to Jerusalem four times for Passover, but that the last time would be one of great affliction for her. He revealed to her many other mysteries, but I have forgotten them.

Mary Cleophas was a handsome, distinguished-looking woman. She spoke with Jesus that morning of her five sons, and entreated him to take them into his own service.

One was a clerk, or a kind of magistrate, named Simon; two were fishermen, James the Less and Judas Thaddeus, and these three were the sons of her first marriage. Alpheus, her first husband, was a widower with one son when she married him. This stepson was named Matthew. She wept bitterly when she spoke of him, for he was a publican. Joseph Barsabbas, who also was at the fishery, was her son by her second husband Sabbas; and, by her third marriage with the fisherman Jonah, she had another son, the young Simeon, still a boy. Jesus consoled her, promising that all her sons would one day follow him. Of Matthew, whom he had already seen when on his way to Sidon, he spoke words of comfort, foretelling that he would one day be one of his best disciples.

The blessed Virgin returned from Nazareth with some of her female relatives to her abode near Capernaum. Servants had come with asses from the latter place to conduct them home. They took several pieces of furniture with them which, after their last journey, had been left behind in Nazareth, various kinds of tapestry and woven stuffs, packages of other things, and some vessels. All were packed in chests formed of broad strips of inner or outer bark, and fastened to the sides of the asses. Mary's house in Nazareth was so ornamented that it had, during her absence, the appearance of a chapel. The fireplace looked like an altar. A chest was placed over it on which stood a flowerpot with a plant growing in it. After Mary's departure this time, the Essenes occupied the house.

Jesus Discourses with Eliud the Essene upon the Mysteries of the Old Testament and the Incarnation

Wednesday, September 7, AD 29 (Elul 10)
Jesus spent much of the day in deep conversation with Eliud. This pious and devout Essene told Jesus of his mystical experiences concerning the coming of the Messiah. Jesus was able to interpret these experiences for Eliud and to answer many of his questions regarding the things he had seen in vision. That evening Jesus and Eliud visited the place where Joseph had worked as a carpenter.

JESUS passed the whole day in most confidential conversation with Eliud, who asked him various questions about his mission. Jesus explained all to the old man, telling him that he was the Messiah, speaking of the lineage of his human genealogy and the mystery of the Ark of the Covenant. I learned then that that mystery had, before the flood, been taken into the ark of Noah, that it had descended from generation to generation, disappearing from time to time, but again coming to light. Jesus said that Mary at her birth had become the Ark of the Covenant of the mystery. Then Eliud who, during the discourse, frequently produced various rolls of writing and pointed out different passages of the prophets which Jesus explained to him, asked why he, Jesus, had not come sooner upon earth. Jesus answered that he could have been born only of a woman who had been conceived in the same way that, were it not for the Fall, all humankind would have been conceived; and that, since the first parents, no married couple had been so pure both in themselves and in their ancestors as Anne and Joachim. Then Jesus unfolded the past generations to Eliud, and pointed out to him the obstacles that had delayed Redemption.

I learned from this conference many details concerning the Ark of the Covenant. Whenever it was in any danger, or whenever there was fear of its falling into enemies' hands, the mystery was removed by the priests; yet still was it, the Ark, so holy that its profaners were punished and forced to restore it. I saw that the family to whom Moses entrusted the special guardianship of the Ark existed until Herod's time. At the Babylonian Captivity, Jeremiah hid the Ark and other sacred things on Mount Sinai. They were never afterward found, but the mystery had been removed. A second Ark was, at a later period, constructed on the first model, but it did not contain the sacred objects that had been preserved in the first. Aaron's rod, and also a portion of the mystery were in the keeping of the Essenes on Horeb. The sacrament of the Blessing was, however—but I know not by what priest—again replaced in the Ark. In the pit, which was afterward the pool of Bethesda, the sacred fire had been preserved. I saw in pictures very many things, which Jesus explained to Eliud, and I heard part of the words, but I cannot recall all.

He related the fact of his having taken flesh of the blessed germ of which God had deprived Adam before his fall. That blessed germ, by means of which all Israel should have become worthy of him, had descended through many generations. He explained how his coming had been so often retarded, how some of the chosen vessels had become unworthy. I saw all this as a reality. I saw all the ancestors of Jesus, and how the ancient patriarchs at their death gave over the Blessing sacramentally to the firstborn. I saw that the morsel and the drink out of the holy cup, which Abraham had received from the angel along with the promise of a son, Isaac, were a symbol of the most holy Sacrament of the New Covenant, and that their invigorating power was due to the flesh and blood of the future Messiah. I saw the ancestors of Jesus receiving this sacrament, in order to contribute to the Incarnation of God; and I saw that Jesus, of the flesh and blood received from his forefathers, instituted a most august sacrament for the uniting of man with God.

Jesus spoke much to Eliud also of the sanctity of Anne and Joachim, and of the supernatural Conception of Mary under the Golden Gate. He told him that not by Joseph had he been conceived, but from Mary according to the flesh; that she had been conceived of that pure Blessing which had been taken from Adam before the Fall, which through Abraham had descended until it was possessed by Joseph in Egypt, after whose death it had been deposited in the Ark of the Covenant, and thence withdrawn to be handed over to Joachim and Anne.

Jesus said that to free man he had been sent in the weakness of humanity; that he received and felt everything like a man; that, like the serpent of Moses in the desert, he would one day be raised up on Mount Calvary where the body of the first man lay buried. He referred also to the sad future that awaited him and to the ingratitude of man.

Eliud simply and confidently asked question after question. Although he understood all that Jesus said better than did the apostles, although looking upon things in a more spiritual sense than they, yet all was not clear to him; he could not rightly comprehend how the mission of Jesus was to be accomplished. He asked Jesus where his kingdom was to be, in Jerusalem, in Jericho, or in Engaddi. Jesus answered that where he himself was, there would his kingdom be, and that he would have no external kingdom.

The old man spoke to Jesus so naturally and simply. He related to him many things of his mother, as if he knew them not, and Jesus listened to him so kindly. He told him of Joachim and Anne, and spoke of the life and death of the latter. Jesus remarked that no woman had ever been more chaste than Anne; that she had married twice after Joachim's death in accordance with the command of God, for it was proper that the number of fruits destined to be produced by this branch should be filled up.

As Eliud recounted the circumstances of Anne's death, I had a vision of the same. I saw her lying on a rather high couch in a back room (something like Mary's) of her own large house. She was unusually animated and talkative, and not at all like a dying person. I saw her blessing her little daughters, also her other relatives, who were in the antechamber. Mary was standing at the head, Jesus at the foot of her bed. Jesus was, at this time, a young man, his beard just beginning to appear. Anne blessed Mary, begged the blessing of Jesus, and continued speaking in a joyous strain. Suddenly she glanced upward, became white as snow, and I saw drops like pearls starting out on her forehead. I cried out: "Ah, she is dying! she is dying!" and, in my eagerness, I wanted to clasp her in my arms.

Then it seemed to me that she came and rested in them. On awaking I still thought that I held her.

Eliud related also many things connected with the virtues of Mary in the temple. As he spoke, I saw it all in vision. I saw that her teacher Naomi was one of Lazarus's relatives. She was about fifty years old and, like all the other women who served in the temple, she was an Essene. I saw that Mary learned from her how to knit. Even as a child, she used to go with Naomi when the latter went to cleanse the different vessels and utensils that had been soiled with the blood of sacrifice. Certain parts of the animal sacrificed were received by them, then cut up and prepared as food for the priests and others who served in the temple; for they depended in part upon that for support. I saw the blessed Virgin at a later period helping in these duties. I saw Zechariah, when it was his turn to serve in the sanctuary, visiting the child Mary. Simeon, also, knew her. And so, as Eliud was recounting it to the Lord, I saw all her pious and lowly serving in the temple.

They spoke, also, of Christ's conception, and Eliud told of Mary's visit to Elizabeth. Eliud mentioned also a spring that Mary had found there; and that, too, I saw.

I saw the blessed Virgin going with Elizabeth, Zechariah, and Joseph from Zechariah's house to another little property belonging to him, and on which there was no water. The blessed Virgin went alone into the garden, a little rod in her hand, and prayed. She pierced the earth with the rod, and a tiny stream gushed out and flowed around a little knoll. When Zechariah and Joseph removed the earth with a spade, an abundant supply rushed forth, and soon formed a most beautiful spring. Zechariah dwelt about five hours southward from Jerusalem, and a little to the west.

In confidential discourse like the above, interrupted only by prayer, Eliud treated with Jesus. He honored him, but quite simply and joyously, looking upon him as a chosen human being. Eliud's daughter did not dwell in the same house with her father, but at some distance in a rocky cavern.

There were about twenty Essenes living on the mountain. The women dwelt apart from the men, about five or six together. All honored Eliud as their superior and daily assembled around him for prayer. Jesus ate with him alone, but very sparingly, their repast consisting of bread, fruit, honey, and fish. Weaving and agriculture formed the chief occupation of these people.

The mountain at whose base the Essenes dwelt was the highest peak of a ridge on one of whose plateaus Nazareth was built. A valley lay between it and the city. On the other side the descent was steep and overgrown with verdure and grapevines. The abyss at its base, the one into which the Pharisees at a later period wanted to precipitate Jesus, was full of all kinds of rubbish, ordure, and bones. Mary's house stood on a hill outside the city, part of it extending into the hill like a cave. The top of the house, however, arose above the hill, on the opposite side of which lay other dwellings.

Mary and the other women accompanied by Kolaya, Lea's son, arrived at her house in the valley of Capernaum. Her female friends in the neighborhood came out to meet her. Mary's dwelling at Capernaum belonged to a man named Levi, who lived in a large house not very far from it. It had been rented from Levi by Peter's family and given over to the holy family; for Peter and Andrew knew the holy family in a general way, also through John the Baptist, whose disciples they were. The house had several buildings attached to it in which relatives of the family and the disciples could stay when visiting the holy family. It appeared to have been chosen on that account. Mary Cleophas had with her her little boy Simeon, the son of her third marriage.

Toward evening Jesus accompanied Eliud from his house to Nazareth. Outside the city walls, where Joseph had had his carpenter shop, lived several people, poor but good, who had been known to Joseph, and among whose sons were some of the playmates of Jesus's childhood.

Eliud took Jesus to visit these people. They offered their guests a morsel of bread and a little fresh water. The water was especially good in Nazareth. I saw Jesus sitting on the ground among them and exhorting them to go to the baptism of John. They acted somewhat shyly in Jesus's regard. They had in the past looked upon him as one of themselves. But now that he was so gravely introduced to them by Eliud, whom they all so highly honored, whose advice they often asked, from whom they were accustomed to seek consolation, and who, moreover, united in persuading them to go to the baptism, they could scarcely reconcile themselves to the position he now held toward them. They had indeed heard of the Messiah, but they could hardly think that Jesus was he.

Jesus and Eliud Walking and Conversing Together

Thursday, September 8, AD 29 (Elul 11)

Together with Eliud, Jesus set off on a journey southward from Nazareth, passing through the valley of Esdrelon, and then turning eastward in the direction of Endor. They arrived at a small village close to a well-known spring. At the synagogue, Jesus taught concerning the Messiah and the kingdom of God, which he affirmed was not of this world. He also expounded many passages from the prophets. That night, he and Eliud stayed at an inn near the synagogue.

THE NEXT day Jesus went with Eliud southward from Nazareth through the valley of Esdrelon on the road to Jerusalem. When about two hours beyond the brook Kishon, they arrived at a village consisting of a synagogue, an inn, and only a few houses. It was one of the environs of the not far distant Endor, and nearby was a celebrated spring. Jesus put up at the inn. The people of the place behaved rather coldly, though not inimically toward him. Eliud was not held in special esteem by them, for they were rather pharisaical. Jesus notified their head men that he intended to teach in the synagogue, but they replied that that was not usual for strangers. Jesus told them that he had a special call to do so and, entering the school, he taught of the Messiah whose kingdom was not of this world, whose coming would not be attended by outward splendor, also of John's baptism. The priests of the synagogue were not favorably inclined toward Jesus. Jesus bade them give him the scriptures. He unrolled them and explained many passages from the prophets.

Eliud's confident communications with Jesus were to me singularly touching. He knew of and believed in his mission and supernatural advent, still without appearing to have a suspicion that he was God himself. He told Jesus quite naturally, as they walked together, many things connected with his youth, what the prophetess Anna had related to him, also what she had heard from Mary after the return from Egypt, for Mary had sometimes visited her in Jerusalem. Jesus, in turn, related to Eliud some things that he did not know, each accompanied with significant interpretation. But all was so natural, so simple, like a dear old man speaking with a beloved young friend.

While Eliud was relating what Anna had heard from Mary and told to him, I saw all in pictures. I rejoiced to find them exactly similar to what I had long before seen and partly forgotten.

Jesus spoke to Eliud also of his journey to the baptism. He had gathered together many people and sent them to the desert near Ophra; but he said that he would go alone by the road past Bethany, where he wanted to speak with Lazarus. He spoke of Lazarus by another general name, which I have forgotten. He mentioned also his father, saying that he had been in war. He said that Lazarus and his sisters were rich, and that they would devote all they had to the advancement of Redemption.

Lazarus had three sisters: the eldest Martha, the youngest Mary Magdalene, and one between them also called Mary. This last lived altogether secluded, her silence causing her to be looked upon as a simpleton. She went by no other name than Silent Mary. Jesus, speaking to Eliud of this family, said, "Martha is good and pious. She will, with her brother, follow me." Of Mary the Silent, he said, "She is possessed of great mind and understanding; but, for the good of her soul, they have been withdrawn from her. She is not for this world, therefore is she now altogether secluded from it. But she has never committed sin. If I should speak to her, she would perfectly comprehend the greatest mysteries. She will not live much longer. After her death, Lazarus and his sister Martha will follow me and devote all that they possess to the use of the community. The youngest sister Mary has strayed from the right path, but she will return and rise to higher sanctity than Martha."

Friday, September 9, AD 29 (Elul 12)

Setting off early, Jesus and Eliud journeyed around Mount Hermon and came to Endor. There they visited a sanatorium—a bathing spot for invalids—where Jesus taught the sick and told two parables. There was no synagogue in Endor, so, for the sabbath, they returned to the synagogue at the village where they had been the previous day.

Eliud spoke also of John the Baptist, but he had not yet seen him and was not yet baptized. Jesus and Eliud spent the night at the inn near the synagogue, and early on the following morning, they journeyed along Mount Hermon toward the somewhat dilapidated city of Endor. Around the inns lay masses of broken walls all the way along the mountain, so broad that a wagon could pass over them. Endor was full of ruins interspersed with gardens. On one side were large, magnificent buildings like palaces, while in other quarters of the city the desolation of war was visible. It seemed to me that the inhabitants were a race apart from the Jews. There was no synagogue in Endor, so Jesus went with Eliud to a large square in which three side buildings containing small chambers were built around a pond. The pond was in the center of a green lawn, and on its waters little barks were sailing. There was a pump nearby, and the place bore the appearance of a health-giving resort. The little chambers around the pond were occupied by invalids. Jesus, accompanied by Eliud, entered one of the buildings. He was hospitably received, and his feet washed. A high seat was erected for him on the lawn, and there he taught the people. The women, who occupied one of the wings, took back seats in the audience. These people were not orthodox Jews. They were more like slaves, cast out and oppressed, who had to pay tribute of all that they earned. After a certain war, they remained behind in the city. I think their leader, Sisara, was defeated not far off, and was then murdered by a woman. His army had been scattered throughout the whole country and reduced to servitude. There were still about four hundred in these parts. Their forefathers had, under David and Solomon, been forced to quarry stones for the building of the temple. They were long accustomed to such work. The deceased King Herod had employed them in building an aqueduct to Mount Zion of several hours in length. They were very compassionate and stood by one another under all circumstances. They wore long coats and girdles. Their pointed caps covered their ears like those of the ancient hermits. They had no communication with the Jews, although they were allowed to send their children to the Jewish schools. But the poor little creatures were so badly treated and so despised that the parents preferred keeping them home.

Jesus felt great compassion for them. He had the sick brought to him. They sat in a kind of bed like my reclining chair (I can still see them), under the movable back of which were supports. When the back was let down, the chair formed a bed.

As Jesus instructed them about the Messiah and baptism and exhorted them to the latter, they answered timidly that they could not lay claim to such a privilege, for that they were only poor outcasts. Then he taught them by the parable of the unjust steward. The clear interpretation he gave of it, I perfectly understood. It haunted me the whole day, but now I have forgotten it. Perhaps I shall recall it again. Jesus also related the parable of the son sent by his father to take possession of his vineyard. He always related that when instructing the poor, neglected pagans. The people prepared a repast for Jesus out in the open air. He invited to it the poor and the sick, and he and Eliud served them at table.

This action greatly impressed his entertainers. That evening Jesus returned with Eliud to the place outside of Nazareth, where he stayed overnight and celebrated the sabbath in the synagogue.

Saturday, September 10, AD 29 (Elul 13)

After the sabbath morning service in the synagogue, Jesus and Eliud returned to Endor. The inhabitants of the town were Canaanites, some of whom secretly worshipped an idol of the goddess Astarte. Jesus reprehended them for this practice. Then, accompanied by Eliud, he returned to the synagogue for the service at the close of the sabbath. That evening, he and Eliud set off back to Nazareth.

The following day, Jesus and Eliud returned to Endor, which was only a sabbath distance from the inn, and there he taught. The inhabitants were Canaanites and, I think, from Shechem; for I heard that day, at least once, the name Shechemite. They had an idol hidden away in a subterranean cavern. By some kind of mechanism on springs it could be made to rise suddenly out of the earth and seat itself on an altar beautifully ornamented and prepared to receive it. They had procured this idol from Egypt, and it was named Astarte, which I understood yesterday to be the same as Esther. The idol had a face round like the moon. On its outstretched arms it held something long and swathed, like the chrysalis of a butterfly, large in the middle and tapering at either end. It may have been a fish. On the back of the idol was a pedestal upon which stood a high pail, or a small half-tub, which extended over the head. In it was something like ears in green husks, also fruits and green leaves. The idol stood in a cask that reached up to the lower part of the body, and all around it were pots of growing plants. These people worshipped their idol in secret, and Jesus in his instructions to them reprehended them for it. They had been accustomed to sacrifice deformed children to the goddess. There was a companion idol belonging to this goddess, the god Adonis, who I think was Astarte's husband.

This nation, as has been said, had been defeated in three parts under their general Sisara, and scattered as slaves throughout the country. They were at this time greatly oppressed and despised. Not very long before Christ, they had excited some disturbance around Herod's castle in Galilee, after which they were still more oppressed.

In the afternoon, Jesus and Eliud returned to the synagogue and there ended the sabbath.

The Jews, meanwhile, were very much displeased at Jesus's visit to Endor. But he reprehended them very severely for their hardheartedness toward their abandoned fellow beings. He exhorted them to a spirit of kindness and urged them to take them to the baptism, which they themselves had, at his recommendation, resolved to receive. The Jews of this place became more favorably inclined toward Jesus after they had heard his instructions. Toward evening he returned to Nazareth with Eliud. I saw them conversing together the whole way, sometimes even pausing to stand and talk. Eliud was again recalling many of the incidents of the flight into Egypt, and I saw them again in vision. He began by asking whether Jesus was not going to extend his kingdom over the good people in Egypt who had been impressed by his presence among them in his childhood.

Here I saw again that the journey of Jesus after the raising of Lazarus through pagan Asia down to Egypt, and which I had seen before, was no dream of mine, for Jesus told Eliud that wherever the seed had been sown, would he before his end reap the harvest.

Eliud knew of the sacrifice of bread and wine, also of Melchizedek; but he knew not what idea to form of Jesus. He questioned him as to whether he was not another Melchizedek. Jesus answered: "No. Melchizedek had to pave the way for my sacrifice. But I shall be the sacrifice itself."

I learned also from that conversation that Naomi, Mary's teacher in the temple, was the aunt of Lazarus, his mother's sister. Lazarus's father was the son of a Syrian king who had, for services in war, received some property as a reward. His wife was a Jewess of distinction. She belonged to the priestly race of Aaron (although Manasseh allied with Anna), and dwelt in Jerusalem. They owned three castles: one in Bethany; one near Herodium; and one at Magdala, on the Sea of Galilee, not far from Tiberias and Gabara. Herod also had a castle in the country near Magdala. Jesus and Eliud spoke also of the scandal Magdalene gave her family.

Jesus in Nazareth

Sunday, September 11, AD 29 (Elul 14)

Jesus and Eliud arrived back at Eliud's home in the early hours of the morning. Jesus's disciples, a number of Essenes, and some other people—including two Pharisees from Nazareth—gathered together to hear his discourses. The Pharisees invited Jesus to come to them and later conducted him to the synagogue. There, he taught concerning Moses and the prophecies of the coming of the Messiah. That night, he stayed at an inn nearby, together with his five disciples.

JESUS went home with Eliud. There they found assembled the five disciples, the Essenes, and many others who were desirous of going to the baptism. Some publicans, also, had come to Nazareth for the same purpose, and several bands had already started for the place of baptism.

Next morning Jesus resumed his instructions. Two of the Pharisees from Nazareth came to him and, in a friendly manner, invited him to go back with them to the school. They had, as they said, heard so much of his teaching in the country around that they were eager to hear him explain the prophets. Jesus went with them. They conducted him to the house of a Pharisee, in which many others were assembled. The five disciples were with their Master. The Pharisees listened very politely to Jesus while he spoke to them in beautiful parables. His teaching appeared to please them greatly, and they led him to the synagogue, where a numerous audience awaited him. Jesus spoke of Moses and explained the prophecies concerning the Messiah. But whenever he dropped any words from which they might infer that he alluded to himself, they showed displeasure. One of the Pharisees spread for him a repast, and he spent the night with his five disciples at an inn near the school.

Monday, September 12, AD 29 (Elul 15)

Today, Jesus addressed a group of tax collectors who were on their way to be baptized by John. Afterward, in the synagogue, he taught a parable and then, on his way out, blessed some children. To the small group of five followers, four others were now added as disciples; these four were friends of or were related to the holy family.

Next day Jesus addressed a crowd of publicans who were journeying just then to receive the baptism. He afterward taught in the synagogue, making use of the similitude of the grain of wheat which must die in the earth before producing its fruit. His words displeased the Pharisees, and they repeated their remarks about the son of the carpenter Joseph. They reproached him also for his communications with publicans and sinners, to which Jesus replied with great firmness. Then they took up the Essenes whom they denominated hypocrites who lived not according to the Law. But Jesus showed them clearly that the Essenes were stricter followers of the Law than the Pharisees, and so the reproach of hypocrisy fell back upon themselves. It was the question of benedictions that had led to the Essenes. Blessings were in common use among them, and the Pharisees were annoyed at seeing Jesus blessing little children. When, for instance, he was entering or leaving the synagogue, he was stopped by many mothers with their children, and his blessing craved for the little ones.

While Jesus dwelt at Nazareth, he had always much to do with the children, who became still and quiet near him. No matter how passionately they cried, his blessing had power to calm them. The mothers, remembering this, now brought their little ones to him to see whether he had become too proud to notice them. There were some among them who kicked violently, rolling over and over on the floor, as if they had cramps, screaming loudly all the while. But Jesus's blessing stilled them instantly. I saw something like a dark vapor going out from some of them. Jesus laid his hand on the heads of the boys and gave them the patriarchs' blessing in three lines, one from the head and one from either shoulder down to the heart where all three united. He blessed the girls in the same way, but without laying his hand on them, though he made a sign on their lips. I thought as I saw him do it that it meant that they should not prattle so much; still, however, it was significant of something else. Jesus passed the night with his disciples in the house of a Pharisee.

To the five followers of Jesus, four others were now added, relatives and friends of the holy family. I think there was a son of one of the three widows among them, and one from Bethlehem, who had found out that he was a descendent of Ruth who had married Boaz in that city. Jesus formally received them to the number of his disciples.

Jesus Rejects Three Rich Youths • He Confounds Many Learned Men in the Synagogue of Nazareth

Tuesday, September 13, AD 29 (Elul 16)

Three youths from wealthy families in Nazareth were sent by their parents to the synagogue to hear a dispute between Jesus and some learned men of Nazareth. This dispute was arranged by the Pharisees to test Jesus's wisdom. Jesus displayed such an extraordinary knowledge that all present were excited by his teaching. Urged on by their parents, who thought that their sons could benefit from absorbing Jesus's wisdom, the three youths then sought to become Jesus's pupils; but Jesus rejected them, which incensed their parents. That night, Jesus stayed again at Eliud's home.

THERE were in Nazareth a couple of rich families who had three sons. In childhood these latter had associated with Jesus. They were now quite cultured and well educated. The parents, who had heard much of Jesus's wisdom and teaching, agreed together that their sons should today hear a specimen of it. They would then offer him money to let the young men travel with him that they might profit by his knowledge. The good people had so high an opinion of their sons that they thought Jesus would gladly become their tutor. So the young men went to the synagogue whither, by the connivance of their wealthy parents and the Pharisees, all the learned men of the city had flocked. They were determined to put Jesus to the test in every way. Among these men were a lawyer and a physician, the latter a tall, portly man with a long beard. He wore a girdle and had some kind of a badge upon one shoulder of his mantle. I saw Jesus, on entering the school, again blessing many children whom their mothers brought to him, among them some afflicted with leprosy, whom he healed. During his discourse he was interrupted in various ways by the literati, who proposed to him all kinds of subtle questions. But his wisdom silenced them.

To the lawyer's speech Jesus answered most wonderfully from the Law of Moses, and when divorce was spoken of, he rejected it entirely. Divorced, husband and wife could never be; but if the former could not in any way live with the latter, he might leave her. Still were they one body, and could not again marry. These words of the Lord greatly displeased the Jews.

The physician asked whether he could tell whether a man was of a dry, matter-of-fact nature or of a phlegmatic disposition, under what planets such a one was born, what simples were good for this or that temperament, and how the human body is formed. Jesus answered him with great wisdom. He spoke of the complexion of some of those present, their diseases and the remedies, and of the human body, with a depth of knowledge quite unknown to the physician. He spoke of life, of the spirit, and how it influences the body, of sicknesses that could be cured only by prayer and amendment, of such as needed medicine for their cure—and that in language so profound, and yet so beautiful, that the physician in astonishment declared himself vanquished and that he had never before heard such things. I think he afterward became one of Jesus's disciples. Jesus described to him the human body with all its members, muscles, veins, nerves, and intestines, their special functions and their various relations one with another, in general terms and yet with such accuracy that his questioner was humbled and silenced.

There was an astrologer present who spoke of the course of the stars. He (Jesus) explained how one constellation ruled another, how different stars possess different influences, and he discoursed upon comets and the signs of the zodiac. Jesus in most appropriate language treated with another upon architecture; with others of trade and commerce with foreign nations, taking occasion at the same time to censure severely the various fashions and frivolities lately introduced from Athens. He condemned likewise the games and juggling now in use among them, and which were also spreading throughout Nazareth and other places. These games were likewise a product of their contact with Athens. Jesus stigmatized them as unpardonable since they that indulge in them look upon them as no sin; consequently, they do no penance for them, and therefore they cannot be pardoned.

His hearers were transported by his wisdom. They begged him to take up his residence among them, offering to give him a house and all that he needed, questioning him also as to why he and his mother had removed to Capernaum. Jesus replied that he could not remain with them, and he spoke of his mission and the duties it imposed. In answer to their question as to why he had gone from among them, he said that it was because of his desire to dwell in a more central locality, etc. But they did not understand his reasons, and they were offended at his rejection of their offer, which they thought a very fine one. They looked upon his words, "mission," and "duties" as the offspring of pride. And so they left the school that evening.

The three youths, who were about the age of twenty, greatly desired to speak with Jesus. But he would not allow them to do so until his nine disciples were present. That annoyed them. Jesus told them that he insisted upon having witnesses to what he might say to them. When at last they were admitted to an audience, they very modestly and humbly laid before him their own and their parents' wishes that he would receive them as his pupils. Their parents, they said, would remunerate him, and as for themselves, they would bear him company in all his labors, they would serve and help him. I saw that Jesus was troubled at having to refuse their request, partly for their own sake, and partly on account of his disciples, for he was obliged to assign reasons for his refusal which they could not as yet comprehend. He replied to the youths that he who gave money to obtain something aimed at gaining some temporal advantage; but that whoever would follow him must abandon all earthly possessions, must leave parents and friends, and that his disciples must neither woo nor marry. He laid down many other hard conditions, so that the young men became very much discouraged. They argued that many of the Essenes were married. Jesus replied that they, the Essenes, acted rightly and in accordance with their laws, but that his doctrine was to accomplish fully that for which theirs only paved the way, and so forth. With this remark and bidding them take time to reflect, he left them.

The disciples were intimidated by his words. His teaching was so severe that they could not understand it, and they grew faint-hearted. But on the way from Nazareth to Eliud's, he bade them not despond, that he had good reasons for talking as he had done, that those youths would only at some distant day, and perhaps never, come to him; but as for themselves, the disciples, they should follow him calmly and be without anxiety. And so they arrived at Eliud's. I do not think he will again go to Eliud's, for great talk and excitement had arisen in Nazareth on his account. The inhabitants were vexed at his not remaining among them. They thought that he had acquired all his knowledge during his travels. "True," they said, "He is a very clever and extraordinary man; but, for a carpenter's son, he is rather conceited." I saw the three young men returning to their homes. Their parents were very much displeased at the objections Jesus made to receiving them. The sons chimed in with the parents, and all talked at random in their indignation against him.

Wednesday, September 14, AD 29 (Elul 17)
The three youths returned to Jesus to request that they might become his pupils. Again, Jesus sent them away. Later, he explained to his disciples that the three youths sought to follow him on account of what they might be able to gain for themselves and were not willing to sacrifice all for love. He then sent the disciples on in advance to the place of baptism, instructing them to travel via Capernaum to let his mother know that he himself would soon go to be baptized. That night, he set off with Eliud for the little town of Chim, southwest of Nazareth.

On the following day, the three youths went again to Jesus and begged once more to be accepted. They promised him perfect obedience and faithful service. But Jesus again dismissed them, and I saw that their inability to seize the meaning of his refusal troubled him. He spoke then with his nine disciples who, by his directions, were to go first to a certain place and afterward to John. On the subject of those whom he had dismissed, Jesus said that they desired to follow him for the sake of what they might gain, that they were not willing to give all for love. But that they, the disciples, sought for nothing, consequently they had been received. He spoke again in significant and beautiful terms of the baptism, telling them to go over to Capernaum and say to his mother that he was going to the baptism. He charged them likewise to speak to the disciples, John, Peter, and Andrew about John (the Baptist) and say to the last named that he (Jesus) was coming.

Jesus with Eliud in the Leper Settlement

Thursday, September 15, AD 29 (Elul 18)
At daybreak, Jesus and Eliud reached Chim. Not far from the town was a small pool in which the lepers of the place washed themselves. Jesus went into a leper's hut and healed him. He and Eliud then made their way south through the valley of Esdrelon. They continued walking after dark, deep in conversation. Around midnight, Jesus said to Eliud that he would reveal himself, and—turning toward heaven—he prayed. A cloud of light enveloped them both and Jesus became radiantly transfigured. Eliud stood still, utterly entranced. After a while, the light melted away, and Jesus resumed his steps, followed by Eliud, who was speechless at what he had beheld.

I SAW Jesus journeying with Eliud in a southwesterly direction from Nazareth, but not exactly on the highroad. He wanted to go to Chim, a leper settlement. They reached it at daybreak, and I saw that Eliud tried to restrain Jesus from entering it, that he might not be defiled; for, as Eliud urged, if it were discovered that he had been there, he would not be allowed to go to the baptism. But Jesus replied that he knew his mission, that he would enter, for there was in it a good man who was sighing for his coming. They had to cross the Kishon. The leper settlement lay near a brook formed by the waters of the Kishon which flowed into a little pond in which the lepers bathed. The water thus used did not return into the Kishon. This settlement was perfectly isolated; no one ever approached it. The lepers dwelt in scattered huts. There were no others in the place, excepting those that attended the infected. Eliud remained at a distance and waited for the Lord. Jesus entered one of the most remote huts wherein lay stretched on the ground a miserable creature entirely enveloped in sheets. He was a good man. I have forgotten how he contracted leprosy. Jesus addressed him. He raised himself, and appeared to be deeply touched at the Lord's deigning to visit him. Jesus commanded him to rise and stretch himself in a trough of water that stood near the hut. He obeyed, while Jesus held his hands extended over the water. The rigid limbs of the leper relaxed, and he was made clean. He then resumed his ordinary dress, and Jesus

River Kishon

commanded him not to speak of his cure until he should have returned from the baptism. He accompanied Jesus and Eliud along the road till Jesus ordered him to go back.

I saw Jesus and Eliud the whole day journeying toward the south through the valley of Esdrelon. Sometimes they conversed together, and at others walked apart as if in prayer and meditation.

The weather was not very pleasant at that time, the sky dark, and fog in the valley. Jesus had no stick. He never carried one. But Eliud had one with a little shovel on it like those of the shepherds. Jesus wore only sandals, though a kind of perfect shoe, consisting of a thick, woven upper of coarse cotton, was in use at the time. Once I saw Jesus and Eliud at noon resting by a well and eating bread.

Jesus Transfigured before Eliud

DURING the night I saw them again walking, sometimes together, sometimes separate. And then I witnessed something extraordinary, an unspeakably lovely vision. While Jesus was walking on ahead, Eliud passed some remarks upon the symmetry and beauty of his person. Jesus replied: "If thou shouldst behold this body two years hence, thou wouldst find in it neither beauty nor symmetry, so greatly will they abuse and maltreat me." But Eliud understood not his words. Above all he could not comprehend why Jesus always spoke of his kingdom as existing in so short a time; for he thought ten, or even twenty years must elapse before it would be founded. He could not bring himself to think otherwise, since his thoughts were all of an earthly kingdom.

When they had gone on a short distance, Jesus paused and bade Eliud, who was following lost in thought, to approach and he would show him who he was, of what nature was his body, and of what kind his kingdom. Eliud drew near to within several steps of Jesus. Then Jesus raised his eyes to heaven and prayed. A cloud, like those seen in a thunderstorm, descended and enveloped both. From without they could not be seen, but over them opened a heaven of light which seemed to descend toward them. Above I saw a city of shining walls, I saw the Heavenly Jerusalem! The whole interior was lit up with a rainbow colored light. I saw a figure like God the Father, and Jesus, his form perfectly luminous and transparent, connected with him by beams of light. Eliud stood awhile gazing upward as if entranced, and then sank prostrate on his face, in which position he remained until the apparition and the light had melted away. Then Jesus resumed his way, and Eliud followed speechless and frightened by what he had seen. It was a vision like the Transfiguration, but I did not see Jesus lifted up.

I think Eliud did not live to see the crucifixion of Christ. Jesus was more confidential toward him than toward the apostles, for Eliud was very enlightened and very familiar with many of the mysteries connected with the family of Jesus. Jesus took him as a friend and companion, and clothed him with authority, so that he did much for his community. He was one of the best instructed of the Essenes. In Jesus's time, the Essenes did not dwell all together on the mountains as formerly; they were more scattered throughout the cities. I had that wonderful vision about twelve o'clock at night.

Friday, September 16, AD 29 (Elul 19)

At dawn, they approached the huts of some shepherds. The shepherds already knew Jesus. Leading Jesus and Eliud to a shed, they washed the feet of the two guests and prepared a meal for them. Afterward, Jesus took leave of Eliud, first blessing him and then embracing him before going on his way. Jesus then traveled to the mountain village of Gur. He celebrated the sabbath there alone in his room at an inn, having requested a roll of the scriptures to be brought to him from the synagogue.

In the morning, I saw Jesus and Eliud arrive at a shepherd field. It was daybreak, and the shepherds were already out of their huts and with the cattle. They came forward to meet Jesus, who was known to them. They cast themselves down before him, and then led him and his companion under a shed where they had their cooking utensils. Here they washed their feet, prepared for them a couch, and set before them bread and little drinking cups. They roasted some turtledoves for their guests. The birds had their nests in the roofs of the huts, and were hopping around in great numbers like hens. And now I saw Jesus dismissing Eliud, who knelt to receive his blessing. The shepherds were present. Jesus told him that he would end his days in peace, that the path which he himself had to walk would be too difficult for him, that he had admitted him to his community, that he had already done his part in the vineyard, and that he should receive his reward in his kingdom. Jesus explained this by the parable of the laborers in the vineyards. Eliud was very grave since the vision of the preceding night, very silent, and deeply impressed. I think he was afterward baptized by the disciples. He accompanied Jesus a part of the way from the shepherd field. The Lord embraced him, and he departed with signs of manly emotion.

The place to which Jesus was going for the sabbath could be seen from here. Some of his relatives once dwelt there. The place to which he now went alone was called Gur. It was built on a mountain. Joseph's brother, who afterward removed to Zebulon and who had had frequent communication with the holy family, once dwelt there. Jesus went unnoticed to an inn, where they washed his feet and presented him food. He had a chamber to himself. He caused a roll of the scriptures to be brought to him from the synagogue, and out of it he read and prayed, sometimes standing, sometimes kneeling, often raising his eyes toward heaven. He did not go to the school. Once I saw some people going to the inn and asking to speak to Jesus, but he would not see them.

A Glance at the Disciples Going to the Baptism

I SAW the disciples whom Jesus had dispatched with messages arrive in Capernaum. They were about five of the best-known. They had an interview with Mary, and then two of them went to Bethsaida for Peter and Andrew. James the Less, Simon, Thaddeus, John, and James the Greater were present. The disciples spoke of the mildness, meekness, and wisdom of Jesus, while the followers of John the Baptist proclaimed with enthusiasm the austere life of their master, and declared that they had never before heard such an interpreter of the law and the prophets. Even John spoke enthusiastically of the Baptist, although he already knew Jesus. His parents had once lived only a couple of hours from Nazareth, and Jesus loved him even as a child. The disciples celebrated the sabbath here.

The next day I saw the nine disciples along with those named above on the road to Tiberias, whence they were to go to John, passing near Ephron and then through the desert toward Jericho. Peter and Andrew particularly distinguished themselves by the zeal with which they spoke of the Baptist. He was, they said, of a noble, priestly race; he had been educated by the Essenes in the wilderness, he would suffer no irregularity around him, he was as rigorous as he was wise. Then Jesus's disciples put forward the mildness and wisdom of their Master, to which the others retorted that many disorders arose from such condescension, and they cited instances in proof of what they said. Jesus's disciples replied that their Master, too, had been educated by the Essenes and that, moreover, he had but lately returned from traveling. But John entered not into this discussion. I did not hear him saying anything more in that strain. They started together for the place of baptism, but after a few hours took different directions. As I listened to their conversation, I thought, "Men were then as they now are."

Saturday, September 17, AD 29 (Elul 20)
On this day, the last sabbath prior to his baptism, Jesus spent the whole day in his room alone in prayer.

(Follow Map 5)

Jesus in Gophna

Sunday, September 18, AD 29 (Elul 21)
Jesus arose before daybreak and proceeded further. Toward evening, he arrived at Gophna on Mount Ephron, north of Jerusalem. After eating a meal at an inn, he was escorted by some relatives and a couple of Pharisees to a house where he stayed overnight.

GUR, where Jesus prayed alone in the inn, lay not very far from a city, Megiddo, and a field of the same name. I have clearly seen that, toward the end of the world, there will be fought in that field a battle with Antichrist. Jesus arose with the dawn, rolled up his couch, laid a coin on it, girded himself, and went forth. His way led him around many towns and villages, but he met no one, put up at no inn. He passed Mount Garizim near Samaria, which lay to the left, as he journeyed southward. Occasionally he ate a few berries and some other fruit, and in the hollow of his hand or with a concave leaf scooped up some water to quench his thirst.

Toward evening, Jesus entered Gophna, a city on Mount Ephron. It was built upon very jagged foundations, some high, some low, numerous gardens and pleasure grounds scattered between the houses. Some relatives of Joachim dwelt here, but they had not maintained intimate communications with the holy family. Jesus put up at an inn, where they washed his feet and gave him some little refreshment. But soon there came to the inn some of his relatives accompanied by a couple of Pharisees of the better sort, and escorted him to their own home, one of the handsomest houses in the city. The city itself was of some importance, and possessed at this time jurisdiction over a portion of the country around. Jesus's relative was an official, and was much employed in writing. I think the city belonged to Samaria. Jesus was received with respect. There were several guests at his relative's house and all, standing or walking, took refreshments in a pleasure garden. Jesus slept here overnight.

It was a day's journey from Gophna to Jerusalem. There was a little river in this region. During the loss of the boy Jesus in the temple, the holy family went to Gophna in search of him; for when they missed him at Michmas, they thought he might perhaps have gone to his relatives there. Mary feared that he had fallen into the little river.

Monday, September 19, AD 29 (Elul 22)
Jesus went to the synagogue and asked for the scriptures of one of the prophets. He then interpreted the prophecies, saying that the time had arrived for the coming of the Messiah. After spending much of the day teaching in the synagogue, Jesus departed from Gophna. That evening, he arrived at the shepherd village of Bethel, where he met up with two groups of people on their way to be baptized by John the Baptist. The patriarch Jacob had lived for a time in the neighborhood of Bethel.

Jesus, having gone to the synagogue, asked for the writings of one of the prophets, and taught of baptism and the Messiah. He proved to his hearers from the prophets, that the time must have arrived for his appearance. He cited events which were to precede his coming, and which had actually been accomplished, alluding especially to one that had happened three years before. I do not now remember whether that particular event was a war, or whether it was that the scepter had passed from Judah. And so he went on enumerating proofs of accomplished signs which were to precede the coming of the Messiah. He mentioned also the multiplication of sects and the irreligious nature of so many of their ceremonies. He told them that the Messiah

Map 5: Journey to the Baptism in the Jordan
September 18–28, AD 29

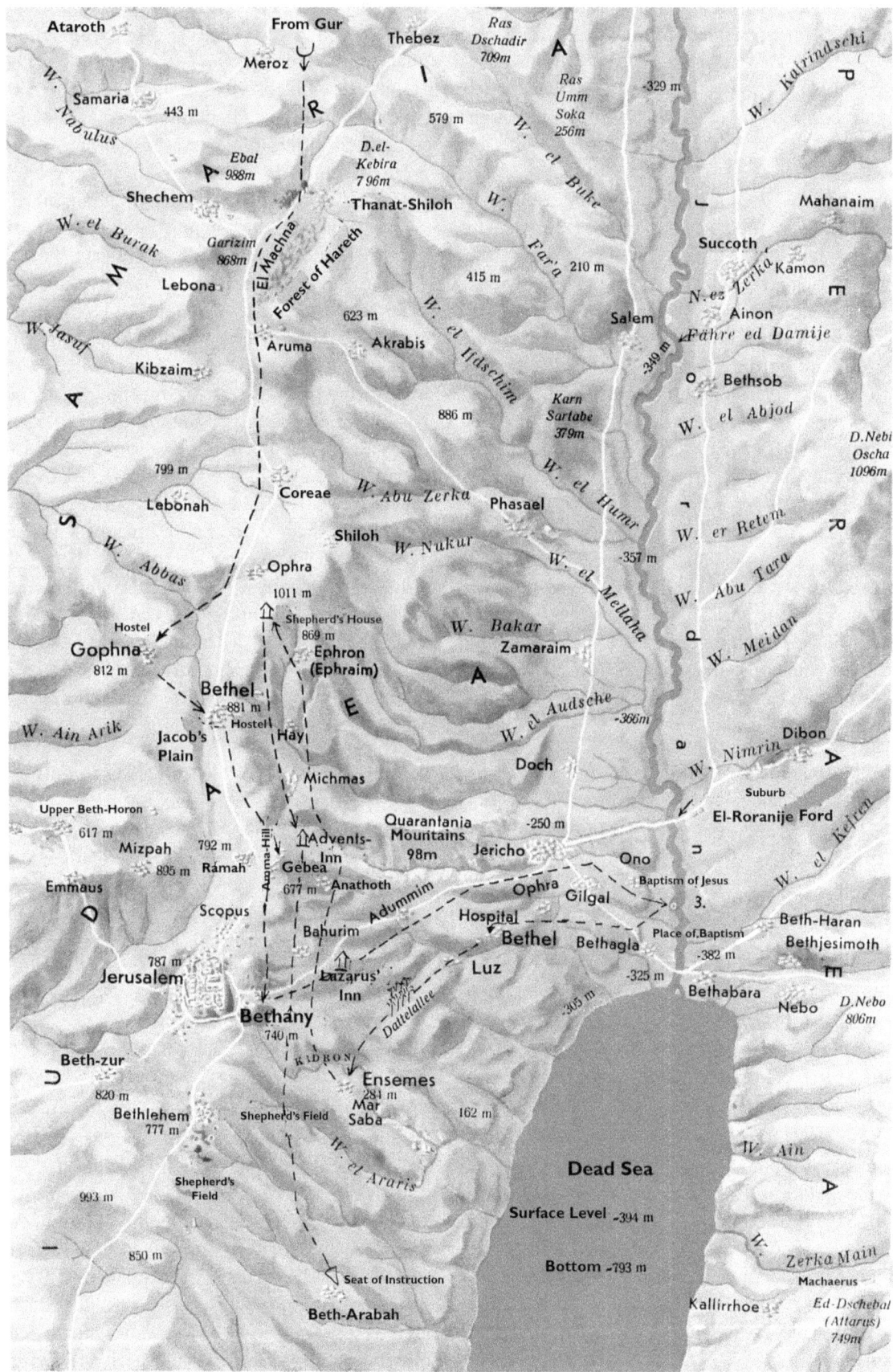

Gophna—Jacob's Town Bethel—Giah—Bethany—Jerusalem—Third Place of Baptism—Place of Convalescence—Bethel—Luz—Ensemes—Shepherd's House—Advent Inn—Beth-Arabah

would be in their midst, and they would not know him. He alluded, in words something like the following, to the connection existing between himself and John: "There will be one who will point him out (the Messiah), but ye will not acknowledge him. Ye wish to see a conqueror, an illustrious personage, a man surrounded by magnificence and eminently learned companions. Ye will not recognize as the Messiah one that comes among you destitute of wealth and authority, unattended by the pomp of worldly splendor and magnificence, one whose companions are unlettered peasants and laborers, whose followers are made up of beggars, cripples, lepers, and sinners."

In this way Jesus spoke at length, interpreting the prophecies, and putting forth clearly the connection between himself and John. Still, he never once said, "I," but spoke of himself in the third person. His instruction occupied the greater part of the day. His relatives concluded that he must be an envoy, a forerunner of the expected Messiah. On his return to their house, they referred to a book in his presence wherein they had recorded all that had happened in the temple to Jesus, the son of Mary, in his twelfth year. They were struck by the similarity between what he had then said and his teaching of today, and on perusal of that record they were still more astonished.

The father of the house was an aged widower. His two daughters, both widows, lived with him. I heard the two daughters talking together of the marriage of Joseph and Mary in Jerusalem, at which they had been present. They recalled the magnificence of that wedding, how well-off Anne had been, but how changed the circumstances of the family had become. They spoke just as people of the world are accustomed to do, a vein of blame and reproach running through their words, as if they of whom they were speaking had greatly degenerated. While thus conversing and, womanlike, recounting the particulars of the wedding and Mary's bridal dress, I saw a circumstantial vision of the whole ceremony and especially of the blessed Virgin's ornaments. Meanwhile the men were hunting up what had been written years before about Jesus and his teaching as a boy in the temple. The parents of Jesus had anxiously sought him here, and it was thus that the news of where and how he was found had reached them. The affair had attracted much attention, especially as he was a relative of theirs.

While his relatives were still expressing surprise at the connection between his former and his present teaching, by which they were even more prejudiced in his favor, Jesus informed them that he must take leave and, in spite of their remonstrances, set out accompanied by several of the men. They had to cross a little river over a bridge of masonry on which trees were growing. They journeyed some hours to a plain covered with meadows. It was here the patriarch Joseph was when Jacob sent him to his brethren in Shechem. The regions from which Jesus had lately come had also been much frequented by Jacob. Late in the evening Jesus entered a shepherd village this side of a small river, and his companions left him. The village lay on both sides of the river, the part on the opposite bank being the larger. The synagogue was on this side. The Lord went to an inn where were assembled two sets of candidates for baptism. They were on their way through the desert to the appointed place. They had spread the news here of Jesus's coming. He conversed with them that evening, and they departed next morning. The servants washed the Lord's feet. He partook of a light repast, and then retired for prayer and rest.

Jesus Condemns Herod's Adultery • The Journey of the Holy Women

Tuesday, September 20, AD 29 (Elul 23)

Jesus went to the synagogue and taught concerning baptism and the nearness of the Messiah. At the evening meal at the inn where he was staying, some of the guests denounced Herod's unlawful connection with his brother's wife. Jesus concurred but said that whoever judged others would himself be judged also. On this day, Anne Catherine also saw Mary, the mother of Jesus, and four of the holy women journeying towards Bethany.

NEXT morning Jesus went to the school, where many were assembled. He spoke, as usual, of the baptism and of the nearness of the Messiah whom they would not acknowledge. He reproached them for their obstinate adherence to old, meaningless customs, on which point these people had a special failing. They were, on the whole, tolerably simple-minded and received his remonstrances well. Jesus requested the high priest of the synagogue to conduct him to the sick. He visited about ten, but cured none; for, in the neighborhood of Jerusalem, he had told Eliud and his five disciples that he would perform no more cures until he had been to the baptism. The sick in this place were mostly dropsical, gouty, and infirm women. Jesus exhorted them and told them separately what religious acts they should perform, according as their infirmities were in part punishment of sin. Some he ordered to purify themselves and go to the baptism.

There was a meal prepared for him at the inn, at which many men of the place were present. Before the hour for it these men spoke of Herod, of his unlawful connection with his brother's wife, blaming him severely and inquiring into Jesus's opinion on the point in question. Jesus heatedly censured Herod's conduct and denounced the sin of adultery, but he told them likewise that if they judged others, they would themselves be judged.

Now there were in this place many sinners. Jesus spoke with them privately and earnestly reproved them for living in adultery. He told many all their secret sins. Trembling with fear, they promised to do penance.

Jesus went from here to Bethany, a distance of perhaps six miles, and again entered a mountainous region. It was the winter season, foggy and cloudy by day, and sometimes white frost by night. Jesus enveloped his head in a scarf, and journeyed straight on toward the east.

I saw Mary and four holy women leaving the house and wending their way through a field near Tiberias. They had with them two servants from the fishery. One went on ahead, the other followed, both laden with baggage which they carried on a pole across the shoulder, a pack in front and another behind. The four women were Johanna Chusa, Mary Cleophas, Mary Salome, and one of the three widows. They, too, were going to Bethany by the usual route, which ran by Shechem to the right. When Jesus passed it, it was on his left. The holy women walked generally in single file, a couple of steps apart. They went in this way probably because most of the roads, excepting the broad highways, were narrow, intended for foot passengers, and led through the mountains. They walked quickly with a firm step, not swaying from side to side, as the country people do here.

Very probably this is because from early youth the inhabitants of that country are accustomed to making long journeys on foot. They had their gowns tucked up to about the middle of the calf, their lower limbs bandaged tightly down to the ankle, and bound to the soles of their feet were thick, padded sandals. Over the head was a veil, the ends of which were fastened into the scarf wound round the neck. This scarf was crossed on the breast, thence carried behind and caught in the girdle; sometimes the wearers ran their hands into its folds and there let them rest. The man, going on before the travelers, prepared the way for them. He opened the hedges, removed stones from the path, laid bridges, gave orders at the inns and, in fine, saw to everything. The one who followed put everything again into its first order.

Jesus in Bethany

Wednesday, September 21, AD 29 (Elul 24)

Jesus left Bethel early and arrived that evening at a little village called Giah on Mount Amma, facing the Gibeon desert. There, he ate a meal and talked with several people who asked him about the prophet from Nazareth. Then he continued on his way, arriving that night at Lazarus' castle in Bethany. He was greeted not only by Lazarus but also by Nicodemus, John Mark, and the aged Obed (a relative of the prophetess Anna), who were guests of Lazarus in Bethany. Among the women gathered there as guests of Martha were Veronica, Mary Mark, and Susanna of Jerusalem. Jesus greeted them all, and they took a meal together before retiring for the night.

ABOUT six miles from Bethany, the road upon which Jesus was traveling again led through a mountainous country. That evening he entered a little village consisting of only one street, about half an hour in length, which ran across a mountain. Bethany was probably still three hours further on. One could see in the distance the region in which it lay, for it was a low plain. From this mountain stretched north and east a desert of about three hours in breadth toward the desert of Ephron. It was between these two deserts that I saw Mary and her companions tonight putting up at an inn.

The mountain is that one upon which Joab and Abisai, in the persecution of Abner, stopped when the latter addressed them. It is called Amma, and lies to the north of Jerusalem. The place where Jesus was faced both north and east. I think it was called Giah. It was opposite the desert Gibeon, which began at the foot of the mountain and stretched off to the desert Ephron. It was about three hours long. Jesus arrived in the evening and entered a house to procure some refreshment. They washed his feet, and set before him a drink and little rolls. Several persons soon gathered around him. As he had just come from Galilee, they questioned him about the teacher from Nazareth, of whom they had heard so much from John and other sources. They asked also whether John's baptism was of any value. Jesus instructed them in his usual style, exhorted them to baptism and penance, and spoke of the prophet from Nazareth and of the Messiah. He said that the latter would appear among them, but they would not acknowledge him, yea, they would even persecute and ill-treat him. They must indeed remark that the time was come for his advent. He would not appear in splendor and triumph. He would be poor and would walk among the simple. The people of this place did not know Jesus, but they received him well and expressed veneration for him. Aspirants to baptism had passed through the place and had spoken of him. After resting about two hours, he continued his journey accompanied by some of the good people.

He arrived in Bethany at night. Lazarus had been perhaps for some days at his house in Jerusalem on the west side of Mount Zion, the same side as Mount Calvary. But he must have heard from the disciples of Jesus's intended visit to Bethany, for he had come thither in time to receive him. The castle in Bethany belonged in reality to Martha; but Lazarus loved to be there, so he and his sister kept house together. They were expecting Jesus, and a repast was in readiness. Martha dwelt in a house on the other side of the courtyard. There were guests assembled in both houses. With Martha were Seraphia (Veronica), Mary

Fields and Vineyards on the Road to Bethany

Mark, and an aged woman of Jerusalem who had been in the temple when Mary entered and had left soon after. She had desired to remain, but God had other designs for her, and she married. With Lazarus were Nicodemus, John Mark, the only son of Simeon, and an old man named Obed, a brother or brother's son of the prophetess Anna. All were, in secret, friends of Jesus, partly through John the Baptist, partly through the holy family, and again through the prophecies of Simeon and Anna in the temple.

Nicodemus was a thoughtful, inquiring man, who was anxiously awaiting Jesus's coming. All had received the baptism of John, and all were secretly assembled here at Lazarus's invitation. Nicodemus afterward served Jesus and his cause, but in secret.

Lazarus had sent some of his servants to meet Jesus on the way. About thirty minutes from Bethany, Jesus came up with a trusty old servant who afterward joined the disciples. The old man prostrated on his face before him, saying, "I am the servant of Lazarus. If I have found favor before thee, my Lord, follow me to his house." Jesus bade him rise, and followed him. He was kind to the old man, but at the same time he conducted himself in accordance with his dignity. It was just that way of acting that gave him such power to attract. People loved the Man, but felt the God. The servant led Jesus to a porch near a fountain at the entrance of the castle, where all had been prepared for washing his feet and changing his sandals. He wore thick, green, padded soles which he now exchanged for a pair of stout ones with low, leather uppers. From that time he continued to wear these latter. The servant dusted and aired his garments. When the washing of his feet was over, Lazarus and his friends appeared, bringing to Jesus a light refreshment and something in a drinking cup. Jesus embraced Lazarus and greeted the others, extending to them his hand. They served him hospitably and escorted him to the house. Sometime after, Lazarus conducted him across the courtyard to Martha's dwelling. The women there knelt veiled before him.[B3] Jesus raised them by the hand, and told Martha that his mother was coming to await there his return from the baptism.

They all went back to Lazarus's, where a meal was awaiting them. It consisted of roasted lamb, doves, vegetables, little rolls, honey, and fruits. On the table were cups, and the guests reclined on leaning stools, two and two. The women ate in an antechamber. Jesus prayed before the meal began and blessed the food. He was very grave, even a little sad. During the repast, he said that a time of trial was approaching, that he was about to begin a toilsome journey, which would come to a bitter end. He exhorted them, if they were his friends, to stand firm, for like himself they would have much to suffer. He spoke so feelingly that they all wept, though they did not perfectly understand him and knew not that he was God.

That want of understanding on the part of those around Jesus is always a subject of wonder to me, since I have seen innumerable testimonies of his Godhead and mission; and I cannot help asking why was not that, which I perceive so clearly, shown to those people. I have seen man created by God, Eve taken from his side and bestowed upon him as a wife, and both fallen from their first innocence. I have seen the Promise of the Messiah, the dispersion of humankind, the wonderful providence of God and his mysteries preparing the way for the coming of the blessed Virgin. I saw the descent of the Blessing from which the Word became flesh running like a path of light through all the generations of Mary's ancestors. At last I saw the angel's message to Mary and the ray of light from the Godhead which penetrated her at the instant the Savior became Man. And after all this, how wonderful did it not seem to me, miserable, unworthy sinner, to see those holy contemporaries and friends of Jesus in his presence—though loving and honoring him—yet possessed by the thought that his kingdom was to be an earthly one; to see them regarding him, indeed, as the promised Messiah, and yet never dreaming that he was God himself. He was to them only the son of Joseph and Mary, his mother. None guessed that Mary was a virgin, for they knew not of her supernatural Immaculate Conception; indeed, they did not even know of the mystery of the Ark of the Covenant. It was already a great deal, and a sign of special grace, that they loved him and acknowledged him. The Pharisees, although they knew of the prophecies of Simeon and Anna at the time of his presentation in the temple, and who had listened to his wonderful teaching in the temple when still only a child, were perfectly obdurate. They had indeed made some inquiries at the time concerning the family of the child and later on concerning his instructors; but they esteemed him and his relatives too poor, too insignificant, too despicable. They wanted a Messiah in every way magnificent. Lazarus, Nicodemus, and many of the followers of Jesus entertained the secret belief that he was called with his disciples to take possession of Jerusalem, to free the Jews from the Roman yoke, and to establish them in a kingdom of their own. Truly, it was then as now, when each man might look upon him as a Savior who would restore his fatherland to freedom and once again establish the beloved old government. Neither was it known at that time that the kingdom which alone can help us, is not of this world of penance. Yes, they indeed rejoiced for the moment in the thought, "Now it will soon be all over with the glory of such or such a tyrant." They did not, however, venture to mention their thoughts to Jesus. They stood in great awe of him; besides, they could read a fulfillment of their hopes in no trace of his behavior, in no word that he uttered.

After the meal, all retired to an oratory where Jesus offered a prayer of thanksgiving that his time, his mission was now to begin. It was extremely affecting, and all shed tears. The women were present, but standing back. They recited together the usual prayers, after which Jesus gave them his blessing, and was conducted by Lazarus to his chamber for the night. This was a large room divided off into alcoves where the men slept; but these alcoves were more beautiful than those of ordinary houses. The beds were not rolled up, as they were in general; they were placed on a kind of stationary platform with a cornice in front ornamented with hangings and fringes. A fine mat was rolled up on the wall by the bed. It could, by means of a pulley, be drawn up or let down before the bed, thus concealing it when not in use, and forming a kind of slanting roof. Beside the bed was a small table, and in a niche of the wall stood a tall water vessel, along with a smaller one for drawing and pouring. A lamp projected from the wall, and on the arm of the same hung a toilet towel. Lazarus lighted the lamp, cast himself on his knees before Jesus, who again blessed him, and departed.

Silent Mary, the simple sister of Lazarus, did not make her appearance. Before others she never uttered a word; but when alone in her room or the garden, she talked aloud to herself and to all the objects around her, as if they had life. It was only before others that she was perfectly mute and still; her eyes cast down, she looked like a statue. On being saluted, however, she inclined and was very polite in all her bearing. When alone, she busied herself in various occupations, attending to her own wardrobe, and keeping all things in order. She was very pious, though she never appeared in the school. She prayed in her own chamber. I think she had visions and conversed with apparitions. Her love for her brother and sisters was unspeakable, especially for Magdalene. From her earliest years she had been what she now was. She had a female attendant, but she was perfectly neat in her person and surroundings with no trace of insanity to be found about her.

No word had as yet been spoken in Jesus's presence in reference to Magdalene, who was then living at Magdala in the height of her grandeur.

On the night that Jesus went to Lazarus's, I saw the blessed Virgin, Johanna Chusa, Mary Cleophas, the widow Lea, and Mary Salome passing the night at an inn between the desert Gibea and the desert Ephron, about five hours from Bethany. They slept under a shed enclosed on all sides by light walls. It contained two apartments. The front one was divided off into two rows of alcoves, of which the holy women took possession; the back served as a kitchen. Before the inn was an open hut in which a fire was burning. Here the male attendants slept or kept watch. The inn-keeper's dwelling was not far distant.

Thursday, September 22, AD 29 (E1u125)
During the morning, Jesus walked about in the courtyards and gardens of the castle, teaching those who were present. Then Martha took Jesus to visit her sister Mary, known as Silent Mary, who lived by herself like a hermit in part of the castle. Jesus was left alone to talk with Silent Mary, who lived in continuous vision of heavenly things. Normally silent in the presence of other people, Mary began to speak of the mysteries of Jesus's incarnation, passion, and death. After saying some prayers, Jesus returned to talk with Martha, who

expressed her deep concern regarding her other sister, Mary Magdalene. At about half-past one, the holy Virgin Mary arrived, accompanied by Johanna Chusa, the widow Lea, Mary Salome, and Mary Cleophas. After a light meal, Jesus and his mother, Mary, retired to talk with one another. In this conversation, Jesus told Mary that he was now going to be baptized and that his real mission would begin with this event. He said that they would meet again briefly in Samaria after the baptism, but that he would then go into the desert for forty days. Mary was much troubled when she heard this, but Jesus answered by saying that he must now fulfill his mission and that she should renounce all personal claims upon him. That evening, Lazarus gave a feast for all who were present. During the meal, Jesus again alluded to the persecutions that lay ahead of him, saying that those who allied themselves with him would suffer with him. The same night, Jesus, accompanied by Lazarus, set off in the direction of Jericho to make his way to the place of baptism.

On the following day, Jesus taught walking about the courtyards and gardens of the castle. He spoke earnestly, feelingly, and lovingly, though his manner was full of dignity and he uttered no unnecessary word. All loved him and followed him, though not without a sentiment of awe. Lazarus approached him the most confidently. The other men were more reserved; they gazed on in admiration.

Jesus's Interview with Silent Mary • His Conversation with His Mother

ACCOMPANIED by Lazarus, Jesus went also to the abode of the women, and Martha took him to her silent sister Mary, with whom he wished to speak. A wall separated the large courtyard from a smaller one, which latter, however, was still quite spacious. In it was an enclosed garden adjoining Mary's dwelling. They passed through a gate, and Jesus remained in the little garden while Martha went to call her silent sister. The garden was highly ornamental. In the center stood a large date tree, and all around were aromatic herbs and shrubs. On one side was a fountain or rather a kind of tiny lake with a stone seat in the center. From the opposite edge to the seat was laid a plank, upon which silent Mary could cross and there sit under an awning and surrounded by the water. Martha went to her and bade her come down into the garden, for there someone was waiting to speak to her. Silent Mary was very obedient. Without a word, she threw her veil around her and followed her sister into the garden. Then Martha retired. Mary was tall and very beautiful. She was about thirty years old. She generally kept her eyes fixed on heaven. If occasionally she glanced to one side where Jesus was, it was only a side glance and vaguely, as if she were gazing into the distance. Even when speaking of herself, she never used the pronoun, "I," but always "thou," as if she saw herself as a second person and spoke accordingly. She did not address Jesus nor cast herself at his feet. Jesus was the first to salute, and they walked together around the garden. Properly speaking, they did not converse together. Silent Mary kept her gaze fixed on high and recounted heavenly things, as if passing before her eyes. Jesus spoke in the same manner of his Father and to his Father. Mary never looked at Jesus, though while speaking she sometimes half turned to the side upon which he was walking. There was more a prayer, a song of praise, a contemplation, a revealing of mysteries than a conversation. Mary appeared as if ignorant of her own existence. Her soul was in another world while her body lived on earth.

Of their speech during that interview, I can remember that, glancing intuitively upon the Incarnation of Christ, they spoke as if gazing upon the most holy Trinity acting in that mystery. Their simple, and yet profoundly significant words I cannot recall. Mary gazing upon it, said, "The Father commissioned the Son to go down to humankind, among whom a Virgin should conceive him." Then she described the rejoicings of the angels, and how Gabriel was sent to the Virgin. And so she ran through the nine angelic choirs, who all came down with the bearer of the glad tidings, just as a child would joyously describe a procession moving before its eyes, praising the devotion and zeal of all that composed it. Then she seemed to glance into the chamber of the Virgin, to whom she spoke words expressive of her hope that she might receive the angel's message. She saw the angel arrive and announce the coming of the Savior. She saw all and repeated all, as if uttering her thoughts aloud, gazing the while into the distance. Suddenly she paused, her eyes fixed on the Virgin who appeared to be recollecting herself before replying to the angel, and said very simply, "Then, thou hast made a vow of virginity? Ah, if thou hadst refused to be the Lord's mother, what would have happened? Would there have been found another virgin?" Then addressing her nation, she exclaimed: "Had the Virgin refused, long wouldst thou, O orphaned Israel, still have groaned!" And now, filled with joy by the Virgin's consent, she burst forth into words of praise and thanksgiving, rehearsed the wonders of Jesus's birth and, addressing the divine child, said, "Butter and honey shalt thou eat." She again repeated the prophecies, recalled those of Simeon and Anna, etc., spoke with the different personages connected with them, and all this as if gazing upon those scenes, contemporary with them. At last, descending to the present, she said, speaking as if alone: "Now goest thou on the painful, bitter way," etc. Although she knew that the Lord was at her side, yet she acted and spoke as if he were no nearer to her than all the other visions just recounted. Jesus interrupted her from time to time with prayer and thanksgiving, praising his Father and interceding for humankind. The whole interview was inexpressibly touching and wonderful.

Jesus left her. Relapsing into her usual silence and exterior apathy, she returned to the house. When Jesus went back to Lazarus and Martha, he said to them something like the following: "She is not without understanding, but her soul is not of this world. She sees not this world, and this world comprehends her not. She is happy. She knows no sin."

Silent Mary, in her altogether spiritual state of contemplation, was really and truly oblivious to all that happened to her or around her. She was always thus abstracted. She had never before spoken in the presence of others as she had just done in that of Jesus. Before all others she kept silence, though not from pride or reserve. No, it was because she saw not those people interiorly, saw not what they saw, but gazed upon Redemption and the things of heaven alone. When at times accosted by a learned and pious friend of the family, she would indeed utter some words audibly, though without understanding a single word of what had been said to her. Not having reference to or connection with the vision upon which she was interiorly gazing at the time, she heard without hearing; consequently her reply, bearing upon what was then engrossing her own attention, mystified her hearers. It was for this reason that she was regarded by the family as a simpleton. Her state necessitated her dwelling alone, for her soul lived not in time. She cultivated her little garden and embroidered for the temple. Martha brought her her work. She was skillful with her needle, which she plied in uninterrupted musing and meditation. She prayed most piously and devoutly, and endured a kind of expiatory suffering for the sins of others, for her soul was often oppressed as if the weight of the whole world was upon her. Her dwelling was comfortably fitted up with sofas and different kinds of furniture. She ate little and always alone. She died of grief at the immensity of Jesus's Passion, which in spirit she foresaw.

Martha spoke to Jesus of Magdalene and her own great anxiety on her account. Jesus comforted her, telling her that Magdalene would certainly be converted, but that she must on no account weary of praying for her and exhorting her to change her life.

At about half-past one the blessed Virgin arrived with Mary Chusa, Lea, Mary Salome, and Mary Cleophas. The servant had in advance announced their approach. Martha, Seraphia, Mary Mark, and Susanna proceeded to that hall at the entrance of the castle where Jesus the day before had been received by Lazarus. They took with them refreshments and the vessels necessary for washing their guests' feet. After welcoming the newly-arrived and performing for them that duty of hospitality, the latter changed their dress, lowered their skirts, and put on fresh veils. All were clothed in undyed wool, yellowish-white or brownish. They partook of a light refreshment, and then accompanied Martha to her house.

Jesus and the men now presented themselves to salute the holy women, after which Jesus retired to converse with the blessed Virgin. He told her most earnestly and lovingly that he was about to begin his career, that he was now going to John's baptism whence he would return and once more be with her for a short time in the region of Samaria, but that then he would retire to the desert for forty days. When Mary heard him speak of the desert, she became very uneasy. She besought him not to go to so frightful a place where he would die of hunger and thirst. Jesus replied that henceforth she should not seek to deter him by human considerations, for he must accomplish what was marked out for him; a very different life was now about to commence for him, and they who would adhere to him must suffer with him; that he must now fulfill his mission, and she must sacrifice all purely personal claims upon him. He added that although he would love her as ever, yet he was now for all humankind. She should do as he said and his heavenly Father would reward her, for what Simeon had foretold was about to be fulfilled—a sword should pierce her soul. The blessed Virgin listened gravely. She was very much troubled, though at the same time strong in her resignation to God, for Jesus was very tender and loving.

That evening Lazarus gave a feast to which Simon the Pharisee, and some others of the sect were invited. The women ate in an adjacent room, which was separated by a grating from the men's dining hall, but within hearing of all that Jesus said. He taught of faith, hope, charity, and obedience. He said that they who desired to follow him must not look back. They should practice what he taught and suffer the trials that might befall them, but that he would never abandon them. He again alluded to the thorny path before him, to the buffetings and persecutions he would have to undergo, and impressed upon them the fact that whoever called themselves his friends would have to suffer with him. His hearers, deeply touched, listened in wonder to his words, but what he said in allusion to his bitter Passion they did not rightly understand. They did not take his words in their simple and literal meaning, but looked upon them as the figurative expressions of prophecy. The Pharisees present, though less favorably disposed than the others, found nothing to carp at in Jesus's speech. This time, however, he spoke very moderately.

Jesus Journeys with Lazarus to the Place of Baptism

THE ENTERTAINMENT over, Jesus rested awhile and then started with Lazarus toward Jericho to the place of baptism. One of Lazarus's servants went on ahead with a lighted torch, for it was night. After walking for about half an hour, they reached an inn belonging to Lazarus where at a later period the disciples often stopped. This inn must not be confounded with that other of which I have often made mention, and at which also the disciples frequently put up. That one was farther on in an opposite direction. The hall in which Jesus and Mary were received by Lazarus on their arrival at his house, was the same in which Jesus was stopping and teaching before the resurrection of Lazarus when Magdalene went to meet him. On arriving at the inn, Jesus removed his sandals and went barefoot. Lazarus, touched with compassion, begged him in consideration of the rough, stony roads not to do so. But Jesus gravely replied: "Let it be thus! I know what it behooveth me to do," and so they entered into the wilderness. The desert, broken up by narrow chasms, stretched out before them a distance of five hours toward Jericho. Then came the fruitful valley of Jericho, also interspersed by wild tracts, about two hours' journey in breadth, whence to John's place of baptism was a journey of another two hours. Jesus walked more quickly than Lazarus, and was often an hour ahead of him. A multitude, among them some publicans whom Jesus had sent from Galilee to the baptism, were now on their return journey. They passed Jesus in the desert, though at some distance, on their way back to Bethany. Jesus stopped nowhere. He passed Jericho on his left and a couple of other places on the way, but paused at none.

Lazarus's friends, Nicodemus, Simeon's son, and John Mark, had spoken but little with Jesus. But to one another they were constantly interchanging words of admiration at his behavior, his wisdom, his human, yes, even his personal attractions. In his absence or when walking behind

Plain of Jericho, with Aqueducts in the Distance

him, they said to one another: "What a man! There never before was such a one, there never again will be another like him! How earnest, how mild, how wise, how discerning, and yet how simple! But I cannot perfectly comprehend his words, though I accept them with the thought, 'He said it!' One cannot look him in the face, for he seems to read one's thoughts. Look at his figure—how majestic in bearing! How swiftly he moves, and yet no undignified haste! Whoever walked like him! How quickly he journeys from place to place, and yet shows no signs of weariness! He is always ready to start again for hours. What a man he has turned out to be!" Then they went on to speak of his childhood, his teaching in the temple, and referred to the dangers attendant on his first voyage, when he had aided the sailors. But not one of them dreamed that he was speaking of the Son of God. They saw that he was greater than all other men, they honored him, and stood in awe of him; still he was to them only a man, though, indeed, a man full of prodigies. Obed of Jerusalem was an aged man, the fraternal nephew of the husband of old Anna the prophetess. He was a pious man, one of the so-called elders at the temple, a member of the Sanhedrin. He was one of the secret disciples of Jesus and, as long as he lived, lent assistance to the community.

JOHN PREACHING PENANCE AND BAPTIZING • BAPTISM IN THE JORDAN • RETRACING THE JOURNEYS OF MARY AND JOSEPH • BEGINNING OF FORTY DAYS' FAST

John Leaves the Desert

JOHN received from on high a revelation concerning the baptism, in consequence of which shortly before leaving the desert he dug a well within reach of the inhabited districts. I saw him on the western side of a steep precipice. On his left ran a brook, perhaps one of the sources of the Jordan which rises on Libanus in a cave between two ridges. It cannot be seen from a distance. To the right lay a level space in the midst of the wilderness, and there he dug a well. I saw him kneeling on one knee and supporting on the other a long roll of bark upon which he was writing with a reed. The sun was darting hot beams upon him as he knelt facing Libanus toward the west. While thus engaged, he became like one entranced. I saw him as if in ecstasy, and standing by him was a man who drew plans and wrote upon the roll. When John returned to consciousness, he read what had been written, and at once set vigorously to work at the well. The bark roll lay beside him on the ground, weighted by a stone at either end to prevent it from rolling together. John often examined it. It seemed as if all he had to do was there marked down.

Side by side with his vision of the well, I beheld a scene in the life of Elijah. I saw him sitting in the desert, sad and dejected, on account of some fault he had committed. At last he fell asleep, and had a dream, in which it seemed to him that a little boy approached and pushed him with a stick, and that he feared falling into a well nearby. The thrusts he received from the child were so violent as to send him rolling forward some steps. At this stage of the dream an angel awoke him and gave him to drink. This took place on the same spot upon which John now dug the well.

I recognized the signification of every layer of earth through which John dug and of every step in the work until its completion. All had some relation to human obduracy and its other characteristics, which he had to overcome before the grace of the Lord could take effect upon humankind. This work of John's was, like all his actions and his whole life, a symbol, a prefiguration. By it the Holy Spirit not only instructed him what he was to do, but he really accomplished in its performance all that the work itself signified, God accepting the good intention which he had thereto associated. The Holy Spirit urged John on in his work, as formerly the inspired prophets.

He removed the sod from a wide circumference and dug out of the hard marl a large circular basin, which he very carefully and beautifully lined with stones, excepting in the center where it was dug to a little water. With the excavated earth, he formed around the basin a rim which he divided into five sections. Opposite the openings between four of these sections and at equal distances around the basin, he planted four slender saplings whose tops were covered with luxuriant foliage. These four trees were of different kinds, each bearing its own signification. But in the center of the basin he set a very choice tree with narrow leaves; its blossoms hung in pyramidal clusters surrounded by a prickly calyx. This tree had long lain partially withered before John's cave. The four little trees were more like slender berry bushes. John protected their roots by little mounds of earth.

When the basin had been excavated down to the well, in which later on the central tree was planted, John hollowed out a channel from the brook near his cave to the basin. Then I saw him gathering reeds in the wilderness, inserting one into the other and, through this conduit (which he covered with earth) conducting the waters of the brook to the basin. The reed pipe could be closed at pleasure.

He had made a path through the bushes down to one of the openings in the basin's rim. It ran all around the basin between it and the four trees I have just described. Before the opening at the entrance there was no tree, and on this side alone was access to the basin free; on all the others the path was hemmed in by bushes and rocks. John planted on the mounds at the foot of the four trees an herb well known to me. I was fond of it when a child and, whenever I found it, I used to transplant it to the neighborhood of my home. It has a tall, succulent stalk and bears brownish-red, globular blossoms. It is a very efficacious remedy for ulcers and such sore throats as that from which I am today suffering. John set around also various other plants and

John Leaves the Desert

young trees. During his labor, he consulted from time to time the bark roll before him, and measured all off with a stick, for it seemed to me that every step of the work, even to the trees that he had planted, was therein sketched. I remember having seen in it a drawing of the middle tree.

John labored thus for several weeks and when he had finished, there was only a small quantity of water in the bottom of the basin. The middle tree, whose leaves had lately been brown and withered, had now become fresh and green. In a vessel formed of the bark of a large tree and whose sides had been smeared with pitch, John now brought water from another well and poured it into the basin. This water was from a well near one of the caves in which John had first dwelt. It had gushed from a rock upon which he struck with the end of his standard. I heard that he could not have built the fountain at that earlier dwelling place of his because it was too rocky there, and that, too, had its own signification. After that he let as much water into the basin from the brook as was necessary. If the reservoir became too full, the water could flow off by the channels in the rim and refresh the vegetation of the surrounding surface.

I saw John stepping into the water up to the waist. With one hand he clasped the tree in the center while he struck the water with a little staff to the end of which he had fastened a cross and pennant. Every stroke sent the water in a spray above his head. At the same time, I saw descending upon him from above a cloud of light and, as it were, an effusion from the Holy Spirit, while angels appeared upon the rim of the basin and addressed to him some words. I saw that this was John's last labor in the desert.

That well was in use even after Jesus's death. When the Christians were obliged to flee, the sick and travelers were baptized there; it was frequented also as a place of devotion. It was at that time, that is during Peter's time, protected by a surrounding wall.

Soon after the completion of the baptismal well, John left the desert for the haunts of men. Wherever he went, he made a wonderful impression. Tall of stature, strong and muscular, though emaciated by fasting and corporal mortification, he presented an extraordinarily pure and noble appearance, his manner simple, straightforward, and commanding. His face was thin and haggard; his expression, grave and austere; his auburn hair in curls over his head, and his beard short. Around his waist was a tunic that reached to the knee, and his rough brown mantle appeared to be of three pieces. The back part was fastened around the waist by a strap, but in front it was open, leaving the breast uncovered and the arms free. His breast was rough with hair almost the color of his mantle, and in his hand he carried a staff bent like a shepherd's crook.

Coming down from the desert, he built first a little bridge over a brook. He took no notice of the crossing that lay at some distance, for he never turned out of his way, but worked straight on wherever he went. There was an old highway in those regions. He was near Cidessa here, and he instructed the people in the neighborhood. They were the first pagans that afterward went to his baptism. They lived in mud huts entirely neglected. They were the descendants of a mixed multitude who, after the destruction of the temple, the last one before Jesus's coming, had settled here. One of the latest of the prophets had foretold to them that they should remain in these parts until a man should come to them, a man like John, who would tell them what they should do. Later on they removed toward Nazareth.

John allowed nothing to prove an obstacle in his way. He walked boldly up to all he met, and spoke of one thing only, penance and the near coming of the Lord. His presence everywhere excited wonder and made the lightest grave. His voice pierced like a sword. It was loud and strong, though tempered with a tone of kindness. He treated all kinds of people as children. The most remarkable thing about him was the way in which he hurried on straight ahead, deterred by nothing, looking around at nothing, wanting nothing. It was thus I saw him hastening on his way through desert and forest, digging here, rolling away stones there, removing fallen trees, preparing resting places, calling together the people who stood staring at him in amazement, yes, even bringing them out of their huts to help him. I saw their looks of astonishment. He tarried long nowhere, but was soon in another place. He went along the Sea of Galilee, around Tarichea, down to the valley of the Jordan, then past Salem, and on through the desert toward Bethel. He passed by Jerusalem. He had never been in the Holy City; he gazed sadly upon it, and uttered lamentations over it. Entirely possessed by the thought of his mission, on he went, earnest, grave, simple, full of the Holy Spirit, crying aloud the selfsame words: "Penance! Prepare! The Lord is nigh!" He entered the shepherd valley, and journeyed on to the place of his birth. His parents were dead, but some youths, his relatives on Zechariah's side, resided there. They were among the first to join him as disciples. When he passed through Bethsaida, Capernaum, and Nazareth, the blessed Virgin did not see him, for since Joseph's death, she seldom went out of the house. But several male relatives of her family were present at his exhortations, and accompanied him some distance on his way.

During the three months immediately preceding the baptism, John twice made the circuit of the country announcing him who was to come. His progress was made with extraordinary vehemence. He marched on vigorously, his movements quick though unaccompanied by haste. His was no leisurely traveling like that of the Savior. Where he had nothing to do, I saw him literally running from field to field. He entered houses and schools to teach, and gathered the people around him in the streets and public places. I saw the priests and elders here and there stopping him and questioning his right to teach, but soon, astonished and full of wonder, they allowed him to proceed on his way.

The expression, "To prepare the way for the Lord," was not wholly figurative, for I saw John begin his mission by actually preparing the way and traversing the roads and different places over which Jesus and his disciples afterward traveled. He cleared them of stones and briars, made paths, laid planks across brooks, cleaned the channels, dug wells and reservoirs, put up seats, resting places, and sheds to afford shade in the various places where later on the Lord rested, taught, and acted. While thus engaged, the earnest, simple-hearted, solitary man—by his rough garments and conspicuous figure—attracted the attention of the people, and excited wonder when he entered the huts sometimes to borrow a tool, sometimes even to claim assistance from the residents. Everywhere he was soon surrounded by a crowd whom he boldly and earnestly exhorted to penance, and to follow the Messiah of whom he announced himself the precursor. I often saw him pointing in the direction in which Jesus was passing at that moment. But yet I never saw Jesus with him, although they were sometimes scarcely one hour apart. Once I saw him at the most only a short hour's distance from Jesus, crying out to the people that he himself was not the looked-for Redeemer, but only his poor precursor; but that there went the Savior, and he pointed to him. John saw the Savior face to face only three times in his whole life. The first time that he did so, was in the desert when the holy family was journeying from Egypt. He had then been hurried by the Spirit to greet his Master whom, years before while still in his mother's womb, he had saluted. He felt the nearness of his Savior, and he knew that he thirsted. The boy prayed and thrust his little staff into the ground, whereupon a plentiful stream sprang forth. He then hurried further on the road and took his stand by the running water, to watch Jesus, Mary, and Joseph as they passed by. When they appeared and as long as they remained in sight, he danced about with joy, waving his little standard.

The second time that John saw Jesus was at the baptism; and third was when, at the Jordan, he rendered testimony to him as he was passing at a distance. I heard the Savior speaking to his apostles of John's great self-command; for even at the baptism he had restrained himself within the bounds of solemn contemplation, although his heart was almost bursting with love and desire. After the ceremony, he was more anxious to abase and humble himself than to yield to his love and seek for Jesus.

But John saw the Lord always in spirit, for he was generally in the prophetic state. He saw Jesus as the accomplishment of his own mission, as the realization of his own prophetic vocation. Jesus was not to John a contemporary, not a man like unto himself. He was to him the Redeemer of the world, the Son of God made man, the Eternal appearing in time, therefore he could in no way dream of associating with him. John felt also that he himself was not like his fellow men, existing in time, living in the world and connected with it; for even in his mother's womb had the hand of the Eternal touched him, and by the Holy Spirit had he, in a way superior to the relations of time, been brought into communication with his Redeemer. As a little boy he had been snatched from the world and, knowing nothing but what appertained to his Redeemer, had remained in the deepest solitude of the wilderness until, like one born anew, earnest, inspired, ardent, he went forth to begin his wonderful mission, unconcerned about aught else. Judea is now to him the desert; and as formerly he had had for companions the fountains, rocks, trees, and animals, as with them he had lived and communed, so now did he treat with men, with sinners, no thought of self arising in his mind. He sees, he knows, he speaks only Jesus. His word is: "He comes! Prepare ye the ways! Do penance! Receive the baptism! Behold the Lamb of God who beareth the sins of the world!" In the desert, blameless and pure as a babe in the mother's womb, he comes forth from his solitude innocent and spotless as a child at the mother's breast. "He is pure as an angel," I heard the Lord say to the apostles. "Never has impurity entered into his mouth, still less has an untruth or any other sin issued from it."

John baptized in different places: first, at Ainon in the neighborhood of Salem; then at Ono opposite Beth-Arabah on the west side of the Jordan, and not far from Jericho. The third place was on the east side of the Jordan, a couple of hours further north than the second. The last time he baptized was at Ainon, whither he had returned. It was there that he was taken prisoner.

The water in which John baptized was an arm of the Jordan formed by a bend of the river to the east, and of about an hour in length. At some places it was so narrow that one could leap over it; at others it was broader. Its course must have changed here and there, for in many places I saw it dry. This bend of the river encircled pools and wells which were fed by its waters. One of these pools, separated by a dam from the arm of the river, formed the baptism place of John at Ainon. Under the dam ran pipes, by means of which the pool could be emptied or filled at pleasure. John himself had so arranged it. On one side of the pool, its waters flowed inland like a creek, and into this extended tongues of land. The aspirants for baptism stood in the water up to the waist between two of these tongues, supporting themselves by a railing that ran along before them. On one tongue stood John. He scooped up water in a shell and poured it on the head of the neophyte, while on the opposite tongue stood one of the baptized with his hand resting on the shoulder of the latter. John himself had laid his hand upon the first. The upper part of the body of the neophytes was not entirely nude; a kind of

River Jordan at Dan

white scarf was thrown around them, leaving only the shoulders bare. Near the pool was a hut into which they retired for unrobing and dressing. I never saw women baptized here. The Baptist wore a long, white garment during the ceremony.

The region in which John baptized was an exceedingly charming and well-watered district called Salem. It lay on both sides of an arm of the Jordan, but Ainon was on the opposite side of the river. It was larger than Salem, further north and nearer the river. Around the numerous creeks and pools of this region were pasture grounds for cattle, and droves of asses grazed in the verdant meadows.

The country around Salem and Ainon was, as it were, free, possessing a kind of privilege established by custom, by virtue of which the inhabitants dared not drive anyone from its borders. John had built his hut at Ainon on the old foundations of what was once a large building, but which had fallen to ruins, and was now covered with moss and overgrown by weeds. Here and there arose a hut. These ruins were the foundations of the tent castle of Melchizedek. Of this place in particular I have had visions, all kinds of scenes belonging to early times, but I can now recall only this, that Abraham once had a vision here. He pulled two stones in position, one as an altar, and upon the other he knelt. I saw the vision that was shown to him—a City of God like the Heavenly Jerusalem, and streams of water falling from the same. He was commanded to pray more for the coming of the City of God. The water streaming from the City spread around on all sides. Abraham had this vision about five years before Melchizedek built his tent castle on the same spot. This castle was more properly a tent surrounded by galleries and flights of steps similar to Mensor's castle in Arabia. The foundation alone was solid; it was of stone. I think that even in John's time, the four corners where the principal stakes once stood were still to be seen. On this foundation, which now looked like a mount overgrown with vegetation, John had built a little reed hut. The tent castle in Melchizedek's time was a public halting place for travelers, a kind of charming resting place by the pleasant waters. Perhaps Melchizedek, whom I have always seen as the leader and counselor of the wandering races and nations, built his castle here in order to be able to instruct and entertain them. But even in his time it had some reference to baptism. It was also the place from which he set out to his building near Jerusalem, to Abraham, and elsewhere. Here it was, also, that he assembled the various races and peoples whom he afterward separated and settled in different districts.

Jacob, too, had once lived at Ainon a long time with his herds. The cistern of the baptism pool was in existence at that early time, and I saw that Jacob repaired it. The ruins of Melchizedek's castle were near the water and the place of baptism; and I saw that in the early days of Christian Jerusalem a church stood on the spot were John had baptized. I saw this church still standing when Mary of Egypt passed that way when retiring into the desert.

Salem was a beautiful city, but it was ruined during a war, I think at the destruction of the temple before the time of Jesus. The last prophet, also, dwelt there awhile.

John, perhaps for about two weeks, had been attracting public attention by his teaching and baptizing, when some messengers sent by Herod from Kallirrhoe came to him. Herod was at that time living in his castle at Kallirrhoe, on the eastern side of the Dead Sea. There were numerous baths and warm springs in the vicinity. Herod wanted John to come to him. But John replied to the messengers: "I have much to occupy me. If Herod wishes to confer with me, let him come himself." After that I saw Herod going to a little city about five miles south of Ainon. He was riding in a low-wheeled chariot, and surrounded by a guard. From its raised seat he could command a view upon all sides as from a canopied throne. He invited John to meet him in the little city. John went to a man's hut outside the city, and thither Herod repaired alone to meet him. Of their interview I remember only that Herod asked John why he dwelt in so miserable an abode at Ainon, adding that he would have a house built for him there. But to this John replied that he needed no house, that he had all he wanted and that he was accomplishing the will of one greater than he. He spoke earnestly and severely, though briefly, standing the while with his face turned away from Herod.

I saw that Simon, James the Less, and Thaddeus, the sons of Mary Cleophas by her deceased husband Alpheus, and Joseph Barsabbas, her son by her second marriage with Sabbas, were baptized by John at Ainon. Andrew and Philip also were baptized by him, after which they returned to their occupations. The other apostles and many of the disciples had already been baptized.

One day many priests and doctors of the Law came to John from the towns around Jerusalem intending to call him to account. They questioned him as to who he was, who had sent him, what he taught, etc. John answered with extraordinary boldness and energy, announced to them the coming of the Messiah and charged them with impenitence and hypocrisy.[B4]

Not long after, multitudes were sent from Nazareth, Jerusalem, and Hebron by the elders and Pharisees to question John upon his mission. They made his having taken possession of the place chosen for baptism a subject of complaint.

Many publicans had come to John. He had baptized them and spoken to them upon the state of their conscience. Among them was the publican Levi, later called Matthew, the son of Alpheus by his first marriage, for he was a widower when he married Mary Cleophas. Levi was deeply touched by John's exhortations, and he amended his life. He was held in low esteem by his relatives. John refused baptism to many of these publicans.

Herod's Soldiers • Deputies from the Sanhedrin • Crowds of Neophytes Come to John

IN Dothan, where Jesus had calmed the raving possessed, Jews and pagans had, since the Babylonian Captivity, dwelt together indiscriminately. On a hill in the vicinity the pagans had their idols and a place of sacrifice. The Jews, roused by the rumor of the advent of the Messiah who was to come from Galilee, would no longer suffer the pagans to dwell among them. The report had been spread both by John himself when journeying through those parts, and by those whom he had there baptized. A neighboring prince of Sidon had dispatched soldiers to the defense of the idols and Herod also sent troops thither to bring the people to order.

These troops were made up of the rabble. I saw them with Herod at Kallirrhoe. They told him that they would first be baptized by John, but this was mere policy. They thought by so doing they would have more success among the people. Herod replied that it was not at all necessary to be baptized by John, especially as he wrought no miracles, and neither were they obliged to recognize his mission, but that they might make inquiries at Jerusalem. Then I saw them going to Jerusalem. They had among them chief men of three different ranks, whose office it was to propose the questions to John, and by that I saw they were of three different sects. They had an interview with the priests in the judgment hall in which Peter afterward denied the Lord. In it sat many judges, and it was full of people. The priests derided the soldiers' question, as to whether they should receive John's baptism or not. Their answer was that they might or they might not, it was all the same. About thirty of the soldiers went to John, who reproved them sharply as if to imply that he had little cause to hope for their amendment. He administered baptism to only a few of them in whom he perceived still a little good. These last also he sternly reproached for their dissimulation.

The multitude gathered at Ainon was very great. John baptized none for several days, being engaged in vehement and zealous preaching. Crowds of Jews, Samaritans, and pagans occupied the hills and ramparts around, separate from one another, some under shelter, some under sheds, and some in the open air. John's pulpit was in the center of the encampment, and all listened to him as he preached. Their number amounted to many hundreds. They came to hear his teaching and receive baptism, after which they departed. Once, in particular, I saw many pagans, also people from Arabia and others from a land still farther east. They brought large asses and sheep with them. They had relatives around the country whom they visited here and there, and at last came to John.

In Jerusalem, the Sanhedrin held a great consultation about John, the result of which was that nine messengers were dispatched to him from three different authorities. Annas sent Joseph of Arimathea, also Simeon's eldest son, and a priest whose office it was to inspect the sacrifices; three members of the council, and three private citizens were also chosen for the mission. Their instructions were to question John as to who he was, and to summon him to appear in Jerusalem; for if his mission was authorized, he should first have presented himself at the temple. They likewise found fault with his unseemly raiment and, moreover, with his administering baptism to the Jews when it was customary to do so only to pagans! Some believed that he was Elijah returned from the other world.

Andrew and John the Evangelist were with the Baptist. Many of the disciples and most of the future apostles excepting Peter, who had already been baptized, and Judas the Traitor (who, however, had been at the fishery around Bethsaida making inquiries concerning Jesus and John) were with John at this time.

For three days, John had not baptized; but he had just resumed that work as the messengers from Jerusalem arrived. They wanted an audience with him right away, but John replied roughly and shortly that they must wait

Stream in Jezreel Valley

until he was ready. When at last they gained a hearing, they represented to him that he acted entirely too independently, that he should present himself at Jerusalem, and should adopt a less unsightly garb. When the envoys departed, Joseph of Arimathea and the son of Simeon remained with John and received from him baptism. There were many present whom John would not baptize; consequently they went to the envoys and charged John with partiality.

The future apostles, returning to their own part of the country, told what they knew of John, and in consequence of his teaching, listened favorably to Jesus.

As Joseph of Arimathea was journeying back to Jerusalem, he met Obed, a relative of Seraphia (Veronica). He was a server in the temple. Joseph, in answer to his questions, told him much about John. Obed then went and received the baptism. As a temple server, he belonged to the number of the secret disciples. It was only at a later period that he followed Jesus openly.

John Receives an Admonition to Go to Jericho

I SAW John crossing the Jordan to baptize the sick. He had only his linen scarf thrown around him and his mantle hanging from his shoulders. At one side hung a leathern bottle of baptismal water; on the other, the shell he used in baptizing. On the shore of the river opposite John's place of baptism were many sick persons who had been brought thither, some in litters and some on a kind of wheelbarrow. They could not be taken across the river on the raft, and so they implored John to come to them. He did so, attended by two of his disciples. He prepared a beautiful basin separated from the river by a dyke. This he did himself, for he always had a spade with him. Through a channel, which he could close at pleasure, he let in the water from the river and then poured into it the bottle of baptismal water that he had brought with him. He instructed the sick and then baptized them, pouring water out of a shell over them as they lay on the edge of the basin. When he had finished, he returned to Ainon by the east bank of the Jordan.

Here I beheld an angel appear to him and tell him to go to the other side of the Jordan near Jericho, for the time was drawing nigh. One would soon arrive there, and he should announce his coming.

At this command, John and his disciples took down their tents at the place of baptism near Ainon. They journeyed for some hours along the east side of the Jordan, then crossed the river, pursued their course along the western bank for a short distance, and again pitched their tents. There was a bathing place here, consisting of pits lined with white masonry and connected with the Jordan by canals that could be opened or closed as needed. There were no islands in this part of the river.

This second baptism place lay between Jericho and Bethagla on the western side of the Jordan and opposite Beth-Arabah, which was situated somewhat further down on the east side of the river. From this place of baptism to Jericho, the distance was about five miles. The direct road led through Bethany and a desert. There was an inn on the route, but built a short distance off from the road. This region was a pleasure resort. The water of the Jordan is beautiful, becoming so clear when allowed to stand. In many places also it is highly odoriferous owing to the blossoms that fall into it from the bushes in full bloom upon its banks. At times it is very shallow, one can see almost to the bottom, and I saw along the shore deep caves hollowed out of the rocks. I like so much to be in the Holy Land, though I never exactly understand the seasons there. When it is winter with us everything there is in full bloom, and in our summer they already have their second harvest. There is also a season of thick mists and heavy rains. There were about one hundred people with John, among them his disciples and numerous pagans. They all set to work preparing the place and building the tent. All sorts of things were brought over from the baptism place at Ainon. All was now better arranged, and the sick were carried thither in beds.

It was in this part of the Jordan that Elijah divided the waters with his mantle and passed over with Elisha, who did the same on his return. Elisha also rested here, and over this same spot the children of Israel crossed.

From the temple of Jerusalem messengers, both Pharisees and Sadducees, were now dispatched to John. He knew through the angel of their coming. When they reached the neighborhood of the Jordan, they sent a courier on before, to summon John to meet them at a place nearby. But he replied by their messenger that, if they wanted to speak with him, they might come to him. They did so, but John paid no attention to them. He went on teaching and baptizing. They listened for awhile and then withdrew. When John had finished, he ordered them to meet him under the shelter or tent that the disciples had erected.

And now, accompanied by his disciples and many others, he went to them. They put all kinds of questions to him, asking whether he was this one or that one, and I saw that he invariably answered in the negative. Then they asked who that one was of whom he spoke so much, for the old prophecies were still remembered, and the rumor was current among the people that the Messiah had come. John answered that among them had arisen one whom they knew not, that he himself had never seen him, and yet before his birth he had been commanded by him to prepare his ways and to baptize him. If they would return at a certain time, he continued, they would behold him there, for he was coming to receive baptism. Then he chided them severely, telling them that they had not come to the baptism, but merely for the purpose of seeing what was going on. They retorted that they now knew who he was, that he was baptizing without a mission, that he was a hypocrite clothed in rough garments, etc., and thus abusing him, they went their way.

Not long after, about twenty other messengers from the Sanhedrin arrived in Jerusalem. They were men of all conditions, among them some priests wearing caps and broad girdles and long scarfs hanging from the arm. The ends of these scarfs were rough as if trimmed with fur. They addressed John very earnestly, telling him that they had been sent to him by the whole Sanhedrin to summon him to appear before the council in order to prove his calling and mission. They urged as a proof of his having none, his want of obedience to the Sanhedrin. I heard John replying in plain terms, bidding them tarry a little while and they should see coming to him the one from whom he had his mission. He told them undisguisedly that the one to whom he so plainly referred had been born in Bethlehem and reared in Nazareth, that he had fled into Egypt, etc., but that he himself had never seen him. The deputies of the Sanhedrin reproached John with maintaining a secret understanding with Jesus, asserting that their communications were carried on by means of trusty messengers. To this John replied that he could not show to their blind eyes the messengers between Jesus and himself, they could not be seen by them. Indignant at his words, the deputies departed.

Multitudes from all sides, pagans as well as Jews, came to John. Herod very often sent people to hear him, and they carried back to their master an account of his teaching.

All things were very beautifully arranged at this place of baptism. John, with the help of his disciples, had put up an immense tent in which the sick and weary found refreshment, and in which also instructions were given. They sang hymns. I heard them singing a psalm that treated of the passage of the children of Israel through the Red Sea.

By degrees there sprang up at this place a little village of huts and tents covered partly with skins, partly with rushes. The concourse of strangers was very great. They came from the most distant countries, even from the land of the three kings. They brought with them numbers of camels, asses, and beautiful, little frolicsome horses. They always journey this way into Egypt. All encamped around John's baptism place to hear his teaching concerning the Messiah and to receive baptism.

From this place they proceeded in crowds to Bethlehem. Not far from the crib cave, off toward the shepherd field, was a well of Abraham. He and Sarah had dwelt for a period in this region, and during an illness he had had an eager craving after some water from this well. But when it was brought to him in a bottle, he mortified himself, denied himself the cooling draught for the love of God. In reward he was cured. The water of this well was hard to raise on account of its great depth. A large tree stood by it, and the well itself was near the spot upon which lay buried Maraha, Abraham's nurse. When he came to these parts, he brought her with him on a camel. This spot had, like Mount Carmel and Horeb, become a place of pilgrimage for devout Jews. The three holy kings had once prayed there.

There were not as yet many Galileans among John's followers, only a few of the subsequent disciples of Jesus. Many went from the region of Hebron, among them numbers of pagans. Therefore did Jesus in his discourses on his way through Galilee so zealously exhort his hearers to go to John's baptism.

Herod's Interview with John • The Celebration of a Festival at the Place of Baptism

THE PLACE at which John taught was about a short hour further on from where he was accustomed to baptize. It was one of the holy memorial places of the Jews, and was surrounded by walls like a garden inside and around which were rush-covered huts. In the center of this enclosure lay a stone upon the spot where the children of Israel, when crossing the Jordan, had first rested the Ark of the Covenant and celebrated a festival of thanksgiving. John had erected his tent for teaching, a large canopy of latticework covered with rushes, over this stone at whose base was the chair from which he taught. Here John was holding forth to his disciples when Herod came marching by, but he continued his discourse undisturbed by his presence.

Herod had gone to Jerusalem to meet his brother's wife, who had repaired thither with her daughter Salome, then about sixteen years old. He desired to marry the mother, and had in vain laid the question of the lawfulness of such a union before the Sanhedrin. The refusal of the council to sanction his desires excited his wrath and, as he feared the public voice, he determined to silence it by the decision of the prophet John. He doubted not that John, in order to win his favor, would approve the step he wished to take.

I saw Herod's cavalcade consisting of himself, Salome, the daughter of Herodias, her female attendants, and about thirty followers marching toward the Jordan. Herod and the women rode in a chariot. He had sent a courier on to John, but the latter would not suffer Herod to come to the place of baptism. He regarded him as a man who, with his women and followers, would defile the sacred ceremonies. He suspended the baptism therefore, and, followed by his disciples, went to the place destined for preaching. Here he spoke boldly on the question which Herod intended to propose. He said that Herod should wait for the one who was to come after him, that he himself would not baptize there much longer, for he must make way for him whose precursor he was.

John's words were so pointedly directed against Herod that the latter could not fail to see that his design was known. However, he caused a large roll of writings on the subject of his suit to be presented to John. The latter would not pollute the hand so often raised in baptism by contact with them, and so they were laid before him. Then I saw Herod and his train indignantly leaving the place. He was still residing at the baths of Kallirrhoe, some hours distant from John's place of baptism. He left behind him some of his followers with the writings in order to compel John to give his sanction to what they contained, but in vain. After Herod's departure, John returned to the place of baptism. The women in Herod's retinue were arrayed magnificently, though with tolerable modesty. Magdalene was more fantastic in her attire.

A three days' festival was now celebrated at the stone of the Ark of the Covenant, where John's teaching tent had been erected. I cannot now say for certain whether it was to commemorate the passage of Israel through the Jordan, or some other event. John's disciples adorned the place with branches of trees, garlands, and flowers. Peter, Andrew, Philip, James the Less, Simon, and Thaddeus were there, and many of the subsequent disciples of Jesus. This spot was always regarded as sacred by the devout among the Jews, but at this time it was rather dilapidated. John had it repaired. He, as well as some of his disciples, were in priestly robes. Over a gray undergarment, the Baptist wore a white robe, long and wide, girded at the waist by a sash woven in yellow and white, the ends fringed. On either shoulder was a setting as if of two curved precious stones, upon which were engraven the names of the twelve tribes of Israel, six on each. On his breast was a square shield, yellow and white, fastened at the corners by fine golden chains. In this shield were set twelve precious stones, each bearing the name of one of the twelve tribes. Around his shoulders hung a long linen scarf like a handtowel. It was a white and yellow stole fringed at the ends. His robe also was fringed with white and yellow silk balls like fruit. His head was uncovered, but under the neck of his robe he wore a narrow strip of woven stuff which could be drawn over the head like a cowl, and which then hung over the forehead in a point.

Before the stone upon which the Ark of the Covenant had rested stood a small altar. It was not exactly square. In the center of the surface was a cavity covered by a grating, and below it a hole for ashes; on the sides were pipes, which looked like horns. There were present many disciples in white garments and broad girdles such as the apostles used to wear in the early assemblies for divine worship. They served at the incense sacrifice. John burned several kinds of herbs, also spices, and I think some wheat on the portable altar of incense. All was decorated with green branches, garlands, and flowers. Crowds of aspirants to baptism were present.

The priestly garments and ornaments of the Baptist had all been prepared at this place of baptism. In those days there dwelt near the Jordan some holy women recluses who worked at all kinds of necessary things and prepared the sacred robes of the Baptist. They were not baptized.

The ceremonies performed by John at this time reminded one of the opening of a new church. He wore a long, white garment when baptizing. He performed no manual labor, with the exception of completing the place for Jesus's baptism. He did all with his own hands, the disciples carrying to him the materials.

I saw John at this place holding forth in a long and vehement discourse. Arrayed in his priestly vestments, he stood above the tent, which was surrounded by galleries like the tents of the kings in Arabia. Tiers of seats were erected within the walls of the enclosure, and on them stood an innumerable crowd of listeners. John spoke of the Savior, who had sent him and whom he had never seen, also of the passage through the Jordan. Incense was again offered in the tent, and fragrant spices.

From Mizpah down into Galilee the news had spread that John was to hold this great meeting for instruction, consequently multitudes of men and women were present. Almost all the Essenes had come. Most of the people were clad in long, white garments. I saw married couples arriving, the wives sitting between panniers of doves on asses which the husbands led. The men offered bread; the women, doves. John stood during the ceremony behind a grating and received the loaves, which were laid on a grated table and the flour still clinging to them removed. They were then piled in pyramids on dishes, blessed by John, and raised on high as if for an offering. It was afterward cut into pieces and distributed among the people, they that came from the greatest distance receiving the largest portions, since they had the most need of it. The flour scraped from the loaves, and the crumbs of the cutting, fell through the grated table on a tray and were burned on the altar. The doves brought by the women were divided also. The ceremony occupied almost half a day. The whole festival lasted during the sabbath and three days inclusively. At its conclusions, I saw John busied again at the place of baptism.

The Island upon which Jesus Received Baptism Rises out of the Jordan

JOHN delivered to his disciples at the Jordan a discourse upon the nearness of the Messiah's baptism. He told them that he had never seen him, "But," said he, "I shall, as a proof of what I say, show unto you the place at which he will receive baptism. Behold, the waters of the Jordan will divide and from their midst an island will arise." At the same moment I beheld the waters of the river dividing and, on a level with its surface appeared a small, white island circular in shape. This happened at the spot over which the children of Israel had crossed the Jordan with the Ark of the Covenant and at which also Elijah had divided the waters with his mantle.

Wonder seized upon the beholders. They prayed and sang praises. John and his disciples laid great stones in the water. Upon them they placed branches and trees, over which they scattered fine, white gravel, thus forming from the shore to the island a bridge beneath which the water could flow. Then they planted twelve small trees around the island, connecting their upper branches in such a way as to form a kind of latticed arbor. Between the trees they set hedges of low bushes, of which numbers were found here and there along the Jordan. They had red and white blossoms, the fruit was yellow with a little crown like the medlar. These hedges looked very beautiful, for some were covered with blossoms, others full of fruit.

The new island, the spot upon which the Ark at the passage through the Jordan rested, appeared to be rocky and the bed of the river deeper than in Joshua's time. But when John called it forth for the place of Jesus's baptism, the water seemed to be much lower, so that I could not determine whether it had sunk or the island had risen.

To the left of the bridge, not in the middle of it, but nearer to the shore of the island, there was a deep hole in which welled up clear water. Some steps led down to it. Nearby rising above the surface of the water lay a smooth, red stone of triangular form, upon which Jesus was to stand, and to the right of it was a slender, fruit-bearing palm tree which he was to clasp with one arm during his baptism. The edge of the well was laid out in ornamental style and very beautifully wrought.

I saw that the Jordan was very much swollen when Joshua led the Israelites through it. The Ark of the Covenant was borne far ahead of the people. Among the twelve carriers and attendants were Joshua, Caleb, and one whose name sounded something like Enoi. When they arrived at the Jordan, the forepart of the Ark, which was usually borne by two, was now taken charge of by one alone, while the others supported the back. As soon as the leader set the foot of the Ark in the river, the rushing waters instantly stood still, rose up like galleries on either side, and continued rising and swelling, until like a mountain they could be seen far away in the region of the city of Zarthan. They flowed toward the Dead Sea, leaving the bed of the river such that the carriers bore the Ark over dry-shod. The Israelites crossed in the same way, but at some distance from the Ark and further down the river.

The Ark of the Covenant was borne by the Levites far into the riverbed to a spot upon which were four square, blood-red stones arranged in order. On either side lay two rows of triangular stones, six in number. They were smooth, as if cut with a chisel. Besides these there were twelve others on each side. The twelve Levites set down the Ark of the Covenant on the four central stones and stepped, six to the right, six to the left, on the twelve lying near. These latter were triangular, the sharp end sunk in the earth.

There were twelve others still further off. They, too, were triangular, very large and massive, and were differently variegated, some of them marked with all kinds of figures and flowers. Joshua caused twelve men from the twelve tribes to be chosen to bear these stones on their shoulders to the shore, and thence to a place at some distance where they were deposited in a double row for a memorial. At a later period a city rose in the neighborhood of this spot. The names of the twelve tribes and of those that bore them were engraved on the stones. Those upon which the Levites stood were still larger than the others and, before the Israelites left the bed of the river, they were turned so that their point stood upward. The stones borne to the shore were no longer to be seen in John's time. Whether they lay buried in the earth or had been destroyed by war, I cannot now say. John, however, had pitched his tent between the sites of the double rows.

At a subsequent period, I think through the influence of Helena, a church was built on the spot.

The place upon which the Ark of the Covenant rested in the Jordan was the exact spot upon which, later on, was the baptismal well of Jesus on the island, which otherwise appeared to be destitute of water.

When the Israelites and the Ark of the Covenant had crossed and the twelve stones had been turned upward, the Jordan began again to flow.

The water in the baptismal well on the island was so low down that from the shore only the head and neck of him that was being baptized could be seen. The descent to the well was by a very gentle slope. The octangular basin, about five feet in diameter, was surrounded by a broad ledge in five sections upon which was standing room for several.

The twelve triangular stones, upon which the Levites had stood, extended to both sides of Jesus's baptismal well, their sharp ends rising out of the ground. In the well itself lay those four red ones upon which the Ark had rested. They were now below the surface of the water though in earlier times, when the waters of the Jordan were low, their points were distinctly visible.

Close to the edge of the well was a three-cornered pyramidal stone resting on the sharp end. It was on this that Jesus was standing at his baptism when the Holy Spirit came upon him. On his right, and close to the edge of the well, arose the slender palm tree which he clasped during the baptism; on his left stood the Baptist. This triangular stone upon which Christ stood was not one of the twelve that surrounded the inside of the well. I think John brought it himself from the shore. There was a mystery connected with it also. It was covered with all kinds of veining and flowers. The other stones, the twelve, were of different colors, and they, too, were pierced by innumerable veinings and covered with flowers. They were larger than those carried to the land. It seems to me that they were precious stones that had been placed there by Melchizedek before the waters of the Jordan had begun to flow. But when he placed them there they were small. He had in this way laid the foundations of many subsequent buildings. These foundations had long lain cancelled by mud and earth, but when brought to light, they became holy places wherein something remarkable happened.

I think also that the gems worn by the Baptist in his breastplate at this feast had been taken either from those twelve stones or from those that had been removed to the shore.

New Embassy from Jerusalem • Herod again Seeks an Interview with John

WHEN John was once more busy at the place of baptism, I again saw about twenty deputies from all the authorities of Jerusalem approaching with the intention of calling him to account. They paused on the spot where the festival had been celebrated and sent word to him to appear, but John heeded not. Next day I saw them distant from the baptism place about a short half-hour. But John would not allow them so much as to enter the circle of the numerous dwellings on the outskirts of the enclosure. This was the circle that was hedged off. When he had finished his labors, I saw him speaking to the envoys, though standing at some distance from them. He spoke in his customary style, paying no attention to the questions put to him, but dwelling upon him who would soon come to be baptized, who was greater than he and whom he had never seen.

Then I saw Herod sitting in a kind of chest upon a mule. He was accompanied by his brother's wife, with whom he was then living. She was magnificently and shamelessly adorned, her hair in curls, her robes wide and flowing. She, too, rode a mule and was attended by a retinue of servants. I saw them coming into the neighborhood of the place of baptism. The wife, without dismounting, halted at some distance; but Herod alighted and approached on foot for a conference with John who, however, would not permit him to come nearer than was absolutely necessary. Herod expostulated with John for having pronounced against him a sentence of excommunication shortly after he laid before him the papers in defense of his unlawful connection. John had excluded him from all share in the baptism and the salvation of the Messiah if he refused to break off his shameful relations with his brother's wife. Herod inquired of John whether he knew a man by the name of Jesus of Nazareth of whom the whole country was talking, whether or not he kept up communication with him, and whether that man was the one whose coming he was constantly announcing. He urged that John need not hesitate to inform him on these points, for that he intended to lay his case before him. John answered that that man would give him (Herod) just as little quarter as he himself did, that he (Herod) was and would always be an adulterer, that he might present his case where he would, but it would always remain adultery. When Herod asked John why he did not approach nearer to him and why he would speak to him only from a distance, John answered: "Thou wast blind before, but thy adultery has made thee still blinder. The nearer I approach to thee, the blinder wilt thou become. But when I shall be in thy power, thou wilt do that of which thou wilt have cause to repent." In these words of John lay the prophecy of his own death. Herod and the wife now left, very much irritated.

The time drew near for Jesus to come to the baptism, and I saw that John was greatly troubled in mind. It was as if his time was now short. His manner of acting was no longer so spirited, and he became deeply depressed. By turns from Jericho, from Jerusalem, and from Herod came people deputed to drive John from the place of baptism. John's followers had pitched their encampment to a great distance around the place. The newcomers demanded of John that he should retire to the other side of the Jordan. Herod's soldiers broke down the hedges of the enclosure and drove the people away; but they did not proceed as far as John's tent, which lay between the two rows formed by the twelve stones. John's words to his disciples on this occasion were anxious and dejected. He earnestly longed for Jesus to present himself at the baptism, for then, as he said, he would retire before him to the opposite side of the Jordan. He told them that he would not much longer be among them, which words troubled them very much, for they did not want him to leave them.

When John was informed of Jesus's approach, he roused himself and with new courage began to baptize. Crowds came to him, chiefly those whom Jesus had exhorted to receive baptism, among them many publicans, also Parmenas and his parents from Nazareth. When John discoursed of the Messiah, saying that for him he himself would soon make room, his words breathed so great humility as to cause real trouble to his disciples. The disciples whom Jesus had left in Nazareth also came to John. I saw them with him in his tent conversing about Jesus. John was so inflamed with ardent love for Jesus that he grew almost impatient at his not proclaiming himself the Messiah openly and in unmistakable terms. When John baptized these disciples, he received the assurance of the nearness of the Messiah. He saw a cloud of light hovering over them, and had a vision of Jesus surrounded by all his disciples. From that moment, John became unspeakably joyous and expectant, constantly glancing into the distance, to see whether or not the Lord was yet in sight.

The island with the baptismal well had grown beautifully green, but no one went to it excepting John occasionally. The path over the bridge was usually kept barred.

Jesus Baptized by John

Friday, September 23, AD 29 (Elul 26)

Jesus went on ahead of Lazarus and arrived at the place of baptism some two hours before him. This place of baptism (the third, as John originally began to baptize further north, near Ainon, and then baptized for a short time near Gilgal) was located on the west side of the Jordan, just south of the village called Ono. A large crowd had already assembled there to hear John's preaching when Jesus arrived around daybreak. John felt Jesus's presence among the crowd. He was fired with zeal and preached with great animation concerning the nearness of the Messiah. Then, he started baptizing. By ten o'clock he had already baptized many people. Jesus now came down to the baptizing pool where John was being helped by Andrew, later the apostle, and by Saturnin, a young Greek of royal blood from the city of Patras, who later was one of Jesus's closest disciples. At the moment of baptism a voice of thunder spoke the words, "This is my beloved Son in whom I am well pleased," and Jesus became transparent with radiant light. Meanwhile, Nicodemus, Obed, John Mark, and Joseph of Arimathea had also arrived to join Lazarus in witnessing the baptism of Jesus. John then told Andrew to announce the baptism of the Messiah throughout Galilee. He himself then continued baptizing and preaching, while Jesus journeyed with his followers in the direction of Jerusalem, traveling until he reached a little place called Bethel, where there was a kind of hospital. (Anne Catherine Emmerich was not sure of the name of this Bethel, east of Jerusalem, which is not to be confused with the shepherd village Bethel, north of Jerusalem, where Jesus had been a few days previously, on Elul 23). In Bethel, Andrew and Saturnin baptized a number of people, following Jesus's instructions. This baptism as Jesus gave it differed in several respects from John's baptizing. Jesus and his disciples then celebrated the sabbath in Bethel.

JESUS, walking more quickly than Lazarus, reached John's place of baptism two hours before him. It was morning twilight when, on the road near the place, he caught up with a crowd of people who also were going to the baptism, and he walked on with them. They did not know him, but they could not keep their eyes off him, for there was something about him very remarkable. When they reached the end of their journey, it was morning. A crowd more numerous than usual was assembled to whom John was with great animation preaching of the nearness of the Messiah and of penance, proclaiming at the same time that the moment was approaching for him to retire from his office of teacher. Jesus was standing in the throng of listeners. John felt his presence. He saw him also, and that fired him with zeal and filled his heart with joy. But he did not on that account interrupt his discourse, and when he had finished he began to baptize. [B5]

He had already baptized very many and it was drawing on to ten o'clock when Jesus in his turn came down among the aspirants to the pool of baptism. John bowed low before him, saying: "I ought to be baptized by thee, and comest thou to me?" Jesus answered: "Suffer it to be so now, for so it becometh us to fulfill all justice that thou baptize me and I by thee be baptized." He said also: "Thou shalt receive the baptism of the Holy Spirit and of blood." Then John begged him to follow him to the island. Jesus replied that he would do so, provided that some of the water with which all were baptized should be poured into the basin, that all present should be baptized at the same place with himself, and that the tree by which he was to support himself should be transplanted to the ordinary place of baptism, that all might share the same conveniences.

The Savior now went with John and his two disciples, Andrew and Saturnin. Andrew had followed those disciples and adherents of the Lord whose conversation between Capernaum and this place has been recorded above. They crossed the bridge to the island and into a little tent that, close to the eastern edge of the baptismal well, had been erected for the purpose of robing and disrobing. The disciples followed the Lord to the island, but at the far end of the bridge the people stood on the shore in great crowds. On the bridge itself three could stand abreast. One of the foremost in the latter position was Lazarus.

The baptismal well lay in a gently inclined, octagonal basin the bottom of which was encircled by a similarly shaped rim connected with the Jordan by five subterranean canals. The water surrounded the whole basin, filling it through incisions made in the rim, three in the northern side serving as inlets, and two on the southern acting as outlets. The former were visible, the latter covered, for at this point were the place of action and the avenue of entrance. For this reason the water did not here surround the well. From this south side, sodded steps led down into it by an inclination of about three feet in depth.

In the water off the southern shore was a red, triangular, sparkling stone sunk close to the margin of the basin, the flat side toward the center of the well, the point toward the land. This side of the well upon which were the steps leading down into it, was somewhat higher than the opposite one. This latter, that is, the north side, was the one with the three inflowing canals. On the southwestern side was a step leading to the somewhat deeper part of the margin and on this side only was there access to the well. In the well, in front of the triangular stone, there stood a green tree which had a slender trunk.

The island was not quite level. It was rather elevated toward the center and in some parts rocky. It was covered with moss and in the middle of it was the wide-spreading tree connected with which were the tops of the twelve trees planted around the edge of the island. Between every two of the trees, was a hedge of several small shrubs.

The nine disciples that were always with Jesus during his last days went down to the well with him and took their stand on the ledge around it. [B6] Jesus entered the tent and there laid off, first, his mantle and girdle; then a yellow, woolen garment which was closed in front by laces; then that narrow, woolen strip which he wore around his neck and crossed over the breast, and which he was accustomed to wind around his head at night and in stormy weather. Retaining his brown, woven undergarment, he stepped forth and descended to the margin of the well, where he drew it off over his head. About his loins was fastened a broad linen band which was also wound around each limb for about half a foot. Saturnin received the garments of the Lord as he disrobed, and handed them to Lazarus, who was standing on the edge of the island.

And now Jesus descended into the well, and stood in the water up to his breast. His left arm encircled the tree, his right hand was laid on his breast, and the loosened ends of the white, linen binder floated out on the water. On the southern side of the well stood John, holding in his hand a shell with a perforated margin through which the water flowed in three streams. He stooped, filled the shell, and then poured the water in three streams over the head of the Lord, one on the back of the head, one in the middle, and the third over the forepart of the head and on the face.

I do not now clearly remember John's words when baptizing Jesus, but they were something like the following: "May Yahweh through the ministry of his cherubim and seraphim, pour out his blessing over thee with wisdom, understanding, and strength!" I cannot say for certain whether these last three words were really those that I heard; but I know that they were expressive of three gifts, for the mind, the soul, and the body respectively. In them was contained all that was needed to convert every creature, renewed in mind, in soul, and in body, to the Lord.

While Jesus ascended from the depths of the baptismal well, Andrew and Saturnin, who were standing to the right of the Baptist around the triangular stone, threw about him a large linen cloth with which he dried his person. They then put on him a long, white baptismal robe. After this Jesus stepped on the red triangular stone which lay to the right of the descent into the well, Andrew and Saturnin each laid one hand upon his shoulder, while John rested his upon his head.

This part of the ceremony over, they were just about mounting the steps when the Voice of God came over Jesus, who was still standing alone and in prayer upon the stone. There came from heaven a great, rushing wind like thunder. All trembled and looked up. A cloud of white light descended, and I saw over Jesus a winged figure of light as if flowing over him like a stream. The heavens opened. I beheld an apparition of the heavenly Father in the figure in which he is usually depicted and, in a voice of thunder, I heard the words: "This is my beloved Son in whom I am well pleased."

Jesus was perfectly transparent, entirely penetrated by light; one could scarcely look at him. I saw angels around him.

But off at some distance on the waters of the Jordan, I saw Satan, a dark, black figure, as if in a cloud, and myriads of horrible black reptiles and vermin swarming around him. It was as if all the wickedness, all the sins, all the poison of the whole region took a visible form at the outpouring of the Holy Spirit, and fled into that dark figure as into their original source. The sight was abominable, but it served to heighten the effect of the indescribable splendor and joy and brilliancy spread over the Lord and the whole island. The sacred baptismal well sparkled and glanced, foundations and margin and waters—a pool of living light. One could see the four stones that had once supported the Ark of the Covenant shining beneath the waters as if in exultation; and on the twelve around the well, those upon which the Levites had stood, appeared angels bending in adoration, for the Spirit of God had before all humankind rendered testimony to the living foundation, to the precious, chosen cornerstone of the church around whom we as so many living stones must build up a spiritual edifice, a holy priesthood, that thereby we may offer an acceptable, spiritual sacrifice to God through his beloved Son in whom he is well pleased.

Jesus then ascended the steps and entered the tent near the baptismal well. Saturnin brought the garments which Lazarus had been holding all this time, and Jesus put them on. When clothed, he left the tent and, surrounded by his disciples, took his stand on the open space near the central tree. John in joyous tones addressed the crowd and bore witness to Jesus that he was the Son of God and the promised Messiah. He cited the prophecies of the patriarchs and prophets now fulfilled, recounted what he had seen, reminded them of the voice of God which they had heard, and informed them that when Jesus returned he himself would retire. John referred also to the sacred memories that graced the spot upon which they were standing on account of the Ark of the Covenant's having rested here when Israel was journeying to the Land of Promise. Now, he continued, had they seen the realization of the Covenant witnessed to by his Father, the almighty God Himself. John referred all to Jesus, and called this day that had beheld the fulfillment of the desire of Israel blessed.

Meanwhile many newcomers had arrived on the spot, and among them some friends of Jesus. I saw in the crowd Nicodemus, Obed, Joseph of Arimathea, John Mark, and others. John bade Andrew announce the baptism of the Messiah throughout Galilee. Then Jesus spoke, confirming in plain and simple words the truth John had proclaimed. He told them that he would withdraw from them for a short time, after which all the sick and afflicted should come to him and he would heal and console them. They should in the meantime prepare themselves by penance and good works. He would withdraw for awhile, and then return to lay the foundations of that kingdom which his Father had given to him. Jesus made use of a parable when thus addressing the crowd, that of a king's son who, before taking possession of his throne, withdrew into solitude, there to prepare himself and implore the assistance of his father.

Among his numerous listeners were some Pharisees, who received his words with ridicule. "Perhaps, after all," they said, "He is not the carpenter's son, but the supposititious child of some king. Is he now about to return to his kingdom? Will he assemble his subjects and march upon Jerusalem?" The idea appeared to them foolish and absurd.

John recommenced his work, and continued throughout the whole day baptizing at the sacred well of Jesus all that were on the island. They were for the most part people who later on joined the community of Jesus. They stepped into the water that covered the rim of the pool, the Baptist standing outside on the edge itself baptizing.

Jesus Travels over Luz and Ensemes to Visit the Two Inns at which the Holy Family Rested on Their Journey to Bethlehem and Their Flight into Egypt

JESUS journeyed that same day with his followers the distance of a couple hours toward Jerusalem to a little, obscure place whose name sounded like Bethel. There was a kind of hospital in the place and in it many sick. Jesus entered, and with his followers partook of some food. Several aged persons approached and saluted him reverently as a prophet, for they had heard from the lately baptized what John had proclaimed of him. Accompanied by his disciples, Jesus visited the sick in their chambers consoling them and telling them that, if they would believe in him, he would come again and cure them. But on this occasion he healed only one sick man, him of the third chamber. The poor man was greatly emaciated, his head covered with ulcers and white eczema. Jesus blessed him and bade him arise. The man obeyed and fell on his knees at Jesus's feet.

Andrew and Saturnin baptized many of this place. Jesus ordered a tub of water, large enough for a child perhaps, to be set on a stool in one of the rooms. I saw him blessing the water and sprinkling something into it with a sprig. I think it was some of the baptismal water from the leathern bottle brought hither by the disciples. They that were to be baptized bared their shoulders to the breast, and lowered their head over the tub while Saturnin baptized them. I think the words he used were dictated to him by Jesus and were different from those employed by John; but I do not remember them clearly.

Saturday, September 24, AD 29 (Elul 27)
After the close of the sabbath, which Jesus celebrated, Andrew took leave of Jesus and departed for Galilee, to proclaim the baptism of the Messiah there. Jesus and those with him then went to the town of Luz.

Sunday, September 25, AD 29 (Elul 28)
In the synagogue at Luz, Jesus held a lengthy discourse, interpreting many things from the Old Testament. He also spoke of the need to forsake all to follow the Messiah and to have no great concern for one's daily needs. Lazarus, who had accompanied Jesus thus far, now parted company with him and returned to Bethany.

Jesus proceeded to a city named Luz and, going into the synagogue, held a long discourse during which he explained very many ancient mysterious symbols from the scriptures. I remember that he spoke of the children of Israel. After crossing the Red Sea, they had on account of their sins wandered so long in the desert, before being allowed to pass through the Jordan and into the Promised Land. Now was the actual fulfillment of what was then only typical, for the baptism in the Jordan had been symbolized by the passage of the Israelites through its waters. If they now remained true and observed God's commands, they should indeed be put into possession of the Promised Land and the City of God. Jesus spoke in a spiritual sense, signifying thereby the Heavenly Jerusalem. But his hearers dreamed only of an earthly kingdom and of deliverance from the Romans. Jesus then spoke of the Ark of the Covenant and of the severity of the Old Law, for whoever approached so near the Ark as to touch it instantly fell dead; but now was the Law fulfilled and grace poured forth in the Son of Man. Now, too, was being fulfilled that of which the angels conducting Tobias back into the Promised Land was a figure; for they who, faithful to the commands of God, had so long pined in captivity were now to be introduced into the freedom of the Law of grace. Jesus referred also to Judith, the widow, who had delivered Bethuel from oppression by cutting off the head of Holofernes, the Assyrian, as he lay sunk in the fumes of wine. Now would the Virgin, foreseen from eternity, become great and exalted, while the proud heads that had once oppressed Bethuel would fall. By this Jesus signified the church and her triumph over the powers of the world.

Still many other similitudes of a like bearing Jesus spoke, all which had now been fulfilled. But he never once said the words: "I am He." He spoke always as of a third person. Then he referred to his followers, saying that they should abandon all things and have no immoderate care for their maintenance, for it was a far greater thing to be regenerated than to find nourishment for the body. But if they would be born again of water and the Holy Spirit, he who had regenerated them would also nourish them. They that follow him, he said, must leave their relatives and live in continence, for it was not now the time for sowing, but for reaping. He spoke of the manna also. The people listened in astonishment and reverence, but interpreted all his teaching in an earthly and material sense.

Lazarus now departed. The other friends of Jesus had already left him at the Jordan. The holy women, too, who had been staying with Susanna in Jerusalem, had gone away through the desert.

Monday, September 26, AD 29 (Elul 29)

Accompanied by twelve disciples, Jesus traveled southward from Luz, healing several sick people on the way. When the group arrived at the little village of Ensemes, Jesus was given a warm welcome. The people there had already heard of the new prophet. Jesus spoke in the synagogue. He repeated John's words concerning the relation of his baptism to the Messiah's (Matthew 3:11), adding: "Whoever despises the precursor's baptism will not honor the Messiah's." That evening Jesus ate a meal with his disciples. Afterward, they prayed together, for it was the close of the month of Elul and the start of the first day of Tishri, the beginning of the civil year in the Jewish calendar.

From Luz Jesus traveled southward with his disciples and crossed the desert. After journeying for some time, they came to a double row of date trees. As they passed under them, the disciples expressed a doubt as to whether they might gather and eat the fruit that had fallen. Jesus told them to eat it without scruple and henceforth not to be so constrained in acting, that they should cultivate purity of soul and holiness of speech rather than take so much account of that which went into the mouth.

I saw Jesus entering some houses that stood in a row off by themselves on the road. He there visited about twelve sick persons whom he consoled and some of whom he cured. Several of these last followed him.

Jesus next entered a little town called Ensemes, whither many had come to meet him. They now presented themselves before him, for it had already been announced that the new prophet was nigh. They came with their children by the hand, saluted him solemnly, and prostrated before him. Jesus told them kindly not to do that. He was conducted to their home by the most distinguished of the place. The Pharisees escorted him thence to the synagogue, for they were well-disposed and rejoiced to have among them a prophet. But when they learned from the disciples that Jesus was the son of Joseph, a carpenter of Nazareth, there arose in their breast all sorts of prejudices against him, for they had at first thought that he was another prophet. When Jesus spoke of the baptism they, in order to ensnare him, asked which baptism was to be preferred, his own or John's. Jesus answered by repeating what John had said of his own baptism and, also, of that of the Messiah. "But," he added, "whoever despises the baptism of the precursor will not honor that of the Messiah." Still Jesus never said: "I am He," but always spoke of himself in the third person, calling himself "The Son of Man," as the Gospel records. In the house to which he had been conducted, he partook of a meal, and before retiring for rest prayed with his disciples.

TISHRI (30 days): September 26/27 to October 25/26, AD 29 Tishri New Moon: September 26 at 5:00 PM Jerusalem time

Tuesday, September 27, AD 29 (Tishri 1)

News of John's baptism of Jesus had spread and there was talk of it everywhere, especially in Jerusalem. Because of this, Jesus avoided the larger towns. He intended to make his public appearance only after the forty days in the wilderness. Before going into the desert, however, he wanted to retrace the steps of Joseph and Mary as they had journeyed to Bethlehem almost thirty years before. Accompanied by his followers, he took the byways Joseph and Mary had taken, stopping occasionally at the places where his parents had halted on their journey. Jesus and his disciples spent the night in a shepherd's house.

From Ensemes Jesus and his followers crossed the brook Kidron into Judah. For the most part he followed the byways and valleys, the indirect routes by which the blessed Virgin and Joseph had journeyed to Bethlehem, and paused at those places where they had put up. The atmosphere was foggy and the season tolerably cool, while in the deep valleys might sometimes be seen snow or frost. On the sunny side, however, all was green and lovely, fruit still hanging on the trees and bushes. The Lord and his disciples ate of it on the way. Jesus avoided the large cities, because there was already much talk everywhere of his baptism, the circumstances attending it, and the testimony of John. The same rumors created a great stir in Jerusalem. Jesus intended to make his public appearance only after his return from the desert of Galilee. He made this little journey into these parts only through affection to certain individuals and with a view to induce them to go to the baptism. He was not always accompanied by all his disciples; sometimes only two were with him. The others scattered among the houses of the shepherds lying off the road, and tried to rectify the notions of the occupants, for all were so partial to John that they looked upon Jesus as merely his assistant, and called him only "The Helper." The disciples related to them the apparition of the Holy

Spirit, the words heard at the baptism, and the testimony rendered by John. They explained that the latter was only the preparer of the way of the Lord, and consequently so ardent and vehement, for it was his to break the way.

As a result of the disciples' exhortations, numbers of the shepherds and weavers dwelling around in the valleys came to Jesus to pay him homage, and to listen under the trees and sheds to his short instructions. Jesus blessed and exhorted them.

Jesus explained to the disciples on the way the meaning of the words they had heard at the baptism, "This is my beloved Son." These words, said Jesus, were spoken by his Eternal Father of all who, free from sin, should receive the baptism of the Holy Spirit.

This region was that through which Joseph and Mary had journeyed to Bethlehem. Joseph was familiar with it, for his father owned meadows in the country around. Joseph had indeed kept clear of Jerusalem by a day and a half's journey, and had shunned the other cities. As the shepherds' houses were to be met all along the road, he made only a few hours a day, for the blessed Virgin found both sitting on the cross-saddle and continual walking very painful.

The chief places to which Jesus went were the houses of two shepherds at which during their journey his parents had asked admission. He went first to the one by whom Mary had been badly received. The master of the house was a rough, old man, and he refused hospitality to Jesus also. He looked like some of the peasants of our own day who say: "What more do I want? I pay my tithes, I go to church," and, for the rest, live as they list. And thus spoke the people of this house in Jesus's time. "What more do we want? We have our Law of Moses given to us by God himself, and more than that we do not need." Then Jesus spoke of the mercy and hospitality exercised by all the holy patriarchs, for where would the Blessing and the Law then be had Abraham repulsed the angels that brought the former? The Lord spoke to them a parable: "He that had refused shelter when she knocked at his door to the travel-wearied virgin, so soon to become a mother, and had scorned the companion of her journey when so meekly seeking admission to the inn, had repulsed the son also along with the salvation that he brought with him." Jesus uttered these words so significantly that I saw them fall like a thunderbolt upon the heart of one present, for this was the house from which Mary and Joseph had been contemptuously repulsed when on their journey to Bethlehem. I recognized it at once. The most aged of the occupants became greatly distressed, for without naming himself, Mary, or Joseph, Jesus had in this parable related what they had done.

Hereupon one of them cast himself at Jesus's feet, begging him to tarry with them and accept refreshment, for, as he said, Jesus must surely be a prophet, since he knew all that had happened here thirty years ago. But Jesus would accept nothing from them. He taught the shepherds who had assembled around him, saying that one action is the type, the kernel of that which follows, that the roots of sin are destroyed by contrition and penance, and that by conversion man would be born anew in the baptism of the Holy Spirit and bring forth fruits of eternal life.

Wednesday, September 28, AD 29 (Tishri 2)
Jesus and his disciples continued on their journey, stopping here and there to teach the workers in the fields. Jesus spoke in terms of the parables of plowing, sowing, and reaping (Luke 9:62; Mark 4:26–29; Matthew 13:24–30). On the way, he appointed Saturnin and another disciple to baptize in the Jordan. Soon, they were to begin to give the baptism of Jesus. That afternoon, Jesus and his followers arrived at the little town of Beth-Arabah. Jesus taught some people who were gathered there in an open square. That evening, he set off again, traveling with his disciples through the night.

From this place Jesus journeyed on through the valleys, teaching here and there as he went. The possessed cried after him, but became silent upon his command.

He arrived at a second shepherd inn which stood on a hill. The holy family had been there also. The man of the house owned numerous herds. In rows of houses along the valleys dwelt shepherds and tent weavers. Stretched in the open air were long strips of stuff upon which the weavers worked one to another. There were many flocks of sheep in this region, and wild animals not a few. The doves went in flocks like hens, and there was another kind of bird, large with a long tail, very numerous here. In the wilderness ran animals with little horns like deer; they were not timid, but mixed up freely with the herds. Jesus was most cordially received. The people of the house with the neighbors and children went out joyously to meet him, and cast themselves down before him. The blessed Virgin and Joseph had been most kindly entertained at this house, which was now kept by a couple of young people, children of the old householder. The latter was still alive, a little, stooped old man who carried a small shepherd staff. Jesus accepted food here: fruits, herbs which they dipped in sauce, and small rolls baked in the ashes. The members of this family were very pious and enlightened.

They introduced Jesus into the room wherein the blessed Virgin had passed the night, and which they had long ago changed into an oratory. It was at first merely a retired corner of the house cut off by only a partition, but later they had so arranged it as to form a separate apartment with an entrance of its own. From a four-cornered, they had changed it into an eight-cornered room; the ceiling running up from the different corners formed a central obtuse point, from which hung a lamp. There was also in the roof an aperture that could be opened at pleasure. In front of the lamp was a narrow table, something like our Communion rail, upon which one could lean when in prayer. The room was very neat and beautiful like a chapel. The venerable old man led Jesus in and pointed out to him the spot in which his Holy Mother had rested, also where Anne, his grandmother had slept; for she, too, had put up here on her journey to visit the blessed Virgin in Bethlehem.

These people knew of the birth of Jesus, the adoration of the three kings, the prophecies of Simeon and Anna in the temple, the flight into Egypt, and of the admirable teaching of Jesus in the temple. Several of these days they commemorated with prayer in their little chapel, for from the very beginning this family had sincerely believed, hoped, and loved. Like the simple peasants that they were, they questioned Jesus as to how things were then in Jerusalem, for they had heard that, among the great ones there, the report was current that the new Messiah would, in quality of king of the Jews, restore to them the scepter and free them from the Roman yoke. They asked Jesus whether, indeed, things would so turn out. Jesus answered their questions by a parable. "A young prince," he said, "had been sent by the king, his father, to take possession of his throne, to restore the sacred mystery, and to free his people from bondage. But they to whom he was sent would not recognize him as the king's son, they persecuted and maltreated him. Nevertheless, he would after a time be exalted, he would draw to himself in the kingdom of his father all that faithfully kept his commandments."

Many accompanied Jesus into the little chapel and there listened to his teaching. He also performed some cures here. The old shepherd conducted him to one of his neighbors who had for long years been confined to bed with the gout. Jesus took her by the hand and commanded her to arise. She obeyed instantly and, casting herself on her knees, thanked the Lord, after which she followed her benefactor to the door. The poor woman had been as crooked and stooped as Peter's mother-in-law.

Jesus asked to be taken down into a deep valley in which were many sick. He cured several, perhaps about ten, and consoled the rest.

John was still baptizing the crowds that continued to present themselves. The tree from Jesus's baptismal pool had been removed to the center of the large pool and had become beautifully green. This latter pool was reached by steps descending from the shore. Many tongues of land jutted out into it, and on them the people in turn took their stand, descending on one side and ascending on the other.

When Jesus left the shepherd house, distant from Jerusalem about five hours, the people followed him. They had associated with the shepherds who had visited Jesus in the crib and, on that account, were so upright in intention.

The Lord and his disciples pursued their journey through byways and retired places. Here and there assembled around him crowds of shepherds and laborers whom he instructed in similitudes borrowed from their own

Threshing Grain

occupations. He exhorted them repeatedly to baptism and penance, and spoke of Redemption and the near coming of the Messiah.

I saw on Jesus's road a fertile spot on the declivity of the mountain and there, engaged in all kinds of field and vineyard labor, were many people. I saw plowing, sowing, planting going on, and heaps of corn being gathered together. It was very fruitful here although, as in other places, frost or snow covered the valleys. The corn was not put up in sheaves. The ears were cut off about one-half a foot in length and then bound together in the center, so that they piled up in heaps. They were not gathered in as had been done long before in the harvest, but were allowed to stand outdoors in heaps high and broad like hills. They were covered with straw when the rainy season came on, and the field was plowed up anew. The ears were afterward cut off with a curved knife, the straw pulled out and thrown on the heaps. Then I saw the gathering in, the ears piled on litters and borne away by four men. The straw remained lying in rows; it was afterward rolled into bundles, I think for burning. In other places they were plowing. The plow had no wheels, but was drawn by men. The one that I saw was like a sled on three sharp heavy runners, between two of which was the place for yoking. Usually the plow was not guided from behind, but asses or men pulled it in front. The fields were plowed both in length and breadth. The harrows used by these people were three-cornered, the broad part in front. They seemed to work quite well. Where the soil was rocky, a little earth spread over it afforded sufficient support for vegetation. The sowers carried their sack slung round the neck, the two ends hanging on their breast. The plants that I saw set out were garlic, and a certain large-leaved plant used for seasoning, I think. One species is called dhurra.

The disciples gathered the people together on the way, and Jesus taught them in parables of plowing, sowing, and reaping. He spoke to the disciples of the seed they would scatter by means of baptism. He appointed two, one of whom was Saturnin, to baptize shortly at the Jordan. He addressed them, saying: "This is the seed. And like unto the people before us, shall ye in two months begin your harvest." Then he spoke of the straw that was to be cast into the fire.

While Jesus was thus teaching, a crowd of laborers from Sichar came in sight along the road, carrying spades, pickaxes, and long poles. They looked like slaves, and appeared to be returning home from work on some public building or road. They halted at some distance and listened with a timid air to the words of Jesus, not daring to approach nearer to the Jews. But Jesus, raising his voice, bade them draw near, telling them that his heavenly Father called all to himself through him; and then he spoke of the equality of all that do penance and receive baptism. The poor creatures were so affected by Jesus's gentle words that, falling on their knees, they implored him to come to Samaria and help them also. Jesus replied that he would indeed go to them, but not just yet, for he must now go away for awhile in order to prepare his kingdom, of which his Father had sent him to take possession.

And now the shepherds again conducted Jesus over all the roads and byways that his mother had traversed. But when they found that he was better acquainted with them than even they themselves, they exclaimed in wonder: "Lord, thou art a prophet! Thou art a filial Son, thus to know and trace the footsteps of thy blessed Mother!"

After Jesus had taught and exhorted the multitude, he went to the little city of Beth-Arabah. It was afternoon when he and his disciples arrived. They proceeded to an open square, and Jesus mounted the stone pulpit under the trees. A crowd gathered around him, and he taught. The people here were men of good will.

(Follow Map 6)

Jesus in the Valley of Shepherds near Bethlehem
Thursday, September 29, AD 29 (Tishri 3)
As the sun was rising, Jesus and his disciples made their way down to the valley of the shepherds near Bethlehem. He was seen from afar by some shepherds, who beheld him in the glory of the light of the rising sun. They quickly summoned more shepherds, who gathered together to greet Jesus and praise him with verses from the Psalms. Jesus told them that he had come to visit them because of the homage the shepherds had paid to him as an infant in the crib. He also recounted the parable of the good shepherd (John 10:1–18).

JESUS, leaving Beth-Arabah, directed his steps, followed by many of his last audience, toward the valley of the shepherds about three and a half hours distant. Once I saw him with the disciples under an open shed, eating corn and red berries, which they had gathered on the way. Then the disciples separated, each taking a different road, Jesus having appointed the place at which they should again join him. As they went along, they told all whom they met about Jesus and exhorted them to penance and baptism, if they had not already been baptized. Many of those whom they thus exhorted followed them to the appointed meeting place, there to listen to the teaching of Jesus. Jesus himself took very circuitous routes, and I often saw him passing half the night alone on the hills in prayer, so that the whole time of the journey was entirely filled up. I heard the disciples beseeching him not to bring on an untimely death by the little care he took of his body, his fasting, his going barefoot, his long night-watches during that cold, damp season. But Jesus reproved them gently and went gravely on his way.

Before daybreak I beheld him and his disciples descending the mountain side into the valley of the shepherds. The shepherds dwelling around already knew of his coming. All had been baptized by John, and some even had had dreams and visions of the approach of the Lord. Several were on the watch for him. They gazed uninterruptedly toward the point whence he might be seen coming down the mountain. Suddenly he appeared in sight. They beheld him shining with glory and surrounded by light, descending into the valley, for many of these simple-hearted people were highly favored with grace. Instantly they sounded

Map 6: Visit to the Valley of the Shepherds near Bethlehem

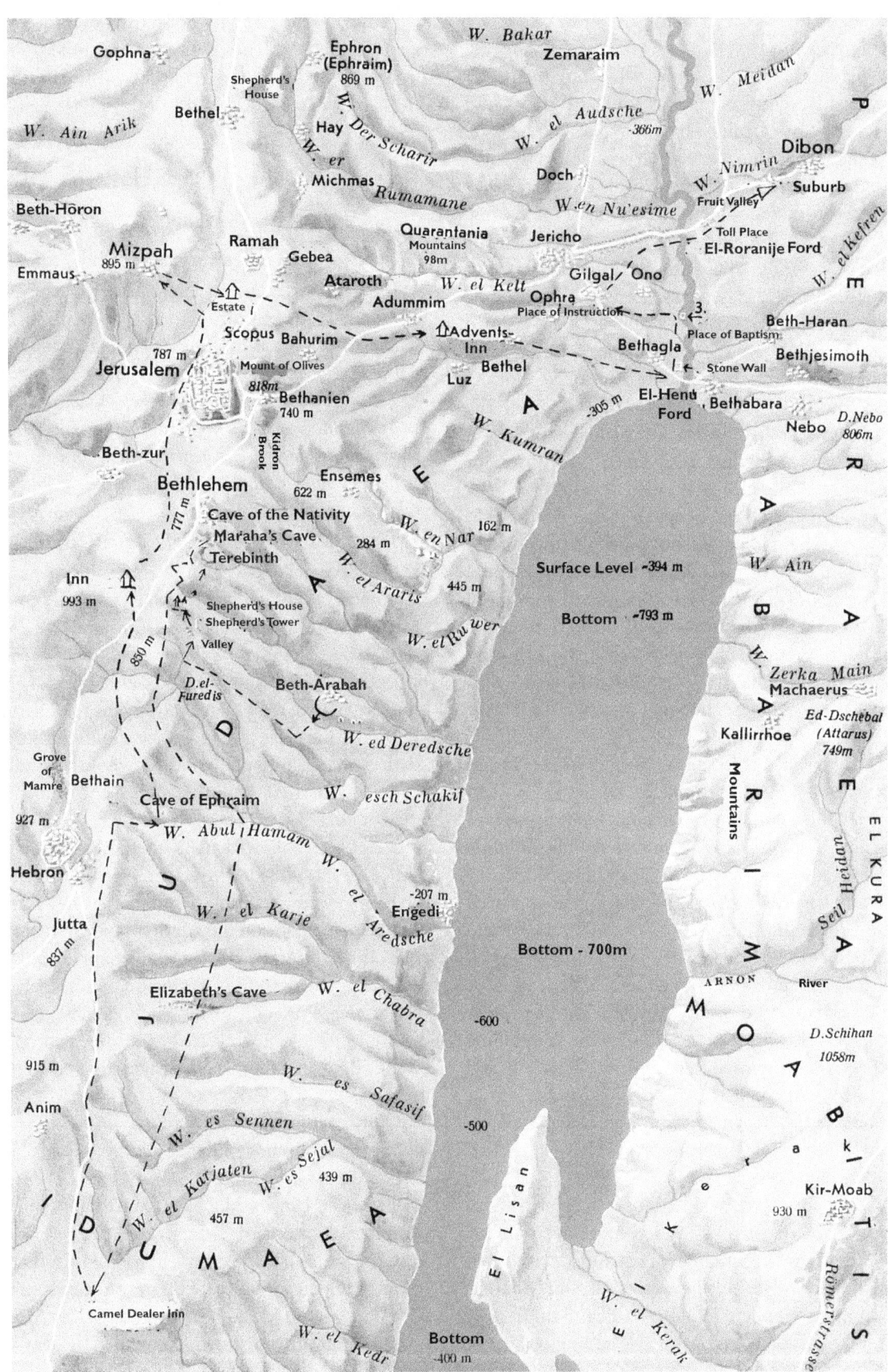

Beth-Arabah—Valley of the Shepherds—Bethlehem—Ruben's Inn—Sarepta—Ephraim's Cave—Mizpah
Third Place of Baptism—Gilgal—Publicans' Place—Suburb of Dibon

a horn, to arouse the more distant dwellers and summon them to the spot. This was their custom at every extraordinary occurrence. All hastened to meet the Lord. They knelt before him, with head lowly bent, their long staves resting in their arms; many of them prostrated flat on their face. They wore short doublets to the knee, mostly of sheepskin, some open on the breast, others closed, their wallets hung on their shoulder. They greeted Jesus in words from the Psalms that foretold the coming of the Messiah and proclaimed Israel's gratitude for the fulfillment of the Promise. Jesus showed them great affection, and congratulated them on their happy state. Here and there he taught in the huts that lay around the broad meadow valley, his instructions turning upon the pastoral life which he treated in parables.

Then, followed by his hearers, he passed farther on through the valley toward Jerusalem to the shepherd tower. This tower stood on an eminence in the center of a field, its foundation being huge fieldstones. It consisted of a very high superstructure of beams, supported in part by the green trees around it. The walls were hung with mats. There were galleries and outside steps around it, and at various distances little, covered standing places like sentry boxes. From a distance it looked like a ship with high masts and spreading sails; it also bore some resemblance to the towers in the land of the three kings from which they watched the stars. The whole country around could be scanned from this tower, even Jerusalem and the mountain upon which Jesus was at a later period tempted by Satan.

The shepherds made use of it to catch their herds and ward off threatening danger. Some of them with their families dwelt around it in a circle of about five hours in circumference, in farmhouses surrounded by gardens and field. But their general rendezvous was in the near neighborhood of the tower. Here they kept their various utensils, and here the herdsmen received their food. All along the base of the tower-hill were huts, and at some distance from it a large enclosed shed wherein the wives of the herdsmen dwelt and prepared the food. These women did not go forth with the rest to meet the Lord and his disciples, but later on they were instructed by Jesus. There were about twenty shepherds living around here. Jesus instructed them, called their attention to the happiness of their state of life, and told them that he had come to visit them because they had greeted him in his infancy and had lovingly treated both himself and his parents. He taught especially in parables of shepherds and herds, telling them that he, too, was a Shepherd, that he had under him other shepherds who till the end of time should gather together, heal, and guide his flocks.

Then the shepherds told Jesus all about the glad tidings brought them by the angels, also about Mary, Joseph, and the child. They had seen, they said, the image of the child in the star that had hovered over the crib cave. They told of the kings and how they in their turn had beheld the shepherd tower in the stars, and of the numerous gifts they had left here on their return to their own country. Many of them had been put to use both in the tower and in the surrounding huts, which were formed of coarse canvas. Some of the old men present had in their youth been at the crib. They repeated the story all over again to Jesus.

Friday, September 30, AD 29 (Tishri 4)

The shepherds conducted Jesus and the disciples in the direction of Bethlehem. They arrived at the dwellings of the sons of the three shepherds who had visited him at his birth. These three shepherds had in the meantime died. Their burial place was an isolated hill where there was a vineyard. After visiting their graves, Jesus and his followers, accompanied by some shepherds, visited the cave where he had been born. As it was now evening, lamps were lit in the cave, where they celebrated the beginning of the sabbath together.

Next day Jesus and the disciples were escorted by the shepherds farther on toward Bethlehem to the dwellings of the sons of the three eldest shepherds to whom the angels at Christ's birth had first appeared, and who first had offered him their homage of veneration. They were now dead and lay buried not far from the dwellings, which were about one hour's distance from the crib cave. Three sons of the old shepherds were still alive and they were themselves old men. They were held in great respect by all the others, their families being something like superiors over the rest, something similar to the three kings among their people. They received Jesus very humbly and joyfully, and led him to the graves of their fathers. The site was an isolated hill covered by a vineyard; the base was surrounded by a kind of covered walk from which opened various caves and cellars. The cave containing the remains of the old shepherds was high up on the hill. The light entering from above disclosed the three graves which lay together in the ground, two parallel, the third lengthwise between them. They were closed by doors. The shepherds opened the graves for Jesus, and I saw the brown faces of the closely enveloped corpses. The space around the coffins was filled with little pebbles. The shepherd crooks lay in the coffins by their owners.

The shepherds also showed Jesus the treasure that they still had from the gifts of the three kings and which was concealed here in the cave. It consisted of little solid bars of gold and whole pieces of very costly stuffs embroidered in gold. They asked Jesus whether or not they should give it to the temple. He answered by telling them to keep it for the community which was to form the new temple, and he foretold to them that there would one day be a church erected over this tomb. On this hill began a vineyard that extended toward Gaza. It was the usual burial-place of the shepherds.

From here the Lord was conducted to the place of his birth in the crib cave distant about an hour. Their way led through a remarkably beautiful meadow valley. Three paths ran through it between tracts of fruit trees trimmed into shape. The shepherds told on the way of the angelic Gloria, and I saw all again in pictures. The angels had appeared in three different places: first, to the three shepherds; then, on the following night, at the shepherd tower; and lastly, at the well near the spot at which Jesus had the day before been welcomed by the shepherds. Around the shepherd tower they appeared in greater numbers, large, wingless figures. The shepherds took Jesus into the tomb cave of Maraha, Abraham's nurse, near the great pine tree.

The Crib Cave, a Place of Devotion among the Shepherds

THE PATH to the crib cave ran along the east, from which side Bethlehem was not directly accessible, since no straight road led thither. The city could scarcely be seen from this side, for it was separated from the valley of the shepherds by dilapidated walls, and massive ruins of similar masonry between which ran deep ravines. The nearest direct entrance into the city was by the south gate that led to Hebron. Leaving this gate, one would have to go around toward the east in order to reach the region of the crib. This region was contiguous to the valley of the shepherds from which one could go to it without entering Bethlehem. Both the crib cave and the adjoining caves belonged to the shepherds, who used them for storing their utensils and sheltering their cattle. No one from Bethlehem had any communication with this region, neither road nor path leading thither. Joseph, whose father's house stood on the south side of the city, had often when a boy visited the shepherds here, concealed himself in the caves from his brothers, and spent therein much time in prayer.

When Jesus now visited the crib in company with the shepherds, it was already very much changed, for they had fitted it up as a place of devotion. No one was allowed to step on the sacred ground; consequently a grated passage had been made around the cave, thus enlarging the space covered by it. Into this passage opened cells hewn in the rock. It was like a cloister. The ground and walls of the cave were covered with the tapestry and carpets left by the kings. They were woven in colors, the principal figure in them being pyramids. Two flights of steps ran from the passage up above the crib cave. The roof of the latter, wherein had once been oblique openings to admit light, had been entirely removed and replaced by a domelike cupola through which the light streamed. By one of the flights mentioned above, one could mount from the dome of the cave to the top of the hill and thence proceed toward Bethlehem. All these changes had been made with the means left by the kings.

The sabbath was just beginning and the lamps had been lighted in the crib cave when the shepherds brought Jesus hither. The crib itself still occupied the same place. Jesus pointed out to the shepherds something that they did not know; that is, the exact spot upon which he was born. He gave them an instruction and they celebrated the sabbath in the cave. He told his hearers that his heavenly Father had chosen this place for his nativity at the time of Mary's Immaculate Conception, and I saw that it had been the theater of several significant events of the Old Testament. Abraham and Jacob had been within its walls, and before them had Seth, the child of Promise, been born therein of Eve after a penance of seven years. An angel appeared to Eve on that occasion, telling her that this was the seed that God had given her in the place of Abel. Seth was for a long time hidden here and nursed, also in the Suckling Cave of Abraham's nurse Maraha; for, as Jacob's sons pursued Joseph, so did the brothers of Seth pursue him. The Suckling Cave was now Maraha's tomb.

The shepherds led Jesus into the adjacent cave also, where for a time the holy family had tarried. The fountain that had sprung up therein on the night of Christ's nativity, they had beautifully enclosed, and they made use of its waters in sickness. Jesus commanded them to take some of the water away with them. On leaving the cave, he visited the shepherds' huts.

Saturday, October 1, AD 29 (Tishri 5)

With his disciples, Jesus visited numerous dwellings in and around the valley of the shepherds. Saturnin baptized some of the more elderly shepherds who could not go to the baptism in the Jordan. Anne Catherine noted that Jesus himself never baptized, but always baptized through his disciples.

Saturnin baptized several aged men who were unable to go to the baptism of John. Into the water which they had brought from the fountain of the cave near the crib, they poured some of Christ's baptismal water from the pool on the island in the Jordan. At John's baptism all confessed their sins publicly; but at that of Jesus each acknowledged his sins privately, gave proofs of contrition, and received pardon. The old men whom Saturnin baptized knelt, their shoulders bared to the breast, their head bowed over a large basin. In this manner they were baptized. The form made use of at this baptism was similar to that employed by John at the baptism of Jesus. But to the word Jehovah and the invocation of the three gifts, was added "and in the name of the One that has been sent."

Jesus Visits Certain Inns, the Halting Places of the Holy Family on Their Flight into Egypt

Sunday, October 2, AD 29 (Tishri 6)

Jesus took leave of the shepherds and of his disciples, saying that he now wanted to be alone for a while, and would visit some people by himself. He arranged to meet with his disciples in a valley on Mount Ephron in two days' time. He then set off alone, southward.

JESUS had spent his nights alone and in prayer. Upon leaving the shepherds he addressed his disciples, telling them that he was now going to make another journey to some people who had hospitably sheltered him and his parents on their flight, that he would cure their sick and convert a sinner, that no footstep of his holy parents should remain unblessed, and that everyone who had shown them compassion and kindness on their flight, he would now seek out and lead to salvation. The mercy and benevolence of all such persons have been to them a pledge and a furtherance of salvation; their effects will continue forever. As now, he said, he was visiting all that had at that time shown charity to him and his, so would his heavenly Father be mindful of all that showed mercy and charity to even the most insignificant of his brethren. Jesus then appointed a place near the city and Mount Ephron, where his disciples were to await his coming.

Monday, October 3, AD 29 (Tishri 7)

Passing through a wild region, Jesus came to an inn belonging to a man called Reuben, who had been there at the time of the holy family's flight into Egypt. Jesus greeted and blessed Reuben, and then healed Reuben's grandchildren, some of whom were sick with leprosy, some of whom were lame.

He now journeyed alone around Herod's dominions toward the desert near Anim, or Enzannim, a few hours from the Dead Sea. His way lay through a wild, though tolerably fertile region where, hedged in by enclosures, were pastured a great many camels divided into droves of forty. There was an inn for the accommodation of travelers through the desert, and to it Jesus went. Several huts and sheds stood nearby, and the proprietors of the inn owned many camels.

This inn was the last in Herod's dominions met by the holy family on their flight into Egypt. The people were a bad set who carried on thievery, but notwithstanding they had received the holy family kindly. The neighboring city contained many disorderly characters who had settled there after some war.

Jesus went to the inn and asked hospitality. The proprietor was a man about fifty years old, called Reuben, who had been there at the time of the flight into Egypt. When Jesus glanced at him and addressed him, grace shot like a ray of light into his breast. The words of Jesus and his salutation fell upon him like a blessing, and deeply moved he exclaimed: "Lord, it is as if the Promised Land enters with thee into my house!" Jesus replied that, if he would believe in the Promise and would not cast away from him its fulfillment, he would indeed share in the Promised Land. Then he spoke of good works and their consequences, telling him that he had now come to announce salvation to him, because he had kindly entertained his mother and his foster-father so many years before when on their flight to Egypt. In like manner does every action, the good as well as the bad, bear its own fruit. At these words of Jesus, the man cast himself trembling on the ground before him, saying: "Lord, whence is this to me, a poor, despised, miserable man, that thou shouldst enter my house?" Jesus answered that he had come to cleanse sinners from their iniquity and lead them back to God. The man still spoke of his own baseness, and said that all the inhabitants of the place belonged to a miserable, lost generation; he also told Jesus of his poor, sick grandchildren. Jesus replied that if he would believe in him and be baptized, he would restore his grandchildren to health. He washed Jesus's feet, and gave him the best he had for his refreshment. When the neighbors came in, he told them who Jesus was and what he had promised. He had a relative among them who was named Issacher.

After that he conducted Jesus to his sick grandchildren who, some from leprosy and some from lameness, had become quite deformed. Jesus commanded the children to rise, and they stood up cured. He visited some women also, who were sick with a flow of blood. Then he ordered a bath to be prepared. They got ready a large vessel of water under a tent. From one of the two flasks that he carried with him strapped to his side under his outer robe, he poured into it some of the baptismal water from the Jordan, and blessed the whole. The sick were then ordered to bathe in it. They did so, and came forth cleansed and thanking the Lord. Jesus did not baptize them himself, although this washing was equivalent to baptism in case of death; but he exhorted them to go seek for the baptism at the Jordan.

When the people questioned Jesus, asking if the Jordan

really possessed special virtue, he answered that the channel of the Jordan had been hollowed out and its course directed; that all holy places of this land had been allotted to special purposes by his heavenly Father long before man had existed there, yea, even before the land or the Jordan had sprung forth from nothing. Very wonderful things spoke Jesus on this subject, and he instructed the women on marriage, inculcating modesty and continency. He pronounced the degeneracy of the people of this place and the pitiful condition of the children, consequences of the illegitimate connections so common among them. He spoke of the parents' share in the corruption of their children, of arresting the evil by penance and satisfaction, and of the second birth in baptism.

Then he recounted to them all the kind offices they had performed for the holy family at the time of their flight, and gave them some information relative to the places at which they had rested and refreshed themselves. Mary and Joseph had with them on their flight a she-ass, as well as the ass upon which the blessed Virgin rode. Jesus showed the people all their actions at the time of the flight, that is all the acts of kindness they had shown the holy family, as so many types of their present turning from sin to salvation. They prepared for the Lord a repast from the best they had. It consisted of a kind of milk thick like white cheese, honey, rolls baked in the ashes, grapes, and birds.

Accompanied by some of these men, Jesus left Ainon and, returning by another route, arrived toward evening at a city built on both sides of a mountain, through which ran a rugged valley full of deep ravines. Both mountain and city bore the name of Ephraim, or Ephron. The mountain faced straight toward Gaza. Jesus had come through the country of Hebron. At some distance from the road that he traveled could be seen a ruined city with a tower still standing, whose name sounded like Malaga. About an hour's distance from this place was the grove Mamre whither the angels bore to Abraham the promise of a son, Isaac; also the double cave that Abraham bought from Ephren, the Hethite, and which afterward formed his tomb. The field that witnessed David's combat with Goliath was not far off.

Tuesday, October 4, AD 29 (Tishri 8)

The disciples met Jesus in a valley on Mount Ephron, some five miles east of Hebron. He conducted them to a nearby cave, where they spent the night. The disciples lit a fire, and Jesus recounted all that had taken place in the cave: that David had been there before his fight with Goliath, and that the holy family had spent a night there on the way to Egypt.

Jesus, his escort having taken leave, wended his way around one side of the double city and met his disciples in the rugged valley road which had been designated by him as the place of meeting. He conducted them out of the winding ravine into a very spacious cave in the wildest part of the mountain, to which no path led. It had afforded a resting place, the sixth in order, to the holy family on their flight into Egypt, and here Jesus and his disciples passed the night.

Jesus told this circumstance to the disciples, impressing upon them the sacred character of the place, while they were busying themselves making a fire. They struck a light by revolving one piece of wood inside another. One of the prophets had frequently spent some time in this cave, in order to give himself more unreservedly to prayer. I think it was Samuel. David, too, while guarding his father's flocks around here, had made the cave a place of prayer and there received commands of God through the ministry of angels. It was while thus engaged that he was admonished to slay Goliath.

When the holy family reached this cave, they were dejected and exhausted. The blessed Virgin wept sadly. They were in want of all things, because they had fled by unfrequented ways, shunning the great cities and customary inns. They spent a whole day here recruiting their strength, and several wonders were vouchsafed them for their refreshment—a fountain sprang up in the cave, and a wild goat bounded in and allowed itself to be milked.

Jesus spoke to the disciples of the great tribulations in store for him and all his followers, of the hardships here endured by himself and his blessed Mother, of the mercy of his heavenly Father, and of the holiness of the place. He added that at some future day there would be a church built on the spot, and he blessed the cave as if consecrating it. The disciples had brought with them some fruit and rolls, and of them all partook.

Jesus Goes toward Mizpah to Visit a Relative of Joseph

Wednesday, October 5, AD 29 (Tishri 9)

Jesus and his followers made their way northward. They visited an inn near Bethlehem and ate a meal there. Traveling further, they went around Jerusalem on the west side of the city until they reached the town of Mizpah, where Judas Maccabeus once had been (1 Maccabees 3:46). Jesus taught in the synagogue. Some of the members of the Sanhedrin had come from Jerusalem as agents. They listened with great interest to what Jesus had to say. After leaving the synagogue, Jesus and his companions journeyed eastward about one hour to the home of Aminadab and Manasseh, who had already been baptized. Here they stayed the night.

WHEN Jesus and his disciples left the cave, they struck off in the direction of Bethlehem. On this side of Ephron they entered an inn that stood among houses built apart, and there, after washing their feet, took some refreshment. The people were good and somewhat inquisitive. Jesus instructed them on penance, the nearness of Redemption, and of what they must do to follow him. They asked him why his mother took that long journey from Nazareth to Bethlehem, since she could have been so comfortably cared for at home. Jesus answered by telling them of the Promise and that he was to be born in poverty at Bethlehem among the shepherds, since like a shepherd he was to gather the flocks together. It was also for this same reason that now, after his heavenly Father's testimony of him, he visited these shepherd regions first.

From here Jesus turned his steps to the south side of Bethlehem about two hours distant, crossed a portion of the shepherd valley, and proceeded around the west side of the city, leaving Joseph's paternal house to the right. Toward evening he entered the now little city of Mizpah, some hours from Bethlehem.

Mizpah could be seen at a great distance, for on the highroads all around the city burned lights in iron lanterns. It was encompassed by walls and towers, and traversed by several streets. Mizpah was long one of the principal places of devotion. Judas Maccabeus had before battle held here a great prayer meeting in which he reminded almighty God of all the outrageous decrees of the enemy, recalled to him his own promises, and exposed the priestly garments before the assembled multitude. Then five angels appeared to him before the city and promised him victory. It was here also that Israel had assembled against the tribe of Benjamin, on account of an outrage and murder committed upon the wife of a traveling Levite. The infamous scene was enacted under a tree, which was afterward walled around, and no one went near it. In Mizpah also Samuel had exercised his office of Judge; and here was found that Essene cloister in which dwelt Manahem, who had foretold the scepter to Herod when the latter was only a boy. This cloister had been built by the Essene Chariot, who lived about one hundred years before Christ. He was a married man from the country of Jericho. He had separated from his wife and both, he for men and she for women, had founded several communities of Essenes. He was a very holy man and died in a cloister founded by him not far from Bethlehem. He was the first to arise from his tomb at the death of Christ and appear to men.

Mizpah was full of inns, and the arrival of a stranger was soon noised about the city; consequently Jesus had scarcely entered the inn when he was surrounded by a crowd. He was conducted to the synagogue where he explained the Law. Some of his hearers were spies whose intentions were insincere. They sought to draw him out, because they had heard of his promise to lead the Gentiles also into the kingdom of God, and that he had spoken among the shepherds about the three kings. Jesus's words on this occasion were very severe. He said that the days of the Promise were completed; and that all who would be born again in baptism, would believe in him whom the Father had sent, and would keep his commandments, should as well as his followers have a share in the kingdom. But from the unbelieving Jews should the Promise be withdrawn and given over to the Gentiles.

I cannot repeat Jesus's words exactly, but they were to this effect: that he knew their intentions, that they were spies, that they might betake themselves to Jerusalem, and there tell all they had heard him say.

Jesus had alluded to Judas Maccabeus and the several important events that had here taken place. His hearers boasted the magnificence of the temple and the superiority of the Jews over the pagans. But Jesus explained to them that the end for which the chosen people had been called and their temple erected was now attained, since the One promised by God through the prophets was now come to establish the kingdom of his heavenly Father, and to raise to him a new temple.

After this instruction, Jesus left Mizpah and went about an hour eastward. He reached first a row of houses, then came to a residence that stood alone and which belonged to one of Joseph's family. Joseph's father had married a widow with one son. This stepson had married and settled in this place, and his descendants now occupied the house alluded to. They had been baptized and had a family of children. They received Jesus cordially and with every mark of deference. Several of the neighbors assembled at the house. Jesus gave an instruction after which he partook of a repast with them. The meal over, he retired with two of the men, Aminadab and Manasseh. They questioned him as to whether he was acquainted with their circumstances and whether they should follow him right away. Jesus replied no, that they should for the present be numbered among his secret disciples. Then they knelt before him, and he blessed them. Prior to his death, they publicly joined the disciples. Jesus stayed here overnight.

Jesus Visits an Inn at which Mary Stopped on her Journey to Bethlehem

Thursday, October 6, AD 29 (Tishri 10)

FROM here Jesus and his disciples went on for a couple of hours till they came to a farmhouse which had been the last stopping place but one on Mary's journey to Bethlehem. It may have been about four hours' distance from the city. The men of the house came out to meet Jesus and, falling down before him on the road, begged him to enter. He was very cordially received. These people went almost daily to John's instructions and were all familiar with the wonders connected with the Lord's baptism. A warm bath was prepared for Jesus, also a repast, and a beautiful couch was made ready for him that night. Jesus taught here.

The woman who had harbored the holy family here thirty years ago was still alive. But she was blind, and had been for many years almost bent double. She lived alone in the main building and her children, who lived nearby, sent her her food. When Jesus had performed his ablutions, he went to see the poor, old woman. He spoke to her of compassion and hospitality, of good works that bear no merit, and of selfishness, placing her present afflictions before her as a punishment of the same. She was deeply touched, confessed her fault, and he cured her. He ordered her to bathe in the water he had just used. She did so, recovered her sight, and became straight and well. But Jesus commanded her to say nothing of her cure.

The people of this place questioned Jesus as to which was the greater, he or John. Jesus answered: "He of whom John gives testimony." Then they spoke of John's zeal and energy, also of the beautiful, manly figure of Jesus himself. Jesus remarked that, three and a half years hence, they would see no beauty in him, they would not even recognize him so disfigured would he be. Of John's zeal and energy he spoke, likening him to one knocking at the house of a sleeping man, to rouse him for the coming of the Lord; to one breaking a path through the wilderness, that the king might safely travel over it; and lastly to an impetuous torrent that rushing along purifies the channel through which it flows.

"Behold the Lamb of God"

Friday, October 7, AD 29 (Tishri 11)

At daybreak, Jesus and his followers set off in the direction of the Jordan. They came close to the place of baptism where John was preaching to the assembled crowd. (This was now John's new place of baptism, somewhat south of the place where he had baptized Jesus.) At that moment, John turned, pointing in the direction of Jesus, who—although far away in the distance—was just visible. He said: "Behold the Lamb of God, who bears the sins of the world." He continued with the words recorded in John 1:30–34. Jesus, however, did not draw nearer but made his way northwest. Nevertheless, two pupils of John—the brothers Aram and Themeni, nephews of Joseph of Arimathea—followed Jesus until they caught up with him and joined his group of disciples. When they arrived at the town of Gilgal, Saturnin and two other disciples began baptizing there. Amid much jubilation from the people of the place, Jesus and his disciples went to the synagogue to celebrate the sabbath.

NEXT morning at daybreak Jesus departed with his disciples, followed by the crowd that had gathered around him. They wended their way toward the Jordan, distant from this point at least three hours. The Jordan flows through a broad valley that rises on either bank for the distance of about half an hour. The stone in the enclosed space whereon the Ark of the Covenant had rested, and where the recent festival was celebrated, was about an hour's distance from John's place of baptism, that is, taking it in a straight line toward Jerusalem. John's hut near the twelve stones was in direction of Beth-Arabah and somewhat more to the south than the stone of the Ark of the Covenant. The twelve stones lay one-half hour from the place of baptism and in the direction of Gilgal. Gilgal was on a gentle slope on the west side of the mountain.

From John's baptismal pool the view up both the shores, which were very fertile, was most lovely. The most delightful region, however, rich in fruits and teeming with abundance, was around the Sea of Galilee. But here, and also around Bethlehem, there were broader meadowlands, more husbandry, and a greater abundance of dhurra, garlic, and cucumbers.

Jesus had already passed the memorial stone of the Ark of the Covenant and was about one quarter of an hour beyond John's tent, before which the latter stood teaching. A gap in the valley disclosed this scene to the distant traveler, and Jesus in passing was for not longer than a couple of minutes visible to the Baptist. John was seized by the Spirit and, pointing to Jesus, he cried out: "Behold the Lamb of God, who bears the sins of the world!" Jesus passed, preceded and followed by his disciples in groups, the multitude lately gathered around him in the rear. It was early morning. The people crowded forward at the words of John, but Jesus had already disappeared. They called after him in acclamations of praise, but he was out of hearing.

When they returned from their fruitless attempt to see

Jesus, the people complained to John that Jesus had so many followers and that, as they had heard, his disciples had already begun to baptize. What, they asked, would be the outcome of all that. John made answer by repeating that he would soon resign his place to Jesus, since he was only a servant and precursor. These words were not at all acceptable to John's followers, who were somewhat jealous of Jesus's disciples.

Jesus now directed his steps toward the northwest, leaving Jericho on the right and proceeding to Gilgal about two hours distant from Jericho. He stopped at many places on the way. The children followed him singing songs of praise, and ran into the houses to bring their parents out.

Jesus in Gilgal, Dibon, Succoth, Aruma, and Bethany

THE REGION known as Gilgal comprised the whole of the elevated country above the low valley of the Jordan, and which was embraced by the inflowing streams of the Jordan for a circumference of five hours. But the city Gilgal, to which Jesus drew near before evening, lay scattered and interspersed by numerous gardens for the distance of about one hour, in the direction of the place to which John had retired to preach and baptize.

Jesus first entered the precincts of a sacred spot open to prophets and doctors of the Law. It was the place where Joshua had communicated something to the children of Israel, namely, the six maledictions and six benedictions that had been revealed to Eliezer and himself by Moses before his death. The circumcision hill of the Israelites was nearby, and it, too, was enclosed by a wall.

I saw on this occasion the death of Moses. He died upon a low, but steep peak of Mount Nebo, which rises between Arabia and Moab. The camp of the Israelites flanked the mount, the outposts extending far into the valley around. A growth like ivy covered the whole mount. It was short and crisp, and grew in tufts like the juniper. Moses was obliged to support himself by it when climbing to the top of the peak. Joshua and Eliezer were with him. Moses had a vision from God that his companions saw not. He delivered to Joshua a roll of writing containing six maledictions and six benedictions, which the latter had to publish to the people when in the Promised Land. Then, having embraced them, he commanded them to depart and not to look back. When they had gone, Moses cast himself upon his knees with outstretched arms, and gently sank upon his side dead. I saw the earth open under him and enclose him as in a beautiful grave. When Moses appeared at the Transfiguration of Jesus on Tabor, I saw that he came from that place. Joshua read the six blessings and six maledictions before the people.

Saturday, October 8, AD 29 (Tishri 12)
Jesus remained for the sabbath in Gilgal. Lazarus, Joseph of Arimathea, and some other friends arrived from Jerusalem to hear him preach. The mood was joyful, and as Jesus was leaving the synagogue the crowd shouted: "The covenant is fulfilled!" Lazarus and the friends from Jerusalem left, and Jesus sent a message through them to his mother in Galilee that she should expect him at Great Chorazin (about ten miles east of Capernaum) at the Feast of Tabernacles.

Many of Jesus's friends awaited him in Gilgal: Lazarus, Joseph of Arimathea, Obed, a son of the widow of Nazareth, and others. There was an inn here, in which they set refreshments before the Lord and his companions after washing their feet.

Before the crowds here assembled, many of whom were on their way to John's baptism, Jesus gave an instruction. The spot chosen for the purpose was near the baths and place of purification built high up on the sloping, terraced shore of an arm of the Jordan. It was shaded by an awning, and all around were pleasure gardens ornamented with trees, shrubs, and green plots. Saturnin and two other disciples who had left John to follow Jesus baptized after Jesus had given an instruction on the Holy Spirit. He taught of the several attributes of the Holy Spirit, and pointed out the marks that distinguish one that has received him.

John's baptism was preceded by only a summary confession of sins accompanied by proofs of contrition and a promise of amendment. But at the baptism of Jesus the acknowledgment of sin was not made in this general way. Everyone accused himself individually and mentioned his chief transgressions. Jesus exhorted to sincerity. He frequently proclaimed the sins of those that, through pride or false shame, concealed them thus to lead them to repentance.

Here also Jesus alluded to the passage over the Jordan and the ceremony of circumcision that had here been performed. It was in memory of this latter circumstance that baptism was now administered here and, through its efficacy, he said, they should henceforth be circumcised in their heart. He spoke likewise of the fulfillment of the Law.

The baptized on this occasion were not immersed in the water, they only inclined their head over it; nor did they put on an entire baptismal garment, a white cloth only was placed on their shoulders. The disciples did not make use of a three-channelled shell like John's; but from the basin over which the neophyte inclined, they dipped up the water three times with the hand. Jesus had previously blessed it and poured into it some from his own baptismal well. About thirty were baptized at this time. They appeared radiant with joy after the ceremony, and declared that they truly felt that they had now received the Holy Spirit.

Jesus then proceeded with his followers amid the acclamations of the multitude to Gilgal, to celebrate the sabbath in the synagogue, a very large, old building on the east side of the city. It was a four-cornered edifice, longer than broad, the angles filled in in such a way as to give it something of the appearance of an octagon. It contained three stories, in each of which was a school. A spiral, exterior flight of steps joined to the wall led up to each, and around each landing ran a little portico. High up in the rounded corners of the building were niches, in which one could stand and view the country far and near. The synagogue stood by itself with gardens cut off on both sides. In front of the entrance was a porch and a teacher's desk similar to that of the temple in Jerusalem, and there was also an open court containing an altar upon which sacrifice had once been offered. There were likewise covered porches for women and children. One could easily detect the similarity of all these arrangements with those of the temple, also that the Ark of the Covenant had once rested here and sacrifices been offered.

The school on the lowest story was the most beautiful in its arrangements. At one end, in the spot corresponding to that occupied by the Holy of Holies in the temple, stood an octagonal pillar around which were compartments containing rolls of writings. A table encircled the base of the pillar, and below that was a vault. Here it was that the Ark of the Covenant had once stood. The pillar was very beautiful, of polished white marble.

In the school on the first story, Jesus taught before the priests, the people, and the doctors of the Law. Among other things he alluded to the fact that here the promised kingdom had been first established, but that idolatry so abominable had been practiced at a later period that scarcely could seven just souls be found among the inhabitants. Nineveh, though five times greater, had been able to produce five just. Gilgal had been spared by God, therefore they should not now repulse him who came to fulfill the Promise: they should do penance and through baptism be born anew. Then taking the rolls from their places around the pillar, Jesus read and explained them.

After that he taught the young men in the school on the second story, and lastly the boys on the third. Coming down, he delivered another instruction to the women in an open space under a porch, and still another to the young maidens. To these last he spoke of modesty and chastity, of repressing curiosity, of modesty in dress, of veiling the hair, and of covering the head in the temple and in the synagogue. He reminded them of the presence of God and the angels in holy places, and that the latter themselves veil their face before the Lord. He told them that in the temple and synagogue there were myriads of angels hovering around the worshippers, and he explained why females should veil the head and hair. The children ran familiarly to Jesus. He blessed them and took them up in his arms. They were very much attached to him. The joy and jubilation over Jesus were general in this place. As he left the school, the people ran from all sides to meet him, crying out, and exclaiming: "The Promise is fulfilled! May it remain with us. May it never forsake us!"

When Jesus had finished his instructions, the people were anxious to bring their sick to him. But he dismissed them, saying that it was neither the time nor the place for that, he must now leave them, for he was called elsewhere. Lazarus and the friends from Jerusalem returned to their homes and Jesus took leave of the blessed Virgin, telling her that he would see her again before he retired into the desert.

Sunday, October 9, AD 29 (Tishri 13)

Agents reported back to the Sanhedrin in Jerusalem about the jubilation Jesus evoked at Gilgal and his baptizing activity there. The Sanhedrin, composed of seventy-one priests and scribes, appointed a committee of twenty to investigate Jesus. They concluded that Jesus was in league with the devil. On this day, Jesus and about twenty followers left Gilgal. Traveling eastward, they crossed the Jordan on a large raft. Coming to a place where many tax collectors lived—they had already been baptized by John—Jesus taught them the parable of the sower (Matthew 13).

The Sanhedrin in Jerusalem again held a long consultation on the subject of Jesus. Everywhere they had spies bribed to give them information of his words and actions. The Sanhedrin consisted of seventy-one priests and doctors, of whom twenty were again divided into fives, thus forming so many subcommittees for deliberating and disputing together. They examined the genealogical register, and could in no way deny that Joseph and Mary were of the House of David and Mary's mother of the race of Aaron. But as they said, these families had fallen into obscurity, and Jesus strolled around with vagrants. He also defiled himself with publicans and pagans, and sought the favor of slaves. They had heard, they said, of the familiar way in which he had spoken lately to the Shechemites, who were returning home from their work in the region of Bethlehem, and they thought that he must have designs to raise an insurrection with the aid of such hangers-on. Some gave it as their opinion that he was very likely an illegitimate child, because he had once proclaimed himself the son of a king. Others declared that he must in some way receive secret training from the devil, for he often retired apart and spent the night alone in the wilderness or on the mountains. They knew what they were saying, for they had already inquired into all this. Among these twenty deliberators were some who knew Jesus and his family very well, who were most favorably inclined toward him, who were indeed his friends in secret. Nevertheless, they did not contradict what was said against him. They kept silence in order to be the better able to serve him and his disciples and to give them information of whatever might come to their knowledge. The majority of the committee concluded at last that Jesus was in communication with the devil from whom he received instruction, and this was the opinion they publicly proclaimed and which was spread throughout Jerusalem.

John's disciples announced to him the baptism that had lately taken place in Gilgal, representing the same as a usurpation of his rights. But in deepest humility John again repeated what he had often told them before; that is, that he would soon give place to his Lord, whose herald and precursor he had been. The disciples could not rightly understand his words.

With about twenty followers, Jesus left Gilgal and moved on to the Jordan, which he crossed on a raft. All around on the beams of the raft were seats, and in the center two concave spaces in which they were accustomed to stand the camels that they might not slip between the beams into the water. Three camels could be so accommodated; but now there were none on board, the Lord and his disciples being the only passengers. It was night, and lighted torches stood in the hollow spaces. Jesus related the parable of the sower which, on the following day, he explained. The passage over the river occupied fifteen minutes at least, for the current at this point was very strong. They had to row some distance up the river, and then drift down to the spot at which they intended to land, and which was not directly opposite their starting point. The Jordan is a singular river; it cannot be crossed at all in many places, and its steep shores are pathless. It makes frequent and sudden bends, and often appears to flow straight past a place around which it is, in reality, bending. Its bed in many places is rocky and its course consequently arrested. Its waters encircle numerous islands as they flow sometimes troubled, sometimes clear, according to the nature of its bed, here and there forming falls. The water of the Jordan is soft and tepid.

They landed near the settlement of the publicans. A highroad from the region of Kedar passed nearby and there, too, a lovely valley took its rise. The publicans, who had already received John's baptism, entertained Jesus; but several of his followers, surprised at their Master's intimacy with these despised people, stood shyly aloof. Jesus and his disciples spent the night here, accepting hospitality from the publicans, who were most deferential to them. Their houses stood on the side of the road that ran through the valley and not far from the Jordan; somewhat further on was the inn for the accommodation of merchants and their camels. There were many tarrying here at the time, on account of the next day's feast, that of Tabernacles; for although most of them were pagans, yet they were obliged to observe the festivals as days of rest. The publicans questioned Jesus as to how they should restore their unjustly acquired goods. He told them that they should be taken to the temple, which however he meant only spiritually, for in reality he designated thereby his own community, the church. There should, he said, be purchased with it a field near Jerusalem for the support of poor widows, and he explained to them why a field, illustrating by the parable of the sower.

Monday, October 10, AD 29 (Tishri 14)
After giving further teaching to the tax collectors, Jesus set off in the direction of Dibon. At the outskirts of the town, he paused to teach. That evening was the start of the Feast of Tabernacles—to celebrate the gathering in of the fruits of the fields—and little booths (tabernacles) had been erected and festooned with bushes, bunches of grapes, and so forth. Jesus and his disciples were offered refreshment. That night, they stayed at an inn not far from the synagogue of Dibon.

Next day Jesus walked with them on the shore and in the country around, teaching again of the sower and the future harvest.[B7] He took his text from the Feast of Tabernacles, which was then beginning, and which commemorated the vintage as well as the ingathering of the fruits of the field. From the publican village, Jesus pressed on further through the valley. On either side of the mountain slope, for the distance of half an hour perhaps, were rows of houses in which the Feast of Tabernacles was being celebrated. These houses extended as far as Dibon, in the environs of which indeed they appeared to be. By their side were erected the booths formed of green branches of trees and adorned with bushes, festoons, and clusters of grapes. On one side of the road were the tabernacles and the little tents of the women; on the other, the huts in which the animals were slaughtered. All the food was carried across the road. The children, adorned with garlands, went in bands from one tabernacle to another, singing and playing upon musical instruments. These last consisted of triangles furnished with rings which they tinkled, triangles spanned by cords, and a wind instrument from which arose spiral tubes.

Jesus paused here and there to teach. Refreshments were offered to him and his disciples, grapes on sticks, two clusters on each. At the further end of this row of houses stood an inn which Jesus entered. Not far from the inn, between it and Dibon, was a broad, open space in the middle of the road. Here, surrounded by trees, arose the large and beautiful synagogue of Dibon.

Tuesday, October 11, AD 29 (Tishri 15)

On the next day Jesus taught in the synagogue, taking again the parable of the sower, alluding to the baptism and the nearness of the kingdom of God. He spoke also of the Feast of Tabernacles and of its celebration here, taking occasion to reprove the people for mixing up pagan customs in their services, for some of the Moabites still dwelt in this place, and with them the Jewish people had intimate relations. When Jesus left the synagogue, he found in the open court numbers of sick who had been borne thither on litters. They cried out as soon as they saw him: "Lord, thou hast been sent from God! Thou canst help us! Help us, Lord!" He cured many. That evening a banquet was prepared in the inn for Jesus and his followers. There were many of the pagan merchants near Jesus when he spoke of the call of the Gentiles, of the star that had appeared in the land of the kings, and of their going to visit the child. Jesus left the place that night alone and went to pray on the mountain.

(Follow Map 7)

Wednesday, October 12, AD 29 (Tishri 16)

Early in the morning the disciples met up with Jesus and journeyed with him northward from Dibon. They passed through Bethsob and paused briefly in Ainon before arriving that evening at the town of Succoth, where Jesus taught in the synagogue, and Saturnin—together with four other disciples—baptized a number of people.

Jesus had engaged to meet his disciples the following morning on the road at the other side of Dibon. Dibon was six hours distant from Gilgal. It was rich in fountains and meadows, gardens and terraces, for it lay in the valley and up both sides of the mountain.

Jesus next went to Succoth where he arrived toward evening. An innumerable multitude gathered around him, among them many sick. He taught in the synagogue, and allowed Saturnin and four other disciples to administer baptism. It took place at a spring in a rocky grotto facing westward toward the Jordan which, however, could not be seen from it as a hill intervened. But the spring was fed from the deep waters of the river. The light fell into the grotto from apertures in the roof. In front of it was an extensive pleasure garden beautifully laid out with small trees, aromatic shrubs, and well-kept lawns. In it was an ancient memorial stone commemorative of an apparition of Melchizedek to Abraham.

Jesus taught here of John's baptism, which he called a baptism of penance, and which would soon be discontinued. In its stead would be received the baptism of the Holy Spirit and the remission of sin. He received from them a kind of general confession of their sins, and then some separately disclosed their predominant passions and transgressions. Many trembled at hearing Jesus accusing them of sins that they thought secret. After the confession Jesus laid his hands upon them as if giving absolution. They were not immersed when receiving baptism. A large basin of water was placed on Abraham's memorial stone, and over it the neophytes bowed with bared shoulders. The baptizers poured the water thrice from the hollow of their hand over the heads of the baptized, who were very numerous at this place.

Abraham had once dwelt at Succoth with his nurse Maraha, and had owned fields in three different localities. Even here he had begun to share with Lot. It was here that Melchizedek first appeared to Abraham in the same way as did the angels. Melchizedek commanded him a threefold sacrifice of doves, long-beaked birds, and other animals, promising to come again and offer bread and wine in sacrifice. He told him what was going to happen to Sodom and to Lot, and pointed out to him several graces for which he should pray. Melchizedek at that time had no longer an earthly abode at Salem. Jacob also dwelt at Succoth.

Thursday, October 13, AD 29 (Tishri 17)

After teaching and healing in Succoth, Jesus and his disciples journeyed further north through the region known as the Decapolis.

Friday, October 14, AD 29 (Tishri 18)

From Succoth Jesus proceeded to Great Chorazin where, at an inn near the city, he had appointed to meet his mother and the holy women. On the way thither he passed through Gerasa where he kept the sabbath, after which he went to an inn in the desert some hours from the Sea of Galilee.

Saturday, October 15, AD 29 (Tishri 19)

The proprietors of the inn dwelt nearby. The inn was still adorned for the Feast of Tabernacles [the sixth day of this Feast was just beginning], for the holy women had rented

Map 7: The Forty Days in the Wilderness
October 11 – November 30, AD 29

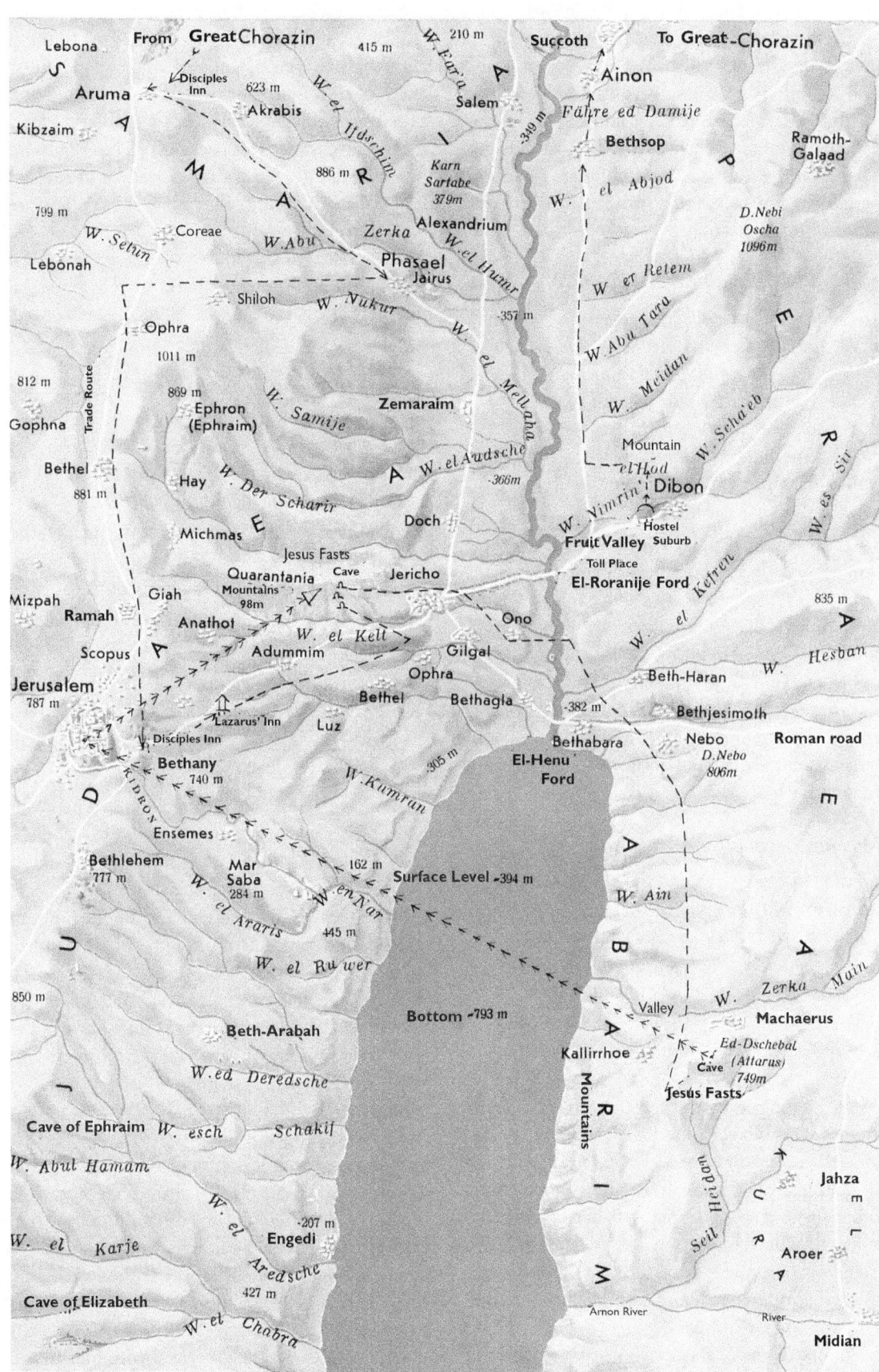

Suburb of Dibon—Bethsop—Ainon—Bethany—Succoth—Gerasa—Near Great Chorazin
Aruma—Phasael—Bethany—Quarantania—Attarus—Jerusalem—Quarantania

it some days previously and put all things in order. The necessary provisions were brought at their expense from Gerasa. Peter's wife was with them, also Susanna of Jerusalem, and all the others excepting Veronica. Jesus had an interview with his mother alone. He told her that he was now on his way to Bethany, whence he would retire to the desert. Mary was grave and anxious. She begged him not to go to Jerusalem for awhile, for she had heard of the council convened on his account.

Sunday, October 16, AD 29 (Tishri 20)

Today, Jesus taught upon a hill. Many men and women from the neighborhood came to hear him. He spoke of his imminent departure and foretold that John's baptizing would soon cease. He also referred to the hard trials that would beset him and his followers. That evening, Jesus set off in a southwesterly direction accompanied by about twenty traveling companions. They journeyed through the night.

Later on Jesus gave an instruction. The place chosen for it was a hill upon which was a stone seat formerly used for the same purpose. There were rows of people from the surrounding country and about thirty women present. They stood apart from the men.

After the instruction Jesus told his followers that he must now leave them for a time and that they, as well as the women, should disband until his return. He spoke of John's baptism soon to cease, and of the bitter persecution awaiting him and his.

Monday, October 17, AD 29 (Tishri 21)

The whole day through, Jesus and the disciples continued on their way. In the evening, they arrived at the town of Aruma, where they stayed at an inn that had been made ready for them by Martha and Susanna of Jerusalem. Some Essenes living nearby came to eat with Jesus and his disciples. That evening, Jesus taught in the synagogue. Judas Iscariot was among the crowd of those who listened.

The preceding evening Jesus had left the inn with about twenty disciples and followers, and journeyed some twelve hours southwest toward the city of Aruma near which an inn for him and his friends was always in readiness. Martha, for whom the journey to Gerasa was her first expedition with the holy women, had prepared this inn for Jesus, and his friends in Jerusalem bore the cost. The steward and servants lived in the neighborhood. The holy women told Jesus of the inn before his departure. The city was about nine hours from Jerusalem and between six and seven from Jericho.

Some Essenes dwelt near the inn. They went to see Jesus, conversed and ate with him. Jesus went to the synagogue and taught of John's baptism, which was a baptism of penance, a preliminary purification, a preparatory action such as was prescribed in the Law. It was different from the baptism of him whom John heralded. They that were baptized by John I did not see again baptized, until after the death of Jesus and the coming of the Holy Spirit when, for the most part, the ceremony was performed at the pool of Bethesda. The Pharisees of this place asked Jesus by what signs they should know the Messiah, and he told them. He gave an instruction on the subject of mixed marriages with the pagans and Samaritans.

Tuesday, October 18, AD 29 (Tishri 22)

Jesus taught again in the synagogue. Later, he went to the town of Phasael and visited the Essene Jairus (not the Jairus mentioned in the Gospels). He ate with Jairus and spent the night at his house.

Judas Iscariot, subsequently the apostle, here heard Jesus preaching. He had come alone and not with the other disciples. After listening to his instructions for two days, and passing remarks on the same with the disaffected Pharisees, he departed for a neighboring village which did not bear a very good name. There he gave an account of what he had heard, talking with an air of importance to a pious man of the place. The latter in consequence invited Jesus to visit him. Judas carried on some kind of traffic. He was much occupied with writing, and held himself in readiness for general services of any kind. When Jesus and his disciples arrived at the aforenamed place, which had been lately built and which on account of its mixed population was not in very good repute, Judas had departed. Herod owned a castle in the neighborhood. Something connected with the Benjaminites must have happened in this place, for there was a tree close at hand surrounded by a wall, and no one went near it. Abraham and Jacob had each offered sacrifice here, and hither had Esau withdrawn when at variance with Jacob on the subject of the Blessing. Isaac at that time was living near Sichar.

The man that had invited Jesus to these parts was called Jairus; he belonged to the married Essenes. He had a wife and several children, among the latter two sons named Ammon and Caleb. He had also a daughter whom Jesus at a later period cured of some disease, but he was not the Jairus of the Gospel. He was a descendant of Chariot the Essene, who had founded the convents near Bethlehem and Mizpah, and he was familiar with many circumstances of Jesus's youth and family. He and his sons went forth to meet Jesus, whom they received with marks of deference. Jairus was, on account of his charity, the chief man of this despised place. He helped the poor and, on certain days, gave instructions to the children and the ignorant, for they had here neither schools nor priests. He likewise cared for the sick. As usual, Jesus taught of the baptism of John, setting it forth as a preparatory baptism of penance, also of the near coming of the kingdom of God.

Wednesday, October 19, AD 29 (Tishri 23)

Jesus remained in Phasael, teaching. With Jairus he visited the sick, and consoled them, but he would not cure any. He promised to return in four months and cure them. In his instructions he alluded to the events that had taken place here, namely, the estrangement of Esau in anger from his brother, and the consequences following upon his rage. It was this that had brought the place into ill-repute. Jesus told of the mercy of the heavenly Father, who would realize all his promises in favor of those that would believe in the one sent by him, would do penance, and be baptized and he showed how penance wards off the consequences of sin. Toward evening, accompanied about halfway by Jairus and his sons, Jesus went with his disciples to Bethany.

Thursday, October 20, AD 29 (Tishri 24)

They stopped at an inn in the vicinity, and there Jesus gave his disciples a long instruction in which he alluded to the trials in store for him and all his followers. He told them that they should now leave him, and weigh well whether they would be able to stand by him in his future sufferings.

Lazarus came out to meet him. The disciples departed for their homes, Aram and Themeni alone accompanying him to Bethany where many friends from Jerusalem were awaiting him, among them the holy women and Veronica. Aram and Themeni were the nephews of Joseph of Arimathea on the mother's side. They had been John's disciples, but had followed Jesus when on his way to Gilgal he had passed John's place of baptism. Jesus gave an instruction at Lazarus's on the baptism of John, on the Messiah, on the Law and its fulfillment, and on the various sects among the Jews.

Friday, October 21, AD 29 (Tishri 25)

Jesus interpreted various passages from the scriptures to the friends gathered together. Later, he had a conversation with Silent Mary, whom he blessed. He then set off in the direction of Jericho. For the first part of the journey, Jesus was accompanied by Lazarus. Lazarus went with Jesus as far as a hostel (that he owned) close to the wilderness. Here they parted company, and Jesus continued on his way alone and barefoot. As the sabbath began, he climbed a mountain—Mount Quarantania—about one hour's distance from Jericho. Here he started his forty-day fast and spent the night in prayer in a cave. Jesus knelt with outstretched arms and prayed to his heavenly Father for strength and courage in all the trials that awaited him.

His friends had brought with them from Jerusalem some rolls of writings from which Jesus explained to them the words of the prophets relative to the Messiah. But only a few were present at this instruction, only Lazarus and some intimate friends.

Jesus consulted with them on the subject of his future abode. They counseled him not to remain in Jerusalem, telling him all that was said of him there. They proposed to him Salem as proper for his residence, since but few Pharisees were in it. Jesus spoke of various places and of Melchizedek, whose figurative priesthood was soon to be realized. Melchizedek had laid out all the roads, founded all the places that in the designs of God the Son of Man was afterward to travel over and evangelize. Jesus concluded by telling them that he would be found mostly around the Sea of Galilee. This conference was held in a retired apartment that opened upon a garden attached to the baths.

Jesus had an interview with the women in a chamber fronting on the road that led to Jerusalem, and which had formerly been occupied by Magdalene. In obedience to Jesus's direction, Lazarus brought his silent sister Mary and left her alone with the Lord, the other women retiring in the meantime to the antechamber.

Silent Mary's bearing toward Jesus was somewhat different from that of the last interview, for she cast herself down before him and kissed his feet. Jesus made no attempt to prevent her, and raised her up by the hand. With her eyes turned heavenward, she, as once before, uttered the most sublime and wonderful things, though in the most simple and natural manner. She spoke of God, of his Son, and of his kingdom just as a peasant girl might talk of the father of the village lord and his inheritance. Her words were a prophecy, and the things of which she spoke she saw before her. She recounted the grave faults and bad management of the wicked servants of the household. The Father had sent his Son to arrange affairs and pay off all debts, but they would receive him badly. He would have to die in great suffering, redeem his kingdom with his own blood, and efface the crimes of the servants, that they might again become the children of his Father. She carried out the allegory in most beautiful language, and yet in as natural a manner as if she were recounting a scene enacted in her presence. At times she was gay, at others sorrowful, calling herself a useless servant and grieving over the painful labors of the Son of the merciful Lord and Father. Another cause of sorrow to her was that the servants would not rightly understand the parable, although so simple and so true. She spoke of the resurrection. The Son, she said, would go to the servants in the subterranean prisons also. He would console them and set them free, because he had purchased their redemption. He would return with them to his Father. But at his second advent, when he would come again to judge, all those that had abused the satisfaction he had made and who would not turn from their evil ways, should be cast into the fire. She then spoke of Lazarus's death and resurrection: "He goes forth from this world," she said, "and gazes upon the things of the other life. His friends weep around him as if he were never to return. But the Son calls him back to earth, and he labors in the vineyard." Of Magdalene too she spoke: "The maiden is in the frightful desert where once were the children of Israel. She wanders in accursed places where all is dark, where never human foot has trod. But she will come forth, and in another desert make amends for the past."

Mary the Silent spoke of herself as of a captive, for her body appeared to her a prison, and she longed to go home. She was so straitened on all sides; not one around her understood her and they were, as it seemed to her, all blind. But, she said, she was willing to wait, she would bear her captivity submissively, for she deserved nothing better. Jesus spoke to her lovingly, consoling her and saying: "After Passover, when I again come here, thou shalt indeed go home." Then as she knelt before him, he raised his hands over her and blessed her. It seemed to me that at the same time he poured over her something from a flask, but I cannot say whether it was oil or water.

Mary the Silent was a very holy person, but none knew or understood her. Her whole life was one uninterrupted vision of the work of redemption, of which she spoke like an innocent child. No one guessed her interior life, and she was regarded as a simpleton. When Jesus signified to her the time of her death, that is, that she should, freed from captivity, at last go home, he anointed her for death.

From this we may conclude that anointing is more necessary for the body than some people generally think. Jesus pitied Silent Mary who, as a reputed simpleton, would have received no embalming. Her holiness was hidden. Jesus dismissed her, and she returned to her abode.

After this Jesus again instructed the men on the baptism of John and that of the Holy Spirit. I do not remember any very great difference between the first named and that bestowed by the disciples of Jesus. The latter, however, was a little more like that which at a later period was to take away sin. Nor did I ever see any of those that had been baptized by John rebaptized before the descent of the Holy Spirit.

The friends from Jerusalem returned to the city before the sabbath, Aram and Themeni going in company with Joseph of Arimathea. Jesus had told them that he would retire awhile in order to prepare for the painful mission before him, that of teaching, but he did not tell them that he was going to fast.

JESUS IN THE DESERT · MARRIAGE FEAST OF CANA · JESUS CELEBRATES PASSOVER IN JERUSALEM FOR THE FIRST TIME

The Forty Days' Fast of Jesus

ACCOMPANIED by Lazarus, Jesus went to the inn belonging to the latter situated near the desert. It was just before the sabbath began. Lazarus was the only one whom Jesus had told that after forty days he would return. From this inn he began his journey into the desert alone and barefoot. He went first, not toward Jericho, but southward toward Bethlehem, as if he wished to pass between the residence of Anne's relatives and that of Joseph's near Mizpah. But he turned off toward the Jordan, shunned the different cities and villages by taking the footpaths around them, and passed that place near which the Ark had once stood and at which John had celebrated the feast.

About one hour's distance from Jericho, he ascended the mountain and entered a spacious grotto. This mountain rises to the southeast of Jericho, and faces Madian across the Jordan.

Jesus began his fast here near Jericho, continued it in different parts of the desert on the other side of the Jordan, and after the devil had borne him to the top of the mountain, concluded it where it had been commenced. From the summit of this mountain, which is in some parts covered with low brushwood, in others barren and desolate, the view is very extended. Properly speaking, it is not so high as Jerusalem, because it lies on a lower level; but rising abruptly from low surroundings, its solitary grandeur is the more striking. The height that commands the whole plateau upon which stand the Holy City and its environs is the Mount of Calvary, the loftiest point of which is almost on a level with the highest parts of the temple. On the south side, the nearest to Bethlehem, Jerusalem is flanked by rocks dangerously steep. There was no gate on this side, the whole being taken up by palaces.

It was night when Jesus climbed that steep, wild mountain in the desert now called Mount Quarantania. Three spurs, each containing a grotto, rise one above another. Jesus climbed to the topmost of all, from the back of which one could gaze down into the steep, gloomy abyss below. The whole mountain was full of frightfully dangerous chasms. Four hundred years before, a prophet, whose name I forget, had sojourned in that same cave. Elijah, also, had dwelt there secretly for a long time and had enlarged it. Sometimes, without anyone's knowing whence he came, he used to go down among the inhabitants of the surrounding district to prophesy and restore peace. About twenty-five Essenes one hundred and fifty years ago dwelt on this mountain. It was at its foot that the camp of the Israelites was pitched when, with the Ark of the Covenant, they marched around Jericho to the sound of trumpets. The fountain whose water Elisha rendered sweet was not far off. St. Helena caused these grottoes to be transformed into chapels. In one of them, I once saw on the wall a picture of the Temptation. At a later period a convent arose on the summit of the mountain. I wondered how the workmen could get up there. Helena erected churches on numerous sacred spots. It was she who built the church over mother Anne's birthplace two hours from Sepphoris. In Sepphoris itself Anne's parents owned a house. How sad that most of these holy places have gone to ruin, some even lost to memory! When as a young girl I used to go before the day through the snows of winter to Coesfeld to church, I used to see all those holy places so plainly. And I often saw how good men, to save them from destruction, would cast themselves flat in the road before the destroying soldiers.

The words of scripture: "He was led by the Spirit into the desert," mean that the Holy Spirit, who descended upon Jesus at the moment of his baptism when he allowed his humanity to be, in some measure, visibly penetrated by the divinity, impelled him to go into the desert to prepare as man in close communication with his heavenly Father for his vocation to suffering.

Saturday, October 22, AD 29 (Tishri 26)

Jesus, kneeling in the grotto with outstretched arms, prayed to his heavenly Father for strength and courage in all the sufferings that awaited him. He saw all in advance, and begged for the grace necessary for each. All his afflictions, all his pains passed before me in vision, and I saw him receiving consolation and merit for every one. A cloud of white light, large like a church, descended and hovered over him. At the end of each prayer spirits approached him. When close to him, they assumed a human form, offered him homage, and presented to him consolation and promises from On High. I saw then that Jesus here in the desert acquired for us all our consolation, all our strength, our help, our victory in temptation; purchased for us merit in struggle and conquest; gave value to our fasting and mortifications; and offered to God the Father all his future labors and sufferings, in order to give worth to the prayers and spiritual works of all his faithful followers in the ages to come. I saw the treasure that he thereby laid up for the church, and which she, in the forty days' fast, opens to her children. During this prayer, Jesus sweat blood.

Sunday, October 23, AD 29 (Tishri 27)

Jesus descended from the mountain (Mount Quarantania) before sunrise. He walked toward the Jordan, which he crossed on a beam of wood, and journeyed east of the town of Bethabara into the wilderness beyond the Dead Sea. Eventually, he reached a very wild mountain range east of Kallirrhoe, where he ascended the forbidding Mount Attarus. This savage, desolate mountain lay about nine hours' distance from Jericho. Here he continued to pray and fast, spending the night in a narrow cave near the summit of the mountain.

From this mountain Jesus went down again toward the Jordan to the country between Gilgal and John's place of baptism, about an hour further on to the south. He crossed that narrow but deep part of the river on a beam, and journeyed on, leaving Bethabara to the right. Crossing several highroads that led to the Jordan, he took the rugged mountain paths from the southeast through the wilderness. Proceeding through the valley leading to Kallirrhoe, he crossed a small stream and climbed a mountain spur a little to the north where Jahza lies in a valley opposite. The children of Israel defeated Sihon, king of the Amorites, here in a battle in which the Israelites were only three against sixteen. But God wrought a miracle in behalf of his people. A frightful noise swept over the Amorites and terrified them.

Jesus was now upon a very wild mountain range about nine hours from the Jordan, and far more savage and desolate than the one near Jericho, almost opposite to which it lies.

Monday, October 24, to Wednesday, November 30, AD 29 (Tishri 28—Kislev 6)

Throughout this period Jesus stayed at the mountain cave on Mount Attarus, praying and fasting. Here he was tempted. The three temptations described in Matthew 4:1–11 and Luke 4:1–13 actually took place on the last three days of the forty-day period (November 27–

29). Throughout the whole period, however, Anne Catherine beheld how Jesus was daily submitted to temptation that then culminated in the three temptations described in the Gospels. On Wednesday, November 30, when Jesus had overcome the last temptation, the twelve angels of the twelve apostles served him heavenly food. These twelve angels were accompanied in turn by the seventy-two angels of the seventy-two disciples. An indescribable blessing and consolation emanated from this heavenly celebration of Jesus's triumphant victory over temptation—a blessing and consolation that was transmitted by the angels to the apostles and disciples.

The divinity of Jesus, as well as his mission, was hidden from Satan. The words: "This is my beloved Son in whom I am well pleased," were understood by Satan as spoken of a mere human being, a prophet. Jesus had already been frequently and in many ways interiorly afflicted. The first temptation that he experienced was: "This nation is so corrupt. Shall I suffer all this and yet not perfect the work for which I came upon earth?" But with infinite love and mercy, he conquered the temptation in the face of all his torments.

Jesus prayed in the grotto sometimes prostrate, again kneeling, or standing. He wore his customary dress, but ungirded, loose and flowing, his feet bare. His mantle, a pair of wallets, and the girdle lay on the ground nearby. Daily was his labor of prayer different; daily did he acquire for us new graces, those of today unlike those of the preceding eve. Were it not for this labor of his, our resistance against temptation would never have been meritorious.

Jesus neither ate nor drank, but I saw him strengthened by angels. He was not emaciated by his long fast, though he became perfectly pale and white.

The grotto was not quite on the summit of the mountain. In it was an aperture through which the wind blew chill and raw, for at that season it was cold and foggy. The rocky walls of the grotto were streaked with colored veins; had they been polished, one would have thought them painted. There was space enough in it to afford room for Jesus, whether kneeling or prostrate, without his being directly under the aperture. The rock outside was overgrown by straggling briars.

One day I saw Jesus prostrate on his face. His unsandaled feet were red, wounded by the rugged roads, for he had come to the wilderness barefoot. At times he arose, and again prayed lying prostrate. He was surrounded by light. Suddenly a sound from heaven was heard, light streamed into the grotto, and myriads of angels appeared bearing with them all kinds of things. I was so afflicted, so overcome, that I felt as if pressed into the rocky wall of the grotto; and, filled with the sensation of one falling, I began to cry out: "I shall fall! I shall fall next to my Jesus!"

And now I beheld the angelic band bending low before Jesus, offering him their homage, and begging leave to unfold to him their mission. They questioned him as to whether it was still his will to suffer as man for the human race, as it had been his will to leave the bosom of his heavenly Father, to become incarnate in the Virgin's womb. When Jesus answered in the affirmative, accepting his sufferings anew, the angels put together before him a high cross, the parts of which they had brought with them. It was in shape such as I always see it, of four pieces, as I always see the winepress of the cross. The upper part of the trunk, that is, the part that arose between two inserted arms, was likewise separate. Five angels bore the lower portion; three, the upper; three, the left and three, the right arm; three, the ledge whereon his feet rested; and three carried a ladder. Another had a basket full of ropes, cords, and tools, while others bore the spear, the reed, the rods, the scourges, the crown of thorns, the nails, the robes of derision—in a word, all that figured in his Passion.

The cross appeared to be hollow. It could be opened like a cupboard, and then it displayed the innumerable instruments of torture with which it was filled. In the central part, where Jesus's heart was broken, were entwined all possible emblems of pain in all kinds of frightful instruments, and the color of the cross itself was heartrending, the color of blood.

The various parts presented different tints symbolic of the pain there to be endured, but all, like so many streams, converged to the heart. The different instruments were likewise symbolical of future pains.

In the cross were also vessels of vinegar and gall, as well as ointment, myrrh, and something like herbs, prefiguring perhaps to Jesus his death and burial.

There were also numbers of open scrolls like billets of about a hand in width. They were of various colors, and on them were written pains and labors to be realized by sufferings of innumerable kinds. The colors were significant of the several degrees and species of darkness which were to be enlightened and dissipated by that suffering. What was utterly lost was typified by black; aridity, dryness, agitation, confusion, negligence were symbolized by brown; red was significant of all that was heavy, earthly, sensual; while yellow betokened effeminacy and horror of suffering. Some of the scrolls were half yellow and half red; they had to be bleached entirely white. There were others white like currents of milk, and the writing on them shone and glittered. They signified the won, the finished.

These colored bands of writing were like the summing

up of all the pains that Jesus would have to endure in his mortal life, all his labors, all that the apostles and others would cause him to suffer.

Then there appeared before him, as in a procession, all those men through whom were to come the most keenly felt sufferings he would have to endure, the malice of the Pharisees, the treason of Judas, the insults of the Jews at his bitter and ignominious death.

The angels arranged all, unfolded all before the Savior, doing all with unspeakable reverence, like priests performing the holiest functions. While thus the entire Passion was unfolded and passed in detail before his gaze, I saw Jesus and the angels weeping.

On another occasion, I saw the angels placing before Jesus the ingratitude of men, the skepticism, the scorn, the mockery, the treachery, the denial of friends and of enemies up to the moment of his death and after it. All passed before him in pictures, as also those sufferings and labors of his that would bear no fruit. But for his consolation, they showed him likewise all that would be gained by them. As these pictures floated past, the angels pointed them out with a motion of the hand.

In all these visions of Jesus's Passion, I always saw his cross composed of five kinds of wood, the arms set in with a wedge under each, and a block upon which the feet were to rest. The piece above the head, on which was the inscription, I saw put on separately, for the trunk of the cross was too low to admit of the writing over the head. It fitted on like the cover on a needle case.

JESUS TEMPTED IN MANY WAYS BY SATAN

SATAN knew not of the divinity of Christ. He took him for a prophet. He had noted his holiness from early youth, as also that of his mother. But Mary took no notice whatever of Satan. She never listened to a temptation. There was nothing in her upon which Satan could fasten. Though the fairest of women, the fairest of virgins, she never thought of a suitor excepting at the holy lottery, at the flowering of the rods in the temple, when there was question of her marriage. That Jesus was wanting in a certain pharisaical severity toward his disciples in non-essential points, puzzled the wicked fiend. He took him for a man, because the so-called irregularities of his disciples scandalized the Jews.

As Satan had often seen Jesus fired with zeal, he thought at one time to irritate him by assuming the appearance of one of the disciples who had followed him thither; and as he had also seen examples of his tenderness of heart, he tried at another time, under the form of a decrepit old man, to excite his compassion; and again as an Essene, to dispute with him. I saw him therefore at the entrance of the grotto under the form of the son of one of the three widows, a youth especially loved by Jesus. He made a noise to attract attention, thinking that Jesus would be displeased at his disciple's following him against his prohibition. Jesus did not look toward him even once. Then Satan put his head in and began to talk, first of one thing, then of another, and at last of John the Baptist who, he said, was very indignant at Jesus for encroaching upon his rights, by allowing his disciples to baptize from time to time.

Foiled in this first ruse, Satan tried another. He sent seven, eight, or nine apparitions of the disciples into the grotto. In they came one after another, saying to Jesus that Eustachius had informed them that he was there, and that they had sought him with so much anxiety. They begged him not to expose his life in that wild abode, not to abandon them. The whole world was talking about him, they continued, and he should not allow such and such things to be said. But Jesus's only reply was: "Withdraw, Satan! It is not yet time," and the phantoms disappeared.

Again Satan drew near under the form of a feeble old man, a venerable Essene, toiling painfully up the steep mountain. The ascent seemed so difficult for him that, really, I pitied him. Approaching the grotto, with a loud groan he fell fainting from exhaustion at its entrance. But Jesus took no notice of him, not even by a glance. Then the old man arose with an effort, and introduced himself as an Essene from Mount Carmel. He had, he said, heard of Jesus and, though almost worn out by the effort, had followed him thither in order to sit with him a little while and converse on holy things. He too knew what it was to fast and to pray, and when two joined their prayers to God, edification became greater. Jesus uttered a few words only, such as: "Retire, Satan! It is not yet time." Then I discovered that it was Satan, for as he turned away and vanished, I saw him becoming dark and horrible to behold. I felt like laughing when I thought of his throwing himself on the ground and of having to pick himself up again.

When Satan next came to tempt Jesus, he assumed the appearance of old Eliud. Satan must have known that his cross and Passion had been shown to Jesus by the angels, for he said that he had had a revelation of the heavy trials in store for him, and that he felt he would not be able to resist them. For a forty days' fast, he continued, Jesus was not in a state; therefore, urged by love for him, he had come to see him once more, to beg to be allowed to share his wild abode and assume part of his vow. Jesus noticed not the tempter, but raising his hands to heaven, he said: "My Father, take this temptation from me!" whereupon Satan vanished in a horrible form.

Jesus was kneeling in prayer when, after a time, I saw

three youths approaching. They were those who, on his first departure from Nazareth, were with him and who subsequently abandoned him. They appeared to approach timidly. They cast themselves on the ground before him, complaining that they could find no rest until he pardoned them. They begged him to have mercy on them, to receive them again to favor, and allow them to share his fast as a penance for their defection, and they promised thenceforth to be his most faithful disciples. They had ventured into the grotto, and they surrounded Jesus with tears and loud lamentation. Jesus rose from his knees, raised his hands to God, and the apparitions vanished.

On another day as he knelt in the grotto praying, I beheld Satan in a glittering robe borne, as it were, through the air up the steepest and highest side of the rock. This precipitous, inaccessible side faced to the east; in it were some apertures opening into the grotto. Jesus glanced not toward Satan, who was now intent on passing himself off for an angel. But he was a poor imitation, for the light that enveloped him was far from transparent. It looked as if it had been smeared on, and his robe was stiff and harsh, while those of the angels are soft and light and transparent. Hovering at the entrance of the grotto, Satan spoke: "I have been sent by thy Father to console thee." Jesus turned not toward him. Then Satan flew around to the steep, inaccessible side of the grotto and, peering in through one of the apertures, called to Jesus to witness a proof of his angelic nature, since he could hover there without support. But Jesus noticed him not. Seeing himself foiled in every attempt, Satan became quite horrible, and made as if he would seize Jesus in his claws through the aperture. His figure grew still more frightful and he vanished. Jesus looked not after him.

Satan came next under the appearance of an aged solitary from Mount Sinai. He was quite wild, almost savage-looking, with his long beard and scanty covering, a rough skin being his only garment. But there was something false and cunning in his countenance as he climbed painfully up the mountain. Entering the grotto, he addressed Jesus, saying that an Essene from Mount Carmel had visited him and told him of the baptism, also of the wisdom, the miracles, and the present rigorous fasting of Jesus. Hearing which, notwithstanding his great age, he had come all the way to see him, to converse with him, for he himself had long experience in the practice of mortification. He told Jesus that he should now desist from further fasting, that he would free him from what remained, and he went on with much more talk in the same strain. Jesus, looking aside, said: "Depart from me, Satan!" At these words, the evil one grew dark and, like a huge, black ball, rolled with a crash down the mountain.

Then I asked myself how it was that Christ's divinity remained so concealed from Satan. And I received the following instruction: I understood clearly that it was the most incomprehensible advantage for men that neither they nor Satan knew of Christ's divinity, and that they were thereby to learn how to exercise faith. The Lord said one word to me that I still remember. "Man," said he, "knew not that the serpent tempting him was Satan; in like manner, Satan was not to know that he who redeemed man was God." I saw too that the divinity of Christ was not made known to Satan until the moment in which he freed the souls from Limbo.

On one of the subsequent days, I saw Satan under the form of a distinguished man of Jerusalem. He approached the cave in which Jesus was praying and told him that sympathy had urged him to come to him, for he felt assured that he was called to give freedom to the Jewish nation. Then he related all the reports, all the discussions rife in Jerusalem on his account, and told him that he had come to offer his support in the good cause. He was one of Herod's officers, he said. Jesus might unhesitatingly accompany him back to Jerusalem, might even take up his abode in Herod's palace, where he could lie concealed, gather his followers around him, and set his undertaking on foot. And he urged him to return with him at once. The pretended officer laid his proposal before Jesus in a multiplicity of words. Jesus looked not toward him, but continued earnestly to pray. Then I saw Satan retreating, his form becoming frightful, fire and smoke bursting from his nostrils, until at last he vanished.

When Jesus began to hunger, and especially to thirst, Satan appeared in the form of a pious hermit and exclaimed: "I am so hungry! I pray thee give me of the fruits growing here on the mountain outside thy grotto. I would pluck none of it without asking the owner" (pretending that he took Jesus for the owner), "then let us sit together and talk of good things." Not at the entrance of the grotto, but on the opposite side, that is, toward the east, and at a little distance, grew figs and berries, and another kind of fruit something like nuts, though with soft shells like those of the medlar. Jesus answered the false hermit: "Depart from me! Thou art from the very beginning the liar. Harm not the fruit!" Then I saw Satan as a little somber figure hurrying off, a black vapor exhaling from him.

But he returned again in the form of a traveler, and asked Jesus for permission to eat of the fine grapes growing nearby, because they were so good for thirst. But Jesus gave him no answer, did not even look at him.

On the following day, Satan tempted Jesus again on the same head, only this time it was with a spring instead of fruit.

SATAN TEMPTS JESUS BY MAGICAL ARTS

SATAN appeared to Jesus in the grotto as a magician and philosopher. He told him that he had come to him as to a wise man, and that he would show him that he, too, could exhibit marvels. Then he showed him hanging on his hand a piece of apparatus like a globe, or perhaps still more like a bird cage. Jesus would not look at the tempter, much less into the globe as Satan desired, but turning his back on him, he left the grotto. I saw that a look into Satan's trickshow disclosed the most magnificent scenes from nature, lovely pleasure gardens full of shady groves, cool fountains, richly laden fruit trees, luscious grapes, etc. All seemed to be within one's reach, and all was constantly dissolving into ever more beautiful, more enticing scenes. Jesus turned his back on Satan, and he vanished.

This was another temptation to interrupt the fast of Jesus, who now began to thirst and to experience the pangs of hunger. Satan did not yet know what to think of him. He was aware, it is true, of the prophecies relating to him and he felt that he exercised power over himself, but he did not yet know that Jesus was God. He did not know even that he was the Messiah whose advent he so dreaded, since he beheld him fasting, hungering, enduring temptation; since he saw him so poor, suffering in so many ways; in a word, since he saw him in all things so like an ordinary man. In this Satan was as blind as the Pharisees. He looked upon Jesus as a holy man whom temptation might lead to a fall.

SATAN TEMPTS JESUS TO TURN STONES INTO BREAD

JESUS was now suffering from hunger and thirst. I saw him several times at the entrance of the grotto. Toward evening one day, Satan in the form of a large, powerful man ascended the mountain. He had furnished himself below with two stones as long as little rolls, but square at the ends, which as he mounted he molded into the perfect appearance of bread. There was something more horrible than usual about him when he stepped into the grotto to Jesus. In each hand he held one of the stones, and his words were to this effect: "Thou art right not to eat of the fruit, for it only excites an appetite. But if thou art the beloved Son of God over whom the Spirit came at baptism—behold! I have made these stones look like unto bread. Do thou change them into bread."[B8] Jesus glanced not toward him, but I heard him utter these words only: "Man lives not by bread!" These were the only words that I caught distinctly. Then Satan became perfectly horrible. He stretched out his talons as if to seize Jesus (at which action I saw the stones resting on his arms), and fled. I had to laugh at his having to take his stones off with him.

SATAN CARRIES JESUS TO THE PINNACLE OF THE TEMPLE, AND THEN TO MOUNT QUARANTANIA • ANGELS MINISTER UNTO JESUS

TOWARD evening of the following day, I saw Satan in the form of a majestic angel sweeping down toward Jesus with a noise like the rushing wind. He was clad in a sort of military dress such as I have seen St. Michael wear. But in the midst of his greatest splendor, one might detect something sinister and horrible. He addressed boasting words to Jesus, something in this strain: "I will show thee who I am, and what I can do, and how the angels bear me up in their hands. Look yonder, there is Jerusalem! Behold the temple! I shall place thee upon its highest pinnacle. Then do thou show what thou canst do, and see whether the angels will carry thee down." While Satan thus spoke and pointed out Jerusalem and the temple, I seemed to see them both quite near, just in front of the mountain. But I think that it was only an illusion. Jesus made no reply, and Satan seized him by the shoulders and bore him through the air. He flew low toward Jerusalem, and placed Jesus upon the highest point of one of the four towers that rose from the four corners of the temple, and which I had not before noticed. The tower to which Satan bore Jesus was on the west side toward Zion and opposite the citadel Antonia.[B9] The mount upon which the temple stood was very steep on that side. The towers were like prisons, and in one of them were kept the costly garments of the high priest. The roofs of these towers were flat, so that one could walk on them; but from the center rose a hollow, conical turret capped by a large sphere, upon which there was standing room for two. From that position, one could view the whole temple below.

It was on the loftiest point of the tower that Satan placed Jesus, who uttered no word. Then Satan flew to the ground, and cried up to him: "If thou art the Son of God, show thy power and come down also, for it is written: 'He has given his angels charge over thee, and in their hands shall they bear thee up, lest perhaps thou dash thy foot against a stone." Jesus replied: "It is written again: Thou shalt not tempt the Lord, thy God." Satan, in a fury, returned to Jesus, who said: "Make use of the power that hath been given thee!"

Then Satan seized him fiercely by the shoulders, and flew with him over the desert toward Jericho.[B10] While standing on the tower, I noticed twilight in the western sky. This second flight appeared to me longer than the first. Satan was filled with rage and fury. He flew with Jesus now

The Forty Days' Fast of Jesus

high, now low, reeling like one who would vent his rage if he could. He bore him to the same mountain, seven hours from Jerusalem, upon which he had commenced his fast.

I saw that Satan carried Jesus low over an old pine tree on the way. It was a large and still vigorous tree that had stood long ago in the garden of one of the ancient Essenes. Elijah had once lived a short time in its vicinity.

The tree was behind the grotto and close by the rugged precipice. Such trees used to be pierced three times in one season, and each time they yielded a little turpentine.

Satan flew with the Lord to the highest peak of the mountain, and set him upon an overhanging, inaccessible crag much higher than the grotto. It was night, but while Satan pointed around, it grew bright, revealing the most wonderful regions in all parts of the world. The devil addressed Jesus in words something like these: "I know that thou art a great teacher, that thou art now about to gather disciples around thee and promulgate thy doctrines. Behold, all these magnificent countries, these mighty nations! Compare with them poor, little Judea lying yonder! Go rather to these. I will deliver them over to thee, if kneeling down thou wilt adore me!" By adoration the devil meant that obeisance common among the Jews, and especially among the Pharisees, when supplicating favors from kings and great personages. This temptation of Satan was similar to that other one in which, under the guise of one of Herod's officers, he had sought to lure Jesus to take up his abode in the castle of Jerusalem, and had offered to assist him in his undertaking. It was similar in kind, though more extended in degree. As Satan pointed around, one saw first vast countries and seas, with their different cities into which kings in regal pomp and magnificence and followed by myriads of warriors were triumphantly entering. As one gazed, these scenes became more and more distinct until, at last, they seemed to be in the immediate vicinity. One looked down upon all their details, every scene, every nation differing in customs and manners, in splendor and magnificence.

Satan pointed out in each the features of special attraction. He dwelt particularly upon those of a country whose inhabitants were unusually tall and magnificent-looking. They were almost like giants. I think it was Persia. Satan advised Jesus to go there above all to teach. He showed him Palestine, but as a poor, little, insignificant place. This was a most wonderful vision, so extended, so clear, so grand, and magnificent!

The only words uttered by Jesus were: "The Lord thy God shalt thou adore and him only shalt thou serve! Depart from me, Satan!" Then I saw Satan in an inexpressibly horrible form rise from the rock, cast himself into the abyss, and vanish as if the earth had swallowed him.

At the same moment I beheld myriads of angels draw near to Jesus, bend low before him, take him up as if in their hands, float down gently with him to the rock, and into the grotto in which the forty days' fast had been begun. [B11] There were twelve angelic spirits who appeared to be the leaders, and a definite number of assistants. I cannot now remember distinctly, but I think it was seventy-two, and I feel that the whole vision was symbolical of the apostles and the disciples. And now was held in the grotto a grand celebration, one of triumph and thanksgiving, and a banquet was made ready. The interior of the grotto was adorned by the angels with garlands of vine leaves from which depended a victor's crown, likewise of leaves, over the head of Jesus. The preparations were made rapidly, though with marvelous order and magnificence. All was resplendent, all was symbolical. Whatever was needed appeared instantly at hand and in its proper place.

Next came the angels bearing a table, small at first but which quickly increased in size, laden with celestial fare. The food and vessels were such as I have always seen on the heavenly tables, and I saw Jesus, the twelve chief spirits, and also the others partaking of refreshment. But there was no eating by the mouth, though still a real participation, a passing of the essence of the fruits into the partakers. All was spiritual. It was as if the interior signification of the aliments entered into the participants, bearing with it refreshment and strength. But it is inexpressible.

At one end of the table stood a large, shining chalice with little cups around it, the whole similar to that which I have always seen in my visions of the institution of the blessed sacrament. But this that I now saw was immaterial, was larger. There was also a plate with thin disks of bread. I saw Jesus pouring something from the large chalice into the cups and dipping morsels of bread into it, which morsels and cups the angels took and carried away. With this the vision ended and Jesus, going out from the grotto, went down toward the Jordan.

The angels that ministered unto Jesus appeared under different forms and seemed to belong to different hierarchies. Those that, at the close of the banquet, bore away the cups of wine and morsels of bread, were clothed in priestly raiment. I saw at the instant of their disappearance all kinds of supernatural consolation descending upon the friends of Jesus, those of his own time and those of after ages. I saw Jesus appearing in vision to the blessed Virgin then at Cana, to comfort and strengthen her. I saw Lazarus and Martha wonderfully touched, while their hearts grew warm with the love of Jesus. I saw Mary the Silent actually fed with the gifts from the table of the Lord. The angel stood by her while she, like a child, received the food. She had been a witness of all the temptations and sufferings of

Jesus. Her whole life was one of vision and suffering through compassion, therefore such supernatural favors caused her no astonishment. Magdalene, too, was wonderfully agitated. She was at the time busied with finery for some amusement. Suddenly anxiety about her life seized upon her, and a longing rose in her soul to be freed from the chains that bound her. She cast the finery from her hands, but was laughed at by those around her. I saw many of the future apostles consoled, their hearts filled with heavenly desires. I saw Nathaniel in his home thinking of all that he had heard of Jesus, of the deep impression he had made upon him, and of how he had cast it out of his mind. Peter, Andrew, and all the others were, as I saw, strengthened and consoled. This was a most wonderful vision.

During Jesus's fast, Mary resided in the house near Capernaum, and had to listen to all kinds of speeches about her divine Son. They said that he went wandering about, no one knew where; that he neglected her; that after the death of Joseph it was his duty to undertake some business for his mother's support, etc. Throughout the whole country the talk about Jesus was rife at this time, for the wonders attendant on his baptism, the testimony rendered by John, and the accounts of his scattered disciples had been everywhere noised abroad. Only once after this, and that was before his Passion, at the resurrection of Lazarus, were reports of Jesus so widespread and active. The blessed Virgin was grave and recollected, for she was never without the internal vision of Jesus, whose actions she contemplated and whose sufferings she shared.

Toward the close of the forty days, Mary went to Cana, in Galilee, and stopped with the parents of the bride of Cana, people of distinction who appeared to be of the first rank. Their beautiful mansion stood in the heart of the clean and well-built city. A street ran through the middle of it, I think a continuation of the highroad from Ptolomais; one could see it descending toward Cana from a higher level. This city was not so irregularly and unevenly built as many others of Palestine. The bridegroom was almost of the same age as Jesus and he managed his mother's household with the cleverness of an old married man. The parents of the young people consulted the blessed Virgin upon all the affairs of their children and showed her everything.

John was at this time constantly occupied in administering baptism. Herod did his best to procure a visit from him, and he likewise sent messengers to draw him out on the subject of Jesus. But John paid very little attention to him, and went on repeating his old testimony of Jesus. From Jerusalem also, messengers were again sent to call him to account concerning Jesus and himself. John answered as usual that he had never laid eyes on him when he began his own career, but that he had been sent to prepare for him the way.

Since Jesus's baptism, John taught that through that baptism and the descent of the Holy Spirit upon him, water had been sanctified and out of it much evil had been cast. Jesus's baptism had been like an exorcism of the water. Jesus had suffered himself to be baptized in order to sanctify water. John's baptism had in consequence become purer and holier. It was for this end that Jesus was baptized in a separate basin. The water sanctified by contact with his divine Person had then been conducted to the Jordan and into the public pool of baptism, and of it also Jesus and his disciples had taken some for baptism in distant towns and villages.

HESHVAN (29 days):
October 26/27 to November 23/24, AD 29
Heshvan New Moon: October 26 at
3:00 AM Jerusalem time

[*Note concerning the calendar: The forty days in the wilderness were "Jewish days," in which the day began at dusk and extended until the following sunset. The 40-day period began with the onset of the sabbath evening of Friday, October 21, which was the beginning of Tishri 26 in the Jewish calendar. The last of the forty days—which equated with Kislev 6 in the Jewish calendar—ended on the evening of Wednesday, November 30. That evening, as Jesus descended from the mountain, Kislev 7 began. Jesus then traveled through the night until he reached the river Jordan.*]

KISLEV (30 days):
November 24/25 to December 23/24, AD 29
Kislev New Moon: November 24
at 2:00 PM Jerusalem time

(Follow Map 8)

Jesus Goes to the Jordan, and Orders Baptism to be Administered

Thursday, December 1, AD 29 (Kislev 7)

AT break of day Jesus went over the Jordan at the same narrow place which he had crossed forty days before. Some logs lay there to facilitate a passage. This was not the usual crossing place, the terminus of the public road, but a neighboring one. Jesus proceeded along the east bank of

Map 8: At the Second Place of Baptism
December 1–19, AD 29

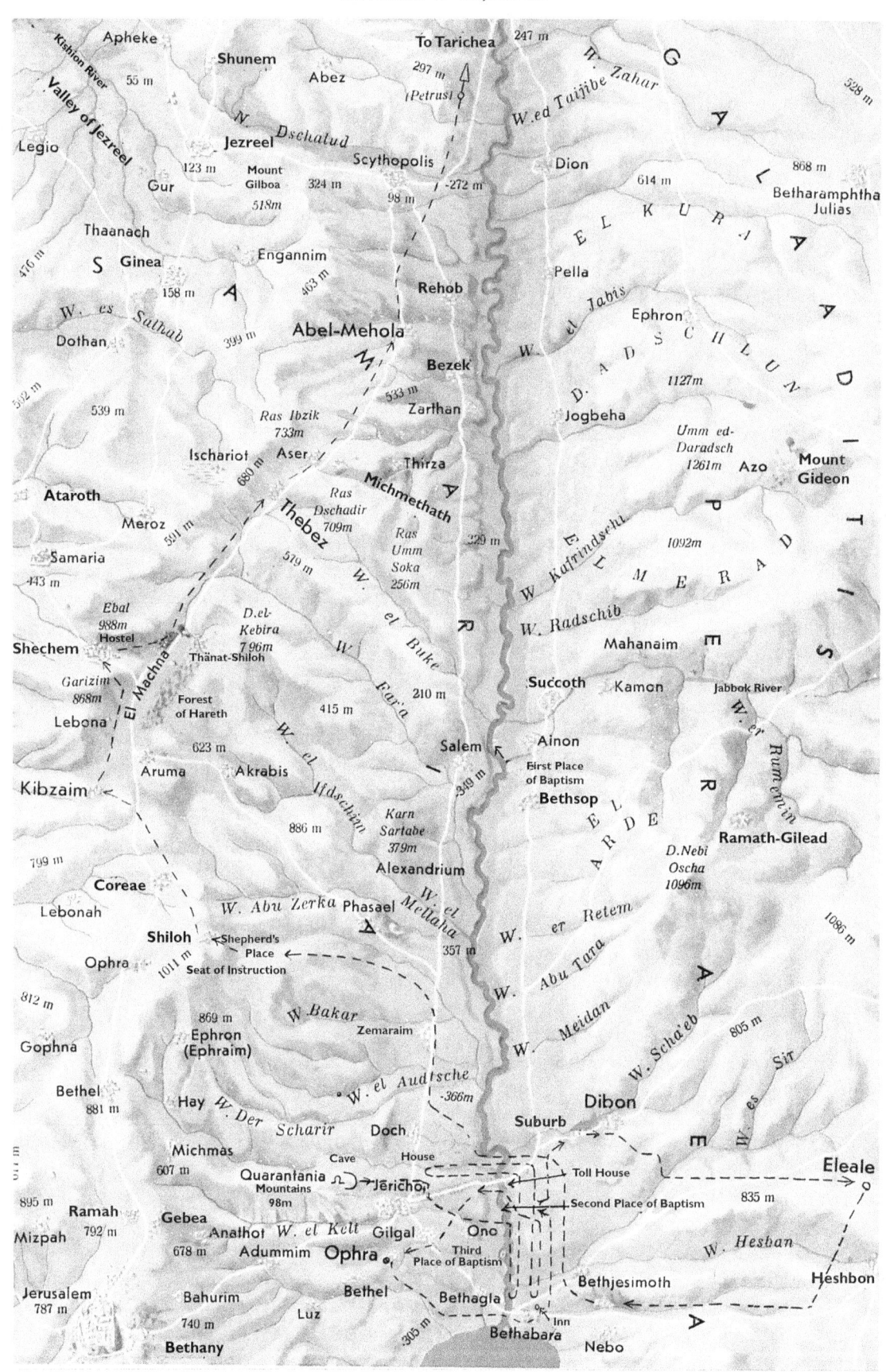

Quarantania—Bethabara—Publicans' Place—Bethabara—Ophra—Second Place of Baptism—Suburb of Dibon—Eleale—Bethjesimoth—Shiloh—Kibzaim—Sychar—Thebez—Abel-Mehola

the river up to a point directly opposite John's place of baptism. John at that moment was busy teaching and baptizing. Pointing straight across the river, he exclaimed: "Behold, the Lamb of God who taketh away the sins of the world." Jesus then turned away from the shore and returned to Bethabara.

Andrew and Saturnin, who had been standing near John, hurried over the river by the same way that Jesus had passed (John 1:35). They were followed by one of the cousins of Joseph of Arimathea, and two others of John's disciples. They ran after Jesus, who, turning, came to meet them, asking what they wanted. Andrew, overjoyed at having found him once more, asked him where he dwelt. Jesus answered by bidding them follow him (John 1:37–39),[B12] and he led them to an inn near the water and outside of Bethabara. There they entered and sat down. Jesus stayed all this day with the five disciples in Bethabara, and took a meal with them. He talked of his teaching mission about to begin and of his intention to choose his disciples. Andrew mentioned to him many of his own acquaintances whom he recommended as suitable for the work, among others Peter, Philip, and Nathaniel. Then Jesus spoke of baptizing here at the Jordan, and commissioned some of them to do so. Whereupon they objected that there was no convenient place around those parts. The only suitable locality was where John was baptizing, and it would never do to interfere with him. But Jesus spoke of John's vocation and mission, remarking that his work was well nigh its completion, and confirming all that John had said of himself and of the Messiah.

Andrew was the first of the future apostles to join Jesus as a disciple.

Jesus alluded also to his own preparation in the desert for the mission of teaching that was before him, and of the preparation necessary before undertaking any important work. Jesus was cordial and confidential toward the disciples, but they were humble and somewhat shy.

Friday, December 2, AD 29 (Kislev 8)

Jesus traveled with his five disciples to the place of the tax collectors where he had been on Tishri 13–14. After teaching there and at another place, he returned to Bethabara for the beginning of the sabbath.

Next morning Jesus went with the disciples from Bethabara to a group of houses that stood near the river ferry. Here he taught in presence of a small audience. After that he crossed the river and taught in a little village of about twenty houses, distant perhaps one hour from Jericho. Crowds of neophytes and John's disciples kept coming and going, to hear his words and report them to the Baptist. It was near midday when Jesus taught here.

After the sabbath Jesus commissioned several of the disciples to cross the Jordan and go up the river to the distance of about one hour from Bethabara, there to prepare a pool for baptism. The site chosen by Jesus was that upon which John, when going down from Ainon, had baptized before he had crossed to the west bank of the river opposite Bethabara.

Saturday, December 3, AD 29 (Kislev 9)

Jesus celebrated the sabbath in Bethabara and taught in the synagogue there.

The people of this place wanted to give Jesus an entertainment, but he would not stay. He crossed the Jordan and returned to Bethabara where he celebrated the sabbath and taught in the synagogue. He ate with the principal of the school and slept in his house.

The baptismal pool which John had used just before he removed near Jericho was soon put in order again by the disciples. It was not quite so large as that just mentioned. It had an elevated margin and a projecting tongue of land on which the baptizer could stand. A small canal surrounded it, and from this the water could be turned into the basin.

There were now as many as three pools for baptism: that above Bethabara, that of Jesus on the lately formed island in the Jordan, and that in use by John.

Sunday, December 4, AD 29 (Kislev 10)

Jesus made his way up the Jordan to the second place of baptism (near Gilgal), where John had baptized for only a short time. Jesus blessed the water. Andrew and Saturnin baptized, and Jesus taught from a nearby grassy mound concerning repentance, baptism, and the coming of the Holy Spirit. Those who came were mainly disciples of John the Baptist. But other followers of John complained about the rivalry presented by Jesus's baptizing. John reminded them that he was merely the forerunner (John 3:26–36). Jesus returned to Bethabara, staying there overnight.

On Jesus's arrival, he poured into the baptismal pool some of the water from the well on the island where he himself had been baptized, and blessed it. Andrew had brought the water with him in a flask. The neophytes became unusually touched and agitated. Andrew and Saturnin administered baptism, but not by complete immersion. The neophytes stood in the water near the edge of the pool, the sponsors' hands upon their shoulders, while the baptizers, dipping the water up in the hollow of their hand, poured it thrice over them, baptizing in the name of the Father and of the Son and of the Holy Spirit. John baptized somewhat differently. He used a three-channeled shell for dipping up the water. Crowds were baptized at this time, most of them from Peraea.

Jesus, standing on a little green hill nearby, instructed the people on penance, baptism, and the Holy Spirit. He said: "When I was baptized, my Father sent down the Holy Spirit and uttered the words, 'This is my beloved Son in whom I am well pleased.' These words are addressed to everyone that loves his heavenly Father and is sorry for his sins. Upon all that will be baptized in the name of the Father and of the Son and of the Holy Spirit, he sends his Holy Spirit. They then become his sons in whom he is well pleased, for he is the Father of all that receive his baptism and to him by the same are born again."

It is always a subject of astonishment to me that the Gospel narratives of the facts in Jesus's life are so short; for instance, it records the meeting of Jesus with Peter as happening close upon Andrew's following Jesus after the testimony of John; while in reality, Peter was at the time not in that part of the country, but in Galilee. But still more wonderful is it to read of the Last Supper and the Passion's following so closely the triumphal entrance of Jesus into Jerusalem, celebrated by us on Palm Sunday, since I always see so many days, and hear Jesus delivering so many instructions, between the two events. So I think that Jesus remained here fourteen days before going to Galilee.

Andrew had not as yet been formally received as a disciple; indeed, Jesus had not even called him. He had come of himself, had offered himself, for he would gladly be near Jesus. He was more eager to serve, more ready to offer service than Peter. Peter was ever ready to quiet himself with the thought: "Oh, I am too weak for that! That is beyond my strength," and so went about his own affairs. Saturnin and the two nephews of Joseph of Arimathea, Aram and Themeni, had, like Andrew, followed Jesus of their own accord.

John's place of baptism was daily becoming less frequented, and many more of his disciples would have gone over to Jesus, had they not been prevented by some others, pertinacious characters, who took it hard that so many of his disciples abandoned John. They complained to him about it, saying that Jesus had no right to baptize in those parts, that he was encroaching upon John's privilege, etc. John had some difficulty in convincing them to the contrary. He told them that they should call to mind his words and how he had always foretold what was now happening. He repeated that his duty was only to prepare the way, which done, he was to desist entirely from the work, and that that would be soon, since the way was almost prepared. But his disciples were greatly attached to him and they would not understand his words. Jesus's baptismal place was already so crowded that he told his disciples they should on the morrow move further down the river.

Monday, December 5, AD 29 (Kislev 11)
Early in the day, Jesus made his way to Ophra, south of Gilgal. He was accompanied by about twenty people, among then Andrew, Saturnin, and the two nephews of Joseph of Arimathea (Aram and Themeni). As he entered the town, some of those possessed cried out: "Here comes the prophet, the Son of God, Jesus Christ, our enemy; he will cast us out!" Jesus commanded them to be silent, whereupon they all became quiet and followed him to the synagogue. He taught there until evening and then retired to an inn.

With about twenty companions, among them Andrew, Saturnin, Aram, and Themeni, Jesus left Bethabara and went over the Jordan at the usual crossing place where the passage was easy. Leaving Gilgal on the right, he went to a very densely settled place called Ophra, situated in a narrow mountain valley. Hither flocked the merchants from the regions beyond Sodom and Gomorrha. With their camels laden with merchandise they passed to the east side of the Jordan, where they were baptized by John. There was at this place a byway leading from Judea to the Jordan. Ophra was in many respects quite forgotten. It was between three and four hours from John's place of baptism, not quite so far from Jericho, and from Jerusalem about seven hours. It was not exposed to the influence of the sun; consequently, though well built, it was cold. The inhabitants were made up of merchants, publicans, and smugglers. They were not exactly wicked, but they were indifferent, and as is often the case among traders and innkeepers, they cleared great profits; it seemed as if they made something off everyone that passed through their city. As yet they had paid little attention to John's baptism; they hungered not after salvation. Things went on here as in places of which it is said: Business thrives there.

When they approached Ophra, Jesus sent the nephews of Joseph of Arimathea on ahead, in order to get the key of the synagogue and to call the people to the instruction. Jesus always entrusted such messages to these youths, for they were very clever and amiable. At the entrance of the city the possessed and lunatics ran around Jesus, crying out: "Here comes the prophet, the Son of God, Jesus Christ, our enemy! He will drive us out!" Jesus commanded them to be silent and to cease their frantic gestures. All became quiet and followed him into the synagogue, to which he had to go from almost one end of the city to the other. There he taught till evening, going out only once to take some refreshment. His theme was, as usual, the nearness of the kingdom of God and the necessity of baptism. In vigorous words he warned the inhabitants to awake from their indifference and fancied security, lest judgement should come upon them. He spoke in strong terms against their usury, their smuggling, and such sins as are common to publicans and merchants. His hearers did not contradict him, though they were not very well disposed. They were captives to their gains. Still, some of them were really touched and very much changed by his teaching. That evening several of the most important men of the city, as well as some of the humblest class, called upon Jesus at the inn. They had resolved to receive baptism, and on the following day they went to John.

Tuesday, December 6, AD 29 (Kislev 12)

Next morning Jesus and his disciples left Ophra and returned to Bethabara. On the way they separated, Andrew and the greater number being sent on ahead by the same route by which they had come; while Jesus with Saturnin and Joseph of Arimathea's nephews went on toward John's place of baptism, taking the same road as at the time upon which John rendered to him the first public testimony after his baptism. On the way he entered some of the houses, taught their occupants, and exhorted them to baptism. They reached Bethabara in the afternoon, where Jesus again delivered an instruction at the place of baptism. Andrew and Saturnin baptized the crowds that succeeded one another. Jesus's teaching was generally the same; that is, that to all that did penance and were baptized his heavenly Father had said: "This is my beloved Son," and that, in truth, all then became God's children.

Most of those who now received baptism were under the jurisdiction of the Tetrarch Philip, who was a good man. His people were tolerably happy, and therefore had thought little about receiving baptism.

Wednesday, December 7, AD 29 (Kislev 13)

Accompanied by three disciples, Jesus journeyed from Bethabara to Dibon, where he had been at the start of the Feast of Tabernacles (Tishri 15). There he taught at the synagogue and also addressed some workers in the fields, speaking of the parable of the sower (Matthew 13:2).

From Bethabara Jesus, with three disciples, went up through the valley to Dibon, where he had lately been for the Feast of Tabernacles. He taught in some houses, also in the synagogue, which was somewhat distant from the city on the road running through the valley. Jesus did not enter Dibon itself. He stayed overnight at a poor, retired inn which indeed was little more than a shed where the field laborers from the country around obtained food and lodging. It was now seed time on the sunny side of the valley, the crops of which were to ripen about Passover. They had to dig the ground here, for it was made up of soil, sand, and stone. They could not use the implement generally employed in breaking up the ground. Part of the standing-out harvest was now gathered in for the first time. The inhabitants of this valley, which was about three hours in length, were good people, of simple habits, and well inclined toward Jesus.

In the synagogue, as also among the field laborers, Jesus related and explained the parable of the sower. He did not always explain his parables. He often related them to the Pharisees without an explanation.

Thursday, December 8, AD 29 (Kislev 14)

Jesus taught all day in a valley near Dibon. Andrew, Saturnin, and the other disciples returned to Ophra to encourage those who had been awakened there by Jesus's teaching.

Andrew and Saturnin with some other disciples went afterward to Ophra, to confirm in their good resolutions those that Jesus had roused by his teaching.

Friday, December 9, AD 29 (Kislev 15)

When Jesus left the inn near Dibon, he started southward for Eleale about four hours distant, taking a road two hours farther to the southeast of the Jordan than that by which he had come thither from Bethabara. He arrived with about seven disciples, and put up with one of the elders of the synagogue.

Saturday, December 10, AD 29 (Kislev 16)

Jesus remained in Eleale for the sabbath and the following night.

When the sabbath began, he taught in the synagogue taking for his subject a parable upon the waving branches of a tree scattering around their blossoms and bearing no fruit. By this parable Jesus intended to rebuke the inhabitants, who for the most part had not become better after having received John's baptism. They allowed the blossoms of penance to be scattered by every wind without bearing fruit. Such were they here. Jesus chose this similitude because these people found their support chiefly in the cultivation of fruit. They had to carry it far away for sale, as no highroad passed near their isolated city. They were also largely engaged in coarse embroidery and the manufacture of covers.

Up to the present Jesus had met no contradiction. The people of Dibon and the country around loved him, and said that never before had they heard such a teacher. The old men always likened him to the prophets of whose teaching they had heard from their forefathers.

Sunday, December 11, AD 29 (Kislev 17)

After the sabbath Jesus went about three hours westward to Bethjesimoth on the east side of a mountain, the sunny side, about one hour from the Jordan. Andrew and Saturnin with some others of John's disciples met him on the way. Jesus spoke to them of the children of Israel who had formerly encamped here, and of Joshua and Moses who had instructed them, applying it to the present time and to his own teaching. Bethjesimoth was not a large place, but it was very fruitful, especially in wine.

Just as Jesus arrived, some demoniacs, who had been confined together in a house, were led out into the open air. All at once they began to rage and to cry: "There he comes, the prophet! He will drive us out!" Jesus turned, enjoined silence upon them, commanded their fetters to fall, and that they should follow him into the synagogue. Their chains fell miraculously and the poor creatures became quite calm. They cast themselves down before Jesus, thanked him, and followed him into the synagogue. There he taught in parables of the culture of the vine and its fruitfulness, after which he visited and cured many sick in their homes. Bethjesimoth did not lie on any highroad. The people had to carry their fruit to market themselves.

Monday, December 12, AD 29 (Kislev 18)

Jesus stayed in Bethjesimoth all day, teaching and healing.

Jesus healed here for the first time since his return from the desert. On account of the cures wrought among them, the people were urgent in their prayers for him to remain. But he departed.

Tuesday, December 13, AD 29 (Kislev 19)

With Andrew, Saturnin, Joseph of Arimathea's nephews [Aram and Themeni], and others, about twelve in all, he went in an oblique line toward the north until he reached the public ferry leading to the highroad of Dibon, over which he had crossed in going from Gilgal to Dibon at the Feast of Tabernacles. It takes tolerably long to cross the river at this point, because the steep bank directly opposite does not afford a landing place. From here Jesus and his little company journeyed on for about an hour over the base of a mountain in the direction of Samaria, until they arrived at a small place consisting of only one row of houses and which had no school.

It was occupied entirely by shepherds and kindhearted people, who were clothed in almost the same style as the shepherds I saw at the crib. Jesus taught in the open air on a little elevation whereon a teacher's chair of stone was erected. The people here had received John's baptism.

Jesus in Shiloh, Kibzaim, and Thebez

Wednesday, December 14, AD 29 (Kislev 20)

Toward evening Jesus and his companions arrived at the town of Shiloh, where there were two synagogues—one belonging to the Pharisees and the other to the Sadducees. A group of Pharisees and Sadducees gathered to dispute with Jesus. They spoke of the voice of thunder at his baptism. Jesus replied that this was the voice of his heavenly Father—the Father of all who repent their sins and are born again through baptism. His hearers were furious at the things he spoke of and left seething with rage.

I NEXT saw Jesus in Shiloh, a city built around a high, steep rock with an extended plateau on a gently rising mountain range. On this plateau, the highest elevation of the mountain range, in early times after the departure from Egypt and during the journey through the desert, the Tabernacle with the Ark of the Covenant had rested. There was a large space surrounded by a wall partly in ruins, and in it might still be seen the remains of the little building that had been erected over the Tabernacle. On the spot whereon the Ark had stood, under a roof which rested upon open arches, was a pillar similar to the one in Gilgal, and under it a kind of vault excavated in the rocky foundation. Not far from the spot occupied by the Ark was a place for offering sacrifice and a covered pit for the reception of the refuse of the slaughter, for they were permitted to offer sacrifice here three or four times in the year. The synagogue also was built on this enclosed space of the plateau, from which was presented a widely extended view. From it one could see the plateau of Jerusalem, the Sea of Galilee, and far over many mountains.

Shiloh itself was a somewhat dilapidated and not very populous city. It possessed two schools, one belonging to the Pharisees, the other to the Sadducees. But the people were not good; they were arrogant, full of self-conceit and false assurance. At some distance from the city gate with its dilapidated towers stood an Essene cloister now fallen to ruin, and nearer to the city was the house wherein the Benjaminites had confined the virgins whom, at the Feast of Tabernacles, they had brought captive to Shiloh.

Jesus with his twelve companions put up at a house at which traveling teachers and prophets were privileged. It was adjoining the schools and dwellings of the Pharisees and scribes, who had a kind of seminary here. About twenty of these scribes in their long robes and girdles, with long, rough tufts hanging from their sleeves, gathered around Jesus. They feigned not to know him, and spoke of Jesus as of a third person, using all kinds of cutting speeches, such as: "Now, how will it be? There are two

Under the Arches

baptisms, that of John and that of Jesus, the carpenter's son of Galilee. Which, now, will be the right baptism?" They went on to say that they had heard also that women attached themselves to the mother of this carpenter's son; for instance, a widow with her two sons. These latter, at the instigation of their mother, joined the followers of Jesus, while she herself went with his mother, and so they traveled about. But as for themselves, they needed not such novelties. They had the Promise and the Law. All this they did not express bluntly and rudely, but with a semblance of mock friendship for Jesus. He answered their pointed speeches by saying that he was the one of whom they were speaking. And when they referred to the voice heard at his baptism, he informed them that it was the voice of his heavenly Father, who was the Father of everyone who would repent of his sins and be regenerated by baptism.

Then, affecting to consider it a very sacred place, they expressed unwillingness to allow Jesus and his disciples to enter the enclosure where formerly the Ark of the Covenant had stood. But Jesus, heedless of their opposition, entered. He reproached them with having, on account of their wickedness, lost the Ark of the Covenant; that now, preserving only the remembrance of it, they were still just as bad; that they had always violated the Law in the past, as well as in the present; and that, as the Ark had been withdrawn from the keeping of their ancestors, so now would the fulfillment of the Law be taken from themselves. As these men showed a desire to dispute with him on some points of the Law, he stood them out, two by two, and interrogated them like children, proposing to them many deep questions in the Law. They were unable to answer; so, confused and angry, muttering and nudging one another with the elbow, they began to slink away. Then Jesus led them to the covered pit in which had been thrown the refuse of the sacrifice. He ordered them to uncover it and told them in a similitude that they were like unto that pit, inwardly full of ordure and rottenness and unfit for sacrifice, though outwardly clean, their unsightliness covered over by a fine exterior. He reminded them that from this very spot, as punishment of the sins of their forefathers, the Holy Ark had been taken away. They all left the place in anger.

Thursday, Dec. 15, AD 29 (Kislev 21)

When Jesus taught in the synagogue, he insisted especially upon the reverence due the aged and love toward parents. He spoke warmly on these points, for the people of Shiloh had long been in the wicked habit of slighting, despising, and disowning their aged parents.

A road led to Shiloh from Bethel on the south. Lebona was not far distant, and to Samaria from Bethel it may have been from eight to nine hours. The prophet Jonah lies buried at Shiloh.

Friday, December 16, AD 29 (Kislev 22)

This morning, Andrew, Saturnin, Aram, and Themeni took leave of Jesus and set off for Galilee. Andrew went to his brother Simon Peter (John 1:41). Jesus and the remaining disciples journeyed to Kibzaim for the sabbath. There, they met Lazarus and his servant, together with Martha, Johanna Chusa, and Simeon's son, who were all on their way to the wedding at Cana.

When Jesus left Shiloh from the opposite side of the city, the northwest, Andrew, Saturnin, and Joseph of Arimathea's nephews separated from him, and proceeded on ahead to Galilee. Jesus with some disciples of John, then in his company, directed his steps to Kibzaim, where he arrived before the sabbath. Kibzaim lay in a valley between two branches of a mountain range that extended through the middle of the country, and assumed in this place almost the exact shape of a wolf's claw. The people were good, hospitable souls, and well-inclined to Jesus, whose coming they were expecting. Kibzaim was a Levitical city. Jesus put up near the school with one of the head men.

There arrived also to salute Jesus, Lazarus, Martha, Johanna Chusa, the son of Simeon (who was employed at the temple), and the old servant of the first named. They were on their way to the wedding at Cana, and had been informed by messengers that they would here meet Jesus. Jesus, from the very first, always treated Lazarus with distinction and as a very dear friend. And yet I never heard him ask: How is such or such a one of thy relatives or acquaintances?

Saturday, December 17, AD 29 (Kislev 23)

After the sabbath morning service, Jesus healed by word of command several people who had been carried to a place in front of the synagogue. He was invited to a meal at the home of a distinguished Levite. At the close of the sabbath Jesus went to Shechem, where he stayed the night at an inn.

Kibzaim was a solitary place hidden away in a corner of the mountain. The inhabitants subsisted chiefly by the cultivation of fruits. The manufacture of tents and carpets was also carried on, and many were engaged in sandal-making. Jesus spent the sabbath here, and cured several sick persons by a word of command. Some were dropsical and others simpletons. They were brought on litters to Jesus and set down in front of the school. Jesus took a repast at the house of a distinguished Levite. After the sabbath he went again to Shechem, where he arrived late, and passed the night at an inn appointed for him. Lazarus and his party went from Kibzaim straight to Galilee.

Sunday, December 18, AD 29 (Kislev 24)

Early this morning, Jesus left Shechem and traveled to Thebez. As he entered the town, those possessed cried out: "Here comes the prophet of Galilee! He has power over us! He will cast us out!" Jesus commanded them to be quiet and they became silent. He taught in the synagogue, healing many. That evening—the start of Kislev 25 in the Jewish calendar—the Feast of the Dedication of the Temple began, which Jesus celebrated here.

Early next morning, Jesus went from Shechem northeastwardly toward Thebez. In Shechem, he could not teach. There were no Jews there. The inhabitants were made up of Samaritans and some others who had settled there either after the Babylonian Captivity, or in consequence of a war. They used to go up to the temple at Jerusalem, though they did not join in the Jewish sacrifices. Near Shechem is that beautiful field which Jacob bought for his son Joseph. A part of it already belonged to Herod of Galilee. A boundary consisting of stakes, a rampart of earth, and a path ran through the valley.

Thebez was quite an important city, traversed by a highway and possessed of considerable trade. Heavily laden camels, their burdens rising high upon their backs, came and went. It was something wonderful to see those animals with their packs like so many little towers, climbing slowly over the mountain, their head at the end of the long neck moving from side to side before their lofty burden. Raw silk formed a chief staple of trade. The people of Thebez were not bad, nor were they prejudiced against Jesus, but they were neither simple nor childlike. They were indifferent, as well-to-do tradespeople often are. The priests and scribes were content with themselves and indifferent to others. As Jesus entered the city, the possessed and the lunatics raised their cry: "There comes the prophet of Galilee! He has power over us! He will drive us away!" Jesus commanded them silence, and instantly they became quiet. Jesus put up near the synagogue whither the crowds followed him, bringing with them their sick, of whom he healed many. That evening he taught in the school and celebrated the Feast of Dedication, which then began. In the school and in all the houses seven lights were lit, also outdoors in the fields and on the roads near the shepherds' huts were little burning tufts of something on the ends of stakes. Thebez was admirably situated on the mountain. At some distance, one could see the mountain road running through it and the laden camels climbing up; but near the city the view was hidden.

Andrew, Saturnin, and Joseph's nephews had already left Shiloh and gone to Galilee. Andrew had been up among his relatives at Bethsaida. He had informed Peter that he had again found the Messiah, who was on his way up to Galilee, and that he would take him (Peter) to him.

All went now to Arbela, called also Betharbel, to see Nathaniel Chased, who was there on business, and to induce him to go with them to celebrate the feast at Gennabris. Chased resided at that time in Gennabris in a high house that, with several others, stood by itself outside the city. The disciples spoke much to him of Jesus. Andrew had purposely taken them there for the feast because he, as well as they, counted upon Nathaniel. They were eager to hear his opinion, but Nathaniel appeared rather indifferent to the whole affair.

Lazarus had brought Martha and Johanna Chusa to Mary then at Capernaum, whither she had come from Cana. They set off again for Tiberias where they hoped to meet Jesus. Simeon's son was one of the escorts, and the bridegroom of Cana went also to meet the Lord. This bridegroom was the son of the daughter of Sobe, the sister of Anne. His name was Nathaniel. He did not belong to Cana, though he was married there. Gennabris was a populous city. A highway ran through it, and there was much business and traffic carried on, especially in silk. It was in the country, a couple of hours from Tiberias, from which it was separated by mountains. To reach it, one had to go

First Formal Call of Peter, Philip, and Nathaniel

Monday, December 19, AD 29 (Kislev 25)

Before daybreak, Jesus left Thebez and traveled north toward Galilee. On the way, he paused briefly in Abel-Mehola, the birthplace of the prophet Elisha, and then continued on again. On the road leading to Tarichea, Jesus encountered Andrew, Simon Peter, and John. Andrew introduced his brother to Jesus. Jesus looked at him and said: "Thou art Simon, the son of Jonah; thou shalt be called Cephas" [which means Peter, the rock] (John 1:42). To John, he said something about seeing him again another time. Peter and John then journeyed on to Gennabris while Jesus, together with his disciples (including Andrew), continued on their way toward Tarichea. By this time, John the Baptist had abandoned his third place of baptism (near Ono) and returned to the second place (near Gilgal), where Jesus had instructed his disciples to baptize.

JESUS departed before daybreak from Thebez. He and his disciples proceeded at first eastward, and then turning to the north, journeyed along the base of the mountain and through the valley of the Jordan toward Tiberias. He passed through Abel-Mehola, a beautiful city, where the mountain extends more to the north. It was the birthplace of Elisha. The city is built on a spur of the mountain, and I noticed the great difference between the fruitfulness of its sunny side and its northern one. The inhabitants were tolerably good. They had heard of the miracles wrought by Jesus at Kibzaim and Thebez, so they stayed with him on the way, begging him to tarry with them and heal their sick. The excitement became almost tumultuous, but Jesus did not stay with them long. This city was about four hours from Thebez. Jesus passed near Scythopolis and on to the Jordan.

As he was journeying from Abel-Mehola, he met near a little city about six hours from Tiberias, Andrew, Peter, and John. Leaving the other friends in Gennabris, these three had come on to meet Jesus. Peter and John were in this part of the country upon some business connected with their fishery. They intended to proceed direct to Gennabris, but Andrew persuaded them to go first to meet the Lord. Andrew presented his brother to Jesus, who among other words said to him: "Thou art Simon, the son of Jonah; thou shalt be called Cephas." This was said at the first salutation. To John, Jesus addressed some words relative to their next meeting. Then Peter and John went out to Gennabris, while Andrew accompanied Jesus into the environs of Tarichea.

John the Baptist had by this time abandoned his place of baptism on this side of the Jordan [near Ono]. He had crossed the river and was now baptizing about one hour to the north of Bethabara, at the place whereon Jesus had lately allowed the disciples to baptize and where John himself had baptized at an earlier period. John had made this change to suit the convenience of the people from the region under Philip the Tetrarch. Philip was a good-natured man. Many of his people desired baptism, but were unwilling to cross the Jordan to receive it. Among them were many of the pagans. The last visit that Jesus made to this part of the country had roused in numbers the desire after baptism. Another reason also influenced John to baptize where Jesus's disciples had lately been similarly engaged, and that was to show that there was no disunion between him and Jesus.

(Follow Map 9)

Tuesday, December 20, AD 29 (Kislev 26)

Jesus and his traveling companions did not go into Tarichea, but stayed at an inn just outside the town. Jesus was visited there by Lazarus, Saturnin, Simeon's son, and the bridegroom Nathaniel, who was to be married at the wedding at Cana. Nathaniel invited Jesus and everyone else to attend his wedding. That evening, they remained at the inn and celebrated the Feast of the Dedication of the Temple, which lasted from the evening of December 18 (start of Kislev 25) to the evening of December 26 (end of Tebeth 2).

When Jesus with Andrew reached the neighborhood of Tarichea, he put up near the lake at a house belonging to Peter's fishery. Andrew had previously given orders for preparations to be made for Jesus's reception. Jesus did not go into the city. There was something dark and repulsive about the inhabitants, who were deeply engaged in usury and thought only of gain. Simon, who here had some employment, had with Thaddeus and James the Less, his brothers, gone for the feast to Gennabris, where James the Greater and John were. Lazarus, Saturnin, and Simeon's son came here to meet Jesus, as also the bridegroom of Cana. The last named invited Jesus and all his company to his marriage.

Wednesday, December 21, AD 29 (Kislev 27)

Today, Jesus wandered about in the neighboring hills with some of his disciples. That evening, they gathered at the inn and prayed together, lighting the candles for the Feast of the Dedication. Andrew busied himself writing letters with a reed upon strips of parchment. These were to be sent by messengers to Philip, Peter, and his half-brother Jonathan, notifying them that Jesus would be in Capernaum for the sabbath.

The principal motive that led Jesus to pass a couple of days in the vicinity of Tarichea was that he desired to give the future apostles and disciples time to communicate to one another the reports circulated about himself, and especially what Andrew and Saturnin had to relate. He desired also that, by more frequent contact, they should better understand one another. While Jesus traversed the country around Tarichea, I saw Andrew remaining in the house. He was busy writing letters with a reed upon strips of parchment. The writings could be rolled into a little hollow, wooden cylinder and unrolled at pleasure. I saw men and youths frequently entering the house, and seeking employment. Andrew engaged them as couriers to convey to Philip and his half-brother Jonathan, also to Peter and the others at Gennabris, letters notifying them that Jesus would go to Capernaum for the sabbath and engaging them to meet him there.

Meanwhile a messenger arrived from Capernaum begging Andrew to solicit Jesus to go thither right away, for a messenger from Kedesh had been there awaiting him for the past few days. This man wanted to ask Jesus for help.

Thursday, December 22, AD 29 (Kislev 28)
Today, Jesus went to Capernaum accompanied by Andrew, Saturnin, Obed, and several other disciples. On the way, Andrew parted company with Jesus and went to meet his half-brother Jonathan, who was with Philip. He told them that Jesus was truly the Messiah. In Capernaum, Jesus and his traveling companions stayed at a house belonging to Nathaniel, the bridegroom. Here a messenger from Kedesh came to see Jesus. His master's son was very ill, and he begged Jesus to come and heal the child. Jesus gave instructions to be followed, whereupon the child was healed without his direct presence.

Accordingly, with Andrew, Saturnin, Obed, and some of John's disciples, Jesus set out from the fisherhouse near Tarichea to Capernaum. This last named city was not close to the lake, but on the plateau and southern slope of a mountain. On the western side of the lake, the mountain formed a valley through which the Jordan flowed into the lake. Jesus and his companions went separately, Andrew with his half-brother Jonathan, and Philip—both of whom had come in answer to his notification—walked together. Jonathan and Philip had not yet met Jesus. Andrew spoke enthusiastically to them. He told them all that he had seen of Jesus, and protested that he was indeed the Messiah. If they desired to follow him, he added, there was no need of their presenting to him a formal petition to that effect; all they had to do was to regard him attentively, and he, seeing their earnest wish, would give them a hint, a word to join his followers.

Mary and the holy women were not in Capernaum itself, but at Mary's house in the valley outside the city and nearer to the lake. It was there that they celebrated the feast. The sons of Mary Cleophas, Peter, James the Greater, and his brother John had already arrived from Gennabris with others of the future disciples. Chased (Nathaniel), Thomas, Bartholomew, and Matthias, however, were not present. But there were many other relatives and friends of the holy family who had been invited to Cana for the wedding, celebrating the sabbath here, because they had been notified that Jesus was expected.

Jesus along with Andrew, Saturnin, some of John's disciples, Lazarus, and Obed, stopped at a house belonging to the bridegroom Nathaniel. Nathaniel's parents were dead. They had left a large patrimony to their son.

The future disciples, just come from Gennabris, experienced a certain shyness in Jesus's company. They were actuated in this by the influence Nathaniel Chased's opinion had over them, and then again by the thought of the wonderful things they had heard of Jesus from Andrew and some others of John's disciples. They were restrained also by their own natural bashfulness and likewise by the remembrance of what Andrew had told them; that is, that they were not to make advances themselves, but merely pay attention to the teaching of Jesus, for that would be sufficient to make them decide to follow him.

For two whole days had the messenger from Kedesh been waiting here for Jesus. Now he approached him, cast himself at his feet, and informed him that he was the servant of a man of Kedesh. His master, he said, entreated Jesus to return with him and cure his little son who was afflicted with leprosy and a mute devil. This man was a most faithful servant; he placed his master's trouble before Jesus in very pathetic words. Jesus replied that he could not return with him, but still the child should receive assistance, for he was an innocent boy. Then he directed the servant to tell his master to stretch himself with extended arms over his son, to recite certain prayers, and the leprosy would disappear. After which, he, the servant himself, should lie upon the boy and breathe into his mouth. A blue vapor would then escape from the boy and he would be freed from muteness. I had a glimpse of the father and servant curing the boy, as Jesus had directed.

There were certain mysterious reasons for the command that the father and the servant should stretch themselves alternately upon the boy. The servant himself was the true

Map 9: The Wedding at Cana
December 19, AD 29– January 2, AD 30

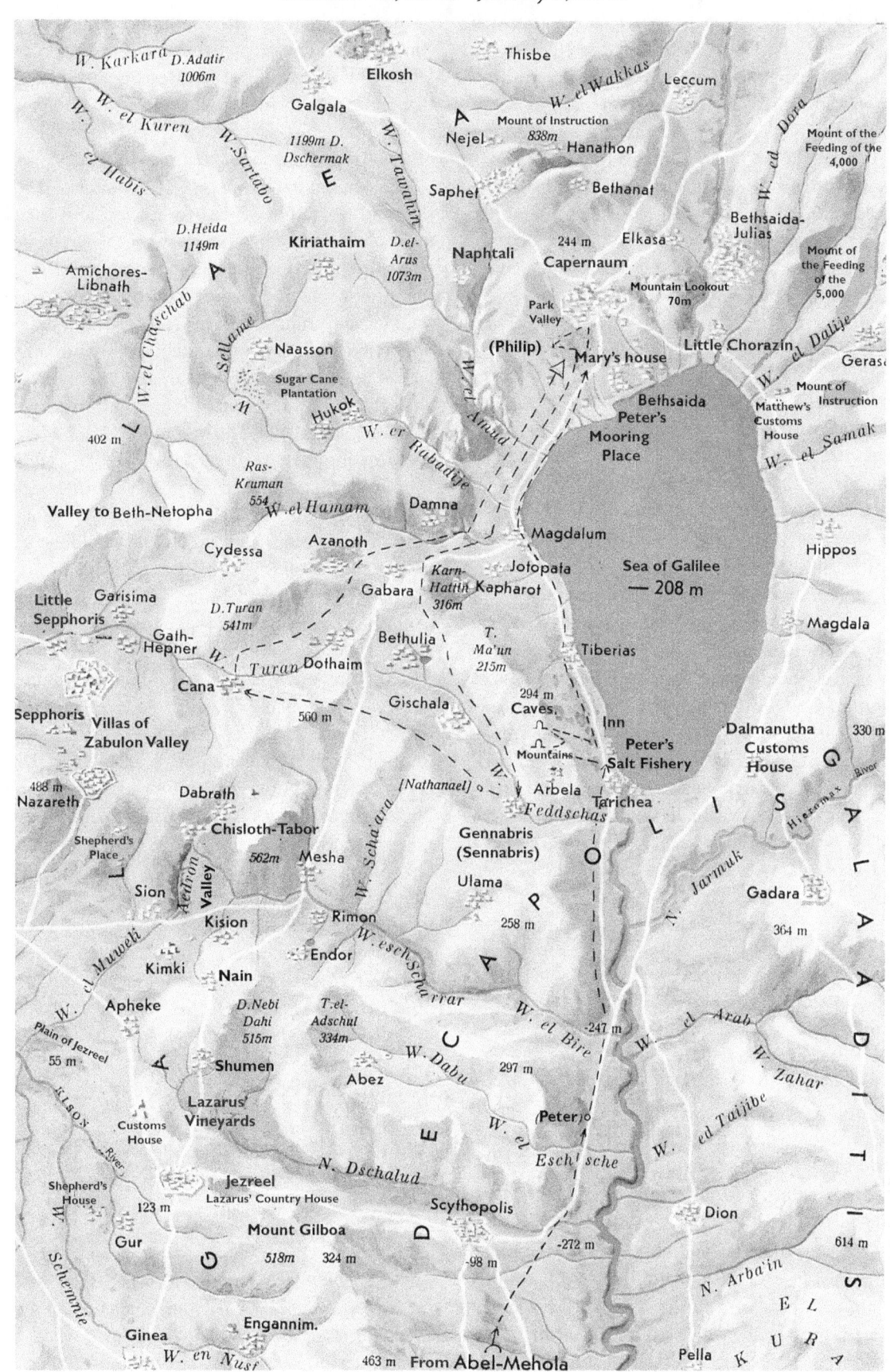

Tarichea—Capernaum—Gennabris—Cana—Capernaum

father of the child, of which fact, however, the master was ignorant. But Jesus knew it. Both had therefore to be instrumental in freeing the child from the penalty of sin.

Kedesh was about six hours from Capernaum, on the boundary toward Tyre and west of Paneas. It was once the capital of the Canaanites, but was now a free city whither the prosecuted might flee from justice. It bordered on a region called Kabul, which had been presented by Solomon to the king of Phoenicia. I saw this region ever dark, gloomy, dismal. Jesus always shunned it when going to Tyre and Sidon. I think robbery and murder were freely carried on in it.

Friday, December 23, AD 29 (Kislev 29)
That evening, at the start of the sabbath, Jesus taught in the synagogue. Many friends and relatives were in attendance, including the holy Virgin Mary. In connection with the lighting of candles at the Feast of Dedication, Jesus spoke of the light that should not be hidden under a bushel (Matthew 5:17).

When on the sabbath Jesus taught in the synagogue, an unusually large crowd was assembled to hear him, and among his audience were all his friends and relatives. His teaching was entirely novel to these people, and quite transporting in its eloquence. He spoke of the nearness of the kingdom of God, of the light that should not be hidden under a bushel, of sowing, and of faith like unto a mustard seed. He taught, not in naked parables, but with explanations. The parables were short examples and similitudes, which he used to explain his doctrine more clearly. I have indeed heard him in his teaching making use of a great many more parables than are related in the Gospel. Those there recorded are such as he most frequently used with explanations more or less varied to suit the occasion.

Saturday, December 24, AD 29 (Kislev 30)
At the close of the sabbath, he and his disciples went for a walk in the little vale nearby. Philip, who was modest and humble, hung back. Jesus turned and said to him: "Follow me" (John 1:43), whereupon Philip, filled with joy, joined the other disciples. That evening, after returning to the town, Jesus visited his mother—several other relatives were also gathered there—and together they celebrated the New Moon festival (start of the month of Tebeth).

Jesus taught again, morning and afternoon, in the synagogue. After the close of the sabbath, Jesus went with his disciples into a little valley near the synagogue. It seemed intended for a promenade or a place of seclusion. There were trees in front of the entrance, as well as in the valley. The sons of Mary Cleophas, of Zebedee, and some others of the disciples were with him. But Philip, who was backward and humble, hung behind, not certain as to whether he should or should not follow. Jesus, who was going on before, turned his head and, addressing Philip, said: "Follow me!" at which words Philip went on joyously with the others. There were about twelve in the little band.

Jesus taught here under a tree, his subject being "Vocation and Correspondence." Andrew, who was full of zeal for his Master's interests, rejoiced at the happy impression made upon the disciples by the teaching of Jesus on the preceding sabbath. He saw them convinced that Jesus was the Messiah, and his own heart was so full that he lost no opportunity to recount to them again and again all that he had seen at Jesus's baptism, also the miracles he had wrought.

I heard Jesus calling heaven to witness that they should behold still greater things, and he spoke of his mission from his heavenly Father.

He alluded also to their own vocation, telling them to hold themselves in readiness. They would, he continued, have to forsake all when he called them. He would provide for them, they should suffer no want. They might still continue their customary occupations, because as the Passover was now approaching he would have to discharge other affairs. But when he should call them, they should follow him immediately. The disciples questioned him unrestrainedly as to how they should manage with regard to their families. Peter, for instance, said that just at present he could not leave his old stepfather, who was also Philip's uncle. But Jesus relieved his anxiety by his answer, that he would not begin before the Passover feast; that only insofar as the heart was concerned, should they detach themselves from their occupations; that exteriorly they should continue them until he called them. In the meantime, however, they should take the necessary steps toward freeing themselves from their different avocations. Jesus then left the valley by the opposite end, and went to his mother's house, one of a row that stood between Capernaum and Bethsaida. His nearest relatives accompanied him, for their mothers also were with Mary.

TEBETH (29 days):
December 24/25, AD 29, to January 21/22,
AD 30, Tebeth New Moon: December 24
at 2:45 AM Jerusalem time

Sunday, December 25, AD 29 (Tebeth 1)
The holy Virgin and her companions set off along the road leading to Cana. Jesus and his disciples went a more circuitous route. They traveled through Gennabris, where Jesus taught in the synagogue. While he

did so, Philip sought out Nathaniel Chased, who worked in Gennabris as a clerk. Philip found Nathaniel and said to him: "We have found him of whom Moses in the Law and also the Prophets wrote, Jesus of Nazareth, the son of Joseph." Nathaniel replied: "Can anything good come from Nazareth?" Philip then said to him: "Come and see" (John 1:45–46). Philip and Nathaniel then set off along the road to Cana, and soon caught up with Jesus. Philip called out: "Master! I bring you here one who has asked: Can anything good come from Nazareth?" Jesus, turning to the disciples, said, as Nathaniel came up to them, "Behold, a true Israelite in whom there is no guile!" (John 1:47). Then followed the exchange of words between Jesus and Nathaniel Chased reported in John 1:48–51. Everyone then went on to Cana, where Jesus was received by the bridegroom, Nathaniel, and by the bride's father, Israel, by her mother, and the holy Virgin.

Very early the next morning, Jesus with his relatives and disciples started for Cana. Mary and the other women went by themselves, taking the more direct and shorter route. It was only a narrow footpath running for the most part over a mountain. The women chose it as being the more private. It was besides wide enough for them, as they usually walked single file. A guide went on ahead, and a servant followed at some distance. Their journey was to the southwest of Capernaum, almost seven hours.

Jesus and his companions took a more circuitous route through Gennabris. The road was broader and better suited to conversation. Jesus taught along the way. He often halted, gave utterance to some truth, and then explained it. This road was more to the south than that which Mary took. It was almost six hours by it from Capernaum to Gennabris, at which place it turned southward, and three hours more took the traveler to Cana.

Gennabris was a beautiful city. It had a school and a synagogue. There was also a school of rhetoric, and the trade carried on was extensive. Nathaniel had his office outside the city in a high house that stood by itself, though there were others at some distance around it. In spite of the invitation received from the disciples to that effect, he did not go into the city to meet Jesus.

Jesus taught in the synagogue and, with some of the disciples, took a luncheon at the house of a rich Pharisee. The rest of the disciples had already continued their journey to Cana. Jesus had commissioned Philip to go to Nathaniel and bring him to meet him on the way.

Jesus was very honorably treated at Gennabris, and the inhabitants were eager to keep him with them longer. They brought forward as a reason for his doing so that he was one of their own countrymen, and also that he should have compassion on their sick. But Jesus soon left them and proceeded to Cana.

Meantime Philip had gone to Nathaniel's office, in which he found several clerks, Nathaniel being in a room upstairs. Philip had never before spoken of Jesus to Nathaniel, since he, Nathaniel, had not accompanied his friends to Gennabris. They were, however, well acquainted with each other, and Philip, full of joy, was enthusiastic when speaking of Jesus. "He is," he said, "the Messiah of whom the prophets have spoken. We have found him, Jesus of Nazareth, the son of Joseph."

Nathaniel was of a bright, lively disposition, energetic and self-reliant, consequently frank and sincere. In reply to Philip's remarks, Nathaniel said: "Can anything very good come from Nazareth?" He knew the reputation of the Nazareans, that they were of a contradictory spirit and were not distinguished for the wisdom of their schools. He thought that a man who had been educated there might indeed shine in the eyes of his credulous and simple-minded friends, but that he could never satisfy his own pretentious claims to learning. But Philip bade him come and see for himself, for Jesus would soon pass that way to Cana. Nathaniel accordingly accompanied Philip down by the short road to that house which stood a little off the highway to Cana. Jesus, with some of his disciples, was standing where the road branched off into the highway. Philip, since Jesus's injunction to follow him, had been as joyous and unrestrained as before he had been timid. Addressing Jesus in a loud voice as they approached, he said: "Rabbi! I bring you here one who has asked: 'What good can come from Nazareth?'" But Jesus, turning to the disciples who were standing around him, said as Nathaniel came forward: "Behold! A true Israelite, in whom there is no guile!" Jesus uttered the words in a kind, affectionate manner. Nathaniel responded: "How dost thou know me?" meaning to say: How knowest thou that I am true and without guile, since we have never before spoken to each other? Jesus answered: "Before Philip called thee, I saw thee when thou wast standing under the fig tree." These words Jesus accompanied by a significant look at Nathaniel intended to recall something to him.

This glance of Jesus instantly awoke in Nathaniel the remembrance of a certain passerby whose warning look had endued him with wonderful strength at a moment in which he was struggling with temptation. He had indeed been standing at the time under a fig tree on the pleasure grounds around the warm baths, gazing upon some beautiful women who, on the other side of the meadow, were playing for fruit. The powerful impression produced by that glance, and the victory which Jesus had then enabled him to gain, were fixed in his memory, though perhaps the form of the man to whom he owed both the one and the other had faded from his mind. Or he may indeed have recognized Jesus without being aware that the warning glance had been designedly given. But now that Jesus reminded him of it and repeated the significant glance, Nathaniel became greatly agitated and impressed. He felt that Jesus in passing had read his thoughts, and had been to him a guardian angel. Nathaniel was so pure of heart that a thought contrary to the holy virtue had power to trouble his soul. He recognized, therefore, in Jesus his Savior and Deliverer. This knowledge of his thoughts was enough for his upright, impetuous, and grateful heart, enough to make him, on the instant, joyfully acknowledge Jesus before all the disciples. Humbling himself before him as he uttered those significant words, Nathaniel exclaimed: "Rabbi! Thou art the Son of God! Thou art Israel's king!" Jesus responded: "Thou believest now because I have said that I saw thee under the fig tree. Verily, thou shalt greater wonders see!" And then turning to all, he said: "Verily! Ye shall see the heavens open and the angels of God ascending and descending over the Son of Man!" The other disciples, however, did not understand the real import of Jesus's words concerning the fig tree, nor did they know why Nathaniel Chased had so quickly declared for Jesus. It was like a matter of conscience hidden from all excepting John, to whom Nathaniel himself entrusted it at the marriage feast of Cana. Nathaniel asked Jesus whether he should at once leave all things and follow him, for that he had a brother, to whom he could make over his employment. Jesus answered him as he had the others on the preceding evening, and invited him to Cana for the marriage feast.

Then Jesus and his disciples proceeded on their way to Cana, Nathaniel Chased meanwhile returning home to prepare for the wedding, for which he set out on the following morning.

The Wedding at Cana

CANA, situated on the west side of a hill, was a clean, pleasant place, not so large as Capernaum, and had a synagogue to which were attached three priests. Near it was the public house at which the wedding was to be held. It had a forecourt planted with trees and shrubs. From this house to the synagogue, the street was adorned with leafy festoons and arches from which hung garlands and fruits. The festal hall extended from the entrance of the house back to and beyond the fireplace, a high wall with ledges in it, which was now adorned like an altar with vases and flowers and gifts for the bride. Almost a third of this spacious hall was behind the fireplace, and there the women sat at the wedding banquet. The beams supporting the upper story were likewise hung with garlands, and there were means of ascent in order to light the lamps fastened to them.

Monday, December 26, AD 29 (Tebeth 2)

In Cana, Jesus stayed at a house belonging to one of Mary's cousins. This cousin was the daughter of Anne's sister Sobe and was also an aunt of Nathaniel the bridegroom. On this day, Jesus spent much time walking and talking with those disciples who later became his apostles.

When Jesus with his disciples arrived near Cana, he was most deferentially received by Mary, the bride's parents, the bridegroom, and others that had come out to meet him. Jesus with his familiar disciples, among them the future apostles, took up his abode in an isolated house belonging to the maternal aunt of the bridegroom.

This aunt also was a daughter of Anne's sister Sobe. She held the mother's place to the bridegroom during the wedding ceremonies. The bride's father was named Israel and was a descendant of Ruth of Bethlehem. He was an opulent merchant, who carried on a large freighting business. He owned warehouses and great inns and storing places along the highroads for supplying caravans with fodder. His employees were numerous, for most of the inhabitants of Cana earned their living by working for him; in fact, all business transactions were wholly in the hands of himself and a few others. The bride's mother was a little lame; she limped on one side and had to be led.

Tuesday, December 27, AD 29 (Tebeth 3)

About a hundred guests had gathered in Cana to attend the wedding. That evening, Jesus taught in the synagogue concerning the significance of marriage, husbands and wives, continence, chastity, and spiritual union. Later, Jesus addressed the bridal pair.

All the relatives of St. Anne and Joachim had come from around Galilee to Cana, in all over one hundred guests. Mary Mark, John Mark, Obed, and Veronica had come from Jerusalem. Jesus himself brought about twenty-five of his disciples with him.

Long ago had Jesus, in his twelfth year at the children's feast held in the house of St. Anne upon his return from the temple, addressed to the bridegroom words full of mysterious significance on the subject of bread and wine. He had told him that at some future day he would be present at his marriage. Jesus's participation in this marriage, like every other action of his earthly career, had, besides its high, mysterious signification, its exterior, apparent, and ordinary motives. More than once had Mary sent messengers to Jesus begging him to be present at it. The friends and relatives of the holy family, judging from a human view, were making such speeches as these: "Mary, the mother of Jesus, is a lone widow. Jesus is roaming the country, caring little for her or his relatives, etc., etc." It was on this account, therefore, that Mary was anxious that her son should honor his friends by his presence at the marriage. Jesus entered into Mary's views and looked upon the present as a fitting opportunity to disabuse them of their erroneous ideas. He undertook also to supply one course of the feast, and so Mary went to Cana before the other guests and helped in the various preparations. Jesus had engaged to supply all the wine for the feast, wherefore it was that Mary so anxiously reminded him that the wine failed. Jesus had also invited Lazarus and Martha to Cana. Martha assisted with Mary in the preparations, and it was Lazarus who defrayed (a circumstance known only to Jesus and Mary) all the expenses assumed by Jesus at the feast. Jesus had great confidence in Lazarus, and willingly received everything from him, while Lazarus was only too happy to give to Jesus. He was up to the last like the treasurer of the community. During the whole feast, he was treated by the bride's father as a person of special distinction, and he even personally busied himself in his service. Lazarus was very refined in his manners, his whole demeanor earnest, quiet, and marked by a dignified affability; he spoke little, and his bearing toward Jesus was full of loving devotedness.

Besides the wine, Jesus had also engaged to supply one course of the banquet, which course consisted of the principal dishes, such as birds of all kinds, fruits, and vegetables. For all these provision had been made. Veronica had brought with her from Jerusalem a basket of the choicest flowers and the most skillfully made confections. Jesus was like the master of the feast. He conducted all the amusements, which he seasoned with his own instructions. He it was, too, who arranged the whole order of the wedding ceremonies. He directed that all guests should amuse themselves on those days according to the customs usual on such occasions, but at the same time draw some lesson of wisdom from their various enjoyments. Among other things, he ordered that twice in the day the guests should leave the house, to amuse themselves in the open air.

Then I saw the wedding guests in a garden, the men and women separate, amusing themselves with conversation and games. The men reclined in circles on the ground. In the center were all kinds of fruit which, according to certain rules, they threw at one another. The thrower aimed at making it fall into certain holes or circles, while the others sought to prevent its doing so. I saw Jesus with cheerful gravity taking part in the game. Frequently he smilingly uttered a word of wisdom that made his hearers wonder. Deeply impressed, they received it in silence, the less quick to perceive its meaning asking for an explanation from their neighbor. Jesus had the inner circle and decided the prizes, which he awarded with beautiful and sometimes quite astonishing remarks. The younger of the guests amused themselves by running and leaping over leafy festoons and heaps of fruit. The women sat apart and played also for fruit, the bride's seat being always between Mary and the bridegroom's aunt.

There was also performed a kind of dance. Children played on musical instruments and sang choruses at intervals. The dancers, both the men and the maidens, held scarfs with which they touched one another when dancing in rows or in rings. Without those scarfs they never touched one another. Those of the bride and bridegroom were black, the others were yellow. At first, the bride and bridegroom danced alone, then all danced together. The maidens wore veils, but partly raised over the face; their dresses were long in the back, but a little raised in front by means of laces. There was no leaping nor springing in the dance, as is customary amongst us. It was more a moving in all kinds of figures, accompanied by frequent swaying of the person and keeping time to the music with the hands, the head, and the whole body. Though perfectly modest and graceful, it reminded me of that swaying of the Pharisaical Jews at prayer. None of the future apostles took part in the dance; but Nathaniel Chased, Obed, Jonathan, and some others of the disciples entered into it. The female dancers were the maidens only. The order observed was quite extraordinary, and a spirit of tranquil joyousness prevailed among the guests.

During those days of rejoicing, Jesus had frequent private interviews with those disciples that were later on to become his apostles. But the others were not neglected. Jesus often walked with them and with all the other guests in the country around and instructed them. The future apostles often explained Jesus's teachings to their companions. This going abroad of the guests facilitated the preparations for the feast indoors. Several of the disciples, however, and even Jesus himself at times, were present at the preparations going on in the house, helping to arrange this or that, and besides, several of them had a part in the bridal procession.

Jesus intended to manifest himself at this feast to all his friends and relatives. He wished also that all whom he had chosen up to the present should become known to one another and to his own relatives. This could be done with greater freedom on such an occasion as this marriage festival.

Jesus taught likewise in the synagogue before the guests

assembled there. He spoke of the enjoyment of lawful pleasures, of the motives through which they might be indulged, and of the moderation and prudent reserve that ought to accompany them. Then he spoke of marriage, of husband and wife, of continence, of chastity, and of spiritual unions. At the close of the instruction, the bridal pair stepped out in front of Jesus, and he addressed each separately.

THE NUPTIAL CEREMONY •
THE WOMEN'S GAME • THE MEN'S LOTTERY

Wednesday, December 28, AD 29 (Tebeth 4)
Today, on the third day (in terms of Jewish days) after Jesus's arrival in Cana, the marriage ceremony took place at about nine o'clock in the morning. Afterward, the guests left the synagogue and assembled for the wedding banquet. Jesus had taken responsibility for arranging the banquet. However, when Mary saw that there was no wine, she said to him: "They have no wine." There then followed the sequence of events that culminated in the miracle of the transformation of water into wine (John 2:4–11). This miracle gave interior strength to all those present who drank of the wine. All became convinced of Jesus's power and of the lofty nature of his mission. Faith entered their hearts, and they became inwardly united as a community. Here, for the first time, Jesus was in the midst of his community. He wrought this miracle on their behalf. This was his first miraculous sign, which found its octave subsequently in the last miracle, that of the Last Supper, at which the apostles received inner strength for their mission. After the banquet, Nathaniel the bridegroom had a private conversation with Jesus in which he expressed his desire to lead a life of continence. His bride came to Jesus with the same wish. Kneeling before Jesus, they took a vow to live as brother and sister for a period of three years. He bestowed his blessing upon them.

ON the third day after Jesus's arrival, at about nine o'clock in the morning, the marriage ceremony was performed.[B13] The bride had been adorned by her bridesmaids. Her dress was something like that worn by the Mother of God at her espousals. Her crown, too, was similar, though more richly ornamented. But her hair was not netted in strands so fine as was that of Mary, the braids were fewer and thicker. When fully attired, she was presented to the blessed Virgin and the other women.

The bride and bridegroom were conducted processionally from the house of festivity to the synagogue and back again. Six little boys and as many little girls with garlands and wreaths headed the procession. Then came six larger boys and six larger girls with flutes and other musical instruments. On their shoulders stood out some kind of stiff material like wings. Twelve young maidens accompanied the bride as bridesmaids, and the same number of youths the bridegroom. Among the latter were Obed, Veronica's son, Joseph of Arimathea's nephews, Nathaniel Chased, and some of John's disciples, but none of the future apostles.

The nuptial ceremony was performed by the priest in front of the synagogue. The rings exchanged by the young pair had been presented to the bridegroom by Mary after Jesus had blessed them for her. I remarked something at this marriage that had escaped me at the nuptials of Joseph and Mary; that is, the priest pierced the left ring finger of both bridegroom and bride with a sharp instrument, just at the place where the ring was to be worn. Then he caught in a glass of wine two drops of blood from the bridegroom and one from the bride. The contents of the glass the young couple then drank in common, and afterward gave away the glass. After this many other articles, such as scarfs and other pieces of clothing, were bestowed upon the poor gathered around. When the bridal pair were reconducted to the festal house, Jesus himself received them.

Before the wedding banquet I saw all the guests again assembled in the garden. The women and maidens sat on a carpet in an arbor and played for fruit. They passed from one to another a little, triangular tablet on the edge of which were inscribed certain letters, and which was provided also with an index. The tablet was rested on the lap, the index twirled, and the point over which it paused determined the prizes.

But for the amusement of the men I beheld a wonderful game, contrived by Jesus himself in the summerhouse. In the center of the house stood a round table with as many portions of flowers, leaves, and fruits placed around the edge as there were players. Jesus had, beforehand and alone, arranged these portions, each with reference to some mysterious signification. Above the surface of the table was a movable disk with a slot in it. The portion of fruit or flowers over which the slot rested when the disk was revolved, became the prize of him who had turned it. In the center of the table, a vine branch laden with grapes rose out of a bundle of ears of wheat. The longer the disk was turned, the higher rose the grapes and wheat. Neither the future apostles nor Lazarus took part in the game. I was told at the time that whoever had received a call to teach or who was to be favored with greater knowledge than his companions, should not engage in the game: he should watch the results and be ready to season them with instructive applications. Thus would gravity and hilarity mutually temper each other.

In this game arranged by Jesus there was something very wonderful and more than fortuitous, for the prize that fell to the players severally was significant of his own individual inclinations, faults, and virtues. This Jesus explained to each as the prize he had won was assigned him. Each prize was, as it were, a parable, a similitude upon the winner himself, and I felt that with the fruit he actually received something interiorly. All were touched and animated by the words of Jesus, perhaps also by the partaking of the fruit whose significant properties were now producing their effect. What Jesus said about each prize was quite unintelligible to all that it did not concern. It was received by the bystanders as only a pleasant, pointed remark. But each felt that the Lord had cast a deeply penetrating glance into his own interior. The same thing happened here as at Jesus's words to Nathaniel relative to that gazing under the fig tree. They had sunk deep into Nathaniel's soul, while from the others their meaning remained hidden.

I remember even yet that mignonette was one among the flowers, and that Jesus, when awarding his prize to Nathaniel Chased, said to him: "Now canst thou understand that I was right in saying to thee: Thou art a true Israelite in whom there is no guile."

I saw one of the prizes producing most wonderful effects. Nathaniel, the bridegroom, won a remarkable piece of fruit. There were two pieces on a single stem: one was like a fig, the other, which was hollow, more like a ribbed apple. They were of a reddish color, the inside white and streaked with red. I have seen similar in Paradise.

I perceived that the bystanders were very much surprised when the bridegroom won that fruit, and that Jesus spoke of marriage and of chastity, and dwelt upon the hundredfold fruit of the latter. And yet in all that Jesus said on these subjects, there was nothing that could shock the Jewish ideas on the score of marriage. Some of the Essene disciples, James the Less for instance, comprehended better than the others the deep significance of his words.

I saw that the guests wondered more over that prize than over any other, and I heard Jesus saying that those fruits could produce effects far greater than was the remarkable signification attached to them. After the bridegroom and bride had eaten the fruit they had won, I saw the former become very much agitated. He grew pale, and a dark vapor escaped from him, after which he looked to me much brighter and purer, yes, even transparent when compared with what he had been before. The bride, too, who at a distance was sitting among the women, became after eating her piece of fruit quite faint. A dark shadow appeared to go out from her. The fruit that the bridal pair ate bore some reference to chastity.

There were certain penances connected with the different prizes. I remember seeing both the bride and bridegroom bringing something away from the synagogue, and performing certain devotions. Nathaniel Chased's prize was a little bunch of sorrel.

In each of the other disciples there awoke after eating their prizes his predominant passion. It struggled a little for the mastery, and then either departed, or the possessor became by the combat strengthened against its assaults. The vegetable kingdom before the Fall was endowed with certain supernatural virtues, but since the taint of sin the power of plants remains for man a secret. The form, the taste, the effects of the various herbs and fruits, are now but simple vestiges of the virtues they possessed before sin touched them. In my visions, I have seen upon the celestial tables fruits such as they were before the Fall. But their peculiar attributes were not always quite clear to me. Such things appear confused to our darkened understanding, rendered even more obtuse by the customs of ordinary life.

When the bride fainted, her attendants relieved her of some of her heaviest ornaments. From her fingers they drew several of her numerous rings. Among them was a gold funnel-shaped shield worn like a thimble on the middle finger. They removed also the bracelets and chains from her arms and breast. The only ornament she retained beside the marriage ring, which the blessed Virgin had given, was a gold pendant from the neck. It was in shape something like an oblong arch on the plain of which was inlaid something in brown, like that of the wedding ring of Mary and Joseph. On that brown ground reclined a figure attentively considering a flower bud which it held in its hand.

The game in the garden was followed by the nuptial banquet. That part of the spacious hall of the festal house on this side of the adorned fireplace was divided into three spaces by two movable screens so low that the guests reclining at the different tables could see one another. In each of these compartments was a long, narrow table. Jesus reclined at the head of the middle one, his feet toward the fireplace. At the same table sat Israel, the bride's father, Lazarus, the male relatives of Jesus, and those of the bride. The other wedding guests, along with the disciples, sat at the two side tables. The women sat in the space back of the fireplace, but where they could hear all that Jesus said. The bridegroom served at table, assisted by the steward, who wore an apron, and by several servants. The women were waited upon by the bride and some maidservants.

When the dishes of food were brought in, a roasted lamb, the feet bound crosswise, was set before Jesus. When the bridegroom brought to Jesus the little case in which lay the carving knife, Jesus bade him recall that children's entertainment after the Passover feast, at which he had related the parable of a marriage, and had foretold to him that he would be present at his (the bridegroom's) marriage. These words were intended for Nathaniel alone. On hearing them, he became very thoughtful, for he had quite forgotten the circumstance. Jesus was at the banquet as he had been during the whole celebration, very cheerful and always ready with a word of instruction. He accompanied every action with an explanation of its spiritual signification, and spoke of hilarity and the enjoyment of the feast. He remarked that the bow must not always be bent, that the field must sometimes be refreshed by rain, and upon each he uttered a parable. As he carved the lamb, most wonderful words fell from his lips. He spoke of separating the lambs from the flocks, not for the greater advantage of the little animals thus chosen, but that they should die. Then he alluded to the process of roasting in which the meat was divested of its rawness by the fire of purification. The carving of each member signified, as he said, the manner in which they who would follow the Lamb should separate from their nearest relatives according to the flesh. When to each one he had reached a piece and all were partaking of it, he said that the lamb had been separated from its companions and cut into pieces, that it might become in them a nourishment of mutual union, so too must he that would follow the Lamb renounce his own field of pasture, put his passions to death, and separate from the members of his family. Then would he become, as it were, a nourishment, a food, to unite by means of the Lamb his fellow men to the heavenly Father. Before every guest was a plate or a little wheaten cake. Jesus set a dark brown plate with a yellow rim before himself, and it was afterward handed around. I saw him at times holding up a little bunch of herbs in his hand, and giving some instruction upon it.

Jesus had engaged to supply the second course of the banquet as well as the wine, and for all this his mother and Martha provided. This second course consisted of birds, fish, honey confections, fruits, and a kind of pastry which Veronica had brought with her. When it was all carried in and set on a side table, Jesus arose, gave the first cut to each dish, and then resumed his place at table. The dishes were served, but the wine failed. Jesus meanwhile was busy teaching. Now when the blessed Virgin, who had provided for this part of the entertainment, saw that the wine failed, she went to Jesus and reminded him that he had told her that he would see to the wine. Jesus, who was teaching of his heavenly Father, replied: "Woman, be not solicitous! Trouble not thyself and me! My hour is not yet come." These words were not uttered in harshness to the blessed Virgin. Jesus addressed her as "Woman," and not as "mother," because, at this moment as the Messiah, as the Son of God, he was present in divine power and was about to perform in presence of all his disciples and relatives an action full of mystery.

On all occasions when he acted as the Incarnate Word, he ennobled those that participated in the same by giving them the title that best responded to the part assigned them. Thus did the holiness of the divine action shed, as it were, some rays upon them and communicate to them a special dignity. Mary was the "Woman" who had brought forth him whom now, as her Creator, she invokes on the occasion of the wine's failing. As the Creator, he will now give a proof of his high dignity. He will here show that he is the Son of God and not the Son of Mary. Later on, when dying upon the cross, he again addressed his weeping mother by the appellation of Woman, "Woman, behold thy son!" thereby designating John.

Jesus had promised his mother that he would provide the wine. And here we see Mary beginning the role of mediatrix that she has ever since continued. She places before him the failure of the wine. But the wine that he was about to provide was more than ordinary wine; it was symbolical of that mystery by which he would one day change wine into his own blood. The reply: "My hour is not yet come," contained three significations: first, the hour for supplying the promised wine; secondly, the hour for changing water into wine; thirdly, the hour for changing wine into his own blood.

But Mary's anxiety for the wedding guests was now entirely relieved. She had mentioned the matter to her Son, therefore she says confidently to the servants: "Do all that he shall tell you."

In like manner does the church, the Bride of Jesus, say to him: "Lord, thy children have no wine." And Jesus replies: "Church" (not Bride), "be not troubled, be not disquieted! My hour is not yet come." Then says the church to her priests: "Hearken to his words, obey all his commands, for he will always help you!"

Mary told the servants to await the commands of Jesus and fulfill them. After a little while Jesus directed them to bring him the empty jugs and turn them upside down. The jugs were brought, three water jugs and three wine jugs, and that they were empty was proved by inverting them over a basin. Then Jesus ordered each to be filled with water. [B14] The servants took them off to the well which was in a vault in the cellar, and which consisted of a stone cistern provided with a pump. The jugs were earthen, large and so heavy that when full it took two men to carry them, one at each handle. They were pierced at intervals from top to bottom by tubes closed by faucets. When the contents to a certain depth were exhausted, the next lower faucet opened to pour out. They were only tipped up on their high feet.

Mary's words to Jesus had been uttered in a low tone, but Jesus's reply, as well as his command to draw water, was given in a loud voice. When the jugs filled with water had been placed, six in number, on the side table, Jesus went and blessed them. As he retook his place at table, he called to a servant: "Draw off now, and bring a drink to the steward!" When this latter had tasted the wine, he approached the bridegroom and said: "Every man at first setteth forth good wine, and when men have well drunk, then that which is worse. But thou hast kept the good wine until now." He did not know that the wine was provided by Jesus as was also this whole course of the feast. That was a secret between the holy family and the family of the bridal pair. Then the bridegroom and the bride's father drank of the wine, and great was their astonishment. The servants protested that they had drawn only water, and that the drinking vessels and glasses on the table had been filled with the same. And now the whole company drank. The miracle gave rise to no alarm or excitement; on the contrary, a spirit of silent awe and reverence fell upon them. Jesus taught much upon this miracle. Among other things, he said that the world presents the strong wine first, and then deceives the partially intoxicated with bad drinks; but it was not so in the kingdom that his heavenly Father had given him. There pure water was changed to costly wine, as lukewarmness should give place to ardor and intrepid zeal. He alluded also to that banquet at which in his twelfth year, after his return from teaching in the temple, he had been present with many of the guests now assembled, and who were then mere boys. He reminded them that he had on that occasion spoken of bread and wine, and had related the parable of a marriage at which the water of tepidity would be changed into the wine of enthusiasm. This, he said, was now fulfilled. He told them that they should witness greater miracles than this; that he would celebrate several Passovers, and at the last would change wine into blood and bread into flesh, and that he would remain with them till the end to strengthen and console. After that meal they should see happen to him things that they could not now understand, even were he to explain them. Jesus did not say all this in plain terms. He hid it under parables, which I have forgotten, though I have given their sense. His listeners were filled with fear and wonder, and the wine produced a change in all. I saw that, not by the miracle alone, but also by the drinking of that wine, each one had received strength, true and interior, each had become changed. This change was similar to that wrought in them at an earlier stage of the entertainment by the eating of the fruit. His disciples, his relatives, in a word, all present were now convinced of Jesus's power and dignity, as well as of his mission. All believed in him. Faith at once took possession of every heart. All became better, more united, more interior. This same effect was produced in all that had drunk of the wine. Jesus at this wedding feast was, as it were, in the midst of his community for the first time. There it was that he wrought that first miracle in their favor and for the confirmation of their faith. It is on that account that this miracle, the changing of water into wine, is recorded as the first in his history; as that of the Last Supper, when his apostles were staunch in the faith, was the last.

At the close of the banquet, the bridegroom went to Jesus and spoke to him very humbly in private. He told him that he now felt himself dead to all carnal desires and that, if his bride would consent, he would embrace a life of continence. The bride also, having sought Jesus alone and expressed her wish to the same effect, Jesus called them both before him. He spoke to them of marriage, of chastity so pleasing in the sight of God, and of the hundredfold fruit of the spirit. He referred to many of the prophets and other holy persons who had lived in chastity, offering their bodies as a holocaust to the heavenly Father. They had thus reclaimed many wandering souls, had won them to themselves as so many spiritual children, and had acquired a numerous and holy posterity. Jesus spoke all this in parables of sowing and reaping. The young couple took a vow of continence, by which they bound themselves to live as brother and sister for the space of three years. Then they knelt before Jesus, and he blessed them.

Thursday, December 29, AD 29 (Tebeth 5)
Jesus taught in the house where the wedding banquet had taken place. Several guests, including Lazarus and Martha, departed from Cana. That evening, in a festive procession, the bride and bridegroom were conducted to their house.

On the evening of the fourth day of the marriage, the bride and bridegroom were conducted to their home in festal procession. Lights arranged so as to form a letter were carried. Children went before carrying on strips of cloth two wreaths of flowers, an open one and a closed one, which they tore to pieces and scattered around in front of the house of the newly-married couple. Jesus had gone on ahead. He received them at the house and blessed them. The priests also were present. Since the miracle wrought by Jesus at the banquet, they had become very humble, and gave him precedence everywhere.

Friday, December 30, AD 29 (Tebeth 6)

Today, most of the remaining guests, including Mary and the other holy women, left Cana. In the evening, with the beginning of the sabbath, Jesus taught in the synagogue concerning the marriage ceremony and the devout sentiments of the bridal pair.

Saturday, December 31, AD 29 (Tebeth 7)

Jesus taught morning and afternoon in the synagogue. When he came out of the synagogue, in the presence of the priests he healed six people and raised from the dead a man who had died as a consequence of falling from a tower. After the close of the sabbath, Jesus and his remaining disciples set off for Capernaum (John 2:12).

On the sabbath spent at Cana, Jesus taught twice in the synagogue. He alluded to the wedding feast and to the obedience and pious sentiments of the bridal couple. On leaving the synagogue, he was accosted by the people, who threw themselves at his feet and implored him to cure their sick.

Jesus performed here two wonderful cures. A man had fallen from a high tower. He was taken up dead, all his limbs broken. Jesus went to him, placed the limbs in position, touched the fractures, and then commanded the man to rise and go to his home. The man arose, thanked Jesus, and went home. He had a wife and children. Jesus was next conducted to a man possessed by the devil, and whom he found chained to a great stone. Jesus freed him. He was next led to a woman, a sinner, who was afflicted by an issue of blood. He cured her, as also some others sick of edema. He healed seven in all. The people had not dared to crowd around him during the marriage festivities; but now that it was rumored that he was going away after the sabbath, they could no longer be restrained. Since the miracle of the marriage feast, the priests did not interfere with Jesus. They allowed him to do all that he wished. The miracles, the cures just related happened in their presence alone, for the disciples were not there.

Jesus in Capernaum and at the Sea of Galilee

THE SABBATH over, Jesus went that night with his disciples to Capernaum, the bridegroom, his father, and several others accompanying him a part of the way. The poor had been bountifully supplied at the marriage feast, for nothing appeared a second time on the table; whatever was left was immediately given away.

Sunday, January 1, and Monday, January 2, AD 30 (Tebeth 8–9)

Jesus stayed in Capernaum, teaching in the synagogue and fasting. (The actual day of fasting celebrated at this time in the Jewish calendar is Tebeth 10. The fast commemorates the beginning of the siege of Jerusalem—see 2 Kings 25:1. This year, AD 30, Tebeth 10 began on Monday evening, and the fast ought to have begun at sunrise on the following day. Anne Catherine, however, referred to two days of fasting). Here in Capernaum, Jesus healed the sick. In between periods of teaching, he remained with his mother.

For two fasting days that occurred immediately after the sabbath, I saw the cooking done in advance.

All the fires were covered, and the windows not absolutely necessary were closed. In the homes of the rich, there were little receptacles on the hearth in which, covered with hot ashes, the food kept warm. Jesus kept these fasts in Capernaum where, too, he taught in the synagogue. Twice a day, the sick were brought to him, and he cured them. The disciples from Bethsaida went home, but some of them afterward returned. Jesus traversed the country around teaching, but in the hours of rest he stayed with Mary.

(Follow Map 10)

Tuesday, January 3, AD 30 (Tebeth 10)

Andrew, Saturnin, Aram, Themeni, and Eustachius were sent by Jesus to the great baptismal place on the Jordan this side of Jericho—the third place of baptism, near Ono. It had been abandoned by John, and the disciples were now to baptize there. Jesus went with them a part of the way, and then turned off to Bethulia, where he cured the sick and taught.

Wednesday, January 4, AD 30 (Tebeth 11)

Jesus, accompanied by the three disciples, walked to Hanathon, seven or eight hours northwest of Capernaum. Near Hanathon there was a mountain used by the prophets in former times. Jesus sent out his three disciples to let the people of the town know that on the following day he would teach on the mountain.

From there he walked back between seven and eight hours toward Hanathon, northwest of Capernaum, in whose vicinity there was a mountain formerly used by the prophets for teaching. It had a gentle elevation of about an hour, and on it was a space arranged in olden times for teaching. It consisted of a high stone seat surrounded by stakes, over which a tent could be stretched as a protection against sun and rain. The space thus enclosed could accommodate a

Map 10: The First Sermon on the Mount
January 3–11, AD 30

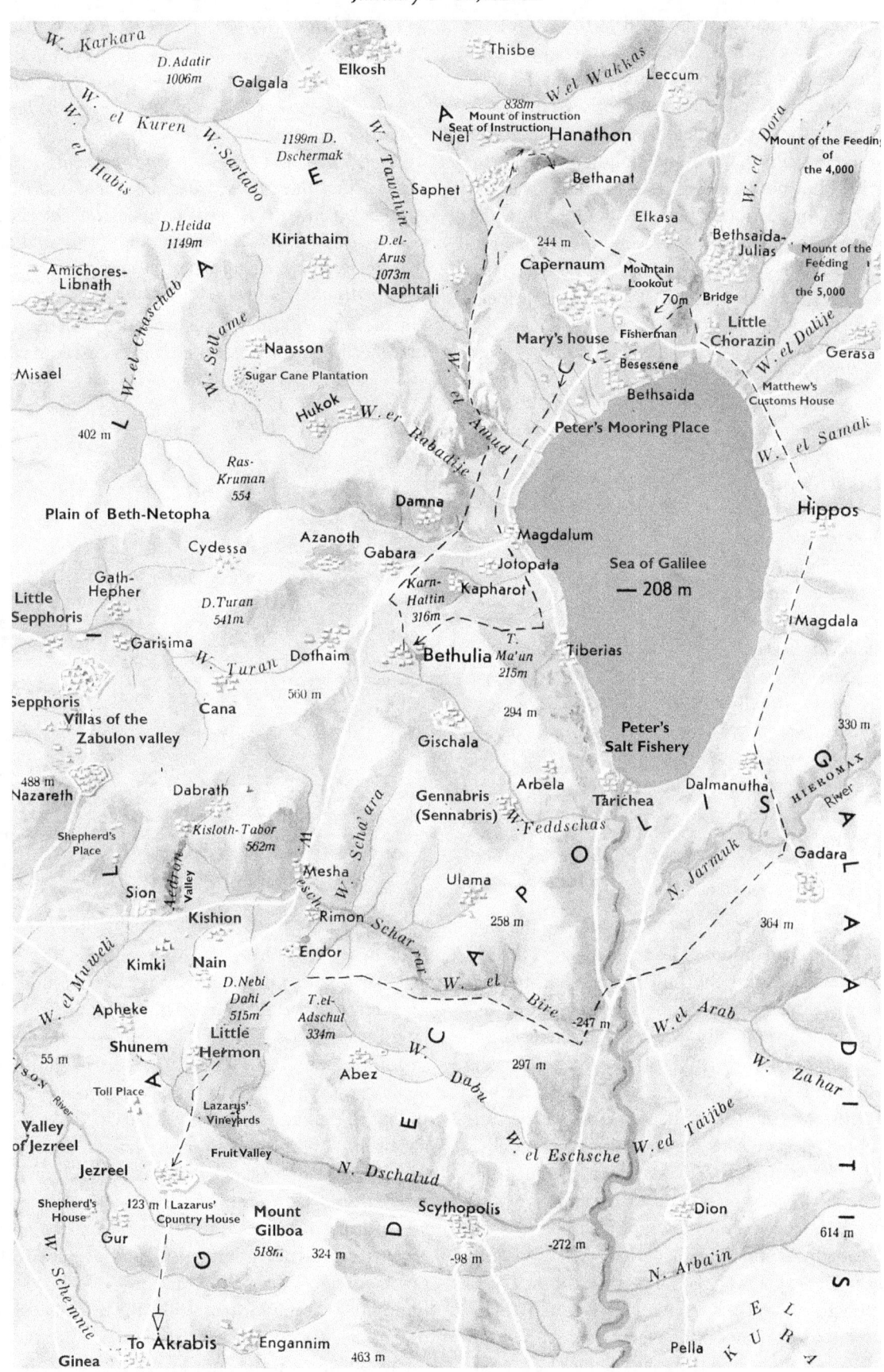

Capernaum—Bethulia—Hanathon—Mount of Instruction—Bethanat—Capernaum
Hippos—Jezreel—Akrabis

large audience. The tent was removed at the end of the instructions. From the mountain ridge arose three hills, one of which was the Mount of Beatitudes. From the place where Jesus taught was a widely extended view: the Sea of Galilee lay below the observer, and he could see far around toward Nazareth. Some parts of the mountain were fertile and inhabited, but not so where Jesus taught. It was surrounded by the foundations of a ruined wall, upon which might still be seen the remains of several towers. Around the mountain lay Hanathon, Bethanat, and Nejel. Their proximity leaves the impression that they were formerly but one large city.

Thursday, January 5, AD 30 (Tebeth 12)

Jesus was on the mountain near Hanathon. Addressing the assembled crowd, he referred to the spirit one receives through baptism. This is the spirit in which—through penance, making amends, and reconciliation—all people can be united and become one with the Father in heaven. He also spoke concerning some of the petitions of his prayer (the Our Father), but without giving the entire prayer. He taught from noon until evening. Then he made his way to Bethanat.

Jesus had with him three disciples: one the son of the widowed aunt of the bridegroom of Cana; the second the son of the other widow; and the third Peter's half-brother Jonathan. The people were summoned by them to Jesus's instruction on the mountain. Jesus taught here of the diverse spirits in men of different places, yea, even of the same family, and of the spirit that they should receive through baptism. By this last spirit, they should all become one; one in penance, satisfaction, and expiation, as well as one with the heavenly Father. Then he gave them some signs by which they might be able to recognize in what degree they had received the Holy Spirit in baptism. He taught also on prayer and individual petitions. I was astonished to hear him explaining several petitions of the Lord's Prayer, although as a whole he had not yet repeated it. This instruction lasted from noon till evening, when he went down to Bethanat and stayed there overnight. The preceding night he had spent in Hanathon.

Friday, January 6, AD 30 (Tebeth 13)

In Bethanat, Jesus and his three disciples were joined by five of John's disciples. Together, they walked southward in the direction of Capernaum. Pausing on a hill about half an hour from the Sea of Galilee, they could see Peter, James, and John in their fishing boats. Jesus indicated that these three fishermen would also join him. After paying a brief visit to his mother at her house between Bethsaida and Capernaum, Jesus and the disciples went to the synagogue in Capernaum to celebrate the start of the sabbath.

On the following day Jesus went from Bethanat toward the lake. Five more of John's disciples had come to Jesus in

Fishing in the Sea of Galilee near Bethanat

Bethanat. They were from Apheke, the native city of St. Thomas, situated in a region to the north on the Mediterranean. They had long been with John; but now they followed Jesus.

Toward noon I saw Jesus and his disciples on a little hill about one half-hour from the lake, between Bethsaida and the spot where the Jordan flows into it. They commanded a view of it upon which they saw Peter, John, and James in their boats. Peter owned a large ship, and on it were his servants; but he was at the time in a small one which he was steering himself. John and James, in company with their father, owned a large ship and several small ones. I saw Andrew's little boat near those of Zebedee, but he himself was at the Jordan. When the disciples took notice of their friends on the lake, they wanted to go down to call them. But Jesus would not allow it. I heard the disciples asking: "How can those men down there still go around fishing after seeing what thou hast done and hearing thy teaching?" But Jesus answered: "I have not yet called them. They, and especially Peter, carry on a large business upon which many depend for subsistence. I have told them to continue it, and in the meantime hold themselves in readiness for my call. Until then I have many things to do. I have also to go to Jerusalem for Passover."

About six and twenty dwellings were on the west side of the hill, occupied principally by peasants and the families of the fishermen. As Jesus approached these houses, a possessed person cried after him: "There he goes! Here he comes! The prophet before whom we must flee!" and soon he was surrounded by a crowd of such creatures, clamoring and raving, who were followed by their keepers. Jesus commanded them to be at peace and to follow him. Then he went up on the hill and taught. There were about one hundred people, including the possessed, around him. He spoke of evil spirits, of how to resist them, and of reformation of life. The possessed were freed from the spirits that held them. They became perfectly calm, they wept, they thanked, and declared that they could now recall nothing of what had happened to them during the time of their possession. Among these poor creatures were some who had been brought chained together from different parts of the country around, their friends having heard that there was on his way thither a prophet as holy as Moses. After all their trouble, they would have missed Jesus had not one broken loose and cried after him.

Saturday, January 7, AD 30 (Tebeth 14)

Jesus taught in the synagogue at Capernaum until the close of the sabbath.

From this place Jesus went to join his mother between Capernaum and Bethsaida, the former of which was a little to the north and not far from the hill mentioned above. That evening when the sabbath began, Jesus taught in the synagogue of Capernaum. A feast was being celebrated that had some reference to Tobias, who had frequented this part of the country and had done much good. He had also bequeathed property to the schools and synagogues. Jesus gave an instruction on gratitude.

Sunday, January 8, AD 30 (Tebeth 15)

After the sabbath, Jesus returned to his mother, with whom he conversed alone far into the night. He spoke of his future movements: he would first go to the Jordan, then celebrate Passover at Jerusalem, afterward call his apostles, and make his public appearance. He predicted the persecution he should endure at Nazareth, alluded to his career after that, and explained in what way she and the other women should bear a part in it. There was at that time in Mary's house a woman already far advanced in years. She was the same poor widowed relative whom Anne had sent to Mary to take the place of a servant to her in the crib cave. She was now so old that Mary rather served her than she Mary.

Monday, January 9, AD 30 (Tebeth 16)

Before sunrise, Jesus set off with his eight disciples to journey to the place of baptism. Passing around the north side of the Sea of Galilee, they then went down the east side, staying overnight at Hippos.

With eight disciples, Jesus set out before break of day on his journey to the place of baptism on the Jordan. Their way ran to the east of the lake and over the hill whence they had seen the boats of the apostles. The Jordan here flows through a deep bed. About one half-hour before its discharge into the lake, the river is spanned by a bridge high and steep. This the Lord and his disciples crossed. On the other side, in a retired corner near the lake, lay a little fishery surrounded by numerous outstretched nets. It was called Little Chorazin. Not quite an hour northward from the lake was Bethsaida-Julias. Great Chorazin was a couple of hours east of the lake, and there dwelt Matthew the publican. Jesus traveled down the eastern shore of the lake and remained overnight in Hippos.

Tuesday, January 10, AD 30 (Tebeth 17)

Today they journeyed on. As they approached Gadara, Jesus healed a man possessed. Toward evening, they reached Jezreel. Here Jesus publicly healed several people in front of the synagogue. However, after only a few hours in Jezreel, they set off on their way again.

Next morning he went on to Gadara, in whose neighborhood he cured a man possessed. The unfortunate creature was being led after him bound, but he freed himself and set up the cry: "Jesus, thou Son of David! Jesus! Whither goest thou? Thou wilt drive us away!" Jesus stood still, commanded the devil to be silent and to depart from the man, indicating at the same time whither he should go.

A couple of hours from Gadara, Jesus again crossed the Jordan, and went on toward the southwest, leaving Scythopolis to the left. He crossed Mount Moreh to Jezreel, a city on the west side of the plain Esdrelon. Jesus cured numbers there openly before the synagogue. But he stayed a few hours only in Jezreel, so that Magdalene, who at the earnest entreaty of Martha had come with her to see Jesus, did not find him on her arrival. She heard only of his miracles from the lips of those whom he had cured. The sisters here separated, and Magdalene retraced her steps to Magdalum.

(Follow Map 11)

Wednesday, January 11, AD 30 (Tebeth 18)
Today, Jesus and his disciples arrived at Akrabis, a shepherd place. Jesus taught in the open air.

Thursday, January 12, AD 30 (Tebeth 19)
Toward evening, Jesus arrived in Hay, not far from Bethel, where he healed several people. He taught, and a number of Pharisees disputed with him, putting such questions as: "When will the Messiah come?"

The next place in which I saw Jesus was Hay, not far from Bethel, and about nine hours distant from the place of baptism. Hay had in ancient times been destroyed, and later partly restored. It was a retired little place. Jesus cured and taught there.

Among the Pharisees of Hay were some that had been present in the temple at the teaching of Jesus in his twelfth year. They now referred to it as to a piece of consummate hypocrisy. He had, they said, in the synagogue of learned men taken his place on the ground among the scholars, disputed with them, and then, as if demanding information on the words of his opponents, had called upon the teachers with such questions as these: "What think you? Tell us, when will the Messiah come?" Having drawn them thus into the manifestation of their opinion, he ended by a show of his own superior knowledge. They now put to Jesus the plain question whether he was not that child.

Jesus Permits Baptism to be Given at the Jordan

Friday, January 13, AD 30 (Tebeth 20)
Toward noon, Jesus and his disciples arrived at the place of baptism near Ono. There he gave instruction to the people who had come to be baptized. That evening, he celebrated the sabbath at the synagogue in Ono.

FROM HAY, Jesus departed for John's former baptismal place, on the Jordan three hours from Jericho. Andrew and many of the disciples had come about an hour's distance to meet him. Several of John's disciples, some also from Nazareth, were here. Some of them went on ahead to the little village of Ono, about an hour's distance from the place of baptism, and gave notice that Jesus would there celebrate the sabbath and cure the sick. They told the people that Jesus was continuing John's work and teaching, and that openly and effectively he perfected that for which John had laid the foundation. Outside of Ono and about one half-hour from the baptismal place there was a private inn for Jesus's accommodation. Lazarus had purchased it for him and had placed there a man to see to the cooking, though Jesus usually took his meals cold. This inn served him as a stopping place when in that part of the country, and from it he went around to the neighboring villages teaching and baptizing.

Saturday, January 14, AD 30 (Tebeth 21)
Today, Jesus taught in the synagogue. He spoke of himself as continuing the work begun by John. He also healed several people.

When he reached Ono for the sabbath, he taught in the synagogue and cured many sick persons who had been brought thither, among them a poor, emaciated woman suffering from an issue of blood.

In these last days, Herod frequently went to John, but the latter always treated him with contempt as an adulterer. Herod interiorly acknowledged that John was right, but his wife was furious against John. John baptized no more, and Jesus was now the whole subject of his preaching. All the candidates for baptism, he sent across the Jordan to him.

Sunday, January 15, AD 30 (Tebeth 22)
While Andrew and Saturnin were baptizing, Jesus gave instruction to the people who had come to the place of baptism. Many had been sent by John, who was now at the second place of baptism, on the east side of the Jordan. John had stopped baptizing, and now only preached, speaking always of Jesus. He also denounced Herod Antipas as an adulterer, thus arousing the fury of Herodias.

At the place of baptism, many changes had been made by the disciples sent thither from Cana, and all in accordance with Jesus's orders. It now presented a festal appearance, and things were better arranged than when John was there. On account of the crowds desirous of crossing, the ferry was removed to a lower point of the river, at a greater distance from that large circular enclosure which John had arranged in the open air around the baptismal pool. The spot upon which Andrew, Saturnin, and the other disciples baptized in turn upon Jesus's command was the little island upon which he himself had been baptized. It was now covered by a large awning. While the disciples baptized, Jesus taught and prepared the aspirants for baptism. The pool in which Jesus had been baptized was now very much changed. The five canals leading from the Jordan into the pool, and which had at first been covered, were now uncovered, and the four stones from the center, as well as the large, three-cornered, red-veined one at the edge upon which Jesus was standing when the Holy Spirit came upon him, had all been removed. They had been taken to the new place of baptism.

Map 11: At the Place of Baptism
January 11–26, AD 30

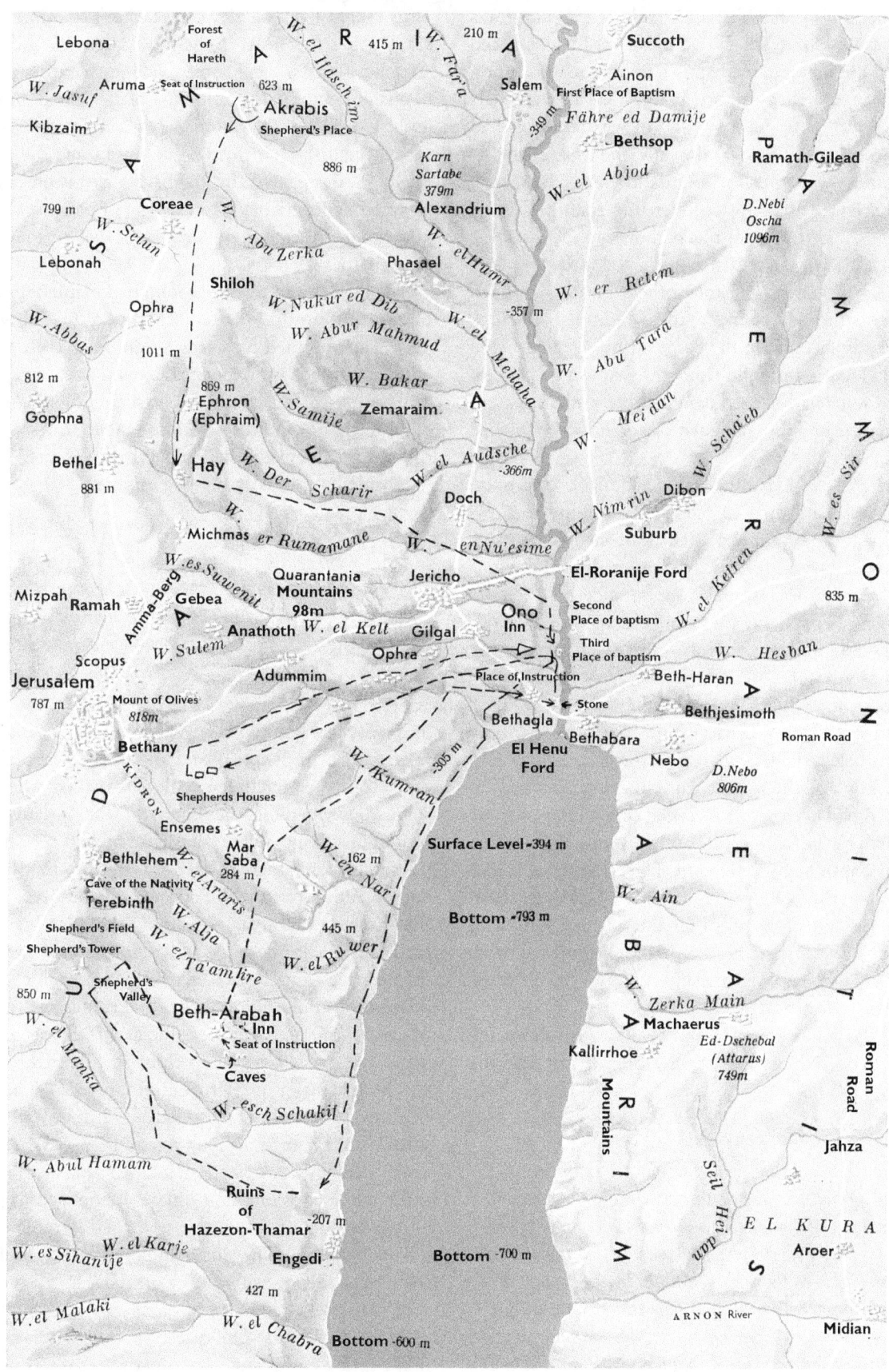

Akrabis—Hay—Third Place of Baptism—Ono—Hazezon-Thamar—Shepherd's Valley
Beth-Arabah—Bethagla—Third Place of Baptism

That the spot upon which Jesus had been baptized was the same as that upon which the Ark of the Covenant had stood, that the stones in the baptism pool were those upon which it had rested in the bed of the Jordan, were facts known only to Jesus and John, and of which neither had spoken. So, too, the Lord was the only one who knew that these stones now formed the foundation of the baptismal basin. The Jews had long forgotten the resting place of these stones, and it was not made known to the disciples. Andrew had hewn a circular basin in the three-cornered stone which rested on the four others in a cavity filled with water which surrounded the stones like a canal. This water, as also that in the basin of the three-cornered stones, had been brought from the baptismal pool of Jesus, and Jesus had blessed it. When the aspirants stood in the canal around the triangular basin, the water reached up to their breast.

Near the place of baptism was a kind of altar upon which lay the baptismal garments. Two of the disciples imposed hands upon the shoulders of the neophytes while Andrew or Saturnin, sometimes another, dipped the hollow hand three times into the basin and poured the water over their head, baptizing them in the name of the Father and of the Son and of the Holy Spirit. The baptizers, as well as those that imposed hands, wore long white robes girdled, and from their shoulders hung long white strips like broad stoles. John was accustomed to baptize from a triple-channeled shell from which the water flowed in three streams, and the words he used were of Jehovah and of him that had been sent, somewhat different from those now uttered by the disciples at baptism. None of those that had been baptized by John were here rebaptized; but I think that after the descent of the Holy Spirit, at the baptism administered at the pool of Bethesda, they were again baptized. Nor were there here any women as yet baptized. The baptism with triple immersions I saw for the first time at the pool of Bethesda.

There was an opening in the awning just above the basin of baptism. The neophytes stood at the side, the baptizer and sponsors on the corner of the stone.

Monday, January 16, AD 30 (Tebeth 23)

Jesus continued to teach at the place of baptism. He spoke of his baptism as a cleansing, while John's baptism had been one of penance. He also referred to a baptism by fire (from the Holy Spirit), which was to come. John's baptism had used the words: "May Yahweh through the ministry of his Seraphim and Cherubim pour out his blessing upon thee with wisdom, understanding, and strength." In contrast, Jesus's baptism was in the name of the Father, the Son, and the Holy Spirit.

Jesus taught from an elevated teacher's stand in the open air. During the heat of the day, a tent or awning was stretched over it. The subjects of Jesus's discourse were baptism, penance, the approach of the kingdom of God, and of the Messiah, whom they should seek not among the distinguished of this world, but among the poor and lowly. He designated this baptism a cleansing, a washing away, while John's baptism was one of penance. He spoke also of a baptism of fire, a baptism of the Spirit, which was yet to come.

The bushes and trees that John had planted in the form of an arbor around the baptismal pool rose above them all. On the pointed top I saw a figure like a little child. It appeared to be rising out of the trunk of a vine, its little arms outstretched in the act of scattering yellow apples with one hand, and roses with the other. It was a remnant of the adornments of the festival that celebrated the commencement of Jesus's baptizing mission.

Tuesday, January 17, AD 30 (Tebeth 24)

Jesus went with several disciples to the ruined city of Hazezon-Thamar on the west side of the Dead Sea, not far from Engedi. The people living there—slaves belonging to wandering tribes—were very poor and humble. They gratefully received Jesus in their midst, and he healed a number of them.

Jesus was now gone with several of his disciples southward from the place of baptism and toward the west of the Dead Sea. He had entered the region in which Melchizedek sojourned when he measured off the Jordan and the mountains. Long before Abraham, he had conducted the patriarch's forefathers thither. But the city that they built had been destroyed with Sodom and Gomorrha. I saw at that time, at about half an hour's distance inland from the Dead Sea, in the midst of a desolate region where immense caves and black, jagged rocks met the gaze, the dilapidated walls and towers in the ruined city Hazezon-Thamar. Where now appears the Dead Sea was before the submersion of those godless cities only the river Jordan. It was here about a quarter of an hour broad. The people, who dwelt in caves and ruined buildings of all kinds at some distance from the sea, were not real Jews. They were slaves belonging to wandering tribes that had settled in those parts, and for whom they were obliged to perform all the field labor. They were poor and humble and very greatly neglected. They looked upon Jesus's arrival among them as an inconceivable favor, and gave him a very loving reception. He cured many of them.

At the present day that region is not so desolate as it was in the time of Jesus, but in very early ages it was indescribably fruitful and lovely. It was in Abraham's time changed by the formation of the Dead Sea from one of the most magnificent regions into a dreary desert. The shores of the Jordan were then walled in with freestone and on them once stood a great number of cities and towns, beautiful mountains and hills rising up between them. The whole region was covered with groves of date palms, vineyards, orchards, and fields of grain, its fruitfulness surpassed description. Previously to the formation of the Dead Sea, the Jordan had, just below its greatest depth, divided into two branches between the cities that were afterward submerged. One of these branches flowed eastward, receiving in its course the waters of many smaller streams; the other watered the desert through which the holy family fled into Egypt, as far as the region of Mara, where Moses had rendered the bitter waters sweet, and where Anne's ancestors had sojourned. There were salt mines in the neighborhood of those cities, but they exercised no deleterious influence upon the waters of the numerous springs around. The tribes dwelling at a considerable distance in this region that afterward became so desolate, used the water of the Jordan and found it excellent.

The remote ancestors of Abraham, who had been settled in Hazezon by Melchizedek, had become very degenerate, and Abraham was, by a second exercise of God's mercy, led to the Promised Land. Melchizedek had been in these parts long before the Jordan existed. He had measured off and determined everything. He often came and went, and sometimes he was accompanied by a couple of men, who appeared to be slaves.

Wednesday, January 18, AD 30 (Tebeth 25)

Jesus made his way through the valley of the shepherds, where he had been one week after his baptism.

Jesus went afterward with his disciples in a direction leading to Bethlehem. After his baptism he crossed the valley of the shepherds. The people depended upon the caravans that passed through for their principal support. It is about four hours from Bethany and on the boundary between Judah and Benjamin.

Thursday, January 19, AD 30 (Tebeth 26)

As Jesus approached Beth-Arabah, many who were possessed ran about, calling out that Jesus was coming. Jesus cast the evil spirits out of these people. Then he and his disciples put up at an inn.

There were in Beth-Arabah many possessed. They ran about outside the city crying out that Jesus was coming. Jesus commanded them to cover themselves, and in a few moments they had made aprons of leaves. Jesus delivered them from the evil spirits and, on entering the city, sent back to them messengers with clothes. There were some among them whose body used suddenly to swell to a great size.

Friday, January 20, AD 30 (Tebeth 27)

Andrew and five disciples had come from the place of baptizing. Also Lazarus, Joseph of Arimathea, and some others had come from Jerusalem to hear Jesus teach in the synagogue on the sabbath. The people of Beth-Arabah were well disposed toward Jesus.

Andrew and five other disciples had left the place of baptism and preceded the Lord to Beth-Arabah in order to announce his coming and to give notice that he would there celebrate the sabbath.

Jesus and his disciples put up at a private inn, one of those free inns, such as in those times were always found in the different cities for the accommodation of traveling teachers and rabbis. Lazarus, Joseph of Arimathea, and others from Jerusalem had come hither to meet Jesus.

Jesus taught in the synagogue, also from a stone seat that stood in a public place intended for such use, and on all the streets and corners, for the crowds were too great for the school to accommodate. He healed numerous sick of different kinds whom the disciples brought to him, making a way for them through the crowd. Lazarus and Joseph of Arimathea stood in the distance.

Saturday, January 21, AD 30 (Tebeth 28)

At the close of the sabbath, Jesus set off to return to the place of baptizing. On the way, he passed through Bethagla. Meanwhile, Lazarus and Joseph of Arimathea traveled to Jerusalem.

At the close of the sabbath, the Lord returned to Ono with his disciples. They passed through the little town of Bethagla, one of the stopping places of the children of Israel after they had crossed the Jordan, for they did not all cross at one and the same place. They went over in bands at different points of the dry bed of the river. When arrived at Bethagla, they arranged their clothing and girded themselves. Jesus passed the stone of the Ark of the Covenant where John had celebrated the feast.

Lazarus and Joseph of Arimathea returned to Jerusalem. Nicodemus had not come. He was more reserved, on account of the office that he held, but he served Jesus in secret, and to the end notified the little community of any danger that threatened.

Sunday, January 22, AD 30 (Tebeth 29)

The next day was the first Feast of the New Moon (close of the month of Tebeth/start of the month of Shebat), and I saw that the serving class and civil functionaries in Jerusalem had a holiday. It was kept as a festival of joy, a day of rest, consequently there was no baptizing on it.

The flags for the Feast of the New Moon were waving from long flagstaffs on the roof of the synagogue. Large knots were made at intervals on the staves between which the folds of the streamers opened in the breeze. The number of knots signified to those at a distance what month had just begun. Such flags were unfurled also as signals of victory or of danger.

SHEBAT (30 days): January 22/23, to February 20/21, AD 30, Shebat New Moon: January 22, at 4:30 PM Jerusalem time

Monday, January 23, AD 30 (Shebat 1)

Because of the New Moon festival there was no baptizing today, but to prepare those who were going to be baptized Jesus taught at the place of baptism. In the evening, at the start of the second day of the month of Shebat, a feast was celebrated to commemorate the death of the wicked king Alexander Jannaeus. Lazarus and Obed arrived.

The whole day Jesus was busy preparing for baptism the people who had gathered there on the eve and encamped around; but there was no baptizing, because a feast was being celebrated in commemoration of the death of a wicked King (Alexander Jannaeus). The place of baptism had been very beautifully arranged and adorned. Andrew and the other disciples began very early on the following day the baptism of those that Jesus had prepared the day before.

Tuesday, January 24, AD 30 (Shebat 2)

Early this morning, Andrew and Saturnin began baptizing. Jesus set off with Lazarus and Obed in the direction of Bethlehem, taking a course between Bethagla and Ophra. Lazarus told Jesus of the reports concerning him that were circulating in Jerusalem. They spent the night with some shepherds.

The preceding evening Lazarus had returned with Obed, Simeon's son, and with them Jesus started very early the next morning for the neighborhood of Bethlehem, passing between Bethagla and Ophra, which was more to the west. Jesus took this journey with Lazarus in order to hear what reports were circulating about himself at Jerusalem, also to give him some instructions, which he was to transmit to the little community, as to how they should conduct themselves under certain circumstances. They took the road once trodden by Joseph and Mary when going to Bethlehem, and in about three hours reached a row of poor, isolated dwellings belonging to shepherds. Lazarus told Jesus all that was being said about him at Jerusalem, and that they spoke of him in a manner partly derisive,

and partly inquisitive. They said that they would see whether he would come to Jerusalem for Passover and, if he did, whether he would as daringly perform his miracles in a great city as among the credulous people of Galilee. He told Jesus also of the spying of the Pharisees and of what they reported of him in different places. Jesus relieved Lazarus's anxiety on these points, and drew his attention to various passages in the prophets wherein all this had been foretold. He said that he would be about eight days longer at the Jordan, would then return to Galilee, then go to Jerusalem for Passover, and after that call his disciples. Jesus consoled Lazarus on the subject of Magdalene, of whom he said that already there had fallen upon her soul a spark of salvation, which would entirely consume her.

They spent the greater part of the day among the shepherd dwellings, at which they were entertained with bread, honey, and fruit. There dwelt here only about twenty-one women of the shepherd class, all widows. Some had grown sons, who supported them in their old age. Their dwellings were merely cells separated from one another by hedges of living brushwood. Some of these women had visited the crib cave at the birth of Christ and offered gifts. Jesus taught here. He entered some of the cells and cured the sick inmates. One was very old and emaciated, and lay upon a couch made of leaves. Jesus led her forth by the hand. The women had a refectory and dormitory in common.

Wednesday, January 25, AD 30 (Shebat 3)

Jesus, Lazarus, and Obed started out in the direction of Ono. Lazarus and Obed left Jesus on the way and returned to Jerusalem. Jesus went on, visiting and healing some sick people on the way. He reached the place of baptism, Ono, around three in the afternoon.

Lazarus and Obed went back to Jerusalem, while Jesus continued visiting and curing the sick. Toward three in the afternoon, I saw him again at the place of baptism.

Thursday, January 26, AD 30 (Shebat 4)

Jesus taught again today, while Andrew and Saturnin continued to baptize.

(Follow Map 12)

Jesus in Adummin and Nebo

Friday, January 27, AD 30 (Shebat 5)

Jesus and many of his disciples walked through Bethagla to Adummin. Here they visited the spot where the parable of the good Samaritan had taken place. Jesus taught this parable to his disciples and to those people from the neighborhood who had come to hear him. In the evening, Jesus celebrated the sabbath in Adummin.

JESUS, with most of his disciples, passed through Bethagla to Adummin, a place hidden away in a frightfully wild, mountainous region, broken by innumerable ravines. The road running along by the rocks was in some places so narrow that even an ass could scarcely tread it. It was about three hours from Jericho, in a district so retired on the boundary between Benjamin and Judah that I never before noticed it. It was wonderfully steep. It was a refugial city for murderers and other malefactors, who found here protection from capital punishment. They were either kept in custody until they reformed or employed in the quarries and in the most painful field labors. The place received on this account the appellation "The path of the red, the bloody." This city of refuge was in existence even before David's time. During the first persecution of the community after Jesus's death, it came to an end. Later on, a convent was built there to serve as a stronghold, or fortress, for the first religious guardians of the Holy Sepulcher. The people subsisted by the culture of the vine and other fruits. It was a frightful wilderness, consisting chiefly of naked rocks, which sometimes toppled from their base, carrying down with them the clinging vines.

The road proper from Jericho to Jerusalem did not run through Adummin, but westward of it, on which side there was no access to the city. But that from Bethagla to Adummin was intersected by another running from the shepherd valley to Jericho, and at about one half-hour's distance from Adummin. Near this crossroad was a very narrow and dangerous pass, designated by a stone as the spot where long before had really happened the fact upon which Jesus based the parable of the good Samaritan and the man that had fallen among robbers. As Jesus was approaching Adummin, he turned a little out of the way with his disciples, to give an instruction on that memorable spot. Seated on the stone chair and surrounded by the disciples and the people of the immediate neighborhood, he taught, taking for his text the incident just quoted. He celebrated the sabbath in Adummin and taught in the synagogue, relating a parable that referred to the advantages offered to malefactors by the refugial city, all which he applied to the grace of doing penance on this earth. He also cured several persons, most of them dropsical.

Saturday, January 28, AD 30 (Shebat 6)

Jesus taught in the synagogue and also healed many people. At the close of the sabbath, he and the disciples returned to the place of baptism.

Sunday, January 29, AD 30 (Shebat 7)

Jesus taught, while Andrew and Saturnin baptized. In the evening, Jesus went with some disciples to Nebo, situated at the foot of Mount Nebo. The disciples brought some water from the baptismal pool in leathern bottles.

Next evening Jesus went with his disciples to the city of Nebo, situated on the opposite side of the Jordan at the foot of Mount Nebo, whose height is such that several hours are necessary to reach the summit. Messengers had previously been sent to implore him to enter the city and teach. The population was a mixed one, Egyptians, Moabites, and Israelites that had in former times defiled themselves with idolatry. They had been aroused by John's preaching, but had not had the courage to go over to Jesus's place of baptism. I think they dared not. On account of some crime of their forefathers (of what kind I no longer remember), they were held by the Jews in great contempt. They dared not go about freely, but to certain places only. They now came to Jesus humbly begging him to baptize among them. The disciples had brought from the baptismal pool water in leathern bottles, which they had left under the care of some guards.

Nebo was about one half-hour from the Jordan, from which it was separated by a mountain, and between five and six hours from Machaerus. The country around was not fertile. To reach Nebo, one must, after crossing the river, climb the mountain and then descend on the other side. Just opposite the place of baptism stands the mountain, affording no place for a landing, and behind was the city Nebo. It was tolerably large, the foundation hilly, and separated by a valley from the mount of the same name. There was still here a pagan temple, but it was closed and something built around it.

Monday, January 30, AD 30 (Shebat 8)

Jesus sat on a special chair—for teachers—in the open air, and prepared people for baptism. They were then baptized with water drawn from the place of baptism.

Jesus, from a teacher's chair and out in the open air, prepared the people for baptism, which the disciples administered. The baptismal basin was placed over a cistern into which the neophytes stepped, and which was filled with water to a certain height. The disciples had brought with them the baptismal robes, rolled up and wrapped around their person, which were put on the neophytes during the ceremony. They floated around them on the water. After the baptism a kind of little mantle was placed on their shoulders. At John's baptism, it was something like a stole and as wide as a hand-towel, but at the baptism of Jesus it was more like a real little mantle on which was fastened a

Map 12: A Raising from the Dead
January 27–February 9, AD 30

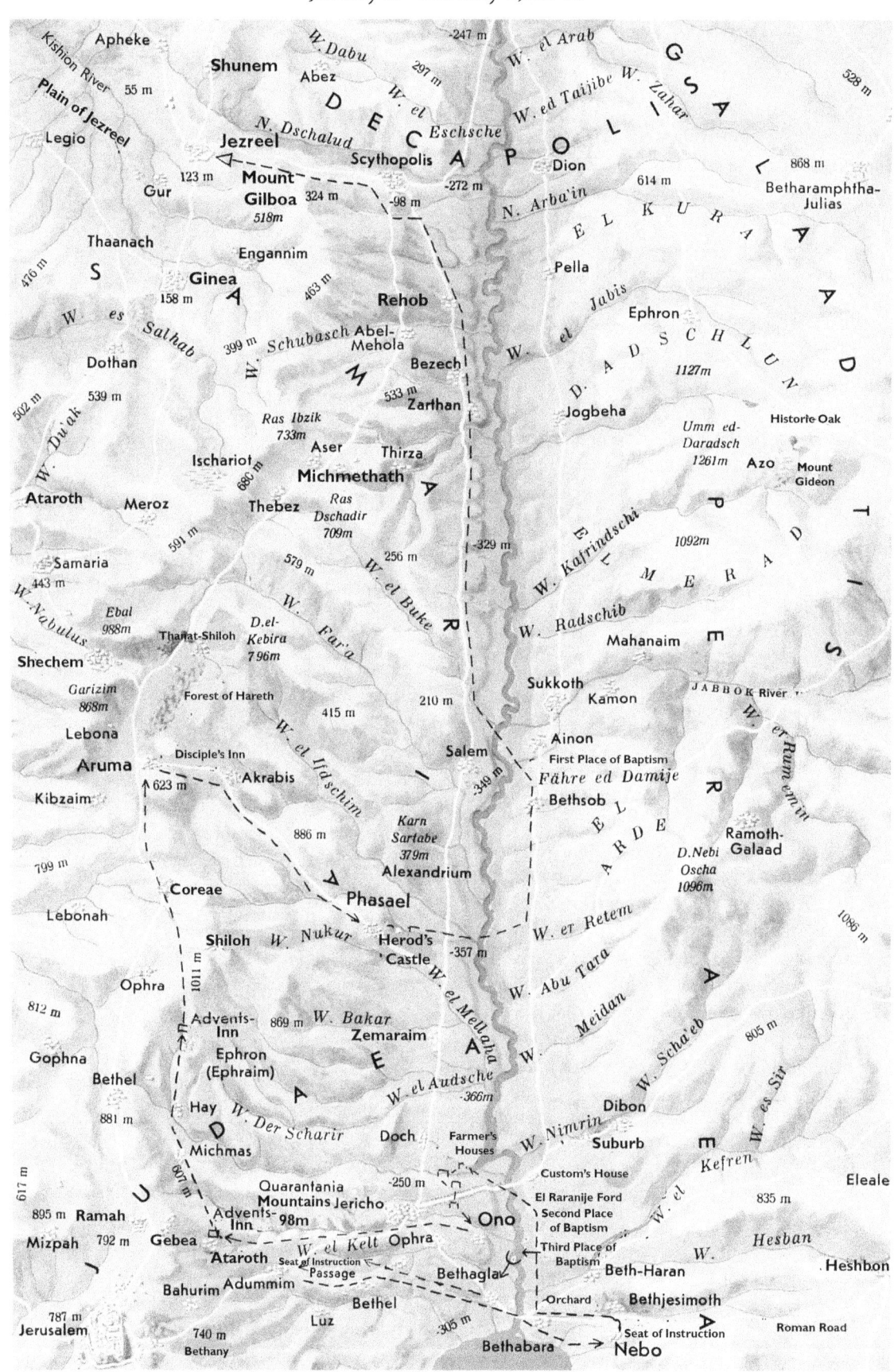

Third Place of Baptism—Wadi el-Kelt—Adunnim—Nebo—Ono—Aruma—Phasael—Jezreel

stole like a lappet trimmed with fringe. Among the newly baptized were mostly tender youths and very old men, for many of the middle-aged were postponed until they should become less unworthy. Jesus healed many sick of fevers and many dropsical who had been carried thither on litters. The possessed among the pagans were not so numerous as among the Jews.

Jesus blessed also the drinking water, which was not good here. It was muddy and brackish. It was collected among the rocks whence it was brought in bottles and poured into a reservoir. Jesus blessed it crosswise, and rested his hand upon several different points of the surface.

Tuesday, January 31, AD 30 (Shebat 9)
This morning Jesus and the disciples left Nebo. They stopped at a place between Nebo and the Jordan. Here Jesus taught. Later that evening, they returned to their inn near the place of baptism.

On their return journey to the inn outside Ono, Jesus and the disciples spent the greater part of the day on the road, only one hour long, from Nebo to the Jordan ferry. Jesus taught the whole way. The road was bordered by huts and tents in which the people from Nebo sold to travelers fruit and distilled wine. It was these vendors that Jesus instructed. Before evening he returned with the disciples to his inn at the place of baptism.

Wednesday, February 1, AD 30 (Shebat 10)
Jesus went afterward through the surrounding district, instructing the peasants singly and in crowds. Among them were many good souls, who during the time that John was baptizing here supplied the crowds with food. Jesus appeared to be seeking out everyone, even those in the most remote corners, for he was soon to leave these parts and go on to Galilee.

Thursday, February 2, AD 30 (Shebat 11)
He stopped for a while at the house of a rich peasant whose fields covered a whole mountain. On one side the harvest was ripe, when on the other they were just about to sow. Jesus taught in a parable of sowing and harvesting (Matthew 13:3, 24).

There was here an old, dilapidated teacher's chair formerly used by the prophets. The peasants had restored it very handsomely, and from it Jesus delivered his instructions.

Several such places for teaching had been restored since John had here baptized. He had ordered it, for that, too, was a part of his preparing the way. These teaching chairs had here, as with us, the pictures of the Stations, quite gone to ruin since the times of the prophets. Elijah and Elisha had frequented this part of the country. Jesus celebrated in Ono the morning of the sabbath, which was followed by a feast that must have had some connection with fruit. I saw whole basketfuls carried during those days into the synagogue and town halls.

The arrangements at the place of baptism had already been taken apart and stowed away by the disciples. Near the spot upon which the stone of the Ark of the Covenant lay there were now scattered around about twenty dwellings. Bethabara was not close to the shore, but about one half-hour from the ferry; one could see it however. From the ferry to John's present place of baptism beyond Bethabara was a good hour and a half's distance.

Friday, February 3, AD 30 (Shebat 12)
I saw Jesus going from house to house at Ono. At first I knew not for what reason, but later I heard that it was on account of the tithes, to the paying of which he was urging the people. He reminded them also of the alms which it was customary to give on the feast of fruit trees now beginning. That evening he celebrated the sabbath in the synagogue, where he taught.

Saturday, February 4, AD 30 (Shebat 13)
After that began the preparations for the new year's fruit festival. Throughout the day, Jesus taught in Ono concerning the threefold meaning of the approaching feast: firstly, it commemorated the rising of the sap in the trees; secondly, because today tithes of all the fruits were offered; and lastly, it was a feast of thanksgiving for the fertility of the soil.

Sunday, February 5, AD 30 (Shebat 14)
The preparations for the new year's "fruits of the trees" festival continued. That evening, with the start of Shebat 15, the festival began. Jesus preached again concerning its meaning.

Monday, February 6, AD 30 (Shebat 15)
They ate much fruit, and gave to the poor whole figures of fruit that were built up on the tables. About twenty new disciples had, up to the present, come to Jesus.

Jesus Cures in Phasael the Daughter of Jairus the Essene • Magdalene's First Call to Conversion

AT the close of the feast, Jesus left Ono with twenty-one disciples and journeyed to Galilee. His way led through the region in which Jacob had owned a field, and among those shepherd houses, from one of which Joseph and Mary had been so harshly turned away on their journey to Bethlehem. He visited the occupants of the inn that had extended hospitality to the holy travelers, and instructed them; with those of the inhospitable one, he stayed overnight and admonished them to be converted. The woman of the house was still alive, though on a sickbed. Jesus cured her.

Tuesday, February 7, AD 30 (Shebat 16)

When Jesus arrived at Aruma, a messenger came to him from Phasael sent by Jairus, the Essene. The messenger told Jesus that Jairus' daughter had died. Jesus left his disciples, arranging to meet them in two days' time in Jezreel, and went with the messenger to Phasael. When he arrived at the home of Jairus, the daughter lay bound in sheets and wrappings ready for burial. Jesus ordered the bindings to be loosened. Then he took the girl's hand, commanding her to rise. She sat up, and rose to stand before him. She was about sixteen years old. Jesus warned those present not to speak of what they had witnessed. (This miracle is not to be confused with the raising from the dead of the daughter of Jairus of Capernaum reported in Mark 5:35–43—see Kislev 3/Kislev 16, AD 30).

Then he passed through Aruma where he had before been. Jairus, a descendant of the Essene Chariot, dwelt in the neighboring and somewhat despised place, Phasael. He had some time previously begged Jesus to cure his sick daughter, and Jesus had promised to do so, though not just then. Although his daughter was dead, Jairus now dispatched a messenger to meet him and remind him of his promise. Jesus sent his disciples on ahead after appointing a certain place [in Jezreel] where they should again meet him, and he himself accompanied Jairus's messenger back to Phasael.

When he entered the house of Jairus, the daughter lay wrapped in the winding-sheet ready for burial, her weeping friends around her. Jesus ordered the neighbors to be called in, and the winding-sheet and linens to be loosened. Then taking the dead girl by the hand, he commanded her to arise. She did so, and stood before him. She was about sixteen years old and not good. She had no love for her father, although he prized her above all things. He was charitable and pious, and shrank not from communication with the poor and despised. That was a source of vexation to his daughter. Jesus roused her from death both of soul and body. She reformed, and some time after joined the holy women. Jesus warned those present not to speak of the miracle they had witnessed. It was through the same desire of secrecy that he had not allowed the disciples to accompany him. This was not the Jairus of Capernaum whose daughter also was, at a later period, raised from the dead by Jesus.

Wednesday, February 8, AD 30 (Shebat 17)

Jesus went eastward from Phasael, crossed the Jordan and walked northward. Then he re-crossed the Jordan north of Salem, and made his way to Jezreel. Thus, he avoided passing through Samaria.

Thursday, February 9, AD 30 (Shebat 18)

Jesus taught in Jezreel [where one month before he had publicly healed the sick] and performed many miracles before a great concourse of people. All the disciples from Galilee were here assembled to meet him. Nathaniel Chased, Nathaniel the bridegroom, Peter, James, John, the sons of Mary Cleophas, all were there.

Lazarus, Martha, Veronica, and Johanna Chusa, who had come before from Jerusalem, had visited Magdalene at her castle of Magdalum to persuade her to go with them to Jezreel in order to see, if not to hear, the wise, the admirable, the most eloquent, and most beautiful Jesus, of whom the whole country was full. Magdalene had yielded to the persuasions of the women and, surrounded by much vain display, accompanied them thither. As she stood at the window of an inn gazing down into the street, Jesus and his disciples came walking by. He looked at her gravely as he passed with a glance that pierced her soul. An unusual feeling of confusion came over her. Violently agitated, she rushed from the inn and, impelled by an overpowering sense of her own misery, hid in a house wherein lepers and women afflicted with an issue of blood found a refuge. It was a kind of hospital under the superintendence of a Pharisee. The people of the inn from which Magdalene had fled, knowing the life she was leading, cried out: "That's the right place for her, among lepers and people tormented with flows of blood!"

But Magdalene had fled to the house of the leprous through that feeling of intense humiliation roused in her soul by the glance of Jesus, for she had made her way into that respectable position among the other women through a motive of pride, not wishing to stand in the crowd of poor, common people. Accompanied by Lazarus, she returned to Magdalum with Martha and the other women. The next sabbath was there celebrated by them, for Magdalum could boast a synagogue.

(Follow Map 13)

Jesus in Capernaum, Gennabris, and Chisloth-Tabor

Friday, February 10, AD 30 (Shebat 19)

TOWARD evening Jesus went for the sabbath to Capernaum, though not till after he had visited his mother. He taught there, and again took up his abode in the house belonging to the bridegroom of Cana. The disciples were gathered here.

Saturday, February 11, AD. 30 (Shebat 20)

Jesus preached all the next day and till the close of the sabbath. Numbers of sick and possessed were brought to him from the country around. He cured them openly before all his disciples, and drove the devils out in presence of an ever-increasing crowd.

Sunday, February 12, AD 30 (Shebat 21)

Messengers came from Sidon begging him to go back with them, but he put them off kindly until a future day. The crowd became so great that at the close of the sabbath Jesus left Capernaum with some of his disciples, and escaped into a mountainous district about an hour to the north of the city. It was situated between the lake and the mouth of the Jordan, and was full of ravines. Into one of these he retired alone to pray. This is the same mountain range from one of whose spurs, when returning lately from the mount of Bethanat with his disciples, they had seen the ships of Peter and Zebedee on the lake.

The disciples that accompanied him went down to the dwellings of the fishermen near the lake in order to apprise them of Jesus's coming. Andrew had stayed behind in Capernaum, teaching and explaining to the assembled multitude.

In the evening Jesus went to his mother's house between Bethsaida and Capernaum, whither had come Lazarus with Martha and the other women from Jerusalem. They were on their way from Magdalum and had called to take leave of Mary before returning to Jerusalem. He said that Martha was too anxious, that Magdalene had been very deeply affected, yet she would, notwithstanding, relapse once more into her old ways. She had not yet laid aside her fine attire, for, as she declared, one in her position could not dress so plainly as the other women, etc.

Monday, February 13, AD 30 (Shebat 22)

As there now began in the city a fast of thanksgiving for the death of a man who, in violation of the Law, had caused certain images to be set up in the temple, Jesus taught again in Capernaum. Again were brought to him the sick, of whom he cured many, and again did messengers come to invite him to other places. There were at this time some very ill-disposed Pharisees around him and they contradicted him on several points. They asked him what would come of all that excitement, for the whole country was in commotion on his account, since he was teaching publicly and daily swelling the numbers of his followers. Jesus rebuked them severely, and told them that he was about to teach and act still more openly.

On that evening began a fast in commemoration of the great victory gained by the other tribes over that of Benjamin, on account of some shameful transgression. I saw that in the country of Phasael, where Jesus had lately raised to life the daughter of Jairus, as also in Aruma, Givea, etc., this day was kept with special strictness, since they had been the theater of those events. I saw that the women in those places made a certain offering and took a prominent part in the fast of atonement.

That night Jesus, with Andrew, Peter, the sons of Mary Cleophas [Judas Thaddeus, Simon, and James the Less] and of Zebedee [James the Greater and John], was conducted by Nathaniel Chased to Gennabris, his own dwelling place. Nathaniel had established there an inn for Jesus. He did not enter Nathaniel's house which, however, he passed on the way to the city. Nathaniel the bridegroom and his wife also visited Capernaum and Jezreel at this time.

Tuesday, February 14, AD 30 (Shebat 23)

Jesus taught in Gennabris, healing some of those who were possessed. In addition to Nathaniel Chased and the seven future apostles, Jonathan—the half-brother of Peter and Andrew—was also in Gennabris.

The place of baptism near Ono was guarded in turn by the inhabitants. Jesus taught in Gennabris and cured some raging possessed. A road for traffic ran through the city. The inhabitants were not so docile as those nearer the lake. Although they did not openly contradict Jesus, yet many received his teaching coldly.

Besides the future apostles, Jonathan, Peter's half-brother, was also in Gennabris. The other apostles had scattered around Capernaum and Bethsaida relating all that they had seen and heard of Jesus.

Wednesday, February 15, AD 30 (Shebat 24)

From Gennabris Jesus went with the future apostles to Bethulia, about three hours distant, five from Tiberias, and not far from Jezreel. It lay on a height so steep that one might fancy it was ready to topple down at any moment. The fragments of its walls were so broad that a wagon could be driven on them. The road from here to Nazareth passed Mount Tabor, from which it was only a couple of hours to the south.

Nathaniel Chased had at this time given over his office in Gennabris to his brother, or cousin. He was, for the future, to follow Jesus.

When Jesus entered Bethulia, the possessed began to cry after him on the street. On arriving at the marketplace, he stood still near a teacher's chair and sent some of his disciples with directions to the superior of the synagogue to have the doors on all sides of the school opened. Others

Map 13: First Journey with the Future Apostles
February 10–23, AD 30

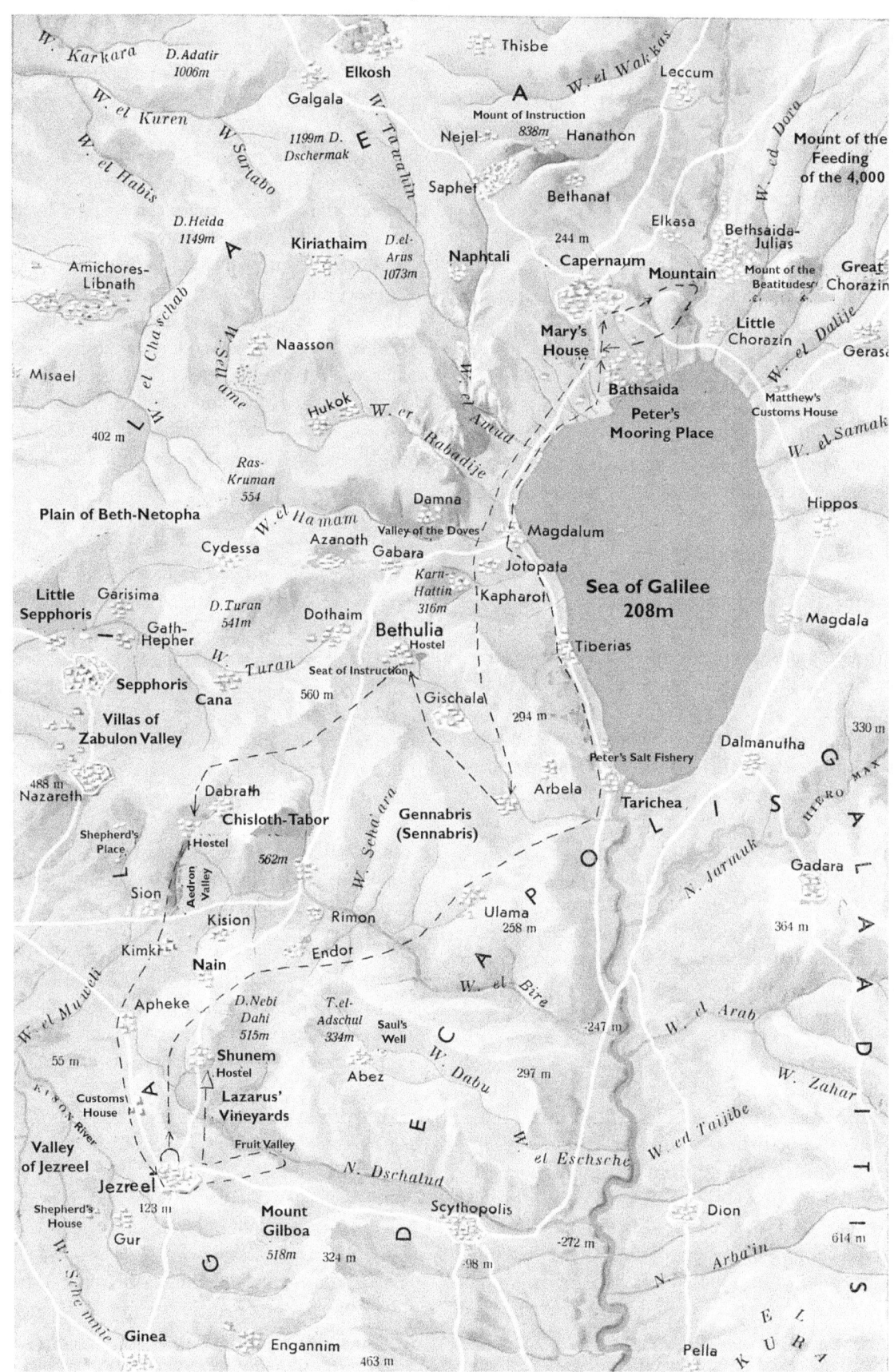

Jezreel—Capernaum—Gennabris—Bethulia—Chisloth-Tabor—Jezreel—Fruit Valley—Shunem

were sent from house to house to call the occupants to the instruction. The synagogue was surrounded by doors between the columns, and it was customary to throw them open when the crowd was exceptionally great. Jesus taught here of the tiny grain of wheat that must be cast into the earth [John 12:24–26]. During his stay he abode in an inn that had been prepared for him.

Thursday, February 16, AD 30 (*Shebat 25*)

The Pharisees in Bethulia feared that Jesus would celebrate the sabbath in their town. Because of this, Jesus left the town and taught at a nearby place where there was a teacher's chair made of stone. During the afternoon he made his way to the town of Chisloth at the foot of Mount Tabor. Word had got around that he would celebrate the sabbath there, and therefore many people flocked to Chisloth to hear him. Andrew and some other disciples had gone on ahead and reserved rooms at an inn for Jesus and his traveling companions. They set up a space in front of the inn, using thick ropes that were run through stakes to hold the crowd back. That evening, Jesus preached from there. Among those listening were several rich merchants of Chisloth. Jesus taught concerning the dangers attached to acquiring wealth. Pointing to one of the thick ropes, made of camel hair, he said: "A rope like this would pass more easily through the eye of a needle than a rich man into the kingdom of heaven" (cf. Matt. 19:24).

The Pharisees here did not indeed openly contradict, but they murmured, and Jesus knew that they did so, because they feared he would celebrate the sabbath among them. He told his disciples this, and that he would keep it about a couple of hours further on, at a place to the northwest toward Tabor. I cannot now recall the name of that place, but the inhabitants were engaged in dyeing silk for fringes and tassels.

Jesus also cured the sick there. All the disciples that had remained behind met here again.

As Jesus, on account of the murmuring of the Pharisees, left Bethulia, he taught outside of the city at the distance of about a quarter of an hour where there was a teacher's chair of stone. Ruined walls lay around, and the place looked as if it might once have belonged to the city proper. At about three in the afternoon, Jesus arrived at Chisloth, which was almost three hours distant, at the foot of Mount Tabor. Andrew and the others had preceded him in order to arrange the inn. A great multitude from the whole country around had gathered at Chisloth, among them numbers of shepherds with their crooks and merchants on their way from Sidon and Tyre. Jesus's miracles and preaching were already noised throughout the land. All crowded to the places where he taught; and when it became known that he purposed celebrating the sabbath at Chisloth, they flocked thither to hear him.

Wherever Jesus now appeared great excitement prevailed. They called after him, cast themselves down before him, and pressed around him in order to be able to touch him; consequently he came and went suddenly and unexpectedly, thus to escape the crowd. Frequently he separated from his disciples on the road, sent them by another route, and went on himself alone. In the towns and villages, they often had to open a way for him through the crowd. Nevertheless he permitted many to draw near and touch him, and many a one was thereby interiorly aroused, converted, or cured.

In the evening Jesus retired to the inn prepared for him by the disciples outside of Chisloth-Tabor, where he had already been twice before. Chisloth was perhaps seven hours from Nazareth, though in a direct line about five. As the roads of this country are so winding, running as they do through the valleys, and as the inhabitants determine distances sometimes by the length of the roads between two places, and sometimes by what it might appear to one gazing down from the mountains, their statistics on that point seldom agree. Galilee was thickly dotted with cities and towns, but from no elevated point could more than a few be seen.

Chisloth-Tabor was chiefly a commercial mart in which were some rich merchants and a great number of poor people. Many of them were dyers of raw silk which was afterward manufactured into fringes and tassels for sacred vestments. These dyers in earlier times were found principally at Tyre on the sea, but later many of them removed here. The rich merchants employed the poor in their factories. I saw here likewise some people who appeared to be slaves.

The disciples, with thick ropes run through stakes, had cut off a space in front of the inn in order to keep back the crowd. It was from that space that Jesus preached. As among his audience there were many of the rich merchants from the city, he taught upon riches and the danger attending the love of gain. Their position, he told them, was more perilous than that of the publicans, who more easily than they would reform. Saying these words, Jesus pointed to the ropes that separated him from the crowd, and uttered the words: "A rope like one of those would go more easily into the eye of a needle than a rich man into the kingdom of heaven." The ropes were camel's hair, as thick as one's arm, and drawn four times through the stakes around the enclosure. The rich people defended themselves by saying that they gave alms out of all their profits. But Jesus replied that alms that have been expressed from the sweat of the poor bring down no blessing. This instruction was not pleasing to his hearers.

Friday, February 17, AD 30 (Shebat 26)

Chisloth was a Levitical town, renowned for its large and magnificent synagogue. Jesus taught in the synagogue most of the day and also that evening. In front of the synagogue he healed a number of children who were brought to him. He also cured several women. After preaching that evening, he and his disciples ate a meal together at the inn where he was staying.

Chisloth was a Levitical city made over by the tribe of Zebulon to the Levites of the race of Merari. The most celebrated school of the whole country was here. It was very large and all its exercises were conducted with solemnity. When on the sabbath Jesus taught in the synagogue, the priests assisted at the discourse. They handed him the rolls of scripture or read the passages that he indicated, upon which he questioned and explained. There was also singing, but not of the Pharisaical kind. I heard the voice of Jesus sweetly sounding among all the others, but I do not remember having heard him singing alone.

Next morning Jesus taught in the school of Chisloth. Andrew instructed the children in an adjacent hall, and recounted to the strangers crowding in all that he had seen and heard of Jesus. Jesus took for his subject vanity and presumption. He performed no cures that day because, as he said, they thought themselves better than others, and attributed to their own merit his coming to teach in their city; whereas he would have them know that he had been led thereto by his knowledge of their misery and his desire to humble and convert them.

The preaching ended, Jesus went out into the court in front of the synagogue, in which there were little cells belonging to it. They were like sentry boxes in a courtyard. Here, he cured of convulsions and other ills numerous children brought to him by their mothers. He cured them because they were innocent. He cured several women also who humbled themselves before him, saying: "Lord, hearken to my fault, my transgression!" They cast themselves down in the hall before him and bewailed their sins. Among them were some afflicted with an issue of blood, and others tormented by evil inclinations from which they implored to be freed.

That evening Jesus celebrated the sabbath in the school and afterward ate at the inn. His future apostles and intimate friends were with him at the same table, and the disciples not engaged in serving were in adjoining apartments.

Saturday, February 18, AD 30 (Shebat 27)

Today, Jesus healed many sick people in front of the synagogue. After the close of the sabbath, a Pharisee, who was so moved by what he had heard of Jesus' teaching that he was converted, invited Jesus and his disciples to dine with him.

The next day he celebrated the sabbath in the synagogue, and in front of it healed many sick. He also visited and cured in their homes many that could not be carried to him. The disciples assisted Jesus in this, bringing the sick, leading them to him, raising them up, and making room for them. They executed his commissions and delivered his messages.

All the traveling expenses, as well as the alms, were up to the present furnished by Lazarus, and Simeon's son Obed kept the accounts.

The little cells before the synagogue that looked like sentry boxes were in the courtyard where, through a grating, the women spoke in private to Jesus. It was the custom for female sinners, penitents, or women that had contracted legal impurity to receive in these cells consolation from the priests.

There was no city upon Mount Tabor, but there were bulwarks, walls, and something like a vacant fortress, whither at times the troops retired. On the evening after the sabbath, Jesus and his most intimate disciples, the future apostles, were entertained by a Pharisee who had been touched and converted by the teaching of Jesus.

Sunday, February 19, AD 30 (Shebat 28)

Next day Jesus, with his disciples, was present at a great banquet, given in his honor in the public feast hall by the most distinguished men of the place. Jesus taught here also, and on the same evening left the city for Jezreel, which was not much more than three hours' distance from Chisloth-Tabor.

Monday, February 20, AD 30 (Shebat 29)

In Jezreel, Jesus's relatives and the disciples from Bethsaida, including Andrew and Nathaniel, took leave of him in order to visit their homes. He indicated to them where they should again meet. About fifteen of the younger disciples still remained with him while he taught here and performed some cures. There were all kinds of religious and secular schools in Jezreel, for it was a large city. Jesus took Naboth's vineyard for the subject of one of his discourses (1 Kings, 21).

Tuesday, February 21, AD 30 (Shebat 30)

Today, Jesus taught in the open at a place about an hour and a half east of Jezreel. Later in the day, Jesus and his disciples made their way to Shunem. That evening, at the inn where they were staying, they celebrated the New Moon festival denoting the start of the month of Adar.

From Jezreel Jesus went one hour and a half southward to a field in a valley, two hours long and as many broad, wherein were numerous orchards surrounded by low hedges. It was an uncommonly productive and charming fruit region. There were numerous tents here standing in couples at different intervals, and occupied by people from Shunem who guarded and gathered in the fruit. I think it was a kind of service that they were obliged to take turns in rendering. About four occupied one tent. The women dwelt together apart from the men, for whom they did the cooking. Jesus instructed these people under a tent. There were here most beautiful springs and abundant streams, which flowed into the Jordan. The principal source came from Jezreel. It formed in the valley a charming spring, over which a kind of chapel was built. From this spring house the stream divided into several others throughout the valley, united with other waters, and at last emptied into the Jordan. There were about thirty custodians whom Jesus instructed, the women remaining at some distance. He taught of the slavery of sin, from which they should free themselves. They were inexpressibly rejoiced and touched that he had come to them. He was so loving and courteous to these poor people that I had to shed tears myself over it. They set before Jesus and the disciples fruit, of which they ate. In some parts of the valley the fruit was already ripe, in others the trees were only in blossom. There were some brown fruits like figs, but growing in clusters like grapes, also yellow plants from which they prepared a kind of pap. In this valley rises Mount Gilboa, and here also was Saul slain in battle against the Philistines.

Jesus in Shunem, Ulama, and Capernaum

IN the evening Jesus went through Jezreel and about three hours further to Shunem, an open place on a hill. Some of the disciples had gone on before, in order to make arrangements with the landlord of the inn at the entrance of the city. The fertile valley through which Jesus had just passed lay to the south of Jezreel. He went through a part of Jezreel without attracting notice, and then turned northward toward Shunem. Near this city, that is, at a distance of one to two hours, are two others, one of which Jesus had passed on his way from Chisloth-Tabor to Jezreel.

The inhabitants of Shunem depended upon weaving for their livelihood. They wove narrow edging of twisted silk, plain or interspersed with flowers. Shunem did not lie in the valley of Esdrelon, but rather where the mountains took their rise.

ADAR (29 days):
February 21/22, to March 21/22, AD 30
Adar New Moon: February 21 at 7:15 AM
Jerusalem time

Wednesday, February 22, AD 30 (Adar 1)
A multitude of people gathered at Shunem to hear Jesus. There was great jubilation at the appearance of the new prophet, sent by God. Jesus taught in the synagogue and visited some homes to heal the sick.

The multitude that here pressed around Jesus was simply astonishing, and it was ever on the increase. The people surrounded him everywhere, cast themselves down before him, crying and shouting that a new prophet had arisen, one sent by God! Many were sincere in their acclamations, but others followed through curiosity and shouted merely to swell the noise. The crowd was so dense that it was almost like an insurrection, and because here in Galilee the

Synagogue Lamp

excitement was daily increasing, Jesus resolved soon to leave it. Shunem was the native city of the beautiful Abishag who had served David in his old age. Elisha also had had an inn here at which he frequently stopped and in which he had recalled the dead son of his hostess to life. A vision of the same was vouchsafed me, that I might know the place. This city possessed also a free inn for certain travelers. It had been founded as a memorial of Elisha. I know not, however, whether it was the house that the prophet once occupied, or whether it was another built upon the same site. Jesus taught on this day in the synagogue and visited many of the houses to console and cure the sick. Shunem was built rather irregularly around a hill whose summit overlooked the city. A road led up the hill. The houses upon it decreased in size with the ascent, the highest being mere huts. The top of the hill was crowned by an open space upon which stood a teacher's seat. It was surrounded by palings over which an awning could be stretched for protection from the sun.

Thursday, February 23, AD 30 (Adar 2)

This morning Jesus went with his disciples to a teacher's chair on the top of a hill. There was great excitement, and he healed many sick people who had been brought there. Jesus spoke of the necessity of repenting, doing penance, and fulfilling the commandments. That afternoon he proceeded to Ulama, where he met up with his other disciples. On his way to the inn, where they were to stay, he healed several people who were possessed.

When Jesus, on the morning of the following day, started with his disciples for the teacher's chair, the whole place was alive with excitement. They had brought numbers of sick in litters, and had placed them all along the road leading up the hill. Jesus ascended through the clamoring multitude, healing as he went. The people had mounted to the roofs, the better to see and hear all that he would do and say. From the teacher's chair on the top of the hill the view was magnificent, stretching off toward Tabor. Jesus inveighed against the pride and presumption of the Shunemites who, instead of being converted, doing penance, and keeping the commandments of God, broke forth into vain shouts over the prophet that had come among them, the sent from God, for they attributed his coming as an honor due their own merit, whereas he had come in order to convince them of their sins.

About three in the afternoon Jesus left Shunem. Taking a northerly direction, he reached, in about three hours, a large and closely built city with a less ancient appearance than Shunem. It was enclosed by walls so broad that trees flourished upon them. This city was called Ulama and was about five hours southeast of Tabor. Arbela was about two hours to the north. The rough roads of the surrounding mountains were covered with sharp, white pebbles, on which account there were made in Ulama numbers of soles to bind as a protection under the feet. The city was built on a mountain, surrounded by other mountains, and in an altogether impassable region. Vines covered those mountains from base to summit. I have seen upon them plants as high as a tree, their tangled branches as thick as one's arm. They produce large, pyriform fruits like gourds, and from them flasks are made. Ulama did not appear so old as other cities; indeed, there was something about it that even made it look unfinished. The inhabitants did not bear the stamp of old Jewish simplicity, they appeared to be aiming at greater culture and refinement. It was as if the Romans or some other nation had formerly sojourned among them. Here as elsewhere, the concourse of people was very great, for they knew that Jesus was about to celebrate the sabbath in Ulama. Several of the disciples had rejoined Jesus, among them Peter's half-brother Jonathan and the sons of the widows. They numbered, in all, twenty. Peter, Andrew, John, James the Less, Nathaniel Chased, and Nathaniel the bridegroom had also come. Jesus had directed them to do so that they might hear his instructions and assist him in his ministrations to the sick, rendered difficult by the turbulence of the multitude. The people had found out the way by which Jesus was to come, and they went forth to welcome him, carrying green branches and strewing leaves. They had stretched across the road long strips of stuff which they lowered for him to step over, while shouts of joy proclaimed the advent of the prophet. The chief officers of the place maintained order and formally saluted Jesus in the name of the city. There were in Ulama many possessed, who clamored violently after Jesus and shouted his name. But he commanded them to be silent. Even at the inn they allowed him no rest. They ran about raging and screaming, until he again ordered them to be silent and had them removed. Ulama had three schools: one of jurisprudence; another for youths; and the third, the synagogue.

(Follow Map 14)

Friday, February 24, AD 30 (Adar 3)

Jesus entered different houses, to cure and to console. Then he taught in the school, speaking especially upon simplicity and of the respect due to parents; for in both of these particulars the people of this place were wanting. He rebuked them severely also for their pride. Vain at the thought of a prophet's coming among them, they were by their presumption depriving themselves of the benefits attached to these days of penance and instruction.

Saturday, February 25, AD 30 (Adar 4)

At the close of the sabbath, Jesus was invited to attend a banquet in his honor.

The sabbath over, the distinguished men of the place gave Jesus an entertainment in the grand public hall. The apostles and disciples that had gone home limited themselves to a mere visit to their relatives. They had then called upon Mary, with whom the holy women were becoming more and more intimate.

The Baptist was still in the same place, his followers constantly diminishing. Herod had several times been to see him and had frequently sent his officers for the same purpose.

Sunday, February 26, AD 30 (Adar 5)

Around nine o'clock in the morning, Jesus and his disciples walked to a place about a quarter of an hour from the town. Many people had already gathered there to hear him; also many sick people had been brought, whom he healed. Jesus taught concerning the death of Moses, which was to be celebrated on Adar 7, a day of fasting. Afterward, he went to a place where those who were possessed dwelt and cured them.

At nine o'clock on the morning after the sabbath, Jesus went with his disciples to a mountain along which was a pleasure garden or bathing place, about a quarter of an hour from the city. The garden was almost as large as the cemetery of Dulmen [Anne Catherine's home village]. It had pavilions and little summer houses, a beautiful fountain, and a place for instruction. Jesus had directed the sick, of whom there were numbers, to be transported thither from the city, for he could not, on account of the crowd, cure in the latter place. The disciples busied themselves in the maintenance of order, and the sick on their litters were placed around under tents and in the pavilions. The crowds that followed from the city were so great that many could not even reach the garden. The magistrates and priests also kept order. Jesus passed from litter to litter curing many. When I say many, I generally mean about thirty. (When I say a few or several, I mean about ten.) Jesus taught and alluded to the death of Moses, whose anniversary would soon be celebrated by a fast day, when their food already cooked would be placed under the ashes, and when they would eat, as was usual on such days, a particular kind of bread. He also referred to the Promised Land and its fertility, which was to be understood not only of the material sustenance of the body, but also of the spiritual nourishment of the soul; for it was also fruitful in prophets and oracles from God, the fruit of which would be penance and the salvation promised to all that would embrace it.

This instruction ended, I saw Jesus going into a building nearby wherein the possessed had been assembled. He entered to find them raging and shouting. They were for the most part young people, some of them only children. Jesus caused them to be placed in a row, commanded silence, and with one word freed them from the evil spirit. Some of them fell fainting. Their parents and friends were present, and to all Jesus addressed some words of exhortation and instruction.

Monday, February 27, AD 30 (Adar 6)

After Jesus had taught in the synagogue, he left Ulama unnoticed, the disciples having gone before him. He knew how to manage that. Without entering any of the cities on the way, they proceeded toward Capernaum. Jesus was about to leave Galilee on account of the great excitement there prevailing.

Tuesday, February 28, AD 30 (Adar 7)

Early this morning, he arrived at his mother's house in Capernaum. She and the other holy women gathered there were veiled because of the fast day commemorating the death of Moses. Jesus talked privately with Mary. He told her that he would soon leave for Judea in order to be in Jerusalem for the Passover. Today, too, Jesus taught in the synagogue in Capernaum.

He traveled with the disciples throughout the night, and arrived at his mother's in the morning. Peter's wife and sister were there, also the bride of Cana and other women. The house that Mary occupied here was for the most part like its neighbors and very roomy. She was never alone. The widows lived nearby and the women from Bethsaida and Capernaum, between which these houses were, gathered around her as also one or other of the disciples. I saw them keeping the fast with signs of mourning, the women being veiled. Jesus taught in the synagogue of Capernaum, the disciples and holy women being present.

Capernaum was situated, measuring in a straight line over the mountain, about one hour from the Sea of Galilee, but two hours if one went through the valley and through Bethsaida on the south. About a good half-hour on the road from Capernaum to Bethsaida were the houses, in one of which Mary dwelt. A beautiful stream flows from Capernaum to the lake. Near Bethsaida it branched off into several arms, rendering the land very fruitful. Mary conducted no household, she owned neither cattle nor fields. She lived as a widow upon the gifts of her friends, engaged in spinning, sewing, knitting with little wooden needles, praying, consoling, and instructing the other women.

Jesus, on the day of his arrival, had a private interview with his mother. She wept over the great danger threatening him on account of the excitement everywhere produced by his teachings and miracles, for she had been informed of all the murmurs and calumnies uttered against him by those that would not presume to say them to his face. But Jesus told her that his time was come, that he would soon leave those parts and go down to Judea where, after Passover, still greater vexation would arise on his account. [B15]

That evening there began in Capernaum a feast of thanksgiving for rain. The synagogue and other public buildings were gaily ornamented with young green trees and pyramids of foliage, while from the galleries on the roof of the synagogue and other large edifices, a wonderful,

Map 14: Travels in Galilee
February 24–March 15, AD 30

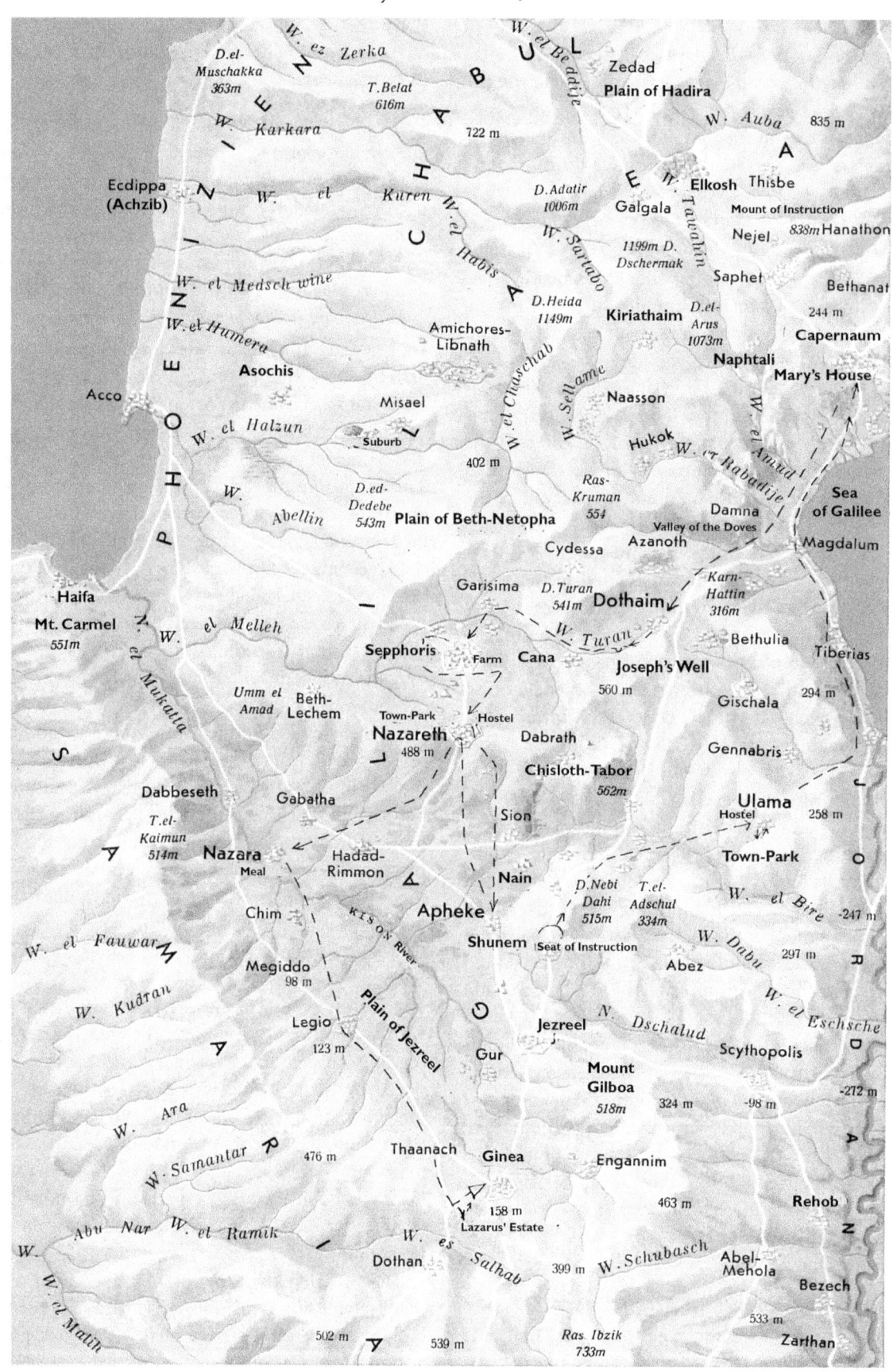

Shunem—Ulama—Capernaum—Dothaim—Sepphoris—Nazareth—Apheke—Nazareth
Nazara—Lazarus's Estate—Ginea

many-toned instrument was sounded. The servants of the synagogue, people like our sextons, played on it. It looked like a bag about four feet in length in which were several pipes and trumpet mouthpieces. When the bag was not distended with wind, these pipes and tubes lay together, one upon another. But when it was inflated by the breath of a man blowing into one of the mouthpieces, two other men raised it up and (either by blowing the breath, or by means of a bellows) introduced air into it. Then by opening and closing the different valves of the pipes, which arose in several directions, a shrill-sounding, many-voiced tone was produced. Those standing at the side of the instrument blew into it at certain intervals.

Wednesday, March 1, AD 30 (Adar 8)

Jesus taught again in the synagogue at Capernaum. In the evening, he took leave of many of his disciples, as he intended to travel to Judea with a small group of only twelve disciples.

Jesus delivered in the synagogue an extremely touching discourse upon rain and drought. In it he told of Elijah, who prayed on Mount Carmel for rain and six times questioned his servant as to what he saw. The seventh time, the servant replied that he saw a little cloud rising out of the sea. It became larger and larger until at last it bore rain to the whole country. Then Elijah journeyed through the whole land. Jesus applied those seven questionings of Elijah to the space of time before the fulfillment of the Promise. The cloud he explained as a symbol of the present and the rain as an image of the coming of the Messiah, whose teaching should spread everywhere and bear new life to all. Whoever thirsted should now drink, and whoever had prepared his field should now receive rain. This was said so touchingly, so impressively that all his hearers, as well as Mary and the other holy women, wept.

The people of Capernaum were at that time very well disposed. There were three priests attached to the synagogue and near it was the house in which they dwelt. Jesus and his intimate disciples often took their meals with them, for a certain degree of hospitality was always extended to the teacher who had taught in the synagogue.

That evening and early the next morning, I heard them playing again on that wonderful instrument. The feast was celebrated all the next day, but only by the children and young people, who enjoyed themselves heartily. The evening of the feast, Jesus took leave of the disciples related to him, as also those from Bethsaida, because early the next day he was to depart from Capernaum and go down into Judea. He took with him only about twelve, those from Nazareth, those from Jerusalem, and those that had come from John.

Jesus in Dothaim and Sepphoris • From a Distance, He Helps the Shipwrecked

Thursday, March 2, AD 30 (Adar 9)

Mary and several holy women accompanied Jesus and a small group of disciples as far as the little place called Dothaim. Entering the town, they were welcomed by a group of men, some of them priests, who invited them to a meal. Jesus told the story of Joseph, who had been sold at a well nearby (Genesis 37:17–28). After the meal, Jesus took leave of his mother, who wept. Then Jesus went with his disciples and some people of Dothaim to Joseph's well and blessed it. Traveling further, Jesus and his disciples arrived toward evening at Sepphoris. Here he stayed with his great-aunt Maraha.

AFTER the feast of thanksgiving, Jesus, with about twelve disciples, traveled in a southeasterly direction from Capernaum, as if between Cana and Sepphoris. Mary and eight of the holy women, among them Mary Cleophas, the three widows, the bride of Cana, and Peter's sister, accompanied him to a little city where they took a meal together and then parted from him. In the neighborhood of this place was the pit into which Joseph was cast by his brethren. The place was called Dothaim. But there was another and a much larger Dothaim (or Dothan) in the valley of Esdrelon, about four hours to the north of Samaria. This Dothaim was a little place, and the people lived chiefly by providing for the wants of the merchants traveling through their city. It lay at the end of a little valley large enough to afford pasturage for about eighty head of cattle. At the other side stood that great building in which Jesus had once calmed the possessed; this time he did not enter. Dothaim is an hour and a half northeast of Sepphoris and between four and five hours from Mount Tabor.

The disciples had gone on before, to prepare the inn. About eight men, some of them priests, came out to meet Jesus and the holy women, and escort them to the public hall of entertainment. No one lived in it, but already everything was prepared for a repast. Before the entrance there was spread in honor of Jesus a carpet upon which he had to walk. They washed his feet. The women ate apart, back of the fireplace. Jesus and the disciples reclined at table and partook of only cold foods, such as little rolls and honey, green salad steeped in sauce, and fruits. Their drink was water mixed with balsam. Little flasks of the same were presented to Jesus and the women to take away with them. The priests from the city remained standing during the repast and served the guests with uncommon love and humility, while Jesus spoke of Joseph, who had here been sold. It was an indescribably touching scene. I could not restrain my tears. It appeared to me so strange that I should behold it so near to me, and yet could not enter as I so longed to do. I wanted to do this and that, but I could not. Immediately after the repast, the holy women departed for Capernaum.

Jesus took leave of his mother in private, and then bade goodbye to the others. I have remarked that when alone Jesus always embraced his mother on his arrival or departure, but before others he merely extended his hand or inclined his head. Mary wept. She was still very youthful looking, tall and delicately built. Her forehead was very high, her nose rather long, her eyes very large and mildly downcast, her lips of a beautiful red, her complexion rather dark, but beautiful, and her cheeks lightly tinged with the color of the rose.

Jesus tarried a while longer teaching in the inn, and the men, who would accept no remuneration for the repast, accompanied him on his departure as far as Joseph's well, which was at that time not such as it was when Joseph was let down into it. Then it was only an empty pit, its mouth surrounded by green bushes and vines, but now it was a spacious, four-cornered reservoir, like a little pool, under a roof supported by pillars. It was full of water and in it was kept an abundance of fish. I saw some that lifted their heads up so curiously, not pointed like those we see. But they were not so large as similar ones in the Sea of Galilee. There was no visible supply of water to the well. There was a fence around it, and it was guarded by people living near. Jesus entered the spring house with his companions. The whole way he had taught of Joseph and his brethren, and he continued the same discourse at the well, which I saw him blessing as he left. His escort now returned to Dothaim, while he and his disciples went on for about a good hour to Sepphoris, where he stopped with the sons of Anne's sister.

Friday, March 3, AD 30 (Adar 10)

However, he was not well received by the learned teachers there who criticized his wandering about the land instead of staying with his mother.

Sepphoris was built on a mountain in the midst of mountains. It was larger than Capernaum, and there were many separate residences standing around in the environs. That evening, at the start of the sabbath, Jesus preached in the synagogue. He was not very well received by the doctors of the synagogue, and I heard wicked people, of whom there were many in this city, calumniating him, saying that he was wandering about instead of staying with his mother.

Saturday, March 4, AD 30 (Adar 11)

Jesus taught again in the synagogue in Sepphoris and visited various homes—mostly of Essene families—to offer encouragement and support to his followers. He spoke with great affection, his words full of love. That night a great storm arose. Jesus prayed with outstretched arms that danger might be averted. Thus, he protected the ships on the Sea of Galilee from afar.

Jesus performed no cures here, and held himself very much aloof; still, on the sabbath he preached in the synagogue and went to an inn nearby for his meals. He visited many private individuals and families, principally Essenes, however, whom he exhorted and consoled, for many of the wicked inhabitants ridiculed and slandered them, on account of their affection for him. Jesus told several of those that lived in the environs, as also some of his own relatives, not to follow him just then, but to remain his friends in secret, and to continue their good works until the end of his career. His relatives did much good here and contributed also to the support of the blessed Virgin, to whom they sent all kinds of necessaries. I saw Jesus conversing with these different families in so affectionate and intimate a way that I have no words to describe it. His deportment, so full of love, touched me to tears.

That night I saw something else that appeared to me surprising and inexpressibly affecting. There happened on that night a great windstorm in the Holy Land, and I saw Jesus with many others in prayer. He prayed with outstretched hands that danger might be averted. Then I had a glance at the Sea of Galilee, which was lashed by the tempest, the ships of Peter, Andrew, and Zebedee being in distress. The apostles were, as I saw, asleep in Bethany, their servants alone being on the ships. And lo! As Jesus stood praying, I saw an apparition of him there upon the ships, now on one, now on the other, and then again upon the raging billows. It was as if he were laboring among them, holding back the vessels, warding off the danger. He was not there in person, for I did not see him going, but he stood above the sufferers, he hovered on the waves. The sailors did not see him, for it was his spirit assisting them in prayer. Nobody knew anything about his being there, though he was really helping them. Perhaps the sailors believed in him and called on him for help.

Jesus in Nazareth • The Three Youths • The Feast of Purim

Sunday, March 5, AD 30 (Adar 12)

Jesus and his disciples made their way to Nazareth. In the evening, Jesus taught at the synagogue. It was the start of the fast day (Adar 13) commemorating Esther. That night another storm arose, and Jesus—through prayer—again helped to avert the danger threatening the people aboard ships on the Sea of Galilee.

FROM Sepphoris Jesus took a byway around some country houses to Nazareth about two hours distant, teaching and consoling as he went. Among the disciples now with him were two or three youths, sons of Essene widows. Arrived at Nazareth, he put up with some acquaintances, and without being remarked visited several good people. The Pharisees, with an outward show of respect but inwardly full of malice, called upon Jesus to ask him what he now purposed doing and why he did not stay with his mother, which questions he answered gravely and sharply. Preparations were going on all around for the fast day observed in remembrance of Esther, also for that of the Feast of Purim immediately to follow. Jesus taught very zealously in the synagogue.

That night I again saw Jesus praying with outstretched arms, and again appearing on the Sea of Galilee to bear help in a storm. This time the distress was much greater, and many more vessels were in danger. I saw Jesus laying his hand on the helm without the helmsman's seeing him.

Monday, March 6, AD 30 (Adar 13)
Today, Jesus was visited by the three rich youths who had sought him out on Elul 16/17. Jesus again refused their request to become his disciples. In the afternoon, he taught in the synagogue. That evening, with the start of Adar 14, the Festival of Purim—a festival of joy—began. Jesus visited the home of the old Essene Eliud, talking with him late into the night.

The three rich youths of Nazareth who had once before vainly preferred their petition to him to be received as disciples came to him again, reiterating their request. They almost knelt to him, but he sent them away after pointing out certain conditions that had to be fulfilled before he would allow them to join his disciples. Jesus knew well that their views were wholly terrestrial, and that they could not understand him. They wanted to follow him because they saw in him a philosopher, a learned Rabbi. After a time spent in his school, they could, as they thought, shine with a more brilliant reputation and do honor to their city Nazareth. They were besides somewhat vexed at seeing him giving the preference to the poor sons of Nazareth rather than to themselves.

Until far into the night I saw Jesus with the old Essene, Eliud of Nazareth. The holy man looked as if he would soon die of old age. He was no longer able for much, indeed he was almost bedridden. Jesus leaned on his arm at the bedside and talked with him. Eliud was entirely absorbed in God.

Tuesday, March 7, AD 30 (Adar 14)
The Festival of Purim was celebrated today with scenes from the Book of Esther enacted by children and maidens. A great banquet was held, which Jesus attended, and presents were given to the poor.

At the commencement of the Festival of Purim, a musical instrument, which stood on three feet, was again played on the roof of the synagogue. It was hollow with pipes running through it, the ends extending both above and below. By pushing the pipes in and out, the music was produced. Children also were playing on harps and flutes. Today in commemoration of Esther, the women and young maidens enjoyed certain rights and privileges in the synagogue. They were not separated from the men, they could even approach where the priests were. There was a procession in the synagogue of children dressed fancifully, some in white, others in red. Then a maiden entered wearing around her neck an ornament somewhat frightful looking. It was a blood-red circle around her throat, as if she had been beheaded, and from it hung on her white garments, numerous knots of blood-red threads like so many streaks of blood from the wounded neck. She wore a magnificent mantle borne by train-bearers, and appeared to be enacting the principal part in some drama. Children and maidens followed her. She wore a high, pointed ornament on the forepart of her head and a long veil. In her hand she carried something, whether a sword or a scepter, I do not know. She was tall, and a maiden of great beauty. I do not know for certain what distinguished character she represented. It might, I think, have been Esther, or again, Judith, though not that Judith who slew Holofernes, for there was with her a maiden, who carried a beautiful basket containing presents for the chief priest. She presented to him many precious little shields, such as the priests wore sometimes on the forehead or the breast. In one corner of the synagogue, concealed by a curtain, lay upon a bed of state the effigy of a man, whose head the maiden struck off and took to the chief priest. Then, making use of the privilege granted to females on that day, she rebuked the priests for the principal faults they had committed during the year. That done, she withdrew. This privilege to rebuke the priests belonged to the women on certain other feasts also.

In the synagogue they read in turn from separate rolls the Book of Esther, Jesus also taking his turn to read. The Jews, especially the children, had little wooden tablets with hammers. When they pulled a string, the hammer struck a name inscribed on the tablet, while at the same time holders uttered some words. They did this as often as the name of Aman was pronounced.

There were also great banquets. Jesus was present at that given to the priests in the grand public hall. The adornments of this feast were similar to those of the Feast of Tabernacles. There were numbers of wreaths, roses as large as one's head, pyramids made up entirely of flowers, and quantities of fruit. A whole lamb was on the table, and I gazed in wonder at the magnificence of the plates, glasses, and dishes. There was one kind of dish, many-colored and transparent, like precious stones. They looked as if formed of interwoven threads of colored glass. There was today a great exchange of gifts, consisting principally of jewels and handsome articles of apparel, such as robes, maniples, veils for the head, and sashes trimmed with tassels. Jesus, too, was presented with a holiday robe trimmed in like manner. But he would not keep it; he passed it to another. Many others likewise bestowed their presents on the poor, who were very bountifully remembered that day.

Wednesday, March 8, AD 30 (Adar 15)

Today, the Festival of Purim continued to be celebrated. This morning Jesus went with his disciples and some priests to the pleasant gardens near Nazareth, where passages from the Book of Esther were read aloud.

After the banquet, Jesus and his disciples walked with the priests to the pleasure gardens, and the beautifully adorned teaching places near Nazareth. They had with them three rolls of writings, and I saw again the Book of Esther, out of which they read in turn. Crowds of youths and maidens followed them, but the latter listened to the discourse only at a distance. I saw also on that day men going around and taking up a tax.

Thursday, March 9, AD 30 (Adar 16)

This morning, Jesus was in the synagogue, where a kind of thanksgiving service took place. Afterward, he disputed with some priests. In the afternoon, he went with his disciples to Apheke.

Friday, March 10, to Sunday, March 12, AD 30 (Adar 17–19)

In the course of the day, Jesus returned to Nazareth, where he celebrated the sabbath. During the night from Sunday to Monday, he made his last visit to the home of the old Essene Eliud, who was close to death.

Jesus at Lazarus's Estate near Thirza and at his Home in Bethany

Monday, March 13, AD 30 (Adar 20)

This morning, Jesus and his disciples left Nazareth. Priests accompanied them part of the way. Some were secretly envious of Jesus because of his knowledge and how he taught. Jesus then set off on the same route that the holy family had taken on the flight to Egypt. He passed first through the little place Nazara. Here he performed a miracle: He bought bread and multiplied it in his hands and distributed it to the poor. Then he made his way to Lazarus's villa near Ginea. He was met by Lazarus, John Mark, Obed, and four other disciples. Together they stayed overnight at Lazarus's villa.

THE PRIESTS of Nazareth could not comprehend where Jesus, in so short an absence, had come by so much knowledge. They could find nothing reprehensible in his teaching, though many were secretly envious of him. They escorted him part of the way when he left Nazareth with his disciples.

Jesus, taking the road traveled by the holy family on the occasion of their flight into Egypt, arrived with his disciples at the little place not far from Legio where the holy family had put up and where lived a set of despised people like slaves. Jesus bought some bread here, and as he divided it, it was multiplied in his hands; but the miracle created no excitement, since he did not tarry long and performed it, as it were, in passing.

Proceeding on his journey, he was met by Lazarus, John Mark, and Obed, who had come for that purpose. With them Jesus went on to Lazarus's villa near Ginea, about five hours distant. They arrived unnoticed and by night, and found all things ready for their reception. The villa was on a mountain toward Samaria, not far from Jacob's field. A very old Jew, who went barefoot and girt, was the steward, an office he had held even when Mary and Joseph stopped here on their journey to Bethlehem. It was at this same villa that Martha and Magdalene, in Jesus's last year when he was teaching in Samaria, showed him hospitality and implored him to come to their brother Lazarus who was sick.

Tuesday, March 14, AD 30 (Adar 21)

Near that estate of Lazarus was the then small city of Thirza, situated in a lovely region about seven hours' journey from Samaria. The morning sun, to which Thirza was exposed, rendered it extremely fruitful in grain, wine, and orchard fruits. The inhabitants were engaged chiefly in agriculture, the products of which they carried to a distance for sale. The city was once large and handsome and the residence of kings, but the palace had been consumed by fire and the city ruined by war. One king, Amri, had made that property of Lazarus his home until the building of Samaria, whither he then removed. The people of Thirza were in Jesus's time very pious and lived very retired in their little, isolated city. I think there are some remains of it even in our own day. The inhabitants were very reserved in their dealings with the Samaritans. Jesus taught in the synagogue of Thirza, but performed no cures.

Jesus at Lazarus's Estate near Thirza and at his Home in Bethany

Wednesday, March 15, AD 30 (Adar 22)
This evening, with the start of Adar 23, Jesus celebrated the beginning of the Feast of the Dedication of the Temple of Zorobabel. It was Zorobabel—of the house of David—who had laid the foundation stone of the temple around 519 BC (Ezra 3). However, this dedication feast was not given the same significance as the Feast of the Maccabees that began on Kislev 25 and lasted for a whole week.

On the sabbath began the Feast of the Dedication of the Temple of Zorobabel. It was not so solemn as the dedication feast of the Maccabees, though in the houses, in the streets, out in the fields among the shepherds, and in the synagogue there were numbers of lights and fires.

Thursday, March 16, AD 30 (Adar 23)
For most of the day, Jesus celebrated the Temple feast in the synagogue. That evening, he and the disciples continued on their way, walking through the night.

Jesus spent the greater part of the day in the synagogue with all the disciples. His meals were taken at Lazarus's, but he ate sparingly. The greatest portion of the food was distributed to the poor of Thirza, of whom there were large numbers. Such distributions were constantly made during his stay. The city still possessed, in ancient walls and towers, some remains of its former greatness. It is probable that the house of Lazarus, which was now fifteen minutes from the city, was formerly comprised within its limits, for the gardens were interspersed with all kinds of ruined walls and foundations. Lazarus inherited this property from his father. Here as elsewhere, he was held in great honor and esteem as a very wealthy and pious, yes, a very enlightened man. His deportment rendered him very distinguished from other men. He was remarkably grave and spoke very little, but that little with great mildness and to the point.

When the feast was over, Jesus left Thirza with Lazarus and the disciples, and proceeded on his journey to Judea. The direction was that taken by Mary and Joseph when going to Bethlehem, though the road was not exactly the same, but it ran through the same region, through the mountains near Samaria. I saw them climbing a high mountain on a night that was lovely, mild and clear, a beneficent dew bathing the whole region. There were about eighteen companions with Jesus, and they walked two and two, some before him, some behind him, and some at his side. When the breadth of the road permitted, Jesus often stood still to instruct them and to pray. A great part of the night was spent on this journey.

(Follow Map 15)

Friday, March 17, AD 30 (Adar 24)
On the way to Bethany, a young man from Samaria approached and cast himself down at Jesus's feet, saying, "Savior of humanity, thou who wilt free Judea and restore her to her former glory. . . ." He begged to become a disciple of Jesus. He was an orphan who had inherited much from his father, and he held some kind of office in Samaria. Jesus said he would talk with him again later. (This second meeting, which took place on Iyyar 17, AD 32, is recorded in Matt. 19:16–22). As the sabbath began, they arrived at the shepherd's inn where Mary and the holy women had stayed (prior to baptism) on their way to Bethany. Jesus celebrated the sabbath there.

Toward morning they rested and took a light repast, after which, carefully shunning the cities and towns, they continued their way over a mountain on which the air blew keen and cold.

Not far from Samaria, I saw Jesus going along with about six of his disciples. A young man from the city cast himself down on the road before him, saying: "Savior of humanity, thou who wilt free Judea and restore her to her former glory," etc. Thinking that Christ was about to found an earthly kingdom, he begged to be received into the number of his followers in the hope of being appointed to some post of distinction. He was an orphan, but had inherited large possessions from his father, and he held some kind of an office in Samaria. Jesus treated him very graciously. He told him that on his return he would say whether he would receive him or not, that he was pleased with his good will and humility, and that he had nothing to say against what he alleged, etc. But I saw that Jesus knew how greatly the young man was attached to his riches and that, wishing to give him a lesson, he would not vouchsafe him an answer until after he had chosen the apostles. The young man came once more to Jesus and that second visit is recorded in the gospel.

In the evening before the sabbath began, I saw them arrive at the shepherd inn between the two deserts, about four or five hours from Bethany. Mary and the holy women stayed there overnight when they went to Bethany, to see Jesus before the baptism. The shepherds from the country around gathered together bringing gifts and other necessaries. The inn was transformed into an oratory, a lamp was lighted, and there they remained. Jesus taught here and celebrated the sabbath. While traveling on this mountainous and lonely road, he stopped likewise at the place where Mary on her journey to Bethlehem had suffered so from the cold and where afterward she had been miraculously warned.

Jesus's First Passover Celebration in Jerusalem

Saturday, March 18, AD 30 (Adar 25)
Jesus and the disciples remained at the inn, where they celebrated the sabbath. After the close of the sabbath, they continued on their way to Bethany. That night Jesus stayed at Lazarus's castle.

Jesus and his disciples spent the whole of the sabbath among these shepherds, who were so happy to have him and so deeply moved by his presence. Even Jesus himself appeared brighter among these simple, innocent people. After the sabbath he went on to Bethany four hours distant.

Jesus's First Passover Celebration in Jerusalem

WHILE at Bethany, Jesus occupied the same room at Lazarus's as formerly. It was the family oratory and was fitted up like a synagogue. In the center stood the usual desk with the prayer rolls and scriptures. Jesus's sleeping chamber was a little room adjoining.

Sunday, March 19, AD 30 (Adar 26)
This morning Jesus and Lazarus went to Jerusalem. By midday, the holy women and friends of Jesus from Jerusalem were gathered together at the house of Mary Mark. They ate a meal together with Jesus, who spoke of the nearness of the kingdom of heaven. That evening, Jesus and Lazarus returned to Bethany.

The morning after his arrival, Martha went to Jerusalem to notify Mary Mark and the other women that Jesus was coming with her brother to the house of the former. Jesus and Lazarus arrived toward midday. There were present at the dinner besides Veronica, Johanna Chusa, and Susanna, the disciples of Jesus and of John belonging to Jerusalem, John Mark, Simeon's sons, Veronica's son, and Joseph of Arimathea's nephews, about nine men in all. Nicodemus and Joseph were not there. Jesus spoke of the nearness of the kingdom of God, of his disciples' call, of their following him, and even hinted at his own Passion.

John Mark's house was beyond the city, on the eastern side and opposite the Mount of Olives. Jesus did not have to enter the city in order to reach it. That evening he returned with Lazarus to Bethany. Here and there in Jerusalem it was noised about that the new prophet of Nazareth was in Bethany, and many rejoiced at the news, though there were others whom it displeased. In the gardens and on the roads of the Mount of Olives there were loitering here and there people, among them some Pharisees, to see Jesus as he passed. They may have heard accidentally or found out in Bethany that he was to return to the city. But no one accosted him. Some hid timidly behind the hedges and peeped out after him. They said to one another: "There is the prophet of Nazareth, Joseph the carpenter's son!"

On account of the approaching feast, numbers were at work in the gardens and on the hedges. All was being arranged and ornamented, the paths cleared, the hedges clipped and tied up. From all sides poor Jews and laboring people with asses laden with baggage were wending their way to Jerusalem. During the feast they labored by the day in the city and gardens. Simon, who later on was forced to help Jesus carry his cross, was one of these people.

Monday, March 20, AD 30 (Adar 27)
Jesus went to Jerusalem again. He visited Obed, the son of Simeon, and ate a meal there. After eating, he walked the streets of Jerusalem. That evening, he returned to Bethany, where Saturnin and some of John's disciples came to him. Nicodemus also came from Jerusalem to hear Jesus.

The next day Jesus was again in Jerusalem. He was at a house near the temple, that of Obed, the son of Simeon, also at another opposite the temple, one in which old Simeon's family had once dwelt. There he partook of a repast that had been prepared and sent by Martha and the other women. The disciples belonging to Jerusalem, about nine in number, and some other devout men were present, but not Nicodemus and Joseph of Arimathea. Jesus spoke very lovingly and earnestly of the near coming of the kingdom of God. He had not yet gone to the temple.

He went fearlessly about the city, clad in a long, white robe of woven material such as prophets usually wore. Sometimes there was nothing remarkable in his appearance, and he passed along without attracting attention, but at other times he looked quite extraordinary, his countenance shining with a supernatural light. When in the evening he returned to Bethany, some of John's disciples came to him, among them Saturnin. They saluted him and told him on the part of John that very few now came to him for baptism, but that Herod still continued to harass him. That same evening Nicodemus went to Bethany and heard at Lazarus's the instruction given by Jesus.

Tuesday, March 21, AD 30 (Adar 28)
This morning Jesus went to Simon the Pharisee's inn in Bethany. Many disciples and holy women gathered there and ate together with Jesus, who spoke of the fulfillment of the prophecies.

On the following morning Jesus went to Simon the Pharisee's, an inn or public house in Bethany. He gave an entertainment at which Nicodemus, Lazarus, John's disciples, and the disciples from Jerusalem met. Martha also and the women of Jerusalem were present. Nicodemus scarcely

Map 15: The First Passover
March 16–May 26, AD 30

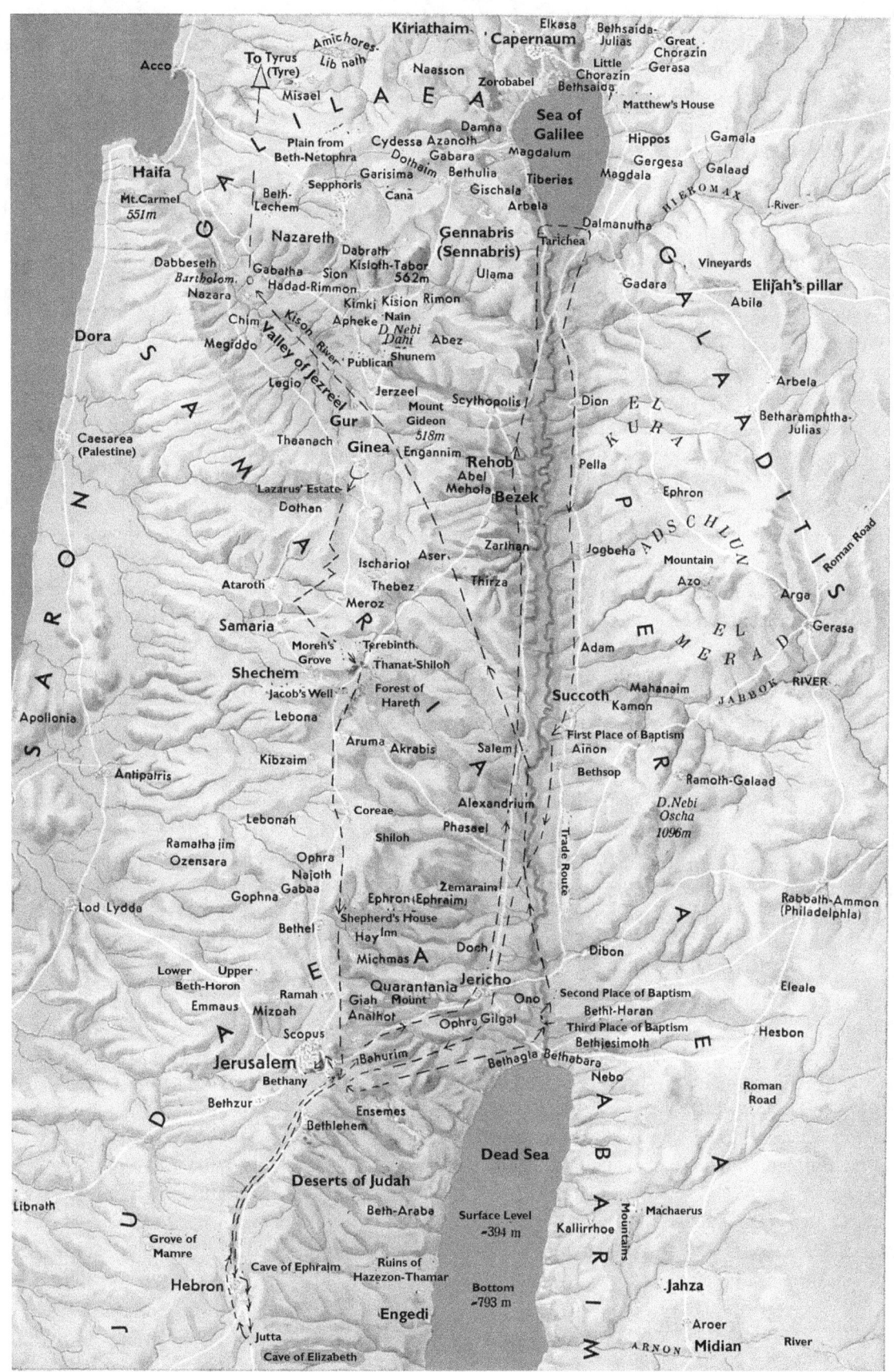

Ginea—Moreh's Grove—Bethany—Jerusalem—Jutta—Hebron—Jerusalem—Bethany—Bahurim
First Place of Baptism—Bethany—Third and Second Place of Baptism—West Galilee

said a word in Jesus's presence. He behaved with reserve and listened in astonishment to his words. But Joseph of Arimathea was more open-hearted, and sometimes even put questions to Jesus. Simon the Pharisee was not a bad man, though as yet very wavering. He held to Jesus's party on account of his friendship for Lazarus, but at the same time he desired to stand well with the Pharisees.

During the meal Jesus made many allusions to the prophets and the fulfilling of their prophecies. He spoke of the wonders attending the conception of John the Baptist, of God's protecting him from Herod's massacre of the children, and of his now being engaged preparing the ways. He drew their attention to man's indifference respecting the completion of the time marked by the prophets. "It was fulfilled thirty years ago, and yet who thinks of it excepting a few devout, simple-minded people? Who now recalls the fact that three kings, like an army from the East, followed a star with childlike faith seeking a newborn king of the Jews, whom they found in a poor child of poor parents? Three days did they spend with these poor people! Had their coming been to the child of a distinguished prince, it would not have been so easily forgotten!" Jesus, however, did not say that he himself was that child.

Wednesday, March 22, AD 30 (Adar 29)

Accompanied by Lazarus and Saturnin, he visited the homes of several poor, pious sick people of the working class in Bethany, and cured about six of them. Some were lame, some dropsical, and others afflicted with melancholy. Jesus commanded those that he cured to go outdoors and sit in the sun. Up to this time there was very little excitement about Jesus in Bethany, and even these cures produced none. The presence of Lazarus, for whom they felt great reverence, kept the enthusiasm of the people in check.

That evening, upon which began the first day of the month Nisan, there was a feast celebrated in the synagogue. It appeared to be the Feast of the New Moon, for there was a kind of illumination in the synagogue. There was a disc like the moon which, during the recitation of prayers, shone with ever-increasing brilliancy, owing to the lights lit one after another by a man behind it.

NISAN (30 days):
March 22/23 to April 20/21, AD 30 Nisan
New Moon: March 22 at 10:45 PM Jerusalem time

Thursday, March 23, AD 30 (Nisan 1)

The next day Jesus was present at divine service in the temple with Lazarus, Saturnin, Obed, and other disciples. A ram was sacrificed. The appearance of Jesus in the temple produced a peculiar excitement among the Jews. The strangest part of it was that each concealed the impression made upon him; no one mentioned to his neighbor the wonderful effect of Jesus's presence upon him. This was a divine dispensation, in order to allow the Savior to fulfill his mission. Had they imparted their thoughts to one another, it would have given rise to open anger; but as it was, hatred and rage struggled with gentler emotions in the hearts of many, while others felt within them an almost imperceptible desire to know Jesus better, and took steps to do so through the mediation of others. This was a fast day in memory of the death of Aaron's children.

Friday, March 24, AD 30 (Nisan 2)

The disciples and many other devout persons were gathered together at Lazarus's. Jesus taught in a large hall in which was a teacher's chair. He continued the discourse begun in the house of Simon the Pharisee in which he had spoken of the three kings, and he drew the attention of his hearers to other facts of the past. He said: "It is now about eighteen years ago since a little *bachir*" (by which Jesus must have meant a young scholar) "argued most wonderfully with the doctors of the Law who, in consequence, were filled with wrath against the child." And then he related to them the teachings of the little *bachir*.

Saturday, March 25, AD 30 (Nisan 3)

This morning Jesus went to celebrate the sabbath in the temple at Jerusalem. He wore a white woven robe with a girdle and a white mantle. He chanted and sang in turn with the others. Around two o'clock in the afternoon, he and his disciples ate a meal together at a place adjoining the temple. Jesus remained at the temple for the rest of the day, returning to Bethany at about nine o'clock in the evening.

Jesus with Obed, who served in the temple, and the other disciples of Jerusalem, went again to the temple for the celebration of the sabbath. They stood two by two among the young Israelites. Jesus wore a white, woven robe with a girdle, and a white mantle like those used by the Essenes, but there was something very distinguished about him. His clothing looked remarkably fresh and elegant, probably because he wore it. He chanted and prayed from the parchment rolls in turn with the others. There were some prayer leaders present. The people were again struck at the sight of Jesus. They were astonished, they wondered at him, though without having said a word to him. Even among themselves they did not speak openly of him, but I saw the wonderful impression made on many. There were three instructions or discourses delivered: one on the children of Israel, another on their departure from Egypt, and a third on the paschal lamb. On one of the altars was a sacrifice of incense. The priest could not be seen, though the fumes and the fire were visible. The fire could be seen through a kind of grating upon which there was something like a paschal lamb surrounded by rays and ornaments through which sparkled the fire. This altar stood near the Holy of Holies, its horns apparently entering it. I saw Pharisees praying, some of them wearing wrapped around one arm a long, narrow band that had perhaps once been used as a veil.

About two in the afternoon, Jesus went with his companions into an apartment in the court of Israel, where a repast of fruit and rolls had been prepared. The rolls were twisted like braids, or plaited hair. A steward had been engaged to see to everything. All necessaries could be bought or ordered in the precincts of the temple itself, and strangers had the right to avail themselves of the privilege. The temple was so large that it seemed like a little city, and in it one could procure everything. During this repast, Jesus gave an instruction. When the men had finished, the women took some refreshment.

I learned on that day what before I had not known; that is, that Lazarus held a position in the temple, as amongst us a burgomaster may also be a church warden. He went around with a box and took up a collection. Jesus and his followers remained the whole afternoon in the temple. I did not see him back in Bethany before about nine o'clock that night. There were innumerable lamps and lights in the temple on this sabbath.

Mary and the other holy women had now left Capernaum to go to Jerusalem. Their route lay toward Nazareth and passed Tabor, from which district other women came to join them, and then off through Samaria. They were preceded by the disciples from Galilee and followed by servants with the baggage. Among the disciples were Peter, Andrew, and their half-brother Jonathan, the sons of Zebedee, the sons of Mary Cleophas, Nathaniel Chased, and Nathaniel the bridegroom.

Sunday, March 26, AD 30 (Nisan 4)

On the fourth of Nisan, Jesus spent the whole morning in the temple with about twenty disciples, after which he taught at Mary Mark's and took a luncheon. He afterward returned to Bethany and went with Lazarus to Simon the Pharisee's. Already many of the lambs brought to the temple had been rejected by the priests.

Monday, March 27, AD 30 (Nisan 5)

This morning, Jesus visited the temple. During the afternoon, he and his disciples went to the house of Joseph of Arimathea, where Jesus taught. Joseph of Arimathea's house was located beyond the city walls, in the northeast, near to the house of John Mark (not to be confused with the house in which the Last Supper took place, which belonged to Joseph of Arimathea and Nicodemus).

Jesus was again in the temple and in the afternoon taught at Joseph of Arimathea's not far from the home of John Mark, and near a stonecutter's yard. It was a retired quarter of the city and little frequented by Pharisees. At this period no one feared to be seen in company with Jesus, for hatred against him had not yet been manifested.

Tuesday, March 28, AD 30 (Nisan 6)

Jesus was in the temple. The Pharisees were angered to see him again. Afterward, he returned to the home of Joseph of Arimathea. Everywhere, preparation was underway for the approaching Feast of the Passover.

Jesus continued to show himself still more freely and boldly throughout Jerusalem and in the temple. He went in with Obed even to the place between the altar of sacrifice and the temple, where an instruction was being delivered to the priests relative to Passover and its ceremonies. The disciples remained back in the court of Israel. The Pharisees were greatly annoyed at seeing him present at that instruction. Jesus also addressed the people on the streets.

The crowds flowing into Jerusalem kept continually increasing, especially workmen, day laborers, servants, and dealers in the necessaries of life. Around the city and on the open places, crowds of huts and tents had been erected for the accommodation of the multitudes flocking for Passover. Many lambs and other cattle had been brought into the city, from the former of which selections had already begun. Numbers of pagans also came to Jerusalem for the feast.

Wednesday, March 29, AD 30 (Nisan 7)

This morning, Jesus taught and healed in Bethany. During the afternoon he went to the temple, remaining there for the evening service. When it was over, and most of the people had gone, Jesus taught his disciples concerning the nearness of the fulfillment of all the prophecies. He hinted at the deeper mystery underlying the sacrifice of the paschal lamb. That night, he traveled southward to John the Baptist's hometown (Jutta).

Jesus taught and cured openly in Bethany, even sick strangers were brought to him. Some relatives of Zechariah from the country of Hebron came to invite him to thither.

He went up again to the temple. When the priests left

after the services, on the place where he was standing among his disciples, Jesus taught them and other good people upon the nearness of the kingdom of God, the Passover solemnity, the approaching fulfillment of all the prophecies and symbols, yes, even of the paschal lamb itself. His words were earnest and severe, and several priests who were still going here and there in the temple, were troubled at his discourse and secretly annoyed. Jesus then went back to Bethany, and that night, accompanied by some of the disciples, left with the envoys for Hebron, about four hours to the south.

Preparations for the feast were actively going on in the temple, and many changes were being made in the interior. Halls and corridors were opened, stands and partitions were removed. The altar could now be approached from many sides, and everything presented quite a different appearance.

Thursday, March 30, AD 30 (Nisan 8)

Jesus went from Jutta to Hebron, where he taught and healed many sick people.

Jesus, with the disciples and Zechariah's relatives, proceeded to Hebron by the route running between Jerusalem and Bethlehem. It was at most a journey of five hours. Passing through Jutta, Jesus entered the neighboring city, Hebron, where he taught and quietly cured many sick.

Friday, March 31, AD 30 (Nisan 9)

Around midday, Jesus left Hebron and made his way back to Bethany in time for the start of the sabbath.

He returned to Bethany for the sabbath. His way led high over mountains, whose exposure to the sun made it very hot. The disciples that had come from John to Jesus in Bethany, now went back to the former.

Saturday, April 1, AD 30 (Nisan 10)

Jesus went to the temple for the sabbath. Together with Obed, he entered the inner court, where the priests and Levites were holding a discourse concerning the Passover festival. The whole assembly was thrown into consternation by the appearance of Jesus, who started to put questions that they could not answer. Jesus told them that the sacrifice of the paschal lamb—meaning the Lamb of God—would soon be fulfilled, so that the temple and its services would then come to an end. The Pharisees were angry and astounded at his whole bearing. They did not undertake anything against him. Although it was forbidden to ordinary people to come into this part of the temple, Jesus had entered it in his capacity as a prophet. That evening, after the close of the sabbath, he returned to Bethany and talked with Lazarus's sister, Silent Mary, about the nearness of the kingdom of God. He blessed her, for she was close to death.

Jesus went to the temple on the sabbath and with Obed penetrated into the court containing the teacher's chair, from which later on he also taught. Priests and Levites were sitting on the circular seats around the chair, from which a discourse on the Passover festival was being delivered. The entrance of Jesus threw the assembly into consternation, especially when he started objections and asked questions to which not one of them could answer. Among other things, he told them that the time was approaching when the symbolical paschal lamb would give place to the reality, then would the temple and its services come to an end. The language of Jesus was figurative, and yet so clear that my thoughts instantly reverted to the words of the Pange lingua, "et antiquum documentum novo cedat ritui."† When they questioned him as to how he knew that, he answered that his Father had told him, but he did not say who that Father was.

The Pharisees were highly displeased, though at the same time full of astonishment. They did not venture to contradict him. Access to that part of the temple was not permitted to all, but Jesus had entered in quality of prophet. In his last year he even taught therein.

After the sabbath, Jesus went to Bethany. I had not as yet seen him conversing with Mary the Silent. Her end, I think, was near, for she appeared greatly changed. She was lying on the ground on a gray carpet, supported in the arms of her maids, and she was in a kind of swoon. She appeared to me to have drawn nearer to this world of ours, as if she had ever been absent in spirit, but now she appeared to have been brought back again to life. She was now to know that this Jesus here in Bethany, who lived in her own time and in her own vicinity, was he who had to suffer so cruelly. She was still alive in order to experience through compassion, in her own person, the sufferings of Jesus, after which she was soon to die.

On the night of Saturday, Jesus visited her and conversed long with her. Part of the time she sat up on her couch, and part of the time walked around her chamber. She had now the perfect use of her senses. She distinguished between the present and the future, she recognized in Jesus the Savior and the Paschal Lamb, and she knew that he was to suffer frightfully. All this made her inexpressibly sorrowful. The world appeared to her gloomy and an insupportable weight. But most of all was she grieved at man's ingratitude, which she foresaw. Jesus

---

† A hymn written by St. Thomas Aquinas. This verse can be translated as "Over ancient forms of worship, newer rites of grace prevail."

spoke long with her of the approach of the kingdom of God and his own Passion, after which he gave her his blessing and left her. She was soon to die. She was tall and extraordinarily beautiful, white as snow and shining with light. Her hands were like ivory, her fingers long and tapering.

Sunday, April 2, AD 30 (Nisan 11)

Next morning, Jesus cured openly in Bethany many that had been brought to him, among them some strangers that had come up for the feast. Some were lame, some were blind. There came to him also several men connected with the temple who called him to account for his actions and conduct. Who, they asked, had authorized him on the preceding day to take part in the conference held in the temple? Jesus answered them very gravely, and again spoke of his Father. The Pharisees dared not enter the lists against him. They felt a certain terror in his presence; they did not know what to make of him. But next day, Jesus taught again in the temple. All the Galilean disciples that had been at the marriage feast in Cana had now come to Jesus. Mary and the holy women were stopping with Mary Mark. Lazarus bought many of the lambs that had been rejected as not fit for the feast and had them slaughtered and divided among the poor day laborers and other workmen.

Jesus Turns the Vendors out of the Courts of the Temple • The Paschal Supper • Death of Mary the Silent

Monday, April 3, AD 30 (Nisan 12)

WHEN Jesus, with all his disciples, went to the temple, he found there, ranged around the court of the suppliants, dealers in green herbs, birds, and all kinds of eatables. In a kindly and friendly manner, he accosted them and bade them retire with their goods to the court of the Gentiles. He admonished them gently of the impropriety of taking up a position where the bleating of the lambs, and the noise of the other cattle would disturb the recollection of the worshippers. With the help of the disciples, he assisted the dealers to remove their tables to the places that he pointed out to them.

Tuesday, April 4, AD 30 (Nisan 13)

A great multitude of people were gathered in Jerusalem. Arriving at the temple, Jesus and his disciples again found the vendors there. Jesus admonished them more severely this time, and set about forcibly removing their tables to the outer court. Some pious Jews approved of his action and called out: "The prophet of Nazareth!" The Pharisees, put to shame by Jesus's action, were angered by the crowd's response. Later, as Jesus left the temple, he healed a cripple. All was quiet on the streets of Jerusalem that evening, for people were busy in their homes cleansing out the leaven and preparing the unleavened bread.

On this day, Jesus cured many sick strangers in Jerusalem, chiefly poor, lame working people who dwelt in the neighborhood of the Cenacle on Mount Zion. There was an astonishingly great multitude gathered in Jerusalem. The city was surrounded by a perfect encampment of huts and tents. On the large, open places ran building after building, forming long streets wherein all things could be had in large quantities, such as tents, everything necessary for their erection, and whatever was needed for the eating of the paschal lamb. There were other stores, also, in which such things could be bought or hired. Crowds of day laborers and poor people from all parts of Israel were busied carrying the above mentioned articles here and there, and putting them up. These people had been at work a long time in Jerusalem, clearing away whatever might block up the streets, clipping the hedges, opening the roads, leveling and measuring off the grounds for encampments, and putting up booths and stalls. In the same way for weeks before, the roads and bad crossing places in the country around were being repaired and made ready for travel. All these preparations referred to the paschal lamb, just as the Baptist's preparing of the ways referred to the true Lamb of God.

When Jesus again went up to the temple with his disciples, he admonished the dealers a second time to withdraw. Since all the passages were open on account of the immolation of the paschal lamb soon to take place, many had again crowded up to the court of the suppliants. Jesus bade them withdraw, and shoved their tables away. He acted with more vehemence than on the last occasion. The disciples opened a way for him through the crowd. Some of the dealers became furious. With violent gesticulations of head and hands they resisted him, and then it was that Jesus, stretching out his hand, pushed back one of the tables. They were powerless against him, the place was soon emptied, and all things carried to the exterior court. Then Jesus addressed to them words of warning. He said that twice he had admonished them to remove their goods, and that if he found them there again, he would treat them still more severely. The most insolent insulted him with: "What will the Galilean, the scholar of Nazareth, dare to do? We are not afraid of him." These taunts began at the moment of their removal. Many were standing around looking at Jesus in amazement. The devout Jews approved his action and praised him in his absence. They also cried out: "The prophet of Nazareth!" The Pharisees, who were ashamed and angry at what had occurred, had for days past privately warned the people to refrain from attaching themselves to the stranger during the feast, not to run after him, nor even to speak much about him. But the people had become more and more interested in Jesus, for there were already many among them who had heard his teaching or had been cured by him.

As Jesus left the temple, he passed a cripple in one of the courts. The man cried after him. Jesus cured him, and he who had been lame going into the temple joyfully proclaimed Jesus as his benefactor. Upon this, great excitement arose.

John the Baptist did not come to the feast. He was not a Jew under the Law, nor was he at all like other men. He was, as it were, a voice clothed with flesh. He had at this time a fresh concourse of aspirants to baptism on account of the multitudes going to Jerusalem.

All was very quiet in Jerusalem that evening. The people were busy in their own homes with cleansing out the leaven and preparing the unleavened bread. All the cooking utensils were covered and hung away. This was done also at Lazarus's on Mount Zion, where Jesus and his followers were to eat the paschal lamb. Jesus himself was present at these preparations, he gave instructions upon them, and all was done by his direction; but the minutiae were not so punctiliously observed as among the other Jews. Jesus explained of what it all was a figure, and how it should be practiced, showing them at the same time what the Pharisees, through want of understanding, had added.

Wednesday, April 5, AD 30 (Nisan 14)

Jesus remained in Bethany today, the day of preparation for the Passover. In the temple, the vendors gathered again. In the afternoon, the paschal lambs were slaughtered. Lazarus, Obed, and Saturnin slaughtered the three lambs that Jesus and the disciples were to eat. The Passover meal took place in the great hall at Lazarus's castle. Jesus taught, and they sang and prayed together until late into the night.

Jesus did not appear in the temple the next day. He remained in Bethany. I thought, as so many vendors had again crowded into the temple, something would surely have happened to them had he been there. That afternoon the paschal lambs were slaughtered in the temple, and that with indescribable order and celerity. Everyone brought his paschal lamb on his shoulder, and took his place in order, for there was room enough for all. There were three courts around the altar in which they could stand, but the space between it and the temple was not open to the people. They that did the slaughtering were behind railings, a table with all that was necessary for their work before them; but they were placed so close to one another that the blood of one lamb sprinkled the neighboring butcher. Their clothes were full of blood. The priests were ranged in several rows up to the altar, passing basins from hand to hand, some full of blood, others empty. Before disemboweling a lamb, the Israelites pressed and kneaded it in a certain way. Then the butcher standing next in order held the animal, while his neighbor with a light grasp easily tore out the intestines.

The flaying was done very expeditiously. They loosened a little piece of skin and fastened it to a round stick provided for the purpose. Then they hung the lamb around their neck, with both hands twisted the stick around, and the skin rolled up on it. Toward evening the slaughter was over. The evening sky was blood-red.

Lazarus, Obed, and Saturnin slaughtered the three lambs that Jesus and his friends were to eat. The meal was taken at Lazarus's on Mount Zion. It was a large building with two wings. The oven for roasting was in the dining hall, but it was very different from the hearth in the Cenacle. It was higher, like the fireplace in Anna and Mary's house, also like that at Cana. In the thick, perpendicular wall that formed it, were holes wherein the lamb was fastened. It was stretched out and pinned in place with wooden skewers, just as if crucified. The hall was beautifully ornamented and the table, at which they ate in three groups, was exactly like a horizontal cross. At the upper and shorter end of the cross, upon which were many dishes of bitter herbs, Lazarus sat. The paschal lambs were placed one on each of the arms of the cruciform table and one toward the middle of the lower beam. Jesus, Peter, Saturnin, and Obed sat as follows: Jesus and Peter opposite each other at the left arm of the table, Obed at the right arm, and Saturnin at the lower beam. Around Jesus stood his relatives and the disciples from Galilee, around Obed and Lazarus those from Jerusalem, while John's disciples gathered around Saturnin. There were present, in all, over thirty.

The Passover supper was very different from Jesus's last Passover supper, more strictly Judaical. Each here held a staff in his hand, was girded as for a journey, and all ate in haste. Jesus had two staves placed crosswise before him. They chanted psalms and, standing, quickly consumed the paschal lambs. Later on they placed themselves at table in a recumbent position. This supper was different also from that customary among the other Jews at this feast. Jesus explained all to the guests, but omitted the ceremonies that had been added by the Pharisees. He carved the three lambs himself and served at table, saying that he did it as their servant. They remained together far into the night, singing and praying.

Jerusalem was so still and solemn during that whole day. The Jews not engaged in the slaughtering of the lambs remained shut up in their houses, which were ornamented with dark green foliage. The immense multitude of people were, after the slaughtering, so busy in the interior of their homes, and all was so still that it produced upon me quite a melancholy impression.

I saw on that day also where all the paschal lambs for the numerous strangers, of whom many were encamped before the gates, were roasted. Both outside and inside the city, there were built on certain places long, low walls, but so broad that one could walk on them. In these walls were furnace after furnace, and at certain distances lived men who attended to them, and received a small remuneration for their services. At these furnaces travelers and strangers could, at the different feasts, or at any other time, roast their meat and cook any kind of food. The consuming of the fat of the paschal lambs went on in the temple far into the night. After the first watch the altar was purified, and the doors thrown open at a very early hour the next morning.

Jesus and his disciples spent the night in prayer and with but little sleep at Lazarus's on Mount Zion. The disciples from Galilee slept in the wings of the building.

YEAR 2

Nisan 15, AD 30, to Nisan 14, AD 31
April 5/6, AD 30, to March 26/27, AD 31

Thursday, April 6, AD 30 (Nisan 15)

Having prayed for much of the night on Mount Zion, at daybreak Jesus and his disciples went to the temple. Jesus taught in the forecourts. Vendors had again erected tables to sell their wares, and Jesus demanded that they withdraw. When they refused, he drew a cord of twisted reeds from the folds of his robe. With this in hand, he overturned their tables and drove the vendors back, assisted by the disciples. Jesus said: "Take these things away; you shall not make my Father's house a house of trade." They replied: "What sign have you to show us for doing this?" Jesus answered them: "Destroy this temple, and in three days I will raise it up." They said: "It has taken forty-six years to build this temple, and you will raise it up in three days?" But he spoke of the temple of his body (John 2:13–21). All this occurred between seven and eight o'clock in the morning.

At daybreak they went up to the temple, which was lighted by numerous lamps, and to which the people were already flocking from all parts with their offerings. Jesus took his stand in one of the courts with his disciples, and there taught. A crowd of vendors had again pressed into the court of the suppliants and even into that of the women. They were scarcely two steps from the worshippers. As they still came crowding in, Jesus bade the newcomers to keep back, and those that had already taken their position to withdraw. But they resisted, and called upon the guard nearby for help. The latter, not venturing to act of themselves, reported what was taking place to the Sanhedrin. Jesus, meantime, persisted in his command to the vendors to withdraw. When they boldly refused, he drew from the folds of his robe a cord of twisted reeds or slender willow branches and pushed up the ring that held the ends confined, whereupon one half of it opened out into numerous threads like a whip. With this he rushed upon the vendors, overthrew their tables, and drove back those that resisted, while the disciples, pressing on right and left, shoved his opponents away. And now came a crowd of priests from the Sanhedrin and summoned Jesus to say who had authorized him to behave so in that place. Jesus answered that, although the holy mystery had been taken away from the temple, yet it had not ceased to be a sacred place and one to which the prayer of so many just was directed. It was not a place for usury, fraud, and for low and noisy traffic. Jesus having alleged the commands of his Father, they asked him who was his Father. He answered that he had no time then to explain that point to men and even if he did they would not understand, saying which he turned away from them and continued his chase of the vendors.

Two companies of soldiers now arrived on the spot, but the priests did not dare to take action against Jesus. They themselves were ashamed of having tolerated such an abuse. The crowd gathered around declared Jesus in the right, and the soldiers even lent a hand to remove the vendors' stands and to clear away the overturned tables and wares. Jesus and the disciples drove the vendors to the exterior court, but those that were modestly selling doves, little rolls, and other needful refreshments in the recesses of the wall around the inner court, he did not molest. After that he and his followers went to the court of Israel. It may have been between seven and eight in the morning when all this took place.

On the evening of this day, a kind of procession went out along the valley of Kidron, to cut the first fruits of the harvest.

Friday, April 7, AD 30 (Nisan 16)

This afternoon, Jesus healed about ten people—some crippled, some mute—in the forecourt of the temple, giving rise to much excitement and jubilation. Summoned to answer for his action, he rebuked his interrogators severely. He then returned to Bethany, where he celebrated the sabbath.

Jesus on one of the succeeding days cured in the court of the temple about ten persons, some lame, some mute, and it gave rise to great excitement, for the cured filled the whole place with their acclamations of joy. Again he was summoned to answer for his conduct, which he did in severe words. The people were enthusiastic in his favor. After the divine service, Jesus and the disciples attended the instruction given in a hall of the temple. The text was from one of the Books of Moses. Jesus offered some objections, for it was a kind of conference in which questions might be raised. He silenced his opponents, and gave an explanation of the disputed points very different from what had before been given.

During all these days Jesus hardly saw his mother. She was staying with Mary Mark, passing the livelong day in anxiety, tears, and prayer on account of the excitement roused by the appearance of her son.

Saturday, April 8, AD 30 (Nisan 17)

Jesus kept the sabbath at Lazarus's, in Bethany, whither he had retired after the tumult occasioned by the cures wrought in the temple. After the sabbath, the Pharisees went to the house of Mary Mark in Jerusalem, thinking to find Jesus there and to take him into custody. They were, however, disappointed. They did not find him, but only his mother and the other holy women whom, as the followers of Jesus, they commanded with harsh words to leave the city. The mother of Jesus and the other women became greatly troubled at hearing this, and in tears hurried to Martha in Bethany. Mary, weeping, entered the room wherein Martha was with her sick sister, Mary the Silent. The latter was again quite rapt in ecstasy. All that she had hitherto seen in spirit, she now beheld about to be fulfilled. She could no longer endure the pain it caused her, and she died in the presence of Mary, Mary Cleophas, Martha, and the other women.

Nicodemus, in spite of the open persecution directed against Jesus, visited him during these days by invitation of Lazarus. I saw Jesus during the night reclining beside him on the ground and instructing him (John 3:1–21). [B16]

Sunday, April 9, AD 30 (Nisan 18)

Before daybreak, Jesus and Nicodemus went to Jerusalem to Lazarus's house on Mt Zion, where Joseph of Arimathea joined them. Later, a whole group of about thirty disciples came. Jesus gave instructions about what the disciples should do during the coming period.

Before daybreak, both started for Jerusalem, where they went to Lazarus's on Zion. Here came Joseph of Arimathea also to see Jesus. He conversed with them. They humbled themselves before him, telling him that they did indeed discern that he was more than human, and they pledged him lasting fidelity. Jesus commanded them secrecy, and they begged him to remember them kindly.

After that all the other disciples who had eaten the paschal lamb with him came to Jesus. He gave them his commands and instructions for the near future. Extending to him their hands, they wept, making use of the narrow scarf they wore around the neck or wound around the head to dry their tears.

Monday, April 10, to Monday, April 17, AD 30 (Nisan 19–26)

Jesus remained concealed at Bethany for part of this week and for the rest of the time at a little place called Bahurim, about one hour's distance north of Bethany.

Tuesday, April 18, to Tuesday, April 25, AD 30 (Nisan 27—Iyyar 4)

Jesus traveled northward through Samaria to the southern end of the Sea of Galilee. He crossed over to the east side of the Jordan and journeyed south of Succoth to the region of Ainon, where John the Baptist had first started baptizing. John himself had now returned to this first place of baptism. Jesus taught some of John's disciples during these days, but he did not meet John.

IYYAR (30 days):
April 21/22 to May 20/21, AD 30 Iyyar
New Moon: April 21, at 2:30 PM Jerusalem time

Wednesday, April 26, to Tuesday, May 2, AD 30 (Iyyar 5–11)

Jesus returned to Bethany and remained concealed at Lazarus's castle, where he was visited again both by Nicodemus and by Joseph of Arimathea.

TISSOT ILLUSTRATIONS
[SECTION B]

The Public Teaching of Jesus

⊕

Nathaniel Under the Fig Tree · · · · · · · · · · · · · · · 426	Jesus Carried Up to a Pinnacle of the Temple · · · 442
The Voice in the Desert · 428	Jesus Transported onto a High Mountain · · · · · · 444
Jesus, Mary Magdalene, and Martha in Bethany · 430	Jesus Ministered to by Angels · · · · · · · · · · · · · · · · 446
John the Baptist and the Pharisees · · · · · · · · · · · 432	The Calling of John and Andrew · · · · · · · · · · · · · 448
John the Baptist Sees Jesus from Afar · · · · · · · · · 434	The Betrothed of Cana · 450
The Baptism of Jesus · 436	The Marriage of Cana · 452
Jesus Teaches the People by the Sea · · · · · · · · · · · 438	Passover Approaches · 454
Jesus Tempted in the Wilderness · · · · · · · · · · · · · 440	Interview between Jesus and Nicodemus · · · · · · 456

Nathaniel Under the Fig Tree [B1]

⊕

JESUS went through Nazareth in going from Capernaum to Hebron, passing through the indescribably beautiful country of Galilee and by the hot baths of Emmaus. These baths were on the declivity of a mountain, about an hour's distance further on from Magdala in the direction of Tiberias.

The meadows were covered with very high, thick grass, and on the declivity stood the houses and tents between rows of fig trees, date palms, and orange trees. The road was crowded, for a kind of national feast was going on. Men and women in separate groups were playing for wagers, the prize consisting of fruit. There Jesus saw Nathaniel, called also Chased, standing among the men under a fig tree. Just at the moment when Nathaniel was struggling against a sensual temptation that had seized him and was glancing over at the women's game, Jesus passed and cast upon him a warning look. Without knowing Jesus, Nathaniel was deeply moved by his glance, and thought: "That man has a sharp eye." He felt that Jesus was more than an ordinary man. He became conscious of his guilt, entered into himself, overcame the temptation, and from that time kept a stricter guard over his senses. I think I saw there, also, Naphtali, known as Bartholomew, and that a glance from Jesus touched him also. [294]

[JOHN 1:44–51]44 Now Philip was from Bethsaida, the city of Andrew and Peter. 45 Philip found Nathaniel, and said to him, "We have found him of whom Moses in the law and also the prophets wrote, Jesus of Nazareth, the son of Joseph." 46 Nathaniel said to him, "Can anything good come out of Nazareth?" Philip said to him, "Come and see." 47 Jesus saw Nathaniel coming to him, and said of him, "Behold, an Israelite indeed, in whom is no guile!" 48 Nathaniel said to him, "How do you know me?" Jesus answered him, "Before Philip called you, when you were under the fig tree, I saw you." 49 Nathaniel answered him, "Rabbi, you are the Son of God! You are the King of Israel!" 50 Jesus answered him, "Because I said to you, I saw you under the fig tree, do you believe? You shall see greater things than these." 51 And he said to him, "Truly, truly, I say to you, you will see heaven opened, and the angels of God ascending and descending upon the Son of man."

THE following is the manner in which we have pictured the scene of Nathaniel under the fig tree, according to a curious and fairly probable though uncertain interpretation.

The gathering in of the figs takes place in Judea in the autumn and is celebrated as a fête, much as is the vintage in the south of France. Parties of friends meet beneath the fig trees, and the picking of the fruit serves as a pretext for happy gatherings. Carpets are brought and spread on the ground, and jars full of cooling drinks are provided, for the heat is still considerable, the season being not yet far advanced.

Sometimes the company on these occasions was very mixed, and this, it would appear, was the case with the group frequented by Nathaniel.

Now one day, near the road skirting the lake between Magdala and Bethsaida, when he found himself under a fig tree, in a company of doubtful reputation, Nathaniel began to be troubled, feeling himself tempted, and on the brink of engaging in an evil course, much like some traveler who takes the wrong path at cross roads. Perhaps this moment was about to influence the whole of his future life and to compromise him forever, when, all of a sudden, the disciples of the new prophet and the new prophet himself passed near the group. Nathaniel raised his head and, looking up, saw Jesus, his tall figure rising above his followers. The two exchanged a long look, and the expression of the Master was so fraught with mystery, so penetrating, that it touched to the very depths the tempted soul of the other, working in it an instantaneous change.

Then Nathaniel, arrested on the edge of what he well knew to be a precipice, felt that he was saved, and he preserved, engraved upon his very heart, the memory of the passing stranger.

Some time passed by, and, when his friends or neighbors spoke to him of the growing reputation of the new prophet, he contented himself with saying, for he did not know him yet: "Can there any good thing come out of Nazareth?" which was a kind of proverb current in the country, referring to the little town hidden in the mountains and of no reputation.

The Voice in the Desert [B2]

⊕

WHEN Jesus returned to Nazareth, he went around among his parents' acquaintances, but he was everywhere coldly received. When he sought to enter the synagogue in order to teach, they turned him away. Then he repaired to the public marketplace and spoke of the Messiah to the crowd, of whom some were Sadducees, others Pharisees. He told them that the Messiah would be different from what each one's ideas pictured. John the Baptist, he called "The voice in the wilderness." Two youths, clothed in long garments and wearing girdles like priests, had followed Jesus from the country of Hebron; but they went not always with him. [297]

[JOHN 1:22–23] 22 They said to him then, "Who are you? Let us have an answer for those who sent us. What do you say about yourself?" 23 He said, "I am the voice of one crying in the wilderness, 'Make straight the way of the Lord,' as the prophet Isaiah said." [MATTHEW 3:3] 3 For this is he who was spoken of by the prophet Isaiah when he said, "The voice of one crying in the wilderness: Prepare the way of the Lord, make his paths straight."

THE desert in which dwelt John the Baptist was three hours' march from Jerusalem, the Terebinth valley shutting in and isolating it. Opposite to it on the west, when the back was turned on Aïn-Karim where Elizabeth dwelt, could be seen on the lofty mountains the villages and towns of Kastoul, perched on a hilltop; Kalounieh, further away in the valley on the right; Soba, scarcely visible in the distance and looking like an eagle's nest, with Shathaf, and other hamlets upon the slopes. It was in the wider portion of this valley that so many struggles took place between the Israelites and Philistines, and it was there that Goliath was killed, smitten in the forehead by the stone from the sling of David.

In these rocky valleys the voice resounds in an extraordinary manner, and even now the traveler is struck with the way in which the long drawn-out melancholy cries of the shepherds ring out in the silent solitudes. The voice echoes back from side to side to a very great distance. Now it so happened that in the fifteenth year of the reign of Tiberius Caesar an unusual and exciting incident occurred again and again at the close of the day, for a voice, a strange appealing voice, resounded through the silence and the gathering shades of night: "Prepare ye the way of the Lord, make His paths straight," "the Savior, the Messiah is near," "repent ye, for the kingdom of Heaven is at hand." This mysterious chanting probably went on till the night was well advanced. It was known that a human being lived alone in the desert, a prophet, no doubt, and the voice having now been heard for some time, people in Jerusalem and the villages round about became curious as to what it might mean, so that groups began to collect and to venture to approach the place from which it came. These groups presently found themselves face to face with a remarkable being, leading a most mysterious life and apparently altogether possessed with the thought of some great approaching event. John the Baptist then began to preach in the wilderness; the crowd ever increasing, when he drew the people after him till he came to the banks of the Jordan, where he baptized many. If we want go get a true idea of the extent of John the Baptist's influence we have only to read what he said to the leaders of the people: the Pharisees and Sadducees. He treated them with an independence and addressed them in terms of a character so strong and searching, that they would never have been tolerated in the mouth of an ordinary man.

Jesus, Mary Magdalene, and Martha in Bethany [B3]

⊕

LAZARUS must have heard from the disciples of Jesus's intended visit to Bethany, for he had come thither in time to receive him. The castle in Bethany belonged in reality to Martha; but Lazarus loved to be there, so he and his sister kept house together. They were expecting Jesus, and a repast was in readiness. Martha dwelt in a house on the other side of the courtyard. There were guests assembled in both houses.... All were, in secret, friends of Jesus, partly through John the Baptist, partly through the holy family, and again through the prophecies of Simeon and Anna in the temple.

Lazarus had sent some of his servants to meet Jesus on the way. About thirty minutes from Bethany, Jesus came up with a trusty old servant who afterward joined the disciples. The old man prostrated on his face before him, saying, "I am the servant of Lazarus. If I have found favor before thee, my Lord, follow me to his house." Jesus bade him rise, and followed him. The servant led Jesus to a porch near a fountain at the entrance of the castle, where all had been prepared for washing his feet and changing his sandals. The servant dusted and aired his garments. When the washing of his feet was over, Lazarus and his friends appeared, bringing to Jesus a light refreshment and something in a drinking cup. Jesus embraced Lazarus and greeted the others, extending to them his hand. They served him hospitably and escorted him to the house. Sometime after, Lazarus conducted him across the courtyard to Martha's dwelling. The women there knelt veiled before him. [327]

[LUKE 10:38] 38 Now as they went on their way, he entered a village; and a woman named Martha received him into her house.

JESUS found at Bethany a pleasant resting-place after his apostolic journeys. There he need fear no wearisome discussions, no plots to catch him unawares, no hateful conspiracies against him. His friends and the holy women would listen to his discourse, and at his feet would sit Mary Magdalene with, perhaps, Johanna Chusa, the woman of Samaria and the Canaanite woman, who were now his followers.

John the Baptist and the Pharisees [B4]

⊕

ONE day many priests and doctors of the Law came to John from the towns around Jerusalem intending to call him to account. They questioned him as to who he was, who had sent him, what he taught, etc. John answered with extraordinary boldness and energy, announced to them the coming of the Messiah, and charged them with impenitence and hypocrisy. [336]

[LUKE 3:10–14] 10 And the multitudes asked him, "What then shall we do?" 11 And he answered them, "He who has two coats, let him share with him who has none; and he who has food, let him do likewise." 12 Tax collectors also came to be baptized, and said to him, "Teacher, what shall we do?" 13 And he said to them, "Collect no more than is appointed you." 14 Soldiers also asked him, "And we, what shall we do?" And he said to them, "Rob no one by violence or by false accusation, and be content with your wages."

WE are able to form a very good idea of the noble way in which John the Baptist fulfilled his mission in the desert. Every class of Jewish society flocked to consult him. As the man sent from God to preach penitence to the people, it was necessary for him to know what must be done to avert the calamities he prophesied. Each one who came to him wished to learn the secret of how to escape the judgment threatening his generation, and to each and all John had the right advice ready, the advice suited to the character and position of the enquirer. It was natural that so energetic and important a preacher should attract the attention of the religious authorities; and therefore, probably at the initiative of the high priest, Pharisees were sent from Jerusalem to enquire into his doctrine.

John the Baptist Sees Jesus from Afar [B5]

⊕

JESUS, walking more quickly than Lazarus, reached John's place of baptism two hours before him. It was morning twilight when, on the road near the place, he caught up with a crowd of people who also were going to the baptism, and he walked on with them. They did not know him, but they could not keep their eyes off him, for there was something about him very remarkable. When they reached the end of their journey, it was morning. A crowd more numerous than usual was assembled, to whom John was with great animation preaching of the nearness of the Messiah and of penance, proclaiming at the same time that the moment was approaching for him to retire from his office of teacher. Jesus was standing in the throng of listeners. John felt his presence. He saw him also, and that fired him with zeal and filled his heart with joy. But he did not on that account interrupt his discourse, and when he had finished he began to baptize. [343]

[JOHN 1:34–36] 34 "And I have seen and have borne witness that this is the Son of God." 35 The next day again John was standing with two of his disciples; 36 and he looked at Jesus as he walked, and said, "Behold, the Lamb of God!"

AT Bethabara, the place where John the Baptist for the first time bore witness to Jesus, the Jordan is wider and not so deep as at its mouth; its waters divide there and it is more often fordable. It was here that the twelve stones were set up, marking the spot where the Children of Israel crossed the Jordan, dryshod, to enter the Promised Land. There, too, David, fleeing from Absalom, passed over the river; while later it must have been here, or near here, that Elijah smote the waters with his mantle "so that they divided hither and thither," when "he and his companion went over on dry ground."

The Baptism of Jesus [B6]

⊕

THE nine disciples that were always with Jesus during his last days went down to the well with him and took their stand on the ledge around it. Jesus entered the tent and there laid off, first, his mantle and girdle; then a yellow, woolen garment which was closed in front by laces; then that narrow, woolen strip which he wore around his neck and crossed over the breast, and which he was accustomed to wind around his head at night and in stormy weather. Retaining his brown, woven undergarment, he stepped forth and descended to the margin of the well, where he drew it off over his head. About his loins was fastened a broad linen band which was also wound around each limb for about half a foot. [343]

[MATTHEW 3:13–17] 13 Then Jesus came from Galilee to the Jordan to John, to be baptized by him. 14 John would have prevented him, saying, "I need to be baptized by you, and do you come to me?" 15 But Jesus answered him, "Let it be so now; for thus it is fitting for us to fulfill all righteousness." Then he consented. 16 And when Jesus was baptized, he went up immediately from the water, and behold, the heavens were opened and he saw the Spirit of God descending like a dove, and alighting on him; 17 and lo, a voice from heaven, saying, "This is my beloved Son, with whom I am well pleased."

THE divine majesty of Jehovah was no longer made manifest in the second Temple; the stone which once upheld the Ark of the Covenant was vacant; the "urim" and the "thummim" had long been silent. But now once more the Divine Majesty reveals Himself and consecrates the Messiah on the banks of the Jordan. Twice more in the life of the Savior will a similar manifestation take place; once on Mount Tabor at the Transfiguration and once in the Temple on the Wednesday of Passion week.

According to the early Gnostics it was at the moment of the baptism that the celestial Eon or first emanation from the Divinity which they call the Christ, descended upon Jesus and made him divine. The Ebionites, in their turn, say that at the moment of the baptism a fire suddenly fell from heaven and set fire to the waters of the Jordan.

Jesus Teaches the People by the Sea [B7]

⊕

JESUS afterward taught on the borders of the lake, not far from Peter's fishery. He had journeyed with the disciples over the mountain back of Mary's and Peter's dwellings in the direction of Bethsaida, and thence had descended to the lake. The shore near Bethsaida was steep, but at the point to which I now allude it gently sloped and afforded an easy landing place. Peter's ship and Jesus's little boat lay here. The latter was small and could at most contain fifteen men. [359]

[MARK 2:13] 13 He went out again beside the sea; and all the crowd gathered about him, and he taught them.

IN the crowd seated at the feet of Jesus and listening to him, men of many different races are to be seen. There are wealthy citizens of Tiberias, an essentially modern town at that period; there are Jews in the black and white abayeh; Africans, with loose mantles, wearing no sash or belt; women of Samaria and from the shores of the Jordan; and lastly, men from the north; for Tiberias was a halting-place for those who traveled from the north to the south, from Persia to Egypt.

Jesus Tempted in the Wilderness [B8]

✠

TOWARD evening one day, Satan in the form of a large, powerful man ascended the mountain. He had furnished himself below with two stones as long as little rolls, but square at the ends, which as he mounted he molded into the perfect appearance of bread. There was something more horrible than usual about him when he stepped into the grotto to Jesus. In each hand he held one of the stones, and his words were to this effect: "Thou art right not to eat of the fruit, for it only excites an appetite. But if thou art the beloved Son of God over whom the Spirit came at baptism—behold! I have made these stones look like unto bread. Do thou change them into bread." Jesus glanced not toward him, but I heard him utter these words only: "Man lives not by bread!" These were the only words that I caught distinctly. Then Satan became perfectly horrible. He stretched out his talons as if to seize Jesus (at which action I saw the stones resting on his arms), and fled. I had to laugh at his having to take his stones off with him. [369]

[LUKE 4:1–4] 1 And Jesus, full of the Holy Spirit, returned from the Jordan, and was led by the Spirit 2 for forty days in the wilderness, tempted by the devil. And he ate nothing in those days; and when they were ended, he was hungry. 3 The devil said to him, "If you are the Son of God, command this stone to become bread." 4 And Jesus answered him, "It is written, 'Man shall not live by bread alone.'"

THE gospel tells us in fact that, before beginning his public ministry, Jesus wished to prepare himself for it by forty days of fasting and prayer. Tradition fixes the scene of his retirement in a cave on a mountain which has received the name of Quarantania, round about which lie numerous stones, not unlike loaves of bread in shape, from which has arisen the idea accepted by many that it was such stones as these that the devil referred to when he said "if thou be the Son of God, command that these stones be made bread." In the background of my picture, and on the other side of the Dead Sea, can be seen Mount Nebo, rising above the chain of heights known as the Mountains of Moab. The rows of trees in the plain mark the course of the Jordan, and the town of Jericho, the ruins of which are so well known, was a little farther to the right.

Jesus Carried Up to a Pinnacle of the Temple [B9]

⊕

TOWARD evening of the following day, I saw Satan in the form of a majestic angel sweeping down toward Jesus with a noise like the rushing wind. He was clad in a sort of military dress such as I have seen St. Michael wear. But in the midst of his greatest splendor, one might detect something sinister and horrible. He addressed boasting words to Jesus, something in this strain: "I will show thee who I am, and what I can do, and how the angels bear me up in their hands. Look yonder, there is Jerusalem! Behold the temple! I shall place thee upon its highest pinnacle. Then do thou show what thou canst do, and see whether the angels will carry thee down."

While Satan thus spoke and pointed out Jerusalem and the temple, I seemed to see them both quite near, just in front of the mountain. But I think that it was only an illusion. Jesus made no reply, and Satan seized him by the shoulders and bore him through the air. He flew low toward Jerusalem, and placed Jesus upon the highest point of one of the four towers that rose from the four corners of the temple, and which I had not before noticed. The tower to which Satan bore Jesus was on the west side toward Zion and opposite the citadel Antonia. [369]

[LUKE 4:9–13] 9 And he took him to Jerusalem, and set him on the pinnacle of the temple, and said to him, "If you are the Son of God, throw yourself down from here; 10 for it is written, 'He will give his angels charge of you, to guard you,' 11 and 'On their hands they will bear you up, lest you strike your foot against a stone.'" 12 And Jesus answered him, "It is said, 'You shall not tempt the Lord your God.'" 13 And when the devil had ended every temptation, he departed from him until an opportune time.

OUR Savior's body was carried in a passive condition by Satan above the temple lit up by the rising sun. At his feet was the Court of the Women with its semicircular staircase having on either side of the steps the entrances to the rooms where the musicians of the temple kept their instruments. On that part of the building which dominated the Gate giving entrance to the Men's Court, above the flights of steps known as the Psalms or Songs for the reason already explained. Herod had a golden eagle placed as a compliment to the Imperial Government. This led to very serious troubles; some young men having had the hardihood to throw down in broad daylight what they looked upon as an idol. Farther away, the Antonia tower or citadel, occupied by a garrison of Roman soldiers, dominated the temple. In the angle of the Court of the Women, shown in my picture, can be seen one of the chambers open to the sky, occupying the four corners. This is the Leper's Chamber, the other three were the Nazarite's Chamber, and the store rooms for the wine, oil, and wood, used in the services of the temple. In our engraving, behind the figure of the evil one, can be seen the gateway of the Porch of the Temple. It was twenty cubits wide by forty high, and its lower half was hidden, as already described, by the Babylonian veil or curtain of four colors. The upper portion of the gateway, above this veil, was open to the air, so that the fumes of the incense burnt within the Holy Place escaped without difficulty.

Jesus Transported by a Spirit onto a High Mountain [B10]

⊕

THEN Satan seized him fiercely by the shoulders, and flew with him over the desert toward Jericho. Satan was filled with rage and fury. He flew with Jesus now high, now low, reeling like one who would vent his rage if he could. He bore him to the same mountain, seven hours from Jerusalem, upon which he had commenced his fast. [369]

[LUKE 4:1, 5] 1 And Jesus, full of the Holy Spirit, returned from the Jordan, and was led by the Spirit 5 And the devil took him up, and showed him all the kingdoms of the world in a moment of time.

TRADITION *indicates Mount Nebo, one of the heights overlooking the mountains of Moab beyond the Dead Sea, as the high mountain to which Jesus was carried in the Temptation. It was to this same mountain that Moses had retired to die, and on it his body, which was never found, was miraculously buried. Mount Nebo commands a very wide-stretching view and from it the tempter could easily have pointed out to Jesus the various directions of all those kingdoms which he offered to him if he would fall down and worship him. Truth to tell, the language employed in the Gospel narrative seems to imply something more than an ordinary view of an ordinary panorama. "He showeth him" it says "all the kingdoms of the world and the glory of them," but what this vision really was we do not know.*

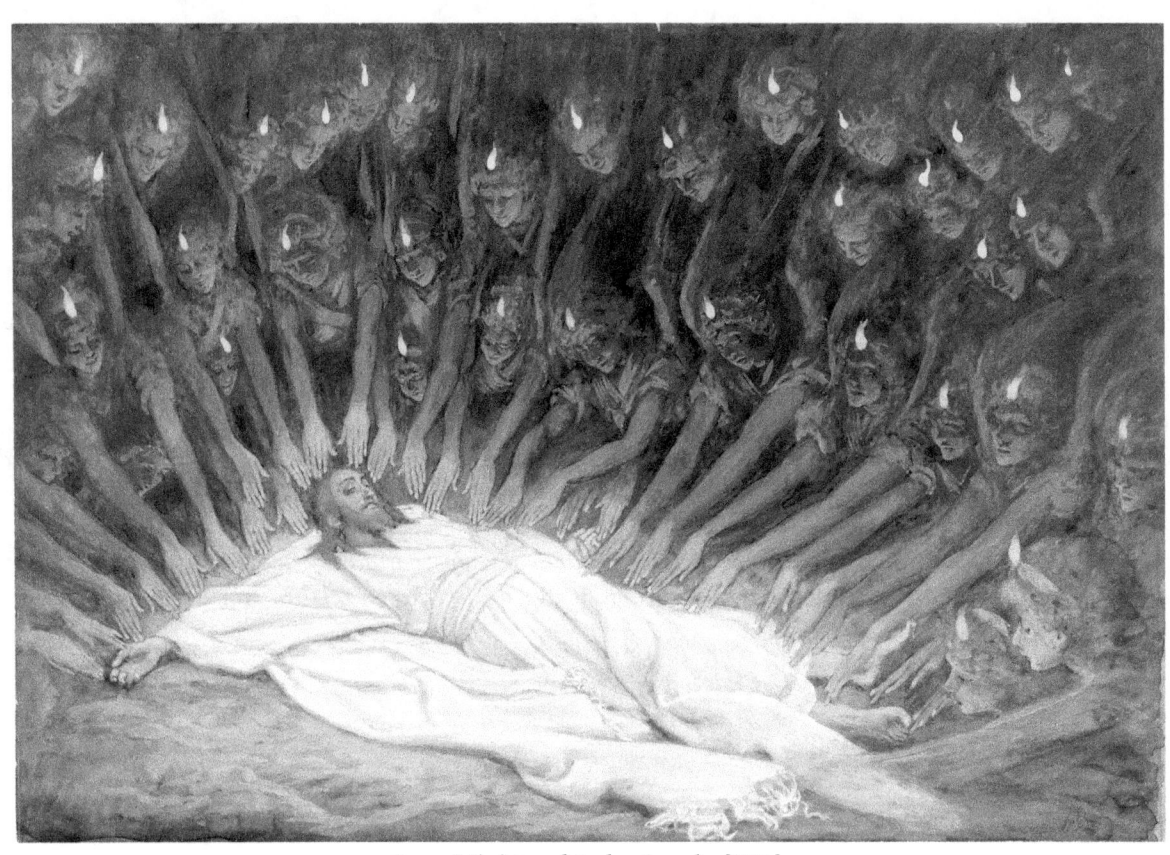
Jesus Ministered to by Angels [B11]

⊕

AT the same moment I beheld myriads of angels draw near to Jesus, bend low before him, take him up as if in their hands, float down gently with him to the rock, and into the grotto in which the forty days' fast had been begun. There were twelve angelic spirits who appeared to be the leaders, and a definite number of assistants. I cannot now remember distinctly, but I think it was seventy-two, and I feel that the whole vision was symbolical of the apostles and the disciples. And now was held in the grotto a grand celebration, one of triumph and thanksgiving, and a banquet was made ready. The angels that ministered unto Jesus appeared under different forms and seemed to belong to different hierarchies. [370]

[MATTHEW 4:11] 11 Then the devil left him, and behold, angels came and ministered to him. [MARK 1:13] 13 And he was in the wilderness forty days, tempted by Satan; and he was with the wild beasts; and the angels ministered to him.

ANGELS came and ministered unto Jesus and in some mysterious way renewed his powers. The strength given to him did not result from the revival of bodily vigor through the natural means of partaking of food and drink; the help sent down from heaven to fortify him for the mission he was about to undertake came from the same divine source as the manifestation which had taken place at his baptism. The forty days' retirement was thus inaugurated by one of the three manifestations from on high which proclaimed our Lord to be the Son of God and revealed his spiritual grandeur; and it closed with yet another heavenly manifestation, this time consecrating his body. Such, at least, is our interpretation of the Gospel narrative.

The Calling of John and Andrew [B12]

⊕

ANDREW and Saturnin, who had been standing near John, hurried over the river by the same way that Jesus had passed (John 1:35). They were followed by one of the cousins of Joseph of Arimathea, and two others of John's disciples. They ran after Jesus, who, turning, came to meet them, asking what they wanted. Andrew, overjoyed at having found him once more, asked him where he dwelt. Jesus answered by bidding them follow him. [373]

[JOHN 1:35–41] 35 Again the next day after John stood, and two of his disciples. 36 And looking upon Jesus as he walked, he saith, Behold the Lamb of God! 37 And the two disciples heard him speak, and they followed Jesus. 38 Then Jesus turned, and saw them following, and saith unto them, What seek ye? They said unto him, Rabbi, (which is to say, being interpreted, Master) where dwellest thou? 39 He saith unto them, Come and see. They came and saw where he dwelt, and abode with him that day for it was about the tenth hour. 40 One of the two which heard John speak, and followed him, was Andrew, Simon Peter's brother. 41 He first findeth his own brother Simon, and saith unto him, We have found the Messiah, which is, being interpreted, the Christ. [Tissot decides, for the purposes of his painting, that the second disciple spoken of here is St. John the Evangelist.]

The Betrothed of Cana [B13]

⊕

ON the third day after Jesus's arrival, at about nine o'clock in the morning, the marriage ceremony was performed. The bride had been adorned by her bridesmaids. Her dress was something like that worn by the Mother of God at her espousals. Her crown, too, was similar, though more richly ornamented. But her hair was not netted in strands so fine as was that of Mary, the braids were fewer and thicker. When fully attired, she was presented to the blessed Virgin and the other women. The bride and bridegroom were conducted processionally from the house of festivity to the synagogue and back again. [386]

[JOHN 2:1–5] 1 On the third day there was a marriage at Cana in Galilee, and the mother of Jesus was there; 2 Jesus also was invited to the marriage, with his disciples. 3 When the wine failed, the mother of Jesus said to him, "They have no wine." 4 And Jesus said to her, "O woman, what have you to do with me? My hour has not yet come." 5 His mother said to the servants, "Do whatever he tells you."

JESUS went to Cana accompanied by his mother, when he had left Nazareth, having been driven out of that town. This Cana, situated three leagues from Nazareth, and five from Tiberias, was called the little Cana, to distinguish it from the large town of the same name, situated near to Sidon. It was built in a valley full of reeds, and it was to this peculiarity of its site that it owed its name. Not far from it, near the waters of Merom, on the north of the Sea of Tiberias, there was a little lake called the Lake of Crocodiles, the borders of which were also celebrated for the beauty of the reeds growing on them. It was one of these reeds, it is said, which was later given to Jesus as a scepter in his Passion.

On his way to Capernaum, then, Jesus passed through Cana, where there was a marriage, to which Jesus, his mother, and the disciples accompanying him, were invited. According to some accounts, the bridegroom, but recently converted, was named Nathaniel. Jesus, as will be well understood, had now become of extreme importance in the life of the man under notice, which will explain at once the invitation sent to him and also the honor with which he and those with him were received and treated at the wedding. In celebtrations of this description, the repast was served of an evening, the betrothed taking their places beneath a canopy of foliage, or sometimes beneath a kind of trellis-work dome, from which, as shown in my picture, were suspended all the ornaments that could be collected.

The Marriage of Cana [B14]

⊕

AFTER a little while Jesus directed them to bring him the empty jugs and turn them upside down. The jugs were brought, three water jugs and three wine jugs, and that they were empty was proved by inverting them over a basin. Then Jesus ordered each to be filled with water. [388]

[JOHN 2:6–11] 6 Now six stone jars were standing there, for the Jewish rites of purification, each holding twenty or thirty gallons. 7 Jesus said to them, "Fill the jars with water." And they filled them up to the brim. 8 He said to them, "Now draw some out, and take it to the steward of the feast." So they took it. 9 When the steward of the feast tasted the water now become wine, and did not know where it came from (though the servants who had drawn the water knew), the steward of the feast called the bridegroom 10 and said to him, "Every man serves the good wine first; and when men have drunk freely, then the poor wine; but you have kept the good wine until now." 11 This, the first of his signs, Jesus did at Cana in Galilee, and manifested his glory; and his disciples believed in him.

Passover Approaches [B15]

☩

JESUS, on the day of his arrival, had a private interview with his mother. She wept over the great danger threatening him on account of the excitement everywhere produced by his teachings and miracles, for she had been informed of all the murmurs and calumnies uttered against him by those that would not presume to say them to his face. But Jesus told her that his time was come, that he would soon leave those parts and go down to Judea where, after Passover, still greater vexation would arise on his account. [409]

[JOHN 2:12–13] 12 After this he went down to Capernaum, with his mother and his brothers and his disciples; and there they stayed for a few days. 13 The Passover of the Jews was at hand, and Jesus went up to Jerusalem.

Interview between Jesus and Nicodemus [B16]

⊕

NICODEMUS was a thoughtful, inquiring man, who was anxiously awaiting Jesus's coming. All had received the baptism of John, and all were secretly assembled at Lazarus's invitation. Nicodemus afterward served Jesus and his cause, but in secret. Nicodemus, and many of the followers of Jesus entertained the secret belief that he was called with his disciples to take possession of Jerusalem, to free the Jews from the Roman yoke, and to establish them in a kingdom of their own. Neither was it known at that time that the kingdom which alone can help us is not of this world of penance. Yes, they indeed rejoiced for the moment in the thought, "Now it will soon be all over with the glory of such or such a tyrant." They did not, however, venture to mention their thoughts to Jesus. They stood in great awe of him; besides, they could read a fulfillment of their hopes in no trace of his behavior, in no word that he uttered. . . .

Lazarus and Joseph of Arimathea returned to Jerusalem. Nicodemus had not come. He was more reserved, on account of the office that he held, but he served Jesus in secret, and to the end notified the little community of any danger that threatened. Nicodemus, in spite of the open persecution directed against Jesus, visited him during these days by invitation of Lazarus. I saw Jesus during the night reclining beside him on the ground and instructing him. [424]

[JOHN 3:1–18] 1 Now there was a man of the Pharisees, named Nicodemus, a ruler of the Jews. 2 This man came to Jesus by night and said to him, "Rabbi, we know that you are a teacher come from God; for no one can do these signs that you do, unless God is with him." 3 Jesus answered him, "Truly, truly, I say to you, unless one is born anew, he cannot see the kingdom of God." 4 Nicodemus said to him, "How can a man be born when he is old? Can he enter a second time into his mother's womb and be born?" 5 Jesus answered, "Truly, truly, I say to you, unless one is born of water and the Spirit, he cannot enter the kingdom of God. 6 That which is born of the flesh is flesh, and that which is born of the Spirit is spirit. 7 Do not marvel that I said to you, 'You must be born anew.' 8 The wind blows where it wills, and you hear the sound of it, but you do not know whence it comes or whither it goes; so it is with every one who is born of the Spirit." 9 Nicodemus said to him, "How can this be?" 10 Jesus answered him, "Are you a teacher of Israel, and yet you do not understand this? 11 Truly, truly, I say to you, we speak of what we know, and bear witness to what we have seen; but you do not receive our testimony. 12 If I have told you earthly things and you do not believe, how can you believe if I tell you heavenly things? 13 No one has ascended into heaven but he who descended from heaven, the Son of man. 14 And as Moses lifted up the serpent in the wilderness, so must the Son of man be lifted up, 15 that whoever believes in him may have eternal life." 16 For God so loved the world that he gave his only Son, that whoever believes in him should not perish but have eternal life. 17 For God sent the Son into the world, not to condemn the world, but that the world might be saved through him. 18 He who believes in him is not condemned; he who does not believe is condemned already, because he has not believed in the name of the only Son of God.

THE rabbis tell us that the Hebrew name of Nicodemus the disciple of Jesus was Bonoi Ben Gorion. He was a priest and a member of the Sanhedrim, or Supreme Council of the Jewish people. His wealth was considerable and his influence very great. It is even said that he was superintendent of the water supply of Jerusalem, and it is to him the story refers telling how every time he went to the temple, he had a fresh carpet spread out for him, giving the old ones to the poor, and never using the same one twice. Nicodemus was by no means what we should call at the present day a parvenu; he was of a very ancient and illustrious race; his family originally came from Jericho, and he himself was a disciple of the celebrated Hillel, who had founded in his own house an academy and school which had become famous.

FROM CLOSE OF FIRST PASSOVER TO CONVERSION OF SAMARITAN WOMAN AT JACOB'S WELL · TRAVELS IN NORTH GALILEE

The Letter of King Abgar

Wednesday, May 3, AD 30 (Iyyar 12)

Around this time (about three weeks after the Passover festival), Jesus went to the place of baptism near Ono, where he himself had been baptized. (This was the third place of baptism chosen by John the Baptist.) His disciples had gathered there, and many people came to hear him. While Jesus was teaching, a messenger from King Abgar of Edessa arrived. The messenger asked Jesus to accompany him back to Edessa, or—if not—if he could at least paint a portrait of him. He produced a letter from the king in which the king described that he was ill, and believed in Jesus as God or the Son of God, and requested to be healed. Jesus replied to the king's letter by miraculously causing a perfect likeness of his countenance to be imprinted on the messenger's paper. The sight of this image later effected a deep transformation in the king's life.

FROM Bethany, where Jesus had for some time remained in concealment, he went to the place of baptism near Ono. The arrangements were still in good order, owing to the care of its custodians. The disciples gathered around Jesus, and crowds of people came streaming in. As Jesus was teaching before the multitude, part of whom were standing, others sitting on wooden platforms in a circle around him, a stranger approached mounted on a camel. He was followed by six attendants, who rode on mules. They halted at the tents, some distance from the place of instruction. It was an embassy from King Abgar, who was sick, and who had sent presents to Jesus with a letter in which he implored him to come to Edessa to cure him. He had had an eruption that had settled in his feet and rendered him lame. Travelers returning to their homes had told him about Jesus and his miracles, of the testimony of John, and the wrath of the Jews at the last Passover solemnity, all which had excited in him a great longing to be cured by Jesus.

The young man commissioned to bear the king's letter to Jesus was an artist, and he had received commands to bring back Jesus's portrait if he would not come himself. I saw him vainly trying to reach Jesus. He pressed sometimes here, sometimes there through the crowd, both to hear the instruction and to paint Jesus's likeness. Then Jesus bade one of the disciples to make room for the man that was going around people unable to push his way to the front, and he pointed out a platform nearby to which he should be conducted. The disciple brought the envoy forward, and placed him and his attendants where they could see and hear. They had with them gifts of woven stuffs, thin plates of gold, and very beautiful lambs.

The envoy, overjoyed at being able at last to see Jesus, at once produced his drawing materials, rested his tablet on his knee, regarded Jesus with great admiration and attention, and set to work. The tablet before him was white as if made of wax. He began by sketching with a pencil the outlines of Jesus's head and beard. Then it looked as if he spread over his work a layer of wax in which to receive the impression of the sketch. After that he resumed his sketching, touched again and again with his pencil, again took the impression, and so continued, but without ever perfecting his work. As often as he glanced at Jesus, he seemed lost in amazement at the countenance he beheld, and was forced to begin anew. Luke did not paint in exactly this way. He used a brush also. The picture this man was producing appeared to me to be somewhat in relief; one could trace it by the touch.

Jesus continued his discourse a while longer, and then sent the disciple to say to the envoy that he might now approach and deliver his message. The envoy came down from the platform whereon he was sitting, followed by his attendants with the presents and lambs. His doublet was short, almost like those of the three kings, and he wore no mantle. The picture at which he had been working was hanging by a strap on his left arm. It was like a shield in the form of a heart. In the right hand he held the king's letter. Casting himself on his knees before Jesus, he bowed low, as did also his attendants, and said: "Thy slave is the servant of Abgar, king of Edessa. He is sick. He sends thee this letter, and prays thee to accept these gifts from him." Then the slaves approached with the presents. Jesus replied to the envoy that the good intentions of his master were pleasing to him, and he commanded the disciples to take the gifts and distribute them among the poorest of the assembled crowd. Then he unfolded the letter and read it. I do not remember all that was in it, but only that the king referred to Jesus's power to raise the dead, and begged him to come and cure him. The part of the letter containing the writing was stiff; the envelope pliable, as if of some kind of stuff, either leather or silk. I saw, too, that it was bound by a string.

When Jesus had read the letter, he turned the other side of the stiff part and, drawing from his robe a coarse pencil out of which he pushed something, he wrote several words in tolerably large characters, and then folded it again. After that he called for some water, bathed his face, pressed the soft stuff in which the letter had been folded to his sacred countenance, and returned it to the envoy. The latter applied it to the picture he had vainly tried to perfect, when behold! The likeness instantly became a facsimile of the original. The artist was filled with delight. He turned the picture, which was hanging by a strap, toward the spectators, cast himself at Jesus's feet, arose, and took leave immediately. But some of his servants remained behind and followed Jesus who, after this instruction, crossed the Jordan to the second place of baptism which John had abandoned. There these new followers were baptized.

I saw the envoy on his way home passing a night outside a city near which were long stone buildings like brick kilns. Very early the next morning some of the workmen hurried to the spot, because they had seen there a bright light like a fire. Something remarkable then took place in connection with the picture, and a great crowd of people gathered on the spot. The artist exhibited to them his picture, as well as the cloth with which Jesus had dried his face, and which, too, had received the imprint of his features. Abgar came some distance through his gardens to meet his envoy. He was indescribably touched at Jesus's letter and the sight of his picture. He immediately amended his life and dismissed the numerous concubines with whom he had sinned.

I saw again that, after the death of Abgar's son, in the reign of a wicked successor, the portrait of Jesus, which had been publicly exposed, was concealed by a pious bishop. He placed it in a niche, a burning lamp before it, and walled up the aperture. After a long time, the picture was discovered, and then it was found that the stone that concealed it from sight also bore its imprint.

Jesus on the Confines of Sidon and Tyre

Thursday, May 4, to Sunday, May 21, AD 30 (Iyyar 13–30)

After leaving the third place of baptism near Ono, Jesus crossed the Jordan and went to the second place of baptism near Gilgal. Many people were baptized there during this period by Andrew, Saturnin, Peter, and James the brother of John (John 3:22). John the Baptist remained at the first place of baptism near Ainon (John 3:23). Several of John's disciples traveled down the Jordan to join Jesus, and a controversy arose between these disciples of John and one who had been baptized by Jesus's disciples—a controversy concerning the difference between the baptisms with regard to purification (John 3:25). Furthermore, as Jesus now had so many disciples, John's remaining disciples complained that everyone was going over to Jesus (John 3:26). John's reply that he had come to bear witness as the forerunner of the Messiah is reported in John 3:26–36. All of these events—the controversy, the testimony of John the Baptist, the multitude that flocked to be baptized by Jesus's disciples—aroused fresh excitement among the Pharisees. They dispatched letters to the elders of all the synagogues in the land, directing them to take Jesus and his disciples into custody.

JESUS went from Ono with the disciples to the middle place of baptism, that above Bethabara and opposite Gilgal. There he permitted Andrew, Saturnin, Peter, and James to baptize. Immense crowds were coming and going, rousing in consequence fresh excitement among the Pharisees. They dispatched letters to the elders of all the synagogues throughout the country, directing them to deliver over Jesus wheresoever he might be found, to take the disciples into custody, to inquire into their teachings, and inflict punishment upon them.

SIVAN (30 days):
May 21/22 to June 19/20, AD 30 Sivan
New Moon: May 21 at 6:00 AM Jerusalem time

Around the beginning of the month of Sivan, Jesus left the place of baptism, and his disciples returned to their homes in different parts of the country. (At the same time, Herod Antipas imprisoned John the Baptist in his castle at Kallirrhoe but let him go again six weeks later, around the middle of the month of Tammuz.) Jesus crossed the Jordan and made his way through Samaria toward Tyre.

(Follow Map 16)

While Jesus was crossing through West Galilee, Andrew brought Bartholomew to meet him. Jesus said: "I know him; he will follow me. I see good in him, and in due course of time I shall call him." Jesus traveled further up the coast of the Mediterranean, passing by Tyre and teaching here and there in the region lying inland between Tyre and Sidon. Later, he turned south again and visited his mother near Capernaum. Then, accompanied by Saturnin and some other disciples, he went to the towns of Adama and Seleucia close to Lake Merom. Here he taught various people privately, rather than appearing publicly in the synagogues. He also healed many.

But Jesus, accompanied by only a few disciples, left the place of baptism, and journeyed through Samaria and Galilee on the confines of Tyre. The rest of the disciples separated and returned to their homes. About the same time, Herod ordered his soldiers to bring John to Kallirrhoe, where he kept him confined for about six weeks in a vault of his castle. Then he set him free.

While Jesus, with a few of his disciples, was crossing the valley Esdrelon on his way through Samaria, Bartholomew passed. Returning home to Debbaseth from the baptism of John, he fell in with some of the disciples, and Andrew spoke to him enthusiastically of the Lord. Bartholomew listened with delight and reverence, and Andrew, whose joy it was to add intelligent men to the number of the disciples, went forward to Jesus and spoke to him of Bartholomew, who was desirous of following him. Just at this moment, Bartholomew passed by. Andrew pointed him out to Jesus who, glancing toward Bartholomew, said to Andrew: "I know him; he will follow me. I see good in him, and I shall call him in time." Bartholomew dwelt in Debbaseth not far from Ptolomais. He was a writer. I saw that he met Thomas soon after, to whom in turn he spoke of Jesus and whom he inclined in his favor.

Jesus had to endure great privations on this hurried journey. Saturnin, or some other one of the disciples, had charge of a basket of bread. Several times I saw Jesus steeping the hard crust in water, in order to be able to eat it.

Tuesday, June 20, AD 30 (Sivan 30)

Toward the end of the month of Sivan, accompanied by a few disciples, Jesus made his way to the city of Tyre. This evening he went to stay at an inn on the outskirts of the city. Here he and his disciples celebrated the New Moon festival that signified the end of the month of Sivan and the beginning of the month of Tammuz.

TAMMUZ (29 days):
June 20/21 to July 18/19, AD 30 Tammuz
New Moon: June 19 at 8:45 PM Jerusalem time

Wednesday, June 21, AD 30 (Tammuz 1)

Today, about twenty of Jesus's disciples arrived at Tyre, having traveled from Galilee. In the evening, they met together with Jesus. He greeted each one of them warmly and told the assembled disciples that he would soon take up his public teaching again.

In Tyre Jesus put up at an inn near the gate on the land side of the city. He had come over a high mountain ridge. Tyre was a very large city. To one approaching from a distant height, it looked as if hanging from a mountain and momentarily in danger of being detached. Jesus did not enter the city. He kept along the wall on the land side where there were not so many people. The wall was very thick. In it was built the inn, and on top of it ran a road. Jesus wore a brownish robe and a white woolen mantle. He went here and there, but only to the houses of the poor built in the wall. Saturnin and one other disciple had come with Jesus to Tyre. Peter, Andrew, James the Less, Thaddeus, Nathaniel Chased, and all the disciples that had been with him at the marriage feast of Cana followed.

Thursday, June 22, AD 30 (Tammuz 2)

Today, the Galilean disciples set off back to Galilee. Jesus went with Saturnin and another disciple to a fruit plantation some two hours northeast of Tyre. Jesus taught the workers there. That night, he stayed in one of their huts.

Friday, June 23, AD 30 (Tammuz 3)

Jesus returned to Tyre. In the evening, he celebrated the sabbath in the Jewish meeting house in Tyre.

Saturday, June 24, and Sunday, June 25, AD 30 (Tammuz 4–5)

On Saturday, Jesus celebrated the sabbath in Tyre. On Sunday, he healed people in the bathing garden of the Jewish meeting house there. Many people were baptized by Saturnin.

The disciples traveled in separate bands, and met Jesus in the Jewish meeting house, situated in another quarter of Tyre, to which led a broad canal bordered with trees.

To this house, with which the school was connected, belonged a large bathing garden, which ran down even to the water that cut off this quarter of the city from the mainland. The bathing garden was surrounded by a wall, inside of which was a quickset hedge of bushes cut in figures. In the middle of the garden was an open portico containing numerous passages and little apartments, and around it was the spacious bathing cistern full of flowing water. There was in the middle of it a pillar with steps and hand supports, by means of which one could descend into the water to any depth. This place was inhabited by aged Jews, who were despised on account of their religion or origin, although they were good, pious men.

It was touching to see Jesus saluting the disciples on their arrival. He passed among them giving his hands first to one, then to another. They were full of respectful confidence, for they regarded him as an extraordinary, supernatural Being. They were indescribably joyous at seeing him again. He delivered to them a long instruction, after which they told him all that had happened to them. They took a meal together consisting of bread, fruit, honey, and fish which the disciples had brought with them.

Map 16: Travels in Northern Galilee
End of May–July 19, AD 30

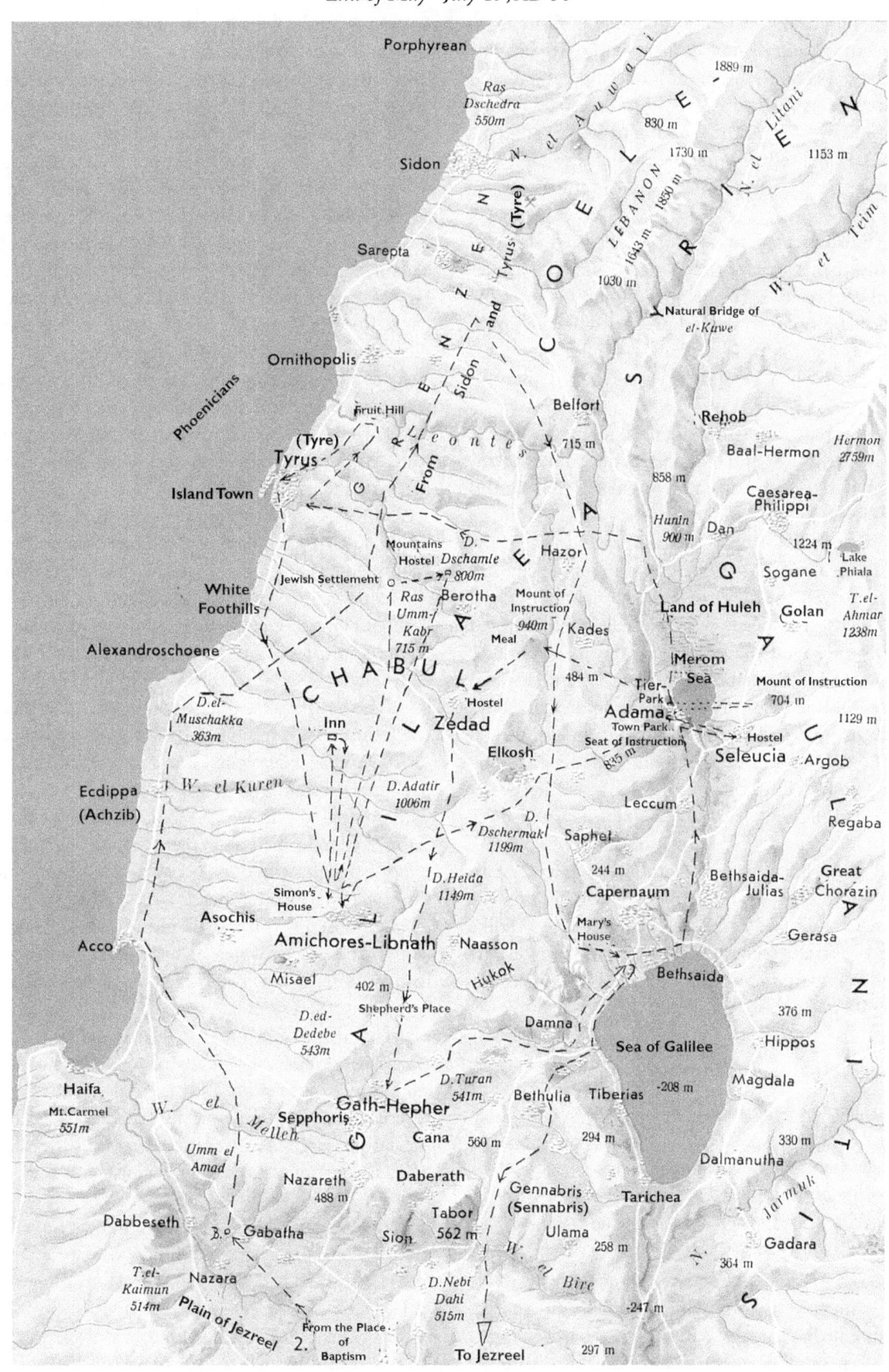

West Galilee—At the Boundaries of Sidon and Tyre—Capernaum—Adama and Seleucia—Tyre
Amichores-Libnath—Land of Chabul—Adama—Seleucia—Adama—Mount of Instruction
near Berotha—Zedad—Gath-Hepher—Capernaum

The disciples, some in Jerusalem, some in Gennabris, were called to account by the Pharisees before large assemblies on the subject of Jesus, his doctrine and designs, and their own dealings with him. They were molested in many ways. Once I saw Peter, Andrew, and John with their hands bound, but a slight effort burst their bonds asunder, as if by a miracle. They were then allowed to return to their homes in peace.

Jesus exhorted them to constancy and told them to begin to free themselves more and more from their avocations, and to spread, as far as they could, his doctrine among the people of their district. He added that he would soon be with them again, and that he would resume his public teaching when he should have rejoined them in Galilee.

After the departure of the disciples, Jesus held in the school of the bathing garden an instruction and exhortation before a numerous assembly of men, women, and children. He spoke of Moses, of the prophets, and of the near coming of the Messiah. He interpreted to them the meaning of the drought that had fallen upon the country in the time of Elijah, the prophet's prayer for rain, the uprising clouds, and the showers that fell, and he showed how all this was soon to be realized. He spoke also of water and of purification, healed many of the sick, and directed them to receive the baptism of John. He cured many boys who had been brought to him on beds. He plunged several of them, holding them by the arms, into the water, Saturnin having poured into it from a bottle some other water that Jesus had blessed. The two disciples baptized these children. There were other boys approaching manhood, who went down into the cistern and, holding to the column, plunged themselves under the water, and in this way were baptized. I noticed here several circumstances unlike what I had generally seen on such occasions. Many of the adults had to remain standing at a distance. The ceremony went on until night closed in.

Jesus in Amichores-Libnath

Monday, June 26, AD 30 (Tammuz 6)

Jesus sent Saturnin and the other disciple with messages to Capernaum and Ainon. Jesus then went alone to the town of Amichores-Libnath, where there was a rich man named Simeon, who revered Jesus greatly. Simeon welcomed Jesus, and they dined together.

WHEN Jesus left Tyre, he proceeded alone on his way. He had sent both the disciples with orders to Capernaum, also to John the Baptist. He went from ten to eleven hours south of Tyre to the city Amichores-Libnath, through which he had already passed on his journey hither. Lake Merom, with the two cities Adama and Seleucia, lay to the east on his left. Amichores-Libnath (Amichores, meaning "city built upon the waters," is sometimes simply called Sichor) was a couple of hours inland from Ptolomais on a small, muddy lake, one side of which was rendered inaccessible by high mountains. From this lake arose the little, sandy stream Belus, which empties into the sea near Ptolomais. The city was so large that I cannot conceive why so little is known of it. The Jewish city Misael was not far off. This is the country that Solomon bestowed upon King Hiram. Sichor was free, though with some little dependence on Tyre. There was much cattle raising going on in these parts. I saw numbers of large sheep with fine wool. They could swim over the water. Beautiful woolen goods were woven here and dyed in Tyre. I saw no tilling of fields, but only the cultivation of orchards. There grew in the water a kind of grain with very large stalks. Bread was made of the grain. I think they were not obliged to sow seed for this plant, it sprang up wild. A road led from Sichor to Syria and Arabia, but there was no highway to Galilee. Jesus had come to Tyre by an indirect route.

There were two great bridges outside of Sichor: the one, high and long to enable the inhabitants to cross when the whole country was inundated; the other lower, affording a convenient passage under the arches formed by the upper one. The houses were built high and so constructed that, when the city was submerged, the people could take refuge on the roofs under tents. Most of the inhabitants were pagans. I saw little flags waving from several buildings with pointed towers, which I took for pagan temples. I was astonished to see here so many Jews, although held in contempt by their neighbors, occupying handsome houses. I think they were exiles.

The house in which Jesus put up was outside the city and on the side by which he had come. He had, however, to cross water to reach it. There was a synagogue nearby. It seemed as if Jesus, on his journey to Tyre, had announced his return by this route, for the people of the house at which he stopped appeared to be expecting him. They came out to meet him and received him with marks of reverence. They were Jews, the father an aged man, and the family large. They occupied a very beautiful house which, like a palace, had many wings, and smaller buildings around it. Through respect for Jesus, the master of the family conducted him not into his own house, but into one of the neighboring dwellings, where he washed his feet and showed him hospitality.

I saw a great procession of all kinds of laboring people, men, women, and lads, a mixed crowd of pagans, some brown, some black (very likely slaves of this man) coming from their work. They filed into a large open place and took their food. They had with them all kinds of shovels and carts, and carried on their shoulders little, light boats like troughs. These last were provided with a seat and rudder, and contained fishing tackle. These laborers were employed in building and repairing bridges and banks. They received food in earthen vessels, also vegetables and birds; the flesh of the latter some of them ate raw. Jesus had them brought before him. He spoke to them kindly, and they were delighted to see such a man.

Two old Jews came to Jesus with some rolls of the scriptures. They took a repast with him, and he explained to them many things that they were very desirous to know. They were instructors of youth.

The rich Jew and master of the house at which Jesus stopped was named Simeon, and was from the region of Samaria. Either he or his forefathers had interested themselves in the temple on Mount Garizim, and had associated with the Samaritans, and were on that account driven from their country. They had settled here.

Tuesday, June 27, AD 30 (Tammuz 7)

Jesus taught at Simeon's house and in a public place in the town.

Jesus taught a whole day at the house of his host in an open court surrounded by columns, over which an awning was stretched. The master of the house came and went. There were gathered in the court very many Jews, men and women of all ages. I did not see Jesus performing any cures; indeed, there were no sick nor cripples. The people here were lank and lean, but very tall. Jesus gave an instruction on baptism, and promised to send some of his disciples hither to baptize. Accompanied by the master of the house, he went out on the road by which the slaves had returned from their work. He spoke to them, encouraged them, and explained to them a parable. There were many good people, who were very much touched. They again received food and wages. It reminded me of the parable that speaks of the lord of the vineyard paying the day laborers. The slaves dwelt in a row of huts about a quarter of an hour from Simeon's. It was some kind of serfdom that they were discharging by their labor for Simeon.

On one of the following days, after Jesus had been preaching from early morn and the Jews had gone away, about twenty pagans came to him. For several days they had been asking to be allowed to do so. Simeon's was about half an hour from the city, and the pagans dared not approach beyond a certain tower or arch. But Simeon himself brought these newcomers to Jesus, whom they saluted reverently and begged to instruct them. He spoke for a long time with them in a hall, so long indeed that the lamps were lighted before he finished. He consoled them, told them in a parable of the holy three kings, and said that light would one day shine upon the pagans.

Wednesday, June 28, AD 30 (Tammuz 8)

Having sent disciples from Capernaum to Ainon, as Jesus had instructed, Saturnin and the other disciple arrived this morning from Capernaum. In Amichores-Libnath, Jesus continued his teaching.

When the two disciples whom Jesus had sent to Capernaum returned to him at Sichor, they told him that the four disciples whom he had summoned were coming.

Thursday, June 29, AD 30 (Tammuz 9)

Jesus and the two disciples went north of Amichores-Libnath to an inn where they met up with Peter, Andrew, James the Less, and Nathaniel Chased. That evening they returned together to Amichores-Libnath. It was a beautiful moonlit night, and Jesus paused from time to time to pray or teach.

Jesus went a journey of from three to four hours over a mountain to meet them, and came up with them at an inn on Galilean territory. There were, besides those that he had called, seven others and among them John. Some women also had come with them, of whom I recognized Mary Mark of Jerusalem and the maternal aunt of the bridegroom Nathaniel. Those called were Peter, Andrew, James the Less, and Nathaniel Chased. Although it was already dark, Jesus walked with the four and the two other disciples back to Sichor, but the seven that had not been called returned to Galilee. It was an exceedingly delightful night—the sky was clear and a delicious fragrance embalmed the air. They walked sometimes all together, sometimes before or after Jesus, who then went on alone. Once they rested in the midst of a very fertile region under trees laden with fruit, and in the neighborhood of green meadows and running brooks. As they started again, there rose up from the meadow a flock of birds that accompanied them on their way. They were almost as large as hens, had red beaks and long pointed wings like those with which angels are painted, and as they flew they kept up the funniest twittering. The birds followed them even into the city, and there lighted among the reeds in the water. They could run on the water like waterfowl. It was a touching sight—the beautiful night, Jesus pausing from time to time to pray or to teach, and the birds settling around the little party of travelers. Thus did they climb the mountain and descend on the other side. Simeon came forward to meet them, washed the feet of all, presented them a cup to drink and a morsel to eat in the vestibule, and then conducted them into his house. The birds, or waterfowl, belonged to Simeon; they flew around like pigeons.

Jesus in Amichores-Libnath

Friday, June 30, AD 30 (Tammuz 10)
Jesus and his disciples all stayed with Simeon at his house where they celebrated the start of the sabbath that evening.

Jesus taught here during the whole day, and in the evening they celebrated the sabbath in Simeon's house, which was very high. Besides Jesus and the disciples, there were present about twenty Jews. The synagogue was in a subterranean vault, and arranged in perfect order. A flight of steps led down to it. A leader sang and read in the synagogue, after which Jesus delivered a discourse. The disciples slept in the same house with Jesus.

Saturday, July 1, AD 30 (Tammuz 11)
Although it was the sabbath, Jesus and his disciples set off early in the morning to journey to a little town in the land of Chabul. They traveled through mountain passes some five or six hours north of Amichores-Libnath. Arriving at their destination—a town where many Jewish exiles lived—Jesus healed about twenty people. He also taught concerning the prophet Elisha. That night, Jesus and his disciples stayed at an inn in the mountains about two hours from the town.

Their sleep was only a few hours long, for the gray dawn found them again on their way. They journeyed through crooked mountain passes to a little Jewish city in the land of Chabul, where dwelt some other Jewish exiles who had frequently implored to be allowed to return to their country, but the Pharisees would not permit it. Long had they sighed for a visit from Jesus, though they deemed themselves unworthy of it, and for that reason had refrained from sending for him. But now Jesus went of his own accord. The winding mountainous roads made it a journey of from five to six hours.

When they neared the little Jewish city, two of the disciples went on ahead to notify the ruler of the synagogue of Jesus's coming. Although it was the sabbath, Jesus had undertaken this journey, for here in the country, when necessity intervened, he did not strictly observe this law. He went to the rulers of the synagogue, who received him with great humility. They washed his feet, also those of the disciples, and offered them a luncheon. Then Jesus had himself taken around to all the sick, about twenty of whom he cured. Among them were people quite deformed and lame, women afflicted with an issue of blood, others blind, dropsical, and leprous, also many children.

As he went along the street, several possessed cried out after him and he freed them from the evil spirit. Order and silence reigned throughout the city. The disciples helped their Master. Some assisted the cured to rise, some instructed the crowd that followed Jesus and gathered around the doors of the houses into which he had entered. Before curing some of the sick, Jesus exhorted them to faith and amendment of life; others who already believed, he cured at once. Raising his eyes to heaven, he prayed over them; some he touched, over others he passed his hand. I saw, too, that he blessed water and sprinkled the people with it, directing the disciples to do the same to the house. In one of the houses he and the disciples accepted a little wine and a morsel of bread.

Many of the cured, rising up, cast themselves at his feet, and then followed him joyously, as we here follow the blessed sacrament, though always reverently and at a distance. But to others again, Jesus gave a command to remain in their homes.

He directed some of the cured to bathe in the water that he had blessed; these were the children and the leprous. Jesus went to a well near the synagogue and blessed it, casting in at the same time salt that he had previously blessed. This well was very deep; a flight of steps led down to it. He taught on this occasion of Elisha, who with salt had rectified the water near Jericho; then he explained the signification of salt. He furthermore commanded that the people, when sick, should use the water of the well for bathing purposes. He always blessed in the form of a cross. While he was thus engaged, the disciples held his mantle, which he sometimes laid off, and handed him the salt that he threw into the water. He performed all these ceremonies with great gravity and recollection.

During this vision, I saw interiorly that a similar power to heal is given to priests. Some of the sick were brought to Jesus on beds, and he cured them. He delivered a discourse in the synagogue, but he took no repast, for the whole day was spent in teaching and healing. On the evening after the sabbath, he left the place with his disciples. On taking leave of the inhabitants, who were distressed to see him go, he ordered them not to follow him, and they obeyed humbly. He had blessed and purified the water for them, because it was bad and full of snakes and animals with thick heads and long tails. About two hours from this place Jesus and his disciples put up at a large inn among the mountains where they ate and slept. On their journey to the Jewish city they had passed this inn at some distance.

Sunday, July 2, AD 30 (Tammuz 12)
Today, Jesus taught and healed a number of people—mainly non-Jews—who came to the inn where he was staying. Toward evening, he and the disciples made their way back to Amichores-Libnath.

The next day, crowds of people bringing their sick gathered in the mountain inn, for they knew that Jesus was come. They were people that lived in huts and caves on opposite sides of the mountain. On the west side, toward Tyre, dwelt the pagans, who also had come; and on the east side, poor Jews. Jesus gave an instruction in which he spoke of purification, of ablutions, and of penance, and cured about thirty persons.

The pagans remained at a distance, and Jesus did not teach them until the others had retired. He addressed to them a consoling instruction that lasted till after midday. These poor people had little gardens and plantations around their caves. Their principal nourishment was sheep's milk, which they made into cheese and ate like bread. The fruits of their gardens, as also those that they gathered growing wild, they carried around the country for sale. Many of them likewise furnished the dwellers, in the little city where Jesus had on the preceding day blessed the water, with good water which they carried thither in leathern bottles. Some other places were provided by them in like manner. There were many lepers among these people, for whom Jesus blessed water in which they might bathe.

Toward evening Jesus returned to Amichores-Libnath, where he again taught and announced that on the following day he would baptize.

Monday, July 3, AD 30 (Tammuz 13)

Many people were baptized with water from a basin in the court of Simeon's mansion in Amichores-Libnath. Jesus blessed the water and instructed the people. They were then baptized by Andrew, Peter, or Saturnin. Toward evening, Jesus and the disciples left and traveled eastward in the direction of Adama. That night they rested under some trees where there was much high grass.

In the court of the large mansion belonging to Simeon, there was a round, shallow basin from which the water overflowed into a surrounding trench. Here, too, the water was not good; it had a bad taste. Jesus blessed it, casting into it at the same time salt in lumps like stones. In this region there was a whole mountain formed of salt.

In that basin, which had previously been drained and cleansed, the baptism of about thirty persons took place. The master of the house with all the males of his household, some other Jews of the place, many of the pagans that had lately been with Jesus, and some of the slaves from the huts, were baptized. These last Jesus had on several different occasions instructed when returned from their work. The pagans were the last to be baptized. They had to prepare themselves for the ceremony by certain purifications. Jesus poured from a flask into the baptismal basin some of the Jordan water, which the disciples always carried with them, and then he blessed it. The trench around the basin was filled high enough for the neophytes to stand in it up to the knees in water.

Before administering baptism, Jesus prepared the aspirants by a long instruction. These latter wore long, gray mantles with hoods over the head, something like the mantles worn in prayer. When about to step into the trench around the basin, they laid aside the mantle. Their loins were covered, as also the back and breast, while from the shoulders fell a little open mantle like a scapular. A disciple laid one hand upon the shoulder of the neophyte, the other upon his head. The baptizer, in the name of the Most High, poured over his head several times from a flat shell water dipped from the basin. First Andrew baptized, then Peter, who was afterward relieved by Saturnin. The pagans were baptized last. The ceremony, including the preparations, continued until near evening.

When the people had retired, Jesus and the disciples left the place separately. They met again on the road and went eastward toward Adama on Lake Merom, resting by night in the beautiful high grass under the trees.

Jesus in Adama • Miraculous Conversion of an Obstinate Jew

Tuesday, July 4, AD 30 (Tammuz 14)

Around midday, they arrived in Adama. After being given a meal by some of the most respected people of the town, Jesus was conducted to the synagogue. Here he spoke of the fulfillment of the divine covenant.

ALTHOUGH Adama did not appear very distant, still Jesus and the disciples had to journey some hours up a river before reaching a crossing place. There was no ferryman, but only a raft of beams, something like a gridiron, which lay on the shore for the accommodation of travelers. Toward noon the little troop reached Adama, which was hemmed in on all sides by water. On the eastern side of the city lay Lake Merom. The city was surrounded by a stream, which was at five different points crossed by bridges. At the bathing gardens, the stream again united with the lake. The steep shores of the low lake were covered with thick reeds and undergrowth, and its waters were muddy except in the middle where those of the Jordan flowed. The country around was infested by wild beasts.

As Jesus, with the disciples, approached the bathing garden near the city, several distinguished men of the place came forward to meet him. They had been awaiting his coming in the garden. They conducted him into the city and to a large open square, in the center of which stood the governor's palace. It had a spacious forecourt, on both sides of which and in the rear ran rows of low buildings. The court was cut off from the street by a railing of shining metal made into various colored plates. Here they washed the feet both of Jesus and the disciples, brushed and shook their mantles, and presented them with a luncheon of small fruits and herbs. It was an old

Lake Merom in the Distance

custom of the people of Adama to conduct all that visited their city to this castle, where they interrogated them. If they were pleased with them, they treated them hospitably in the hope of attracting blessings upon themselves; but if they were not favorably impressed by their guests, they did not hesitate to cast them into prison. Adama, with about twenty little districts, belonged to a province under the jurisdiction of one of the Herods. The inhabitants of the city were Samaritan Jews who, in consequence of their schism, had embraced sundry perverse notions. Still, there was no idolatry practiced among them, and pagans living here had to carry on their idol worship in secret.

After that, Jesus was conducted by the men that had received him outside the city to the synagogue, a building of three stories. There he found a great part of the Jews assembled, the women in the background. First they prayed and chanted canticles to God, that to his honor they might understand all that Jesus was about to say to them. Then Jesus began his discourse. He spoke of the divine Promises, of their mutual dependence and their realization, and of grace which, he said, was never allowed to go to waste. If he to whom, on account of the merit of his ancestors, some grace was given, would not receive it, it was passed on to the next most deserving. He told them also of a good action performed by their ancestors in this city so long before that it was to them almost unknown, but the happy results of which they were still experiencing. Their forefathers had once harbored some strangers and exiles.

Jesus and the disciples put up at a large inn near the gate by which they had entered the city.

In the neighborhood of the bathing garden outside, though more to the south, was a place for teaching. It consisted of a green hill in the center of a large, open space in which were trees planted in rows five deep, whose dense shade afforded protection from the sun. On the hill and overshadowed by a tree, was a teacher's chair beautifully hewn out of stone. It was a very delightful place and was known as the "Place of Grace," because the people believed that here a great favor had once upon a time been accorded them. To the north of the city was another place of which there was a popular saying expressive of some great calamity that had come upon them.

Wednesday, July 5, AD 30 (Tammuz 15)
The disciples went from house to house inviting people to attend a discourse that Jesus would give the following day. That evening, a great banquet was held at the public hall in honor of Jesus.

The disciples went into the houses throughout the city, inviting the people to the "Place of Grace," where Jesus was about to deliver a great discourse. On the evening before, a banquet was given in the public hall of the governor's court. About fifty citizens were present and five tables were spread. Jesus was at that of the most distinguished, and the disciples were scattered among the guests at the other tables. I think Jesus and the disciples also contributed something to the entertainment. Plants like little trees in pots adorned the table. Jesus taught during the meal, going from table to table and speaking to all the guests. When the tables were cleared of all but their ornamental foliage, and grace said, all present ranged in a half-circle before Jesus, who delivered an instruction and invited them to come next morning to the "Place of Grace," where he would discourse to them more at length.

Thursday, July 6, AD 30 (Tammuz 16)

Jesus discoursed for much of the day—from around nine in the morning to four in the afternoon—at a place on a hill with a stone teacher's chair overshadowed by a tree. First, he prayed to the heavenly Father; then, he spoke of penance and baptism, and of Moses and the giving of the Law. At the end of his discourse, when many people had already left, an elderly man with a long beard stepped forward and said: "Allow me now to speak with you. You have enumerated twenty-three truths when, in reality, there are twenty-four." He then proceeded to relate them one after the other. Jesus replied: "You say that there are twenty-four truths and that I have taught only twenty-three. But you have already added three to my number, for I taught only twenty." And Jesus counted up twenty truths according to the letters of the Hebrew alphabet. But the old man would by no means acknowledge his error. Jesus spoke of the evil of obstinacy and of the disastrous consequences attached to making arbitrary additions to the truth. As he spoke, the old man turned pale, then yellow, and became shrunken on one side. Bewailing his plight, the old man acknowledged his error and implored Jesus to have mercy on him. Jesus responded to his entreaties, restoring him to his former condition. The old man cast himself down at Jesus's feet and—as a result of this conversion—became one of Jesus's most faithful followers.

Next day toward nine in the morning, Jesus set out with the disciples for the place of instruction, where over one hundred distinguished men were gathered under the shade of the trees. In the outer circle were some women also. On the way thither, Jesus and the disciples arrived at the palace of the governor who, in magnificent robes and attended by his officers, was just about setting out for the same place. But Jesus commanded him not to go in such array, but to make his appearance like the other men in a long mantle and penitential garb. The mantle was of dyed wool. They wore also a scapular of one piece in the back but open on the breast, the two held in place over the shoulders by a narrow strap. The two pieces, front and back, were black with the names of the seven capital sins wrought into them in different colors. The women were veiled. When Jesus stepped up on the teacher's chair, the people bowed reverently. The governor and the most distinguished men of the city stood close to the chair.

The disciples, standing in the outer circles, had each around him a group of men and women receiving instructions. Jesus first raised his eyes to heaven and prayed aloud to his Father, from whom all graces flow, that his teaching might fall upon hearts repentant and sincere. He directed the people to repeat his words after him, which they did. His discourse lasted without interruption from nine in the morning till about four in the afternoon. Once only there was a pause, during which they brought him a little refreshment, a glass of wine and a morsel of bread. The listeners came and went, according as their business in the city demanded. Jesus taught of penance and baptism, of which he here spoke principally as of a spiritual purification and cleansing. No women were baptized before Pentecost, though among the children admitted to baptism were little girls of from five to eight years old, but no grown girls. The mysterious signification connected with this, I no longer remember. Jesus spoke also of Moses, of the broken tables of the Law, of the golden calf, and of the thunder and lightning on Sinai.

When he had made an end of speaking and the instruction was quite finished, many of the people including the governor having returned to the city, a tall, prepossessing old Jew with a long beard stepped boldly up to the teacher's chair and thus addressed Jesus: "Allow me now to speak with thee. Thou hast enumerated twenty-three truths when, in reality, there are twenty-four," and he proceeded to name them one after another and to argue with Jesus on the point. But Jesus replied: "Desiring thy conversion, I have suffered thee here. I might have sent thee away before the whole crowd, since thou didst come hither uninvited. Thou sayest that there are twenty-four truths, and that I have taught only twenty-three. But thou hast already added three to my number, for I taught twenty only." And then Jesus counted up twenty truths according to the letters of the Hebrew alphabet, although it was by the same manner of reckoning that his opponent had proved that there were twenty-four. He then spoke upon the sin and punishment of those that add something to the truth. But the old Jew would by no means acknowledge his error, and he was supported by some present who were glad to hear Jesus contradicted. But Jesus said to him: "Thou hast a beautiful garden. Bring me some of the best and soundest of its fruits. They will rot away as a sign that thou art in the wrong! Thou hast an erect, robust body.

Thou shalt grow crooked if thou art wrong, that thou mayest see how the noblest gifts are ruined and deformed as soon as additions are made to the truth! But if thou canst show forth some such prodigy, we shall admit that there are twenty-four truths."

Thereupon the old Jew hurried with his associates to the garden, but a short way off. In it was to be found all that was rare and costly in the shape of fruits, plants, and flowers. All kinds of choice animals and birds were there in cages, and in the center was a large basin in which were kept rare fish for the delight of the beholder. The old man, with the help of his friends, quickly gathered the most magnificent fruits, yellow apples, and bunches of ripe grapes, which they put into two little baskets; the small fruits they put into a cut-glass dish that looked as if made of threads of colored glass intersecting one another. Besides that, he took with him in latticed baskets various birds and rare animals of the size of a hare, or a little kitten.

All this time Jesus continued to speak of the evil of obstinacy and of the ruinous consequences attendant upon arbitrary additions to the truth.

When now the old Jew and his companions placed around Jesus's chair the rare flowers and animals in the baskets and cages, intense excitement prevailed in the crowd. But when he proudly and obstinately maintained his first assertion, the words of Jesus were fulfilled in all that he had brought. The fruit began to stir and from all sides broke forth horrible maggots and worms that soon devoured it, so that of a magnificent apple, nothing more could be seen than a tiny piece of peel on the head of a squirming maggot. The beautiful birds and other rare animals began to grow faint and exude matter from which were formed worms that turned and gnawed their flesh, now become red and raw. The sight was so disgusting that the crowd, which had pressed forward through curiosity, began to turn away with expressions of horror, and this all the more as the old Jew, turning pale and perfectly yellow, became shrunken on one side.

At this miracle the people set up a frightful noise and clamor, and the old Jew bewailing himself acknowledged his error and implored Jesus for mercy. There was so great a tumult that the governor of the city, who had returned home, had to be called to quell the disturbance. As for the old Jew, he loudly proclaimed his fault and confessed that he had indeed tampered with the truth.

In consideration of the man's vehement sorrow and his entreaties to all present to pray for him that he might be cured, Jesus blessed the fruits and animals that had been brought to him. All were immediately restored to their first state, including the man himself, who cast himself in tears at Jesus's feet, giving thanks.

He was so truly converted that he became one of the most faithful of Jesus's followers and the instrument of many other conversions. In a spirit of penance, he shared with the poor a great part of the magnificent fruits of his garden. This miracle made a deep impression upon all that had now returned from the city, whither they had gone to take something to eat. And indeed such a miracle was necessary here; for these people, as is often the case among nations of mixed origin, were obstinate in maintaining opinions that had been proved to them to be erroneous. They sprang from Samaritans who had entered into mixed marriages with pagans, and who had in consequence been banished from Samaria. They were fasting today not on account of the destruction of the temple of Jerusalem, but on account of their own expulsion from Samaria. They indeed acknowledged and lamented their having fallen into error, but at the same time they cared not to abandon it.

They had given Jesus an extraordinarily gracious reception, because many signs contained in an old tradition received by them from the pagans had been fulfilled, and in accordance with the same, they were now expecting some great favor from God to befall them.

This promise had been made at the place afterward named the "Place of Grace." I know only this, that these pagans had once in great affliction prayed on that spot with hands raised to heaven, and that it had been foretold to them that when new streams should flow into the lake and another into the bathing spring, when the city should have extended as far as the spring, then should the favor be received. And now all these signs had been fulfilled. There flowed at this time, I think, five new streams either all into the lake, or some into it and some into the Jordan nearby. Another sign was fulfilled in the taking place of some change in an arm of the Jordan, and a new stream of good water had begun to flow into the well at the "Place of Grace."

It was at this place that Jesus was about to baptize and it was, very probably, to this that all the prophecies concerning the water referred. The water here, too, was bad. The city had also extended entirely on this side. The northern side lay low and black, full of exhalations arising from its marshes; only some poor pagan outcasts dwelt there in little huts. But toward the southeast of the city were many new houses, gardens, and buildings all the way to the "Place of Grace." The place was low and the country around level. By a change in the river banks and the sudden elevation of a mountain, an arm of the Jordan had bent its course westwardly as far as the garden, where it united with a little stream, and then flowed back into its bed. This bend covered a considerable area. The waters of the Jordan flowing hither constituted one of the aforementioned signs.

Friday, July 7, AD 30 (Tammuz 17)

Today was a day of fasting to commemorate the breaking of the Tablets of the Law and also the breaking down of the walls of Jerusalem by the Babylonians (2 Kings 25:4). Jesus taught in the synagogue at Adama. That evening, with the start of the sabbath, he again taught in the synagogue.

As Jesus on the following day was again teaching in the synagogue, in the center of which stood a magnificent chest containing the rolls of the Law, the Jews entered barefoot. Ablutions were prohibited on that day, therefore after the instruction of the preceding eve, they had washed and bathed. Above the clothes of the day before they wore in the synagogue a long, black mantle with a hood and train. It was open at the sides and fastened with cords. On the right arm hung two rough, black maniples, and on the left arm one. They prayed and chanted in a mournful tone, enveloped themselves for awhile in sacks, open in front, and prostrated face downward in the galleries around the synagogue. The women practiced similar penances in their homes.

The fires had been covered the day before. Not till evening did I see any meal taken, and then it was at an uncovered table in the inn where Jesus ate with his disciples alone. The others took theirs in the large hall of the court. The meal consisted entirely of cold foods brought from the governor's house. Jesus spoke words of instruction on the subject of eating. Many people, among them the lame and crippled, came in turn to the table upon which were some shallow dishes filled with ashes. The old Jew who had been converted gave many of the best of his magnificent fruits to the poor.

Saturday, July 8, AD 30 (Tammuz 18)

Jesus taught in the synagogue. After the close of the sabbath, he went with his disciples and about ten other people to a house in the mountains north of Adama, where they shared a meal. He told them that he would soon leave Adama. He recounted, among other things, the parable of the unjust steward (Luke 16:1).

On the next day also, the sabbath, Jesus again taught in the synagogue and after the instruction walked with his disciples and about ten Jews to the mountain north of the city. The country in that direction was wild and savage. The little party tarried awhile under the trees in front of a house and partook of some food and drink offered them by its inmates.

Jesus gave his companions all kinds of rules for their direction for, as he said, he would soon leave them to return but once again. Among other things, he exhorted them not to make so many motions when at prayer, a custom here carried to excess; and above all, not to be so severe toward sinners and pagans, to be more lenient to them. Thereupon he related the parable of the unjust steward, proposing it to them in the form of an enigma. They wondered at it, and he asked them why the conduct of the steward should be praised. It appeared to me that Jesus symbolized the synagogue by the unjust steward and the other debtors by the pagans and the various sects. The synagogue should reduce the debt of the sects and pagans while she is furnished with power and grace; that is, while she undeservedly and unjustly possesses opulence in order that, when she is herself about to be ejected, she may flee to the mediation of the kindly treated debtors.

The Parable of the Unjust Steward

EVEN as a child, I saw this and the other parables passing like living scenes before my eyes, and I used to think that, here and there, I recognized occasional figures from them in the life around me. And so it happened also with this steward whom I have always seen as a hunchback with a reddish beard, a receiver of revenues. I used to see him running very briskly and rapidly among the undertenants, making them sign their contracts with a pen. I saw the unjust steward living in a tent castle, in the desert of Arabia, not far from the place where the children of Israel murmured. His lord, who dwelt far away across Mount Lebanon, owned here on the frontiers of Palestine a corn and olive plantation. On either side of the field lived two peasants to whom it was rented. The steward was a diminutive, humpbacked fellow, very cunning and full of expedients. He thought: "The lord will not come yet awhile," and so he feasted freely and let things go as they would. The two peasants were pretty much of the same stamp, and spent their time in carousing. All of a sudden I saw the lord coming. Far over a high mountain range, I saw a magnificent city and palace from which a most beautiful road led straight to the plantation. Then I saw the king and his whole court coming down with a great caravan of camels and little, low chariots drawn by asses. I saw all this very much as I see paths coming down from the Heavenly Jerusalem. The king was a heavenly king who owned a wheat and olive field on this earth. But he came in the manner of the patriarchal kings, attended by a great retinue. I saw him coming down from on high, for that little fellow, the steward, had been accused to him of dissipating his revenues.

The lord's debtors were two persons in long coats buttoned all the way down. The steward wore a little cap. The castle of the latter was nearer the desert than the wheat and olive plantation, on either side of which the peasants lived. That was more toward the land of Canaan, and formed a triangle with the castle. And now came the lord down over the cornfield. The two debtors had squandered the fruits of the field with the steward, although toward their dependents they were hard and exacting. They were two bad parish priests, and the steward a bishop far from good; or again, it was like a worldling putting his affairs in order. The steward, having espied the coming of his lord while yet he was a long way off, fell into the greatest anxiety. He prepared a grand feast, and became very active and servile. When the lord arrived, he thus addressed the steward: "Why, what is this that I hear of thee, that thou dost squander my property! Render an account, for thou shalt no longer be my steward!" Then I saw the steward hurriedly summoning the two peasants. They presented themselves carrying rolls, which they opened. He questioned them as to the amount of their indebtedness, for of that he was utterly ignorant, and they showed it to him. With the crooked reed that he held in his hand, he made them quickly change the sum to a lesser amount, for he thought: "When I shall be discharged, I shall find shelter with them and have whereon to live, for I cannot work."

I saw now the peasants sending their servants to the lord with camels and asses laden with sacks of corn and baskets of olives. They that had charge of the olives carried money also, little metal bars done up in packages, larger or smaller according to their sum, and fastened together with rings. But the lord, glancing at the packages, saw by what he had before received that these were far too small, and from the false account rendered he understood the design of the steward. Turning to his courtiers, he said with a laugh: "See, the man is shrewd and cunning. He intends to make friends of those under him. The children of the world are wiser in their doings than the children of light, who rarely do for good what the former do for evil, who rarely take as much trouble for a reward as this man has done for punishment." Then I saw that the hunchbacked knave was discharged from his office and banished into the desert. The soil there was metallic (yellow, hard, unfruitful ferruginous sand, ocher), its only vegetation the alder tree. He was at first quite confounded and troubled, but I saw that he afterward set to work to chop wood and to build. The two peasants also were sent away, though to them somewhat better places amidst the sand of the desert were allotted. But the poor underservants, formerly the victims of cruel extortion, were now entrusted with the care of the field.

Jesus and the Disciples Invited to Teach and Baptize in Seleucia

Sunday, July 9, AD 30 (Tammuz 19)

Jesus and the disciples went from house to house in Adama, inviting the people to be baptized and to attend the discourse in two days' time.

JESUS and the disciples separated and went in different directions throughout the whole city of Adama. Jesus took the central portions for himself, while the disciples went to the most distant quarters even as far as the homes of the pagans. They stopped at almost every house inviting the people, who were already prepared, to go on the following day to the baptism, and on the day after to the great instruction that Jesus was to deliver in a larger grassy enclosure on the other side of the lake near Seleucia. The invitations were accompanied by words of instruction. The disciples were thus occupied until dusk, when they left the city and proceeded along the western side of the lake to where some fishing vessels were lying. They went on board, and instructed the fishermen who were fishing by torchlight on the broad side of the lake below the spot where the Jordan flowed into it. The glare of the torches allured the fish, which were then taken with hooks and darts. The disciples told the fishermen to bring their fish over to the green square near Seleucia, where the instruction was to be held, and they should be well rewarded. The green square, of which they made mention, was a kind of zoological garden surrounded by a wall and a hedge. Wild animals taken alive were confined there, consequently it was provided with all kinds of dens and cages for that purpose. The place belonged to Adama and was about one hour and a half from Seleucia.

Monday, July 10, AD 30 (Tammuz 20)

Jesus gave instruction to the people who came to be baptized. Following the instruction, four of the disciples baptized them at a reservoir that served as a baptismal well.

When morning dawned, Jesus joined the disciples, and they went back to the city together by a roundabout way on which were several huts. Invitations and instructions were given at these huts as at the other houses. Arrived at the city, Jesus and the disciples went to the residence of the governor, which stood in an open square, and there took some refreshment. The repast consisted of little rolls joined in pairs, and small fish with upright heads. These last were served in a many-colored, shining glass dish formed like a ship. Jesus laid one of the fishes on a roll before each of the disciples. All around the edge of the table were cavities hollowed out like plates, and into them the portions were put.

Jesus and the Disciples Invited to Teach and Baptize in Seleucia

After the repast, Jesus gave an instruction in the hall opening on the court in presence of the governor and his household, all of whom were to be baptized. After that he went to the place of instruction outside the city where he found many already waiting for him, and there too he taught in preparation for baptism. The people in bands came and went by turns, proceeding from this place to the synagogue where they prayed, sprinkled their head with ashes, and did penance. They repaired afterward to the bathing garden near the "Place of Grace," where two by two they performed their ablutions in a bathhouse separated from each other by a curtain.

When the last band had left the place of instruction, Jesus and his disciples followed. The baptismal well was that into which the water from the arm of the Jordan flowed. The basin here, as in other places, was surrounded by a canal so broad as to afford a passage for two, and from it five conduits connected with the basin. These conduits could be opened or closed at pleasure, and at the side of each ran a path over the little canal. In the center of the basin rose a stake which, by a crosspiece that reached to the bank, could be made to open and close the basin.

This reservoir with its five canals had not been especially constructed for the baptism. The number five was a frequent recurrence in Palestine, and the five aqueducts leading to the pool of Bethesda, to John's fountain in the desert, to the baptismal well of Jesus, bore reference no doubt to the five sacred wounds, or to some other mystery of religion.

Jesus here gave instructions as an immediate preparation for baptism. The neophytes were clothed in long mantles which they laid aside at the moment of stepping into the canal, retaining only the covering for the loins and the little scapular on the breast. [C1] Water from the basin had been let into the canal. On the pathways over it stood the baptizers and the sponsors. The water was thrice poured from a shallow dish over the head in the name of Jehovah and him whom he had sent. Four disciples baptized at the same time, two others imposing hands as sponsors. This ceremony, with the instructions of Jesus in preparation for it, lasted until evening. Many of the aspirants to baptism were not admitted to its reception.

Tuesday, July 11, AD 30 (Tammuz 21)

At daybreak, the disciples crossed the lake to Seleucia, a fortified town inhabited by Roman soldiers and a few oppressed Jews. The disciples invited the people to attend a discourse of Jesus. The people assembled at a teaching place on a hill at some distance from the town. When Jesus arrived, he spoke concerning nourishment of the body and the soul. Afterward, he went to Seleucia, where he was served a meal as a guest of the most distinguished people of the town. Here he taught: "Not what goes into the mouth defiles a person, but what comes out" (Matthew 15:11). The inhabitants of Seleucia were deeply impressed by his teaching and asked him to stay. He did not stay there himself but allowed Andrew and Nathaniel Chased to do so.

At daybreak next morning, the disciples embarked for Seleucia and the appointed place nearby. The lake at some distance from Adama took the figure of a violin, narrowing off to about fifteen minutes in breadth. Seleucia, a city of only moderate importance, was however a well-fortified place, being surrounded by two walls and an intervening rampart. On the northern side, especially, it was so steep as to be wholly inaccessible; in that quarter the pagan soldiers dwelt. The women lived to themselves in a separate part of the city in long rows of buildings, each occupying a private apartment. The few Jews here residing were very greatly oppressed. They lived in miserable holes in the walls, and had to perform the lowest and most painful labors on the canals and marshes.

I saw no synagogue here but only a round temple, which stood on a circle of pillars upon which were enormous figures in the attitude of supporting the building. In the center was an immense column, in which were the steps that led up into the edifice. Underneath were subterranean vaults, wherein the urns containing the ashes of the dead were deposited. Nearby was a somber-looking place in which they were accustomed to consume the bodies of their dead. In the temple were idols of serpents with human faces, human figures surmounted by dogs' heads, and one holding the moon and a fish.

The soil around these parts was not very productive, though the inhabitants were remarkably industrious. They made all kinds of cordage for the harness of horses as well as various kinds of armor, everything necessary for military equipment.

The disciples went around in Seleucia inviting the people to the instruction and to partake of the repast prepared at the appointed place. Meanwhile, Jesus went for the same purpose through the pagan quarters at Adama. Then the disciples repaired to the grassy enclosure of the zoological garden, which was beautifully sodded and filled with flowers and bushes, and there, with the fishermen who kept their fish in a cistern, prepared the meal. The tables were broad beams about two feet wide, that had been drawn up out of the lake. Back of the garden were furnaces in which the fish were roasted. It appeared as if meals were often prepared here, for in the caves around were kept a number of flat stone plates, which looked as if formed by nature, and upon which the dishes of food were served up. There were at this repast bread, fish, herbs, and fruit.

When all had been prepared and about a hundred of the pagan men were assembled, Jesus came over the lake. He was followed by about twelve Jews, the governor, and several pagans from Adama. He taught on a hill. The governor and the other Jews took part in the management of the repast and served at table with the disciples. Jesus taught of man's twofold composition, body and soul, and of the nourishment of both the one and the other. The people were free either to listen to his instruction or to partake of the meal. Jesus granted that permission to try them. Some went straight to the table and others soon followed, so that about a third only remained to hear. Jesus taught of the vocation of the pagans and told about the three kings, whose history was not unknown to these people.

When the meal and instruction were over, Jesus went toward evening with the disciples and Jews to Seleucia, an hour and a half to the south and at some distance from the lake. The people had already returned thither. Here Jesus and his party were received by the most distinguished men of the city, and a luncheon was served for their refreshment. After that they were conducted into the city and Jesus saluted and instructed the pagan women, who had assembled in a square not far from the gate in order to see him. They were clothed as Jewesses, though not so modestly veiled. Like most of the people of this region, they were not tall, but stout and robust.

Jesus entered a large public hall wherein a banquet had been prepared in his honor. There was a great deal of feasting going on in these parts. Jesus, the disciples, and the Jews sat by themselves at one of the tables. At first, the Jews were unwilling to partake of the entertainment. But Jesus told them that what entered the mouth did not sully the man, and added that they who would not eat with him, would not follow his doctrine. He taught unweariedly during the whole of the entertainment.

The pagans used tables higher than those of the Jews and also small single ones. They sat cross-legged on cushions, like the people in the land of the three kings. The food servings consisted of fish, herbs, honey, fruit, also flesh meat roasted brown.

Jesus so impressed them by his teaching that they were very much grieved when he had to leave. They begged him so earnestly to remain with them that he allowed Andrew and Nathaniel to do so. The pagans were very curious when there was question of novelty. It was already dusk when he left them.

The houses in which the women dwelt faced on a broad street, though their rear was built in the wall or the rampart of the fortification. Some of them were very beautiful, separated at intervals by gardens and squares in which the women carried on their domestic affairs and did their washing. Jesus addressed them in their usual meeting place.

In Seleucia, also, Jesus spoke of the baptism as of a purification; and when they wished to detain him longer, he told them that they were at present incapable of understanding more.

Wednesday, July 12, AD 30 (Tammuz 22)

From Seleucia Jesus returned to Adama. In the synagogue a feast of thanksgiving was celebrated by the newly baptized, who occupied the places of honor and chanted canticles of praise. Numbers of others were baptized when Andrew and Nathaniel Chased returned from Seleucia. The converted Jew exhibited naught but humility and a desire to render assistance to Jesus, delighted to act as servant and messenger on all occasions.

Thursday, July 13, AD 30 (Tammuz 23)

Peter, Andrew, and some other disciples went off to visit other places in the region to invite people to attend a sermon that Jesus would give on a mountain near Berotha on the day following the sabbath. Jesus stayed in Adama and, accompanied by Saturnin and the remaining disciples, visited the sick to heal and comfort them.

A great number of sick had been unable to attend Jesus's instructions and the baptism; consequently, with Saturnin and the disciple who was related to him, he went to hunt them up in their homes. The other disciples started for the cities Azor, Kedesh, Berotha, and Thisbe, all from two to three hours north of Adama, in order to invite the inhabitants to the instruction which Jesus was going to deliver on a gently rising mountain on the road from Kedesh to Berotha. On the top of that mountain, which was covered with vegetation, and in an open space surrounded by a wall, stood a chair used from remote times for teaching. In some places the disciples went to the chief magistrates and called upon them to invite the people to the instruction that the prophet from Galilee would deliver on the mountain the day after the sabbath, while in others they themselves went to the houses and invited the occupants to the instruction.

Meanwhile, Jesus was going around in Adama among the rich and the poor, Jews and pagans, healing the dropsical, the lame, the blind, and those afflicted with an issue of blood. I was especially surprised at the sight of ten possessed men and women, all of them pure Jews. I never saw so many possessed among the pagans. Some of these ten were of distinguished families. They were confined in grated chambers in their own houses, either in the house or the forecourt. As Jesus was coming toward them, they began crying and raging in a frightful manner, but on a nearer approach, they became quiet and stared at him perplexedly. I saw him, by his glance alone, driving all the devils from them. They left them under a visible form, a vapor which afterward assumed the shadow of an abominable human figure, and then disappeared. The bystanders were amazed at the sight; the former possessed turned pale and sank down unconscious. Jesus addressed some words to them, took them by the hand, and commanded them to rise. Then, as if coming out of a dream, they sank on their knees giving thanks, and rose up changed men. Jesus then exhorted them and mentioned the faults they should correct.

When the disciples returned to Adama, they took a meal with Jesus at the chief magistrate's. They had purchased fish and bread at the places they had visited, and ordered them to be delivered at the mount of instruction. The food was intended for the audience. Jesus received presents from many people and various places. I saw little bars of gold that looked like twigs. These gifts were devoted to the purchase of food for the multitude. Jesus had not broken his fast since the last meal taken at Seleucia.

Friday, July 14, AD 30 (Tammuz 24)

This evening, Jesus celebrated the sabbath at the large synagogue in Adama.

On the sabbath he taught in the synagogue of Adama. There was here also a party formed against Jesus. They sent two Pharisees to where John was teaching in order to hear what he had to say about Jesus, and thence to Bethabara and Capernaum to inform some of their friends that he was now going around among them baptizing and making disciples. When these messengers returned, they spoke against Jesus and spread the calumnies they had heard, but their efforts gained no adherents to their own party.

Saturday, July 15, AD 30 (Tammuz 25)

After the close of the sabbath, Jesus, at a meal, was asked by some of the town elders what he thought of the Essenes. Jesus answered that there was nothing to reproach in their way of life.

Once the magistrates of Adama interrogated Jesus as to what he thought of the Essenes. They wanted to tempt him, because they pretended to have remarked in his sentiments some similarity to those of that sect, and also because James the Less, his relative and who was then with him, was an Essene. They brought all kinds of accusations against them, condemning chiefly their retired life and their celibacy. Jesus answered in very general terms: One could, he said, find nothing to reproach in those people; if they were called to such a life, they deserved great praise. Everyone has his own vocation; were a cripple to aim at walking upright, he would hardly succeed. When the magistrate objected that so few families were raised up by them, Jesus enumerated a great many Essene families and spoke of their well-bred children. He alluded to the married state, first of the good, then of the bad. He neither took part with the Essenes, nor did he accuse them. The people did not comprehend him, though they saw that he had family connections among the Essenes and kept up contact with them.

Jesus Preaching on the Mountain near Berotha

Sunday, July 16, AD 30 (Tammuz 26)

Before daybreak, Jesus and his disciples left Adama and went to a nearby mountain, where it had been made known beforehand that he would teach on the day after the sabbath. A multitude had already gathered there and, as Jesus arrived, he was greeted with cries such as: "Thou art the true prophet, the helper!" Shortly after nine, Jesus began to teach. He spoke of, among other things, the parable of the sowing of the seed (Matthew 13:24–30; see page 364). He taught until evening. After a communal meal, he blessed the people and left. Peter, Andrew, James the Less, and Nathaniel Chased then returned to Capernaum and Bethsaida. After parting company with them, Jesus, Saturnin, and the other remaining disciple made their way to Zedad, where they stayed that night at an inn.

BEFORE daybreak of the night between the sabbath and Sunday, Jesus left Adama. He had taken leave of the people after the exercises of the sabbath, though without saying that he was not to return, and he now went with his disciples and several of the Jews to the mountain appointed for the instruction. He left Adama by the gate through which he had entered, and that was over a bridge. Had they gone by another, they would have had to ferry over the river that ran from Azor to Kedesh, and which near Adama flowed into the Jordan. They left Kedesh to the right, and proceeded westward over gently rising mountain terraces. This region had high mountain ridges that formed great plateaus. There were fewer ravines and isolated peaks than in southern Palestine. Thisbe was to the left of the little troop on very high ground. Tobias once lived in Thisbe and had there given in marriage his wife's brother, or brother-in-law. He had also been in Amichores, the water city. He might have taken up his abode there permanently,

Jesus Preaching on the Mountain near Berotha

Parable of the Pharisee and the Publican

[LUKE 18:9–14] 9 He also told this parable to some who trusted in themselves that they were righteous and despised others: 10 "Two men went up into the temple to pray, one a Pharisee and the other a tax collector. 11 The Pharisee stood and prayed thus with himself, 'God, I thank thee that I am not like other men, extortioners, unjust, adulterers, or even like this tax collector. 12 I fast twice a week, I give tithes of all that I get.' 13 But the tax collector, standing far off, would not even lift up his eyes to heaven, but beat his breast, saying, 'God, be merciful to me a sinner!' 14 I tell you, this man went down to his house justified rather than the other; for every one who exalts himself will be humbled, but he who humbles himself will be exalted."

were it not that he preferred to go into captivity, in order to be useful to his people. Elijah, too, had been in Thisbe, and Jesus had once before journeyed through it.

The multitude was already gathered upon the mountain. On the preceding evening, people had gone thither after the sabbath and put the place in order. On the summit was an enclosed space in which stood a teacher's chair. The people living on the sides of the mountain had been busied preparing for the tents, and already the stakes and cords were at hand. They had carried them up and stretched the awnings over the teacher's chair and other available spots around. The place was one of historic interest, for Joshua had here celebrated a feast of thanksgiving after his successful siege of the Canaanites. Water had been transported hither in leathern bottles, and bread and fish in baskets. These baskets were like our beehives; they could be placed one above another, and in the several compartments various things could be put without danger of mixing.

As Jesus was going up through the crowd to the summit of the mountain, shouts greeted him on every side: "Thou art the true prophet! The helper!" etc., and as he passed along, they bowed low before him. It may have been nine o'clock when he reached the summit, for it was six to seven hours from Adama to this place.

Many possessed had been led up the mountain. They were raging and shouting. When Jesus saw them, he commanded them silence, and by his command and the glance of his eye, they became calm and were freed from the evil one.

When Jesus had reached the tribune and the crowd had been brought to order and silence by the disciples, he first invoked his heavenly Father, from whom come all good gifts, the people likewise praying. Then he began his instruction. He made allusion to what had there occurred, spoke of the children of Israel, of Joshua's once appearing in these parts and freeing them from the Canaanites and from paganism, and of the destruction of Azor. Of all these events Jesus explained the spiritual meaning. Thus came truth and light to them anew, with grace and mildness to free them from the power of sin. He exhorted them not to resist as did the Canaanites, that God's punishment might not come upon them as it had done upon Azor. He also related a parable of which he again made use on a later occasion. It is in the book of the Gospels, I think, something about wheat and husbandry. He taught also of penance and the coming of the kingdom, speaking significantly of himself and the heavenly Father as he had done in the neighboring towns.

The sons of Johanna Chusa and Veronica came here to Jesus. They had been sent by Lazarus, to warn him against the two spies whom the Pharisees had dispatched from Jerusalem to Adama. The disciples brought them to Jesus during a pause in the instruction. He told them not to be at all disquieted on his account, that he would fulfill his mission, and he thanked them for their devotedness, etc. The spies sent by the Pharisees were also on the mountain with the disaffected Jews from Adama. Jesus did not address them, but he said aloud in the course of his instruction that enemies would lie in wait for him and persecute him, still they would not succeed in hindering him from accomplishing what the Father in heaven had entrusted to him. He would soon appear among them again to announce the kingdom of God and the truth.

Many mothers were present with their children, demanding Jesus's blessing. But the disciples were disquieted and thought, on account of the presence of the spies, that he should not give it. Jesus, however, reproved them for their anxiety, saying that he regarded the intention of the mothers as good, and that the children would thereby derive benefit, and so he went down through the rows that they formed and gave them his benediction.

The instruction lasted from ten in the morning till near evening, when the people were ranged in order to take some food. On one side of the mountain there were grated fires whereon the fish were roasted. The order observed was beautiful. Not only the inhabitants of each separate city encamped together, but even the residents of the same streets were divided into families with their neighbors. To the guests of each street, one man was appointed to bring and divide the food. Each person or one person in each group, had a leather cover which, being spread out, served for plates. They had with them also such things as are used at table: bone knives and spoons with jointed handles. Some had brought gourds, others cups of bark, in which they received water from the leathern bottles, while others, there and then, quickly formed for themselves such cups if they had not done so on the way. The superintendents received the food from the disciples, and divided each portion among the four or five sitting together, laying the fish and bread on the leathern cover before them. Jesus had blessed the food before it was divided, and by virtue of that blessing it was multiplied, otherwise it would have been far from sufficient for the two thousand for whom it was intended. Each group received a small portion only, but all were satisfied after eating, and much remained over to be collected into baskets and carried off by the poor.

There were some Roman soldiers going around among the crowd. They either knew Lentulus in Rome, or had instructions from him, for he had soldiers under his command. Perhaps they had been charged to bring him information of Jesus, for they went to the disciples and begged

Jesus Preaching on the Mountain near Berotha

The Sower

[MATTHEW 13:3–12] 3 And he told them many things in parables, saying: "A sower went out to sow. 4 And as he sowed, some seeds fell along the path, and the birds came and devoured them. 5 Other seeds fell on rocky ground, where they had not much soil, and immediately they sprang up, since they had no depth of soil, 6 but when the sun rose they were scorched; and since they had no root they withered away. 7 Other seeds fell upon thorns, and the thorns grew up and choked them. 8 Other seeds fell on good soil and brought forth grain, some a hundredfold, some sixty, some thirty. 9 He who has ears, let him hear."

some of the blessed bread, to take with them to Lentulus. On receiving it, they stowed it away in the knapsacks that hung from their shoulders.

It was already dark and torches lighted when the meal was over. Jesus blessed the multitude and left the mountain with the disciples, from whom, however, he soon separated. They took a shorter route back to Bethsaida and Capernaum, while he with Saturnin and that disciple, his relative, went southward to a city lying off from Berotha, called Zedad, and spent the night at an inn outside the city.

Jesus Passes Through Gath-Hepher to Capernaum

Monday, July 17, AD 30 (Tammuz 27)

For the entire day and through the following night Jesus and the two disciples continued on their way. That night, John the Baptist was arrested again by Herod's soldiers at the place of baptism near Ainon. He was locked up, first in the tower of Herod's castle at Hesebon, and then was brought to Machaerus.

ON the night between Monday and Tuesday, I saw Jesus in the mountains with Saturnin and that other disciple. As he walked alone in prayer and they questioned him about it, he spoke to them of prayer in private, illustrating by the example of the serpent and scorpion: "Were a child to ask for a fish, the father would not give him a scorpion," etc.

Tuesday, July 18, AD 30 (Tammuz 28)

After visiting some small shepherd places, Jesus, Saturnin, and the other disciple arrived at Gath-Hepher. Here Jesus continued his healing work. Then he traveled to Capernaum, arriving at his mother's house that evening. There Mary and about seven holy women, together with Lazarus, Obed, Aram, Themeni, Nathaniel the bridegroom, and several other disciples awaited him. They discussed John's imprisonment. Jesus spoke of it as a sign for the beginning of his public work, the next step of which would be his going to Bethany.

During these days, I saw him again in various little places among the shepherds healing and exhorting, also in Gath-Hepher, Jonas's birthplace, and where some of his own relatives lived. He wrought cures in this latter place also, and then toward evening went as far as Capernaum.

How indefatigable was Jesus! With what ardor he inspired the disciples and apostles! At first they were often overcome by fatigue; but now what a difference! The disciples while traveling along the highways went forward to meet some and to hunt up the others, to instruct them themselves or invite them to attend Jesus's instructions.

Lazarus, Obed, Joseph of Arimathea's nephews, the bridegroom of Cana, and some other disciples, had arrived at Mary's house near Capernaum. There were present also about seven women, relatives and friends, awaiting the return of Jesus. They went in and out the house and gazed along the road, to catch the first sight of him. And now came some of John's disciples with the news of their master's imprisonment, which filled the hearts of the little company with anxiety. The disciples then went on to meet Jesus, with whom they came up not far from Capernaum, and made known to him their errand. He consoled them, and continued his way to his mother's alone. He had sent his disciples on in advance. Lazarus came out to meet him, and washed his feet in the vestibule.

When Jesus entered the apartment, the men bowed low before him. He greeted them, and went up to his mother, to whom he stretched out his hands. She, too, most lovingly and humbly inclined to him. There was no rushing into each other's arms; their meeting was full of tender and ingenuous reserve, which touched all present and made upon them the holiest impression. Then Jesus turned toward the other women, who lowered their veils and sank on their knees before him. He was accustomed to give his blessing at such meetings and leavetakings.

I saw now a repast made ready, and the men reclining around the table, the women at one end sitting cross-legged. They spoke indignantly of John's imprisonment, but Jesus rebuked them. He said that they should not be angry and pass sentence upon it, for that it had to be. Were John not removed from the scene, he himself would not be able to begin his work and go to Bethany. Then he told them of the people among whom he had been. Of Jesus's coming, none knew excepting those present and the confidential disciples. Jesus slept with the other guests in a side building. He appointed the disciples to meet him after the next sabbath at a house, high and solitary, in the neighborhood of Beth-Horon.

Wednesday, July 19, AD 30 (Tammuz 29)

This morning, Jesus comforted Mary and told her not to be downcast about his coming journey to Judea. Around midday, he set off with Lazarus and about five other disciples. They passed by Bethulia and continued on their way southward. At dusk, the New Moon festival was celebrated at synagogues throughout the land, indicating the start of the month of Ab. Jesus and his companions walked through the night.

I saw Jesus conversing with Mary alone. She was weeping at the thought of his exposing himself to danger by going to Jerusalem. He comforted her, telling her that she must not be anxious, that he would accomplish his mission, and that the sorrowful days had not yet come. He encouraged her to persevere in prayer and exhorted the others to refrain from all comments and judgments upon John's imprisonment and the action of the Pharisees against himself, for such proceedings on their part would only increase the danger—adding that the Pharisees' manner of acting was permitted by divine Providence, though they were thereby working out their own destruction.

Some mention was made of Magdalene also. Jesus again told them to pray for her and think of her kindly, for she would soon be converted and become so good as to be an example for many.

That morning, Jesus went to Bethany with Lazarus and about five of the disciples belonging to Jerusalem. It was the beginning of the Feast of the New Moon, and I saw floating from the synagogues of Capernaum and other places long streamers of knotted drapery and festoons of fruit on the principal houses.

John the Baptist Arrested by Herod and Imprisoned at Machaerus

HEROD had once before caused the Baptist to be arrested at the place of baptism and brought to him, where he kept him in custody some weeks in the hope of intimidating him and leading him to a change of sentiment. But through fear of the immense crowds that were hurrying to hear John, he had released him. John then retired to the place where he had formerly baptized near Ainon and opposite Salem. It was one hour and a half east of the Jordan and about two hours south of Succoth. The baptismal well was in the region of a lake, about a quarter of an hour long, from which two streams, after bathing the foot of a hill, flowed into the Jordan. On this hill were the remains of an old castle, whose towers were still habitable, and scattered around were gardens and walks and other dwellings. Between the lake and the hill was John's baptismal well. In the center of the spacious, caldron-shaped summit of the hill, John's disciples had raised an awning over a terraced elevation formed of stone, and it was there that he taught. This region was under Philip's jurisdiction. But it ran like a point into Herod's country, who on that account was somewhat reserved in executing his designs against John.

An uncommonly great concourse of people had assembled to hear John: whole caravans from Arabia on camels and asses, and hundreds of people from Jerusalem and all Judea, both men and women. The crowds came and went by turns, covered the caldron-shaped plateau, encamped at the base of the hill, and stood on the heights around. The most beautiful order was established and maintained by John's disciples. Those nearest the preacher reclined on the ground, those behind them sat on their heels, while the outer rows stood; in this way all could see. The pagans were separated from the Jews, and the men from the women, who always stood back in the last row. On the slope of the hill were other groups squatting, head and arms resting on their knees, or again, clasping one knee and lying or sitting on the other hip.

Since his return from Herod, John was as if penetrated by a new spirit. His voice sounded usually sweet, and yet was so powerful and far-reaching that every word was understood. He again wore his mantle of skins, and was more roughly clothed than at Ono, where he had sometimes appeared in a flowing robe. His teaching was of Jesus and his persecution in Jerusalem. Pointing toward Upper Galilee where Jesus was at that instant going about working miraculous cures, John said: "But he will soon reappear in those parts. His persecutors will gain nothing over him until his mission shall have been fulfilled."

Herod also and his wife came with a guard of soldiers to John's place of instruction. He had traveled from his castle of Livias twelve hours, passing near Dibon where he had to cross two branches of a little river. As far as Dibon the road was good, but after that it became very rough and difficult, properly speaking fit only for foot-passengers and beasts of burden. Herod rode upon a long, narrow chariot on which one could recline or sit sideways. There were several with him. The wheels proper were heavy, low, round disks without spokes, though there were other larger ones and rollers at the back. The road was so uneven that on one side the chariot rested on the high wheels, and on the other upon low ones. The journey was a painful one. Herod's wife, along with her ladies in waiting, rode upon a similar chariot. They were drawn by asses preceded and followed by soldiers and courtiers.

Herod had undertaken this journey because John was now preaching again, and that more boldly and zealously than before. He was anxious to hear him and learn whether he said anything personally against himself. His wife was only waiting for an opportunity to excite him to extreme measures against John; she hid her crafty designs, however, under a fair appearance. Herod had still another motive in making this journey. He knew that the Arabian king Aretas, father of his repudiated first wife, had come hither to John and, to escape observation, had mingled with the disciples. He wanted to see whether Aretas had any design to stir up the people against himself. His first wife, a good and very beautiful lady, had returned to her father who, having heard of John's teaching and of his opposition to Herod's unlawful desires, had come to satisfy himself of the truth of what had been told him. But anxious to attract no attention, he was dressed simply, like John's disciples, with whom he identified himself.

Herod alighted at the old castle on the hill and sat during John's instruction upon the graded terrace in front. His wife, surrounded by her guards and attendants, sat on cushions under an awning. John was preaching in a loud voice and at that moment crying out to the people that they should not be scandalized at Herod's second union, that they should honor him without imitating him. These words pleased Herod at first, though on second thought they irritated him. The force with which John spoke was indescribable. His voice was like thunder, and yet sweet and intelligible. He seemed to be exerting himself for the last time. He had already warned his disciples that his days were drawing to a close, but that they should not abandon him, they should visit him when in prison. For three days he had neither eaten nor drunk. The whole time had been spent in teaching, proclaiming aloud his testimony to Jesus, and in rebuking Herod for his adultery. The disciples implored him to discontinue and take a little nourishment, but he listened not; he was wholly under the spirit of inspiration.

The view from the height upon which John taught was uncommonly beautiful. One could see off in the distance the Jordan, the cities lying around, fields, and orchards. There must have been here in days gone by a great building, for I could still see stone arches like those of bridges, overgrown with thick green moss. Two of the towers of the castle at which Herod stopped had been lately restored, and it was in them that he lodged. This region was rich in springs and the baths were kept in perfect order. The water that supplied them was brought through a skillfully constructed, vaulted canal from the hill upon whose summit John taught. The baptismal pool was oval in form and encircled by three beautiful green terraces through which five pathways were cut. This region was indeed much smaller, but richer in appearance than that of Bethsaida at Jerusalem, which is here and there rendered unsightly and impure by reeds and by the leaves that fall into it from the surrounding trees. The baptismal pool lay behind the hill, and about one hundred and fifty feet beyond was the great pond in which were numbers of fish. They seemed to be crowding to the side at which John was teaching, as if they wanted to hear. On the pond were little skiffs, trunks of trees hollowed out, large enough at most for two men only, with seats in the middle for fishing. John ate only a little poor honey. When he took food with his disciples, it was always in very small quantities. He prayed alone, and spent much of the night gazing up to heaven.

John knew that the time of his arrest was near; therefore had he spoken as if under inspiration and as if taking leave of his auditors. He had announced Jesus more clearly than ever. He was now coming, he said; consequently he himself should retire and they should go to Jesus. He, John, was soon to be apprehended. They were, he continued addressing his audience, a hard and indocile people. They should recall how he had come at first and prepared the ways for the Lord. He had built bridges, made foot paths, cleared away stones, arranged baptismal pools, and conducted thither the water. He had a difficult task, struggling against stony earth, hard rocks, and knotty wood. And these labors he had had to continue toward a people stubborn, obdurate, and unpolished. But they whom he had stirred up should now go to the Lord, to the well-beloved Son of the Father. They whom he received would be truly received; they whom he rejected should indeed be rejected. He was coming now to teach, to baptize, to perfect what he himself had prepared. Then turning toward Herod, John earnestly reproached him several times before the people for his scandalous connection.

Herod, who both reverenced and feared him, was inwardly furious, though preserving a cool exterior.

The instruction was ended and the crowd began to disperse on all sides, the people from Arabia and Aretas, Herod's father-in-law, going with them. Herod had not caught sight of him. Herod's wife had already gone, and now he himself departed, concealing his rage and taking a friendly leave of John.

John sent several disciples to different quarters with messages, dismissed the others, and retired to his tent to give himself up to prayer. It was already dark and the disciples had departed, when about twenty soldiers, after placing guards on all sides, surrounded the tent and one entered. John told him that he would follow quietly, that he knew his time had come and that he must make way for Jesus, they needed not to fetter him, for he would willingly accompany them, and that, in order to avoid a tumult, they should lead him away with as little noise as possible. And so the twenty men hurried him off at a rapid pace. He had only his rough mantle of skins thrown about him, and his staff in his hand. Some of his disciples met him as he was being led away. He took leave of them with a glance, and bade them visit him in his imprisonment. But soon the disciples and people mobbed together and cried aloud: "They have arrested John!" and then arose weeping and lamentations. They wanted to follow, but they knew not what direction to take, for the soldiers had turned quickly out of the usual way and proceeded southward by an unknown route. Intense excitement, grief, and mourning prevailed. The disciples scattered and fled in all quarters just as they did later, at the time of Jesus's arrest, and the news was soon spread throughout the whole country.

After marching with the soldiers the whole night, John was conducted first to a tower at Hesebon. Toward morning some soldiers of the place came to meet the prisoner, for it was already known there that John had been arrested, and the people were gathering together in groups. The soldiers who had charge of John seemed to be a kind of bodyguard to Herod. They wore helmets, their breasts and shoulders protected by armor formed of metal plates and rings, and they bore long lances in their hands.

The people of Hesebon gathered in crowds before John's prison, and the guards had enough to do to drive them off. The upper part of the tower had several exterior openings. John stood in his prison crying in a voice loud enough to be heard without. His words were to this effect, that he had prepared the ways, had broken rocks, had directed streams, had dug fountains, had built bridges; he had had to cope with obstacles the most adverse and contradictory, and it was owing to the obstinacy of those whom he now addressed that he had been arrested. But they should turn to him whom he had announced, to him who would soon come by the paths he himself had made straight. When the Master approached, then should they who had prepared his way withdraw, and all should turn to Jesus, the latchets of whose shoes he himself was not worthy to loose. "Jesus," he continued, "is the Light, the Truth, and the Son of the Father," etc. He called upon his disciples to visit him in his confinement, for no one would yet venture to lay hands upon him, his hour was not yet come. John uttered the above in a voice as loud and distinct as if he were addressing the multitude from an orator's stand. Again and again the guard dispersed the crowd, but the throng soon reassembled, and John's instructions recommenced.

He was afterward led by the soldiers from Hesebon to the prison of Machaerus, the access to which was up a high and steep mountain. He rode with several in a low, narrow, covered chariot like a box, drawn by asses. Arrived at Machaerus, the soldiers conducted him up the steep mountain path to the fortress. But they did not enter by the principal gate, but through a postern in the wall nearby, which overhanging moss almost concealed. Traversing a passage somewhat inclined, they reached a brazen door which opened into another that ran under the gateway of the fortress, and thence led into a large underground vault. It was lighted from above and was clean, though destitute of every kind of comfort.

From the place of baptism, Herod went to his castle of Herodium, which had been built by Herod the Elder, and where once, for mere sport, he had caused some persons to be drowned in a pond. Here, filled with dejection, Herod hid himself away and would see nobody, although many had already presented themselves to express to him their disapproval of John's arrest. A prey to inquietude, he shut himself up in his own apartments.

After some time John's disciples, provided they came in small numbers, were allowed to approach the prison, converse with him, and pass things to him through the grating. But if many came together, they were turned away by guards. John ordered the disciples to go on baptizing at Ainon, until Jesus came to establish himself there for the same purpose. The prison was large and well-lighted, but its only resting place was a stone bench. John was very serious. His countenance always wore an expression of thoughtfulness and sadness. He looked like one that loved and heralded the Lamb of God, but who knew the bitter death in store for him.

Jesus in Bethany • Inns Established for the Accommodation of Jesus and the Disciples on their Journeys • The Pearl Lost and Found

AB (30 days): July 19/20 to August 17/18, AD 30, Ab New Moon: July 19 at 9:45 AM Jerusalem time

(Follow Map 17)

Thursday, July 20, AD 30 (Ab 1)
Early this morning Jesus and his disciples arrived at an inn, east of Jezreel, belonging to Lazarus. There they breakfasted before traveling on. Later in the day, they passed by Salem and, further south, crossed the Jordan. That night, they slept at a shepherd's place not far from the river, more or less west of Dibon.

WITH Lazarus and the five disciples belonging to Jerusalem, Jesus traversed the road from Capernaum to Bethany through the region of Bethulia. But to Bethulia itself, which lay high in the distance, they did not go. Their way ran around it toward Jezreel, outside of which Lazarus owned a kind of accommodation inn with a garden.

The disciples had gone on ahead and prepared a luncheon. One of the trusty servants of Lazarus had charge of the place. It was early in the morning when they washed their feet here, shook the dust from their clothes, ate something, and took a little rest. From Jezreel they went over a little river, leaving Scythopolis and afterward Salem to the left, crossed a mountain spur, and approached the Jordan. Continuing their course southward, they crossed the river below Samaria and, because it was already night, rested some hours on an eminence of the river's bank where some faithful shepherds dwelt.

Map 17: The Conversation at Jacob's Well
July 20–29, AD 30

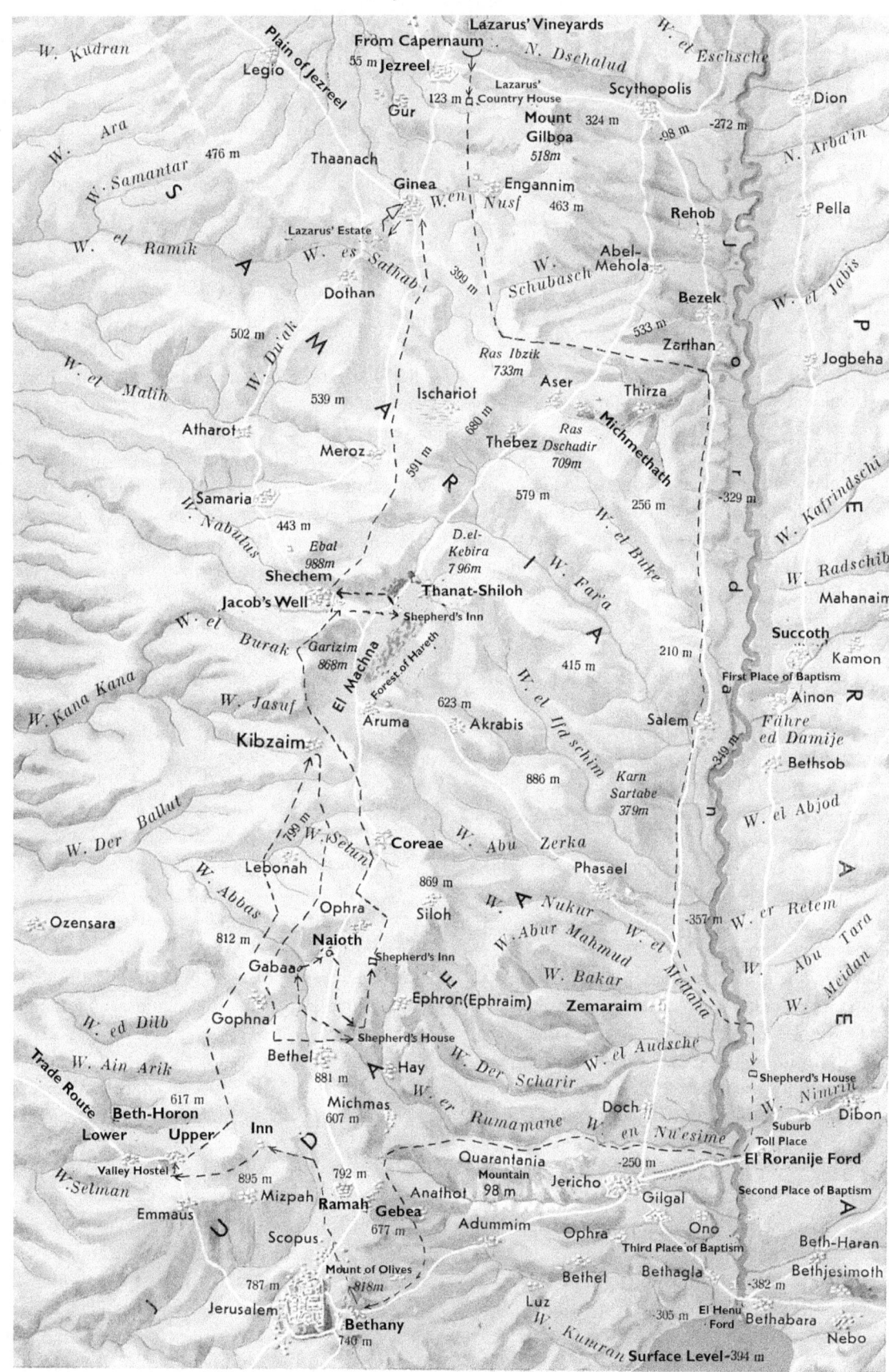

Capernaum—Lazarus's Estate near Jezreel—Bethany—Upper Beth-Horon—Kibzaim
Boundary of Judea/Samaria—Jacob's Well—Shechem—Ginea

Friday, July 21, AD 30 (Ab 2)

Jesus and Lazarus re-crossed the Jordan before the sun rose. Proceeding onward, they reached Bethany late that afternoon. The entire group of Jesus's friends and supporters were gathered at Lazarus's castle, expectantly awaiting their arrival. After eating together, they celebrated the start of the sabbath. That night, when all was still in the castle, Jesus went to the Mount of Olives, to the cave in the garden of Gethsemane, where he was to pray on the night before the Passion began. Now he prayed to his heavenly Father for strength to fulfill his mission. He returned to Lazarus's castle before daybreak.

Before daybreak next morning they started again and directed their steps between Hay and Gilgal through the desert of Jericho. Jesus and Lazarus journeyed together, while the disciples went ahead by another route. Jesus and Lazarus walked the whole day by unfrequented paths without touching at any place, not even at the inn that Lazarus owned on this side of the desert. When within a few hours of Bethany, Lazarus went on ahead and Jesus continued his journey alone.

There were assembled at Bethany with Lazarus and the five disciples from Jerusalem, about fifteen disciples and followers of Jesus and seven women: Saturnin, Nicodemus, Joseph of Arimathea, his nephews, Simeon's sons, and those of Johanna Chusa, Veronica, and Obed respectively. Among the women were Veronica, Johanna Chusa, Susanna, Mary Mark the widow of Obed, Martha, and the discreet old servant of the last named, who afterward joined the holy women who cared for the wants of the Lord and his disciples. All were gathered in a large, subterranean vault of Lazarus's castle, quietly and, it seemed, secretly awaiting the coming of Jesus.

Toward evening he arrived and entered the garden by a back gate. Lazarus went out to meet him in a reception hall, where he washed his feet. There was here a deep basin connected with the house by pipes, through which Martha poured tepid water for the use of their guest. Jesus, sitting on the rim of the basin, immersed his feet, which Lazarus washed and dried. After that he shook out Jesus's garments, put on his feet fresh sandals, and handed him a little food and drink.

Then Jesus accompanied Lazarus through a long, shady walk up to the house and down into the vaulted chamber. The women drew their veils and bowed low on their knees before him, while the men inclined profoundly. Jesus greeted all and blessed them, after which they took their place at table. The women sat on cushions at one side of the table, their feet crossed under them.

Nicodemus was remarkably impressed and very desirous of hearing every word of Jesus. The men spoke indignantly of John's imprisonment. But Jesus said that it had to be, it was the will of God, and that they should not speak of such things in order not to attract attention and thereby give rise to danger. If John had not been removed from the scene of action, he himself would not yet have been able to labor here. The blossoms must fall, if the fruit is to appear.

Then they spoke angrily of the spying and persecution set on foot by the Pharisees, whereupon Jesus again commanded them to be at peace. He deplored the action of the Pharisees and related the parable of the unjust steward. The Pharisees, too, were unjust stewards, though not so prudent as the subject of the parable, therefore would they have no resource on the day of reckoning.

After the meal, they retired to another apartment, where lamps were lighted. Jesus prayed aloud, and they began the exercises of the sabbath. After that Jesus conversed awhile with the men, and all retired to rest.

When silence reigned in the house and the inmates were sunk in slumber, Jesus arose from his couch and went out unperceived to the cave on the Mount of Olives in which, on the day before his bitter Passion, he would wrestle in prayer. He prayed several hours to his heavenly Father for strength to accomplish his work, and before daybreak returned unnoticed to Bethany.

Saturday, July 22, AD 30 (Ab 3)

Jesus and his disciples remained for the sabbath and the following evening at Lazarus's castle. Jesus spoke of his experiences in Adama. He also related the parable of the good Samaritan (Luke 10:25–27). That night, he prayed again alone on the Mount of Olives.

The sons of Obed, who were servers in the temple, now returned with some others to Jerusalem, but the rest of the guests remained quietly in the house, and none but themselves knew of Jesus's presence.

During the meal today, Jesus told them of his stay among the people of Upper Galilee, at Amead, Adama, and Seleucia. And as the men in their zeal vehemently inveighed against the sects, he reproved them for their bitterness, and related to them a parable. He told them of a man who on the way to Jericho had fallen among robbers, and who had received more pity from a Samaritan than from a Levite. I have always heard this parable related in the same way, though with different applications. He spoke also of the calamities about to befall Jerusalem.

At night when all were asleep, Jesus went again to pray in the cave on the Mount of Olives. He shed many tears and endured intense fear and anguish. He was like a son going forth to great labors, and who first threw himself on the bosom of his father to receive strength and comfort. My guide told me that whenever Jesus was in Bethany and had an hour to spare, he used to go to that cave to pray. This was a preparation for his last agony on the Mount of Olives. It was also shown to me that Jesus chiefly on the Mount of Olives prayed and sorrowed, because Adam and Eve when driven from Paradise had here first trodden the inhospitable earth. I saw them in that cave sorrowing and praying, and it was on this mountain, which Cain was cultivating for the first time, that he became so enraged as to resolve to kill Abel. I thought of Judas. I saw Cain murdering his brother in the vicinity of Mount Calvary, and on the Mount of Olives called by God to account for the same. Daybreak found Jesus back again in Bethany.

Sunday, July 23, AD 30 (Ab 4)

Today, as Jesus explained his intention to teach throughout the land, Lazarus and the women made plans how best to help Jesus in his mission. They thought of setting up inns for Jesus and the disciples at certain places and of supplying provisions and clothes. After eating a meal together, everyone gathered in the castle's subterranean hall. Here Jesus spoke of how God in his mercy had sent to his people one prophet after another, but each had been disowned and mistreated. Now, however, the people would reject the Supreme Grace: Jesus predicted what would befall them. He summarized this teaching in the parable of the vineyard owner and the evil tenants (Matthew 21:33–43). Later, he told the parable of the lost coin and also hinted at Mary Magdalene when he referred to the "joy before the angels of God over one sinner who repents" (Luke 15:8–10). Jesus then retired to pray alone again on the Mount of Olives. He returned shortly before midnight and—with Lazarus and Saturnin—set off for Beth-Horon, where he was expected to teach the following day.

The sabbath over, that took place on account of which principally Jesus had come to Bethany. The holy women had heard with sorrow what hardships Jesus and his followers had had to endure upon their journeys, and that Jesus especially, on his last hurried journey to Tyre, had suffered such want; they had heard of his having to soften the hard crusts, which Saturnin had begged on the way, in order to be able to eat them. They had therefore offered to establish inns and furnish them with all that was necessary. Jesus accepted their offer, and came hither to make with them the necessary arrangements. As he now declared that he would henceforth publicly teach everywhere, Lazarus and the women again offered to establish inns, especially since the Jews in the cities around Jerusalem, instigated by the Pharisees, would furnish nothing to him and his disciples. They also begged the Lord to signify to them the principal stopping places on his journeys and the number of his disciples, that they might know how many inns would be needed and what quantity of provisions to supply.

Jesus replied by giving them the route of his future journeys, also the stopping places, and the probable number of disciples. It was decided that about fifteen inns should be made ready and entrusted to the care of confidential persons, some of them relatives either of Lazarus or of the holy family. They were scattered throughout the whole country, with the exception of the district of Cabul toward Tyre and Sidon.

The holy women then consulted together as to what district each should see to and what share each should take in the new establishments, to supply furniture, covers, clothes, sandals, etc., to provide for washing and repairing, and to attend to the furnishing of bread and other necessaries. All this took place before and during the meal. Martha was in her element.

After the meal Jesus, Lazarus, the other friends, and the holy women assembled secretly in another of the subterranean halls. Jesus sat on a raised seat at one side of the hall, the men standing and sitting around him; the women were on the opposite side on steps covered with carpets and cushions. Jesus spoke of the mercy of God to his people. He had sent them prophets one after another whom they had disowned and ill-treated; now they would reject the Supreme Grace, and he predicted what would betide them. After he had dwelt upon this at length, some of his hearers said to him: "Lord, relate this to us in a beautiful parable," and Jesus told them the parable of a king who after all his servants had been killed by the unfaithful vinedressers, sent his son into the vineyard where he too was murdered.

Some of the men withdrew at the close of this instruction and Jesus went with others into the hall and walked up and down. Martha, who was passing to and fro, approached him and had a long talk about her sister Magdalene. She related what she had heard of her from Veronica, and her own consequent anxiety.

While Jesus was walking up and down the hall with the men, the women sat playing a kind of lottery for the benefit of their new undertaking. On the elevated platform was a table on rollers around which they sat. The plane of the table, which projected into five angles like the rays of a star, covered a box about two inches in depth. From the five points to the center of this partitioned box, ran deep furrows on the surface, and between them were slits connecting the interior. Each of the women had some long strings of pearls and many other little precious stones. Each in turn placed some of them in one of the furrows on the table. Then, resting a delicate little bow on the outer end of the furrow, she shot a tiny arrow at the nearest pearl or stone. The shock received by this one communicated itself to the rest, which rolled into the other furrows or dropped through the holes into the compartments in the interior of the box. When all the pearls and stones had been shot from the surface, the table, which was upon rollers, was agitated to and fro, by which movement the contents fell into other little compartments which could be drawn out at the edge. Each of these little drawers had previously been assigned to one of the players, so that when the holy women drew them out, they saw at once what they had won for their new undertaking or which jewel they had lost.

Obed had died not long before and his widow was still mourning for him. Before the baptism, he had been at Lazarus's with Jesus.

During the game the holy women lost a very precious pearl that had fallen down among them. All moved back and looked for it most carefully. When at last they found it and were expressing their joy, Jesus came over to them and related the parable of the lost drachma and the joy of the owner upon finding it again. From their pearl, lost, carefully sought, and joyfully found, he drew a new similitude to Magdalene. He called her a pearl more precious than many others that, from the lottery table of holy love, had fallen and were going to destruction. "With what joy," he exclaimed, "will ye find again the precious pearl!" Then the women, deeply moved, asked: "Ah, Lord! Will that pearl be found again?" and Jesus answered: "Seek ye more earnestly than the woman in the parable sought the lost drachma, or the shepherd his stray sheep." Profoundly touched at this answer, all promised to seek after Magdalene more diligently than after their lost pearl, and assured him that their joy upon finding her would far exceed what they now felt. Some of the women begged the Lord to receive among his disciples the young man of Samaria who, after Passover, had besought this favor of him on the road to that city. They praised his great wisdom and virtue. I think he was related to one of them. But Jesus replied that he could not count upon him as he was blinded by love of riches.

That evening several of the men and women began their preparations to go to Beth-Horon, where Jesus was to preach next day. That night Jesus again retired secretly to the Mount of Olives and prayed with his whole heart and soul, after which he went with Lazarus and Saturnin to Beth-Horon, about six hours off.

Monday, July 24, AD 30 (Ab 5)

Early this morning, on the outskirts of Beth-Horon, they met up with Peter, Andrew, James the Greater, John, Judas Thaddeus, James the Less, and Philip. Around eight o'clock, Jesus and his disciples came to the synagogue. It was already full of people waiting in expectation to hear him. He spoke of the persecution of the prophets and the imprisonment of John the Baptist. He spoke too of his own future persecution and of the judgment and woe that would come upon Jerusalem. After healing various people in the town, Jesus and his disciples left Beth-Horon and journeyed to Kibzaim. That night, they stayed at a large house belonging to a shepherd.

It was then one hour past midnight. They cut through the desert on their way. When about two hours distant from Beth-Horon, they were met by the disciples whom Jesus had appointed to join him there, and who had arrived at the inn near Beth-Horon the day before. They were Peter, Andrew, and their half-brother Jonathan, James the Greater, John, James the Less, and Judas Thaddeus, who was with them now for the first time, Philip, Nathaniel Chased, also the bridegroom of Cana, and one or two of the widow's sons. Jesus rested with them under a tree in the desert for a long time, and gave them an instruction. He spoke again on the parable of the lord of the vineyard who had sent his son to the vinedressers. At the conclusion of the discourse, they proceeded to the inn and took something to eat. Saturnin had received from the women a purse of money with which to procure provisions for the little party.

Jesus in Beth-Horon • *Hardships and Privations of the Disciples*

IT was toward eight o'clock in the morning when Jesus arrived in Beth-Horon. A couple of the disciples went to the dwelling of the elders and demanded the keys of the synagogue, as their Master wanted to deliver an instruction; others scattered through the streets and summoned the people to the school, while Jesus went with the rest to the synagogue, which was soon filled with auditors. He taught again in severe terms on the parable of the lord of the vineyard whose servants were murdered by the unfaithful vinedressers, whose son whom he had sent to them shared the same fate, and who at last gave the vineyard into the hands of others. He spoke likewise of the persecution of the prophets and the imprisonment of John, saying that they would persecute him also and lay hands upon him, and he ended by predicting the judgment and woe that were to come upon Jerusalem. This discourse occasioned great excitement among the Jews. Some rejoiced, while others muttered angrily to one another: "Whence came this man so unexpectedly here? No one knew of his arrival!" And some who had heard that there were women, followers of Jesus, at the inn in the valley, went out to question them on the designs of their Master. Jesus cured several that were sick of a fever, and after some hours left the city.

Veronica, Johanna Chusa, and Obed's widow had arrived at the inn and prepared a luncheon. Jesus and the disciples partook of it standing, after which they girded themselves and recommenced their journey. Jesus taught on this same day in Kibzaim on similar subjects as at Beth-Horon, also in some small shepherd settlements. All the disciples were not present in Kibzaim, but they met again at a large house belonging to a shepherd. It was surrounded by outbuildings and stood on the confines of Samaria. Mary and Joseph had been hospitably received there on their journey to Bethlehem, after having vainly sought admittance elsewhere. Here Jesus and the disciples, about fifteen in all, ate and slept. Lazarus and the women had returned to Bethany.

Tuesday, July 25, AD 30 (Ab 6)
Jesus and the disciples journeyed on, passing through Gabaa and Naioth. Jesus taught and healed as he traveled on his way. That night, they stayed again at a shepherd's place.

On the next day Jesus and the disciples sometimes together, sometimes in separate groups, passed rapidly through several large cities and small towns that lay in a district of some hours in extent. Gabaa and Naioth, about four hours from Kibzaim, were among them. In none of these places did Jesus take time to go to the synagogues to teach, but instructed the crowds that gathered to hear him on hills in the open air, on the public places, and in the streets. Several of the disciples remained with Jesus, while the others scattered through the valleys and shepherd villages to call the dwellers to the places which Jesus was to pass. The whole day's work was performed with incredible hardship and fatigue, with constant going from place to place. Jesus cured many sick, some of whom were carried to him, but others cried out themselves for his aid. There were some lunatics among them. Many possessed ran clamoring after him, but he commanded them to be silent and to retire.

What made that day's work still more wearisome, was the bad dispositions of the people and the insults of the Pharisees. These places, being near Jerusalem, were full of people who had taken part against Jesus. It was then as it is now in little places, they talk of everything without understanding anything. It was to such people that Jesus suddenly appeared with his band of disciples and his grave and denunciatory preaching. He repeated the instructions delivered at Beth-Horon, spoke of the graces now offered for the last time, after which would come the day of justice, and again alluded to the ill-usage of the prophets, the imprisonment of John, and the persecution directed against himself. He brought forward above all the parable of the lord of the vineyard, who had now sent his son. He said that the kingdom would soon come and the king's son would enter into possession of it. He often cried, "Woe!" to Jerusalem and to them that would not receive his kingdom, would not do penance. These severe and menacing discourses were interrupted by many acts of charity and by the cure of the sick. In this way, Jesus journeyed from place to place.

The disciples had much to endure, and it was often very hard for them. On reaching a town or village and announcing the coming of Jesus, they often heard the scornful words: "What! Is he coming again! What does he want? Whence comes he? Has he not been forbidden to preach?" And they laughed at them, derided and insulted them. There were, indeed, a few that rejoiced to hear of Jesus's coming, but they were very few. No one ventured to attack Jesus himself, but wherever he taught, surrounded by his disciples, or proceeded along the street followed by them, the crowd shouted after them. They stopped the disciples and plied them with impertinent questions, pretending that they had misunderstood or only half comprehended his severe words, and demanding an explanation. Meanwhile other cries resounded, cries of joy at some cure just wrought by Jesus. This scandalized the crowd and they fell back and left him. And so he continued till evening these rapid and fatiguing marches without rest or refreshment.

I noticed how weak and human the disciples still were in the beginning. If during Jesus's instructions, they were questioned as to his meaning, they shook their head as if they had not understood what he really meant. Nor were they satisfied with their condition. They thought to themselves: "Now we have left all things, and what have we for it but all this tumult and embarrassment? Of what kind of a kingdom is he always speaking? Will he really gain it?" These were their thoughts. They kept them concealed in their own breast, though often manifesting discouragement in their countenance. John alone acted with the simplicity of a child. He was perfectly obedient and free from constraint. And yet the disciples had seen and were still witnessing so many miracles!

It was indeed touching to think that Jesus knew all their thoughts, and yet acted as if wholly ignorant of them. He changed nothing in his manner, but calmly, sweetly, and earnestly went on with his work.

Jesus journeyed far into the night of that day. When on this side of a little river that forms the boundary of Samaria, he and his disciples stopped for the night among

Shechem at the Foot of Mount Garizim

some shepherds from whom they received little or nothing. The river water was not fit for drinking. It was a narrow stream and here, not far from its source at the foot of Gerizim, made a rapid turn toward the west.

Jesus at Jacob's Well near Sichar • Dinah the Samaritan Woman

Wednesday, July 26, AD 30 (Ab 7)

While the other disciples were otherwise engaged, Jesus went to Jacob's well, accompanied by Andrew, James the Greater, and Saturnin. Toward midday, they arrived at the hill on which the well-house was located. Jesus sent the three disciples to Shechem to buy provisions and sat down near the well. Then there took place the encounter with the Samaritan woman—named Dinah—as described in the Gospel of Saint John 4:1–42.

ON the following day Jesus crossed the little river and, leaving Mount Garizim to the right, approached Shechem. Andrew, James the Greater, and Saturnin accompanied him, the others having scattered in different directions. Jesus went to the Well of Jacob, on a little hill in the inheritance of Joseph to the north of Mount Garizim and south of Mount Ebal. Shechem lay about a quarter of an hour to the west in a valley which ran along the west side of the city for about an hour. About two good hours northward from Sichar stood the city of Samaria upon a mountain.

Several deeply rutted roads ran from different points around the little hill and up to the octangular buildings that enclosed Jacob's well, which was surrounded by trees and grassy seats. The springhouse was encircled by an open arched gallery under which about twenty people could find standing room. Directly opposite the road that led from Shechem and under the arched roof was the door, usually kept shut, that opened into the springhouse proper. There was an aperture in the cover of the latter, which could be closed at pleasure. The interior of the little springhouse was quite roomy. The well was deep and surrounded by a stone rim high enough to afford a seat. Between it and the walls, one could walk around freely. The well had a wooden cover, which when opened disclosed a large cylinder just opposite the entrance and lying across the well. On it hung the bucket, which was unwound by means of a winch. Opposite the door was a pump for raising the water to the top of the wall of the springhouse, whence it flowed out to the east, south, and west under the surrounding arches into three little basins dug in the earth. They were intended for travelers to perform their ablutions and wash their feet, also for watering beasts of burden.

It was toward midday when Jesus and the three disciples reached the hill. Jesus sent them on to Shechem to procure food, for he was hungry, while he himself ascended the hill alone to await them. The day was hot, and Jesus was very tired and thirsty. He sat down a short distance from the well on the side of the path that led up from Shechem. Resting his head upon his hand, he seemed to be patiently waiting for someone to open the well and give him to drink. And now I saw a Samaritan woman of about thirty years, a leathern bottle hanging on her arm, coming up the hill from Shechem to draw water. She was beautiful, and I remarked how briskly and vigorously, and with what long strides she mounted the hill. Her costume appeared somewhat studied, and there was an air of distinction about it. Her dress was striped blue and red embroidered with large yellow flowers; the sleeves above and below the elbow were fastened by yellow bracelets, and were ruffled at the wrist. She wore a white stomacher ornamented with yellow cords. Her neck was entirely concealed by a yellow woolen collar thickly covered with strings of pearl and coral. Her veil, very fine and long, was woven of some rich, woolen material. It hung down her back, but by means of a string could be drawn together and fastened around her waist. When thus worn, it formed a point behind and on either side folds in which the elbows could comfortably rest. When both sides of the veil were fastened on the breast, the whole of the upper part of her person was enveloped as if in a mantle. Her head was bound with fillets that entirely concealed the hair. From her headdress there arose above the forehead something like a little tower or a crown. Tucked up behind it lay the forepart of the veil which, when let down over her face, reached to the breast.

She had her large, brownish goat or camel-hair apron with its open pockets, thrown up over her right arm, so that the leather bottle hanging on that arm was partly concealed. This apron was similar to those usually worn at such work as drawing water. It protected the dress from the bucket and water bottle.

The bottle was of leather, and like a seamless sack. It was convex on two sides, as if lined with a firm, arched, wooden surface; but the two others, when the bottle was empty, lay together in folds like those of a pocketbook. On the two firm sides were leather-covered handles through which ran a leather strap used for carrying it on the arm. The mouth of the bottle was narrow. It could be opened like a funnel for receiving the contents, and closed again like a work pouch. When empty, the bottle hung flat on the side, but when filled it bulged out, holding as much as an ordinary water bucket.

It was under this guise that I saw the woman briskly ascending the hill, to get water from Jacob's well for herself and others. I took a fancy to her right away. She was so kind, so frank, so openhearted. She was called Dinah, was the child of a mixed marriage, and belonged to the sect of Samaritans. She lived in Shechem, but it was not her birthplace. Her peculiar circumstances were unknown to the inhabitants, among whom she went by the name of Salome. Both she and her husband were very much liked on account of their open, friendly, and obliging manners.

The windings of the path by which she mounted the hill prevented Dinah's seeing the Lord until she actually stood before him. There was something startling in the sight as he sat there exhausted and all alone on the path leading to Jacob's well. He wore a long, white robe of fine wool like an alb, bound with a broad girdle. It was a garment such as the prophets wore, and which the disciples usually carried for him. He made use of it only on solemn occasions when he preached, or fulfilled some prophecy.

Dinah coming thus suddenly upon Jesus was startled. She lowered her veil and hesitated to advance, for the Lord was sitting full in her path. I saw passing through her mind the characteristic thoughts: "A man! What is he doing here? Is it a temptation?" She saw that Jesus was a Jew as, beaming with benevolence, he graciously drew his feet back, for the path was narrow, with the words: "Pass on, and give me to drink!"

These words touched the woman, since the Jews and the Samaritans were accustomed to exchange only glances of mutual aversion, and so she still lingered, saying: "Why art thou here all alone at this hour? If anyone should happen to see me here with thee, he would be scandalized." To which Jesus answered that his companions had gone on to the city to purchase food. Dinah said: "Indeed! The three men whom I met? But they will find little at this hour. What the Shechemites have prepared for today, they need for themselves." She spoke as if it were either a feast or a fast that day in Sichar, and named another place to which they should have gone for food.

But Jesus again said: "Pass on, and give me to drink!" Then Dinah passed by him. Jesus arose and followed her to the well, which she unlocked. While going thither, she said: "How canst thou, being a Jew, ask a drink from a

Samaritan?" And Jesus answered her: "If thou didst know the gift of God and who he is that sayeth to thee: 'Give me to drink,' thou wouldst perhaps have asked of him, and he would have given thee living water."

Then Dinah loosened the cover and the bucket, meanwhile saying to Jesus, who had seated himself on the rim of the well: "Sir, thou hast nothing wherein to draw, and the well is deep. Whence then hast thou living water? Art thou greater than our father Jacob who gave us this well, and drank thereof himself and his children and his cattle?" [C2] As she uttered these words, I had a vision of Jacob's digging the well and the water's springing up. The woman understood Jesus's words to refer to the water of this well and so, as she was speaking, she put the bucket on the cylinder, which turned heavily, lowered it and drew it up again. She pushed up her sleeves with the bracelets until they puffed out high above the elbow, and in this way with bare arms she filled her leather bottle out of the bucket. Then, taking a little vessel made of bark and shaped like a horn, she filled it with water and handed it to Jesus, who, sitting on the rim of the well, drank it and said to her: "Whosoever drinketh of this water, shall thirst again, but he that shall drink of the water that I shall give him, shall not thirst forever. Yes, the water that I will give him, shall become in him a fountain of water springing into life everlasting."

Dinah replied eagerly: "Sir, give me that living water, that I may no more thirst nor have to come with so much fatigue to draw." She was struck by his words "living water" and had a presentiment, though without being fully conscious of it, that Jesus meant by the "living water" the fulfillment of the Promise. And so it was under prophetic inspiration that she uttered her heartfelt prayer for that living water. I have always felt and understood that those persons with whom the Redeemer treated are not to be considered as mere individuals. They perfectly represented a whole race of people, and they did so, because they belonged to the plenitude of time. And so in Dinah the Samaritan there stood before the Redeemer the whole Samaritan sect, so long separated from the true faith of Israel, from the fountain of living water.

Jesus at the well of Jacob thirsted after the chosen souls of Samaria, in order to refresh them with the living waters from which they had cut themselves off. It was that portion of the rebellious sect still open to salvation that here thirsted after this living water and, in a certain way, reached out an open hand to receive it. Samaria spoke through Dinah: "Give me, O Lord, the Blessing of the Promise! Help me to obtain the living water from which I may receive more consolation than from this temporal well of Jacob, through which alone we still have communication with the Jews."

When Dinah had thus spoken, Jesus said to her: "Go home, call thy husband, and come back hither!" and I heard him give the command twice, because it was not to instruct her alone that he had come. In this command the Redeemer addressed the whole sect: "Samaria, call hither him to whom thou belongest, him who by a holy contract is lawfully bound to thee." Dinah replied to the Lord: "I have no husband!"

Samaria confessed to the Bridegroom of souls that she had no contract, that she belonged to no one. Jesus replied: "Thou hast said well, for thou hast had five husbands, and he with whom thou now livest is not thy husband. Thou hast spoken truly." In these words the Messiah said to the sect: "Samaria, thou speakest the truth. Thou hast been espoused to the idols of five different nations, and thy present alliance with God is no marriage contract." Here Dinah, lowering her eyes and hanging her head, answered: "Sir, I see that thou art a prophet," and she drew down her veil. The Samaritan sect recognized the divine mission of the Lord, and confessed its own guilt.

As if Dinah understood the prophetic meaning of Jesus's words: "and he with whom thou livest is not thy husband," that is, thy actual connection with the true God is imperfect and illegal, the religion of the Samaritans has by sin and self-will been separated from God's covenant with Jacob; as if she felt the deep significance of these words, she pointed toward the south, to the temple not far off on Mount Garizim, and said questioningly: "Our Fathers adored on that mountain, and you say that Jerusalem is the place where men must adore?" Jesus replied with the words: "Woman! Believe me, the hour cometh when neither in Gerizim nor in Jerusalem wilt thou adore the Father." In this reply he meant to say: "Samaria, the hour cometh when neither here nor in the sanctuary of the temple will God be adored, because he walks in the midst of you," and he continued: "You adore that which you know not, but we adore that which we know, for salvation is of the Jews." Here he related to her a similitude of the wild, unfruitful suckers of trees, which shoot forth into wood and foliage, but produce no fruit. It was as if he had said to the sect: "Samaria, thou hast not security in thy worship. Thou hast no union, no sacrament, no pledge of alliance, no Ark of the Covenant, no fruit. The Jews, from whom the Messiah will be born, have all these things, the Promise, and its fulfillment."

And again Jesus said: "But the hour cometh and now is when the true adorers will adore the Father in spirit and in truth, for the Father wills such to adore him. God is a spirit, and they that adore him must adore him in spirit, and in truth." By these words the Redeemer meant: "Samaria, the hour cometh, yea, it now is, when the Father by true adorers will be honored in the Holy Spirit and in the Son, who is the Way and the Truth."

Dinah replied: "I know that the Messiah cometh. When he is come, he will tell us all things." In these words here at the well of Jacob, spoke that portion of the Samaritan sect, which might lay some legitimate claim to the Promise: "I hope for, I believe in the coming of the Messiah. He will help us." Jesus responded: "I am he, I who now speak to thee!"

By this he said to all Samaria that would be converted: "Samaria! I came to Jacob's well athirst for thee, thou

whom she met what had happened to her. It was strictly forbidden to leave the well of Jacob open, but what cared Dinah now for the well of Jacob! What cared she for her bucket of earthly water! She had received the living water, and her loving, joyous heart was longing to pour its refreshing streams over all her neighbors. But as she was hurrying out of the springhouse, she ran past the three disciples who had come with the food and had already been standing for some time at a little distance from the door, wondering what their Master could have to say for

Hill of Samaria

water of this well. And when thou didst give me to drink, I promised thee living water that would never let thee thirst again. And thou didst, hoping and believing, make known to me thy longing for this water. Behold, I reward thee, for thou hast allayed my thirst after thee by thy desire after me! Samaria, I am the fountain of living water. I who now speak to thee, am the Messiah."

As Jesus pronounced the words: "I am the Messiah," Dinah, trembling with holy joy, gazed at him in amazement. But suddenly recovering herself, she turned and, leaving her water bottle standing and the well open, she fled down the hill to Shechem, to tell her husband and all

so long with a Samaritan woman. But through reverence for him, they forebore to question. Dinah ran down to Shechem and with great eagerness said to her husband and others whom she met on the street: "Come up to Jacob's well! There you will see a man that has told me all the secret actions of my life. Come, he is certainly the Christ!"

Meanwhile the three disciples approached Jesus, who was still by the well, and offered him some rolls and honey out of their basket, saying: "Master, eat!" Jesus arose and left the well with the words: "I have meat to eat which you know not." The disciples said to one another: "Hath any man brought him to eat?" and they thought to themselves: "Did that Samaritan woman give him to eat?" Jesus would not stop to eat, but began descending the hill to Shechem. The disciples followed, eating. Jesus said to them as he went on before: "My meat is to do the will of him that sent me, that I may perfect his work." By that he meant, to convert the people of Shechem, after whose salvation his soul hungered. He spoke much more to the same purport.

When near the city, Dinah the Samaritan again appeared hurrying back to meet Jesus. She joined him respectfully, but full of joy and frankness, and Jesus addressed many words to her, sometimes standing still and sometimes moving slowly forward. He unfolded to her all her past life with all the dispositons of her soul. She was deeply moved and promised that both she and her husband would abandon all and follow him. He pointed out to her many ways by which she could do penance for her sins and repair her scandals.

Dinah was an intelligent woman of some standing in the world, the offspring of a mixed marriage, a Jewish mother and a pagan father, born upon a country seat near Damascus. She had lost her parents at an early age, and had been cared for by a dissolute nurse by whom her evil passions had been fostered. She had had five husbands one after another. Some had died of grief, others had been put out of the way by her new lovers. She had three daughters and two half-grown sons, all of whom had remained with the relatives of their respective fathers when their mother was obliged to leave Damascus.

Dinah's sons at a later period joined the seventy-two disciples. The man with whom she was now living was a relative of one of her former husbands. He was a rich merchant. As Dinah followed the Samaritan religion, she had induced the man to remove to Shechem, where she superintended his household and lived with him, though without being espoused to him. They were looked upon in Shechem as a married couple. The husband was a vigorous man of about thirty-six years with a ruddy face and a reddish beard. There were many things in Dinah's life similar to those of Magdalene's, but she had fallen more deeply than the latter. Still I once saw that in the beginning of Magdalene's evil career at Magdalum, one of her lovers lost his life at the hand of a rival. Dinah was an uncommonly gifted, open-hearted, easily influenced, pleasing woman of great vivacity and impetuosity, but she was always disturbed in conscience. She was living now more respectably, that is with this her reputed husband, in a house that stood alone and surrounded by a moat, near the gate leading from Shechem to the spring house. Though not held in contempt by the inhabitants, still they did not have much communication with her. Her manners were different from theirs, her costume elaborate and studied, all which, however, they pardoned in her as she was a stranger.

While Jesus was speaking with Dinah, the disciples followed at some distance, wondering what he could have to say to the woman. "We have brought him food, and that with a good deal of difficulty. Why, now, does he not eat?"

When near Shechem, Dinah left the Lord and hurried forward to meet her husband and many of the citizens, who came pouring out of their houses, all curiosity to see Jesus. Full of joy, they exulted and shouted salutations of welcome to him. Jesus, standing still, motioned with his hand for silence, and addressed them kindly for some moments, telling them among other things to believe all that the woman had told them. Jesus was so remarkably gracious in his words, his glance was so bright and penetrating that all hearts beat more quickly, all were borne toward him, and they were pressing in their solicitations for him to enter and teach in their city. He promised that he would do so, but for the present passed on.

This scene took place somewhere between three and four o'clock in the afternoon.

While Jesus was thus addressing the Samaritans outside the gate, all the other disciples, among them Peter, who in the morning had gone on commissions in a different direction, returned to their Master. They were surprised and not any too well pleased to see him talking so long with the Samaritans. They felt somewhat embarrassed at it, for they had been reared in the preconceived idea that they were to have no communication with these people, consequently they had never before seen anything like this. They felt tempted to take scandal at it. They reflected upon the hardships of yesterday and the day before, on all the scorn and insult, on the cruel treatment that they had endured. They had expected an easier time, since the women of Bethany had advanced so much money for that end. Seeing now this business with the Samaritans, they thought to themselves it was certainly no wonder when things went on in this way that they were not better received. Their heads were always full of extravagant, worldly fancies of the kingdom that Jesus was to establish, and they thought if all this should become known in Galilee, they would indeed be derided.

Peter had in Samaria a long conversation with that young man who wanted to join the disciples, but was still wavering. He afterward spoke with Jesus on the subject.

Jesus went with them all about a half-hour around the city to the north, and there rested under some trees. On the way thither the Lord had been conversing with them about the harvest, a subject which he now continued. He said, "There is a proverb often on the lips, 'yet four months, and the harvest cometh.' Sluggards are ever desirous of putting off their work, but they should look around and see all the fields standing white for the harvest." Jesus meant the Samaritans and others who were ripe for conversion. "Ye, disciples, are called to the harvest, though ye have not sown. Others have sown, namely, the prophets and John and I myself. He that reapeth, receiveth wages and gathereth fruit for eternal life, that both he that soweth and he that reapeth may rejoice together. For in this is the saying true, that it is one man that soweth and it is another that reapeth. I have sent you to reap that in which you did not labor. Others have labored and you have entered into their labors." In this way Jesus spoke to the disciples in order to encourage them to the work. They rested only a short time and then separated, Andrew, Philip, Saturnin, and John remaining with Jesus, while the others went on to Galilee passing between Thebez and Samaria.

Jesus, leaving Shechem to the right, journeyed about an hour southward to a field around which were scattered twenty shepherd huts and tents. In one of the larger huts, the blessed Virgin and Mary Cleophas, the wife of James the Greater, and two of the widows were awaiting him. They had been there the whole day, having brought with them food and little flasks of balsam. They now prepared a meal. On meeting his mother, Jesus extended both hands to her, while she inclined her head to him. The women saluted him by bowing their head and crossing their hands on their breast. There was a tree in front of the house, and under it they took the meal.

Among the shepherds dwelling around these parts were the parents of the youths whom Jesus, after the raising of Lazarus, took with him on his journey to Arabia and Egypt. These people had come to Bethlehem in the suite of the three holy kings, had on account of the hasty departure of the latter remained behind in this country, and had married some of the shepherds' daughters in the valley near Bethlehem. Shepherd settlements like that just mentioned were frequent in the winding valleys between this place and Bethlehem. The people dwelling here cultivated also the field of Joseph's inheritance which they had rented from the Shechemites. There were many of them gathered here, but no Samaritans.

The first noteworthy incident that took place here was the blessed Virgin's begging Jesus to cure a lame boy whom some of the neighboring shepherds had brought thither. They had before doing so implored Mary's intercession. Such things happened very often, and it was quite affecting to see her asking Jesus for these favors. Jesus commanded that the boy should be brought, and the parents bore him on a little litter to the door of the house in which Jesus was. The child was about nine years old. Jesus addressed some words of exhortation to the parents and, as they fell back, somewhat timidly awaiting the result, the disciples gathered around Jesus. He spoke to the boy, leaned a little over him, then took him by the hand and raised him up. The boy jumped out of the litter, took a few steps, and then ran into the arms of his parents, who cast themselves with him at Jesus's feet. The crowd uttered cries of joy, but Jesus reminded them to thank the heavenly Father. He then addressed a short instruction to the assembled shepherds and took with the disciples a light repast, which the women had prepared in an arbor under the great tree in front of the house. Mary and the women sat apart at the end of the table. I am under the impression that this house was taken for one of the private inns, and was prepared and served by the holy women of Capernaum.

There approached now, and that rather timidly, several persons from Shechem, among them Dinah, the woman of the well. They did not venture to draw near, because they were not accustomed to have dealings with the Jewish shepherds. Dinah, however, made bold to advance first, and I saw her talking with the women and the blessed Virgin. After the repast, Jesus and the disciples took leave of the holy women, who immediately set about preparing for their return journey to Galilee, whither Jesus himself was to go the next day but one.

Jesus now returned with Dinah and the other Samaritans to Shechem, a city not very large, but with broad streets and open squares. The Samaritan house of prayer was a finer looking building, more ornamented than the synagogues of small Jewish places. The women of Shechem were not so reserved as the Jewish women; they communicated more freely with the men. As soon as Jesus entered Shechem, he was surrounded by a crowd. He did not go into their synagogue, but taught walking around here and there on the streets, and in one of the squares where there was an orator's chair. Everywhere was the concourse of people very great, and they were full of joy at the Messiah's having come to them.

Dinah, though very much moved and very recollected, was of all the women the one that approached nearest to Jesus. Her neighbors now looked upon her with special regard, as she had been the first to find Jesus. She sent the man with whom she was living to Jesus, who spoke to him a few words of exhortation. He stood before Jesus quite embarrassed and ashamed of his sins. Jesus did not tarry long in Shechem, but went out by the opposite gate and taught here and there among the houses and gardens that extended for some distance along the valley. He put up at an inn distant from Shechem a good half-hour, promising, however, to return to the city on the following day and give them an instruction.

Thursday, July 27, AD 30 (Ab 8)

Jesus taught at Shechem for the whole day, expounding again upon the theme of the persecution of the prophets that is summarized in the parable of the vineyard owner and the evil tenants (Matthew 21:33–43). Dinah, the Samaritan woman, spoke to Jesus concerning her future, for she had resolved to dedicate herself to his work, to help Jesus and the disciples in whatever way she could.

When Jesus went again to Shechem, he taught the whole day, dividing the time between the orator's chair in the city and the hills outside, and in the evening he taught again in the inn. From the whole country around came crowds to hear him, and they followed him from place to place. The cry was: "Now he is teaching here! Now he is teaching there!" The young man of Samaria also listened to the instructions, but he did not speak with Jesus.

Dinah was everywhere foremost, everywhere made her way through the crowd to Jesus. She was very attentive, very earnest, and deeply impressed. She had had another interview with Jesus and was now about to separate from her reputed husband. They had resolved for Jesus's sake to consecrate all their riches to the poor and the good of the future church. Jesus told them how to proceed in the affair. Many of the Samaritans were profoundly touched by what they had seen and heard, and they said to Dinah: "Thou hast spoken truly. We have now heard him ourselves. He is the Messiah!" The good woman was quite out of herself, and so in earnest, so joyous! I have always loved her dearly.

Here as in former places, Jesus took for the subjects of his discourse: the imprisonment of John, the persecution of the prophets, the precursor charged to prepare the ways, and the son sent to the vineyard, but who was murdered by the wicked servants. He declared plainly that the Father had sent him. He taught also upon all that he had said to the woman at the well, namely, the living water, Mount Garizim, salvation from the Jews, the nearness of the kingdom and the judgment, and the punishment inflicted upon the wicked servants who had put to death the son of the lord of the vineyard. Many of his hearers questioned him as to where now they should be baptized and cleansed, since John was imprisoned. Jesus answered that John's disciples were again baptizing near Ainon across the Jordan, and that, until he himself should appear there with his disciples to give baptism, they should go thither. On the following day, accordingly, crowds flocked to Ainon.

Next day Jesus taught at the inn and on the surrounding hills. His audience consisted of laborers, of all kinds of people, and those slaves whom, after his baptism, he had once consoled in the field of the shepherds near Bethabara. There were present also many spies sent by the Pharisees from the environs around. They listened to him with anger in their hearts, stuck their heads together, and muttered jeeringly. But they did not attempt to accost him, and he took no notice of them. Several Samaritan doctors and others remained unmoved by his words, receiving them into a disaffected heart.

Jesus in Ginea and Ataroth • He Confounds the Wickedness of the Pharisees

Friday, July 28, AD 30 (Ab 9)

This morning, having stayed the night at an inn outside Shechem, Jesus taught at the inn and later on the surrounding hills. In the afternoon, he journeyed to Ginea accompanied by his disciples. The sabbath had already begun when they arrived, so they went straight to the synagogue. After the service, they made their way to a place belonging to Lazarus situated some three-quarters of an hour south of Ginea. They stayed overnight there.

WHEN Jesus with his five disciples left the inn near Shechem, he journeyed leaving Thebez to the right and Samaria to the left, six hours further on to the city of Ginnaea, or Ginea, situated in a valley on the boundary of Samaria and Galilee. Late in the evening they entered Ginea, their garments still tucked up and, as the sabbath had begun, they went straight to the synagogue. The disciples who had journeyed on before them were likewise present. On leaving the synagogue, they went all together to a country seat belonging to Lazarus, and which lay up among the mountains. Nearby was Little Thirza, where Jesus had already put up, and where also Mary and Joseph on their journey to Bethlehem had received lodgings. The steward, a man whose manners breathed the simplicity of ancient times, had many children. Jesus and his disciples spent the night there. The country seat may have been about three-quarters of an hour distant from Ginea. The holy women, on their return journey from Shechem, had spent the night in Thebez. The day of Jesus's arrival here, the day before the sabbath, was a fast in expiation of the murmuring of the children of Israel.

Saturday, July 29, AD 30 (Ab 10)

Jesus preached at the synagogue in Ginea, and entered into a dispute with twelve Pharisees, who asked him what it meant that Jonah was three days and three nights in the belly of the whale. Jesus explained that it meant that the Messiah would be slain and would remain three days in the grave, and then arise again from the dead (Matthew 12:38–42).

On the sabbath Jesus taught in the synagogue. The passages read from holy scripture referred to the journey through the wilderness, the parcelling out of the land of Canaan, and to something in Jeremiah. Jesus interpreted all as bearing reference to the nearness of the kingdom of God. He spoke of the murmuring of the children of Israel in the desert, saying that they would have taken a much shorter way to the Promised Land, had they kept the commandments that God gave them on Sinai, but on account of their sins they were obliged to wander, and they that murmured died in the desert. And so, too, would they among his present hearers wander in the desert and die therein, if they murmured against the kingdom that was now at hand and with it the final mercy of God. Their life had been an image of that wandering in the desert, but they should now go by the shortest way to the promised kingdom of God, which would be pointed out to them. He referred also to the dissatisfaction of the children of Israel with the judgeship of Samuel, their clamoring after a king, and their receiving one in Saul. Now, when the prophecy was fulfilled, when on account of their impiety the scepter had passed from Judah, they were again sighing for a king and for the re-establishment of the kingdom. God would send them a king, their true king, just as the lord of the vineyard had sent his own son after his servants had been murdered by the unfaithful vinedressers. But in the same way would they, too, expel their king and put him to death. He also explained those verses of the Psalms that speak of the cornerstone rejected by the builders, applying them to the son of the lord of the vineyard, and spoke of the punishment that would fall upon Jerusalem. The temple, he said, would not exist much longer, and Jerusalem itself would soon be unrecognizable. He referred likewise to Elijah and Elisha.

There were twelve obstinate Pharisees at this instruction, and when it was over they disputed with Jesus. They pointed to a roll of parchment, and asked what was meant by Jonas's lying three days in the whale's belly. [C3] Jesus answered: "In like manner will your king, the Messiah, lie three days in the grave, descend into Abraham's bosom, and then rise again." They laughed at that. Then three of the Pharisees came forward and, full of hypocrisy, said: "Venerable Rabbi, you speak always of the shortest way. Tell us, which is that shortest way?" Jesus answered: "Know ye the Ten Commandments given on Sinai?" They answered: "Yes." He went on: "Observe the first of them, and love your neighbor as yourself. Lay not upon those under you heavy burdens that you do not impose upon yourselves. That is the way!" They replied: "We know all that!" Jesus rejoined: "That ye know all this and yet do nothing of it, constitutes your guilt, therefore will ye be chastised." And he reproached them for burdening the people with unnecessary prescriptions while they themselves did not observe the Law itself, for that was especially the case in this city. He alluded also to the priestly robes prescribed by God to Moses, and of their mysterious signification. He convicted them of their non-fulfillment of these matters, for which they substituted many perversions and external forms. The Pharisees were highly exasperated, but they could not get the better of Jesus. They repeated to one another: "He is the prophet from Nazareth! The carpenter's son, forsooth!" Most of them left the synagogue before Jesus had concluded his discourse. One only remained till the end and invited Jesus and his disciples to a repast. He was better than the rest, though still a lurker.

Some sick persons had been brought and placed outside the synagogue, and the Pharisees requested Jesus to cure them, that thereby they might see a sign. But Jesus refused to perform any cure, saying that they would not believe in him, therefore they should see no sign. Their real aim was to tempt him to heal on the sabbath, that they might have something for which to bring an action against him.

(Follow Map 18)

Sunday, July 30, AD 30 (Ab 11)

As Jesus taught this morning, many children were gathered in a park close by the place belonging to Lazarus where Jesus was staying. Around midday, he set off together with three disciples to Ataroth, where a group of Sadducees tried to trick Jesus into raising from the dead someone who had been dead already eight days. Jesus exposed their plot, however. He then traveled on to a place on a hill near Engannim, where he stayed overnight.

When the sabbath was over, most of the disciples from Galilee returned to their homes, but Jesus with Saturnin and two other disciples went back to Lazarus's country seat. How touching to see him giving instructions to the children of the steward and those of the neighbors, first to the boys and then to the girls. He spoke of obedience to parents and of reverence for old age. The Father in heaven had appointed for them their fathers; as much as they honored them, so much also would they honor their heavenly Father. He spoke likewise of the children of the sons of Jacob and of those of Israel, telling how they had murmured and for that reason had not been allowed to enter the Promised Land, a land that was so beautiful. Then he pointed to the fine trees and fruits in the garden, and told them of the heavenly kingdom promised to them that keep the commandments of God. It was far more glorious and beautiful than the lovely garden in which they were; that garden, compared with the heavenly one, was nothing more than a desert. They must then be obedient and submit thankfully to the decrees of God in their regard; they must never murmur, that thereby they might not be excluded from the kingdom of heaven; they must not doubt concerning the beauty of that kingdom, as the Israelites did in the desert; they must believe it to be far above, yes, a thousand times more magnificent than what they then saw before them; and lastly, they should have it often in their thoughts, in order to merit it by their daily toil and labors. During these instructions Jesus had the smaller ones right in front of him. He lifted some of them up to his breast, or encircled a couple of them with his arms.

From Lazarus's country seat, Jesus went with the three disciples again southward about four hours, back toward Ataroth, one of the chief cities of the Sadducees, lying among the mountains. The Sadducees of this place, like the Pharisees of Gennabris, had in consequence of what had taken place at Passover persecuted the disciples, imprisoned several of them and tormented them with judicial interrogatories. Some of them also had lately been in Shechem and had listened insidiously to Jesus's instructions in which he had censured the harshness of the Pharisees and Sadducees toward the Samaritans. They had then resolved upon a plan to ensnare Jesus, and it was in pursuance of the same that they had engaged him to celebrate the sabbath of Ataroth. But he knew of their doings, and so went by a different route to Ginea. They had, however, concerted with the Pharisees of Ginea and, on the morning of the sabbath, they sent messengers to say to Jesus: "Thou hast taught beautiful things concerning the love of one's neighbor. Thou sayest that one should love his neighbor as himself. Come, then, to Ataroth and heal one of our sick. If thou showest us this sign, we, as well as the Pharisees of Ginea, will all believe in thee and we shall spread thy doctrines throughout the country."

Jesus knew their wickedness and the plot they had laid to entrap him. The man whom, as they pretended, they wanted him to cure, had already for several days lain stiff and dead, but they declared to all the people of the city that he was only in a trance. His wife herself did not know that he was dead. Had Jesus raised him up, they would have said that he was not dead. They went to meet Jesus and conducted him to the house of the dead man, who had been one of the leaders of the Pharisees and had been most active in annoying the disciples. They were carrying the corpse on a litter out into the street as Jesus came up. There were about fifteen Sadducees and a crowd of people standing around. The corpse presented quite a fine appearance, for they had opened and embalmed it, the better to deceive Jesus. But Jesus said: "This man is dead and dead he will remain." They replied that he was only in a trance, and if he was indeed dead, he had only just now died. Jesus responded: "He denied the resurrection of the dead, therefore he will not now arise! Ye have filled him with spices, but behold, with what spices! Uncover his breast!" Thereupon I saw one of them raise the skin like a lid from the dead man's breast, when there broke forth a swarm of worms, squirming and straining to get out. The Sadducees were furious, for Jesus rehearsed aloud and openly all the dead man's sins and delinquencies, saying that these were the worms of his bad conscience, which he had in life covered up, but which were now gnawing at his heart. He reproached them with their deceit and evil design, and spoke very severely of the Sadducees and of the judgment that would fall upon Jerusalem and upon all that would not accept salvation. They hurried the corpse back again into the house. The scene was one of frightful alarm and confusion. As Jesus with the disciples was going to the gate of the city, the excited rabble cast stones after them. They were incited thereto by the Sadducees whom the discovery of the worms and their own wickedness had infuriated.

Among the wicked mob, there were, however, some well-intentioned persons who shed tears. In a bystreet lived some infirm women sick with an issue of blood. They believed in Jesus, and from a distance implored his aid, for, as unclean, they dared not approach him. Knowing their need, he compassionately went through their street. When he had passed, they followed in his footsteps kiss-ing them. He looked around upon them, and they were healed.

Jesus went on for almost three hours to a hill in the neighborhood of Engannim, a place lying almost in a line with Ginea, though in another valley some hours to the south. It was on the direct route to Nazareth through Endor and Nain, about seven hours from the latter.

Jesus spent the night on this hill, in the shed of a public inn where, too, he took some refreshment brought from Galilee by the disciples who had come thither to meet him. They were Andrew, the bridegroom Nathaniel, and two servants of the so-called centurion of Capernaum. They urged Jesus to hurry, as the man's son was so ill. Jesus replied that he would go at the right time.

This centurion was a retired officer who had once been

Map 18: The Healing of the Nobleman's Son
July 29–August 7, AD 30

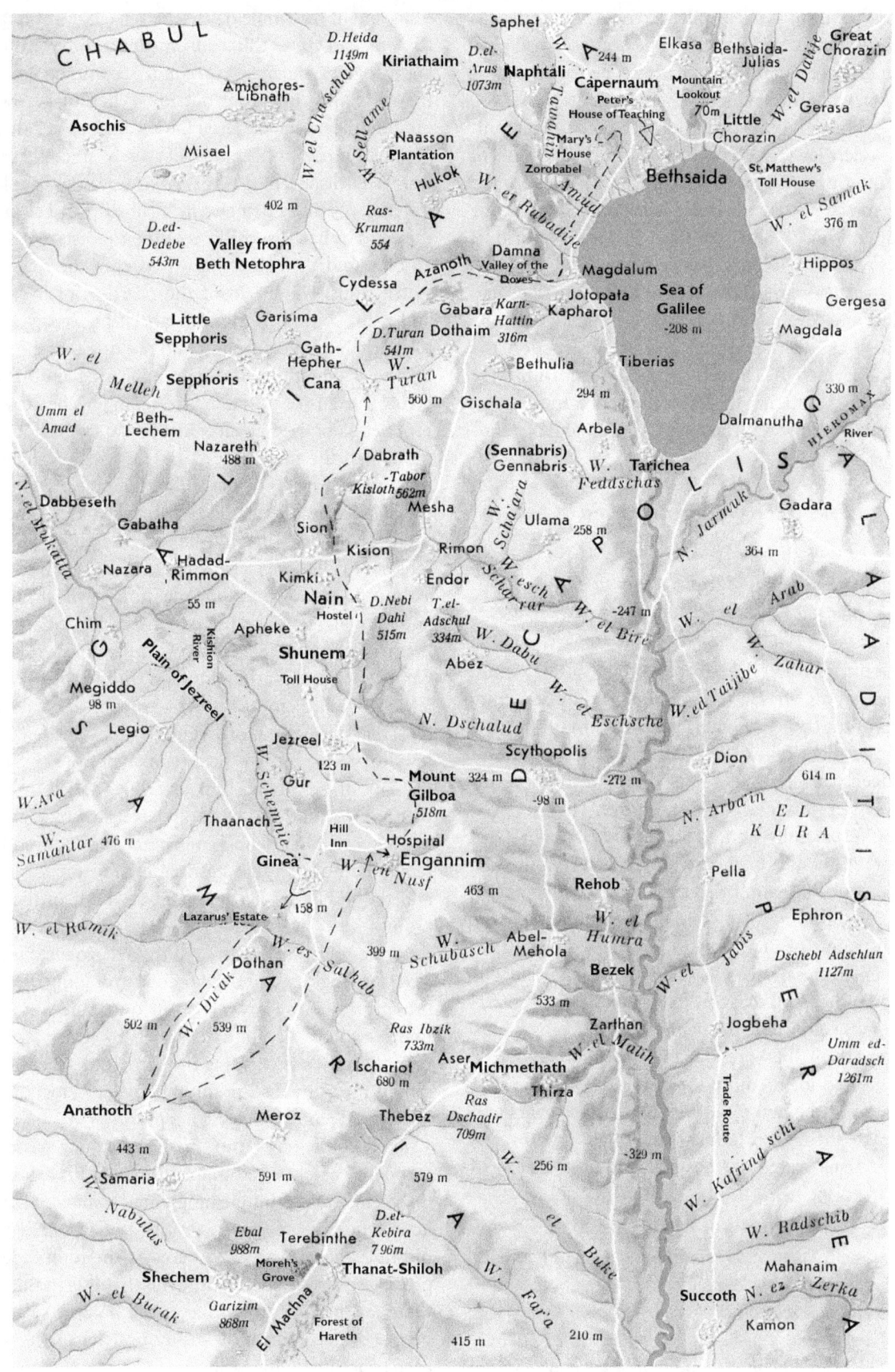

Ginea—Ataroth—Engannim—Nain—Cana—Capernaum—Bethsaida

governor of a part of Galilee under Herod Antipas. He was a well-disposed man and, in the late persecution, had protected the disciples against the Pharisees; he had also provided them with money and other necessaries. As yet, however, he was not quite believing, although he put faith in the miracles. He was very desirous of one in behalf of his son, both through natural affection and also to put the Pharisees to shame. The disciples likewise were eager for it, saying with him: "Then the Pharisees will be furious! Then they will see who he is that we follow!"

It was in this spirit that Andrew and Nathaniel had undertaken the commission to Jesus, who knew well the bottom of their heart. He gave another instruction the next morning when the two servants of the centurion were converted. They were pagan slaves, and had brought food with them. They now returned with Andrew and Nathaniel to Capernaum.

Jesus in Engannim and Nain

Monday, July 31, AD 30 (Ab 12)

Jesus and three of his disciples went to Engannim, where he had some distant relatives who were Essenes. He taught in the synagogue and was well received.

FROM the inn on the hill Jesus proceeded to Engannim, which was not far off. He was accompanied by Saturnin, by the son of the bridegroom of Cana's maternal aunt, and by the son of the widow of Obed of Jerusalem, a youth of about sixteen years. Jesus had some distant relatives in this place. They were Essenes of Anne's family. They received Jesus very respectfully and as an intimate friend. They dwelt apart at one side of the city, and led a very pure life, many of them being unmarried and living together as in a cloister. They, however, no longer strictly observed the ancient discipline of the Essenes; they dressed like others and frequented the synagogue. They supported in Engannim a kind of hospital that was full of the sick and suffering of all sects, and where the poor were fed at long tables. They received all that presented themselves, supported them, and cared for them. In the dormitories of the sick, they always put the bed of a bad man between two good ones that, by their exhortations, they might try to make him better. Jesus visited this hospital, and healed some of the sick.

Tuesday, August 1, AD 30 (Ab 13)

Many came to hear Jesus speak today as he taught in the synagogue. He spoke of the deeds of Elijah, and mentioned the three holy kings who had come from the East. When he had finished speaking, he healed many sick people. Later, he slipped away from the crowd and withdrew to pray alone in the hills.

Jesus taught the whole day in the synagogue of Engannim. Crowds had come thither from the country around, and because the synagogue could not accommodate them all, they remained in troops outside. When one crowd came out, another went in. Jesus taught here as at other places on this journey, only not so severely since these people were well-disposed. It was then as now, the people of the different localities being well- or ill-disposed according to the good or bad dispositions of their priests.

Jesus told them that he would cure the sick after the instructions. He taught of the nearness of the kingdom and of the coming of the Messiah, citing passages from the scriptures and the prophets and proving that the time had arrived. He mentioned Elijah, his words and his visions, giving the date of the latter, and telling his hearers that the prophet had raised an altar in a grotto to the honor of the mother of the future Messiah. He made a calculation of the time which could be no other than the present, warned them that the scepter had been taken from Judah, and recalled to them the journey of the three kings. Jesus referred to all these facts in a general way, as if speaking of a third person, making no mention at all of his mother and himself. He spoke also of compassion, recommending them to treat the Samaritans kindly, and explained the parable of the Samaritan, though without mentioning Jericho. He told them of his own experience of the Samaritans, that they were more willing to assist the Jews than the Jews them. He related the circumstance of the Samaritan woman, of her giving him to drink (a piece of courtesy that a Jew would not so easily have shown a Samaritan), and how well her people in general had received him. He taught here also of the chastisement in store for Jerusalem and the publicans, of whom some dwelt in the country around.

While Jesus was teaching in the synagogue, numbers of sick from the city and the whole surrounding district were brought thither. They were laid on litters and cushions under awnings all along the streets by which Jesus was to pass, their friends standing by them. It was the rule that all sick of the same disease should be placed together. It was like a great fair of suffering people.

Jesus came out from the instruction, passed along through the sick, who humbly implored his aid, and while instructing and admonishing cured about forty persons, lame, blind, mute, gouty, dropsical, fever-stricken, etc. I did not see any possessed here. As the multitude was so great, Jesus went upon a little hill that was in the city, and there taught; but the throng at last became such that the people pressed into houses, mounted to the roofs, and even broke down the walls.

Seeing this confusion, Jesus disappeared in the crowd,

left the city, and took a steep byway into the mountains where there was a solitary place. [C4] His three disciples followed, but after long seeking found him not till night. He was praying. They asked him how they, too, should occupy themselves in prayer, and he gave them in few words some petitions of the "Our Father," for instance: "Hallowed be thy Name! Forgive us our trespasses as we forgive those that trespass against us, and deliver us from evil!" He added: "Now say these words and put them in practice," and he gave them on this point some admirable instructions. They were very faithful in following his injunction whenever he did not converse with them or when he walked alone.

The disciples always carried with them now some food in pouches, and when other wayfarers passed, even off on the byways, they hurried after them in obedience to the words of Jesus, and shared with them, especially if they were poor, whatever they needed.

Engannim was a Levitical city. It was built on the declivity of a valley that extended toward Jezreel across the claw of a mountain range that ran in an easterly direction. A brook flowed northward through the valley. The inhabitants carried on spinning and the manufacture of cloth for priests' vestments. They made also tassels, silk fringes, and balls for trimming the borders of these robes, upon which the women sewed. The people here were very good.

Jesus passed Jezreel and Endor, and toward evening arrived at Nain, going unnoticed to an inn outside the city.

Wednesday, August 2, AD 30 (Ab 14)

Accompanied by three disciples, Jesus went to the town of Nain. There he met the widow of Nain—Maroni—whose sister was married to James the Greater. Maroni introduced Jesus to another widow who, like herself, wished to serve his work and help the community of his followers.

The widow of Nain, the sister of the wife of James the Greater, had been informed by Andrew and Nathaniel of Jesus's near approach, and she was awaiting his arrival. With another widow she now went out to the inn to welcome him. They cast themselves veiled at his feet. The widow of Nain begged Jesus to accept the offer of the other good widow, who wished to put all she possessed into the treasury of the holy women for the maintenance of the disciples and for the poor, whom she herself also wanted to serve. Jesus graciously accepted her offer, while he instructed and consoled her and her friend. They had brought some provisions for a repast, which along with a sum of money they handed over to the disciples. The latter was sent to the women at Capernaum for the common treasury.

Jesus took some rest here with the disciples. He had on the preceding day taught in Engannim with indescribable effort and had cured the sick, after which he had journeyed thence to Nain, a distance of about seven hours. The widow, lately introduced to Jesus, told him of another woman named Mary who likewise desired to give what she possessed for the support of the disciples. But Jesus replied that she should keep it till later when it would be more needed. This woman was an adulteress, and had been, on account of her infidelity, repudiated by her husband, a rich Jew of Damascus. She had heard of Jesus's mercy to sinners, was very much touched, and had no other desire than to do penance and be restored to grace. She had visited Martha, with whose family she was distantly related, had confessed to her her transgression, and begged her to intercede for her with the mother of Jesus. She gave over to her also a part of her wealth. Martha, Johanna Chusa, and Veronica, full of compassion for the sinner, interested themselves in her case, and took her at once to Mary's dwelling at Capernaum. Mary looked at her gravely and allowed her to stand for a long time at a distance. But the woman supplicated with burning tears and vehement sorrow: "O Mother of the prophet! Intercede for me with thy Son, that I may find favor with God!" She was possessed by a mute devil and had to be guarded, for in her paroxysms she could not cry for help and the devil drove her into fire or water. When she came again to herself, she would lie in a corner weeping piteously. Mary sent in behalf of the unhappy creature a messenger to Jesus, who replied that he would come in good time and heal her.

Women Carrying Water

SUPPLEMENTS

✥

Olive Trees in Hinnom Valley

North Walls of Jerusalem

MYSTICISM, MIRACLES, AND WONDERS

The Miracles of Jesus Regarding Himself

Theophany in the Life of Jesus

Holy Scripture records three theophanies in Jesus's earthly life: at the *Baptism* by John (Matt. 3:16–17) on September 23, AD 29; at the *Theophany in the Temple* (John 12:27–28) on March 20, AD 33; and at the *Transfiguration on Mount Tabor* (Matt. 17:1–5) on April 3/4, AD 31. On each of these occasions, through the sounding of a heavenly voice, the First Person of the Trinity bore witness to the divinity of the Second Person in Jesus the human being:

The Baptism in the Jordan

Theophany in the Temple: The Voice from on High

At the *Baptism* with the words, "And when Jesus was baptized, he went up immediately from the water, and behold, the heavens were opened and he saw the Spirit of God descending like a dove, and alighting on him; and lo, a voice from heaven, saying, *This is my beloved Son, with whom I am well pleased*"—witnessing thereby to the natural divine sonship of the divine human being and our status as God's children by adoption effected through baptism.

At the *Theophany in the Temple* through the words, "Now is my soul troubled. And what shall I say? 'Father, save me from this hour'? No, for this purpose I have come to this hour. 'Father, glorify thy name.' Then a voice came from heaven, *I have glorified it, and I will glorify it again*"—for the heavenly Father already glorified his only-begotten Son. He did so in the eternal intra-trinitarian creation, in the *Birth* of Jesus through the Gloria-singing angels, at the *Baptism* through the same witnessing voice, and in the *countless miracles* worked by Jesus. And the same Father will further glorify him. He will do so on Mount Tabor through the *Transfiguration*, at the *Passion* through the triumph of Jesus over the devil, at the *Resurrection* through the victory over death, at the *Ascension* through his participation in the rulership of the Father, and finally, in the *Conversion* of all who are of good will.

At the *Transfiguration* on Mount Tabor this same voice says, "And after six days Jesus took with him Peter and James and John his brother, and led them up a high mountain apart. And he was transfigured before them, and his face shone like the sun, and his garments became white as light. And behold, there appeared to them Moses and Elijah, talking with him. And Peter said to Jesus, 'Lord, it is well that we are here; if you wish, I will make three booths here, one for you and one for Moses and one for Elijah.' He was still speaking, when lo, a bright cloud overshadowed them, and a voice from the cloud said, *This is my beloved Son, with whom I am well pleased; listen to him.*" This was said to strengthen the faith of the three apostles who were present for the sake of their apostolic efficacy.†

Transfiguration

The essence of all genuine Christian mysticism lies in a select pre-revelation of the final goal. And so the two transfigurations of Jesus during his time on earth signify climaxes of this mysticism. For to make steady progress along a difficult path one must at least dimly descry the goal, just as the archer can confidently let fly his arrow only if his target is clearly in view. Thus does the apostle Thomas say to Jesus (John 14:5), "Lord, we do not know where you are going; how can we know the way?" Now, Christ's goal was not the glorification of the soul only, but of the body also; and it is this goal that he reveals to some of his companions by transfiguring himself in his body before them.

The first witness to a transfiguration, on the night of September 15/16, AD 29 on the Plain of Jezreel (today's Merdsch Ibn Amir), is Jesus's friend Eliud, the old Essene from Nazareth. As Jesus walks before him, Eliud remarks how well-formed and beautiful is his body. Jesus speaks to him of his coming Passion, when his body will lose all its beauty. As they pause in their journey at midnight, Jesus tells Eliud he wishes to show him who he is and what will become of his body and his kingdom.

Deep in prayer, the Master looks up to the heavens. A cloud descends and envelops them, and then a heavenly glow lights up in the heights and descends upon them. The figure of Jesus appears all shimmering and quite transparent. At first Eliud stands looking upward as if in profound ecstasy. Then he sinks down, pressing his face against the ground until the light, and all other aspects of

Jesus Transfigured

the manifestation, have passed away. Jesus continues on his way, and Eliud follows behind, speechless and in awe of what he has seen.

The next three to witness Jesus transfigured are the apostles Peter, James the Greater, and John—Peter, in his love for Christ and in the power of the primacy accorded

---

† Note that in her visions of the transfiguration Anne Catherine saw also the prophet Malachi together with Moses and Elijah.

him, as representative of the Church Militant; James the Greater, through his privilege as the first martyr among the apostles, as representative of the Suffering Church; and John, in his heartfelt personal love for the Lord, his virginal nature, and his calling as the visionary of the Apocalypse, as representative of the Church Triumphant.

On the afternoon of April 3, AD 31, Jesus climbs Mount Tabor with the three. They have no provisions, for Jesus has forbidden them to bring any, saying that they will be satiated to overflowing (cf. Ps. 16:15).

Jesus does not take the nearest way to the top but pauses frequently at the different caves and places made memorable by the sojourn of the prophets. There he unites with them in prayer and explains to them manifold mysteries, presumably as an indication of the progressive stages of divine revelation through the prophets as forerunners of his appearance.

Once atop the mountain, Jesus summons his companions to pray on their knees with upraised hands. They kneel in a half-circle around him. He kneels also, while leaning against a projecting rock, and speaks—praying and teaching them the Lord's Prayer, interspersing the several petitions with verses from the Psalms and with instructions, wonderfully profound and sweet, upon the mysteries of Creation and Redemption. His words are extraordinarily loving, like those of one inspired, and the disciples are by them wholly inebriated.

John, Peter, and James Kneel at the Transfiguration

In the beginning of his instruction, Jesus tells them he will show them who he is, that they will behold him glorified, so they might not waver in faith when his enemies mock and maltreat him—when they will behold him in death, shorn of all glory.

The sun sets and it is dark, but the apostles have not remarked the fact, so entrancing are Jesus's words and bearing. He becomes brighter and brighter, and apparitions of angelic spirits hover around him. Peter sees them, for he interrupts Jesus with the question, "Master, what does this mean?" Jesus answers "They serve me!" Peter, quite out of himself, stretches forth his hands, exclaiming "Master, are we not here? We will serve thee in all things!"

Jesus meantime continues to shine with ever-increasing splendor, until he becomes as if transparent. The circle around them is so lit up in the darkness of night that each little plant can be distinguished on the green sod as if in clear daylight. The three apostles are so penetrated, so ravished that, when the light reaches a certain degree, they cover their heads, prostrate themselves on the ground, and there remain lying.

It is about midnight when this glory reaches its height. There is a shining pathway reaching from heaven to earth, and on it angelic spirits of different choirs, all in constant movement.

The apostles lie, ravished in ecstasy rather than in sleep, prostrate on their faces.

Then I see three shining figures approaching Jesus in the light. Their coming appears perfectly natural. It is like that of one who steps from the darkness of night into a place brilliantly illuminated. Two of them appear in a more definite form, a form more like the corporeal. They address Jesus and converse with him. They are Moses and Elijah. The third apparition speaks no word; it is more ethereal, more spiritual. That is Malachi.

I hear Moses and Elijah greet Jesus, and I hear him speaking to them of his Passion and of Redemption. Their being together appears perfectly simple and natural. Moses and Elijah do not look aged nor decrepit, as when they left the earth. They are, on the contrary, in the bloom of youth.

Moses tells Jesus how rejoiced he is to see him who had led himself and his people out of Egypt, and who is now once more about to redeem them. He refers to the numerous types of the Savior in his own time, and utters deeply significant words upon the paschal lamb and the Lamb of God. Elijah is quite the opposite of Moses. He appears to be more refined, more lovable, of a sweeter disposition.

But both Elijah and Moses are very dissimilar from the apparition of Malachi, for in the former one can trace something human, something earthly in form and countenance; yes, there is even a family likeness between them. Malachi, however, looked quite different. There is in his appearance something supernatural. He looks like an angel, like the personification of strength and repose. He is more tranquil, more spiritual than the others.

Jesus speaks with them of all the sufferings he has endured up to the present, and of all that still awaits him. He relates the history of his Passion in detail, point by point. Elijah and Moses frequently express their emotion and joy. They constantly refer to the types of the mysteries of which Jesus is speaking, and praise God for having from all eternity dealt in mercy toward his people. But Malachi keeps silence.

The disciples raise their heads, gaze long upon the glory of Jesus, and behold Moses, Elijah, and Malachi.

When in describing his Passion Jesus comes to his exaltation on the cross, he extends his arms at the words: "So shall the Son of Man be lifted up!" His face is turned toward the south, he is entirely penetrated with light, and his robe flashes with a bluish white gleam. He, the prophets, and the three apostles—all are raised above the earth.

With Arms Extended

And now the prophets separate from Jesus, Elijah and Moses vanishing toward the east, Malachi westward into the darkness.

When the three apostles have returned to their usual waking state, a cloud of white light descends upon them, like the morning dew floating over the meadows.

I see the heavens open above Jesus and the vision of the most holy Trinity, God the Father seated on a throne. He looks like an aged priest, and at his feet are crowds of angels and celestial figures.

A stream of light descends upon Jesus, and the apostles hear above them, like a sweet, gentle sighing, a voice pronouncing the words: "This is my beloved Son in whom I am well pleased. Hear ye him!"

Fear and trembling fall upon them. Overcome by the sense of their own human weakness and the glory they behold, they cast themselves face downward on the earth. They tremble in the presence of Jesus, in whose favor they have just heard the testimony of his heavenly Father.

Jesus goes to them, touches them, and says: "Arise, and fear not!" They arise, and behold Jesus alone. It is now approaching three in the morning.

While going down, Jesus talks of what has taken place, and impresses upon the disciples that they should tell no one of the vision they have seen, until the Son of Man shall have risen from the dead.

The Luminosity of Jesus's Figure

Occasionally those present also see a supernatural luminousness around the figure of Jesus. For instance, at his baptism by John, Jesus is completely permeated with light and looks as if transparent when the voice from heaven sounds. And as he descends a mountain on the morning of September 29, AD 29, into the valley of the shepherds of Bethlehem, some shepherds see him glowing and surrounded by light—for many of these simple people are blessed. During his second walking on the Sea of Galilee in the night of January 29/30, AD 31, his figure is also luminous. And on June 21, AD 31, Jesus glows as if surrounded by a bright cloud as, filled with ecstasy and joy, he prays within the circle of his apostles and disciples on a hill just

Luminous Figure of Jesus Walking on the Sea

in front of the teaching mountain near Gabara: "I praise you, Father, Lord of heaven and earth, because you have hidden these things from the wise and the intelligent but revealed them to infants." (Matt. 11:25)

Miracles Involving the World of Nature

Miracles Involving Lifeless Matter

As all creation, including lifeless matter, is subject to the power of God, so do his miracles directly affecting matter also bear witness to Jesus, whose divinity leads to the salvation of human beings.

Stilling a Storm

Three times Jesus miraculously stills a storm on the Sea of Galilee. On two of these occasions (the nights of March 4/5 and 5/6, AD 30) he does so from a distance—from Sepphoris and from Nazareth.

While standing in prayer at these two places, Jesus appears as though hovering over the imperiled boats, and also lays his hand upon the helmsman's wheel, without however being seen by those in the boat—and each time the storm immediately subsides. On the third occasion (the night of November 21/22, AD 30), when the disciples awaken Jesus far out at sea, it is through his words that he stills the storm. (Matt. 8:23–27)

Twice Jesus walks upon the moving waters of the sea without wetting his feet, and both times beckons Peter to join him upon the water. At dusk on the evening of December 7/8, AD 30, well out at sea, Jesus walks upon the water past the boat, still quite distant. The disciples see the figure, but not knowing whether it is he or a ghost, cry out loudly in fear, whereupon the Master comes to them. (Matt. 14:22–33)

Jesus walks upon the sea for the second time, from the northeast toward the southwest, on the night of January 29/30, AD 31. He is glowing, and a shimmer surrounds him, so that his figure appears reflected upside down in the water. After passing opposite Peter's boat, Jesus proceeds diagonally between two night-watch boats with torches burning; and as he does so, those on board cry out in fear and blow their horns, thinking him a ghost. The apostles on Peter's boat, just then steering by the light of a

Walking on the Sea, as Peter Sinks

night-watch boat to resume their course, look up and see Jesus drawing near. He seems to float along more quickly than one walking. As he nears the boat, the water stills and all happens again as before, with Peter venturing forth upon the waves but finally sinking—until both climb aboard by a small ladder at the side.

Opening the locked door of a synagogue, and the gate at the place of teaching in the temple by simply laying on his hands also reveals Jesus's power over inanimate matter. Likewise the miraculous changing of water into wine, which takes place on December 28, AD 29 at the wedding of Cana. (John 2:6–11)

Through his touch, Jesus five times multiplies food. The first occasion takes place on March 13, AD 30 in Nazara (at the northern end of the Plain of Jezreel), when he buys bread for slaves who are working, and distributes it to them. But there is no great uproar on this occasion, primarily because he immediately continues toward Ginea.

Multiplying of Food

The second increase occurs following the Sermon on the Mount, which takes place between Berotha and Kades-Nephthali on July 16, AD 30. Here Jesus blesses the portions of bread and fish before they are distributed to the listeners. These portions, brought from neighboring cities, are not nearly sufficient for the several thousand present, but after being blessed by Jesus all are filled, with even many baskets of scraps left over for the poor to take home with them.

Jesus for the third time miraculously multiplies food on December 4, AD 30, as can be read in the itinerary for this date.

The feeding of the five thousand known through the gospels takes place on January 29, AD 31, between four o'clock and five o'clock in the evening. (Matt. 14:15 ff.) Jesus makes small cuts into the five loaves with a bone knife; and the fish, which have been split lengthwise, he divides into crosspieces. After that he takes one of the loaves in his hands, raises it on high and prays. He does the same with one of the fish. Jesus now blesses the bread, the fish, and also some honey, and begins to break the cross-sections of bread into pieces, and these again into smaller portions. Every portion immediately increases to the original size of the loaf, and on its surface appear, as before, dividing lines. Jesus then breaks the individual pieces into portions sufficiently large to satisfy a man, and gives with each a piece of fish.

Saturnin of Patras, who is by his side, lays the piece of fish upon the portion of bread, and a young disciple of the Baptist, a shepherd's son who later on became a bishop, lays upon each a small quantity of honey. There is no perceptible diminution in the fish, and the honeycomb appears to increase.

Thaddeus lays the portions of bread upon which are the fish and honey in flat baskets that are then borne away to those most in need. As soon as the empty baskets are brought back, they are exchanged for full ones—and so the work goes on for about two hours until all are fed.

The apostles and disciples are for the most part occupied in carrying the baskets here and there and in distributing their contents, but the whole while all are silent and filled with amazement at the sight of such a multiplication.

Jesus works in the same way also on the occasion of the miraculous feeding of the four thousand (Matt. 15:32 ff.) on March 15, AD 31, which takes place after a sermon on a more elevated mountainside to the northeast, near Bethsaida-Julias.

Finally, the miracle with the fruit should be mentioned, which can be read about in the present book under the date of July 6, AD 30.

The Draught of Fish and the Fig Tree

The miracle of Peter's abundant catch of fish is described under the date of November 26, AD 30, and the cursing of a fig tree under July 30, AD 32 and March 20, AD 33. (Matt. 21:18) In the case of the cursings of a barren fig tree, in each instance the Master hungers—yet in truth his hunger is for the souls of the Jews and for their conversion. The nourishment Jesus seeks is souls who desire him, as is the case also of his desiring water of Dinah the Samaritan woman at Jacob's well on July 26, AD 30.

Abundant Catch of Fish

But the fig tree is a visible sign also of the Old Law, just as the grape vine is a visible sign of the New Law—this being the point of the parable Jesus relates after laying the curse on the barren fig tree on July 30, AD 32 (Luke 13:6–9), as also the explanation of this given by St. Thomas Aquinas (see L. 13, 6 of his *Commentary on Matthew* 21:18).

The Healings of Jesus

Jesus's Assessment of the Value of Healings

Jesus never regards miraculous healing as an end in itself, or as the means to some mere practical advantage. Such healings hold no value for him if they serve to awaken respect for him only in the moment, but fail to convert people from their sins. When on January 17, AD 33, in Shechem, the apostles ask Jesus to go on to Nazareth and there make known his power and his mission, he is unwilling, for as he says, miracles avail nothing if those who witness them do not look further and reform themselves. Indeed, he adds, what has he accomplished with his signs and miracles—even such miracles as the feeding of the five thousand and the raising of Lazarus—if the people know of these and yet desire still more? Signs and miracles work no lasting good if in the end they offer people a means to forget how sinful and loveless they are—in which case teaching is far more salutary than miracles.

The Impression Made by His Miracles

Jesus's humility and earnest bearing when healing the sick is truly wondrous, and especially astonishing is his patience and physical endurance as he moves among long rows of the sick—often for hours at a time—pausing with each in a loving way, admonishing, comforting, healing, and offering pastoral advice. Nor is there anything overt or alarming in his gestures. All transpires quietly and naturally. Only among some of the unbelieving, and especially those hostile to him, do his miracles elicit fear.

Healing the Sick Along the Road

The Logistics of the Healings

It is no wonder that as news of the healings spreads, many sick gather wherever Jesus is to appear. Scarcely has his next stop been made known than multitudes of the sick are brought there from huts and villages throughout the region. In cities, the sick are laid out on stretchers with cushions—often with awnings set over them—before houses fronting the streets where it is said Jesus will pass by. For major sermons in the open air—upon hills and teaching mountains, as well as at bathing places—Jesus makes prior arrangements through his disciples for the sick to be brought and arranged in rows according to type of illness. In the case of synagogues where Jesus is to speak,

Healing the Sick Before a City Gate

it becomes customary to lay out the sick in the plaza before the entrance. On larger city squares, or in front of city gates, long rows of tents are usually set up to shield the sick from the sun as they await Jesus.

Different Types of Healings

Jesus does not heal always in the same way; but even so, his manner of healing unerringly differs from that of all other miracle-workers before him in that—through his personal union with the Godhead—he is capable of immediately healing each and every illness simply by willing it so.

But it was not the intention of Jesus to redeem people merely through his divine power, but also through the mystery of his human incarnation; and this is why he often includes in his miracle-working a feature that relates to his human nature, to the soul-condition of the one to be healed, and to useful instruction for his disciples.

Sometimes Jesus heals at a distance through prayer, or then again by a glance; sometimes he commands, other times he lays on his hands; sometimes he bends over the sick, other times he takes them in his arms; on one occasion he may command the sick person to bathe, but another time mix his spittle and some earth and with it rub the eyes of the blind. Upon some of the sick he breathes; others he blesses. Some are healed merely by touching him, others he heals without turning to them directly.

Just as the Son of God, in becoming a human being, chose the body of the purest of all creation—not assuming his humanity in any unnatural way—so does he make use often of the simplest and, through his spirit's blessing, purest of created things as the means for healing: often, for example, water and oil that have been blessed, and then later—as the sick one convalesces—bread and grape juice that have been blessed. Jesus heals in these different ways also as a means to instruct the disciples through example in the proper form for each treatment, according to the type of sickness or soul malady to be healed.

The Miraculous Process of Healing

The healing processes that Jesus sets in motion—that is, the immediate effects of his initial healing act—take different forms also, each appropriate to the particular condition of the one to be healed. For example, a hunchback is not in an instant upright nor a crooked bone suddenly straight. We should not take this to mean that Jesus could not effect such sudden alterations, did he so will. Rather, he avoids what is sudden, for his miracles are meant not as spectacles but as works of mercy and emblems of his mission—namely reconciliation, forgiveness, teaching, liberation, and redemption.

Jesus does not shatter the order of nature, but merely relaxes its strictures. He does not sever knots, but unties them. He can release all because he possesses every key. He unlocks the chains and bonds of temporal privation and punishment with manifold keys of love, then teaches and heals and helps in endless ways, finally opening the gate of atonement to heaven, and also to limbo, with the key of keys—the cross.

What Jesus Requires for Healing

Just as the Master desires of those who would partake of his redemption that they be co-workers alongside him, so must the one to be healed evince faith, hope, love, repentance, and reform as evidence of their cooperation and worthiness, in order to be set in the way of convalescence. And so in each healing Jesus offers just the right treatment to enlist the participation of the recipient's soul, whereby the sickness and its healing together form a visible sign for spiritual sickness (sin and its punishment) and for spiritual healing (pardon on God's part and reform on the part of the one healed).

The Psychological Effects of Healing

With all of Jesus's healings, a kind of transition takes place in the psyche of the one to be healed according to type of sickness or sin. For a few moments a stillness and inwardness comes over those for whom he prays or upon whom he lays his hands, and then they arise convalescing as if out of a momentary faint. It is immediately clear that those healed have experienced a comforting grace, for they are noticeably strengthened in their soul, more mature—not only stronger in faith and filled with joy, but more seriously reflective about moral reformation of their individual conduct of life. Yet it sometimes happens that this better mood does not endure, and some prior indiscretion returns to take its place, so that the person relapses into the previous sickness.

As for the interior effects called forth in onlookers, a distinction must be made between the healing of pagans and the healing of Jews, in that the miracles Jesus works among the former are more striking and singular. In this respect they are more like the healings wrought among the pagans by the apostles and saints of later times, which also are more conspicuous in nature, often contradicting the normal course of nature. For pagans in general stood in greater need of a shock, whereas the need for the Jews was more that of a release. This is also undoubtedly why Jesus told his apostles and disciples that in his name they would do still greater things than he.

Jesus and the Lepers

When healing lepers, Jesus does not linger, but neither does he pass quickly on. With some he initiates the approach, turning off the path and hurrying to them like a loving friend bent on rescue. Others he sidesteps, leaving them to follow after him pleading earnestly, sometimes at great length, before he heals them.

He leaves behind his companions, and initially even the disciples, during such healings so as not to expose them to the terrifying fear of infection. Yet upon his return (November 17, AD 30) to the waiting disciples after healing a leper, Jesus tells them that if one has faith and a pure heart, even lepers can be touched.

At his touch the lepers' sores quickly dry and fall away as scales; the red spots that remain fade, but at differing rates according to the nature and merit of the one healed. Some he commands to lie down by their huts in a washing trough, and then heals them by holding his hands over the water. Others wash themselves in water Jesus has used to bathe his own feet, and they are healed.

Healing Lepers in the Open Air

The law of the land requires that any who have recovered from leprosy must present themselves to the nearest priest or Pharisee to have their chests examined, and Jesus often turns this requirement to advantage by invoking it after healing lepers at places where he wishes to benefit the officials in question with a confirmation of his teaching. It is notable that when healing lepers, Jesus often lets fall the remark that those in question contracted their disease through thoughtless sins against the sixth commandment.

Mysticism, Miracles, and Wonders

The lepers mostly live in groups in areas staked out or marked off in some other way to indicate the range of movement allowed them. None venture near them, and any communications are entered into from afar. Food is provided at designated locations in bowls which after such use are not taken back but destroyed and buried. The same is done with any utensils provided, which are for this reasons always of the poorest quality. The lepers mostly wear long, ungirded white robes with hoods to which is affixed a black cloth (with eye-holes) to cover the face.

Healing the Man with a Withered Hand

Gout and the Lame

When Jesus heals those suffering from gout, they are immediately relieved of their pain and can begin to move about like the healthy, but the growth does not simply disappear, rather does it fade away gradually—though usually quite quickly. When Jesus touches the lame, their muscles are made whole: they sit up, meekly raise themselves, throw themselves down before Jesus, and are healed. Yet the full strength and suppleness of the limbs returns only after a while, sometimes within hours, sometimes within days. When healing lame or stiff arms and hands, Jesus slowly moves them up and down, then strokes them, and soon they are again mobile; growths, however, disappear after several hours.

Cramps and Broken Bones

Those suffering from cramps are immediately healed, and their fevers broken; however, they are not simply refreshed in the blink of an eye and fully restored, but recover rather more like wilted plants after a rain. After such a healing, Jesus occasionally instructs those affected to sit in the sun. In the case of broken limbs, the bones fuse together as Jesus takes hold of the break. On December 2, AD 30, in the synagogue at Capernaum, Jesus bids the man with the withered hand approach, takes his hand, and after bending the fingers straight, says "Stretch out your hand!" The man stretches out his hand, and it is healed.

Healings of the Blind, Deaf, and Mute

With the blind, Jesus usually puts some spittle on his thumbs, placing them then over the eyes while looking up in prayer. On March 16, AD 31, he touches the eyes of a

Healing Two Blind Men in Capernaum

blind man with his tongue, lays his hand upon him, and asks whether he sees anything. The man opens his eyes, staring, and says, "I see people as big as trees walking by." Jesus puts his hands on his eyes and has him look again—and he sees normally. This manner of healing is apportioned to the boastfulness of the man healed, which is why Jesus forbids him to go straightaway to the city and boast of his healing (Mark 8:22–26). Jesus also once uses oil to heal two blind men, as can be read above under the date December 1, AD 30.

When healing the deaf, Jesus puts his fingers into their ears; with the mute, his thumbs and forefingers under the tongue; and with the deaf and mute, both. When the mute are healed, their speech is at first slurred, but soon they cry out in joy, and talk and sing. In the case of group healings in institutions for the deaf, those healed sing a poignant, single-toned psalm of thanksgiving improvised in a remarkable way under the influence of a kind of grace. (See September 19, AD 30.)

Flows of Blood and Dropsy

Women with flows of blood Jesus does not touch, but heals with a glance. In one instance, on October 14, AD 30, he has the one to be healed kiss the sash or girdle of his robe, and speaks to the effect that "I heal you through the mystery" (or it may have been: I heal you in the intention) in which this girdle has been worn from beginning, and will be worn to the end." With others he lays the ends of his sash upon their heads. Then again, some are healed suddenly by secretly touching his cloak, or by following in his tracks.

When, on December 1, AD 30, Jesus says—on the way to the house of Jairus after the widow with a flow of blood, Enue from Caesarea-Philippi, touches the seam of his cloak—"Someone touched me; for I notice that power has gone forth from me" (Luke 8:46), this signifies the same healing power of which the Evangelist Luke (6:19) says: "And all in the crowd were trying to touch him, for power came out from him and healed all of them."

Of this, Dionysius the Carthusian, in his *Commentary to the Gospel of Luke*, Article 22, writes "This power, however, proceeded from the divinity of Christ as its first and principal cause, and from the humanity of Christ as its secondary and instrumental cause, for the humanity of Christ was the ensouled instrument of his divinity, even as our bodies are the instruments of our souls."

In the case of those suffering from dropsy (both those able to stagger up to him on their own, and those borne to him on a litter), on most occasions Jesus places his hands upon the head and stomach, and then, as he speaks some words, they are able to stand erect and go forth quite at their ease, while water issues forth from them in the form of sweat.

Enue Touches the Seam of Jesus's Cloak

The Sick Whom Jesus Does Not Heal

Jesus could of course cure any of the sick, but he does so only for those who believe and repent, often warning them against relapse. Such as these, who believe and repent, he heals in a trice, even the seriously ill who are carried to him; indeed he himself seeks out such as these in hospitals and private houses, taking into account that their severe suffering renders them the more easily overpowered in their will. The mildly ill he heals quickly only if it will benefit their souls.

Other ailing ones, however, who sin somewhat less only because their suffering and discomfort distract them—and do not truly repent—Jesus either turns away, admonishing them to reform, or only alleviates in such wise that their souls will continue to be tamed if only through the effects of their physical limitations.

Some, whose suffering Jesus has already several times relieved in this way and who have relapsed in body and soul, approach him on November 11, AD 30, calling out as he passes, "Lord, Lord! You heal all these severely ill ones, but heal not us!" Then Jesus asks, "Why do you not stretch out your hands to me?" and they immediately stretch out their hands to him. But he says: "Yes, you stretch out these hands, but I cannot embrace the hands of your heart, which you hold back and clench, for you are full of darkness." Then he teaches more on these things and at length heals only those who truly repent.

In some cities where he goes to teach, Jesus performs no healings at all, indicating the reason for this by taking the inhabitants to task for feeling self-important just because he is teaching in their city—as if he had come for the sake of their own inflation. Neither does he heal those who wish only to test his miraculous power, or to boast afterwards about his healings. Yet does he not hold such things against the innocent, but heals them secretly in the night, or returns another time to heal them.

Freedom from Possession

Possession and External Influences

Just as, through its unitary ordering principle, the cosmos and all its aspects stand in a particular relationship with human beings—as does the body likewise with the soul, and the human state in general with animals, plants, and minerals—so also do the stars and the immaterial created substances we call angels and demons stand in relationship with and influence the earth and human beings.

Good spirits or angels serve human beings in their striving to keep the straight path toward God, their ultimate goal. Evil spirits, those fallen away from God whom we call devils or demons or evil spirits, may sometimes overpower human beings in various ways. And God allows this, either to punish those who strive toward evil, or to exalt the virtue of those who stand firm with the help of divine grace in face of such attacks—for in this they dispense on the one hand just punishment to the evil spirits, while on the other they serve to further exalt divine mercy and holiness.

When according to God's wise dispensation an evil spirit overpowers the body of a human being and indwells it—thereby wreaking violent, torturous effects upon that person's bodily organs and lower powers of soul—we speak of *possession* in the proper sense of the word.

When however an evil spirit exercises its influence on human beings from without (that is, does not indwell them), fomenting in them unrest and a tendency toward sin, we speak of *external influences*.

Both these forms of evil action may affect morally sound human beings also, which is why we must further distinguish between *malevolent* and *benevolent* possession or external influence.

That Jesus when walking the earth encountered so many possessed can be explained by his special relationship to the devil, the "prince of this world"—for God incarnated in the flesh precisely to the end of driving out the devil from this world (John 12:31). And to make this campaign against satan the more visible, God permits the devil to run riot in a very obvious way, before being compelled—amid the witness of loud cries against "the Holy One of God" (Mark. 1:24)—to yield to the power of the Christ.

Benevolent Possession

The possessed are often taken along to public teachings of Jesus, where they rage and throw themselves about in an appalling way. But as soon as Jesus commands them to be quiet, they become still. After some time, however, they can be still no longer and resume their thrashing about.

Curing a Raging Possessed

Then Jesus motions with his hand and they fall still again. When he is finished teaching, and commands satan to go forth from the possessed, they slump together for a few moments as though in a faint and then awaken full of good cheer and thankfulness, oblivious to their former state.

Such persons as these, whom we call the benevolently possessed, have fallen into this state through no fault of their own. In place of an evil person who may for a time remain unaffected through the grace and patience of God, the devil will sometimes take possession of some innocent, weak individual with a mysterious relationship to the evil person. In such cases it is as though the good take upon themselves, at least in part, the punishment of the evil, for insofar as we are all members of one body, here too a healthy limb may fall prey—through some secret, inner relationship—to the fault of another, diseased, limb.

Malevolent Possession

Whereas the benevolently possessed merely suffer from time to time, and may otherwise be quite devout, the malevolently possessed are fearsome and more or less in league with satan.

It was the practice in Palestine at the time of Jesus to confine the malevolently possessed in houses with bars. Should Jesus come near such a place, the inmates would commence to rave. Sometimes they might break loose from their fetters and dash into the Master's path, crying, "Here he comes, the prophet, he wants to drive us out," or "What do you want here? What business have you here?" or "Jesus of Nazareth! What have we to do with you? You have come to drive us out. We know you are the Holy One of God!"

It might also happen that some among such possessed would shout out—despite the violent blows of those charged with their confinement—the whole salvation story of Jesus. On such occasions Jesus commands the malevolently possessed to be quiet. Sometimes he commands that their fetters fall away, and miraculously they do. Or he commands them to lie quietly upon the ground until he has finished teaching. When finally he calls out, "Satan, depart," those present often see escaping something like a dark vapor that gathers into a hideous human shadow and disappears.

The Effect of Being Freed

The malevolently possessed who have been freed usually collapse into unconsciousness. Jesus addresses them, grips them by the hand, and commands them to rise. They awaken as out of a dream, sink down upon their knees, give

"Satan, depart!"

thanks, and are completely changed. Thereupon Jesus admonishes them, points out the previous errors of their ways which they are to reform, and occasionally admonishes also any relatives and acquaintances of the released person who may be present.

All witnesses to such incidents are astonished at the power of Jesus. Those favorably inclined say "Surely this man possesses the power of the prophets of old, for even the spirits hasten to his bidding." Opponents, however, especially the Pharisees, noise about that "He drives the devils out with the power of Beelzebub, the prince of devils. Now do we know why he goes to the hills and mountains in the night."

Raisings from the Dead

Jesus's Power to Awaken the Dead

As Jesus himself said (John 10:18), he with the power to give his life and take it back again, possesses equally the power, on the basis of his divinity and merely through his word, to reunite the souls of others—who had been separated from their body in death—with that body again into one unified nature.

Thus does Jesus prove himself Lord over life and death, establishing in this way, already in advance as a prefiguration, the possibility of his own eventual resurrection from death. At the same time, his raising of the dead is a visible sign or symbol of the soul's arising from the death of mortal sin—both original sin and personal sin—to supernatural life through justification and healing, thereby confirming the right and power of Jesus to forgive through his word the sins of others.

Different Forms of Raising from the Dead

On February 7, AD 30, Jesus commands that the burial sheets and garments of the sixteen-year-old daughter of the Essene Jairus of Phasael be loosened. He takes the dead girl by the hand and commands her to arise, whereupon she raises herself up from her bed and stands. Thus is she awakened from the death of the soul. No disciple is present, and Jesus commands that the miracle be kept hidden.

At Gadara, on September 23, AD 30, Jesus calls to life a three-year-old child of heathen parents, who was poisoned by berries, by holding it to his chest and breathing into its face, whereupon the child opens its eyes and stirs. Jesus raises the child on high and commands the two disciples present—Joseph Barsabbas and Nathaniel Chased—to lay their hands on the child's head and bless it.

Towards nine o'clock on the morning on November 13, AD 30, before the gate of Nain, Jesus sprinkles, with water he has blessed, the people standing by the corpse of the youth Martialis (son of Maroni, the widow of Nain), to whom in death he says, "Young man, I tell you, arise!" The young man raises himself into a sitting position, looking around with curiosity and amazement, stands up, and says, "What has happened, how came I here?"

On November 18 and December 1, AD 30, Jesus raises Salome, the daughter of another Jairus, who is head of the synagogue of Capernaum. The first time the girl is only half-dead, which is why Jesus says beforehand that the girl is not dead but only sleeping. He lifts her from her bed, takes her in his arms, breathes upon her, lays her down again on the bed, takes hold of her arm above the hand—as would a doctor—and says, "Young girl, I tell you, arise!" whereupon the twelve-year-old raises herself.

The Master holds her by the hand, she opens her eyes and pulls herself out of bed with the hand of Jesus, who then leads her (for she is still weak and unsteady) into the arms of her waiting parents, commanding them to give her something to eat and also to make no undue commotion over the matter. Peter, James the Greater, and John are present.

Raising of the Daughter of Jairus

Shortly thereafter, Salome relapses, in punishment both for her parents (who remained unbelieving after the first miracle) and for her own foolishness, and now truly dies. Upon the imprecations of the father, Jesus then awakens Salome a second time by sprinkling her corpse with water that has been blessed, praying, and speaking to her (as he takes her hand) the same words he had spoken the first time.

After Salome is raised the second time, Jesus gravely admonishes the parents (who now convert completely) and warns Salome about sensual desire and sin. He has bread and grapes brought, which he blesses and offers to the girl, telling her that in future she should live no longer according to the flesh, following the desires of her sinful blood, but eat rather of the bread of life, the word of God—that she should repent, believe, pray, and do works sacred to God. Witness to these raisings from death are the apostles Peter, James the Greater, John, Matthew, and the disciple Saturnin.

In the early morning of July 26, AD 32, Jesus stands before the coffin of his friend Lazarus of Bethany. The apostles take away the coffin's finely woven cover so that the wrapped corpse is visible. Jesus looks up and prays, then calls out in a strong voice, "Lazarus, come forth!"

At his call the corpse raises itself into a sitting position, and the crowd outside the tomb presses closer. Jesus commands the apostles to turn the crowd away, and they drive them to the front of the cemetery. The apostles remaining by Jesus take away the cloth from the face of Lazarus, who looks as if half asleep, free his hands and feet from the winding sheet, and bring a cloak. Lazarus then climbs out of the coffin and walks through the tomb, swaying like a shadow, the cloak wrapped about him.

Like a somnambulist he walks past Jesus out the door of the tomb, where his sisters and the other women step back timidly as if before a spirit, and without touching him fall to the ground upon their faces. Jesus follows Lazarus from the tomb and takes hold of his hands in a friendly but also solemn way. All proceed to the castle. Lazarus walks tentatively, looking still like a corpse dressed in grave clothes.

Raising of Lazarus

What Jesus bestows upon him when they arrive is, in part, the subject of what follows.

The Bestowal of Supernatural Gifts

Remarkable Conversions

The remarkable conversions wrought by Jesus during his earthly life must be accounted among his mystical acts and miracles. Along with St. Thomas Aquinas, we reckon in general that miraculous healings and raisings of the dead, as well as exorcisms from possession of various sorts, are instances of release from evil, whereas conversions and blessings are to be accounted sharings of the good.

One could debate the relative significance attached to these actions, for as a practical matter reversals of the evils of sickness, possession, and death are in some ways more remarkable than the conferred goods of health, normalcy, and life; but in the end, conversions and blessings, and the thereby conferred gifts of repentance and holiness, are of the greater significance.

The many conversions effected by Jesus, including the remarkable case of Mary Magdalene, are described in considerable detail in the visions of the ministry of Jesus. What remains to be emphasized here is that the great conversions he accomplished during his ministry unfold in different ways depending on and corresponding to the soul-types of those converted.

Thus Magdalene must with great force and an extraordinary spirit of repentance first struggle and pass through several relapses before she is fully converted. Dinah the Samaritan woman is quickly converted—in no time as it were—in response to the words that reveal Jesus to her as the Messiah. Mara the Suphanite's conversion extends over a longer period and with more yearning, but when it occurs, is sudden and complete.

In the case of others, their path to conversion may fluctuate much, and over an extended period. Judas is always vacillating in this way, and in the end perishes. Some are shaken and converted by no more than a glance from Jesus; others through certain words spoken during his sermon, or by being miraculously released from sickness or death or possession; again others, like Nicodemus, through a private conversation or other blessing from Jesus.

Most however are converted by hearing Jesus's teachings, by beholding his healing of the sick, and by the impression that the entire lofty, yet so loving, being of Jesus makes upon them.

Of course the two final causes of all conversions are first and principally the will of the heavenly Father together with the will and prayer of Jesus, and secondly (but just as essential and necessary) the free-will decision made by the one who converts.

The Blessings of Jesus

It is remarkable how often and on how many different occasions Jesus blesses. He blesses human beings, many of them children. He blesses food before its enjoyment. He blesses water, to purify and improve its taste if impure, salty, or bitter—or to use for sprinkling at a baptism. He blesses the oil the apostles and disciples employ to heal the sick when traveling. He sometimes blesses plots of ground to liberate them from dangerous animals. He blesses vineyards, that they may flourish.

Blessing Mother and Child

With some blessings, Jesus's intention is directed toward freedom from evil: from natural and physical evil, from human and moral evil, or from demonic influences. Other blessings are directed toward bestowing good, or providing certain graces and consecrations. In most cases, however, the two species of blessing are closely bound up with one another, as for example in blessing children.

The Outward Form of Blessing

Jesus blesses undrinkable water with the sign of the cross, lingering over certain places on the water's surface with his hand. When blessing water that he will thereafter sprinkle on people, or instruct the disciples to sprinkle on a house, he always makes use of salt.

When Jesus blesses loudly crying or unruly children, they become immediately still. Sometimes other children present may writhe, suffer cramps, or violently call out; but after his blessing they also grow quiet. Sometimes a dark vapor takes leave of them.

Blessing a Young Boy

In the case of boys, Jesus lays his hand upon their heads and blesses them in the manner of the patriarchal blessing, which consisted of three lines or strokes—from head and shoulders down to where these lines came together. The same is done with the girls, except for the laying of the hand on the head, which in their case is replaced with a sign made on the mouth (against the evil of gossip). Many of the children Jesus blesses receive an interior grace and later become Christians.

When Jesus greets friends in the castle of Lazarus or in the house of his mother, he blesses them. He blesses also, when taking leave of them, friends such as the old Essene Eliud of Nazareth, and in Bethany the sister of Lazarus, Silent Mary. When taking him as a disciple, Jesus blesses the kneeling tax collector Levi as he gives him the new name Matthew.

When Jesus journeys to Cyprus in early April 26, AD 31, he stands at ship's mast blessing land and sea. Earlier, on April 24, AD 31, in the land of Cabul between northwest Galilee and Tyre, when he was approached for help against dangerous lizard-like animals, Jesus blesses the region and through his word banishes the creatures to a swamp.

Sometimes he commands lepers to bathe in water he has blessed. On July 1, AD 30, while blessing a fountain in Amichores-Libnath, the disciples hold Jesus's cloak (which on such occasions he often lays aside) and provide him salt, which he casts into the water. He does all this with much gravity, teaching the while from the prophet Elisha, who healed the water at Jericho with salt (2 Kings 2:19–22).

Sharing Gifts of Grace

Apart from bestowing the grace of his vocation as it proceeded simply and with no special outward sign from his divine will, Jesus on several occasions gathers together the apostles and disciples to share with them his power to heal the sick, drive out evil spirits, and forgive sins.

It is to Andrew and the disciple Saturnin that Jesus first gives authority to baptize, and he does so on September 23, AD 29, the very day of the baptism of Jesus by John.

A year later, on September 2, AD 30, in Bezek on the Jordan, while the disciples are as usual assisting by lifting, setting upright, and unbandaging the sick, Jesus lays hands for the first time upon the heads of Andrew, John, and Joseph Barsabbas, then takes their hands in his and commands them in his name to do for a portion of the sick present what he himself is doing. To this task they straightaway turn, healing many.

On December 4, AD 30, Jesus gathers together all twelve newly-appointed apostles at a beautiful green and isolated place on the north shore of the Sea of Galilee, and there—as related in Matthew 10:1—names Simon Peter, James the Greater, and John, "Sons of Thunder." Thereafter he speaks movingly about their future apostolic missions and bestows upon them the power to heal and drive out evil spirits. To the other disciples present he grants full authority to baptize, along with the laying on of hands. This power he grants them with a blessing. All weep, and Jesus is also much affected. On December 28, AD 30, Jesus again bestows his blessing upon several apostles as a renewed strengthening and further increase of grace.

Three days later, on December 31, AD 30, all the apostles and disciples gather at the foot of Mount Tabor, where Jesus blesses the oil to be used by them for healing the sick, then again blesses them as he sends them forth two-by-two in three directions.

The Disciples Baptize

Some time later, on February 5, AD 31, while on the north shore of the Sea of Galilee, Jesus divides the disciples into several classes, setting the elder and better instructed before the younger and more recently arrived. He disposes the apostles in pairs (Peter and John first) around the elder disciples in the circle, and behind these, the disciples according to rank. Then he lays hands once more upon the apostles in this favored placement; the disciples, however, he only blesses. Everything takes place in great stillness and deep emotion, and without disagreement or chagrin of any kind on the part of those present.

Eleven days later, somewhat north of Naphtali, Jesus imparts freely to the apostles and disciples the grace to heal and to drive out demons. On this occasion there is no laying on of hands, but Anne Catherine beholds rays of different colors streaming out to each, according to their particular gift or disposition; for their part, they say "Lord, we feel a power in us, your words are truth and life," and each now understands immediately and with no need for prior reflection how in each situation they should heal.

Jesus Sends the Disciples Out in Pairs

The Purpose and Character of Jesus's Miracles

What is the Ultimate Purpose of Jesus's Miracles?

In the end, Jesus intended his miracles to confirm, through sufficiently telling signs, the truth of his becoming human and his divinity. For divinity can be amply proven only through what is unique to God. And God alone can alter the laws of nature when and where and how He will; for He alone, with His free will, instituted these laws for the general unfolding of world events.

From this it follows that the divine is most clearly proven through works that are beyond nature, as for example that the blind see, lepers are restored to health, and the dead raised again to life upon a word. Of such kind were the miracles of Jesus, establishing his divinity—to those who might ask (Luke 7:20) "Are you the one who is to come, or are we to wait for another?"—by responding (Luke 7:22) "the blind receive their sight, the lame walk, the lepers are cleansed, the deaf hear, and the dead are raised."

Have Not Others Worked Miracles Also?

To be sure, the biblical prophets and later Christian saints worked genuine miracles also, but those of Jesus were different and far more divine. Of other miracle-workers one reads (and as they themselves also attest) that they accomplished their miracles through prayer alone and not out of their own self-power, whereas the power whereby Jesus worked miracles he invoked, as it were, from within himself. Furthermore, Jesus not only worked miracles himself but shared with many others the power to perform similar—and sometimes even more remarkable—miracles, by simply calling upon his name. And again, Jesus performed not only corporeal miracles but spiritual miracles also, which were in fact far greater, namely, that through Christ himself, or through invoking his name, was bestowed the Holy Spirit—through whom hearts caught fire with the emotion of divine love, through whom the intellect apprehended the science of the divine, and through whom, that they might carry the divine truth to all, knowledge of different tongues was granted even to the simplest of folk.

ALPHABETICAL GAZETTEER TO THE MAPS OF THE JOURNEYS OF JESUS, THE HOLY FAMILY, AND OTHERS

The following index includes not only the names of places visited by Jesus (which are in italics) but also gives translations of Arabic terms appearing on the geographical maps. For example, Ain is Arabic for "spring." In the case of many of the place names a translation (" ") is given of the name, relating to its meaning. Also, the approximate location is indicated, and the dates [ ] upon which, according to the usage in this text, Jesus visited the place. The dates are written [year month day] so that, for example, [29 Dec. 19] signifies December 19 in the year AD 29. In describing the location, place names are referred to as they appear on the maps in this book and, if known, present-day designations (Hebrew or Arabic) are given in parentheses. Note that all distances, given in miles, are approximate, even if this is not explicitly stated.

Abel-Mehola ("dance meadow"). Approximately 7 miles south of Scythopolis (Bet She'an). Birthplace of the prophet Elisha. [29 Dec. 19; 30 Aug. 28–30]

Abez, Ebez ("height" or "lead mine"). 6 miles northwest of Scythopolis (Bet She'an). Saul's well was immediately east of Abez. It was here that Saul was wounded and died. [30 Oct. 31–Nov. 1]

Abila, Abila Decapoleos. 16 miles southeast of the Sea of Galilee, 10 miles east of Gadara. Elijah's pillar of instruction was close by. [30 Sept.18–21]

Abram ("sublime father"). 11 miles west of the Sea of Galilee, north of present-day Eilabun. [30 Dec. 19–23]

Adama ("red earth"). On the southwest shore of Lake Merom. [30 mid-June & Jul. 4–15]

Adummim, Adommim ("red ascent"). Between Jerusalem and Jericho. [30 Jan. 27–28]

Ainon ("spring" or "well"). 2 miles east of the Jordan and 2 miles south of Sukkoth = Succoth. Close to the first place of baptism of John the Baptist. [29 Oct. 12; 30 Sept. 4, 29–30; 30 Oct. 3]

Akrabis, Accrabata, Acrabeta, present-day Agraba. 8 miles southeast of Sichem = Shechem (Nablus). [30 Jan. 11 & Oct. 3–4]

Alexandrium. 18 miles north of Jericho and 5 miles east of the Jordan. [33 Jan. 24 & Feb. 9, 17–18]

Amichores-Libnath, Amead-Sichor, Sichor-Libnath, Sihor, Labanath. Sichor signifies the "Nile" and Labanath means "white" (the town was often flooded). 13 miles east of Ptolemais (Akko). [30 Jun. 26–Jul. 3]

Anathoth (named after Anathot, the son of Bechor; see Jeremiah 1:1). Present-day Anata, 3 miles northeast of Jerusalem. Birthplace of the prophet Jeremiah. [31 Jan. 7]

Antipatris (built by Herod the Great and named after his father, Antipater). 10 miles northeast of Japha (Jaffa, near Tel Aviv). [31 Jan. 4]

Apheke, Aphec ("stream"). Present-day Afula, 2 miles southwest of Nain (Nein). Place of birth of the apostle Thomas. [30 Mar. 9]

Ard = land.

Arga. Close to present-day Suf, about 3 miles northwest of Gerasa and 15 miles east of the Jordan. [30 Sept. 8–10]

Argob. About 5 miles southeast of Lake Merom. [31 Mar. 7–8; Jul. 26–27]

Aruma, Ruma. 5 miles southeast of Shechem (Nablus). [29 Oct. 18; 30 Feb. 7 & Oct. 13–15]

Aser-Michmethath (Aser="blessed", Michmethat "hidden corner"). Present-day Tayasir, 12½ miles south of Scythopolis (Bet She'an) and 11 miles northeast of Shechem (Nablus). [30 Oct. 18–22; 31 Jan. 22]

Ataroth ("glorious crown"?). Present-day ruins Attara, 19 miles east of the Mediterranean Sea and 3 miles northwest of Samaria (Sabastiya). [30 Jul. 30; 31 Mar. 30–31]

Attarus. Mount Attarus, southeast of Herod's fortress Machaerus and about 10 miles east of the Dead Sea. Jesus spent most of the forty days in the wilderness in a cave on Mount Attarus. [29 Oct. 22–Nov. 30]

Azanoth. In the region of the Horns of Hittin, 6 miles northwest of Tiberias. [30 Dec. 26; 31 Jun. 10]

Azo. Present-day Ajlun, 12 miles east of the Jordan. [30 Sept. 10–12. On Sept. 12, Jesus Christ visited the fishing lake 3 miles north of Azo]

Bach = stream.

Bahurim ("chosen"). East of the Mount of Olives, on the old road leading from Jerusalem to Jericho. [30 Apr. 10–17; 31 Sept. 28–30]

Beersheba ("well of the seven"). [33 Jan. 8]

517

Bethabara ("house of crossing"). Just north of the point of influx of the Jordan into the Dead Sea. [29 Dec. 3; 32 May 17–18; 33 Feb. 10–14]

Bethagla. Present-day Ain Hajla, 4½ miles southeast of Jericho. [30 Jan. 21]

Beth-Anoth, Bethanoth ("house of Anoth"). The ruins Bet Enun, 2½ miles northeast of Hebron. [31 Jan. 10; 32 Jun. 25; 33 Jan. 9–10]

Bethan. Close to present-day Akbara, 6 miles northwest of Capernaum. [30 Dec. 15]

Bethanat. 2½ miles east of Saphet (Safad, Zefat). [30 Jan. 5–6 & Dec.13–14]

Bethany (Eizariya) ("house of the poor"). Place of residence of Lazarus. [29 May 30, & Sept. 21–22, & Oct. 20–21: 30 Mar. 19–Apr. 17 & Apr. 26–May 2 & Jul. 21–23; 31 Jan. 7, 18, 20 & Mar. 24–28; 32 Jul. 25–26; 33 Feb. 2–4, 6–8 & Feb. 19–Apr. 2]

Beth-Arabah ("house of the steppe"). 6 miles west of the Dead Sea and 12 miles northeast of Hebron. [29 Sept. 28; 30 Jan. 19–20]

Betharamphtha-Julias, Amatha. 16 miles east of the Jordan and 21 miles east of Scythopolis (Bet She'an). [30 Sept. 15–18]

Bethel, Luz ("house of God"). Present-day Beitin, 10 miles north of Jerusalem. In the neighborhood of Bethel Jacob had his vision of the heavenly ladder (Genesis 28:12). [29 Sept. 19–20; 33 Jan. 21–22]

Bethel. 11 miles east of Jerusalem. A small place with a hospital, where Jesus spent the Sabbath after the baptism in the Jordan. [29 Sept. 23–24]

Bethjesimoth, Bethsimoth ("desert houses"). Present-day ruins Suweima, about 1 mile northeast of where the Jordan flows into the Dead Sea. [29 Dec. 11–12; 32 May 23–27]

Beth-Lechem. Present-day Bet Lehem, 6 miles northwest of Nazareth. However, it does not seem likely that this Beth-Lechem is the place which, according to Anne Catherine Emmerich's description, Jesus Christ visited on June 10 in AD 31.

Bethlehem ("house of bread"). Birthplace of Jesus. [29 Sept. 30; 30 Jan. 18]

Beth-Horon, Bethoron ("house of caves"). Two towns: Upper and Lower Beth-Horon. Lower Beth-Horon is present-day Beit Ur et Tahta, and Upper Beth-Horon is present-day Beit Ur el Fauqa, approximately 10 miles northwest of Jerusalem. [30 Jul. 24; 31 Jan. 5–6]

Bethsaida, Bezatha ("house of fishing or hunting"). Not to be confused with Bethsaida-Julias on the other side of the Jordan. The exact location of this little fishing village cannot be found, as the shoreline of the Sea of Galilee was changed significantly by an earthquake. From Anne Catherine Emmerich's description, Bethsaida was on the shore of the Sea of Galilee about 2½ miles southeast of Capernaum. Now the ruins of Capernaum are close to the shoreline on the north side of the lake. Bethsaida was the home town of the apostles Peter, Andrew, and Philip. [29 Aug. 5; 30 Aug. 7 & Nov. 23; 31 Mar. 16 & Apr. 7 & Jun. 14–15, 23; 32 Aug. 2–3]

Bethsaida-Julias. Present-day ruins at et-Tell on the east side of the Jordan, 2½ miles north of the place of influx of the Jordan into the Sea of Galilee. [30 Nov. 19; 31 Mar. 7–17 & Apr. 11 & Jun. 25]

Bethsop ("house of Ysop"). 1 mile east of the Jordan and 23 miles north of the Dead Sea. [29 Oct. 12]

Bethulia. A mountain stronghold about 6 miles west of Tiberias. [29 May 29 & Aug. 19–21; 30 Jan. 3 & Feb. 15–16 & Aug. 20–22; 31 Jan. 24 & Mar. 19]

Beth-zur, Bethsur ("home of rock"). Present-day Beit Sahur close to Bethlehem. The three kings passed through this place on their way from Jerusalem to Bethlehem. [31 Jan. 16–17]

Bezek. 1 mile west of the Jordan and 10 miles south of Scythopolis (Bet She'an). [30 Sept. 1–3]

Bosra, Beestra ("house of Astarte"). Present-day Busra, some 55 miles east of the Jordan, about 25 miles east of Edrai (Der'a). [31 Jul. 2]

Caesarea-Philippi. Paneas (Baniyas) was the earlier name of this place, reminding us of the nearby grotto of Pan. The town was built by Philip, a son of Herod the Great, and was named Caesarea in honor of Emperor Tiberius. 5 miles northwest of Lake Phiala. [31 Mar. 4–7]

Cana ("place of reeds"). Present-day Kafr Kanna, 3 miles northeast of Nazareth. Hometown of Nathaniel the bridegroom, at whose wedding Jesus Christ changed water into wine (John 2:1–11). [29 Jun. 30 & Dec. 25–31; 30 Aug. 3; 31 Feb. 4 & Jun. 19–20]

Capernaum, Kafr Nahum ("village of Nahum"). The ruins of Capernaum are on the northwest shore of the Sea of Galilee. In her visions Anne Catherine Emmerich always saw Capernaum about 2½ miles from the shoreline. She indicated that an earthquake significantly changed the shoreline of the Sea of Galilee: "The waters of the lake poured into the valley and came almost up to Capernaum, which previously was about half an hour from the shoreline. The house of Peter and that of the Holy Virgin—close to Capernaum, toward the lake— remained standing. The Sea of Galilee moved violently, the waters surging over the shoreline here and there, and receding elsewhere. The shoreline was changed significantly, approximating to its present form, and is no longer recognizable as it was." (WJW, 466) [29 May 29, Jun. 20, Aug. 4, 8–9, Dec. 22–24; 30 Jan. 1–2, 6–7, Feb. 10–13, Mar. 1, mid–June, Jul. 18–19, Aug. 4–7, 9–11, Nov. 9–11, 17–19, Nov. 24–Dec. 10; 31 Jan. 26–Feb. 17, Apr. 5–13, Jun. 14–17, 22; 33 Jan. 26]

Carmel = Mount Carmel. Mountain range near Haifa, overlooking the Mediterranean, rising to 1,730 feet above sea level. Elijah lived for some time on Mount Carmel and it was here that he defeated the prophets of Baal (I Kings 18:17–46). [29 Jul. 23–24]

Chabul, Cabul, Chabalon. A stretch of land east of the Mediterranean, between Akko and Tyre, bordering on Galilee. [30 end of May & Jul. 1–2]

Chim. 16 miles southeast of Hepha (Haifa). [29 Sept. 15]

Chirbet = ruin.

Chisloth-Tabor, Chesulloth. Present-day Iksal, west of Mount Tabor and 2 miles southeast of Nazareth. [29 Jul. 25, Aug. 31–Sept. 1; 30 Feb. 16–19; 30 Dec. 28–29; 31 Apr. 3]

Chorazin. Anne Catherine Emmerich saw two places: Great Chorazin and Little Chorazin. Great Chorazin she saw about 6 miles northeast of the place where the Jordan flows into the Sea of Galilee, and Little Chorazin approximately 1 mile from the place of influx of the Jordan. [29 Oct. 15–16; 30 Nov. 22; 31 Mar. 11–12; 32 Aug. 1]

Coreae. 15 miles west of the Jordan and 20 miles north of Jerusalem. [30 Oct. 6–8; 31 Mar. 22]

Cydessa, Cydassa, Cedesa. 11 miles northwest of Tiberias. [31 Feb. 6]

Cyprus. Island in the Mediterranean visited by Jesus Christ for five weeks. [31 Apr. 26–May 30]

Daberath, Dabaritta. Present-day Dabburiya, 5 miles east of Nazareth, at the northwest side of Mount Tabor. [30 Nov. 1–4]

Dalmanutha. "Jesus went to the district of Dalmanutha" (Mark 8:10). A small village at the southeast end of the Sea of Galilee, and close by a tax/customs place. [31 Jan. 30 & Mar. 15]

Damna, Dimnah. 2 miles west of Magdalum/Sea of Galilee. [30 Dec. 27; 31 Jan. 25 & Jun. 11]

Dan ("judge"), previously named Lais (Lesem). 2 miles west of Caesarea-Philippi. [31 Jan. 27—Feb. 13]

Datheman, Dathema. Present-day Ataman, 4½ miles north of Edrai (Der'a), 30 miles east of the Jordan. [31 Jul. 8]

David's Way, running south of Bosra (Busra) [31 Jul. 6]

Dibon. 5 miles east of the Jordan and 10 miles north of the Dead Sea. 1 mile west of Dibon was the suburb of Dibon. [29 Oct. 10–11 & Dec. 7–8]

Dion, Dium, Dia. 7½ miles east of Scythopolis (Bet She'an), 3 miles east of the Jordan. [30 Sept. 25–27]

Dothaim ("two wells"). 7½ miles west of Tiberias. [29 Jun. 15 & Aug. 31; 30 Mar. 2 & Dec. 24–25; 31 Apr. 4–5]

Dothan. 9 miles north of Samaria (Sabastiya). [30 Oct. 27–29]

Dschebal/Dschebl = range of mountains/mountain.

Edon. Heathen town with a Jewish settlement, east of Kedar. [32 Aug. 13–15]

Edrai ("my strength"). Present-day Der'a, about 30 miles east of the place where the Jordan flows out of the Sea of Galilee, in the direction of Bosra (Busra), which is some 25 miles further east. [31 Jun. 29–30]

Eleale, El'aleh ("God's path"). Present-day El'Al, 1 mile northeast of Hesbon (Hisban). [29 Dec. 9–10]

Elkasa, a village 2 miles northeast of Capernaum. [31 Feb. 9]

Elkese, Elkosh. 5 miles northwest of Saphet (Zefat, Safad). Birthplace of the prophet Nahum. [30 Dec. 14]

Endor, Ain-dor ("spring of Dor"). Present-day 'En Dor, 7 miles southeast of Nazareth. [29 Sept. 8–10; 30 Oct. 30]

Engannim ("garden spring"). 7½ miles southwest of Scythopolis (Bet She'an). [30 Jul. 31–Aug. 1]

Ensemes, Ain-Semes ("spring of the sun"). 10 miles northeast of Bethlehem. [29 Sept. 26]

Ephron. 8 miles east of the Jordan and 20 miles south of the Sea of Galilee. [30 Sept. 13–14]

Ephron or Ephraim. Present-day Taiyiba, 14 miles west of the Jordan and 12 miles north of Jerusalem. [32 Aug. 26; 33 Jan. 19–20 & Feb. 15]

First Place of Baptism, where John the Baptist first started baptizing people. Close to Ainon.

Gabaa. 20 miles west of the Jordan and 14 miles north of Jerusalem. [30 Jul. 25]

Gabara. Present-day ruins of Madin, 6 miles northwest of Tiberias. [30 Nov. 6–9; and on the Mount of Instruction near Gabara on 30 Apr. 18–20 & 31 Jun. 21]

Gadara, Gadar. The present-day site Hamat Gader, 5 miles southeast of where the Jordan flows out from the Sea of Galilee. [30 Sept. 21–24]

Galgala ("circle"). Close to the present-day site Gush Halav, 6 miles northwest of Saphet (Zefat, Safad). [30 Dec. 14]

Garisma, Garis, Garsis. 14 miles west of the Sea of Galilee and 2 miles north of Sepphoris (Zippori). [31 Apr. 20–22]

Gath-Hepher, (Geth = "wine-press"). 11 miles west of the Sea of Galilee and 3 miles east of Sepphoris (Zippori). Present-day Mash-had. Birthplace of the prophet Jonah. [30 Jul. 18 & Dec. 28]

Golan ("exodus"). In the region of the present-day ruins of Summaka, 6 miles south of Caesarea-Philippi (Baniyas). [31 Feb. 28]

Gennabris, Ginnabris, Sennabris. 2 miles west of the place where the Jordan flows out from the Sea of Galilee. Nathaniel Chased lived here. [29 Dec. 25; 30 Feb. 14 & Aug. 25–26]

Gerasa. 5 miles east of where the Jordan flows into the Sea of Galilee. [29 Oct. 14; 30 Aug. 16]

Gergesa. 5 miles, east of the Sea of Galilee, approximately the location of present-day Eli'Al. [30 Dec. 6]

Gessur. Town with a Roman garrison, about 12½ miles northeast of Caesarea-Philippi (Baniyas). [31 Feb. 20–24]

Gebea, Gibea, Gibeath ("hill"). Close to or perhaps identical with present-day Jaba, 6 miles north of Jerusalem. [29 Sept. 21]

Gilead. 7½ miles east of the Sea of Galilee. [30 Aug. 14]

Gilgal. 2 miles southeast of Jericho. [29 Oct. 7–8]

Ginea = Ginnim, Ain-Gannim ("garden spring"). Present-day Jenin, midway between Nazareth and Shechem (Nablus). An estate, which Lazarus had inherited from his father, was close to Ginea and was put at the disposal of the disciples. [30 Mar. 14–16 & Jul. 28–29; 32 Jul. 8–21]

Gischala, Gis-Halab. 3 miles west of Tiberias. Here there was a fortress with Roman soldiers. The birthplace of Antigonus (founder of the Sadducees) and of the rebel John of Gischala and also of Saul (later the apostle Paul). [30 Nov. 5–6; 31 Feb. 5]

Gophna. Present-day Jifna, 12 miles north of Jerusalem. [29 Sept. 18–19]

Gur. A village 2 miles southwest of Jezrael (Yizre'el), 15 miles west of the Jordan. [29 Sept. 16–17]

Hadad-Rimmon, Adaremmon, Maximianopolis. 5 miles southwest of Nazareth. [31 Apr. 1–2]

Hain Mambre = Mambre grove. The site of the present-day sacred oak of Abraham, 3 miles north of Hebron. [31 Jan. 10]

Hain Moreh = Moreh's grove ("Moreh's oak"). 2½ miles northeast of Shechem (Nablus). Here there was a sacred tree, where God appeared to Abraham. At this tree Mary prayed on her journey from Nazareth to Bethlehem. [30 Mar. 17 & Oct. 15, 18]

Hanathon ("place of grace"). 5 miles north of Capernaum. [30 Jan. 4–5 & Dec. 10]

Hareth. A wood where David once sought refuge from Saul. 3 miles east of Shechem (Nablus). [30 Oct. 11]

Hay, ha'Ai ("pile of stones"). The present-day ruins Haiyan near Deir-Dibwan, 10 miles northeast of Jerusalem. [30 Jan. 12]

Hazezon-Thamar, Asesonthamar ("row of palms"). An earlier name for En Gedi on the west shore of the Dead Sea. The town of Hazezon-Thamar was destroyed along with the destruction of Sodom and Gomorrha, which were located in the (what is now desert) region close to the Dead Sea. At the time of Jesus the ruins of Hazezon-Thamar still existed. [30 Jan. 17]

Hebron ("friend of God"). 17½ miles south of Jerusalem. The town of Abraham ("friend of God"). See also Hain Mambre, Jutta, and Machpelah, all in the area of Hebron. [29 Jun. 3; 30 Mar. 30–31; 31 Jan. 11–12]

Heliopolis. Present-day site adjoining Cairo in Egypt. Taking flight to Egypt, the Holy Family lived at Heliopolis (or close to Heliopolis) before returning to Israel. Jesus

Christ visited Heliopolis three months prior to the crucifixion.[33 Jan. 2–4]

Haifa. On the Mediterranean. Jesus Christ landed at the harbor of Haifa upon his return from Cyprus. [31 May 31]

Hermon. Mount Hermon in the north, on the border between Lebanon and Syria, 27 miles southwest of Damascus, height 9,232 feet. Jesus passed by Mount Hermon on his journey to Sidon and Sarepta. [29 Jul. 8]

Hieromax. A river flowing down from Gilead into the Jordan just south of the Sea of Galilee. [29 Jun. 7]

Hippos, Hippene. Present-day site of Susitha, just east of 'En Gev on the east shore of the Sea of Galilee. [30 Jan. 9]

Hukok, Hucuca. Present-day Huqoq, 5 miles west of Capernaum. [30 Dec. 11–13]

Ischariot = *Iscariot* ("man from Keriyot or Karioth"). In the region of present-day Aqaba, 12 miles west of the Jordan and 10 miles northeast of Shechem (Nablus). Home town of Judas Iscariot. [30 Oct. 27]

Jacob's well. One mile east of Shechem (Nablus). Mentioned in John 4:6 as the place where the conversation between Jesus Christ and the Samaritan woman took place. [29 Jul. 30; 30 Jul. 26; 33 Jan. 13]

Jericho. One of the most ancient archeological sites in the world, 5 miles west of the Jordan. Captured when its walls fell after the Hebrews marched around the city, it was destroyed by Joshua (Joshua 6). [32 May 29–Jun. 10; 33 Jan. 20–21]

Jerusalem, Salem ("peace"). [29 May 31 & Nov. 30; 30 Mar. 20–Apr. 9; 31 Jan. 19–20 Mar. 25–28; 32 Jul. 27; 33 Feb. 19–Apr.3]

Jezreel. Present-day Yizre'el, about 10 miles south of Nazareth. [29 Aug. 27–28; 30 Feb. 9 & 20]

Jogbeha ("high place"). 2 miles east of the Jordan and 24 miles south of the Sea of Galilee. [30 Sept. 27–28]

Jotopata, Jotapata. A town and fortress of the Herodians (followers of Herod). 3 miles northwest of Tiberias. [30 Aug. 27]

Jutta. Present-day Yatta, 5 miles south of Hebron. Birthplace of John the Baptist. [31 Jan. 8–9, 13]

Kades-Nephthali (Kedes = "consecrated, holy"). 5 miles northwest of Lake Merom. [31 Feb. 11]

Kafr = village.

Kamon. About 5 miles east of the Jordan and 29 miles north of the Dead Sea. [30 Sept. 5]

Kapharot. A small place 3 miles northwest of Tiberias. [31 Apr. 20]

Kedar. A heathen town about 100 miles northeast of the Sea of Galilee. There was a Jewish settlement in this town. [32 Aug. 8–13, 15–18 & Sept. 5–9]

Kibzaim. 19 miles east of the Jordan and 25 miles north of Jerusalem. [29 Dec. 16–17; 30 Jul. 24]

Kimki, Chimki. A shepherd village 6 miles south of Nazareth.[29 Sept. 2–4]

Kiriathaim. A Levite town 8 miles west of Capernaum. [30 Dec. 17–19]

Kishion, Kiseon, Kedes. A small place at the southern foot of Mount Tabor, 6 miles southeast of Nazareth. [29 Aug. 25]

Kition. Town with a nearby harbor on the southeast side of the island of Cyprus. Upon completion of his five-week stay on the island, Jesus Christ set sail from the harbor of Kition. [31 May 23 & 30]

Kore. A small place between Edrai (Der'a) and Bosra (Busra), 38 miles east of the place where the Jordan flows out from the Sea of Galilee. [31 Jul. 1]

Kyrenia. Town on the north side of the island Cyprus, which Jesus Christ visited in the spring of AD 31. [31 May 25–26]

Kythrea, northern Cyprus. [31 May 4–8]

Lake Merom. Present-day Hula Reserve 12 miles north of the Sea of Galilee.

Lake Phiala. Present-day Berekhat Ram, 4 miles southeast of Caesarea-Philippi (Baniyas). [31 Feb. 24–25]

Lebona. A small place at the southern foot of Mount Garizim, 17 miles west of the Jordan and 27 miles north of Jerusalem. [31 Jan. 21]

Lebonah. Near present-day Lubban Shaqiya, 17 miles west of the Jordan and 20 miles north of Jerusalem. [31 Mar. 21–22]

Leccum. One mile west of the Jordan and 8 miles north of the Sea of Galilee. [31 Apr. 9–10]

Leppe. A village west of Mallep (present-day Bellapaise) on the north side of the island of Cyprus. [31 May 13]

Libnath, Libna, Lebna, Labana, Lobna. A town of Levites, 17 miles west of Hebron. [31 Jan. 16]

Luz. Not to be confused with Jacob's town Bethel, present-day Beitin, formerly Luz. This place Luz was a village 9 miles west of the place of influx of the Jordan into the Dead Sea. [29 Sept. 25]

Machpelah. Machpelah's cave is mentioned in Genesis 23:9 & 17; 49:29–30. A large cave located north of the old town of Hebron. The patriarchs Abraham, Isaac, and Jacob, and also others, were buried in this cave. [31 Jan. 10]

Midian. A large town of Madianites with a Jewish quarter, 12 miles east of the Dead Sea. [32 May 20]

Magdala ("tower"). On the east side of the Sea of Galilee in the region of present-day 'En Gev. [30 Dec. 4–7]

Magdalum. Now generally referred to as Magdala, present-day Migdal, on the west side of the Sea of Galilee. [29 Aug. 10]

Mahanaim. This historical town of Levites is on the north side of the River Jabbok (Yaboq), 6 miles east of the Jordan. [30 Sept. 5]

Mallep. A Jewish colony on the north side of the island of Cyprus. Present-day Bellapaise. It was here that Jesus Christ spent much of the time during his five-week visit to Cyprus. [31 May 9–20, 26–28]

Megiddo, Magiddo. 17 miles southeast of Haifa on the southwest side of the Jezreel valley. [30 Nov. 14–15]

Merdsch = plain.

Meroz ("refuge"). 15 miles west of the Jordan and 30 miles north of Jerusalem. [30 Oct. 23–26]

Misael ("who is like God"), also named Masal. An ancient Levite town 10 miles east of Akko, in the region of present-day Bet Kerem. [31 Jun. 1–4]

Mizpah ("lookout"), also named Maspha. Present-day Nabi Samwil (Shemu'el), supposedly the home town and place of birth and death of the prophet Samuel. [29 Oct. 5]

Mozian. Ancient city east of the Tigris and Euphrates. [32 Oct. 7–8]

Mount of the Apostles. 16 miles south of Tiberias. [33 Jan. 28]

Naasson ("big snake"). About 12½ miles west of where the Jordan flows into the Sea of Galilee. [30 Dec. 19]

Nain ("beautiful"), also named Naim. Present-day Nein, 6 miles southeast of Nazareth. The home town of the rich widow Maroni, whose son was raised from the dead (Luke 7:11). Maroni became one of the holy women. [30 Aug. 2, Nov. 13–14; 31 Jun. 7–9]

Nazara. A Samaritan town at the northwest end of the Jezreel valley, 12½ miles southeast of Haifa. The Holy Family stopped here upon returning from Egypt. [30 Mar. 13]

Nazareth. The home town of Jesus. According to Anne Catherine Emmerich, Nazareth had five gates and the house of Joseph and Mary was close to the north gate. Joseph's carpentry was close by. [29 May 29, Jul. 31–Aug. 2, Sept. 5–7, 11–14; 30 Mar. 5–12, Aug. 11–12; 33 Jan. 27]

Nebo, Nabo. At the foot of Mount Nebo, 9 miles east of the north end of the Dead Sea. [30 Jan. 29–30; 32 May 18]

Naphtali ("my battle"). A little place 4 miles west of Capernaum. [31 Feb. 8]

Nobah. 14 miles northeast of Lake Merom. [31 Feb. 25–27]

Nobah in Hauran. A heathen town with a Jewish quarter populated mainly by Rechabites who settled there upon returning from the Babylonian captivity. In the neighborhood of present-day Behem, 20 miles east of Bosra (Busra) and 8 miles northeast of Salcha (Salkhad). [31 Jul. 3]

Ono. In the neighborhood of the present-day ruins of a Johannite monastery named Kasr el-Jehud, 1 mile northwest of the place of the baptism in the Jordan (see "Third Place of Baptism") and 3 miles southeast of Jericho. [30 Jan. 13— 14, Feb. 3–6]

Ophra, Ophera ("dust"?). In the region of present-day Mazra'at, some 16 miles north of Jerusalem. [30 Oct. 8–9]

Ornithopolis ("bird town"). Located close to the shore of the Mediterranean Sea, between Sarepta (Sarafand) and Tyre (Sour). Pliny refers to the town Ornithon between Tyre and Sarepta (*Hist. nat.* V, 18). Here there was a small Jewish colony north of the town. The Syrophoenician woman, whose possessed daughter was healed (Matthew 15:22), lived in Ornithopolis. It was from the harbor of Ornithopolis that Jesus Christ set sail for his visit to the island of Cyprus on the evening of April 25, AD 31. [31 Feb. 15–16, Apr. 25]

Ozensara, Uzzen Se'ereh ("Sarah's town"). Between Jerusalem and Tel Aviv, 19 miles northwest of Jerusalem. [29 Sept. 18; 31 Jan. 4]

Peraa = Perea. Stretch of land to the east of the Jordan, running down to the Dead Sea.

Phasael. Present-day El-Fasayil, 5 miles west of the Jordan and 22 miles northeast of Jerusalem. [29 Oct. 9; 30 Feb. 7]

Quarantania = Mount Quarantania. Present-day Quruntul, 7½ miles west of the Jordan and 7½ miles northeast of Jerusalem. It was here that Jesus Christ spent the first night of the forty days of temptation in the wilderness, before he went to Mount Attarus. [29 Oct. 21]

Ramah ("heights"). Present-day Ram, 5 miles north of Jerusalem. [31 Mar. 28]

Ramath-Gilead ("heights in Gilead"), also called Ramath-Mizpa, or sometimes Hag Gilead. Present-day Salt, 11 miles east of the Jordan and 25 miles north of the Dead Sea. [30 Sept. 5–7]

Ras (abbreviated R.) = foothills.

Rehob. About 14 miles north of Lake Merom. [31 Feb. 19] *Regaba*. 10 miles southeast of Lake Merom. [31 Mar. 1–4, 9–10] *Rimon*. About 2 miles southeast of Mount Tabor. [31 Jun. 10]

Salamis. Ancient port on the east coast of the island of Cyprus. It was here that Jesus Christ landed on April 26, AD 31, upon crossing the Mediterranean from the harbor of Ornithopolis. Salamis was destroyed by an earthquake in the fourth century AD [31 Apr. 26–May 1, 29]

Salcha, Selcha. Present-day Salkhad in Hauran, 15 miles east of Bosra (Busra), 74 miles east of the Jordan and at a latitude corresponding to 12½ miles south of the Sea of Galilee. [31 Jul. 5]

Salem ("peace"). About 1½ miles west of the Jordan and 24 miles north of the Dead Sea. According to Anne Catherine Emmerich, Melchizedek had built here prior to laying the foundations for another Salem (= Jerusalem). [30 Oct. 11–12]

Saphet, Sephet. Present-day Safad/Zefat, 8 miles northwest of Capernaum. [30 Dec. 15–17]; Mount of Instruction between Hanathon and Saphet: [30 Jan. 4–5, Dec. 10; 31 Jun. 24]

Sarepta, Sarephat, Zarphat. Present-day Sarafand on the Mediterranean, north of Ornithopolis and Tyre (Sour). It was in Sarepta that the prophet Elijah raised the son of a widow from the dead (I Kings 17:9). [29 Jul. 9, 22; 31 Feb. 17–18]

Second Place of Baptism. This was the second place where John the Baptist baptized people. (See First Place of Baptism and Third Place of Baptism.) The second place of baptism was located on the east side of the Jordan, more or less opposite (but slightly to the north of) the third place of baptism. It was at the third place of baptism, on the west side of the Jordan and close to the village of Ono, that the baptism of Jesus took place.

Seleucia. A garrison town of heathen soldiers about 3 miles southeast of Lake Merom. [30 mid-June & Jul. 11]

Sepphoris, Saphorim. Present-day ruins Zippori, 3 miles north of Nazareth. Sepphoris had three synagogues: one for the Pharisees, one for the Sadducees, and one for the Essenes. Little Sepphoris lay northeast of Greater Sepphoris. Sepphoris was the hometown of Anna, the mother of Mary of Nazareth. [29 Aug. 14–18; 30 Mar. 2–4; Little Sepphoris: 30 Aug. 8–10]

Shechem = Sichem. Present-day Nablus. Jacob's well is located 1 mile east of Shechem. [29 Dec. 17; 30 Jul. 26–27; 33 Jan. 16–17]

Shiloh ("place of rest"). Present-day ruins of Shillo, 19 miles north of Jerusalem. [29 Dec. 14–15; 30 Oct. 4–5]

Shunem = present day Sulam (Shumen) 9 miles southeast of Nazareth. [30 Feb. 22–23; 31 Jan. 1–2]

Sichar. A heathen town with a Jewish settlement, near Kedar, some 100 miles northeast of the Sea of Galilee. [32 Aug. 19–Sept. 4]

Sichem (see Shechem).

Sidon, Zidon ("fortress"). Present-day Saida on the Mediterranean, 21 miles north of Tyre (Sour). [29 Jul. 8]

Sion. Not Mount Zion in Jerusalem but a small place southwest of Mount Tabor. [31 Jun. 6–7]

Sogane. About 4 miles south of Caesarea-Philippi (Baniyas). [31 Mar. 18–19]

Succoth. ("huts"). 2 miles east of the Jordan and 27½ miles north of the Dead Sea. [29 Oct. 12–13; 30 Oct. 1–2]

Tabor. Mount Tabor, 1,929 feet, located 5 miles southeast of Nazareth. It was on this mountain that the Transfiguration took place (Matthew 17:1), around midnight April 3/4, AD 31. [31 Apr. 3–4]

Tarichea. Located close to the place where the Jordan flows

Alphabetical Gazetteer

out from the Sea of Galilee. [29 Dec. 20–21; 30 Aug. 13; 31 Jan. 30, Apr. 16]

Terebenthe = hill of terebinth trees.

Thaanach ("sandy ground"). Present-day ruins Ta'nakh, 13 miles southwest of Nazareth. [31 Jun. 5]

Thanat-Shiloh. Present-day ruins of Ta'na, 6 miles east of Shechem (Nablus). [30 Oct. 16–18; 31 Jan. 2–3, Mar. 29; 33 Jan. 29]

Thantia, Thainata. On the Roman road between Bosra (Busra) and Philadelphia (Rabbath Ammon), 22 miles south of Bosra, 33 miles northeast of Philadelphia, 46 miles east of the Jordan. [31 Jul. 6–7]

Thebez. Present-day Tubas, 10 miles northeast of Shechem (Nablus). [29 Dec. 18]

Third Place of Baptism, where the Baptism in the Jordan took place, 3 miles north of the place of influx of the Jordan into the Dead Sea.

Thirza ("lovely"). Between Thebez (Tubas) and the Jordan, 15½ miles northeast of Shechem (Nablus). [31 Jan. 23]

Tyre, Zor ("rock"). Present-day ruins of Sour on the Mediterranean, 21 miles south of Sidon (Saida). Here there was a Jewish community, which Jesus Christ visited in the year AD 30. [30 Jun. 20–25]

Ulama. Present-day village of Ullama, 5½ miles southwest of the place where the Jordan flows out from the Sea of Galilee. [30 Feb. 23–27]

Ur. Ancient Chaldean city close to the Euphrates, about 160 miles northwest of the place where the Euphrates flows into the Persian Gulf. The hometown of the patriarch Abraham. [32 Oct. 10–12]

Valley of the Doves, 6 miles northwest of Tiberias.

Wadi (abbreviated W.) = valley.

Zebulon valley (Zabulon valley). Valley to the north of Nazareth, between Nazareth and Sepphoris. [29 Aug. 12, 24; 30 Aug. 10–11]

Zedad. A small town in Northern Galilee, 12½ miles west of Lake Merom. [30 Jul. 16–17]

Zorobabel. The nobleman whose adopted son was healed by Jesus Christ (John 4:47). Jesus was often a guest at Zorobabel's estate at Capernaum. [30 Aug. 20, Nov. 9, 11, 17; 31 Jan. 26, 31, Apr. 14, Jun. 12, 16]

SOME TOPOGRAPHICAL CORRECTIONS:

Map 25: Gath-Hepher should be shown 5 miles further to the northwest of the route.

On all the maps the place Coreae should be somewhat further northeast, adjoining Wadi Far'a = Far'a valley.

The village of Jutta should appear on all the maps just southeast of Hebron.

The place Thanat-Shiloh should appear a little further to the southeast on all the maps.

www.ingramcontent.com/pod-product-compliance
Lightning Source LLC
Chambersburg PA
CBHW081156230426
43666CB00016B/2832